EYEWITNESS TRAVEL

SPAIN

THE INTERNATIONAL SCHOOL OF AMSTERDAM

EYEWITNESS TRAVEL

SPAIN

LONDON, NEW YORK,
MELBOURNE, MUNICH AND DELHI
www.dk.com

PROJECT EDITOR Nick Inman
ART EDITORS Jaki Grosvenor, Janis Utton
EDITORS Catherine Day, Lesley McGave, Seán O'Connell
DESIGNERS Susan Blackburn, Dawn Davies-Cook,
Joy Fitzsimmons, Helen Westwood

MAIN CONTRIBUTORS
John Ardagh, David Baird, Mary-Ann Gallagher, Vicky Hayward,
Adam Hopkins, Lindsay Hunt, Nick Inman, Paul Richardson,
Martin Symington, Nigel Tisdall, Roger Williams

PHOTOGRAPHERS
Max Alexander, Joe Cornish, Neil Lukas, Neil Mersh,
John Miller, Kim Sayer, Linda Whitwam, Peter Wilson

ILLUSTRATORS
Stephen Conlin, Gary Cross, Richard Draper, Isidoro González-Adalid
Cabezas (Acanto Arquitectura y Urbanismo S.L.), Claire Littlejohn,
Maltings Partnership, Chris Orr & Assocs, John Woodcock

Reproduced by Colourscan (Singapore)
Printed and bound by South China Printing Co. Ltd, China

First published in Great Britain in 1996
by Dorling Kindersley Limited 80 Strand, London WC2R 0RL

Reprinted with revisions 1997, 1999, 2000, 2001,
2002, 2003, 2004, 2005, 2006, 2007, 2008, 2009

Copyright 1996, 2009 © Dorling Kindersley Limited, London
A Penguin Company

ALL RIGHTS RESERVED. NO PART OF THIS PUBLICATION MAY BE
REPRODUCED, STORED IN A RETRIEVAL SYSTEM, OR TRANSMITTED IN ANY
FORM OR BY ANY MEANS, ELECTRONIC, MECHANICAL, PHOTOCOPYING,
RECORDING OR OTHERWISE, WITHOUT THE PRIOR WRITTEN PERMISSION
OF THE COPYRIGHT OWNER.

A CIP CATALOGUE RECORD IS AVAILABLE FROM THE BRITISH LIBRARY.

ISBN 978-1-40533-378-8

*Front cover main image: Caseras village,
Andalusia, Southern Spain*

We're trying to be cleaner and greener:

- we recycle waste and switch things off
- we use paper from responsibly managed
forests whenever possible
- we ask our printers to actively reduce
water and energy consumption
- we check out our suppliers' working
conditions – they never use child labour

**Find out more about our values and
best practices at www.dk.com**

**The information in this
DK Eyewitness Travel Guide is checked regularly.**
Every effort has been made to ensure that this book is as up-to-date
as possible at the time of going to press. Some details, however,
such as telephone numbers, prices, opening hours, gallery hanging
arrangements and travel information, are liable to change. The
publishers cannot accept responsibility for any consequences arising
from the use of this book, nor for any material on third-party
websites, and cannot guarantee that any website address in this
book will be a suitable source of travel information. We value the
views and suggestions of our readers very highly.
Please write to: Publisher, DK Eyewitness Travel Guides,
Dorling Kindersley 80 Strand, London WC2R 0RL.

CONTENTS

HOW TO USE THIS
GUIDE **6**

King Alfonso X the Learned

INTRODUCING
SPAIN

DISCOVERING
SPAIN **10**

PUTTING SPAIN ON
THE MAP **14**

A PORTRAIT
OF SPAIN **18**

SPAIN THROUGH
THE YEAR **40**

THE HISTORY
OF SPAIN **46**

NORTHERN SPAIN

INTRODUCING
NORTHERN SPAIN **74**

GALICIA **84**

ASTURIAS AND
CANTABRIA **100**

THE BASQUE
COUNTRY, NAVARRA
AND LA RIOJA **114**

BARCELONA

INTRODUCING
BARCELONA **138**

OLD TOWN **142**

EIXAMPLE **158**

MONTJUÏC **168**

FURTHER AFIELD **174**

BARCELONA STREET
FINDER **179**

SHOPPING AND
ENTERTAINMENT
IN BARCELONA **186**

Grapes growing in La Mancha, the world's largest expanse of vineyards

EASTERN SPAIN

INTRODUCING
EASTERN SPAIN **198**

CATALONIA **206**

ARAGÓN **226**

VALENCIA AND
MURCIA **242**

Statue of Alfonso XII, Madrid

MADRID

INTRODUCING
MADRID **266**

OLD MADRID **268**

BOURBON MADRID **282**

FURTHER AFIELD **300**

MADRID STREET
FINDER **307**

SHOPPING AND
ENTERTAINMENT IN
MADRID **316**

MADRID PROVINCE **326**

CENTRAL SPAIN

INTRODUCING
CENTRAL SPAIN **336**

CASTILLA Y LEÓN **346**

CASTILLA-LA
MANCHA **378**

EXTREMADURA **400**

SOUTHERN SPAIN

INTRODUCING
SOUTHERN SPAIN **416**

SEVILLE **426**

SEVILLE STREET
FINDER **447**

SHOPPING AND
ENTERTAINMENT IN
SEVILLE **454**

ANDALUSIA **458**

SPAIN'S ISLANDS

INTRODUCING SPAIN'S
ISLANDS **504**

THE BALEARIC
ISLANDS **506**

THE CANARY
ISLANDS **528**

TRAVELLERS' NEEDS

WHERE TO STAY **554**

RESTAURANTS AND
BARS **602**

SHOPPING **654**

ENTERTAINMENT **656**

OUTDOOR ACTIVITIES
AND SPECIALIST
HOLIDAYS **658**

SURVIVAL GUIDE

PRACTICAL
INFORMATION **664**

TRAVEL INFORMATION
674

PHRASE BOOK **719**

Iglesia de Santa
María del
Naranco in
Asturias

HOW TO USE THIS GUIDE

This guide helps you to get the most from your visit to Spain. It provides detailed practical information and expert recommendations. Introducing Spain maps the country and sets it in its historical and cultural context. The five regional sections, plus Barcelona and Madrid, describe important sights, using maps, photographs and illustrations. Features cover topics from food and wine to fiestas and beaches. Restaurant and hotel recommendations can be found in Travellers' Needs. The Survival Guide has tips on everything from transport to using the telephone system.

BARCELONA, MADRID AND SEVILLE

These cities are divided into areas, each with its own chapter. A last chapter, *Further Afield*, covers peripheral sights. Madrid Province, surrounding the capital, has its own chapter. All sights are numbered and plotted on the chapter's area map. Information on each sight is easy to locate as it follows the numerical order on the map.

Sights at a Glance lists the chapter's sights by category: Churches and Cathedrals, Museums and Galleries, Streets and Squares, Historic Buildings, Parks and Gardens.

2 Street-by-Street Map
This gives a bird's-eye view of the key areas in each chapter.

Stars indicate the sights that no visitor should miss.

All pages relating to Madrid have green thumb tabs. Barcelona's are pink and Seville's are red.

A locator map shows where you are in relation to other areas of the city centre.

1 Area Map
For easy reference, sights are numbered and located on a map. City centre sights are also marked on Street Finders: Barcelona (pages 179–85); Madrid (pages 307–315); Seville (pages 447–53).

A suggested route for a walk is shown in red.

3 Detailed information
The sights in the three main cities are described individually. Addresses, telephone numbers, opening hours, admission charges, tours, photography and wheelchair access are also provided, as well as public transport links.

1 Introduction
The landscape, history and character of each region is outlined here, showing how the area has developed over the centuries and what it has to offer to the visitor today.

SPAIN AREA BY AREA

Apart from Barcelona, Madrid and Seville, the country has been divided into 12 regions, each of which has a separate chapter. The most interesting cities, towns and villages, and other places to visit are numbered on a *Regional Map*.

2 Regional Map
This shows the road network and gives an illustrated overview of the whole region. All interesting places to visit are numbered and there are also useful tips on getting to, and around, the region by car and public transport.

Fiesta boxes highlight the best traditional fiestas in the region.

Each area of Spain can be quickly identified by its colour coding, shown on the inside front cover.

3 Detailed information
All the important towns and other places to visit are described individually. They are listed in order, following the numbering on the Regional Map. *Within each town or city, there is detailed information on important buildings and other sights.*

For all top sights, a Visitors' Checklist provides the practical information you will need to plan your visit.

4 Spain's top sights
These are given two or more full pages. Historic buildings are dissected to reveal their interiors. The most interesting towns or city centres are shown in a bird's-eye view, with sights picked out and described.

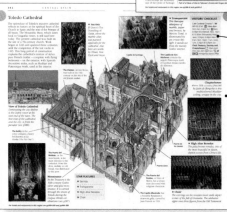

INTRODUCING SPAIN

DISCOVERING SPAIN 10–13
PUTTING SPAIN ON THE MAP 14–17
A PORTRAIT OF SPAIN 18–39
SPAIN THROUGH THE YEAR 40–45
THE HISTORY OF SPAIN 46–71

DISCOVERING SPAIN

Few countries offer more choice to the visitor than Spain, with its lush forests and wild mountain peaks, its busy cities crammed with great art and architecture and the endless stretch of laid-back beach resorts. To find out what you

A ceramic plate made in Seville

want from a trip to Spain amid all this variety, you need to know where to look. These pages offer an at-a-glance guide on where to go, with the different characteristics of each region, city or island group explained and the main sights highlighted.

Finisterre beach, Galicia

GALICIA

- Verdant landscapes
- Santiago de Compostela
- Dramatic coastlines
- Rural idylls

The northwest corner of Spain is the wettest and, because of this, also the greenest region of the country. The medieval city of **Santiago de Compostela** (see pp90–93) draws large numbers of visitors as it stands at the end of a legendary pilgrimage route and centres on an awe-inspiring cathedral. The other great attraction is the

long, heavily indented coastline. One stretch of this, the **Rías Baixas** (see p95), has just the right blend of beaches, low-key holiday resorts and scenery. Inland, Galicia has hills, meadows, forests, monasteries and handsome old towns where time seems slowed down and you can be sure to get away from the crowds.

CANTABRIA AND ASTURIAS

- Picos de Europa mountains
- Enigmatic cave art
- Ancient churches of Oviedo
- Medieval towns

These two regions form the central part of the green north coast. Both are composed of inland uplands descending to a gentle coastline punctuated by pretty bays and good beaches. The two regions share Spain's most approachable mountain range, the **Picos de Europa** (see pp108–109), whose canyons and summits are a draw for

hikers. Prehistory and history are other regional fortes. The most famous of many caves painted by early humans are those of **Altamira** (see p112). The exquisite, pre-Romanesque churches of **Oviedo** (see pp106–7) and the town of **Santillana del Mar** (see p112), seemingly frozen in the Middle Ages, are also worth a visit.

The stunning titanium façade of Museo Guggenheim, Bilbao

THE BASQUE COUNTRY, NAVARRA AND LA RIOJA

- Museo Guggenheim
- San Sebastián beaches
- Pamplona bullrunning
- Superb Riojan wines

The futuristic **Museo Guggenheim** (see pp120–21) has put the city of Bilbao on the map and introduced the Basque Country to a wealth of new visitors, and its two neighbouring regions attract tourists in search of rural Spain. The pride of the Basque's short coast is **San Sebastián** (see p122), a well-established resort on an

Parque Nacional de los Picos de Europa, Cantabria

◁ *Rooftops, Fortna Lux, Mallorca (1969) by Frederick Gore*

almost perfectly rounded bay. Navarra is made up of picturesque green Pyrenean foothills and valleys in the north and charming little towns, castles and Romanesque churches in the south. Its capital, **Pamplona** *(see pp132–3)* – scene of the famous bullrunning festival in July – stands in the middle. For wine-lovers, La Rioja, the smallest region of Spain, is the place to visit.

BARCELONA

- **Gaudí and Modernisme**
- **Contemporary art**
- **Medieval streets**
- **Exhilarating nightlife**

For most people, Barcelona is synonymous with Modernisme, and in particular the enchanting buildings of Antoni Gaudí. It is also famed for its innovation and design, and leads Spain in contemporary art and architecture. At the heart of this city of cutting-edge creativity is the Gothic Quarter, with its well preserved medieval architecture. Barcelona's draw is also in its shops, bars, clubs and street life – any visit has to include a stroll down **Las Ramblas** *(see pp150–51)*.

Barcelona can easily be combined with a beach holiday in one of the resorts a short way north or south of the city.

CATALONIA

- **Cava wine region**
- **Beautiful beaches**
- **Poblet and Montserrat**
- **Dalí masterpieces**

This self-assured region with its own language stretches from the Pyrenees in the north to the rice fields of the Ebro delta in the south, taking in vineyards which produce the famous *cava* sparkling wine. The **Costa Brava** *(see p217)*, a rugged mix of cliffs and bays, is its most attractive strip of coast but the Costa Daurada,

The sculptured rooftop chimneys of Casa Milà ("La Pedrera"), Barcelona

around the Roman city of **Tarragona** *(see pp224–5)*, also has popular resorts. Catalonia also has two of Spain's greatest monasteries: **Poblet** *(see pp222–3)* and **Montserrat** *(see pp218–9)*.

The city of **Figueres** *(see p215)* is the birthplace of Surrealist artist Salvador Dalí, and many of his works can be viewed here.

ARAGÓN

- **Pyrenean grandeur**
- **Ordesa National Park**
- **San Juan de la Peña**
- **Mudéjar architecture**

Aragón is one of the least known regions of Spain, but rewarding to explore. Its sights are grouped to the north and south, with **Zaragoza** *(see pp236–7)*, the country's fifth largest city, in the centre. The Pyrenees and their foothills hold most appeal, particularly the awesome canyons and cliffs of the **Ordesa National Park** *(see pp232–3)*. Also worth seeking out is the secluded monastery of **San Juan de la Peña** *(see p234)*. The mountains are popular for walking, skiing and a range of other sports.

Teruel province in the south is known for its Mudéjar architecture, along with several historic towns, most notably **Albarracín** *(see p241)* and **Teruel** *(see pp240–41)*.

Sculpture in Jaca cathedral, Aragón

VALENCIA AND MURCIA

- **City of Arts and Sciences**
- **Costa Blanca beaches**
- **Baroque architecture**
- **Spectacular fiestas**

These two regions take up the middle of Spain's Mediterranean coast and enjoy a pleasant climate. Valencia city is drawing increasing numbers of visitors to its gleaming white **City of Arts and Sciences** *(see p253)*. The Costa Blanca, a popular coastline, has a range of resorts, from the brash **Benidorm** *(see p260)* to quieter places like **Xàbia** *(see p255)*. The region of Murcia is distinguished by its Baroque architecture and the coastal lagoon of **Mar Menor** *(see p262)*. Both regions have spectacular fiestas, such as the lively Fallas festival in **Valencia** *(see p255)*.

A stretch of golden beach in Calp, Costa Blanca

The imposing San Lorenzo de El Escorial palace, Madrid province

MADRID

• **World famous art museums**
• **Royal residences**
• **Historic squares and streets**
• **Vibrant nightlife**

Spain's capital has three of the world's greatest art museums within an easy stroll of each other: the **Museo del Prado** *(see pp292–5)*, the **Thyssen-Bornemisza** *(see pp288–9)* and the **Centro Reina Sofia** *(see pp298–9)*. Art can also be seen in Madrid's three magnificent royal palaces, two of them – the **Escorial** *(see pp330–31)* and **Aranjuez** *(see p333)* – involving pleasurable day trips into nearby countryside.

The medieval part of the city, meanwhile, is a dense tangle of streets around two squares dotted with many attractive bars and cafés. Madrid is known for its buzzing nightlife, and is also a great place to come for the finest in Spanish cuisine.

CASTILLA Y LEÓN

• **Historic cities**
• **Gothic cathedral of Burgos**
• **Defiant castles**

Distances between sights can be daunting in the country's largest region, but five historic cities reward the intrepid visitor: the harmonious Renaissance university city of **Salamanca**

Detail, Salamanca University

(see pp358–61); **Segovia** *(see pp364–5)* with its towering Roman aqueduct and exquisite royal castle; **Burgos** *(see pp370–73)* built around a Gothic cathedral; **León** *(see pp353–5)*, its cathedral famous for its stained-glass windows; and **Ávila** *(see pp362–3)*, ringed by medieval walls. En route between these cities there are vast empty tracts of land but you are rarely out of sight of a castle, a distinguishing feature of this part of Spain.

CASTILLA-LA MANCHA

• **Historic architecture**
• **Dramatically sited towns**
• **Don Quixote's windmills**

This region is not an obvious choice for many tourists but it does have one of Spain's most attractive cities – **Toledo** *(see pp388–91)*, crammed with interesting architecture from the Middle Ages. Two unusually sited towns also worth a visit are **Cuenca** *(see pp384–5)* perched on a ravine and **Alcalá del Júcar** *(see p395)*, where some of the houses have been extended into the soft rock of the chalky hills into which they are built.

Although daunting at first, the plains of **La Mancha** *(see pp379–99)*, well known for Spain's most famous fictional character, Don Quixote, has a certain charm in its quirky landscape of windmills and castles.

EXTREMADURA

• **Birds and wildflowers**
• **Roman theatre at Mérida**
• **Mansions of Cáceres**
• **Monastery of Guadalupe**

Although not a huge tourist destination, Extremadura has a lot to offer any visitor. With the lowest population density of any region, it has a corresponding richness in wildlife – in spring and summer the countryside is full of wildflowers and storks can be seen nesting on rooftops and church spires.

Extremadura also has a formidable collection of historic monuments, such as the Roman theatre at **Mérida** *(see pp410–11)*, which still hosts performances today, and the cluster of Renaissance mansions at **Cáceres** *(see pp408–9)*. The other place to see is **Guadalupe monastery** *(see pp406–7)*, though a long trek up winding mountain roads is required to get to it.

SEVILLE

• **Cathedral and La Giralda**
• **Moorish Real Alcázar**
• **Bars and bullfighting**
• **Semana Santa (Easter Week)**

This lively southern city on the Guadalquivir River combines the glories of Moorish and Christian Spain in its great cathedral and

The parade of the Virgin during Semana Santa, Seville

La Giralda, its bell tower *(see pp436–7)*, and in the lavishly decorated royal palace of the **Real Alcázar** *(see pp440–41)*.

Visitors also flock to Seville to relish the exciting atmosphere, particularly in the whitewashed streets of the Santa Cruz quarter and, when there's a fight on, in the **Plaza de Toros de la Maestranza** *(see p430)*, Spain's most famous bullring.

Seville is even more animated during the intense celebrations of *Semana Santa* (Holy Week) *(see p431)* and the passionate April Fair that follows, when the city hums to the sound of *Sevillanas*, its own brand of flamenco.

The Alhambra Palace, Granada

ANDALUSIA

- **Flamenco rhythms**
- **Sun and sea**
- **The Alhambra in Granada**
- **Doñana national park**

Stretching from the Atlantic to the Mediterranean across the south of the Iberian peninsula, this is Spain's second largest region and easily the most varied. It is the home to all things "typically Spanish": sherry *(see pp420–21)*, flamenco *(see pp424–5)*, guitars, tapas, gypsies, bullfighting, white towns and the Costa del Sol *(see pp472–3)*. Blazing Mediterranean sunshine makes it a good place for beach holidays, but it is not short of countryside or grandiose monuments either.

Coves d'Arta, Mallorca

The superb Moorish architecture of Granada's **Alhambra Palace** *(see pp490–91)* and the **Mezquita** in Cordoba *(see pp480–81)* continue to dazzle visitors. The region's landscapes vary enormously from the wildlife refuge of **Doñana** *(see pp464–5)* to Europe's only desert in **Almería** *(see p501)*.

THE BALEARIC ISLANDS

- **Beaches, cliffs and coves**
- **Pretty Ibizan villages**
- **Minorcan monuments**

This archipelago off Spain's eastern Mediterranean coast has long been regarded as a holiday playground for Europe. However, as well as beaches, there is plenty of interest to discover. **Mallorca** *(see pp514–21)*, the largest island, has impressive mountains and caves as well as a splendid Gothic cathedral in the capital, **Palma** *(see pp520–21)*.

Despite its reputation for a busy nightlife, **Ibiza** *(see pp510–12)* also has secluded coves, and quiet countryside dotted with pretty villlages. **Menorca** *(see pp522–3)* boasts prehistoric monuments, handsome small towns and a spectacular horse-riding fiesta *(see p523)*.

THE CANARY ISLANDS

- **Subtropical vegetation**
- **Volcanic landscapes**
- **Beaches and watersports**

Most visitors are drawn to the Canaries by their reliable subtropical warmth – despite many of the beaches being composed of black sand. The islands have a great contrast of scenery from luxuriant vegetation to spectacular volcanic formations.

La Gomera, **La Palma** and **El Hierro** *(see pp532–3)* are small but with wonderful scenery making for good hiking. **Lanzarote** *(see pp548–51)*, a choice place for beach holidays, is dry and still volcanically active. **Fuerteventura** *(see pp546–7)* also has beautiful beaches but with a windy climate. **Tenerife** *(see pp534–6)* and **Gran Canaria** *(see pp542–5)* offer the most variety, with northern coasts swathed in banana plantations and lively tourist spots in the hot and sunny south.

A cactus park in San Nicolás de Tolentino, Gran Canaria

Putting Spain on the Map

Spain, in southwestern Europe, covers the greater part
of the Iberian Peninsula. The third largest country in
Europe, it includes two island groups: the Canaries in the
Atlantic and the Balearics in the Mediterranean, and two
small territories in North Africa. Its southernmost point
faces Morocco across a strait,
making Spain a
bridge between
continents.

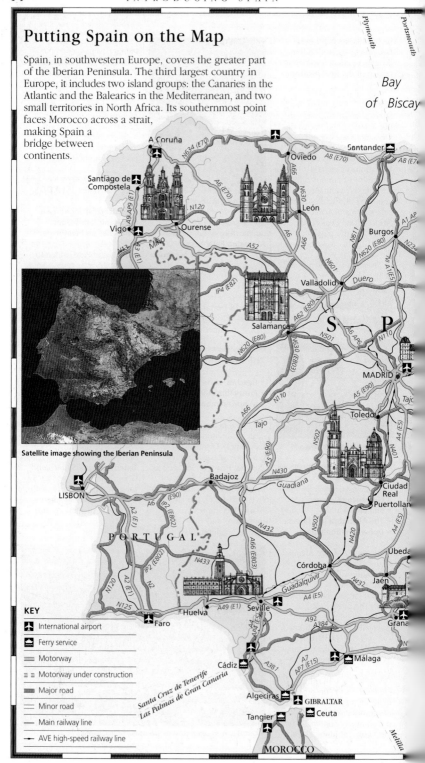

Satellite image showing the Iberian Peninsula

KEY

✈	International airport
⚓	Ferry service
▭	Motorway
▭	Motorway under construction
▭	Major road
▭	Minor road
—	Main railway line
→	AVE high-speed railway line

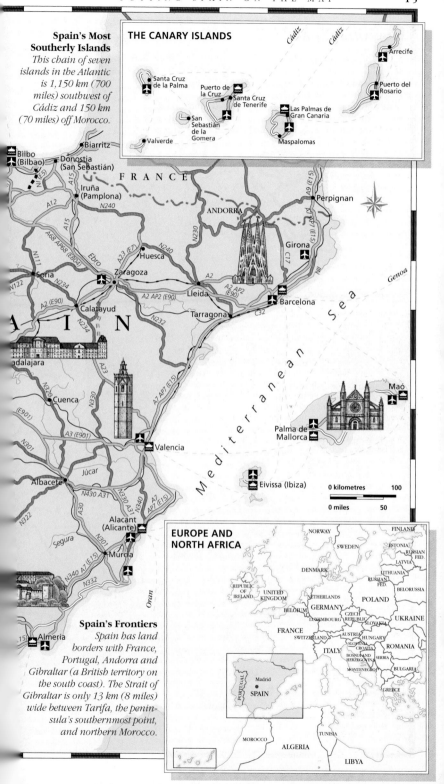

Spain's Most Southerly Islands
This chain of seven islands in the Atlantic is 1,150 km (700 miles) southwest of Cádiz and 150 km (70 miles) off Morocco.

THE CANARY ISLANDS

Cádiz

Cádiz

Arrecife

Santa Cruz de la Palma

Puerto de la Cruz

Santa Cruz de Tenerife

Puerto del Rosario

San Sebastián de la Gomera

Las Palmas de Gran Canaria

Valverde

Maspalomas

Biarritz

Bilbo (Bilbao)

Donostia (San Sebastián)

Iruña (Pamplona)

F R A N C E

ANDORRA

Perpignan

Huesca

Girona

Zaragoza

Lleida

Barcelona

Calatayud

Tarragona

Soria

A I N

Cuenca

Maó

adalajara

Valencia

Palma de Mallorca

Albacete

Alacant (Alicante)

Eivissa (Ibiza)

Murcia

M e d i t e r r a n e a n   S e a

Genoa

Almería

0 kilometres   100

0 miles   50

Spain's Frontiers
Spain has land borders with France, Portugal, Andorra and Gibraltar (a British territory on the south coast). The Strait of Gibraltar is only 13 km (8 miles) wide between Tarifa, the peninsula's southernmost point, and northern Morocco.

EUROPE AND NORTH AFRICA

NORWAY

SWEDEN

FINLAND

ESTONIA

RUSSIAN FED.

DENMARK

LATVIA

LITHUANIA

RUSSIAN FED.

BELORUSSIA

REPUBLIC OF IRELAND

UNITED KINGDOM

NETHERLANDS

POLAND

GERMANY

BELGIUM

LUXEMBOURG

CZECH REPUBLIC

SLOVAKIA

UKRAINE

FRANCE

SWITZERLAND

AUSTRIA

HUNGARY

ROMANIA

SLOVENIA

CROATIA

ITALY

BOSNIA AND HERZEGOVINA

SERBIA

BULGARIA

MONTENEGRO

PORTUGAL

SPAIN

Madrid

GREECE

MOROCCO

ALGERIA

TUNISIA

LIBYA

Regional Spain

Spain has a population of 45 million and receives more than 58 million visitors a year. It covers an area of 504,780 sq km (194,900 sq miles). Madrid is the largest city, followed by Barcelona and Valencia. The country is dominated by a central plateau drained by the Duero, Tagus (Tajo) and Guadiana rivers. This book divides Spain into 15 areas, but officially it has 17 independent regions called *comunidades autónomas*.

GETTING AROUND

Spain's regional capitals and islands are linked by regular flights and there is a shuttle service between Madrid and Barcelona. The TALGO and AVE high-speed trains provide fast rail services and are backed up by regional and local rail networks. Some motorways have expensive tolls, but are fast. The Balearic and Canary islands are served by regular ferries. Be aware that Spain has just changed its road numbering system. Some of the roads featured here may differ from new road signs.

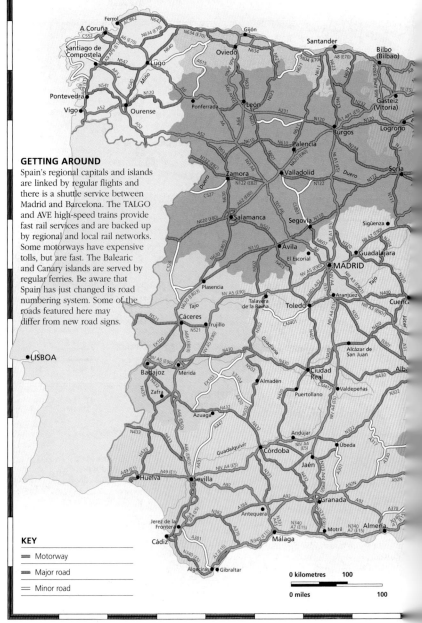

KEY

━━━ Motorway

━━━ Major road

══ Minor road

0 kilometres   100

0 miles   100

Eyewitness Spain Regions

Each of the chapters in this guide has a colour code. The chapters are grouped into five sections: Northern, Eastern, Central and Southern Spain and Spain's Islands; and two cities: Madrid and Barcelona.

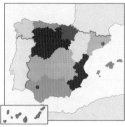

KEY TO COLOUR CODING

Northern Spain

- Galicia
- Asturias and Cantabria
- The Basque Country, Navarra and La Rioja

Eastern Spain

- Barcelona
- Catalonia
- Aragón
- Valencia and Murcia

Central Spain

- Madrid
- Castilla y León
- Castilla-La Mancha
- Extremadura

Southern Spain

- Seville
- Andalusia

Spain's Islands

- The Balearic Islands
- The Canary Islands

ostia
Sebastián)
Iruña
(Pamplona)
Huesca
Tudel
Zaragoza
Lleida
La Seu
d'Urgell
Figueres
Girona
Vic
Manresa
Barcelona
Reus
Tarragona
Tortosa
Ebro
Teruel
Castelló de la Plana
Sagunt
Valencia
Turia
Alcoi
Benidorm
Alacant
(Alicante)
Elx
Murcia
Cartagena
nansa
THE BALEARIC
ISLANDS
Ciutadella
Menorca
Maó
Mallorca
Palma de
Mallorca
Manacor
Cabrera
Ibiza
Eivissa (Ibiza)
Formentera
THE CANARY ISLANDS
Lanzarote
Arrecife
La Palma
Santa Cruz
de la Palma
Fuerteventura
Puerto del
Rosario
Puerto de
la Cruz
Santa Cruz
de Tenerife
Tenerife
La Gomera
San Sebastián
de la Gomera
Las Palmas
de Gran Canaria
Gran Canaria
Maspalomas
El Hierro
Valverde

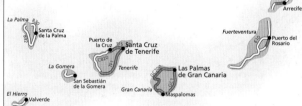

Spain's Atlantic Territories

The Canary Islands, in the Atlantic Ocean off the coast of Africa, are an integral part of Spain. They are one hour behind the rest of the country.

A PORTRAIT OF SPAIN

The familiar images of Spain – flamenco dancing, bullfighting, tapas bars and solemn Easter processions – do no more than hint at the diversity of the country. Spain has four official languages, two major cities of almost equal importance and a greater range of landscapes than any other European country. These remarkable contrasts make Spain an endlessly fascinating country to visit.

Separated from the rest of Europe by the Pyrenees, Spain reaches south to the coast of North Africa. It has both Atlantic and Mediterranean coastlines, and includes two archipelagos – the Balearics and the Canary Islands.

The climate and landscape vary from snow-capped peaks in the Pyrenees, through the green meadows of Galicia and the orange groves of Valencia, to the desert of Almería. Madrid is the highest capital in Europe, and Spain its most mountainous country after Switzerland and Austria. The innumerable sierras have always hindered communications. Until railways were

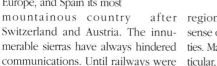

Statue of Don Quixote and Sancho Panza, Madrid

built it was easier to move goods from Barcelona to South America than to Madrid.

In early times, Spain was a coveted prize for foreign conquerors including the Phoenicians and the Romans. During the Middle Ages, much of it was ruled by the Moors, who arrived from North Africa in the 8th century. It was reconquered by Christian forces, and unified at the end of the 15th century. A succession of rulers tried to impose a common culture, but Spain remains as culturally diverse as ever. Several regions have maintained a strong sense of their own independent identities. Many Basques and Catalans, in particular, do not consider themselves to

Landscape with a solitary cork tree near Albacete in Castilla-La Mancha

◁ **The outlandishly dressed *Peliqueiros* who take to the streets during Carnival in Laza, Galicia**

Peñafiel castle in the Duero valley (Castilla y León), built between the 10th and 13th centuries

be Spanish. Madrid may be the nominal capital but it is closely rivalled in commerce, the arts and sport by Barcelona, the main city of Catalonia.

THE SPANISH WAY OF LIFE

The inhabitants of this very varied country have few things in common except for a natural sociability and a zest for living. Spaniards commonly put as much energy into enjoying life as they do into their work. The stereotypical "mañana" (leave everything until tomorrow) is a myth, but time is flexible in Spain and many people bend their work to fit the demands

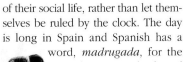

"Vinegar Face" in Pamplona's Los Sanfermines fiesta

of their social life, rather than let themselves be ruled by the clock. The day is long in Spain and Spanish has a word, *madrugada*, for the time between midnight and dawn, when city streets are often still lively.

Spaniards are highly gregarious. In many places people still go out in the evening for the *paseo*, when the streets are crowded with strollers. Eating is invariably communal and big groups often meet up for tapas or dinner. Not surprisingly, Spain has more bars and restaurants per head than any other country in Europe.

Underpinning Spanish society is the extended family. Traditionally, the state in Spain has been very inefficient at providing public services – although this has improved in the last 20 years. The Spanish have therefore always relied on their families and personal connections, rather than institutions, to find work or seek assistance in a crisis. This attitude has sometimes led to a disregard for general interests – such as the environment – when they have conflicted with private ones.

Most Spaniards place their family at the centre of their lives. Three generations may live together under one roof, or at least see each other often. Even

Tables outside a café in Madrid's Plaza Mayor

lifelong city-dwellers refer fondly to their *pueblo* – the town or village where their family comes from and where they return whenever they can. Children are adored in Spain and, consequently, great importance is attached to education. The family in Spain, however, is under strain as couples increasingly opt for a higher income and better lifestyle rather than a large family. One of the most striking transformations in modern Spain has been in the birth rate, from one of the highest in Europe, at 2.72 children for every woman in 1975, to just 1.37 children for every woman in 2006.

The windmills and castle above Consuegra, La Mancha

Virgin of Guadalupe
in Extremadura

Catholicism is still a pervasive influence over Spanish society, although church attendance among those under 35 has declined in recent years to below 20 per cent. The images of saints watch over some shops, bars and lorry drivers' cabs. Church feast days are marked by countless traditional fiestas, which are enthusiastically maintained in modern Spain.

SPORT AND THE ARTS

Spanish cultural life has been reinvigorated in recent years. Spanish-made films – notably those of cult directors Pedro Almodóvar and Alejandro Amenabar – have been able to compete with Hollywood for audiences, and the actor Javier Bardem won an Oscar in 2008. The overall level of reading has risen (but only one in ten buy a daily newspaper), and contemporary literature has steadily gained a wider readership. The performing arts have been restricted by a lack of facilities, but recent major investments have provided new venues, regional arts

A matador plays a bull in the Plaza de Toros de la Maestranza, Seville

Poster for a Pedro Almodóvar film

independent channels and regional TV stations. Sports are one of the mainstays of TV programming. Spanish sportsmen and women have been very successful – for example, tennis player Rafael Nadal and Formula 1 driver Fernando Alonso. Such role models have encouraged participation in sport and new facilities have been provided to meet this demand. Most popular are basketball and, above all, soccer.

Bullfighting has enjoyed renewed popularity since the late 1980s. For aficionados, a *corrida* is a unique occasion that provides a link to Spain's roots, and the noise, colour and argumentative attitude of the crowd are as much of an attraction as the bullfight itself.

centres and new symphony orchestras. The country has produced many remarkable opera singers including Montserrat Caballé, Plácido Domingo and José Carreras. Spain has also excelled in design, particularly evident in the interior furnishings shops of Barcelona.

Spaniards are the most avid TV-watchers in Europe after the British. There are now 16 state-owned TV channels in Spain, as well as

SPAIN TODAY

In the last 40 years Spain has undergone more social change than anywhere else in western Europe. Until the 1950s, Spain was predominantly a poor, rural country, in which only 37 per cent of the population lived in towns of over 10,000 people. By the 1990s, the figure was 65 per cent. As people flooded into towns and cities many rural areas became depopulated. The 1960s saw the beginning of spec-

A farmer with his crop of maize hanging to dry on the outside of his house in the hills of Alicante

Beach near Tossa de Mar on the Costa Brava

Basque terrorist group ETA is a constant thorn in the side of Spanish democracy.

During the 1980s Spain enjoyed an economic boom as service industries and manufacturing expanded. Even so, GDP remains a little below the European Union average and growth has been very unevenly spread around the country. Agriculture is an important industry but while it is highly developed in some regions, it is inefficient in others. Tourism provides approximately ten per cent of the country's earnings. Most tourists still come for beaches. But increasingly, foreign visitors are drawn by Spain's rich cultural heritage and spectacular countryside. Anyone who knows this country, however, will tell you that it is the Spanish people's capacity to enjoy life to the full that is Spain's biggest attraction.

tacular economic growth, partly due to a burgeoning tourist industry. In that decade, car ownership increased from 1 in 100 to 1 in 10.

After the death of dictator General Franco in 1975 Spain became a constitutional monarchy under King Juan Carlos I. The post-Franco era, up until the mid-1990s, was dominated by the Socialist Prime Minister Felipe González. As well as presiding over major improvements in roads, education and health services, the Socialists increased Spain's international standing. The PSOE could not continue forever, however, and in 1996 revelations of a series of scandals lost the PSOE the election. Spain joined the European Community in 1986, triggering a spectacular increase in the country's prosperity. The country's fortunes seemed to peak in the extraordinary year of 1992, when Barcelona staged the Olympic Games and Seville hosted a world fair, Expo '92.

With the establishment of democracy, the 17 autonomous regions of Spain have acquired considerable powers. Several have their own languages, which are officially given equal importance to Spanish (strictly called Castilian). A significant number of Basques favour independence, and the

King Juan Carlos I and Queen Sofía

Demonstration for Catalan independence

Architecture in Spain

Spain has always imported its styles of architecture: Moorish from North Africa, Romanesque and Gothic from France and Renaissance from Italy. Each style, however, was interpreted in a distinctively Spanish way, with sudden and strong contrasts between light and shady areas; façades alternating between austerity and extravagant decoration; and thick walls pierced by few windows to lessen the impact of heat and sunlight. Styles vary from region to region, reflecting the division of Spain before unification. The key design of a central patio surrounded by arcades has been a strong feature of civil buildings since Moorish times.

The 15th-century Casa de Conchas in Salamanca *(see p361)*

ROMANESQUE AND EARLIER (8TH–13TH CENTURIES)

Romanesque churches were mainly built in Catalonia and along the pilgrim route to Santiago *(see p83).* Their distinctive features include round arches, massive walls and few windows. Earlier churches were built in Pre-Romanesque *(see p106)* or Mozarabic *(see p352)* style.

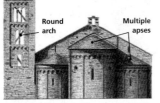

Round arch

Multiple apses

The Romanesque Sant Climent, Taüll *(p201)*

MOORISH (8TH–15TH CENTURIES)

The Moors *(see pp52–3)* reserved the most lavish decoration for the interior of buildings, where ornate designs based on geometry, calligraphy and plant motifs were created in *azulejos* (tiles) or stucco. They made extensive use of the horseshoe arch, a feature inherited from the Visigoths *(see pp50–1).* The greatest surviving works of Moorish architecture *(see pp422–3)* are in Southern Spain.

The **Salón de Embajadores** *in the Alhambra (see p490) has exquisite Moorish decoration.*

GOTHIC (12TH–16TH CENTURIES)

Gothic was imported from France in the late 12th century. The round arch was replaced by the pointed arch which, because of its greater strength, allowed for higher vaults and taller windows. External buttresses were added to prevent the walls of the nave from leaning outwards. Carved decoration was at its most opulent in the Flamboyant Gothic style of the 15th century. After the fall of Granada, Isabelline, a late Gothic style, developed. Meanwhile, Moorish craftsmen working in reconquered areas created the highly decorative hybrid Christian-Islamic style Mudéjar *(see p55).*

Gothic arched window

Rose window

Pointed arch

Tracery

Flying buttress

The nave *of León Cathedral (see pp354–5), built in the 13th century, is supported by rib vaulting and is illuminated by the finest display of stained glass in Spain.*

Sculptural decoration *above the doorways of León cathedral's south front depicted biblical stories for the benefit of the largely illiterate populace.*

RENAISSANCE (16TH CENTURY)

Around 1500 a new style was introduced to Spain by Italian craftsmen and Spanish artists who had studied in Italy. The Renaissance was a revival of the style of Ancient Rome. It is distinguished by its sense of symmetry and the use of the round arch, and Doric, Ionic and Corinthian columns. Early Spanish Renaissance architecture is known as Plateresque because its fine detail resembles ornate silverwork (*platero* means silversmith).

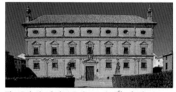

The Palacio de las Cadenas *in Úbeda (see p497) has a severely Classical façade.*

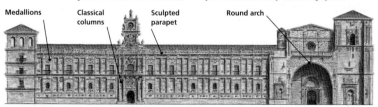

Medallions • Classical columns • Sculpted parapet • Round arch

The Hostal de San Marcos in León *(see p353)*, one of Spain's finest Plateresque buildings

BAROQUE (17TH–18TH CENTURIES)

Baroque was driven by a desire for drama and movement. Decoration became extravagant, with exuberant sculpture and twisting columns. Although the excessive Baroque style of Churrigueresque is named after the Churriguera family of architects, it was their successors who were its main exponents.

The ornamentation *on the Baroque façade of Valladolid University (see p366) is concentrated above the doorway.*

Finials • Statues on parapet

The façade of the Museo Municipal in Madrid *(pp304–5)*

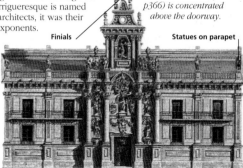

MODERN (LATE 19TH CENTURY ONWARDS)

Modernisme *(see pp140–1)*, a Catalan interpretation of Art Nouveau, is seen at its best in Barcelona. Its architects experimented with a highly original language of ornament. In recent decades, Spain has seen an explosion of bold, functionalist architecture in which the form of a building reflects its use and decoration is used sparingly.

Torre de Picasso in Madrid

Casa Milà, *in Barcelona (see p165), was built in 1910 by Modernisme's most famous and best-loved architect, Antoni Gaudí, who drew much of his inspiration from nature.*

Curving parapet • Spiral chimney • Decorative ironwork

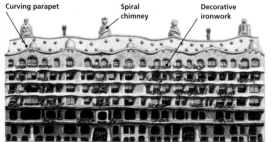

Vernacular Architecture

Window in Navarra

As well as its cathedrals and palaces, Spain has a great variety of charming vernacular buildings. These have been constructed by local craftsmen to meet the practical needs of rural communities and to take account of local climate conditions, with little reference to formal architectural styles. Due to the high expense involved in transporting raw materials, builders used whatever stone or timber lay closest to hand. The three houses illustrated below incorporate the most common characteristics of village architecture seen in different parts of Spain.

A cave church in Artenara *(see p545)*, on Gran Canaria

STONE HOUSE

The climate is wet in the north and houses like this one in Carmona *(see p111)*, in Cantabria, are built with overhanging eaves to shed the rain. Wooden balconies catch the sun.

Detail of stonework

Family and farm *often share rural houses. The ground floor is used to stable animals, or store tools and firewood.*

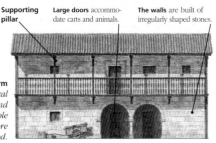

Supporting pillar

Large doors accommodate carts and animals.

The walls are built of irregularly shaped stones.

TIMBER-FRAMED HOUSE

Spain, in general, has few large trees and wood is in short supply. Castilla y León is one of the few regions where timber-framed houses, such as this one in Covarrubias *(see p370)*, can be found. These houses are quick and cheap to build. The timber frame is filled with a coarse plaster mixed from lime and sand, or adobe (bricks dried in the sun).

Half-timbered wall

The ends of the beams supporting the floorboards are visible.

Stone plinths below upright timbers provide protection from damp.

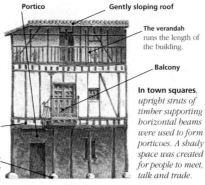

Portico

Gently sloping roof

The verandah runs the length of the building.

Balcony

In town squares, *upright struts of timber supporting horizontal beams were used to form porticoes. A shady space was created for people to meet, talk and trade.*

WHITEWASHED HOUSE

Houses in the south of Spain – often built of baked clay – are regularly whitewashed to deflect the sun's intense rays. Andalusia's famous white towns *(see p468)* exemplify this attractive form of architecture.

Clay-tiled roof

Windows *are small and few in number, and deeply recessed, in order to keep the interior cool.*

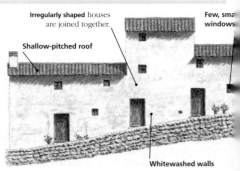

Irregularly shaped houses are joined together.

Shallow-pitched roof

Few, sma windows

Whitewashed walls

THE PLAZA MAYOR

Almost every town in Spain centres on a main square, the plaza mayor, like this one in Pedraza de la Sierra *(see p365)*, near Segovia. More than a market square, it acts as a focus for local life. It is usually overlooked by the church, the town hall, shops and bars and the mansions of aristocratic families.

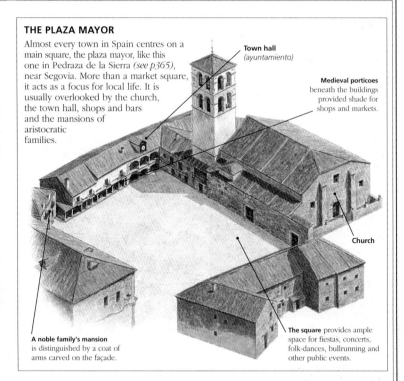

Town hall *(ayuntamiento)*

Medieval porticoes beneath the buildings provided shade for shops and markets.

Church

A noble family's mansion is distinguished by a coat of arms carved on the façade.

The square provides ample space for fiestas, concerts, folk-dances, bullrunning and other public events.

RURAL ARCHITECTURE

A variety of distinctive buildings dots the countryside.

Where the rock is soft and the climate hot, subterranean dwellings have been excavated. Insulated from extremes of temperature, they provide a comfortable place to live.

Hórreos, granaries raised on stone stilts to prevent rats climbing up into the grain, are a common sight in Galicia (where they are stone-built) and Asturias (where they are made of wood). In fields you will often see shelters for livestock or for storing crops, such as the *teitos* of Asturias.

Windmills provided power in parts of Spain where there was little running water but plentiful wind, like La Mancha and the Balearic Islands.

Almost everywhere in the Spanish countryside you will come across *ermitas*, isolated chapels or shrines dedicated to a local saint. An *ermita* may be opened only on the patron saint's feast day.

Cave houses in Guadix near Granada *(see p493)*

Teito in Valle de Teverga in Asturias *(see p105)*

Hórreo, a granary, on the Rías Baixas *(see p95)* **in Galicia**

Windmill above Consuegra *(see p394)* **in La Mancha**

Farming in Spain

Spain's varied geography and climate have created a mosaic of farming patterns ranging from lush dairylands to stony hillsides where goats graze. Land can be broadly divided into *secano*, or dry cultivation (used for olives, wheat and vines), and much smaller areas of *regadío*, irrigated land (planted with citrus trees, rice and vegetables). Farming in many parts is a family affair relying on traditional, labour-intensive methods but it is becoming increasingly mechanized.

Donkey in Extremadura

Plains of cereals *make up much of the farmland of the central meseta of Spain. Wheat is grown in better-watered, more fertile western areas; barley is grown in the drier south.*

Cork oaks thrive in Extremadura and western Andalusia.

MADRID

SEVILLA

0 kilometres   2
0 miles   100

Sheep *grazed on the rough pastures of Central Spain are milked to make cheese, especially* manchego, *which is produced in La Mancha (see p339).*

THE AGRICULTURAL YEAR

	Jul–Aug Wheat harvested in Central Spain	**Sep** Rice harvest in Eastern Spain. Grape harvest at its height	**Oct** Maize harvested in Northern Spain	**Dec–Mar** Olives for making oil picked
			Oct–Nov Table olives picked	
Spring	**Summer**		**Autumn**	**Winter**
Mar–Apr Orange trees in blossom on Mediterranean coast			**Nov–Dec** Oranges picked	**Feb** Almond trees in blossom
	Jun–Aug Haymaking in Northern Spain	**Sep** Start of wild mushroom season	**Dec** Pigs are slaughtered when cold weather arrives	

The high rainfall *and mild summers of Northern Spain make it suitable for dairy farming. Farms are often small, especially in Galicia, one of the country's most under-developed regions. Crops such as maize and wheat are grown in small quantities.*

Wine is produced in many parts of Spain *(see pp606–7)*. The country's best sparkling wine grapes are grown in Catalonia.

BARCELONA ●

Rice is grown in the Ebro delta, in the Marismas del Guadalquivir, around L'Albufera near Valencia and also at Calasparra in Murcia.

Cork oaks are stripped of their bark every ten years

CROPS FROM TREES

The almond, orange and olive create the three most characteristic landscapes of rural Spain but several other trees provide important crops. Wine corks are made from the bark of the cork oak. Tropical species, such as avocado and cherimoya, a delicious creamy fruit little known outside Spain, have been introduced to the so-called Costa Tropical of Andalusia *(see p483)*; and bananas are a major crop of the Canary Islands. Elsewhere, peaches and loquats are also grown commercially. Figs and carobs – whose fruit is used for fodder and as a substitute for chocolate – grow semi-wild.

Oranges, *lemons and clementines are grown on the irrigated coastal plains beside the Mediterranean. The region of Valencia is the prime producer of oranges.*

Almonds *grow on dry hill-sides in many parts of Spain. The spring blossom can be spectacular. The nut, enclosed by a fleshy green skin, is used in a variety of sweetmeats including the Christmas treat turrón (see p201).*

Olive trees *grow slowly and often live to a great age. The fruit is harvested in winter and either pickled in brine for eating as a to extract the oil which is widely used in Spanish cuisine.*

Sweet oranges *are grown in dense, well-irrigated groves near the frost-free coasts. The sweet smell of orange blossom in spring-time is unmistakeable. Trees of the bitter orange are often planted for shade and decoration in parks and gardens.*

Olive trees *are planted in long, straight lines across large swaths of Andalusia, especially in the province of Jaén. Spain is the world's leading producer of olive oil.*

Spain's National Parks

Few other countries in western Europe have such unspoiled scenery as Spain, or can boast tracts of wilderness where brown bears live and wolves hunt. More than 200 nature reserves protect a broad range of ecosystems. The most important areas are the 13 national parks, the first of which was established in 1918. Natural parks (*parques naturales*) regulated by regional governments, are also vital to the task of conservation.

Giant orchid

Clear mountain river, Ordesa

MOUNTAINS

Much of Spain's finest scenery is found in the mountains. Rivers have carved gorges between the peaks of the Picos de Europa. Ordesa and Aigüestortes share some of the most dramatic landscapes of the Pyrenees, while the Sierra Nevada has an impressive range of indigenous wildlife.

Rough terrain in the Picos de Europa

Eagle owls *are Europe's largest owl, easily identified by their large ear tufts. At night they hunt small mammals and birds.*

Chamois *are well adapted to climbing across slopes covered in scree. They live in small groups, always alert to predators, and feed on grass and flowers.*

WETLANDS

Wetlands, including coastal strips and freshwater marshes, are ever-changing environments. Seasonal floods rejuvenate the water providing nutrients for animal and plant growth. These areas are rich feeding grounds for birds. Spain's best-known wetland is Doñana. Tablas de Daimiel, in La Mancha, is much smaller.

Lynx, *endangered by hunting and habitat loss, can occasionally be spotted in Doñana (see pp464–5).*

Black-winged stilts, *with their long, straight legs, are adept at stalking tiny freshwater crustaceans.*

Laguna del Acebuche, Parque Nacional de Doñana

ISLANDS

Cabrera, off Mallorca, is home to rare plants, reptiles and seabirds, such as Eleonara's falcon. The surrounding waters are important for their marine life.

Cabrera archipelago, Balearic Islands

Lizards *are often found in rocky terrain and on cliff faces.*

NATIONAL PARKS

① Mountains

⑤ Wetlands

⑦ Islands

⑨ Woods and Forests

⑪ Volcanic Landscapes

MOUNTAINS

① Picos de Europa *pp108–9*

② Ordesa y Monte Perdido *pp232–3*

③ Aigüestortes y Estany de Sant Maurici *p211*

④ Sierra Nevada *p485*

WETLANDS

⑤ Tablas de Daimiel *p399*

⑥ Doñana *pp464–5*

ISLANDS

⑦ Archipiélago de Cabrera *p517*

⑧ Islas Atlánticas de Galicia *p95*

WOODS AND FORESTS

⑨ Cabañeros *p387*

⑩ Garajonay *p533*

VOLCANIC LANDSCAPES

⑪ Caldera de Taburiente *p532*

⑫ Teide *pp538–9*

⑬ Timanfaya *pp548–9*

VISITORS' CHECKLIST

All but one of the national parks are managed by the Ministerio de Medio Ambiente. **Tel** *915 97 60 00. Parque Nacional d'Aigüestortes y Estany de Sant Maurici is administered jointly with Catalonia's Department of Environment.* **Tel** *973 62 40 36. Most, but not all, of Spain's national parks have visitors' centres.*

WOODS AND FORESTS

Deciduous broad-leaved forests grow in the northwest of Spain, and stands of Aleppo and Scots pine cover many mountainous areas. On the central plateau there are stretches of open woodland of evergreen holm oak and cork oak in the Parque Nacional de Cabañeros. Dense, lush *laurasilva* woodland grows in the Parque Nacional de Garajonay, on La Gomera, one of the smaller Canary Islands.

Parque Nacional de Garajonay

Black vultures *are the largest birds of prey in Europe, with an enormous wingspan of over 2.5 m (8 ft).*

Hedgehogs, *common in woodlands, root among fallen leaves and grass to find worms and slugs.*

VOLCANIC LANDSCAPES

Three very different parks protect parts of the Canary Islands' amazing volcanic scenery. Caldera de Taburiente on La Palma is a volcanic crater surrounded by woods. Mount Teide in Tenerife has unique alpine flora, and Lanzarote's Timanfaya is composed of barren but atmospheric lava fields.

Rabbits *are highly opportunistic, quickly colonizing areas in which they can burrow. In the absence of predators, populations may increase, damaging fragile ecosystems.*

Colonizing plant species, Mount Teide (Tenerife)

Canaries *belong to the finch family of songbirds. The popular canary has been bred from the wild serin, native to the Canaries.*

Spanish Art

Three Spanish painters stand out as milestones in the history of Western art. Diego de Velázquez was a 17th-century court portrait painter and his *Las Meninas* is a seminal work. Francisco de Goya depicted Spanish life during one of its most violent periods. The prolific 20th-century master, Pablo Picasso, is recognized as the founder of modern art. To these names must be added that of El Greco who was born in Crete but who lived in Spain, where he painted religious scenes in an individualistic style. The work of these and Spain's many other great artists can be seen in world-renowned galleries, especially the Prado *(see pp292–5)*.

Self-portrait of Velázquez

The king and queen, reflected in a mirror behind the painter, may be posing for their portrait.

In his series, Las Meninas *(1957), Picasso interprets the frozen gesture of the five-year-old Infanta Margarita. Altogether, Picasso produced 44 paintings based on Velázquez's canvas. They can be seen in Barcelona's Museu de Picasso (see p153).*

RELIGIOUS ART IN SPAIN

The influence of the Catholic Church on Spanish art through the ages is reflected in the predominance of religious imagery. Many churches and museums have Romanesque altarpieces or earlier icons. El Greco *(see p391)* painted from a highly personal religious vision. Baroque religious art of the 17th century, when the Inquisition *(see p274)* was at its height, often graphically depicts physical suffering and spiritual torment.

The Burial of the Count of Orgaz by El Greco (see p390)

LAS MENINAS *(1656)*
In Velázquez's painting of the Infanta Margarita and her courtiers, in the Prado *(see pp292–5)*, the eye is drawn into the distance where the artist's patron, Felipe IV, is reflected in a mirror.

TIMELINE OF GREAT SPANISH ARTISTS

1285–1348 Ferrer Bassá	1390–1410 Pere Nicolau	The Saviour *by José de Ribera*		1598–166 Francisco de Zurbará
1363–95 Jaume Serra	1428–1460 Luis Daimau			1591–1652 José de Ribera
1300		**1400**	**1500**	
	1388–1424 Luis Borrassa	1474–95 Bartolomé Bermejo		1565–162 Francisco Ribalta
		1450–1504 Pedro Berruguete		1599–16 Diego Velázqu
Virgin and Child *by Ferrer Bassá*	1427–52 Bernat Martorell	1541–1614 El Greco		

José Nieto, the queen's chamberlain, stands in the doorway in the background of the painting.

Court jester

Salvador Dalí's painting of the *Colossus of Rhodes* (1954)

MODERN ART

The early 20th-century artists Joan Miró (*see p172*), Salvador Dalí (*see p215*) and Pablo Picasso (*see p152*) all belonged to the Paris School. More recent artists of note include Antonio Saura and Antoni Tàpies (*see p164*). Among many great Spanish art collections, the Centro de Arte Reina Sofia in Madrid (*see pp298–9*) specializes in modern art. Contemporary artists are accorded great prestige in Spain. Their work is to be seen in town halls, banks and public squares, and many towns have a museum dedicated to a local painter.

Collage (1934) by Joan Miró

The Family of King Charles IV *was painted in 1800 by Francisco de Goya (see p239), nearly 150 years after* Las Meninas. *Its debt to Velázquez's painting is evident in its frontal composition, compact grouping of figures and in the inclusion of a self-portrait.*

The Holy Children with the Shell *by Murillo*	**1893–1983** Joan Miró	**1904–89** Salvador Dalí	
	1881–1973 Pablo Picasso	**1923–** Antoni Tàpies	
1746–1828 Francisco de Goya	**1863–1923** Joaquín Sorolla		
1700	**1800**	**1900**	
1642–93 Claudio Coello		**1887–1927** Juan Gris	
18–82 Bartolomé eban Murillo	Jug and Glass *(1916) by Juan Gris*	**1930–1998** Antonio Saura	

Literary Spain

The best-known work of Spanish literature, *Don Quixote* is considered the first modern novel, but Spain has produced many major works over the last 2,000 years. The Roman writers Seneca, Lucan and Martial were born in Spain. Later, the Moors developed a flourishing, but now little-known, literary culture. Although Spanish (Castilian) is the national tongue, many enduring works have been written in the Galician and Catalan regional languages. Basque literature, hitherto an oral culture, is a more recent development. Many foreign writers, such as Alexandre Dumas, Ernest Hemingway and Karel Capek, have written accounts of their travels in Spain.

The 14th-century *El Libro de Buen Amor*

MIDDLE AGES

As the Roman empire fell, Latin evolved into several Romance languages. The earliest non-Latin literature in Spain derives from an oral tradition that arose before the 10th century. It is in the form of *jarchas*, snatches of love poetry written in Mozarab, the Romance language that was spoken by Christians living under the Moors.

In the 12th century, the first poems appeared in Castilian. During the next 300 years, two separate schools of poetry developed. The best-known example of troubadour verse is the anonymous epic, *El Cantar del Mío Cid*, which tells of the heroic exploits of El Cid *(see p370)* during the Reconquest. Works of clerical poetry – for example, Gonzalo de Berceo's *Milagros de Nuestra Señora*, relating the life of the Virgin – convey a moral message.

Spanish literature evolved in the 13th century after Alfonso X the Learned *(see p55)* replaced Latin with Castilian

Alfonso X the Learned (1221–84)

Romance (later called Spanish) as the official language. Under his supervision a team of Jews, Christians and Arabs wrote scholarly treatises. The king himself was a poet, writing in Galician Romance.

The first great prose works in Spanish appeared in the 14th and 15th centuries. *El Libro de Buen Amor*, by an ecclesiastic, Juan Ruiz, is a tale of the love affairs of a priest, interleaved with other stories. Fernando de Rojas uses skilful characterization in *La Celestina* to tell a tragic love story about two nobles and a scheming go-between. This was an age in which tales of chivalry were also popular.

GOLDEN AGE

The prolific Golden Age dramatist, Félix Lope de Vega

The 16th century hailed the start of Spain's Golden Age of literature. But it was also a period of domestic strife. This found expression in the picaresque novel, a Spanish genre originating with the anonymous *El Lazarillo de Tormes*, a bitter reflection on the misfortunes of a blind man's guide.

Spiritual writers flourished under the austere climate of the Counter-Reformation. St John of the Cross's *Cántico Espiritual* was influenced by oriental erotic poetry and the Bible's *Song of Songs*.

The 17th century saw the emergence of more great talents. The life and work of Miguel de Cervantes *(see p333)* straddles the two centuries of the Golden Age. He published his masterpiece, *Don Quixote*, in 1615. Other important writers of the time include Francisco de Quevedo and Luis de Góngora.

Corrales (public theatres) appeared in the 17th century, opening the way for Lope de Vega *(see p290)*, Calderón de la Barca and other dramatists.

Don Quixote's adventures portrayed by José Moreno Carbonero

18TH AND 19TH CENTURIES

Influenced by the French Enlightenment, literature in the 18th century was seen as a way to educate the people. Such was the aim, for instance, of Leandro Fernández de Moratín's comedy *El Sí de las Niñas*. This period saw the development of journalism as well as the emergence of the essay as a literary form. Romanticism had a short and late life in Spain. *Don Juan Tenorio*, a tale of the legendary irrepressible Latin lover by José Zorrilla, is the best-known Romantic play.

José Zorrilla (1817–93)

The satirical essayist Larra stands out from his contemporaries at the beginning of the 19th century. Towards the end of the century, the novel became a vehicle for realistic portrayals of Spanish society. Benito Pérez Galdós, regarded by many to be Spain's greatest novelist after Cervantes, studied the human condition in his *Episodios Nacionales*. The heroine in Clarín's *La Regenta* is undone by the reactionary prejudices of provincial town society.

20TH CENTURY

Writers at the turn of the century, including Pío Baroja *(see p64)*, Miguel de Unamuno and Antonio Machado, described Spain as falling behind the rest of Europe. Ramón María del Valle-Inclán wrote highly satirical plays that created the foundations of modern Spanish theatre. In poetry, the Nobel Prize winner, Juan Ramón Jiménez, strived for pureness of form.

The so-called "Generation of 27" combined European experimental art with Spain's traditional literary subjects. The best-known of them is the poet and playwright Federico García Lorca who was executed by a Fascist firing squad in 1936 *(see p67)*. He drew on the legends and stereotypes of his native Andalusia to make universal statements in his poems and plays, such as *Yerma*.

In the aftermath of the Civil War, many intellectuals who had backed the Republic were forced into exile. The Franco regime tried to create its own propagandist culture. Yet the finest literature of the period was written in spite of the political climate. Camilo José Cela's *La Colmena*, a description of everyday life in the hungry, postwar city of Madrid, set a mood of social realism that inspired other writers.

Since the 1960s, the novel has become increasingly popular due to

Poster for a Lorca play

the emergence of writers like Joan Benet, Julio Llamazares, Antonio Muñoz Molina, José Manuel Caballero Bonald, Juan Marsé and the best-selling Carlos Ruiz Zafón.

The 20th century has also witnessed a surge of great Spanish literature from Latin America. Prominent authors include Jorge Luis Borges and Gabriel García Márquez.

Camilo José Cela, Nobel Prize-winning novelist, by Alvaro Delgado

The Art of Bullfighting

Poster for a bullfight

Bullfighting is a sacrificial ritual in which men (and also a few women) pit themselves against an animal bred for the ring. In this "authentic religious drama", as poet García Lorca described it, the spectator experiences vicariously the fear and exaltation felt by the matador. Although some Spaniards oppose it on grounds of its cruelty, nowadays it is as popular as ever. Many Spaniards see talk of banning bullfighting as striking at the essence of their being, for they regard the *toreo*, the art of bullfighting, as a noble part of their heritage. Bullfights today, however, are often debased by practices which weaken the bull, especially shaving its horns to reduce its aim.

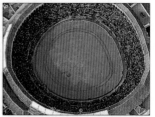

Plaza de Toros de la Maestranza, *Seville. This ring is regarded, with Las Ventas in Madrid, as one of the top venues for bullfighting in Spain.*

The matador wears a *traje de luces* (suit of lights), a colourful silk outfit embroidered with gold sequins.

The passes are made with a *muleta*, a scarlet cape stiffened along one side.

Well treated at the ranch, *the* toro bravo *(fighting bull) is specially bred for qualities of aggressiveness and courage. As aficionados of bullfighting point out in its defence, the young bull enjoys a full life while it is being prepared for its 15 minutes in the ring. Bulls must be at least four years old before they fight.*

THE BULLFIGHT

The *corrida* (bullfight) has three stages, called *tercios*. In the first one, the *tercio de varas*, the matador and *picadores* (horsemen with lances) are aided by *peones* (assistants). In the *tercio de banderillas*, *banderilleros* stick pairs of darts in the bull's back. In the *tercio de muleta* the matador makes a series of passes at the bull with a *muleta* (cape). He then executes the kill, the *estocada*, with a sword.

The matador *plays the bull with a* capa *(red cape) in the* tercio de varas. Peones *will then draw the bull towards the* picadores.

Horses are now padded.

Picadores *goad the bull with steel-pointed lances, testing its bravery. The lances weaken the animal's shoulder muscles.*

THE BULLRING

The *corrida* audience is seated in the *tendidos* (stalls) or in the *palcos* (balcony), where the *presidencia* (president's box) is situated. Opposite are the *puerta de cuadrillas*, through which the matador and team arrive, and the *arrastre de toros* (exit for bulls). Before entering the ring, the matadors wait in a corridor (*callejón*) behind *barreras* and *burladeros* (barriers). Horses are kept in the *patio de caballos* and the bulls in the *corrales*.

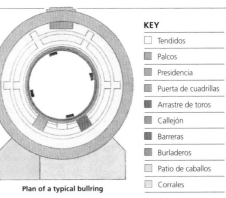

Plan of a typical bullring

KEY

☐	Tendidos
■	Palcos
■	Presidencia
■	Puerta de cuadrillas
■	Arrastre de toros
■	Callejón
■	Barreras
■	Burladeros
☐	Patio de caballos
☐	Corrales

Banderillas, barbed darts, are thrust into the bull's already weakened back muscles.

Manolete *is regarded by most followers of bullfighting as one of the greatest matadors ever. He was eventually gored to death by the bull Islero at Linares, Jaén, in 1947.*

The bull may go free if it shows courage – spectators wave white handkerchiefs, asking the *corrida* president to let it leave the ring alive.

Joselito *is one of Spain's leading matadors today. He is famous for his purist approach and for his flair and technical skill with both the* capa *and the* muleta.

Banderilleros *enter to provoke the wounded bull in the* tercio de banderillas, *sticking pairs of* banderillas *in its back.*

The bull weighs about 500 kg (1,100 lbs).

The matador *makes passes with the cape in the* tercio de muleta, *then lowers it and thrusts in the sword for the kill.*

The estocada recibiendo *is a difficult kill, rarely seen. The matador awaits the bull's charge rather than moving to meet it.*

The Fiestas of Spain

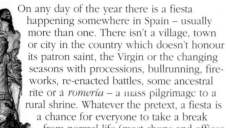

On any day of the year there is a fiesta happening somewhere in Spain – usually more than one. There isn't a village, town or city in the country which doesn't honour its patron saint, the Virgin or the changing seasons with processions, bullrunning, fireworks, re-enacted battles, some ancestral rite or a *romería* – a mass pilgrimage to a rural shrine. Whatever the pretext, a fiesta is a chance for everyone to take a break from normal life (most shops and offices close) and let off steam, with celebrations sometimes going on around the clock.

The Passion, Semana Santa

Many *romerías* wind through the countryside during the year

SPRING FIESTAS

The end of winter and the start of spring are marked by Valencia's great fire festival, Las Fallas *(see p255)*, in which huge papier-mâché sculptures are set alight in a symbolic act of burning the old in order to make way for the new.

Alcoi's noisy mock battles between costumed armies of Moors and Christians in April *(see p255)* are the most spectacular of the countless fiestas which commemorate the battles of the Reconquest.

Seville's great April Fair *(see p431)*, is the biggest celebration held in Andalusia.

During Los Mayos, on 30 April and the following days, crosses are decorated with flowers in parts of Spain.

EASTER

Easter is an important fiesta and most communities observe it in some form with pomp and solemnity.

It is heralded by the processions of Palm Sunday. The most impressive of these is in

Elx, where intricate sculptures are woven from blanched leaves cropped from the most extensive forest of palm trees in Europe *(see p261)*.

The best Semana Santa (Easter Week) processions are those held in Seville *(see p431)*, Málaga, Murcia and Valladolid. Brotherhoods of robed men carry *pasos*, huge sculptures depicting the Virgin, Christ or scenes of the Passion, through the streets. They are accompanied by people dressed as biblical characters or penitents, in tall conical hats. In some towns passion plays are acted out. In others, people carry heavy crosses. Sometimes the centuries-old ritual of self-flagellation can be witnessed.

SUMMER FIESTAS

The first major fiesta of the summer is Pentecost (also known as Whitsun), in May or June, and its most famous celebration is at El Rocío *(see p463)*, where many thousands of people gather in a frenzy of religious devotion.

At Corpus Christi (in May or June) the consecrated host is carried in procession through many cities in an ornate silver monstrance. The route of the procession is often covered with a carpet of flowers. The main Corpus Christi celebrations take place in Valencia, Toledo and Granada.

On Midsummer's Eve, bonfires are lit all over Spain, especially in the areas along the Mediterranean coast, to

The Brotherhood of Candlemas, Semana Santa (Easter Week) in Seville

herald the celebration of St John the Baptist on 24 June.

During Los Sanfermines *(see p128)* in Pamplona in July, young people run through the streets in front of six bulls.

The Virgin of Carmen, who is revered as the patron of fishermen, is honoured in many ports on 16 July.

The important Catholic holiday of Assumption Day, 15 August, is marked by a huge number and variety of fiestas.

AUTUMN FIESTAS

There are few fiestas in autumn, but in most wine regions the grape harvest is fêted. The annual pig slaughter has become a jubilant public event in some villages, especially in Extremadura. In Galicia it is traditional to roast chestnuts on street bonfires.

On All Saints' Day, 1 November, people remember the dead by visiting cemeteries to lay flowers, especially chrysanthemums, on graves.

CHRISTMAS AND NEW YEAR

Nochebuena (Christmas Eve) is the main Christmas celebration, when families gather for an evening meal before attending Midnight Mass, known as *misa del gallo* (Mass of the rooster). During the Christmas period, *belenes* (crib scenes) of painted figurines abound. You may also see a "living crib", peopled by costumed actors.

The losers end up in the harbour in Denia's July fiesta *(see p255)*

Spain's "April Fools' Day" is 28 December, the Day of the Holy Innocents, when people play practical jokes on each other. Clown-like characters may act out the role of mayor and make fun of passers-by.

To celebrate New Year's Eve *(Noche Vieja)*, crowds gather beneath the clock in Madrid's central square, the Puerta del Sol *(see p272)*. Traditionally people eat 12 grapes, one on each chime of midnight, to bring good luck for the year.

Spanish children do not receive their Christmas presents until Epiphany, on 6 January.

WINTER FIESTAS

Animals hold centre stage in a variety of fiestas on 17 January, the Day of St Anthony, patron saint of animals, when pets and livestock are blessed by priests.

St Agatha, the patron saint of married women, is honoured on 5 February when women, for once, are the protagonists of many fiestas. In Zamarramala (Segovia), for example, women take over the mayor's privileges and powers for this particular day *(see p368)*.

St Anthony's Day in Villanueva de Alcolea (Castellón province)

CARNIVAL

Carnival, in February or early March (depending on the date of Easter), brings a chance for a street party as winter comes to an end and before Lent begins. The biggest celebrations are held in Santa Cruz de Tenerife *(see p536)* – comparable with those of Rio de Janeiro – and in Cádiz *(see p463)*. Carnival was prohibited by the Franco regime because of its licentiousness and frivolity. It ends on or after Ash Wednesday with the Burial of the Sardine, a "funeral" in which a mock sardine, representing winter, is ritually burned or buried.

A spectacularly costumed choir singing during Carnival in Cádiz

SPAIN THROUGH THE YEAR

estivals, cultural events and sports competitions crowd the calendar in Spain. Even small villages have at least one traditional fiesta, lasting a week or more, when parades, bullfights and fireworks displays replace work *(see pp38–9)*. Many rural and coastal towns celebrate the harvest or fishing catch with a gastronomic fair at which you can sample local produce.

Matador with a cape playing a bull

Music, dance, drama and film festivals are held in Spain's major cities throughout the year. Meanwhile, the country's favourite outdoor sports – football, basketball, cycling, sailing, golf and tennis – culminate in several national and international championships. It is a good idea to confirm specific dates of events with the local tourist board as some vary from year to year.

SPRING

Life in Spain moves outdoors with the arrival of spring, and terrace-cafés begin to fill with people. The countryside is at its best as wild flowers bloom, and irrigation channels flow to bring water to the newly sown crops. The important Easter holiday is a time of solemn processions throughout the country.

MARCH

International Vintage Car Rally *(mid- or end-Mar)*, from Barcelona to Sitges. **Las Fallas** *(15–19 Mar)*, Valencia *(see p255)*. A spectacular fiesta which also marks the start of the bullfighting *(see pp36–7)* season.
Fiestas Castellón de la Plana *(end Feb or mid-Mar)*. All in honour of Mary Magdalene.

APRIL

Religious Music Week *(week before Easter)*, Cuenca.

Feria del Caballo (Festival of the Horses) in Jerez de la Frontera

Trofeo Conde de Godó *(mid-Apr)*, Barcelona. Spain's international tennis championship.
Moors and Christians *(21–24 Apr)*, Alcoi *(see p258)*. Costumed celebration of the Christian victory over the Moors in 1276.
April Fair *(two weeks after Easter)*, Seville. Exuberant Andalusian fiesta *(see p431)*.
Feria Nacional del Queso *(late Apr/early May)*, Trujillo (Cáceres). A festival celebrating Spanish cheese *(see p407)*.

MAY

Feria del Caballo *(first week)*, Jerez de la Frontera. Horse fair showing Andalusia at its most traditional, with fine horses, and beautiful women in flamenco dresses.
Spanish Motorcycle Grand Prix *(Mar)*, Jerez de la Frontera race track.
Fiestas de San Isidro *(8–15 May)*, Madrid *(see p290)*. Bullfights at Las Ventas bullring are the highlights of the taurine year.
National Flamenco Competition *(mid-May, every third year: 2010, 2013)*, Córdoba. Song, dance and guitar performances.
Spanish Formula One Grand Prix *(May/Jun)*, Montmeló circuit, Barcelona. International motor race.
A Rapa das Bestas *(Jun, Jul and Aug)*, villages of Pontevedra province (Galicia). Wild horses are rounded up so that their manes and tails can be cut *(see p99)*.

Onlookers lining the street during the Vuelta Ciclista a España

San Sebastián, one of the most popular resorts on the north coast

SUMMER

August is Spain's big holiday season. The cities empty as Spaniards flock to the coast or to their second homes in the hills. Their numbers are swelled by millions of foreign tourists, and beaches and camp sites are often full to bursting. As the heat starts in the centre and south, entertainment often takes place only in the evening, when the temperature has dropped. In late summer the harvest begins and there are gastronomic fiestas everywhere to celebrate food and drink, from the fishing catches of the north coast to the sausages of the Balearic Islands.

JUNE

International Festival of Music and Dance *(mid-Jun–early Jul)*, Granada. Classical music and ballet staged in the Alhambra and the Generalife.
Grec Arts Festival *(Jun–Aug)*, Barcelona. Both Spanish and international theatre, music and dance.
Copa del Rey *(Apr–Jun)* Football cup final.

JULY

Classical Theatre Festival *(Jul–Aug)*, Mérida. Staged in the Roman theatre and amphitheatre *(see p410)*.
Guitar Festival *(first two weeks)*, Córdoba. Performances range from classical to flamenco *(see pp424–5)*.
International Classical Theatre Festival of Almagro *(end Jun–end Jul)*. Spanish and classical repertoire performed in one of the oldest theatres in Europe *(see p399)*.

The pouring and tasting of cider in Asturias's Cider Festival

Cider Festival *(second Sat)*, Nava (Asturias). Includes traditional cider-pouring competitions and parties throughout the town.
International Festival of Santander *(Aug)*. Celebration of music, dance and theatre.
Pyrenean Folklore Festival *(late Jul/early Aug, odd years only)*, Jaca (Aragón). Display of folk costumes, music and dance.
International Jazz Festivals in San Sebastián *(third week)*, Getxo *(first week)* and Vitoria *(mid-Jul)*.

AUGUST

Certamen Internacional de Habaneras y Polifonía *(late Jul–early Aug)*, Torrevieja (Alicante). Musical competition of 19th-century seafarers' songs.
HM the King's International Cup *(first week)*, Palma de Mallorca. Sailing competition in which Juan Carlos I participates.
Descent of the Río Sella *(first Sat)*. Canoe race in Asturias from Arriondas to Ribadesella *(see p107)*.
Assumption Day *(15 Aug)* The Assumption is celebrated throughout the country.

Participants in the Descent of the Río Sella canoe race

Semanas Grandes *(early–mid-Aug)*, Bilbao and San Sebastián. "Great Weeks" of sporting and cultural events.
Misteri d'Elx *(11–15 Aug)*, Elx *(see p265)*. Unique liturgical drama performed in a church and featuring spectacular special effects.

Vines and the village of Larouco in the Valdeorras wine region of Galicia *(see p78)* in autumn

AUTUMN

Autumn usually brings rain after the heat of summer, and with the high tourist season over, a large number of resorts practically close down. Harvest festivities continue, however, and the most important celebrations are in honour of the grape. The first pressings are blessed and, in some places, wine is served for free.

Wild mushrooms

In woodland areas, freshly picked wild mushrooms start to appear in various dishes on local restaurant menus. The hunting season begins in the middle of October and runs until February. Autumn is also the start of the new drama and classical music seasons in the major cities of Spain.

SEPTEMBER

Vuelta Ciclista a España *(Sep)*. Annual bicycle race around Spain.
International Folklore Gala *(late Aug/early Sep)*, Ronda (Málaga). Music and dancing.
Grape Harvest *(first week)*, Jerez de la Frontera. Celebration of the new crop in the country's sherry capital.
Madrid Autumn Festival *(mid-Sep–mid-Nov)*. Drama, dance and music by national and foreign companies.
San Sebastián Film Festival *(last two weeks)*. Gathering of film-makers *(see p123)*.
Bienal de Arte Flamenco *(last two weeks, even years only)*, Seville. Top flamenco artists perform.

OCTOBER

Día de la Hispanidad *(12 Oct)*. Spain's national holiday marks Columbus's discovery

of America in 1492. The biggest celebration in the country is the exuberant fiesta of Día del Pilar in Zaragoza *(see p239)*, which marks the end of the bullfighting year.

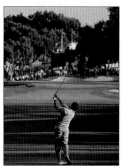

Driving down the fairway in the Volvo Masters Golf Championship

Moors and Christians *(mid-Oct)*, Callosa D'en Sarria (Alicante). Parades in honour of the local madonna.
Saffron Festival *(late Oct)*, Consuegra (Toledo).
Volvo Masters Golf Championship *(late Oct, early Nov)*, Valderrama

NOVEMBER

All Saints' Day *(1 Nov)*. The start of the *matanza* (pig slaughter) in rural Spain.
Os Magostos *(11 Nov)*. Chestnut-harvest fairs in Galicia.
Latin American Film Festival *(last two weeks)*, Huelva *(see p462)*.

Lana Turner on centre-stage at the San Sebastián Film Festival

PUBLIC HOLIDAYS

Besides marking the national holidays below, each region *(comunidad autónoma)* celebrates its own holiday and every town and village has at least one other fiesta each year. If a holiday falls on a Tuesday or a Thursday shops, offices and monuments may also be closed on the intervening Monday or Friday, making a long weekend called a *puente* ("bridge").

Año Nuevo *(New Year's Day)* (1 Jan)
Día de los Tres Reyes *(Epiphany)* (6 Jan)
Jueves Santo *(Maundy Thursday)* (Mar/Apr)
Viernes Santo *(Good Friday)* (Mar/Apr)
Día de Pascua *(Easter Sunday)* (Mar/Apr)
Día del Trabajo *(Labour Day)* (1 May)
Asunción *(Assumption Day)* (15 Aug)
Día de la Hispanidad *(National Day)* (12 Oct)
Todos los Santos *(All Saints' Day)* (1 Nov)
Día de la Constitución *(Constitution Day)* (6 Dec)
Inmaculada Concepción *(Immaculate Conception)* (8 Dec)
Navidad *(Christmas Day)* (25 Dec)

Assumption Day in La Alberca (Salamanca)

WINTER

Winter varies greatly from region to region. In the mountains, snowfalls bring skiers to the slopes; while in lower areas, olive and orange picking are in full swing. The higher parts of Central Spain can become very cold. Andalusia, the east coast and the Balearic Islands have cool nights but often sunny days. The winter warmth of the Canary Islands brings the high tourist season. Christmas is a special time of celebration – an occasion for families to re-unite, share food and attend religious celebrations.

Skiers in the Sierra de Guadarrama, north of Madrid *(see p329)*

"El Gordo", the largest Spanish lottery prize, being drawn

DECEMBER

El Gordo *(22 Dec)*. Spain's largest lottery prize, "the Fat One", is drawn *(see p622)*.
Noche Buena *(24 Dec)* is a family Christmas Eve, fol-lowed by Midnight Mass.
Santos Inocentes *(28 Dec)*, Spain's version of April Fools' Day, when people play tricks.
Noche Vieja *(31 Dec)*. New Year's Eve is most celebrated in Madrid's Puerta del Sol.

JANUARY

Canary Islands International Music Festival *(Jan–Feb)*. Classical concerts are held on La Palma and Tenerife.
Opera Season *(Jan–Apr)*, Palacio de la Música y Con-gresos Euskelduna, Bilbao.

Día de los Tres Reyes *(6 Jan)*. On the eve of the Epiphany, the Three Kings parade through town, throwing sweets to the children.

FEBRUARY

Festival of Ancient Music *(Feb–Mar)*, Seville. Played on period instruments.
ARCO *(mid-Feb)*, Madrid. International contemporary art fair attracting galleries from across the world.
Pasarela Cibeles (Fashion Week) *(mid-Feb)*, Madrid. Women's and men's fashion shows in the capital.
Carnival *(Feb/Mar)*. Final fiesta before Lent, with col-ourful costumes. Those in Santa Cruz de Tenerife and Cádiz are among the best.

The Climate of Spain

Spain's large landmass, with its extensive high plateaus and mountain ranges, and the influences of the Mediterranean and Atlantic produce a wide range of climatic variation, especially in winter. The north is wettest year round, while the eastern and southern coasts and the islands have mild winters, while winter temperatures in the interior are often below freezing. Summers everywhere are hot, except in upland areas.

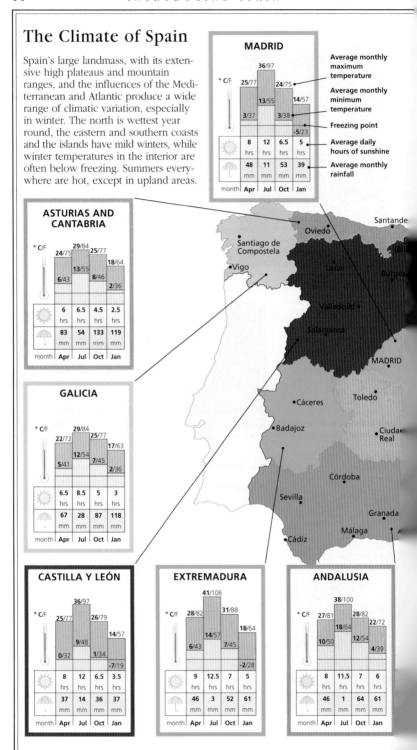

MADRID

- Average monthly maximum temperature
- Average monthly minimum temperature
- Freezing point
- Average daily hours of sunshine
- Average monthly rainfall

°C/F	Apr	Jul	Oct	Jan
max	25/77	36/97	24/75	14/57
min	3/37	13/55	3/38	-5/23
☀ hrs	8	12	6.5	5
☂ mm	48	11	53	39

ASTURIAS AND CANTABRIA

°C/F	Apr	Jul	Oct	Jan
max	24/75	29/84	25/77	18/64
min	6/43	13/55	8/46	2/36
☀ hrs	6	6.5	4.5	2.5
☂ mm	83	54	133	119

GALICIA

°C/F	Apr	Jul	Oct	Jan
max	22/72	29/84	25/77	17/63
min	5/41	12/54	7/45	2/36
☀ hrs	6.5	8.5	5	3
☂ mm	67	28	87	118

CASTILLA Y LEÓN

°C/F	Apr	Jul	Oct	Jan
max	25/77	36/97	26/79	14/57
min	0/32	9/48	1/34	-7/19
☀ hrs	8	12	6.5	3.5
☂ mm	37	14	36	37

EXTREMADURA

°C/F	Apr	Jul	Oct	Jan
max	28/82	41/106	31/88	18/64
min	6/43	14/57	7/45	-2/28
☀ hrs	9	12.5	7	5
☂ mm	46	3	52	61

ANDALUSIA

°C/F	Apr	Jul	Oct	Jan
max	27/81	38/100	28/82	22/72
min	10/50	18/64	12/54	4/39
☀ hrs	8	11.5	7	6
☂ mm	46	1	64	61

Santander
Oviedo
Santiago de Compostela
Vigo
León
Burgos
Valladolid
Salamanca
MADRID
Toledo
Cáceres
Badajoz
Ciudad Real
Córdoba
Sevilla
Granada
Málaga
Cádiz

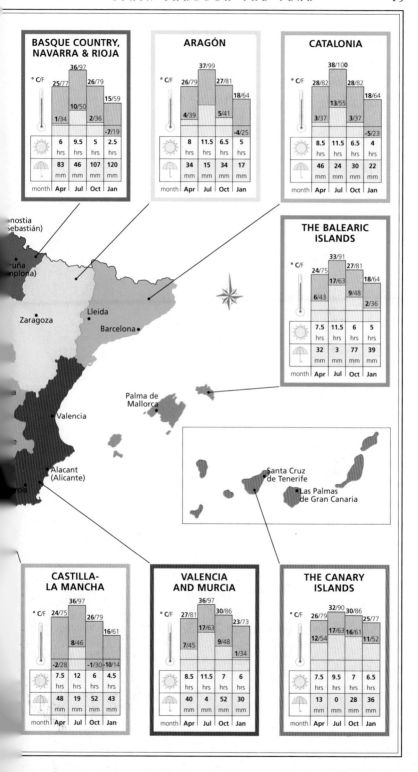

BASQUE COUNTRY, NAVARRA & RIOJA

°C/F

36/97
25/77 26/79
10/50 15/59
1/34 2/36
-7/19

	6 hrs	9.5 hrs	5 hrs	2.5 hrs
	83 mm	46 mm	107 mm	120 mm
month	Apr	Jul	Oct	Jan

ARAGÓN

°C/F

37/99
26/79 27/81
18/64
4/39 5/41
-4/25

	8 hrs	11.5 hrs	6.5 hrs	5 hrs
	34 mm	15 mm	34 mm	17 mm
month	Apr	Jul	Oct	Jan

CATALONIA

°C/F

38/100
28/82 28/82
13/55 18/64
3/37 3/37
-5/23

	8.5 hrs	11.5 hrs	6.5 hrs	4 hrs
	46 mm	24 mm	30 mm	22 mm
month	Apr	Jul	Oct	Jan

THE BALEARIC ISLANDS

°C/F

33/91
24/75 27/81
17/63 18/64
6/43 9/48
2/36

	7.5 hrs	11.5 hrs	6 hrs	5 hrs
	32 mm	3 mm	77 mm	39 mm
month	Apr	Jul	Oct	Jan

nostia
Sebastián)

ruña
mplona)

Zaragoza • Lleida •
Barcelona •

Palma de
Mallorca

• Valencia

• Alacant
(Alicante)

Santa Cruz
de Tenerife
• Las Palmas
de Gran Canaria

CASTILLA- LA MANCHA

°C/F

36/97
24/75 26/79
16/61
8/46
-2/28 -1/30 -10/14

	7.5 hrs	12 hrs	6 hrs	4.5 hrs
	48 mm	19 mm	52 mm	43 mm
month	Apr	Jul	Oct	Jan

VALENCIA AND MURCIA

°C/F

36/97
27/81 30/86
17/63 23/73
7/45 9/48
1/34

	8.5 hrs	11.5 hrs	7 hrs	6 hrs
	40 mm	4 mm	52 mm	30 mm
month	Apr	Jul	Oct	Jan

THE CANARY ISLANDS

°C/F

32/90 30/86
26/79 25/77
17/63 16/61
12/54 11/52

	7.5 hrs	9.5 hrs	7 hrs	6.5 hrs
	13 mm	0 mm	28 mm	36 mm
month	Apr	Jul	Oct	Jan

THE HISTORY OF SPAIN

The Iberian Peninsula, first inhabited around 800,000 BC, has long been subject to foreign influences. From the 11th century BC it was colonized by sophisticated eastern Mediterranean civilizations, starting with the Phoenicians, then the Greeks and Carthaginians.

The Romans arrived in 218 BC to fight the Carthaginians, thus sparking off the Second Punic War. They harvested the peninsula's agricultural and mineral wealth and established cities with aqueducts, temples and theatres.

Pre-Columbian gold statue

With the fall of the Roman Empire in the early 5th century AD, Visigothic invaders from the north assumed power. Their poor political organization, however, made them easy prey to the Moors from North Africa. In the 8th century, the peninsula came almost entirely under Moorish rule. Europe's only major Muslim territory, the civilization of Al Andalus excelled in mathematics, geography, astronomy and poetry. In the 9th and 10th centuries Córdoba was Europe's leading city.

From the 11th century, northern Christian kingdoms initiated a military reconquest of Al Andalus. The marriage, in 1469, of Fernando of Aragón and Isabel of Castile, the so-called Catholic Monarchs, led to Spanish unity. They took Granada, the last Moorish kingdom, in 1492. Columbus discovered the Americas in the same year, opening the way for the Spanish conquistadors, who plundered the civilizations of the New World.

The succeeding Habsburg dynasty spent the riches from the New World in endless foreign wars. Spain's decline was exacerbated by high inflation and religious oppression. Although the Enlightenment in the late 18th century created a climate of learning, Spain's misfortunes continued into the next century with an invasion by Napoleon's troops and the loss of her American colonies. A new radicalism began to emerge, creating a strong Anarchist movement. The political instability of the late 19th and early 20th centuries led to dictatorship in the 1920s and a republic in the 1930s, which was destroyed by the Spanish Civil War. Victorious General Franco ruled by repression until his death in 1975. Since then Spain has been a constitutional monarchy.

Bullfighting in Madrid's Plaza Mayor in the 17th century

◁ Moors paying homage to Fernando and Isabel, the 15th-century Catholic Monarchs

Prehistoric Spain

Helmet of Celt-Iberian warrior

The Iberian Peninsula was first inhabited by hunter-gatherers around 800,000 BC. They were eclipsed by a Neolithic farming population from 5000 BC. First in a wave of settlers from over the Mediterranean, the Phoenicians landed in 1100 BC, to be followed by the Greeks and Carthaginians. Invading Celts mixed with native Iberian tribes (forming the Celtiberians). They proved a formidable force against the Romans, the next conquerors of Spain.

SPAIN IN 5000 BC

☐ *Neolithic farming settlements*

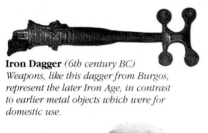

Iron Dagger *(6th century BC)*
Weapons, like this dagger from Burgos, represent the later Iron Age, in contrast to earlier metal objects which were for domestic use.

The 28 bracelets have perforations and moulded decorations.

Small silver bottle

Stone Age Man
This skull belongs to a Palaeolithic man, who hunted deer and bison with tools made of wood and stone.

Incised geometric pattern

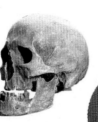

La Dama de Elche
Dating from the 4th century BC, this stone statue is a fine example of Iberian art. Her austere beauty reveals traces of Greek influence.

THE VILLENA TREASURE

Discovered in 1963 during works in Villena, near Alicante, this Bronze Age find consists of 66 dazzling objects mostly of gold, including bowls, bottles and jewellery *(see p260).* The treasure dates from around 1000 BC.

TIMELINE

800,000 BC *Homo erectus* arrives in Iberian Peninsula	**35,000 BC** Cro-Magnon man evolves in Spain	**2500 BC** Los Millares *(p501)* is inhabited by early metal-workers with belief in the afterlife
300,000 BC Tribes of *Homo erectus* live in hunting camps in Soria and Madrid		

1800–110 Civilization of El A an advanced agri society, flourish southeast

800,000 BC	2500	2000

500,000 BC Stones used as tools by hominids (probably *Homo erectus*)	**100,000–40,000 BC** Neanderthal man in Gibraltar	**5000 BC** Farming begins in Iberian Peninsula

18,000–14,000 BC Drawings by cave dwellers at Altamira (Cantabria), near Ribadesella (Asturias) and at Nerja (Andalusia)

Bison cave drawing, Altamira

Greek Ceramic Vase
The Greek colonizers brought new technology, including the potter's wheel, as well as refined artistic ideals. Ceramics, such as this 6th-century BC vase depicting the Labours of Hercules, provided sophisticated models.

The largest of the treasure's five bottles, made of silver, stands 22.5 cm (9 in) high.

Bowls of beaten gold may have originated in southwest Spain.

Brooches with separate clasps

The smaller pieces are of unknown use.

WHERE TO SEE PREHISTORIC SPAIN

The most famous cave paintings in Spain are at Altamira *(see p112)*. There are dolmens in many parts of the country; among the largest are those at Antequera *(see p475)*. The Guanches – the indigenous inhabitants of the Canary Islands – left behind more recent remains *(see p547)*.

La Naveta d'es Tudons *is one of the many prehistoric stone monuments scattered across the island of Menorca (see p527).*

An excavated Celtic village, *with its round huts, can be seen near A Guarda in Pontevedra (see p97).*

Astarte *(8th century BC) Worship of Phoenician deities was incorporated into local religions. One of the most popular was the fertility goddess Astarte, shown on this bronze from the kingdom of Tartessus.*

Phoenician gold ornament

1100 BC Phoenicians believed to have founded modern-day Cádiz

600 BC Greek colonists settle on northeast coast of Spain

228 BC Carthaginians occupy southeast Spain

1500 **1000** **500**

1200 BC The "talaiotic" people of Menorca erect three unique types of stone building: *taulas, talaiots* and *navetas*

Taula *in Menorca*

775 BC Phoenicians establish colonies along the coast near Málaga

300 BC *La Dama de Elche* is carved (p296)

700 BC Semi-mythical kingdom of Tartessus thought to be at its height

Carthaginian glass necklace

Romans and Visigoths

The Romans came to Spain to fight the Carthaginians and take possession of the Iberian Peninsula's huge mineral wealth. Later, Hispania's wheat and olive oil became mainstays of the empire. It took 200 years to subdue the peninsula, which was divided in three provinces: Tarraconensis, Lusitania and Baetica. In time, cities with Roman infrastructure developed. The fall of the empire in the 5th century left Spain in the hands of the

Roman vase

Visigoths, invaders from the north. Politically disorganized, they fell victim to the Moors in 711.

SPAIN (HISPANIA) IN 5 BC

☐ *Tarraconensis*

☐ *Lusitania*

☐ *Baetica*

Trajan *(AD 53–117)*
Trajan was the first Hispanic Roman emperor (AD 98–117). He improved public administration and expanded the empire.

Portico overlooking the gardens

Good acoustics at every level

A Classical façade served as a backdrop for tragedies. Additional scenery was used for comedies.

Seneca *(4 BC–AD 65)*
Born in Córdoba, the Stoic philosopher Seneca lived in Rome as Nero's adviser.

The *orchestra*, a semicircular open space for the choir

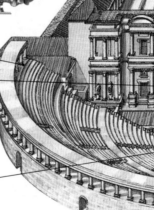

Visigothic Relief
This crude Visigothic stone carving, based on a Roman relief, is in the 7th-century church of Quintanilla de las Viñas, near Burgos (p370).

The auditorium seated over 5,000. The audience was placed according to social status.

TIMELINE

218 BC Scipio the Elder lands with a Roman army at Emporion *(p216)*. The Second Punic War begins

c.200 BC Romans reach Gadir (modern Cádiz) after driving Carthaginians out of Hispania

155 BC Lusitanian Wars begin. Romans invade Portugal

26 BC Emerita Augusta (Mérida) is founded and soon becomes capital of Lusitania

19 BC Augustus takes Cantabria and Asturias, ending 200 years of war

200 BC	100	AD 1	AD

219 BC Hannibal takes Saguntum *(p249)* for Carthaginians

Hannibal

133 BC Celt-Iberian Wars culminate in destruction of Numantia, Soria *(p377)*

61 BC Julius Caesar, governor of Hispania Ulterior, begins final conquest of northern Portugal and Galicia

82–72 BC Roman Civil War. Pompey founds Pompaelo (Pamplona) in 75 BC

AD 74 Empe Vespasian gr Latin status t towns in His completing process of Romanizatic

Gladiator Mosaic

Mosaics were used as decoration both indoors and out. Themes range from mythical episodes to portrayals of daily life. This 4th-century AD mosaic shows gladiators in action and has helpful labels to name the fighters and show who is dead or alive.

WHERE TO SEE ROMAN SPAIN

Like Mérida, Tarragona *(see p224)* has extensive Roman ruins and Itálica *(see p476)* is an excavated town. A magnificent Roman wall rings Lugo in Galicia *(see p99)*. Built in Trajan's rule, the bridge over the Tagus at Alcántara *(see p410)* has a temple on it.

Emporion *a Roman town, was built next to a former Greek colony in the 3rd century BC. The ruins include grand villas and a forum (see p216).*

Segovia's Roman aqueduct (see p365), *a huge monument with 163 arches, dates from the end of the 1st century AD.*

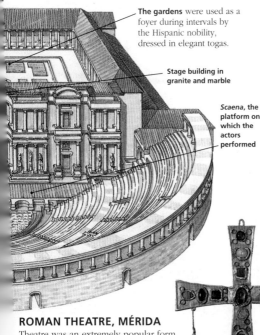

The gardens were used as a foyer during intervals by the Hispanic nobility, dressed in elegant togas.

Stage building in granite and marble

Scaena, the platform on which the actors performed

ROMAN THEATRE, MÉRIDA

Theatre was an extremely popular form of entertainment in Hispania. This reconstruction shows the theatre at Mérida *(see p410)*, built in 16–15 BC.

Visigothic Cross

Although Visigothic kings seldom ruled long enough to make an impact on society, the early Christian Church grew powerful. Fortunes were spent on churches and religious art.

Mosaic from Mérida

415 Visigoths establish their court at Barcelona

409 Vandals and their allies cross Pyrenees into Tarraconensis

446 Romans attempt to win back rest of Hispania

476 Overthrow of the last Roman emperor leads to end of Western Roman Empire

200	300	400	500

258 Franks cross Pyrenees into Tarraconensis and sack Tarragona

312 Christianity officially recognized as religion under rule of Constantine, the first Christian emperor

The Codex Vigilianus, a Christian manuscript

589 Visigothic King Reccared converts from Arianism to Catholicism at Third Council of Toledo

Al Andalus: Muslim Spain

The arrival of Arab and Berber invaders from North Africa, and their defeat of the Visigoths, gave rise to the most brilliant civilization of early medieval Europe. These Muslim settlers, often known as the Moors, called Spain "Al Andalus". A rich and powerful caliphate was established in Córdoba and mathematics, science, architecture and the decorative arts flourished. The caliphate eventually broke up into small kingdoms or *taifas*. Meanwhile small Christian enclaves expanded in the north.

Alhambra Vase
(see p467)

SPAIN IN AD 750

☐ *Extent of Moorish domination*

The palace, dating from the 11th century, was surrounded by patios, pools and gardens.

Water Wheel
Moorish irrigation techniques, such as the water wheel, revolutionized agriculture. New crops, including oranges and rice, were introduced.

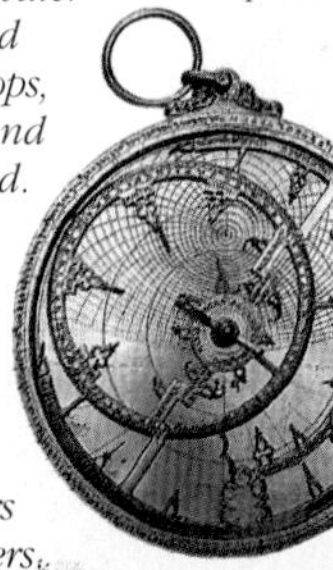

Astrolabe
Perfected by the Moors around AD 800, the astrolabe was used by navigators and astronomers.

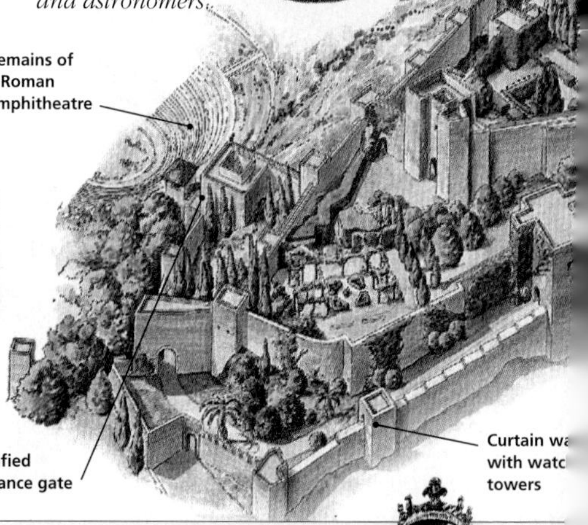

Remains of a Roman amphitheatre

Silver Casket of Hisham II
In the Caliphate of Córdoba, luxury objects of brilliant craftsmanship were worked in ivory, silver and bronze.

Fortified entrance gate

Curtain wa
with watc
towers

TIMELINE

711 Moors, led by Tariq, invade Spain and defeat Visigoths at battle of Guadalete

732 Moors' advance into France is halted by Charles Martel at Poitiers

778 Charlemagne's rearguard defeated by Basques at Roncesvalles *(p134)*

785 Building of great mosque at Córdoba begins

Charlemagne (742–814)

750

800

850

722 Led by Pelayo, Christians defeat Moors at Covadonga *(p109)*

756 Abd al Rahman I proclaims independent emirate in Córdoba

744 Christians under Alfonso I of Asturias take León

Pelayo (718–37)

822 Abd al Rahman II begins 30-year rule marked by patronage of the arts and culture

c.800 Tomb of St James (Santiago) is supposedly discovered at Santiago de Compostela

Puerta de Sabbath in Córdoba's Mezquita
Wealth and artistic brilliance were lavished on mosques, especially in Córdoba (see pp480–1). Calligraphy was a major element in decoration.

WHERE TO SEE MOORISH SPAIN

The finest Moorish buildings are in Andalusia, mainly in the cities of Córdoba *(see pp478–9)* and Granada *(see pp486–92)*. Almería *(see p501)* has a large, ruined *alcazaba* (castle). In Jaén *(see p493)* there are Moorish baths. Further north, in Zaragoza, is the castle-palace of La Aljafería *(see p237).*

Medina Azahara (see p477), *sacked in the 11th century but partly restored, was the final residence of Córdoba's caliphs.*

Torre del Homenaje, the keep, was built by Abd al Rahman I (756–88).

Baths

Patio with Moorish decoration

ALCAZABA AT MÁLAGA

An *alcazaba* was a castle built into the ramparts of a Moorish city, often protected by massive concentric walls. In Málaga *(see p474)* – the principal port of the Moorish kingdom of Granada – the vast Alcazaba was built in the 8–11th centuries on the site of a Roman fortress, and incorporated massive curtain walls and fortified gates.

Moorish Sword
A fine example of late Moorish craftsmanship, this sword has a golden pommel. The blade is inscribed with Arabic writing.

Warrior Helmet
Practical as well as ornate, this Islamic nobleman's helmet, made of iron, gold and silver, incorporates inscriptions, a coat of arms and chain mail.

905 Emergent Navarra becomes Christian kingdom under Sancho I

976 Al Mansur, military dictator, usurps caliphal powers and sacks Barcelona. Córdoba Mezquita finished

1010 Medina Azahara sacked by Berbers

900

950

1000

913 Christian capital is established at León

936 Building of Medina Azahara palace starts near Córdoba

Bronze stag from Medina Azahara

1013 Caliphate of Córdoba breaks up. Emergence of *taifas*: small, independent Moorish kingdoms

The Reconquest

The infant Christian kingdoms in the north – León, Castile, Navarra, Aragón and Catalonia – advanced south gradually in the 11th century, fighting in the name of Christianity to regain land from the Moors. After the fall of Toledo in 1085, the struggle became increasingly a holy war. Militant North African Muslims – Almoravids and Almohads – rallied to the Moorish cause and ultimately took over Al Andalus in the 12th century. As the Christians pushed further south, soon only Granada remained under Moorish control.

Cross of the Knights of St James

SPAIN IN 1173

☐ *Christian kingdoms*

■ *Al Andalus*

Golden Goblet
The exquisite goblet (1063) of Doña Urraca, daughter of Alfonso VI, shows the quality of medieval Christian craftsmanship.

Fernando I
Fernando formed the first Christian power bloc in 1037 by uniting León with Castile, which was emerging as a major military force.

Armies of Castile, Aragón and Navarra

The Almohads fight until the bitter end, although many comrades lay slain.

LAS NAVAS DE TOLOSA
The Christian victory over the Almohads in the battle of Las Navas de Tolosa (1212) led to Moorish Spain's decline. The army of Muhammad II al Nasir was no match for the forces of Sancho VII of Navarra, Pedro II of Aragón and Alfonso VIII of Castile. A stained-glass window in Roncesvalles *(see p134)* depicts the battle.

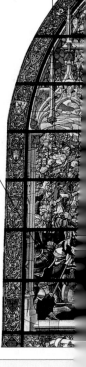

Alhambra, Palace of the Nasrids
Moorish art and architecture of singular beauty continued to be produced in the Nasrid kingdom of Granada. Its apogee is the exquisite Alhambra (see pp490–1).

TIMELINE

1037 León and Castile united for first time under Fernando I

1065 Death of Fernando I precipitates fratricidal civil war between his sons

1086 Almoravids respond to pleas for help from Moorish emirs by taking over *taifas* (splinter states)

Uniforms of military orders

1158 Establishment of the Order of Calatrava, the first military order of knights in Spain

	1050	1100	1150

El Cid

1085 Toledo falls to Christians under Alfonso VI of Castile

1094 The legendary El Cid *(see p370)* captures Valencia

1137 Ramón Berenguer IV of Catalonia marries Petronila of Aragón, uniting the two kingdoms under their son, Alfonso II

1143 Portugal becomes separate kingdom

1147 Almohads arrive in Al Andalus and make Seville their capital

1212 Comb Christian fo defeat Almo at battle o Navas de To

Cantigas of Alfonso X *(1252–84)*
This detail of a manuscript by Alfonxo X portrays the confrontation between Moorish and Christian cavalry. Alfonso the Learned encouraged his scholars to master Arab culture and translate ancient Greek manuscripts brought by the Moors.

Sancho VII of Navarra leads the Christian forces.

St James (Santiago)
Known as the Moorslayer, St James is said to have miraculously intervened at the Battle of Clavijo in 844. This powerful figurehead is the patron saint of Spain.

WHERE TO SEE MUDÉJAR SPAIN

The Mudéjares – Muslims who remained in territories under Christian occupation – created a distinctive architectural style distinguished by its ornamental work in brick, plaster and ceramics. Aragón, particularly Zaragoza *(see pp236–7)* and Teruel *(see pp240–41)*, boasts some of the finest Mudéjar buildings. Seville's Reales Alcázares is an exquisitely harmonious collection of patios and halls built under Pedro I *(see pp440–1)*.

The Mudéjar tower *of Teruel cathedral combines both brick and colourful ceramics to highly decorative effect.*

Santa María la Blanca (see p393), *a former synagogue and church, shows the fusion of cultures in medieval Toledo.*

Foundation of
~~Salam~~anca University

1230 Fernando III reunites Castile and León

Crest of Castile and León

1385 Portuguese defeat Castilians at Aljubarrota, crushing King Juan's aspirations to throne of Portugal

1388–9 Treaties end Spanish phase of Hundred Years War

1250	1300	1350	1400

1250 Toledo at its height as a centre of translation and learning, influenced by Alfonso X the Learned

1386 Invasion of Galicia by the English, ended by Bayonne Treaty

1232 Granada becomes capital of future Nasrid kingdom. Building of the Alhambra begins

Alfonso X

1401 Work starts in Seville on what was then the world's largest Gothic cathedral

The Catholic Monarchs

The foundation of the Spanish nation-state was laid by Isabel I of Castile and Fernando II of Aragón *(see p70)*. Uniting their lands in military, diplomatic and religious matters, the "Catholic Monarchs", as they are known, won back Granada, the last Moorish kingdom, from Boabdil. The Inquisition gave Spain a reputation for intolerance, yet in art and architecture brilliant progress was made and the voyages of Columbus opened up the New World.

Fernando of Aragón

SPAIN'S EXPLORATION OF THE NEW WORLD

— *Route of Columbus's first voyage*

Tomb of El Doncel (15th century)
This effigy of a page who died in the fight for Granada combines ideals of military glory and learning (see p383).

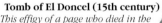

Boabdil, the grief-stricken king, moves forward to hand over the keys to Granada.

Alhambra

The Inquisition
Active from 1478, the Inquisition (see p274) persecuted those suspected of heresy with increasing vigour. This member of the Brotherhood of Death took victims to the stake.

Baptizing Jews
After the Christian reconquest of Granada, Jews were forced to convert or leave Spain. The conversos (converted Jews) were often treated badly.

THE FALL OF GRANADA *(1492)*
This romantic interpretation by Francisco Pradilla (1846–1921) reflects the chivalry of Boabdil, ruler of Granada, as he surrenders the keys of the last Moorish kingdom to the Catholic Monarchs, Fernando and Isabel, following ten long years of war.

TIMELINE

1454 Enrique IV, Isabel's half-brother, accedes to throne of Castile

1465 Civil war erupts in Castile

1478 Papal bull authorizes Castilian Inquisition with Tomás de Torquemada as Inquisitor General

Torquemada

1450	1460	1470	1480

1451 Birth of Isabel of Castile

Fernando and Isabel on 15th-century gold coin

1469 Marriage of Fernando and Isabel in Valladolid unites Castile and Aragón

1474 Death of Enrique IV leads to civil war; Isabel triumphs over Juana la Beltraneja, Enrique's supposed daughter, to become queen

1479 Fernando becomes Fernando II of Aragón

Columbus Arriving in the Americas

The Catholic Monarchs financed Columbus's daring first voyage partly because they hoped for riches in return, but also because they expected him to convert infidels.

Boabdil

As the forlorn king left Granada, his mother reputedly said, "Don't cry as a child over what you could not defend as a man".

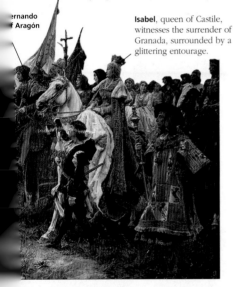

Fernando of Aragón

Isabel, queen of Castile, witnesses the surrender of Granada, surrounded by a glittering entourage.

Crown of Isabel

Worn at the surrender, Isabel's crown is now in her final resting place, the Capilla Real in Granada (see p486).

WHERE TO SEE GOTHIC ARCHITECTURE IN SPAIN

Spain has many great Gothic cathedrals, especially in Seville *(pp436–37)*, Burgos *(pp372–3)*, Barcelona *(pp148–9)*, Toledo *(pp392–3)* and Palma de Mallorca *(pp520–1)*. Secular buildings from this era include commodity exchanges like La Lonja in Valencia *(p251)* and castles *(pp344–5)*.

León cathedral (pp354–5) *has a west front covered in statuary. Here Christ is seen presiding over the Last Judgment.*

1494 Treaty of Tordesillas divides the New World territories between Portugal and Spain

1496 Foundation of Santo Domingo, on Hispaniola, first Spanish city in the Americas

1509 Cardinal Cisneros' troops attack Oran in Algeria and temporarily occupy it

Cardinal Cisneros

1490

1500

1510

1492 Fall of [Gra]nada after ten-[year] war. Columbus [re]aches America. [Exp]ulsion of Jews from Spain

1502 Unconverted Moors expelled from Spain

Columbus's ship, the Santa María

1504 Following death of Isabel, her daughter Juana la Loca becomes queen of Castile with Fernando as regent

1516 Death of Fernando

1512 Annexation of Navarra, leading to full unification of Spain

The Age of Discovery

Following Columbus's arrival in the Bahamas in 1492, the conquistadors went into Central and South America, conquering Mexico (1519), Peru (1532) and Chile (1541). In doing so, they destroyed Indian civilizations. In the 16th century, vast quantities of gold and silver flowed across the Atlantic to Spain. Carlos I and his son Felipe II spent some of it on battles to halt the spread of Protestantism in Europe, and in the Holy War against the Turks.

Aztec god (c.1540)

SPANISH EMPIRE IN 1580

☐ *Dominions of Felipe II*

Mapping the World
This 16th-century German map reflects a new world, largely unknown to Europe before the era of conquistadors.

Galleons were armed with cannons as a defence against pirates and rival conquerors.

Aztec Mask
In their great greed and ignorance, the Spanish destroyed the empires and civilizations of the Aztecs in Mexico and the Incas in Peru.

The lookout was essential for spotting enemies and making landfall.

Forecastle

Seville
Granted the trading monopoly with the Americas, Seville, on the banks of the Guadalquivir, was Europe's richest port in the early 16th century.

TIMELINE

1519 Magellan, Portuguese explorer, leaves Seville under Spanish patronage to circumnavigate the globe	**1520-21** Revolt by Castilian towns when Carlos I appoints foreigner, Adrian of Utrecht, as regent	**1532** Pizarro takes Peru with 180 men and destroys Inca empire	**1554** International Ca alliance created by ma of future king Fe with Mary Tud Er

Pizarro

1520	**1530**	**1540**

1519 Conquest of Mexico by Cortés. Carlos I crowned Holy Roman Emperor Charles V

Conquistador Hernán Cortés

1540 Father Bartolomé de las Casas writes book denouncing the oppression of Indians

Bartolomé de las Casas

Defeat of the Spanish Armada
Spain's self-esteem suffered a hard blow when its "invincible" 133-ship fleet was destroyed in an attempt to invade Protestant England in 1588.

NEW WORLD CROPS

Not only did Spain profit from the gold and silver brought across the ocean from the Americas, but also from an amazing range of new crops. Some, **Cacao plant** including potatoes and maize, were introduced for cultivation in Spain while others, such as tobacco and cacao, were mainly grown in native soil. Cocoa, from cacao beans, gained favour as a drink.

Peruvian with exotic New World fruit

Armour of Felipe II
Felipe II (1556–98) was a cunning administrator, who claimed to rule the world with paper rather than military might.

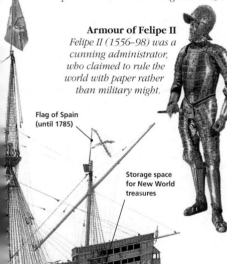

Flag of Spain (until 1785)

Storage space for New World treasures

SPANISH GALLEON

Although sturdily built to carry New World treasure back to Spain, these ships were hard to manoeuvre except with the wind behind. They were often no match for smaller, swifter pirate vessels.

Carlos I *(1516–56)*
During his tumultuous 40-year reign, Carlos I (Holy Roman Emperor Charles V) often led his troops on the battlefield.

57 First of a series of ~~par~~tial bankruptcies of Spain

1561 Building of El Escorial, near Madrid, begins

El Escorial (see pp330–31)

1588 Spanish Armada fails in attack on Britain

1560	1570	1580	1590

1561 Madrid becomes capital of Spain

1571 Spanish victory over Turks in naval battle of Lepanto

1580 Portugal unites with Spain for the next 60 years

8 Moriscos (converted Moors) ~~th~~e Alpujarras (Granada) rebel ~~agains~~t high taxes and persecution

1569 Bible published for first time in Castilian

The Golden Age

Spain's Golden Age was a time of great artistic and literary achievement led by the painters – El Greco and Velázquez *(see pp32–3)* – and writers *(see pp34–35)*, especially Cervantes and the prolific dramatists, Lope de Vega and Calderón de la Barca. This brilliance occurred, however, against a background of economic deterioration and ruinous wars with the Low Countries and France. Spain was gradually losing its influence in Europe and the reigning house of Habsburg entered irreversible decline.

THE SPANISH EMPIRE IN EUROPE IN 1647

☐ Spanish territories

Don Quixote and Sancho Panza
Cervantes' satire on chivalrous romance, Don Quixote, contrasts the fantasy of the main character with his servant's realism.

A clock is a reminder of the inevitable passage of time.

The knight is dressed in mid-17th-century fashion.

Money represents worldly wealth.

Duke of Lerma
This bronze statue depicts the Duke of Lerma (c.1550–1625), a favourite of King Felipe III.

THE KNIGHT'S DREAM *(1650)*
This painting, attributed to Antonio de Pereda, is on a familiar Golden Age theme: human vanity. A young gentleman sits asleep beside a table piled with objects symbolizing power, wealth and mortality. The pleasures of life, we are told, are no more real than a dream.

TIMELINE

Felipe III

1600 Capital temporarily moves to Valladolid

1605 Publication of first of two parts of Cervantes' Don Quixote

1609 Felipe III orders the expulsion of the Moriscos

1619 Construction of Plaza Mayor, Madrid

1609 Lope de Vega publishes poem on the art of comic drama

1621 Low Countries war resumes after 12-year truce

1625 Capture of Breda, Netherlands, after one-year siege

1622 Velázquez moves from Seville to Madrid to become court painter the following year

Lope de Vega (1562–1635)

1643 Fall Count-D Olivares. Sp heavily defea by Franc battle of Ro

1640 Secession of Portugal, amalgamated with Spain since 1580

1600	1610	1620	1630	1

Fiesta in the Plaza Mayor in Madrid
This famous square (see p273) became the scene for pageants, royal celebrations, bullfights and executions, all overlooked from the balconies.

SEVILLE SCHOOL OF ART

Seville's wealth, together with the patronage of the Church, made it a centre of the arts, second only to the royal court. Velázquez, who was born in Seville, trained under the painter Pacheco. Sculptor Juan Martínez Montañés and painters Zurbarán and Murillo created great works which are displayed in the Museo de Bellas Artes *(see p430).*

San Diego de Alcalá Giving Food to the Poor (c.1646) by Murillo

An angel warns that death is near.

The banner says, "It [death] pierces perpetually, flies quickly and kills".

A mask symbolizes the Arts.

Expulsion of the Moriscos
Although they had converted to Christianity, the last Moors were still expelled in 1609.

Weapons represent power.

skull on the book ws death triumphant r learning.

Surrender of Breda
Spain took the Dutch city of Breda on 5 June 1625 after a year-long siege. The event was later painted by Velázquez.

1652 Spanish troops regain Catalonia, following 12-year war with France	*Calderón de la Barca*	**1669** Calderón de la Barca's last work, La Estátua de Prometeo, is published		**1683–4** Louis XIV attacks Catalonia and Spanish Netherlands		
1650	**1660**	**1670**	**1680**	**1690**	**1700**
8 Holland achieves pendence from n by Treaty of phalia, ending hirty Years War	**1659** Peace of the Pyrenees signed with France. Louis XIV marries Felipe IV's daughter María Teresa, leading to Bourbon succession in Spain		*Coin from the reign of Felipe IV*	**1700** Death of Carlos II brings Habsburg line to an end. Felipe V, the first Bourbon king, ascends the throne

Bourbons to First Republic

The War of the Spanish Succession ended in triumph for the Bourbons, who made Spain a centralized nation. Their power was at its height during the reign of the enlightened despot, Carlos III. But the 19th century was a troubled time. An invasion by revolutionary France led to the War of Independence (Peninsular War). Later came the Carlist Wars – caused by another dispute over the succession – liberal revolts and the short-lived First Republic.

Isabel II

SPAIN IN 1714

☐ *Domain after Treaty of Utrecht*

The Enlightenment
The Enlightenment brought new learning and novel projects. On 5 July 1784 this Montgolfier balloon rose above Madrid.

A Franciscan friar is among the innocent victims.

Queen María Luisa
The dominating María Luisa of Parma, portrayed by Goya, forced her husband Carlos IV to appoint her lover, Manuel Godoy, prime minister in 1792.

Spanish rebel faces death in a gesture of crucifixion.

Battle of Trafalgar
The defeat of the Franco-Spanish fleet by the British admiral, Lord Nelson, off Cape Trafalgar in 1805 was the end of Spanish sea power.

Hundreds of live were taken in th executions, whi lasted several d

TIMELINE

1702–14 War of the Spanish Succession. Spain loses Netherlands and Gibraltar by Treaty of Utrecht

1724 Luis I (son of Felipe V) gains throne when his father abdicates, but dies within a year; Felipe V reinstated

1767 Carlos III expels Jesuits from Spain and Spanish colonies

1700	1720	1740	1760

1714 Siege and reduction of Barcelona by Felipe V

Felipe V, the first Bourbon king (1700–24)

Count of Floridablanca (1728–1808)

1762–3 English government declares war on Spanish over colonies in America

1782 Count of Floridablanca he to recover Menorca from Engla

Carlos III Leaving Naples
When Fernando VI died without an heir in 1759, his half-brother Carlos VII of Naples was put on the Spanish throne as Carlos III. His enlightened reign saw the founda- tion of academies of science and art and the beginning of free trade.

French soldiers, operating on orders from Marshal Murat, execute Spanish patriots.

General Prim *(1814–70)*
General Prim was one of 19th-century Spain's most influential figures. He forced the abdication of Isabel II, and pursued liberal poli- cies until assassinated in Madrid.

French infantry helmet

THE 3RD OF MAY BY GOYA *(1814)*

On 2 May 1808, in reaction to Napoleon's occupation of Spain, the people of Madrid rose in vain against the occupying French forces. The next day the French army took its revenge by executing hundreds of people, both rebels and bystanders. These events sparked off the War of Independence.

Baroque Magnificence
The sacristy of the Monasterio de la Cartuja in Granada is typical of Spanish Baroque, more sumptu- ous than anywhere else in Europe.

| 1805 Battle of Trafalgar. Nelson defeats French and Spanish at sea | 1809 Wellington's troops join with Spanish to triumph over French at Talavera | | 1841–3 María Cristina, followed by General Espartero, acts as regent for Isabel II |
| | *Duke of Wellington* | | 1868 Revolution under General Prim forces Isabel II into exile. Amadeo I is king for three years from 1870 |

| **1800** | **1820** | | **1840** | **1860** |

| 1808–14 Joseph Bonaparte on throne. War of Independence | 1824 Peru is the last South American country to gain independence | 1833–9 First Carlist War | 1836 Mendizábal seizes monastic property for the Spanish state | *Carlist soldiers* |
| 1812 Promulgation of liberal constitution in Cádiz leads to military uprising | | | 1847–9 Second Carlist War | |

Republicans and Anarchists

Spain's First Republic lasted only a year (1873) and consumed four presidents. The late 19th century was a time of national decline, with Anarchism developing in reaction to rampant political corruption. The loss of Cuba, in 1898, was a low point for Spain, although there was a flurry of literary and artistic activity in the following years. The country's increasing instability was briefly checked by the dictatorship of Primo de Rivera. Spanish politics, however, were becoming polarized. Alfonso XIII was forced to abdicate and the ill-fated Second Republic was declared in 1931.

Primo de Rivera

THE LEGACY OF SPANISH COLONIZATION IN 1900

☐ *Spanish-speaking territories*

Anarchist Propaganda
Anarchism was idealistic, though often violent. This poster states, "Anarchist books are weapons against Fascism".

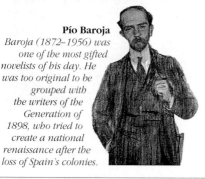

Workers unite, calling for radical social reform.

Pío Baroja
Baroja (1872–1956) was one of the most gifted novelists of his day. He was too original to be grouped with the writers of the Generation of 1898, who tried to create a national renaissance after the loss of Spain's colonies.

POWER TO THE PEOPLE
Political protest was rife under the Second Republic, as shown by this Communist demonstration in the Basque Country in 1932. Industrial workers banded together, forming trade unions to demand better pay and working conditions, and staging strikes. The Spanish Communist Party developed later than the Anarchists, but eventually gained more support.

TIMELINE

1873 Declaration of First Republic, lasting only one year

First Republic's last president, Emilio Castelar (1832–99)

1888 Universal Exhibition in Barcelona creates new buildings and parks, such as the Parc de la Ciutadella

1897 Prime Minister Cán del Castillo assassinated an Italian Anarchist

1870

1880

1890

1875 Second Bourbon restoration puts Alfonso XII on throne

Alfonso XII and Queen María

1893 Anarchists bomb opera-goers in the Barcelona Liceu

1898 Cuba and Philippines gain independence from Spain following the Spanish-American War

1870–75 Third Carlist War

Tragic Week
Led by Anarchists and Republicans, workers in Barcelona took to the streets in 1909 to resist a military call-up. The reprisals were brutal.

Universal Exhibitions
In 1929, Seville and Barcelona were transformed by exhibitions promoting art and industry. The fairs brought international recognition.

The banner appeals for working-class solidarity.

Picasso
Born in Málaga in 1881, the artist Pablo Picasso spent his formative years as a painter in the city of Barcelona (see p148) before moving to Paris in the 1930s.

Cuban War of Independence
Cuba began its fight for freedom in 1895, led by local patriots such as Antonio Maceo. In the disastrous campaign, Spain lost 50,000 soldiers and most of its navy.

The Garrotte
Convicted Anarchists were executed by the garrotte – an iron collar that brutally strangled the victim while crushing the neck.

1912 Prime Minister José Canalejas murdered by Anarchists in Madrid	*Second Republic election poster* **1921** Crushing defeat of Spanish army at Anual, Morocco	**1931** Proclamation of Second Republic with a two-year coalition between Socialists and Republicans	**1933** General election returns right-wing government
1910	**1920**	**1930**	
1909 Semana Trágica (Tragic Week) in Barcelona. Workers' revolt against conscription for Moroccan Wars quashed by Government troops	**1923** Primo de Rivera stages victorious coup to become military dictator under Alfonso XIII	**1930** Primo de Rivera resigns after losing military support **1931** Republicans win local elections, causing Alfonso XIII to abdicate	**1934** Revolution of Asturian miners suppressed by army under General Franco

Civil War and the Franco Era

Nationalist generals rose against the government in 1936, starting the Spanish Civil War. The Nationalists, under General Franco, were halted by the Republicans outside Madrid, but with support from Hitler and Mussolini they inched their way to victory in the north and east. Madrid finally fell in early 1939. After the war, thousands of Republicans were executed in reprisals. Spain was internationally isolated until the 1950s, when the United States brought her into the western military alliance.

Franco

SPAIN ON 31 JULY 1936

☐ *Republican-held areas*

■ *Nationalist-held areas*

Franco's Ideal World
Under Franco, Church and state were united. This poster shows the strong influence of religion on education.

POR LAS ARMAS

La Patria el Pan y la Justicia.

Nationalist Poster
A Nationalist poster adorned with Fascist arrows reads "Fight for the Fatherland, Bread and Justice".

Anguished mother with dead child

Composition reflecting total chaos

GUERNICA *(1937)*
On behalf of advancing Nationalists, the Nazi Condor Legion bombed the Basque town of Gernika *(see p118)* on 26 April 1937 – a busy market day. This was Europe's first air raid on civilians, and inspired Picasso's shocking *Guernica* *(see p299)*. Painted for a Republican Government exhibition in Paris, it is full of symbols of disaster.

TIMELINE

1936 Republican Popular Front wins the general election on 16 January. On 17 July, Nationalist generals rise against Republicans	**1938** On 8 January, Republicans lose battle for Teruel in bitter cold	**1945** By end of World War II, Spain is diplomatically and politically isolated
	1939 In March, Madrid, Valencia and Alicante fall in quick succession to Franco's troops	**1947** Spain declared monarch with Franco as regent
1935	**1940**	**1945**	**1950**
1936 Nationalists declare Franco head of state on 29 September	**1939** Franco declares end of war on 1 April and demands unconditional surrender from Republicans	**1953** Deal wi permits American on Spanish s exchange f
1937 On 26 April, Nazi planes bomb Basque town of Guernica (Gernika-Lumo)	**1938** On 23 December, Nationalists bomb Barcelona	

Soldiers surrender to Nationalist tro

GARCIA LORCA

Federico García Lorca (1898–1936) was Spain's most brilliant dramatist and lyric poet of the 1920s and 1930s. His homosexuality and association with the left, however, made him a target for Nationalist assassins. He was shot by an ad hoc firing squad near his home town of Granada.

Scene from his play *Blood Wedding*

Anarchist Poster
Anarchists fought for the Republic, forming agricultural collectives behind the lines. Their influence waned when they were discredited by the Communist Party.

A wounded horse representing the Spanish people

Witnesses to the massacre stare in wonder and disbelief.

Crucifixion gesture

The flower is a symbol of hope in the midst of despair.

The Hungry Years
Ration cards illustrate the post-war period when Spain nearly starved. Shunned by other nations, she received aid from the US in 1953 in return for accepting military bases.

Spanish Refugees
As the Nationalists came closer to victory, thousands of artists, writers, intellectuals and other Republican supporters fled Spain into indefinite exile.

1962 Tourism on the Mediterranean coast is boosted by official go-ahead

Sunbathers

1969 Franco declares Prince Juan Carlos his successor

1973 ETA assassinates Admiral Carrero Blanco, Franco's hard-line prime minister

1960	1965	1970	1975

1959 Founding of ETA, Basque separatist group

Spain joins United Nations

Franco's funeral, 23 November 1975

1970 "Burgos trials" of the regime's opponents outrage world opinion

1975 Death of Franco results in third Bourbon restoration as Juan Carlos is proclaimed king

Modern Spain

Franco's death left Spain's political future hanging in the balance. But few people wanted to preserve the old regime and the transition from dictatorship to democracy proved surprisingly swift and painless. The previously outlawed Socialist Workers' Party, under Felipe González, won the general election in 1982 and set about modernizing Spain. Considerable power has since been devolved to the regions. A major threat facing central government has been the persistent violence of ETA, the Basque separatist organization. Spain's international relations have been strengthened by her membership of NATO and the European Union.

Contemporary Spanish fashion

SPAIN TODAY

☐ *Spain*

▨ *Other European Union states*

Castilla and León's modern pavilion was one of EXPO's 150 pavilions built to innovative designs.

Hi-tech floodlight

Coup d'Etat, 23 February 1981
Civil Guard colonel, Antonio Tejero, held parliament at gunpoint for several hours. Democracy survived because King Juan Carlos refused to support the rebels.

Anti-NATO Protest Rally
When Spain joined NATO in 1982, some saw it as a reversal of Socialist ideals. To others it represented an improvement in Spain's international standing.

EXPO '92
Over 100 countries were represented at the Universal Exposition, which focused world attention on Seville in 1992. The many pavilions displayed scientific, technological and cultural exhibits.

TIMELINE

Spanish royal family

1977 First free elections return centrist government under Adolfo Suárez. Political parties, including Communists, are legalized

1981 Military officers stage attempted coup d'etat to overthrow democracy

1983 Semi-autonomous regional governments are established to appease Basque Country and Catalonia

1992 Barcelona and Seville Expo place Spain firmly community of m European natio

1980	1985	1990

1982 Landslide electoral victory brings Socialist Workers' Party (PSOE), under Felipe González, to power. Football World Cup held in Spain

1986 Spain joins EC (now EU) and NATO

1992 Spain celebrates quincentenary of Columbus's voyage to America

199 Corrup scan rock long-ser governm

Felipe González Elected
In 1982 the Spanish Socialist Workers' Party (PSOE) leader was elected prime minister. González transformed Spain during his 13 years in power.

Tourism
From 1959–73 the number of annual visitors to Spain grew from 3 million to 34 million, transforming once-quiet coasts and islands.

Leaning blue tower rises above Andalusia's pavilion.

Ana Belén
Spanish women have enjoyed ever greater freedom and opportunity since the advent of democracy. In a 1980s opinion poll, they voted the singer and actress, Ana Belén, the woman they most admired.

El País
Founded in Madrid in 1976, the liberal daily El País is the best-selling newspaper in Spain. During the transition to democracy it had a great influence on public opinion.

EL PAÍS

onorail
ied visitors
nd the site.

Barcelona Olympic Games
The opening ceremony of the Barcelona Olympics included stunning displays of music, dance and colourful costumes.

Cobi, Barcelona Olympic Mascot

2000 Spain celebrates 25 years of democracy and reign of Juan Carlos I

2004 Madrid is hit by the worst terrorist attacks in Spain's modern history in March. Bombs detonated on the city's trains killed 191 people

2008 José Luis Rodríguez Zapatero of the Spanish Socialist Party is re-elected on 9 March

2000	2005	2010	2015

1998 ETA, the Basque separatist terrorist group, announces a ceasefire that lasts a year

e general election on 3 March,
oses to a coalition led by Aznar

2004 José Luis Rodríguez Zapatero of the Spanish Socialist Party comes into power on 14 March

José Luis Rodríguez Zapatero

Rulers of Spain

Spain became a nation-state under Isabel and Fernando, whose marriage eventually united Castile and Aragón. With their daughter Juana's marriage, the kingdom was delivered into Habsburg hands. Carlos I and Felipe II were both capable rulers, but in 1700 Carlos II died without leaving an heir. After the War of the Spanish Succession, Spain came under the French Bourbons, who have ruled ever since – apart from an interregnum, two republics and Franco's dictatorship. The current Bourbon king, Juan Carlos I, a constitutional monarch, is respected for his support of democracy.

1665–1700
Carlos II

1479–1516
Fernando, King
of Aragón

1474–1504 Isabel,
Queen of Castile

1516–56 Carlos I of Spain
(Holy Roman Emperor
Charles V)

1598–1621 Felipe III

1400	1450	1500	1550	1600	1650
INDEPENDENT KINGDOMS		HABSBURG DYNASTY			
1400	1450	1500	1550	1600	1650

1469 Marriage of
Isabel and Fernando
leads to unification
of Spain

1504–16 Juana la
Loca (with
Fernando as regent)

1621–65 Felipe IV

Fernando and Isabel, the Catholic Monarchs

UNIFICATION OF SPAIN

In the late 15th century the two largest kingdoms in developing Christian Spain – Castile, with its military might, and Aragón (including Barcelona and a Mediterranean empire) – were united. The marriage of Isabel of Castile and Fernando of Aragón in 1469 joined these powerful kingdoms. Together the so-called Catholic Monarchs defeated the Nasrid Kingdom of Granada, the last stronghold of the Moors (*see pp56–7*). With the addition of Navarra in 1512, Spain was finally unified.

1556–98
Felipe II

1843–68 Isabel II reigns, following the regency of her mother María Cristina (1833–41) and General Espartero (1841–3)

1814–33 First Bourbon restoration, following French rule: Fernando VII

1871–3 Break in Bourbon rule: Amadeo I of Savoy

1724 Luis I reigns after Felipe V's abdication, but dies within a year

1759–88 Carlos III

1931–9 Second Republic

1939–75 General Franco Head of State

1875–85 Second Bourbon restoration: Alfonso XII

0	1750	1800	1850	1900	1950

URBON DYNASTY   BOURBON   BOURBON

0	1750	1800	1850	1900	1950

1808–13 Break in Bourbon rule: Napoleon's brother, Joseph Bonaparte, rules as José I

1746–59 Fernando VI

1788–1808 Carlos IV

1724–46 Felipe V reinstated as king upon the death of his son, Luis I

1902–31 Alfonso XIII

1886–1902 María Cristina of Habsburg-Lorraine as regent for Alfonso XIII

1873–4 First Republic

24
V

1868–70 The Septembrina Revolution

1975 Third Bourbon restoration: Juan Carlos I

NORTHERN SPAIN

INTRODUCING NORTHERN SPAIN 74–83

GALICIA 84–99

ASTURIAS AND CANTABRIA 100–113

THE BASQUE COUNTRY, NAVARRA
AND LA RIOJA 114–135

Introducing Northern Spain

Increasing numbers of visitors are discovering the quiet, sandy beaches and deep green landscapes of Northern Spain. The Atlantic coast, from the Pyrenees to the Portuguese border, is often scenic but at its most attractive in the cliffs and rías of Galicia. Inland, the mild, wet climate has created lush meadows and broad-leaved forests, making this area ideal for a peaceful, rural holiday. The famous medieval pilgrimage route to the city of Santiago de Compostela crosses Northern Spain, its way marked by magnificent examples of Romanesque architecture. Plentiful seafood and dairy produce, and the outstanding red wines of La Rioja, add to the pleasure of a tour through this part of Spain.

Oviedo (see p106) *has a number of Pre-Romanesque churches, most notably the graceful Santa María del Naranco, and a fine Gothic cathedral.*

Lugo

A Coruña

Asturias

GALICIA
(see pp84–85)

ASTURIAS AND CANTABRIA
(see pp100–13)

Ourense

Pontevedra

The Rías Baixas (see p95) *is one of Spain's prettiest coastlines. Scattered around its pretty towns and villages are many quaint hórreos, grain stores, raised on stone stilts.*

Santiago de Compostela (see pp90–3) *attracts thousands of pilgrims and tourists each year. Its majestic cathedral was one of the most important shrines in medieval Christendom.*

The Picos de Europa *mountain range (see pp108–9) dominates the landscape of Asturias and Cantabria. Rivers have carved deep gorges through the mountains and there are many footpaths through a variety of spectacular scenery.*

0 kilometres   50

0 miles   25

◁ **The coast of Galicia, south of Cabo Fisterra**

Santillana del Mar (see p112), *with its well-preserved medieval streets, is one of the most picturesque towns in Spain. The Convento de Regina Coeli houses a small museum containing a collection of painted wooden figures and other works of religious art.*

San Sebastián (see p122), *the most elegant holiday resort in the Basque Country, is sited around a beautiful horseshoe bay of golden sandy beaches. The city hosts international arts events, including Spain's premier film festival.*

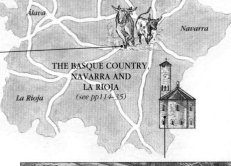

Cantabria

Vizcaya

Guipúzcoa

Álava

Navarra

THE BASQUE COUNTRY,
NAVARRA AND
LA RIOJA
(see pp114–35)

La Rioja

Pamplona (see pp132–3), *the capital of Navarra since the 9th century, is best known for its annual fiesta, Los Sanfermines. The highlight of each day of riotous celebration is the* Encierro, *in which bulls stampede through the streets of the city.*

The Monasterio de Leyre (see p135), *founded in the early 11th century, was built in a lonely but attractive landscape. The monastery was once the burial place of the kings of Navarra and its crypt is among the finest examples of early Romanesque art in Spain.*

The Flavours of Northern Spain

The wild, wet north of Spain is as famous for its rain as it is for its culinary excellence. The rain keeps the pastures lush and green – perfect dairy farming terrain – and the Atlantic provides an incredible variety of seafood. The Basques, in particular, are celebrated chefs, and the region boasts some of the finest restaurants in Europe, along with gastronomic societies (called *txokos*) in every village. Inland and in the remoter regions you'll find old-fashioned country cooking – roast lamb and tender young beef, slow-cooked stews – and traditionally made cheeses.

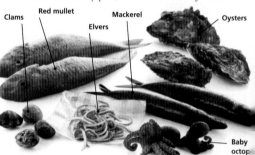
Idiazábal cheese

Pulpo a la gallega, Galicia's signature dish

GALICIA

The westernmost tip of Spain, battered by the Atlantic into a series of plunging *rías*, is famous for its extraordinary wealth of seafood – from staples like cod to unusual delicacies like barnacles (*percebes*), which look like tiny dinosaur feet. Every bar will serve up a plate of *pulpo a la gallega* or a dish of

pimientos del padrón (one in every dozen has a spicy kick). Inland, you'll find tender veal, free-range chicken and delicate soft cheeses such as such as delicious *tetilla*.

ASTURIAS AND CANTABRIA

The bay-pocked coastline provides delicious fresh fish, often served simply grilled (try the fabulous sardines offered in almost every port)

or slowly simmered in casseroles. Inland, the lush green pastures form Spain's dairy country – most Spanish milk, cream and some of its finest cheeses come from this region. Try Asturian Cabrales, a pungent blue cheese, best accompanied by a glass of local cider. The mountains provide succulent meat and game, often traditionally stewed with beans, as in the celebrated Asturian dish of *fabada*.

Clams   Red mullet   Mackerel   Oysters

Elvers

Baby octop

Fish and seafood from the waters of northern Spain

REGIONAL DISHES AND SPECIALITIES

Unsurprisingly, seafood rules supreme along the coastline, from the ubiquitous octopus in a piquant sauce served in Galicia, to the extraordinary spider crabs, which are a sought-after delicacy in the Basque Lands. The verdant pastures and rich farmland provide a wealth of fresh vege- tables, including Navarra's justly famous asparagus, along with all kinds of wonderful cheeses. Slow-cooked stews, an Asturian speciality, are particularly good in the mount- ains, along with tender lamb and outstanding game in season. The renowned wines from La

Cherries

Rioja are excellent, but those of adjoining Navarra are less pricey and often equally interesting. The crisp whites of Galicia and the Basque Lands are the perfect accompani- ment to the fresh seafood, and throughout the North you'll find powerful liqueurs flavoured with local herbs.

Bacalao al Pil Pil *Salted cod is slowly cooked with olive oil, chilli and garlic to create thi classic Basque dish.*

Array of *pinxos* laid out in a bar in the Basque Country

BASQUE COUNTRY

The Basque Country is a paradise for gourmets, renowned throughout Spain for the excellence of its natural produce and the creative brilliance of its chefs. Basque cuisine leans towards seafood, of which there is a dazzling variety: humble salted cod and hake (made extraordinary with delicious sauces) are most common, but sought-after delicacies include elvers (baby eels) and spider crab. Basque wines, drunk young and tart, are the perfect counterpoint. Bar counters groan with platters of *pintxos* (crusty bread with gourmet toppings), each one of them a miniature work of art, and the Basques also make wonderful cheeses, including delicate, smoky Idiazábal.

NAVARRA AND LA RIOJA

The fertile farmland of land-locked Navarra produces a spectacular array of fruit and vegetables such as aspara-gus, artichokes, cherries, chestnuts and peppers

Red peppers strung up to dry in the sun outside a house

(often hung in pretty strings to dry and used to flavour *embutidos*, or cured meats). In the Navarrese mountains, lamb is the most popular meat and you will find *cordero al chilindrón* (lamb stew) featuring on almost every menu. In season, you'll also find richly flavoured game, including partridge, hare and pheasant.

Tiny La Rioja is Spain's most famous wine region, producing rich, oaky reds and whites *(see pp78–9)*. The cuisine of La Rioja borrows from the neighbouring Basque Country and Navarra, with lamb featuring heavily, along with seafood and top-quality local vegetables.

ON THE MENU

Angulas a la Bilbaína Baby eels cooked in olive oil with garlic – a Basque delicacy.

Cocido Montañés Cantabrian stew of pork, spicy sausage, vegetables – and a pig's ear.

Fabada Asturiana Asturian beans stewed with cured meats and pork.

Pimientos del padrón A Gal-lego dish of green peppers fried in olive oil with rock salt.

Pulpo a la Gallega Octopus, cooked until tender in a spicy paprika sauce.

Trucha a la Navarra Trout, stuffed with ham and quickly grilled or fried.

mpanada Gallega *The perfect picnic snack, these olden pastries are stuffed ith all kinds of fillings.*

Chilindrón de Cordero *A rich, hearty stew from the mountains of Navarra, this is made with succulent lamb.*

Leche Frita *"Fried milk" is a scrumptious, custardy dessert from Cantabria. Simple but utterly delicious.*

Wines of Northern Spain

Spain's most prestigious wine region, La Rioja, is best known for its red wines, matured to a distinctive vanilla mellowness. Some of the most prestigious bodegas were founded by émigrés from Bordeaux, and Rioja reds are similar to claret. La Rioja also produces good white and rosé wines. Navarra reds and some whites have improved dramatically, thanks to a government research programme. The Basque region produces a tiny amount of the prickly, tart *txacoli (chacolí)*. Larger quantities of a similar wine are made further west in Galicia, whose best wines are full-bodied whites.

Repairing barrels in Haro, La Rioja

Ribeiro, *a popular wine of Galicia, is slightly fizzy. It is often served in white porcelain bowls* (cuencos).

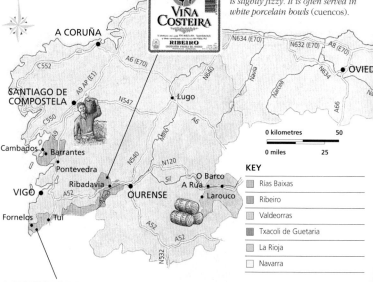

KEY

- ▨ Rías Baixas
- ▨ Ribeiro
- ▨ Valdeorras
- ▨ Txacoli de Guetaria
- ▨ La Rioja
- ▢ Navarra

Lagar de Cervera *is from Rías Baixas, a region known for producing Spain's most fashionable white wines.*

WINE REGIONS

The wine regions of Northern Spain are widely dispersed. Cradled between the Pyrenees and the Atlantic are the important regions of Rioja and Navarra. La Rioja is divided into the sub-regions of Rioja Alavesa, Rioja Alta and Rioja Baja, divided by the Río Ebro. The river also cuts through the wine region of Navarra. To the north are some of the vineyards of the Basque country: the miniscule Txacoli de Guetaria region. In the far west lie the four wine regions of rugged, wet Galicia: Rías Baixas, Ribeiro, Valdeorras, and the newly created Ribera Sacra.

Wine village of El Villar de Álava in Rioja Alta

Gathering the grape harvest in the traditional way in Navarra

Remelluri, *one of the new single-estate "Château" Riojas, from the vineyards of Rioja Alavesa, is soft and not too oaky.*

Chivite, *from a family bodega in Navarra, is made entirely from Tempranillo and aged in the barrel, resulting in a style similar to Rioja.*

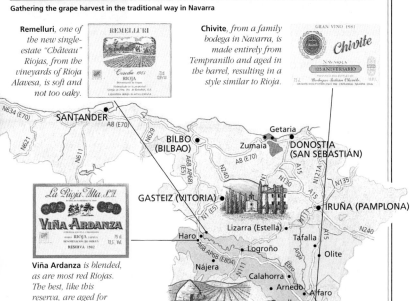

Viña Ardanza *is blended, as are most red Riojas. The best, like this reserva, are aged for two or more years in American oak casks.*

KEY FACTS ABOUT WINES OF NORTHERN SPAIN

Location and Climate
La Rioja and Navarra are influenced by both Mediterranean and Atlantic weather systems. The hillier, northwestern parts receive some Atlantic rain while the hot Ebro plain has a Mediterranean climate. The Basque region and Galicia are both cool, Atlantic regions with high rainfall. Soils everywhere are stony and poor, except in the Ebro plain.

Grape Varieties
The great red grape of La Rioja and Navarra is Tempranillo. In Rioja it is blended with smaller quantities of Garnacha, Graciano and Mazuelo, while in Navarra Cabernet Sauvignon is permitted and blends well with Tempranillo. Garnacha, also important in Navarra, is used for the excellent *rosados* (rosés). Whites of Navarra and Rioja are made mainly from the Viura grape. Galicia has many local varieties, such as Albariño, Loureira and Treixadura, which is now taking over from the inferior Palomino.

Good Producers
Rías Baixas: Fillaboa, Lagar de Fornelos, Morgadío, Santiago Ruiz. *Ribeiro:* Cooperativa Vinícola del Ribeiro. *La Rioja:* Bodegas Riojanas (Canchales, Monte Real), CVNE (Imperial, Viña Real Oro), Faustino Martínez, Federico Paternina, Marqués de Cáceres, Marqués de Murrieta, Martínez Bujanda, Remelluri, La Rioja Alta (Viña Ardanza). *Navarra:* Bodega de Sarría, Guelbenzu, Julián Chivite (Gran Feudo), Magaña, Ochoa, Príncipe de Viana.

Forests of the North

Much of Spain was once blanketed by a mantle of trees. Today, just ten per cent of the original cover remains, mostly in the mountainous north, where rainfall is high and slopes too steep for cultivation. Large areas of mixed deciduous forest – mainly beech, Pyrenean oak and chestnut, with some ash and lime – dominate the landscape, particularly in Cantabria and the Basque Country. The undergrowth of shrubs and flowering plants provides habitats for many insects, mammals and birds. The forests are also the refuge of Spain's last brown bears *(see p104).*

Purple emperor butterfly

Forest in Northern Spain in autumn

REGENERATION OF THE FOREST

Dead materials – leaves, twigs and the excrement and bodies of animals – are broken down by various organisms on the forest floor, especially fungi, bacteria and ants. This process releases nutrients which are absorbed by trees and other plants, enabling them to grow.

Fly agaric mushrooms

Lichens *grow slowly and are sensitive to pollution. Their presence in a forest often indicates that it is in good health.*

The stag beetle *takes its name from the huge antler-like mandibles of the male. Despite their ferocious appearance, these beetles are harmless to humans.*

Millipede and fungus on a woodland floor

BEECH FOREST

Beech, the dominant species in the Cantabrian mountains and Pyrenees, grows on well-drained soils. Some trees retain their distinctive copper-red leaves through the winter. Beech mast (nuts) are collected to feed to pigs.

Beech leaf and mast

The thick crown shuts out light, inhibiting undergrowth.

Long, thin orange buds

Male golden orioles, *among the most colourful European birds, are hard to spot because they spend much of their time in the thick cover provided by old woodlands. Females and juveniles are a duller yellow-green with a brownish tail.*

Beech martens *are nocturnal. By day, they sleep in a hollow tree or another animal's abandoned nest. At night they feed on fruit, birds and small mammals.*

DISTRIBUTION OF BROAD-LEAVED FORESTS

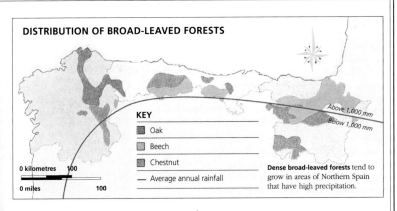

KEY

- Oak
- Beech
- Chestnut
- — Average annual rainfall

Above 1,000 mm

Below 1,000 mm

Dense broad-leaved forests tend to grow in areas of Northern Spain that have high precipitation.

0 kilometres 100

0 miles 100

CHESTNUT FOREST

Chestnut trees grow on well-drained acidic soils. They have slender yellow flowers and in summer produce their fruit, which is eaten by wild boar, dormice, squirrels and mice. The wood is hard and durable but splits easily.

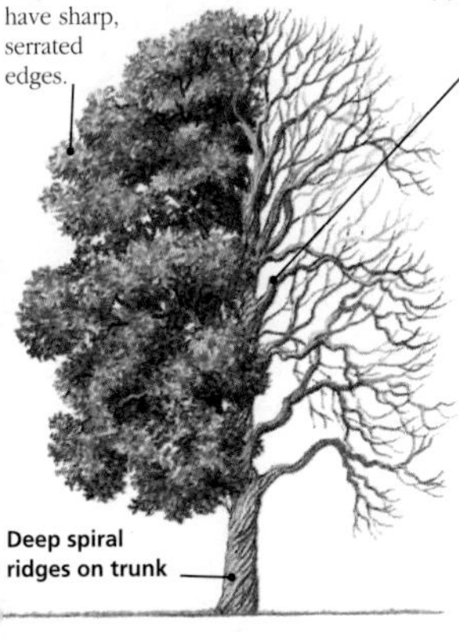

Leaf and chestnut

OAK FOREST

Three main species of oak tree – pedunculate, Pyrenean and the evergreen holm oak – dominate the ancient woodlands of the north. Over 300 species of animal, such as wild boar, squirrels and nuthatches, feed off oaks.

Oak leaf and acorn

Large leaves have sharp, serrated edges.

Few massive, spreading branches

Deep spiral ridges on trunk

Grey twigs ending in numerous buds

The pipistrelle bat *is a nocturnal species common in woodlands. It catches and eats small insects in flight. Larger insects are taken to a perch. The bat hibernates in winter in a hollow tree or cave.*

The jay, *a member of the crow family, is a common but somewhat shy woodland bird with a distinctively raucous cry. It can be identified in flight by its white rump, black tail and above all by its bright blue wing patch.*

Blue tits *feed mainly in the tree canopy of broad-leaved woods and rarely come down to the ground. The male and female have similar, distinctive plumage. They may raise the back feathers of the crown if alarmed.*

Red squirrels *bury large numbers of acorns during autumn to last through winter, since these diurnal creatures do not hibernate. Many of the acorns are left to sprout into seedlings.*

The Road to Santiago

According to legend the body of Christ's apostle James was brought to Galicia. In AD 813 the relics were supposedly discovered at Santiago de Compostela, where a cathedral was built in his honour *(see pp92–3)*. In the Middle Ages half a million pilgrims a year flocked there from all over Europe, crossing the Pyrenees at Roncesvalles *(see p134)* or via the Somport Pass *(see p230)*. They often donned the traditional garb of cape, long staff and curling felt hat adorned with scallop shells, the symbol of the saint. The various routes, marked by the cathedrals, churches and hospitals built along them, are still used by travellers today.

St James on horseback

19th-century painting of the Pórtico da Gloria of Santiago Cathedral

Astorga *(see p352), once a Roman city, was an important halt on the pilgrim route in the Middle Ages. The museum within its cathedral has a collection of gold and silver plate including a 13th-century gold filigree cross.*

A certificate *is given to pilgrims covering 100 km (62 miles) of the route on foot, or 200 km (125 miles) on horseback.*

O Cebreiro *(see p99)* has a 9th-century church and some of the ancient *pallozas* the pilgrims often used for shelter.

León *was one of the main pilgrim stops. Its cathedral (see pp354–5) contains one of Spain's finest collections of stained glass.*

Ponferrada's huge Templar castle stands close to the town centre *(see p352).*

Scallop shells, staffs and gourds to carry water are symbols of the pilgrimage.

| 0 kilometres | 50 |
| 0 miles | 50 |

SANTIAGO DE COMPOSTELA
Maritime Route
Portuguese Route
Silver Route
A Coruña
Ribadeo
Oviedo
Vilar de Donas
Ligonde
O Cebreiro
Villafranca del Bierzo
LEÓN
Ponferrada
Astorga
Hospital de Órbigo
Sahagú
PORTO LISBOA
Vigo • Tui
SALAMANCA

ROMANESQUE CHURCH ARCHITECTURE

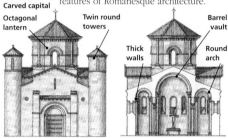

The Romanesque style of architecture *(see p24)* was brought to Spain from France during the 10th and 11th centuries. As the pilgrimage to Santiago became more popular, many glorious religious buildings were constructed along its main routes. Massive walls, few windows, round heavy arches and barrel vaulting are typical features of Romanesque architecture.

Carved capital

Octagonal lantern   **Twin round towers**

Thick walls

Barrel vault

Round arch

Façade

Cross-section

San Martín de Frómista *(see p368), built in the 11th century, is the only complete example of the "pilgrimage" style of Romanesque. The nave and aisles are almost the same height and there are three parallel apses.*

Parallel apses   **Aisle**   **Nave**

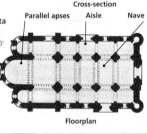

Floorplan

Pamplona's (see p132) *Gothic cathedral was one of the pilgrims' first stops after crossing the Pyrenees at Roncesvalles.*

Santo Domingo de la Calzada's *(see p128)* pilgrim hospital is now a parador.

Puente la Reina (see p131) *takes its name from the 11th-century humpbacked bridge (puente), built for pilgrims and still used by pedestrians.*

Santander

Donostia (San Sebastián)   PARIS

hern Route   Bilbo (Bilbao)

LE PUY VEZELAY

Valcarlos

Orreaga (Roncesvalles)

ARLES

Frómista preserves one of the finest Romanesque churches on the French route.

Iruña (Pamplona)

Lizarra (Estella)

Puente la Reina   Sangüesa   Jaca

San Juan de Ortega   Santo Domingo de la Calzada   *French Route*

San Juan de la Peña

sta   Nájera   Logroño

BURGOS

Burgos has a magnificent Gothic cathedral *(see pp372–3).*

ROUTES TO SANTIAGO

Several traditional pilgrimage roads converge on Santiago de Compostela. The main road from the Pyrenees is known as the French Route, with the Aragonese Route as a variation.

GALICIA

LUGO · A CORUNA · PONTEVEDRA · OURENSE

Remote in the northwest corner of the peninsula, Galicia is the country's greenest region. In its hilly interior, smallholdings are farmed by traditional methods. Galicia is Spain's main seafaring region – three of its four provinces have an Atlantic coastline, and its cuisine is based on superb seafood. The Galicians, whose origins are Celtic, are fiercely proud of their culture and language.

Much of Galicia still has a medieval quality. Some inland farms are divided into plots too tiny or steep for tractors to work, so oxen and horses are used for ploughing. Grain is stored in quaint, pillared granaries called *hórreos*. The misty, emerald countryside abounds with old granite villages and is dotted with *pazos* – traditional stone manor houses.

The discovery of the supposed tomb of St James the Apostle, in the 9th century, confirmed medieval Santiago de Compostela as Europe's most important religious shrine after St Peter's in Rome. Pilgrims and tourists still follow this ancient route of pilgrimage across Northern Spain.

The Galician coast is incised by many fjordlike rías; the loveliest of these are the Rías Baixas in the west. Elsewhere it juts defiantly into the Atlantic in rocky headlands, such as Cabo Fisterra, Spain's most westerly point. Many people still make a living from the sea. Vigo in Pontevedra is the most important fishing port in Spain.

Galicia's official language, used on most signs, is *gallego*. It has similarities to the language of Portugal, which borders Galicia to the south. The Celtic character of this haunting land is still evident in the Galicians' favourite traditional instrument, the bagpipes.

Staple crops – maize, cabbages and potatoes – growing on the harsh land around Cabo Fisterra

The west façade of Santiago de Compostela's cathedral, overlooking the Praza do Obradoiro

Exploring Galicia

Santiago de Compostela is Galicia's major tourist attraction. This beautiful city is the centrepiece of a region with many fine old towns, especially Betanzos, Mondoñedo, Lugo and Pontevedra. The resorts along the coastline of the wild Rías Altas, with their backdrop of forest-covered hills, offer good bathing. The Rías Baixas, the southern part of Galicia's west coast, has sheltered coves and sandy beaches, and excellent seafood in abundance. Travelling through the interior, where life seems to have changed little in centuries, is an ideal way to spend a peaceful, rural holiday.

Musicians dressed in
traditional costumes
playing in Pontevedra

SIGHTS AT A GLANCE

Baiona ⑪
Betanzos ③
O Cebreiro ㉑
Celanova ⑭
A Coruña ④
Costa da Morte ⑤
A Guarda ⑫
Lugo ⑳
Monasterio de Oseira ⑱
Monasterio de Ribas de Sil ⑰
Mondoñedo ②
Ourense ⑯
Padrón ⑦
Pontevedra ⑨
Rías Altas ①
Santiago de Compostela
   pp90–1 ⑥
A Toxa ⑧
Tui ⑬
Verín ⑮
Vigo ⑩
Vilar de Donas ⑲

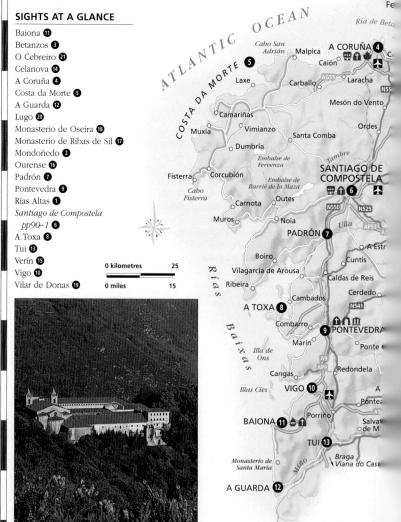

The isolated monastery at Ribas de Sil

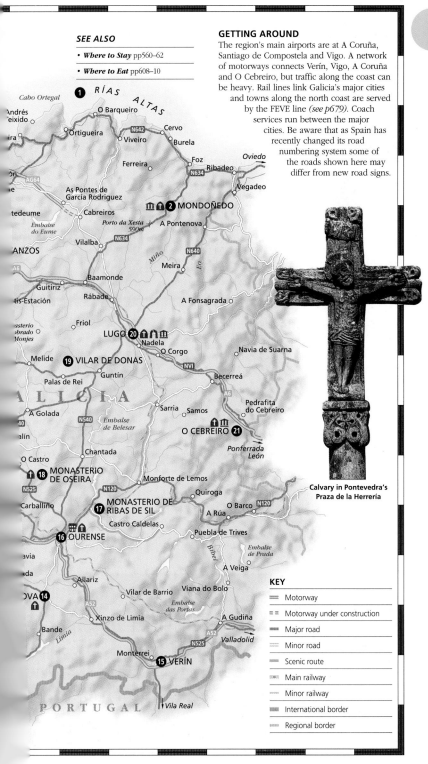

SEE ALSO

- **Where to Stay** pp560–62
- **Where to Eat** pp608–10

GETTING AROUND

The region's main airports are at A Coruña, Santiago de Compostela and Vigo. A network of motorways connects Verín, Vigo, A Coruña and O Cebreiro, but traffic along the coast can be heavy. Rail lines link Galicia's major cities and towns along the north coast are served by the FEVE line (see p679). Coach services run between the major cities. Be aware that as Spain has recently changed its road numbering system some of the roads shown here may differ from new road signs.

Calvary in Pontevedra's Praza de la Herrería

KEY

▬▬	Motorway
▪ ▪	Motorway under construction
▬▬	Major road
⋯	Minor road
▬▬	Scenic route
▪◢▬	Main railway
----	Minor railway
▬▬	International border
▪▪▪	Regional border

Carved coat of arms on a house-front in Mondoñedo

Rías Altas ❶

Lugo & A Coruña. 🚹 *10,000.* 🚉
Ribadeo. 🚌 *Viveiro.* 🛈 *Foz, 982 14
06 75.* 🚍 *Tue.*

Deep rías are interspersed
with coves and headlands
along the beautiful north coast
from Ribadeo to A Coruña.
Inland are hills covered with
forests of pine and eucalyptus.
Many of the small resorts and
fishing villages are charming.

The lovely, winding **Ría de
Ribadeo** forms the border with
Asturias. To the west of it is the
small fishing port of **Foz**, which
has two good beaches. Nearby,
the 10th-century Iglesia de San
Martín de Mondoñedo, standing
alone on a hill, contains carvings of biblical scenes on its
transept capitals – note the
story of Lazarus. **Viveiro**, a
summer holiday resort 35 km
(22 miles) away, is a handsome
old town surrounded by Renaissance walls and gateways,
typically Galician glassed-in
balconies or *galerías*, and a
Romanesque church. Near the
pretty fishing village of O
Barqueiro is the headland of
Estaca de Bares, with its
lighthouse and wind turbines.

Westward along the coast,
the lovely **Ría de Ortigueira**
leads to the fishing port of
the same name, characterized
by neat white houses. Around
this area there are also many
wild and unspoiled beaches.

High cliffs rise out of the
sea near the village of **San
Andrés de Teixido**, whose
church is the focal point for

pilgrims on 8 September. According to legend, those who
fail to visit the church in their
lifetime will come back to it
as an animal in the afterlife.
The village of **Cedeira**, which
sits on a quiet bay, is a rich
summer resort with neat lawns,
modern houses with *galerías*,
and a long, curving beach.

Mondoñedo ❷

Lugo. 🚹 *5,500.* 🚉 🛈 *Plaza de la
Catedral 34, 982 50 71 77.* 🚍 *Thu.*
🎉 *Nuestra Señora de los Remedios
(1st Sun after 8 Sep), San Lucas (18
Oct), As Quendas (1st May).*

This delightful town is set in a
fertile inland valley. Stately
houses with carved coats of
arms and *galerías* are in the
main square. This is dominated
by the **cathedral**, a building of
golden stone in a mix of
styles. It has 18th-century
Baroque towers, a Roman-
esque portal with
a 16th-century
stained-glass
rose window
and 17th-century
cloisters. A statue
in a chapel in
the cathedral,
Nuestra Señora
la Inglesa, was
rescued from St
Paul's Cathedral
in London. The
Museo Diocesano, which is
entered through the cathedral,
contains works by Zurbarán
and El Greco.

🏛 **Museo Diocesano**
Plaza de la Catedral. **Tel** *686 416 111.*
◻ *9am–1pm, 4:30pm–8pm daily.* 🖼

Betanzos ❸

A Coruña. 🚹 *13,000.* 🚉
🛈 *Plaza de Galicia 1, 981 77 66 66.*
🚍 *Tue, Thu & Sat.* 🎉 *San
Roque (14–25 Aug).*

The handsome town of
Betanzos lies in a fertile valley
slightly inland. Its broad main
square has a replica of the
Fountain of Diana at Versailles.
In its steep narrow streets are
fine old houses and Gothic
churches. The **Iglesia de
Santiago**, built in the 15th
century by the tailors' guild,
has a statue of St James on
horseback above the door. The
Iglesia de San Francisco, dated
1387, has statues of wild boars
and a heraldic emblem of
Knight Fernán Pérez de
Andrade, whose 14th-century
tomb is inside the church. For
centuries his family were the
overlords of the region.

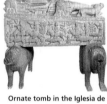

Ornate tomb in the Iglesia de
San Francisco in Betanzos

Environs: 20 km (12 miles)
north is the large,
though pretty,
fishing village
of **Pontedeume**,
with its narrow,
hilly streets. Its
medieval bridge
still carries the
main road to the
large industrial
town of **Ferrol**,
to the north.
Originally a
medieval port, Ferrol became
an important naval base and
dockyard town in the 18th
century, and its Neo-Classical
buildings survive from that
time. General Franco (*see
pp66–7*) was born in Ferrol
in 1892.

Pavement cafés in Betanzos' Plaza de García Hermanos

Stone cross standing above the perilous waters of the Costa da Morte

A Coruña ❹

A Coruña. 🏘 *246,000.* ✈ 🚌 🚉
🛈 *Plaza de María Pita, 618 79 06
65.* 🎭 *Fiestas de María Pita (Aug).*
www. turismocoruna.com

This proud city and busy port
has played a sizeable role in
Spanish maritime history.
Felipe II's doomed Armada
sailed from here to England
in 1588 *(see p59)*. Today, the
sprawling industrial suburbs
contrast with the elegant
town centre, which is laid out
on an isthmus leading to a
headland. The **Torre de
Hércules**, Europe's oldest
working lighthouse, is a
famous local landmark. Built
by the Romans and rebuilt in
the 18th century, it still flashes
across the deep. Climb its 242
steps for a wide ocean view.

On the large, arcaded Praza
María Pita, the city's main
square, is the handsome town
hall. The sea promenade of
a Marina is lined with tiers of
glass-enclosed balconies or
galerías. Built as protection
against the strong winds, they
explain why A Coruña is often
referred to as the City of Glass.
The peaceful, tiny Prazuela
a Bárbaras is enchanting.

A Coruña has several fine
Romanesque churches, such as
the **Iglesia de Santiago**, with
a carving of its saint on horseback situated beneath the

tympanum, and the **Iglesia de
Santa María**. This church, featuring a tympanum carved with
the Adoration of the Magi, is
one of the best-preserved 12th-
century buildings in Galicia.

The quiet Jardín de San
Carlos contains the tomb of
the Scottish general Sir John
Moore who was killed in
1809 as the British army
evacuated the port during
Spain's War of Independence
from France *(see p62).*

The lofty Torre de Hércules
lighthouse at A Coruña

Costa da Morte ❺

A Coruña. 🚌 *A Coruña, Malpica,
Santiago de Compostela.* 🛈 *Dársena
de la Marina s/n, 981 22 18 22.*

From Malpica to Fisterra the
coast is wild and remote. It is
called the "Coast of Death"
because of the many ships
lost in storms or smashed on
the rocks by gales over the
centuries. But the headlands
are majestic and the sunsets
beautiful. Inland, the countryside is breezy and open. There
are no coastal towns, only simple villages, where fishermen
gather gastronomic *percebes*
(barnacles), destined for the
region's restaurants.

One of the most northerly
points of the Costa da Morte,
Malpica, has a seabird sanctuary. Laxe has good beaches
and safe bathing. **Camariñas**,
one of the most appealing
places on this coast, is a fishing
village where women make
bobbin-lace in the streets.
Beside the lighthouse on
nearby Cabo Vilán, a group of
futuristic wind turbines, tall
and slender, swirl in graceful
unison – a haunting sight.

To the south is Corcubión,
exuding a faded elegance,
and lastly, **Cabo Fisterra**
"where the land ends". This
cape, with its lighthouse, is a
good place to watch the sun
go down over the Atlantic.

Street-by-Street: Santiago de Compostela ❻

In the Middle Ages Santiago de Compostela was Christendom's third most important place of pilgrimage *(see pp82–3)*, after Jerusalem and Rome. Around the Praza do Obradoiro is an ensemble of historic buildings that has few equals in Europe. The local granite gives a harmonious unity to the mixture of architectural styles. With its narrow streets and old squares, the city centre is compact enough to explore on foot. Two other monuments worth seeing are the Convento de Santo Domingo de Bonaval, to the east of the centre and the Colegiata Santa Maria la Real del Sar, a 12th-century Romanesque church, located to the east of the city.

Vegetable stall in Santiago market

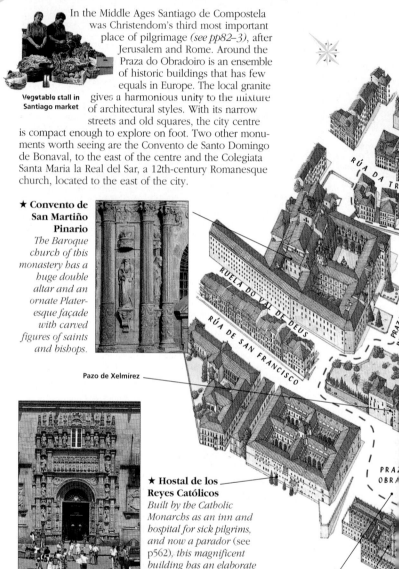

RÚA DA TRO

RUELA DO VAL DE DEUS

RÚA DE SAN FRANCISCO

PRAZA

**PRA
OBRA**

★ Convento de San Martiño Pinario

The Baroque church of this monastery has a huge double altar and an ornate Plater-esque façade with carved figures of saints and bishops.

Pazo de Xelmírez

★ Hostal de los Reyes Católicos

Built by the Catholic Monarchs as an inn and hospital for sick pilgrims, and now a parador (see p562), this magnificent building has an elaborate Plateresque doorway.

Praza do Obradoiro

This majestic square is one of the world's finest and the focal point for pilgrims arriving in the city. The cathedral's Baroque façade dominates the square.

The Pazo de R
with its Class
façade, was b
1772 and ho
the town hal

Convento de San Paio de Antealtares

This is one of the oldest monasteries in Santiago. It was founded in the 9th century to house the tomb of St James, now in the cathedral.

VISITORS' CHECKLIST

A Coruña. 94,000. ✈ 12 km (6 miles) north. 🚉 Calle Hórreo 75a, 902 24 02 02. 🚌 Plaza Camilo Díaz Valiño, 981 54 24 16. 🛈 Calle Rúa do Vilar 63, 981 55 51 29. 🏛 Wed (animal), Thu. 🎉 Semana Santa (Easter Week), Santiago Day (25 July). www.santiagoturismo.com

Praza da Quintana, under the cathedral clock tower, is one of the city's most elegant squares.

Praza das Praterias

The Silversmiths' Doorway of the cathedral opens on to this charming square with Fuente dos Cavalos in the centre.

KEY

– – – Suggested route

– – – Pilgrims' route

Rúa Nova is a handsome arcaded old street leading from the cathedral to the newer part of the city.

To tourist information

| 0 metres | 100 |
| 0 yards | 100 |

Colegio de San Jerónimo

STAR SIGHTS

★ Convento de San Martiño Pinario

★ Hostal de los Reyes Católicos

★ Cathedral

★ Cathedral

This grand towering spectacle has welcomed pilgrims to Santiago for centuries. Though the exterior has been remodelled over the years, the core of the building has remained virtually unchanged since the 11th century.

Santiago Cathedral

With its twin Baroque towers soaring high over the Praza do Obradoiro, this monument to St James is a majestic sight, as befits one of the great shrines of Christendom (see pp82–3). The present building dates from the 11th–13th centuries and stands on the site of the 9th-century basilica built by Alfonso II. Through the famous Pórtico da Gloria is the same interior that met pilgrims in medieval times. The choir, designed by Maestro Mateo, has been completely restored.

The gigantic botafumeiro

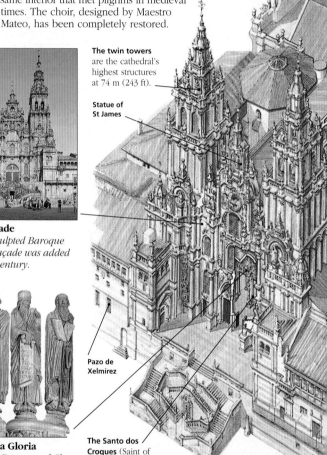

"Passport" – proof of a pilgrim's journey

★ West Façade
The richly sculpted Baroque Obradoiro façade was added in the 18th century.

The twin towers are the cathedral's highest structures at 74 m (243 ft).

Statue of St James

Pazo de Xelmírez

★ Pórtico da Gloria
The sculpted Doorway of Glory, with its statues of apostles and prophets, is 12th century.

The Santo dos Croques (Saint of Bumps) has greeted pilgrims since the 12th century. Touching this statue with the forehead is said to impart luck and wisdom.

STAR FEATURES

- ★ West Façade
- ★ Pórtico da Gloria
- ★ Porta das Praterias

Cathedral Museum
Visitors can view items from excavations made over the years, as well as the cathedral's cloister, chapterhouse, library, reliquary chapel and crypt.

The **botafumeiro**, a giant censer, is swung high above the altar by eight men during important services.

Mondragon Chapel (1521) contains fine wrought-iron grilles and vaulting.

Clock Tower

Cloisters

Chapterhouse

VISITORS' CHECKLIST

Praza do Obradoiro. **Tel** 981 58 35 48. 7am–9pm daily. 7:30am, 8:30am, 9am, 10am, 11am, noon, 1pm, 6pm, 7:30pm daily. tours of rooftops and Pazo de Xelmírez (tickets and reservations in museum). **Museum Tel** 981 56 93 27. daily. lunch, Sun pm, 1 & 6 Jan, 25 Jul, 15 Aug, 25 Dec.

High Altar
Visitors can pass behind the ornate high altar to embrace the silver mantle of the 13th-century statue of St James.

★ **Porta das Praterias**
The 12th-century Silver-smiths' Doorway is rich in bas-relief sculptures of biblical scenes.

Crypt
The relics of St James and two disciples are said to lie in a tomb in the crypt, under the altar, in the original 9th-century foundations.

Padrón ❼

A Coruña. 🚶 9,000. 🚉 🚌 🛈
Avenida Compostela, 627 21 07 77.
🛥 Sun. 🎪 Santiago (24–5 Jul).

This quiet town on the Río Ulla, known for its piquant green peppers, was a major seaport until it silted up. Legend has it the boat carrying the body of St James to Galicia (*see p82*) arrived here. The supposed mooring stone, or *padrón*, lies below the altar of the church by the bridge.

The leafy avenue beside the church features in the poems of one of Galicia's greatest writers, Rosalia de Castro (1837–85). Her home, where she spent her final years, has been converted into a museum.

Environs

The estuary town of Noia (Noya) lies on the coast 20 km (12 miles) west. Its Gothic church has a finely carved portal. East of Padron is Pazo de Oca, a manor house, with a crenellated tower, idyllic gardens and a lake.

🏛 **Museo Rosalia de Castro**
La Matanza. **Tel** 981 81 12 04.
⬜ Tue–Sun. 📷 ♿

The picturesque gardens and lake of Pazo de Oca

A Toxa ❽

Near O Grove. 🚌 🛈 Praza do Corgo,
O Grove, 986 73 14 15. 🛥 Fri.

A tiny pine-covered island joined to the mainland by a bridge, A Toxa (La Toja) is one of the most stylish resorts in Galicia. The *belle époque* palace-hotel (*see p561*) and luxury villas add to the island's elegant atmosphere. A Toxa's best-known landmark is the small church covered with scallop shells. Across the bridge is O Grove (El Grove), a thriving family resort and fishing port on a peninsula, with holiday hotels and flats alongside glorious beaches.

Pontevedra ❾

Pontevedra. 🚶 80,000. 🚉 🚌
🛈 Calle General Gutiérrez Mellado 1,
986 85 08 14. 🛥 1st, 8th, 15th &
23rd of each month. 🎪 Fiestas de la
Peregrina (second week in Aug).

Pontevedra lies inland, at the head of a long ría backed by green hills. The delightful old town is typically Galician and has a network of cobbled alleys and tiny squares with granite calvaries, flower-filled balconies and excellent tapas bars. On the south side of the old town are the Gothic **Ruinas de Santo Domingo**. It is now a museum with Roman steles and Galician coats of arms and tombs. To the west, the 16th-century **Iglesia de Santa María la Mayor** contains a magnificent Plateresque (*see p25*) façade that includes richly carved figures of oarsmen and fishermen at the top.

On the **Praza de la Leña**, two 18th-century mansions form the **Museo de Pontevedra**, one of the best museums in Galicia. The Bronze Age treasures found locally are superb. Among the paintings on display are 15th-century Spanish primitives, and canvases by Zurbarán and Goya. The top floor holds a collection of drawings and paintings by Alfonso Castelao, Galician artist and nationalist who forcefully depicted the misery endured by his people during the Spanish Civil War.

🏛 **Museo de Pontevedra**
Calle Pasantería 2–12. **Tel** 986 85 1
55. ⬜ Oct–May: 10am–2pm, 4–
7pm Tue–Sat, 11am–2pm Sun; Jun–
Sep: 10am–2pm, 4:30–8:30pm Tue–
Sat, 11am–2pm Sun.

Scallop-covered roof of the church on A Toxa island

Rías Baixas

This southern part of Galicia's west coast consists of four large rías or inlets between pine-covered hills. The beaches are good, the scenery is lovely, the bathing safe and the climate much milder than on the wilder coast to the north. Though areas such as Vilagarcía de Arousa and Panxón have become popular holiday resorts, much of the Rías Baixas (Rías Bajas) coastline is unspoiled, such as the quiet stretch from Muros to Noia. This part of the coastline provides some of Spain's most fertile fishing grounds. Mussel-breeding platforms are positioned in neat rows along the rías, looking like half-submerged submarines; and in November, the women harvest clams.

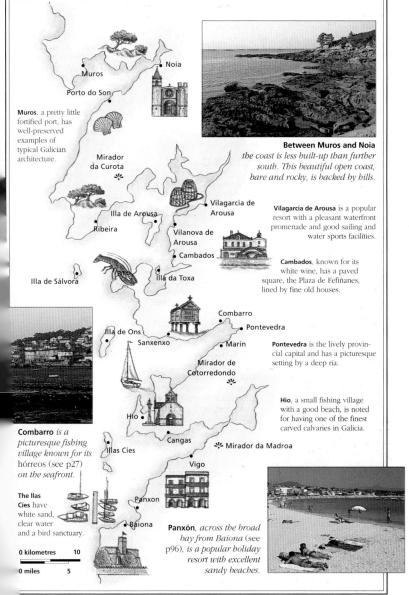

Muros, a pretty little fortified port, has well-preserved examples of typical Galician architecture.

Between Muros and Noia
the coast is less built-up than further south. This beautiful open coast, bare and rocky, is backed by hills.

Vilagarcía de Arousa is a popular resort with a pleasant waterfront promenade and good sailing and water sports facilities.

Cambados, known for its white wine, has a paved square, the Plaza de Fefiñanes, lined by fine old houses.

Pontevedra is the lively provincial capital and has a picturesque setting by a deep ría.

Hío, a small fishing village with a good beach, is noted for having one of the finest carved calvaries in Galicia.

Combarro *is a picturesque fishing village known for its hórreos (see p27) on the seafront.*

The Ilas Cíes have white sand, clear water and a bird sanctuary.

Panxón, *across the broad bay from Baiona (see p96), is a popular holiday resort with excellent sandy beaches.*

Muros
Noia
Porto do Son
Mirador da Curota
Illa de Arousa
Ribeira
Illa de Sálvora
Vilagarcia de Arousa
Vilanova de Arousa
Cambados
Illa da Toxa
Combarro
Pontevedra
Illa de Ons
Sanxenxo
Marin
Mirador de Cotorredondo
Hío
Cangas
Mirador da Madroa
Illas Cíes
Vigo
Panxon
Baiona

0 kilometres 10
0 miles 5

Cannons on the battlements of Monterreal fortress, Baiona

Vigo ⓾

Pontevedra. 🏛 295,000. ✈ 🚉
🚢 🛈 *Calle Teófilo Llorente 5, 986
22 47 57.* 🚢 *Wed, Sun.* 🎭 *Cristo
de los Afligidos (3rd Sun in Jul), Cristo
de la Victoria (1st Sun in Aug).*
www.turismodevigo.org

Galicia's largest town is
also the biggest fishing port
in Spain. It is situated in an
attractive setting near the
mouth of a deep ría spanned
by a high suspension bridge,
and is surrounded by wooded
hills. Vigo is not
noted for its old
buildings but does
have striking
modern sculptures
such as Juan José
Oliveira's horses
statue in the Praza de
España. The oldest part
of the town, Barrio
del Berbes, is near
the port and used
to be the sailors'
quarter. Its
cobbled alleys
are full of
bars,

Bronze sculpture by Oliveira in
Vigo's Praza de España

where you can find some
of the finest tapas. The
Mercado de la Piedra, near
the port, sells reasonably
priced fish and shellfish.

Baiona ⓫

Pontevedra. 🏛 12,000. 🚉 🛈
Paseo Ribeira, 986 68 70 67.
🚢 *Mon in Sabaris (nearby).* 🎭 *Santa
Liberata (20 Jul), Virgen de la Anunciada
(1st Sun in Aug).* **www**.baiona.org

The Pinta, one of the caravels
from the fleet of Christopher
Columbus, arrived at this
small port on 1 March 1493,
bringing the first news of the
discovery of the New World.
Today Baiona (Bayona), which
is sited on a broad bay, is a
popular summer resort, its
harbour a mix of pleasure
and fishing boats. The 12th to
17th-century **Iglesia Antigua
Colegiata de Santa María** is
Romanesque with Cistercian
influences. Symbols on the
arches indicate the local guilds
that helped build the church.

A royal fortress once stood
on Monterreal promontory, to
the north of town. Sections of
its defensive walls remain, but
the interior has been converted
into a smart parador *(see
p560)*. A walk around the
battlements offers superb
views of the coast.

On the coast a short dis-
tance to the south is a huge
granite and porcelain statue of
the **Virgen de la Roca** sculpted
by Antonio Palacios in 1930. It
is possible for visitors to climb
up inside the statue.

A Guarda ⓬

Pontevedra. 🏛 10,000. 🚉 🛈 *Praza
do Reló 1, 986 61 45 46.* 🚢 *Sat.* 🎭
*Monte de Santa Tecla (second week of
Aug).* **www**.concellodaguarda.com

The little fishing port of A
Guarda (La Guardia) has a
reputation for good seafood
and is particularly well known
for the quality of its lobsters.

On the slopes of Monte de
Santa Tecla are the remains of
a Celtic settlement of some
100 round stone dwellings
which are dated around
600–200 BC. The **Museo de
Monte de Santa Tecla** is
situated on a nearby hilltop.

Environs
About 10 km (6 miles) north,
the tiny Baroque **Monasterio
de Santa María** stands by the
beach at Oia. Semi-wild horses
roam the surrounding hills and,
in May and June, are rounded
up for branding in a series of
day-long fiestas *(see p98)*.

🏛 **Museo de Monte de
Santa Tecla**
A Guarda. **Tel** *986 61 45 46.*
⭘ *Tue–Sun.* 🎟 *for hilltop access.*

Circular foundations of Celtic
dwellings at A Guarda

Tui ⓭

Pontevedra. 🏛 17,000. 🚉 🚉
🛈 *Calle Colon 2, 986 60 17 89.* 🚢
Thu. 🎭 *San Telmo (week after Easte
Descent of the Rio Miño (Aug).*

Spain's main frontier town
with Portugal, Tui (Tuy)
stands on a hillside above t
Río Miño. Its graceful old
streets curve up to an old qu
ter and the 12th-century hillt
cathedral. The two countrie
were often at war during the
Middle Ages, and as a resu
the church is built in the st

Unloading the catch in Spain's largest fishing port, Vigo

FISHING IN SPAIN

The Spanish eat more sea-food per head of population than any other European nation except Portugal. Half of this is caught by Galician fishing fleets. Some 90,000 fishermen and 20,000 boats land over a million tonnes of fish and shellfish a year, much of this caught offshore where sardines, tuna, lobster and clams are plentiful. In recent years, the stocks in the seas around Spain have become depleted by over-fishing, forcing deep-sea trawlers to travel as far as Canada and Iceland.

altarpiece and Gothic choir stalls. In the garden is the 10th-century Mozarabic **Iglesia de San Miguel**.

Environs

At **Santa Comba de Bande**, 26 km (16 miles) to the south, is an even older little church. The features of this 7th century Visigothic (*see pp50–1*) church include a lantern turret and a horseshoe arch that has carved marble pillars.

Verín ⓯

Ourense. 🏠 14,000. 🚌 🚹
Avenida San Lazaro 26–8, 988 41 16 14. 🛒 *3rd, 11th & 23rd of month.*
🎭 *Carnival (Feb).*

Though it stands amid vine-yards, Verín produces more than wine. Its mineral springs have given it a thriving bottled water industry. The town has many old houses with arcades and glass balconies (*galerías*).

of a fortress, with towers and battlements. It has a cloister and choir stalls and a richly decorated west porch.

Nearby is the **Iglesia de San Telmo**, dedicated to the patron saint of fishermen, whose Baroque ornamentation shows a Portuguese influence. Near the cathedral is an iron bridge, the **Puente Internacional**, built by Gustave Eiffel in 1884 to stretch across the river to Valença do Minho in Portugal.

The Romanesque **Iglesia de Santo Domingo**, situated beside the Parque de la Alameda, contains ivy-covered cloisters and tombs with delicately carved effigies. The church overlooks the river, which is used in August for the Descent of the Río Miño, a canoe race and fiesta.

Celanova ⓮

Ourense. 🏠 6,200. 🚌 🚹 *Plaza Mayor 1, 988 43 22 01.* 🛒 *Thu.*
🎭 *San Roque (15 Aug).*

On the main square of this little town is the massive **Monasterio de San Salvador**, also known as the Monasterio de San Rosendo, after its founder. Founded during the 10th century and later rebuilt, it is mainly Baroque, though one of its two lovely cloisters is Renaissance. The enormous church of this Benedictine monastery has an ornate

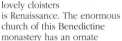
Ceramic tiled floor of the Iglesia de San Miguel

The **Castillo de Monterrei**, built during the wars with Portugal, is 3 km (2 miles) to the west. Inside its three rings of walls are a 15th-century keep, an arcaded courtyard, and a 13th-century church with a delicately carved portal. The castle once housed a monastery and hospital (now a hostal for the pilgrims).

Castillo de Monterrei, standing high above the town of Verín

GALICIA'S FIESTAS

Os Peliqueiros *(Carnival, Feb/Mar)*, Laza (Ourense). Dressed up in grinning masks and outlandish costumes, with cowbells tied to their belts and brandishing sticks, Os Peliqueiros take to the streets on Carnival Sunday. They are licensed to lash out at onlookers, who are forbidden to retaliate. On Carnival Monday morning a battle takes place, with flour, water and live ants used as ammunition. Laza's carnival comes to on end on the Tuesday with a reading of the satirical "Donkey's Will" and the burning of an effigy.

The outrageous costumes of *Os Peliqueiros* in Laza

Flower pavements *(Corpus Christi, May/Jun)*, Ponteareas (Pontevedra). The streets of the town along which the Corpus Christi procession passes are carpeted with intricate designs made from brightly coloured flower petals.

A Rapa das Bestas *(Jun–Aug)*, Oia (Pontevedra). Semi-wild horses are rounded up by local farmers for their manes and tails to be cut. What was once a chore is now a popular fiesta.

St James's Day *(25 Jul)*, Santiago de Compostela. On the night before, there is a firework display in the Praza do Obradoiro. The celebrations are especially wild when 25 July falls on a Sunday.

Ourense ⑯

Ourense. 🏙 *110,000.* 🚆 🚌
🛈 *Calle Burgas 12, 988 36 60 64.*
🗓 *7th, 17th & 25th of each month.*
🎭 *Os Maios (early May); Corpus Christi (one week in Jun).*

The old quarter of Ourense was built around the city's well-known thermal springs, Fonte as Burgas. Even today, these spout water at a temperature of 65°C (150°F) from three fountains.

This old part of the town is the most interesting, particularly the small area around the arcaded Plaza Mayor. Here the **cathedral**, founded in 572 and rebuilt in the 12th–13th centuries, has a vast gilded reredos by Cornelis de Holanda. On the triple-arched doorway are carved figures reminiscent of the Pórtico da Gloria at Santiago *(see p92)*. Nearby is the elegant 14th-century cloister, the **Claustro de San Francisco**.

One of the city's landmarks is the 13th-century **Puente Romano**, a seven-arched bridge which crosses the Río Miño, north of the town. It is built on Roman foundations and is still used by traffic.

Environs
Allariz, 25 km (16 miles) south, and Ribadavia, to the west, have old Jewish quarters with narrow streets and Romanesque churches. Ribadavia is also noted for its Ribeiro wines – a dry white and a port-like red *(see p78)* – and has a wine museum.

Ornate Gothic reredos in the cathedral at Ourense

Monasterio de Ribas de Sil ⑰

Ribas de Sil. 🚆 *San Esteban de Sil.*
🚌 *from Ourense.* **Tel** *988 01 01 10.*
🔵 *daily.*

Near its confluence with the Miño, the Río Sil carves a deep curving gorge in which dams form two reservoirs of dark green water. A hairpin road winds to the top of the gorge, where the Romanesque-Gothic Monasterio de Ribas de Sil is situated high on a crag above the chasm. Recently restored and converted into a parador *(see p558)*, it has an enormous glass wall in one of the three cloisters and fine views.

The Río Sil winding its way through the gorge

The grandiose Monasterio de Oseira surrounded by the forests of the Valle de Arenteiro

Monasterio de Oseira ⑱

Oseira. 🚗 🚌 *from Ourense.*
Tel *988 28 20 04.* ◯ *10am–noon
Mon–Sat, 3:30–6:30pm daily
(until 5:30pm Oct–Mar).* 📷 📹

This monastery stands on its own in a wooded valley near the hamlet of Oseira, named after the bears *(osos)* that once lived in this region. It is a grey building with a Baroque façade dating from 1709. On the doorway is a statue of the Virgin as nurse, with St Bernard kneeling at her feet. The interior of the 12th–13th-century church is typically Cistercian in its simplicity.

Fresco of a *dona* in the monastery Vilar de Donas

Vilar de Donas ⑲

Lugo. 🚗 *80.* 🛈 *Palas de Rey, Avda Compostela 47, 982 38 07 40.*
Church ◯ *Jul–Sep: Tue–Sun, rest of year ask for the key.* 📷 *Jul–Sep. San Antonio (13 Jun), San Salvador (6 Aug).*

This hamlet on the Road to Santiago *(see pp82–3)* has a small church, just off the main road. Inside are tombs of some of the Knights of the Order of Santiago. Also found inside are frescoes painted by the nuns who lived here until the 15th century.

The Cistercian **Monasterio Sobrado de los Monjes**, to the northwest, has a medieval kitchen and chapterhouse, and a church with unusual domes.

Lugo ⑳

Lugo. 🏛 *95,000.* 🚗 🚌 🛈 *Praza de la Constitución s/n, 982 29 73 47.* 🏛 *Tue.* 🎉 *San Froilán (4–12 Oct).*
www.lugo.es/turismo

Capital of Galicia's largest province, Lugo was also an important centre under the Romans. Attracted to the town by its thermal springs, they constructed what is now the finest surviving **Roman wall** in Spain. The wall, which encircles the city, is about 6 m (20 ft) thick and 10 m (33 ft) high with ten gateways. Six of these give access to the top of the wall, from where there is a good view of the city.

Inside the wall, the old town is lively, with pretty squares. In the **Praza de Santo Domingo** is a black statue of a Roman eagle, built to commemorate Augustus' capture of Lugo from the Celts in the 1st century BC. The large, Romanesque **cathedral** is modelled on that of Santiago. It features an elegant Baroque cloister, and a chapel containing the alabaster statue of Nuestra Señora de los Ojos Grandes (Virgin of the Big Eyes). The **Museo Provincial** exhibits local Celtic and Roman finds, a life-size model of a farm kitchen, modern Galician paintings and a statue of a peasant woman holding a miniature priest.

Environs
The stone hamlet of **Santa Eulalia**, situated in lovely open country to the west, conceals a curious building, discovered in 1924: a tiny temple, with lively, bright frescoes of birds and leaves. Though its exact purpose is unknown, it is thought to be an early Christian church and has been dated at around the 3rd century AD.

🏛 **Museo Provincial**
Praza da Soidade. **Tel** *982 24 21 12.* ◯ *10:30am–2pm, 4:30–8pm Mon–Sat; 11am–2pm Sun.* 📷 *Sat pm, Sun in Aug.* ♿

O Cebreiro ㉑

Lugo. 🏛 *16.* 🚌 🛈 *982 36 70 25.* 🎉 *Santa María Real (8 Sep), Santo Milagro (9 Sep).*

Up in the hills in the east of Galicia, close to the border with León, is one of the most unusual villages on the Road to Santiago. Its 9th-century church was supposedly the scene of a miracle in 1300 when the wine was turned into blood and the bread into flesh. Near the church there are several *pallozas*, round thatched stone huts of a Celtic design. Some have been restored, and one of them is now a folk museum.

🏛 **Museo Etnográfico**
O Cebreiro. ◯ *11am–2pm, 3–6pm (to 7pm in summer) Wed–Sun.*

Painted gourd in O Cebreiro's museum

ASTURIAS AND CANTABRIA

ASTURIAS · CANTABRIA

The spectacular Picos de Europa massif sits astride the border between Asturias and Cantabria. In this rural region cottage crafts are kept alive in villages in remote mountain valleys and forested foothills. There are many ancient towns and churches, and pretty fishing ports on the coasts. Cave paintings, such as those at Altamira, were made by people living here about 18,000 years ago.

Asturias is proud that it resisted invasion by the Moors. The Reconquest of Spain is held to have begun in 718 when a Moorish force was defeated by Christians at Covadonga in the Picos de Europa.

The Christian kingdom of Asturias was founded in the 8th century, and in the brilliant, brief artistic period that followed many churches were built around the capital, Oviedo. Some of these Pre-Romanesque churches still stand. Today, Asturias is a province and a principality under the patronage of the heir to the Spanish throne. In the charming, unspoiled Asturian countryside cider is produced and a quaint dialect, *bable,* is spoken.

Cantabria centres on Santander, its capital, a port and an elegant resort. It is a mountainous province with a legacy of Romanesque churches in isolated spots. It also has well-preserved towns and villages such as Santillana del Mar, Carmona and Bárcena Mayor.

Mountains cover more than half of both provinces, so mountain sports are a major attraction. Expanses of deciduous forests remain in many parts, some sheltering Spain's last wild bears. Along the coasts are pretty fishing ports and resorts, such as Castro Urdiales, Ribadesella and Comillas, and sandy coves for bathing. Both the coastal plains and uplands are ideal for quiet rural holidays.

eaceful meadow around Lago de la Ercina in the Picos de Europa massif

One of the pretty cobbled streets of Santillana del Mar, Cantabria

Exploring Asturias and Cantabria

The most obvious attraction in this area is the group of mountains that straddles the two provinces – the Picos de Europa. These jagged peaks offer excellent rock climbing and rough hiking, and in certain parts can be explored by car or bicycle. These and several other nature reserves in the area are home to rare species of flora and fauna, including the capercaillie and brown bear. The coast offers many sandy coves for bathing. Santander and Oviedo are lively university cities with a rich cultural life. There are innumerable unspoiled villages to explore, especially the ancient town of Santillana del Mar. Some of the earliest examples of art exist in Cantabria, most notably at Altamira, where the cave drawings and engravings are among the oldest to be found in Europe.

Typical flower-covered balcony in the village of Bárcena Mayor

A view along the crowded beach of Playa del Camello, Santander

For additional map symbols *see back flap*

SIGHTS AT A GLANCE

Alto Campoo ⓯
Avilés ⑤
Cangas de Onís ⑩
Castro de Coaña ②
Castro Urdiales ㉑
Comillas ⑬
Costa Verde ③
Cuevas de Altamira ⑯
Gijón ⑥
Laredo ⑳
Oviedo ⑦
Parque Nacional de los Picos
  de Europa pp108–9 ⑪
Potes ⑫
Puente Viesgo ⑱
Ribadesella ⑨
Santander ⑲
Santillana del Mar ⑰
Taramundi ①
Teverga ④
Valdediós ⑧
Valle de Cabuérniga ⑭

Cantabrian dairy farmers loading hay on to their cart

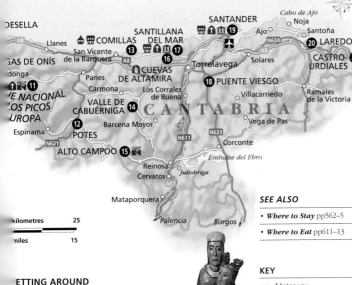

SEE ALSO

• **Where to Stay** pp562–5
• **Where to Eat** pp611–13

GETTING AROUND

The main road through the region is the N634. Most other major roads follow the directions of the valleys and run north to south. Minor roads are generally good but can be slow and winding. The private FEVE railway, which follows the coast from Bilbao to Ferrol in Galicia, is both useful and extremely scenic. A twice-weekly Brittany Ferries service links Santander with Plymouth. Asturias has a small international airport near Avilés. Spain has just changed its road numbering system so some roads featured here may differ from new road signs.

Carved figure in the Convento de Regina Coeli, Santillana del Mar

KEY

═══ Motorway
═ ═ Motorway under construction
▬▬ Secondary road
═══ Minor road
▬▬ Scenic route
╼═╾ Main railway
─── Minor railway
▬▬ Regional border
△ Summit

Craftsman making knife blades in a forge at Taramundi

Taramundi ❶

Asturias. 800. Avenida de
Galicia s/n, 985 64 68 77, 985 64 67
02 (Mon). San José (19 Mar).
www.taramundi.net

Situated in the remote Los
Oscos region, this small
village houses a rural tourism
centre which organizes forest
tours in four-wheel drive
vehicles and has several hotels
and holiday cottages to rent.
Taramundi has a tradition of
wrought-iron craftsmanship.
Iron ore was first mined in
the area by the Romans. There
are approximately 13 forges in
and around the village, where
craftsmen can still be seen
making traditional knives with
decorated wooden handles.

Environs
About 20 km (12 miles) to the
east, at **San Martín de Oscos**,
there is an 18th-century palace.
At **Grandas de Salime**, 10 km
(6 miles) further southeast, the
Museo Etnográfico has displays
showing local crafts, traditional
life and farming.

🏛 **Museo Etnográfico**
Avenida el Ferreiro 17. **Tel** 98 562
72 43. Tue–Sun.

Castro de Coaña ❷

Asturias. 5km from Navia.
Tel 985 97 84 01. Tue–Sun.

One of the best-preserved prehistoric sites of the Cantabrian
area, Castro de Coaña was
later occupied by the Romans.
Set on a hillside in the Navia
valley are the remains of its
fortifications and the stone

foundations of oval and
rectangular dwellings, some
of which stand head high.
Inside can be found hollowed-
out stones which are thought
to have been used for
crushing corn.
   The museum on the site
displays many of the finds
that have been unearthed at
Castro de Coaña. Among
the interesting remains on
display are pottery, tools
and Roman coins.

Circular stone foundations of
dwellings at Castro de Coaña

THE BROWN BEAR

The population of Spain's brown
bears *(Ursus arctos)* has dwind-
led from about 1,000 at the
beginning of the 20th century
to about 80. Hunting by man
and the destruction of the
bear's natural forest habitat have
caused the decline. But now,
protected by nature reserves
such as Somiedo, where most of
the bears in Asturias are found,
together with new conservation
laws, it is hoped this magnificent
omnivore will thrive again.

One of the few remaining
bears in the forests of Asturia

Costa Verde ❸

Asturias. Avilés. Oviedo,
Gijón. Aviles, Calle Ruiz Gomez
21, 985 54 43 25.

The aptly named "green coast"
is a succession of attractive
sandy coves and dramatic
cliffs, punctuated by deep
estuaries and numerous
fishing villages. Inland, there
are lush meadows, and pine
and eucalyptus forests,
backed by mountains. This
stretch of coastline has been
less spoiled than most in
Spain; the resorts tend to be
modest in size, like the hotels.
   Two pretty fishing ports,
Castropol and **Figueras**, stand
by the eastern shore of the
Ría de Ribadeo, forming the
border with Galicia. To the east
are other picturesque villages
such as Tapia de Casariego and
Ortiguera, in a small rocky
cove. Following the coast,
Luarca lies beside a church and
a quiet cemetery on a headland,
and has a neat little harbour
packed with red, blue and white
boats. The village of **Cudillero** is
even more delightful – outdoor
cafés and excellent seafood
restaurants crowd the tiny plaza
beside the port, all of which are
squeezed into a narrow cove.
Behind, white cottages are
scattered over the steep hillsides.
   Further along the coast is
the rocky headland of Cabo
de Peñas where, in the fishing
village of **Candas**, bullfights
are sometimes held on the
sand at low tide. East of Gijón
Lastres is impressively located
below a cliff, and **Isla** has a
broad open beach. Beyond
Ribadesella is the lively town

Church and cemetery overlooking the sea from the headland at Luarca

of **Llanes**. Among the attractions of this old fortified seaport, with its dramatic mountain backdrop, are ruined ramparts and good beaches.

Teverga ❹

Asturias. 🏔 *1,900.* 🚌 *La Plaza.* ⓘ *Dr García Miranda, s/n, San Martin de Teverga, Tel 985 76 42 93 (Easter, 15 Jun–15 Sep, Sat & Sun all year), Tel 985 76 42 02 (rest of year).*

This area is rich in scenery, wildlife and ancient churches. Near the southern end of the Teverga gorge is **La Plaza**. Its church, Iglesia de San Pedro de Teverga, is a fine example of Romanesque architecture. West of La Plaza is **Villanueva**, with its Romanesque Iglesia de Santa María. The 20 km (12 mile) Senda del Oso path skirts the edge of a bear enclosure.

Environs
The large **Parque Natural de Somiedo** straddles the mountains bordering León. Its high meadows and forests are a sanctuary for wolves, brown bears and capercaillies, as well as a number of rare species of wild flowers.

The park has 4 glacial lakes, and is peppered with herdsmen's traditional thatched huts, known as *teitos (see p27)*.

Avilés ❺

Asturias. 🏔 *84,000.* ✈ 🚆 🚌 ⓘ *Calle Ruiz Gómez 21, 985 54 43 25.* 🕌 *Mon.* 🎭 *San Agustin (28 Aug).*

Avilés became the capital of Asturias' steel industry during the 19th century, and is still ringed by big factories. Even though it is sometimes criticized for having little to offer

the visitor, the town hides a medieval heart of some character, especially around the Plaza de España. The **Iglesia de San Nicolás Bari** is decorated with ancient frescoes and has a Renaissance cloister. The **Iglesia de Padres Franciscanos** contains a fine 14th-century chapel and holds the tomb of the first Governor of the US state of Florida. All around are arcaded streets. The international airport outside Avilés serves all Asturias.

Gijón ❻

Asturias. 🏔 *275,000.* 🚆 🚌 ⓘ *Puerto Deportivo, Espigón Central de Fomento, 985 34 17 71.* 🕌 *Sun.* 🎭 *San Antonio (13 Jun); La Virgen de Begoña (15 Aug).*

The province's largest city, this industrial port has been much rebuilt since the Civil War when it was bombarded by the Nationalist navy. The city's most famous son is Gaspar Melchor de Jovellanos, an eminent 18th-century author, reformer and diplomat.

Gijon's old town is on a small isthmus and headland. It centres on the arcaded Plaza Mayor and the 18th-century **Palacio de Revillagigedo**, a Neo-Renaissance folly. The beach, near the city centre, is popular in summer.

🏛 **Palacio de Revillagigedo**
Plaza del Marqués 2. **Tel** 985 34 69 21. ⭕ *for temporary exhibitions. At other times phone for reservations.* ♿

The pretty 12th-century Iglesia de San Pedro at La Plaza

Oviedo ❼

🏙 215,000. 🚌 🚆 ℹ *Plaza de la Constitución 4, 984 08 60 60.* 🗓 *Thu, Sat & Sun.* 🎉 *San Mateo (14–21 Sep).* **www**.oviedo.es

Oviedo, a university city and the cultural and commercial capital of Asturias, stands on a raised site on a fertile plain. The nearby coal mines have made it an important industrial centre since the 19th century. It retains some of the atmosphere of that time, as described by Leopoldo Alas ("Clarín") in his great novel *La Regenta (see p35).*

In and around Oviedo are many Pre-Romanesque buildings. This style flourished in the 8th–10th centuries and was confined to a small area of the kingdom of Asturias, one of the few enclaves of Spain not invaded by the Moors.

The nucleus of the medieval city is the stately Plaza Alfonso II, bordered by a number of handsome old palaces. On this square is situated the Flamboyant Gothic **cathedral** *(see p24)* with its high tower and asymmetrical west façade. Inside are tombs of Asturian kings and a majestic 16th-century gilded reredos. The cathedral's supreme treasure is the Cámara Santa, a restored 9th-century chapel containing statues of Christ and the apostles. The

Cross of Angels in the treasury of Oviedo cathedral

chapel also houses many works of 9th-century Asturian art including two crosses and a reliquary – all made of gold, silver and precious stones.

Also situated in the Plaza Alfonso II is the **Iglesia de San Tirso**. This church was originally constructed in the 9th century, but subsequent restorations have left the east window as the only surviving Pre-Romanesque feature.

Sited behind the cathedral is the **Museo Arqueológico**, housed in the old Benedictine monastery of San Vicente, with its fine cloisters. It contains local prehistoric, Romanesque and Pre-Romanesque treasures.

The **Museo de Bellas Artes**, in Velarde Palace, has a good range of Asturian and Spanish paintings, such as Carreño's portrait of Carlos II *(see p70)* and others by Greco, Goya, Dalí, Miró and Picasso.

Two of the most magnificent Pre-Romanesque churches are

SANTA MARÍA DEL NARANCO

This church, on Mount Naranco, was originally built as a summer palace for Ramiro I in the 9th century. It is one of the finest examples of Pre-Romanesque or Asturian architecture, a style characterized by the slender proportions of its buildings and their original and graceful ornamentation.

The Hall has an unusually high ceiling.

Vaultings of this size were a technical achievement and not adopted throughout Europe until the 11th century.

Arcaded galleries at both ends of the building were designed to let in an enormous amount of light and were an architectural innovation.

Columns carved with *soqueado* or rope effect, were typical of the Pre-Romanesque style.

Church overlooking the sea at Ribadesella

on Mount Naranco, to the north.
Santa María del Naranco has
a large barrel-vaulted hall on
the main floor and arcaded
galleries at either end. Some of
the intricate reliefs on the door
jambs of the nearby **San
Miguel de Lillo** show acrobats
and animal tamers in a circus.

The early 9th-century church
of **San Julián de los Prados**
stands on the road leading
northeast out of Oviedo. The
largest of Spain's surviving Pre-
Romanesque churches, it is
noted for the frescoes which
cover all of its interior.

🏛 **Museo Arqueológico**
Calle San Vicente 5. **Tel** 985 21 54
05. 🕐 *Renovations in progress so
call ahead.*

🏛 **Museo de Bellas Artes**
Calle Santa Ana 1. **Tel** 985 21 30
61. 🕐 *Tue–Sun.* ♿

Valdediós ⑧

Asturias. 👥 150. 🛈 *Monasterio de
Santa María, 985 89 23 24.* **Monastery**
🕐 *11:15am–1pm Tue–Sun.*

Set alone in a field near this
hamlet, the tiny 9th-century
Iglesia de San Salvador is a
jewel of Pre-Romanesque art.

Its ceiling has vivid Asturian
frescoes, and by the portal are
recesses where pilgrims slept.
The church in the **Monasterio
de Santa María** next door is
13th-century Cistercian, with
cloisters from the 16th century.

Environs
To the north, the resort town
of **Villaviciosa** lies amid apple
orchards and has glass-fronted
mansions in its narrow streets.
In nearby **Amandi**, the hilltop
Iglesia de San Juan has a 13th-
century portal and delicate
carvings and friezes.

**Iglesia de San Salvador de
Valdediós in its idyllic setting**

Ribadesella ⑨

Asturias. 👥 6,000. 🚂 🚌 🛈 *Paseo
Princesa Letizia, 985 86 00 38.* 🚢
Wed. 🎉 *Descent of the Río Sella (first
Sat of Aug).* **www**.ribadesella.com

This enchanting little seaside
town bestrides a broad
estuary. On one side is the lively
old seaport full of tapas bars
below a clifftop church. Across
the estuary is a holiday resort.
A multicoloured flotilla of kay-
aks arrives here from Arriondas
(upstream) in an international
regatta that is held every year
on the first Saturday in August.

On the edge of town is the
Cueva de Tito Bustillo. This
cave is rich in stalactites but is
best known for its many prehistoric drawings, which were
discovered in 1968, some
dating from around 18,000 BC.
These include red and black
pictures of stags and horses.
To protect the paintings, only
360 visitors are allowed in
per day; tickets are given out
from 10am every day and
may be booked in advance.
There is a museum on the site.

🛖 **Cueva de Tito Bustillo**
Ribadesella. **Tel** 985 86 11 20.
🕐 *Wed–Sun.* ⚫ *caves: Sep–Mar.* ♿

Cangas de Onís ⑩

Asturias. 👥 6,500. 🚌 🛈 *Plaza del
Ayuntamiento 1, 985 84 80 05.* 🚢
Sun. 🎉 *San Antonio (13 Jun), Fiesta
del Pastor (25 Jul).*

Cangas de Onís, one of the
gateways to the Picos de
Europa *(see pp108–9),* is
where Pelayo, the 8th-century
Visigothic nobleman and hero
of the Reconquest, set up his
court. The town has a Romanesque bridge and the 8th-
century chapel of Santa Cruz.

Environs
About 3 km (2 miles) east in
Cardes is the **Cueva del Buxu**,
which has engravings and rock-
drawings over 10,000 years old.
Only 25 visitors, in groups of
five, are allowed in each day.

🛖 **Cueva del Buxu**
Tel 608 17 54 67 (mobile).
📅 *10:30am, 11:30am, 12:30pm,
3:15pm, 4:15pm Wed–Sun.* ♿ *free
on Wed. Reservations essential.*

Parque Nacional de los Picos de Europa ⑪

Lefebvre's
Ringlet

These beautiful mountains were reputedly christened the "Peaks of Europe" by returning sailors for whom this was often the first sight of their homeland. The range straddles three regions – Asturias, Cantabria and Castilla y León – and has diverse terrain. In some parts, deep winding gorges cut through craggy rocks while elsewhere verdant valleys support orchards and dairy farming. The celebrated creamy blue cheese, Cabrales *(see p77)*, is made here. The Picos offer rock climbing and upland hiking as well as a profusion of flora and fauna. Tourism in the park is well organized.

Covadonga
The Neo-Romanesque basilica, built between 1886 and 1901, stands on the site of Pelayo's historic victory.

Lago de la Ercina
Together with the nearby Lago Enol, this lake lies on a wild limestone plateau above Covadonga and below the peak of Peña Santa.

RIBADESELLA — Cangas de Onís — AS114

DESFILADERO DE — Covadonga

N625

Sella

LAGO ENOL — LAGO DE LA ERCINA

LOS BEYOS

N625

Posada de Valdeó
Cares

Oseja de Sajambre — Puerto de Panderruedas — LE244

Puerto de Pontón

RIAÑO

Desfiladero de los Beyos
This deep, narrow gorge with its high limestone cliffs winds spectacularly for 10 km (6 miles) through the mountains. Tracing the route of the Río Sella below, it carries the main road from Cangas de Onís to Riaño.

KEY

═	Major road
═	Minor road
--	Footpath
—	National park boundary
🚠	Cable car
ℹ	Tourist information
Ⓟ	Parador
☀	Viewpoint

Desfiladero del Río Cares
The River Cares forms a deep gorge in the heart of the Picos. A dramatic footpath follows the gorge, passing through tunnels and across high bridges up to 1,000 m (3,280 ft) above the river.

dramatic view of the mountains of the Picos de Europa

ulnes, one of the remotest villages in Spain, enjoys he views of Naranjo de Bulnes and can now be cessed by an underground funicular railway from ente Poncebos as well as by foot.

VISITORS' CHECKLIST

Casa Dago, Cangas de Onís, 985 84 86 14. Oviedo to Cangas de Onís. **Fuente Dé cable car Tel** *942 73 66 10.* Jul–Sep: 9am–8pm daily, Oct–Jun: 10am–6pm daily. one week in Jan.

PELAYO THE WARRIOR

A statue of this Visigothic nobleman who became king of Asturias guards the basilica at Covadonga. It was close to this site, in 722, that Pelayo and a band of men – though vastly out-numbered – are said to have defeated a Moorish army. The victory inspired Christians in the north of Spain to reconquer the peninsula *(see pp53–5)*. The tomb of the warrior is in a cave which has become a shrine, also containing a painted image of the Virgin.

Pelayo's statue

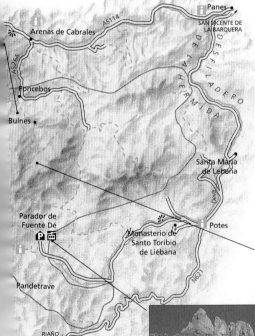

Naranjo de Bulnes, with its tooth-like crest, is in the heart of the massif. At 2,519 m (8,264 ft) it is one of the highest summits in the Picos de Europa.

Fuente Dé Cable Car

The 900-m (2950-ft) ascent from Fuente Dé takes visitors up to a wild rocky plateau pitted with craters. From here there is a spectacular panorama of the Picos' peaks and valleys.

Statue of the Virgin, San Vicente de la Barquera

ASTURIAS AND CANTABRIA'S FIESTAS

La Folía (*first Sun after Easter*), San Vicente de la Barquera (Cantabria). The statue of the Virgen de la Barquera is said to have arrived at San Vicente in a boat with no sails, oars or crew. Once a year, it is put in a fishing boat decorated with flags and flowers, which sails at the head of a procession to bless the sea. Groups of young girls, called *picayos,* stand on the shore singing traditional songs of the region in honour of the Virgin. La Folía usually takes place on the first Sunday after Easter, depending on local tides. **Fiesta del Pastor** (*25 Jul*), near Cangas de Onís (Asturias). Regional dances are performed at this festival beside the shores of Lake Enol in the Picos de Europa National Park. **Battle of the Flowers** (*last Fri of Aug*), Laredo (Cantabria). Floats adorned with flowers are paraded through this small resort. A flower-throwing free-for-all follows the procession. **Nuestra Señora de Covadonga** (*8 Sep*), Picos de Europa (Asturias). Huge crowds converge on the shrine of Covadonga (*see p108*) to pay homage to the patron saint of Asturias.

Potes ⓬

Cantabria. 🏛 *1,500.* 🚉 *Plaza de la Serna (bus station), 942 73 07 87.* 🚌 *Mon.* 🎉 *Ntra. Sra. de Valmayor (15 Aug), Santísima Cruz (14 Sep).*

A small ancient town, with old balconied houses lining the river, Potes is the main centre of the eastern Picos de Europa. It is situated in the broad Valle de Liébana, whose fertile soil yields prime crops of walnuts, cherries and grapes. A potent spirit called *orujo* is made in the town. The **Torre del Infantado**, in the main square, is a defensive tower built in the 15th century.

Environs

Between Potes and the coast runs a gorge, the **Desfiladero de la Hermida**. Halfway up it is **Santa María de Lebeña**, a 10th-century Mozarabic (*see p335*) church.

West of Potes is the monastery church of **Santo Toribio de Liébana**, one of the most revered spots in the Picos de Europa. Founded in the 7th century, it became known throughout Spain a century later when it received reputedly the largest fragment of the True Cross. An 8th century monk, St Beatus of Liébana, wrote the *Commentary on the Apocalypse.* The restored Romanesque monastic buildings were rebuilt in the 1200s, and are now occupied by Franciscan monks.

Comillas ⓭

Cantabria. 🏛 *2,500.* 🚉 *Plaza Joaquín del Piélago 1, 942 72 25 91.* 🚌 *Fri.* 🎉 *El Cristo (16 Jul).* **Palacio** 🕐 *Jul– 9 Sep: 10am–9pm daily; 10 Sep–Jun: 10:30am–2pm, 4–7:30pm Wed–Sun.* 📷 *only.* 🎫

This pretty resort is known for its unusual buildings by Catalan Modernista architects (*see pp140–1).* Antonio López y López, the first Marquis of Comillas, hired Joan Martorell to design the **Palacio Sobrellano** (1881), a huge Neo-

Stone bridge and houses in the ancient town of Potes

Surviving Classical columns among the ruins of the Roman town of Juliobriga, near Reinosa

Gothic edifice. Comilla's best-known monument is Gaudí's *(see p164)* **El Capricho**, now a restaurant (see p611). It was designed for a rich business-man from 1883–9 and is a Mudéjar-inspired fantasy with a minaret-like tower covered in green and yellow tiles. Another of the town's Mod-ernista buildings is the **Universidad Pontificia**, which overlooks the sea from a hilltop. It was designed by Joan Martorell to plans by Domènech i Montaner *(see p140)*.

Wall tile on the façade of El Capricho

Environs
The fishing port of **San Vicente de la Barquera** has arcaded streets, ramparts and the Gothic Romanesque church of Nuestra Señora de los Ángeles.

Valle de Cabuérniga ⓮

Cantabria. 🚌 *Bárcena Mayor.* 🚹 *Ayuntamiento de Tojos, 942 70 60 87, Ayuntamiento de Cabuerniga 942 70 60 01.*

Two exceptionally picturesque towns, notable for their superb examples of rural architecture, draw visitors to the Cabuérniga valley. A good road takes you to the once-remote **Bárcena Mayor**. Its cobbled streets are furnished with old lamps and filled with boutiques, and restaurants serving regional dishes. The pretty houses have

flower-covered balconies and cattle byres.

Carmona is an old, unspoil-ed village approximately 20 km (12 miles) to the northwest of Bárcena Mayor. Its solid stone houses, with pantiled roofs and wooden balcon-ies, are typically Cantabrian *(see p26)*. Woodcarv-ing, the traditional craft of the region, is still practised in this village, where men work outside their houses on a variety of artifacts including bowls, fiddles, *albarcas* (clogs) and chairs. The 13th-century Palacio de los Mier, a manor house in the centre of the village, has been restored and is now a hotel.

The extensive, wild beech woods near **Saja** have been designated a nature reserve.

Traditional balconied houses in Bárcena Mayor

Alto Campoo ⓯

Cantabria. 🚶 *1,900.* 🚉 🚌 🚹 *Estación de Montaña, 942 77 92 23 (am only).* 🎉 *Nuestra Señora de las Nieves (5 Aug), San Roque (16 Aug).*

Sited high in the Cantabrian mountains, this winter resort lies below the Pico de Tres Mares (2,175 m/7,000 ft), the "Peak of the Three Seas", so called because the rivers rising near it flow into the Mediterr-anean, the Atlantic and the Bay of Biscay. The Río Ebro, one of Spain's longest rivers, rises in this area and its source, at Fontibre, is a beauty spot. A road and a chair lift reach the summit of Tres Mares for a breathtaking panorama of the Picos de Europa and other mountain chains. The resort is small, with 23 pistes totalling 27 km (17 miles) in length, and has few facilities for après-ski.

Environs
Reinosa, some 26 km (16 miles) to the east of Alto Campoo, is a handsome market town with old stone houses. Further southeast is Retortillo, a hamlet where the remains of **Juliobriga**, a town built by the Romans as a bastion against the wild tribes of Cantabria, can be seen.

The main road south out of Reinosa leads to **Cervatos**, where the former collegiate church has erotic carvings on its façade. This novel device was meant to deter the villagers from pleasures of the flesh.

At **Arroyuelo** and **Cadalso**, to the southeast, are two churches built into rock faces in the 8th and 9th centuries.

One of the many paintings of bison at Altamira

(see p564). The **Museo Diocesano** is housed in the restored Convento de Regina Coeli, east of the town centre, and has a collection of painted carvings of religious figures.

🏛 **Museo Diocesano**
El Cruce. *Tel* 942 84 03 17.
⬛ Tue–Sun (daily Jul & Aug). ▨

Puente Viesgo ⑱

Cantabria. 🚶 2,600. 🚌 ℹ *Calle Manuel Pérez Mazo 2, 942 59 81 05 (town hall).* 🎉 *La Perolá (20 Jan), San Miguel (28–9 Sep).*

The spa of Puente Viesgo is best known for **El Monte Castillo**, a complex of caves dotted around the limestone hills above the town. Decorated by prehistoric man, it is thought the late Palaeolithic cave dwellers used the deep interior as a sanctuary. They left drawings of horses, bison and other animals, and some 50 hand prints – almost always the left hand. The colours used to create the images were made from minerals in the cave.

Environs
The lush Pas valley, to the southeast, is home to transhumant dairy farmers, the Pasiegos. In the main town of **Vega de Pas**, you can buy two Pasiego specialities – *sobaos*, or sponge cakes (see p77), and *quesadas*, a sweet which is made from milk, butter and eggs. In **Villacarriedo** there is a handsome 18th-century mansion, with two Baroque façades of carved stone hiding a medieval tower.

🏰 **El Monte Castillo**
Puente Viesgo. *Tel* 942 59 84 25. ⬛ Wed–Sun (Apr–Oct: Tue–Sun). ▨ ▨

Cuevas de Altamira ⑯

Cantabria. *Tel* 942 81 80 05 🚌 *Santillana del Mar.* **Caves** ⬤ **Museum** ⬜ 9:30am–6pm Tue–Sat (to 8pm May–Oct), 9:30am–3pm Sun. ⬤ 24, 25 & 31 Dec, 1 & 6 Jan, 1 May, 16 Sep. ▨ (advance booking recommended; see website). ♿ ▨ **http://**museodealtamira.mcu.es

These caves contain some of the world's finest examples of prehistoric art. The earliest engravings and drawings, discovered in 1879, date back to around 16,000 BC (see p48). Public entry to the caves is no longer permitted, but the on-site museum contains a replica of the caves. Similar sites that remain open to the public can be found at nearby Puente Viesgo, Ribadesella (see p107) in Asturias and at Nerja (see p483) in Andalusia.

Carved figure of Christ in the Convento de Regina Coeli

Santillana del Mar ⑰

Cantabria. 🚶 4,000. 🚌 ℹ *Calle Jesus Otero 20, 942 81 88 12.* 🎉 *Santa Juliana (28 Jun), San Roque (16 Aug).* **www.**santillana-del-mar.com

Set just inland, belying its name, this town is one the prettiest in Spain. Its ensemble of 15th- to 18th-century stone houses survives largely intact.

The town grew up around a monastery, which was an important pilgrimage centre, the Romanesque **La Colegiata**. The church houses the tomb of the local early-medieval martyr St Juliana, and contains a 17th-century painted reredos and a carved south door. In its lovely cloisters, vivid biblical scenes have been sculpted on the capitals. On the town's two main cobbled streets there are houses built by local noblemen. These have either fine wooden galleries or iron balconies, and coats of arms inlaid into their stone façades. In the past, farmers used the open ground floors as byres for stabling their cattle.

In the enchanting **Plaza Mayor**, in the centre of town, is a mansion-turned-parador

Main façade of La Colegiata in Santillana del Mar

The Palacio de la Magdalena in El Sardinero

Santander ⓳

Cantabria. 🏠 180,000. ✈ 🚉 🚌 ⛴ ℹ Jardines de Pereda, s/n, 942 20 30 00. 🚢 Mon–Thu. 🎭 Santiago (25 Jul).

Cantabria's capital, a busy port, enjoys a splendid site near the mouth of a deep bay. The town centre is modern – after being ravaged by fire in 1941 it was reconstructed. The **cathedral** was rebuilt in Gothic style, but retains its 12th-century crypt. The **Museo de Bellas Artes** houses work by Goya as well as other artists of the 19th and 20th centuries. The town's **Museo de Prehistoria y Arqueología** displays finds from caves at Altamira and Puente Viesgo (see p112), such as Neolithic axe heads, and Roman coins, pottery and figurines. The **Museo Marítimo** has rare whale skeletons and 350 species of local fish. Call to check opening times.

The town extends along the coast around the Península de la Magdalena, a headland on which there is a park, a small zoo and the **Palacio de la Magdalena** – a summer palace built for Alfonso XIII in 1912, reflecting the resort's popularity at the time with the Royal Family.

The seaside suburb of **El Sardinero**, north of the headland, is a smart resort with a long graceful beach, backed by gardens, elegant cafés and a majestic white casino. In July and August El Sardinero plays host to a major theatre and music festival.

🏛 **Museo de Bellas Artes**
Calle Rubio 6. *Tel* 942 20 31 20.
🕐 Mon–Sat. 🎫

🏛 **Museo de Prehistoria y Arqueología**
Calle Casimiro Sainz 4. *Tel* 942 20 71 09. 🕐 Tue–Sun. 🚻 🎫

🏛 **Museo Marítimo**
C/ San Martin de Bajamar. *Tel* 942 27 49 62. 🕐 Tue–Sun. 🎫 📷

Laredo ⓴

Cantabria. 🏠 13,000. 🚉 ℹ Calle Lopez Seña, 942 61 10 96. 🎭 Batalla de Flores (last Fri of Aug), Carlos V's last landing (3rd week in Sep)

The excellent long, sandy beach of this small town has made it one of Cantabria's most popular bathing resorts. The attractive old town has narrow streets with balconied houses leading up to the 13th-century **Iglesia de Santa María la Asunción**, with its Flemish altar and bronze lecterns. One of the highlights of the year in Laredo is the colourful fiesta of the Battle of the Flowers (see p110).

Castro Urdiales ㉑

Cantabria. 🏠 30,000. 🚉 ℹ Avenida de la Constitución 1, 942 87 15 12. 🚢 Thu. 🎭 Coso Blanco (1st Fri of Jul), Semana Grande (Jun), San Andrés (last Fri of Nov). **Iglesia** 🕐 daily.

Castro Urdiales, a busy fishing town and popular holiday resort, is built around a picturesque harbour. Above the port, on a high promontory, stands the pinkish Gothic **Iglesia de Santa María**, as big as a cathedral. Beside it the recently restored castle, said to have been built by the Knights Templar, has been converted into a lighthouse. Handsome glass-fronted houses, or galerías, line the promenade. The small town beach often becomes crowded but there are bigger ones to the west, such as the Playa de Ostende.

Environs
Near the village of **Ramales de la Victoria**, 40 km (25 miles) south, are prehistoric caves containing etchings and engravings, reached by a very steep mountain road.

Small boats moored in the harbour at Castro Urdiales

THE BASQUE COUNTRY, NAVARRA AND LA RIOJA

VIZCAYA · GUIPUZCOA · ÁLAVA · LA RIOJA · NAVARRA

Green hills meet Atlantic beaches in the Basque Country, land of an ancient people of mysterious origin. Navarra, also partly Basque, was a powerful medieval kingdom. The beautiful western Pyrenees form part of its charming countryside. The vineyards of La Rioja, to the south, produce many of Spain's finest wines.

The Basques are a race apart – they will not let you forget that theirs is a culture different from any in Spain. Although the Basque regional government enjoys considerable autonomy, there is a strong separatist movement seeking to sever links with the government in Madrid.

The Basque Country (Euskadi is the Basque name) is an important industrial region. The Basques are great deep-sea fishermen and fish has a major role in their imaginative cuisine, regarded by many as the best in Spain.

Unrelated to any other tongue, the Basque language, *Euskera*, is widely used on signs and most towns have two names; the fashionable resort of San Sebastián, for example, is known to locals as Donostia. *Euskera* is also spoken in parts of Navarra, which is counted as part of the wider (unofficial) Basque Country. Many of its finest sights – the towns of Olite and Estella, and the monastery of Leyre – date from the Middle Ages when Navarra was a kingdom straddling the Pyrenees. Pamplona, its capital, is best known for its daredevil bullrunning fiesta, which is held in July.

As well as its vineyards and bodegas, La Rioja is a region of market gardens. Among its many historic sights are the cathedral of Santo Domingo de la Calzada and the monasteries of San Millán de la Cogolla and Yuso.

Basque farmhouse near Gernika-Lumo in the Basque Country

A street in the village of Roncal, in the foothills of the Navarrese Pyrenees

Exploring the Basque Country, Navarra and La Rioja

These green, hilly regions have diverse attractions. The Pyrenees in Navarra offer skiing in winter and climbing, caving and canoeing the rest of the year. The cliffs of the Basque Country are broken by rocky coves, rías, and wide bays with beaches of fine yellow sand, interspersed with fishing villages. Inland, minor roads wind through wooded hills, valleys and gorges, past lonely castles and isolated homesteads. In La Rioja, to the south, they cross vineyards, passing villages and towns clustered round venerable churches and monasteries.

The scenic Río Cárdenas valley below the village of San Millán de la Cogolla in La Rioja

KEY

===	Motorway
= =	Motorway under construction
===	Major road
===	Minor road
===	Scenic route
====	Main railway
----	Minor railway
▬	International border

SEE ALSO

- **Where to Stay** pp565–8
- **What to Eat** pp613–17

0 kilometres

0 miles

For additional map symbols *see back flap*

SIGHTS AT A GLANCE

Bilbao (Bilbo) ❶
Castillo de Javier ㉙
Castillo de Mendoza ❾
Las Cinco Villas
   del Valle de Bidasoa ㉔
Costa Vasca ❸
Elizondo ㉕
Enciso ⑯
Estella (Lizarra) ㉒

Gernika-Lumo ❷
Haro ⑪
Hondarribia (Fuenterrabía) ❺
Laguardia ⑩
Logroño ⑮
Monasterio de Leyre ㉘
Monasterio de La Oliva ⑱
Nájera ⑭
Olite ⑳
Oñati ❼
Pamplona (Iruña) ㉓

Puente la Reina ㉑
Roncesvalles (Orreaga) ㉖
Sangüesa ㉚
San Millán de la Cogolla ⑬
San Sebastián (Donostia) ❹
Santo Domingo de la Calzada ⑫
Santuario de Loiola ❻
Tudela ⑰
Ujué ⑲
Valle de Roncal ㉗
Vitoria (Gasteiz) ❽

GETTING AROUND
The main road in the north is the A8 (E5). The A68 AP68 (E804) runs southwards from Bilbao via Haro and follows the Ebro Valley. Motorway spurs extend to Vitoria and Pamplona. The rail network connects the cities and the larger towns, and most towns are served by coach. Bilbao has an international airport. As Spain has recently changed its road numbering system some roads featured here may differ from new road signs.

The fashionable Playa de Ondarreta, one of San Sebastián's three beaches

Buildings overlooking the Río Nervión in Bilbao

Bilbao ❶

Vizcaya. 🏙 353,000. ✈ 🚇 🚌 ⛴
ℹ️ Pl. Ensanche 11, 944 79 57 60.
🎉 Santiago (25 Jul), La Asunción (15 Aug), Semana Grande (late-Aug).
www.bilbao.net/bilbaoturismo

Bilbao (Bilbo) is the centre of Basque industry, Spain's leading commercial port and the largest Basque city. It is surrounded by high, bare hills. Its suburbs spread 16 km (10 miles) along the Río Nervión (Nerbioi) to its estuary. The river between Las Arenas and the fishing port of Portugalete is crossed via the **Puente Colgante** (a UNESCO World Heritage site). This iron transporter bridge, built in 1888, has a suspended cabin for cars and passengers. On the east bank of the estuary is Santurtzi (Santurce), from where ferries sail to the UK (see p676).

Bilbao has flourished as an industrial city since the mid-19th century, when iron ore began to be extracted from deposits northwest of the city. Soon, steelworks and chemical factories became a major part of the local landscape.

The city is not beautiful, but it is prosperous and its once heavy pollution is now much reduced. An urban development scheme has introduced pieces of fascinating modernist architecture to break up the monotone industrial sprawl.

By the river, however, is the city's medieval heart, the casco viejo, built in the 14th century. Here, amid alleys lively with tapas bars, is the arcaded Plazuela de Santiago and the **Catedral Basílica de Santiago**. The **Museo Arqueológico, Etnográfico e Histórico Vasco** displays Basque art, folk artifacts and photographs of Basque life. In the cloister is the Idol of Mikeldi, an animal-like carving dating from the 3rd–2nd century BC.

In the newer town is the large **Museo de Bellas Artes** (Museum of Fine Art), one of Spain's best art museums. It displays art ranging from 12th-century Basque and Catalan pieces to works by modern artists of international fame, including Vasarely, Kokoschka, Bacon, Delaunay and Léger. There are also paintings by Basque artists.

The jewel in the area's cultural crown is the **Museo Guggenheim Bilbao** (see

pp120–1), which opened in 1997. The museum is part of a redevelopment of the city which includes the expansion of its port and the new metro system, designed in a futuristic style by Norman Foster. Another striking new building is the **Palacio de la Música y Congresos Euskalduna**. Designed to resemble a ship, it has a number of auditoriums, one seating 2,200 people and is the home of the Bilbao Symphony Orchestra.

West of the city, a funicular railway ascends to the village of La Reineta and a panorama across the dockyards.

🏛 **Museo Arqueológico, Etnográfico e Histórico Vasco**
Plaza Miguel Unamuno 4. **Tel** 94 415 54 23. ⏰ Tue–Sun. ⏺ public hols. 🎟 (except Thu). ♿

🏛 **Museo de Bellas Artes**
Plaza del Museo 2. **Tel** 94 439 60 60. ⏰ Tue–Sun. 🎟 (except Wed). 📷 ♿

🎭 **Palacio de la Música y Congresos Euskalduna**
Avenida Abandoibarra 4. **Tel** 94 403 50 00. ⏰ for concerts. 🎟 📷 ♿

Gernika-Lumo ❷

Vizcaya. 🏙 16,000. 🚇 🚌
ℹ️ Artekalea 8, 94 625 58 92.
🛍 Mon & Sat. 🎉 Aniversario del Bombardeo de Guernica (26 Apr), San Roke (14–18 Aug).

This little town is of great symbolic significance to the Basques. For centuries, Basque leaders met in democratic assembly under an oak on a hillside here. On 26 April 1937 Gernika-Lumo (Guernica) was the target of the world's first saturation bombing raid, carried out by Nazi aircraft at the request of General Franco. Picasso's powerful painting (see pp66–7) of this outrage can be seen in Madrid (see p299).

The town has since been rebuilt and is rather dull. But in a garden, inside a pavilion and closely guarded, is the 300-year-old petrified trunk of the oak tree, the Gernikako Arbola, or Oak of Gernika, symbol of the ancient roots of the Basque people. Younger oaks, nurtured from its acorns, have been planted beside it. The Basque people make visits to this ancient tree as i

Zuloaga's Condesa Mathieu de Noailles (1913), Bilbao Museum of Fine Art

Basque fishermen depicted in the stained-glass ceiling of the Casa de Juntas in Gernika-Lumo

on a pilgrimage. The **Casa de Juntas**, nearby, is a former chapel where the parliament of the province of Vizcaya reconvened in 1979, when the Basque provinces regained their autonomy. In one room a stained-glass ceiling depicts the Oak of Gernika with Basque citizens debating their rights.

The Europa Park, next door, has peace sculptures by Henry Moore and Eduardo Chillida.

Environs

Five km (3 miles) northeast of Gernika, near Kortézubi (Cortézubi), are the **Cuevas de Santimamiñe**. On the walls of a small chamber are drawings in charcoal of bison and other animals made by Cro-Magnon cave dwellers around 11,000 BC. They were discovered in 1917. The drawings cannot be seen, but a guide leads visitors down the Long Gallery, an underground passage full of oddly shaped stalagmites and stalactites, some of them shot through with brilliant colours. This is one of several huge cave complexes in this area – most are closed to the public.

Casa de Juntas
Allende Salazar. **Tel** 94 625 11
. ⬤ daily. ⬤ 1, 6 Jan, 16 Aug, 25, 31 Dec. ⬤ ⬤

Cuevas de Santimamiñe
rio Basondo, Kortézubi. **Tel** 944 65
57. ⬤ Tue–Sun ⬤ phone ahead.

Costa Vasca ❸

Vizcaya & Guipúzcoa. ⬤ *Bilbao.* ⬤ *Bilbao.* ⬤ *Getxo, 94 491 08 00.*

The Basque country's 176 km (110 miles) of coastline is heavily indented: rugged cliffs alternate with inlets and coves, the whole backed by wooded hills. Some of the fishing villages are over-developed, but the scenery inland is attractive.

There are good beaches north of Algorta (near Bilbao). **Plentzia** is a pleasant estuary town with a marina. Eastwards on the coast is **Bakio**, a large fishing village also known for its beaches. Beyond it the BI3101, a dramatic corniche road, winds high above the sea past the tiny island hermitage,

Anglers on the quayside at Lekeitio, a port on the Costa Vasca

San Juan de Gaztelugatxe, and Matxitxaco, a headland lighthouse. It passes Bermeo, a port with a fishery museum, the **Museo del Pescador**, and Mundaka, a small surfing resort. On the serene Ría de Guernica there are two sandy beaches, **Laida** and **Laga**.

Lekeitio, a fishing port to the east, has a pretty shoreline. Old Basque houses line the seafront below the 15th-century church of Santa María. One long beach, good for swimming, sweeps round the village of **Saturrarán** and the old port of **Ondarroa**. The Lekeitio–Ondarroa road is pleasantly planted with pines.

Zumaia is a beach resort with an old quarter. In the **Museo de Ignacio Zuloaga**, the former home of the well-known Basque painter who lived from 1870–1945, colourful studies of Basque rural and maritime life are on display. **Getaria**, along the coast, is a trawler port with lively cafés. and the 14th-century Iglesia de San Salvador. **Zarautz**, once a fashionable resort, has sizeable beaches and elegant mansions.

🏛 **Museo del Pescador**
Plaza Torrontero 1. **Tel** 94 688 11 71.
⬤ Tue–Sun. ⬤ public hols. ⬤ ⬤
🏛 **Museo de Ignacio Zuloaga**
Santiago Etxea 4, Zumaia. **Tel** 943
86 23 41. ⬤ Apr–Sep: 4–8pm
Wed–Sun. ⬤ ⬤ ⬤

Bilbao: Museo Guggenheim

The Museo Guggenheim Bilbao is the jewel in the city's cultural crown. The building itself is a star attraction: a mind-boggling array of silvery curves by the American architect Frank Gehry, which are alleged to resemble a ship or a flower. The Guggenheim's collection represents an intriguingly broad spectrum of modern and contemporary art, and includes works by Abstract Impressionists such as Willem de Kooning and Mark Rothko. Most of the art shown here is displayed as part of an ongoing series of temporary exhibitions and shows from the permanent collections of the Guggenheim museums in New York, Venice and Berlin.

Roofscape
The Guggenheim's prow-like points and metallic material make it comparable to a ship.

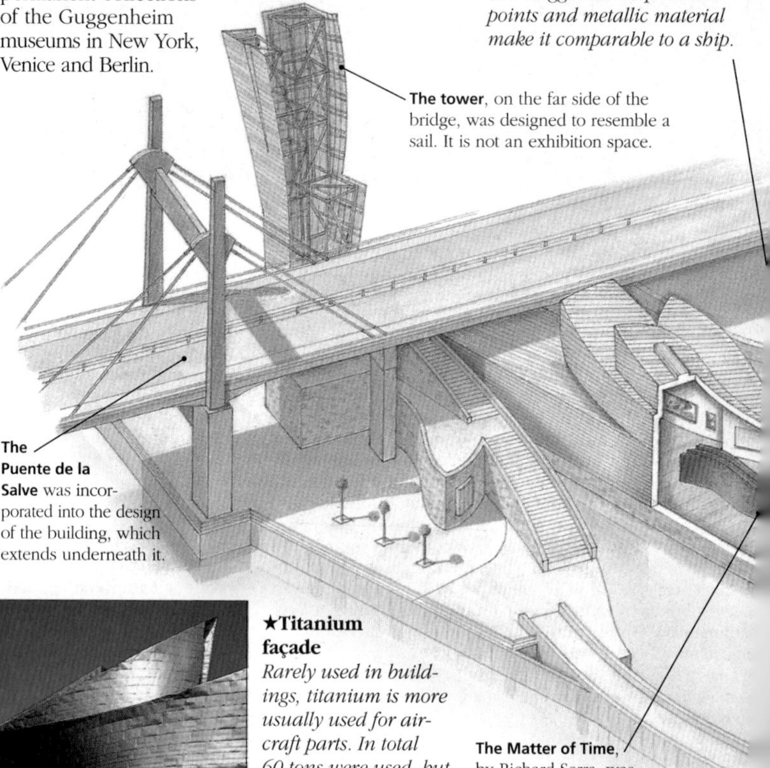

The tower, on the far side of the bridge, was designed to resemble a sail. It is not an exhibition space.

The Puente de la Salve was incorporated into the design of the building, which extends underneath it.

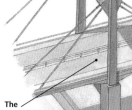

★Titanium façade
Rarely used in buildings, titanium is more usually used for aircraft parts. In total 60 tons were used, but the layer is only 3 mm (0.1 inches) thick.

The Matter of Time, by Richard Serra, was created in hot-rolled steel. It is over 30 m (100 ft) long.

Arcelor Gallery
Dominated by Richard Serra's The Matter of Time, this gallery is the museum's largest. The fish motif, seen in the flowing shape, is one of architect Frank Gehry's favourites.

★ Atrium
The space in which visitors to the museum first find themselves is the extraordinary 60-m (165-ft) high atrium. It serves as an orientation point and its height makes it a dramatic setting for exhibiting large pieces.

VISITORS' CHECKLIST

Avenida Abandoibarra 2.
Tel *944 35 90 00.* ⊗ *Moyua.*
🚌 *1, 10, 11, 13, 18, 27, 38, 48, 71.* ⏱ *10am–8pm Tue–Sun (daily Jul, Aug).* 📷 🚫 🚻 ♿ 📷
🅿 🍴 📷 **www**.guggenheim-bilbao.es

Puppy, by American artist Jeff Koons, is a 13-m (43-ft) West Highland terrier with a coat of flowers watered by an internal irrigation system. It has become a favourite icon of the city.

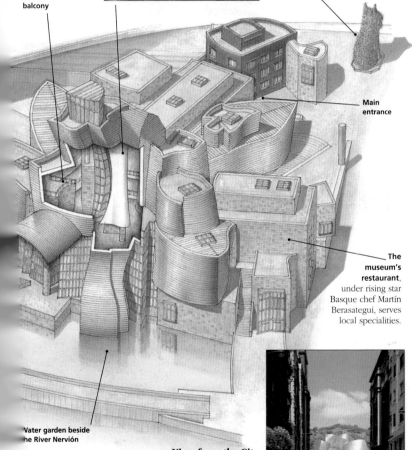

Second-floor balcony

Main entrance

The museum's restaurant, under rising star Basque chef Martín Berasategui, serves local specialities.

Water garden beside the River Nervión

★ STAR FEATURES

★ Titanium façade

★ Atrium

View from the City
Approaching along the Calle de Iparraguirre, the Guggenheim, stands out amid traditional buildings.

San Sebastián's Playa de Ondarreta, with its view across the bay

San Sebastián ④

Guipúzcoa. 185,000. Hondarribia (20 km). Reina Regente 3, 943 48 11 66. Sun. San Sebastián (20 Jan); Semana Grande (week of 15 Aug). **www**.sansebastianturismo.com

Gloriously situated on a neat, shell-shaped bay, San Sebastián (Donostia) is the most elegant and fashionable Spanish seaside resort. At either end of the bay is a tower-topped hill – Monte Urgull in the east and Monte Igueldo in the west. Between the two, in the mouth of the bay, lies a small island, the Isla de Santa Clara.

San Sebastián became a smart resort in the late 19th century. It still has many luxury shops and one of Spain's grandest hotels, the María Cristina (*see p567*), but San Sebastián is now primarily a family resort.

The city is renowned for its great summer arts festivals. The theatre festival is held in May, jazz festivals are held in July, a classical music festival in August, and the San Sebastián International Film Festival in September. The Semana Grande in August is the city's principle fiesta.

Cuisine also plays a huge part in local life: many Basque men in San Sebastián belong to gastronomic clubs where they gather to cook, eat, drink and talk. Even these days, women are seldom invited to such gatherings.

The Old Town

San Sebastián's fascinating old town, called the Parte Vieja, is wedged between the bay and the Río Urumea. The alleys of the old town, packed with restaurants and tapas bars, are intensely animated at night. In the large local fish market, stalls piled high with delicacies testify to the key role of fish in the life of the town.

The heart of the old town is the **Plaza de la Constitución**, a handsome, arcaded square with coloured shutters. The numbers on the balconies date from when the square was used as a bullring – organizers sold a ticket for each numbered place. Nearby is the 16th-century church of **Iglesia de San Vicente**.

Monte Urgull rises behind the old town. On the summit are a statue of Christ and the ruined **Castillo de Santa Cruz de la Mota**, with old cannons.

Beaches

San Sebastián's two principal beaches follow the bay round to **Monte Igueldo**. The **Playa de Ondarreta** is the more fashionable of the two, while the **Playa de la Concha** is the larger. Between them is the **Palacio Miramar**, built in 1889 by the Basque architect, José Goicoa, to designs by Selden Wornum, a British architect. The palace, built for Queen María Cristina, established San Sebastián as an aristocratic resort. The gardens are open to the public.

At the water's edge near the Playa de Ondarreta is a striking group of modern iron sculptures, *The Comb of the Winds* by Eduardo Chillida. A road and a funicular railway, built in 1912, lead to the top of Monte Igueldo, where there is a small amusement park.

To the east of the Playa de la Concha is the surfer's favourite beach, **Playa de la Zurriola**, which is overlooked by the hill, **Monte Ulía**.

Aquarium

Plaza Carlos Blasco de Imaz 1. *Tel* 943 44 00 99. Oct–Mar: 10am–7pm (until 8pm Sat & Sun); Jul–Aug: 10am–9pm daily; Apr–Jun & Sep: 10am–8pm daily. 25 Dec & 1 Jan.
This remodelled aquarium boasts a 360° underwater tunnel, where visitors can view over 5,000 fish, including four species of shark. Tickets allow entry to a Naval Museum with exhibits of Basque naval history

The Comb of the Winds by Eduardo Chillida

Josep Maria Sert's murals of Basque life in the Museo de San Telmo

Kursaal

Avenida de Zurriola 1. *Tel 943 00 30 00.*

These giant cubes stand out as the most prominent feature on Zurriola beach, especially when lit up at night. Designed by Rafael Moneo, the cubes contain large auditoriums, for most of the year home to conferences and concerts.

🏛 Museo de San Telmo

Plaza Zuloaga. *Tel 943 48 15 80.* for renovation until 2010.

This is a large museum in a 16th-century monastery below Monte Urgull. In the cloister is a collection of Basque funerary columns dating from the 5th–17th centuries.

The museum also contains displays of furniture, tools and other artifacts, and paintings by local Basque artists: 19th-century works by Antonio Ortiz Echagüe, modern paintings by Ignacio Zuloaga, portraits

by Vicente López and masterpieces by El Greco. The chapel holds 11 murals by the Catalan artist Josep Maria Sert, depicting Basque legends, culture and the region's seafaring life.

🏛 Chillida-Leku

Caserío Zabalaga, B° Jáuregui 66, Hernani. *Tel 943 33 60 06.* Tue (except Jul & Aug). www.museochillidaleku.com

Set in a 16th-century farmhouse surrounded by gardens, this new museum displays a permanent collection of 140 sculptures by the acclaimed Basque artist Eduardo Chillida.

Environs

5 km (3 miles) east of San Sebastián is **Pasai Donibane**, a picturesque fishing village consisting of a jumble of houses with a cobbled main street, which has some good fish restaurants.

The waterfront of the tiny fishing village of Pasaia Donibane

Old balconied houses in the upper town, Hondarribia

Hondarribia ❺

Guipúzcoa. 16,000. ✈ ❶ Calle Javier Ugarte 6, 943 64 54 58. La Kutxa Entrega (25 Jul), Alarde (6–8 Sep).

Hondarribia (Fuenterrabía), the historic town at the mouth of the Río Bidasoa, was attacked by the French over many centuries. The upper town is protected by 15th-century walls and entered via their original gateway, the handsome **Puerta de Santa María**. They enclose alleys of old houses with carved eaves, balconies and coats of arms.

The streets cluster round the church of **Nuestra Señora de la Asunción y del Manzano**, with its massive buttresses, tall Baroque tower, and, inside, a gold reredos. At the town's highest point is the 10th century **castle**, now a parador (see p566).

Hondarribia has seafront cafés in La Marina, its lively fishermen's quarter. It is also a seaside resort, with beaches stretching to the north.

Environs

A hill road climbs westwards to the shrine of the Virgin of Guadalupe. Further along this road are panoramic views of the coast and the mountains. From the **Ermita de San Marcial**, which stands on a hill 9 km (6 miles) to the south, there are views of the Bidasoa plain straddling the border – the French towns are neatly white, the Spanish ones are greyer.

SAN SEBASTIÁN FILM FESTIVAL

This festival, founded in 1953, is one of the five leading European annual film festivals. It is held in late September, drawing more than 200,000 spectators. The special Donostia Prize is awarded as a tribute to the career of a star or director: recent winners include Francis Ford Coppola, Richard Gere and Woody Allen. Visiting celebrities have included Quentin Tarantino, Greta Scacchi and William Hurt. Prizes also go to individual new films. An early winner was Hitchcock's *Vertigo*. The festival's website is www.sansebastianfestival.com

Lauren Bacall receiving an award

The Renaissance façade of the former Basque university in Oñati

Santuario de Loiola ❻

Loiola (Guipúzcoa). **Tel** 943 02 50 00. 🔲 ⭕ 10am–1pm, 3–7pm daily.
www.santuariodeloyola.org

Saint Ignatius of Loiola (San Ignacio de Loyola), founder of the Jesuits, was born in the 1490s in the Santa Casa (holy house), a stone manor near Azpeitia. In the 17th century it was enclosed by the Basílica de San Ignacio, and the rooms in which the aristocratic Loiola family lived were converted into chapels. The Chapel of the Conversion is the room in which Ignatius, as a young soldier, recovered from a war injury, and had a profound religious experience.

A diorama depicts episodes in the saint's life: dedicating his life to Christ at the Monastery of Montserrat (see pp218–9); writing his *Spiritual Exercises* in a cave at Manresa; his imprisonment by the Inquisition; and his pilgrimage to the Holy Land. The basilica, built from 1681–1738, has a Churrigueresque dome and a circular nave with rich carvings.

Oñati ❼

Guipúzcoa. 🏠 11,000. 🔲 🔽
C/ San Juan 14, 943 78 34 53. 🔼
Sat. 🎭 Corpus Christi (May/Jun), San
Miguel (29 Sep). **www**.oinati.org

This historic town in the Udana Valley has a distinguished past. In the First Carlist War, 1833–9 (see p63), it was a seat of the court of Don Carlos, brother of King Fernando VII and pretender to the throne. Its former **university**, built in about 1540, was for centuries the only one in the Basque Country. It has a Renaissance façade, decorated with statues of saints, and an elegant patio.

In the Plaza de los Fueros is the **Iglesia de San Miguel**, a Gothic church with a stone cloister in Gothic-Flemish style. It contains the tomb of Bishop Zuázola of Ávila, the founder of the university. Opposite is the Baroque **town hall** (ayuntamiento).

Environs
A mountain road ascends 9 km (6 miles) to the **Santuario de Arantzazu**, below the peak of Aitzgorri. In 1469 it is believed a shepherd visualized the Virgin here. Over the door of the church built in the 1950s, are sculptures of the apostles by Jorge Oteiza.

🏛 **Universidad de Sancti Spiritus**
Avenida de la Universidad Vasca.
Tel 943 78 34 53. ⭕ Mon–Sun
for guided tours (phone Oñati
tourist information in advance). 🚫

The imposing Santuario de Loiola, with its Churrigueresque cupola

THE FOUNDING OF THE JESUIT ORDER

The Society of Jesus was founded in Rome in 1539 by Saint Ignatius and a group of priests who were dedicated to helping the poor. Pope Paul III soon approved the order's establishment, with Ignatius as Superior General. The order, which grew wealthy, vowed military obedience to the Pope and became his most powerful weapon against the Reformation. Today, there are approximately 20,000 Jesuits working, mainly in education, in 112 countries.

Saint Ignatius of Loiola

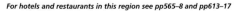

Basque Culture

The Basques may be Europe's oldest race. Anthropologists think they could be descended from Cro-Magnon people, who lived in the Pyrenees 40,000 years ago. The dolmens and carved stones of their ancestors are evidence of the Basques' pagan roots.

Long isolated in their mountain valleys, the Basques preserved their unique language, myths and art for millennia, almost untouched by other influences.

Basque policeman

Many families still live in the isolated, chalet-style stone *caseríos*, or farmhouses, built by their forebears. Their music and high-bounding dances are unlike those of any other culture, and their cuisine is varied and imaginative.

The *fueros* or ancient Basque laws and rights were suppressed under General Franco, but since the arrival of democracy in 1975 the Basques have had their own parliament and police force, having won great autonomy over their own affairs.

THE BASQUE REGION

☐ *Areas of Basque culture*

The national identity *is symbolized by the region's flag:* La Ikurriña. *The white cross symbolizes Christianity. The green St Andrew's Cross commemorates a battle won on his feast day.*

Bertsolaris *are bards. They improvise witty, sometimes humorous songs, whose verses relate current events or legends. Bertsolaris sing, unaccompanied, to gatherings in public places, such as bars and squares, often in competition. This oral tradition has preserved Basque folklore, legends and history. No texts were written in* Euskera (Basque) *until the 16th century.*

The Basque economy *has always relied on fishing and associated industries, such as shipbuilding and agriculture. In recent history, heavy industries have made this region prosperous.*

Traditional sports *are highly respected in Basque culture. In pelota (frontón), teams hit a ball at a wall then catch it with a wicker scoop or their hands. Sports involving strength, such as log-splitting and weightlifting, are the most popular.*

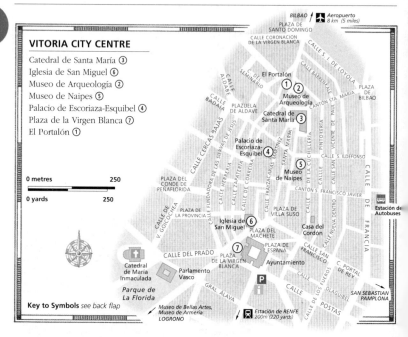

VITORIA CITY CENTRE

Catedral de Santa María ③
Iglesia de San Miguel ⑥
Museo de Arqueología ②
Museo de Naipes ⑤
Palacio de Escoriaza-Esquibel ④
Plaza de la Virgen Blanca ⑦
El Portalón ①

0 metres   250
0 yards   250

Key to Symbols *see back flap*

Vitoria ❽

Alava. 🏠 *230,000.* ✈ 🚉 🚌 ℹ
Plaza General Loma, 945 16 15 98.
🛒 *Thu.* 🎭 *Romería de San
Prudencio (27–28 Apr), Fiestas de la
Virgen Blanca (4–9 Aug).*
www.vitoria-gasteiz.org/turismo

Vitoria (Gasteiz), the seat of the Basque government, was founded on a hill – the province's highest point and the site of an ancient Basque town, Gasteiz. Vitoria's oldest part, El Campillo, was rebuilt in 1200 after a fire. The city later grew rich on the iron and wool trades.

The old town focuses on the **Plaza de la Virgen Blanca**, with its monument to a battle fought nearby in 1813, when the British Duke of Wellington defeated the French. Around the plaza are old houses with *miradores* (glazed balconies).

On the hillside above the plaza is the Gothic **Iglesia de San Miguel**. An outside niche contains a statue of the Virgen Blanca (White Virgin), Vitoria's patron saint. A big festival *(see p132)* starts before her feast day, which is on 5 August. On the wall of San Miguel facing the **Plaza del Machete** there is a recess with a replica of the machete on which the city's rulers swore to uphold the laws or be slain.

The old town has several Renaissance palaces, including the 16th-century **Palacio de Escoriaza-Esquibel**, with its Plateresque *(see p25)* patio. Around it is a charming area of alleys linked by steep steps.

The city has two cathedrals. The oldest, currently under restoration, is the Gothic **Catedral de Santa María**, with a sculpted west porch. Close by, in Calle Correría, a street of old houses, is **El Portalón**, a merchant's house and hostel from the 15th century. The building, which is full of Basque country furniture and art, is now a restaurant.

Among the city's later architectural gems are an arcaded street, **Los Arquillos**, and the adjoining **Plaza de España**, also arcaded. They were built in the late 18th century to link the old town with the new quarter then being built. South of the old town is the Neo-Gothic **Catedral Nueva de María Inmaculada**, begun in 1907 and finished in 1973.

🏛 Museo de Arqueología
Calle Correría 116. **Tel** *945 18 19 ..*
◯ *Tue–Sun.* ⬤ *Good Fri, 25 Dec.*
🎫 *reservations required.*
The exhibits in this museum, in a 16th-century half-timbered house, include dolmens erected more than 4,000 years ago, Roman sculptures found in Álava, and medieval artifacts.

The quiet Plaza de España in the centre of Vitoria

For hotels and restaurants in this region see pp565–68 and pp613–17

The Gothic west door of Vitoria's Catedral de Santa María

🏛 Museo Fournier de Naipes

Palacio de Bendaña, C/ Cuchillería 54. **Tel** 945 18 19 20. ⬤ Tue–Sun. 📷 am only; call 945 18 19 18 to book. ♿

The grandson of Heraclio Fournier, who founded a playing cards factory in Vitoria in 1868, displays his collection of more than 6,000 items in this museum. The oldest exhibits are late 14th-century Italian cards. Among the many sets of tarot cards are some designed by Salvador Dalí in the 1980s.

🏛 Museo de Armería

Paseo Fray Francisco 3. **Tel** 945 18 19 25. ⬤ Tue–Sun. 📷 call 945 18 19 18 for guided tours. ♿

The weapons here range from prehistoric axes to 20th-century pistols. Medieval armour and an exhibit on the 1813 Battle of Vitoria are also on display.

🏛 Museo Diocesano de Arte Sacro

Catedral Nueva de María Inmaculada, Calle Monseñor Cadena y Eleta s/n. **Tel** 945 15 06 31. ⬤ 10am–2pm, 4–6:30pm Tue–Fri, 10am–2pm Sat, 11am–2pm Sun & public hols. 📷 call ahead. ♿

The design of this museum is considerate to the surrounding cathedral. Exhibits of religious art are displayed in sections related to their medium.

Castillo de Mendoza **⑨**

Mendoza (Álava). **Tel** 945 18 16 17. ⬤ to the public until the end of 2009.

In the centre of Mendoza village, 10 km (6 miles) west of Vitoria, stands this small, square, much restored fortress dating from the 13th century. There are marvellous views from the tops of the four towers. Once a ducal residence, the thick-walled castle now houses the **Museo Heráldica**.

In it are displayed the coats of arms of noble Alavese families and items relating to them.

Environs

On the A2622 Pobes–Tuesta road are the **Salinas de Añana**, a group of saltpans fed by mineral springs. The nearby village of **Tuesta** boasts a Romanesque church. Inside are capitals carved with historical scenes, and a medieval wood sculpture of St Sebastian.

Laguardia **⑩**

Álava. 🏘 1,500. 🚉 Plaza San Juan 1, 945 60 08 45. 🚌 Tue. 🎉 San Juan and San Pedro (23–29 Jun).

This little wine town is the capital of La Rioja Alavesa, a part of southern Álava province where Rioja wines (see pp78–9) have been produced for centuries. It is a fertile, vine-clad plain, sheltered by high hills to the north. There are fine panoramic views from the road that climbs up to the Herrera pass. Laguardia is a medieval hill town, its encircling ramparts, towers and fortified gateways visible from afar. Along its steep, narrow cobbled streets there are many **bodegas** (wine cellars), offering wine tastings and tours throughout the year. It is usually necessary to make a booking in advance.

The Gothic **Iglesia de Santa María de los Reyes** has an austere façade and an unusual inner portal. The Virgin and Child are delicately sculptured on this door.

Virgin and child statue in Laguardia

vineyards near Laguardia, capital of La Rioja Alavesa, a wine-producing region since the Middle Ages

Haro ⑪

La Rioja. 🚶 *11,500.* 🚉 🚌 ℹ️
*Plaza Monseñor Florentino Rodriguez,
941 30 33 66.* 🚌 *Tue & Sat.* 🍷 *Wine
Battle (29 Jun), San Felices,
San Pedro (24–29 Jun), Virgen de la
Vega (8 Sep).* **www**.haro.org

A graceful town on the Río
Ebro, Haro has a lively old
quarter with wine taverns and
mansions. It is crowned by
the hilltop **Iglesia de Santo
Tomás**, a Gothic church with
a Plateresque *(see p25)* portal.

Haro is the centre for the
vineyards and bodegas of the
Rioja Alta wine region, which
is higher and cooler than the
Rioja Baja *(see pp78–9)*. The
clay soil and the climate –
Haro is sheltered by a sierra
to the north – create the conditions in which the famous
regional wines are produced.
Many bodegas run tours and
tastings. To join one, you may
need to book ahead at the
bodega. There may be a small
charge. The cafés in the old
town offer local wines and
tapas at low prices and a
convivial atmosphere.

A wine-throwing orgy is the
climax of the area's fiesta *(see
p132)* held every June.

Tomb of St Dominic in the cathedral of Santo Domingo de la Calzada

**Rows of Rioja vines on the rolling
hills near Haro**

Santo Domingo de la Calzada ⑫

La Rioja. 🚶 *6,500.* 🚌 ℹ️ *Calle
Mayor 70, 941 34 12 30.* 🚌 *Sat.*
🍷 *Día del Patron (12 May), Fiestas
del Santo (25 Apr–15 May).*

This town on the Road to
Santiago de Compostela *(see
pp82–3)* is named after the
11th-century saint who built
bridges and roads *(calzadas)*
to help pilgrims. The same
saint also founded a hospital,
which now serves as a
parador *(see p567)*.

Miracles performed by the
saint are recorded in carvings
on his tomb in the town's
part-Romanesque, part-Gothic
cathedral, and in paintings on
the wall of the choir. The
most obvious and bizarre
record is a sumptuously decorated cage set in a wall in
which, for centuries, a live
cock and hen have been kept.
The cathedral has a carved
walnut reredos at the high
altar, the last work, in 1541,
of the artist Damià Forment.
The restored 14th-century
ramparts of the town are also
worth seeing.

THE COCK AND HEN OF ST DOMINIC

A live cock and hen are kept in the cathedral of
Santo Domingo de la Calzada as a tribute to the
saint's miraculous life-giving powers. Centuries ago,
it is said, a German pilgrim refused the advances of
a local girl, who denounced him as a thief. He was
hanged as a consequence, but later his parents found
him alive on the gallows. They rushed to a judge, who
said, dismissively, "Nonsense, he's no more alive
than this roast chicken on my plate". Whereupon, the
chicken stood up on the plate and crowed.

The cock and hen in their decorated cage

San Millán de la Cogolla ⑬

La Rioja. 🏘 *300.* ⓘ *Monasterio de Yuso (open Tue–Sun), Portería de Yuso, piso de abajo, 941 37 32 59; Monasterio de Suso, 941 37 30 82 (for reservations).* 🎉 *Traslación de las Reliquias (26 Sep), San Millán (12 Nov).* **www.fsanmillan.com**

This village grew up around two monasteries. On a hillside above the village is the **Monasterio de San Millán de Suso**. It was built in the 10th century on the site of a community founded by St Emilian, a shepherd hermit, in 537. The church, hollowed out of pink sandstone, has Romanesque and Mozarabic features. It contains the carved alabaster tomb of St Emiliano.

The **Monasterio de San Millán de Yuso** is below it, in the Cárdenas Valley. It was built between the 16th and 18th centuries. The part-Renaissance church has Baroque golden doors and a rococo sacristy, where 17th-century paintings are hung.

In the treasury there is a collection of ivory plaques. They were once part of two 11th-century jewelled reliquaries, which were plundered by French troops in 1813. Medieval manuscripts are also displayed in the treasury. Among them is a facsimile of one of the earliest known texts in Castilian Romance *(see p34)*. It is a commentary by a 10th-century Suso monk on a work by San Cesáreo de Arles, the *Glosas Emilianenses.*

ᴇ Monasterio de San Millán de ᴏ in the Cárdenas valley

Cloister of the Monasterio de Santa María la Real, Nájera

Nájera ⑭

La Rioja. 🏘 *8,000.* 🚉 ⓘ *Plaza de San Miguel, s/n, 941 36 00 41.* 🚌 *Thu.* 🎉 *San Prudencio (28 Apr), Santa María la Real (16–17 Sep).*

The old town of Nájera, west of Logroño, was the capital of La Rioja and Navarra until 1076, when La Rioja was incorporated into Castile. The royal families of Navarra, León and Castile are buried in the **Monasterio de Santa María la Real**. It was founded in the 11th century beside a sandstone cliff where a statue of the Virgin was found in a cave. A 13th-century Madonna can be seen in the cave, beneath the carved choir stalls of the 15th-century church.

The 12th-century carved tomb of Blanca of Navarra, the wife of Sancho III, is the finest of many royal sarcophagi.

🛈 Monasterio de Santa María la Real
Nájera. **Tel** *941 36 10 83.*
🕐 *Tue–Sun.* 🎟

Logroño ⑮

La Rioja. 🏘 *145,000.* 🚉 🚌 ⓘ *Paseo del Espolón, Príncipe de Vergara 1, 941 29 12 60.* 🎉 *San Bernabé (11 Jun), San Mateo (21 Sep).*

The capital of La Rioja is a tidy, modern city of wide boulevards and smart shops. It is the commercial centre of a fertile plain where quality vegetables are produced, in addition to Rioja wines.

In Logroño's pleasant old quarter on the Río Ebro is the Gothic **cathedral**, with twin towers. Above the south portal of the nearby **Iglesia de Santiago el Real**, which houses an image of the patron saint Our Lady of Hope, is an equestrian statue of St James as Moorslayer *(see p55)*.

Environs
About 50 km (30 miles) south of Logroño, the N111 winds through the dramatic **Iregua Valley**, through tunnels and gorges, to the Sierra de Cameros.

The ornate Baroque west door of Logroño Cathedral

Enciso ⑯

La Rioja. 🏘 *175.* 🚌 *from Logroño.* ⓘ *Plaza Mayor, 941 39 60 05.* 🎉 *San Roque (16 Aug).*

Near this remote hill village west of Calahorra is Spain's "Jurassic Park". Signposts point to the *huellas de dinosaurios* (dinosaur footprints). Embedded in rocks overhanging a stream are the prints of many giant, three-toed feet, up to 30 cm (1 ft) long. They were made around 150 million years ago, when dinosaurs moved between the marshes of the Ebro valley, at that time a sea, and these hills. Prints can also be seen at other locations in the area.

Environs
Arnedillo, 10 km (6 miles) to the north, is a spa with thermal baths once used by Fernando VI. In **Autol**, to the east, there are two unusual limestone peaks.

The intricately carved portal of Tudela Cathedral

Tudela ⑰

Navarra. 🏛 33,000. 🚗 🚊
ℹ️ Calle de Juicio 4, 948 84 80 58.
🗓 Sat. 🎭 Santa Ana (26–30 Jul).

Navarra's second city is the great commercial centre of the vast agricultural lands of the Ebro valley in Navarra, the Ribera. Much of Tudela consists of modern developments, but its origins are ancient. Spanning the Ebro is a 13th-century bridge with 17 irregular arches. The old town has two well-preserved Jewish districts.

The **Plaza de los Fueros** is old Tudela's main square. It is surrounded by houses with wrought-iron balconies. On some of their façades are paintings of bullfights, a reminder that the plaza was formerly used as a bullring.

The **cathedral**, begun in 1194, exemplifies the religious toleration under which Tudela was governed after the Reconquest.

It is Early Gothic, with a carved portal depicting the Last Judgement. There is a Romanesque cloister, and beside the cathedral sits a 9th-century chapel that is thought to have once been a synagogue.

Environs
To the north is the **Bárdenas Reales**, an arid area of limestone cliffs and crags. About 20 km (12 miles) west of Tudela is the spa town of **Fitero**, with the 12th-century Monasterio de Santa María.

Monasterio de La Oliva ⑱

Carcastillo (Navarra). **Tel** 948 72 50 06. 🚌 from Pamplona. ◯ daily. 🎫

French Cistercian monks built this small monastery on a remote plain in the 12th century. The church is simple, in typical Cistercian style, but adorned with rose windows.

One of the cloisters in the Monasterio de La Oliva

The serene cloister, dating from the 14th and 15th centuries, adjoins a 12th-century chapter-house. The church also has a 17th-century tower. Today, the monks survive by selling local honey and cheese, their own wine, and by accepting paying guests (see p556).

Ujué ⑲

Navarra. 🏛 220. ℹ️ Plaza Municipal, 948 73 90 46. 🎭 Virgen de Ujué (8 Sep).

One of Spain's least spoiled hill villages, Ujué commands a high spur at the end of a winding road. It has quaint façades, cobbled alleys and steep steps. The **Iglesia de Santa María** is in Gothic style with a Romanesque chancel and an exterior lookout gallery. The ruined fortifications around the church offer views of the Pyrenees.

On the Sunday after 25 April, pilgrims in black capes visit the Virgin of Ujué, whose Romanesque image is displayed in the church.

Olite ⑳

Navarra. 🏛 3,500. 🚗 ℹ️ Pl. de Teobaldos 10, 948 74 17 03. 🛒 Wed. 🎭 Medieval Markets (late Aug), Exaltación de la Santa Cruz (14–20 Sep).

The historic town of Olite was founded by the Romans and later chosen as a royal residence by the kings of Navarra. Part of the town's old walls can be seen. They enclose a

THE KINGDOM OF NAVARRA

Navarra emerged as an independent Christian kingdom in the 10th century, after Sancho I Garcés became king of Pamplona. Sancho III the Great expanded the kingdom, and at his death, in 1035, Navarra stretched all the way from Ribagorza in Aragón to Valladolid. Sancho VI the Wise, who reigned 1150–94, recognized the independent rights (fueros) of many towns. In 1234, Navarra passed by marriage to a line of French rulers. One, Carlos III, the Noble, built Olite Castle. His grandson, Carlos de Viana, wrote the *Chronicle of the Kings of Navarra* in 1455. In 1512 Navarra was annexed by Fernando II of Castile, as part of united Spain, but it kept its own laws and currency until the 1800s.

Prince Carlos de Viana, Carlos III's grandson

For hotels and restaurants in this region see pp565–8 and pp613–17

delightful jumble of steep, narrow streets and little squares, churches and the **Monasterio de Santa Clara**, begun in the 13th century. The houses along the Rúa Cerco de Fuera and the Rúa Mayor were built between the 16th and 18th centuries.

The castle, the **Palacio Real de Olite**, was built in the early 15th century by Carlos III, and has earned Olite its nickname "the Gothic town". It was heavily fortified, but was brilliantly decorated inside by Mudéjar artists with *azulejos* (ceramic tiles) and marquetry ceilings. The walkways were planted with vines and orange trees, and there was an aviary and a lions' den.

During the War of Independence *(see pp62–3)* the castle was burned to prevent it falling into French hands. Since 1937, however, it has been restored to a semblance of its former glory. Part of it houses a parador *(see p567)*.

Today, the castle is a complex of courtyards, passages, steep stairs, large halls, royal chambers, battlements, towers and turrets. From the "windy tower" monarchs were able to watch tournaments.

Adjoining the castle is a 13th-century former royal chapel, the **Iglesia de Santa María**, with its richly carved Gothic portal.

Olite is in the Navarra wine region *(see pp78–9)* and the town has several bodegas.

♠ **Palacio Real de Olite**
Plaza de Carlos III. **Tel** 948 74 00 35. ○ daily. 🎟

e battlements and towers of the 'acio Real de Olite

The five-arched, medieval pilgrims' bridge at Puente la Reina

Puente la Reina ㉑

Navarra. 🏘 2,600. 🚌 c/ Mayor 105, 948 34 08 45. 🛒 Sat. 🎉 Santiago *(25–30 Jul).*

Few towns along the Road to Santiago de Compostela *(see pp82–3)* evoke the past as vividly as Puente la Reina. The town takes its name from the graceful, humpbacked pedestrian bridge over the Río Arga. The bridge was built for pilgrims during the 11th century by royal command.

On Puente la Reina's narrow main street is the **Iglesia de Santiago**, which has a gilded statue by the west door showing the saint as a pilgrim. On the edge of town is the **Iglesia del Crucifijo**, another pilgrim church which was built in the 12th century by the Knights Templar. Contained within the church is a

Distinctive crucifix in Puente la Reina

Y-shaped wooden crucifix of a sorrowful Christ with arms upraised, which is said to have been a gift from a German pilgrim in the 14th century.

Environs
Isolated in the fields about 5 km (3 miles) to the east is the 12th-century **Iglesia de Santa María de Eunate**. This octagonal Romanesque church may once have been a cemetery church for pilgrims, as human bones have been unearthed here. Pilgrims would shelter beneath the church's external arcade. West of Puente la Reina is the showpiece hill village of **Cirauqui**. It is also charming, if rather over-restored. Chic little balconied houses line tortuously twisting alleys linked by steps. The Iglesia de San Román, built in the 13th century on top of the hill, has a sculpted west door.

BASQUE COUNTRY, NAVARRA AND LA RIOJA'S FIESTAS

Los Sanfermines (*6–14 Jul*), Pamplona (Navarra). In the famous *encierro* (bullrunning) six bulls are released at 8am each morning to run from their corral through the narrow, cobbled streets of the old town. On the last night of this week-long, non-stop party, crowds with candles sing Basque songs in the main square. The event gained worldwide fame after Ernest Hemingway described it in his novel, published in 1926, *The Sun Also Rises*.

Bulls scattering the runners in Pamplona

Wine Battle (*29 Jun*), Haro (La Rioja). People dressed in white clothes squirt each other with wine from leather drinking bottles in the capital of the Rioja Alta wine region. **Danza de los Zancos** (*22 Jul and last Sat of Sep*), Anguiano (La Rioja). Dancers on stilts, wearing ornate waistcoats and yellow skirts, hurtle down the stepped alley from the church to the main square. **La Virgen Blanca** (*4 Aug*), Vitoria (Álava). A dummy holding an umbrella (the *celedón*) is lowered from San Miguel church to a house below – from which a man in similar dress emerges. The mayor fires a rocket and the crowds in the square light cigars.

Pilgrims drinking from the wine tap near the monastery at Irache

Estella ❷

Navarra. 🏘 *14,000.* 🚌 🛈 *Calle de San Nicolás 3, 948 55 63 01.* 🛒 *Thu.* 🎎 *San Andrés (starts Fri before first Sun in Aug).*

In the Middle Ages Estella (Lizarra) was the centre of the royal court of Navarra and a major stopping point on the pilgrims' Road to Santiago de Compostela (*see pp82–3*). The town was a stronghold of the Carlists (*see p63*) in the 19th century. A memorial rally is held here on the first Sunday of May every year.

The most important monuments in Estella are sited on the edge of town, across the bridge over the Río Ega. Steps climb steeply from the arcaded Plaza de San Martín to the remarkable **Iglesia de San Pedro de la Rúa**, built on top of a cliff from the 12th to 14th century. It features a Cistercian Mudéjar-influenced, sculpted doorway. The carved capitals are all that now remain of the Romanesque cloister, which was destroyed when a castle overlooking the church was blown up in 1592. The **Palacio de los Reyes de Navarra**, on the other side of the Plaza de San Martín, is a rare example of civil Romanesque architecture.

In the town centre, on Plaza de los Fueros, **Iglesia de San Juan Bautista** has a Romanesque porch. The north portal of the **Iglesia de San Miguel** has Romanesque carvings of St Michael slaying a dragon.

Environs

The **Monasterio de Nuestra Señora de Irache**, 3 km (2 miles) southwest of Estella, was a Benedictine monastery which sheltered pilgrims on their way to Santiago. The church is mainly Transitional Gothic in style, but it has Romanesque apses and a cloister in Platteresque style. It is capped by a remarkable dome.

A bodega next to the monastery provides pilgrims with wine from a tap in a wall.

A small road branches off the NA120 north of Estella and leads to the **Monasterio de Iranzu**, built in the 12th–14th century. The graceful austerity of its church and cloisters are typically Cistercian features.

The Lizarraga Pass, further up the NA120, offers views of attractive beech woods.

Pamplona ❸

Navarra. 🏘 *200,000.* ✈ 🚆 🚌 🛈 *C/Hilarión Eslava 1, 848 420 420.* 🎎 *Sanfermines (6–14 Jul), San Saturnino (29 Nov).* **www**.pamplona.net

The old fortress city of Pamplona (Iruña) is said to have been founded by the Roman general, Pompey. In the 9th century it became the capital of Navarra. This fairly busy city explodes into even more life in July during the fiesta of Los Sanfermines, with its daredevil bullrunning.

From the old **city walls** (*murallas*) you can get a good overview of Pamplona. The nearby **cathedral**, which

Sumptuous interior of the Palacio de Navarra, Pamplona

Stone tracery in the elegant cloister of Pamplona cathedral

is built in ochre-coloured stone, looks down on a loop in the Río Arga. It was built on the foundations of its 12th-century predecessor, and is mainly Gothic in style, with twin towers and an 18th-century façade. Inside there are lovely choir stalls and the alabaster tomb of Carlos III and Queen Leonor.

The southern entrance to the cloister is the beautifully carved, medieval Puerta de la Preciosa. The cathedral priests would gather here to sing an antiphon (hymn) to La Preciosa (Precious Virgin) before the night service.

The Museo Diocesano in the cathedral's 14th-century kitchen and refectory displays Gothic altarpieces, polychrome wood statues from all over Navarra, and a French 13th-century reliquary of the Holy Sepulchre.

West of the cathedral is the old town, cut through with many alleys. The neo-classical **Palacio del Gobierno de Navarra** lies in the Plaza del Castillo and is the seat of the Navarrese government. Outside, a statue of 1903 shows a symbolic woman upholding the *fueros* (historic laws) of Navarra (*see p130*). North of the palace is the medieval **Iglesia de San Saturnino**, built on the site where St Saturninus is said to have baptized some 40,000 pagan townspeople, and the Baroque **town hall** (*ayuntamiento*).

Beneath the old town wall, in a 16th-century hospital with a Plateresque doorway, is the **Museo de Navarra**. This is a museum of regional archaeology, history and art. Exhibits include Roman mosaics and an 11th-century, Islam-inspired ivory casket. There are murals painted during the 14th–16th centuries, a portrait by Goya, and a collection of paintings by Basque artists.

To the southeast is the city's massive 16th-century **citadel**, erected by Felipe II's reign. It is designed with five bastions in a star shape. Beyond it are the spacious boulevards of the new town, and also the university's green campus.

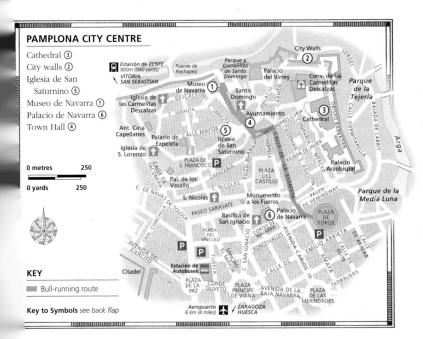

Sculpture in Pamplona depicting the *encierro*

🏛 **Museo de Navarra**
C/Santo Domingo 47. **Tel** 848 42 64 92. ◯ Tue–Sun. 🗖 ⮐

🏛 **Palacio de Navarra**
Avenida Carlos III 2. **Tel** 848 42 71 27. ◯ by appointment. ⮐

PAMPLONA CITY CENTRE

Cathedral ③
City walls ②
Iglesia de San Saturnino ⑤
Museo de Navarra ①
Palacio de Navarra ⑥
Town Hall ④

0 metres 250
0 yards 250

KEY

▬▬ Bull-running route

Key to Symbols *see back flap*

Basque houses in the picturesque town of Etxalar, Valle de Bidasoa

Las Cinco Villas del Valle de Bidasoa ㉔

Navarra. 🚌 Pamplona, San Sebastián. 🛈 Bera, 948 63 12 22 / 948 63 00 05. **www**.turismo.navarra.es

Five attractive Basque towns lie in or near this valley, the most northerly being **Bera** (Vera). The houses in **Lesaka** have wooden balconies under deep eaves. The road south passes hills dotted with white farmsteads to reach **Igantzi**, (Yanci), with its red-and-white houses. **Arantza** is the most remote town. Since the 12th century, pigeons have been caught in huge nets strung across a pass above **Etxalar** (Echalar). From the summit of La Rhune, on the French border above the valley, there is a great view of the Pyrenees.

Elizondo ㉕

Navarra. 🏘 3,000. 🚌 🛈 Tourist office, 948 58 12 79. 🗓 Thu. 🎉 Santiago (25 Jul), Feria (late Oct).

This is the biggest of a string of typical Basque villages in the very beautiful valley of Baztán. By the river are noble houses bearing coats of arms. **Arizkun**, further up the valley, has old fortified houses and a 17th-century convent. The **Cueva de Brujas**, in Zugarramurdi, was once a meeting place for witches.

The forested countryside around Roncesvalles

Canopy over the Virgin and Child in the Colegiata Real

Roncesvalles ㉖

Navarra. 🏘 24. 🛈 Roncesvalles, Antiguo Molino, s/n, 948 76 03 01. 🎉 Día de la Virgen de Roncesvalles (8 Sep).

Roncesvalles (Orreaga), on the Spanish side of a pass through the Pyrenees, is a major halt on the Road to Santiago (see pp82–3). Before it became associated with the pilgrim's way, Roncesvalles was the site of a major battle in 778, in which the Basques of Navarra slaughtered the rearguard of Charlemagne's army as it marched homeward. This event is described in the 12th-century French epic poem, *The Song of Roland*.

The 13th-century **Colegiata Real**, which has served travellers down the centuries, has a silver-plated Virgin and Child below a high canopy. In the graceful chapterhouse, off the cloister, is the white tomb of Sancho VII the Strong (1154–1234), looked down upon by a stained-glass window of his great victory, the Battle of Las Navas de Tolosa (see pp54–5). Exhibits in the church museum include "Charlemagne's chessboard", an enamelled reliquary which is so-called because of its chequered design.

Valle de Roncal ㉗

Navarra. 🚌 from Pamplona. 🛈 Roncal, Paseo Julian Gayarre, s/n, 9 47 52 56. **www**.valled128roncal.es

Running perpendicular to the Pyrenees, this valley is largely reliant on sheep, and the village of **Roncal** is known for its cheeses. Because of relative isolation of the valley, the inhabitants have preserved their own identity and local costumes are worn during fiestas. The ski resort of **Isaba**, further up the valley, has a museum of local life and history. A spectacular road winds from Isaba to the tree-lined village of Ochagavia in the parallel **Valle de Salazar**. To the north, the **Selva de Irati**, one of Europe's largest woodlands, spread over the Pyrenees into France, below the snowy summit of Monte Ori at 2,017 m (6,617 ft).

Colourful balconies of houses in the village of Roncal

Monasterio de Leyre 28

Yesa (Navarra). **Tel** 948 88 41 50. Yesa. ⬜ daily. ⬤ 1 Jan & 25 Dec.

The monastery of San Salvador de Leyre is situated high above a reservoir, alone amid grand scenery, backed by limestone cliffs. The abbey has been here since the 11th century when it was a great spiritual and political centre. Sancho III and his successors made it the royal pantheon of Navarra. The monastery began to decline in the 12th century. It was abandoned from 1836 until 1954, when it was restored by Benedictines. They turned part of it into a modestly priced hotel (see p568). To see the monastery you must join one of the tours run every morning and afternoon.

The big 11th century church has a Gothic vault and three lofty apses. On its west portal are weatherworn carvings of strange beasts, as well as biblical figures. The Romanesque crypt has unusually short columns with chunky capitals. The monks' Gregorian chant (see p376) during services is wonderful to hear.

Castillo de Javier 29

Javier (Navarra). **Tel** 948 88 40 24. from Pamplona. ⬜ daily.

St Francis Xavier, the patron saint of Navarra, a missionary and a co-founder of the Jesuit order (see p124), was born in this 13th-century castle in 1506. It has since been restored and is now a Jesuit spiritual centre. Of interest are the saint's bedroom and a museum in the keep devoted to his life. In the oratory is a 13th-century polychrome Christ on the cross and a macabre 15th-century mural of grinning skeletons entitled *The Dance of Death*.

Crucifix in the oratory of the Castillo de Javier

Sangüesa 30

Navarra. 🚶 5,000. 🚌 ℹ️ Calle Mayor 2, 948 87 14 11 (closed Mon in winter). 🗓️ Fri. 🎉 San Sebastián (11 Sep).

Since medieval times this small town beside a bridge over the Río Aragón has been a stop on the Aragonese pilgrimage route to Santiago (see pp82–3).

The richly sculpted south portal of the **Iglesia de Santa María la Real** is a 12th- and 13th-century treasure of Romanesque art (see p24). It has many figures and details depicting the Last Judgement and society in the 13th century.

The Gothic **Iglesia de Santiago** and the 12th- to 13th-century Gothic **Iglesia de San Francisco** are also worth seeing. On the main street the 16th-century **town hall** (ayuntamiento) and the square beside it, stand on sites that were once part of the medieval palace of the Prince of Viana and a residence of the kings of Navarra. The library beside the square is housed in what remains of the palace and is open to the public.

Environs
To the north of Sangüesa there are two deep, narrow gorges. The most impressive of them is the **Hoz de Arbayún**, whose limestone cliffs are inhabited by colonies of vultures. It is best seen from the NA178 north of Domeño. The **Hoz de Lumbier** can be seen from a point on the A-21.

roughly carved columns in the crypt of the Monasterio de Leyre

BARCELONA

INTRODUCING BARCELONA 138–141
OLD TOWN 142–157
EIXAMPLE 158–167
MONTJUÏC 168–173
FURTHER AFIELD 174–178
BARCELONA STREET FINDER 179–185
SHOPPING IN BARCELONA 186–189
ENTERTAINMENT IN BARCELONA 190–195

Introducing Barcelona

Barcelona, one of the Mediterranean's busiest ports, is more than the capital of Catalonia. In culture, commerce and sport it not only rivals Madrid, but also considers itself on a par with the greatest European cities. The success of the 1992 Olympic Games, staged in the Parc de Montjuïc, confirmed this to the world. Although there are plenty of historical monuments in the Old Town (Ciutat Vella), Barcelona is best known for the scores of buildings in the Eixample left by the artistic explosion of Modernisme *(see pp140–41)* in the decades around 1900. Always open to outside influences because of its location on the coast, not too far from the French border, Barcelona continues to sizzle with creativity: its bars and the public parks speak more of bold contemporary design than of tradition.

Casa Milà (see p165) *is the most avant-garde of all the works of Antoni Gaudí (see p164). Barcelona has more Art Nouveau buildings than any other city in the world.*

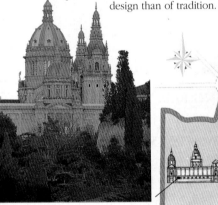

Palau Nacional (see p172), *on the bill of Montjuïc, dominates the monumental halls and fountain-filled avenue built for the 1929 International Exhibition. It now houses the Museu Nacional d'Art de Catalunya with an exceptional collection of medieval art, rich in Romanesque frescoes.*

MONTJUÏC
(see pp168–73)

Montjuïc Castle (see p173) *is a massive fortification dating from the 17th century. Sited on the crest of the bill of Montjuïc, it offers panoramic views of the city and port, and forms a sharp contrast to the ultra-modern sports balls built nearby for the 1992 Olympic Games.*

Christopher Columbus
surveys the waterfront from the top of a 60-m (200-ft) column (see p156) in the heart of the Port Vell (Old Port). From the top, visitors can look out over the new promenades and quays that have revitalized the area.

0 kilometres   1

0 miles   0.5

◁ The Ramblas and the Old Town stretching out behind Barcelona's monument to Columbus

The Sagrada Família
(see pp166–7), *Gaudí's unfinished masterpiece, begun in 1882, rises above the streets of the Eixample. Its polychromatic ceramic mosaics and sculptural forms inspired by nature are typical of his work.*

EIXAMPLE
(see pp158–67)

Barcelona Cathedral (see pp148–9) *is a magnificent 14th-century building in the heart of the Barri Gòtic (Gothic Quarter). It has 28 side chapels, which encircle the nave and contain some splendid Baroque altarpieces. The keeping of white geese in the cloisters is a centuries-old tradition.*

OLD TOWN
(see pp142–57)

Parc de la Ciutadella (see p154), *between the Old Town and the Vila Olímpica, has something for everyone. The gardens full of statuary offer relaxation, the boating lake and the zoo are fun, while the two museums within its gates cover geology and zoology.*

Las Ramblas (see pp150–51) *is the most famous street in Spain, alive at all hours of the day and night. A stroll down its length to the seafront, taking in its palatial buildings, shops, cafés and street vendors, makes a perfect introduction to Barcelona life.*

Gaudí and Modernisme

Chimney, Casa Vicens

Towards the end of the 19th century a new style of art and architecture, Modernisme, a variant of Art Nouveau, was born in Barcelona. It became a means of expression for Catalan nationalism and counted Josep Puig i Cadafalch, Lluís Domènech i Montaner and, above all, Antoni Gaudí i Cornet *(see p164)* among its major exponents. Barcelona's Eixample district *(see pp158–67)* is full of the highly original buildings that they created for their wealthy clients.

All aspects of decoration *in a Modernista building, even interior design, were planned by the architect. This door and its tiled surround are in Gaudí's 1906 Casa Batlló (see p164).*

A dramatic cupola *covers the central salon, which rises through three floors. It is pierced by small round holes, inspired by Islamic architecture, giving the illusion of stars.*

Upper galleries are richly decorated with carved wood and cofferwork.

The spiral carriage ramp *is an early sign of Gaudí's predilection for curved lines. He would later exploit this to the full in the wavy façade of his masterpiece, the Casa Milà (see p165).*

THE EVOLUTION OF MODERNISME

1859 Civil engineer Ildefons Cerdà i Sunyer submits proposals for expansion of Barcelona

1878 Gaudí graduates as an architect

1900 Josep Puig i Cadafalch builds Casa Amatller *(see p164)*

1903 Lluís Domènech i Montaner builds Hospital de la Santa Creu i de Sant Pau *(see p165)*

Hospital detail

1850	1865	1880	1895	1910	1925

1883 Gaudí takes over design of Neo-Gothic Sagrada Família *(see pp166–7)*

Detail of Sagrada Família

1888 Barcelona Universal Exhibition gives impetus to Modernisme

1912 Casa Milà completed

1905 Domènech i Montaner builds Casa Lleó Morera *(see p164)*. Puig i Cadafalch builds Casa Terrades *(see p165)*

1926 Gaudí dies

Bizarrely decorated chimneys *became one of the trademarks of Gaudí's later work. They reach a fantastic extreme on the gleaming, humpbacked roof of the Casa Batlló.*

Elaborate wrought iron lamps light the grand hall.

Ceramic tiles decorate the chimneys.

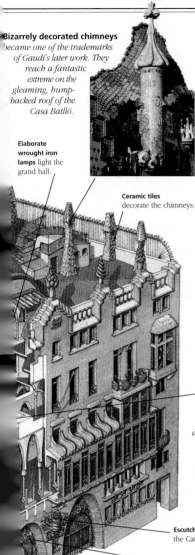

GAUDÍ'S MATERIALS

Gaudí designed, or collaborated on designs, for almost every known media. He combined bare, undecorated materials – wood, rough-hewn stone, rubble and brickwork – with meticulous craftwork in wrought iron and stained glass. Mosaics of ceramic tiles were used to cover his fluid, uneven forms.

Stained-glass window in the Sagrada Família

Mosaic of ceramic tiles, Parc Güell *(see p178)*

Detail of iron gate, Casa Vicens *(see p164)*

Ceramic tiles on El Capricho *(see p111)*

Parabolic arches, *used extensively by Gaudí, show his interest in Gothic architecture* (see p24). *These arches form a corridor in his 1890 Col·legi de les Teresianes, a convent school in the west of Barcelona.*

Escutcheon alludes to the Catalan coat of arms.

ALAU GÜELL *(1889)*

audí's first major building in the centre the city *(see p151)* established his ernational reputation for outstandgly original architecture. Built for his e-long patron, the industrialist Eusebi iell, the mansion stands on a small ot of land in a narrow street, making e façade difficult to view. Inside, audí creates a sense of space by using ved screens, galleries and recesses. s unique furniture is also on display.

Organic forms *inspired the wrought iron around the gates to the palace. Gaudí's later work teems with wildlife, such as this dragon, covered with brightly coloured tiles, which guards the steps in the Parc Güell.*

OLD TOWN

The Old Town, traversed by the city's most famous avenue, Las Ramblas, is one of the most extensive medieval city centres in Europe. The Barri Gòtic contains the cathedral and a maze of streets and squares. Across from the Via Laietana, the El Born neighbourhood is dominated by the Santa Maria del Mar church and is replete with 14th-century mansions. This area is bounded by the leafy Parc de la Ciutadella, home to the city's zoo. The revitalized seafront is a stimulating mix of old and new. Trendy shops and restaurants make up the fashionable marina, contrasted with the old maritime neighbourhood of Barceloneta and the new Olympic port.

SIGHTS AT A GLANCE

Museums and Galleries
Museu d'Art Contemporani **8**
Museu Frederic Marès **2**
Museu de Geologia **21**
Museu Marítim and Drassanes **28**
Museu Picasso **13**
Museu de la Xocolata **17**
Museu de Zoologia **20**

Streets and Districts
Barceloneta **24**
El Born **12**
Carrer Montcada **15**
Las Ramblas **9**
El Raval **7**

Harbour Sights
Golondrinas **27**
Port Olímpic **23**
Port Vell **25**

Churches
Basílica de Santa Maria del Mar **14**
Cathedral (pp148–9) **6**

Historic Buildings
Casa de l'Ardiaca **1**
Casa de la Ciutat **4**
Conjunt Monumental de la Plaça del Rei **3**
La Llotja **11**
Mercat del Born **16**
Palau de la Generalitat **5**
Palau de la Música Catalana **10**

Monuments
Arc del Triomf **18**
Monument a Colom **26**

Parks and Gardens
Parc de la Ciutadella **19**
Parc Zoològic **22**

GETTING THERE
The area is well served by metro lines 1, 3 and 4; Jaume I station is in the heart of the Barri Gòtic. Many buses pass the Plaça de Catalunya, the centre of the modern city.

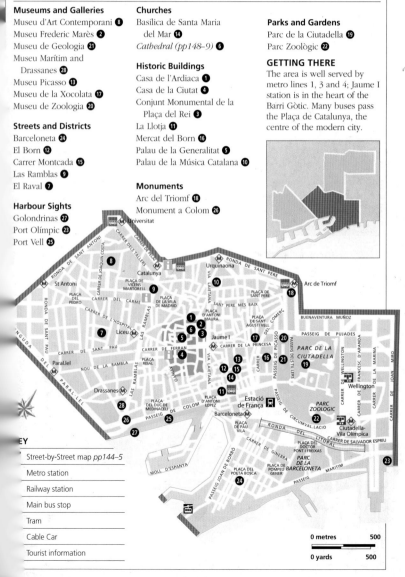

KEY

	Street-by-Street map *pp144–5*
Ⓜ	Metro station
	Railway station
	Main bus stop
	Tram
	Cable Car
	Tourist information

Stunning floral mosaic pillars in the Palau de la Música Catalana

Street-by-Street: Barri Gòtic

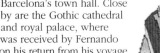

Wax candle,
Cereria
Subirà

The Barri Gotic (Gothic Quarter) is the true heart of Barcelona. The oldest part of the city, it was the site chosen by the Romans in the reign of Augustus (27 BC–AD 14) on which to found a new *colonia* (town), and has been the location of the city's administrative buildings ever since. The Roman forum was on the Plaça de Sant Jaume, where now stand the medieval Palau de la Generalitat, Catalonia's parliament, and the Casa de la Ciutat, Barcelona's town hall. Close by are the Gothic cathedral and royal palace, where Columbus was received by Fernando and Isabel on his return from his voyage to the New World in 1492 *(see p57).*

Casa de l'Ardiaca
Built on the Roman city wall, the Gothic-Renaissance archdeacon's residence now houses Barcelona's historical archives ❶

To Plaça de Catalunya

SANT SEVER

CARRER DEL BISBE

★ Cathedral
The façade and spire are 19th-century additions to the original Gothic building. Among the artistic treasures inside are medieval Catalan paintings ❻

Palau de la Generalitat
The seat of Catalonia's governor has superb Gothic features, which include the chapel and a stone staircase rising to an open-air, arcaded gallery ❺

PLAÇA DE SANT JAUM

CARRER DE FERRAN

To Las Ramblas

Casa de la Ciutat
Barcelona's town hall was built in the 14th and 15th centuries. The façade is a Neo-Classical addition. In the entrance hall stands Three Gypsy Boys *by Joan Rebull (1899–1981), a 1976 copy of a sculpture he originally created in 1946* ❹

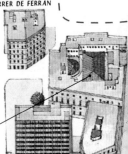

KEY

– – – Suggested route

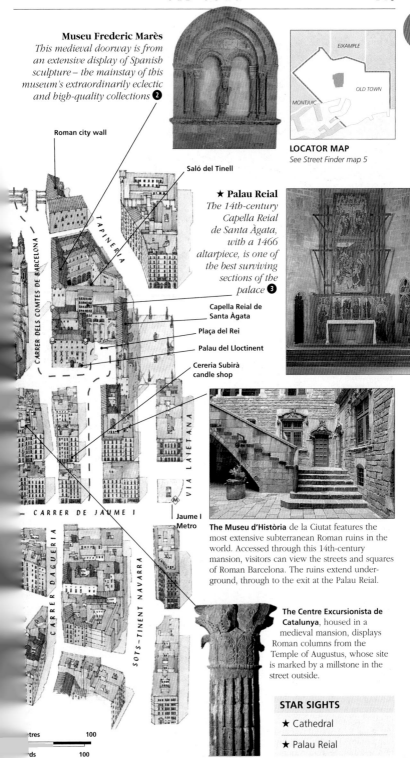

Museu Frederic Marès
This medieval doorway is from an extensive display of Spanish sculpture – the mainstay of this museum's extraordinarily eclectic and high-quality collections ❷

Roman city wall

Saló del Tinell

LOCATOR MAP
See Street Finder map 5

★ **Palau Reial**
The 14th-century Capella Reial de Santa Àgata, with a 1466 altarpiece, is one of the best surviving sections of the palace ❸

Capella Reial de Santa Àgata

Plaça del Rei

Palau del Lloctinent

Cereria Subirà candle shop

CARRER DELS COMTES DE BARCELONA

TAPINERIA

CARRER DE JAUME I

Jaume I Metro

VIA LAIETANA

CARRER DAGUERIA

SOTS–TINENT NAVARRA

The Museu d'Història de la Ciutat features the most extensive subterranean Roman ruins in the world. Accessed through this 14th-century mansion, visitors can view the streets and squares of Roman Barcelona. The ruins extend underground, through to the exit at the Palau Reial.

The Centre Excursionista de Catalunya, housed in a medieval mansion, displays Roman columns from the Temple of Augustus, whose site is marked by a millstone in the street outside.

STAR SIGHTS

★ Cathedral

★ Palau Reial

tres   100

ds   100

Decorated marble letterbox, Casa de l'Ardiaca

Casa de l'Ardiaca ❶

Carrer de Santa Llúcia 1. **Map** 5 B2.
Tel 93 318 11 95. ⊕ Jaume I.
🕘 9am–8:45pm Mon–Fri, 9am–1pm
Sat. ⬤ public hols.
www.bcn.es/arxiu/arxiuhistoric

Standing beside what was
originally the Bishop's
Gate in the Roman wall is
the Archdeacon's House.
It was built in the 12th
century, but its present
appearance dates from
around 1500 when it was
remodelled and a colon-
nade added. In 1870 this
was extended to form
the Flamboyant Gothic
(see p24) patio around a
fountain. The Modernista
architect Domènech i Montaner
(1850–1923) added the fanciful
marble letterbox, carved with
three swallows and a tortoise,
beside the Renaissance portal.
Upstairs is the Arxiu Històric
de la Ciutat (City Archives).

Museu Frederic Marès ❷

Plaça de Sant Iu 5. **Map** 5 B2.
Tel 93 256 35 00. ⊕ Jaume I.
🕘 10am–7pm Tue–Sat, 10am–3pm
Sun. ⬤ 1 Jan, Good Fri, 1 May, 25 &
26 Dec. 🎫 (free first Sun of each
month & Wed pm). ♿ 🎫 by appt.
www.museumares.bcn.es

The sculptor Frederic Marès i
Deulovol (1893–1991) was also
a traveller and collector, and
this extraordinary museum is a
monument to his eclectic
taste. The building is part of
the Royal Palace complex and
was occupied by 13th-century
bishops, 14th-century counts

of Barcelona, 15th-century
judges, and 18th-century nuns,
who lived here until they
were expelled in 1936.
Marès, who had a
small apartment in the
building, opened this
museum in 1948. It
is one of the most
fascinating in the
city and has an out-
standing collection
of Romanesque and
Gothic religious art.
In the crypt there
are stone sculptures
and two complete
Romanesque por-
tals. Exhibits on
the three floors
above range
through clocks,
crucifixes, costumes, antique
cameras, pipes, tobacco jars
and postcards to an amusement room full of toys.

Virgin, Museu Frederic Marès

Conjunt Monumental de la Plaça del Rei ❸

Plaça del Rei. **Map** 5 B2. **Tel** 93 256
21 00. ⊕ Jaume I. 🕘 Apr–Sep:
10am–8pm Tue–Sat, 10am–3pm Sun;
Oct–Mar: 10am–2pm, 4–8pm Tue–
Sat, 10am 3pm Sun. ⬤ 1 Jan, 1
May, 24 Jun, 25 Dec. 🎫 free for
under 16s on 1st Sat of each month,
after 3pm. 🎫 by appointment.

The Conjunt Monumental de
la Plaça del Rei encompasses
the Palau Reial (Royal Palace)
and the Museu d'Història de
la Ciutat. The Royal Palace was
the residence of the count-
kings of Barcelona from its
foundation in the 13th century.
The complex includes the
14th-century Gothic Saló del
Tinell, a vast room with arches
spanning 17 m (56 ft). This is

Gothic nave of the Capella de Santa Àgata, Palau Reial

BARCELONA'S EARLY JEWISH COMMUNITY

Hebrew tablet

From the 11th to the 13th centuries Jews
dominated Barcelona's commerce and
culture, providing doctors and founding
the first seat of learning. But in 1243, 354
years after they were first documented in
the city, violent anti-Semitism led to the
Jews being consigned to a ghetto, El Call.
Ostensibly to provide protection, the
ghetto had only one entrance, which led
into the Plaça de Sant Jaume. Jews were
heavily taxed by the monarch, who
viewed them as "royal serfs"; but in return they also received
privileges, as they handled most of Catalonia's lucrative trade
with North Africa. However, official and popular persecution
finally led to the disappearance of the ghetto in 1401, 91
years before Judaism was fully outlawed in Spain (see p57).
Originally there were three synagogues. The main one,
Sinagoga Mayor at No. 5 Carrer de Marlet, is said to be the
oldest in Europe. A 14th-century Hebrew tablet is embedded
in the wall which reads: "Holy Foundation of Rabbi Samuel
Hassardi, for whom life never ends".

where Isabel and Fernando *(see p70)* received Columbus on his return from America. It is also where the Holy Inquisition sat, believing the walls would move if lies were told.

On the right, built into the Roman city wall, is the royal chapel, the Capella de Santa Àgata, with a painted wood ceiling and an altarpiece (1466) by Jaume Huguet. Its bell tower is formed by part of a watchtower on the Roman wall. Stairs on the right of the altar lead to the 16th-century tower of Martí the Humanist (who reigned from 1396–1410), the last of the count-kings of Barcelona.

The main attraction of the Museu d'Història lies underground. Entire streets and squares of old Barcino are accessible via a lift and walkways suspended over the ruins of Roman Barcelona. The site was discovered when the Casa Clariana-Padellàs, the Gothic building from which you enter, was moved here stone by stone in 1931, as demonstrated by an extraordinary photo of the original dig towards the end of the exhibit. The water and drainage systems, baths, homes with mosaic floors, dye works, laundries and even the old forum now make up the most extensive and complete subterranean Roman ruins in the world.

Casa de la Ciutat ❹

Plaça de Sant Jaume 1. **Map** 5 A2.
Tel 934 02 73 00. 🚇 *Jaume I, Liceu.*
⬜ *10am–1:30pm Sun & public hols; 10am–8pm 12 Feb & 23 Apr, or by appointment (93 402 73 64).* 📷 ♿

The magnificent 14th-century city hall *(ajuntament)* faces the Palau de la Generalitat. Flanking the entrance of the Casa de la Ciutat are statues of Jaime (Jaume) I, who granted the city rights to elect councillors in 1249, and Joan Fiveller, who levied taxes on court members in the 1500s.

Inside is the huge council chamber, the 14th-century Saló de Cent, built for the city's 100 councillors. The Saló de les Cròniques, on the first floor, was commissioned for the 1929 International Exhibition and decorated by Josep-Marià Sert with murals of momentous events in Catalan history.

Palau de la Generalitat ❺

Plaça de Sant Jaume 4. **Map** 5 A2.
Tel 93 402 46 00. 🚇 *Jaume I.*
⬜ *23 Apr (St Jordi's Day), 2nd & 4th Sun of every month: 10:30am–1:30pm.* ♿ 📷 **www**.gencat.es

Since 1403, the Generalitat has been the seat of the Catalonian Governor. Above

The Italianate façade of the Palau de la Generalitat

the entrance, in its Renaissance façade, is a statue of Sant Jordi (St George) – the patron saint of Catalonia – and the Dragon. The late Catalan-Gothic courtyard is by Marc Safont (1416).

Among the fine interiors are the Gothic chapel of Sant Jordi, also by Safont, and Pere Blai's Italianate Saló de Sant Jordi. At the back, one floor above street level, lies the *Pati dels Tarongers*, the Orange Tree Patio, by Pau Mateu, which has a bell tower built by Pere Ferrer in 1568.

The Catalan president has offices here as well as in the Casa dels Canonges. The two buildings are connected by a bridge across Carrer del Bisbe, built in 1928 and modelled on the famous Bridge of Sighs in Venice.

magnificent council chamber, the Saló de Cent, in Casa de la Ciutat

Barcelona Cathedral ❻

This compact Gothic cathedral, with a Romanesque chapel (Capella de Santa Llúcia) and beautiful cloister, was begun in 1298 under Jaime (Jaume) II, on the foundations of a site dating back to Visigothic times. It was not finished until the late 19th century, when the main façade was completed. A white marble choir screen, sculpted in the 16th century, depicts the martyrdom of St Eulàlia, the city's patron. Next to the font, a plaque records the baptism of six Caribbean Indians, whom Columbus brought back from the Americas in 1493.

Statue of St Eulalia

The twin octagonal bell towers date from 1386–93. The bells were installed in this tower in 1545.

The main façade
was not completed until 1889, and the central spire until 1913. It was based on the original 1408 plans of the French architect Charles Galters.

Nave Interior
The Catalan-style Gothic interior has a single wide nave with 28 side chapels. These are set between the columns supporting the vaulted ceiling, which rises to 26 m (85 ft).

★ Choir Stalls
The top tier of the beautifully carved 15th-century stalls contains the coats of arms (1518) of the 12 knights of the Order of Toisón del Oro.

Capella del Santíssim Sagrament
This small chapel houses the 16th-century Christ of Lepanto crucifix.

Capella de Sant Benet
This chapel, dedicated to the founder of the Benedictine Order and patron saint of Europe, houses a magnificent altarpiece showing The Transfiguration *by Bernat Martorell (1452).*

VISITORS' CHECKLIST

Plaça de la Seu. **Map** 5 A2.
Tel *93 310 71 95.* Jaume I.
17, 19, 45. 8am–7:30pm
daily. free 8am–12:45pm,
5:15–7:30pm 1–5pm (2-5pm
Sun).
Sacristy Museum
9am–1pm, 5–7pm daily.
numerous services daily.

★ Crypt
In the crypt, beneath the main altar, is the alabaster sarcophagus (1339) of St Eulàlia, martyred for her beliefs by the Romans during the 4th century AD.

★ Cloisters
The fountain, set in a corner of the Gothic cloisters and decorated with a statue of St George, provided fresh water.

Porta de Santa Eulàlia, entrance to Cloisters

The Sacristy Museum has a small treasury. Pieces include an 11th-century font, tapestries and liturgical artifacts.

Capella de Santa Llúcia

STAR FEATURES

★ Choir Stalls

★ Crypt

★ Cloisters

TIMELINE

559 Basilica dedicated to St Eulàlia and Holy Cross		**1339** St Eulàlia's relics transferred to alabaster sarcophagus		**1913** Central spire completed
	877 St Eulàlia's remains brought here from Santa Maria del Mar	**1046–58** Romanesque cathedral built under Ramon Berenguer I	**1889** Main façade completed, based on plans dating from 1408 by architect Charles Galters	

400	700	1000	1300	1600	1900

4th century Original Roman (paleo-Christian) basilica built

985 Building destroyed by the Moors

1257–68 Romanesque Capella de Santa Llúcia built

1493 Indians brought back from the Americas are baptized

1298 Gothic cathedral begun under Jaime II

Plaque of the Indians' baptism

El Raval ❼

Map 2 F3. 🚇 Catalunya, Liceu.

The district of El Raval lies to the west of La Rambla and includes the old red-light area near the port, which was once known as the Barri Xinès (Chinese quarter).

From the 14th century, the city hospital was in Carrer de l'Hospital, which still has some herbal and medicinal shops. Gaudí (see p160) was brought here after being fatally hit by a tram in 1926. The buildings now house the Biblioteca de Catalunya (Catalonian Library), but the elegant former dissecting room has been fully restored.

Towards the port in Carrer Nou de la Rambla is Gaudí's Palau Güell (see p141). At the end of Sant Pau is the city's most complete Romanesque church, the 12th-century Sant Pau del Camp, where resident Franciscan monks still sing a plainsong mass.

Museu d'Art Contemporani ❽

Plaça dels Angels 1. **Map** 2 F2. **Tel** 93 412 08 10. 🚇 Universitat, Catalunya. 🕐 11am–7:30pm Mon & Wed–Fri (Jul–Sep: 11am–8pm Mon, Wed & Fri; to midnight Thu), 10am–8pm Sat, 10am–3pm Sun & public hols. ⬛ 1 Jan, 25 Dec. 🈳 ♿ 📷 6pm Mon (in English). **www**.macba.es **Centre de Cultura Contemporània** Montalegre 5. **Tel** 93 306 41 00. **www**.cccb.org

This dramatic, glass-fronted building was designed by the American architect Richard Meier. Its light, airy galleries act as the city's contemporary art mecca. The permanent collection of predominantly Spanish painting, sculpture and installation from the 1950s onwards is complemented by temporary exhibitions from foreign artists such as the US painter Susana Solano and South African photojournalist David Goldblatt.

Next to the MACBA, a remodelled 18th-century hospice houses the **Centre de Cultura Contemporània**, a lively arts centre that hosts major arts festivals and regular shows.

Las Ramblas ❾

The historic avenue of Las Ramblas (Les Rambles in Catalan) is busy around the clock, especially in the evenings and at weekends. Newsstands, caged bird and flower stalls, tarot readers, musicians and mime artists throng the wide, tree-shaded central walkway. Among its famous buildings are the Liceu Opera House, the huge Boqueria food market and some grand mansions.

Exploring Las Ramblas

The name of this long avenue, also known as Les Rambles, comes from the Arabic *ramla*, meaning the dried-up bed of a seasonal river. The 13th-century city wall followed the left bank of such a river that flowed from the Collserola hills to the sea. Convents, monasteries and the university were built on the other bank in the 16th century. As time passed, the riverbed was filled in and those buildings demolished, but they are remembered in the names of the five consecutive Rambles that make up the great avenue between the Port Vell and Plaça de Catalunya.

Palau Güell C/ Nou de la Rambla 3–5. **Map** 2 F3. **Tel** 93 317 39 74. 🚇 Liceu. 🕐 partially open until 2010. Free entry to ground floor & basement: 10:30am–2:30pm Tue–Sat. ♿ Ground floor only. **Museu de Cera** Pg de la Banca 7. **Map** 2 F4. **Tel** 93 317 26 49. 🚇 Drassanes. 🕐 Jul–Sep: 10am–10pm daily; Oct–Jun: 10am–1:30pm & 4–7:30pm Mon–Fri, 11am–2pm & 4:30–8:30pm Sat, Sun & public hols. 🈳 ♿

The monument to Columbus at the bottom of the tree-lined Ramblas

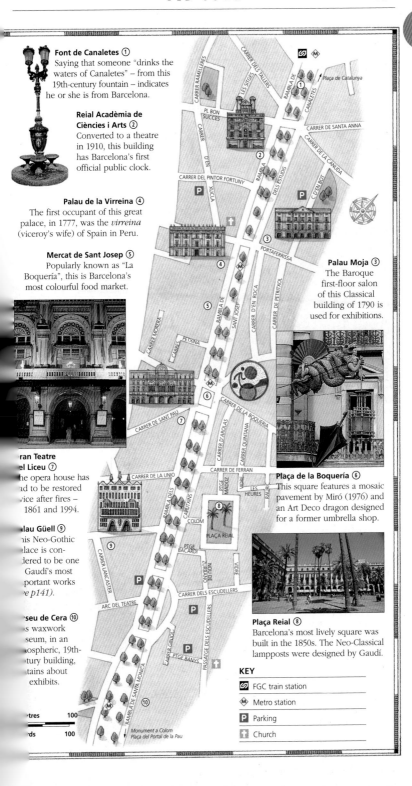

Font de Canaletes ①
Saying that someone "drinks the waters of Canaletes" – from this 19th-century fountain – indicates he or she is from Barcelona.

Reial Acadèmia de Ciències i Arts ②
Converted to a theatre in 1910, this building has Barcelona's first official public clock.

Palau de la Virreina ④
The first occupant of this great palace, in 1777, was the *virreina* (viceroy's wife) of Spain in Peru.

Mercat de Sant Josep ⑤
Popularly known as "La Boquería", this is Barcelona's most colourful food market.

ran Teatre
el Liceu ⑦
he opera house has
ad to be restored
vice after fires –
1861 and 1994.

alau Güell ⑨
his Neo-Gothic
alace is con-
lered to be one
Gaudí's most
portant works
e p141).

rseu de Cera ⑩
s waxwork
seum, in an
ospheric, 19th-
tury building,
tains about
exhibits.

Palau Moja ③
The Baroque first-floor salon of this Classical building of 1790 is used for exhibitions.

Plaça de la Boquería ⑥
This square features a mosaic pavement by Miró (1976) and an Art Deco dragon designed for a former umbrella shop.

Plaça Reial ⑧
Barcelona's most lively square was built in the 1850s. The Neo-Classical lampposts were designed by Gaudí.

KEY

🔄	FGC train station
Ⓜ	Metro station
🅿	Parking
✝	Church

etres — 100
ds — 100

Monument a Colom
Plaça del Portal de la Pau

Glorious stained-glass dome, Palau de la Música Catalana

Palau de la Música Catalana ❿

Carrer de Sant Francesc de Paula 2. **Map** 5 B1. **Tel** 90 244 28 82. Ⓜ Urquinaona. ☐ 10am–3:30pm daily (10am–6pm Easter & Aug); and for concerts. 📷 ♿ limited 🎫 on the hour (book ahead). **www**.palaumusica.org

This is a real palace of music, a Modernista celebration of tilework, sculpture and glorious stained glass. It is the only concert hall in Europe lit by natural light. Designed by Lluís Domènech i Montaner, it was completed in 1908. Although a few extensions have been added, the building still retains its original appearance. The elaborate red-brick façade is hard to appreciate fully in the confines of the narrow street. It is lined with mosaic-covered pillars topped by busts of the great composers Palestrina, Bach and Beethoven. The large stone sculpture of St George and other figures at the corner of the building portrays an allegory from Catalan folksong by Miquel Blay.

But it is the interior of the building that is truly inspiring. The auditorium is lit by a huge inverted dome of stained glass depicting angelic choristers. The sculptures of composers Wagner and Clavé on the proscenium arch that frames the stage area were designed by Domènech but finished by Pau Gargallo. The stunning "Muses of the Palau", the group of 18 highly stylized, instrument-playing maidens are the stage's backdrop. Made of terracotta and trencadís (broken pieces of ceramic), the muses have become the building's most admired feature.

The work of Josep Anselm Clavé (1824–74) in promoting Catalan song led to the creation of the Orfeó Català choral society in 1891, a focus of Catalan nationalism and the inspiration behind the Palau.

Although the Orfeó is now based at the more state-of-the-art L'Auditori in Plaça de les Glòries (see p191), there is a concert at the Palau nearly every night; it is the main venue for the city's jazz and guitar festivals and national and international symphony orchestras regularly grace its flamboyant stage.

The Palau's new era began with the completion of the work carried out by the top local architect Oscar Tusquets. An underground concert hall and an outdoor square for summer concerts were added, consolidating the Palau's reputation as Barcelona's most loved music venue.

La Llotja ⓫

Carrer del Consolat de Mar 2. **Map** 5 B3. **Tel** 902 44 84 48. Ⓜ Barceloneta, Jaume I. 🚫 to the public (except twice a year, days vary).

La Llotja (meaning commodity exchange) was built in the 1380s as the headquarters of the Consolat de Mar. It was remodelled in Neo-Classical style in 1771 and housed the city's stock exchange until 1994, the original Gothic hall acting as the main trading room. It can still be seen through the windows.

The upper floors housed the Barcelona School of Fine Arts from 1849 to 1970, attended by Picasso and Miró. It is now occupied by local government offices.

Statue of Poseidon in the courty of La Llotja

El Born ⑫

Map 5 B3. Ⓜ *Jaume I.*

Named after the jousting sessions that once took place in its central boulevard, El Born is a tiny pocket of the La Ribera district. The village-like atmosphere of the neighbourhood makes it popular with local residents and young urbanites. Trendy bars, fashion and design shops are juxtaposed with medieval architecture. The 14th century mansions of Carrer Montcada have remained intact and now house high-calibre galleries and museums, whilst the tiny, pedestrianised streets and squares fanning out from the Mercat del Born are the centre of the city's café culture. The numerous bars and restaurants are a magnet for revellers, much to the annoyance of the full-time residents who voice their complaints visually through the banners hanging from El Born's balconies.

Museu Picasso ⑬

Carrer Montcada 15–23. **Map** 5 B2.
Tel 932 56 30 00. Ⓜ *Jaume I.*
◻ 10am–8pm Tue–Sun. ᠍ *(free under age 16 & 1st Sun of month).*
◪ 6pm Thu & noon Sat (free and in English), book in advance, email museupicasso_reserves@bcn.cat ᠍

One of Barcelona's most popular attractions, the Picasso Museum is housed in five adjoining medieval palaces on Carrer Montcada: Berenguer d'Aguilar, Baró de Castellet, Meca, Mauri and Finestres.

The museum opened in 1963 showing works donated by Jaime Sabartes, a friend of Picasso. Following Sabartes' death in 1968, Picasso himself donated paintings, including early examples. These were complemented by graphic works, left in his will, and 141 ceramic pieces given by his widow, Jacqueline.

The strength of the 3,000-piece collection are Picasso's early works. These show how, even at the ages of 15 and 16, he was painting major works such as *The First Communion* (1896) and *Science and Charity* (1897). There are only a few pictures from his Blue and Rose periods. The most famous work is his series of 44 paintings, *Las Meninas,* inspired by Velázquez's masterpiece.

Basílica de Santa Maria del Mar ⑭

Plaza Sta Maria 1. **Map** 5 B3.
Tel 93 310 23 90. Ⓜ *Jaume I.*
◻ 9am–1:30pm, 4:30–8pm daily *(Sun from 10am).*

The city's favourite church, with superb acoustics for concerts, is the only example of a church entirely in the Catalan Gothic style. It took just 55 years to build, with money donated by merchants and shipbuilders. The speed – unrivalled in the Middle Ages – gave it a unity of style both inside and out. The west front has a 15th-century rose window of the Coronation of the Virgin. More stained glass, from the 15th–18th centuries, lights the nave and aisles.

The choir and furnishings were burned in the Civil War *(see p67),* adding to the sense of space and simplicity.

A wedding service in the Gothic interior of Santa Maria del Mar

PABLO PICASSO IN BARCELONA

Picasso (1881–1973) was born in Málaga and was almost 14 when he came to Barcelona, where his father had found a job in the city's art academy. Picasso enrolled, and was a precocious talent among his contemporaries. He was a regular visitor to Els Quatre Gats, an artists' café still in existence in Carrer Montsió, where he held his first exhibition. He also exhibited in Sala Parks, a gallery still functioning in Carrer Petritxol. The family lived in Carrer Mercé and Picasso had a studio in Carrer Nou de la Rambla. It was among the prostitutes of Carrer d'Avinyò that he found inspiration for the work that many art historians see as the wellspring of modern art, *Les Demoiselles d'Avignon* (1906–7). Picasso left Barcelona for Paris in his early twenties and initially returned several times. After the Civil War his opposition to Franco kept him in France, but he designed a frieze for Barcelona's College of Architects in 1962 and was persuaded to allow the city to open a museum of his work, which it did the following year.

Pablo Picasso, *Self-Portrait* in charcoal (1899–1900)

Renaissance-style 17th-century façades lining Carrer Montcada

Carrer Montcada ⑮

Map 5 B3. 👤 *Jaume I.* **Centre del Disseny** at No. 12. **Tel** 93 310 45 16. ☐ 10am–6pm Tue–Sat, 10am–3pm Sun & public hols. ⬤ 1 Jan, 1 May, 24 Jun, 25 & 26 Dec. 🎫 (free 1st Sun of each month). ♿

The most authentic medieval street in the city is a narrow lane, overshadowed by gargoyles and roofs that almost touch overhead. The Gothic palaces that line it date back to Catalonia's expansion in the 13th century. Almost all of the buildings were modified over the years, particularly during the 17th century. Only Casa Cervelló-Guidice at No. 25 retains its original façade.

The **Centre del Disseny** in Palau del Marquès de Lliò has temporary exhibitions on product design, architecture, visual communication and fashion. At No. 22 is the city's best-known champagne and *cava* bar, El Xampanyet.

The entrance to the Centre del Disseny

Mercat del Born ⑯

Map 5 C3. 👤 *Jaume I, Barceloneta.*

This covered market, with its ornate iron work and crystal roof, was inspired by the original Les Halles in Paris and it was Barcelona's principal wholesale market until the early 70s when it outgrew its location. The street names in the vicinity reflect what went on in Barcelona's former mercantile hub: L'Argenteria was lined with silversmiths, Flassaders was where you went for a weaved blanket and Vidrieria was once lit up with glass blowers' torches. A few of these establishments remain, but they are rapidly being replaced by tourist-friendly boutiques.

The market itself has been the focus of a fierce debate. When work started in 2002 to convert the space into a library, extensive remains dating from the 1700s were discovered. The architectural importance of the subterranean streets and homes were questioned, but the historical significance of the dig sealed the market's fate as a future cultural centre. In 1714 Barcelona fell to French-Spanish forces in the War of Succession *(see p62)*, with particularly heavy losses in El Born, and became an occupied city. This key event in Catalonia's history is remembered each year on September 11th in flag-waving celebrations centred near the market.

Museu de la Xocolata ⑰

Comerç 36. **Map** 5 C2. 👤 *Jaume I, Arc de Triomf.* **Tel** 93 268 78 78. ☐ 10am–7pm Mon, Wed–Sat, 10am–3pm Sun & pub hols. ⬤ 1 Jan, 1 May, 25 & 26 Dec. 🎫 📷 by appointment. ♿ 💻 **www**.pastisseria.com/ct/portadamuseu

Founded by Barcelona's chocolate and pastry-makers union, this museum celebrates the history of one of the most universally-loved foodstuffs: from the discovery of cocoa in South America to the invention of the first chocolate machine in Barcelona. This is executed through old posters, photographs and footage. The real thing is displayed in a homage to the art of the *mona*. A Catalan invention, this was a traditional easter cake that over the centuries evolved into an edible sculpture. Every year, pastissers compete for the most imaginative piece, decorating their chocolate versions of well-known buildings or folk figures with jewels, feathers and other materials. The museum café serves chocolate temptations.

The pink brick façade of the late 19th-century Arc del Triomf

Arc del Triomf ⑱

Passeig Lluís Companys. **Map** 5 C1. 👤 *Arc de Triomf.*

The main gateway to the 1888 Universal Exhibition, which filled the Parc de la Ciutadella, was designed by Josep Vilaseca i Casanovas. It is built of brick in Mudéjar *(see p55)* style, with sculpted allegories of crafts, industry and business. The frieze by Josep Reynés on the main façade represents the city welcoming foreign visitors.

Parc de la Ciutadella ⑲

Avda del Marquès de l'Argentera. **Map** 6 D2. 👤 *Barceloneta, Ciutadella-Vila Olímpica.* ☐ 8am–10:30pm daily. ♿

This popular park has a boating lake, orange groves and parrots living in the palm trees. It was once the site of a massive star-shaped citadel, built for Felipe V between 1715 and 1720 following a 13-month siege of the city. The fortress was intended to house soldiers to keep law and order, but was never used for this purpose. Converted into a prison, the citadel became notorious during the Napoleonic occupation *(see p63)*, and, during the 19th-century liberal repressions, it was hated as a symbol of centralized power. In 1878, under General Prim, whose statue stands in the middle of the park, the citadel was pulled down and the park given to the city, to become, in 1888, the venue of the Universal Exhibition *(see p64)*. Three buildings survived: the Governor's Palace, now a school; the chapel; and the arsenal, occupied by the Catalan parliament.

The park offers more cultural and leisure activities than any other in the city and is particularly popular on Sunday afternoons when people gather to play instruments, dance and relax, or visit the museums and zoo. A variety of works by Catalan sculptors such as Marès, Arnau, Carbonell, Clarà, Llimona, Gargallo, Dunyach and Fuxà, can be seen in the park, alongside work by modern artists such as Tàpies and Botero.

The gardens in the Plaça de Armes were laid out by the French landscape gardener Jean Forestier and centre on a cascade based around a triumphal arch. It was designed by architect Josep Fontseré, with the help of Antoni Gaudí, then still a young student.

One of the galleries inside the spacious Museu de Zoologia

Museu de Zoologia ⑳

Passeig de Picasso. **Map** 5 C2. *Tel* 93 319 69 12. 🚇 Arc de Triomf or Jaume I. 🕐 10am–2:30pm Tue–Sun & public hols (Thu & Sat to 6:30pm). 🎫 combined ticket with the Museu de Geologia. ♿ 🎫 free 1st Sun each month. **www**.museuzoologia.bcn.es

At the entrance to the Parc de la Ciutadella is the Castell dels Tres Dragons (Castle of the Three Dragons), named after a play by Frederic Soler.

This crenellated brick edifice was built by Lluís Domènech i Montaner for the 1888 Universal Exhibition. His inspiration was Valencia's Gothic commodities exchange. He later used it as a workshop for Modernista design. Since 1937 it has housed the Zoological Museum, which is part of the Museu de Ciències Naturals.

Museu de Geologia ㉑

Parc de la Ciutadella. **Map** 5 C3. *Tel* 93 319 69 12. 🚇 Arc de Triomf, Jaume I. 🕐 10am–2:30pm Tue–Sun & public hols (Thu & Sat till 6:30pm). 🎫 combined ticket with the Museu de Zoologia. 🎫 free 1st Sun each month.

Also part of the Museu de Ciències Naturals is Barcelona's oldest museum. It opened in 1882, the year the Parc de la Ciutadella became a public space. It has a large collection of fossils and minerals. Beside it is the Hivernacle, a glasshouse by Josep Amargós, and the Umbracle, a conservatory by the park's architect, Josep Fontseré. Both date from 1884.

Parc Zoològic ㉒

Parc de la Ciutadella. **Map** 6 D3. *Tel* 93 225 67 80. 🚇 Ciutadella-Vila Olimpica. 🕐 Nov–Feb: 10am–5pm, Mar–May & Oct: 10am–6pm, Jun–Sep: 10am–7pm. 🎫 ♿ **www**.zoobarcelona.com

This zoo was laid out in the 1940s to a relatively enlightened design – the animals are separated by moats instead of bars. Dolphin and whale shows are held in one of the aquariums. The zoo is very child-friendly with pony rides, electric cars and a train. Roig i Soler's 1885 sculpture by the entrance, *The Lady with the Umbrella* has become a symbol of Barcelona.

Ornamental cascade in the Parc de la Ciutadella designed by Josep Fontseré and Antoni Gaudí

Smart boats and the twin skyscrapers at the Port Olímpic

Port Olímpic ㉓

Map 6 F4. Ⓜ *Ciutadella-Vila Olímpica.*

The most dramatic rebuilding for the 1992 Olympics was the demolition of the old industrial waterfront and the laying out of 4 km (2 miles) of promenade and pristine sandy beaches. Suddenly Barcelona seemed like a seaside resort. At the heart of the project was a 65-ha (160-acre) new estate of 2,000 apartments and parks called Nova Icària. The area is still popularly known as the Vila Olímpica because the buildings originally housed the Olympic athletes.

On the sea front there are twin 44-floor blocks, two of Spain's tallest skyscrapers, one occupied by offices and the other by the Arts hotel (see p569). They stand beside the Port Olímpic, which was also built for 1992. The main reason for visiting are the two levels of restaurants in a wonderful setting around the marina.

Barceloneta ㉔

Map 5 B5. Ⓜ *Barceloneta.*

Barcelona's fishing "village", which lies on a triangular tongue of land jutting into the sea just below the city centre, is renowned for its fish restaurants and port-side cafés.

Barceloneta was built by the architect and military engineer Juan Martín de Cermeño in 1753 to rehouse people made homeless by the construction,

just inland, of a large fortress, La Ciutadella (see p154). Since then it has housed largely workers and fishermen. Laid out on a grid system with narrow houses of two or three floors, in which each room has a window on the street, the area has a friendly air.

In the small Plaça de la Barceloneta, at the centre of the district, is the Baroque church of Sant Miquel del Port, also by Cermeño. A market is often held in the square here.

Today, Barceloneta's fishing fleet is still based in the nearby industrial docks by a small clock tower. On the opposite side of this harbour is the Torre de Sant Sebastià, terminus of the cable car that runs right across the port, via the World Trade Centre, to Montjuïc.

Port Vell ㉕

Map 5 A4. Ⓜ *Barceloneta, Drassanes.* **Aquàrium** *Tel* 93 221 74 74.
Ⓞ Oct–May: 9:30am–9pm Mon–Fri, 9:30am– 9:30pm Sat, Sun & public hols; Jun & Sep: 9:30am–9:30pm daily; Jul–Aug: 9:30am–11pm daily.
🖼 ♿ 🍴 www.aquariumbcn.com

The city's new leisure port is at the foot of Las Ramblas, just beyond the old customs house. This was built in 1902 at the Portal de la Pau, the former maritime entrance to the city, where steps lead into the water. To the south, the Moll de Barcelona, with a new World Trade Centre, serves as the passenger pier for visiting liners. In front of the customs house, Las Ramblas is linked to the yacht clubs on the Moll

d'Espanya by a swing bridge and pedestrian jetty. The Moll d'Espanya (moll meaning quay, wharf or pier) has a shopping and restaurant complex, the Maremàgnum, plus an IMAX cinema and the largest aquarium in Europe.

The Moll de la Fusta (Timber Wharf), with terrace cafés, has red structures inspired by Van Gogh's painting of the bridge at Arles. At the end of the wharf stands *El Cap de Barcelona (Barcelona Head)*, a 20-m (66-ft) sculpture by Pop artist Roy Lichtenstein.

Monument a Colom ㉖

Plaça del Portal de la Pau. **Map** 2 F4. *Tel* 93 302 52 24. Ⓜ *Drassanes.*
Ⓞ Nov–Apr: 10am–6:30pm daily; May–Oct: 9am–8:30pm daily. 🖼

The Columbus Monument in the Portal de la Pau (the "Gate of Peace") was designed by Gaietà Buigas for the 1888 Universal Exhibition.

The 60-m (200-ft) cast iron monument marks the spot where Columbus stepped ashore in 1493 after discovering America, bringing with him six Caribbean Indians. He was accorded a state welcome by the Catholic Monarchs in the Saló del Tinell (see p146). The Indians' conversion to Christianity is commemorated in the cathedral (see pp148–9).

A lift provides visitors with access to a viewing platform at the top of the monument, where a bronze statue points out to sea.

Fishing boat moored at the quayside of Barceloneta

A *golondrina* departing from the Plaça del Portal de la Pau

Golondrinas ⑳

Plaça del Portal de la Pau. **Map** 2 F5.
Tel *93 442 31 06.* Ⓜ *Drassanes.*
◯ *times variable – phone ahead.*
www.lasgolondrinas.com

Sightseeing trips around Barcelona's harbour can be made on small double-decker boats called *golondrinas* (literally "swallows"). They moor beside the steps of the Plaça del Portal de la Pau in front of the Columbus Monument.

Tours last around half an hour. The boats go out beneath the steep, castle-topped hill of Montjuïc towards the industrial port. They usually stop off at the breakwater, which reaches out to sea from Barceloneta, to allow passengers to disembark for a stroll.

An alternative one-and-a-half-hour trip takes in Barcelona Harbour, the commercial port and beaches and stops off at the Port Olímpic.

Museu Marítim and Drassanes ⑳

Avinguda de les Drassanes.
Map 2 F4. ***Tel*** *93 342 99 20.*
Ⓜ *Drassanes.* ◯ *10am–8pm daily.*
● *1 & 6 Jan, 25 & 26 Dec.*

The great galleys that made Barcelona a major seafaring power were built in the sheds of the Drassanes (shipyards), which now house the maritime museum. These royal dry docks are the largest and most complete surviving medieval complex of their kind in the world. They were founded in the mid-13th century, when dynastic marriages uniting the kingdoms of Sicily and Aragón meant that better maritime communications between the two became a priority. Three of the yards' four original corner towers survive.

Among the vessels to slip from the Drassanes' vaulted halls was the *Real*, flagship of Don Juan of Austria, Charles V's illegitimate son, who led the Christian fleet to victory against the Turks at Lepanto in 1571 (*see p59*). The museum's showpiece is a full-scale replica decorated in red and gold.

The *Llibre del Consulat de Mar*, a book of nautical codes and practice, is a reminder that Catalonia was once the arbiter of Mediterranean maritime law. The expertise of its sailors is also evident in the collection of Pre-Columbian charts and maps, including one of 1439 which was used by Amerigo Vespucci.

Stained-glass window in the Museu Marítim

BARCELONA'S FIESTAS

La Mercè (*24 Sep*). The patroness of Barcelona, Nostra Senyora de la Mercè (Our Lady of Mercy), whose church is near the port, is honoured for a week around 24 September with masses, concerts and dances. The biggest events are the *correfoc* – a procession of people dressed as devils and monsters, illuminated by fireworks – and the *piro musical* – an impressive firework display with music held at the Font Màgica in Montjuïc.

Firework display during the fiesta of La Mercè

Els Tres Tombs (*17 Jan*). Horsemen, dressed in top hats and tails, ride three times through the streets in honour of St Anthony, the patron saint of animals.
La Diada (*11 Sep*). Catalonia's "national" day is an occasion for singing the Catalan anthem and separatist demonstrations.
Dia de Sant Ponç (*11 May*). Stalls along Carrer Hospital sell herbs, honey and candied fruit on the day of the patron saint of beekeepers and herbalists.
Festa Major (*mid-Aug*). Each district hosts its own *festa* in which streets compete to outdo each other in the inventiveness and beauty of their decorations. The most spectacular displays take place in the old district of Gràcia.

EIXAMPLE

Barcelona claims to have the greatest collection of Art Nouveau buildings of any city in Europe. The style, known in Catalonia as Modernisme, flourished after 1854, when it was decided to pull down the medieval walls to allow the city to develop into what had previously been a construction-free military zone.

The designs of the civil engineer Ildefons Cerdà i Sunyer (1815–76) were chosen for the new expansion *(eixample)* inland. These plans called for a rigid grid system of streets, but at each intersection the corners were chamfered to allow the buildings there to overlook the junctions or squares. The few exceptions

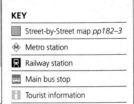

Jesus of the Column, Sagrada Família

to this grid system include the Diagonal, a main avenue running from the wealthy area of Pedralbes down to the sea, and the Hospital de la Santa Creu i de Sant Pau by Modernista architect Domènech i Montaner (1850–1923). He hated the grid system and deliberately angled the hospital to look down the diagonal Avinguda de Gaudí towards Antoni Gaudí's church of the Sagrada Família, the city's most spectacular Modernista building *(see pp166–7)*. The wealth of Barcelona's commercial elite, and their passion for all things new, allowed them to give free rein to the age's most innovative architects in designing their residences as well as public buildings.

SIGHTS AT A GLANCE

Museums and Galleries
Fundació Antoni Tàpies ❷

Churches
Sagrada Família pp166–7 ❻

Modernista Buildings
Casa Milà, "La Pedrera" ❸
Casa Terrades, "Casa de les Punxes" ❹
Hospital de la Santa Creu i de Sant Pau ❺
Illa de la Discòrdia ❶

KEY

▨	Street-by-Street map *pp182–3*
Ⓜ	Metro station
🚆	Railway station
🚌	Main bus stop
ℹ	Tourist information

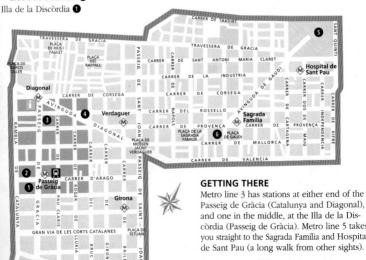

GETTING THERE

Metro line 3 has stations at either end of the Passeig de Gràcia (Catalunya and Diagonal), and one in the middle, at the Illa de la Discòrdia (Passeig de Gràcia). Metro line 5 takes you straight to the Sagrada Família and Hospital de Sant Pau (a long walk from other sights).

0 metres	500
0 yards	500

Nativity façade of the Sagrada Família – the only façade to be more or less completed in Gaudí's lifetime

Street-by-Street: Quadrat d'O

The hundred or so city blocks centring on the Passeig de Gràcia are known as the Quadrat d'Or, "Golden Square", because they contain so many of Barcelona's best Modernista buildings *(see pp140–41)*. This was the area within the Eixample favoured by the wealthy bourgeoisie, who embraced the new artistic and architectural style with enthusiasm, not only for their residences, but also for commercial buildings. Most remarkable is the Illa de la Discòrdia, a single block contain-

Perfume bottle, Museu del Perfum

ing houses by Modernisme's most illustrious exponents. Many interiors can be visited by the public, revealing a feast of stained glass, ceramics and ornamental ironwork.

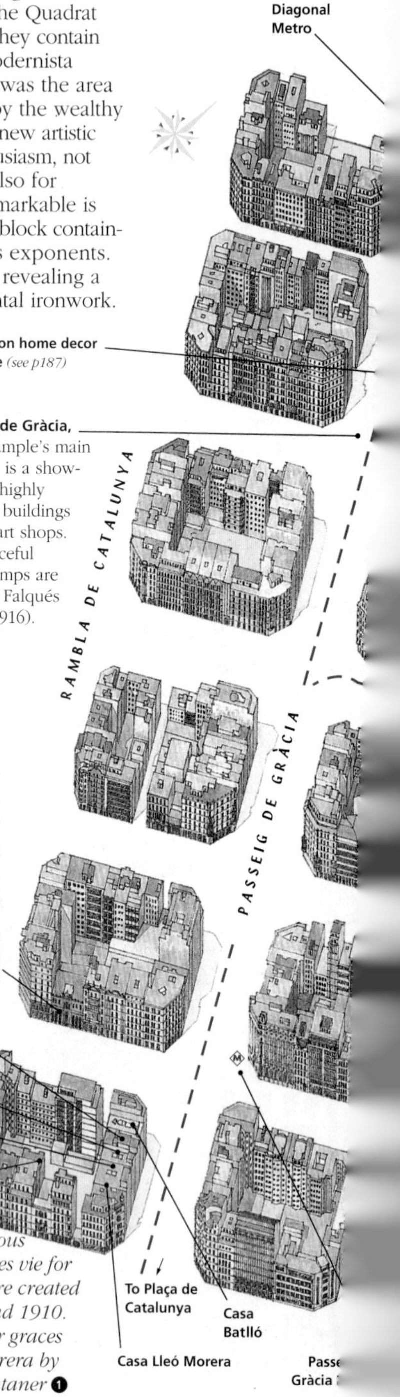

Diagonal Metro

Vinçon home decor store *(see p187)*

Passeig de Gràcia, the Eixample's main avenue, is a show-case of highly original buildings and smart shops. The graceful street lamps are by Pere Falqués (1850–1916).

RAMBLA DE CATALUNYA

PASSEIG DE GRÀCIA

Fundació Tàpies
Topped by Antoni Tàpies' wire sculpture Cloud and Chair, this 1879 building by Domènech i Mon-taner houses a wide variety of Tàpies' paintings, graphics and sculptures ❷

Casa Amatller

Museu del Perfum

Casa Ramon Mulleras

★ **Illa de la Discòrdia**
In this city block, four of Barcelona's most famous Modernista houses vie for attention. All were created between 1900 and 1910. This ornate tower graces the Casa Lleó Morera by Domènech i Montaner ❶

To Plaça de Catalunya

Casa Batlló

Casa Lleó Morera

Passe Gràcia

For hotels and restaurants in this region see pp568–70 and pp617–20

Sumptuous interior of the Casa Lleó Morera, Illa de la Discòrdia

Illa de la Discòrdia ❶

Passeig de Gràcia, between Carrer d'Aragó and Carrer del Consell de Cent. **Map** 3 A4. 🚇 Passeig de Gràcia. **Institut Amatller d'Art Hispanic Tel** 93 487 72 17. 🕐 Mon–Fri am. 📷 📷 only, call for reservations. **Casa Batlló Tel** 93 216 03 06. 🕐 9am–8pm daily. 📷

The most famous group of Modernista (see pp140–1) buildings in Barcelona amply illustrates the range of styles involved in the movement. The city block in which they stand has been dubbed the Illa de la Discòrdia, "Block of Discord", owing to the startling visual argument between them.

The three most famous houses, on Passeig de Gràcia, were remodelled in Modernista style from existing houses early in the 20th century, but named after their original owners.

No. 35 is **Casa Lleó Morera** (1902–6), the first residential work of Lluís Domènech i Montaner. The ground floor was gutted to create a shop in 1943, but the Modernista interiors upstairs still exist.

Beyond the next two houses, one of which is a beauty shop, is **Casa Amatller**, designed by Puig i Cadafalch in 1898. Its façade is a harmonious blend of styles, featuring Moorish and Gothic windows. The stepped gable roof is dotted with tiles. Inside the wrought-iron main doors is a fine stone staircase beneath a stained-glass roof. The rest of the building is

occupied by the **Institut Amatller d'Art Hispanic**.

The third house is Antoni Gaudí's **Casa Batlló** (1904–6), the only house that is completely open to the public. Its façade has heavily tiled walls and curving iron balconies pierced with holes to look like masks or skulls. The hump-backed, scaly-looking roof is thought to represent a dragon, with St George (the patron saint of Catalonia) as a chimney.

Fundació Antoni Tàpies ❷

Carrer d'Aragó 255. **Map** 3 A4. **Tel** 93 487 03 15. 🚇 Passeig de Gràcia. 🕐 10am–8pm Tue–Sun & public hols. 🔴 1 & 6 Jan, 25 & 26 Dec. 📷 📷 by appointment (932 07 58 62). 🔖

Antoni Tàpies, born in 1923, is Barcelona's best-known living artist. Inspired by Surrealism, his abstract work is executed in a variety of materials, including concrete and metal (see p160). It is not easy to appreciate at first, but the exhibits should help those interested obtain a clearer perspective, even if there are not enough here to gain a full understanding of the artist's work. They are housed in the first domestic building in Barcelona to be built with iron (1880), designed by Domènech i Montaner.

ANTONI GAUDÍ (1852–1926)

Born in Reus (Tarragona) into a family of artisans, Gaudí was the leading exponent of Catalan Modernisme. Following a stint as a blacksmith's apprentice, he studied at Barcelona's School of Architecture. Inspired by a nationalistic search for a romantic medieval past, his work was supremely original. His first major achievement was the Casa Vicens (1888) at No. 24 Carrer de les Carolines. But his most celebrated building is the extravagant church of the Sagrada Família (see pp166–7), to which he devoted his life from 1914. He gave all his money to the project and often went from house to house begging for more, until his death a few days after being run over by a tram.

Decorated chimney pot, Casa Vicens

◁ **Extraordinary sculptured and ceramic-encrusted chimneys of Gaudí's Casa Milà**

The rippled façade of Gaudí's apartment building, Casa Milà

Casa Milà ❸

Passeig de Gràcia 92. **Map** 3 B3.
Tel 90 240 09 73. Ⓜ Diagonal.
◯ daily. Mar–Oct: 9am–8pm; Nov–
Feb: 9am–6:30pm. ◉ public hols.
(temporary exhibitions free.)
http://obrasocial.caixacatalunya.es

Usually called "La Pedrera" "the stone quarry"), the Casa Milà is Gaudí's greatest contribution to Barcelona's civic architecture, and his last work before he devoted himself entirely to the Sagrada Família (see pp166–7).

Built between 1906 and 1910, "La Pedrera" completely departed from the established construction principles of the time and, as a result, was ridiculed and strongly attacked by Barcelona's intellectuals.

Gaudí designed this corner apartment block, eight storeys high, around two circular courtyards. The intricate ironwork balconies, by Josep Maria Jujol, are like seaweed against the wave-like walls of white dressed stone. There are no straight walls in the building. The Milà family had an apartment on the first floor. The top floor now houses the Gaudí Museum. Regular guided tours from an office on the ground floor take in the extraordinary roof, where the multitude of sculpted air ducts and chimneys look so threatening that they have been dubbed the *espanta-ixes*, the witch-scarers.

Casa Terrades ❹

Avinguda Diagonal 416. **Map** 3 B3.
Ⓜ Diagonal. ◉ to public.

This free-standing, six-sided apartment block by Modernista architect Puig i Cadafalch gets its nickname, "Casa de les Punxes" (House of the Points), from the spires on its six corner turrets, which are shaped like witches' hats. It was built between 1903 and 1905 by converting three existing houses on the site and was Puig's largest work. It is an eclectic mixture of medieval and

Spire on the main tower, Casa Terrades

Renaissance styles. The towers and gables are influenced in particular by north European Gothic architecture. However, the deeply carved, floral stone ornament of the exterior, in combination with red brick as the principal building material, are typically Modernista.

Hospital de la Santa Creu i de Sant Pau ❺

Carrer de Sant Antoni Maria Claret 167.
Map 4 F1. **Tel** 93 256 25 04. Ⓜ Hospital de Sant Pau. **Grounds** ◯ daily.
Daily tours in English at 10:15am and 12:15pm, call to arrange any other time. **www**.santpau.es

Lluís Domènech i Montaner began designing a new city hospital in 1902. Totally innovative in concept, his scheme consisted of 26 Mudéjar-style pavilions set in large gardens, as he disliked huge wards and believed that patients would recover better amid fresh air and trees. All the connecting corridors and service areas were hidden underground.

Also believing art and colour to be therapeutic, he decorated the pavilions profusely. The turreted roofs were tiled with ceramics, and the reception pavilion embellished with sculptures by Pau Gargallo and mosaic murals. The vast project was completed after Domènech's death, in 1930, by his son Pere.

Statue of the Virgin, Hospital de la Santa Creu i de Sant Pau

Sagrada Família ⑥

A carved whelk

Europe's most unconventional church, the Temple Expiatori de la Sagrada Família, is an emblem of a city that likes to think of itself as individualistic. Crammed with symbolism inspired by nature and striving for originality, it is Gaudí's *(see pp140–1)* greatest work. In 1883, a year after work had begun on a Neo-Gothic church on the site, the task of completing it was given to Gaudí who changed everything, extemporizing as he went along. It became his life's work and he lived like a recluse on the site for 14 years. He is buried in the crypt. At his death only one tower on the Nativity façade had been completed, but work resumed after the Civil War and several more have since been finished to his original plans. Work continues today, financed by public subscription.

Bell Towers
Eight of the 12 spires, one for each apostle, have been built. Each is topped by Venetian mosaics.

THE FINISHED CHURCH

Gaudí's initial ambitions have been kept over the years, using various new technologies to achieve his vision. Still to come is the central tower, which is to be encircled by four large towers representing the Evangelists. Four towers on the Glory (south) façade will match the existing four on the Passion (west) and Nativity (east) façades. An ambulatory – like an inside-out cloister – will run round the outside of the building.

Tower with lift

The apse was the first part of the church Gaudí completed. Stairs lead down from here to the crypt below.

The altar canopy, designed by Gaudí, is still waiting for the altar.

★ Passion Façade
This bleak façade was completed from 1986 to 2000 by artist Josep Maria Subirachs. A controversial work, its sculpted figures are angular and often sinister.

Main entrance

Spiral Staircases
Steep stone steps – 400 in each – allow access to the towers and upper galleries. Majestic views reward those who climb or take the lift.

VISITORS' CHECKLIST

C/ Mallorca 401. **Map** 4 E3.
Tel 93 207 30 31. Sagrada Familia. 19, 43, 51.
daily. Apr–Sep: 9am–8pm; Oct–Mar: 9am–6pm (to 2pm public hols). numerous services are held daily. ground floor. **www.** sagradafamilia.org

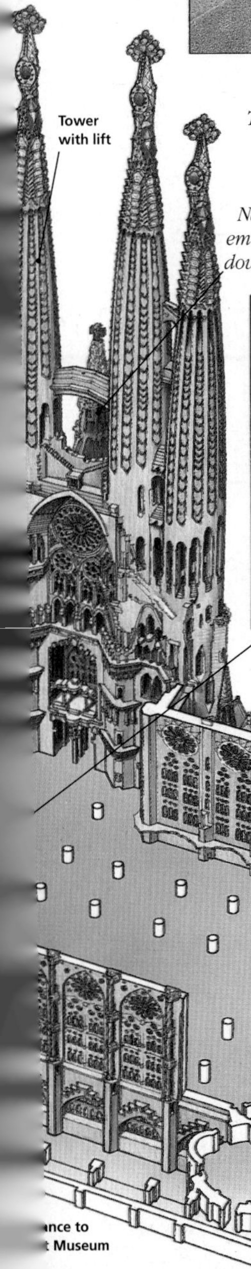

Tower with lift

★ **Nativity Façade**
The most complete part of Gaudí's church, finished in 1930, has doorways which represent Faith, Hope and Charity. Scenes of the Nativity and Christ's childhood are embellished with symbolism, such as doves representing the congregation.

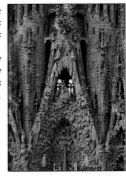

★ **Crypt**
The crypt, where Gaudí is buried, was begun by the original architect, Francesc de Paula Villar i Lozano, in 1882. This is where services are held. On the lower floor a museum traces the careers of both architects and the church's history.

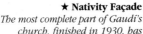

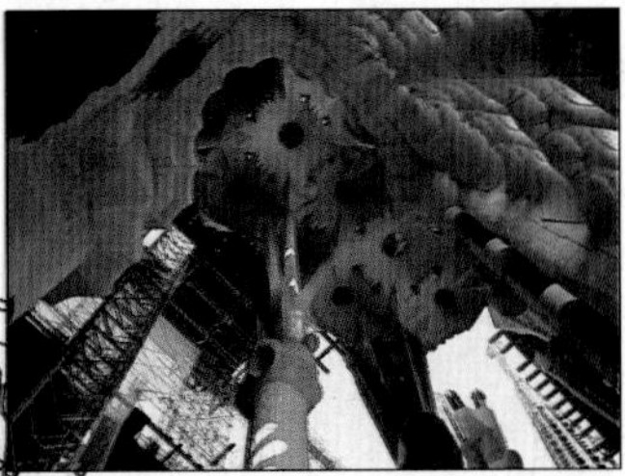

Nave
In the nave, which is still under construction, a forest of fluted pillars will support four galleries above the side aisles, while skylights let in natural light.

...nce to
...t Museum

STAR FEATURES

★ Passion Façade

★ Nativity Façade

★ Crypt

MONTJUÏC

The hill of Montjuïc, rising to 213 m (699 ft) above the commercial port on the south side of the city, is Barcelona's biggest recreation area. Its museums, art galleries, gardens and nightclubs make it a popular place in the evenings as well as during the day.

There was probably a Celtiberian settlement here before the Romans built a temple to Jupiter on their Mons Jovis, which may have given Montjuïc its name – though another theory suggests that a Jewish cemetery on the hill inspired the name Mount of the Jews.

The absence of a water supply meant that there were few buildings on Montjuïc until the castle was erected on the top in 1640.

Statue, gardens of the Palau Nacional

The hill finally came into its own as the site of the 1929 International Fair. With great energy and flair, buildings were erected all over the north side, with the grand Avinguda de la Reina Maria Cristina, lined with huge exhibition halls, leading into it from the Plaça d'Espanya. In the middle of the avenue is the Font Màgica (Magic Fountain), which is regularly illuminated in colour. Above it is the Palau Nacional, home of the city's historic art collections. The Poble Espanyol is a crafts centre housed in copies of buildings from all over Spain. The last great surge of building on Montjuïc was for the 1992 Olympic Games, which left Barcelona with international-class sports facilities.

SIGHTS AT A GLANCE

Historic Buildings
Castell de Montjuïc **7**

Modern Architecture
Estadi Olímpic de Montjuïc **8**
Pavelló Mies van der Rohe **4**

Museums and Galleries
Fundació Joan Miró **1**
Museu Arqueològic **2**
Museu Nacional d'Art de Catalunya **3**

Squares
Plaça d'Espanya **6**

Theme Parks
Poble Espanyol **5**

GETTING THERE

Apart from the exhibition halls near Espanya Metro station, reaching Montjuïc's attractions on foot involves a steep climb. Buses 61 and 50 will take you up the hill from Plaça d'Espanya. For the castle, take the funicular (9am–8pm daily in winter, to 10pm in summer) from Metro Paral·lel, then the cable car (10am–6pm daily in winter, to 9pm in summer).

KEY

▨	Street-by-Street map pp170–71
Ⓜ	Metro station
🚡	Cable car station
🚟	Funicular railway station
🚌	Main bus stop
ℹ	Tourist information

metres | 500

yards | 500

ARC DE MONTJUIC

hanging colours of the Font Màgica (Magic Fountain) on the grand avenue leading up to Montjuïc

Street-by-Street: Montjuïc

Montjuïc is a spectacular vantage point from which to view the city. It has a wealth of art galleries and museums, an amusement park and an open-air theatre. The most interesting buildings lie around the Palau Nacional, where Europe's greatest Romanesque art collection is housed. Montjuïc is approached from the Plaça d'Espanya between brick pillars based on the campanile of St Mark's in Venice, which give a foretaste of the eclecticism of building styles. The Poble Espanyol illustrates the traditional architecture of Spain's regions, while the Fundació Joan Miró is boldly modern.

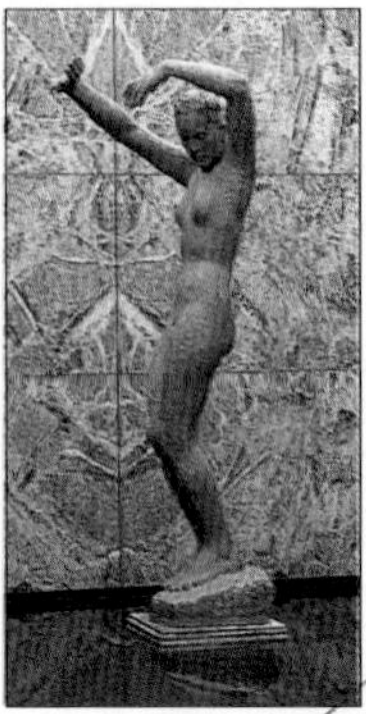

Pavelló Mies van der Rohe
This statue by Geo[...] Kolbe (see p173) *stands serenely in the steel, glass, sto[...] and onyx pavilion built in the Bauha[...] style as the Germa[...] contribution to th[...] 1929 Internation[...] Exhibition* ❹

AVINGUDA DEL MARQUES DE COMILLAS
AVINGUDA DELS MONTANYANS
PASSEIG DE LES
AVINGUDA DE LESTADI
To Montjuïc castle and Olympic stadium

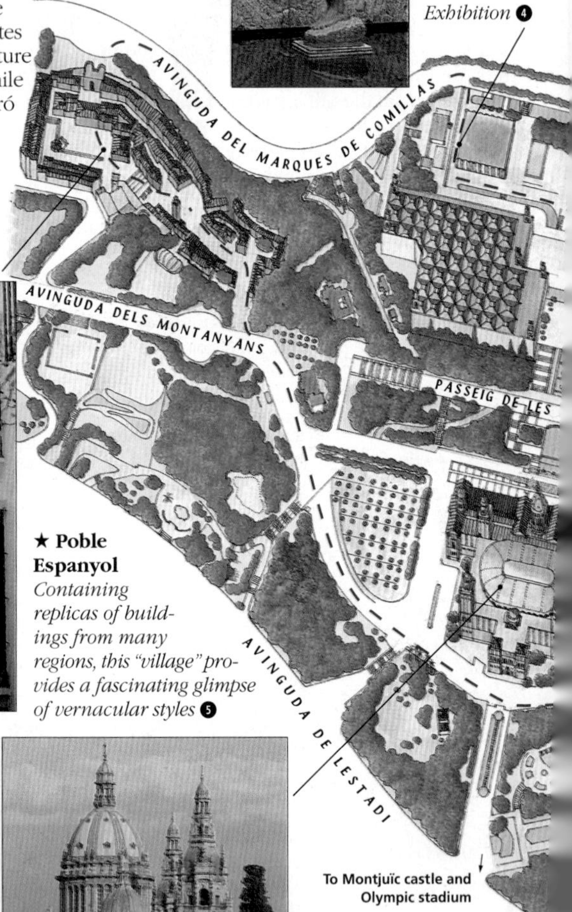

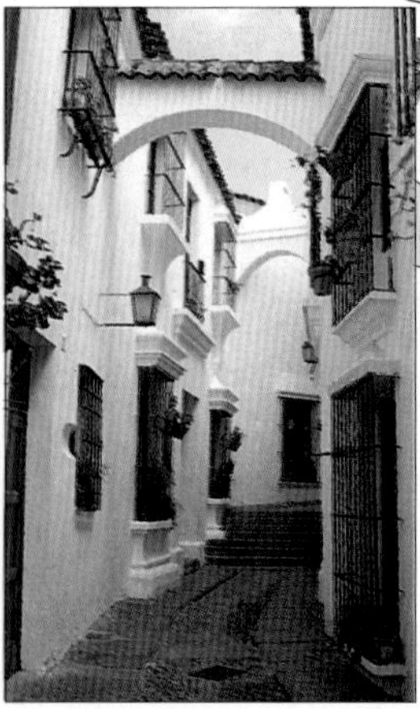

★ Poble Espanyol
Containing replicas of buildings from many regions, this "village" provides a fascinating glimpse of vernacular styles ❺

★ Museu Nacional d'Art de Catalunya
Displayed in the National Palace, the main building of the 1929 International Exhibition, is Europe's finest collection of early medieval frescoes. These were a great source of inspiration for Joan Miró (see p172) ❸

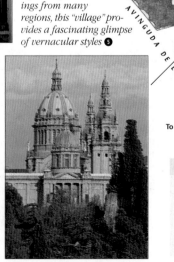

STAR SIGHTS

- ★ Poble Espanyol
- ★ Museu Nacional d'A[...] de Catalunya
- ★ Fundació Joan Miró

For hotels and restaurants in this region see pp568–70 and pp617–20

Fountains and cascades descend in terraces from the Palau Nacional. Below them is the Font Màgica (Magic Fountain). On summer evenings, from Thursday to Sunday, its jets are programmed to a multi-coloured music and light show. This marvel of water-and-electrical engineering was originally built by Carles Buigas (1898–1979) for the 1929 International Exhibition.

LOCATOR MAP
See Street Finder map 1

ça d'Espanya

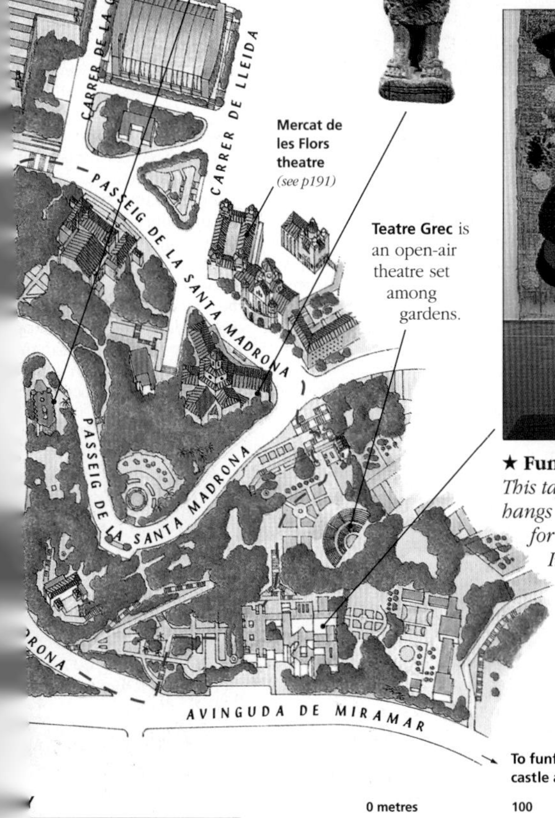

Museu Etnològic displays artifacts from Oceania, Africa, Asia and Latin America.

Museu Arqueològic
The museum displays important finds from prehistoric cultures in Catalonia and the Balearic Islands. The Dama de Ibiza, *a 4th-century sculpture, was found in Ibiza's Carthaginian necropolis (see p511)* ❷

Mercat de les Flors theatre
(see p191)

Teatre Grec is an open-air theatre set among gardens.

★ **Fundació Joan Miró**
This tapestry by Joan Miró hangs in the centre he created for the study of modern art. In addition to Miró's works in various media, the modern building by Josep Lluís Sert is of architectural interest ❶

CARRERS I TAULET

CARRER DE LA GUARDA-URBANA

CARRER DE LLEIDA

PASSEIG DE LA SANTA MADRONA

PASSEIG DE LA SANTA MADRONA

DRONA

AVINGUDA DE MIRAMAR

To funfair, Montjuïc castle and cable car

– – Suggested route

0 metres 100

0 yards 100

Flame in Space and Naked Woman (1932) by Joan Miró

Fundació Joan Miró ❶

Parc de Montjuïc. **Map** 1 B3. **Tel** 93 443 94 70. ⊛ Espanya, then bus 50, 55 or Parallel, then Montjuïc funicular. ☐ Jul–Sep: 10am–8pm Tue–Sat; Oct–Jun: 10am–7pm Tue–Sat; all year: 10am–9:30pm Thu, 10am–2:30pm Sun & public hols. ● 1 Jan, 25, 26 Dec. 📷 ♿ **www**.bcn.fjmiro.cat

Joan Miró (1893–1983) studied at the fine art school at La Llotja (*see p152*). From 1919, he spent much of his time in Paris. Though opposed to Franco, he returned to Spain in 1940 and lived mainly in Mallorca, where he died.

An admirer of primitive Catalan art and Gaudí's Modernisme (*see p140*), Miró always remained a Catalan painter but developed a Surrealistic style, with vivid colours and fantastical forms suggesting dream-like situations.

In 1975, after the return of democracy to Spain (*see p68*), his friend, the architect Josep Lluís Sert, designed the stark, white building to house a permanent collection of paintings, sculptures and tapestries lit by natural light. Miró himself donated the works and some of the best pieces on display include his *Barcelona Series* (1939–44), a set of 50 black-and-white lithographs. Periodic exhibitions of other artists' work are also held.

Museu Arqueològic ❷

Passeig Santa Madrona 39–41. **Map** 1 B3. **Tel** 93 424 65 77. ⊛ Espanya, Poble Sec. ☐ 9:30am–7pm Tue–Sat, 10am–2:30pm Sun & public hols. ● 1 Jan, 25, 26 Dec. 📷 (free 11 Feb, 23 Apr, 18 May, 11 & 24 Sep). ♿ **www**.mac.es

Housed in the Renaissance-inspired 1929 Palace of Graphic Arts, the museum shows artifacts from prehistory to the Visigothic period (AD 415–711). Highlights are finds from the Greco-Roman town of Empúries (*see p216*) and Iberian silver treasure. There is also a splendid collection of Visigothic jewellery.

Museu Nacional d'Art de Catalunya ❸

Parc de Montjuïc, Palau Nacional. **Map** 1 A2. **Tel** 93 622 03 76. ⊛ Espanya. 🚌 PM, 55. ☐ 10am–7pm Tue–Sat, 10am–2:30pm Sun & public hols. ● 1 Jan, 1 May, 25 Dec. 📷 📷 ♿ 📷 by appt (93 622 03 75), free 1st Sun each month. **www**.mnac.es

The austere Palau Nacional was built for the 1929 International Exhibition, but in 1934 it was used to house an art collection that has since become the most important in the city.

The museum has probably the world's greatest display of Romanesque (*see pp24–25*) items, centred around a series of magnificent 12th-century frescoes taken from Catalan Pyrenean churches. The most remarkable are the wall paintings from Sant Climent de Taüll (*see p24*) and from Santa Maria de Taüll (*see p211*).

There is also an expanding Gothic collection, covering the whole of Spain but particularly good on Catalonia, and a collection of notable Baroque and Renaissance works from all over Europe.

The museum has made way for an entire body of 20th-century art, furniture and sculpture, previously on show at the Museu d'Art Modern in the Ciutadella park. These new additions offer a rare opportunity to view more than a millennium of Catalan artistic activity in a single location.

12th-century *Christ in Majesty,* **Museu Nacional d'Art de Catalu...**

Morning by Georg Kolbe (1877–1945), Pavelló Mies van der Rohe

Pavelló Mies van der Rohe ❹

Avinguda del Marqués de Comillas. **Map** 1 B2. **Tel** 93 423 40 16. 🚇 Espanya. 🚌 50. ◯ 10am–8pm daily. ◯ 1 Jan, 25 Dec. 🎫 under 18s free. 📷 5–7pm Wed & Fri in English. www.miesbcn.com

If the simple lines of the glass and polished stone German Pavilion look modern today, they must have shocked visitors to the International Exhibition in 1929. Designed by Ludwig Mies van der Rohe (1886–1969), director of the avant-garde Bauhaus School, it includes his famous *Barcelona Chair*. The building was demolished after the exhibition, but a replica was built in the centenary of his birth.

Poble Espanyol ❺

Avinguda del Marqués de Comillas. **Map** 1 A2. **Tel** 93 508 63 00. 🚇 Espanya. ◯ 9am–8pm Mon, 9am–2am Tue–Thu, 9am–4am Fri (to 5am Sat), 9am–midnight Sun. 🎫 📷 www.poble-espanyol.com.

The idea behind the Poble Espanyol (Spanish Village) is to display Spanish architectural styles and crafts. It was laid out for the 1929 International Exhibition, but has proved enduringly popular. Building styles from all over Spain are illustrated by 116 houses. These are arranged on streets radiating from a main

square and were created by many well-known architects and artists of the time. The village was refurbished at the end of the 1980s and is now a favorite place to visit for both tourists and native Barcelonins.

Resident artisans produce a wide range of crafts including hand-blown glass, ceramics, sculpture, Toledo damascene (*see p390*) and Catalan canvas sandals. The Torres de Ávila, which form the huge main entrance, have been converted into one of the city's most popular nightspots, with an interior by designers Alfredo Arribas and Javier Mariscal.

View from Palau Nacional downhill towards the Plaça d'Espanya

Plaça d'Espanya ❻

Avinguda de la Gran Via de les Corts Catalanes. **Map** 1 B1. 🚇 Espanya. **Magic Fountain Music and Light Show**: May–Sep: 9–11:30pm Thu–Sun; Oct–Apr: 7–9pm Fri–Sat.

The fountain in the middle of this road junction, the site of public gallows until they were transferred to Ciutadella in 1715, is by Josep Maria Jujol, one of Gaudí's followers. The 1899 bullring to one side is by Font i Carreras, but Catalans have never taken to bullfighting and the arena is now used as a music venue.

On the Montjuïc side of the roundabout is the Avinguda de la Reina Maria Cristina. This is flanked by two 47-m (154-ft) high brick campaniles by Ramon Raventós, modelled on the bell towers of St Mark's in Venice. The avenue, lined with exhibition buildings, leads up to Carles Buigas's illuminated *Font Màgica* (Magic Fountain) in front of the Palau Nacional.

Castell de Montjuïc ❼

Parc de Montjuïc. **Map** 1 B5. **Tel** 93 329 86 13. 🚇 Paral·lel, then funicular & cable car. 🚌 PM from Plaça Espanya. **Museum** ◯ Dec–Feb: 9:30am–5pm Tue–Fri (7pm Sat–Sun); Apr–Oct: 9:30am–8pm daily; Mar & Nov: 9:30am–6:30pm Tue–Fri (8pm Sat–Sun). 🎫

The summit of Montjuïc is occupied by an 18th-century castle, first built in 1640 but destroyed by Felipe V in 1705. The present fortress was built for the Bourbon family. During the War of Independence it was captured by the French. After the Civil War it became a prison, where the Catalan leader Lluís Companys was executed in 1940. The castle is now a military museum, but it will be converted into a Centre for the Peace in 2010.

Estadi Olímpic de Montjuïc ❽

Passeig Olímpic 17–19. **Map** 1 A3. **Tel** 93 426 20 89. 🚇 Espanya, Poble Sec. 🚌 50, 61. ◯ May–Sep: 10am–8pm daily; Oct–Apr: 10am–6pm daily. **Museum** ◯ as for the Estadi. ♿ 📷

The Neo-Classical façade has been preserved from the stadium, built by Pere Domènech i Roura for the 1936 Olympics, cancelled at the onset of the Civil War. The arena was refitted to a capacity of 70,000 for the 1992 Olympics Nearby are the steel-and-glass **Palau Sant Jordi** indoor stadium, by Japanese architect Arata Isozaki, and swimming pools by Ricardo Bofill.

Entrance to the refurbished 1992 Olympic Stadium

FURTHER AFIELD

The radical redevelopment of Barcelona's outskirts in the late 1980s and early 1990s gave it a wealth of new buildings, parks and squares. The city's main station, Sants, was rebuilt and the neighbouring Parc de l'Espanya Industrial and Parc de Joan Miró were created, containing lakes, modern sculpture and futuristic architecture. The Parc de Clot, beyond the new national theatre *(see p191)*, is also of striking modern design. In the west of the city, where the streets start to climb steeply, are the historic royal palace and monastery of Pedralbes, and Gaudí's famous Parc Güell, dating from 1910. Beyond is the Serra de Collserola, the city's closest rural area. Two funiculars provide an exciting way of reaching its heights, which offer superb views of the city. Tibidabo, the highest point, with a funfair, the Neo-Gothic church of the Sagrat Cor and a modern steel-and-glass communications tower, is a favourite place among Barcelonins for a day out.

Parc Güell gateway signs

SIGHTS AT A GLANCE

Museums and Galleries
Cosmocaixa – Museu de la Ciència ❽
Museu del Futbol Club Barcelona ❸

Historic Buildings
Monestir de Pedralbes ❺
Palau Reial de Pedralbes ❹

Modern Buildings
Torre de Collserola ❻

Parks and Gardens
Parc de l'Espanya Industrial ❷
Parc Güell ❾
Parc de Joan Miró ❶

Theme Parks
Tibidabo ❼

0 metres	500
0 yards	500

KEY

■	Barcelona City Centre
▢	Built-up area
🚉	Railway station
🚠	Funicular railway station
▬	Motorway
▬	Major road
═	Minor road

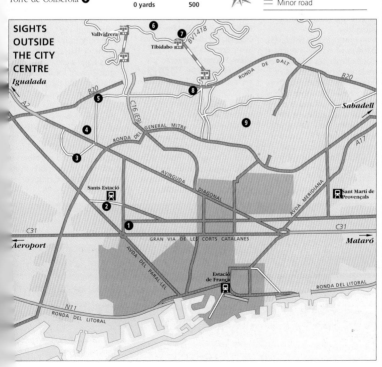

SIGHTS OUTSIDE THE CITY CENTRE

Vallvidrera
Tibidabo
BV1418
RONDA DE DALT
Igualada
B20
B20
A2
CT6 (E9)
RONDA DEL GENERAL MITRE
Sabadell
A17
AVINGUDA DIAGONAL
Sants Estació
AVDA MERIDIANA
Sant Martí de Provençals
C31
GRAN VIA DE LES CORTS CATALANES
C31
Aeroport
Mataró
AVDA DEL PARAL·LEL
Estació de França
RONDA DEL LITORAL
N11
RONDA DEL LITORAL

Dona i Ocell (1983) by Joan Miró in the Parc de Joan Miró

Parc de Joan Miró ❶

Carrer d'Aragó 1. Ⓜ *Tarragona.*

Barcelona's 19th-century slaughterhouse *(escorxador)* was transformed in the 1980s into this unusual park, hence its alternative name, Parc de l'Escorxador.

It is constructed on two levels, the lower of which is devoted to football pitches interspersed with landscaped sections of palms, pines, eucalyptus trees and flowers. The upper level is completely paved and is dominated by a magnificent 1983 sculpture by the Catalan artist Joan Miró *(see p172)* entitled Dona i Ocell (Woman and Bird). Standing 22 m (72 ft) high in the middle of a pool, its surface is coated with colourful pieces of glazed tile.

Parc de l'Espanya Industrial ❷

Plaça de Joan Peiró. Ⓜ *Sants-Estació.*

This modern park, designed by the Basque architect Luis Peña Ganchegui, owes its name to the textile mill that used to stand on the 5-hectare (12-acre) site.

Laid out in 1986 as part of Barcelona's policy to provide more open spaces within the city, the park has canals and a rowing lake – with a Classical statue of Neptune at its centre. Tiers of steps rise around the lake like an amphitheatre and on one side a row of ten futuristic watchtowers dominates the entire area. Their only function is to serve as public viewing platforms and lamp standards.

Six contemporary sculptors are represented in the park, among them Andrés Nagel, whose huge metal dragon incorporates a children's slide.

Museu del Futbol Club Barcelona ❸

Avda de Aristides Maillol.
Tel 93 496 36 08. Ⓜ *Maria Cristina, Collblanc.* ◯ 10am–6:30pm Mon–Sat (to 8pm mid-Apr–mid-Oct), 10am– 2:30pm Sun & public hols. ◉ 1 & 6 Jan, 25 Dec. 🎫 ♿ 🎥 of the stadium. **www**.fcbarcelona.com

Camp Nou, Europe's largest football stadium, is home to the city's famous football club, Barcelona FC (Barça, as it is known locally). Founded in 1899, it is one of the world's richest soccer clubs, and has more than 100,000 members. The stadium is a magnificent,

Line of watchtowers in the Parc de l'Espanya Industrial

sweeping structure, built in 1957 to a design by Francesc Mitjans. An extension was added in 1982 and it can now comfortably seat 100,000 fans.

The club's popular museum displays club memorabilia and trophies on two floors, and has a souvenir shop. There are also paintings and sculptures of famous club footballers commissioned for the Blaugrana Biennial, an exhibition held in celebration of the club in 1985 and 1987. *Blau-grana* (blue-burgundy) are the colours of Barça's strip. The club's flags were used as an expression of local nationalist feelings during the Franco dictatorship, when the Catalan flag was banned.

As well as hosting its own high-profile matches (mainly at weekends), Camp Nou also accommodates affiliated local soccer clubs and promotes a number of other sports in its sports centre, ice rink and mini-stadium.

View across Camp Nou stadium, prestigious home of the Futbol Club Barcelona

For hotels and restaurants in this region see pp568–70 and pp617–20

Palau Reial de Pedralbes ❹

Avinguda Diagonal 686. 🚇 *Palau Reial.* 🅿️ *to the public.* **Museu de Ceràmica, Museu de Arts Decoratives & Museu Textil i d'Indumentària** *Tel* 93 280 50 24. ⬜ *10am–6pm Tue–Sat, 10am–3pm Sun & public hols.* ⬤ *1 Jan, 1 May, 24 Jun, 25 & 26 Dec.* 📷 *(free first Sun of each month).* ♿ 📷 *by appointment*

The Palace of Pedralbes was once the main house on the estate of Count Eusebi Güell. In 1919 he offered it to the Spanish royal family. The first visit was from Alfonso XIII in 1926, before which the interior was refurbished.

Three fascinating museums and the gardens are open to the public. The Museu de Arts Decoratives, opened in 1937, displays period furniture and fine household items from the Middle Ages to the present. A genealogical tree traces the 500-year dynasty of the countkings of Barcelona.

The Museu de Ceràmica has displays of historic Catalan and Moorish pottery and modern ceramics, including works by Miró and Picasso *(see p152).* The permanent collection of the Textil Museum was also moved here in 2008.

The gardens are well laid out with small ponds and paths. Just behind them, in Avinguda de Pedralbes, is the entrance to the original Güell estate. It guarded by a black wrought-iron gate, its top forged into a dragon, and two gate houses, by Gaudí *(see pp140–1).*

Madonna of Humility, Monestir de Santa Maria de Pedralbes

Monestir de Santa Maria de Pedralbes ❺

Baixada del Monestir 9. *Tel* 93 203 94 08. 🚆 *Reina Elisenda or bus 22, 63 or 64.* ⬜ *Oct–Mar: 10am–2pm Tue–Sat; Apr–Sep: 10am–5pm Tue–Sat, 10am–3pm Sun.* 📷 *by appt (93 256 21 22).* ⬤ *1 Jan, Good Friday, 1 May, 24 Jun, 25 Dec.* 📷 *(free first Sun of each month and for under age 16).* ♿ *ground floor only.*

Approached through an arch in its walls, the monastery of Pedralbes still has the air of a living enclosed community. This is heightened by its furnished cells, kitchens, infirmary and refectory. But the nuns of the Order of St Clare moved to an adjoining building in 1983. The monastery was founded in 1326 by Elisenda de Montcada de Piños, fourth wife of Jaime II of Catalonia and Aragón. Her tomb lies between the church and the cloister. On the church side her effigy is dressed in royal robes; on the other as a nun.

The monastery is built around a three-storey cloister. The main rooms encircling the cloister include a dormitory, a refectory, a chapterhouse, an abbey and day cells. Numerous works of art, as well as liturgical ornaments, pottery, furniture, altar cloths and gold and silver work, are on display.

The most important room in the monastery is the Capella (chapel) de Sant Miquel, with murals of the *Passion* and the *Life of the Virgin*, both painted by Ferrer Bassa in 1346, when Elisenda's niece, Francesca Saportella, was abbess.

Torre de Collserola ❻

Carretera de Vallvidrera al Tibidabo. *Tel* 93 406 93 54. 🚠 *Peu de Funicular, then Funicular de Vallvidrera & bus 111.* ⬜ *11am–2:30pm, 3:30–6pm Wed–Sun (to 7pm Apr–Sep); 2:30–3:30pm Sat, Sun.* ⬤ *25, 26, 31 Dec, 1, 6 Jan.* 📷 *(combined ticket with Monument a Colom).* ♿ **www**.torredecollserola.com

In a city that enjoys thrills, the ultimate ride is offered by the communications tower near Tibidabo mountain *(see p178).* A glass-sided lift swiftly reaches the top of this 288-m (944-ft) tall structure standing on the summit of a 445-m (1,460-ft) hill.

The tower was designed by English architect Norman Foster for the 1992 Olympic Games. Needle-like in form, it is a tubular steel mast on a concrete pillar. There are 13 levels. The top one has an observatory with a powerful telescope, and a public viewing platform with a 360° view encompassing Barcelona, the sea and the mountains.

BARCELONA V REAL MADRID

C Barcelona

Més que un club is the motto of Barcelona FC: "More than a club". More than anything else it has been a symbol of the struggle of Catalan nationalism against the central government in Madrid. To fail to win the league is one thing. To come in behind Real Madrid is a complete disaster. Each season the big question is which of the two teams will win the title. Under the Franco regime in a memorable episode in 1941, Barça won 3–0 at home. At the return match in Madrid, the crowd was so hostile that the police and referee "advised" Barça to prevent trouble. Demoralized by the intimidation, they lost 11–. Loyalty is paramount: one Barça player who left to join Real Madrid received death threats.

Real Madrid

Merry-go-round, Tibidabo

Tibidabo **7**

Plaça del Tibidabo 3–4. *Tel 93 211 79 42.* ☎ *Avda Tibidabo, then Tramvia Blau & Funicular.* 🚌 *111.* **Amusement Park** ◯ *variable – phone ahead for times.* ◉ *Oct–Apr: Mon–Fri.* ♿ **Temple del Sagrat Cor.** *Tel 93 417 56 86.* ◯ *10am–8pm daily.* ♿ **www**.tibidabo.es

The heights of Tibidabo are reached by the Tramvia Blau (Blue Tram), Barcelona's one last surviving tram, and a funicular railway. The name, inspired by Tibidabo's views of the city, comes from the Latin *tibi dabo* (I shall give you) – a reference to the Temptation of Christ when Satan took him up a mountain and offered him the world spread at his feet.

The hugely popular Parc d'Atraccions first opened in 1908. The rides were completely renovated in the 1980s. While the old ones retain their charm, the newer ones provide the latest in vertiginous experiences. Their hilltop location at 517 m (1,696 ft) adds to the thrill. Also in the park is the Museu d'Automates, displaying automated toys, juke boxes and gaming machines.

Tibidabo is crowned by the Temple Expiatori del Sagrat Cor (Church of the Sacred Heart), built with religious zeal but little taste by Enric Sagnier between 1902 and 1911. A lift takes you up to the feet of an enormous figure of Christ.

Just a short bus ride away is another viewpoint worth visiting – the Torre de Collserola (*see p177*).

Cosmocaixa – Museu de la Ciència **8**

Carrer Teodor Roviralta 55. *Tel 93 212 60 50.* ☎ *Avinguda del Tibidabo, then Tramvia Blau.* 🚌 *17, 22, 58.* ◯ *10am–8pm Tue–Sun.* ◉ *1 & 6 Jan, 25 Dec.* 🎟 *(free first Sun of every month).* ♿

The new science museum offers hands-on experiences. One of the most modern of its kind, all forms of matter from Inert to Living and Intelligent are questioned and explored over its five subterranean galleries. Above ground is an extensive garden and play area.

Parc Güell **9**

Carrer d'Olot. *Tel 010 (from Barcelona).* Ⓜ *Lesseps.* 🚌 *24.* ◯ *summer 10am–9pm daily, winter 10am–6pm daily.* ♿ **Casa-Museu Gaudí.** *Tel 93 219 38 11.* ◯ *Apr–Sep: 10am– 8pm daily; Oct–Mar: 10am– 6pm daily.* ◉ *1 Jan.* 🎟 *(combined ticket with Sagrada Familia).*

Designated a World Heritage Site by UNESCO, the Parc Güell is Antoni Gaudí's *(see pp140–1)* most colourful creation. He was commissioned in the 1890s by Count Eusebi Güell to design a garden city on 20 hectares (50 acres) of the family estate. Little of the grand design for decorative public buildings and 60 houses among landscaped gardens became reality. What we see today was completed between 1910 and 1914, and the park opened in 1922.

Most atmospheric is the Room of a Hundred Columns, a cavernous covered hall of 84 crooked pillars, which is brightened by glass and ceramic mosaics. Above it, reached by a flight of steps, flanked by ceramic animals, is the Gran Plaça Circular, an open space with a snaking balcony of coloured mosaics, said to have the longest bench in the world.

Two pavilions at the entry are by Gaudí, but the Casa-Museu Gaudí, a gingerbread-style house where Gaudí lived from 1906–26, was built by Francesc Berenguer.

Mosaic-encrusted chimney by Gaudí at the entrance of the Parc Güell

BARCELONA STREET FINDER

The map references given with the sights, shops and entertainment venues described in the Barcelona section of the guide refer to the street maps on the following pages. Map references are also given for Barcelona hotels (see 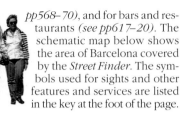 pp568–70), and for bars and restaurants (see pp617–20). The schematic map below shows the area of Barcelona covered by the *Street Finder*. The symbols used for sights and other features and services are listed in the key at the foot of the page.

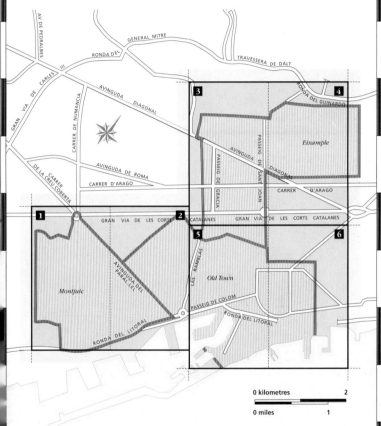

0 kilometres 2

0 miles 1

KEY TO STREET FINDER

▪ Major sight	🚢 Golondrina boarding point	🚓 Police station
▪ Place of interest	🚡 Cable car	✝ Church
▪ Other building	🚟 Funicular railway station	⊠ Post office
⮂ Main railway station	🚃 Tram	═ Railway line
🅾 Local (FF CC) railway station	🚕 Taxi rank	▪ Pedestrianized street
Ⓜ Metro station	🅿 Parking	
🚌 Main bus stop	🛈 Tourist information	**SCALE OF MAP PAGES**
🚍 Coach station	✚ Hospital with casualty unit	0 metres 250
		0 yards 250

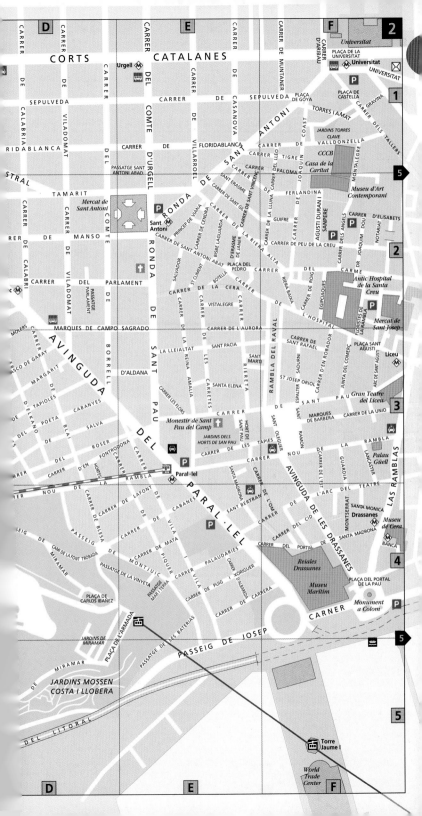

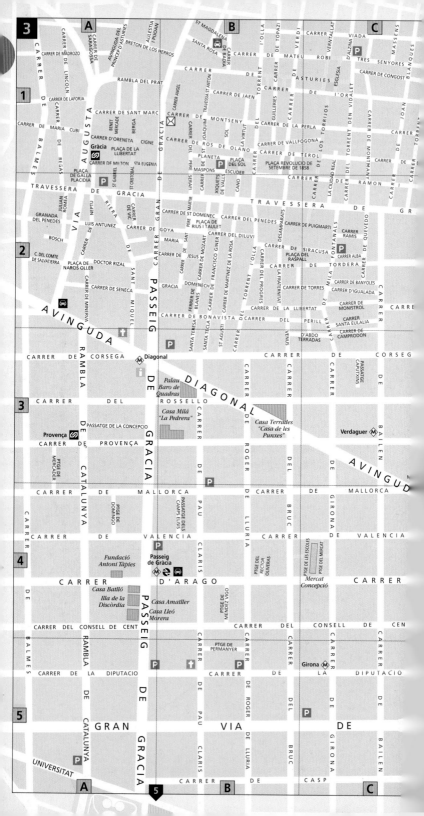

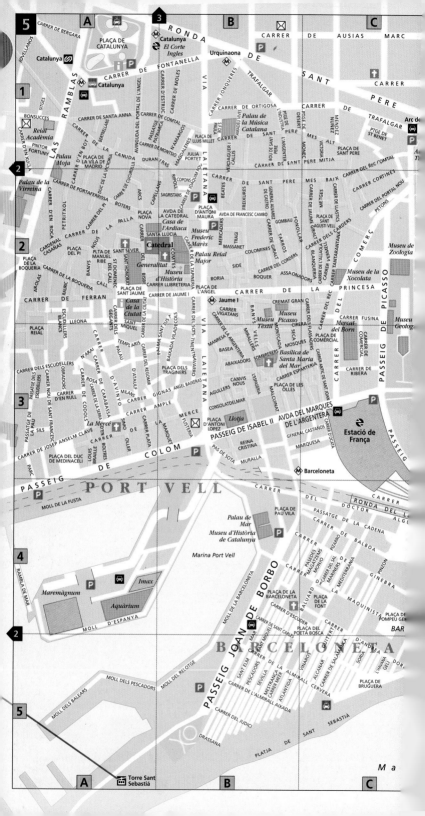

SHOPPING IN BARCELONA

Barcelona is known for its style and sophistication, and can be neatly divided into distinctive shopping districts – Passeig de Gràcia for designer stores and old shops with beautiful Modernista frontages, Barri Gòtic for eclectic antiques and boutiques, El Born for serious fashion divas, and El Raval for markets and museum shops. Though these categories are not fixed, they do provide a useful rule of

Wall tile outside
La Manual Alpargatera

thumb, and help define the city when time is limited. There are numerous food markets as well – 44 in all – and a scattering of flea markets such as the Parisian-style Els Encants and the charming Sant Cugat antiques fair. There is something for everyone in Barcelona – from high-street fashion and unique boutiques to local shops selling traditional crafts. Note that all shops are closed on Sundays.

Some of the beautifully displayed confectionery at Escribà

MARKETS

Barcelona has an impressive range of markets selling a wide variety of things. Everyone should explore **La Boquería** on Las Ramblas, one of the of the most spectacular food markets in Europe. The small and lively Plaça del Pi is also home to a food market selling cheese, honey and sweets. It is held on the 1st and 3rd Friday, Saturday and Sunday of each month.

On Sunday mornings, coin and stamp stalls are set up in the Plaça Reial, while antiques are sold in Plaça Nova on Thursdays. The city's main flea market, **Encants Vells**, takes place on Monday, Wednesday, Friday and Saturday. It offers a variety of goods including jewellery and clothing.

In December, a Christmas street market is held near the cathedral, where Christmas trees, figurines and other decorative items are sold.

FOOD AND DRINK

Barcelonians are proud of their culinary heritage, and rightly so. The land produces superlative vegetables and fruits, flavourful meats and a huge array of cheeses. The bountiful sea offers fresh fish and other seafood, and the wine-growing regions of the Penedès and the Priorat make some of the best vintages in the world. As if all this wasn't enough, chocolate shops, candy makers and patisseries also do their best to complete the feast.

La Boquería food market, is the obvious place to start a gastronomical journey, but Barcelona's numerous specialist food shops are not to be ignored either.

Origins 99.9% in El Born specializes in strictly Catalan products – jars of small, dusky Arbequina olives, truffle-scented salt, vinegars, oils and home-made preserves. Around the corner, **La Botifarría de**

Santa María stocks wonderful artisan charcuterie and a lip-smacking selection of homemade sausages. These include inventive combinations such as pork and cuttlefish, beef and beetroot and lamb and wild mushroom. **Casa Gispert** is the stop for top-grade dried fruit and nuts, as well as coffee toasted in-house. The fabulous **Formatgeria La Seu** is a walk-in dairy where you can choose from a great seasonal collection of cheeses made by small producers.

Xocoa is the trendiest of the many chocolate-makers in the city, with its retro packaging and fun shapes, including chocolate CDs and giant keys. **Escribà Pastisserie** is more extravagant, with magnificently sculpted cakes and life-size chocolate model of famous personalities. **Caca Sampaka**, an innovative swe shop, is owned by chef Albe Adrià, and offers amazing off-the-wall fillings such as anchovy, black olive and blu

Mouthwatering fruit stalls in La Boquería market

cheese, as well as more familiar herb, spice and floral flavours. **Antiga Casa Mauri** is ideal for those who want to sample traditional Spanish sweets such as *turrón* (nougat made with almonds). **Caelum**, where all the sweetmeats are made by nuns, sells lovely *yemas* (a sweet made with egg yolks) and *mazapans* (marzipan treats) and other tasty confections. **Papabubble**, a gorgeous wood-panelled shop, adds modern touches to old-fashioned sweets. You can watch the sweet chefs preparing these handmade concoctions.

For the best breads in town, visit **Bopan** near Rambla de Catalunya. This smart café has its own versions of many different types of bread, ranging from Continental favourites to African specialities.

For sheer scope, you can't beat **Lavinia**, the biggest wine shop in Spain, which stocks thousands of labels from all over the world. In El Born, **Vila Viniteca** sells a formidable range of Spanish and Catalan wines. You can find cheap and cheerful table wines here, as well as decadently expensive Priorats and Riojas. Also remember that leaving Barcelona without a bottle of the nation's beloved Catalan champagne, *cava*, would be verging on the sacrilegious. You can buy it everywhere, but for something truly special, head for **Xampany**, which specializes in wonderful artisan *cavas* from the Penedés wine producing region.

DEPARTMENT STORES AND GALERÍAS

The Plaça Catalunya branch of **El Corte Inglés**, the largest department store chain in Spain, is a Barcelona landmark. It is a handy place with everything under one roof, including plug adaptors and services such as photographic development. There are other branches around the city. The *galerías* (fashion malls), built mostly during the 1980s, are hugely popular.

Menswear department in Adolfo Domínguez

Bulevard Rosa on the Passeig de Gràcia has hundreds of stores selling clothes and accessories. On the Avinguda Diagonal is **L'Illa**, a large, lively shopping mall containing chain stores as well as specialist retailers.

HIGH STREET AND SPORTS FASHION

Ubiquitous Spanish fashion houses, Zara and Mango, have stores all over the city, with both flagships on the Passeig de Gràcia. They are great for good value basics, work-wear and fashionable party dresses. Both also offer a decent menswear range.

Those looking for more upmarket buys can rely on **Massimo Dutti** and **Adolfo Domínguez**. Both labels offer classically styled, elegant and fairly affordable clothing for men and women.

For more individualized fashion, try one of the smaller, independent shops in El Born and the Barri Gòtic. Carrer d'Avinyó, a lively street in the Old Town, is particularly good for such clothing and droves of hipsters flock to it. **Custo Barcelona** is one of the city's most famous design labels. Both branches of this store are in the Old Town, and are piled high with the trademark bright prints and daringly mismatched coats and skirts.

Finally, football fans can head for FC Barcelona's official store, the **Botiga del Barca**. It stocks every conceivable item of merchandise related to the team, including stripes, scarves, boots, balls and keychains.

SPANISH AND INTERNATIONAL DESIGNER LABELS

Independent design house **Giménez & Zuazo** offers truly unique clothing for women, and is well worth seeking out if reasonably priced couture is what you are looking for.

The Barri Gotic has several stores that stock a range of top designer labels. **Loft Avignón** is excellent for menswear, with seasonal collections from Vivienne Westwood, Dolce & Gabbana and many others.

Host to big designer labels such as Gucci, Chanel and Caroline Herrera, Avenida Diagonal and the Passeig de Gràcia are where fashionistas like to go shopping. **Loewe** stocks sleek luxury luggage, and is also a reputed name in fashion.

The stylishly sparse display of furniture at Vinçon (*see p188*)

SECOND-HAND AND VINTAGE FASHION

The diminutive Carrer Riera Baixa in El Raval is home to many interesting second-hand stores. Once a theatre, the vintage shop **Lailo** sells whimsical collectibles such as costumes from the Liceu opera house and 1950s bathing suits. Across the road is **Mies & Felj**, which specializes in fashions from the 1960s and 70s, vintage sportswear, Chinese dresses and brightly patterned curtains.

JEWELLERY, BAGS AND ACCESSORIES

Barcelona has plenty of tiny, Aladdin's Cave-type shops to help put together the perfect outfit. **Platamundi** has top quality silver pieces at good prices, both imported and by local designers. Visit **Rafa Teja Atelier** for embroidered jackets, patchwork scarves, appliqué handbags and hand-painted silk kerchiefs in sumptuous textures and colours.

Take a bit of the city's street-life home – literally – with a Demano handbag. Recycled polyester PVC from banners and placards is transformed into bags in this endeavour by three designers and the city hall. The innovative and eco-friendly range is available from stockists all over town.

With around 650 designers on its books, **Hipótesis** stores many unique pieces. It stocks jewellery as well as scarves and bags. Materials as diverse as white gold, wood, platinum, buttons and beads have been used to create a number of interesting designs.

HATS AND SHOES

Patterned leather shoes and decorative soles from the cult Mallorcan shoemaker, **Camper**, can be purchased cheaper in Barcelona than anywhere else outside of Spain. **La Manual Alpargatera** is another cult classic, beloved by Sardana dancers (see p225) and celebrities alike for its exquisite, individually fitted espadrilles and straw hats. **Le Shoe** is

the place for the discerning buyer willing to spend lavishly for superbly classy stilettos. The store has a collection of gorgeous Miu Mius, Jimmy Choos and Manolo Blahniks.

For the best in designer sports shoes, head to **Czar** in the Born. Their hip selection includes Puma, Paul Smith, Rizzo, Fluxa and Le Coq Sportif.

For trendily old-fashioned hats, go to **Sombrerería Obach** where you will find classics ranging from Basque berets to stetsons and hand-woven Montecristi Panamas.

BOOKS AND MUSIC

Arguably the finest specialist travel bookshop in Spain, **Altaïr** stocks a stupendous range of maps, travel guides and coffee-table books for anyone who loves to live on the move. If you are simply looking for some holiday reading, try **Casa del Llibre**, the city's biggest bookstore for books and magazines in English.

Barcelona has become a hot spot for music collectors, largely due to Sonár, the city's annual electronica festival. **Wah Wah Discos** and **Discos Revolver** are good for stocking up on the latest club tunes and old vinyl, while **FNAC** has a wide variety of books, CDs and DVDs.

UNUSUAL GIFTS AND KNICK-KNACKS

Barcelona is a wonderful city for unearthing intriguing knick-knacks and one-of-a-kind gifts. **Sabater Hnos. Fábrica de Jabones** sells homemade soaps, which come in all shapes and smells, from traditional lavender to delicious chocolate. The risqué **La Condonería** (the condom emporium) stocks condoms in every shape, size, colour and flavour possible.

Cereria Subirà is the city's oldest shop, and sells a phenomenal array of decorative and votive candles in a variety of beautiful designs.

Arlequí Màscares specializes in hand-painted, papier-

mâché folk masks such as Italian Commedia dell'Arte masks, glossy French party masks, Japanese Noh masks and many others.

ARTS AND ANTIQUES

Antiques aficionados will be delighted by what Barcelona has to offer. Equivalent to an antiques shopping mall, the Bulevard dels Antiquaris, in Passeig de Gràcia, is home to over 70 shops filled with vintage relics and every sort of antique imaginable. These range from ancient coins to tin drums and 19th-century candelabras.

Carrer del Call in the Barri Gòtic is another such hub with plush shops, including **L'Arca de l'Àvia**, which sells antique lace, dolls and fine furniture. **Heritage** is a purveyor of semi-precious stone jewellery and antique silks. Also check out the several **Artur Ramon** shops on Carrer de la Palla for 18th- and 19th-century ceramics, and 14th-century paintings.

Sala Parés, the city's oldest and most prestigious gallery, exhibits Catalan artists, both past and present. For pictures that won't break the bank, try the **Boutique Galería Picasso** for prints, lithographs and posters of works by the great Spanish masters, Picasso, Dalí and Miró.

INTERIORS

L'Appartamente is an eclectic gallery and shop that exhibits and sells furniture ranging from funky lamps to stylish folding armchairs. **Zara Home** has four basic styles in its collection: classic, ethnic, contemporary and white, all at very reasonable prices. **Dom**, on the other hand, is more trendy and quirky, with its metallic bead curtains and inflatable sofas in shocking neon shades.

Vinçon is the star among Barcelona's design stores, and a favourite with fans of gizmos and gadgets. Housed in a 1900s apartment, it is filled with everything from French Creuset cookware to straight-edged tumblers and silk bean bags and futons.

DIRECTORY

MARKETS

La Boquería
Las Ramblas 101.
Map 5 A2.

Encants Vells
Plaça de les Glóries.
Map 4 F5.

FOOD AND DRINK

Antiga Casa Mauri
C/ Flassaders 32.
Map 5 C2.
Tel 933 10 04 58.

Bopan
Rambla de Catalunya 119.
Map 3 A3.
Tel 932 37 35 23.

Cacao Sampaka
C/ Consell de Cent 292.
Map 3 A4.
Tel 932 72 08 33.

Caelum
C/ Palla 8. **Map** 5 A2.
Tel 933 01 69 93.

Casa Gispert
C/ Sombrerers 23.
Map 5 B3.
Tel 933 19 75 35.

Escribà Pastisseries
Las Ramblas 83.
Map 5 A1.
Tel 933 01 60 27.

Formatgeria La Seu
C/ Dagueria 16.
Map 5 B3.
Tel 934 12 65 48.

La Botifarrería de Santa María
Carrer Santa María 4.
Map 5 B3.
Tel 933 19 97 84.

Lavinia
Av Diagonal 605.
Map 3 A2.
Tel 933 63 44 45.

Origins 99.9%
C/ Vidrería 6.
Tel 933 10 75 31.

Papabubble
C/ Ample 28.
Map 5 A3.
Tel 932 68 86 25.

La Viniteca
C/ Agullers 7.
Map 5 B3.
Tel 933 10 19 56.

Xampany
C/ Valencia 200. **Map** 3 A4
Tel 934 53 93 38 .

Xocoa
C/ Vidrería 4.
Map 5 B2.
Tel 933 19 63 71.

DEPARTMENT STORES AND GALERÍAS

Bulevard Rosa
Passeig de Gràcia 55. **Map** 3 A4. **Tel** 933 78 91 91.

El Corte Inglés
Plaça de Catalunya 14.
Map 5 B1.
Tel 933 06 38 00.

La Illa
Avinguda Diagonal 545.
Tel 934 44 00 0.

HIGH STREET AND SPORTS FASHION

Adolfo Domínguez
Passeig de Gràcia 89.
Map 3 A2–A5.
Tel 932 15 13 39.

Botiga del Barca
Maremàgnum (Moll d'Espanya). **Map** 5 A4.
Tel 932 25 80 45.

Custo Barcelona
Plaça de les Olles 7.
Map 5 B3.
Tel 932 68 78 93.

Massimo Dutti
Portal de L'Angel 16.
Map 5 A1.
Tel 933 01 89 11.

SPANISH AND INTERNATIONAL DESIGNER LABELS

Giménez & Zuazo
C/ Elisabets 20.
Map 2 F2.
Tel 934 12 33 81.

Loewe
Passeig de Gràcia 35.
Map 3 A2–A5.
Tel 932 16 04 00.

Loft Avignón
C/ Avinyó 22. **Map** 5 A3.
Tel 933 01 24 20.

SECOND-HAND AND VINTAGE FASHION

Lailo
C/ Riera Baixa 20.
Map 2 F2.
Tel 934 41 37 49.

Mies & Felj
C/ Riera Baixa 4.
Map 2 F2.
Tel 934 42 07 55.

JEWELLERY, BAGS AND ACCESSORIES

Hipótesis
Rambla de Catalunya 105.
Map 3 A3.
Tel 932 15 02 98.

Platamundi
Plaça Sta. María 7.
Map 5 B3.
Tel 933 10 10 87.

Rafa Teja Atelier
C/ Sta. María 18.
Map 5 B3.
Tel 933 10 27 85.

HATS AND SHOES

Camper
C/ Elizabets 9.
Map 2 F2.
Tel 933 42 41 41.

Czar
Passeig del Born 20.
Map 5 C3.
Tel 933 10 72 22.

La Manual Alpargatera
C/ Avinyó 7.
Map 5 A3.
Tel 933 01 01 72.

Le Shoe
C/ Tenor Viñas 4.
Map 3 A2–A5.
Tel 932 00 54 20.

Sombrerería Obach
Carrer del Call 2.
Map 5 A2.
Tel 933 18 40 94.

BOOKS AND MUSIC

Altaïr
Gran Via 616.
Map 3 A4.
Tel 933 42 71 71.

Casa del Llibre
Passeig de Gràcia 62.
Map 3 A2–A5.
Tel 932 72 34 80.

Discos Revolver
Tallers 11.
Map 5 A1.
Tel 933 02 16 85.

FNAC
Plaça de Catalunya 4.
Map 3 A4.
Tel 933 44 18 00.

Wah Wah Discos
Riera Baixa 14.
Map 2 F2.
Tel 934 42 37 03.

UNUSUAL GIFTS AND KNICK-KNACKS

Arlequí Màscares
C/ Princesa 7. **Map** 5 B2.
Tel 932 68 27 52.

Cereria Subirà
Baixada Llibreteria 7.
Map 5 A2.
Tel 933 15 26 06.

La Condonería
Plaça Sant Josep Oriol 7.
Map 5 A2.
Tel 933 02 77 21.

Sabater Hnos. Fábrica de Jabones
Pl Sant Felip Neri 1,
Barri Gòtic
Map 5 B2.
Tel 933 01 98 32.

ARTS AND ANTIQUES

Artur Ramón
C/ Palla 23. **Map** 5 A2.
Tel 933 02 59 70.

Boutique Galería Picasso
C/ Tapinería 10. **Map** 5 B2. **Tel** 933 10 49 57.

Heritage
C/ Banys Nous 14.
Map 5 A2.
Tel 933 17 85 15.

L'Arca de l'Àvia
C/ Banys Nous 20.
Map 5 A2.
Tel 933 02 15 98.

Sala Parés
C/ Petritxol 5. **Map** 5 A2.
Tel 933 18 70 08.

INTERIORS

L'Appartement
C/ Enric Granados 44.
Map 3 A4.
Tel 934 52 29 04.

Dom
Consell de Cent 248,
Eixample. **Map** 3 A4.
Tel 934 52 17 68.

Vinçon
Passeig de Gràcia 96.
Map 3 A2–A5.
Tel 932 15 60 50.

Zara Home
Rambla de Catalunya 71.
Map 3 A4.
Tel 934 87 49 72.

ENTERTAINMENT IN BARCELONA

Barcelona has one of the most colourful and alternative live arts scenes in Europe, offering a variety of entertainment, from the spectacular Modernista masterpiece the Palau de la Música and the gilded Liceu opera house, to small independent theatres hosting obscure Catalan comedies and dark Spanish dramas. But there's also much to see

Busker in the Barri Gòtic

simply by walking around the city. Street peformances you may stumble upon range from the human statues on Las Ramblas to excellent classical, ragtime and jazz buskers in the squares. In addition, there are a series of weekend-long musical and arts fiestas that run throughout the year, many of which now attract international performers from all over Europe and beyond.

The magnificent interior of the Palau de la Música Catalana

ENTERTAINMENT GUIDES

The most complete guide to what's going on each week in Barcelona is the *Guía del Ocio*, out every Thursday. This guide also includes cinema listings. The Friday *La Vanguardia* features the entertainment supplement *Què Fem?* Barcelona's free English-language magazine, *Metropolitan*, also offers extensive details of cultural events going on in town.

SEASONS AND TICKETS

Theatre and concert seasons for the main venues run from September to June, with limited programmes at other times. The city's varied menu of entertainment reflects its rich, multi-cultural artistic heritage. In summer, the city hosts the **Festival del Grec**, a showcase of international music, theatre and dance, held at open-air venues.

There is also a wide variety of concerts to choose from during the **Festa de la Mercè**, held in September. The **Festival del Sónar**, which takes place in June, has become Europe's biggest electronic music festival, drawing musicians from around the world. The **Clàssics als Parcs**, held in June and July, presents classical music in serene surroundings.

The simplest way to get theatre and concert tickets is to buy them at the box office, although tickets for many theatres can also be bought from branches of Caixa de Catalunya and the Caixa savings banks, or from ServiCaixa machines. Tickets for the Grec festival are sold at tourist offices and at the Palau de la Virreina.

THEATRE AND DANCE

Most theatre in Barcelona is performed in Catalan and English-language productions are still in short supply. However, many Catalan and

Spanish shows are well worth seeing, regardless of language constraints. There are some good independent theatre groups, such as Els Comediants and La Cubana, that perform at the **Llantiol Teatre** in El Raval. They offer a thrilling mélange of theatre, music, mime and elements from traditional Mediterranean fiestas. Also staged at the tiny Llantiol is a weekly repertoire of alternative shows, comedy, magic and other off-the-cuff performances designed to attract a mixed crowd, from the city's growing expatriate community to local arts lovers. Similarly, the **L'Antic Teatre** in La Ribera is a cultural centre and bar with a scruffy, but pleasant, summer roof-terrace and small vegetarian restaurant. It hosts a number of alternative production companies, such as the Argentinian company 4D Òptic.

Las Ramblas and Paral.lel are the main hubs of the city's bigger and more mainstream

Outrageous stage show at one of Barcelona's many clubs

The façade of the modern Teatre Nacional de Catalunya

heatres. The **Teatre Tívoli**
s a gargantuan theatre where
igh-quality productions,
ance and musical recitals
y Catalan, Spanish and
ternational stars are held.
he **Teatre Poliorama** on
as Ramblas, meanwhile, is
nown more for musicals,
ccasional operas and
ontemporary flamenco
erformances. The **Teatre**
polo is good for big-bang
usicals such as Queen's
We Will Rock You" and
BBA's "Mamma Mia!"
For serious theatre-lovers,
e **Teatre Nacional de**
atalunya (TNC) is an impos-
g, columned affair designed
the Catalan architect
card Bofill, with state-of-
e-art facilities and a weighty
e-up of Spanish and
atalan directors. Good for
ant-garde performances
d music is the **Mercat de**
Flors, a converted flower
rket in the Montjuïc area
t it is known as Barcelona's
ty of Theatre". This is
same part of town that
tains Barcelona's drama
ool and the **Teatre Lliure**,
haps Barcelona's best-
ed independent theatre.
Iodern dance has always
n popular in Barcelona
performances can often
caught at the city's main
tres. The **Teatre Victòria**
Avinguda del Paral.lel is
d for ballet and more
sical dance productions,
the **Liceu** opera house.

ERA AND CLASSICAL
SIC

ra and classical music
oved by Catalans who
up with near-religious
rence. Indeed, many

of the great artists of the
20th century were locals,
including the celebrated
cellist Pau Casals and
opera singers José Carreras
and Montserrat Caballé.

The city of Barcelona is
also home to some of the
most spectacular venues in
the world, including the
glamorous, gilded **Gran Teatre**
del Liceu, which first opened
its doors in 1847. The opera
house has been a continuing
beacon of Catalan arts for
more than 150 years, with a
rich and dramatic history of
fire and bomb attacks. It
burned down for the third
time in 1994, but careful
renovations have restored it
to its former glory. Despite its
misfortunes, it has sustained a
stellar line-up of the greatest
composers in the world.
Among them are Puccini and
Tchaikovsky, as well as
Catalan composers such as
Felip Pedrell, Vives and Enric
Granados. Sergei Diaghilev's
Russian ballets were also
staged here.

The whimsical fancy of
the **Palau de la Música**
Catalana is another of
Barcelona's architectural
triumphs (*see p152*). A
jewel-bright vision by the
Modernista master Lluís
Domènech i Montaner, this
sublime concert hall has a
dedicated audience, and
performers who vie to play
here. This is also the main
venue for the city's jazz and
guitar festivals, as well as
national and international
symphony orchestras.

Both venues, the Gran
Teatre del Liceu and Palau
de la Música Catalana, can
be visited on daytime guided
tours, but booking tickets

for a production is the
best way to experience
the ambience.

Modern, but no less
important as a shrine to the
Catalan arts scene, **L'Auditori**
de Barcelona was built to
accommodate growing
demands for better facilities
and to attract ever greater
numbers of world-class
musicians. It began primarily
as a place for classical concerts
and orchestral recitals, but
has since begun to embrace
giants of jazz, pop and rock.

It is also worth keeping
abreast of regular choral
music that is performed
at the city's churches and
cathedrals. Most notable
among these are the **Església**
Santa Maria del Pi, the main
cathedral on Plaça del Pi, and
the **Basílica Santa Maria del**
Mar, particularly around
Christmas and Easter.

Packed house at the gigantic Nou
Camp stadium

SPORTS

The undoubted kings of sport
in Catalonia are **FC Barcelona**,
known locally as Barça. They
have the largest football
stadium in Europe, Camp
Nou (*see p176*), and a
fanatical following.

Tickets for Barça home
matches in the national
league (*La Liga*), the King's
Cup (*Copa del Rey*) and
Champions League can
be purchased at the FC
Barcelona ticket offices
(in person or by telephone),
at ServiCaixa machines, or
perhaps most conveniently,
they can be bought online.
Barcelona also has a high-
ranking basketball team.

AMUSEMENT PARK

In summer, Barcelona's giant amusement park on the summit of **Tibidabo** (see p178) is extremely busy and is usually open till the early hours on weekends. Getting there by tram, funicular or cable car is even more fun.

FILM

In recent years, directors such as Alejandro Amenábar (*The Sea Inside*), Catalan writer and director Isabel Coixet (*My Life Without You*) and, of course, Spain's bad boy of film, Pedro Almodóvar (*All About My Mother* and *Bad Education*) have revitalized Spanish cinema. Today, Barcelona has become the venue for many independent film festivals. The biggest event of the year is the International Film Festival in Sitges, which is held in October.

Most cinemas dub films in Spanish or Catalan, but there are an increasing number of VO (original version) venues that screen Hollywood block-busters as well as independent art-house movies.

The **Icària Yelmo Cineplex** is the town's biggest multi-screen VO complex, built around an American-style mall, with a variety of fast-food eateries and shops. The **Renoir Floridablanca**, a relatively new cinema on the edge of El Raval and the Eixample, screens a range of European and international movies, usually with Spanish or Catalan subtitles. In Gràcia, **Verdi** and **Verdi Park** feature good independent movies, with an interesting selection of foreign films. During summer, both the Castell de Montjuïc and the Piscina Bernat Picornell, the Olympic swimming pool in Montjuïc, host a number of open-air cinema screenings.

The two-screen **Méliès** is a gem showcasing art-house movies, Hollywood classics, B&W horrors and anything by Fellini or Alfred Hitchcock. For children, there is the **IMAX Port Vell**, which shows the usual 3-D roller coaster knuckle-biters,

Everest expeditions and squid-entangled journeys to the bottom of the sea.

It's worth knowing that the prices for movie tickets are lower on Monday nights and for weekend matinées. Some cinemas offer midnight and early-hour screenings.

LIVE MUSIC: ROCK, JAZZ AND BLUES

In terms of popular music, Barcelona may not compare to London, whose endless clubs, pubs, stadiums and music emporiums make it one of the best places for live music. However, it doesn't do too badly, given its size. The city attracts a star-studded cast that ranges from pop stars such as Kylie Minogue and Madonna to contemporary jazz musicians such as the Brad Mehldau Quartet, hip-hoppers, rappers and world groove mixers, country singers and good old-fashioned rock and rollers.

In 2004, two of the city's most iconic jazz venues – La Boite and La Cova del Drac – closed down, much to the disbelief of residents. What will fill the gap remains to be seen, but for now Barcelona still has a clutch of tiny, intimate venues. The cellar-like **Jamboree** attracts a number of jazz heavyweights as well as more experimental outfits and solo artists such as the saxophonist Billy McHenry.

Another good bet is the **Jazz Sí Club**, a more obscure destination but much beloved by aficionados of the genre. It doubles up as a jam session space for students from the nearby music school. The narrow, crowded and smoky **Harlem Jazz Club** is one of the city's longest surviving clubs for alternative and lesser-known jazz troupes.

One of the two major venues for pop and rock maestros is **Bikini**, Barcelona's very own Studio 54. It opened in 1953, preceding the New York icon by a year. This veteran of the scene, which is open from midnight onwards, is still going strong with a robust line-up of big-name bands and a cocktail of

different club nights. The other, **Razzmatazz**, arguably the city's most important live music venue, has played host to big-name pop bands Blur and Pulp, and more recently, Welsh rappers Goldie Lookin Chain. Club sessions go on until dawn in Razz Club and The Loft, next door. This trendy club also holds rock and jazz concerts several nights a week.

For a touch of unbeatable glam, **Luz de Gas** is a glitzy ballroom that oozes old-fashioned atmosphere with its lamp-lit tables, chandeliers and a features lists of bands and shows that enjoyed their heyday here in the 1970s and 80s. It's not quite cabaret, but gets close, though not as close as the infamous **El Cangrejo**. This club features outrageous drag cabaret, with shockingly attired queens in full make-up and sequins miming along to numbers by Sara Montiel (the Spanish sex symbol) and back-chatting with the crowd. If your taste is for the small and subtle, the **Bar Pastis** is a miniscule bar, decorated with dusty bottles and yellowing posters from French musicals. French love ballads are performed live here most nights of the week.

FLAMENCO

One of the best places to catch a Flamenco show is **El Tablao de Carmen**, a stylish restaurant serving both Catalan and Andalusian dishes. The venue is named after Carmen Amaya, a famous dancer who performed for King Alfonso XIII in 1929, in the very spot where it now stands. Various dinner and show packages are available.

For a less formal ambience, **Los Tarantos** is an atmospheric nightspot with live flamenco and Latin music every night of the week.

Those who would like to try their hand at Flamenco can visit **Flamenco Barcelona**, a shop and cultural activity centre that specialises in the passionate dance. They offer Flamenco and guitar lessons, as well as live shows at weekends.

DIRECTORY

FESTIVALS

Classics als Parcs
Tel 010.
www.bcn.es/parcsijardins

Festa de la Mercè
see 157.

Festival del Grec
Tel 010.
Contact any tourist office.

Festival del Sónar
Palau de la Virreina.
sonar@sonar.es
www.sonar.es

TICKETS

Palau de la Virreina
Las Ramblas, 99.
Map 5 A1.
Tel 933 16 10 00.

Serviticket
Tel 902 33 22 11.
www.serviticket.com

TelEntrada
Tel 902 10 12 12.
www.telentrada.com

Tourist Office
Plaça de Catalunya.
Map 5 A1.
Tel 932 85 38 34.
www.barcelonaturisme.com

THEATRE AND DANCE

L'Antic Teatre
C/ Verdaguer i Callís 12.
Map 5 A1.
Tel 933 15 23 54.

Sant Antiol Teatre
C/ Riereta 7.
Map 2 E2.
Tel 933 29 90 09.

Teatre Lliure
Plaça Margarida Xirgu 1.
Tel 932 89 27 70.
www.teatrelliure.com

Mercat de les Flors
C/ de Lleida 59.
Map 1 B2.
Tel 934 26 18 75.
www.mercatflors.org

Teatre Apolo
Av del Paral.lel 57.
Map 1 B1.
Tel 934 41 90 07.
www.teatreapolo.com

Teatre Nacional de Catalunya (TNC)
Plaça de les Arts 1.
Tel 933 06 57 00.
www.tnc.es

Teatre Poliorama
Las Ramblas 115.
Map 5 A1.
Tel 933 17 75 99.
www.teatrepoliorama.com

Teatre Tívoli
C/ Casp 10–12.
Map 3 B5.
Tel 934 12 20 63.

Teatre Victòria
Av del Paral.lel 67–9.
Map 1 B1.
Tel 934 43 29 29.

OPERA AND CLASSICAL MUSIC

L'Auditori de Barcelona
C/ de Lepant 150.
Map 4 E1.
Tel 932 47 93 00.
www.auditori.org

Gran Teatre del Liceu
Las Ramblas 51–9.
Map 2 F3.
Tel 934 85 99 00.
www.liceubarcelona.com

Església Santa Maria del Pi
Plaça del Pi.
Map 5 A2.
Tel 933 18 47 43.

Basílica Santa Maria del Mar
Plaça de Santa Maria.
Map 5 B3.
Tel 933 10 23 90.

Palau de la Música Catalana
C/ Palau de la Música 4-6.
Map 5 B1.
Tel 902 44 28 82.
www.palaumusica.org

SPORTS

FC Barcelona
Camp Nou,
Avda Aristides Maillol.
Tel 934 96 36 00.
www.fcbarcelona.com

AMUSEMENT PARK

Tibidabo
Plaça del Tibidabo, 3.
Tel 932 11 79 42.
www.tibidabo.es

FILM

Icària Yelmo Cineplex
C/ Salvador Espriu 61.
Map 6 E4.
Tel 932 21 75 85.
www.yelmocineplex.es

IMAX Port Vell
Moll d'Espanya.
Map 5 A4.
Tel 932 25 11 11.

Méliès
C/ Villarroel 102.
Map 2 E1.
Tel 934 51 00 51.

Renoir Floridablanca
C/ Floridablanca 135.
Map 1 C1.
Tel 902 88 89 02.
www.cinesrenoir.es

Verdi
C/ Verdi 32.
Map 3 B1.
Tel 932 38 79 90.
www.cines-verdi.com

Verdi Park
C/ Torrijos 49.
Map 3 C2.
Tel 932 38 79 90.

LIVE MUSIC: ROCK, JAZZ AND BLUES

Bar Pastis
C/ Santa Mónica 4.
Map 2 F4.
Tel 933 18 79 80.

Bikini
Deu I Mata 105.
Tel 933 22 08 00.
www.bikinibcn.com

El Cangrejo
C/ Montserrat 9.
Map 2 F4.
Tel 933 01 29 78.

Harlem Jazz Club
C/ Comtessa de Sobradiel 8.
Tel 933 10 07 55.

Jamboree
Plaça Reial 17. **Map** 5 A3.
Tel 933 19 17 89.
www.masimas.com

Jazz Sí Club
C/ Requesens 2.
Tel 933 29 00 20.
www.tallerdemusics.com

Luz de Gas
C/ Muntaner 246.
Map 2 F1.
Tel 932 09 77 11.
www.luzdegas.com

Razzmatazz
C/ Pamplona 88.
Map 4 F5.
Tel 932 72 09 10.
www.salarazzmatazz.com

FLAMENCO

El Tablao de Carmen
Avda Marqués de Comillas s/n. **Map** 1 B1.
Tel 933 25 68 95.
www.tablaodecarmen.com

Flamenco Barcelona
Marqués de Barberá 6.
Map 2 F3.
Tel 934 43 66 80.

Los Tarantos
Plaça Reial 17.
Map 5 A3.
Tel 933 19 17 89.

Nightlife

If New York is the city that never sleeps, then Barcelona is the one that never goes to bed and those with energy can party around the clock, all week. It has one of the most varied scenes, with something for everybody. Old-fashioned dance halls rub shoulders with underground drum and bass clubs and trashy techno discos, and club-goers are either glammed-up or grunged-out. Each *barrio* (neighbourhood) offers a different flavour.

NIGHTLIFE

In the summer the beaches become party havens when the *chiringuitos* (beach bars) spring back into life. Wander from Platja de Sant Sebastià in Barceloneta, all the way to Bogatell (a few kilometres beyond the Hotel Arts) and you'll find people dancing barefoot on the sand to the tune of Barcelona's innumerable DJs. Way uptown (above the Diagonal), the city's most glamorous terraces morph into social hubs while the Barri Gòtic – lively at the best of times – becomes one massive street party throughout the summer. If you want to hang with the locals, the demolition of some of El Raval's less salubrious streets has meant that the neighbourhood has become much safer and easier to move about. The underground vibe, however, remains steadfastly intact with tiny hole-in-the-wall-style bars where folks drink and boogie till the early hours. Similarly Gràcia has a bohemian, studenty ambience. If it's an alternative scene you seek Poble Sec has a handful of "ring-to-enter" joints and the city's only serious drum and bass club, **Plataforma**. The city also has a thriving and friendly gay scene, most notably within the Eixample Esquerra, also known as the Gay Eixample, boasting numerous late-night drinking holes, discothèques, saunas and cabarets.

BARRI GÒTIC

The Plaça Reial is overrun with tourists banging on tin drums and whooping it up, but if you're looking for more grown-up fun, check out

Fantástico Club. Pop and electro music combine with candy-coloured decor to make this club a hit. Underground and cosmopolitan are words that best describe **Club Fellini**, which has three rooms with different music and decor in each. Jazz lovers shouldn't miss the daily concerts at **Jamboree**, one of Spain's mythical jazz clubs. Later, the venue becomes one of the most popular funk and hip-hop discos in town. The nightclub **New York** has come over all loungey in a recent revamp and these days is inclined towards more commercially gratifying tunes. The vibe here is more disco.

EL RAVAL

Designer clubs proliferate in Barcelona these days. With slinky red, black and white decor and a specially-designed underlit bar, **Zentraus** is one of the best-looking clubs in the neighbourhood. A restaurant until midnight or so, the tables are cleared away once the DJ sessions get underway. **Moog** is more extreme, with blaring, heart-pumping techno for aficionados of the genre. The stark industrial interior gives it the character of a New York nightclub in the mid-1990s. Likewise, the state-of-the-art sound system ensures a thumping, ear-bleedingly good night out. Going back in time, check out the old-school ambience of **El Cangrejo**, where in 1924 the famous copla singer Carmen Amaya made her debut. The club still has an excellent list of performers, and you can see drag shows on Friday and Saturday nights (the most famous ones by Carmen de Mairena) followed by pop revival DJ sessions. Other nights feature a 70s and 80s music theme.

PORT VELL AND PORT OLÌMPIC

Beach parties aside, this area continues to be a hub for creatures of the night. The Port Olìmpic itself is nothing but bars and boats, while **Maremagnum** has a clutch of music bars and cocktail bars. The **Sugar Club** (another *salsitas* offspring) is the newest kid on the block, which offers a splash of sophistication, not to mention society, to the downtown scene. **C.D.L.C.** in front of the Hotel ArtsV, however, still manages to draw celebrities staying nearby.

EIXAMPLE

One of the city's best loved discos, **City Hall**, is a multiple space and terrace, where you can pick and choose your groove according to your mood. It has different theme every night from Saturday night-fever discos to Sunday chill-outs. **Buda Barcelona** is quite literally oozing with glitz and glamour, beloved b models and their entourages It is a place where anything goes from dancing on the b tops to dancing with your to off. For a more understated type of glamour, **Astoria** is housed in a converted cinen and therefore bags the title for the best projections in town. **Dow Jones** is Barcelona's "drinks stock exchange" where the prices of drinks rise and fall throughout the evening according to demand.

POBLE SEC

The most alternative nightli has come to roost in the "dry village," though in nar only. The bars are wet and the music is happening. **Apolo** is another old-fashioned music hall, though it attracts a more independen breed of DJ and performer Expect anything from soul gypsy folk singers from Marseille, to the legendary purveyor of deep funk, Ke Darge. Further into the village, **Mau Mau** is an alternative club and cultural centre with a firm eye on what's new and happening. This could mean local DJs, Japanese musicians such as the cultish Cinema Dub Monks, alternative cinema, and multimedia art installations. If it's of the here and now, chances are Mau Mau's on it. For the seriously hardcore and lovers of high-speed garage, **Plataforma** is Barcelona's only serious drum and bass club, hosting DJs from far and wide in a huge concrete warehouse.

GRÀCIA AND TIBIDABO

Tiny and always packed, the **Mond Bar** attracts music-lovers from all over, wishing to dip into tunes from the past. Resident DJs delight a

20-something crowd with their swing-back to the 1970s sessions of northern soul and Motown. And high up above the rest, **Elephant** offers the best in mansion-house clubbing experiences, with chill-out lounges, two dance floors, a VIP area, sprawling terraces, and prices to suit the altitude.

OUT OF TOWN

The mega-clubs are located away from the city centre and from anyone trying to sleep. Most of them are only open on Friday and Saturday nights. The big boys are based in Poble Espanyol where folks can party until the sunrise. **La Terrrazza** is a summer club which hosts rave-like parties under the stars. It takes its name from

the giant terrace it occupies. Nearby on Plaça Espanya, after much bated breath, the Ibiza-style **Space** finally opened in 2004 and is still very popular. Don't even think about getting in without an appropriately glamorous outfit, and remember, less is most definitely more.

Further out of town you will find the world's most famous nightclub, **Pacha**. What most people don't realize, however, is that it was born in Barcelona and continues to stage the most sensational nights out. Alternatively, **Liquid** is the only summer club in the city with a swimming pool (from June to September). The only drawback is that should you wish to leave before the party's over, finding a taxi can be a big problem.

DIRECTORY

BARRI GÒTIC

Club Fellini
La Rambla 27, Barri Gòtic.
Map 2 F3.
Tel 93 272 49 80.

Fantástico Club
Passatge Escudellers 3,
Barri Gòtic. **Map** 5 A3.
Tel 93 317 54 11.

Jamboree
Plaça Reial 17,
Barri Gòtic.
Map 5 A3.
Tel 93 319 17 89.

New York
C/Escudellers 5,
Barri Gòtic.
Map 5 A3.
Tel 93 318 87 30.

EL RAVAL

El Cangrejo
C/Montserrat 9. **Map** 2
F3. *Tel* 90 301 29 78.

Moog
Arc del Teatre 3,
Raval.
Map 2 F4.
Tel 93 301 72 82.
www.masimas.com

Zentraus
Rambla de Raval 41,
El Raval.
Map 2 F3.
Tel 93 443 80 78.
www.zentraus.com

PORT VELL AND PORT OLÌMPIC

C.D.L.C.
Passeig Marítim 32,
Port Olimpic.
Map 6 E4.
Tel 93 224 04 70.
www.cdlcbarcelona.com

Sugar Club
Moll de Barcelona s/n,
Port Vell.
Tel 93 508 83 25.
www.sugarclub-barcelona.com

EIXAMPLE

Astoria
C/Paris 193,
Eixample.
Tel 93 414 47 99.
www.grupocostaeste.com

Buda Barcelona
C/Pau Claris 92,
Eixample.
Map 3 B3.
Tel 93 318 42 52.

City Hall
Rambla Catalunya 2–4,
Eixample.
Map 3 A3.
Tel 93 317 21 77.
www.cityhall-bcn.com

Dow Jones
C/Bruc 97.
Map 3 B4.
Tel 93 207 60 45.

POBLE SEC

Apolo
C/Nou de la Rambla 113,
Poble Sec.
Map 2 D4.
Tel 93 441 40 01.
www.sala-apolo.com

Mau Mau
C/Fontrodona 33,
Poble Sec.
Map 2 D3.
Tel 93 441 80 15.
www.
maumaunderground.com

Plataforma
C/Nou de la Rambla 145,
Poble Sec.
Map 2 D4.
Tel 93 329 00 29.

GRÀCIA AND TIBIDABO

Elephant
Passeig des Til.lers 1,
Tibidabo.
Tel 93 203 75 46.
www.elephantbcn.com

Mond Bar
Plaza del Sol 21, Gràcia.
Map 3 B1.
www.mondclub.com

OUT OF TOWN

La Terrrazza
Poble Espanyol, Avda
Marquès de Comillas.
Map 1 B1.
Tel 93 423 12 85.
www.nightsungroup.com

Liquid
Complex Esportiu
Hospitalet Nord,
C/Manuel Azaña.
www.liquidbcn.com

Pacha
Avda. Gregorio
Marañón 17.
Tel 93 334 32 33.
www.clubpachabcn.com

Space
C/Tarragona 141–147.
Tel 93 426 84 44.
www.spacebarcelona.com

EASTERN
SPAIN

INTRODUCING EASTERN SPAIN 198–205

CATALONIA 206–225

ARAGÓN 226–241

VALENCIA AND MURCIA 242–263

Introducing Eastern Spain

Eastern Spain covers an extraordinary range of climates and landscapes, from the snowbound peaks of the Pyrenees in Aragón to the beaches of the Costa Blanca and Costa Cálida, popular for their winter warmth and sunshine. The region has a wealth of historical sights including ancient monasteries near Barcelona, magnificent Roman ruins in Tarragona, Mudéjar churches and towers in Aragón and the great cathedrals of Valencia and Murcia. Away from the busy coasts, the countryside is often attractive but little visited.

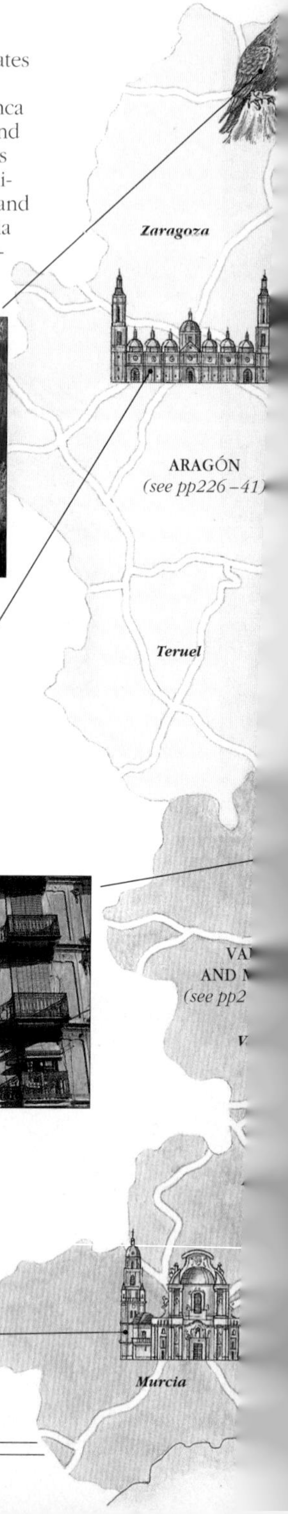

Zaragoza

ARAGÓN
(see pp226–41)

Teruel

Ordesa National Park (see pp232–3) *in the Pyrenees has some of the most dramatic mountain scenery in Spain. It makes excellent walking country.*

Zaragoza (see pp236–7) *has many striking churches, especially the cathedral, the Basílica de Nuestra Señora del Pilar, and the Mudéjar-style Iglesia de la Magdalena.*

Valencia (see pp250–53) *is Spain's third largest city. It has an old centre of narrow streets overlooked by venerable houses and monuments, such as El Miguelete, the cathedral's conspicuous bell tower. The city hosts a spectacular festival, Las Fallas, in March.*

VA
AND N
(see pp2

Murcia Cathedral (see p262), *built in the 14th century, has a Baroque façade and belfry, and two ornate side chapels – one in late-Gothic style and the other Renaissance. The cathedral museum houses Gothic altarpieces and other fascinating exhibits.*

| 0 kilometres | 50 |
| 0 miles | 50 |

Murcia

◁ **The 12th-century monastery at Gerri de la Sal in Catalonia**

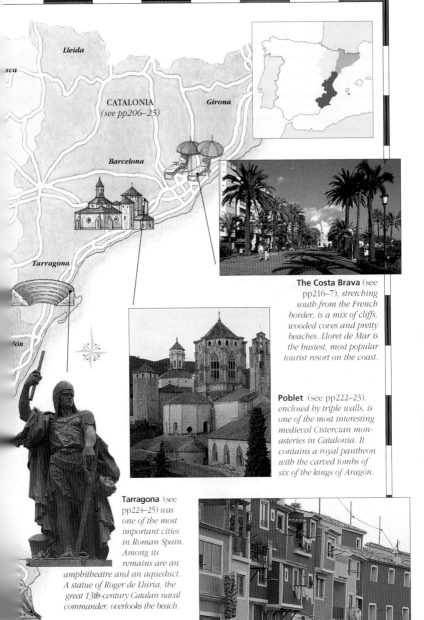

CATALONIA
(see pp206–25)

Lleida

Girona

Barcelona

Tarragona

The Costa Brava (see pp216–7), *stretching south from the French border, is a mix of cliffs, wooded coves and pretty beaches. Lloret de Mar is the busiest, most popular tourist resort on the coast.*

Poblet (see pp222–23), *enclosed by triple walls, is one of the most interesting medieval Cistercian monasteries in Catalonia. It contains a royal pantheon with the carved tombs of six of the kings of Aragón.*

Tarragona (see pp224–25) *was one of the most important cities in Roman Spain. Among its remains are an amphitheatre and an aqueduct. A statue of Roger de Llúria, the great 13th-century Catalan naval commander, overlooks the beach.*

The Costa Blanca (see pp258–61) *is an attractive coast, as well as a popular holiday destination. Calp is overshadowed by a huge rock, the Penyal d'Ifach. In La Vila Joiosa, a line of houses has been painted in striking colours to make them visible to sailors at sea.*

The Flavours of Eastern Spain

The current stars of Spain's culinary firmament are Catalans like Ferran Adriá or Carme Ruscalleda, whose creativity and innovation have brought them international acclaim. Fashionable new eateries and traditional country inns alike still place the emphasis firmly on fresh local ingredients. Along with adjoining Murcia and Catalonia, Valencia produces a huge array of fruit, vegetables, seafood, meat and game, all heaped colourfully in local markets. Rice is the key ingredient in paella and its many local variations. In land-locked Aragón, country cooking is key, with dishes that recall the Arabic occupation more than a thousand years ago.

Valencian rice

Fresh octopus lie on the ice of a fish-seller's stall

Spain's finest chefs create culinary fireworks in their celebrated restaurants, but Catalan cuisine, even at its most experimental, is essentially simple and relies on the wonderful freshness of its produce.

ARAGÓN

In land-locked, mountainous Aragón, the emphasis is firmly on meat – particularly lamb, but also beef, rabbit and free-range chicken, often served simply grilled or slowly simmered in earthen-ware pots. There is also much excellent charcuterie, including hams and cured sausages, some flavoured with spices, which are often used to flavour the hearty stews popular in the mountainous north. River trout and eels are regularly found on local menus and,

CATALONIA

The incredible variety of fresh produce in Catalonia is a reflection of the varied landscape – the Mediterranean provides all manner of fish and shell-fish, the inland plains offer a wealth of vegetables and fields of golden rice, and the mountains contribute meat, game and wild mushrooms (a Catalan obsession).

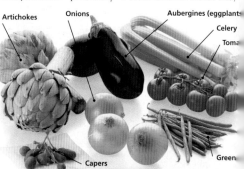

Artichokes **Onions** **Aubergines (eggplants** **Celery** **Toma** **Capers** **Green**

A range of fresh vegetables grown in eastern Spain

REGIONAL DISHES AND SPECIALITIES

Candied fruits

The lush Mediterranean coastline, backed by fertile plains and cool mountains, offers an extraordin-ary abundance of fresh produce here. From the sturdy stews of land-locked Aragón and the traditional cured meats of inland Murcia, to the celebrated seafood paellas and other rice dishes of Valencia, this is a region that dazzles with the variety of its cuisine. Spring and summer bring tiny broad beans, asparagus, and all manner of other vegetables and fruits. In autumn and winter, the annual pig slaughter is followed by the preparation of hams and cured meats, mushrooms proliferate on shady hills, and gamey stews keep out the winter cold. Seafood remains a constant, whether in *zarzuela de mariscos* (a rich shellfish stew), or the Murcian favourite of sea bream baked in a salty crust.

Suquet de peix *A Catalan stew of fresh, firm-fleshed fish, flavoured with tomato garlic and toasted almond*

Spectacular harvest of wild autumn mushrooms in a local market

perhaps unusually so far north, the ancient Arabic heritage can still be tasted in exquisite local sweets and desserts, from candied fruits to heavenly *guirlache*, made from almonds and sugar.

VALENCIA

Valencia, the "Orchard of Spain", is magnificently lush and fertile. Most famous for its oranges, it also produces countless other fruits and vegetables, partnered in local recipes with Mediterranean seafood and mountain lamb, rabbit and pork. In spring, hillsides blaze with cherry and almond blossom and, in autumn, the golden rice fields are spectacular. Spain's signature dish, paella, is a Valencian invention – the local plump *bomba* rice is perfect for soaking up juices.

MURCIA

Tiny, arid Murcia is almost a desert in parts but, thanks to irrigation methods introduced by the Arabs more than a thousand years ago, it has become one of the largest

An *embutidos* (cured meats) producer shows off his wares

fruit- and vegetable-growing regions in Europe. The mountainous hinterland is famous for its flavoursome *embutidos* (cured meats), especially *morcilla* (black pudding/blood sausage) and *chorizo* (spicy, paprika-flavoured cured sausage), along with excellent rice which has earned its own DO *(denominación de origen)*. Along the coast, you can enjoy a wide range of fresh Mediterranean seafood, including sea bream baked in a salt crust, or lobster stew from the Mar Menor. The Arabic heritage lingers particularly in the desserts, flavoured with saffron, pine nuts and delicate spices.

ON THE MENU

Arroz Negro A Valencian rice dish; squid ink gives the distinctive dark colour.

Caldero Murciano Fishermen's stew, flavoured with saffron and plenty of garlic.

Dorada a la Sal Sea bream baked in a salty crust to keep the fish moist and succulent.

Fideuá A paella made with shellfish and tiny noodles instead of rice.

Guirlache An Aragonese sweet, made of toasted whole almonds and buttery caramel.

Migas con Tropezones Crusty breadcrumbs fried with garlic, pork and spicy cured sausage.

ella *In Spain's best-known dish, ingredients include saffron, round* bomba *rice, and meat, fish and shellfish.*

Lentejas al estilo del Alto Aragón *Lentils are slowly cooked with garlic, chunks of ham and black sausage.*

Crema Catalana *This hugely popular dessert is an eggy custard topped with a flambéed sugar crust.*

Wines of Eastern Spain

Spain's eastern seaboard offers a wide spread of wines of different styles. Catalonia deserves pride of place, and here the most important region is Penedès, home of *cava* (traditional-method sparkling wine) and some high-quality still wine. In Aragón, Cariñena reds can be good, and Somontano, in the Pyrenees, has fine, international-style varietals. Valencia and Murcia provide large quantities of easy-drinking reds, whites and *rosados* (rosés). Most notable among these are the rosés of Utiel-Requena, the Valencian Moscatels and the strong, full-bodied reds made in Jumilla.

Cabernet Sauvignon vines

Somontano *has had remarkable success because of the COVISA company's cultivation of international grape varieties such as Chardonnay and Pinot Noir.*

Monastery of Poblet and Las Murallas vineyards in Catalonia

```
0 kilometres              100
0 miles            50
```

KEY FACTS ABOUT WINES OF EASTERN SPAIN

Location and Climate
The climate of Eastern Spain varies mainly with altitude – low-lying parts are hot and dry; it also gets hotter the further south you go. The wine regions of Catalonia have a Mediterranean climate along the coast, which becomes drier futher inland. The middle Penedès is a favoured location with a range of climates which suits many grape varieties. Somontano has a cooler, altitude-tempered climate. Valencia and Murcia can be, in contrast, unrelentingly hot.

Grape Varieties
The most common native red grape varieties planted in much of Eastern Spain are Garnacha, Tempranillo – which is called Ull de Llebre in Catalonia – Monastrell and Cariñena. Bobal makes both reds and, to a greater extent, rosés in Utiel-Requena. For whites, Catalonia has Parellada, Macabeo and Xarel·lo (the trio most commonly used for *cava*), while in Valencia, Merseguera and Moscatel predominate. In the regions furthest to the southeast, Airén and Pedro Ximénez are sometimes found. French grape varieties, such as Chardonnay, Merlot Cabernet Sauvignon and Sauvignon Blanc, flourish in the regions of Penedès, Costers del Segre and Somontano.

Good Producers
Somontano: COVISA (Viñas del Vero), Viñedos del Altoaragón. **Alella:** Marqués de Alella, Parxet **Penedès:** Codorníu, Conde de Caralt, Freixenet, Juvé y Camps Masía Bach, Mont-Marçal, René Barbier, Miguel Torres. **Costers del Segre:** Castell de Remei, Raimat. **Priorato:** Cellers Scala Dei, Masía Barril. **Valencia:** Vicente Gandía. **Utiel-Requena:** C. Augusto Egli. **Alicante:** Gutiérrez de la Vega. **Jumilla:** Asensio Carcelén (Sol y Luna), Bodegas Vitivino.

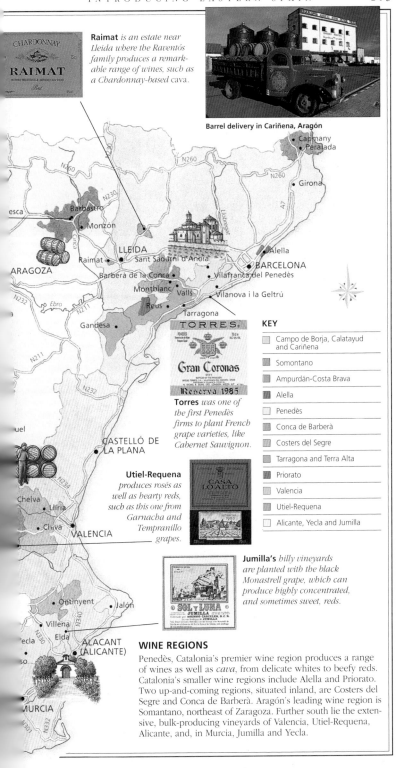

RAIMAT *is an estate near Lleida where the Raventós family produces a remarkable range of wines, such as a Chardonnay-based cava.*

Barrel delivery in Cariñena, Aragón

KEY

- Campo de Borja, Calatayud and Cariñena
- Somontano
- Ampurdán-Costa Brava
- Alella
- Penedès
- Conca de Barberà
- Costers del Segre
- Tarragona and Terra Alta
- Priorato
- Valencia
- Utiel-Requena
- Alicante, Yecla and Jumilla

Torres *was one of the first Penedès firms to plant French grape varieties, like Cabernet Sauvignon.*

Utiel-Requena *produces rosés as well as hearty reds, such as this one from Garnacha and Tempranillo grapes.*

Jumilla's *hilly vineyards are planted with the black Monastrell grape, which can produce highly concentrated, and sometimes sweet, reds.*

WINE REGIONS

Penedès, Catalonia's premier wine region produces a range of wines as well as *cava*, from delicate whites to beefy reds. Catalonia's smaller wine regions include Alella and Priorato. Two up-and-coming regions, situated inland, are Costers del Segre and Conca de Barberà. Aragón's leading wine region is Somontano, northeast of Zaragoza. Further south lie the extensive, bulk-producing vineyards of Valencia, Utiel-Requena, Alicante, and, in Murcia, Jumilla and Yecla.

Flowers of the Matorral

Yellow bee orchid

The Matorral, a scrubland rich in wild flowers, is the distinctive landscape of Spain's eastern Mediterranean coast. It is the result of centuries of woodland clearance, during which the native holm oak was felled for timber and to provide land for grazing and cultivation. Many colourful plants have adapted to the extremes of climate here. Most flower in spring, when hillsides are daubed with pink and white cistuses and yellow broom, and the air is perfumed by aromatic herbs such as rosemary, lavender and thyme. Buzzing insects feed on the abundance of nectar and pollen.

Spanish broom *is a small bush with yellow flowers on slender branches. The black seed pods split when dry, scattering the seeds on the ground.*

The century plant's flower stalk can reach 10 m (32 ft).

Aleppo pine

Rosemary

Jerusalem sage, *an attractive shrub which is often grown in gardens, has tall stems surrounded by bunches of showy yellow flowers. Its leaves are greyish-white and woolly.*

Rose garlic *has round clusters of violet or pink flowers at the end of a single stalk. It survives the summer as the bulb familiar to all cooks.*

Common thy *is a low-gro aromatic he which is wi cultivated in the kitch*

FOREIGN INVADERS

Several plants from the New World have managed to colonize the bare ground of the *matorral*. The prickly pear, thought to have been brought back by Christopher Columbus, produces a delicious fruit which can be picked only with thickly gloved hands. The rapidly growing century plant, a native of Mexico which has tough spiny leaves, sends up a tall flower shoot only when it is 10–15 years old, after which it dies.

Prickly pear in fruit

Flowering shoots of the century plant

The mirror orchid, *a small plant that grows on grassy sites, is easily distinguished from other orchids by the brilliant metallic blue patch inside the lip, fringed by brown hairs.*

— Temperature   ☐ Rainfall

J F M A M J J A S O N D

CLIMATE CHART

Most plants found in the *matorral* come into bloom in the warm, moist spring. The plants protect themselves from losing water during the dry summer heat with thick leaves or waxy secretions, or by storing moisture in bulbs or tubers.

WILDLIFE OF THE MATORRAL

The animals that live in the *matorral* are most often seen early in the morning, before the temperature is high. Countless insects fly from flower to flower, providing a source of food for birds. Smaller mammals, such as mice and voles, are active only at night when it is cooler and there are few predators around.

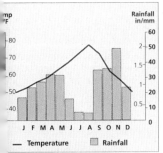

Holm oaks *are very common in Eastern Spain. The leaves are tough and rubbery to prevent water loss.*

The strawberry tree *is an evergreen shrub with glossy serrated leaves. Its edible, strawberry-like fruit turns red when ripe.*

Ladder snakes *feed on small mammals, birds and insects. The young are identified by a black pattern like the rungs of a ladder, but adults are marked with two simple stripes.*

Tree heather

Scorpions *hide under rocks or wood by day. When disturbed, the tail is curled quickly over the body in a threatening gesture. The sting, lethal to small animals, can cause some irritation to humans.*

Grey-leaved cistus, *growing on sunny sites, has crumpled petals and bright yellow anthers.*

Narrow-leaved cistus *exudes a sticky aromatic gum used in perfumes.*

The Dartford warbler, *a skulking bird that has dark plumage and a cocked tail, sings melodiously during its mating display. Males are more vividly coloured than females.*

The swallow-tail butterfly *is one of the most conspicuous of the great many insects living in the matorral. Bees, ants and grasshoppers are also extremely common.*

Star clover *is a low-growing annual whose fruit develops into a star-shaped seed head. Its flowers are often pale pink.*

CATALONIA

LLEIDA · ANDORRA · GIRONA
BARCELONA PROVINCE · TARRAGONA

*C*atalonia is a proud nation-within-a-nation, which was once, under the count-kings of Barcelona-Aragón, one of the Mediterranean's great sea powers. It has its own semi-autonomous regional government and its own language, Catalan, which has all but replaced Spanish in place names and on road signs throughout the region.

The Romans first set foot on the Iberian Peninsula at Empúries on Catalonia's Costa Brava ("wild coast"). They left behind them great monuments, especially in and around Tarragona, the capital of their vast province of Tarraconensis. Later, Barcelona emerged as the region's capital, economically and culturally important enough to rival Madrid.

In the 1960s the Costa Brava became one of Europe's first mass package-holiday destinations. Although resorts such as Lloret de Mar continue to draw the crowds, former fishing villages such as Cadaqués remain relatively unspoiled on this naturally attractive coast.

Inland, there is a rich artistic heritage to be explored. Catalonia has several spectacular monasteries, especially Montserrat, its spiritual heart, and Poblet. There are also many medieval towns, such as Montblanc, Besalú and Girona – which contain a wealth of monuments and museums.

In the countryside there is a lot to seek out, from the wetland wildlife of the Río Ebro delta to the vineyards of Penedès (where most of Spain's sparkling wine is made). In the high Pyrenees rare butterflies brighten remote mountain valleys, and little hidden villages encircle exquisite Romanesque churches.

Aigüestortes y E. Sant Maurici National Park in the central Pyrenees, in the province of Lleida

A fisherman inspects his nets in Cadaqués on the Costa Brava

Exploring Catalonia

Catalonia includes a long stretch of the
Spanish Pyrenees, whose green, flower-
filled valleys hide picturesque villages
with Romanesque churches. The Parc
Nacional d'Aigüestortes and Vall d'Aran are
paradises for naturalists, while Baqueira-
Beret offers skiers reliable snow. Sun-
lovers can choose between the rugged
Costa Brava or the long sandy stretches of
the Costa Daurada. Tarragona is rich in
Roman monuments. Inland are the
monasteries of Poblet and Santes Creus and
the well-known vineyards of Penedès.

Isolated houses in the countryside
around La Seu d'Urgell

KEY

═══	Motorway (highway)
━━	Other highway
━	Main road
═	Minor road
▬	Scenic route
▬▬	Main railway
—	Minor railway
▬	International border
▬	Regional border
△	Summit

GETTING AROUND

A tunnel near Puigcerdà has
made the central Catalan
Pyrenees easily accessible.
Buses, more frequent in
summer, connect most towns.
The main north-south railway
hugs the coast from Blanes
southwards. Other lines run
from Barcelona through Vic,
Lleida and Tortosa. Be aware
that Spain has recently
changed its road numbering
system and that some of the
old signs and numbers may
still exist in rural areas, on old
maps and in old road atlases.

Pau
Toulouse

1 VALL D'ARAN

3 BAQUEIRA-BERET

VIELHA 2 Arties   Pica d'I

PARC NACIONAL
D'AIGÜESTORTES   Esterri d'A

N230   5

Boi   Llavorsi

4 VALL DE BOI   Tossa
2437

Pont de Suert   Sort   L
D'U

N260

La Pobla de Segur

Coll d
Tremp   Embassament   Narg
de Talarn

Isona   Embass
d' Oll

Embalse
de Canelles   El Segre   Pont

Artesa de Seg

Alfarràs   Agramunt   C A

N230   Balaguer
Almacelles   Belcaire d'Urgell

Bell-lloc
N240   d'Urgell   Tàrrega

LLEIDA 24   A2   Bellpuig
Alcarràs   AP2   Juneda   Belianes   Sa
de
les Borges Blanques

Seròs   MONTBLANC

Zaragoza   25   26
Maials   La Granadella   POBLET
N240
La Bisbal de Falset

Flix   Alcover

Ascó   Falset   N420   Reus   Torred
31
Batea   Móra d'Ebre   Móra la   TA
Gandesa   Nova   Cambrils
Salou
Ebro   Rasquera   Cap de
Salou
Xerta   L'Hospitalet   C
de l'Infant
El Perelló   L'Ametlla de Mar

TORTOSA 32   Golf de
Sant Jordi

L'Aldea   33
Amposta   Cap Tortosa
DELTA
Sant Carles de la Ràpita   DE L'EBRE

Ulldecona   N340   La Banya

Alcanar

Valencia

SEE ALSO

• **Where to Stay** pp571–

• **Where to Eat** pp620–

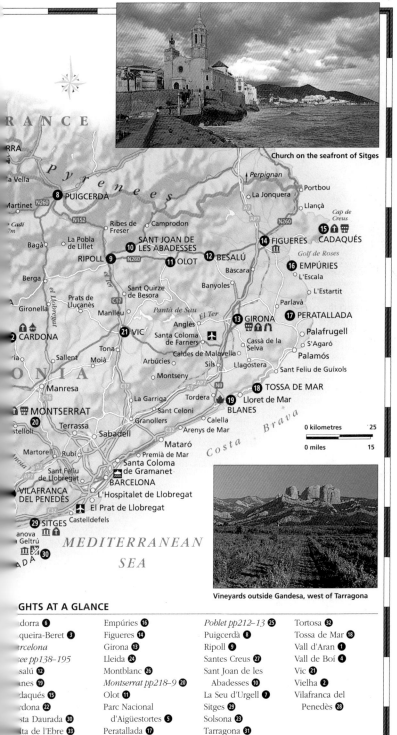

Church on the seafront of Sitges

Vineyards outside Gandesa, west of Tarragona

Map labels:
FRANCE
Pyrenees
PUIGCERDÀ 8
Martinet N260
Cadí 7m
Bagà
La Pobla de Lillet
Ribes de Freser
Camprodon
SANT JOAN DE LES ABADESSES 10
RIPOLL 9
OLOT 11
BESALÚ 12
FIGUERES 14
CADAQUÉS 15
Cap de Creus
Golf de Roses
EMPÚRIES 16
L'Escala
L'Estartit
Parlavà
PERATALLADA 17
Palafrugell
S'Agaró
Palamós
Sant Feliu de Guíxols
La Jonquera
Portbou
Llançà
Perpignan
Berga
Gironella
CARDONA 2
Sallent
Tona
Moià
Manresa
MONTSERRAT
Terrassa
Sabadell
Martorell
Rubí
Sant Feliu de Llobregat
VILAFRANCA DEL PENEDÈS
SITGES 29
BARCELONA
L'Hospitalet de Llobregat
El Prat de Llobregat
Castelldefels
Sant Quirze de Besora
Manlleu
Prats de Lluçanès
VIC 21
Santa Coloma de Farners
Anglès
GIRONA 13
Cassà de la Selva
Caldes de Malavella
Arbúcies
Sils
Llagostera
Montseny
La Garriga
Sant Celoni
Granollers
Tordera
BLANES 19
Lloret de Mar
TOSSA DE MAR 18
Calella
Arenys de Mar
Mataró
Premià de Mar
Santa Coloma de Gramanet
Bàscara
Banyoles
Pantà de Sau
El Ter
Costa Brava
MEDITERRANEAN SEA

0 kilometres   25
0 miles   15

SIGHTS AT A GLANCE

Andorra 6
Baqueira-Beret 3
Barcelona
  see pp138–195
Besalú 12
Blanes 19
Cadaqués 15
Cardona 22
Costa Daurada 30
Delta de l'Ebre 33

Empúries 16
Figueres 14
Girona 13
Lleida 24
Montblanc 26
Montserrat pp218–9 20
Olot 11
Parc Nacional d'Aigüestortes 5
Peratallada 17

Poblet pp212–13 25
Puigcerdà 8
Ripoll 9
Santes Creus 27
Sant Joan de les Abadesses 10
La Seu d'Urgell 7
Sitges 29
Solsona 23
Tarragona 31

Tortosa 32
Tossa de Mar 18
Vall d'Aran 1
Vall de Boí 4
Vic 21
Vielha 2
Vilafranca del Penedès 28

The Vall d'Aran, surrounded by the snow-capped mountains of the Pyrenees

BUTTERFLIES OF THE VALL D'ARAN

A huge variety of butterflies and moths is found high in the mountains and valleys of the Pyrenees. In particular, the isolated Vall d'Aran is the home of several unique and rare subspecies. The best time of year to see the butterflies is between May and July.

Grizzled Skipper
(Pyrgus malvae)

Checkered Skipper
(Carterocephalus palaemon)

Clouded Apollo
(Parnassius mnemosyne)

Vall d'Aran ❶

Lleida N230. 🚌 Vielha. 🛈 Vielha 973 64 06 88. **http**://torisme.aran.org

This Valley of Valleys – *aran* means valley – is a beautiful 600-sq km (230-sq mile) haven of forests and flower-filled meadows, surrounded by towering mountain peaks.

The Vall d'Aran was formed by the Riu Garona, which rises in the area and flows out to France as the Garonne. With no proper link to the outside world until 1924, when a road was built over the Bonaigua Pass, the valley was cut off from the rest of Spain for most of the winter. Snow still blocks the narrow pass from November to April, but today access is easy through the Túnel de Vielha from El Pont de Suert.

The fact that the Vall d'Aran faces north means that it has a climate similar to that found on the Atlantic coast. Many rare wild flowers and butterflies flourish in the perfect conditions created by the damp breezes and shady slopes. It is also a noted habitat for many species of narcissus.

Tiny villages have grown up beside the Riu Garona, often around Romanesque churches, notably at **Bossòst**, **Salardú**, **Escunhau** and **Arties**. The valley is also ideal for outdoor sports such as skiing and is popular with walkers.

Vielha ❷

Lleida. 🏘 2,000. 🚌 🛈 Carrer Sarriulera 10, 973 64 01 10. 🛒 Thu. 🎉 Fiesta de Vielha (8 Sep), Feria de Vielha (8 Oct).

Now a modern ski resort, the capital of the Vall d'Aran preserves relics of its medieval past. The Romanesque church of **Sant Miquel** has an octagonal bell tower, a tall, pointed roof and a super wooden 12th-century crucifix the *Mig Aran Christ*. It once formed part of a larger carving since lost, which represented the Descent from the Cross. The **Museu de la Vall d'Aran** is a museum devoted to Aranese history and folklore

🏛 **Museu de la Vall d'Aran**
Carrer Major 26. **Tel** 973 64 18 15
🕐 Tue–Sun. 🔴 public hols. 🖼 ⚠

Mig Aran Christ (12th-century), Sant Miquel church, Vielha

Baqueira-Beret ❸

Lleida. 🚶 100. 🚌 🛈 *Baqueira-Beret, 973 63 90 10.* 🎭 *Romeria de Nuestra Señora de Montgarri (2 Jul).* **www**.baqueira.es

This extensive ski resort, one of the best in Spain, is popular with both the public and the Spanish royal family. There is reliable winter snow cover and a choice of over 40 pistes at altitudes from 1,520 m to 2,470 m (4,987 ft to 8,105 ft).

Baqueira and Beret were separate mountain villages before skiing became popular, but now form a single resort. The Romans took full advantage of the thermal springs located here; nowadays they are appreciated by tired skiers.

Vall de Boí ❹

Lleida N230. 🚌 *La Pobla de Segur.* 🚌 *Pont de Suert.* 🛈 *Barruera, 973 69 40 00.* **www**.vallboi.com

This small valley on the edge of the Parc Nacional d'Aigüestortes is dotted with tiny villages, many of which are built around magnificent Catalan Romanesque churches. Dating from the 11th and 12th centuries, these churches are distinguished by their tall belfries, such as the **Església de Santa Eulàlia** at Erill-la-Vall, which has six floors.

The two churches at Taüll, **Sant Climent** *(see p24)* and **Santa Maria**, have superb frescoes. Between 1919 and 1923 the originals were taken for safekeeping to the Museu Nacional d'Art de Catalunya in Barcelona *(see p172)* and replicas now stand in their place. You can climb the towers of Sant Climent for superb views of the surrounding countryside.

Other churches in the area worth visiting include those at Erill, for its fine ironwork, Barruera, and **Durro**, which has another massive bell tower.

At the head of the valley is the hamlet of **Caldes de Boí**, popular for its thermal springs and ski facilities. It is also a good base for exploring the Parc Nacional d'Aigüestortes, the entrance to which is only 5 km (3 miles) from here.

The tall belfry of Sant Climent church at Taüll in the Vall de Boí

Parc Nacional d'Aigüestortes ❺

Lleida. 🚌 *La Pobla de Segur.* 🚌 *Pont de Suert, La Pobla de Segur.* 🛈 *Barruera, 973 69 61 89.*

The pristine mountain scenery of Catalonia's only national park *(see pp30–1)* is among the most spectacular to be seen in the Pyrenees.

Established in 1955, the park covers an area of 102 sq km (40 sq miles). Its full title is Parc Nacional d'Aigüestortes i Estany de Sant Maurici, named after the lake *(estany)* of Sant Maurici in the east and the Aigüestortes (literally, twisted waters) area in the west. The main village is the mountain settlement of Espot, on the park's eastern edge. Dotted around the park are waterfalls and the sparkling, clear waters of around 150 lakes and tarns which, in an earlier era, were scoured by glaciers to depths of up to 50 m (164 ft).

The finest scenery is around Sant Maurici lake, which lies beneath the twin shards of the Serra dels Encantats, (Mountains of the Enchanted). From here, there is a variety of walks, particularly along the string of lakes that lead north to the towering peaks of Agulles d'Amitges. To the south is the dramatic vista of Estany Negre, the highest and deepest tarn in the park.

Early summer in the lower valleys is marked by a mass of pink and red rhododrons, while later in the year wild lilies bloom in the forests of fir, beech and silver birch.

The park is also home to a variety of wildlife. Chamois (also known as izards) live on the mountain screes and in the meadows, while beavers and otters can be spotted by the lakes. Golden eagles nest on mountain ledges, and grouse and capercaillie are found in the woods.

During the summer the park is popular with walkers, while in winter, the snow-covered mountains are ideal for cross-country skiing.

A crystal-clear stream, Parc Nacional d'Aigüestortes

THE CATALAN LANGUAGE

Catalan has now fully recovered from the ban it suffered under Franco's dictatorship and has supplanted Castilian (Spanish) as the language in everyday use all over Catalonia. Spoken by more than eight million people, it is a Romance language akin to the Provençal of France. Previously it was suppressed by Felipe V in 1717 and only officially resurfaced in the 19th century, when the Jocs Florals (medieval poetry contests) were revived during the rebirth of Catalan literature. A leading figure of the movement was the poet Jacint Verdaguer (1845–1902).

Catalonia's national emblem

it nevertheless has a fine view right down the beautiful Cerdanya valley, watered by the trout-filled Riu Segre. Puigcerdà, very close to the French border, was founded in 1177 by Alfonso II as the capital of Cerdanya, which shares a past and its culture with the French Cerdagne. The Spanish enclave of **Llívia**, an attractive little town with a medieval pharmacy, lies 6 km 4 miles) inside France.

Cerdanya is the largest valley in the Pyrenees. At its edge is the nature reserve of **Cadí-Moixeró**, which has a population of alpine choughs.

Andorra ❻

Principality of Andorra. 🏔 77,000.
🚌 Andorra la Vella. ℹ Plaça de la Rotonda, Andorra la Vella, 00 376 82 71 17. **www**.andorra.ad

Andorra occupies 464 sq km (179 sq miles) of the Pyrenees between France and Spain. In 1993, it became fully independent and held its first ever democratic elections. Since 1278, it had been an autonomous feudal state under the jurisdiction of the Spanish bishop of La Seu d'Urgell and the French Count of Foix (a title adopted by the President of France). These are still the ceremonial joint heads of state.

Andorra's official language is Catalan, though French and Castilian are also spoken. The currency changed from the peseta to the Euro in 2002.

For many years Andorra has been a tax-free paradise for shoppers, reflected in the crowded shops of the capital **Andorra la Vella**. Les Escaldes (near the capital), as well as Sant Julià de Lòria and El Pas de la Casa (near the Spanish and French borders), have also become shopping centres.

Most visitors never see Andorra's rural charms, which match those of other parts of the Pyrenees. The region is excellent for walkers. One of the main routes leads to the **Cercle de Pessons**, a bowl of lakes in the east, and past Romanesque chapels such as **Sant Martí** at La Cortinada. In the north is the picturesque Sorteny valley where traditional farmhouses have been converted into snug restaurants.

La Seu d'Urgell ❼

Lleida. 🏔 13,000. 🚌 ℹ Avda Valles de Andorra 33, 973 35 15 11.
🕑 Tue & Sat. 🎉 Fiesta Mayor (Aug).

This ancient Pyrenean town was made a bishopric by the Visigoths in the 6th century. Feuds between the bishops of Urgell and the Counts of Foix over land ownership led to the emergence of Andorra in the 13th century.

The 12th-century **cathedral** has a much venerated Romanesque statue of Santa Maria d'Urgell. The **Museu Diocesà** contains medieval works of art and manuscripts, including a 10th-century copy of St Beatus of Liébana's *Commentary on the Apocalypse (see p110)*.

🏛 Museu Diocesà
Plaça del Deganat. **Tel** 973 35 32 42.
🕑 daily. ⬤ public hols. 📷 ♿

Carving, La Seu d'Urgell cathedral

Puigcerdà ❽

Girona. 🏔 9,000. 🚌 🚏 ℹ Carrer Querol 1, 972 88 05 42.
🕑 Sun. 🎉 Fiesta de l'Estany (third Sun of Aug). **www**.puigcerda.com

Puig is Catalan for hill. Although Puigcerdà sits on a relatively small hill compared with the encircling mountains, which rise to 2,900 m (9,500 ft),

Portal of Monestir de Santa Maria

Ripoll ❾

Girona. 🏔 11,000. 🚌 🚏 ℹ Plaça Abat Oliba, 972 70 23 51.
🕑 Sat. 🎉 Fiesta Mayor (11–12 May). **www**.elripolles.com

Once a tiny mountain base from which raids against the Moors were made, Ripoll is now best known for the **Monestir de Santa Maria**, built in AD 888. The town has been called "the cradle of Catalonia" as the monastery was both the power base and cultural centre of Guifré el Pélos (Wilfred the Hairy), founder of the 500-year dynasty, the House of Barcelona. He is buried in the monastery.

In the later 12th century, the huge west portal gained a series of intricate carvings, which are perhaps the finest Romanesque carvings in Spain. They depict historical and biblical scenes. The two-storey cloister is the only other part of the original monastery to have survived wars and anticlerical purges. The rest is a 19th-century reconstruction.

The medieval town of Besalú on the banks of the Riu Fluvià

Sant Joan de les Abadesses ⑩

Girona. 🏠 *3,600.* 🚌 🛈 *Plaza de Abadía 9, 972 72 05 99.* 🚍 *Sun.* 🎉 *Fiesta Mayor (second Sun of Sep).* www.santjoanlesabadesses.com

A fine, 12th-century Gothic bridge arches over the Riu er to this unassuming market town, whose main attraction is its **monastery**. Founded in AD 885, it was a gift from Guifré, first count f Barcelona, to his daughter, e first abbess. The church is nadorned except for a uperb wooden calvary, *The escent from the Cross*. Made 1150, it looks modern; part it, a thief, was burnt in the vil War and replaced with ch skill that it is hard to tell nich is new. The monas- y's museum has Baroque d Renaissance altarpieces.

-century calvary, Sant Joan de badesses monastery

Environs
To the north is **Camprodon**, a small town full of grand houses, and shops selling local produce. The region is especially noted for its *llonganisses* (sausages).

Olot ⑪

Girona. 🏠 *32,000.* 🚌 🛈 *Hospici 8, 972 26 01 41.* 🚍 *Mon.* 🎉 *Corpus Christi (Jun), Fiesta del Tura (8 Sep).* www.olot.org/turisme

This small market town is at the centre of a landscape pockmarked with the conical hills of extinct volcanoes. But it was an earthquake in 1474 which last disturbed the town, destroying its medieval past.

During the 18th century the town's textile industry spawn-ed the "Olot School" of art: finished cotton fabrics were printed with drawings, and in 1783 the Public School of Drawing was founded.

Much of the school's work, which includes sculpted saints and paintings such as Joaquim Vayreda's *Les Falgueres*, is in the **Museu Comarcal de la Garrotxa**, housed in an 18th-century hospice. There are also pieces by Modernista sculptor Miquel Blay, whose damsels support the balcony at No. 38 Passeig Miquel Blay.

🏛 **Museu Comarcal de la Garrotxa**
Calle Hospici 8. **Tel** *972 27 91 30.* 🕙 *Tue–Sun.* ⬤ *1 Jan, 25 Dec.* 🎫 ♿

Besalú ⑫

Girona. 🏠 *2,300.* 🚌 🛈 *Plaça de la Llibertat 1, 972 59 12 40.* 🚍 *Tue.* 🎉 *Sant Vicenç (22 Jan), Fiesta Mayor (last weekend of Sep).* 🎫 www.ajuntamentbesalu.org

A magnificent medieval town, with a striking approach across a fortified bridge over the Riu Fluvià, Besalú has two fine churches. These are the Romanesque **Sant Vicenç** and **Sant Pere**, the sole remnant of Besalú's Benedictine mon-astery. It was founded in AD 948, but pulled down in 1835.

In 1964 a **mikvah**, a ritual Jewish bath, was discovered. It was built in 1264 and is one of only three of that period to survive in Europe. The tourist office organizes guided visits to all the town's attractions.

To the south, the sky-blue lake of **Banyoles**, where the 1992 Olympic rowing contests were held, is ideal for picnics.

Sausage shop in the mountain town of Camprodon

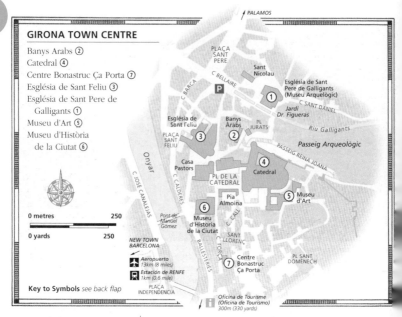

GIRONA TOWN CENTRE

Banys Arabs ②
Catedral ④
Centre Bonastruc Ça Porta ⑦
Església de Sant Feliu ③
Església de Sant Pere de
  Galligants ①
Museu d'Art ⑤
Museu d'Història
  de la Ciutat ⑥

0 metres 250

0 yards 250

Key to Symbols see back flap

Girona ⓭

Girona. 🎎 90,000. ✈ 🚂 🚌 ℹ
Rambla de la Llibertat 1, 972 22 65
75. 🛍 Tue, Sat. 🎉 El Pedal (last fortnight of Sep), San Narciso (late Oct).
www.ajuntament.gi/turisme

This handsome town puts on
its best face beside the Riu
Onyar, where tall, pastel-
coloured buildings rise above
the water. Behind them, in
the old town, the Rambla de
la Llibertat is lined with busy
shops and street cafés.

The houses were built in the
19th century to replace sections of the city wall damaged
during a seven-month siege
by French troops in 1809. Most
of the rest of the ramparts, first

raised by the Romans, are still
intact and have been turned
into the **Passeig Arqueològic**
(Archaeological Walk), which
runs right around the city.

The starting point of the
walk is on the north side of
the town, near the **Església de
Sant Pere de Galligants**
(St Peter of the Cock Crows).
The church now houses the
city's archaeological collection.

From here a narrow street
into the old part of town
passes through the north gate,
where huge Roman
foundation stones are still
visible. They mark the route
of the Via Augusta, the road
which originally ran from
Tarragona to Rome. The most
popular place of devotion for

the people of Girona is the
Església de Sant Feliu. The
church, begun in the 14th
century, was built over the
tombs of St Felix and St
Narcissus, both patrons of the
city. Next to the high altar are
eight Roman sarcophagi
embedded in the apse wall.

Despite their name, the
nearby **Banys Arabs** (Arab
Baths), lit by a fine octagonal
lantern, were built in the late
12th century, about 300 years
after the Moors had left.

🏛 Centre Bonastruc Ça Porta

Carrer de la Força 8. **Tel** 972 21 6
61. 🔲 daily. 🌑 public hols 🖾 🈁
🖾 **www**.ajuntament.gi/turisme
Amid the maze of alleyways
and steps in the old town is
the former, partially restored
Jewish quarter of El Call. The
Centre Bonastruc Ça Porta
gives a history of Girona's
Jews, who were expelled in
the late 15th century.

🔒 Cathedral

🔲 10am–8pm daily (summer:
until 7pm Sun–Fri, 4:30pm Sat).
www.lacatedraldegirona.com
The style of Girona Cathedral
solid west face is pure Cata
Baroque, but the rest of the
building is Gothic. The sin
nave, built in 1416 by Guil
Bofill, is the widest Gothic
span in Christendom. Behi

Painted houses crowded along the bank of the Riu Onyar in Girona

For hotels and restaurants in this region see pp571–74 and pp620–24

the altar is a marble throne known as "Charlemagne's Chair" after the Frankish king whose troops took Girona in 785. In the chancel is a 14th-century jewel-encrusted silver and enamel altarpiece. Among the Romanesque paintings and statues in the cathedral's museum are a 10th-century illuminated copy of St Beatus of Liébana's *Commentary on the Apocalypse*, and a 14th-century statue of the Catalan king, Pere the Ceremonious.

The collection's most famous item is a large, well preserved 11th- to 12th-century tapestry, called *The Creation*.

Tapestry of *The Creation*

Museu d'Art
Pujada de la Catedral 12.
Tel 972 20 38 34. ☐ Tue–Sun.
● 1, 6 Jan, 25–26 Dec. 🎟 &
www.museuart.com

This former episcopal palace is one of Catalonia's best art galleries, with works ranging from the Romanesque period to the 20th century. Items from churches destroyed through war or neglect give an idea of church interiors long ago. Highlights are 10th-century carvings, a silver-clad altar from the church at Sant Pere de Rodes and a 12th-century beam from Cruïlles.

Museu d'Història la Ciutat
Carrer de la Força 27. **Tel** 972 22 22
☐ 10am–2pm, 5–7pm
Tue–Sat, 10am–2pm Sun. 🎟

The city's history museum is housed in an 18th-century former convent. Parts of the cemetery are preserved, including the recesses where the bodies of members of the Capuchin Order were placed while decomposing. The collection includes old *sardana* (see p225) instruments.

Figueres ⑭

Girona. 🚋 40,000. 🚂 🚌 🅿 *Plaça del Sol*, 972 50 31 55. 🛒 *Thu.* 🎉 *Santa Cruz (3 May), San Pedro (29 Jun).*
www.figueresciutat.com

Figueres is in the north of the Empordà (Ampurdán) region, the fertile plain that sweeps inland from the Gulf of Roses. Every Thursday, the market here fills with fruit and vegetables from the area.

The **Museu de Joguets** (Toy Museum) is housed on the top floor of the old Hotel de Paris, on the Rambla, Figueres' main street. Inside are exhibits from all over Catalonia. At the lower end of the Rambla is a statue of Narcís Monturiol i Estarriol (1819–85), claimed to be the inventor of the submarine.

A much better-known son of the town is Salvador Dalí, who founded the **Teatro-Museo Dalí** in 1974. The most visited museum in Spain after the Prado, the galleries occupy Figueras's old main theatre. Its roof has an eye-catching glass dome. Not all the work shown is by Dalí, and none of his best-known works are here.

Rainy Taxi, a monument in the garden of the Teatro-Museu Dalí

But the displays, including *Rainy Taxi* – a black Cadillac being sprayed by a fountain – are a monument to the man who, fittingly, is buried here.

Museu del Joguet
Calle Sant Pere 1. **Tel** 972 50 45 85.
☐ daily. ● Mon in winter. 🎟 &

Teatre-Museu Dalí
Plaça Gala-Salvador Dalí.
Tel 972 67 75 00. ☐ Oct–Jun: Tue–Sun; Jul–Sep: daily. ● 1 Jan, 25 Dec. 🎟
www.dali-estate.org

THE ART OF DALI

Salvador Dalí e Domènech was born in Figueres in 1904 and mounted his first exhibition at the age of 15. After studying at the Escuela de Bellas Artes in Madrid, and dabbling with Cubism, Futurism and Metaphysical painting, the young artist embraced Surrealism in 1929, becoming the movement's best-known painter. Never far from controversy, the self-publicist Dalí became famous for his hallucinatory images – such as *Woman-Animal Symbiosis* – which he described as "hand-painted dream photographs". Dalí's career also included writing and film-making, and established him as one of the 20th century's greatest artists. He died in his home town in 1989.

Ceiling fresco in the Wind Palace Room, Teatro-Museu Dalí

Cadaqués

Girona. 🏃 *3,000*. 🚇 🛈 *Carrer Cotxe 2 (972 25 83 15)*. 🚢 *Mon.* 🎉 *Fiesta major de Verano (first week of Sep), Santa Esperança (18 Dec).*

This pretty resort is overlooked by the Baroque **Església de Santa Maria**. In the 1960s it was dubbed the "St Tropez of Spain", due to the young crowd that sought out Salvador Dalí in nearby Port Lligat. The house where he lived from 1930 until his death in 1989 is known as the **Casa-Museu Salvador Dalí**. Visitors can see the painter's workshop, the library, private bedrooms and the garden area and swimming pool. Book in advance as group visits are permitted only in small numbers. In summer, a "bus-train" takes visitors there from (but not back to) Cadaqués.

🏛 **Casa-Museu Salvador Dalí**
Port Lligat. **Tel** *972 25 10 15. Reservations required, email pllgrups@dali-estate.org.* ● *early Jan–mid-Mar.* 🖥 *www.salvador-dali.org*

Empúries

Girona. 🚇 *L'Escala.* **Tel** *972 77 02 08.* ● *Easter, Jun–Sep: 10am–8pm daily; Oct–May: 10am–6pm daily.* 🖥 *ruins.* 🗓 *by appt.* **www.mac.es**

The ruins of this Greco-Roman town *(see p51)* are beside the sea. Three settlements were built between the 7th and 3rd centuries BC: the old town (Palaiapolis); the new town (Neapolis); and the Roman

An excavated Roman pillar in the ruins of Empúries

town. The **old town** was founded by the Greeks in 600 BC as a trading port. It was built on what was a small island, and is now the site of the hamlet of Sant Martí de Empúries. In 550 BC this was replaced by a larger town on the shore which the Greeks named Emporion, meaning "trading place". In 218 BC, the Romans landed at Empúries and built a city next to the new town.

A nearby museum exhibits some of the site's finds, but the best are in Barcelona's Museu Arqueològic *(see p172).*

Peratallada

Girona. 🏃 *400*. 🛈 *C/Unió 3, Ajuntament de Forallac, Vullpellac (972 64 55 22).* 🎉 *Feria Peratallada (last weekend in Apr or first in May), Festa Major (6 & 7 Aug), Medieval Market (first weekend in Oct).* **www**.forallac.com

This tiny village is stunning and only a short inland trip from the Costa Brava. Together with Pals and Palau Sator it forms part of the "Golden Triangle" of medieval villages. Its mountain-top position gives some dramatic views of the area. A labyrinth of cobbled streets wind up to the well-conserved castle and lookout tower, whose written records date from the 11th century. Both counts and kings made doubly sure of fending off any attackers by constructing a sturdy wall enclosing the entire village that even today limits the nucleus from further expansion, ensuring it retains its medieval character.

Looking south along the Costa Brava from Tossa de Mar

Tossa de Mar

Girona. 🏃 *5,000*. 🚇 🛈 *Avinguda Pelegrí 25, 972 34 01 08.* 🚢 *Thu.* 🎉 *Fiesta de Verano (29 Jun–2 Jul), Fiesta de Invierno (22 Jan).* **www**.infotossa.com

At the end of a corniche, the Roman town of Turissa is one of the prettiest along the Costa Brava. Above the new town is the **Vila Vella** (old town), a protected national monument. In the old town, the **Museu Municipal** has a collection of local archaeological finds and modern art including *The Flying Violinist*, by the artist Marc Chagall.

🏛 **Museu Municipal**
Plaça Roig y Soler 1. **Tel** *972 34 07 09.* ● *winter: Tue–Sun; summer: daily.* 🖥

Blanes

Girona. 🏃 *38,000*. 🚇 🚇 🛈 *Passeig de Catalunya 21, 972 33 0. 48.* 🚢 *Mon.* 🎉 *El Bilar (6 Apr), Si Ana (late Jul).* **www**.blanes.net

The working port of Blanes has one of the longest beach on the Costa Brava, but the highlight of the town is the **Jardí Botànic Mar i Murtra**. These fine gardens, designe by Karl Faust in 1928, are sp tacularly sited above cliffs. There are 7,000 species of M iterranean and tropical plan

🌿 **Jardí Botànic Mar i Murt**
Passeig Karl Faust 10. **Tel** *972 33 08 26.* ● *daily.* ● *1 & 6 Jan, 24 & 25 Dec.* 🖥 🗓 🛢

The Costa Brava

The Costa Brava ("wild coast") runs for some 200 km (125 miles) from Blanes northwards to the region of Empordà (Ampurdán), which borders France. It is a mix of pine-backed sandy coves, golden beaches and crowded, modern resorts. The busiest resorts – Lloret de Mar, Tossa de Mar and La Platja d'Aro – are to the south. Sant Feliu de Guíxols and Palamós are still working towns behind the summer rush. Just inland there are medieval villages to explore, such as Peralada, Peratallada and Pals. Wine, olives and fishing were the mainstays of the area before the tourists came in the 1960s.

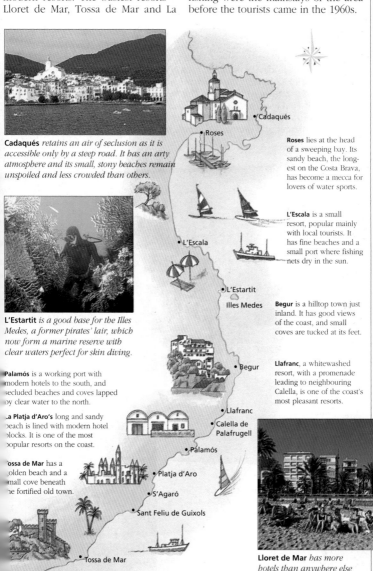

Cadaqués *retains an air of seclusion as it is accessible only by a steep road. It has an arty atmosphere and its small, stony beaches remain unspoiled and less crowded than others.*

Roses lies at the head of a sweeping bay. Its sandy beach, the longest on the Costa Brava, has become a mecca for lovers of water sports.

L'Escala is a small resort, popular mainly with local tourists. It has fine beaches and a small port where fishing nets dry in the sun.

L'Estartit *is a good base for the Illes Medes, a former pirates' lair, which now form a marine reserve with clear waters perfect for skin diving.*

Begur is a hilltop town just inland. It has good views of the coast, and small coves are tucked at its feet.

Llafranc, a whitewashed resort, with a promenade leading to neighbouring Calella, is one of the coast's most pleasant resorts.

Palamós is a working port with modern hotels to the south, and secluded beaches and coves lapped by clear water to the north.

La Platja d'Aro's long and sandy beach is lined with modern hotel blocks. It is one of the most popular resorts on the coast.

Tossa de Mar has a golden beach and a small cove beneath the fortified old town.

• Cadaqués
• Roses
• L'Escala
• L'Estartit
  Illes Medes
• Begur
• Llafranc
• Calella de Palafrugell
• Pálamós
• Platja d'Aro
• S'Agaró
• Sant Feliu de Guixols
• Tossa de Mar
• Lloret de Mar
• Blanes

0 kilometres 10
0 miles 5

Lloret de Mar *has more hotels than anywhere else on the coast. But there are unspoiled beaches nearby, such as Santa Cristina.*

Monestir de Montserrat ⑳

A Benedictine monk

The "Serrated Mountain" (*mont serrat*), its highest peak rising to 1,236 m (4,055 ft), is a magnificent setting for Catalonia's holiest place, the Monastery of Montserrat, which is surrounded by chapels and hermits' caves. A chapel was first mentioned in the 9th century, the monastery was founded in the 11th century and in 1811, when the French attacked Catalonia in the War of Independence (*see p63*), it was destroyed and the monks killed. Rebuilt and repopulated in 1844, it was a beacon of Catalan culture during the Franco years. Today Benedictine monks live here. Visitors can hear the Escolania singing the *Salve Regina i Virolai* (the Montserrat hymn) in the basilica at 1pm and 7pm Monday to Friday, 6:45pm Monday to Thursday and noon and 6:45pm on Sundays, except in the summer and during the Christmas period.

Plaça de Santa Maria
The focal points of the square are two wings of the Gothic cloister built in 1477. The modern monastery façade is by Françesc Folguera.

Gothic cloister

Funicular to the holy site of Santa Cova

The Museum has a collection of 19th- and 20th-century Catalan paintings and many Italian and French works. It also displays liturgical items from the Holy Land.

The Way of the Cross
This path passes 14 statues representing the stations of the Cross. It begins near the Plaça de l'Abat Oliba.

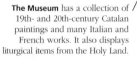

STAR FEATURES

★ Basilica Façade

★ Black Virgin

View of Montserrat
The complex includes cafés and a h... A second funicular transports visito... to nature trails above the monaste...

★ **Basilica Façade**
Agapit and Venanci Vallmitjana sculpted Christ and the apostles on the basilica's Neo-Renaissance façade. It was built in 1900 to replace the Renaissance façade of the original church, consecrated in 1592.

VISITORS' CHECKLIST

Montserrat (Barcelona province).
Tel *93 877 77 01.* 🚠 *Aeri de Montserrat, then cable car; Monistrol–Enllaç, then rack railway.* 🚌 *from Barcelona.* **Basilica** 🕐 *Oct–Jun: 7:30am–7:30pm daily; Jul–Sep: 7:30am–8:15pm daily.* ✝ *from 9am Mon–Fri, from 7:30am Sat, from 8am Sun & religious hols.* 🖼 **Museum** 🕐 *10am–6pm Mon–Fri, 9:30am–6:30pm Sat–Sun & public hols.* 📷 ♿ 🎧
www.abadiamontserrat.cat

★ **Black Virgin**
La Moreneta looks down from behind the altar. Protected behind glass, her wooden orb protrudes for pilgrims to touch.

Basilica Interior
The sanctuary in the domed basilica is adorned by a richly enamelled altar and paintings by Catalan artists.

The rack railway, opened in 2003, follows the course of a historic rail line built in 1880.

Cable car to Aeri de Montserrat station

THE VIRGIN OF MONTSERRAT

The small wooden statue of La Moreneta (the dark one) is the soul of Montserrat. It is said to have been made by St Luke and brought here by St Peter in AD 50. Centuries later, the statue is believed to have been hidden from the Moors in the nearby Santa Cova (Holy Cave). Carbon dating suggests, however, that the statue was carved around the 12th century. In 1881 Montserrat's Black Virgin became patroness of Catalonia.

The blackened Virgin of Montserrat

Inner Courtyard
On one side of the courtyard is the baptistry (1902), with sculptures by Carles Collet. Pilgrims may approach the Virgin through a door to the right.

Vic ㉑

Barcelona. 🏘 *39,000.* 🚉 🚌 🛈
Calle Ciutat 4, 93 886 20 91. 🚐 *Tue
& Sat.* 🎭 *Mercat del Ram (Sat before
Easter), Sant Miquel (5–15 Jul), Música
Viva (Sep), Mercat Medieval (6–10
Dec).* **www**.victurisme.net

Market days – Tuesdays and
Saturdays – are the best time
to go to this small country
town. This is when the
renowned local sausages
(embotits) are piled high in
the large Gothic Plaça Major,
along with other produce from
the surrounding plains.

In the 3rd century BC Vic
was the capital of an ancient
Iberian tribe, the Ausetans. The
town was then colonized by
the Romans – the remains of
a Roman temple survive today.
Since the 6th century the town
has been a bishop's see. In the
11th century, Abbot Oliva
commissioned the El Cloquer
tower, around which the
cathedral was built in the 18th
century. The interior of the
cathedral is covered with vast
murals by Josep Maria Sert
(1876–1945). They are painted
in reds and golds, and represent scenes from the Bible.

Adjacent to the cathedral is
the **Museu Episcopal de Vic**,
which has one of the best
collections of Romanesque
artifacts in Catalonia. Its large
display of mainly religious art
and relics includes bright,
simple murals and wooden
sculptures from rural churches.
Also on display are 11th- and
12th-century frescoes.

Cardona dominating the surrounding area from its hilltop site

🏛 Museu Episcopal
Plaça Bisbe Oliba. **Tel** 93 886 93
60. ◻ Tue–Sun. ● 25 & 26 Dec,
1 & 6 Jan. ♿ 📷 📷

Cardona ㉒

Barcelona. 🏘 *5,000.* 🚌 🛈
Avinguda Rastrillo, 93 869 27 98. 🚐
Sun. 🎭 *Fiesta Mayor (2nd Sun of
Sep).* **www**.ajcardona.org

The 13th-century castle of the
dukes of Cardona, constables
to the crown of Aragón, is set
on the top of a hill. The castle
was rebuilt in the 18th century
and is now a parador *(see
p558).* Beside the castle is an
early 11th-century church, the
Església de Sant Vicenç,
where the dukes are buried.

The castle gives views of the
town below and of the Mon-
tanya de Sal (Salt Mountain),
a huge salt deposit beside the
Riu Cardener which has been
mined since Roman times.

12th-century altar frontal, Museu Episcopal de Vic

Solsona ㉓

Lleida. 🏘 *9,000.* 🚌 🛈 Carrelera de
Bassella 1, 973 48 23 10. 🚐 Tue & Fr
🎭 Carnival (Feb); Corpus Christi
(May/Jun), Fiesta Mayor (8–11 Sep).
www.elsolsonesinvita.com

Nine towers and three gateways remain of Solsona's
fortifications. Inside the walls
is an ancient town of noble
mansions. The cathedral has
black stone Virgin. The
Museu Diocesà i Comarcal
contains Romanesque paintings and archaeological finds

🏛 Museu Diocesà i
Comarcal
Plaça Palau 1. **Tel** 973 48 21 01. ◻
Tue–Sun. ● 1 Jan & 25, 26 Dec. ♿

Lleida ㉔

Lleida. 🏘 *130,000.* 🚉 🚌 🛈 Pla
Ramón Berenguer IV, s/n, 902 10 1
10. 🚐 Thu & Sat. 🎭 Sant Anastas
(11 May), Sant Miquel (29 Sep).
www.lleidatur.es

Dominating Lleida (Lérida),
the capital of Catalonia's on
landlocked province, is **La
Suda**, a large, ruined fort
taken from the Moors in 11
The old cathedral, **La Seu
Vella**, founded in 1203, is s
ated within the walls of the
fort, high above the town.
was transformed into barra
by Felipe V in 1707 but toc
sadly, is desolate. It remain
imposing, however, with
Gothic windows in the clois

A lift descends from the
Vella to the Plaça de Sant J
in the town below. This sq
is at the mid-point of a bus

street sweeping round the foot of the hill. The new cathedral is here, as are manorial buildings such as the rebuilt 13th-century town hall, the **Paeria**.

Poblet 25

See pp222–3.

Montblanc 26

Tarragona. 🐾 7,000. 🚆 📥
🛈 *Antigua Iglesia de Sant Françesc, 977 86 17 33.* 🚌 *Tue, Fri.* 🎉 *Fiesta Mayor (8–11 Sep), Fiesta Medieval (2 weeks in Apr).*

The medieval grandeur of Montblanc lives on within its walls, which are considered to be Catalonia's finest piece of military architecture. At the **Sant Jordi** gate, St George allegedly slew the dragon. The **Museu Comarcal de la Conca de Barberà** has interesting displays on local crafts.

🏛 **Museu Comarcal de la Conca de Barberà**
Carrer Josa 6. **Tel** *977 86 03 49.* 🕐 *Tue–Sun & public hols.* 🖼

Santes Creus 27

Tarragona. 🐾 150. 🛈 *Plaça de Sant Bernat 1, 977 63 81 41.* 🚌 *Sat, Sun.* 🎉 *Sta Llúcia (13 Dec).*

Home to the the prettiest of the "Cistercian triangle" monasteries is the tiny village of Santes Creus. The other two,

Vallbona de les Monges and Poblet *(see pp222–3)*, are nearby. The **Monestir de Santes Creus** was founded in 1150 by Ramon Berenguer IV *(see p54)* during his reconquest of Catalonia. The Gothic cloisters are decorated with figurative sculptures, a style first permitted by Jaime II, who ruled from 1291 to 1327. His finely carved tomb, along with that of other nobles, is in the 12th-century church, which has a beautiful rose window.

🔒 **Monestir de Santes Creus**
Tel *977 63 83 29.* 🕐 *Tue–Sun.* 🖼 *(free Tue).* 🎫 *by appointment* ♿

Vilafranca del Penedès 28

Barcelona. 🐾 35,000. 🚆 📥
🛈 *Carrer Cort 14, 93 818 12 54.* 🚌 *Sat.* 🎉 *Fiesta Mayor (29 Aug–2 Sep).* **www**.turismevilafranca.com

This busy market town is set in the heart of Catalonia's main wine-producing region *(see pp202–3)*. The **Museu del Vi** (Wine Museum), in a 14th-century palace, documents the history of the area's wine trade. Local bodegas can be visited for wine tasting.

Eight km (5 miles) to the north is **Sant Sadurni**, the capital of Spain's sparkling wine, *cava (see pp606–7)*.

🏛 **Museu del Vi**
Plaça Jaume I. **Tel** *93 890 05 82.* 🕐 *for renovation until end 2009.* 🖼

Anxaneta climbing to the top of a tower of castellers

CATALONIA'S FIESTAS

Human Towers *(various dates and locations).* The province of Tarragona is famous for its *castellers* festivals, where teams of men stand on each others' shoulders in an effort to build the highest human tower. Each tower, which can be up to seven people high, is topped by a small boy called the *anxaneta*. *Castellers* can be seen in action in many towns, especially Vilafranca del Penedès and Valls.
Dance of Death *(Maundy Thu)*, Verges (Girona). Men dressed as skeletons perform a macabre dance.
St George's Day *(23 Apr).* Lovers give each other a rose and a book on the day of Catalonia's patron saint. The book is in memory of Cervantes, who died on this day in 1616.
La Patum *(Corpus Christi, May/Jun)*, Berga (Barcelona province). Giants, devils and bizarre monsters parade through the town.
Midsummer's Eve *(23 Jun).* Celebrated all over Catalonia with bonfires and fireworks.

Monestir de Santes Creus, surrounded by poplar and hazel trees

Monestir de Poblet 🄐

The Monastery of Santa Maria de Poblet is a haven of tranquillity and a resting place of kings. It was the first and most important of three Cistercian monasteries, known as the "Cistercian triangle" *(see p221)*, that helped to consolidate power in Catalonia after it had been recaptured from the Moors by Ramon Berenguer IV. In 1835, during the Carlist upheavals, it was plundered and seriously damaged by fire. Restoration of the impressive ruins, now largely complete, began in 1930 and monks returned in 1940.

The dormitory is reached by stairs from the church. The vast 87-m (285-ft) gallery dates from the 13th century.

The 12th-century refectory is a vaulted hall with an octagonal fountain and a pulpit.

View of Poblet
The abbey, its buildings enclosed by fortified walls that have hardly changed since the Middle Ages, is in an isolated valley near the Riu Francolí's source.

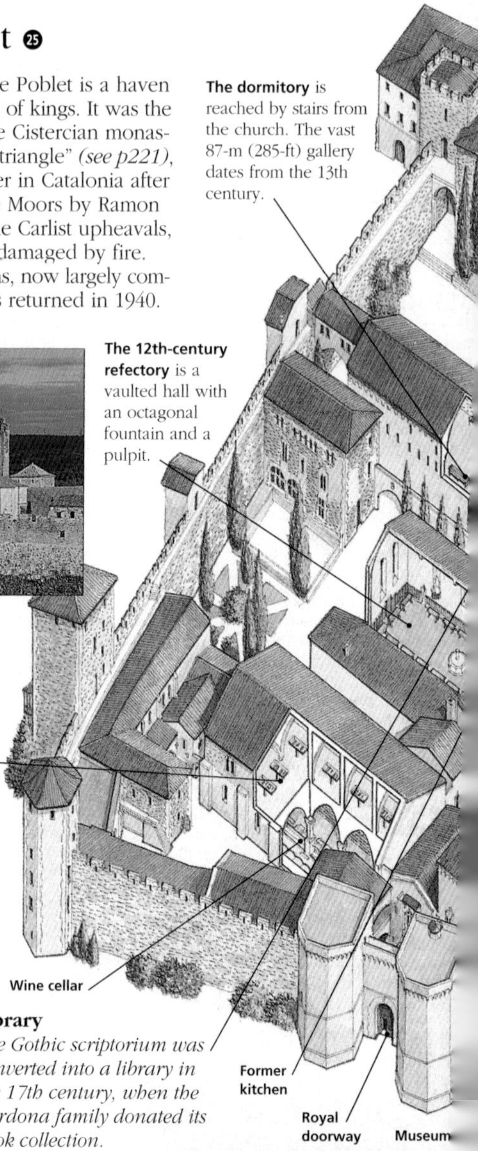

Museum

Wine cellar

Library
The Gothic scriptorium was converted into a library in the 17th century, when the Cardona family donated its book collection.

Former kitchen

Royal doorway   Museum

TIMELINE

Royal tombs

1150 Santes Creus founded – third abbey in Cistercian triangle	**14th century** Main cloister finished			
1156 Founding of monastery at Vallbona de les Monges		**1479** Juan II, last king of Aragón, buried here		**1940** Monks return

1100	1300	1500	1700	1900

	1196 Alfonso II is the first king to be buried here	**1336–87** Reign of Pere the Ceremonious, who designates Poblet a royal pantheon		**1952** Tombs reconstructed. Royal remains returned
	1150 Poblet monastery founded by Ramon Berenguer IV		**1835** Disentailment (p45) of monasteries. Poblet ravaged	

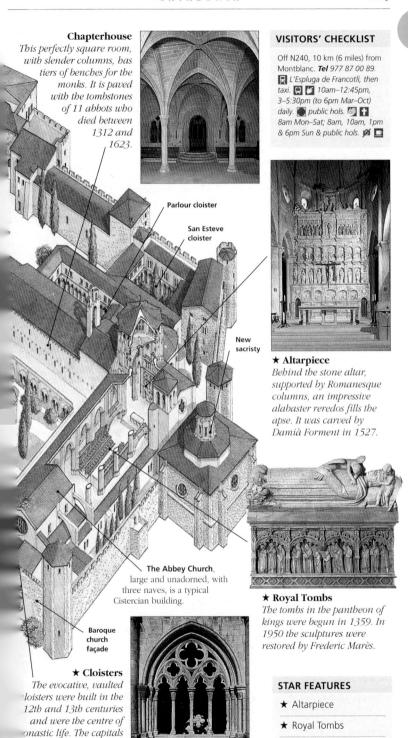

Chapterhouse
This perfectly square room, with slender columns, has tiers of benches for the monks. It is paved with the tombstones of 11 abbots who died between 1312 and 1623.

VISITORS' CHECKLIST

Off N240, 10 km (6 miles) from Montblanc. **Tel** 977 87 00 89. L'Espluga de Francolí, then taxi. 10am–12:45pm, 3–5:30pm (to 6pm Mar–Oct) daily. public hols. 8am Mon–Sat; 8am, 10am, 1pm & 6pm Sun & public hols.

Parlour cloister

San Esteve cloister

New sacristy

★ **Altarpiece**
Behind the stone altar, supported by Romanesque columns, an impressive alabaster reredos fills the apse. It was carved by Damià Forment in 1527.

The Abbey Church, large and unadorned, with three naves, is a typical Cistercian building.

★ **Royal Tombs**
The tombs in the pantheon of kings were begun in 1359. In 1950 the sculptures were restored by Frederic Marès.

Baroque church façade

★ **Cloisters**
The evocative, vaulted cloisters were built in the 12th and 13th centuries and were the centre of monastic life. The capitals are beautifully decorated with carved scrollwork.

STAR FEATURES

★ Altarpiece

★ Royal Tombs

★ Cloisters

Palm trees lining the waterfront at Sitges

Sitges ㉙

Barcelona. 🏘 *26,000.* 🚆 🚌 ℹ️
C/ Sínia Morera 1 (93 810 93 40). 🏨
Thu. 🎭 *Carnival (Feb–Mar) Festa major
(22–27 Aug).* **www**.sitgestour.com

There are no less than nine
beaches to choose from at
this seaside town. It has a
reputation as a gay resort but
is just as popular with all.
Lively bars and restaurants
line its main boulevard, the
Passeig Marítim, and there are
many examples of *modernista*
architecture amongst the '70s
apartment blocks. Modernista
artist Santiago Rusiñol (1861–
1931) spent much time here
and bequeathed his quirky
collection of ceramics,
sculptures, painting and ornate
iron-work to the **Museu Cau
Ferrat**. It lies next to Sitges's
landmark, the 17th century
church of **Sant Bartomeu i
Santa Tecla**.

🏛 Museu Cau Ferrat
Carrer Fonollar. **Tel** *93 894 03 64.*
🕐 *Tue–Sun.* 🌑 *public hols.* 🎫 🖼

Costa Daurada ㉚

Tarragona. 🚆 🚌 *Calafell, Sant Vicenç
de Calders, Salou.* ℹ️ *Tarragona (977
23 03 12).* **www**.costadaurada.org

The long, sandy beaches of
the Costa Daurada (Golden
Coast) run along the shores of
Tarragona province. **El Vendrell**
is one of the area's active ports.
The **Museu Pau Casals** in Sant
Salvador (El Vendrell) is dedi-
cated to the famous cellist.

Port Aventura, south of
Tarragona, is one of Europe's
largest theme parks and has
many exotically-themed
attractions, such as Polynesia
and Wild West. **Cambrils and
Salou** to the south are the liveliest resorts – the others are
low-key, family holiday spots.

🏛 Museu Pau Casals
Avinguda Palfuriana 67.
Tel *977 68 42 76.* 🕐 *Tue–Sun.* 🖼

📷 Port Aventura
Autovia Salou–Vila-seca. **Tel** *902 20
22 20.* 🕐 *mid-Mar–6 Jan.* 🖼 ♿

Tarragona ㉛

Tarragona. 🏘 *130,000.* ✈️ 🚆 🚌
ℹ️ *Carrer Major 39 (977 25 07 95).*
🏨 *Tue, Thu & Sun.* 🎭 *Sant Magí
(19 Aug), Santa Tecla (23 Sep).*
www.tarragonaturisme.es

Tarragona is now a major
industrial port, but it has
preserved many remnants of its
Roman past. As the capital of
Tarraconensis, the Romans
used it as a base for the conquest of the peninsula in the
3rd century BC (*see pp50–1*).

The avenue of Rambla
Nova ends abruptly on the
clifftop Balcó de Europa, in
sight of the ruins of the
Amfiteatre Romà and the
ruined 12th-century church
of **Santa Maria del Miracle**.

Nearby is the Praetorium,
a Roman tower that was
converted into a palace in
medieval times. It now
houses the **Pretori i Circ
Romans**. This displays Roman
and medieval finds, and gives
access to the cavernous
passageways of the excavated
Roman circus, built in the 1st
century AD. Next to the
Praetorium is the **Museu
Nacional Arqueològic**,
containing the most important
collection of Roman artifacts
in Catalonia. It has an
extensive collection of bronze

The remains of the Roman amphitheatre, Tarragona

tools and beautiful mosaics, including a *Head of Medusa*. Among the most impressive remains are the huge Pre-Roman stones on which the Roman wall is built. An archaeological walk stretches 1-km (half-a-mile) along the wall. Behind the wall lies the 12th-century **cathedral**, built on the site of a Roman temple. This evolved over many centuries, as seen from the blend of styles of the exterior. Inside is an alabaster altarpiece of St Tecla, carved by Pere Joan in 1434. The 13th-century cloister has Gothic vaulting, but the doorway is Romanesque.

In the west of town is a 3rd- to 4th-century Christian cemetery (ask about opening times in the archaeological museum).

Environs

The **Aqüeducte de les Ferreres** lies just outside the city, next to the A7 motorway. This 2nd-century aqueduct was built to bring water to the city from the Riu Gaià, 30 km (19 miles) to the north. The **Arc de Berà**, a 1st-century triumphal arch on the Via Augusta, is 20 km (12 miles) northeast on the N340.

The bustling, provincial town of **Reus** lies inland from Tarragona. Although its airport serves the Costa Daurada, it is often overlooked by holiday-makers. However there is some fine *modernista* architecture to be seen here, notably some early work by Antoni Gaudí who was born in Reus. The Pere Mata Psychiatric Institute was designed by Domènech i Montaner before his master-piece, the Hospital de la Santa Creu i de Sant Pau *(see p165)*.

Museu Nacional Arqueològic de Tarragona
Plaça del Rei 5. **Tel** 977 23 62 09.
☐ Tue–Sun. 🕹 (senior citizens and under 18s free). 👍 **www**.mnat.es

Pretori i Circ Romans
Plaça del Rei. **Tel** 977 24 19 52.
☐ Tue–Sun. 🕹

Tortosa ❸❷

Tarragona. 🚶 30,000. 🚆 Carrilet 1, 977 44 96 48. 🚌 Mon. 🎉 Nuestra Señora de la Cinta (late Aug & early Sep). **www**.turismetortosa.com

A ruined castle and medieval walls are clues to Tortosa's historical importance. Sited at the lowest crossing point on the Riu Ebre (Río Ebro), it has been strategically significant since Iberian times. The Moors held the city from the 8th century until 1148. The old Moorish castle, known as La Zuda, is all that remains of their defences. It has been renovated as a parador *(see p573)*. The Moors also built a mosque in 914. Its

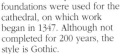

Ruins of the Palaeo-Christian Necropolis

foundations were used for the cathedral, on which work began in 1347. Although not completed for 200 years, the style is Gothic.

Tortosa was badly damaged in 1938–39 during one of the fiercest battles of the Civil War *(see pp64–7)*, when the Ebre formed the front line between the opposing forces.

Delta de L'Ebre ❸❸

Tarragona. 🚆 Aldea. 🚌 Deltebre, Aldea. 🛈 Deltebre 977 48 96 79. **www**.ebre.com/delta

The delta of the Riu Ebre is a prosperous rice-growing region and wildlife haven. Some 70 sq km (27 sq miles) have been turned into a nature reserve, the **Parc Natural del Delta de L'Ebre**. In Deltebre there is an information centre and an interesting **Eco-Museu**, with an aquarium containing species found in the delta.

The main towns in the area are **Amposta** and **Sant Carles de la Ràpita**, both of which serve as good bases for exploring the reserve.

The best sites for seeing wildlife are along the shore, from the Punta del Fangar in the north to the Punta de la Banya in the south. Everywhere is accessible by car except Illa de Buda. Flamingoes breed on this island and other water birds, such as avocets, can be seen from tourist boats that leave from Riumar and Deltebre.

🏛 **Eco-Museu**
Carrer Martí Buera 22. **Tel** 977 48 96 79. ☐ Tue–Sun. 🕹 1 & 6 Jan, 25 & 26 Dec. 🕹 👍 👍

THE SARDANA

Catalonia's national dance is more complicated than it appears. The success of the Sardana depends on all of the dancers accurately counting the complicated short- and long-step skips and jumps, which accounts for their serious faces. Music is provided by a *cobla*, an 11-person band consisting of a leader playing a three-holed flute *(flabiol)* and a little drum *(tabal)*, five woodwind players and five brass players. When the music starts, dancers join hands and form circles. The Sardana is performed during most local fiestas *(see p221)* and at special day-long gatherings called *aplecs*.

A group of Sardana dancers captured in stone

ARAGÓN

HUESCA · ZARAGOZA · TERUEL

Stretching almost half the length of Spain, and bisected by the Ebro, one of the country's longest rivers, Aragón takes in a wide variety of scenery, from the snow-capped summits of Ordesa National Park in the Pyrenees to the dry plains of the Spanish interior. This largely unsung and undervisited region contains magnificent Mudéjar architecture and many unspoiled medieval towns.

From the 12th–15th centuries Aragón was a powerful kingdom, or, more accurately, a federation of states, including Catalonia. In its heyday, in the 13th century, its dominions stretched across the Mediterranean as far as Sicily. By his marriage to Isabel of Castile and León in 1469, Fernando II of Aragón paved the way for the unification of Spain.

After the Reconquest, Muslim architects and craftsmen were treated more tolerantly here than elsewhere, and they continued their work in the distinctive Mudéjar style, building with elaborate brickwork and patterned ceramic decoration. Their work can be seen in churches all over Aragón and there are outstanding examples in the cities of Teruel and the capital, Zaragoza, Spain's fifth largest city, which stands on the banks of the Ebro.

The highest peaks of the Pyrenees lie in Huesca province. Some of the region's finest sights are in the Pyrenean foothills, which are crossed by the Aragonese variation of the pilgrims' route to Santiago de Compostela. Probably the most spectacular of them is the monastery of San Juan de la Peña – half-concealed beneath a rock overhang – which was founded in the 9th century.

The climate of the region varies as much as the landscape: winters can be long and harsh and summers hot.

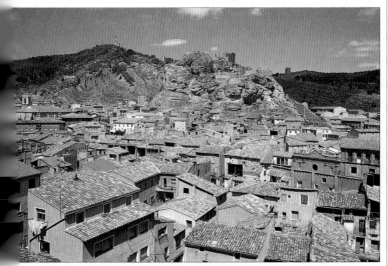

view of the rooftops and medieval walls of Daroca

orla village church, on the edge of Ordesa National Park

Exploring Aragón

The landscapes of Aragón range from the high Pyrenees, north of Huesca, through the desiccated terrain around Zaragoza to the forested hills of Teruel province. The cities of Teruel and Zaragoza have some of the most striking Mudéjar monuments in Spain. There are many small, picturesque preserved towns in the region. Ordesa National Park contains stunning mountain scenery, but it can only be visited fully after the snow melts in spring, and even then much of it has to be explored on foot. Pretty Los Valles offers less dramatic but equally enjoyable landscapes and is a popular tourist destination. Other attractive places include the impressively sited Castillo de Loarre and Monasterio de San Juan de la Peña, and the waterfalls of Monasterio de Piedra.

Stone carving, San Juan de la Peña

The Puerto de Somport, near Panticosa

SIGHTS AT A GLANCE

Agüero **9**
Ainsa **6**
Albarracín **27**
Alcañiz **22**
Alquézar **12**
Benasque **5**
Calatayud **18**
Castillo de Loarre **10**
Daroca **20**
Fuendetodos **21**
Graus **14**
Huesca **11**
Jaca **7**
Monasterio de Piedra **19**
Monasterio de San Juan
  de la Peña **8**

Monasterio de Veruela **16**
Mora de Rubielos **25**
*Parque Nacional de Ordesa
  pp232–3* **4**
Puerto de Somport **3**
Rincón de Ademuz **28**
Santuario de Torreciudad **13**
Sierra de Gúdar **24**
Sos del Rey Católico **1**
Tarazona **15**
Teruel **26**
Valderrobres **23**
Los Valles **2**
Zaragoza **17**

Sigüe
N240
Emb.
de V
SOS DEL REY CATÓLICO **1**
Uncastillo
Sádaba
Valareña
Ejea de
Caballe

Burgos
TARAZONA **15**
Gallur
Tauste
Parque
Natural de
Moncayo
16
MONASTERIO DE VERUELA
Alagón
N122
N232
Tierga
Épila
ZARA
Torrelapaja
A2
La Almunia de Doña Godina
CALATAYUD
FUEND
Ariza
Ateca
18
Cariñena
Jalón
Madrid
N234
N330
19
MONASTERIO DE PIEDRA
DAROCA **20**
Huecha
Calamocha
Se
lo
Caminreal
N211
Monreal
del Campo
Peral
Alfa
N330
A23
Orihuela del
Tremedal
Alfar
Cella
ALBARRACÍN **27**
TERUEL
Montes
Universales
La F
N330
28
RIN
AD

↑ Lourdes

3 PUERTO DE SOMPORT

Monte Perdido
3355m

N330

Torla ○ ❄ **4**

A **7** Sabinanigo

PARQUE NAC. DE ORDESA

Bielsa

Pico de Aneto
3404m △

5 BENASQUE

N260

Castejón de Sós

N260

MONASTERIO DE SAN JUAN DE LA PEÑA

Boltaña **6** AÍNSA

Campo

N230

10

Arguís

Sierra de Guara

SANTUARIO DE TORRECIUDAD

Roda de Isábena

CASTILLO PARRE

N330

Arguís

ALQUÉZAR 12

14 GRAUS

13

HUESCA **11**

Angüés

N240

N123

Benabarre

Grañén

Huerto

Barbastro

Tardienta

Alcubierre

Monzón ○

Chica

N230

Sariñena

Binéfar

N240

Tamarite de Litera

A R A G Ó N

Ontiñena

Lleida
Barcelona →

AP2 A2

Pina de Ebro

Bujaraloz

NIII

Fraga

Ebro

Embalse de Mequinenza

Mequinenza

N211

Escatrón

Caspe

Fayón

Martín

Híjar

Maella

N232

22 ALCAÑIZ

Andorra

Calanda

Valjunquera

N211

VALDERROBRES **23**

Castellote

Monroyo

Guadalope

N232

Mirambel

Cantavieja

E GÚDAR

arroya
0m

DE RUBIELOS

0 kilometres 20

bielos de Mora

0 miles 20

SEE ALSO

• *Where to Stay* pp574–6

• *Where to Eat* pp624–6

GETTING AROUND

Zaragoza is linked by motorway to the Basque Country, Navarra, Madrid and Barcelona. Major roads link the region's main cities with each other, and Teruel with Valencia. Many minor roads have been improved and may be fast and uncongested in the flatter, central areas. The principal railway lines run from Zaragoza to Madrid and Barcelona, both of which are linked by high-speed AVE trains, and to Valencia. Coaches are infrequent, except between the main population centres. Zaragoza has a small international airport. Be aware that as Spain has recently changed its road numbering system some of the roads featured here may differ from new road signs.

KEY

═══	Motorway
═ ═	Motorway under construction
▬▬▬	Major road
═══	Minor road
▬▬▬	Scenic route
▭▭▭	Main railway
-----	Minor railway
▬▬▬	International border
▭▭▭	Regional border
△	Summit

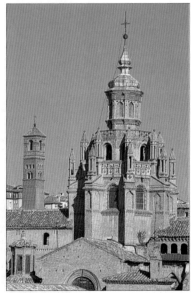

Mudéjar tower of Iglesia de Santa Magdalena, Tarazona

The town hall, Sos del Rey Católico

Sos del Rey Católico ❶

Zaragoza. 🏠 700. 🚌 🛈 *Palacio de Sada, Madrigal de las Altas Torres s/n, 948 88 85 24. Closed Mon–Tue in winter.* 🚌 *Fri.* 🎭 *Fiestas mayores (third Wed of Aug).*

Fernando of Aragón – the so-called "Catholic King" who married Isabel of Castile, thereby uniting Spain (*see pp56–7*) – was born in this small town in 1452, hence its distinguished royal name.

The **Palacio de Sada**, the king's reputed birthplace, with a beautiful inner courtyard, is among the town's grandest stone mansions. It stands in a small square amid a maze of narrow cobbled streets. At the top of the town are the remnants of a castle and the **Iglesia de San Esteban**. The church's font and carved capitals are noteworthy, as are the 13th-century frescoes in two of the crypt's apses. From here there are fine views over the surrounding hills.

The Gothic-arched **Lonja** (commodities exchange) and the 16th-century **town hall** (*ayuntamiento*) are located on the adjacent main square.

Environs
The "Cinco Villas" are five towns recognized by Felipe V for their loyalty during the War of the Spanish Succession (*see p62*). **Sos del Rey Católico** is the most appealing of these. The others are Ejea de los Caballeros, Tauste, Sádaba and **Uncastillo**. This last town, 20 km (12 miles) to the southeast, has a fortress and a Romanesque church, the Iglesia de Santa María.

Los Valles ❷

Huesca. 🚌 *Jaca.* 🚌 *from Jaca to Hecho.* 🛈 *Carretera de Oza, Hecho (ayuntamiento) 974 37 50 02 (in winter); 974 37 55 05 (in summer).*

The delightful valleys of Ansó and Hecho, formed by the Veral and Aragón Subordán rivers respectively, were isolated until recently due to poor road links. Their villages have retained traditional customs and a local dialect called *cheso*, passed down the generations. Now the area's crafts and costumes have made it popular with tourists. The Pyrenean foothills and forests above the valleys are good for walking, fishing and cross-country skiing.

Ansó lies in the prettiest valley, which becomes a shadowy gorge where the Río Veral and the road next to it squeeze between vertical crags and through rock tunnels. Many of its buildings have stone façades and steep, tiled roofs. The Gothic church (16th century) has a museum dedicated to local costume. Pieces of modern sculpture lie scattered beside the tourist information office of **Hecho**, from an open-air festival previously held in the village. The bucolic village of **Siresa**, which contains the 11th-century church of San Pedro, lies to the north of Hecho.

Puerto de Somport ❸

Huesca. 🚌 *Somport, Astun or Jaca.* 🛈 *Pl Ayuntamiento 1, Canfranc, 974 37 31 41 (closed Sun–Mon).*

Just inside the border with France, the Somport Pass was for centuries a strategic crossing point for the Romans and Moors, and for medieval pilgrims en route to Santiago de Compostela (*see pp82–3*). Today the austere scenery is specked with holiday apartments built for skiing. **Astún** is modern and well organized while **El Formigal**, to the east, is a stylish, purpose-built resort. Non-skiers can enjoy the scenery around the Panticosa gorge. **Sallent de Gállego** is popular for rock-climbing and fishing.

Steep, tiled roofs of Hecho, with a typical pepperpot chimney

Rough and craggy landscape around Benasque

Parque Nacional de Ordesa ❹

See pp232–3.

Benasque ❺

Huesca. 🏔 *2,000.* 🛈 *Calle de San Sebastián 5, 974 55 12 89.* 🚌 *Tue.* 🎎 *San Marcial (30 Jun), San Pedro (29 Jun).*

Tucked away in the northeast corner of Aragón, at the head of the Esera valley, the village of Benasque presides over a ruggedly beautiful stretch of Pyrenean scenery. Although the village has expanded greatly to meet the holiday trade, a sympathetic use of wood and stone has resulted in buildings which complement the existing older houses. A stroll through the old centre filled with aristocratic mansions is a delight.

The most striking buildings in Benasque are the 13th-century **Iglesia de Santa María Mayor**, and the **Palacio de los Condes de Ribagorza**. The latter has a Renaissance façade. Above the village rises the Maladeta massif. There are magnificent views from its ski slopes and hiking trails. Several real mountain peaks, including **Posets** and **Aneto**, exceed 3,000 m (9,800 ft).

Environs

For walkers, skiers and climbers, the area around Benasque has a great deal to offer. The neighbouring resort of **Cerler** was developed with care from a rustic village into a popular base for skiing and other winter sports.

At Castejón de Sos, 14 km (9 miles) south of Benasque, the road passes through the **Congosto de Ventamillo**, a scenic rocky gorge.

Aínsa ❻

Huesca. 🏔 *2,000.* 🚌 🛈 *Cruce de Carreteras, Avda Pirinaica 1, 974 50 07 67.* 🚌 *Tue.* 🎎 *San Sebastián (20 Jan), Fiestas Mayores (14 Sep).*

The capital of the kingdom of Sobrarbe in medieval times, Ainsa has retained its charm. The Plaza Mayor, a broad cobbled square, is surrounded by neat terraced arcades of brown stone. On one side stands the belfry of the **Iglesia de Santa María** – consecrated in 1181 – and on the other the restored castle.

Jaca ❼

Huesca. 🏔 *13,000.* 🚉 🚌 🛈 *Plaza de San Pedro 11, 974 36 00 98.* 🚌 *Fri.* 🎎 *La Victoria (first Fri of May), Santa Orosia San Pedro (25–29 Jun).* **www**.jaca.es

Jaca dates back as far as the 2nd century AD. In the 8th century the town bravely repulsed the Moors – an act which is commemorated in the festival of La Victoria – and in 1035 became the first capital of the kingdom of Aragón. Jaca's 11th-century **cathedral**, one of Spain's oldest, is much altered inside. Traces of its original splendour can be seen on the restored south porch and doorway, where carvings depict biblical scenes. The dim nave and chapels are decorated with ornate vaulting and sculpture. A museum of sacred art, in the cloisters, contains a collection of Romanesque and Gothic frescoes and sculptures from local churches. The streets that surround the cathedral form an attractive quarter.

Sculpture in Jaca cathedral

Jaca's only other significant tourist sight is its 16th-century **citadel**, a fort decorated with corner turrets, on the edge of town. Today the town serves as a principal base for the Aragonese Pyrenees.

The arcaded main square of Ainsa with the Iglesia de Santa María

Parque Nacional de Ordesa ❹

Pirineo
Aragonés
Ordesa y
Monte Perdido
Valle de Ordesa
Valle de Bujaruelo

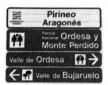

Signpost in Ordesa National Park

Within its borders the Parque Nacional de Ordesa y Monte Perdido combines all the most dramatic elements of Spain's Pyrenean scenery. At the heart of the park are four glacial canyons – the Ordesa, Añisclo, Pineta and Escuain valleys – which carve the great upland limestone massifs into spectacular cliffs and chasms. Most of the park is accessible only on foot: even then, snow during autumn and winter makes it inaccessible to all, except those with specialist climbing equipment. In high summer, however, the crowds testify to the park's well-earned reputation as a paradise for walkers and nature lovers alike.

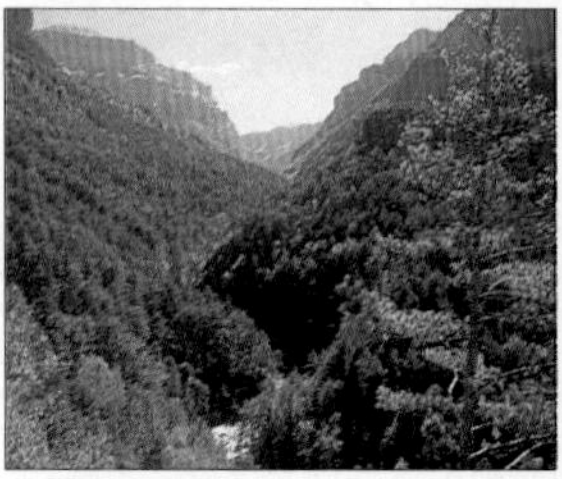

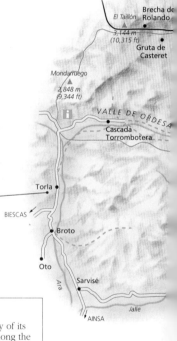

Valle de Ordesa
The Río Arazas cuts through fores limestone escarpments, providing some of Ordesa's most popular wa

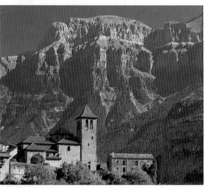

Torla
This village, at the gateway to the park, huddles beneath the forbidding slopes of Mondarruego. With its core of cobbled streets and slate-roofed houses around the church, Torla is a popular base for visitors to Ordesa.

Brecha d
Rolando
El Taillón
3,144 m
(10,315 ft)
Gruta de
Casteret
Mondarruego
2,848 m
(9,344 ft)
VALLE DE ORDESA
Cascada
Torrombotera
Torla
BIESCAS
Broto
Oto
Ara
Sarvisé
AINSA

0 kilometres 2

0 miles

KEY

- Major road
- Minor road
- Footpath
- Spanish/French border
- National park boundary
- Tourist information
- Viewpoint

PYRENEAN WILDLIFE

Ordesa is a spectacle of flora and fauna, with many of its species unique to the region. Trout streams rush along the valley floor, where slopes provide a mantle of various woodland harbouring all kinds of creaturès, including otters, marmots and capercaillies (large grouse). On the slopes, flowers burst out before the snow melts, with gentians and orchids sheltering in crevices and edelweiss braving the most hostile crags.

Higher up, the Pyrenean chamois is still fairly common; but the unique Ordesa ibex, or mountain goat, became extinct in 2000. The rocky pinnacles above the valley are the domain of birds of prey, among them the huge bearded vulture, itself now almost extinct.

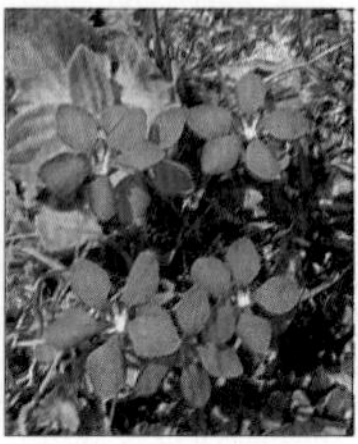

Spring gentian ***(Gentiana verna)***

For hotels and restaurants in this region see pp574–6 and pp624–6

View from Parador de Bielsa

The parador (see p574), at the foot of Monte Perdido, looks out at stunning sheer rock faces streaked by waterfalls.

VISITORS' CHECKLIST

i *Visitors' centre (open all year round), Torla, 974 48 64 72.*
□ *Change at Sabiñánigo for Torla.* **□** *Sabiñánigo.*

Parador de Bielsa

erdido

m
3 ft)

ugio de Góriz

VALLE DE PINETA

Cinca

BIELSA

SIERRA DE LAS TUCAS

scada
la de Caballo

Soaso

Vellos

CAÑÓN DE AÑISCLO

GARGANTA DE ESCUAIN

Revilla

Escuaín

BIELSA

Tella

Nerín

Bestué

Vellos

Puértolas

Cola de Caballo

The 70-m (230-ft) "Horse's Tail" waterfall makes a scenic stopping point near the northern end of the long hike around the Circo Soaso. It provides a taste of the spectacular scenery found along the route.

Hikers in Ordesa National Park

TIPS FOR WALKERS

Several well-marked trails follow the valleys and can be easily tackled by anyone reasonably fit, though walking boots are a must. The mountain routes may require climbing gear so check first with the visitors' centre and get a detailed map. Pyrenean weather changes rapidly – beware of ice and snow early and late in the season. Overnight camping is permitted, but only for a single night above certain altitudes.

ñon or Garganta de Añisclo
*ide path leads along this beautiful, steep-sided
ge, following the wooded course of the turbulent
Vellos through dramatic limestone scenery.*

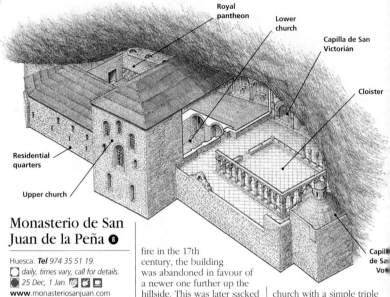

Royal pantheon

Lower church

Capilla de San Victorián

Cloister

Residential quarters

Upper church

Capilla de San Voti

Monasterio de San Juan de la Peña ❽

Huesca. **Tel** 974 35 51 19.
◯ daily, times vary, call for details.
● 25 Dec, 1 Jan. ▥ ▦ ▣
www.monasteriosanjuan.com

Set under a bulging rock, this monastery was an early guardian of the Holy Grail *(see p250)*. In the 11th century it underwent reformation in Cluniac style, and was the first monastery to introduce the Latin Mass in Spain. After a fire in the 17th century, the building was abandoned in favour of a newer one further up the hillside. This was later sacked by Napoleon's troops, although the Baroque façade survives.

The church of the old monastery is on two floors. The lower one is a primitive rock-hewn crypt built in the early 10th century. The upper floor contains an 11th-century church with a simple triple apse hollowed out of the side of the cliff. The well-preserve Romanesque pantheon contains the stacked tombs of the early Aragonese kings. The exterior cloister is San Juan d la Peña's *pièce de résistance*, the capitals of its columns carved with biblical scenes.

Agüero ❾

Huesca. ▨ 160. ▮ San Jaime 1, 974 38 04 89. ▧ San Roque (15–19 Aug).

The picturesque setting of this attractive village, clustered against a dramatic crag of eroded pudding stone, amply rewards a brief detour from the main road. The most important reason for visiting Agüero, however, is to see the 12th-century **Iglesia de Santiago**. This Romanesque church is reached by a long stony track leading uphill just before the village.

The capitals of the columns in this unusual triple-naved building are carved with fantastical beasts as well as scenes from the life of Jesus and the Virgin Mary. The beautiful carvings on the doorway display biblical events, including scenes from the Epiphany and Salome dancing ecstatically. The lively, large-eyed figures are attributed to the mason responsible for the superb carvings in the mon tery at San Juan de la Peña.

Castillo de Loarre ❿

Loarre (Huesca). **Tel** 974 34 21 61
▤ Ayerbe. ▦ from Huesca.
◯ daily. ● 25 Dec, 1 Jan. ▥ ▣

The ramparts of this sturdy fortress stand majestically above the road approachin from Ayerbe. The fortress i so closely moulded around the contours of a rock that night or even in poor visib it could be easily mistaken a natural outcrop. On a cle day, the hilltop setting is stupendous, with clear vie of the surrounding orchar and reservoirs of the Ebro plain. Inside the curtain

Village of Agüero, situated under a rocky crag

walls lies a complex founded some time in the 11th century on the site of what had originally been a Roman settlement. It was later remodelled under Sancho I (Sancho Ramírez) of Aragón, who established a religious community here, placing the complex under the rule of the Order of St Augustine.

Within the castle walls is a Romanesque church with such decorative details as alabaster windows, a chequered frieze and carved capitals.

Sentry paths, iron ladders and flights of steps ramble precariously around the castle's towers, dungeons and keep.

The formidable Castillo de Loarre looming above the surrounding area

Huesca ⓫

Huesca. 50,000. Plaza López Allué, 974 29 21 70. Tue, Thu & Sat. San Vicente (22 Jan); San Lorenzo (9–15 Aug).

...arpiece by Damià Forment, in ...esca cathedral

...unded in the 1st century ..., the independent state of ...ca (present-day Huesca) ...d a senate and an advanced ...ucation system. From the ... century, the area grew into ...Moorish stronghold. In 1096 ...was captured by Peter of ...gón and was the region's ...ital until 1118, when the ...e passed to Zaragoza. ...uesca is now the provincial ...ital. The pleasant old town ...a Gothic **cathedral**. The ...led west front is surmount-...by an unusual wooden ...ery in Mudéjar style. Above ...nave is slender-ribbed star ...ting studded with golden ...es. The cathedral's best ...ure is an alabaster altar-...e by the master sculptor,

Damià Forment. On the altarpiece, a series of energetic Crucifixion scenes in relief are highlighted by illumination.

Opposite the cathedral is the Renaissance **town hall** (*ayuntamiento*). Inside hangs *La Campana de Huesca*, a gory 19th-century painting depicting the town's most memorable event: the beheading of a group of troublesome nobles in the 12th century by order of King Ramiro II. The massacre occurred in the former Palacio de los Reyes de Aragón, later the university and now the superb **Museo Arqueológico Provincial**, containing archaeological finds and a collection of art.

🏛 Museo Arqueológico Provincial
Plaza de la Universidad 1. **Tel** 974 22 05 86. 10am–2pm, 5–8pm Tue–Sat, 10am–2pm Sun & public hols. 1 & 6 Jan, 24, 25, & 31 Dec.

Alquézar ⓬

Huesca. 310. Calle Nueva 14, 974 31 89 40. San Sebastián (20 Jan); San Ipolito (12 Aug).

This moorish village attracts much attention because of its spectacular setting. Its main monument, the stately 16th-century **collegiate church**, dominates a hill jutting above the strange rock formations of the canyon of the Río Vero. Inside, the church's cloisters have capitals carved with biblical scenes. Next to it is the chapel built after Sancho I recaptured Alquézar from the Moors. Nearby are the ruined walls of the original *alcazar*, which gives the village its name.

Santuario de Torreciudad ⓭

Huesca. **Tel** 974 30 40 25. to El Grado from Barbastro. daily.

This shrine was built to honour the devotion of the founder of the Catholic lay order of Opus Dei – San Jose María Escrivá de Balaguer – to the Virgin. It occupies a promontory, with picturesque views over the waters of the **Embalse de El Grado** at Torreciudad. The huge church is made of angular red brick in a stark, modern design.

Inside, the elaborate modern altarpiece of alabaster, sheltering a glittering Romanesque Virgin, is in contrast to the bleak, functional nave.

Environs
The small town of **Barbastro**, which lies 30 km (18 miles) to the south, has an arcaded *plaza mayor* and a 16th-century cathedral with an altar by Damià Forment.

The ruins of Alquézar Castle, rising above the village

Houses with frescoed façades on the Plaza de España, Graus

Graus ⓮

Huesca. 🏘 3,500. 🚊 🛈 Calle Fermin Mur 25, 974 54 61 63. 🚌 Mon. 🎉 Santo Cristo, San Vicente Ferrer (12–15 Sep); Feria de San Miguel (29 Sep).

Concealed in the heart of Graus's old town lies the unusual **Plaza de España**, surrounded by stone arcades and columns. It has brightly frescoed half-timbered houses and a 16th-century city hall. The home of the infamous Tomás de Torquemada, the Inquisitor General (see p56) is in the narrow streets of the "Barrichos", the old quarter. At fiesta time, Graus is a good spot to see Aragonese dancing.

Environs
About 20 km (12 miles) northeast, the hill village of **Roda de Isábena** has the smallest cathedral in Spain. Dating from 1067, this striking building has a 12th-century cloister off which is a chapel with 13th-century frescoes. North of the village is the picturesque Isábena valley.

Tarazona ⓯

Zaragoza. 🏘 11,000. 🚊 🛈 Plaza San Francisco 1, 976 64 00 74. 🚌 (every other Thu. 🎉 San Atilano (27 Aug–1 Sep). www.tarazona.org

Mudejar towers stand high above the earth-coloured, mottled pantiles of this ancient bishopric. On the outskirts of the old town is the **cathedral**, all turreted finials and pierced brickwork with Moorish cloister tracery and Gothic tombs. In the upper town on the

other side of the river, more churches, in typical Mudéjar style, can be found amid the maze of narrow hilly streets. More unusual perhaps are the former bullring, now a circular plaza enclosed by houses, and the splendid Renaissance **town hall** (ayuntamiento). The town hall, built of golden stone, has a façade carved with mythical giants and a frieze showing Carlos V's homage to Tarazona.

Monasterio de Veruela ⓰

Vera de Moncayo (Zaragoza). **Tel** 976 64 90 25. 🚊 Vera de Moncayo. ⏰ Wed–Mon. 🎉 🛇 🛈 by appt.

This isolated Cistercian retreat, set in the green Huecha valley near the Sierra de Moncayo, is one of the greatest monasteries in Aragón. Founded in the 12th century by French monks, the huge abbey church has a mixture of Romanesque and Gothic

features. Worn green and blue Aragonese tiles line the floor of its handsomely vaulted triple nave. The well-preserved cloisters sprout exuberantly decorated beasts, heads of human beings and foliage in the Gothic style (see p24). The plain, dignified chambers make a suitable venue for art exhibitions in the summer.

Environs
In the hills to the west the small **Parque Natural de Moncayo** rises to a height of 2,315 m (7,600 ft). Streams race through the woodland of this nature reserve, which throngs with bird life. A tortuous potholed road leads to a chapel at 1,600 m (5,250 ft).

Zaragoza ⓱

Zaragoza. 🏘 655,000. ✈ 🚊 🚌 🛈 Plaza del Pilar, 902 20 12 12. 🚌 Wed, Sun. 🎉 San Valero (29 Jan); Cincomarzada (5 Mar); San Jorge (23 Apr), Virgen del Pilar (12 Oct). www.zaragozaturismo.es

A Celtiberian settlement called Salduba existed on the site of the present city; but it is from the Roman settlement of Cesaraugusta that Zaragoza takes its name. Its location on the fertile banks of the Río Ebro ensured its ascendancy, now Spain's fifth largest city and the capital of Aragón.

Badly damaged during the War of Independence (see p62), the city was largely rebuilt but the old centre retains some interesting buildings. Most of the main sights are grouped around Plaza del Pilar. The most impresssive

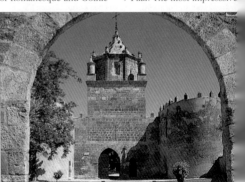

Entrance and tower of the Monasterio de Veruela

them is the **Basílica de Nuestra Señora del Pilar**, with its huge church sporting 11 brightly tiled cupolas. Inside, the Santa Capilla (Lady Chapel) by Ventura Rodríguez contains a small statue of the Virgin on a pillar amid a blaze of silver and flowers. Her skirt-like *manta* is changed every day, and pilgrims pass behind the chapel to kiss an exposed part of the pillar. The basílica also has frescoes by Goya.

Nearby, on the square, stand the **town hall** *(ayuntamiento)*, the 16th century Renaissance **Lonja** (commodities exchange) and the **Palacio Arzobispal**.

Occupying the east end of the square is Zaragoza's cathedral, **La Seo**, displaying a great mix of styles. Part of the exterior is faced with typical Mudéjar brick and ceramic decoration, and inside are a fine Gothic reredos and splendid Flemish tapestries.

Close by is the flamboyant Mudéjar bell tower of the **Iglesia de la Magdalena**, and remains of the Roman forum. Parts of the **Roman walls** can also be seen at the opposite side of the Plaza del Pilar, near the **Mercado de Lanuza**, a market with sinuous ironwork in Art Nouveau style.

Some of the cupolas of the Basílica de Nuestra Señora del Pilar

The **Museo Camón Aznar** in the Pardo's Palace exhibits the eclectic collection of a wealthy local art historian, whose special interest was Goya. The top floor contains a collection of his etchings. Minor works by artists of other periods can be seen, as well as good contemporary art. The **Museo de Zaragoza** has a Goya room and archaeological artifacts.

The **Museo Pablo Gargallo** is a showroom for the Aragonese sculptor after whom it is named, who was active at the beginning of the 20th century. One of the most important monuments in Zaragoza lies on the busy road to Bilbao. The **Aljafería** is an enormous Moorish palace built in the 11th century. A courtyard of lacy arches surrounds a sunken garden and a small mosque.

🏛 **Museo Camón Aznar**
Calle Espoz y Mina 23. *Tel* 976 39 73 28. ⬤ for renovation until 2010.

🏛 **Museo de Zaragoza**
Plaza de los Sitios 6. *Tel* 976 22 21 81. ◻ Tue–Sun. ♿

🏛 **Museo Pablo Gargallo**
Plaza de San Felipe 3. *Tel* 976 72 49 23. ⬤ for renovation until mid–2009.

ZARAGOZA CITY CENTRE

Basílica de Nuestra Señora del Pilar ④
La Seo (Cathedral) ⑦
Lonja ⑥
Mercado de Lanuza ②
Museo Camón Aznar ⑤
Museo Pablo Gargallo ③
Palacio Arzobispal ⑧
Roman walls ①

0 metres 150
0 yards 150

Key to Symbols *see back flap*

Gateway through the medieval walls of Daroca

Calatayud ⑱

Zaragoza. 🏘 21,000. 🚇 🚌
ℹ Plaza del Fuerte, 976 88 63 22.
🗓 Tue. 🎉 San Roque (14–17 Aug),
Virgen de la Peña (6–10 Sep).

The huge Moorish fortress
and minaret-like church towers
are visible from miles around.
Only ruins are left of the 8th-
century Arab castle of the ruler,
Ayub, which gave the town its
name. The church of **Santa
María la Mayor** has a Mudéjar
tower and an elaborate
façade in the Plateresque style.
The 17th-century Baroque-
style church of **San Juan Real**
holds paintings by Goya.
   The ruins of the Roman settlement of Bilbilis are east of
Calatayud, near Huérmeda.

Monasterio de Piedra ⑲

3 km (2 miles) south of Nuévalos.
Tel 902 19 60 52. 🚇 Calatayud. 🚌
from Zaragoza. ◯ daily. 🎬 🎫 ♿
www.monasteriopiedra.com

Built on the site of a Moorish
castle conquered by Alfonso
II of Aragón and given to
Cistercian monks in the 12th

century, this monastery was
damaged in the 19th century
and subsequently rebuilt. Some
of the 12th-century buildings
remain, including the chapterhouse, refectory and hostel.
   In the damp cellars, the
monks once distilled strong
potions of herbal liqueur. This
was allegedly the first place in
Europe where drinking chocolate, from Mexico, was made
(see p59), and there is now a
chocolate exhibition.
   The park in which the monastery stands is a nature reserve
full of grottoes and waterfalls.
A hotel is now located in the
old monastery buildings.

Daroca ⑳

Zaragoza. 🏘 2,300. ℹ Plaza de
España 4, 976 80 01 29. 🗓 Thu.
🎉 Santo Tomás (7 Mar).

An impressive array of battlemented medieval walls
stretches approximately 4 km
(2 miles) around this old Moorish stronghold. Although parts
of the walls have decayed,
some of the 114 towers and
gateways are still a remarkable sight, particularly from
the main road to Zaragoza.
   The **Colegial de Santa
María**, a church in the Plaza
España, houses the Holy Cloths
from the Reconquest (see pp
54–55). After a surprise attack
by the Moors in 1239, priests
celebrating Mass bundled the
consecrated bread into the
linen sheets used for the altar.
Upon being unwrapped, the
cloths were miraculously
stained with blood.

Environs
The agricultural town of
Monreal del Campo, 42 km
(26 miles) south of Daroca,
has a saffron museum. To-
wards Molina de Aragón, 20
km (12 miles) from Daroca,
the **Laguna de Gallo Canta**, a
lake and wildlife refuge.

Fuendetodos ㉑

Zaragoza. 🏘 180. ℹ Cortes de
Aragón 7, 976 14 38 67. 🎉 San
Roque (last Sat of May), San Bartolo
(24 Aug). **www**.fuendetodos.org

This small village was the
birthplace of one of Spain's
best-known artists of the lat

Interior of Goya's cottage in Fuendetodos

Castle-parador above Alcañiz

...8th and early 19th centuries, Francisco de Goya. The **Casa-Museo de Goya** is a neat cottage said to have been the painter's home. It has been restored and furnished in a style appropriate for the period.

Environs

Lying 14 km (9 miles) east of Fuendetodos is **Belchite**, the site of one of the most horrific battles of the Spanish Civil War *(see pp66–7)*, for control of the strategic Ebro valley. Remains of the old, shell-torn town have been left tottering as a monument to the horrors of war.

In **Cariñena**, 25 km (16 miles) west of Fuendetodos, bodegas offer the opportunity to sample and buy the excellent, full-bodied red wine for which the region is justly renowned *(see pp202–3)*.

Casa-Museo de Goya
Calle Zuloaga 3. **Tel** 976 14 38 30.
☐ 11am–2pm, 4–7pm Tue–Sun.

Alcañiz ❷

Teruel. 🏠 16,000. 🚉 ℹ *Calle Mayor 1, 978 83 12 13.* 🗓 *Tue.* 🎉 *Fiestas Patronales (8–13 Sep).*

From a distance, two buildings rise above the town of Alcañiz. One is the **castle**, which was the headquarters of the Order of Calatrava. This historic building has been converted into a parador *(see p574)*. The keep, the Torre del Homenaje, has a collection of 14th-century frescoes depicting the conquest of Valencia by Jaime I.

The other building is the **Iglesia de Santa María**. This church, on the sloping Plaza de España, has a Gothic tower and a Baroque façade.

On the same square are the elegantly galleried **Lonja** (commodities exchange), with its lacy Gothic arches, and the town hall *(ayuntamiento)*, with one Mudéjar and one Renaissance façade.

FRANCISCO DE GOYA

Self-portrait by Goya

Born in Fuendetodos in 1746, Francisco de Goya specialized in designing cartoons for the tapestry industry *(see p306)* in his early life, and in decorating churches such as Zaragoza's Basílica del Pilar with vivacious frescoes. In 1799 he became painter to Carlos IV, and depicted the king and his wife María Luisa with unflattering accuracy *(see p33)*. The invasion of Madrid by Napoleon's troops in 1808 *(see pp62–3)* and its attendant horrors had a profound and lasting effect on Goya's temperament, and his later works are imbued with cynical despair and isolation. He died in Bordeaux in 1828.

ARAGÓN'S FIESTAS

Las Tamboradas
(Maundy Thursday and Good Friday), Teruel province. During Easter Week, brotherhoods of men wearing long black robes beat drums in mourning for Christ. Las Tamboradas begins with "the breaking of the hour" at midnight on Thursday in Híjar. The Tamborada in Calanda begins the following day at midday. The solemn drum rolls continue for several hours. Aching arms and bleeding hands are considered to be signs of religious devotion.

Young drummer in Las Tamboradas, Alcorija

Carnival *(Feb/Mar)*, Bielsa (Huesca). The protagonists of this fiesta, known as *Trangas*, have rams' horns on their heads, blackened faces and teeth made of potatoes. They are said to represent fertility.
Romería de Santa Orosia *(25 Jun)*, Yebra de Basa (Huesca). Pilgrims in folk costume carry St Orosia's skull to her shrine.
Día del Pilar *(12 Oct)*, Zaragoza. Aragón's distinctive folk dance, the *jota*, is performed everywhere during the city's festivities in honour of its patroness, the Virgin of the Pillar *(see p237)*. On the Día del Pilar there is a procession with cardboard giants, and a spectacular display of flowers dedicated to the Virgin.

Alcalá de la Selva Castle, overlooking the town

Valderrobres ㉓

Teruel. 🏠 *2,200.* 🚌 ⓘ *Avda Cortes de Aragón 7, 978 89 08 86.* 🚌 *Sat.* 🎉 *San Roque (mid-Aug).*

Just inside Aragón's border with Catalonia, the town of Valderrobres overlooks the trout-filled Río Matarraña. Dominating the town is the restored **castle**, which was formerly a palace for Aragonese royalty. Below it stands the imposing Gothic **Iglesia de Santa María la Mayor**, with a huge rose window in Catalan Gothic style. The arcaded plaza has a pleasing town hall *(ayuntamiento)* completed in the late 16th century.

Environs
Near Valderrobres is the mountain chain of **La Caixa**. At 14 km (9 miles) are the mountain passes of Beceite.

🏰 **Castillo de Valderrobres**
⬜ *Jul–Sep: Tue–Sun, Oct–Jun: Fri–Sun & public hols.* 🎫 📷

Sierra de Gúdar ㉔

Teruel. 🚌 *Mora de Rubielos.* 🚌 *Alcalá de la Selva.* ⓘ *Plaza de la Iglesia 4, Alcalá de la Selva, 978 80 10 00.*

This range of hills, northeast of Teruel, is a region of pine woods and jagged limestone outcrops erupting from scrub-covered slopes. At 2,028 m (6,653 ft), **Peñarroya** is the highest point. Nearby Valdelinares, Spain's highest village, is a ski station. From the access roads there are panoramic views of the hills. Especially noteworthy are the views from the towns of **Linares de Mora** and **Alcalá**

de la Selva, which has a castle set against a backdrop of rock faces. Its Gothic-Renaissance church, with shell motifs and twisted columns, shelters the shrine of the Virgen de la Vega.

Mora de Rubielos ㉕

Teruel. 🏠 *1,650.* ⓘ *Diputación 2, 978 80 61 32 (summer); 978 80 00 00 (winter).* 🚌 *Mon & Fri.* 🎉 *San Miguel (28 Sep–1 Oct).*

Dominated by one of the best-preserved castles in Aragón, Mora de Rubielos displays the remains of the old walled city with its bridges and a medieval old town. There is a fine 17th century town hall and the **collegiate church** of Santa María.

Environs
Rubielos de Mora, lying 14 km (9 miles) to the southeast, is worth exploring simply for its well-preserved stone and timber buildings. Among the balconied houses is an Augustinian convent with a Gothic reredos.

Teruel ㉖

Teruel. 🚶 *34,000.* 🚌 🚌 ⓘ *Calle San Francisco 1, 978 64 14 61.* 🚌 *Thu.* 🎉 *Día del Sermón de las Tortillas (Tue of Easter week), La Vaquilla del Ángel (mid-Jul), Feria del jamón (mid-Sep).* **http://**turismo.teruel.net

This industrial town has been the scene of much desperate fighting throughout the centuries. It began with the Romans, the first to capture and civilize Celtiberian Turba.

During the Reconquest the town became a strategic frontier prize. In 1171 Alfonso II recaptured Teruel for Christian Spain, but many Muslims continued to live peacefully in the city, which they embellished with beautiful Mudéjar towers. The last mosque was closed only at the height of the Inquisition *(see p274)*, in 1502. More recently, during the terrible, freezing winter of 1937, the bitterest battle of the Civil War *(see pp66–7)* was fought here. There were many thousands of casualties.

The old quarter is home to the wedge-shaped Plaza del Torico, with a monument of

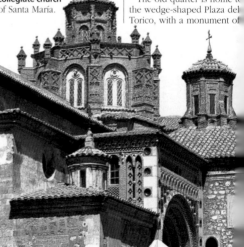

Tiled towers and rooftops of Teruel Cathedral

…alconied café above Albarracín's main square

Many have been restored to their medieval form. Just outside the town are the caves of Navazo and Callejón, with their prehistoric rock paintings. Reproductions can be seen in Teruel's Museo Provincial.

Environs
In the surrounding **Montes Universales**, which rise to 1,935 m (6,348 ft), is the source of the Tagus, one of Spain's longest rivers. From fertile cereal plains to crumbling rocks, this area is a colourful mixture of poplars, junipers and thick pine woods, with poppies in spring. At **Cella**, northeast of Albarracín, the Río Jiloca has its source.

…all bull, the city's emblem. …ithin walking distance lie the …ve remaining Mudéjar towers. …ost striking are those of **San …lvador** and **San Martín**, …oth dating back to the 12th …ntury. The latter has multi-…tterned brickwork studded …th blue and green ceramics. …Beside the **Iglesia de San …dro** are the tombs of the …nous Lovers of Teruel. The …**thedral** has more colourful …déjar work, including a …tern dome of glazed tiles, …d a tower completed in the …h century. The dazzling …fered ceiling is painted with …ly scenes of medieval life.

…he **Museo Provincial**, one …Aragón's best museums, is …sed in an elegant mansion. …as a large collection of ce-…ics, testifying to an industry …which Teruel has long been …wn. North of the centre is …**Acueducto de los Arcos**, a …-century aqueduct.

Museo Provincial
…ay Anselmo Polanco 3. **Tel** 978 …1 50. ☐ Tue–Sun. ☐

pink buildings. Standing on a ridge behind the town are the defensive walls and towers which date from Muslim times.

There is a good view of the town from below the **Palacio Episcopal** (Bishop's Palace). Inside the neighbouring 16th-century **cathedral**, which is topped by a belfry, there is a Renaissance carved wooden altarpiece depicting scenes from the life of St Peter. The treasury museum contains 16th-century Brussels tapestries and enamelled chalices.

Some of Albarracín's sturdy beamed and galleried houses have an unusual two-tier structure. The ground floor is limestone, and the overhanging upper storey is covered in rough coral-pink plasterwork.

Rincón de Ademuz ㉘

Valencia. 🏠 1,200. 🚌 Ademuz.
🛈 Plaza del Ayuntamiento 1, 978 78 20 00. ☐ Wed. 🎉 Fiestas de Agosto (15 Aug), Fiestas de la Virgen del Rosario (early Oct).

This remote enclave south of Teruel belongs to the Comunidad Valenciana (see p243); but is effectively an island of territory, stranded between the borders of Aragón and Castilla-La Mancha. The area has not prospered in recent years, but still has an austere charm and some peaceful tracts of country scattered with red rocks.

…arracín ㉗

…l. 🏠 1,100. 🚌 🛈 Calle …ación 4, 978 71 02 51. ☐ 🎉 Los Mayos (30 Apr–1 May), …s Patronales (8–17 Sep). …w.albarracin.org

…easy to see why this pic-…que town earned an …national award for histor-…reservation. A dramatic …bove the Río Guadalaviar … perfect setting for this …tive cluster of mellow

THE LOVERS OF TERUEL

According to legend, in 13th-century Teruel two young people, Diego de Marcilla and Isabel de Segura, fell in love and wished to marry. She came from a wealthy family, but he was poor, and her parents forbade the match. Diego was given five years in which to make his fortune and establish a name for himself. At the end of this time he returned to Teruel, laden with wealth, only to find his bride-to-be already married to a local nobleman. Diego died of a broken heart and Isabel, full of despair at his death, died the following day.

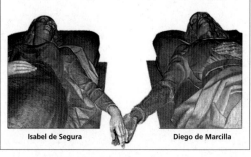

Isabel de Segura   Diego de Marcilla

VALENCIA AND MURCIA

CASTELLÓN · VALENCIA · ALICANTE · MURCIA

Today, the central region of Spain's eastern Mediterranean coast is an important holiday destination – the beaches of the Costa Blanca, the Costa del Azahar and the Costa Cálida draw millions of tourists annually. Centuries ago, Muslim settlers made these regions bloom, and the fertile fields and citrus groves of the coastal plains are still Spain's citrus orchard and market garden.

These productive lands have been occupied for more than 50,000 years. The Greeks, Phoenicians, Carthaginians and Romans all settled here before the Moors arrived, trading the products of land and sea.

The provinces of Castellón, Valencia and Alicante (which make up the Comunidad Valenciana) were reconquered from the Moors by a Catalan army. The language these troops left behind them developed into a dialect, *valenciano*, which is widely spoken and increasingly seen on signposts. Murcia, to the south, is one of Spain's smallest autonomous regions.

The population is concentrated on the coast where the historic towns and cities of Valencia, Alicante and Cartagena have been joined by modern package holiday resorts, such as Benidorm and La Manga del Mar Menor. Inland, where tourism has barely reached, the landscape rises into the chains of mountains that stand between the coast and the plateau of Central Spain. The scenery inland ranges from picturesque valleys and hills in the Maestrat, in the north of Castellón, to the semi-desert terrain around Lorca in southern Murcia.

The warm climate encourages outdoor life and exuberant fiestas. Most famous of these are Las Fallas of Valencia; the mock battles between Moors and Christians staged in Alcoi; and the lavish, costumed Easter processions in Murcia and Lorca.

ll terraces of olive and almond trees ascending the hillsides near Alcoi

he Penyal d'Ifach, rising directly out of the sea to tower above the Costa Blanca near Calp

Exploring Valencia and Murcia

The coasts of Valencia and Murcia are popular for seaside
holidays and ideal for water sports almost all year round.
Principal resorts include Benidorm, Benicassim, La Manga del
Mar Menor and Oropesa. Some coastal towns such as Peñíscola,
Gandía, Denia, Alicante and Cartagena have charming old
quarters, castles and other sites well worth visiting. Close to the
sea are several scenic nature reserves: the freshwater lagoon of
L'Albufera, and, on the Costa Blanca, the saltpans of Santa Pola
and the striking limestone crag of the Penyal d'Ifach.

Inland, the region offers excursions to such undiscovered
beauty spots as El Maestrat and the mountains around Alcoi,
as well as the undervisited historic towns of Xàtiva and Lorca.
The two regional capitals, Valencia and Murcia, are both lively
university cities with fine cathedrals and numerous museums.

Fishing nets strung out in the lagoon of L'Albufera

GETTING AROUND

The region's principal roads are the A7 (AP7) motorway
and the N332 along the coast. Other motorways connect
Valencia with Madrid, A3 (E901), and Alicante with Madrid,
N330 A31. There are main rail lines from Alicante, Valencia
and Murcia to Madrid and Barcelona, but the rest of the rail
network is rather fragmented and buses are often quicker
than trains. A scenic narrow-gauge railway line along the
Costa Blanca connects Denia to Alicante via Benidorm. The
region's international airports are at Alicante and Valencia.
Be aware that as Spain has recently changed its road
numbering system some of the roads featured
here may differ from new road signs.

KEY

▬▬	Motorway
▪▪	Motorway under construction
▬▬	Major road
▬	Secondary road
▬	Scenic route
▬▬	Main railway
—	Minor railway
▬	Regional border
△	Summit

La Balma · La Poble de Benifassà · La Sènia
Forcall
Mirambel
lavieja — **2 MORELLA**
EL MAESTRAT
ranca del Cid — Ares del Maestre — Sant Mateu — Barcelona — Vinaròs
Albocácer — Benicarló
3 PENÍSCOLA
riagolosa 1813m — Alcossebre
Cabanes — Torreblanca
VILLAFAMÉS 5 — Oropesa **4**
za — Alcora — Benicasim — N340
ONDA 7 — **CASTELLÓ 6 DE LA PLANA**
La Val d'Uxio — Burriana
8 COVES DE SANT JOSEP
A23
10 SAGUNT
Pucol
MONASTERIO 11 DE EL PUIG
rna
12 VALENCIA
te
Catarroja
13 L'ALBUFERA
Alginet — Sueca
NQ
Alzira — Cullera
Tavernes de la Valldigna
4 XÀTIVA — **15 GANDÍA**
Oliva
inyent — Pego
Agres
16 DENIA
17 XÀBIA
20 — **19 GUADALEST**
Calp
Callosa d'en Sarrià — Altea
Xixona — **18 PENYAL D'IFACH**
21 BENIDORM
N332 — La Vila Joíosa
El Campello
23 ALICANTE (ALACANT)
Costa Blanca
LCHE)
nta Pola
24 ILLA DE TABARCA
amar del Segura
EVIEJA
R

0 kilometres 25
0 miles 20

E ALSO

Where to Stay pp576–9

Where to Eat pp626–9

COSTA DEL AZAHAR

Lemon groves outside Denia

SIGHTS AT A GLANCE

Alicante (Alacant) ㉓
L'Albufera ⑬
Alcoi ⑳
Alto Turia ⑨
Benidorm ㉑
Caravaca de la Cruz ㉝
Cartagena ㉚
Castelló de la Plana ⑥
Costa del Azahar ④
Costa Cálida ㉛
Coves de Sant Josep ⑧
Denia ⑯
Elx (Elche) ㉕
Gandía ⑮
Guadalest ⑲
Illa de Tabarca ㉔
Lorca ㉜

El Maestrat ①
Mar Menor ㉙
Monasterio de El Puig ⑪
Morella ②
Murcia ㉘
Novelda ㉒
Onda ⑦
Orihuela ㉖
Peñíscola ③
Penyal d'Ifach ⑱
Sagunt ⑩
Torrevieja ㉗
Valencia pp250–53 ⑫
Vilafamés ⑤
Xàbia ⑰
Xàtiva ⑭

Costa Blanca

One of the many coves on Xàbia's rugged coast

The unbroken medieval wall surrounding the historic hilltop town of Morella in El Maestrat

El Maestrat ❶

Castellón & Teruel. 🚌 *Morella.*
ℹ️ *Morella, 964 17 30 32.*

Crusading warlords of the Knights Templar and the Knights of Montesa – known as *maestres* (masters) – gave their name to this lonely upland region. To rule over this frontier land, which straddles the border between Valencia and Aragón, they built fortified settlements in dramatic defensive positions, often on rocky crags. The best preserved of them is **Morella**, the principal town. **Forcall**, not far from Morella, has two 16th-century mansions on its porticoed

The Torre de la Sacristía, in the restored village of Mirambel

square. To the south, the village of **Ares del Maestre** is spectacularly sited beneath a 1,318-m (4,300-ft) high rock.

Cantavieja is the most important town in the Aragonese part of El Maestrat (where it is known as El Maestrazgo). It has a handsome, arcaded square. The walled village of **Mirambel**, nearby, has been meticulously restored to its medieval condition.

There are several spooky but fascinating shrines to the Virgin in El Maestrat, notably the cave of La Balma at **Zorita**, which is reached via a rocky ledge.

The scenery in most parts is striking: fertile valleys alternate with breathtaking cliffs and bare, flat-topped mountains overflown by eagles and vultures. Tourism is developing very slowly here: there are few places to stay and the roads can be windy and slow.

Morella ❷

Castellón. 👥 *2,800.* 🚌 ℹ️ *Plaza de San Miguel, 964 17 30 32.* 📅 *Sun.* 🎉 *Fiestas patronales (mid–late Aug).*

Built on a high, isolated outcrop and crowned by a ruined castle, Morella cuts a dramatic profile. Its unbroken medieval walls retain six gateways, which lead into a fan-shaped maze of streets and

steep, tapering alleys, many of which are shaded by the eaves of ancient houses. The main street is lined with shad[ed] porticoes. In the upper part o[f] town is the **Basílica de Santa María la Mayor**. Its unique raised choirloft is reached by a finely carved spiral staircase

MORELLA'S MIRACLE

A plaque on the wall of Morella's Calle de la Virgen marks the house in which St Vincent Ferrer is said to have performed a bizarre miracle in the early 15th century. A housewife, distraught at having no meat to offer the saint, cut up her son and put him in the cooking pot. When St Vincent discovered this, he reconstituted the boy – except for one of his little fingers, which his mother had eaten to see if the dis[h] was sufficiently salted.

Peñíscola ❸

Castellón. 🏘 7,000. 🚌 ℹ️ *Paseo Marítimo, 964 48 02 08.* 🚌 *Mon.* 🎉 *Fiestas Patronales (2nd week Sep).* **www**.peniscola.org

The fortified old town of Peñíscola clusters around the base of a castle built on a rocky promontory, surrounded on three sides by the sea. This labyrinth of narrow winding streets and white houses is enclosed by massive ramparts. These are entered by either the Fosch Gate – reached by a ramp from the Plaza del Caudillo – or through the San Pedro Gate, from the harbour. Some visitors are drawn to the town because the 1961 Hollywood blockbuster *El Cid* was filmed there.

The **Castell del Papa Luna** was built on the foundations of an Arab fortress in the late 13th century by the Knights Templar. Their cross is carved above the door. It later became the residence of the papal pretender Pedro de Luna, cardinal of Aragón. He was elected Pope Benedict XIII during the Great Schism that split the Catholic Church at the end of the 14th century. Although he was deposed by the Council of Constance in 1414, he continued to proclaim his right to the papacy until his death as a nonagenarian in 1423.

Castell del Papa Luna
Calle Castillo. **Tel** *964 48 00 21.* ☐ *daily.* ● *1 & 6 Jan, 9 Sep, 9 Oct, 25 Dec.* 🎟️ 📷

Sunset view of the beach and old town of Peñíscola

Costa del Azahar ❹

Castellón. 🚆 *Castelló de la Plana.* 🚌 *Castelló de la Plana.* ℹ️ *Castelló de la Plana, 964 35 86 88.*

The "Orange Blossom Coast" of Castellón province is named after the dense citrus groves of the coastal plain. The three principal resorts are Oropesa, Peñíscola and Benicàssim, where handsome old villas have been supplemented by modern hotels and other tourist amenities. Alcossebre also has a popular beach. Vinaròs – the most northerly point – and Benicarló are key fishing ports supplying prawns and date-mussels to local restaurants.

Sculpture in the Casa del Batle

Vilafamés ❺

Castellón. 🏘 1,900. 🚌 ℹ️ *Plaza del Ayuntamiento 2, 964 32 99 70.* 🚌 *Fri.* 🎉 *San Miguel (late Mar), Patronales (mid-Aug).*

This medieval town climbs from a flat plain along a rocky ridge to the restored round keep of its castle. The older, upper part of the town is a warren of sloping streets filled with sturdy houses.

A 15th-century mansion houses the **Casa del Batle**, a museum of contemporary art. The works on display date from 1959 to the present.

🏛 Casa del Batle
Calle Diputación 20. **Tel** *964 32 91 52.* ☐ *Tue–Sun.* 🎟️

Castelló de la Plana's planetarium, close to the beach

Castelló de la Plana ❻

Castellón. 🏘 167,500. 🚌 🚆 ℹ️ *Plaza María Agustina 5, 964 35 86 88.* 🚌 *Mon.* 🎉 *Fiesta de la Magdalena (3rd Sun of Lent).*

Originally founded on high ground inland, the capital of Castellón province was relocated nearer to the coast in the 13th century.

The city centre, the Plaza Mayor, is bordered by the market, the cathedral, the town hall and **El Fadrí**, a 58-m (190-ft) high octagonal bell tower begun in 1590 and finished in 1604.

The **Museo Provincial de Bellas Artes** contains a collection of artifacts dating from the middle Palaeolithic era, paintings from the 14th to the 19th centuries and modern ceramics from the region. Most of the older works come from the nearby convents, because the government seized many church possessions during the 19th century. An important collection of paintings that are attributed to Francisco de Zurbarán are also on display here.

In **El Planetario** there are demonstrations of the night sky, the solar system and the nearest stars. Two rooms hold temporary exhibits.

🏛 Museo Provincial de Bellas Artes
Avda Hermanos Bou 28. **Tel** *964 72 75 00.* ☐ *10am–8pm Tue–Sat, 10am–2pm Sun.* 🚻 🎟️ *by appt.* 📷

🔭 El Planetario
Paseo Marítimo 1, El Grao. **Tel** *964 28 29 68.* ☐ *11am–2pm, 4:30–8pm Tue–Sat, 11am–2pm Sun.* ● *Sep.* 🎟️ *(planetarium).* 🚻

Onda ❼

Castellón. 🏛 24,000. 🚌 ℹ️
Calle la Cossa, 964 60 28 55.
🚏 *Thu.* 🎉 *Feria del Santísimo
Salvador (6 Aug).*

Onda, home to a thriving
ceramics industry, is overlooked by a ruined **castle**,
which was known to its
Moorish founders as the
"Castle of the Three Hundred
Towers". The castle houses a
museum of local history.

However, the main reason
to visit Onda is to take a
look at the **Museo de Ciencias
Naturales El Carmen**, a natural
history museum belonging to
a Carmelite monastery.

The collection was begun in
1952 by the monks for their
own private scientific study.
It was only opened to the
public a decade later. The
clever use of subdued lighting
lends dramatic effect to the
10,000 plant and animal
specimens which are
exhibited over three floors.
Objects include large stuffed
animals placed in naturalistic
settings, butterflies and other
insects, shells, fossils, minerals
and grisly, preserved
anatomical specimens.

🏛 **Museo de Ciencias
Naturales El Carmen**
Carretera de Tales. **Tel** 964 60 07 30.
⏰ *Tue –Sun.* ⚫ *20 Dec–6 Jan.* 🎫

Two butterfly exhibits in the Museo
El Carmen

**Boat ride through the winding
Coves de Sant Josep**

Coves de
Sant Josep ❽

Vall d'Uixó (Castellón). **Tel** *964 69
05 76.* 🚌 *Vall d'Uixó.* ⭕ *daily.*
⚫ *25 Dec, 1 & 6 Jan* 🎫

The caves of St Joseph were
first explored in 1902. The
subterranean river that formed
them, and which still flows
through them, has been chart-
ed for almost 3 km (2 miles).
However, its source has not
yet been discovered and only
part of this distance can be
explored on a visit.

Boats take visitors along the
serpentine course of the river.
You may have to duck to avoid
projections of rock on the way.
Sometimes the narrow caves
open out into large chambers
such as the *Sala de los Murcié-
lagos* (Hall of the Bats – the
bats left when the floodlights
were installed). The water is at
its deepest – 12 m (39 ft) – in
the *Lago Azul* (Blue Lake). You
can explore a further 250 m
(820 ft) along the *Galería
Seca* (Dry Gallery) on foot.
The caves are often closed to
visitors after heavy rain.

Alto Turia ❾

Valencia. 🚌 *Chelva.* ℹ️ *CV35
Valencia–Ademúz km 73, 96 163 50 84.*

The attractive wooded hills of
the upper reaches of the Río
Turia in Valencia (Alto Turia)
are popular with hikers and
day-trippers. **Chelva**, the main
town, has an unusual clock
on its church, which shows

not only the hour but the day
and month as well. The town
is overlooked by the **Pico del
Remedio** (1,054 m/ 3,458 ft),
from the summit of which
there is a fine panoramic view
of the region. In a valley near
Chelva, at the end of an
unsurfaced but drivable track,
are the remains of a Roman
aqueduct, **Peña Cortada**.

The most attractive and interesting village in Alto Turia is
Alpuente, situated above a dry
gorge. Between 1031 and 1089
when it was captured by El
Cid *(see p370)*, Alpuente was
the capital of a small *taifa*, a
Moorish kingdom. In the 14th
century it was still important
enough for the kingdom of
Valencia's parliament to meet
here. The town hall is confined to a small tower over a
14th-century gateway, which
was later extended in the 16th
century by the addition of a
rectangular council chamber.

Requena, to the south is
Valencia's main wine town.
Further south, Valencia's other
principal river, the Xúquer
(Júcar), carves tremendous
gorges near Cortes de Pallás
on its way past the **Muela de
Cortes**. This massive, wild
plateau and nature reserve is
crossed by one small road
and a lonely dirt track.

LA TOMATINA

The highpoint of the annual
fiesta in Buñol (Valencia) is a
sticky food fight on the last
Wednesday of August, which
attracts thousands of visitors
dressed in their worst clothes.
Lorry loads of ripe tomatoes
are provided by the town
council at 11am for
participants to hurl at each
other. No one in range of
combatants is spared:
foreigners and photographers
are prized targets.

The battle originated in
1944. Some say it began with
a fight between friends.
Others say irreverent locals
pelted civic dignitaries with
tomatoes during a procession.
Increasing national and
international press coverage
means that more people
attend, and more tomatoes are
thrown, every year.

Sagunt's ruined fortifications, added to by successive rulers of the town

Iberians, the Carthaginians, the Romans and the Moors. The ruins of the castle are divided into seven divisions, the highest being La Ciudadella, and the most important Armas.

♦ **Castillo de Sagunt**
○ *Tue–Sun.*

Monasterio de El Puig ⓫

El Puig (Valencia). *Tel* 96 147 02 00. ▦ ▤ *El Puig.* ○ *Tue–Sat.* 🈺 🈯 only, 10 & 11am, noon, 4 & 5pm.

This Mercedarian monastery was founded by King Jaime I of Aragón, who conquered Valencia from the Moors in the 13th century. The monastery is now home to a collection of paintings from between the 16th and 18th centuries and the Museo de la Imprenta y de la Obra Gráfica (Museum of Printing and Graphic Art). The museum commemorates the printing of the first book in Spain – thought to have been in Valencia in 1474 – and illustrates the development of the printing press. Exhibits include printers' blocks and a copy of the smallest printed book in the world.

Sagunt ⓰

Valencia. 🏛 64,000. ▦ ▤ ◻ Pl Cronise Chabret, 96 266 22 13. ▤ Wed. 🎆 Fallas (15–19 Mar), Fiestas end Jul–Aug).

Sited near the junction of two Roman roads, Sagunt (Sagunto) played a crucial role in Spain's ancient history. In 219 BC Hannibal, the Carthaginian commander in southern Spain, stormed and sacked Rome's ally Saguntum. All the inhabitants of the town were said to have died in the assault, the last throwing themselves on to bonfires rather than fall into the hands of Hannibal's troops. The incident sparked off the Second Punic War, a disaster for the

Carthaginians, which ended with Rome's occupation of the peninsula *(see pp50–1)*.

The town still contains several reminders of the Roman occupation, including the 1st-century AD **Roman theatre**. Built out of limestone in a natural depression on the hillside above the town, it has been controversially restored using modern materials. The theatre is now used as a venue for music, plays and Sagunt's annual theatre festival.

The ruins of the **castle**, sprawling along the crest of the hill above the modern-day town, mark the original site of Saguntum. Superimposed on each other are the excavated remains of various civilizations, including the

Messy participants throwing tomatoes at each other in the annual fiesta of La Tomatina

Valencia ⑫

Spain's third largest city is sited in the middle of the *huerta*: a fertile plain of orange groves and market gardens, which is one of Europe's most intensively farmed regions. With its warm coastal climate, Valencia is known for its exuberant outdoor living and nightlife. In March the city stages one of Spain's most spectacular fiestas, Las Fallas *(see p255)*, in which giant papier-mâché sculptures are burned in the streets. Modern Valencia is a centre for trade and manufacturing, notably ceramics. A ferry service connects the city with the Balearic Islands.

Flowers in honour of Valencia's patroness, Virgen de los Desamparados

Exploring Valencia

Valencia stands on the course of the Río Turia. The city centre and the crumbling old quarter of El Carmen are on the right bank. Most of the monuments are within walking distance of the Plaza del Ayuntamiento, the triangular main square, which is presided over by the town hall.

The city was founded by the Romans in 138 BC and later conquered by the Moors. It was captured by El Cid *(see p370)* in 1096, retaken by the Moors, and finally recaptured by Jaime I, the Conqueror, in 1238, to become absorbed into the kingdom of Aragón.

The three finest buildings in Valencia were built during its economic and cultural heyday in the 14th and 15th centuries: the Torres de Serranos, a gateway that survived the demolition of the medieval walls in the 19th century, La Lonja and the cathedral.

🏛 Palau de la Generalitat

Plaza de Manises. *Tel 96 386 34 61.*
◯ *Mon–Thu and by prior appt only.*
This palace, which is now used by the Valencian regional government, was built in Gothic style between 1482 and 1579 but added to in the 17th and 20th centuries. It surrounds an enclosed stone patio from

which two staircases ascend to splendidly decorated rooms.

The larger of the two Salas Doradas (Golden Chambers), on the mezzanine level, has a multicoloured coffered ceiling and tiled floor. The walls of the parliament chamber are decorated with frescoes.

⛪ Basílica de la Virgen de los Desamparados

Pl de la Virgen. *Tel 96 391 86 11.*
◯ *7:20am–2pm, 4:30pm–9pm daily.*
The ornately dressed statue of Valencia's patroness, the Virgin of the Helpless, stands above an altar in this 17th-century church, lavishly adorned with flowers and candles. She is honoured during Las Fallas by La Ofrenda ("the Offering"), a display of flowers in the square outside the church.

⛪ Cathedral

Plaza de la Reina *Tel 96 391 81 27.*
◯ *Nov–Mar 7:30am–8:30pm daily.*
Museo ◯ *daily (except Sun pm).*
Miguelete ◯ *daily.* 🎫 🔵 *2–5pm Sun.* 🎫 *daily (except Sun pm in winter)*
Built originally in 1262, the cathedral has been added to over the ages, and its three doorways are all in different styles. The oldest is the Romanesque Puerta del Palau but the main entrance is the 18th-century Baroque portal, the Puerta de los Hierros.

A unique court meets on Thursdays at noon in front of the other doorway, the Gothic Puerta de los Apóstoles. For an estimated 1,000 years, the Water Tribunal has settled disputes between farmers over irrigation in the *huerta*.

The Miguelete, the cathedral's bell tower on Plaza de la Reina

Inside the cathedral, a chapel holds an agate cup, claimed to be the Holy Grail. According to legend it arrived in Valencia from Jerusalem by way of San Juan de la Peña monastery in Aragón *(see p234)*.

The cathedral's bell tower, the **Miguelete**, is Valencia's main landmark. The cathedral also houses a museum.

La Lonja

Plaza del Mercado. **Tel** *96 352 54 78 ext. 4153.* ◯ *Tue –Sun.*

An exquisite Late Gothic hall, built between 1482 and 1498 as a commodities exchange, La Lonja now hosts cultural events. The outside walls are decorated with gargoyles and other grotesque figures. The high ceiling of the transactions hall is formed by star-patterned vaulting, which is supported on graceful spiral columns.

Mercado Central

Plaza del Mercado 6. **Tel** *96 382 91 00.* ◯ *8am–3pm Mon–Sat.*

This huge iron, glass and tile Art Nouveau building, with its parrot and swordfish weather-

Ornate toilet sign outside Valencia's Mercado Central

vanes, opened in 1928 and is one of the largest and most attractive markets in Europe. Every morning its 350 or so stalls are filled with a bewildering variety of food.

Museo Nacional de Cerámica Gonzalez Martí

Poeta Querol 2. **Tel** *96 351 63 92.* ◯ *Tue–Sun.* ● *1 Jan, 1 May, 24, 25 & 31 Dec.* (free Sat pm & Sun).

Spain's Ceramics Museum is housed in the mansion of the Marqués de Dos Aguas, an 18th-century fantasy of coloured plasterwork. The

VISITORS' CHECKLIST

Valencia. 🚗 798,000. ✈ 8 km (5 miles) SW. 🚉 C/ Játiva 24, 902 24 02 02. 🚌 Avda Menéndez Pidal 13, 96 346 62 66. 🚢 96 367 43 91. 🛈 Plaza de la Reina 19, 963 15 39 31. 🏬 Mon–Sat. 🎉 Las Fallas (15–19 Mar). **www**.comunidadvalenciana.com

doorway is edged by a carving by Ignacio Vergara. The 5,000 exhibits include prehistoric, Greek and Roman ceramics and pieces by Picasso.

Colegio del Patriarca

Calle Nave 1. **Tel** *96 351 41 76.* ◯ *11am–1:30pm daily.*

This seminary was built in 1584. The walls and ceiling of the church are covered with frescoes by Bartolomé Matarana. During Friday morning Mass, the painting above the altar, *The Last Supper* by Francisco Ribalta, is lowered to reveal a sculpture of the crucifixion by an anonymous 15th-century German artist.

VALENCIA CITY CENTRE

Basílica de la Virgen de los Desamparados ②
Cathedral ③
Centre Cultural la Beneficència ⑫
Colegio del Patriarca ⑦
Estación del Norte ⑬
Instituto Valenciano de Arte Moderno (IVAM) ⑪
Jardines del Río Turia ⑧
La Lonja ④
Mercado Central ⑤
Museo Nacional de Cerámica Gonzalez Martí ⑥
Museo de Bellas Artes ⑨
Palau de la Generalitat ①
Torres de Serranos ⑩

0 metres 250
0 yards 250

Key to Symbols *see back flap*

The Palau de la Música, Valencia's prestigious concert hall

Beyond the Centre

The centre of the city is bordered by the Gran Vía Marqués del Túria and the Gran Vía Ramón y Cajal. Beyond these lie the 19th-century suburbs laid out on a grid plan.

The best way to get around beyond the centre is by the metro, one line of which is a tramway to the beaches of El Cabañal and La Malvarrosa.

⚜ Jardines del Río Túria

Where once there was a river there is now a 10-km (6-mile) long strip of gardens, sports fields and playgrounds crossed by 19 bridges. In a prominent position above the riverbed stands the Palau de la Música, an international-class concert hall built in the 1980s. The centrepiece of the nearby children's playground is the giant figure of Gulliver pinned to the ground and covered with steps and slides. Jardín de Cabecera is a new garden that aims to recreate the Túria River's original landscape.

Ecce Homo by Juan de Juanes in the Museo de Bellas Artes

With particular emphasis placed on water, the garden on the former riverbed has a lake, beach, waterwheel, waterfall and riverside wood.

The best of Valencia's other public gardens stand near the banks of the river. The largest of them, the Jardines del Real – known locally as Los Viveros – occupy the site of a royal palace which was torn down in the Peninsular War. The Jardín Botánico, created in 1802, is planted with 7,000 species of shrubs and trees.

🏛 Museo De Bellas Artes

Museo San Pio V, Calle San Pio V 9. **Tel** 96 387 03 00. ◯ 10am–8pm Tue–Sun. ● 1 Jan, Good Fri, 25 Dec. ♿ 🅿

An important collection of 2,000 paintings and statues dating from the 14th to the 19th centuries is housed in this former seminary, which was built between 1683 and 1744.

Valencian art dating from the 14th and 15th centuries is represented by a series of golden altarpieces by Alcanyis, Pere Nicolau and Maestro de Bonastre. Velázquez's self-portrait and works by Bosch, El Greco, Murillo, Ribalta, Van Dyck and the local Renaissance painter Juan de Juanes hang on the first floor. On the top floor there are six paintings by Goya and others by important 19th- and 20th-century Valencian artists: Ignacio Pinazo, Joaquín Sorolla and Antonio Muñoz Degrain. A large collection of the latter's hallucinatory coloured paintings are gathered together in one room, among them the disturbing *Amor de Madre*.

⚓ Torres de Serranos

Plaza de los Fueros. **Tel** 96 391 90 70. ◯ Tue–Sun. ▨ (free Sun).

Erected in 1391 as a triumphal arch in the city's walls, this gateway combines defensive and decorative features. Its two towers are crowned with battlements and lightened by delicate Gothic tracery.

🏛 Instituto Valenciano de Arte Moderno (IVAM)

Calle Guillem de Castro 118. **Tel** 96 386 30 00. ◯ 10am–8pm Tue–Sun. ▨ (free Sun). 🎫 by appointment. ▨ 🖥 ♿ www.ivam.es

The Valencian Institute of Modern Art is one of Spain's most highly respected spaces for displaying contemporary art. The core of its permanent collection is formed by the work of Julio Gonzalez, one of the most important sculptors of the 20th century. All art forms are represented in its temporary exhibitions, with an emphasis on photography and photomontage. One of the eight galleries, Sala Muralles, incorporates a stretch of the old city walls.

Art Nouveau-style column in the Estación del Norte

🚂 Estación del Norte

Calle Játiva 24. **Tel** 963 52 85 73. ◯ daily.

Valencia's mainline railway station was built from 1906 in a style inspired by Austri Art Nouveau. The exterior i decorated with orange and orange blossom flower mot whilst inside, ceramic mura and stained glass in the foy and cafeteria depict the life and crops of the *huerta* an L'Albufera (*see p254*).

The hemispherical IMAX cinema at the Ciutat de les Arts i de les Ciències

🏛 Ciutat de les Arts de les Ciències

Avenida Autovia del Saler 1–7. **Tel** 90 210 00 31. ⬤ 10am–7pm daily (to 9pm 1 Jul–15 Sep). 🅿 🛈 📷 ♿ www.cac.es

The futuristic complex of the City of Arts and Sciences stands at the seaward end of the Río Túria gardens. It is made up of five stunning buildings, four of them designed by Valencian architect Santiago Calatrava.

The Palau de les Arts, the final building to be added to the complex, has a concert hall with four performance spaces including an open-air theatre. On the other side of the Puente de Monteolivete is Hemisfèric, an architectural icon by Calatrava on the theme of vision, consisting of a blinking eye. The "eyeball" is an auditorium equipped as an IMAX cinema and planetarium. Next to this is the Museu de les Ciències Príncipe Felipe, a science museum contained within a structure of glass and gleaming white steel arches. The displays inside are mainly geared towards visiting school parties. Opposite the museum is l'Umbracle, a giant pergola of parabolic arches covering the complex's car park.

The last part of the "city" is an aquarium, the Oceanogràfic, designed by architect Felix Candela as a series of lagoons and pavilions linked up by bridges and tunnels.

🏛 Museo de Historia de Valencia

Calle Valencia 42, Mislata. **Tel** 963 701 105. ⬤ Tue–Sun. 📷 (free Sat, Sun). ♿

Valencia's history museum is housed in the 19th-century cistern, which used to supply the city with water, now an atmospherically-lit labyrinth of brick, pillars and arches. The displays tell the story of the city's development, as experienced by ordinary people, from its foundations by the Romans to the present day. In each section there is a "time machine", a full-sized screen on which a typical scene of daily life is reproduced in the language of the visitor's choice.

El Cabañal and La Malvarrosa Beaches

To the east of the city, the beaches of El Cabañal and La Malvarrosa are bordered by a broad and lively esplanade about 2 km (1 mile) long. Although these two former fishermen's districts were carelessly developed in the 1960s and 1970s, they retain some quaint, traditional houses tiled on the outside to keep them cool in summer. The light of La Malvarrosa inspired the Impressionist painter Joaquín Sorolla (see p305). The Paseo de Neptuno, near the port, is lined with restaurants, many of which specialize in paella.

Environs

The intensively farmed plain of the *huerta* is a maze of fields planted with artichokes and *chufas*, the raw ingredient of *horchata*.

Manises, near the airport, is renowned for its ceramics, which are sold in shops and factories. There is also a ceramics museum.

VALENCIA'S SUMMER SPECIALITY

In summer, the bars and cafés of Valencia offer a thirst-quenching drink unique to the area. *Horchata*, a sweet, milky drink produced mainly in the nearby town of Alboraia, is made from *chufas* (earth almonds). It is served semi-frozen or in liquid form and usually eaten with *fartons* – soft, sweet bread sticks – or *rosquilletas* – crunchy biscuit sticks. The oldest *horchatería* in the city centre is Santa Catalina, off the Plaza de la Virgen.

Painted tiles showing woman serving *horchata*

Fishing boats on the shore of the freshwater lake, L'Albufera

L'Albufera ⑬

Valencia. 🚌 ℹ️ *Carretera del Palmar, Raco de l'Olla, 96 162 73 45.*

A freshwater lake situated on the coast just south of Valencia, L'Albufera is one of the prime wetland habitats for birds in Eastern Spain.

It is cut off from the sea by a wooded sandbar, the Dehesa, and fringed by a network of paddy fields, which produce a third of Spain's rice.

L'Albufera is fed by the Río Turia and connected to the sea by three channels, which are fitted with sluice gates to control the water level. The lake reaches a maximum depth of 2.5 m (8 ft), and is gradually shrinking because of natural silting and the reclamation of land. In the Middle Ages the lake encompassed an area over ten times its present size.

Over 250 species of birds – including large numbers of egrets and herons – have been recorded in the lake's reed beds and marshy islands, the *matas*. L'Albufera was declared a nature reserve in 1986 to protect its birdlife. Many birds can be seen with binoculars from the shores of the lake.

A visitors' centre at Raco de l'Olla provides information on the ecology of lake, the paddy fields and the Dehesa.

Xàtiva ⑭

Valencia. 👥 *29,000.* 🚌 🚍 ℹ️ *Alameda de Jaime I 50, 96 227 33 46.* 🚌 *Tue & Fri.* 🎆 *Las Fallas (16– 19 Mar); Fira de agosto (14–20 Aug).*

Along the narrow ridge of Mount Vernissa, above Xàtiva, run the ruins of a once-grand **castle** of 30 towers. It was largely destroyed by Felipe V in the War of the Spanish Succession *(see p62)*. Felipe also set fire to the town, which continues to wreak its revenge in an extraordinary way – by hanging Felipe's full-length portrait upside down in the **Museo Municipal**.

Until the attack, Xàtiva was the second town of the kingdom of Valencia. It is thought

Felipe V's full-length portrait hanging upside down in Xàtiva

to have been founded by the Iberians. Under the Moors it became prosperous, and in the 12th century it was the firs European city to make paper

Among the sights in the streets and squares of the old town are a former hospital with a Gothic–Renaissance façade, and a Gothic fountain in the Plaça de la Trinidad.

The oldest church in Xàtiva is the **Ermita de San Feliú** (Chapel of St Felix) on the road up to the fortress. It dates from around 1262 and is hung with a number of 14th- to 16th-century icons.

⚓ **Castillo de Xàtiva**
Subida del Castillo. **Tel** *96 227 42 74.* ⭘ *Tue–Sun.* 🎫

🏛 **Museo Municipal**
Carrer de la Corretgeria 46. **Tel** *96 227 65 97.* ⭘ *Tue–Sun.* 🎫 ♿

Gandía ⑮

Valencia. 👥 *78,000.* 🚌 🚍 ℹ️ *Calle Marqués de Campo, 96 287 88.* 🚌 *Thu, Sat.* 🎆 *Las Fallas (16– 19 Mar).* **www.**gandiaturismo.cc

In 1485, Rodrigo Borja (wh became Pope Alexander VI was granted the title of Du of Gandía. He founded the Borgia clan and, together v his children, was later impl ed in murder and debauch

For hotels and restaurants in this region see pp576–9 and pp626–9

Rodrigo's great-grandson later redeemed the family name by joining the Jesuit order. He was canonized as St Francis Borja by Pope Clement X in 1671.

The house in which he was born and lived, the **Palau Ducal** (Duke's Palace), is now owned by the Jesuits. Its simple Gothic courtyard belies the richly decorated chambers within, especially the Baroque Golden Gallery. The small patio has a tiled floor depicting the four elements of earth, air, fire and water.

🏛 Palau Ducal
Duc Alfons el Vell 1. **Tel** 96 287 14 65. ⭕ daily. 🈹 🎫

The ornate and gilded interior of the Palau Ducal, Gandía

Denia 🔟

Alicante. 🏠 42,500. 🚉 🚌 🚢 🛈 Plaza Oculista Buigues 9, 96 642 23 67. 🚢 Mon, Fri. 🎉 Fiestas Patronales (early Jul). **www**.denia.net

This town was founded as a Greek colony. It takes its name from the Roman goddess Diana – a temple in her honour was excavated here. In the 11th century it became the capital of a short-lived Muslim kingdom, whose dominion extended from Andalusia to the Balearic Islands. It is now a fishing port and holiday resort. The town centre spreads around the base of a hill. A large **castle**, once an Arab fortress, on its summit overlooks the harbour. The entrance gate, the Portal de la Vila, survives, but it was altered in the 17th century.

The Palacio del Gobernador (Governor's House), within the castle, contains an archaeological museum, which shows the development of Denia from 200 BC to the 18th century.

North of the harbour is the sandy beach of Las Marinas. To the south is the rocky and less developed Las Rotas beach, which is good for snorkelling.

🏰 Castillo de Denia
Calle San Francisco. **Tel** 96 642 06 56. ⭕ daily. ⬤ 1 Jan, 25 Dec. 🈹 🈳

Xàbia 🔟

Alicante. 🏠 30,000. 🚉 🛈 Plaza de la Iglesia 6, 96 579 43 56. 🚢 Thu. 🎉 San Juan (24 Jun), Moros Y Cristianos (third weekend of Jul), Bous a la Mar (first week of Sep). **www**.xabia.org

Pirates and smugglers once took advantage of the hiding places afforded by the cliffs, caves, inlets and two rocky islands along Xàbia's coastline.

The town centre is perched on a hill a short way inland, on the site of an Iberian walled settlement. Many of the buildings lining its streets are made from the local Tosca sandstone. The 16th-century **Iglesia de San Bartolomé** was fortified to serve its congregation as a refuge in times of invasion. It has openings over the door through which missiles could be dropped on to attackers.

The seafront at Cabo de San Antonio is overlooked by ruined 17th- and 18th-century windmills, and the beaches are free of the high-rise apartment blocks that spoil many resorts.

Entrance to the Gothic Iglesia de San Bartolomé in Xàbia

The ceremonial burning of Las Fallas on St Joseph's Day

VALENCIA AND MURCIA'S FIESTAS

Las Fallas (15–19 Mar). Huge papier-mâché monuments (fallas) are erected in the crossroads and squares of Valencia around 15 March and ceremonially set alight on the night of the 19th, St Joseph's Day. Costing thousands of euros each, the fallas depict satirical scenes. During the fiesta, the city echoes to the sound of fire crackers.

Good Friday, Lorca (Murcia). The "blue" and "white" brotherhoods compete to outdo each other in pomp and finery during a grand procession of biblical characters.

Moors and Christians (21–24 Apr), Alcoi (Alicante). Two costumed armies march into the city, where they perform ceremonies and fight mock battles in commemoration of the Reconquest.

Bous a la Mar (early Jul), Denia (Alicante). People dodge bulls on the quay until one or the other falls into the sea (see p39).

Misteri d'Elx (11–15 Aug), Elx (Alicante). This choral play, in the Iglesia de Santa María, has spectacular special effects.

La Tomatina (last Wed of Aug), Buñol (Valencia). Thousands of participants pelt each other with ripe tomatoes (see pp248–9).

The Costa Blanca

Less hectic than the Costa del Sol *(see pp472–3)* and with warmer winters than the Costa Brava *(see p217),* the Costa Blanca occupies a prime stretch of Spain's Mediterranean coastline. Alicante, with its airport and mainline railway station, is the arrival and departure point for most tourists. Between Alicante and Altea there are long stretches of sandy beach, which have been heavily built up with apartment blocks and hotels. North of Altea there are more fine beaches, but they are broken by cliffs and coves. South from Alicante, as far as the resort of Torrevieja, the scenery is drier and more barren, relieved only by the wooded sand dunes of Guardamar del Segura.

Gandía marks the southern end of the Costa de Valencia, whose extensive beaches of fine sand and shallow water are popular with the Spanish.

Denia's Las Marinas beach is a flat, sandy strip lined by hotels. The rocky Les Rotes beach is good for snorkelling.

Xàbia's busiest beach is El Arenal. Most of the resort's coastline is punctuated by cliffs and coves.

Altea is a resort with an unspoiled, whitewashed old town on a hilltop. Beneath it is a long, shingle beach.

Santa Pola *is still a working fishing port, but its long, sandy beaches are very popular.*

Benidorm's liveliest beach, Levante, is considered to be one of the ten best beaches in the world. Poniente is further from the town centre.

Platja de Sant Joan has a long strip of seamless sand bordered by a road and a narrow-gauge railway, which gives easy access to the beach.

The Illa de Tabarca attracts day-trippers for its natural beauty and clear waters, good for snorkelling.

Guardamar del Segura has one of the coast's least busy beaches. It is bordered by windswept sand dunes covered with aromatic pine woods.

Torrevieja is a very popular package holiday resort with sweeping, sandy beaches to the south. It has been highly developed in recent years.

Alicante's *city centre is served by the popular Postiguet beach. Nearby are vast, sandy beaches, such as La Albufereta and Sant Joan.*

Map labels: Gandia, Oliva, Denia, Xàbia, Moraira, Calp, Altea, Benidorm, La Vila Joiosa, El Campello, Platja de Sant Joan, Alacant (Alicante), Santa Pola, Illa de Tabarca, Guardamar del Segura, Torrevieja

0 kilometers   25
0 miles   25

Penyal d'Ifach ⑱

Alicante, Calp. 🚌 Calp. 🚌 Calp.
🅸 Avda de los Ejércitos Españoles
44, Calp, 96 583 69 20.

When viewed from afar,
the rocky outcrop of the
Penyal d'Ifach seems to rise
vertically out of the sea. One
of the Costa Blanca's most
dramatic sights, this 332-m
(1,089-ft) tall block of limestone looks virtually unclimb-
able. However, a short tunnel,
built in 1918, allows walkers
access to the much gentler
slopes on its seaward side.

Allow about two hours for
the round trip, which starts at
the visitors' centre above Calp
harbour. It takes you up gentle
slopes covered with juniper
and fan palm, with the waves
crashing below. As you climb,
and at the exposed summit,
there are spectacular views of
a large stretch of the Costa
Blanca. On a clear day you can
see the hills of Ibiza (see p510).

The Penyal d'Ifach is also
home to 300 types of wild
plant, including several rare
species. Migrating birds use it
as a landmark, and the salt
flats below it are an important
habitat for them. The rock
was privately owned until
1987, when the regional
government acquired it and
turned it into a nature reserve.
Situated below the rock is
the Iberian town of Calp, renowned for its beaches.

Guadalest ⑲

Alicante. 👥 200. 🅸 Avenida de
Alicante, 96 588 52 98. 🎉 Fiestas de
Jóvenes (1st week of Jun), Virgen
la Asunción (14–17 Aug).

Despite drawing coach loads
of day-trippers from Benidorm, the pretty mountain
village of Castell de Guadalest
remains relatively unspoiled.
This is largely because its old-
part is accessible only on
foot by a single entrance: a
winding tunnel cut into the rock
on which the castle ruins and
church's distinctive belfry
precariously perched.
Guadalest was founded by the
Moors, who carved the
surrounding hillsides into ter-

The magnificent limestone rock Penyal d'Ifach

races and planted them with
crops. These are still irrigated
by the original ditches constructed by the Moors. The
village was badly damaged by
earthquakes in 1644 and 1748.

From the **castle** there are
fine views of the surrounding
mountains. Access to the castle
is through the Casa Orduña.

The **Museo de Micro-
Miniaturas**, displays a micro-
scopic version of Goya's *Fusil-
amiento 3 de Mayo* painted
on a grain of rice, his *The
Naked Maja (see p293)*, painted on the wing of a fly, and a
sculpture of a camel passing
through the eye of a needle.

🏛 Museo de Micro-
Miniaturas
Calle de la Iglesia 5. **Tel** 96 588 50
62. ◯ daily (until 9pm Apr–Sep). 🖼

The belfry of Guadalest, perched
on top of a rock

Alcoi ⑳

Alicante. 👥 61,000. 🚌 🚉 🅸 San
Lorenzo 2, 965 53 71 55. 🛒 Wed &
Sat 🎉 Los Reyes Parade (5 Jan),
Moors and Christians (21–24 Apr).
www.alcoiturisme.com

Sited at the confluence of
three rivers and surrounded by
high mountains, Alcoi is an
industrial city. But it is best
known for its mock battles
between Moors and Christians
(see p255) and its *peladillas* –
almonds coated in sugar.

On the slopes above it is
Font Roja (the red spring), a
nature reserve and shrine,
marked by a towering statue
of the Virgin Mary.

Environs
To the north of Alcoi is the
Sierra de Mariola, a mountain
range famed for its herbs. The
best point of access is the village
of **Agres**. A scenic route runs
from here to the summit of
Mont Cabrer at 1,390 m (4,560
ft). It passes two ruined *neveras*
– pits once used to store ice
for preserving fish and meat.

The bullring of **Bocairent**,
10 km (6 miles) west of Agres,
was carved out of rock in 1813.
A nearby cliff is pockmarked
with **Les Covetes dels Moros**
("the Moors' Caves"), but their
origin remains a mystery.

Benidorm

Alicante. 🕴 *69,000.* 🚉 🚌 🛈
*Avda Martínez Alejos 16, 96 585 13
11.* 🚢 *Wed, Sun.* 🎭 *Virgen del
Carmen (16 Jul), Las Fallas (16–19 Mar),
Fiestas Patronales (second weekend in
Nov), Moros y Cristianos (late Sep,
early Oct).* **www**.benidorm.org

With forests of skyscrapers
overshadowing its two long
beaches, Benidorm is more
reminiscent of Manhattan than
the obscure fishing village it
once was in the early 1950s.

Benidorm boasts more ac-
commodation than any other
resort on the Mediterranean,
but its clientele has changed
since the 1980s when its name
was synonymous with "lager
louts". A huge public park and
open-air auditorium used for
cultural events, the **Parque de
l'Aigüera**, is emblematic of
the facelift Benidorm has gone
through in recent years. The
town now attracts more elderly
holidaymakers from the north
of Spain than English youths.
Even so, the top attractions
are still said to be sex, sun,
nightclubs and "English" pubs.

A park on a promontory
between the Levante and
Poniente beaches, the **Balcón
del Mediterráneo**, ends in a
giant waterspout – a single-jet
fountain. From here there is a
panoramic view of the town.
A short way out to sea is the
Illa de Benidorm, a wedge-

Main staircase with floral lamp in
the Casa Modernista, Novelda

shaped island served by ferries from the harbour. The
island is being converted into
a nature reserve for sea birds.

Environs
La Vila Joiosa (Villajoyosa), to
the south, is much older than
Benidorm. Its principal sight is
a line of brightly painted houses that overhang the riverbed.
They were painted in such
vivid colours, it is said, so that
their fishermen owners would
be able to identify their homes
when they were out at sea.

The older part of **Altea**, to
the north of Benidorm, stands
on a hill above modern beach-
front developments. It is a
delightful jumble of white
houses, narrow streets and
alleys, and long flights of steps
arranged round a prominent,
blue-domed church.

The old town of Altea, dominated by its domed church

Novelda ㉒

Alicante. 🕴 *27,000.* 🚉 🚌
🛈 *Calle Mayor 6, 96 560 92 28.* 🚢
Wed, Sat. 🎭 *Santa María Magdalena
(19–25 Jul).* **www**.novelda.es

The industrial town of
Novelda is dominated by its
many marble factories. But it
is the exquisitely preserved
Art Nouveau house, the **Casa
Modernista**, that is of special
interest. It was built in 1903
and and rescued from
demolition in 1970. The
building's three floors are furnished in period style. There
are few straight lines or functional shapes and almost
every inch of wall-space has
some floral or playful motif.

Environs: Villena's town hall
has a collection of Bronze
Age gold objects, the **Tesoro
de Villena** *(see pp48–9).*

🚩 **Casa Modernista**
Calle Mayor 24. **Tel** 965 60 02 37
🕙 *10am–2pm Mon–Sat.* 🗝 *by app.*

🏛 **Tesoro de Villena**
City Hall, Plaza de Santiago 1. **Tel**
965 80 11 50. 🕙 *Tue–Sun am.* 🛗

Alicante ㉓

Alicante. 🕴 *320,000.* ✈ 🚉 🚌
🛈 *Avenida Rambla de Méndez Núñ
23, 965 20 00 00.* 🚢 *Thu, Sat.* 🎭
Hogueras (20–24 Jun).
www.alicanteturismo.com

A port and seaside resort b
around a natural harbour,
Alicante (Alacant) is the pri
cipal city of the Costa Blan
Both the Greeks and Roma
established settlements here
In the 8th century the Moo
refounded the city under th
shadow of Mount Benacan
The summit of this hill is n
occupied by the **Castillo de
Santa Bárbara**, which dates
mainly from the 16th centu
From its top battlements th
is a view over the whole c
The focus of the city is t
Explanada de España, a pa
lined promenade along the
waterfront. The 18th-centu
town hall *(ayuntamiento)*
worth seeing for the Salón
Azul (Blue Room). A meta
disc on the marble staírca
used as a reference point

'achts moored in Alicante harbour, beside the Explanada de España

measuring the sea level all
round Spain. A fine collection
f 20th-century art can be seen
the small **Museo de Arte**
ontemporáneo. Local artist
usebio Sempere (1924–85)
ssembled works by Dalí,
iró, Picasso *(see pp32–3)*,
nd others. The museum is
rrently closed for restoration.

Castillo de Santa Bárbara
aya del Postiguet. **Tel** 965 15 29
. ◯ daily. 🎦 (for elevator only).

Ayuntamiento
aza del Ayuntamiento 1. **Tel** 96
4 91 00. ◯ 9am–2pm Mon–Fri.

Museo de Arte
ontemporáneo.
aza de Santa María 3. **Tel** 96 514
59. ● closed till 2010.

a de Tabarca ㉔

ante. 🚢 from Santa Pola/Alicante.
Santa Pola, 966 69 22 76.

e best point of departure
the Illa de Tabarca is
ta Pola. This small, flat
nd is divided into two parts:
ony, treeless area of level
und known as *el campo*
e countryside), and a walled
lement, which is entered
ugh three gateways. The
ement was laid out on a
plan in the 18th century,
he orders of Carlos III, to
r pirates.

barca is a popular place
vim or snorkel and it can
crowded in the summer.
sh and salt have long been
ortant to the economy of
a Pola. A Roman fish salt-
orks has been excavated
, and outside the town are
e modern saltpans.

Elx ㉕

Alicante. 👥 220,000. 🚉 🚌 ℹ️
Parque Municipal, 96 665 81 95. 🖂
Mon, Sat. 🎭 Misteri d'Elx (11–15
Aug). **www**.turismedelx.com

The forest of over 300,000
palm trees that surrounds Elx
(Elche) on three sides is said
to have been planted by the
Phoenicians around 300 BC.
Part of it has been enclosed
as a private garden called
the **Huerto del Cura**. Some
of the palms – one with a
trunk which has divided
into eight branches – are
dedicated to various
notable people, such as the
Empress Elizabeth of Austria,
who visited here in 1894.
　The first settlement in the
area, around 5000 BC, was
at La Alcudia, where a 5th-
century BC Iberian stone bust
of a priestess, *La Dama de
Elche (see p48)*, was discovered
in 1897. The original is in
Madrid, but there are several
replicas scattered around Elx.
　The blue-domed Baroque
church, the **Basílica de Santa
María**, was built in the 17th
century to house the **Misteri
d'Elx** *(see p41)*. Next to it is
La Calahorra, a Gothic tower,
which is a surviving part of
the city's defences.
　A clock on the roof next to
the town hall has two 16th-
century mechanical figures,
which strike the hours on bells.

🌴 **Huerto del Cura**
Porta de la Morera 49. **Tel** 96 545
19 36. ◯ daily. 🎦 ♿ 📷
www.huertodelcura.com

🏯 **La Calahorra**
Calle Uberna. ● closed to public.

Orihuela ㉖

Alicante. 👥 80,000. 🚉 🚌 ℹ️ Calle
Francisco Die 25, 96 530 27 47. 🖂
Tue. 🎭 Moros y Cristianos (10–17 Jul).

In the 15th century Orihuela
was prosperous enough for
Fernando and Isabel to stop
and collect men and money on
their way to do battle against
the Moors at Granada. The
Gothic **cathedral** contains
Velázquez's *The Temptation
of St Thomas Aquinas*. Among
the exhibits in the **Museo
San Juan de Dios**
archaeological museum is a
processional float bearing a
17th-century statue of a she-
devil, *La Diablesa*.

🏛 **Museo San Juan de Dios**
Calle del Hospital. **Tel** 96 674 31
54. ◯ Tue–Sun. ♿ 📷

La Diablesa, Orihuela

Torrevieja ㉗

Alicante. 👥 94,000. ℹ️ Plaza Ruiz
Capdepont, 96 570 34 33. 🖂 Fri.
🎭 Habaneras (22–30 Jul).

During the 1980s, Torrevieja
grew at a prodigious rate as
thousands of Europeans
purchased homes here. Before
tourism, the town's source of
income was sea salt. The salt
works are the most productive
in Europe and the second most
important in the world.
　Torrevieja stages a festival of
habaneras, melodic songs originating in Cuba, brought back
to Spain by salt exporters.

Capilla del Junterón, Murcia

Murcia ㉘

Murcia. 🏠 425,000. 🚉 🚌 🛈 *Plaza Cardenal Belluga, Ayuntamiento Building, 902 10 10 70/968 35 87 49.* 🚆 *Thu.* 🎭 *Semana Santa (Easter Week).* **www**.murciaturistica.es

A regional capital and university city on the River Segura, Murcia was founded in 825 by the Moors, following successful irrigation of the surrounding fertile plain.

The centre of the modern city is the 18th-century square, **La Glorieta**. The pedestrianized Calle de la Trapería, linking the cathedral and the former marketplace (now the Plaza Santo Domingo), is the city's main street.

On it stands the **Casino**, a gentlemen's club founded in 1847. Visitors can usually ask the doorman's permission to look round but the club is closed for renovation until 2009. It is entered through an Arab-style patio, fashioned on the royal chambers of the Alhambra. The huge ballroom has a polished parquet floor and is illuminated by five crystal chandeliers.

Work on the **cathedral** began in 1394 over the foundations of Murcia's central mosque, and it was finally consecrated in 1467. The large tower was added much later and constructed in stages from the 16th to the 18th centuries. The architect Jaime Bort built the main, Baroque façade between 1739 and 1754.

The cathedral's finest features are two exquisitely ornate side chapels. The first, the Capilla de los Vélez, is in Late Gothic style and was built between 1490 and 1507. The second, the Renaissance Capilla del Junterón, dates from the early 16th century.

The **cathedral museum** displays grand Gothic altarpieces, a frieze from a Roman sarcophagus and the third-largest monstrance in Spain.

Francisco Salzillo (1707–83), one of Spain's greatest sculptors, was born in Murcia, and a museum in the **Iglesia de Jesús** (Church of Jesus) exhibits nine of his *pasos* – sculptures on platforms. These

Arab-style patio, Murcia Casino

are carried through the streets of the city on Good Friday morning. The figures are so lifelike that a fellow sculptor is said to have told the men carrying a *paso*: "Put it down, it will walk by itself".

The folk museum, the **Museo Etnológico de la Huerta de Murcia**, stands beside a large water wheel – a 1955 copy in iron of the original 15th-century wooden wheel. The three galleries display agricultural and domestic items, some of them 300 years old. A traditional, thatched Murcian farmhouse (*barraca*) forms part of the museum.

🎰 **Casino**
Calle Trapería 18. **Tel** 968 21 53 99.
🔴 *for renovation until 2009.* 🈺 &

🏛 **Museo Etnológico de la Huerta de Murcia**
Avda Principe. **Tel** 968 89 38 66. 🔒 Tue–Sun. ● *public hols.* &

Mar Menor ㉙

Murcia. ✈ *San Javier.* 🚉 *to Cartagena, then bus.* 🚌 *La Manga.* 🛈 *La Manga, 968 14 61 36.* **www**.marmenor.net

The elongated, high-rise holiday resort of La Manga, built on a long, thin, sandy strip, separates the Mediterranean and the Mar Menor, literally "the Smaller Sea".

Really a large lagoon, the sheltered Mar Menor can be 5°C (9°F) warmer than the Mediterranean in summer. Its high mineral concentrations first drew rest-cure tourists in the early 20th century. They stayed at the older resorts of Santiago de la Ribera and Los Alcázares, which still have pretty wooden jetties.

From either La Manga or Santiago de la Ribera you can make a ferry trip to the Isla Perdiguera, one of the five islands in the Mar Menor.

The old saltpans at Lo Pagan, near San Pedro del Pinatar, now a nature reserve.

The resort of Los Alcázares on the edge of the Mar Menor

View of the domes and spires of Cartagena's town hall from the seafront

Cartagena ③⓪

Murcia. 🏘 200,000. ✈ San Javier. 🚂 🚌 ⛴ 🚏 Plaza Almirante Bastar-eche, 968 50 64 83. 🛒 Wed. 🎭 Semana Santa (Easter Wk), Carthagin-ians and Romans (last two weeks Sep).

The first settlement founded in the natural harbour of Cartagena was constructed in 223 BC by the Carthaginians, who called it *Quart Hadas* (New City). After conquering the city in 209 BC, the Romans renamed it *Cartbago Nova* (New Carthage). Although the city declined in importance in the Middle Ages, its prestige increased in the 18th century when it became a naval base. You can get an overview of the city from the park, which surrounds the ruins of the Castillo de la Concepción, Cartagena's castle. On the quayside below is a prototype submarine designed by Isaac Peral in 1888. The city hall, opposite, marks the end of the Calle Mayor, a street over-looked by balconies and lined with handsome buildings. Ex-cavations in the city include a Roman street and the **Muralla Bizantina** (Byzantine Wall), built between 589 and 590. The **Museo Nacional de Arqueología Marítima** has an interesting collection of ancient Roman and Greek jars.

Muralla Bizantina
Calle Doctor Tapia Martínez.
968 50 79 66.
Tue–Sat.

Museo Nacional de Arqueología Marítima
Paseo Alfonso XII. **Tel** 968 12 11 66.
for renovation until 2010.

Costa Cálida ③①

Murcia. 🚂 Murcia. 🚌 Murcia. 🚏 C/ Antonio Cortijos, Águilas, 968 49 32 85. **www**.murciaturistica.es

The most popular resorts of Murcia's "Warm Coast" are around the Mar Menor. Be-tween Cabo de Palos and Cabo Tinoso the few small beaches are dwarfed by cliffs. The resorts of the southern part of the coast are relatively quiet. There are several fine beaches at Puerto de Mazarrón; and at nearby Bolnuevo the wind has eroded soft rocks into strange shapes. The growing resort of Águilas marks the southern limit of the coast, at the border with Andalusia.

Lorca ③②

Murcia. 🏘 90,000. 🚂 🚌 🚏 Calle Lope Gisbert, 968 44 19 14. 🛒 Thu. 🎭 Semana Santa (Easter Week), Feria (3rd week of Sep), Día de San Clemente (23 Nov).

The fertile farmland around Lorca, Murcia's third most important town, is an oasis in one of the most arid areas of Europe. Lorca was an important staging post on the Via Heraclea, as witnessed by the Roman milepost standing in a corner of the Plaza San Vicente. During the wars between Moors and Christians in the 13th to 15th centuries, Lorca became a frontier town between Al Andalus and the Castilian territory of Murcia. Its castle dates from this era, although only two of its original 35 towers remain. After Granada fell the town lost its importance and, except for one surviving gateway, its walls were demolished.

The centre of the town, the Plaza de España, is lined with handsome stone buildings. One side is occupied by the **Colegiata de San Patricio** (Church of St Patrick), built between 1533 and 1704, the only church in Spain dedicated to the Irish saint. At the head of the square is the town hall. A former prison, it was built in two blocks between 1677 and 1739, and later connected by an arch that spans the street.

Caravaca de la Cruz ③③

Murcia. 🏘 26,000. 🚏 Calle de las Monjas 17, 968 70 24 24. 🛒 Mon, 3rd Sun of month (crafts). 🎭 Vera Cruz (1–5 May). **www**.caravaca.org

A town of ancient churches, Caravaca de la Cruz's fame lies in its castle which houses the **Santuario de la Vera Cruz** (Sanctuary of the True Cross). This is where a double-armed cross is said to have appeared miraculously in 1231 – twelve years before the town was seized by Christians. The highlight of the Vera Cruz fiesta is the Race of the Wine Horses, which commemorates the lifting of a Moorish siege of the castle and the appearance of the cross. The cross was dipped in wine, which the thirsty defenders then drank and recovered their fighting strength.

Environs
Just to the north, among the foothills on Murcia's western border, is the village of **Moratalla**, a jumble of steep streets and brightly painted houses lying beneath a 15th-century castle. **Cehegín**, east of Caravaca, is a partially preserved 16th- and 17th-century town.

Roman milepost topped by a statue of St Vincent, Lorca

MADRID

INTRODUCING MADRID 266–267

OLD MADRID 268–281

BOURBON MADRID 282–299

FURTHER AFIELD 300–306

MADRID STREET FINDER 307–315

SHOPPING IN MADRID 316–319

ENTERTAINMENT IN MADRID 320–325

MADRID PROVINCE 326–333

Introducing Madrid

Spain's capital, a city of over three million people, is situated close to the geographical centre of the country, at the hub of both road and rail networks. Because of its distance from the sea and its altitude – 660 m (2,150 ft) – the city endures cold winters and hot summers, making spring and autumn the best times to visit. Madrid's attractions include three internationally famous art galleries, a royal palace, grand public squares and many museums filled with the treasures of Spain's history. The city is surrounded by its own small province, the Comunidad de Madrid, which takes in the Sierra de Guadarrama and one of Spain's most famous monuments, the palace of El Escorial.

The Palacio Real (see pp276–7
the royal palace built by Spain's
first Bourbon kings, dominates
the western part of Old Madrid
Its lavishly decorated chambers
include the throne room.

The Plaza Mayor (see p273),
Old Madrid's great 17th-century
square, has been a focal point
of the city since the days when
it was used as a public arena
for bullfights, trials by the
Inquisition and executions
(see p274). An equestrian
statue of Felipe III stands in
the middle of the square.

OLD MADRID
(see pp268–81)

MADRID PROVINCE
(see pp308–9)

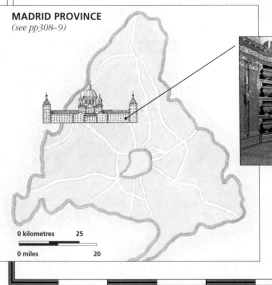

0 kilometres   25

0 miles   20

El Escorial (see pp330–31), th
massive, architecturally auste
monastery-palace built by Fel
II, has some sumptuous apart
ments decorated with great
works of art. Marble sarcoph
in the octagonal Royal Panth
contain the mortal remains o
most Spanish monarchs.

◁ Sculpted fountain of the Goddess Cybele in the Plaza de Cibeles, with the City Hall and main post office beh

The Museo Thyssen-Bornemisza (see pp288–9), one of the most important privately assembled art collections in the world, was sold to Spain in 1993. The 18th-century palace houses major works by Titian, Rubens, Goya, Van Gogh and Picasso.

The Plaza de Cibeles (see p286), one of the city's most impressive squares, is ringed by distinctive buildings, including the 19th-century Banco de España and Madrid's main post office, with sculptures on its white façade.

BOURBON MADRID
(see pp282–99)

The Parque del Retiro (see p297) has leafy paths and avenues, and a boating lake overlooked by a majestic colonnade. It is an ideal place in which to relax between visits to the great art galleries and museums of Bourbon Madrid.

The Museo del Prado (see pp292–5) is one of the world's greatest art galleries. It has important collections of paintings by Velázquez and Goya, whose statues stand outside the main entrances.

0 metres	500
0 yards	500

The Centro de Arte Reina Sofía (see pp298–9), an outstanding museum of 20th-century art, is entered by highly original exterior glass lifts. Inside, the star exhibit is Guernica, Picasso's famous painting of the horrors of the Civil War.

OLD MADRID

When Felipe II chose Madrid as his capital in 1561, it was a small Castilian town of little real significance. In the following years, it was to grow into the nerve centre of a mighty empire.

According to tradition, it was the Moorish chieftain Muhammad ben Abd al Rahman who established a fortress above the Río Manzanares. Magerit, as it was called in Arabic, fell to Alfonso VI of Castile between 1083 and 1086. Narrow streets with houses and medieval churches began to grow up on the higher ground behind the old Arab *alcazar* (fortress), which was replaced by a Gothic palace in the

Drawer designed for storing herbs, Palacio Real

15th century. When this burned down in 1734, it was replaced by the present Bourbon palace, the Palacio Real.

The population had scarcely reached 20,000 when Madrid was chosen as capital, but by the end of the century it had more than trebled. The 16th-century city is known as the "Madrid de los Austrias", after the reigning Habsburg dynasty. During this period royal monasteries were endowed and churches and private palaces were built. In the 17th century, the Plaza Mayor was added and the Puerta del Sol, the "Gate of the Sun", became the spiritual and geographical heart not only of Madrid but of all Spain.

SIGHTS AT A GLANCE

Historic Buildings
Palacio Real pp276–7 ❾

Museums and Galleries
Real Academia de
  Bellas Artes ⓮

Churches and Convents
Catedral de la
  Almudena ❼
Colegiata de San Isidro ❷
Iglesia de San Nicolás ❺

Monasterio de las
  Descalzas Reales ⓭
Monasterio de la
  Encarnación ❿

Streets, Squares and Parks
Campo del Moro ❽
Gran Vía ⓬
Plaza de España ⓫
Plaza Mayor ❹
Plaza de Oriente ❻

Plaza de la Villa ❸
Puerta del Sol ❶

GETTING THERE
The metro is the fastest and easiest way to get to Old Madrid. Take line 1 to Gran Vía or Sol; alternatively, lines 2, 3, 5, and 10 are good for getting to the main sights. Buses 15, 51, 52 and 150 to the Puerta del Sol are useful.

KEY

- Street-by-Street map *pp270–71*
- Metro station
- Main bus stop
- Tourist information

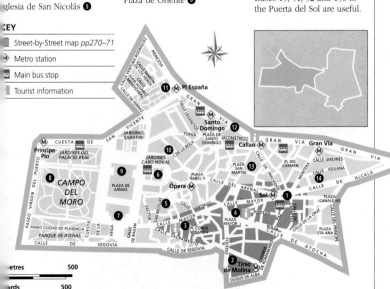

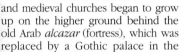

Monument to Cervantes by Lorenzo Coullaut-Valera in the Plaza de España

Street-by-Street: Old Madrid

Stretching from the charming Plaza de la Villa to the busy Puerta del Sol, the compact heart of Old Madrid is steeped in history and full of interesting sights. Trials by the Inquisition *(see p274)* and executions were once held in the Plaza Mayor. This porticoed square is Old Madrid's finest piece of architecture, a legacy of the Habsburgs *(see pp58–61)*. Other buildings of note are the Colegiata de San Isidro and the Palacio de Santa Cruz. For a more relaxing way of enjoying Old Madrid, sit in one of the area's numerous cafés or browse among the stalls of the Mercado de San Miguel.

★ **Plaza Mayo**
This beautiful century square competes with Puerta del Sol the focus of Ol Madrid. The arcades at the of the three-sto buildings are with cafés and craft shops ❹

The Mercado de San Miguel is housed in a 19th-century building with wrought-iron columns. The market has several excellent delicatessens and a restaurant.

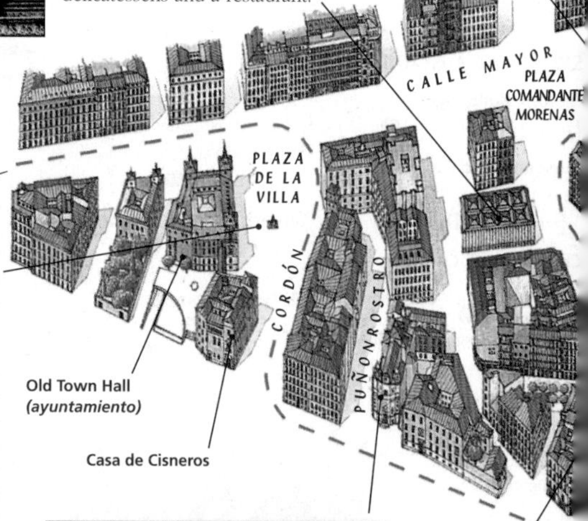

CALLE MAYOR

PLAZA COMANDANTE MORENAS

PLAZA DE LA VILLA

To Palacio Real

CORDÓN

PUÑONROSTRO

Old Town Hall (ayuntamiento)

Casa de Cisneros

Arco de Cuchilleros

★ **Plaza de la Villa**
The 15th-century Torre de los Lujanes is the oldest of several historic buildings standing on this square ❸

STAR SIGHTS

★ Plaza Mayor

★ Plaza de la Villa

★ Puerta del Sol

The Basílica Pontifici San Miguel is an imposing 18th-cent church with a beau façade and a gracef interior. It is one of few churches in Sp inspired by the Ital Baroque style.

0 metres

0 yards

LOCATOR MAP
See Street Finder map 4

★ **Puerta del Sol**
With its shops and cafés, the Puerta del Sol is one of the city's liveliest areas. This sign for Tío Pepe, a brand of sherry, has become synonymous with the square ❶

Iglesia de San Ginés

Sol Metro

Equestrian statue of Carlos III

To Bourbon Madrid

CALLE DEL ARENAL

PUERTA DEL SOL

CALLE DE ALCALÁ

Casa de Correos

CALLE MAYOR

CALLE DE POSTAS

CALLE CORREOS

CALLE PAZ

CALLE DE CARRETAS

BARCELONA

ESPOZ Y MINA

PLAZA PROVINCIA

PLAZA DE JACINTO BENAVENTE

SALVADOR

DUQUE DE RIVAS

CALLE DE LA COLEGIATA

Tirso de Molina Metro

— Suggested route

The Palacio de Santa Cruz was built as the court prison in the 17th century. This Baroque *(see p25)* palace is now occupied by the Foreign Ministry.

Colegiata de San Isidro
This was Madrid's provisional cathedral until La Almudena was completed (see p275). It is named after the city's patron, St Isidore, a local 12th-century farmer ❷

Kilometre Zero, the centre of Spain's road network, Puerta del Sol

Puerta del Sol ●

Map 4 F2. ⓜ *Sol.*

Noisy with traffic, chatter and policemen's whistles, the Puerta del Sol makes a fitting centre for Madrid. This is one of the city's most popular meeting places, and huge crowds converge here on their way to the shops and sights in the old part of the city.

The square marks the site of the original eastern entrance to the city, once occupied by a gatehouse and castle. These disappeared long ago and in their place came a succession of churches. In the late 19th century the area was turned into a square and became the centre of café society.

Today the "square" is shaped like a half moon. A recent addition is the imposing statue of Carlos III. The southern side of the square is edged by an austere red-brick building, originally the city's post office, built in the 1760s under Carlos III. In 1847 it became the headquarters of the

The bronze bear and strawberry tree of Madrid, Puerta del Sol

Ministry of the Interior. The clocktower, which gives the building much of its identity, was added in 1866. During the Franco regime *(see pp 66–7)*, the police cells beneath the building were the site of many human rights abuses. In 1963, Julián Grimau, a member of the underground Communist party, allegedly fell from an upstairs window and miraculously survived, only to be executed shortly afterwards.

The building is now home to the regional government and is the focus of many festive events. At midnight on New Year's Eve crowds fill the square to eat a grape on each stroke of the clock, a tradition supposed to bring good luck for the year. Outside a symbol on the ground marks Kilometre Zero, considered the centre of Spain's huge road network.

The buildings opposite are arranged in a semicircle and contain modern shops and cafés. On the corner of Calle del Carmen is a bronze statue of the symbol of Madrid – a bear reaching for the fruit of a *madroño* (strawberry tree).

The Puerta del Sol has witnessed many important historical events. On 2 May 1808 the uprising against the occupying French forces began here, but the crowd, pitted against the well-armed French troops, was crushed *(see p63)*. In 1912 the liberal prime minister José Canalejas was assassinated in the square and, in 1931, the Second Republic *(see p 65)* was proclaimed from the balcony of the Ministry of the Interior.

Repair works will be undertaken until 2009 and there may be some disruption.

Colegiata de San Isidro ●

Calle Toledo 37. **Map** 4 E3.
Tel *91 369 20 37.* ⓜ *La Latina.*
⬚ *8am–1pm, 6–8pm Mon–Sat, 9am–2:30pm, 6–8:30pm Sun.*

Built in the Baroque style *(see p25)* for the Jesuits in the mid-17th century, this twin-towered church served as Madrid's cathedral until La Almudena *(see p275)* was completed in 1993.

After Carlos III expelled the Jesuits from Spain in 1767 *(see p62)*, Ventura Rodríguez was commissioned to redesign the interior of the church. It was then rededicated to Madrid's patron saint, St Isidore, and two years later the saint's remains were moved here from the Iglesia de San Andrés. San Isidro was returned to the Jesuits during the reign of Fernando VII (1814–33).

Altar in the Colegiata de San Isidro

Plaza de la Villa ●

Map 4 D3. ⓜ *Ópera, Sol.*

The much restored and frequently remodelled Plaza de la Villa is one of the most atmospheric spots in Madrid. Some of the city's most historic secular buildings are situated around this square.

The oldest building is the early 15th-century Torre de los Lujanes, with its Gothic portal and Mudéjar-style horse shoe arches. François I of France was allegedly imprisoned in it following his defeat at the Battle of Pavia in 1525. The Casa de Cisneros was built in 1537 for the nephew

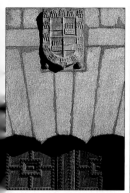

Portal of the Torre de los Lujanes

of Cardinal Cisneros, founder of the historic University of Alcalá (see pp332–33). The main façade, on the Calle de Sacramento, is an excellent example of the Plateresque style (see p25).

Linked to this building, by an enclosed bridge, is the old town hall (ayuntamiento). Designed in the 1640s by Juan Gómez de Mora, architect of the Plaza Mayor, it exhibits the same combination of steep roofs with dormer windows, steeple-like towers at the corners and an austere façade of brick and stone. Before construction was finished – more than 30 years later – the building had acquired hand-some Baroque doorways. A balcony was later added by Juan de Villanueva, the architect of the Prado (see p292–5), so that the royal family could watch Corpus Christi processions passing by.

Plaza Mayor ❹

Map 4 E3. Ⓜ Sol.

The Plaza Mayor forms a splendid rectangular square, with balconies and pinnacles, dormer windows and steep slate roofs. The square, with its theatrical atmosphere, is very Castilian in character. Much was expected to happen here and a great deal did – bullfights, executions, pageants and trials by the Inquisition (see p44) – all watched by crowds, often in the presence of the reigning king and queen. The great public scene was the

beatification of Madrid's patron, St Isidore, in 1621. In the same year, the execution of Rodrigo Calderón, secretary to Felipe III, was held here. Although hated by the Madrid populace, Calderón bore himself with such dignity on the day of his death that the phrase "proud as Rodrigo on the scaffold" survives to this day. Perhaps the greatest occasion of all, however, was the arrival here – from Italy – of Carlos III in 1760.

The square was started in 1617 and built in just two years, replacing slum houses. Its architect, Juan Gómez de Mora, was successor to Juan de Herrera, designer of Felipe II's austere monastery-palace, El Escorial (see pp330–31). Mora echoed the style of his master, softening it slightly. The square was later reformed by Juan de Villanueva. The fanciest part of the arcaded construction is the

Casa de la Panadería (bakery). Its façade, recently and crudely reinvented, is decorated with allegorical paintings. Madrid's main tourist office is sited here.

The equestrian statue in the centre is of Felipe III, who ordered the square's construc-tion. Started by the Italian Giovanni de Bologna and finished by his pupil Pietro Tacca in 1616, the statue was moved here in 1848 from the Casa de Campo (see p302). Today the square is lined with cafés, and is the venue for a collectors' market on Sundays (see p317). The square's southern exit leads into Calle de Toledo towards the streets where the Rastro, Madrid's famous flea-market (see p302), is held. A flight of steps in the southwest corner takes you under the Arco de Cuchilleros to the Calle de Cuchilleros, where there are some mesones, traditional restaurants.

Allegorical paintings on the Casa de la Panadería, Plaza Mayor

The Spanish Inquisition

The Spanish Inquisition was set up by Fernando and Isabel in 1480 to create a single, monolithic Catholic ideology in Spain. Protestant heretics and alleged "false converts" to Catholicism from the Jewish and Muslim faiths were tried, to ensure the religious unity of the country. Beginning with a papal bull, the Inquisition was run like a court, presided over by the Inquisitor-General. However, the

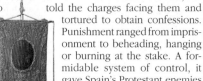

Inquisition banner

defendants were denied counsel, not told the charges facing them and tortured to obtain confessions. Punishment ranged from imprisonment to beheading, hanging or burning at the stake. A formidable system of control, it gave Spain's Protestant enemies a major propaganda weapon by contributing to the *Leyenda Negra* (Black Legend) which lasted, along with the Inquisition, into the 18th century.

A Protestant heretic appears before the royal family, his last chance to repent and convert.

A convicted defendant, forced to wear a red *sanbenito* robe, is led away to prison.

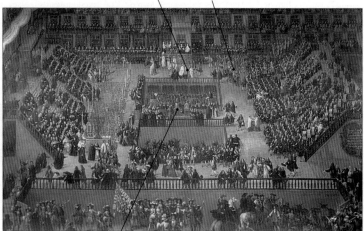

Those who have refused to confess are sentenced in public by day, and then executed before nightfall.

Torture *was widely used by the Inquisitors and their assistants to extract confessions from their victims. This early 19th-century German engraving shows a man being roasted on a wheel.*

AUTO-DE-FÉ IN THE PLAZA MAYOR

This painting by Francisco de Ricci (1683) depicts a trial, or *auto-de-fé* – literally, show of faith – held in Madrid's main square on 30 June 1680. Unlike papal inquisitions elsewhere in Europe, it was presided over by the reigning monarch, Carlos II, accompanied by his queen.

The Procession of the Flagellants *(c.1812) by Goya shows the abiding influence of the Inquisition on the popular imagination. The penitents in the picture are wearing the tall conical hats of heretics tried by the Inquisition. These hats can still be seen in Easter Week processions (see p38) throughout Spain.*

Iglesia de San Nicolás de Bari ❺

Plaza de San Nicolás 1. **Map** 3 C2.
Tel *91 559 40 64.* Ópera.
8:30am–1:30pm Mon,
6:30–8:30pm Tue–Sat, 10am–
1:30pm, Sun.

The first mention of the church of San Nicolás is in a document of 1202. Its brick tower, with horseshoe arches, is the oldest surviving ecclesiastical structure in Madrid. It is thought to be 12th-century Mudéjar in style, and may have originally been the minaret of a Moorish mosque.

Plaza de Oriente ❻

Map 3 C2. Ópera.

During his days as king of Spain, Joseph Bonaparte *(see p63)* carved out this stirrup-shaped space from the jumble of buildings to the east of the Palacio Real *(see pp276–7),* providing the view of the palace enjoyed today.

The square was once an important meeting place for state occasions; kings, queens and dictators all made public appearances on the palace balcony facing the plaza. The many statues of early kings that stand here were originally intended for the palace roof, but proved too heavy. The equestrian statue of Felipe IV in the centre of the square is by Italian sculptor Pietro

View of the Catedral de la Almudena and the Royal Palace

Tacca, and is based on drawings by Velázquez. Facing the palace, across the square, is the imposing Teatro Real, or Teatro de la Ópera, inaugurated in 1850 by Isabel II.

Catedral de la Almudena ❼

Calle Bailén 8 –10. **Map** 3 B2.
Tel *91 542 22 00.* Ópera.
9am–8:30pm daily (10am–2pm,
5–9pm Sat, Sun).

Dedicated to the city's patron, the cathedral was begun in 1879 and completed over a century later. The cathedral's Neo-Gothic grey and white façade is similar to that of the Palacio Real, which stands opposite. The crypt houses a 16th-century image of the Virgen de la Almudena.

Further along the Calle Mayor is the site of archaeological excavations of the remains of Madrid's Moorish and medieval city walls.

The first royal wedding took place in the cathedral between Prince Felipe and Letizia Ortíz in May 2004.

Equestrian statue of Felipe IV, by Pietro Tacca, Plaza de Oriente

Campo del Moro ❽

Map 3 A2. Príncipe Pío.
Oct–Mar: 10am–6pm daily; Apr–
Sep: 9am–8pm daily. 1 & 6 Jan, 1
& 15 May, 12 Oct, 9 Nov, 24–25 &
31 Dec and for official functions.
www.patrimonionacional.es

The Campo del Moro (the "Field of the Moor") is a pleasing park, rising steeply from the Río Manzanares to offer one of the finest views of the Palacio Real *(see pp276–7).*

The park has a varied history. In 1109 a Moorish army, led by Ali ben Yusuf bivouacked here, hence the name. The park went on to become a jousting ground for Christian knights. In the late 19th century it was used as a lavish playground for royal children. Around the same time it was landscaped in what is described as English style, with winding paths, grass and woodland, fountains and statues. It was reopened to the public in 1931 under the Second Republic *(see p65),* closed again under Franco, and not reopened until 1978.

For hotels and restaurants in this region see pp579–82 and pp629–32

Palacio Real 🄈

Madrid's vast and lavish Royal Palace was built to impress. The site, on a high bluff over the Río Manzanares, had been occupied for centuries by a royal fortress, but after a fire in 1734, Felipe V commissioned a truly palatial replacement. Construction lasted 17 years, spanning the reign of two Bourbon monarchs, and much of the exuberant decor reflects the tastes of Carlos III and Carlos IV *(see p71)*. The palace was used by the royal family until the abdication of Alfonso XIII in 1931. The present king, Juan Carlos I, lives in the more modest Zarzuela Palace outside Madrid, but the Royal Palace is still used for state occasions.

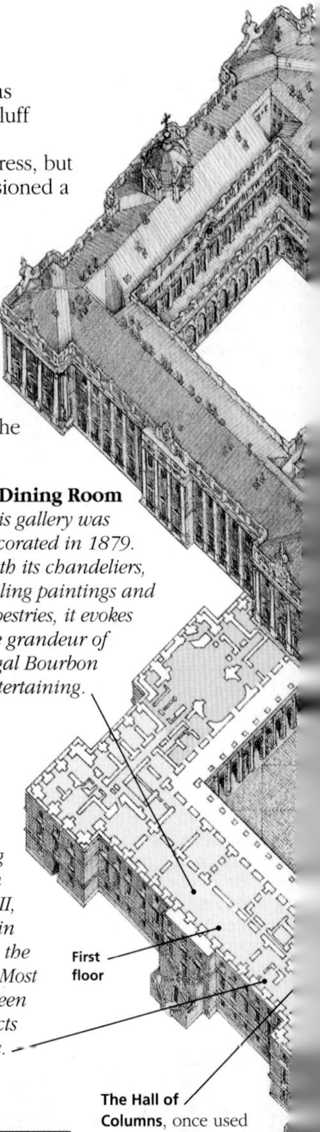

Statue of Carlos III

★ Dining Room
This gallery was decorated in 1879. With its chandeliers, ceiling paintings and tapestries, it evokes the grandeur of regal Bourbon entertaining.

★ Porcelain Room
The walls and ceiling of this room, built on the orders of Carlos III, are entirely covered in royal porcelain from the Buen Retiro factory. Most of the porcelain is green and white, and depicts cherubs and wreaths.

First floor

The Hall of Columns, once used for royal banquets, is decorated with 16th-century bronzes and Roman imperial busts.

★ Gasparini Room
Named after its Neapolit[an] designer, the Gasparin[i] Room is decorated with lavish rococo chinoiseri[e]. The adjacent antecham[ber] with painted ceiling an[d] ornate chandelier, hous[es] Goya's portrait of Carlos

---

STAR FEATURES

★ Gasparini Room

★ Porcelain Room

★ Dining Room

★ Throne Room

For hotels and restaurants in this region see pp579–82 and pp629–32

Plaza de Armas
The square in front of the main entrance also gives access to the Royal Armoury. The outstanding collection of weaponry includes the suits of armour belonging to Charles V and Felipe II.

Entrance Hall
A marble staircase by ...atini, next to the statue of ...os III as a Roman emperor, ...ads to the main floor. The painted rococo ceiling by Giaquinto vividly depicts allegorical scenes.

Billiards room

Hall of the Halberdiers

Entrance

Plaza de Armas

★ Throne Room
This room maintains the original decor of Carlos III. There are two gold and scarlet thrones and mirrors made in the royal glass factory of La Granja.

...ury

VISITORS' CHECKLIST

Calle de Bailén. **Map** 3 C2. **Tel** 91 454 88 00. Ópera. 3, 25, 39, 148. 9am–6pm Mon–Sat, 9am–3pm Sun (opens 30 minutes later on winter weekends; closes 1hr earlier in winter & public hols). for official functions. (free Wed for EU citizens). **www** patrimonionacional.es

Pharmacy
This unique collection includes decorated Talavera pottery storage jars and herb drawers. The Pharmacy Museum has recipe books detailing medications prescribed for the royal family.

KEY TO FLOORPLAN

☐ Exhibition rooms

☐ Entrance rooms

☐ Carlos III rooms

☐ Chapel rooms

☐ Carlos IV rooms

Visitors' centre

Entrance to the Convento de la Encarnación

Monasterio de la Encarnación ⑩

Plaza de la Encarnación 1. **Map** 3 C3.
Tel 91 454 88 00. ⚐ Ópera, Santo
Domingo. ◻ 10:30am–12:45pm,
4–5:45pm Tue–Thu & Sat, 10:30am–
12:45pm Fri, 11am–1:45pm Sun &
public hols. ◼ 1 & 6 Jan, 1 & 15
May, 27 Jul, 9 Nov, 24, 25 & 31 Dec.
◪ (free Wed for EU residents). ♿
▣ www.patrimonionacional.es

Standing in a delightful tree-
shaded square, this tranquil
Augustinian convent was
founded in 1611 for Margaret
of Austria, wife of Felipe III.
The architect, Juan Gómez de
Mora, also built the Plaza
Mayor *(see p273)* and the
façade clearly reveals his work.

Still inhabited by nuns, the
convent has the atmosphere
of old Castile, with its blue and
white Talavera tiles, wooden
doors, exposed beams and
portraits of royal benefactors.
Inside is a collection of 17th-
century art, with paintings
by José de Ribera and Vincente
Carducho lining the walls.
Polychromatic wooden
statues include *Cristo Yacente*
(*Lying Christ*), by Gregorio
Fernández.

The convent's main attraction
is the reliquary chamber with a
ceiling painted by Carducho. It
is used to store the skulls and
bones of saints. There is also a
phial containing the dried
blood of St Pantaleon. According to a popular myth, the
blood liquefies each year on 27
July, the anniversary of the

saint's death. Should the blood
fail to liquefy, it is said that
disaster will befall Madrid. The
church was rebuilt by Ventura
Rodríguez after a fire in 1767.

Plaza de España ⑪

Map 1 C5. ⚐ Plaza de España.

One of Madrid's busiest
traffic intersections and most
popular meeting places is the
Plaza de España, which slopes
down towards the Palacio Real
(see pp276–7) and the Sabatini
Gardens. In the 18th and 19th
centuries the square was
occupied by military barracks,
built here because of the
square's close proximity to
the palace. However, further
expansion of Madrid resulted
in its becoming a public space.

The square acquired its
present appearance during the
Franco period *(see pp66–7)*,
with the construction, on the
northern side, of the massive
Edificio España between 1947
and 1953. Across the square is
the Torre de Madrid (1957),
known as *La Jirafa* (the

Giraffe), which, for a while,
was the tallest concrete
structure in the world. The most
attractive part of the square is
its centre, occupied by a
massive stone obelisk built in
1928. In front of it is a statue of
the author Cervantes *(see p333)*.
Below him, Don Quixote *(see
pp394–5)* rides his horse
Rocinante while the plump
Sancho Panza trots alongside
on his donkey. On the left-
hand side is Dulcinea, Don
Quixote's sweetheart.

Gran Vía ⑫

Map 2 D5. ⚐ Plaza de España,
Santo Domingo, Callao, Gran Vía.

A main traffic artery of the
modern city, the Gran Vía
was inaugurated in 1910. Its
construction spanned several
decades and required the
demolition of large numbers
of run-down buildings and
small lanes between the Calle
de Alcalá and the Plaza de
España. This somewhat hap-
hazard road-building scheme
soon became the subject of

Stone obelisk with statue of Miguel de Cervantes, Plaza de España

◁ **Night-time traffic on the Gran Vía, seen from the Plaza de España**

One of the many 1930s buildings ...ining the Gran Vía

...arzuela – a comic opera – ...hat most *Madrileño* of art ...orms *(see p320)*. Nowadays, ...he Gran Vía is at the centre ...f city life and, following a ...uch-needed restoration ...rogramme, has become an ...rchitectural showpiece.

The most interesting build-
...gs are clustered at the Alcalá
...nd, starting with the Corin-
...ian columns, high-level
...atuary and tiled dome of the
...dificio Metrópolis *(see p284)*.
A temple with Art Nouveau
...osaics on its upper levels
...owns No. 1 Gran Vía. One
...iking feature of buildings at
...is end of the street is colon-
...ded galleries on the upper
...ors, imitating medieval
...agonese and Catalan archi-
...cture. Another is the fine
...ought-iron balconies and
...rved stone details, such as
...e gargoyle-like caryatids at
.... 12. This part of the Gran
... has a number of old-world
...nish shops.

...n the Red de San Luis, an
...ersection of four major
...ds, is the Telefónica build-
.... The first skyscraper to be
...cted in the capital, built
...ween 1926 and 1929, it
...sed a sensation. Beyond
...e, the Gran Vía becomes
...ch more American in
...racter, with cinemas,
...ist shops and many cafés.
...pposite Callao metro
...on, on the corner of the
...e Jacometrezo, is another
...l-known building, the Art
...o Capitol cinema and
...o hall, built in the 1930s.

Monasterio de las Descalzas Reales ⓱

Plaza de las Descalzas 3. **Map** 4 E2.
Tel 91 454 88 00. Ⓜ *Sol, Callao.*
🕙 *10:30am–12:30pm, 4–5:30pm
Tue–Thu & Sat, 10:30am–12:30pm
Fri, 11am–2:30pm Sun & public hols.*
🔲 *1 & 6 Jan, 1 & 15 May, 9 Nov, 24,
25 & 31 Dec.* 🎫 🎟 *(free Wed
for EU residents).*
www.patrimonionacional.es

Madrid's most notable
religious building has a fine
exterior in red brick and
granite. This is one of the few
surviving examples of 16th-
century architecture in the city.

Around 1560, Felipe II's
sister, Doña Juana, decided to
convert the original medieval
palace which stood here into
a convent for nuns and women
of the royal household. Her
high rank, and that of her
fellow nuns, accounts for the
massive store of art and wealth
of the Descalzas Reales (Royal
Barefoot Sisters).

The stairway has a fresco of
Felipe IV's family looking
down, as if from a balcony,
and a fine ceiling by Claudio
Coello and his pupils. It leads
up to a small first-floor cloister,
which is ringed with chapels
containing works of art relating
to the lives of the former nuns.
The main chapel houses Doña
Juana's tomb. The Sala de

Decorated chapel, Monasterio de
las Descalzas Reales

Tapices contains a series of
tapestries, one woven in 1627
for Felipe II's daughter, Isabel
Clara Eugenia. Another, *The
Triumph of the Eucharist,* is
based on cartoons by Rubens.
Major paintings on show
include works by Brueghel the
Elder, Titian and Zurbarán.

Fray Pedro Machado by Zurbarán

Real Academia de Bellas Artes ⓲

Calle Alcalá 13. **Map** 7 A2.
Tel 91 524 08 64. Ⓜ *Sevilla, Sol.*
🕙 *9am– 2pm Mon, 9am–7pm Tue–
Fri, 9am–2:30pm Sat, Sun.* 🔲 *some
public hols.* 🎫 *(free Wed).* 🎟 *by
appt.* ♿ **http**://rabasf.insde.es

Famous former students of
this arts academy, housed in
an 18th-century building by
Churriguera *(see p25)*, include
Dalí and Picasso. Its art
gallery's collection includes
works such as drawings by
Raphael and Titian. Among the
old masters are paintings by
Rubens and Van Dyck. Spanish
artists from the 16th to the 19th
centuries are well represented,
with magnificent works by
Ribera, Murillo, El Greco and
Velázquez. One of the highlights is Zurbarán's *Fray Pedro
Machado*, typical of the artist's
paintings of monks.

An entire room is devoted
to Goya, a former director of
the academy. On show here
are his painting of a relaxed
Manuel Godoy *(see p62)*, the
Burial of the Sardine (see p39),
the grim *Madhouse*, and a
self-portrait painted in 1815.

BOURBON MADRID

To the east of Old Madrid, there once lay an idyllic district of market gardens known as the Prado, the "Meadow". In the 16th century a monastery was built and later the Habsburgs extended it to form a palace (see p297), of which only fragments now remain; the palace gardens are now the popular Parque del Retiro. The Bourbon monarchs chose this area to expand and embellish the city in the 18th century. They built grand squares with fountains, a triumphal gateway, and what was to become the Museo del Prado, one of the world's greatest art galleries. A more recent addition to the area is the Centro de Arte Reina Sofía, a collection of modern Spanish and international art.

SIGHTS AT A GLANCE

Historic Buildings
Ateneo de Madrid ⓭
Café Gijón ⓯
Casa de Lope de Vega ⓾
Congreso de los Diputados ⓮
Estación de Atocha ㉑
Hotel Ritz ❶
Real Academia de la
   Historia ⓫
Teatro Español ⓬

Museums and Galleries
Centro de Arte Reina
   Sofía pp298–9 ㉒
Museo Arqueológico
   Nacional ⓲
Salón de Reinos ❼
Museo Nacional de
   Artes Decorativas ❻
Museo del Prado pp292–5 ❾
Museo Thyssen-
   Bornemisza pp288–9 ❸

Churches
Iglesia de San Jerónimo
   el Real ❽

Monuments
Puerta de
   Alcalá ❺

Streets, Squares and Parks
Calle de Serrano ⓱
Parque del Retiro ⓳
Plaza Cánovas del Castillo ❷
Plaza de Cibeles ❹
Plaza de Colón ⓰
Real Jardín Botánico ⓴

GETTING THERE
The metro is the fastest and easiest way to get to and around Bourbon Madrid. Lines 1, 2 and 4 serve all of the main sights. Useful buses include routes 2, 14, 15, 21, 27, 34, 74, and 146 to the Plaza de Cibeles.

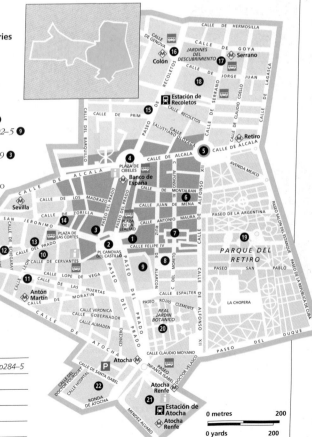

KEY

	Street-by-Street map pp284–5
◈	Metro station
▤	Railway station
▥	Main bus stop
❓	Tourist information

The expansive Parque del Retiro, which once formed the gardens of a Habsburg palace

Street-by-Street: Paseo del Prado

Façade of Banco de España

In the late 18th century, before the museums and lavish hotels of Bourbon Madrid took shape, the Paseo del Prado was laid out and soon became a fashionable spot for strolling. Today the Paseo's main attraction lies in its museums and art galleries. Most notable are the Museo del Prado (just south of the Plaza Cánovas del Castillo) and the Museo Thyssen-Bornemisza, both displaying world-famous collections. Among the grand monuments built under Carlos III are the Puerta de Alcalá, the Fuente de Neptuno and the Fuente de Cibeles, which stand in the middle of busy roundabouts.

The Paseo del Prado, based on the Piazza Navona in Rome, was built by Carlos III as a centre for the arts and sciences in Madrid.

Banco de España Metro

The Edificio Metrópolis (*see p281*), on the corner of Gran Vía and Calle de Alcalá, was built in 1905. Its façade is distinctively Parisian.

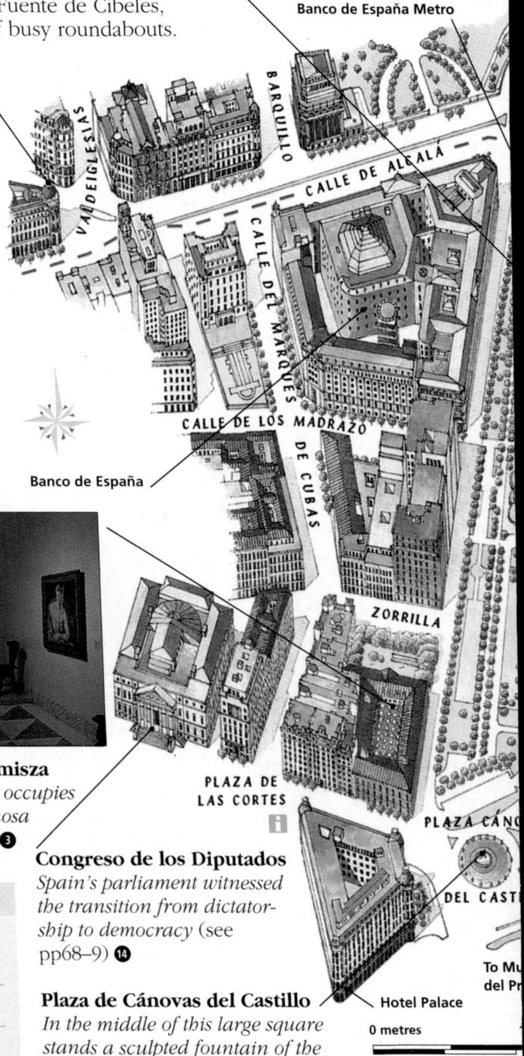

Banco de España

★ Museo Thyssen-Bornemisza
This excellent art collection occupies the Neo-Classical Villahermosa Palace, completed in 1806 ❸

STAR SIGHTS

★ Museo Thyssen-Bornemisza

★ Puerta de Alcalá

★ Plaza de Cibeles

PLAZA DE LAS CORTES

Congreso de los Diputados
Spain's parliament witnessed the transition from dictatorship to democracy (see pp68–9) ⓮

Plaza de Cánovas del Castillo
In the middle of this large square stands a sculpted fountain of the god Neptune in his chariot ❷

Hotel Palace

0 metres

0 yards   100

For hotels and restaurants in this region see pp579–82 and pp629–32

★ Puerta de Alcalá
Sculpted from granite, this former gateway into the city is especially beautiful when floodlit at night ❺

LOCATOR MAP
See Street Finder maps 7–8

BOURBON MADRID

OLD MADRID

Palacio de Comunicaciones and City Hall

Palacio de Linares

CALLE DE ALCALÁ

PLAZA DE LA INDEPENDENCIA

ALFONSO XI

CALLE DE MONTALBÁN

CALLE DE MENA

CALLE JUAN DE MENA

CALLE DE

CALLE ANTONIO MAURA

CALLE DE ALFONSO XII

RUÍZ DE ALARCÓN

MORETO

PE IV

★ Plaza de Cibeles
A fountain with a statue of the Roman goddess Cybele stands in this square ❹

The Museo Nacional de Artes Decorativas
This museum, near the Retiro, was founded in 1912 as a showcase for Spanish ceramics and interior design ❻

Salón de Reinos
The former army museum, this part of the old Retiro Palace will form part of the Prado Museum ❼

Casón del Buen Retiro
(see p295)

tel Ritz
h its Belle Époque *rior, the Ritz is one of most elegant hotels in in* ❶

The Monumento del Dos de Mayo commemorates the War of Independence against the French *(see p63).*

KEY

– – – Suggested route

Hotel Ritz ❶

Plaza de la Lealtad 5. **Map** 7 C2.
Tel 91 701 67 67. ⓜ *Banco de
España.* 🅿 ♿ www.ritz.es

A few minutes' walk from the
Prado, this hotel is said to be
Spain's most extravagant. It
was part of the new breed of
hotels constructed as luxury
accommodation for the
wedding guests of Alfonso
XIII in 1906.

The opulence of the Ritz
(see p581) is reflected in its
prices. Each of the 158 rooms
is beautifully decorated in a
different style, with carpets
made by hand at the Real
Fábrica de Tapices *(see p306)*.

At the start of the Civil War
(see pp66–7) the hotel was
converted into a hospital, and
it was here that the Anarchist
leader Buenaventura Durruti
died of his wounds in 1936.

The Fuente de Neptuno

Plaza Cánovas del Castillo ❷

Map 7 C3. ⓜ *Banco de España.*

This busy roundabout is
named after Antonio Cánovas
del Castillo, one of the
leading statesman of 19th-
century Spain *(see p64)*, who
was assassinated in 1897.

Dominating the plaza is the
Fuente de Neptuno – a
fountain with a statue depicting Neptune in his chariot,
being pulled by two horses.
The statue was designed in
1780 by Ventura Rodríguez as
part of Carlos III's scheme to
beautify eastern Madrid.

**Visitors admiring the works of art
in the Museo Thyssen-Bornemisza**

Museo Thyssen-Bornemisza ❸

See pp288–9.

Plaza de Cibeles ❹

Map 7 C1. ⓜ *Banco de España.*
**Casa de América exhibition
room** *Tel* 91 595 48 00.
◯ 11am–8pm Mon–Sat,
noon–3pm Sun. ⬤ Aug.

As well as being one of
Madrid's best-known land-
marks, the Plaza de Cibeles is
also one of the most beautiful.

The Fuente de Cibeles stands
in the middle of the busy traffic island at the junction of the
Paseo del Prado and the Calle
de Alcalá. This fine sculpted
fountain is named after Cybele,
the Graeco-Roman goddess of
nature, and shows her sitting in
her lion-drawn chariot. Designed in the late 18th century by
José Hermosilla and Ventura

Rodríguez, it is considered a
symbol of Madrid. Around the
square rise four important
buildings. The most impressive
is the main post office, the
Palacio de Comunicaciones,
mockingly known as "Our
Lady of Communications". Its
appearance – white, with high
pinnacles – is often likened to
a wedding cake. It was built
between 1905 and 1917 on
the site of former gardens. At
the end of 2007 it became the
new home of the town hall.

On the northeast side of the
square is the stone façade of
the Palacio de Linares, built by
the Marquis of Linares at the
time of the second Bourbon
restoration of 1875 *(see p64)*.
Once threatened with demolition, the palace was repriev-
ed and converted into the Casa de
América, and now hosts art
exhibitions by Latin American
artists. It is also used as a
venue for theatrical
performances and lectures.

In the northwest corner of
the Plaza de Cibeles, surrounded by attractive gardens, is the
heavily guarded Army Headquarters, which is housed in
the buildings of the former
Palacio de Buenavista. The
palace was commissioned by
the Duchess of Alba in 1777,
though its construction was
twice delayed by fires.

On the opposite corner is
the Banco de España, constructed between 1884 and 1891.
Its design was inspired by the
Venetian Renaissance style,
with delicate ironwork adorning the roof and windows.
Much-needed renovation work
has returned the bank to its
late 19th-century magnificence.

The Fuente de Cibeles, with the Palacio de Linares in the background

For hotels and restaurants in this region see pp579–82 and pp629–32

through the central arch of the Puerta de Alcalá

erta de Alcalá ❺

8 D1. 🚇 Retiro.

ceremonial gateway is
grandest of the monu-
ts erected by Carlos III in
ttempt to improve the
s of eastern Madrid. It
designed by Francesco
tini to replace a smaller
que gateway, which had
built by Felipe III for
ntry into Madrid of his
Margarita de Austria.
nstruction of the gate
n in 1769 and lasted nine
. It was built from granite
o-Classical style, with a
pediment and sculpted
s. It has five arches –
central and two outer
gular ones.

il the mid-19th century
ateway marked the city's
nmost boundary. It now
s in the busy Plaza de la
endencia, and is best
when floodlit at night.

Museo Nacional de Artes Decorativas ❻

Calle Montalbán 12. **Map** 8 D2.
Tel 91 532 64 99. 🚇 Retiro, Banco
de España. ⬚ 9:30am–3pm Tue–Sat
(5–8pm Thu), 10am–3pm, Sun & public hols. 📷 (free Sun). 📷 guided tour
Sun. ♿

Housed in a 19th-century
palace near the Parque del
Retiro, the National Museum
of Decorative Arts contains an
interesting collection of
furniture and *objets d'art*. The
exhibits are mainly from
Spain and date back as far as
Phoenician times.

There are also some
excellent ceramic pieces from
Talavera de la Reina (see
p386), and ornaments from
the Far East.

Refurbishment and reorganisation work is due to begin in
2009, so some rooms may be
closed during this period.

Salón de Reinos ❼

Calle Méndez Núñez 1. **Map** 8 D3.
🚇 Retiro, Banco de España
⬤ closed for refurbishment until
2015.

The Salón de Reinos (Hall
of Kingdoms) is one of the
two remaining parts of the
17th-century Palacio del
Buen Retiro and gets its
name from the shields of
the 24 kingdoms of the
Spanish monarchy, part of
the decor supervised by
court painter Velázquez (see
p32). In the time of Felipe
IV, the Salón was used for
diplomatic receptions and
official ceremonies.

The Salón de Reinos is
currently undergoing an
extensive refurbishment
to restore the interiors to
their former glory. It will
ultimately become part of
the Prado (see pp292–5).
Among the exhibits to be
housed in the new gallery
will be five equestrian
portraits by Velázquez, and
Zurbarán's series of ten
paintings on the life of
Hercules, along with other
17th-century royal paintings.
It is hoped that the building
will be open by 2015.
Despite this closure, the
Palacio del Buen Retiro is
worth visiting to admire its
impressive facade. The
original Palacio was built
for King Felipe IV in 1637
on a large stretch of land
situated next to the Monastery
of San Jeronimo.

**The sword of El Cid, *La Tizona*, will
be in the Salón de Reinos**

Museo Thyssen-Bornemisza ●

This magnificent museum is based on the collection
assembled by Baron Heinrich Thyssen-Bornemisza and
his son, Hans Heinrich, the preceding baron. In 1992 it
was installed in Madrid's 18th-century Villahermosa
Palace, and was sold to the nation the following year.
From its beginnings in the 1920s, the collection was
intended to illustrate the history of Western art, from
Italian and Flemish primitives, through to 20th-century
Expressionism and Pop Art. The museum's collection,
consisting of more than 1,000 paintings, includes masterpieces by Titian, Goya, Van Gogh and Picasso. Carmen
Thyssen's collection of mainly impressionist art opened
to the public in 2004. It is regarded by many critics as
the most important private art collection in the world.

**★ Our Lady of the Dry
Tree** (c.1450)
*This tiny painted
panel is by Bruges
master Petrus
Christus. The
letter A hanging
from the tree
stands for "Ave
Maria".*

★ Harlequin with a Mirror
*The figure of the harlequin was
a frequent subject of Picasso's.
The careful composition in
this 1923 canvas, which is
thought by some to represent
the artist himself, is typical of
Picasso's "Classical" period.*

GALLERY GUIDE
*The galleries are arranged
around a covered central
courtyard, which rises the full
height of the building.
The top floor starts with early
Italian art and goes through
to the 17th-century. The
first floor continues
the story with
17th-century
Dutch works
and ends with
German Express-
ionism. The ground
floor is dedicated to
20th-century paintings.*

STAR PAINTINGS

★ Harlequin with a
  Mirror by Picasso

★ Our Lady of the Dry
  Tree by Christus

★ The Toilet of Venus
  by Rubens

Hotel Room (1931)
*Edward Hopper's painting is a study of
urban isolation. The solitude is made
less static by the suitcases and the
train timetable on the woman's knee.*

**Portrait
of Baron
Thyssen-
Bornemisza**
*This informal p
of the previous
against the bac
ground of a W
painting, was p
by Lucian Freu*

★ **The Toilet of Venus**
This reflection of ideal beauty was painted by the Flemish master Rubens between 1606 and 1611. The picture illustrates his luscious use of colour and form.

VISITORS' CHECKLIST

Paseo del Prado 8. **Map** 7 C2. **Tel** 91 369 01 51. Ⓜ Banco de España, Sevilla. 🚌 1, 9, 14, 20, 27, 37, 45. ◯ 10am–7pm Tue–Sun; Jul & Aug: also 7pm–11pm Tue–Sat for temporary exhibitions. ● 1 Jan, 1 May & 25 Dec. 🗒 👍 🖬 🗂 🛆 🚻 www.museothyssen.org

St Casilda *(c.1630)*
Francisco de Zurbarán is known for his depictions of monks and saints. In this work, St Casilda's brightly coloured robe stands out against the plain background.

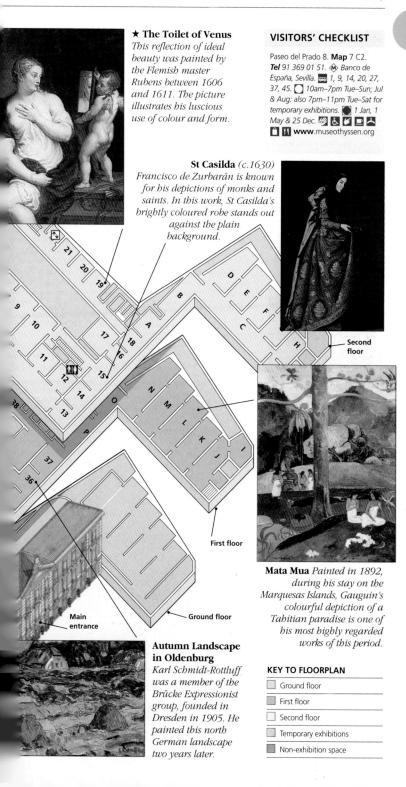

Second floor

First floor

Ground floor

Main entrance

Mata Mua *Painted in 1892, during his stay on the Marquesas Islands, Gauguin's colourful depiction of a Tahitian paradise is one of his most highly regarded works of this period.*

KEY TO FLOORPLAN

☐ Ground floor
☐ First floor
☐ Second floor
☐ Temporary exhibitions
☐ Non-exhibition space

Autumn Landscape in Oldenburg
Karl Schmidt-Rottluff was a member of the Brücke Expressionist group, founded in Dresden in 1905. He painted this north German landscape two years later.

Iglesia de San Jerónimo el Real ⑧

Calle del Moreto 4. **Map** 8 D3. **Tel** 91 420 35 78. Ⓜ Banco de España. ⬜ Oct–Jun: 10am–1pm, 5:30–8:30pm daily, (6–8:30pm Jul–Sep). ♿

Built in the 16th century for Queen Isabel, but since remodelled, San Jerónimo is Madrid's royal church. From the 17th century it became virtually a part of the Retiro palace which once stood here *(see p297)*. The church was originally attached to the Hieronymite monastery. The cloister and part of the atrium form part of a new building at the Prado Museum.

The church was the setting for the marriage of Alfonso XIII and Victoria Eugenia of Battenberg in 1906. King Juan Carlos I's coronation was also held here in 1975.

Museo del Prado ⑨

See pp292–5.

Casa de Lope de Vega ⑩

Calle Cervantes 11. **Map** 7 B3. **Tel** 91 429 92 16. Ⓜ Antón Martín. ⬜ 9:30am–1:30pm Tue–Fri, 10am–2pm Sat. ⬛ Aug, Christmas week, Easter & public hols. 🈺 (free Sat). 🚫 📷

Félix Lope de Vega, a leading Golden Age writer *(see p34)*, moved into this sombre house in 1610. Here he wrote over two-thirds of his plays,

Félix Lope de Vega

thought to total almost 1,500. Meticulously restored in 193[ ] using some of Lope de Vega[ ] own furniture, the house giv[ ] a great feeling of Castilian li[ ] in the early 17th century. A dark chapel with no extern[al] windows occupies the cent[re] separated from the writer's bedroom by only a barred window. The small garden at the rear is planted with the flowers and fruit trees mentioned by the writer in [his] works. He died here in 163[ ]

Castizos during San Isidro

MADRID'S FIESTAS

San Isidro *(15 May)*. Madrid's great party around 15 May is in honour of St Isidore, the humble 12th-century farmworker who became the city's patron. With a *corrida* every day, this is Spain's biggest bullfighting event. Throughout the city there are also art exhibitions, open-air concerts and fireworks. Many people dress in *castizo (see p302)* folk costume for the occasion.

The Passion *(Easter Saturday)*, Chinchón. A passion play is performed in the town's atmospheric arcaded Plaza Mayor.

Dos de Mayo *(2 May)*. This holiday marks the city's uprising against Napoleon's troops in 1808 *(see p63)*.

New Year's Eve. The nation focuses on the Puerta del Sol *(see p272)* at midnight as crowds gather to swallow a grape on each chime of the clock.

Statue of Goya in front of the Prado

unlit balcony of the magnificent Teatro Español

Congreso de los Diputados ⑭

Plaza de las Cortes. **Map** 7 B2. **Tel** 91 390 60 00. Ⓜ Sevilla. ☐ 10:30am–12:30pm Sat, by appt Mon–Fri. ☐ Aug & public hols. 🚫 ♿

This imposing yet attractive building is home to the Spanish parliament, the Cortes. Built in the mid-19th century on the site of a former convent, it is characterized by Classical columns, heavy pediments and guardian bronze lions. It was here, in 1981, that Colonel Tejero of the Civil Guard held the deputies at gunpoint on national television, as he tried to spark off a military coup *(see p68)*. His failure was seen as an indication that democracy was now firmly established in Spain.

Real Academia de la Historia ⑪

Calle León 21. **Map** 7 A3. **Tel** 91 29 06 11. Ⓜ Antón Martin. 🚫 ☐ For exhibitions 4–7pm Mon–Fri, am–2pm Sat–Sun.

The Royal Academy of History an austere brick building uilt by Juan de Villanueva in '88. Its location, in the so-lled Barrio de las Letras riters' Quarter), is apt. n 1898, the great intellectual d bibliophile, Marcelino enéndez Pelayo, became director of the academy, living re until his death in 1912. e library holds more than),000 books. A museum housing the ademy's pictures and anues is due to open in 2009.

Villanueva. Engraved on it are the names of great Spanish dramatists, including that of celebrated writer Federico García Lorca *(see p35)*.

Ateneo de Madrid ⑬

Calle del Prado 21. **Map** 7 B3. **Tel** 91 429 17 50. Ⓜ Antón Martin, Sevilla. ☐ by appointment only – apply in writing. **Library** ☐ 9am–12:45pm Mon–Sat, 9am–8:45pm Sun.

Formally founded in 1835, this learned association has liberal political leanings. It is similar to a gentlemen's club in atmosphere, with a grand stairway and panelled hall hung with the portraits of famous fellows. Closed down during past periods of repression and dictatorship, it is still a mainstay of liberal thought in Spain. Many leading Socialists are members, along with writers and other Spanish intellectuals.

eatro Español ⑫

e del Príncipe 25. **Map** 7 A3. **Tel** 91 14 80. Ⓜ Sol, Sevilla. ☐ for per-nances from 7pm Tue–Sun. ♿

minating the Plaza Santa a is the Teatro Español, e of Madrid's oldest and st beautiful theatres. From 3 many of Spain's finest 's, by leading dramatists ne time such as Lope de da, were first performed in Corral del Príncipe, which nally stood on this site. In 2 this was replaced by the ro Español. The Neo-sical façade, with pilasters medallions, is by Juan de

Bronze lion guarding the Cortes

Café Gijón ⑮

Paseo de Recoletos 21. **Map** 5 C5. **Tel** 91 521 54 25. Ⓜ Banco de España. ☐ 7:30am–1:30am Mon–Fri, 8am–2am Sat & public hols, 8am–1:30am Sun. ♿

Madrid's café life *(see pp320–5)* was one of the most attractive features of the city from the turn of the 20th century, right up to outbreak of the Civil War. Of the many intellectuals' cafés which once thrived, only the Gijón survives. Today the café continues to attract a lively crowd of *literati*. With its cream-painted wrought-iron columns and black and white table tops, it is perhaps better known for its atmosphere than for its appearance.

Carving on the façade of the Ateneo de Madrid

Museo del Prado ㉑

The Prado Museum contains the world's greatest assembly of Spanish painting – especially works by Velázquez and Goya – ranging from the 12th to 19th centuries. It also houses impressive foreign collections, particularly of Italian and Flemish works. The Neo-Classical building was designed in 1785 by Juan de Villanueva on the orders of Carlos III, and it opened as a museum in 1819. The Spanish architect Rafael Moneo has constructed a new building, over the adjacent church's cloister, where the temporary exhibitions are located. Some galleries may be closed temporarily due to ongoing reorganisation.

★ Velázquez Collection
The Triumph of Bacchus *(1629), Velázquez's first portrayal of a mythological subject, shows the god of wine (Bacchus) with a group of drunkards.*

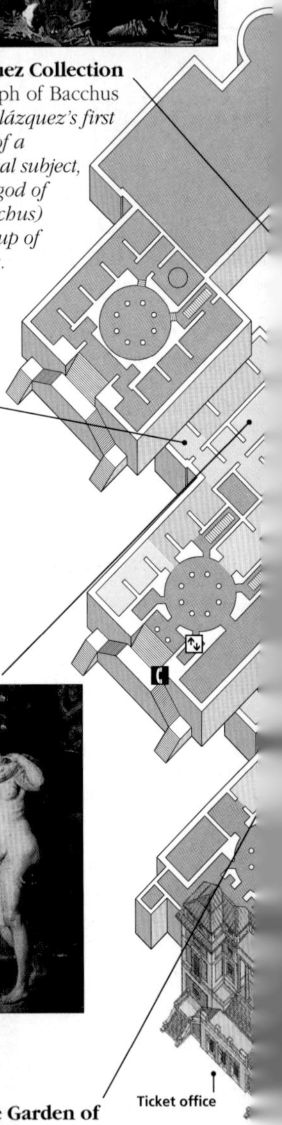

The Adoration of the Shepherds *(1612–14)*
This dramatic work shows the elongated figures and swirling garments typical of El Greco's style. It was painted during his late Mannerist period for his own funerary chapel.

The Three Graces
(c.1635)
This was one of the last paintings by the Flemish master Rubens, and was part of the artist's personal collection. The three women dancing in a ring – the Graces – are the daughters of Zeus, and represent Love, Joy and Revelry.

STAR EXHIBITS

★ Velázquez Collection

★ Goya Collection

Ticket office

The Garden of Delights *(c.1505)*
Hieronymus Bosch (El Bosco in Spanish), one of Felipe II's favourite artists, is especially well represented in the Prado. This enigmatic painting depicts paradise and hell.

GALLERY GUIDE

The museum's permanent collection is arranged over the three main floors, although some paintings may not be on show, or galleries may be closed due to ongoing renovation; check the website for more details. The permanent collection is accessed via the Velazques entrance, however, visitors to the temporary exhibitions should use the Jerónimos entrance.

Second floor

First floor

VISITORS' CHECKLIST

Paseo del Prado. **Map** 7 C3.
Tel 91 330 28 00. Atocha, Banco de España. 10, 14, 19, 27, 34, 37, 45. 9am–8pm Tue–Sun & public hols. 1 Jan, Good Fri, 1 May, 25 Dec. (free 6–8pm Tue–Sat, 5–8pm Sun and for those aged under 18 or over 65).
www.museodelprado.es

★ Goya Collection
In The Clothed Maja *and* The Naked Maja *(both c.1800), Goya tackled the taboo subject of nudity, for which he was later accused of being obscene.*

Murillo entrance

Ground floor

The Martyrdom of St Philip
(c.1639) José de Ribera moved from his native Valencia to Naples as a young man. There he was influenced by Caravaggio's dramatic use of light and shadow, known as chiaroscuro, as seen in this work.

Velazques entrance

The Annunciation
Fra Angelico's work of c.1427 is a high point of Italy's Early Renaissance, as illustrated by the detailed architectural setting and deep perspective of the interior.

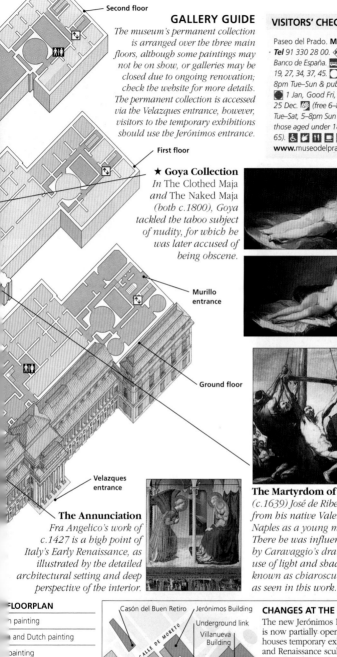

FLOORPLAN

- painting
- and Dutch painting
- painting
- painting
- painting
- re
- ary Exhibitions
- ibition space

Casón del Buen Retiro / Jerónimos Building
CALLE DE MORETO — Underground link — Villanueva Building
Jerónimos entrance
CALLE DE FELIPE IV
PASEO DEL PRADO
Salón de Reinos

CHANGES AT THE PRADO
The new Jerónimos Building is now partially open and houses temporary exhibitions and Renaissance sculptures, as well as a shop, restaurant, café, auditorium and cloakroom. In the future the Salón de Reinos *(see p285)* will become part of the Prado.

■ Museum Buildings
□ Due to open in 2015

Exploring the Prado's Collection

The importance of the Prado is founded on its royal collections. The wealth of foreign art, including many of Europe's finest works, reflects the historical power of the Spanish crown. The Low Countries and parts of Italy were under Spanish domination for centuries. The 18th century was an era of French influence, following the Bourbon accession to the Spanish throne. The Prado is worthy of repeated visits, but if you go only once, see the Spanish works of the 17th century.

Saturn Devouring One of his Sons (1820–23) by Francisco de Goya

St Dominic of Silos Enthroned as Abbot (1474–7) by Bermejo

SPANISH PAINTING

Right up to the 19th century, Spanish painting focused on religious and royal themes. Although the limited subject matter was in some ways a restriction, it also offered a sharp focus that seems to have suited Spanish painters.

Spain's early medieval art is represented somewhat sketchily in the Prado, but there are some examples, such as the anonymous mural paintings from the Holy Cross hermitage in Maderuelo, which show a Romanesque heaviness of line and forceful characterization.

Spanish Gothic art can be seen in the Prado in the works of Bartolomé Bermejo and Fernando Gallego. The sense of realism in their paintings was borrowed from Flemish masters of the time.

Renaissance features began to emerge in the works of painters such as Pedro de Berruguete, whose *Auto-de-fé* is both chilling and lively. *St Catherine*, by Fernando Yáñez de la Almedina, shows the influence of Leonardo da Vinci, for whom Yáñez probably worked while training in Italy.

What is often considered as a truly Spanish style – with its highly-wrought emotion and deepening sombreness – first started to emerge in the 16th century in the paintings of the Mannerists. This is evident in Pedro Machuca's fierce *Descent from the Cross* and in the Madonnas of Luis de Morales, "the Divine". The elongation of the human figure in Morales' work is carried to a greater extreme by Domenikos Theotocopoulos, who is better known as El Greco *(see p391)*. Although many of his master pieces remain in his adopted town of Toledo, the Prado has an impressive collection, including *The Nobleman with his Hand on his Chest*.

The Golden Age of the 17 century was a productive tim for Spanish art. José de Riber who lived in (Spanish) Naple followed Caravaggio in com ining realism of character wi the techniques of *chiaroscu* (use of light and dark) and tenebrism (large areas of da colours, with a shaft of light Another master who used th method was Francisco Ribal whose *Christ Embracing St Bernard* is here. Zurbarán, known for still lifes and po traits of saints and monks, i also represented in the Prac

This period, however, is b represented by the work of Diego de Velázquez. As Spa leading court painter from h late twenties until his death, produced scenes of heighten realism, royal portraits, and religious and mythological paintings. Examples of all of these are displayed in the Prado. Perhaps his greatest work is *Las Meninas (see p.*

Another great Spanish painter, Goya, revived Spa art in the 18th century. He first specialized in cartoon for tapestries, then became court painter. His work we on to embrace the horrors war, as seen in *The 3rd of May in Madrid (see p63)*, culminated in a sombre se known as *The Black Painti*

Still Life with Four Vessels (c.1658–64) by Francisco de Zurbarán

FLEMISH AND DUTCH PAINTING

Spain's long connection with the Low Countries naturally resulted in an intense admiration for the so-called Flemish primitives. Many exceptional examples of Flemish and Dutch art now hang in the Prado. *St Barbara*, by Robert Campin, has a quirky intimacy, while Rogier van der Weyden's *The Deposition* is an unquestioned masterpiece. Most notable of all, however, are Hieronymus Bosch's weird and eloquent inventions. The Prado has some of his major paintings, including the *Temptation of St Anthony* and *The Haywain*. Works from the 16th century include the *Triumph of Death* by Brueghel the Elder. There are nearly 100 canvases by the 17th-century Flemish painter Peter Paul Rubens, including *The Adoration of the Magi*. The most notable Dutch painting on display is Rembrandt's *Artemisia*, a portrait of the artist's wife. Other Flemish and Dutch artists featured at the Prado are Antonis Moor, Anton Van Dyck and Jacob Jordaens, considered one of the finest portrait painters of the 17th century.

ITALIAN PAINTING

The Prado is the envy of many museums, not least for its vast collection of Italian paintings. Botticelli's dramatic wooden panels telling the *Story of Nastagio*

David Victorious over Goliath (c.1600) by Caravaggio

degli Onesti, a vision of a knight forever condemned to hunt down and kill his own beloved, were commissioned by two rich Florentine families and are a sinister high point.

Raphael contributes the superb *Christ Falls on the Way to Calvary* and the sentimental *The Holy Family of the Lamb*. *Christ Washing the Disciples' Feet*, an early work by Tintoretto, is a profound masterpiece and reveals the painter's brilliant handling of perspective.

Caravaggio had a profound impact on Spanish artists, who admired his characteristic handling of light, as seen in *David Victorious over Goliath*. Venetian masters Veronese and Titian are also very well represented. Titian served as court painter to Charles V, and few works express the drama of Habsburg rule so deeply as his sombre painting *The Emperor Charles V at Mühlberg*. Also on display are works by Giordano and Tiepolo, the master of Italian

Rococo, who painted *The Immaculate Conception* as part of a series intended for a church in Aranjuez.

FRENCH PAINTING

Marriages between French and Spanish royalty in the 17th century, culminating in the Bourbon accession to the throne in the 18th century, brought French art to Spain. The Prado has eight works attributed to Poussin, among them his serene *St Cecilia* and *Landscape with St Jerome*. The magnificent *Landscape with the Embarkation of St Paula Romana at Ostia* is the best work here by Claude Lorrain. Among the 18th-century artists featured are Antoine Watteau and Jean Ranc. *Felipe V* is the work of the royal portraitist Louis-Michel van Loo.

St Cecilia (c.1627–8) by the French artist Nicolas Poussin

GERMAN PAINTING

Although German art is not especially well represented in the Prado, there are a number of paintings by Albrecht Dürer, including his classical depictions of Adam and Eve. His lively *Self-Portrait* of 1498, painted at the age of 26, is undoubtedly the highlight of the small but valuable German collection in the museum. Lucas Cranach is also featured and works by the late 18th-century painter Anton Raffael Mengs include some magnificent portraits of Carlos III.

Deposition (c.1430) by Rogier van der Weyden

Floor mosaic in the Museo Arqueológico Nacional

Plaza de Colón ⑯

Map 6 D5. Ⓜ *Serrano, Colón.*

This large square, one of Madrid's focal points, is dedicated to Christopher Columbus (Colón in Spanish).

It is overlooked by huge tower blocks, built in the 1970s to replace the 19th-century mansions which stood here.

On the south side is a palace housing the National Library and Archaeological Museum. The Post-Modernist skyscraper of the Heron Corporation towers over the square from the far side of the Paseo de la Castellana.

The real feature of the square, however, is the pair of monuments dedicated to the discoverer of the Americas. The prettiest, and oldest, is a Neo-Gothic spire made in 1885, with Columbus at its top, pointing west. Carved reliefs on the plinth give highlights of his discoveries. Across the square is the second, more modern monument – a cluster of four large concrete shapes inscribed with quotations about Columbus's journey to America *(see p57).*

Constantly busy with traffic, the plaza may seem an unlikely venue for cultural events. Beneath it, however, is an extensive complex, recently renamed the Centro Cultural

Statue of Columbus, Plaza de Colón

Fernan Gómez. Exhibitions are held in its prestigious exhibition halls. The complex also includes lecture rooms, a theatre and a café.

Calle de Serrano ⑰

Map 8 D1. Ⓜ *Serrano.*

Named after a 19th-century politician, Madrid's smartest shopping street runs north from the Plaza de la Independencia, in the district of Salamanca, to the Plaza del Ecuador, in the district of El Viso. The street is lined with shops *(p316)* – many specializing in luxury items – housed in old-fashioned mansionblocks. Several of the country's top designers, including Adolfo Domínguez and Purificación García, have boutiques towards the north, near the ABC Serrano *(see p317)* and the Museo Lázaro Galdiano *(see p305).* Branches of the Italian shops Versace, Gucci and Armani, as well as the French Chanel, can be found on the Calle de José Ortega y Gasset. Lower down the Calle de Serrano, towards Serrano metro station, are two branches of El Corte Inglés. On the Calle de Claudio Coello, which runs parallel with Serrano, there are several lavish antique shops, in keeping with the area's up-market atmosphere.

Museo Arqueológico Nacional ⑱

Calle Serrano 13. **Map** 6 D5. **Tel** *91 577 79 12.* Ⓜ *Serrano.* 🚌 *5, 14, 21, 27, 45.* ◯ *9:30am–8pm Tue–Sat, 9:30am–3pm Sun.* ⬤ *public hols.* 🎫 *(free during refurbishment).* ♿ 🎥 ⛪ 📷

The museum is being extensively refurbished until 2010, and rooms will be closed on a rotating basis. However, with hundreds of exhibits, ranging from prehistoric times to the 19th century, this museum is still one of Madrid's best. Founde by Isabel II in 1867, it consis mainly of material uncovered during excavations all over Spain, as well as pieces from Egypt, Ancient Greece and the Etruscan civilization.

Highlights of the earliest finds include an exhibition o the ancient civilization of El Argar in Andalusia *(see p48)* and a display of jewellery uncovered at the Roman settlement of Numantia, near Soria *(see p377).*

Another area is devoted to the period between Roman and Mudéjar Spain. Iberian culture is also represented, with two notable sculptures *La Dama de Elche (see p48* and *La Dama de Baza.* The Roman period is illustrated with some impressive mosai including *Monks and Season* from Hellín (Albacete), and *Bacchus and his Train, fro* Zaragoza.

Outstanding pieces from the Visigothic period inclu several 7th-century gold vo crowns from Toledo provi

On show from the Islam era is pottery uncovered fr Medina Azahara in Andalu *(see p477),* and metal obje

Romanesque exhibits inc an ivory crucifix carved in for Fernando I of Castilla-Le and the *Madonna and Chi* from Sahagún, considered a masterpiece of Spanish art.

Steps outside the museu entrance lead undergroun an exact replica of the Alta caves in Cantabria *(see p1* – complete with their pain of the Paleolithic era.

Parque del Retiro ⑲

Map 8 E3. **Tel** 91 409 23 36. Ⓜ *Retiro, Ibiza, Atocha.* ⏺ at night. ♿

The Retiro Park, in Madrid's smart Jerónimos district, takes its name from Felipe IV's royal palace complex, which once stood here. Today, all that remains of the palace is the **Casón del Buen Retiro** (*see p295*) and the **Salón de Reinos** (*see p287*).

Used privately by the royal family from 1632, the park became the scene of elaborate pageants, bullfights and mock naval battles. In the 18th century it was partially opened to the public, provided visitors were formally dressed, and in 1869 it was fully opened. Today, the Retiro remains one of the most popular places for relaxing in Madrid.

A short stroll from the park's northern entrance down the tree-lined avenue leads to the pleasure lake, where rowing boats can be hired. On one side of the lake is a half-moon colonnade in front of which an equestrian statue of Alfonso XII rides high on a column. Opposite, portrait painters and fortune-tellers ply their trade. To the south of the lake are two palaces. The Neo-Classical **Palacio de Velázquez** and the **Palacio de Cristal** (Crystal Palace) were built by Velázquez Bosco in 1883 and 1887 respectively as venues for exhibitions held in that year.

Statue of Bourbon King Carlos III in the Real Jardín Botánico

Real Jardín Botánico ⑳

Plaza de Murillo 2. **Map** 8 D4. **Tel** 91 420 30 17. Ⓜ *Atocha.* ⏺ 10am–dusk daily. ⏺ 1 Jan, 25 Dec. 🎫 ♿ **www**.rjb.csic.es

South of the Prado (*see pp292–5*), and a suitable place for resting after visiting the gallery, are the Royal Botanical Gardens. Inspired by Carlos III, they were designed in 1781 by Gómez Ortega, Francesco Sabatini and Juan de Villanueva, architect of the Prado.

Interest in the plants of South America and the Philippines took hold during the Spanish Enlightenment (*see p62*), and the neatly laid out beds offer a huge variety of flora, ranging from trees to herbs.

Estación de Atocha ㉑

Plaza del Emperador Carlos V. **Map** 8 D5. **Tel** 902 240 202. Ⓜ *Atocha RENFE.* ⏺ 6am–1am daily. ♿

Madrid's first railway service, from Atocha to Aranjuez, was inaugurated in 1851. Forty years later Atocha station was replaced by a new building, which was extended in the 1980s. The older part of the station, built of glass and wrought iron, now houses an indoor palm garden. Next to it is the terminus for high-speed AVE trains to Seville, Toledo, Córdoba, Zaragoza, Lleida, Barcelona, Málaga, Valladolid, Segovia and France by 2010 (*see p678*).

The Ministerio de Agricultura, opposite, is a splendid late 19th-century building.

Entrance of Madrid's Estación de Atocha, busy with travellers

Monument of Alfonso XII (1901), facing the Retiro's boating lake

Museo Nacional Centro de Arte Reina Sofía ㉒

The highlight of this museum of 20th-century art is Picasso's *Guernica*. There are, however, other major works by influential artists, including Miró. The collection is housed in Madrid's former General Hospital, built in the late 18th century. Major extensions, designed by Jean Nouvel, were inaugurated in 2005, allowing the permanent collection to extend over three floors. The new glass buildings include two temporary exhibition rooms, a library, a restaurant, a café, an art shop and an auditorium.

Portrait II (19
Joan Miró's hu
work shows ele
of Surrealism,
was painted m
than ten years
his true Surrea
period ended.

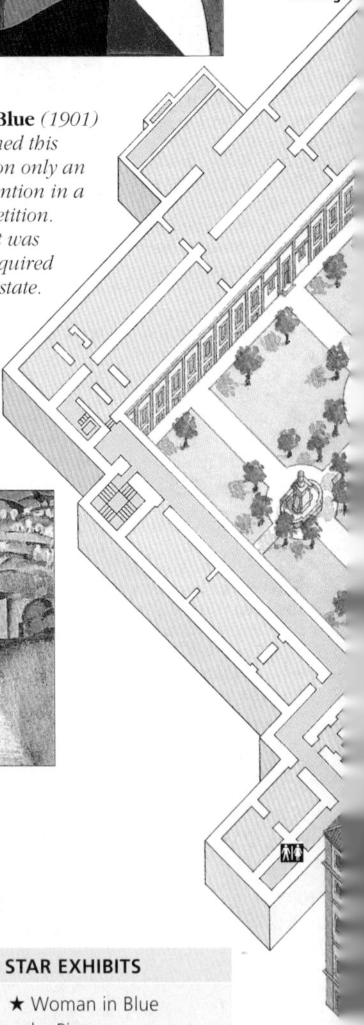

Nouvel
building

★ Woman in Blue *(1901)*
Picasso disowned this work after it won only an honourable mention in a national competition. Decades later it was located and acquired by the Spanish state.

Landscape at Cadaqués
Salvador Dalí was born in Figueres in Catalonia. He became a frequent visitor to the town of Cadaqués, on the Costa Brava (see p217), where he painted this landscape in the summer of 1923.

Accident
Alfonso Ponce de León's disturbing work, painted in 1936, prefigured his death in a car crash later that same year.

STAR EXHIBITS

★ Woman in Blue
by Picasso

★ La Tertulia del Café
de Pombo by Solana

★ Guernica by Picasso

★ **La Tertulia del Café de Pombo** *(1920)*
*José Gutiérrez Solana depicts a gathering of
intellectuals* (tertulia) *in a famous café in
Madrid, which no longer exists.*

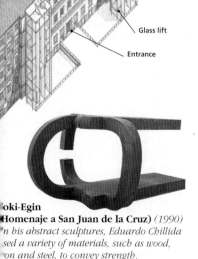

Glass lift

Entrance

ʻoki-Egin
Homenaje a San Juan de la Cruz) *(1990)*
*ʼn his abstract sculptures, Eduardo Chillida
sed a variety of materials, such as wood,
ʼon and steel, to convey strength.*

VISITORS' CHECKLIST

Calle Santa Isabel 52. **Map** 7 C5.
Tel 91 774 10 00. Atocha.
6, 14, 19, 27, 45, 55, 86.
10am–9pm Mon & Wed–Sat,
10am–2:30pm Sun. 1 Jan,
24, 25, 31 Dec & some public
hols. (free Sat pm & Sun).
www.museoreinasofia.mcu.es

GALLERY GUIDE

*The permanent collection
is in the Sabatini Building,
arranged around a court-
yard. The displays of 20th
century art occupy four floors,
with individual rooms
allocated to significant artists
such as Dalí, Miró and
Picasso. However, there are
plans to rearrange the
collection in chronological
order, so visitors may
experience some disruption.
Two temporary exhibition
rooms are located in the new
Nouvel building.*

KEY TO FLOORPLAN

Exhibition space

Non-exhibition space

Visitors admiring *Guernica*

★ PICASSO'S *GUERNICA*

The most famous single work of the
20th century, this Civil War protest
painting *(see pp66–7)* was commissioned by the Spanish Republican
government in 1937 for a Paris exhibition. The artist found his inspiration
in the mass air attack of the same year
on the Basque town of Gernika-
Lumo *(see p118)*, by German pilots
flying for the Nationalist air force. The
painting hung in a New York gallery
until 1981, reflecting the artist's wish
that it should not return to Spain until
democracy was re-established. It was
moved here from the Prado in 1992.

FURTHER AFIELD

Several of Madrid's best sights, including some interesting but little-known museums, lie outside the city centre. The axis of modern Madrid is the Paseo de la Castellana, a long, wide avenue lined by skyscraper offices and busy with traffic. A journey along it gives a glimpse of Madrid as Spain's commercial and administrative capital. La Castellana skirts the Barrio de Salamanca, an upmarket district of stylish boutiques, named after the 19th-century aristocrat who built it, the Marquis de Salamanca.

Statue in Plaza de Cascorro

The districts around Old Madrid, especially Malasaña and La Latina, offer a more typically authentic *Madrileño* atmosphere. On Sundays, some of the old streets are crowded with bargain-hunters at the sprawling second-hand market, El Rastro. If you need to escape from the bustle of the city for a while, west of Old Madrid, across the Río Manzanares, is Madrid's vast, green recreation ground, the Casa de Campo, with its pleasant pine woods, boating lake, amusement park and zoo.

SIGHTS AT A GLANCE

Historic Buildings
Palacio de Liria ⑨
Real Fábrica de Tapices ⑯
Templo de Debod ⑥

Churches and Convents
Ermita de San Antonio de la Florida ⑤

Museums and Galleries
Museo de América ⑦
Museo Cerralbo ⑧
Museo Lázaro Galdiano ⑬

Museo Municipal ⑪
Museo Sorolla ⑫

Streets, Squares and Parks
Casa de Campo ④
La Latina ②
Malasaña ⑩
Paseo de la Castellana ⑭
Plaza de la Paja ③
Plaza de Toros de Las Ventas ⑮
El Rastro ①

0 kilometres   2
0 miles   1

KEY

■ Main sightseeing area
□ Parks and open spaces
🚉 Railway station
═ Motorway
━ Major road
═ Minor road

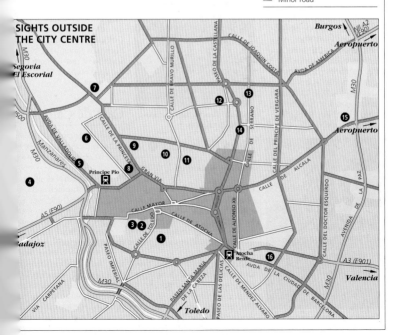

SIGHTS OUTSIDE THE CITY CENTRE

Mudéjar arches and tilework on the exterior of the Plaza de Toros de Las Ventas

El Rastro ❶

Calle Ribera de Curtidores. **Map** 4
E4. ⊛ *La Latina, Embajadores.* ◻
10am– 2pm Sun & public hols.

Madrid's celebrated flea
market *(see p317)*, established
in the Middle Ages, has its
hub in the Plaza de Cascorro
and sprawls downhill towards
the Río Manzanares. The
main street is the Calle Ribera
de Curtidores, or "Tanners'
Riverbank", once the centre of
the slaughterhouse and
tanning industry.

Although some people claim
that the Rastro has changed a
great deal since its heyday
during the 19th century, there
are still plenty of *Madrileños*,
as well as tourists, who shop
here. They come in search of
a bargain from the stalls which
sell a huge range of wares –
anything from new furniture
to second-hand clothes. The
wide range of goods and the
lively crowds in the Rastro
make it an ideal way to spend
a Sunday morning.

The Calle de Embajadores is
the market's other main street.
It runs down past the dusty
Baroque façade of the Iglesia
de San Cayetano, designed by
José Churriguera and Pedro
de Ribera. Its interior has been
restored since fire destroyed
it during the Civil War.

Further along the street is
the former Real Fábrica de
Tabacos (the Royal Tobacco
Factory), begun as a state
enterprise in 1809. Its female
workers had a reputation for
taking a hard-line stance in
industrial disputes.

**Shoppers browsing around the
Rastro flea market**

La Latina ❷

Map 4 D4. ⊛ *La Latina.*

The district of La Latina,
together with the adjacent
Lavapiés, is considered to be
the heart of *castizo* Madrid.
This term is used to describe
the culture of the traditional
working classes of Madrid –
that of the true *Madrileño*.

La Latina runs along the
city's southern hillside from
the Plaza Puerta de Moros,
southwards through the streets
where the Rastro is held. To
the east it merges with
Lavapiés. La Latina's steep
streets are lined with tall,
narrow houses, renovated to
form an attractive neighbourhood. There are old-fashioned
bars around the Plaza del
Humilladero, although the
streets to the east of La Latina,
in the Lavapiés district, have
sadly become notorious for
petty crime.

**Bottles of wine for sale in an old-
style bar in Lavapiés**

Plaza de la Paja ❸

Map 4 D3. ⊛ *La Latina.*

Once the focus of medieval
Madrid, the area around the
Plaza de la Paja – literally
Straw Square – is extremely
atmospheric and many
interesting buildings are
located on the square.

Climbing upwards from the
Calle de Segovia, a glimpse
left along the Calle Príncipe
Anglona yields a view of the
Mudéjar-style brick tower of
the Iglesia de San Pedro,
dating from the 14th century.

Interior of San Francisco el Grande

Up past the fountain, the
Plaza de la Paja ends with the
harsh stone walls of the
Capilla del Obispo, or
Bishop's Chapel, belonging
originally to the adjoining
Palacio Vargas. The superb
Plateresque altarpiece is by
Francisco Giralte. Up to the
left, the Baroque, cherub-
covered dome of the Iglesia
de San Andrés stands out.

Nearby is a small cluster of
interlinked squares, ending in
the Plaza Puerta de Moros, a
reminder of the Muslim community which once occupied
the area. From here, a right
turn leads to the domed bulk
of San Francisco el Grande, an
impressive landmark. Inside
the church is a painting by
Goya and his brother-in-law
Francisco Bayeu. The choir-
stalls were moved here from
the monastery of El Paular
(see pp328–9).

Casa de Campo ❹

Avenida de Portugal. **Tel** 91 463
63 34. ⊛ *Batán, Lago, Príncipe Pío,
Casa de Campo.* ◻ for cars at night.

This former royal hunting
ground, with pines and
scrubland stretching over 1,7
ha (4,300 acres), lies in southwestern Madrid. Its wide range
of amenities make it a popular
daytime recreation area. Attractions include a boating lake, a
zoo, and an amusement park,
the Parque de Atracciones *(see
p321)*. Sports enthusiasts can
make use of the swimming
pool and jogging track. In the
summer the park is also used
as a venue for rock concerts.

Egyptian temple of Debod, with two of its original gateways

engineers involved in the project. The temple is carved with shallow reliefs, and stands in a line with two of its original three gateways. They are situated on high ground above the Río Manzanares, in the gardens of the Parque del Oeste. From the park there are sweeping views over the Casa de Campo to the Guadarrama mountains.

The park is the site of the former Montaña barracks, which were stormed by the populace at the start of the Civil War in 1936.

Further to the west, below the brow of the hill, there is an attractive rose garden.

Ermita de San Antonio de la Florida **5**

Glorieta San Antonio de la Florida 5.
Tel 91 542 07 22. **⊛** Príncipe Pío.
9:30am–8pm Tue–Fri, 10am–2pm
& Sun. **⬤** public hols. **⬤ &**
www.munimadrid.es

Goya enthusiasts should not miss a visit to the Neo-Classical Ermita de San Antonio de la Florida, built during the reign of Carlos IV. The present church stands on the site of two previous ones, and is dedicated to St Anthony. It is named after the pastureland of la Florida, on which the original church was built.

Goya took four months, in 1798, to paint the cupola. It depicts the resurrection of a murdered man who rises in order to prove the innocence of the falsely accused father of St Anthony. The characters in it are everyday people of the late 18th century: lurking, low-life types and lively *majas (see p33)* – shrewd but elegant

women. The fresco is considered by many art critics to be among Goya's finest works.

The tomb of the artist is housed in the chapel. His remains were brought here from Bordeaux, where he died in exile in 1828 *(see p239)*.

Templo de Debod **6**

Paseo de Pintor Rosales. **Map** 1 B5.
Tel 91 366 74 15. **⊛** Ventura
Rodríguez, Plaza de España.
⬤ 10am–2pm Sat–Sun; Apr–
Sep: 10am–2pm, 6–8pm Tue–
Fri; Oct–Mar: 9:45am–1:45pm,
4:15–6:15pm Tue–Fri.
⬤ public hols.
www.munimadrid.es

The Egyptian temple of Debod, built in the 2nd century BC, was rescued from the area flooded by the Aswan Dam and given to Spain as a tribute to Spanish

Museo de América **7**

Avenida de los Reyes Católicos 6.
Tel 91 549 26 41. **⊛** Moncloa. **⬤**
9:30am–3pm Tue–Sat, 10am–3pm Sun.
⬤ some public hols. **⬤** (free Sun).
& http://museodeamerica.mcu.es

This handsome museum houses artifacts related to Spain's colonization of parts of the Americas. Many of the exhibits, which range from prehistoric times to the present, were brought back to Europe by early explorers of the New World *(see pp58–9)*.

The collection is arranged on the first and second floors, and individual rooms are given a cultural theme such as society, communication and religion. There is documentation of the Atlantic voyages by the first explorers, and examples of the objects which they found. The highlight of the museum is perhaps the rare Mayan *Códice Trocortesiano* (AD 1250–1500) from Mexico, a type of parchment illustrated with hieroglyphics of scenes from everyday life. Also worth seeing are the solid gold funereal ornaments from Colombia, the Treasure of the Quimbayas (AD 500–1000), and the collection of contemporary folk art from some of Spain's former American colonies.

Piece of the Treasure of the Quimbayas

Museo Cerralbo ❽

Calle Ventura Rodríguez 17.
Map 1 C5. **Tel** 91 547 36 46. 🚇
Plaza de España, Ventura Rodríguez.
⬤ closed for refurbishment and
reorganisation until 2009; call ahead
for details. 🎫 (free Wed & Sun). 🚫

This 19th-century mansion
near the Plaza de España is a
monument to Enrique de
Aguilera y Gamboa, the 17th
Marquis of Cerralbo. A com-
pulsive collector of art and
artifacts, he bequeathed his
lifetime's collection to the
nation in 1922, stipulating that
the exhibits be arranged
exactly as he left them. They
range from Iberian pottery to
18th-century marble busts.

One of the star exhibits is El
Greco's magnificent *The
Ecstasy of Saint Francis of
Assisi*. There are also paintings
by Ribera, Zurbarán, Alonso
Cano and Goya, which hang
in the Picture Gallery.

The focal point of the main
floor is the ballroom, lavishly
decorated with mirrors. A large
collection of weaponry is on
display on this floor.

Palacio de Liria ❾

Calle la Princesa 20. **Tel** 91 547 53
02. 🚇 Ventura Rodríguez. ⬤ write
a year in advance for permission. 🎫
obligatory. 🚫

The lavish but much restored
Palacio de Liria was completed
by Ventura Rodríguez in 1780.
Once the residence of the
Alba family, and still owned
by the Duchess, it can be
visited by appointment only.

The palace houses the Albas'
outstanding collection of art,
and Flemish tapestries. There
are paintings by Titian, Rubens
and Rembrandt. Spanish art is
particularly well represented,
with major works by Goya,
such as his 1795 portrait of the
Duchess of Alba, as well as
examples of work by El Greco,
Zurbarán and Velázquez.

Behind the palace is the
Cuartel del Conde-Duque, the
former barracks of the Count-
Duke Olivares, Felipe IV's
minister. They were built in
1720 by Pedro de Ribera,
who adorned them with a
Baroque façade. The barracks
now house a cultural centre.

Rooftops in the Malasaña district

Malasaña ❿

Map 2 F5. 🚇 Tribunal, Bilbao.

A feeling of the authentic
old Madrid pervades this
district of narrow, sloping
streets and tall houses. For
some years it was the centre
of the *movida*, the frenzied
nightlife which began after
the death of Franco.

A walk along the Calle San
Andrés leads to the Plaza de
Dos de Mayo. In the centre
a monument to artillery offic
Daoíz and Velarde, who defended the barracks which
stood here at the time of the
uprising against the French
1808 *(see p63)*.

On Calle de la Puebla is t
Iglesia de San Antonio de l
Alemanes. The church was
founded by Felipe III in the
17th century as a hospital fo
Portuguese immigrants, and
was later given over for use
German émigrés. Inside, th
walls are decorated with 18
century frescoes by Giorda

Museo Municipal

Calle de Fuencarral 78. **Map** 5 A
Tel 91 701 18 63. 🚇 Tribunal.
⬤ 9:30am–8pm Tue–Fri, 10am–
Sat & Sun (Aug: 9:30am–2:30pm
Tue–Sun). ⬤ public hols. 🚫 🎫
appt. **www**.munimadrid.es

The Municipal Museum is
worth visiting just for its
Baroque doorway *(see p25*
by Pedro de Ribera, argua
the finest in Madrid. Hous
in the former hospice of S

Main staircase of the exuberant Museo Cerralbo

Ferdinand, the museum was inaugurated in 1929.

Upstairs is a series of bird's-eye views and maps of Madrid. Among them is Pedro Teixeira's map of 1656, thought to be the oldest of the city. There is also a model of Madrid, made in 1830 by León Gil de Palacio.

Modern exhibits include a reconstruction of the collage-filled study of Ramón Gómez de la Serna, a key figure of the famous literary gatherings in the Café de Pombo *(see p299)*. The museum is undergoing refurbishment until 2009 or 2010 so many parts of the collection will be closed.

Sorolla's former studio in the Museo Sorolla

Baroque façade of the Museo Municipal, by Pedro de Ribera

Museo Sorolla ⓬

Paseo del General Martínez Campos. **Tel** 91 310 15 84. Ⓜ Rubén Darío, Iglesia, Gregorio Marañón. 9:30am–3pm Tue–Sat (to 6pm Sun), 10am–3pm Sun; (free Sun).

The former studio-mansion of Valencian Impressionist painter Joaquín Sorolla has been left virtually as it was when he died in 1923.

Although Sorolla is perhaps best known for his brilliantly lit Mediterranean beach scenes, the changing styles of his paintings are well represented in the museum, with examples of his gentle portraiture and series of works representing people from different parts of Spain. Also on display are various objects amassed during the artist's lifetime, including Spanish tiles and

ceramics. The house, constructed in 1910, has an Andalusian-style garden designed by Sorolla himself.

Museo Lázaro Galdiano ⓭

Calle Serrano 122. **Tel** 91 561 60 84. Ⓜ Rubén Darío, Gregorio Marañón. ☐ 10am–4:30pm Wed–Mon ⏾ public hols. free on Sun. by appt. **www.flg.es**

This art museum is housed in the former mansionhome of the editor and financier José Lázaro Galdiano, and consists of his private collection of fine and applied art, bequeathed to the nation in 1947. The

Charles V's fob watch

collection ranges from the 6th to the 20th century and contains items of exceptional quality, ranging from less familiar Goya portraits to a mass of fob watches, including a cross-shaped pocket-watch worn by Charles V when hunting.

Among the most beautiful objects are a series of Limoges enamels, miniature sculptures, and *The Saviour*, a portrait attributed to Leonardo da Vinci. The Museo features paintings by English artists Constable, Turner, Gainsborough and Reynolds, as well as 17th-century paintings by the likes of Spanish painters Madrazo, Zurbarán, Ribera, Murillo and El Greco.

Poster for Almodóvar's Women on the Verge of a Nervous Breakdown

LA MOVIDA

With Franco's death in 1975 came a new period of personal and artistic liberty. For the young, this was translated into the freedom to stay out late, drinking and sometimes sampling drugs. The phenomenon was known as *la movida*, "the action", and it was at its most intense in Madrid. Analysts at the time saw it as having serious intellectual content, and *la movida* has had a few lasting cultural results, like the emergence of satirical film director Pedro Almodóvar.

Torre de Picasso towering over the Paseo de la Castellana

Paseo de la Castellana ⑭

🚇 *Santiago Bernabéu, Cuzco, Plaza de Castilla, Gregorio Marañón, Colón.*

The busy traffic artery which cuts through eastern Madrid comprises several parts. Its southernmost portion – the Paseo del Prado *(see pp284–5)* – starts just north of the Estación de Atocha *(see p297)*. The oldest section of the road, it dates from the reign of Carlos III, who built it as part of his embellishment of eastern Madrid *(see p297)*. At the Plaza de Cibeles, the avenue becomes the handsome Paseo de Recoletos, which boasts fashionable cafés, including the Café Gijón *(see p291)*.

The Plaza de Colón marks the start of the Paseo de la Castellana, whose pavement cafés have become a focal point for young Madrid's social life. This northernmost section has several notable examples of modern architecture, including the huge grey Nuevos Ministerios building, completed under Franco. Further on, before reaching the Plaza de Lima, is the Torre de Picasso *(see p25)*, one of Spain's tallest buildings. East of the square is the Estadio Bernabéu, home of Real Madrid Football Club *(see p177)*. The building that dominates the Paseo, however, is the Puerta de Europa, locally known as "Torres Kio": twin glass blocks on either side of the road, built at an angle as if leaning toward each other.

Plaza de Toros de Las Ventas ⑮

Calle Alcalá 237. **Tel** *91 356 22 00.* 🚇 *Ventas.* ☐ *for bullfights & concerts.* 🎫 *every half hour from 10am to 1:30pm Tue–Sun (91 556 92 37).* **Museo Taurino Tel** *91 725 18 57.* ☐ *Mar–Oct: 9:30am–2:30pm Tue–Fri, 10am–1pm Sun; Nov– Feb: 9:30am–2pm Mon–Fri.* ♿

Whatever your opinion of bullfighting, Las Ventas is undoubtedly one of the most beautiful bullrings in Spain. Built in 1929 in Neo-Mudéjar style, it replaced the city's original bullring which stood near the Puerta de Alcalá. With its horsehoe arches around the outer galleries and the elaborate tilework decoration, it makes an attractive venue for the *corridas* held during the bullfighting season, from May to October. The statues outside the bullring are monuments to two renowned Spanish bullfighters: Antonio Bienvenida and José Cubero.

Adjoining the bullring is the Museo Taurino. Memorabilia includes portraits and sculptures of famous matadors, as well as the heads of several bulls killed during fights at Las Ventas. Visitors can view close up the tools of the bullfighter's trade: capes and *banderillas* – sharp darts used to wound the bull *(see pp36–7)*. For some people, the gory highlight of the exhibition is the blood-drenched *traje de luces* worn by the legendary Manolete during his fateful

bullfight at Linares in Andalusia in 1947. Also on display is a costume which belonged to Juanita Cruz, a female bullfighter of the 1930 who was forced, in the face of prejudice, to leave Spain. In September and October, the bullring hosts rock concerts.

Real Fábrica de Tapices ⑯

Calle Fuenterrabía 2. **Tel** *91 434 05 51.* 🚇 *Menéndez Pelayo.* ☐ *10am 2pm Mon–Fri.* ☐ *Public hols & Aug* 📧 www.realfabricadetapices.com

Founded by Felipe V in 1721 the Royal Tapestry Factory is the sole survivor of several factories which were opened by the Bourbons *(see pp62–)* during the 18th century. In 1889 the factory was relocat to this building just south of the Parque del Retiro.

Visitors can see the makin of the carpets and tapestries by hand, a process which h changed little. Goya and his brother-in-law Francisco Bay created drawings, or cartoo which were the inspiration tapestries made for the roya family. Some of the cartoon are on display here; others can be seen in the Museo c Prado *(see pp292–5)*. Some the tapestries can be seen a El Pardo *(see p332)* and at Escorial *(see pp330–31)*. Now days one of the factory's m tasks is making and repairi the beautiful carpets decora the Hotel Ritz *(see p286)*.

Plaza de Toros de Las Ventas, Madrid's beautiful bullring

MADRID STREET FINDER

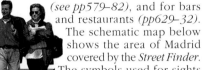

The map references given with the sights, shops and entertainment venues described in the Madrid section of the guide refer to the street maps on the following pages. Map references are also given for Madrid hotels *(see pp579–82)*, and for bars and restaurants *(pp629–32)*. The schematic map below shows the area of Madrid covered by the *Street Finder*. The symbols used for sights and other features are listed in the key at the foot of the page.

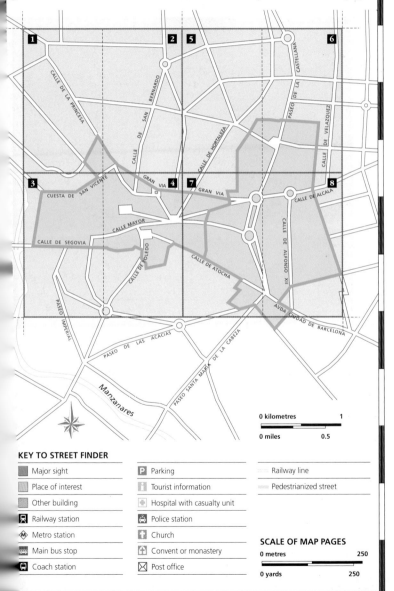

KEY TO STREET FINDER

■ Major sight	**P** Parking	⸺ Railway line
■ Place of interest	**ℹ** Tourist information	▰▰ Pedestrianized street
■ Other building	✚ Hospital with casualty unit	
🚆 Railway station	🚔 Police station	**SCALE OF MAP PAGES**
Ⓜ Metro station	✝ Church	0 metres 250
🚌 Main bus stop	✝ Convent or monastery	0 yards 250
🚍 Coach station	⊠ Post office	

0 kilometres   1
0 miles   0.5

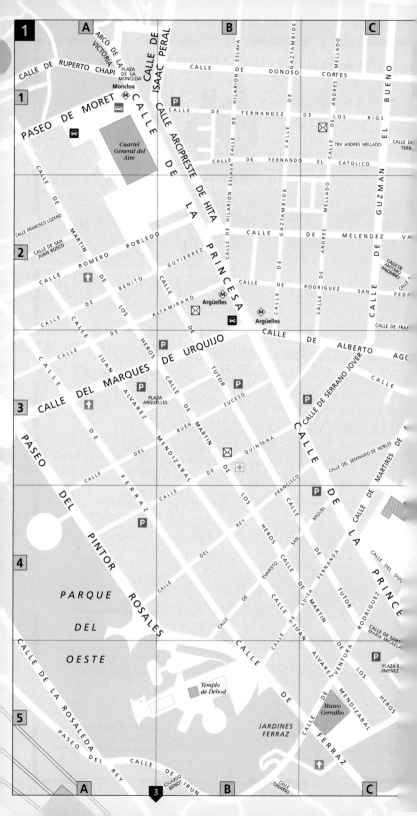

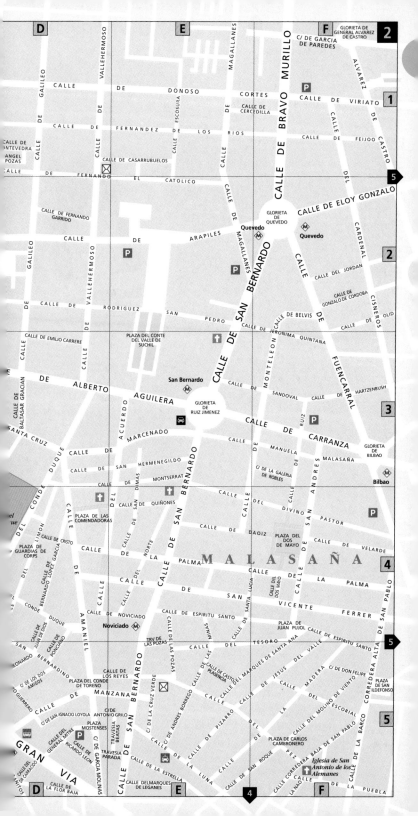

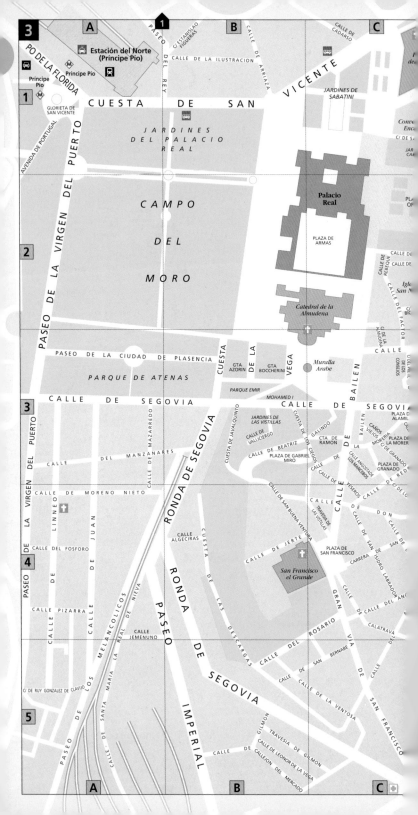

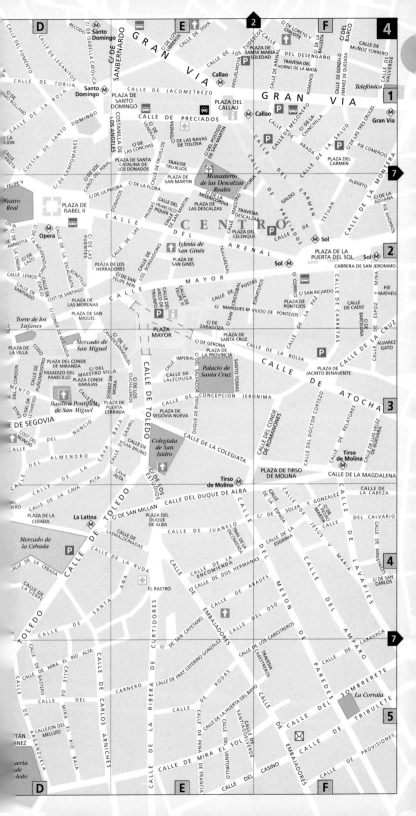

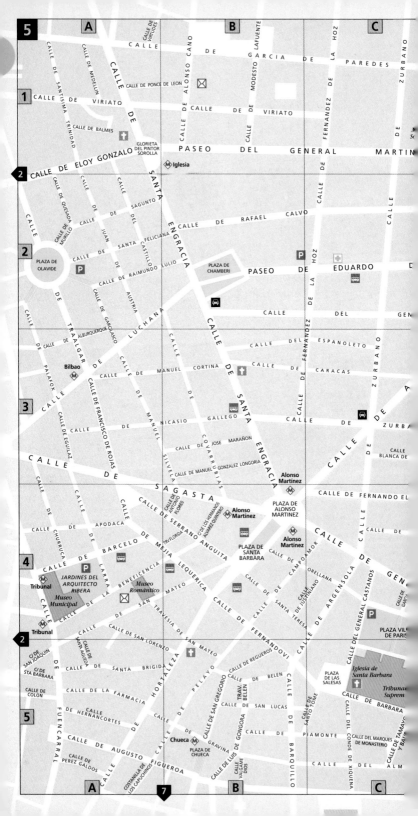

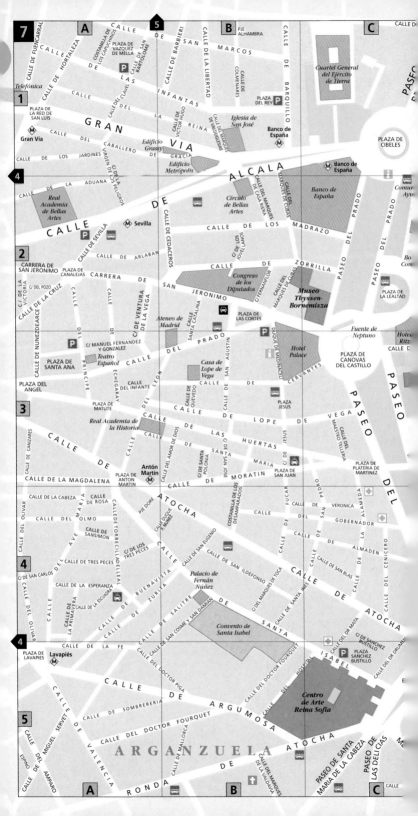

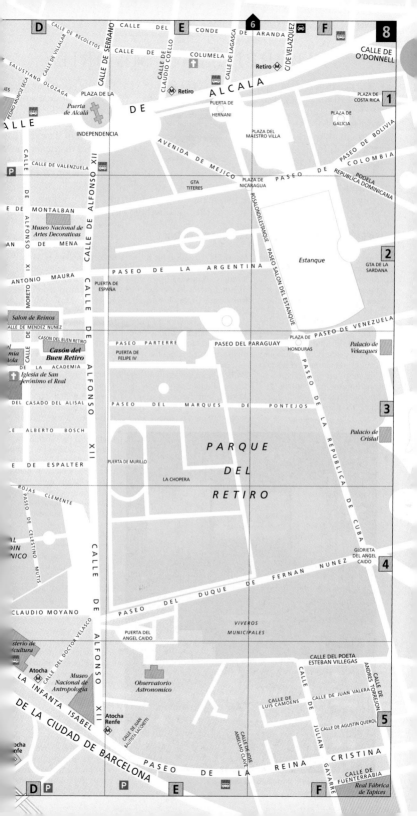

SHOPPING IN MADRID

Madrid is a shoppers' paradise, where designer stores compete for attention with small, quirky shops. Madrid still has more independent and family-run shops than most European capitals, so it should not be hard to pick up some truly original gifts. There are two main shopping hearts in the city – the

Selection of cakes

crowded and popular street around the pedestrianize Preciados and the Plaza de Sol, and Calle de la Princes and adjacent streets. Th Salamanca district is host t designer brands as well a up-market antiques, while for the la est streetware visit the Chueca distric The colourful food markets dotte around the city are well worth a visit

OPENING HOURS

Due to Spanish meal times, shopping hours in Madrid are different from many other European cities. Most shops are open from 10am to 2pm and 5 to 8pm, though larger stores tend to stay open during lunch and close at 10pm. Small shops often close on Saturday afternoon. Shopping centres, department stores and big shops are permitted to open on the first Sunday of the month. Many small shops close for a month (usually August) in the summer.

FOOD AND DRINK

Madrid is a paradise for gourmet food shopping. Strongly scented saffron, matured ewe's cheese or a fruity extra-virgin olive oil all make ideal gifts. Spain has a deep-rooted tradition of pork products, ranging from whole hams to sausages of every shape and size. The best and most expensive ham is Ibérico, from the small, black-hoofed Iberian pig. In Old Madrid, branches of Museo del Jamón have an enormous range of Spanish hams,

cheeses and cured sausages The department store **El Corte Inglés** has its own department dedicated to gourmet delicacies, as well as a supermarket for more general groceries. There are smaller delicatessens in nearly every district. In the Salamanca area visit **Mantequerías Bravo**, famou for its excellent cheeses, preserves and sweets.

If you are looking for goo wine, head to **Reserva y Ca** an outlet with a long histor of selling Spanish and Portuguese wines. It also organizes tasting sessions. **Lavinia**, in the Salamanca district, is said to be Europ biggest wine shop, with m than 1,500 brands available For a truly authentic Madrileño souvenir, try **La Violeta**, famous for its fragrant violet sweets.

MARKETS

A favourite local activity is shopping at the street, or markets, where you can spend a pleasant few hou browsing for antiques, second-hand clothes, pott handicrafts and furniture. Some markets are focused on only one item, such as the Sunday morning stam postcard and coin market under the arches of Plaza Mayor, or the Cuesta de Moyano at the Atocha en Paseo de Prado, where st selling second-hand book are set up daily. The legendary El Rastro Sund flea market *(see p302).* is must for any visitor to Ma not only for the variety o goods to be found, from

The enticing frontage of the Museo del Jamón

...side one of the many antique shops in the streets around El Rastro

...tiques to trendy garments, ...it also for its lively ...mosphere. It gets really ...owded from 12 noon ...wards, with bargain- ...nters rubbing shoulders ...th those out to enjoy a pre- ...nch apéritif at the numerous ...rs of the La Latina area. ...careful, however, as pick- ...ckets frequent the market. ...visit the handicrafts market ...Plaza Comendadoras on ...urdays from 11am to 9pm ...diverse pieces by Madrid's ...sts. The best place for ...ntings is the street market ...ar Sol on Sunday mornings, ...ganized by the art ...ociation, Taller Abierto. ...is worth visiting the ...ourful Mercado de San ...guel in Plaza San Miguel. ...up in a refurbished early ...h-century building, the ...rket stalls offer an array of ...duce and delicious ...catessen items, including ...ditional cured meats and ...nish cheeses.

NUAL FAIRS

...contemporary art fair, ...O, takes place in February. ...ther you want to buy or ...ly browse, it provides a ...t opportunity to catch up ...he latest trends in the art ...d.

...the week prior to Madrid's ...a de San Isidro (*see p40*) ...h begins on 15th May, you ...buy earthern cookware ...wine jugs at the Feria ...Cerámica held in the ...a de las Comendadores in ...colourful district of ...saña. The Feria del Libro, ...at the end of May, is an

impressive outdoor bookfair. Hundreds of stalls are set up in the Parque del Retiro, and publishers and bookshop owners exhibit their wares for two weeks, with book signings taking place as well.

On the Paseo de Recoletos, the Feria de Artesanos takes place every December, selling all kinds of crafts, making it ideal for Christmas shopping. Throughout December, the Plaza Mayor is the venue for a traditional Christmas fair – the Mercado de Artículos Navideños, where Christmas bric-à-brac can be picked up.

ANTIQUES AND ARTS

The commercial galleries and antiques shops of Madrid are all conveniently located around the Calle Barquillo in the Alonso Martínez district, along the streets of Serrano, Velázquez, Jorge Juán and Claudio Coello. For cutting-edge Spanish art, head to the **Juana de Aizpuru** gallery, considered to be one of Madrid's top galleries for contemporary art.

Antique shops can also be found in El Rastro flea market, mainly along Calle de la Ribera de Curtidores. **Hidalgo** is a classic that sells unusual collectors' items, such as keys, metal boxes and corkscrews.

For specialist antique outlets, ranging from 18th-century lacquered furniture, to Spanish paintings from the 16th to 18th centuries, visit **María García Cavestany** and **Theotokopoulos**. On

Calle Lagasca an antique centre, **Centro de Anticuarios**, hosts some of Madrid's top dealers under one roof. There are also opportunities for pricier antique shopping along the streets of the Prado, Santa Catalina and in the Mercado Puerta de Toledo. In Madrid, art and antiques auctions are held by both Spanish and inter- national firms, including Sotheby's and Christie's.

SHOPPING CENTRES AND DEPARTMENT STORES

Among the best shopping centres, or *centros comerciales*, are the tempting and expen- sive malls of the elegant Salamanca neighbourhood. **El Jardín de Serrano** is a high-quality *galleria*, housed in two restored 19th-century palaces that stocks fashion, jewellery, gifts and accessories. **ABC Serrano** has a range of shops that includes home furniture as well as designer fashions and gifts.

If you want more variety at a cheaper price, visit the huge **La Vaguada** on the north side of Madrid, or **El Corte Inglés**, a national institution with branches throughout the city. The latter also has a travel agency and offers services such as photo development and shoe repairs. Also good value for money are the shops in the new **Príncipe Pío** shopping centre, located in the former Northern Railway Station. Shops, restaurants and cinemas sit under the original glass and iron roof.

Sunday morning in the busy Rastro flea market

FASHION

The Spanish chain stores **Zara** and **Mango** have now become international phenomena, offering easy-to-wear clothes for women at very good prices. Zara also caters to men and children. Both stores have branches all over the city. For up-market fashion there are many well-known Spanish designers, such as **Amaya Arzuaga** and **Antonio Miró**, who have their own shops in Madrid, mainly in the Salamanca district.

Those in favour of a more unusual or original look should try **Ágata Ruiz de la Prada**'s creations (for children and adults), while the minimalist **Antonio Pernas'** shop specializes in more classic styles.

For high-quality designer menswear check out **Roberto Verino**, **Antonio Miró**, **Adolfo Domínguez** or **Caramelo**. These shops also offer women's clothes. Another popular, reasonably-priced Spanish chain store for men is **Springfield**. At the top end of the market is the **Loewe** store for men, where a silk tie with a Spanish art motif makes a stylish gift.

The Chueca district is the best place for the latest in streetwear, with offbeat local designers and second-hand shops on almost every corner. Many outlets also sell international brands at reduced prices.

SHOES AND LEATHER GOODS

Madrid is a haven for those with a shoe fetish. You will find every type of shoe here, from the traditional espadrille sold at **Antigua Casa Crespo** to the popular Majorcan **Camper** shoes. For comfort, try **Yanko** for their soft and snug shoes that feel like slippers, while for sophistication, opt for the elegant **Farrutx**. If you are after trendy flip-flops head to Jocomomola in Callejón de Jorge Juan. For something a little different, visit the avant-garde **Excrupulus Net** in Chueca, or **Bravo** for some of the best national and international labels. For trainers or other budget buys, visit the shops along Calle de Fuencarral, or go to **Los Guerrilleros** in Puerta del Sol.

Spain undoubtedly produces some of the best quality leather in the world. The ultimate in bags and leather goes under the prestigious label of **Loewe**, whose products are sold all over the world. Another impressive (and perhaps more budget friendly) national brand is **Salvador Bachiller**, where you will find quality leather and exclusively designed bags, suitcases, wallets and other accessories. If you are looking for a touch of the more traditional Andalusian style, take a look at the range of the handbags and belts for sale at **El Caballo**.

JEWELLERY

In Calle Serrano and Gran Vía you will find both small shops, stacked with trays of gold studs, chains and bracelets, and grand, more exclusive jewellers. Man-made "Majorica" pearls, as well as the cultivated variety, can be found all over Madrid, including at the department store El Corte Inglés.

The innovative Catalan **Tous** is popular among the young for its ubiquitous teddy-bear logo. If you are interested in original, simple designs, visit the acclaimed jeweller **Joaquín Berao**. His shop resembles an art gallery devoted to tastefully designed pieces. Museum shops are also a good place to shop for designer jewellery. Look out for original pieces from Verili, sold at the main museums in the city.

CRAFTS AND DESIGN

Traditional crafts such as woven baskets or embroidered linen are hard to find in Madrid and those that are available often tend to be Asian imports. However, lovely and inexpensive ceramics are widely available, though sometimes the more colourful pieces are from Morocco. A wide choice of ceramics can be found at **Cántaro**, near the Plaza de España. Well stocked in regional styles, the shop also carries so-called "extinct" ceramics – traditional styles of pottery no longer regularly produced. Many shops around Puerta del Sol stock embroidered tablecloths and shawls, but be aware that the authentic pieces can be quite expensive.

In the Mercado de Puerta de Toledo, you will find **Artesanos de la Villa**, an association of more than a 100 craft workshops that sell all kind of traditional and modern crafts such as pottery, leather goods, glassware and metalwork.

For contemporary design, head to **Víctimas del Celuloide**, an original shop with a great variety of unusual goods, from Chinese chopsticks to kits to make-your-own silicone lamps. It is the perfect place to find something a little different.

BOOKS AND MUSIC

The giant French-owned **FNAC** book and video store has an extensive selection of books and magazines in English and other languages as does **Casa del Libro**. **Booksellers**, a little further afield, stocks English classics though only a limited selection of new books. The second-hand bookstalls of Mercado del Libro near the Parque del Retiro are good for cheap paperbacks and, sometimes, rare volumes. books can be found at one the best specialist art book shops, **Gaudí**, near Chueca.

For all types of music, g to the FNAC or one of the El Corte Inglés branches, either in Calle de Preciado or Paseo de la Castellana.

For flamenco buffs, the specialist **El Flamenco Vive** stocks the widest selection of books, guitars and CDs in the world.

DIRECTORY

FOOD AND DRINK

Lavinia
C/ de José Ortega y
Gasset 16.
Map 6 F3.
Tel 914 26 06 04.

La Violeta
Plaza Canalejas 6.
Map 7 A2.
Tel 915 22 55 22.

Museo del Jamón
Carrera de San
Jerónimo 6. **Map** 5 A1.
Tel 915 21 03 46.

**Mantequerías
Bravo**
C/ de Ayala 24.
Map 6 E4.
Tel 915 76 76 41.

Reserva y Cata
C/ del Conde de
Xiquena 13.
Map 5 C5.
Tel 913 19 04 01.

ANTIQUES AND ARTS

**Centro de
Anticuarios**
C/ de Lagasca 36.
Tel 915 77 37 52.
Map 6 E5.

Hidalgo
Galerías Piquer, shop 23.
C/ la Ribera de Curtidores
29.
Map 4 E5.
Tel 915 30 56 53.

Juana de Aizpuru
C/ Barquillo 44.
Map 5 B5.
Tel 913 10 55 61.

**María García
Prevestany**
C/ Jorge Juan 14.
Map 6 E5.
Tel 915 77 76 32.

Theotokopoulos
C/ Alcalá 97. **Map** 8 E1.
Tel 915 75 84 66.
www.theoarte.com

SHOPPING CENTRES AND MALLS

ABC Serrano
C/ Serrano 61.
Map 4 F2.
Tel 915 77 50 31.
www.abcserrano.com

El Corte Inglés
C/ Preciados 1–3.
Map 4 F2.
Tel 913 79 80 00.
www.elcorteingles.es
One of several branches.

El Jardín de Serrano
C/ Goya 6–8.
Map 1 A1.
Tel 915 77 00 12.
www.jardindeserrano.es

La Vaguada
Av Monforte de Lemos 36.
Tel 917 30 10 00.
www.enlavaguada.com

Príncipe Pío
Estación del Norte.
Map 3 A1.
Tel 917 58 00 40.
www.ccprincipepio.com

FASHION

Adolfo Domínguez
C/ Serrano 18.
Map 6 E4.
Tel 915 77 82 80.

**Ágata Ruiz de la
Prada**
C/ Serrano 27.
Map 6 E4.
Tel 913 19 05 01.

Amaya Arzuaga
C/ Lagasca 50.
Map 6 E5.
Tel 914 26 28 15.

Antonio Miró
C/ Lagasca 65.
Map 6 E5.
Tel 914 26 02 25.

Antonio Pernas
C/ Claudio Coello 46.
Map 6 E4.
Tel 915 78 16 76.

Caramelo
C/ Serrano 19.
Map 6 E4.
Tel 914 35 01 77.

Mango
C/ de la Princesa 68.
Map 1 B2.
Tel 915 43 92 67.
One of several branches.

Roberto Verino
C/ Serrano 33.
Map 6 E4.
Tel 914 26 04 75.

Springfield
C/ Fuencarral 107.
Map 2 F3.
Tel 914 47 59 94.
One of several branches.

Zara
C/ Preciados 18.
Map 4 F2.
Tel 915 21 09 58.
One of several branches.

SHOES AND LEATHER GOODS

**Antigua Casa
Crespo**
C/ del Divino Pastor 29.
Map 2 F4.
Tel 915 21 56 54.

Bravo
C/ Serrano 42.
Map 6 E4.
Tel 914 35 27 29.
One of several branches.

Camper
C/ de la Princesa 75.
Map 1 B2.
Tel 902 36 45 98.
www.camper.es

El Caballo
C/ Lagasca 55.
Map 6 E5.
Tel 915 76 40 37.

Excrupulus Net
C/ del Almirante 7.
Map 5 V5.
Tel 915 21 72 44.

Farrutx
C/ Serrano 7.
Map 8 D1.
Tel 915 76 94 93.

Loewe
C/ Serrano 26.
Map 6 E4.
Tel 915 77 60 56.

Los Guerrilleros
Plaza de la Puerta del
Sol 5.
Map 4 F2.
Tel 915 21 27 08.

Salvador Bachiller
Gran Vía 65.
Map 2 D5.
Tel 915 59 83 21.

Yanko
C/ de Lagasca 52.
Map 6 F4.
Tel 915 76 16 78.

JEWELLERY

Joaquín Berao
C/ Claudio
Coello 35.
Map 6 E5.
Tel 915 77 28 28.

Tous
C/ Serrano 86.
Map 6 E3.
Tel 915 77 48 37.

CRAFTS AND DESIGN

**Artesanos de
la Villa**
Mercado Puerta de Toledo,
2nd floor.
Map 4 D5.
Tel 913 64 05 38.

Cántaro
Calle de la Flor Baja 8.
Map 2 D5.
Tel 915 47 95 14.

**Víctimas del
Celuloide**
C/ Santiago 4.
Map 4 D2.
Tel 915 47 61 35.

BOOKS AND MUSIC

Booksellers
C/ Fernández de la
Hoz 40.
Tel 914 42 79 59.

Casa del Libro
Gran Vía 29.
Map 4 F1.
Tel 902 02 64 02.
www.casadellibro.com

El Flamenco Vive
C/ del Conde de Lemos 7.
Map 4 D2.
Tel 915 47 39 17.

FNAC
C/ Preciados 28.
Map 4 E1.
Tel 915 95 61 00.
www.fnac.es

Gaudí
C/ Argensola 13.
Map 5 C4.
Tel 913 08 18 29.

ENTERTAINMENT IN MADRID

As a major European capital, Madrid takes its arts and entertainment very seriously, hosting the finest and most diverse dance, music and theatre productions from around the world. Vibrant art, music and film festivals are held around the year, supplemented by a pulsating nightlife, raucous street parties and lively cafés.

Flamenco guitarist in Parque del Retiro

Even traditional art forms, such as flamenco, bullfighting and Madrid's version of the operetta, *zarzuela*, are characterized by flamboyance and spectacle. Football is also a major draw, and Real Madrid is a hugely celebrated team. Between fiestas, flamenco, football and much more, the revelry never stops in Madrid.

Madrid's Teatro Real *(see p322)*

ENTERTAINMENT GUIDES

Madrid's entertainment guides are mostly in Spanish. *Guía del Ocio*, a handy weekly guide to what's on in the city, comes out every Friday and can be bought from kiosks. Three daily newspapers have entertainment supplements on Friday as well: *El Mundo, ABC* and *El País*.

The English-language monthly, *InMadrid*, publishes cultural listings and reviews of the latest bars and clubs. It is available in bookshops, record stores and **Barajas Airport** information office.

Information on forthcoming events can also be obtained from one of the tourist information offices in the city, where English will be spoken. The tourist board also publishes *Es Madrid*, a free, bilingual brochure.

SEASONS AND TICKETS

There is always something going on in Madrid's theatres and stadiums, but the cultural season is at its peak from Sep-

tember to June. May's Fiesta de San Isidro, Madrid's patron saint festival, and the Festival de Otoño, a music, theatre and dance festival held from October to November, attract many big Spanish and international names. Tickets can be bought in advance from **Entradas.com** or Telentrada.com.

In July and August, Madrid hosts Veranos de la Villa (book through tourist offices), a special programme that includes art exhibitions, jazz, opera, flamenco, cinema and drama at various venues.

Tickets for a number of events can be bought at **FNAC** and **El Corte Inglés** stores and websites. Many other reliable internet sites also sell tickets. Check the websites of venues too, since many of them offer online booking services.

CAFES, BARS AND TERRACES

Madrid's social life revolves around an endless array of cafés, bars and summer terraces. These venues are

perfect places to relax and people-watch. Especially popular areas for *terraceo* (doing the rounds of various terraces) are Plaza de Santa Ana, Paja, Chueca and Dos de Mayo. The glamorous crowd often spend evenings strolling down avenues, such as Paseo de la Castellana and Rosales, stopping now and then to nip into a terrace bar or café.

Madrid has retained many of its old grand cafés. **Café Comercial**, a city landmark, an excellent meeting place with its wonderful early 20th century ambience. **Café del Círculo de Bellas Artes** is housed in a cultural foundation, and is an institution in itself. It is ideal for coffee or lunch after spending a day pursuing cultural interests. Of the literary cafés, the famous **Café Gijón** *(see p291)* should not be missed.

In the evening, it is almost essential to head to a *taberna* where you can order a *ración*, the more substantial version

Dancing the night away at the Joy Madrid Discoteque *(see p324)*

xterior of the historic Café Gijón

f tapas, and accompany it
ith a good local wine. Go
r a *taberna* crawl and visit
e the older and most
teresting establishments
ch as **Taberna Antonio**
ánchez, which is well known
r its history and the quality
f its tapas. **Cervecería La**
rdosa is popular with both
urists and locals, and
berna Maceiras is favoured
r its Galician wines and
her specialities.

ULLFIGHTING

hough bullfighting *(see*
36–7) is not as popular as
used to be in many other
rts of Spain, it continues to
ive in Madrid. The **Plaza**
 Toros de las Ventas is the
st important ring in the
rld, holding *corridas*
ery Sunday from March to
tober. In May, during the
sta de San Isidro, there
 corridas every day, with
ne of the biggest names
rticipating in the spectacle.
he Las Ventas box office
pen on Fridays from 10am
2pm and from 5pm to
n. You can also purchase
ets from abroad through
Taquilla Toros website,
d collect them at the box
ce up to two hours
ore the fight.

OTBALL

rid is very proud of its
n, **Real Madrid** *(see p177)*,
the players are celebrities
pain. With a capacity of
00, their home stadium
iago Bernabéu is one of
greatest theatres of the
e. Tickets can be bought
he phone, or through the
um's internet site.
r those wishing to visit
stadium, guided tours are
lucted on Mondays and
rdays between 10am and
(10:30am to 6:30pm on

Sundays and holidays); on days
when there are matches times
may vary. Tickets can be
bought at the box office with
no need to book in advance.
    Real Madrid's rivals, **Atlético**
de Madrid, are based at the
Vicente Calderón stadium.

DANCE

Madrid's dance scene has
come a long way over
recent years, with inter-
national companies and
local talent performing
regularly around the city.
Madrid is the home of
Spain's prestigious Ballet
Nacional de España and
the more contemporary
Compañía Nacional de
Danza, directed by the
world famous dancer and
choreographer Nacho
Duato. Víctor Ullate's Ballet
de la Comunidad de Madrid
presents a more avant-
garde mix of classical and
contemporary dance.
    A good time to experience
Madrid's rich dance tradition is
around April, when the annual
En Danza festival takes place.
Both Spanish and international
dancers perform at this time.
    The **Teatro Albéniz** is the
main venue for ballet, although
it is due to close in 2009. The
two other major venues are
the **Teatro Madrid** and the
Teatro Real where opera is
usually performed. Smaller
venues such as **Cuarta Pared**
occasionally present alternative dance performances.
    Details can usually be
found in the entertainment
listings or on the individual
venues' website.

FLAMENCO

Although flamenco origin-
ated in Andalusia *(see*
pp424–5), Madrid is often
seen as its spiritual home
and some of the best
flamenco dancers and
musicians regularly perform
here. The scene is
sparklingly vibrant, and
interpretations of the art
range from the traditional
to the daringly innovative,
inspired by dancers such
as Joaquín Cortés.
    Most *tablaos* (flamenco
venues) offer drinks and
dinner with the show. Do
note, however, that the show
may sometimes feature only
singing and not the familar
rhythmic dancing.
    Café de Chinitas and **Corral**
de la Moreria are among the
older and better *tablaos* in
town, but are somewhat
touristy. Also well worth a
visit are **Arco de Cuchilleros**
and **Casa Patas**.
    Flamenco bars such as
Cardamomo are full of
boisterous young people,
but are a fun way of
experiencing the sound and
feel of flamenco. Two bars
that feature regular, spontaneous performances are
the atmospheric **Candela** and
La Soleá. Note that as these
places are frequented by local
flamenco aficionados, visitors
should be respectful of the art.
    Take into account that
although bars are fun and a
good introduction to the art
of flamenco, some of the
best dance troupes, singers
and players usually perform
at the city's theatres.

Las Ventas bullring on the day of a bullfight

CLASSICAL MUSIC, OPERA AND ZARZUELA

Madrid's **Auditorio Nacional de Música** is home to Spain's national orchestra, Orquesta Nacional, as well as its national choir, Coro Nacional de España. With two concert halls, the auditorium also hosts many high-profile performances.

The illustrious and recently renovated **Teatro Real** is best known as the home of the city's opera company. It also houses Orquesta Sinfónica de Madrid, Spain's oldest orchestra with a rich history dating back to more than a century. The magnificent Real is the best place to watch top-class international and national opera performances. Tickets for a show can be bought at a maximum of two weeks in advance by phone or from the website and can be collected at the box office up to half an hour before the show begins.

The **Teatro Monumental** is the main venue for the excellent Orquesta Sinfónica y Coro de RTVE, the orchestra and choir of Spain's state television and radio company. The **Centro Cultural Conde Duque** hosts classical concerts among many other art events.

Those who want to experience a Spanish, especially a *Madrileño*, take on the operetta, should definitely make time to see a *zarzuela* being performed. The origins of this lively form of musical drama-cum-social satire can be traced back to early 17th-century Madrid, and the tradition is still going strong. With both spoken and sung parts as well as dancing, the *zarzuela* can be comic, ribald and even romantic. It is always enjoyable to watch.

The best productions are usually staged at the **Teatro de la Zarzuela**. Other theatres also host *zarzuela* performances occasionally. Check listings for details.

Look our for details on free, outdoor concerts in the papers. The Teatro Real always opens the opera season with a live transmission of the first show on massive video screens in Plaza de Oriente.

ROCK, JAZZ AND WORLD MUSIC

Madrid's music scene is eclectic and energetic, mixing top international pop stars with independent local bands performing at a variety of venues. Madrid's increasingly multicultural mix has ensured an explosion of Latin American and African sounds recently, as well as intersting fusions of both with more familiar Spanish sounds. In the 1980s, the heady days of *la movida* (*see p305*) gave birth to Spanish pop and the momentum continues to this day with Madrid remaining the centre of the country's music scene.

For rock music, **Sala la Riviera**, located next to the Manzanares river, has an excellent and well-deserved reputation. It has hosted major international stars such as Bob Dylan, the Cranberries and guitarist Joe Satriani among countless others. **Honky Tonk**, in the Chamberí district, often has performances from local bands, so keep an eye out for posters advertising events, some of which are free.

Siroco has devoted itself to discovering new alternative and indie bands, and also doubles as a club with live music performances.

One of Europe's best jazz clubs, **Café Central**, with its Art Deco elegance, is one place that should not be missed. Also popular is the lively **Populart** jazz and blues venue.

Musicians from all over the world representing a range of musical genres can be heard at **El Sol**. One of the most important clubs of the *Movida Madrileña* (*see p305*), El Sol is the only one that continues to promote the underground style of music of the 1980s.

There are plenty of other well-reputed venues in the city that feature live music daily. The best way to keep abreast of the latest events is to check out weekly listings and to keep an eye out for adverts on the street.

THEATRE

Madrid has a theatrical tradition that stretches back to the Golden Age of the 17th century, with writers such as Lope de Vega and Calderón de la Barca creating a canon of work that is still performed today.

One of the most prestigious theatres in the city, the **Teatro de la Comedia** is traditionally home to the Compañía Nacional de Teatro Clásico, which stages classic works by Spanish playwrights. However since the Comedia is under renovation, the company is now performing at the **Teatro Pavón** (until the year 2009).

Another one of the most highly regarded theatres is the **Teatro María Guerrero**, which presents Spanish modern drama, as well as foreign plays.

For contemporary and alternative theatre, Madrid has a thriving network of fringe venues such as **Cuarta Pared** and **Círculo de Bellas Artes**.

For musicals, try **Teatro Nuevo Apolo** or **Teatro Häagen-Dazs** Other venues such as **La Latina** and **Teatro Muñoz Seca** specialize in comedy productions.

A wide range of Spanish and international theatrical talent take part in the annual Festival de Otoño in October and November.

CINEMA

Spanish cinema (*see p192*) has earned great international acclaim in recent years. For those with a grasp of the language, Spanish film is a rewarding experience, especially enjoyed at one of the grand film theatres along Gran Vía, such as **Capitol**, which has screened films since the early 1900s.

Non-Spanish movies can be seen in their original-language versions at **Verdi Ideal**, **Golem** and **Renoir**. Screenings will be found listed in newspapers and listings magazines. Note that tickets cost less on the *día del espectador*, which is usually on Monday or Wednesday.

DIRECTORY

TOURIST OFFICES

Comunidad de Madrid Tourist Office
C/ Duque de Medinacelli 2.
Map 7 B3.
Tel 902 100 007.

Municipal Tourist Office
Pl Mayor 27. **Map** 4 E3.
Tel 915 88 16 36.

TICKETS

El Corte Inglés
Tel 902 40 02 22.
www.elcorteingles.com

Entradas.com
Tel 902 48 84 88.

FNAC
Tel 902 10 06 32.
www.fnac.es

Tel Entrada
Tel 902 10 12 12.
www.telentrada.com

CAFES, BARS AND TERRACES

Café Comercial
Glorieta de Bilbao 7.
Map 4 F2.
Tel 915 21 56 55.

Café del Círculo de Bellas Artes
C/ Alcalá 42. **Map** 4 E3.
Tel 915 21 69 42.

Café Gijón
Paseo de Recoletos 21.
Map 7 C1.
Tel 915 21 54 25.

Cervecería La Ardosa
C/ Colón 13. **Map** 5 A5.
Tel 915 21 49 79.

Taberna Maceiras
C/ de Jesús 7. **Map** 7 B3.
Tel 914 29 15 84.

Taberna Antonio Sánchez
C/ de Mesón de Paredes 13.
Map 4 F5.
Tel 915 39 78 26.

BULLFIGHTING

Las Ventas
C/ Alcalá 237.
Tel 913 56 22 00.
www.las-ventas.com

Taquilla Toros
www.taquillatoros.com

FOOTBALL

Atlético de Madrid
Estadio Vicente Calderón,
Paseo de la Virgen del Puerto 67.
Tel 902 26 04 03. www.clubatleticodemadrid.com

Real Madrid
Estadio Santiago Bernabéu, C/ Concha Espina 1.
Tel 913 98 43 00.
www.realmadrid.es

DANCE

Cuarta Pared
C/ del Ercilla 17.
Tel 915 17 23 17.
www.cuartapared.es

Teatro Albéniz
C/ de la Paz 11.
Map 4 F2.
Tel 915 31 83 11.

Teatro Madrid
Avda de la Ilustración s/n.
Map 3 B1.
Tel 917 40 52 74.
www.teatromadrid.com

FLAMENCO

Arco de Cuchilleros
C/ de los Cuchilleros 7.
Map 4 E3.
Tel 913 64 02 63.

Café de Chinitas
C/ Torija 7. **Map** 4 D1.
Tel 915 59 51 35.

Candela
C/ Olivar 7.
Map 7 A4.
Tel 914 67 33 82.

Cardamomo
C/ Echegaray 15.
Map 7 A2.
Tel 913 69 07 57.

Casa Patas
C/ Cañizares 10.
Map 7 A3.
Tel 913 69 04 96.

Corral de la Morería
C/ de la Morería 17.
Map 3 C3.
Tel 913 65 84 46.

La Soleá
C/ Cava Baja 34.
Map 4 D4.
Tel 913 66 05 34.

CLASSICAL MUSIC OPERA AND ZARZUELA

Centro Cultural Conde Duque
C/ del Conde Duque 9.
Map 2 D4.
Tel 915 88 58 34.

Auditorio Nacional de Música
C/ del Príncipe de Vergara 146. **Tel** 913 37 01 40.
www.auditorionacional.mcu.es

Teatro Häagen-Dazs
C/ Atocha 18. **Map** 4 F3.
Tel 914 20 37 97.

Teatro Monumental
C/ Atocha 65. **Map** 7 A3.
Tel 914 29 12 81.

Teatro Real
Pl de Oriente. **Map** 4 D2.
Tel 915 16 06 60.
www.teatro-real.com

Teatro de la Zarzuela
C/ de los Jovellanos 4.
Map 7 B2.
Tel 915 24 54 00. http://teatrodelazarzuela.mcu.es

ROCK, JAZZ AND WORLD MUSIC

Café Central
Pl del Ángel 10. **Map** 7 A3. **Tel** 913 69 41 43.
www.cafecentralmadrid.com

El Sol
C/ Jardines 3. **Map** 7 A1.
Tel 915 32 64 90.
www.elsolmad.com

Honky Tonk
C/ de Covarrubias 24.
Map 5 B3.
Tel 914 45 68 86.

Populart
Huertas 22. **Map** 7 A3.
Tel 914 29 84 07.
www.populart.es

Sala La Riviera
Paseo Virgen del Puerto s/n. **Tel** 913 65 24 15.

Siroco
C/ de San Dimas 3.
Map 2 E4.
Tel 915 93 30 70.
www.siroco.es

THEATRE

Bellas Artes
Marqués de Casa Riera 2.
Map 7 B2.
Tel 915 32 44 37.

La Latina
Pl de la Cebada 2.
Map 4 D4.
Tel 913 65 28 35.

Lope de Vega
Gran Vía 57. **Map** 4 E1.
Tel 915 47 20 11.

Teatro de la Comedia
C/ del Príncipe 14.
Map 7 A2.
Tel 915 21 49 31.

Teatro María Guerrero
C/ de Tamaya y Baus 4.
Map 5 C5.
Tel 913 10 15 00.

Teatro Muñoz Seca
Pl del Carmen 1.
Map 4 F1.
Tel 915 23 21 28.

Teatro Nuevo Apolo
Pl Tirso de Molina 1.
Map 4 F3.
Tel 913 69 06 37.

Teatro Pavón
C/ de Embajadores 9.
Map 4 E4.
Tel 915 28 28 19.

CINEMA

Golem
C/ de Martín de los Heros 14. **Map** 1 A1.
Tel 902 22 16 22.

Capitol
Gran Vía 41. **Map** 4 E1.
Tel 902 33 32 31

Ideal
C/ del Doctor Cortezo 6.
Map 4 F3.
Tel 902 22 09 22.

Renoir
C/ de Martín de los Heros 12. **Map** 1 C5.
Tel 902 22 91 22.

Verdi
C/ Bravo Murillo 28.
Tel 914 47 39 30.

Nightlife

Madrid's reputation as the city that never sleeps persists, despite recent political measures for earlier closing times. In fact, partygoers in Madrid are known as *gatos* (cats) around Spain because of their nocturnal habits. The best nightlife is concentrated around specific districts, each with its own unique atmosphere and a wealth of places for people to get down to one of Madrid's best talents: *la marcha* (partying). Things hot up first in the Huertas area, moving on to Malasaña, Bilbao, Lavapiés and Chueca into the early hours of the morning. You don't need to go to a club for dancing as *Madrileños* also dance to DJs and live music in smaller clubs, called *pubs* – all sorts of musical tastes are catered to more than amply *(see p322)*. Expect to find places crowded from Thursday to Sunday. Also prepare for late nights because things don't get going for *gatos* until midnight.

SANTA ANA AND HUERTAS

With many tapas bars, cafés and terraces, the Huertas area is the perfect place to begin preparing for the wild night ahead. The atmosphere is made by the crowd, which is a heady amalgam of ages, looks and origins. If you want to stay in one area, this is a good choice.

There are several little bars overlooking the lively Plaza de Santa Ana. Pop into any one of them to begin the night. **Viva Madrid** attracts a vivacious crowd of locals and foreigners. **Cardamomo**, a famous *taberna*, is a mandatory stop for any bar crawl. There is live flamenco at least once a week.

For late-night dancing, try the house DJs at **Joy Madrid Discoteque** or the extravagant 19th-century **Palacio Gaviria** near Sol, resplendent in its Baroque decor. Near Atocha, you will find the spectacular seven-floor **Kapital**, which features every kind of music, and a rooftop bar that allows drinkers to gaze at the starlit sky. **Populart**, also a hugely popular club, features live jazz and occasional shows by Latin and world music bands. Weekends can get crowded.

It is a local tradition to end the night with hot chocolate and *churros* (dough sticks) in one of the cafés around Plaza del Sol. The **Chocolatería San Ginés** is open all night.

ALONSO MARTÍNEZ AND BILBAO

This is one of the city's most animated areas. You will find hundreds of great haunts that play music ranging from R&B to Spanish pop.

To begin with, try some of the local bars around Plaza de Santa Bárbara, such as the **Cervecería Santa Bárbara**, the perfect place to start the night with a *caña* (beer). Later on (if you can get past the queues), try the glamorous club **Alegoría**, with its eclectic decor and pop music, where you can dance until late with the beautiful people. Alternatively, you can head for **Pachá**, one of Madrid's most famous discotheques. There are also plenty of live-music venues around, such as **Clamores**, one of Madrid's many temples of jazz music. However, note that areas such as Huertas are more active during weekdays.

ARGÜELLES AND MONCLOA

This area is a favourite haunt of students, thanks to its proximity to the halls of residence of one of Madrid's major universities. The celebrated "basements of Argüelles" are huge double-storeyed patios with several bars and discotheques. The atmosphere is fresh and young.

Another popular district is Moncloa, which has a more mature crowd, as well as several places where you can listen to local Spanish pop and dance tunes, such as **La Sal**, which is also a venue for concerts.

CHUECA

The Chueca district dominates Madrid's gay scene. As well as having a large resident gay community, there are plenty of trendy late-night bars and clubs where gays and non-gays party together. In fact, what sets Chueca apart from other gay neighbourhoods in the world is the *mezcla*, the tolerant gay/straight mix.

The heart of the area is the Plaza de Chueca, packed with crowds visiting the terraces in the summer. Close by are mixed bars such as **Liquid** and **Acuarela**, with its camp, religious artefact decor. The Gay Pride Week in late June focuses around this area, though there are also plenty of well-established gay bars elsewhere in the city.

MALASAÑA

Malasaña was the centre of *la movida* in the Madrid of the 1980's *(see p305)*, and still has an alternative flavour that attracts many young bohemian types. The hub of this cosmopolitan district is the Dos de Mayo square. However, the characteristic atmosphere of the area is changing rapidly into a more design driven space. An example is the **La Ida** bar which has cultivated a revolutionary, arty atmosphere. **Bar & Co** is a typical Malasaña venue, where local bands play weekly. You can relax there after 3am if you don't feel like clubbing.

Tupperware, a fusion of past and present, is a rock bar with an ultra pop decor where you can also listen to garage, indie and pop music.

LAVAPIÉS

Once the Jewish quarter of Madrid, the narrow streets of Lavapiés are rich with an eclectic mix of races and cultures. One of the most fascinating and diverse dist

n town, the locals' old habit
of sitting outside their doors
on summer nights continues as
does the multiracial crowd on
the terraces of Calle de
Argumosa A vibrant fusion of
rtists, immigrants, hipsters
nd squatters results in some
of the most brilliant music,
rt, food, alternative theatre
nd nightlife in the city.
La Escalera de Jacob holds
oncerts, theatre performances
nd inter-cultural workshops.
he endearingly eccentric bar,
a Colonia de San Lorenzo,
osts Verbena de San Lorenzo,
street party with live bands,
ancing, stalls and freely
owing drink.

A LATINA

ill the best district in town
r cosy little hideaways and
pas bars, La Latina is an
pecially good place to go
Sundays after wandering
ound the Rastro flea market.

For an excellent cocktail,
head to **Delic**, and for a
cultural experience try **Anti
Café**, where you can listen to
unique DJs, poetry, drama
and jazz on Sundays. For a
taste of the best delicatessen
tapas, visit **Corazón Loco**,
where top quality wines are
available at reasonable prices.
Another worthwhile bar is
Taberna del Tempranillo,
which also serves a variety of
Spanish wines, cheeses and
ham. In the exquisite **María
Pandora** bar, you can try a
selection of champagnes and
cavas, surrounded by books
and antiques. Afterwards, you
can dance until late at **Berlín
Cabaret**, a modern nightclub
that runs a 1930s cabaret
from Monday to Thursday.

AZCA

With a skyline punctuated by
the highest buildings, this is
one of the most modern areas

in town. Near the Paseo de
la Castellana and the Santiago
Bernabéu stadium, this
financial district has a
multitude of clubs and bars
doing brisk business in
basements.

If visitors feel the urge to
dance to the sensuous
rhythms of salsa, Calle Orense
is definitely the best place to
head to. Avenida de Brasil is
also full of large clubs,
however, these tend to
be a little overcrowded.

Around the Chamartín train
station nearby, you will find
the centre of the hardcore
clubbing scene, which
vibrantly unfolds late at night.
Of the many clubs in the
area, **Macumba** is generally
considered to have the most
cutting-edge sound and
lighting equipment in Europe.
It is particularly famous for
its "Space of Sound" sessions
from 10am to 12pm one
Sunday a month.

DIRECTORY

ARS, CLUBS
ND CAFES

cuarela
/ Gravina 10.
Map 5 B5.
el *915 22 21 43.*

legoría
/ Villanueva 2.
ap 6 D5.
el *915 57 27 85.*

nti Café
nión 2.
ap 4 E2.
l *915 59 41 63.*

ar & Co
Barco 34.
ap 2 F5.
l *915 21 24 47.*

erlín Cabaret
stanilla de San
dro 11.
l *913 66 20 34.*

rdamomo
De Echegaray 17.
ap 7 A3.
913 69 07 57.

**rvecería Santa
rbara**
Santa Bárbara 8.
913 19 04 49.

**Chocolatería
San Ginés**
Pasadizo de San Ginés,
C/ Arenal 11.
Map 4 E2.
Tel 913 65 65 46.

Clamores
C/ Alburquerque 14.
Map 5 A3.
Tel 914 45 79 38.

Corazón Loco
C/ de Almendro 22.
Map 4 D3.
Tel 913 66 57 83.

Delic
Pl De La Paja s/n.
Map 4 D3.
Tel 913 64 54 50.

**Joy Madrid
Discoteque**
C/ Arenal 11.
Map 4 E2.
Tel 913 66 37 33.

Kapital
C/ Atocha 125.
Map 7 C4.
Tel 914 20 29 06.

**La Colonia de
San Lorenzo**
C/ Salitre 38.
Map 7 A5.

**La Escalera de
Jacob**
C/ de Lavapiés 11.
Map 4 F4.
Tel 649 43 32 54.

La Ida
C/ Colón 11.
Map 5 A5.
Tel 915 22 91 07.

La Sal
C/ Guzmán el
Bueno 98.
Tel 915 34 86 91.

Liqüid
C/ Barquillo 8.
Map 7 B1.
Tel 915 32 74 28.

Macumba
Agustín de Foxá s/n,
Estación de Charmartín.
Tel 917 33 35 05.

María Pandora
Pl Gabriel Miró 1.
Map 3 B3.
Tel 913 66 45 67.

Pachá
C/ de Barceló 11.
Map 5 A4.
Tel 914 47 01 28.

Palacio Gaviria
C/ de Arenal 9.
Map 4 E2.
Tel 915 26 60 69.

Populart
Huertas 22.
Map 7 A3.
Tel 914 29 84 07.

**Taberna del
Tempranillo**
C/ de la Cava Baja 38.
Tel 913 64 15 32.

Tupperware
C/ Corredera
Alta de San Pablo 26.
Tel 914 48 50 16.

Viva Madrid
C/ Manuel
Fernández González 7.
Tel 914 29 36 40.

MADRID PROVINCE

Madrid province (the Comunidad de Madrid) sits high on Spain's central plateau. There is plenty of superb scenery and good walking country in the sierras to the north, which are a refuge for city dwellers who go there to ski in winter or cool down during the torrid summers. In the western foothills of these mountains stands El Escorial, the royal palace-cum-monastery built by Felipe II, from which he ruled his empire. Close by is the Valle de los Caídos, the war monument erected by Franco. The smaller royal palace of El Pardo is on the outskirts of Madrid, and south of the city is the 18th-century summer palace of Aranjuez, set in lush parkland. Historic towns include Alcalá de Henares, which has a Renaissance university building, and Chinchón, where taverns cluster around a picturesque arcaded market square.

SIGHTS AT A GLANCE

Towns and Cities
Alcalá de Henares ❾
Buitrago del Lozoya ❷
Chinchón ❿
Manzanares el Real ❼

Historic Buildings
El Escorial pp330–31 ❻
Monasterio de Santa María de
　El Paular ❸
Palacio de El Pardo ❽

Palacio Real de Aranjuez ⓫
Santa Cruz del Valle de los
　Caídos ❺

Mountain Ranges
Sierra Centro de Guadarrama ❹
Sierra Norte ❶

KEY

▢	Madrid city
▢	Madrid province
✈	Barajas Airport
═	Motorway
═	Major road
═	Minor road
-·-	Province boundary

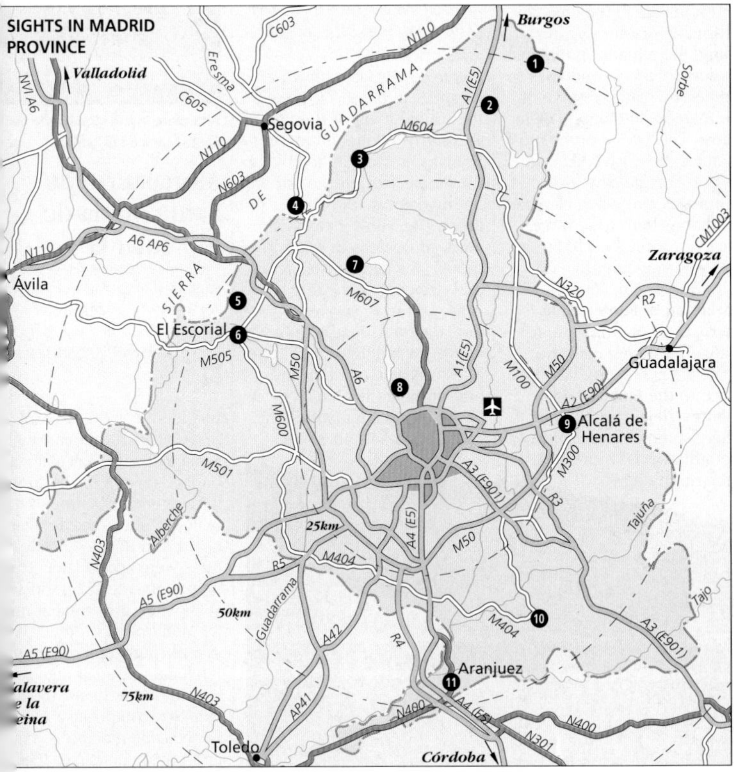

0 kilometres　　25
0 miles　　　　20

SIGHTS IN MADRID PROVINCE

Celebration of Mass in the church of the Monasterio de Santa María de El Paular

The village of Montejo de la Sierra in the Sierra Norte

Sierra Norte ❶

Madrid. 🚉 Montejo. 🛈 Calle Real 64, Montejo, 91 869 70 58.

The black slate hamlets of the Sierra Norte, which were once known as the Sierra Pobre (Poor Sierra), are located in the most attractively rural part of Madrid province.

At **Montejo de la Sierra**, the largest village in the area, an information centre organizes riding, the rental of traditional houses (*see p555*), and visits to the nearby nature reserve of the **Hayedo de Montejo de la Sierra**. This is one of the most southern beech woods (*see p80*) in Europe, and a relic of a previous era, when climatic conditions here were more suitable for the beech. From Montejo, you can drive on to picturesque hamlets such as **La Hiruela** or **Puebla de la Sierra**, both of which are set in lovely walking country.

The drier southern hills slope down to the **Embalse de Puentes Viejas**, a reservoir where summer chalets cluster around artificial beaches. On the eastern edge of the sierra is the village of **Patones**, which is thought to have escaped invasion by the Moors and Napoleon's troops because of its isolated location.

Buitrago del Lozoya ❷

Madrid. 🏠 1,850. 🚉 🛈 Calle Tahona 11, 91 868 16 15. 🚌 Sat. 🎉 La Asunción and San Roque (15–16 Aug), Cristo de los Esclavos (14–15 Sep).

Picturesquely sited above a meander in the Río Lozoya is the walled town of Buitrago del Lozoya. Founded by the Romans, it was fortified by the Arabs, and became an important market town in medieval times. The 14th-century Gothic-Mudéjar castle is in ruins, although the gatehouse, arches and stretches of the original Arab wall have survived. Today, the castle is used as a venue for bullfights and hosts a festival of ancient theatre and music in the summer.

The old quarter, within the walls, retains its charming atmosphere. The church of **Santa María del Castillo**, dating from the 14–15th century, has a Mudéjar tower and ceilings which were moved here from the old hospital. The **town hall** (*ayuntamiento*), in the newer part of Buitrago, preserves a 16th-century processional cross. In the basement is the **Museo Picasso**. The prints, drawings and ceramics were collected by the artist's friend Eugenio Arias.

🏛 Museo Picasso
Plaza de Picasso 1. **Tel** 91 868 00 5 15. 🕐 Mon, Wed pm & Sun pm.

Altarpiece in the Monasterio de Santa María de El Paular

Monasterio de Santa María de El Paular ❸

Southwest of Rascafría on M604. **Tel** 91 869 14 25. 🚉 Rascafría. 🕐 noon, 1pm, 5pm Mon–Sat (except 5pm on Thu); Sun: times v 📷 obligatory.

Founded in 1390 as Castile first Carthusian monastery, Santa María de El Paular sta on the site of a medieval ro hunting lodge. Although it mainly Gothic in style, Plat esque and Renaissance fea tures were added later. The monastery was abandoned 1836 when government mi ter Mendizábal ordered the sale of church goods (*see p* It fell into disrepair until its toration in the 1950s. Today complex comprises a work Benedictine monastery, ch and private hotel (*see p58*.
The church's delicate ala

Buitrago del Lozoya, standing next to the river

er altarpiece, attributed to Flemish craftsmen, dates from the 15th century. Its panels depict scenes from the life of Jesus. The lavish Baroque *camarín* (chamber), behind the altar, was designed by Francisco de Hurtado in 1718.

Every Sunday, the monks sing an hour-long Gregorian chant in the church. If they are not busy, they will show you the cloister's Mudéjar brick vaulting and double sun-clock.

The monastery is a good starting point for exploring the country towns of **Rascafría** and **Lozoya**. To the southwest is the nature reserve of **Lagunas de Peñalara**.

Sierra Centro de Guadarrama ④

Madrid. 🚉 *Puerto de Navacerrada, Cercedilla.* 🚌 *Navacerrada, Cercedilla.* 🛈 *Navacerrada, 91 856 03 08.*

The central section of the Sierra de Guadarrama was little visited until the 1920s, when the area was first linked by train to Madrid. Today, the granite slopes are planted with pines and specked by holiday chalets. Villages such as **Navacerrada** and **Cercedilla** have grown into popular resorts for skiing, mountain-biking, rock-climbing and horse riding. Walkers wanting to enjoy the pure mountain air can follow marked routes from Navacerrada.

The **Valle de Fuenfría**, a nature reserve of wild forests, is best reached via Cercedilla. It has a well-preserved stretch of the original Roman road, as well as several picnic spots and marked walking routes.

The gigantic cross at Valle de los Caídos

cerrada pass in the Sierra de Guadarrama

Santa Cruz del Valle de los Caídos ⑤

North of El Escorial on M600. *Tel 91 890 56 11.* 🚌 *from El Escorial.* ◷ *Tue–Sun.* ⬤ *some public hols.* 🎫 *(free Wed for EU residents).* 📷 **www.patrimonionacional.es**

General Franco had the Holy Cross of the Valley of the Fallen built as a memorial to those who died in the Civil War *(see pp66–7)*. The vast cross is located some 13 km (8 miles) north of El Escorial *(see pp330–31)*, and dominates the surrounding countryside. Some Spanish people find it too chilling a symbol of the dictatorship to be enjoyable, while for others its sheer size is rewarding.

The cross is 150 m (490 ft) high and rises above a basilica carved 250 m (820 ft) deep into the rock by prisoners. A number of them died during the 20-year-plus project. A funicular connects the basilica with the base of the cross, but access to the top of the cross is not permitted.

Next to the basilica's high altar is the plain white tomb-stone of Franco, and, opposite, that of José Antonio Primo de Rivera, founder of the Falange Española party. A further 40,000 coffins of soldiers from both sides in the Civil War lie here out of sight, including those of two unidentified victims.

El Escorial

Fresco by Luca Giordano

Felipe II's imposing grey palace of San Lorenzo de El Escorial stands out against the foothills of the Sierra de Guadarrama to the northwest of Madrid. It was built between 1563 and 1584 in honour of St Lawrence, and its unornamented severity set a new architectural style which became one of the most influential in Spain. The interior was conceived as a mausoleum and contemplative retreat rather than a splendid residence. Its artistic wealth, which includes some of the most important works of art of the royal Habsburg collections, is concentrated in the museums, chapterhouses, church, royal pantheon and library. In contrast, the royal apartments are remarkably humble.

★ Royal Pantheon
The funerary urns of Spanish monarchs line the marble mausoleum.

Main entrance

Bourbon Palace

Architectural Museum

Sala de Batallas

Basílica
The highlight of this huge decorated church, is the lavish altarpiece. The chapel houses a superb marble sculpture of the cruci-fiction by Cellini.

The Alfonso XII College
was founded by monks in 1875 as a boarding school.

Patio de los Reyes

Entrance to Basilica onl

★ Library
This impressive array of 40,000 books incorporates Felipe II's personal collection. On display are precious manuscripts, including a poem by Alfonso X the Learned. The 16th-century ceiling frescoes are by Tibaldi.

STAR FEATURES

★ Library

★ Royal Pantheon

★ Museum of Art

The royal apartments, on the second floor of the palace, consist of Felipe II's modestly decorated living quarters. His bedroom opens directly on to the high altar of the basilica.

★ **Museum of Art**
Flemish, Italian and Spanish paintings hang in the museum, located on the first floor. One of the highlights is The Calvary, *by 15th-century Flemish artist Rogier van der Weyden.*

VISITORS' CHECKLIST

Avda de Juan de Borbón y Battemberg. *Tel 91 890 59 04.*
🚇 from Atocha, Chamartin. 🚌 661, 664 from Moncloa. ◯ Apr– Sep: 10am–6pm Tue–Sun; Oct–Mar 10am–5pm Tue–Sun ● 1 & 6 Jan, 1 May, 10 Aug, 12 Sep, 24, 25 & 31 Dec. 🎟 (free Wed for EU residents). 🕇 9:30am daily; 7pm, 8pm Sat & Sun. 🗹 🖼 ⬜ 🛈

The Patio de los Evangelistas is a temple by Herrera. The Jardín de los Frailes makes a nice walk.

Chapterhouses
On display here is Charles V's portable altar. The ceiling frescoes depict monarchs and angels.

The monastery was founded in 1567, and has been run by Augustinian monks since 1885.

The Glory of the Spanish Monarchy by Luca Giordano
This beautiful fresco, above the main staircase, depicts Charles V and Felipe II, and scenes of the building of the monastery.

The Building of El Escorial
When chief architect Juan Bautista de Toledo died in 1567 he was replaced by Juan de Herrera, royal inspector of monuments. The plain architectural style of El Escorial is called desornamentado, *literally,* "unadorned".

Climber resting on a rock face of La Pedriza, near Manzanares el Real

Manzanares el Real ❼

Madrid. 🏠 6,140. 🚌 ℹ️ *Plaza de la Constitución, 639 17 96 02 (Sat–Sun).* 🛒 *Tue & Fri.* 🎉 *Fiesta de Verano (early Aug), Cristo de la Nave (14 Sep).*

The skyline of Manzanares el Real is dominated by its restored 15th-century castle. Although the castle has some traditionally military features, such as double machicolations and turrets, it was used mainly as a residence by the Dukes of Infantado. Below the castle is a 16th-century church, a Renaissance portico and fine

capitals. Behind the town, bordering the foothills of the Sierra de Guadarrama, is **La Pedriza**, a mass of granite screes and ravines, very popular with climbers. It now forms part of an attractive nature reserve.

Environs
Colmenar Viejo, 12 km (7.5 miles) to the southeast of Manzanares, has a superb Gothic-Mudéjar church.

Palacio de El Pardo ❽

El Pardo, northwest of Madrid off the A6. *Tel 91 376 15 00.* 🚌 *601 from Moncloa.* 🕐 *daily.* ⚫ *Sun pm, during royal visits & on public hols.* 🎫 *(free Wed for EU residents).* **www**.patrimonionacional.es

This royal hunting lodge and palace, set in parkland just outside Madrid's city limits, boasts General Franco among its former residents. A guided tour takes visitors round the moated palace's Habsburg wing and the identical 18th-century extension, designed by Francesco Sabatini.

The Bourbon interior is heavy with frescoes, gilt mouldings and tapestries, many woven to designs by Goya *(see p306).* Today the palace hosts visiting heads of

state and entertains royal guests. Surrounding the palace and the 18th-century village of El Pardo is a vast forest of holm oak. The area is popular for picnicking, and some game animals still run free.

Façade of Colegio de San Ildefonso in Alcalá de Henares

Alcalá de Henares

Madrid. 🏠 200,000. 🚌 🚌 ℹ️ *Callejón Santa María, 91 889 26 94.* 🛒 *Mon, Wed.* 🎉 *Feria de Alcalá (late Aug).* 🎫 *weekend city tours.*

At the heart of a modern industrial town is one of Spain's most renowned university quarters. Founded in 14 by Cardinal Cisneros, Alcalá

Lavish 18th-century tapestry inside the Palacio de El Pardo

university became one of the foremost places of learning in 16th-century Europe. The most historic college, **San Ildefonso**, survives. Former students include Golden Age playwright Lope de Vega *(see p290)*. In 1517 the university produced Europe's first polyglot bible, with text in Latin, Greek, Hebrew and Chaldean.

Alcalá's other sights are the cathedral and the **Casa-Museo de Cervantes**, birthplace of the Golden Age author. The newly restored 9th-century neo-Moorish palace, **Palacio de Laredo** has splendid decorations.

Casa-Museo de Cervantes
Calle Mayor 48. **Tel** 91 889 96 54.
☐ Tue–Sun. ☐ public hols.

Chinchón ⑩

Madrid. 🏠 4,860. ☐ ℹ️ Plaza Mayor 6, 91 893 53 23. ☐ Sat. 🎭 Semana Santa (Easter Week), San Roque (2–18 Aug). **www**.ciudadchinchon.com

Chinchón is arguably Madrid province's most picturesque town. The 15–16th-century, typically Castilian, porticoed **Plaza Mayor** has a splendidly theatrical air. It comes alive for the Easter passion play, acted out by the townspeople *(see p90)*, and during the August bullfights. The 16th-century church, perched above the square, has an altar painting by Goya, whose brother was a priest here. Just off the square is the 18th-century Augustinian monastery, which has been converted into a **parador** with

Chinchón's unique porticoed Plaza Mayor

a peaceful patio garden *(see p582)*. A ruined 15th-century castle is on a hill to the west of town. Although it is closed to the public, there are views of Chinchón and the countryside from outside it.

Chinchón is a popular weekend destination for *Madrileños*, who come here to sample the excellent chorizo and locally produced anís *(see p607)* in the town's many taverns.

Palacio Real de Aranjuez ⑪

Plaza de Parejas, Aranjuez. **Tel** 91 891 07 40. ☐ ☐ ☐ 10am– 6:15pm Tue–Sun, gardens until 8:30pm (Oct–Mar: until 5:15pm, gardens until 6:30pm). ☐ some public hols. ☐ (free Wed for EU residents). ☐ ☐

The Royal Summer Palace and Gardens of Aranjuez grew up around a medieval hunting lodge standing beside a natural weir, the meeting point of the Tagus and Jarama rivers.

Today's palace of brick and white stone was built in the 18th century and later redecorated by the Bourbons. A guided tour takes you

through numerous Baroque rooms, among them the Chinese Porcelain Room, the Hall of Mirrors and the Smoking Room, modelled on the Alhambra in Granada. It is worth visiting Aranjuez to walk in the 300 hectares (740 acres) of shady royal gardens which inspired Joaquín Rodrigo's *Concierto de Aranjuez*. The Parterre Garden and the Island Garden, between the rivers, survive from the original 16th-century palace.

Between the palace and the River Tagus is the 18th-century Prince's Garden, decorated with sculptures, fountains and lofty trees from the Americas. In the garden is the Casa de Marinos (Sailors' House), a museum housing the launches once used by the royal family for trips along the river. At the far end of the garden is the Casa del Labrador (Labourer's Cottage), a decorative royal pavilion built by Carlos IV.

The town's restaurants are popular for the exceptional quality of their asparagus and strawberries. In summer, a 19th-century steam train, built to carry strawberries, runs between here and the capital.

MIGUEL DE CERVANTES

Miguel de Cervantes Saavedra, Spain's greatest literary figure *(see p34)*, was born in Alcalá de Henares in 1547. After fighting in the naval Battle of Lepanto (1571), he was held captive by the Turks for more than five years. In 1605, when he was almost 60 years old, the first of two parts of his comic masterpiece *Don Quixote (see p395)* was published to popular acclaim. He continued writing novels and plays until his death in Madrid on 23 April 1616, the same day that Shakespeare died.

Gardens surrounding the Royal Palace at Aranjuez

CENTRAL SPAIN

INTRODUCING CENTRAL SPAIN 336–345

CASTILLA Y LEÓN 346–377

CASTILLA–LA MANCHA 378–399

EXTREMADURA 400–413

Introducing Central Spain

Much of Spain's vast central plateau, the *meseta*, is covered with wheat fields or dry, dusty plains, but there are many attractive places to explore. Central Spain's mountains, gorges, forests and lakes are filled with wildlife. A deep sense of history permeates the towns and cities of the tableland, reflected in some stunning architecture: the Roman ruins of Mérida, the medieval mansions of Cáceres, the Gothic cathedrals of Burgos, León and Toledo, the Renaissance grandeur of Salamanca, and castles almost everywhere.

León Cathedral (see p354–5), *an outstanding Gothic building, was completed during the 14th century. As well as many glorious windows of medieval glass, it has superb carved choir stalls depicting biblical scenes and everyday life.*

León

CASTILLA Y LEÓN
(see pp346–7)

Zamora

Salamanca (see pp358–61) *is the site of some of the finest Renaissance and Plateresque architecture in Spain. Among the city's most notable buildings are the university, its façade a mass of carved detail; the old and new cathedrals (built side by side); and the handsome Plaza Mayor, built in warm golden sandstone.*

Salamanca

Ávila

Cáceres

EXTREMADURA
(see pp400–13)

The Museo Nacional de Arte Romano *in Mérida (see p410) houses Roman treasures. The city has a well-preserved Roman theatre.*

Badajoz

0 kilometres   50

0 miles

◁ **Roofs and walls in the old part of Toledo**

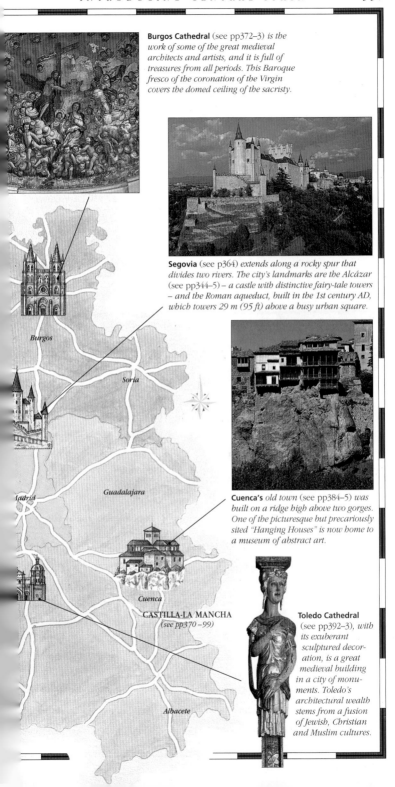

Burgos Cathedral (see pp372–3) *is the work of some of the great medieval architects and artists, and it is full of treasures from all periods. This Baroque fresco of the coronation of the Virgin covers the domed ceiling of the sacristy.*

Segovia (see p364) *extends along a rocky spur that divides two rivers. The city's landmarks are the Alcázar (see pp344–5) – a castle with distinctive fairy-tale towers – and the Roman aqueduct, built in the 1st century AD, which towers 29 m (95 ft) above a busy urban square.*

Burgos

Soria

Madrid

Guadalajara

Cuenca's *old town (see pp384–5) was built on a ridge high above two gorges. One of the picturesque but precariously sited "Hanging Houses" is now home to a museum of abstract art.*

Cuenca

CASTILLA-LA MANCHA
(see pp370–99)

Toledo Cathedral (see pp392–3), *with its exuberant sculptured decor-ation, is a great medieval building in a city of monu-ments. Toledo's architectural wealth stems from a fusion of Jewish, Christian and Muslim cultures.*

Albacete

The Flavours of Central Spain

Madrid is famous for its extremes of temperature – a climate that has given rise to the rueful local saying "nine months of winter and three months of hell". The surrounding regions suffer the same extremes, and their traditional cuisines reflect both the wintry cold and the dusty, scorched terrain. Meat predominates as roasts and stews and in warming soups, thickened with beans and pulses, which thrive despite the weather. Cured hams, spicy sausages and pungent cheeses are excellent accompaniments to the strong local wine. The finest ham is from Extremadura, where black-footed (*pata negra*) pigs forage freely among the oaks.

Manchego cheese

A chef preparing *gambas al ajillo*, a popular tapas dish

MADRID

Restaurants in Madrid, as befits the Spanish capital, offer cuisine from every corner of the country. Curiously, considering its distance from the ocean, the capital is famed for its seafood, flown in freshly every day. Madrileños

appreciate every part of an animal, particularly when it comes to pork, and Madrid menus regularly feature brains, ears, pigs' trotters, and *callos a la Madrileña* (tripe) is a classic local dish. Sturdy stews, such as the celebrated *cocido Madrileño*, keep out the bitter winter cold. The *tapeo* – a bar crawl between tapas bars – is an institution in the city, and each bar has its own speciality dish.

CASTILLA Y LEON

Spread out high on a plain, searingly hot in summer, an bitingly cold in winter, Castilla y León is famous fo its roasted meats, served in *asadores* (grillhouses). The most celebrated local dish i *cochinillo* (suckling pig), b pork, chicken, game in season and lamb are also popular. These are often combined with local pulses and lentils in hearty soups

Pinto beans   **White (butter) beans**

Castillian garbanzos (chickpeas)

(kid be

Black beans

Ar

Beans and pulses, key ingredients in the cooking of central Spain

REGIONAL DISHES AND SPECIALITIES

The cuisine of Spain's often wild and remote interior is characterized by warming soups and stews; traditionally made hams, cured meats and cheeses; plenty of filling beans and pulses; and flavourful fruit and vegetables. On the high plains of Castilla y León, locals keep out the winter cold with succulent roasted meats, and Extremaduran ham is the best you'll taste. In Don Quijote country, a glass of robust local wine and

Fresh figs

a chunk of Manchegan cheese is sheer delight. Fancy restaurants with fashionable food are few and far between, but welcoming, old-fashioned inns offer simple and tasty home-cooking. Madrid, of course, is the exception: here you'll find every possible cuisine, along with excellent seafood, which is harder to find anywhere else in this landlocked region.

Cocido Madrileño *This ric stew is traditionally eaten two stages: first the broth, then the meat and vegeta*

…cking the stamens from crocus flowers to make saffron

…d stews, which are given
…tra flavour with local
…butidos (cured meats). The
…gion also produces de-
…ious cheeses such as soft
…rgos, often served with
…ney, *membrillo* (quince
…y) or nuts for dessert. Local
…nes are robust and simple,
…good accompaniment to the
…ong flavours of the regional
…isine of Castilla y León.

CASTILLA LA MANCHA

…is is Don Quijote country:
…pty, flat, dusty and
…ttered with windmills.
…cal inns and taverns serve
…ditional country cooking,
…h plenty of hearty soups,
…bstantial casseroles and
…ply grilled local meat,
…ltry and seasonal game.
…nchegan *gazpacho*, unlike
…cold, vegetable soup,
…daluz namesake, is a hefty
…w made with whatever
…at is available. A common

accompaniment to it is *pisto*,
a ratatouille-like dish made
with a range of tasty, fresh
local vegetables. The Arabs
brought with them saffron,
which is still grown around
Consuegra, and their influence
also lingers on in Toledo's
famous marzipan sweets and
the fragrant Alajú almond
soup from Cuenca.

Cured hams hanging in an
embutidos **shop**

EXTREMADURA

Wild, beautiful Extremadura
sees few visitors and, in
many places, life continues
virtually untouched by the
21st century. Endless rolling
fields dotted with holm oak
shelter the acorn-fed, black-
footed pigs that make Spain's
most highly prized hams
(*jamón Ibérico*). Thanks to
the deeply rooted hunting
tradition, partridge, hare and
wild boar regularly feature
on local menus along with
river fish such as tench and
trout. There are some
delicious cheeses, as well as
perfumed local honey and
wonderful fruit, particularly
cherries, peaches and figs.

ON THE MENU

Chocolate con Churros The
typical Spanish breakfast –
thick hot chocolate with
sugary strips of fried batter for
dipping, originated in Madrid.

Cochinillo The speciality of
Segovia: 21-day-old suckling
pig, roasted until so tender it
can be cut with a plate.

Gazpacho Manchego
Sometimes called a galiano,
this is a rich stew traditionally
made with hare and partridge.

Macarraca Extremaduran
salad of chopped ripe tomatoes
with peppers, onion and garlic.

Tortilla de Patata A simple
potato omelette, now a staple
in restaurants all over Spain.

…ndigas *Meatballs –*
…ly country fare from
…igh plain of Castilla y

Migas Extremeñas *Chunks
of country bread are fried up
with peppers, pork and
chorizo or cured sausage.*

Yemas *A delicious treat
from Ávila, these lemony,
custardy cakes are made
with egg yolks and sugar.*

Wines of Central Spain

The wines of Central Spain originate in either the small, high-quality regions of northwest Castilla y León or in the vast wine-producing plains of La Mancha and Valdepeñas. Ribera del Duero has become Spain's most fashionable red wine region, with its aromatic, rich yet fine reds made from Tinto Fino grapes (the local name for Tempranillo) and, more recently, lighter, fruity wines. Rueda makes a good white wine, made from the Verdejo grape. La Mancha and Valdepeñas both produce lots of simple white wine, and reds which can be mellow and fruity.

Harvesting Viura grapes at Rueda

Artesian well for irrigating vines in La Mancha

Toro *makes the most powerful and fiery of all red wines from the ubiquitous Tempranillo grape.*

Villafranca
del Bierzo
Cacat
Ponferrada

ZA

SALAMA

N620

KEY FACTS ABOUT WINES OF CENTRAL SPAIN

Location and Climate
Ribera del Duero, Rueda and Toro are all high-lying areas with extreme climates – very hot summer days combined with cool nights, and cold winters. The marked difference of temperature between day and night helps to preserve the acidity in the grapes. Both La Mancha and Valdepeñas are extremely hot and dry areas. In recent years, droughts have caused a severe shortage of grapes.

Grape Varieties
The Tempranillo grape – also known as Tinto Fino, Tinto del Toro and Cencibel – produces nearly all the best red wines of Central Spain. Cabernet Sauvignon is permitted in some regions; it is used in some Ribera del Duero wines and occasionally

surfaces as a single varietal, as at the estate of the Marquis of Griñón in Méntrida. Verdejo, Viura and Sauvignon Blanc are used for white Rueda. The white Airén grape predominates in the vineyards of Valdepeñas and La Mancha.

Good Producers
Toro: Fariña (Gran Colegiata). **Rueda:** Álvarez y Diez, Los Curros, Marqués de Riscal, Sanz. **Ribera del Duero:** Alejandro Fernández (Pesquera), Boada, Hermanos Pérez Pascuas (Viña Pedrosa), Ismael Arroyo (Valsotillo), Vega Sicilia, Victor Balbás. **Méntrida:** Marqués de Griñón. **La Mancha:** Fermín Ayuso Roig (Estola), Vinícola de Castilla (Castillo de Alhambra). **Valdepeñas:** Casa de la Viña, Félix Solís, Luis Megía (Marqués de Gastañaga), Los Llanos.

Traditional earthenware t... used for fermenting wine

0 kilometres	100
0 miles	100

Vineyard near Moral de Calatrava in Valdepeñas

Pesquera *is made by Alejandro Fernández, the second most notable producer in the Ribera del Duero region, after Vega Sicilia.*

KEY

	Bierzo
	Cigales
	Toro
	Rueda
	Ribera del Duero
	Vinos de Madrid
	Méntrida
	La Mancha
	Valdepeñas
	Almansa

Marqués de Griñón *is an intense Cabernet Sauvignon wine with a deep colour, made on a vast estate outside Toledo. Although officially a* Vino de Mesa *(see p607), its quality is as high as a DO wine.*

Señorío de los Llanos *is produced in Valdepeñas. Its fine reds – made from Cencibel (Tempranillo) and aged in oak – are of excellent value.*

NE REGIONS

wine regions of Ribera del Duero, Toro and Rueda, are situated on ote, high plateaus, straddling the Río Duero. To the northwest lies isolated region of Bierzo, whose wines have more in common with hbouring Valdeorras in Galicia. Some wine is produced around rid, and southwest of the capital is the largely undistinguished on of Méntrida. Most of Central Spain's wine is produced in La cha – the world's largest single wine region – and in the smaller ave of Valdepeñas, which produces a great deal of "vino de mesa".

Birds of Central Spain

The vast and varied wild habitats of Central Spain are home to the richest avifauna in the peninsula. White storks' nests are a common sight on the church towers and chimneypots of towns. Grebes, herons and shovelers can be seen in the marshlands; the distinctive hoopoe is often spotted in woods; and grasslands are the nesting grounds of bustards and cranes. The mountains and high plains are the domain of birds of prey such as the imperial eagle, peregrine falcon and vultures. Deforestation, changing agricultural practices and hunting have all taken their toll in recent decades. Today, almost 160 bird species are the subject of conservation initiatives.

Bee-eater

MIGRATION ROUTES

— Cranes
— Storks
— Raptors
— Wildfowl

MARSHLAND AND WET MEADOW

Wetlands, such as Lagunas de Ruidera (see p397), on the edge of the plains of La Mancha, are vital feeding grounds for a wide range of waterfowl, some of which may remain in Spain throughout the year. Other migratory species use such sites as stopover points to feed, rest and build up enough energy to enable them to complete their journeys.

WOODLAND AND SCRUB

Habitats in areas of woodland, such as the Parque Nacional de Cabañeros (see p387), and scrub support many species, such as rollers and woodpeckers, throughout the year. Food is plentiful and there are many places to roost and nest. Early in the morni is the best time for spotting some of the rar species, such as the bluethroat.

Little egrets *are recognized by their snow white plumage and graceful slow flight. They feed largely on frogs, snails and small fish.*

Rollers *are common found in woodland, often nesting in tree stumps or holes left b woodpeckers. Their f includes grasshoppe crickets and beetles.*

Shovellers *feed on the water surface with a characteristic shovelling motion. The male has brightly coloured plumage but the female is a dull brown.*

Hoopoes *can be easily identified by their striking plumage and by the crest which can be raised if the bird is alarmed. They feed on ground insects.*

STORKS

Both the white and the (much rarer) black stork breed in Spain. They can be recognized in flight by their slow, steady wingbeats and may occasionally be seen soaring on thermals, usually during migrations. During the breeding season they put on elaborate courtship displays, which involve "dancing", wing-beating and bill-clapping. Their large nests, made of branches and twigs and lined with grasses, are constructed on roofs, towers, spires and chimneypots, where they are easy to watch. They feed on insects, fish and amphibians. Stork populations are threatened by wetland reclamation and the use of pesticides.

The endangered black stork

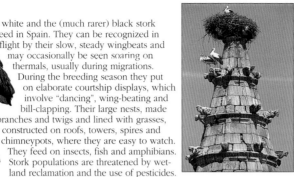

Nesting on a monastery roof

GRASSLAND AND FIELD

Many of Spain's natural grasslands have been ploughed over to plant cereals and other crops. Remaining vestiges are rich in wild grasses and flowers and are ideal habitats for species such as bustards and larks.

Cranes perform elegant courtship dances and are stately birds in flight, their long necks extended to the limit. They are omnivores, feeding on amphibians, crustaceans, plants and insects.

Great bustards nest in shallow depressions formed in open grassland and cultivated fields. Spain is home to half of the world's population.

MOUNTAIN AND HIGH PLAIN

Some of Spain's most spectacular birds of prey live in mountain ranges, such as the Sierra de Gredos (see p362), and the high plains of Central Spain. The broad wingspans of eagles and vultures allow them to soar on currents of warm air as they scan the ground below for prey and carrion.

Imperial eagles, with their vast wingspan of 2.25 m (7 ft), are extremely rare – only around 100 pairs are left in the whole of Spain.

Griffon vultures, a gregarious species, nest in trees and on rocky crags, often using the same place from year to year. Their broad wingspans can exceed 2 m (6 ft).

The Castles of Castile

The greatest concentration of Spain's 2,000 castles is in Castilla y León (now part of Castile), which derived its name from the word *castillo*, or castle. In the 10th and 11th centuries this region was the battleground between Moors and Christians. Villages and towns were fortified as protection against one side or the other. Most of the surviving castles in Castile, however, were built as noble residences after the area had been reconquered and there was no longer a military purpose for them. Fernando and Isabel *(see pp56–7)* banned the building of new castles at the end of the 15th century; many existing ones were converted to domestic use.

13th-century fresco of the siege of a castle

Coca Castle *(see p365)*, a classic Mudéjar design in brick

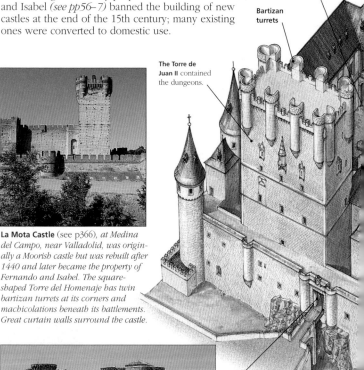

The Torre de Juan II contained the dungeons.

Patio de armas (courtyard)

Bartizan turrets

La Mota Castle (see p366), *at Medina del Campo, near Valladolid, was originally a Moorish castle but was rebuilt after 1440 and later became the property of Fernando and Isabel. The square-shaped Torre del Homenaje has twin bartizan turrets at its corners and machicolations beneath its battlements. Great curtain walls surround the castle.*

The barbican, with the coat of arms of the Catholic Monarchs carved over the gate, contains the portcullis and guards' watchrooms.

Belmonte Castle (see p394) *was buil in the 15th century as the stronghol of the quarrelsome Marquis of Viller Juan Pacheco. Late-Gothic in style, has a sophisticated, hexagonal grou plan, with a triangular bailey.*

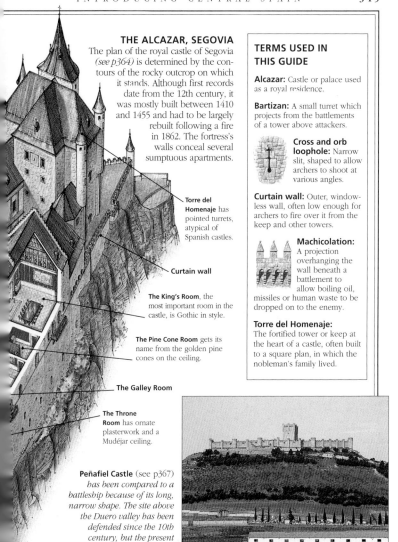

THE ALCAZAR, SEGOVIA

The plan of the royal castle of Segovia *(see p364)* is determined by the contours of the rocky outcrop on which it stands. Although first records date from the 12th century, it was mostly built between 1410 and 1455 and had to be largely rebuilt following a fire in 1862. The fortress's walls conceal several sumptuous apartments.

Torre del Homenaje has pointed turrets, atypical of Spanish castles.

Curtain wall

The King's Room, the most important room in the castle, is Gothic in style.

The Pine Cone Room gets its name from the golden pine cones on the ceiling.

The Galley Room

The Throne Room has ornate plasterwork and a Mudéjar ceiling.

TERMS USED IN THIS GUIDE

Alcazar: Castle or palace used as a royal residence.

Bartizan: A small turret which projects from the battlements of a tower above attackers.

Cross and orb loophole: Narrow slit, shaped to allow archers to shoot at various angles.

Curtain wall: Outer, windowless wall, often low enough for archers to fire over it from the keep and other towers.

Machicolation: A projection overhanging the wall beneath a battlement to allow boiling oil, missiles or human waste to be dropped on to the enemy.

Torre del Homenaje: The fortified tower or keep at the heart of a castle, often built to a square plan, in which the nobleman's family lived.

Peñafiel Castle (see p367) *has been compared to a battleship because of its long, narrow shape. The site above the Duero valley has been defended since the 10th century, but the present castle is 15th-century.*

...IE CASTLES OF ...ASTILLA Y LEÓN

...me of Central Spain's ...est surviving castles ...n be visited today. ...few, such as Ciudad ...drigo *(see p357)*, ...ve been turned into ...urious paradors *(see ...558–9)*.

Torrelobatón
Zamora
Valladolid
Peñaranda de Duero
Calatañazor
Simancas
Peñafiel
Cuéllar
Gomaz
Buen Amor
Coca
Pedraza
Berlanga de Duero
La Mota
Turégano
Salamanca
Segovia
Arévalo
Avila
MADRID
Ciudad Rodrigo

0 kilometres 100
0 miles 50

CASTILLA Y LEÓN

LEÓN · ZAMORA · SALAMANCA · ÁVILA · SEGOVIA
VALLADOLID · PALENCIA · BURGOS · SORIA

*A*wesome *expanses of ochre plains stretch to hills crowned with the castles that cover this vast region. Through Spain's history, these central provinces have had a major influence on its language, religion and culture. Their many historic cities preserve some of the country's most magnificent architectural sights.*

The territories of the two rival medieval kingdoms of Castile and León, occupying the northern half of the great plateau in the centre of Spain, now form the country's largest region, or *comunidad autónoma*.

Castile and León were first brought together under one crown in 1037 by Fernando I; but the union was not consolidated until the early 13th century. The kingdom of Castile and León was one of the driving forces of the Reconquest. El Cid, the legendary hero, was born near Burgos.

Wealth pouring in from the wool trade and the New World, reaching a peak in the 16th century, financed the many great artistic and architectural treasures that can be seen today in the cities of Castilla y León. Burgos has an exuberantly decorated Gothic cathedral. León Cathedral is famous for its wonderful stained glass. At the heart of the monumental city of Salamanca is the oldest university in the peninsula. Segovia's aqueduct is the largest Roman structure in Spain and its Alcázar is the country's most photographed castle. Ávila is surrounded by an unbroken wall, built by Christian forces against the Moors. In Valladolid, the regional capital, a superb collection of multicoloured sculpture is displayed in a magnificent 15th-century building.

Beyond the cities, in Castilla y León's varied countryside, there are many attractive small towns which preserve outstanding examples of the region's vernacular architecture.

...eal fields and vineyards covering the fertile Tierra de Campos in Palencia province

...e battle-scarred castle of Calatañazor (Soria), site of a Christian victory against the Moors in 1002

Exploring Castilla y León

Covering the northern part of Central Spain's vast tableland, Castilla y León has a huge variety of sights. Many – the University of Salamanca, the Alcázar and aqueduct of Segovia, the medieval walls of Ávila, the monastery at Santo Domingo de Silos, and the great cathedrals of Burgos and León – are well known. Other historic towns and villages worthy of a detour include Ciudad Rodrigo, Covarrubias, Pedraza de la Sierra and Zamora. This region also has beautiful mountainous countryside in the Sierra de Francia, Sierra de Bejar and Sierra de Gredos.

0 kilometres   50

0 miles   30

SIGHTS AT A GLANCE

Aguilar de Campoo 25
Astorga 5
Ávila 13
El Bierzo 1
Briviesca 26
El Burgo de Osma 32
Burgos pp370–1 28
Castillo de Coca 18
Ciudad Rodrigo 9
Covarrubias 27
Cuevas de Valporquero 6
Frómista 24
La Granja de San Ildefonso 14
León pp353–5 7
Lerma 29
Medinaceli 34
Medina del Campo 19
Medina de Rioseco 22
Palencia 23
Pedraza de la Sierra 16
Peñaranda de Duero 31
Ponferrada 3
Puebla de Sanabria 4
Salamanca pp358–61 11
Santo Domingo de Silos 30
Segovia 15
Sepúlveda 17
Sierra de Gredos 12
Soria 33
Tordesillas 20
Valladolid 21
Villafranca del Bierzo 2
Zamora 8

Tour

Sierra de Francia and
  Sierra de Bejar 10

SEE ALSO

• *Where to Stay* pp582–5

• *Where to Eat* pp633–6

Puerto de Somiedo 1486m
Puerto de Leitariegos 1525m
Oviedo
Puerto de Pajares 1379m
CUEVAS VALPOR
6
N630
Boñar
Vegarienza
La Robla
Lugo
Sierra de Ancares
EL BIERZO
1
Toreno
N630
N VILLAFRANCA DEL BIERZO
2
Corullón
NVI
A6
AP66
LEÓN
7
Man
as M
A66
A12
AP71
A231
PONFERRADA
3
Las Médulas
Montes de León
ASTORGA
5
Orbigo
N120
El Teleno 2183m
Valencia de Don Juan
Esla
N60
San Martín de Castañeda
PUEBLA DE SANABRIA
4
Eria
La Bañeza
NVI
N630
Mayorga
A66
Vigo
N525
Benavente
A52
Tera
Valderas
N610
A6
MEDI RIC
N631
Embalse de Ricobayo
CAST
Alcañices
N122
Fonfría
Villardefrades
San Pedro de la Nave
ZAMORA
8
N630
TO
Tor
Duero
A11
N122
Castronuño
Fermoselle
Corrales
MEDINA DEL
Embalse de Almendra
Trabanca
Buen Amor
N6
Ca
Duero
Ledesma
Madri
A
Vitigudino
Tormes
SALAMANCA
11
N501
Huebra
N620
Alba de
La Fuente de San Esteban
A62
Águeda
Vecinos
CIUDAD RODRIGO
9
Tamames
N630
Tormes
Guarda
SIERRA DE FRANCIA
Piedrahíta
El Bodón
Peña de Francia 1732m
Sistema
La Alberguería de Argañán
Sotoserrano
10
Béjar
Cáceres
Pico Almanzor 2592m
Ar
Sa

GETTING AROUND

Madrid makes a convenient springboard
for touring in Castilla y León. The major
cities of the region are connected by rail
but the coach is often a quicker
alternative. If you intend exploring rural
areas or visiting small towns it is advisable
to hire a car. Be aware that as Spain has
only recently changed its road numbering
system some of the roads featured here
may differ from new road signs.

Sunflowers growing in Burgos province

KEY

═══	Motorway
= =	Motorway under construction
▬▬	Major road
═══	Secondary road
▬▬	Scenic route
▬✕▬	Main railway
——	Minor railway
▰▰▰	International border
▰▰▰	Regional border
△	Summit

Peñaranda de Duero castle

El Bierzo ❶

León. 🚉 *Ponferrada.* 🚌 *Ponferrada.*
ℹ️ *Ponferrada, 987 42 42 36.*
www.ccbierzo.com

This northwestern region of León province was at one time the bed of an ancient lake. Sheltered by hills from the worst extremes of Central Spain's climate, its sun-soaked, alluvial soils make for fertile orchards and vineyards. Over the centuries, the area has also yielded rich mineral pickings including coal, iron and gold. Many hiking routes and picnic spots are within reach of the main towns of Ponferrada and Villafranca del Bierzo.

In the eastern section, you can trace the course of the old Road to Santiago *(see pp82–3)* through the **Montes de León**, past the pilgrim church and medieval bridge of Molinaseca. Turning off the road at the remote village of Acebo you pass through a deep valley where there are signs pointing to the **Herrería de Compludo**, a fascinating water-powered 7th-century ironworks. The equipment is still in working order and is demonstrated regularly.

The **Lago de Carucedo**, to the southwest of Ponferrada, is an ancient artificial lake. It acted as a reservoir in Roman times, a by-product of a vast gold-mining operation. Using slave labour, millions of tonnes

A palloza in the Sierra de Ancares

of alluvium were washed from the hills of Las Médulas by a complex system of canals and sluice gates. The ore was then panned, and the gold dust collected on sheep's wool. It has been estimated that more than 500 tonnes of precious metal were extracted from the hills between the 1st and 4th centuries AD. These ancient workings lie within a memorable landscape of wind-eroded crags, and hills pierced by tunnels and colonized by gnarled chestnut trees. You can best appreciate the area from a viewpoint at Orellán, which is reached via a rough, steep track. **Las Médulas**, a village south of Carucedo, is another place to go for a fine view.

To the north of the NVI highway lies the Sierra de Ancares, a wild region of rounded, slate

mountains marking the borders of Galicia and Asturias. Part of it now forms the **Reserva Nacional de los Ancares Leoneses**, an attractive nature reserve. The heathland dotted with oak and birch copses is home to deer, wolves, brown bears and capercaillies.

Several isolated villages high in the hills contain *pallozas* – primitive, pre-Roman stone dwellings thatched with rye. One of the most striking collections of these huts can be found in the isolated village of **Campo del Agua**, in the west.

🏛 **Herrería de Compludo**
Compludo. **Tel** *987 69 54 21.*
⏱ *Tue–Sun.* 📷

Villafranca del Bierzo ❷

León. 👥 *3,700.* 🚉 ℹ️ *C/ Díez Ovel 10, 987 54 00 28.* 🚌 *Tue & Fri.* 🎉 *Santo Tirso (28 Jan), Spring Fiesta (1 May), Fiesta del Cristo (14 Sep).*
www.villafrancadelbierzo.com

Emblazoned mansions line the ancient streets of this delightful town. The solid, early 16th-century, drum-towered castle is still inhabited. Near the Plaza Mayor a number of imposing churches and convents compete for attention. Particularly worth seeing are the fine sculptures adorning the north portal of the simple Romanesque **Iglesia de Santiago**. At the church's

Craggy, tree-clad hills around the ancient gold workings near the village of Las Médulas

Puerta del Perdón (Door of Mercy), pilgrims who were too weak to make the final gruelling hike across the hills of Galicia could obtain dispensation. Be sure to sample the local speciality, cherries in *aguardiente*, a spirit.

Environs
One of the finest views over El Bierzo is from **Corullón**, to the south. This pretty village with grey stone houses is set in a sunny location above the broad, fertile basin of the Río Burbia where the vines of the Bierzo wine region flourish (*see pp78–9*). Two churches, the late 11th-century San Miguel and the restored, Romanesque San Esteban, are worth a visit. Down in the valley, the Benedictine monastery at **Carracedo del Monasterio** stands in splendour. Founded in 990, it was once the most powerful religious community in El Bierzo.

The imposing Templar castle of Ponferrada

Puerta del Perdón of Villafranca's Iglesia de Santiago

Ponferrada ❸

Léon. 🏛 70,000. 🚃 🚌 🛈 C/ Gil y Carrasco 4, 987 42 42 36. 🏛 Wed & 🎉 Virgen de la Encina (8 Sep). www.ponferrada.org.

A medieval bridge reinforced with iron (*pons ferrata*), erected for the benefit of pilgrims on their way to Santiago de Compostela, gave this town its name. Today, prosperous on both iron and coal deposits, Ponferrada has expanded into a sizeable town.

Most of its attractions are confined to the small old quarter. Ponferrada's majestic **castle**

was constructed between the 12th and 14th centuries by the Knights Templar to protect pilgrims. During the Middle Ages it was one of the largest fortresses in northwest Spain.

Standing on the main square is the Baroque **town hall** (*ayuntamiento*). One entrance to the square is straddled by a tall clock tower which sits above one of the gateways of the medieval wall. Nearby is the Renaissance **Basílica de la Virgen de la Encina**. The older **Iglesia de Santo Tomás de las Ollas** is hidden away in the town's village-like northern suburbs. Mozarabic, Romanesque and Baroque elements combine in the architecture of this simple church. The 10th-century apse has beautiful horseshoe arches. Ask at the nearest house for the key.

Environs
A drive through the idyllic **Valle de Silencio** (Valley of Silence), south of Ponferrada, follows a poplar-lined stream past several bucolic villages. The last and most beautiful of these is **Peñalba de Santiago**. The 10th-century Mozarabic church of Santiago de Peñalba has horseshoe arches above its double portal.

Puebla de Sanabria ❹

Zamora. 🏛 1,700. 🚌 🛈 Castillo de Puebla de Sanabria, Muralla del Mariquillo s/n, 980 62 07 34. 🏛 Fri. 🎉 Candelas (last weekend in Jan), Las Victorias (8 & 9 Sep).

This attractive old village lies beyond the undulating broom and oak scrub of the Sierra de la Culebra. A steep cobbled street leads past stone and slate houses with huge, overhanging eaves and walls bearing coats of arms, to a hilltop church and castle.

The village has become the centre of a popular inland holiday resort based around the largest glacial lake in Spain, the **Lago de Sanabria**, now a nature park. Among the many activities available are fishing, walking and water sports.

Most routes beckon visitors to Ribadelago, but the road to the quaint hill village of **San Martín de Castañeda** gives better views. There's a small visitors' centre for the nature reserve in San Martín's restored monastery. The village is very traditional – you may see cattle yoked to carts, and women dressed completely in black.

The 12th-century church and 15th-century castle of Puebla de Sanabria

The nave of Astorga Cathedral

Astorga ❺

León. 🏛 12,500. 🚊 🚌 ℹ️ Plaza Eduardo de Castro 5. **Tel** 987 61 82 22. 🗓 Tue. 🎭 Roman Festival (end Jun), Santa Marta (late Aug).

The Roman town of Asturica Augusta was a strategic halt on the Vía de la Plata (Silver Road), a Roman road linking Andalusia and northwest Spain. Later it came to form a stage on the pilgrimage route to Santiago (see pp82–3).

Soaring above the ramparts in the upper town are Astorga's two principal monuments, the cathedral and the Palacio Episcopal. The **cathedral** was built between the 15th and the 18th centuries and displays a variety of architectural styles ranging from its Gothic apse to the effusive Baroque of its two towers, which are carved with various biblical scenes. The gilt altarpiece by Gaspar Becerra is

a masterpiece of the Spanish Renaissance. Among the many fine exhibits found in the cathedral's museum are the 10th-century carved casket of Alfonso III the Great, the jewelled Reliquary of the True Cross and a lavish silver monstrance which is studded with enormous emeralds.

Opposite the cathedral is a fairy-tale building of multiple turrets and quasi-Gothic windows. The unconventional **Palacio Episcopal** (Bishop's Palace) was designed at the end of the 19th century by Antoni Gaudí, the highly original Modernista architect (see p164), for the incumbent bishop, a fellow Catalan, after a fire in 1887 had destroyed the previous building. Its bizarre appearance as well as its phenomenal cost so horrified the diocese that no subsequent bishops ever lived in it. Today it houses an assembly of medieval religious art devoted to the history of Astorga and the pilgrimage to Santiago. Roman relics, including coins unearthed in the Plaza Romana, are evidence of Astorga's importance as a Roman settlement. The palace's interior is decorated with Gaudí's ceramic tiles and stained glass.

Reliquary of the True Cross

🏛 **Palacio Episcopal**
Pl Eduardo de Castro. **Tel** 987 61 68 82. ☐ Tue–Sun. ● Mon, Sun pm, public hols. 📷

Cuevas de Valporquero ❻

Valporquero. **Tel** 987 57 64 08. 🚌 from León. ☐ Oct–Dec, Mar: 10am–4pm Thu–Sun, public hols; Apr–Sep: 10am–2pm, 3:30–7pm daily (Thu–Sun, public hols in Apr). 📷

This complex of limestone caves – technically a single cave with three separate entrances – is directly beneath the village of Valporquero de Torío. The caves were formed in the Miocene period between 5 and 25 million years ago. Severe weather conditions in the surrounding mountains make the caverns inaccessible between December and Easter. Less than half of the huge system, which stretches 3,100 m (10,200 ft) under the ground, is open to the public. Guide tours take parties through an impressive series of galleries in which lighting picks out the beautiful limestone concretions. Iron and sulphur oxides have tinted the rocks many subtle shades of red, grey and black. The massive Gran Rotonda, covering an area of 5,600 sq m (18,350 sq ft) and reaching a height of 20 m (65 ft), is the most stunning.

As the interior is cold, and the surface often slippery, it is advisable to wear warm clothes and sturdy shoes.

Illuminated stalactites hanging from the roof of one of the chambers in the Cuevas de Valporquero

León **❼**

León. 🏠 *150,000.* 🚉 ✈
🛈 *Plaza de la Regla 4, 987 23 70 82.*
🗓 *Wed & Sat.* 🎉 *San Juan and San
Pedro (21–29 Jun), San Froilán (5 Oct).*
www.turismocastillayleon.com

Founded as a camp for the
Romans' Seventh Legion,
León became the capital of a
kingdom in the Middle Ages.
As such it played a central
role in the early years of the
Reconquest *(see pp52–3)*.

The city's most important
building – apart from its great
cathedral *(see pp354–5)* – is
the **Colegiata de San Isidoro**,
built into the Roman walls
which encircle the city. A separate entrance leads through
to the Romanesque **Panteón
Real** (Royal Pantheon), the
last resting place of more than
20 monarchs. It is superbly
decorated with carved capitals and 12th-century frescoes
illustrating a variety of biblical
and mythical subjects, as well
as scenes of medieval life.

The alleyways in the picturesque old quarter around the
Plaza Mayor are interspersed
with bars and cafés, decrepit
mansions and churches. Two
well-preserved palaces stand
near to the Plaza de Santo
Domingo: the **Casa de los
Guzmanes**, with its elegantly
arcaded Renaissance patio, and
Antoni Gaudí's unusually
restrained **Casa de Botines**.
The **Hostal de San Marcos**
is a fine example of Spanish
Renaissance architecture *(see

Frescoes in Basílica de San Isidoro showing medieval seasonal tasks

p25)*. Founded during the 12th
century as a monastery lodging
pilgrims going to Santiago, the
present building was begun in
1513 as the headquarters of the
Knights of Santiago. The main
hall has a fine 16th-century
coffered ceiling. A parador
(see p558) now occupies
the main part of the Hostal.
The **Museo de León** has many
treasures including a haunting
little ivory crucifix, the *Cristo

de Carrizo*. The **MUSAC**,
Museo de Arte Contemporáneo
de Castilla y León, has a
radical, interactive approach
to exhibiting contemporary art.

Environs
Around 30 km (20 miles) east
of León is the **Iglesia de San
Miguel de Escalada**. Dating from
the 10th century, it is one of the
finest surviving churches built
by the Mozarabs – Christians
influenced by the Moors. It has
Visigothic panels and stately
horseshoe arches resting on
carved capitals. At **Sahagún**, 70
km (40 miles) southeast of
León, are the Mudéjar churches
of San Tirso and San Lorenzo,
with triple apses and belfries. A
colossal ruined castle overlooks
the Río Esla beside **Valencia de
Don Juan**, 40 km (25 miles)
south of León.

🏛 **Museo de León**
Edificio Pallarés, Plaza Santo
Domingo. **Tel** 987 24 50 61.
⭕ *Tue–Sun.* 🎫 *(free Sat & Sun).*
🏛 **MUSAC**
Avenida de los Reyes Leoneses
24). **Tel** 987 09 00 00.
⭕ *Tue–Sun.*

THE MARAGATOS

Astorga is the principal town of
the Maragatos, an ethnic group
of unknown origin, thought to
be descended from 8th-
century Berber invaders. By
marrying only among
themselves, they
managed to preserve
their customs through the
centuries and keep them-
selves apart from the rest
of society. Although the
demise of their traditional
trade of mule-driving has
changed their way of life, the
Maragatos still keep to their
communities. Their costumes
can be seen during fiestas.

Maragatos dressed in
traditional costume

León Cathedral

Carved detail from the choir

The master builders of this Spanish Gothic cathedral *par excellence (see p24)* were inspired by French techniques of vaulting and buttressing. The present structure of golden sandstone, built on the site of King Ordoño II's 10th-century palace, was begun in the mid-13th century and completed less than 100 years later.

It combines a slender but very high nave with the huge panels of stained glass which are the cathedral's most magnificent feature. Although it has survived for 700 years, today there is concern about air pollution attacking the soft stone.

West Rose Window
This largely 14th century window depicts the Virgin & Child, surrounded by twelve trumpet-blowing angels.

The 13th- to 14th-century cloister galleries are decorated with Gothic frescoes by Nicolás Francés.

The silver reliquary is an ornate chest dating from the 16th century.

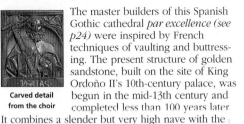

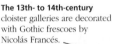

Cathedral Museum
Pedro de Campaña's panel, The Adoration of the Magi, *is one of the many magnificent treasures displayed in the museum.*

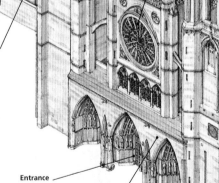

Entrance

★ West Front
The three portals are decorated with 13th-century carvings. The[...] above the Portada de Juicio *depict a scene from the Last Judgme[...] where the Blessed pas[...] into paradise.*

Inside the Cathedral

The plan of the building is a Latin cross. The tall nave is slender but long, measuring 90 m (295 ft) by 40 m (130 ft) at its widest. To appreciate the dazzling colours of the stained glass it is best to visit on a sunny day.

VISITORS' CHECKLIST

Plaza de Regla. *Tel* 987 87 57 70. ☐ Jun–Sep: 8:30am–1:30pm & 4–8pm; Oct–Jun: 8:30am–1:30pm & 4–7pm daily. ✝ 9am, noon, 1pm & 6pm daily, plus 11am & 2pm Sun. 🅿 🕭 Museum ☐ 9:30am–1pm, 4–6:30pm (7pm Jul–Sep) Mon–Sat (except Sat pm Oct–Jun). 🈁 🅿

The altarpiece
includes five original panels created by Gothic master Nicolás Francés.

The Virgen Blanca
is a Gothic sculpture of a smiling Virgin. The original is kept in this chapel. A copy stands by the west door.

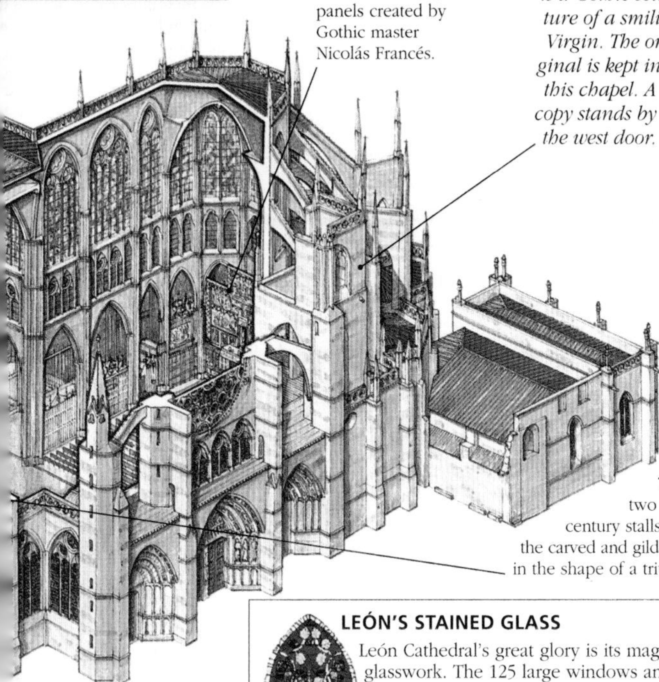

The choir has two tiers of 15th-century stalls. Behind it is the carved and gilded retrochoir, in the shape of a triumphal arch.

Stained Glass
The windows, covering an area of 1,800 sq metres (19,350 sq ft), are the outstanding feature of the cathedral.

STAR FEATURES

West Front

Stained Glass

LEÓN'S STAINED GLASS

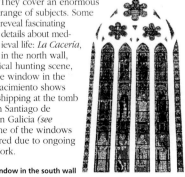

León Cathedral's great glory is its magnificent glasswork. The 125 large windows and 57 smaller, round ones date from every century from the 13th to the 20th. They cover an enormous range of subjects. Some reveal fascinating details about medieval life: *La Cacería*, in the north wall, depicts a typical hunting scene, while the rose window in the Capilla del Nacimiento shows pilgrims worshipping at the tomb of St James in Santiago de Compostela in Galicia *(see pp92–3)*. Some of the windows may be covered due to ongoing restoration work.

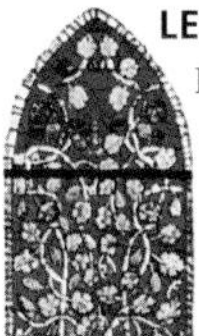

Window with plant motif

A large window in the south wall

Zamora ❽

Zamora. 🏠 67,000. 🚊 🚌 ℹ️
*Avenida Príncipe de Asturias 1, 980 53
18 45.* 🏪 *Tue.* 🎭 *Semana Santa
(Easter Week), San Pedro (23–29
Jun).* **www**.turismocastillayleon.com

Little remains of Zamora's
past as an important strategic
frontier town. In Roman times,
it was on the Vía de la Plata
(see p352), and during the
Reconquest was fought over
fiercely. The city has now
expanded far beyond its
original boundaries, but the
old quarter contains a wealth
of Romanesque churches.

The ruins of the **city walls**,
built by Alfonso III in 893, are
pierced by the Portillo de la
Traición (Traitor's Gate),
through which the murderer
of Sancho II passed in 1072.
The 16th-century **parador** *(see
p585)* is in an old palace with
a Renaissance courtyard
adorned with coats of arms.

Two other palaces, the **Casa
de los Momos** and the **Casa
del Cordón**, have ornately

carved façades and windows.
Zamora's most important
monument is its unique
cathedral, a 12th-century
structure built in Romanesque
style but with a number of
later Gothic additions. The
building's most eyecatching
feature is its striking, scaly,
hemispherical dome. Inside,
there are superb iron grilles
and Mudéjar pulpits surround

**Peaceful gardens of the Colegiata
de Santa María in Toro**

Juan de Bruselas' 15th-century
choir stalls. The allegorical
carvings of nuns and monks
on the misericords and arm-
rests were once considered
risqué. The museum, off the
sober cloisters, has a collection
of 15th- and 16th-century
Flemish tapestries. These
illustrate biblical passages and
classical and military scenes.

Nearby, several churches exhibit features characteristic of
Zamora's architectural style,
notably multi-lobed arches and
heavily carved portals. The best
are the 12th-century **Iglesia de
San Ildefonso** and the **Iglesia
de la Magdalena**.

Another reason for visiting
Zamora is for its lively Easter
Week celebrations, when elaborate *pasos* (sculpted floats) are
paraded in the streets. Otherwise they can be admired in
the **Museo de Semana Santa**.

Environs
The 7th-century Visigothic
church of **San Pedro de la
Nave**, 23 km (14 miles) northwest of Zamora, is Spain's

Sierra de Francia
and Sierra de Béjar ❿

These attractive schist hills buttress the
western edges of the Sierra de Gredos
(see p362). Narrow roads wind their way
through picturesque chestnut, olive and
almond groves, and quaint rural villages
of wood and stone. The highest point of
the range is La Peña de Francia, which,
at 1,732 m (5,700 ft), is easily recognizable
from miles around. The views from the
peak, and from the roads leading up to
it, offer a breathtaking panorama of the
surrounding empty plains and rolling hills.

La Peña de Francia ①
Crowning the peak is a
windswept Dominican
monastery sheltering a
blackened, Byzantine-
style statue of the
Virgin and Child.

La Alberca ②
This pretty and much-
visited village sells local
honey, hams and handi-
crafts. On 15 August each
year it celebrates the
Assumption with a
traditional mystery
play performed
in costume.

CIUDAD ROD.

SA202

SA201

COR

Las Batuecas ③
The road from
Alberca career
into a green va
the monastery
Luis Buñuel m
film *Tierra sin*
(Land without

| 0 kilometres | 5 |
| 0 miles | 5 |

KEY

▦▦▦ Tour route

═══ Other roads

🔆 Viewpoint

The unmistakable peak of La Peña de Francia

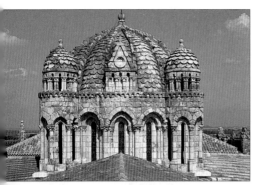

sh-scale tiling on dome of Zamora Cathedral

dest church. Carvings adorn
capitals and friezes. **Toro**, 30
n (18 miles) east of Zamora, is
the heart of a wine region
ee pp 340–1). The highlights
its **Colegiata de Santa María**
e the Gothic west portal and
ine 16th-century Hispano-
emish painting, *La Virgen de
Mosca*. In 1476, the forces of
bel I *(see pp56–7)* secured a
tory over the Portuguese at
ro, confirming her succes-
n to the Castile throne.

Ciudad Rodrigo ❾

Salamanca. 🏠 *14,000.* 🚍 🚉 **ℹ**
Plaza de Amayuelas 5, 923 46 05 61.
🗓 *Tue, Sat.* 🎭 *San Sebastián
(20 Jan), Carnaval del Toro (before
Lent), Easter week.*
www.turismociudadrodrigo.com

Despite its lonely setting –
stranded on the country's
western marches miles from
anywhere – this lovely old
town is well worth a detour.

Its frontier location inevitably
gave rise to fortification, and
its robust 14th-century castle is
now an atmospheric **parador**
(see p583). The prosperous
15th and 16th centuries were
Ciudad Rodrigo's heyday.
During the War of Inde-
pendence *(see pp62–3)*, the
city, then occupied by the
French, was besieged for two
years before falling to the
Duke of Wellington's forces.

The golden stone buildings
within the ramparts are delightful. The main monument is the
cathedral, whose belfry still
bears the marks of shellfire
from the siege. The exterior
has a shapely curved balustrade and accomplished portal
carvings. Inside, it is worth
seeing the cloisters and the
choir stalls, carved with lively
scenes by Rodrigo Alemán.
The main attraction of the
adjacent 16th-century **Capilla
de Cerralbo** (Cerralbo Chapel)
is a 17th century altarpiece.
Off the chapel's south side is
the quiet, arcaded Plaza del
Buen Alcalde.

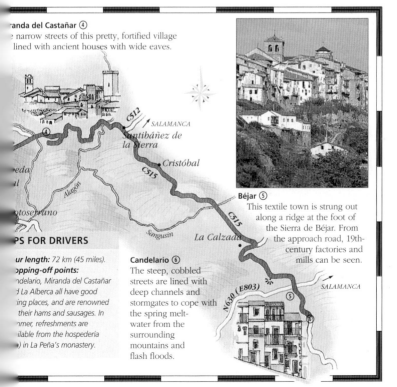

randa del Castañar ④
e narrow streets of this pretty, fortified village
lined with ancient houses with wide eaves.

C512 ↗ SALAMANCA
*Santibáñez de
la Sierra*
• *Cristóbal*
C515

eda
l
Alagón
otoserrano

C515

Sangusin La Calzada

Béjar ⑤
This textile town is strung out
along a ridge at the foot of
the Sierra de Béjar. From
the approach road, 19th-
century factories and
mills can be seen.

PS FOR DRIVERS

ur length: 72 km (45 miles).
opping-off points:
ndelario, Miranda del Castañar
d La Alberca all have good
ing places, and are renowned
their hams and sausages. In
mer, refreshments are
ilable from the hospedería
) in La Peña's monastery.

Candelario ⑥
The steep, cobbled
streets are lined with
deep channels and
stormgates to cope with
the spring melt-
water from the
surrounding
mountains and
flash floods.

N630 (E803)   ↗ SALAMANCA
⑤

Street-by-Street: Salamanca ⓫

Shell detail, façade of the Casa de las Conchas

The great university city of Salamanca is Spain's finest showcase of Renaissance and Plateresque architecture. Founded as an Iberian settlement in pre-Roman times, the city fell to Hannibal in 217 BC. Pre-eminent among its artists and master crafts-men of later years were the Churriguera brothers *(see p25)*. Their work can be seen in many of Salamanca's golden stone build-ings, notably in the Plaza Mayor. Other major sights are the two cathedrals and the 13th-century university, one of Europe's oldest and most distinguished.

The Casa de las Concha is easily identifiable fro stone scallop shells tha its walls. It is now a li

The Palacio de Monterrey is a Renaissance mansion.

Convento de las Ursulas   Casa d Muer

CALLE DE LA COMPAÑÍA

CALLE DE SERRANOS

CALLE DE LOS LIBREROS

CALLE VERACRUZ

★ **Universidad**
In the centre of the university's elaborate façade is this medal-lion, carved in relief, which depicts the Catholic Monarchs.

★ **Catedral Vieja and Catedral Nueva**
Despite being in different architectural styles, the adjoining old and new cathedrals blend well together. This richly coloured altarpiece painted in 1445 is in the old cathedral.

Puente Romano
The Roman bridge across the Río Tormes, built in the 1st century AD, retains 15 of its original 26 arches. It provides an excellent view of the city.

STAR SIGHTS

★ Universidad

★ Catedral Vieja and Catedral Nueva

★ Plaza Mayor

0 metres   100
0 yards   100

Museo de Art Nouveau y Art Decó

KEY

– – – Suggested ro

PAS

★ Plaza Mayor

This 18th-century square is one of Spain's largest and grandest. On the east side is the Royal Pavilion, decorated with a bust of Felipe V, who built the square.

VISITORS' CHECKLIST

Salamanca. 165,000. 15 km (9 miles) east. Paseo de la Estación, 902 24 02 02. Avda de Filiberto Villalobos 71, 923 23 67 17. Plaza Mayor 32, 923 21 83 42; Casa de las Conchas C/ Compañía 2, 923 26 85 71. Sun. San Juan de Sahagún (10–12 Jun), Virgen de la Vega (8 Sep). www.salamanca.es

The **Palacio de Fonseca** (also known as the Palacio de la Salina) was built in 1538 by Archbishop Alonso de Fonseca.

Torre del Clavero

This 15th-century tower still has its original turrets. They are adorned with the coats of arms of its founders, and Mudéjar trelliswork.

Iglesia-Convento de San Esteban

The Plateresque façade of the church is carved with delicate relief. Above the door is a frieze decorated with medallions and coats of arms.

Convento de las Dueñas

Sculptures on the capitals of the beautiful two-storey cloister show demons, skulls and tormented faces, which contrast with serene carvings of the Virgin.

PLAZA MAYOR

CALLE DE SAN PABLO

CALLE DEL CONSUELO

GRAN VIA

PLAZA DEL CONCILIO DE TRENTO

ARROYO SANTO DOMINGO

PERABÉ

Exploring Salamanca

The majority of Salamanca's monuments are located inside the city centre, which is compact enough to explore on foot. The university, the Plaza Mayor, and the old and new cathedrals are all unmissable.

🔒 Catedral Vieja and Catedral Nueva

Unusually, the new cathedral (built during the 16th–18th centuries) did not replace the old, but was constructed beside it. It combines a mix of architectural styles, being mainly Gothic, with Renaissance and Baroque additions. The west front has elaborate Late Gothic stonework.

The 12th- to 13th-century Romanesque old cathedral is entered through the new one. The highlight is a wonderful altarpiece of 53 panels, painted in lustrous colours by Nicolás Florentino. It frames a statue of Salamanca's patron saint, the 12th-century Virgen de la Vega, which was crafted in Limoges enamel. In the vault above it is a fresco depicting scenes from the Last Judgment, which is also by Florentino.

The 15th-century Capilla de Anaya (Anaya Chapel) contains the superb 15th-century alabaster tomb of Diego de Anaya, an archbishop of Salamanca.

Façade of Salamanca University, on the Patio de las Escuelas

🏛 Universidad

Patio de las Escuelas 1. **Tel** 923 29 44 00. ◯ daily. ● 25 Dec, 1, 6 Jan and for official functions. 🈂 (free Mon am). www.usal.es

The university was founded by Alfonso IX of León in 1218, making it the oldest in Spain. The 16th-century façade of the Patio de las Escuelas (Schools Square) is a perfect example of the Plateresque style *(see p25)*. Opposite is a statue of Fray Luis de León, who taught theology here. His former lecture room is preserved in its original style. The Escuelas Menores building houses a huge zodiac fresco, *The Salamanca Sky*.

🏛 Plaza Mayor

This magnificent square was built by Felipe V to thank the city for its support during the War of the Spanish Succession *(see p62)*. Designed by the Churriguera brothers *(see p2* in 1729 and completed in 175 it was once used for bullfigh but nowadays is a delightful place to stroll or shop. With the harmonious blend of arca ed buildings and cafés are th Baroque town hall and, opp site, the Royal Pavilion, from where the royal family used to watch events in the squa The Plaza Mayor is built of warm golden sandstone, and especially resplendent at du

Royal Pavilion in Salamanca's beautiful Plaza Mayor

🔒 Iglesia-Convento de San Esteban

The 16th-century church of Dominican monastery is pa ularly interesting for its su ornamented façade. The r on the central panel, com ed by Juan Antonio Ceron 1610, depicts the stoning Stephen, to whom the mo tery is dedicated. Above t a frieze, delicately carved figures of children and ho

The interior of the large single-nave church is equ stunning. The ornate altarp of twisted gilt columns de rated with vines, is the w of José Churriguera and c from 1693. Below it is on Claudio Coello's last pain another representation of martyrdom of St Stephen

The double-galleried Cl de los Reyes, completed Plateresque style in 1591 capitals which are carved the heads of the prophet

Salamanca's double cathedral, towering over the city

ulpted shells on the walls of the Casa de las Conchas

Casa de las Conchas

lle de la Compañia 2. **Tel** 923 26 93
. ☐ daily. **Library** ☐ Mon–Sat.
e name of this mansion –
ouse of the Shells – derives
om the golden stone scallop
ells that cover most of its
lls. The shells are a symbol
the Order of Santiago, one
whose knights, Rodrigo
as Maldonado, built the
nsion at the start of the 16th
tury. He also adorned the
lding with his family's coat
arms. It is now a library.

Convento de las Dueñas

a del Concilio de Trento. **Tel** 923
4 42. ☐ 9:30am–12:45pm,
–6:45pm daily. 📷
main feature of this Do-
ican convent, beside San
ban, is its Renaissance
ble cloister, whose tranquil
dens seem strangely at odds
the grotesques carved on
capitals. The cloister also
erves tiled Moorish arches.

asa Lis Museo Art
veau y Art Deco

Gibraltar 14. **Tel** 923 12 14 25.
e–Sun. 📷 (free Thu am). ♿ 🏛
important art collection,
ed in a 19th-century build-
includes paintings, jew-
y and furniture from all
Europe. Individual rooms
evoted to porcelain and
ges enamel, and stained-
work by Lalique.

legio de los Irlandeses

le Fonseca 4. **Tel** 923 29
☐ daily.
rchbishop of Toledo,
so de Fonseca, built this
ssance palace in 1519
he coat of arms of the

Fonseca family appears over
the main entrance. Its name
arises from the fact that it
became a seminary for Irish
priests at the end of the 16th
century. The interior Italianate
courtyard has a first-floor gallery and a chapel. Today the
building is used as council
and university offices.

🔒 Convento de las Úrsulas

Calle de las Úrsulas 2. **Tel** 923 21 98
77. ☐ daily. 📷
In the church of this convent
is the superbly carved tomb of
its founder, Alonso de Fonseca,
the powerful 16th-century
Archbishop of Santiago. The
museum includes fine paintings by Luis de Morales.

🏛 Casa de las Muertes

Calle Bordadores. ⬤ to public.
The House of the Dead takes
its name from the small skulls
that embellish its façade. Grotesques and other figures also
feature, and there is a cornice

Skull carving on the façade of the
Casa de las Muertes

decorated with cherubs. The
façade is a wonderfully accomplished example of the early
Plateresque style.
   The adjacent house is where
author and philosopher Miguel
de Unamuno died in 1936. The
Casa-Museo de Unamuno, next
door to the university, contains
information about his life.

🏛 Torre del Clavero

Plaza de Colón.
The tower is the last vestige of
a palace that once stood here.
It was built around 1480 and
is named after a former resident, the key warden *(clavero)*
of the Order of Alcántara.

Tower opposite Casa de las Muertes

Environs

Northwest of the city, the Río
Tormes leads through the
fortified old town of **Ledesma**,
across lonely countryside to
the Arribas del Duero, a series
of massive reservoirs near to
the Portuguese border.
   Dominating the town of
Alba de Tormes, 20 km (12
miles) east of Salamanca, is the
Torre de la Armería, the only
remaining part of the castle of
the Dukes of Alba. The Iglesia
de San Juan was built in the
12th century in Romanesque
style. The Iglesia-Convento de
las Madres Carmelitas was
founded by St Teresa of Ávila
in 1571, and is where her
remains are now kept.
   The castle of **Buen Amor**,
26 km (16 miles) to the north,
was founded in 1227. Later, it
was converted into a palace
and used by the Catholic
Monarchs while fighting
Juana la Beltraneja (see p56).

Sierra de Gredos ⑫

Ávila. 🚌 *Navarrendonda.* ℹ️
*Navarrendonda C/Del Rio, s/n, 920 34
80 01 or 920 34 52 52 (Jul & Aug).*

This great mountain range,
west of Madrid, has abundant
wildlife, especially ibex and
birds of prey. Some parts
have been developed to cater
for weekenders who come skiing, fishing, hunting or hiking.
Tourism here isn't a recent
phenomenon – Spain's first
parador opened in Gredos in
1928 (*see p584*). Despite this,
there are many traditional villages off the beaten track.

The slopes on the south side
of the range, extending into
Extremadura, are fertile and
sheltered, with pinewoods, and
apple and olive trees. The
northern slopes, in contrast,
have a covering of scrub and
a scattering of granite boulders.

A single main road, the
N502, crosses the centre of the
range via the Puerto del Pico, a
pass at 1,352 m (4,435 ft), leading to Arenas de San Pedro,
the largest town of the Sierra
de Gredos. On this road is the
castle of **Mombeltrán**, built at
the end of the 14th century.

Near Ramacastañas, south of
the town of Arenas de San
Pedro, are the limestone caverns of the **Cuevas del Águila**.

The sierra's highest summit,
the Pico Almanzor (2,592 m,
8,500 ft) dominates the west.
Around it lies the **Reserva
Nacional de Gredos**, protecting the mountain's wildlife.

The Toros de Guisando near El Tiemblo in the Sierra de Gredos

Near El Tiemblo, in the east,
stand the **Toros de Guisando**,
four stone statues resembling
bulls, believed to be of Celt-
iberian origin (*see pp48–9*).

Ávila ⑬

Ávila. 🏘️ *57,000.* 🚉 🚌 ℹ️ *Plaza
Pedro Davila 4, 920 21 13 87.*
Walls ⏰ *Tue–Sun.* 🎫 📷 *Fri.* 🎉
*San Segundo (2 May); Sta Teresa
(15 Oct).* **www.**turismo
castillayleon.com

At 1,131 m (3,710 ft)
above sea level, Ávila de
los Caballeros ("of the
Knights") is the highest
provincial capital in
Spain. In winter access
roads can be blocked
with snow, and at night
the temperature plummets.
The centre of the city is
encircled by the finest-
preserved **medieval
walls** in Europe. The
walls are open to visitors.
One of the best views of the
walls is from Los Cuatro Postes

Tuna in Ávila

(Four Posts) on the road to
Salamanca. Built in the 12th
century, the walls are over
2 km (1 mile) long. They are
punctuated by 88 sturdy
turrets, on which storks can be
seen nesting in season. The
ground falls away very steeply
from the walls on three sides,
making the city practically
impregnable. The east side,
however, is
relatively flat
and therefore
had to be fortified
more heavily. The
oldest sections of
the wall are here.
They are guarded by
the most impressive
of the city's nine gate-
ways, the **Puerta de
San Vicente**. The apse
of the **cathedral** also
forms part of the wall.
The cathedral's warlike
(and unfinished) ex-
terior, decorated with
beasts and scaly wild
men, is an unusual design.
The interior is a mixture of
Romanesque and Gothic styles

The superbly preserved 11th-century walls, punctuated with 88 cylindrical towers, which encircle Ávila

For hotels and restaurants in this region see pp582–5 and pp633–6

using an unusual mottled red and white stone. Finer points to note are the carvings on the retrochoir and, in the apse, the tomb of a 15th-century bishop known as El Tostado, "the Tanned One", because of his dark complexion.

Many churches and convents in Ávila are linked to St Teresa, who was born in the city. The **Convento de Santa Teresa** was built on the site of her home within the walls and she also lived for more than 20 years in the **Monasterio de la Encarnación** outside the walls. There is even a local sweetmeat, *yemas de Santa Teresa*, named after the saint. The **Basílica de San Vicente**, also located just outside the eastern walls, is Ávila's most important Romanesque church, distinguished by its ornamental belfry. It was begun in the 11th century but has some Gothic features which were added later. The west door-

Cloisters of the Real Monasterio de Santo Tomás in Ávila

way is often compared to the Pórtico da Gloria of Santiago cathedral (*see p92*). Inside, the carved tomb of St Vincent and his sisters depicts their hideous martyrdom in detail. Another Romanesque-Gothic church worth seeing is the **Iglesia de San Pedro**.

Some way from the centre is the **Real Monasterio de Santo Tomás**, with three cloisters. The middle one, carved with the yoke and arrow emblem of the Catholic Monarchs, is the most beautiful. The last cloister leads to a museum displaying chalices and processional crosses. The church contains the tomb of Prince Juan, the only son of Fernando and Isabel. In the sacristy lies another historic figure: Tomás de Torquemada, head of the Inquisition (*see p56*).

In Ávila, you may see groups of *tunas* – students dressed in traditional costume walking the town's streets while singing songs and playing guitars.

La Granja de San Ildefonso ❶

Segovia. **Tel** 921 47 00 19. 🚌 *from Madrid or Segovia.* ⬜ *10am daily; closing times vary from 6–9pm depending on the month.* ⬤ *1, 6 & 23 Jan, 1 May, 25 Aug, 24, 25 & 31 Dec.* 🆓 *(free Wed for EU residents).* ⬛ www.patrimonionacional.es

This sumptuous royal pleasure palace is set against the backdrop of the Sierra de Guadarrama mountains, standing on the site of the old Convento de Jerónimos.

In 1720, Felipe V embarked on a project to create a fine palace. A succession of different artists and architects contributed to the rich furnishings inside and the splendid gardens without.

A guided tour meanders through countless impressive salons decorated with ornate *objets d'art* and Classical frescoes against settings of marble, gilt and velvet. Huge glittering chandeliers, produced in the local crystal factory, hang from the ceiling. In the private apartments there are superb court tapestries. The church is fittingly adorned in lavish high Baroque style, and the Royal Mausoleum contains the tomb of Felipe V and his queen.

In the gardens, stately chestnut trees, clipped hedges and statues frame a complex series of pools. On 30 May, 25 July and 25 August each year all of the spectacular fountains are set in motion. Four fountains run every Wednesday, Saturday and Sunday at 5:30 pm.

Beautiful gardens and palace of San Ildefonso

ST TERESA OF JESUS

Teresa de Cepeda y Ahumada (1515–82) was one of the Catholic Church's greatest mystics and reformers. When aged just seven, she ran away from home in the hope of achieving martyrdom at the hands of the Moors, only to be recaptured by her uncle on the outskirts of the city. She became a nun at 19 but rebelled against her order. From 1562, when she founded her first convent, she travelled around Spain with her disciple, St John of the Cross, founding more convents for the followers of her order, the Barefoot Carmelites. Her remains are in Alba de Tormes near Salamanca (*see p361*).

Statue of St Teresa in the cathedral museum

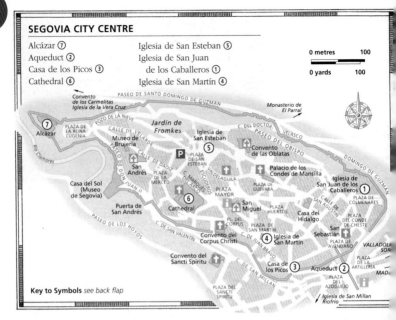

SEGOVIA CITY CENTRE

Alcázar ⑦
Aqueduct ②
Casa de los Picos ③
Cathedral ⑥
Iglesia de San Esteban ⑤
Iglesia de San Juan
de los Caballeros ①
Iglesia de San Martín ④

0 metres   100
0 yards   100

Segovia ⑮

Segovia. 🏛 60,000. 🚉 🚌 ℹ️
Plaza del Azoguejo 1, 921 46 67 21.
📅 Thu & Sat. 🎉 San Pedro (29
Jun), San Frutos (25 Oct).
www.turismodesegovia.com

Segovia is the most spectacularly sited city in Spain. The
old town is set high on a rocky
spur and surrounded by the
Río Eresma and Río Clamores.
It is often compared to a ship –
the Alcázar on its sharp crag
forming the prow, the pinnacles of the cathedral rising
like masts, and the aqueduct
trailing behind like a rudder.
The view of it from the valley
below at sunset is magical.

The **aqueduct**, in use until
the late 19th century, was
built at the end of the 1st century AD by the Romans, who
turned the ancient town into
an important military base.

The **cathedral**, dating from
1525 and consecrated in 1678,
is the last great Gothic church
in Spain. It was built to replace
the old cathedral, which was
destroyed in 1520 during the
revolt of the Castilian towns
(see p58). The cloister, however, survived and was rebuilt
on the new site. The pinnacles,
flying buttresses, tower and
dome form an impressive

silhouette, while the interior
is light and elegantly vaulted.
Graceful ironwork grilles enclose the side chapels. The
chapterhouse museum, with a
coffered ceiling, houses 17th-
century Brussels tapestries.

At the city's western end is
the **Alcázar** (see pp344–5).
Rising sheer above crags with
a multitude of gabled roofs,
turrets and crenellations, it
appears like the archetypal
fairy-tale castle. The present
building is mostly a fanciful
reconstruction following a fire
in 1862. It contains a museum
of weaponry and a series of

elaborately decorated room
Notable churches include
Romanesque **San Juan de lo
Caballeros**, which has an o
standing sculptured portico
San Martín with its beautifu
arcades and capitals, and **S
Miguel**, where Isabel the
Catholic was crowned Que
of Castille. Just inside the c
walls is the **Casa de los Picc
a mansion whose unique
façade is adorned with
diamond-shaped stones.

Environs

The vast palace of **Riofrío**,
km (7 miles) to the southw

The imposing Gothic cathedral of Segovia

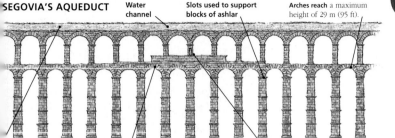

SEGOVIA'S AQUEDUCT

Water channel

Slots used to support blocks of ashlar

Arches reach a maximum height of 29 m (95 ft).

Water from the Río Frío flowed into the city, filtered through a series of tanks along the way.

Two tiers of arches – a total of 728 m (2,400 ft) in length – were needed to cope with the ground's gradient.

In this niche a statue of the Virgin Mary replaces an earlier inscription relating to the founding of the aqueduct.

Segovia's distinctive Alcázar, towering over the city

set in a deer park. It was built as a hunting lodge in 1752, and has richly decorated rooms.

Alcázar de Segovia
Plaza de la Reina Victoria Eugenia. *Tel* 921 46 07 59. ☐ daily. ● 1 & 6 Jan, 25 Dec. 🎟 (free EU residents 3rd Tue of each month). 🚻 🗗
Palacio de Riofrío
Tel 921 47 00 19. ☐ Tue–Sun. (free Wed EU residents).

Pedraza de la Sierra ⑯

Segovia. 🏠 500. 🚌 C/ Real 3, 921 50 86 66. 🎪 Nuestra Señora la Virgen del Carrascal (8 Sep) 🌐 www.pedraza.info.

The aristocratic little town of Pedraza de la Sierra is perched high over rolling countryside. Within its medieval walls, old streets lead past mansions to its porticoed **Plaza Mayor** *(see p20)*. The huge **castle**, standing on a rocky outcrop, was owned by Basque artist Ignacio Zuloaga (1870–1945).

The castle museum shows some of his works. On the first and second Saturdays of July, candlelit concerts are held in Plaza Mayor.

Environs
The main sight at **Turégano**, 30 km (19 miles) west, is a large hilltop castle with the 15th-century Iglesia de San Miguel.

Sepúlveda ⑰

Segovia. 🏠 1,350. 🚌 Plaza del Trigo 6, 921 54 02 37. 🛒 Wed. 🎪 Los Toros (last week of Aug).

Spectacularly sited on a slope above the Río Duratón, this picturesque town offers views of the Sierra de Guadarrama. Parts of its medieval walls and castle survive. Of its several Romanesque churches, the **Iglesia del Salvador**, behind the main square, is notable for possessing one of the oldest atria in Spain (1093).

Environs
Winding through a canyon haunted by griffon vultures is the Río Duratón, 7 km (4 miles) west of Sepúlveda. This area of striking beauty has been designated a natural park, the **Parque Natural de las Hoces del Duratón**.

Ayllón, 45 km (28 miles) northeast of Sepúlveda, has an arcaded main square and the Plateresque *(see p25)* Palacio de Juan de Contreras of 1497.

The Iberian and Roman ruins at **Tiermes**, 28 km (17 miles) further southeast, have been partially excavated, and finds can be seen in Soria's Museo Numantino *(see p377)*.

Castillo de Coca ⑱

Coca (Segovia). *Tel* 617 57 35 54. ☐ daily. ● 1st Tue of month. 🎟 🗗

Built in the late 15th century for the influential Fonseca family, Coca castle *(see p344)* is one of Castilla y León's most memorable fortresses. It was used more as a residential palace than a defensive castle, although its turrets and battlements are a fine example of Mudéjar military architecture. The complex moated structure comprises three concentric walls around a massive keep. It is now a forestry school, with a display of Romanesque woodcarvings.

Environs
The 14th-century castle of **Arévalo** in Avila, 26 km (16 miles) southwest, is where Isabel I spent her childhood. The porticoed Plaza de la Villa is surrounded by some attractive half-timbered houses.

Massive keep of the 15th-century Castillo de Coca

Medina del Campo ⑲

Valladolid. 🏠 *21,000.* 🚌 🚃
ℹ️ *Plaza Mayor 48, 983 81 13 57.*
🚌 *Sun.* 🎭 *San Antolín (1–8 Sep).*
www.turismomedina.net

Medina became wealthy in medieval times on the proceeds of huge sheep fairs and is still an important agricultural centre today. The vast brick Gothic-Mudéjar **Castillo de la Mota** *(see p344)*, on its outskirts, began as a Moorish castle but was rebuilt in 1440. The town transferred the castle's ownership to the Crown in 1475. Isabel I and her daughter Juana "la Loca" ("the Mad") both stayed here. Later, it served as a prison – Cesare Borja was incarcerated here from 1506–08. In a corner of the Plaza Mayor stands the modest house (built over an arch) where Isabel died in 1504.

Environs

Towering over the plains, some 25 km (16 miles) to the south of Medina del Campo, are the walls of **Madrigal de las Altas Torres**, which owes its name to the hundreds of bastions that marked the old wall; only 23 remain. In 1451 Isabel was born here in a palace that later became the Monasterio de las Agustinas in 1527.

⛪ **Castillo de la Mota**
Tel *983 80 10 24.* 🕐 *daily.*
⬤ *public hols.*

Tordesillas ⑳

Valladolid. 🏠 *9,500.* 🚌 🚃 ℹ️ *Casas del Tratado, 983 77 10 67.* 🚌 *Tue.*
🎭 *Fiestas de la Peña (mid-Sep).*
www.tordesillas.net

This pleasant town is where the historic treaty between Spain and Portugal was signed in 1494, dividing the lands of the New World *(see p57)*. A fateful oversight by the Spanish map makers left the immense prize of Brazil to Portugal.

The town's main place to visit is the **Monasterio de Santa Clara**. It was constructed by Alfonso XI around 1340 and

Castillo de la Mota at Medina del Campo

then converted by his son Pedro the Cruel into a stunning residence for his mistress, María de Padilla. Pining for her native Andalusia, she had the convent decorated with fine Moorish arches, baths and tiles. Most impressive are the beautiful patio and the main chapel. There is a fantastic display of royal musical instruments, including the portable organ of Juana "la Loca".

In the old quarter, the **Iglesia de San Antolín** now houses a fascinating religious art museum, which displays paintings as well as a collection of liturgical objects.

🏛 **Monasterio de Santa Clara**
Tel *983 77 00 71.* 🕐 *Tue–Sun.* 📷
(free Wed for EU citizens).

🏛 **Iglesia de San Antolín**
Calle Postigo. **Tel** *983 77 09 80.*
🕐 *Tue–Sun.* 📷

Moorish patio in the Monasterio de Santa Clara, Tordesillas

Valladolid ㉑

Valladolid. 🏠 *333,000.* 🚌 🚃
ℹ️ *Acera de Recoletos, 983 21 93 10.* 🚌 *Wed, Sat, Sun.* 🎭 *San Pedro Regalado (13 May); Virgen d[e] San Lorenzo (8 Sep), Easter week.*
www.asomateavalladolid.com

The Arabic city of Belad-Walid (meaning "Land of th[e] Governor") is located at the confluence of the Río Esgue[va] and Río Pisuerga. Although [it] has become sprawling and industrialized, Valladolid ha[s] some of Spain's best Renais[s]ance art and architecture.

Fernando and Isabel *(see pp56–7)* were married in th[e] Palacio Vivero in 1469 and, following the completion o[f] the Reconquest in 1492, th[ey] made Valladolid their capita[l]. Less spectacularly, Columb[us] died here, alone and forgot[ten] in 1506. In 1527 Felipe II w[as] born in the Palacio de los Pimentel. José Zorrilla, wh[o] popularized the legendary [Don] Juan in his 1844 play *(see p.[ ])* was also born in the city.

The Baroque façade *(see p25)* of the city's 15th-cen[tury] **university** was begun in 1[7 ?] by Narciso Tomé. He later created the Transparente o[f] Toledo Cathedral *(see p39[ ])*.

The **Iglesia de San Pablo** [has] a spectacular façade, embe[l]lished with angels and coa[t of] arms in Plateresque style. Among the other notewo[rthy] churches are **Santa María Antigua**, with its Romane[sque] belfry, and the **Iglesia de Las Angustias**, where Juan de Juni's fine sculpture of the Virgen de los Cuchillos (Virgin of the Knives) is on display.

Casa de Cervantes
alle Rastro. *Tel 983 30 88 10.*
◻ Tue–Sun. ◉ public hols.
(free Sun am).

he author of *Don Quixote* (see p35) lived in this simple house with white-washed walls from 1603 to 1606. The ooms have been restored nd contain some of ervantes' original furnishings.

Cathedral
alle Arribas 1. *Tel 983 30 43 62.*
◻ Mon. by appointment.
ork started on the unfinished thedral in 1580 by Felipe II's vourite architect, Juan de errera, but gradually lost mo-ntum over the centuries. urrigueresque *(see p25)* ourishes on the façade are in ntrast to the sombre, square-ared interior, whose only eeming flamboyance is a an de Juni altarpiece. The seo Diocesano inside, how-er, contains some fine pieces religious art and sculpture.

Museo Nacional de cultura
enas de S Gregorio 1–2. *Tel 983 03 75.* ◻ Tue–Sun. ◉ public . (free Sat pm & Sun am). ://museoescultura.mcu.es

s art collection, usually in Colegio de San Gregorio, moved to the nearby acio de Villena until reno-ions finish. The display sists mainly of wooden

e of Colegio de San orio, Valladolid

Berruguete's *Natividad*, in Museo Nacional de Escultura, Valladolid

religious sculptures from the 13th–18th centuries. They include Juan de Juni's emotive depiction of the burial of Christ and *Recumbent Christ* by Gregorio Fernández. An Alonso Berruguete altarpiece, and walnut choir stalls by Diego de Siloé and other artists, are among the other fine works to be found here.

The building itself is worthy of attention, particularly the Plateresque staircase, the chapel by Juan Güas, and the patio of twisted columns and delicate basket arches. The façade is a fine example of Isabelline *(see p24)* sculpture, portraying a mêlée of naked children scrambling about in thorn trees, hairy wild men, and strange birds and beasts.

🏛 Patio Herreriano Museo de Arte Contemporáneo Español
Calle Jorge Guillén 6. *Tel 983 36 27 71.*
◻ 11am–8pm Tue–Fri, 10am–8pm Sat, 10am–3pm Sun. ◉ Mon.
This private collection of contemporary Spanish art opened in 2002, housed in the former Monastery of San Benito with its fine cloisters. More than 1,000 works by 200 Spanish artists, including work by Joan Miró, Eduardo Chillida, Antoni Tàpies and Miquel Barceló.

Environs
The moated grey castle that dominates the village of **Simancas**, 11 km (7 miles) southwest of Valladolid, was converted by Charles V into Spain's national archive. The

Visigothic church in the village of Wamba, 15 km (9 miles) to the west, contains the tomb of King Recceswinth.

An unusual long, narrow 15th-century castle on a ridge overlooks the wine town of Peñafiel, 60 km (40 miles) east of Valladolid *(see p345)*.

Medina de Rioseco ㉒

Valladolid. 🏚 5,000. 🚍 ℹ
Dársena del Canal de Castilla, 983 72 03 19. 🛒 Wed. 🎉 San Juan (24 Jun), Virgen del Castillviejo (8 Sep), Easter week.
www.medinaderioseco.com

During the Middle Ages this town grew wealthy from the profitable wool trade, enabling it to commission leading artists, mainly of the Valladolid school, to decorate its churches. The dazzling star vaulting and superb wood-work of the **Iglesia de Santa María de Mediavilla**, in the centre of town, are evidence of this. Inside, the Los Bena-vente Chapel is a *tour de force*, with a colourful stucco ceiling by Jerónimo del Corral (1554), and an altarpiece by Juan de Juni.

The interior of the **Iglesia de Santiago** is stunning, with a triple altarpiece designed by the Churriguera brothers of Salamanca *(see p25)*.

The ancient buildings on Medina de Rioseco's main street, the Calle de la Rúa, are supported on wooden pillars, forming shady porticoes.

Altarpiece by Juan de Juni, Iglesia de Santa María de Mediavilla

CASTILLA Y LEON'S FIESTAS

El Colacho (*Sun after Corpus Christi, May/ Jun*), Castrillo de Murcia (Burgos). Babies born during the previous 12 months are dressed in their best Sunday clothes and laid on mattresses in the streets. Crowds of people, including the anxious parents, watch as *El Colacho* – a man dressed in a bright red and yellow costume – jumps over the babies in order to free them from illnesses, especially hernias. He is said to represent the devil fleeing from the sight of the Eucharist. This ritual is thought to have originated in 1621.

El Colacho **jumping over babies in Castrillo de Murcia**

St Agatha's Day (*Sun closest to 5 Feb*), Zamarramala (Segovia). Every year two women are elected as mayoresses to run the village on the day of St Agatha, patron saint of married women. They ceremonially burn a stuffed figure representing a man.
Good Friday, Valladolid. The procession of 28 multi-coloured sculptures, which depict various scenes of the Passion, is one of the most spectacular in Spain.
Fire-walking (*23 Jun*), San Pedro Manrique (Soria). Men, some carrying people on their backs, walk barefoot over burning embers. It is said that only local people can do this without being burned.

The beautiful carved retrochoir of Palencia Cathedral

Palencia ㉓

Palencia. 🏛 *82,000*. 🚊 🚌 🛈 Calle Mayor 105, 979 74 00 68. 🚢 Tue, Wed. 🎭 Virgen de la Calle (2 Feb). **www**.palencia-turismo.com

In medieval times, Palencia was a royal residence and the site of Spain's first university, founded in 1208. The city gradually diminished in importance following its involvement in the failed revolt of the Castilian towns of 1520 (*see p58*).

Although Palencia has since expanded considerably on profits from coal and wheat, its centre, by the old stone bridge over the Río Carrión, remains almost village-like.

The city's main sight is the **cathedral**, known as *La Bella Desconocida* (the Unknown Beauty). It is especially worth a visit for its superb works of art, many the result of Bishop Fonseca's generous patronage. The retrochoir, exquisitely sculpted by Gil de Siloé and Simon of Cologne, and the two altarpieces, are also noteworthy. The altarpiece above the high altar was carved by Philippe de Bigarny early in the 16th century. The inset panels are by Juan de Flandes, Isabel I's court painter. Behind the high altar is the Chapel of the Holy Sacrament, with an altarpiece dating from 1529 by Valmaseda. In this chapel, high on a ledge to the left, is the colourful tomb of Doña Urraca of Navarra. Below the retrochoir, a Plateresque (*see p25*) staircase leads down to the fine Visigothic crypt.

Environs
Baños de Cerrato,12 km (7 miles) to the south, boasts the tiny Visigothic Iglesia de San Juan Bautista, founded in 661. It is alleged to be the oldest intact church in Spain. Carved capitals and horseshoe arches decorate the interior.

Frómista ㉔

Palencia. 🏛 1,000. 🛈 C/ Arquitect Aníbal 2, 979 81 01 80. 🚢 Fri. 🎭 Patrón de Frómista (week after Easter). **www**.citfromista.com

This town on the Road to Santiago de Compostela (*see pp82–3*) is the site of one of Spain's purest Romanesque churches. The **Iglesia de San Martín** is the highlight of the town, partly due to a restoration in 1904, leaving the church, dating from 1066, entirely Romanesque in style. The presence of Pagan and Roman motifs suggest it may have pre-Christian origins.

Environs
Carrión de los Condes, 20 km (12 miles) to the northwest, also on the Road to Santiago. The frieze on the door of the Iglesia de Santiago depicts religious figures but local artisans. There are carvings of bulls on the façade of the 12th-century Iglesia de Santa María del Camino. The Convento de San Zoilo has a Gothic cloister and offers simple accommodation.

Located at **Gañinas**, 20 km (12 miles) to the northwest (just south of Saldaña), is the well-preserved Roman villa.

Interior of the Iglesia de San Ju Bautista at Baños de Cerrato

Posada of the Monasterio de Santa María la Real, Aguilar de Campoo

a Olmeda. It has a number of impressive mosaics, including hunting scene with lions and gers. Finds from the villa are isplayed in the archaeological useum located in the Iglesia e San Pedro in Saldaña.

Villa Romana La Olmeda
edrosa de la Vega. ◯ *Tue–Sun.*
23 Dec–31 Jan. ticket cludes archaeological museum.

guilar de Campoo ㉕

encia. 7,570. *Plaza aña 30, 979 12 36 41.* *Tue.* San Juan y San Pedro (24–29 Jun); meria de la Virgen del Llano (1st Sun ep).* **www**.aguilardecampoo.com

uated between the parched ains of Central Spain and e lush green foothills of the ntabrian Mountains is the fortified town of Aguilar

de Campoo. In the centre of its ancient porticoed main square is the impressive bell tower of the **Colegiata de San Miguel**. In this church is a mausoleum containing the tomb of the Marquises of Aguilar.

Among the other places of interest are the **Ermita de Santa Cecilia**, and the restored Romanesque-Gothic **Monasterio de Santa María la Real**, which has a small, friendly *posada* (inn), ideal for a night's stay.

Environs
Six km (4 miles) south, at **Olleros de Pisuerga**, is a church built in a cave. From the parador at **Cervera de Pisuerga**, 25 km (15 miles) northwest of Aguilar, there are stunning views, and tours of the **Reserva Nacional de Fuentes Carrionas**. This is a rugged region overlooked by Curavacas, a 2,540-m (8,333-ft) peak.

Briviesca ㉖

Burgos. 7,000. *Calle Duque de Frias 9, 947 59 39 39.* first Sat of month. *Feria de San José (19 Mar), Santa Casilda (9 May).*

This little walled town, in the northeast of Burgos province, has an arcaded main square and several dignified mansions. The best known of its churches is the **Convento de Santa Clara**, with its 16th-century walnut reredos carved with religious scenes. In 1387 Juan I of Aragón created the title Príncipe de Asturias for his son, Enrique, in the town. The Santuario de Santa Casilda, situated outside Briviesca, has a collection of votive objects.

Environs
Oña, 25 km (15 miles) north, is an attractive town. A Benedictine monastery was founded here in 1011.

Overlooking a fertile valley, 20 km (12 miles) further north-east, is the little hilltop town of **Frías**. Its castle overlooks cobbled streets and pretty old houses. Crossing the Río Ebro is a fortified medieval bridge, still with its central gate tower.

At **Medina de Pomar**, 30 km (20 miles) north of Oña, there is a 15th-century castle, once the seat of the Velasco family. Inside are the ruins of a palace with fine Mudéjar stucco decoration and Arabic inscriptions.

medieval bridge over the Río Ebro at Frías, with its central gate tower

Flemish triptych inside the collegiate church in Covarrubias

Covarrubias 27

Burgos. 🚶 700. 🚉 🖬 *Calle Monseñor Vargas, 947 40 64 61 (Mar–Dec).* 🛒 *Tue.* 🎉 *San Cosme and San Damián (26–27 Sep).*

Named after the reddish caves on its outskirts, Covarrubias stands on the banks of the Río Arlanza. Medieval walls surround the charming old centre with its arcaded half-timbered houses *(see p26)*. The distinguished **collegiate church** (closed Tue) shows the historical importance of Covarrubias: here is the tomb of Fernán González, first independent Count of Castile, and one of the great figures in Castilian history. By uniting several fiefs against the Moors in the 10th century, he started the rise in Castilian power that ensured the resulting kingdom of Castile would play a leading role in the unification of Spain. The church museum contains a newly-restored Flemish triptych of the Adoration of the Magi, attributed to the school of Gil de Siloé, and a 17th-century organ.

Environs
A short distance east along the Río Arlanza lies the ruins of the 11th-century Romanesque monastery of San Pedro de Arlanza. At Quintanilla de las Viñas, 24 km (15 miles) north of Covarrubias, is a ruined 7th-century Visigothic church. The reliefs on the columns of the triumphal arch are remarkable, depicting sun and moon symbols that may be pagan.

Burgos 28

Burgos. 🚶 170,000. 🚉 🖬 *Plaza de Alonso Martínez 7, 947 20 31 25.* 🛒 *Tue, Wed, Sun.* 🎉 *San Lesmes (30 Jan); Pedro and San Pablo (29 Jun).* **www.**turismoburgos.org

Founded in 884, Burgos has played a significant political and military role in Spanish history. It was the capital of the united kingdoms of Castile and León from 1073 until losing that honour to Valladolid after the fall of Granada in 1492 *(see pp56–7)*. During the 15th and 16th centuries Burgos grew rich from the wool trade and used its riches to finance most of the great art and architecture which can be seen in the city today. Less auspiciously, Franco chose Burgos as his headquarters during the Civil War *(see pp66–7)*.

The city's strategic location on the main Madrid–France highway and on the route to Santiago *(see pp82–3)* ensure many visitors; but even without this Burgos would justify a long detour. Despite its size and extremes of climate, it is one of most agreeable provincial capitals in Castilla y León.

Approach via the bridge of Santa María, which leads into the old quarter through the **Arco de Santa María**, a gateway carved with statues of various local worthies. The main bridge into the city, however, is the Puente de San Pablo, where a statue commemorates the city's hero, El Cid. Not far

from the bridge stands the **Casa del Cordón**, a 15th-century palace (now a bank) which has a Franciscan cord motif carved over the portal. A plaque declares that this is the spot where the Catholic Monarchs welcomed Columbus on his return, in 1497, from the second of his famous voyages to the Americas.

The lacy, steel-grey spires of the **cathedral** *(see pp312–3)* are a prominent landmark from almost anywhere in the city. On the rising ground behind it stands the recently-restored **Iglesia de San Nicolás**, whose main feature is a superb altarpiece by Simon of Cologne (1505). The crowded carvings vividly depict a number of scenes from the life of St Nicholas. Other churches worth visiting are the **Iglesia de San Lorenzo**, with its superb Baroque ceiling, and the **Iglesia de San Esteban** (currently being refurbished and due to open in 2009), which has a museum of altarpieces. The

The Arco de Santa María in Burgos adorned with statues and turrets

EL CID (1043–99)
Rodrigo Díaz de Vivar was born into a noble family in Vivar del Cid, north of Burgos, in 1043. He served Fernando I, but was banished from Castile after becoming embroiled in the fratricidal squabbles of the king's sons, Sancho II and Alfonso VI. He switched allegiance to fight for the Moors, then changed side again, capturing Valencia for the Christians in 1094, ruling the city until his death. For his heroism he was named El Cid, from the Arabic *Sidi* (Lord). He was a charismatic man of great courage, but it was an anonymous poem, *El Cantar del Mío Cid*, in 1180, that immortalized him as a romantic hero of the Reconquest *(see pp54–5)*. The tombs of El Cid and his wife, Jimena, are in Burgos cathedral.

Statue of El Cid in Vivar del Cid

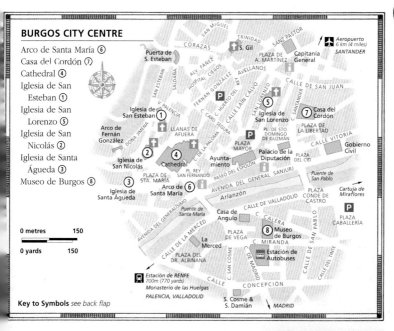

BURGOS CITY CENTRE

Arco de Santa María ⑥
Casa del Cordón ⑦
Cathedral ④
Iglesia de San
Esteban ①
Iglesia de San
Lorenzo ⑤
Iglesia de San
Nicolás ②
Iglesia de Santa
Águeda ③
Museo de Burgos ⑧

| 0 metres | 150 |
| 0 yards | 150 |

Key to Symbols *see back flap*

---

lesia de Santa Águeda is the
ace where El Cid made
ng Alfonso VI swear that he
ayed no part in the murder
his elder brother, King
ncho II *(see p356)*.
Across the river, the palace
the Casa de Miranda
uses the archaeological
ction of the **Museo de
rgos**, with finds from the
man city of Clunia. Nearby,
Casa de Angulo** contains
Fine Arts section, whose
ze exhibits are Juan de
dilla's tomb by Gil de Siloé,
d a Moorish casket in
amelled ivory.

ted tomb of Juan de Padilla by
Siloé, in Museo de Burgos

Two religious houses, on the
outskirts of Burgos, are worth
visiting. Just west of the city is
the **Real Monasterio de
Huelgas**, a late 12th-century
Cistercian convent founded by
Alfonso VIII. One of the most
interesting parts is the **Museo
de Ricas Telas**, a textile
museum containing ancient
fabrics from the convent's
many royal tombs. Other highlights include a Romanesque
cloister dating from the late
12th century, and the Gothic
cloister of San Fernando, decorated with Moorish designs.
In the Capilla de Santiago is a
curious wooden figure of St
James holding a sword, with
which, according to tradition,
royal princes were dubbed
Knights of Santiago.

To the east of Burgos is the
Cartuja de Miraflores, a Carthusian monastery founded
during the 15th century. The
church includes two of Spain's
most notable tombs, attributed
to Gil de Siloé. One holds the
bodies of Juan II and Isabel
of Portugal; the other contains
that of their son, Prince
Alfonso. The altarpiece by Gil
de Siloé, allegedly gilded with
the first consignment of gold
brought back to Spain from
the New World, is spectacular.

Polychrome altarpiece by Gil de
Siloé, in Cartuja de Miraflores

🏛 **Museo de Burgos**
Calle Calera 25. **Tel** 947 26 58 75.
⬜ *Tue–Sun.* 🎟 *(free Sat & Sun).* ♿

⛪ **Real Monasterio de
Huelgas**
Calle de las Huelgas. **Tel** 947 20 16 30.
⬜ *Tue–Sun.* 🎟 📷 *free on Wed.*

⛪ **Cartuja de Miraflores**
Ctra Burgos-Cardeña, km 3. ⬜ *daily.*

Environs
Ten km (6 miles) southeast of
Burgos is the **Monasterio de
San Pedro de Cardeña**. El Cid
led his family to safety here
while he rode into exile after
King Alfonso VI had banished
him from the territory of Castile.

Burgos Cathedral

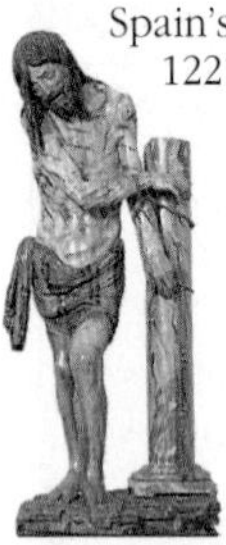

Spain's third-largest cathedral was founded in 1221 by Bishop Don Mauricio under Fernando III. The groundplan – a Latin cross – measures 84 m (92 yds) by 59 m (65 yds). Its construction was carried out in stages over three centuries and involved many of the greatest artists and architects in Europe. The style is almost entirely Gothic, and shows influences from Germany, France, and the Low Countries. First to be built were the nave and cloisters, while the intricate, crocketed spires and the richly decorated side chapels are mostly later work. The architects cleverly adapted the cathedral to its sloping site, incorporating stairways inside and out.

Christ at the Column, by Diego de Siloé

West Front
The lacy, steel-grey spires soar above a sculpted balustrade depicting Castile's early kings.

★ Golden Staircase
This elegant Renaissance staircase by Diego de Siloé (1519–1522) links the nave with a tall door (kept locked) at street level.

STAR FEATURES

- ★ Golden Staircase
- ★ The Crossing
- ★ Constable's Chapel

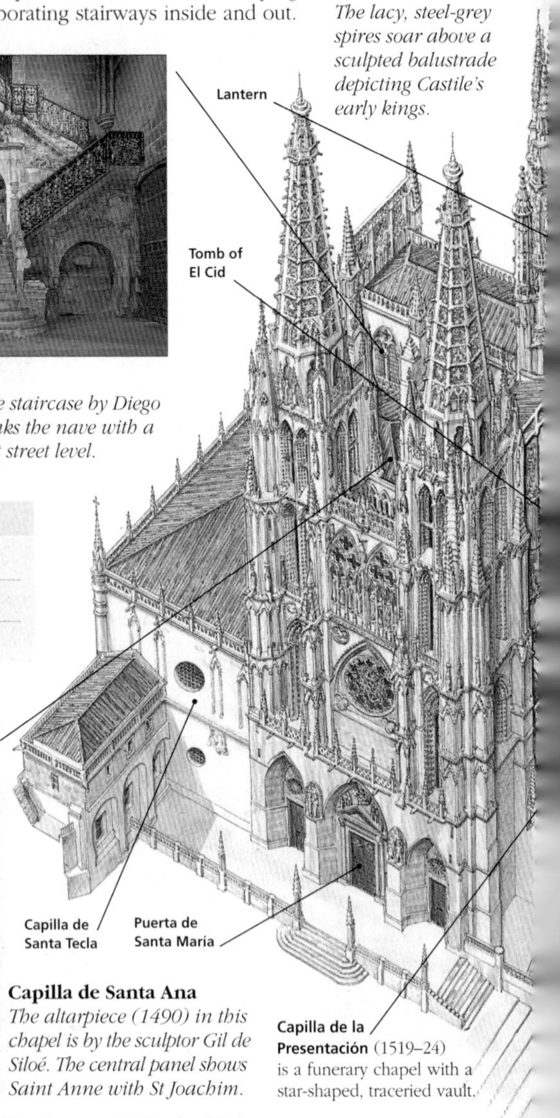

Lantern

Tomb of El Cid

Capilla de Santa Tecla

Puerta de Santa María

Capilla de Santa Ana
The altarpiece (1490) in this chapel is by the sculptor Gil de Siloé. The central panel shows Saint Anne with St Joachim.

Capilla de la Presentación (1519–24) is a funerary chapel with a star-shaped, traceried vault.

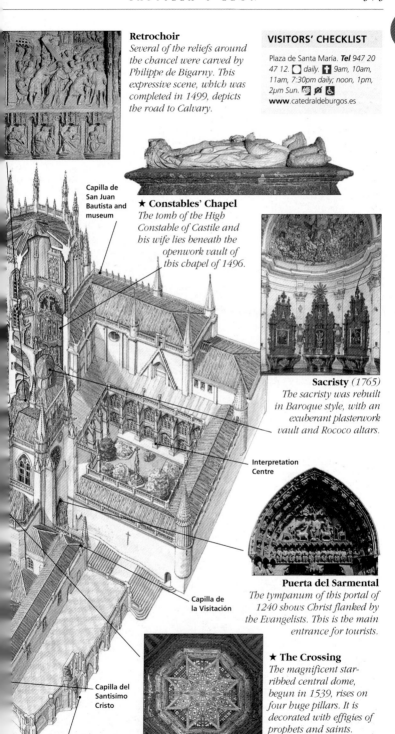

Retrochoir

Several of the reliefs around the chancel were carved by Philippe de Bigarny. This expressive scene, which was completed in 1499, depicts the road to Calvary.

VISITORS' CHECKLIST

Plaza de Santa María. **Tel** 947 20 47 12. ☐ daily. ♦ 9am, 10am, 11am, 7:30pm daily; noon, 1pm, 2pm Sun. ▨ ∅ ♿
www.catedraldeburgos.es

Capilla de San Juan Bautista and museum

★ Constables' Chapel

The tomb of the High Constable of Castile and his wife lies beneath the openwork vault of this chapel of 1496.

Sacristy *(1765)*
The sacristy was rebuilt in Baroque style, with an exuberant plasterwork vault and Rococo altars.

Interpretation Centre

Puerta del Sarmental
The tympanum of this portal of 1240 shows Christ flanked by the Evangelists. This is the main entrance for tourists.

Capilla de la Visitación

★ The Crossing

The magnificent star-ribbed central dome, begun in 1539, rises on four huge pillars. It is decorated with effigies of prophets and saints. Beneath it is the tomb of El Cid and his wife.

Capilla del Santisímo Cristo

Reception and Information Centre

Lerma ㉙

Burgos. 2,900.
Calle Audiencia 6, 947 17 70 02.
Wed. Nuestra Señora de
la Natividad (8 Sep).
www.citlerma.com

The grandiose appearance of
this town is largely due to the
ambition of the notorious first
Duke of Lerma (see p60),
Felipe III's corrupt favourite
and minister from 1598–1618.
He misused vast quantities of
Spain's new-found wealth on
new buildings in his home
town – all strictly Classical in
style, in accordance with prevailing fashion. At the top of
the town, the **Palacio Ducal**,
built in 1605 as his residence,
has been transformed into
a parador.

There are good views over
the Río Arlanza from the archways near to the **Convento de
Santa Clara** and also from the
Colegiata de San Pedro
church, which has a bronze
statue of the Duke's uncle.

**The narrow, sloping streets of the
old town of Lerma**

**Cloisters of the Monasterio de
Santo Domingo de Silos**

Monasterio de Santo Domingo de Silos ㉚

Santo Domingo de Silos (Burgos).
Tel 947 39 00 49. from Burgos.
Tue–Sat, Sun pm. 9am,
7pm Mon–Sat, noon Sun.

St Dominic gave his name to
the monastery that he rebuilt
in 1041 over the ruins of an
old abbey destroyed by the
Moors. It is a place of spiritual
and artistic pilgrimage, and its
tranquil setting has inspired
countless poets.

Others come to admire the
beautiful Romanesque cloisters,
whose capitals are sculpted in
a great variety of designs, both
symbolistic and realistic. The
carvings on the corner piers
depict various scenes from the
Bible and the ceilings are coffered in Moorish style. The
body of St Dominic rests in a
silver urn, supported by three

Romanesque lions, in a chape
in the north gallery. The old
pharmacy, just off the cloister
has a display of jars from
Talavera de la Reina (see p386.

The Benedictine communit
holds regular services in Greg
orian chant in the Neo-Classica
church by Ventura Rodríguez
The monastery offers accommodation for male guests.

Environs
To the southwest lies the
Garganta de la Yecla (Yecla
Gorge), where a path leads t
a narrow fissure cut by the
river. To the northeast, the
peaks and wildlife reserve
of the **Sierra de la Demanda**
extend over into La Rioja.

**The 15th-century castle of
Peñaranda de Duero**

Peñaranda de Duero ㉛

Burgos. 600. Calle
Trinquete 7, **Tel** 947 55 20 63.
Santiago (25 Jul); Santa Ana (.
Jul); Virgen de los Remedios (8 Se

The castle of Peñaranda w
built during the Reconques
(see pp54–5) by the Castili
who had driven the Moors
back south of the Río Due.
From its hilltop site, there
views down to one of the r
charming villages in old Ca
where pantiled houses clu
around a huge church. Th
main square is lined with p
coed, timber-framed build
and the superb Renaissanc
Palacio de Avellaneda. Fra
its main doorway are vari
heraldic devices, and insi
a patio which has double

GREGORIAN PLAINCHANT
At regular intervals throughout the
day, the monks of Santo Domingo
de Silos sing services in plainchant,
an unaccompanied singing of Latin
texts in unison. The origins of
chant date back to the beginnings
of Christianity, but it was Pope
Gregory I (590–604) who codified
this manner of worship. It is an
ancient and austere form of music
which has found a new appeal
with modern audiences. In 1994 a
recording of the monks became a
surprise hit all over the world.

**Manuscript for an 11th-
century Gregorian chant**

...rtain walls and drum towers of Berlanga de Duero castle

...lleries and fine decorated ...ilings. On Calle de la Botica ...a 17th-century **pharmacy**.

...virons
...the old quarter of **Aranda ... Duero**, 18 km (10 miles) to ...e west, the **Iglesia de Santa ...aría**, has an Isabelline ...cade (see p24).

Palacio de Avellaneda
...za Condes de Miranda 1.
...947 55 20 13. ☐ Tue–Sun.
...only (every half hour).

Burgo de ...sma ☻

...a. 🏠 5,000. 🚆 Plaza Mayor 9,
...36 01 16. ☐ Sat. 🚩 San Pedro
...Osma (2 Aug), Virgen del Espino
...San Roque (14–19 Aug).

...e most interesting sight in ...attractive village is the ...hedral. Although it is mostly ...hic (dating from 1232), with ...naissance additions, the tall ...er is Baroque (1739). Its ...sures include a Juan de ...altarpiece and the tomb ...he founder, San Pedro de ...na. The museum has a ...able collection of illumi-...d manuscripts and codices. ...orticoed buildings line the ...ets and the Plaza Mayor, ...storks nest on the Baroque ...pital de San Agustín.

...rons
...rlooking the Río Duero ...ormaz, 12 km (7 miles) ...n, is a massive castle ...28 towers. There are also ...eval fortresses at **Berlanga ...uero**, 20 km (12 miles)

further southeast, and at **Calatañazor**, 25 km (16 miles) northeast of El Burgo de Osma, near to where the Moorish leader al Mansur was killed in 1002 (see p53).

Soria ☻

Soria. 🏠 37,000. 🚆 C/Medinaceli 2,
975 21 20 52. ☐ Thu. 🚩 San Juan
(24 Jun).

Castilla y León's smallest pro-vincial capital stands on the banks of the Río Duero. Soria's stylish, modern parador (see p557) is named after the poet Antonio Machado (1875–1939, see p35), who wrote in praise of the town and the surrounding plains. Many of the older buildings are gone, but notable among those re-maining are the imposing rus-set **Palacio de los Condes de Gómara**, and the handsome **Concatedral de San Pedro**, both built in the 16th century.

The **Museo Numantino**, opposite the municipal gar-dens, displays a variety of finds from the nearby Roman ruins of Numantia and Tiermes (see

p365). Across the Duero is the ruined monastery of **San Juan de Duero**, with a 13th-century cloister of interlacing arches.

Environs
North of Soria are the ruins of **Numantia**, whose inhabitants endured a year-long Roman siege in 133 BC before defiantly burning the town and themselves (see p50). To the northwest is the Sierra de Urbión, a range of pine-clad hills with a lake, the **Laguna Negra de Urbión**.

🏛 **Museo Numantino**
Paseo de Espolón. **Tel** 975 22 14
28. ☐ Tue–Sun. 🎫 (free Sat &
Sun). ♿

Medinaceli ☻

Soria. 🏠 800. 🚆 🛈 Campo de
San Nicolás, 975 32 63 47. 🚩 Beato
Julián de San Agustín (28 Aug);
Cuerpos Santos (13 Nov).

Only a triumphal arch remains of Roman Ocilis, perched on a high ridge over the Río Jalón. Built in the 1st century AD, it is the only one in Spain with three arches. It has been adopted as the symbol for ancient monu-ments on Spanish road signs.

Environs
Lying just to the east are the red cliffs of the Jalón gorges. On the Madrid–Zaragoza road is the Cistercian monastery of **Santa María de Huerta**, founded in the 12th century. Its glories include a 13th-century Gothic cloister and the superb, crypt-like Monks' Refectory.

🏠 **Monasterio de Santa María de Huerta**
Tel 975 32 70 02. ☐ daily. 🎫 ♿

Decorative arches in the cloister of the monastery of San Juan de Duero

CASTILLA–LA MANCHA

GUADALAJARA · CUENCA · TOLEDO · ALBACETE · CIUDAD REAL

*L*a Mancha's empty beauty, its windmills and medieval castles, silhouetted above the sienna plains, was immortalized by Cervantes in Don Quixote's epic adventures. Its brilliantly sunlit, wide horizons are one of the classic images of Spain. This scarcely visited region has great, scenic mountain ranges, dramatic gorges and the two monument-filled cities of Toledo and Cuenca.

You will always find a castle nearby in this region – as the name Castilla suggests. Most were built in the 9th–12th centuries, when the region was a battleground between Christians and Moors. Others mark the 14th- and 15th-century frontiers between the kingdoms of Aragón and Castile. Sigüenza, Belmonte, Alarcón Molina de Aragón and Calatrava La Nueva are among the most impressive.

Toledo, which was the capital of Visigothic Spain, is an outstanding museum city. Its rich architectural and artistic heritage derives from a coalescence of Muslim, Christian and Jewish cultures with medieval and Renaissance ideas and influences.

Cuenca is another attractive city. Its old town is perched above converging gorges; on two sides it spills down steep hillsides. Villanueva de los Infantes, Chinchilla, Alcaraz and Almagro are towns of character built between the 16th and 18th centuries. Ocaña and Tembleque each has a splendid *plaza mayor* (main square).

La Mancha's plains are brightened by natural features of great beauty in its two national parks – the Tablas de Daimiel, and Cabañeros, within the Montes de Toledo. Rimming the plains are beautiful upland areas: the olive groves of the Alcarria; Cuenca's limestone mountains; and the peaks of the Sierra de Alcaraz. The wine region of La Mancha is the world's largest expanse of vineyards. Around Consuegra and Albacete fields turn mauve in autumn as the valuable saffron crocus blooms.

Windmills above Campo de Criptana on the plains of La Mancha

Old houses in Cuenca, a city dramatically located over two gorges

Exploring Castilla-La Mancha

The historic city of Toledo is Castilla-La Mancha's major tourist destination. Less crowded towns with historical charm include Almagro, Oropesa, Alcaraz and Guadalajara. At Sigüenza, Calatrava, Belmonte and Alarcón there are medieval castles, reminders of the region's eventful past. Some towns on the plains of La Mancha, such as El Toboso and Campo de Criptana, are associated with the adventures of Don Quixote (*see p395*). The wooded uplands of the Serranía de Cuenca, the Alcarria and the Sierra de Alcaraz provide picturesque scenic routes. A haven for bird lovers is the wetland nature reserve of the Tablas de Daimiel.

The village of Alcalá del Júcar

SIGHTS AT A GLANCE

Alarcón ⑳
Albacete ㉒
Alcalá del Júcar ㉑
Alcaraz ㉔
La Alcarria ④
Almagro ㉚
Atienza ①
Belmonte ⑲
Calatrava la Nueva ㉙
Campo de Criptana ⑰
Consuegra ⑯
Cuenca pp384–5 ⑦
Guadalajara ⑤
Illescas ⑩
Lagunas de Ruidera ㉕
Molina de Aragón ③
Montes de Toledo ⑬
Oropesa ⑫
Segóbriga ⑧
Serranía de Cuenca ⑥
Sigüenza ②
Tablas de Daimiel ㉛
Talavera de la Reina ⑪
Tembleque ⑮
El Toboso ⑱
Toledo pp388–93 ⑭
Uclés ⑨
Valdepeñas ㉗
Valle de Alcudia ㉜
Villanueva de los Infantes ㉖
Viso del Marqués ㉘

Tours

Sierra de Alcaraz ㉓

SEE ALSO

- **Where to Stay** pp586–8
- **Where to Eat** pp636–8

Cattle grazing on the isolated plains of La Mancha

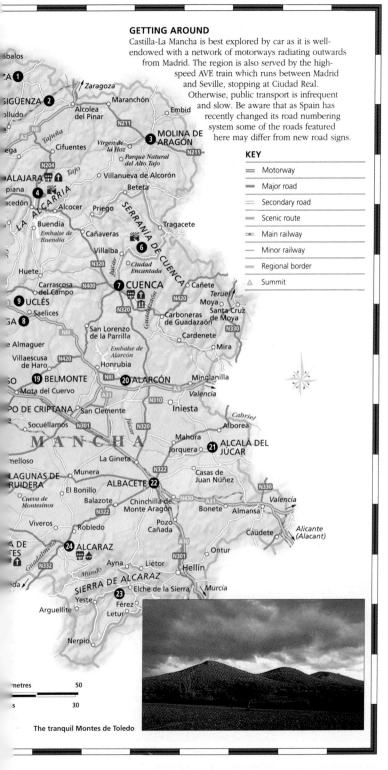

GETTING AROUND

Castilla-La Mancha is best explored by car as it is well-endowed with a network of motorways radiating outwards from Madrid. The region is also served by the high-speed AVE train which runs between Madrid and Seville, stopping at Ciudad Real. Otherwise, public transport is infrequent and slow. Be aware that as Spain has recently changed its road numbering system some of the roads featured here may differ from new road signs.

KEY

▬	Motorway
▬	Major road
▬	Secondary road
▬	Scenic route
▭	Main railway
—	Minor railway
▬	Regional border
△	Summit

The tranquil Montes de Toledo

Atienza ❶

Guadalajara. 🏠 500. 🚹 Cervantes 22, 949 39 90 01. 🚆 Fri. 🎉 La Caballada (Pentecost Sun).

Rising high above the valley it once protected, Atienza contains vestiges of its medieval past. Crowning the hill are a ruined 12th-century castle. The arcaded Plaza Mayor and the Plaza del Trigo are joined by an original gateway. The **Museo de San Gil**, a religious art museum, is in the church of the same name. The **Iglesia de Santa María del Rey**, at the foot of the hill, displays a Baroque altarpiece.

Environs

Campisábalos, to the west, has an outstanding 12th-century Romanesque church. The **Hayedo de Tejera Negra**, further west, is a nature reserve of beech woods.

🏛 **Museo de San Gil**
C/ San Gil.
Tel 949 39 90 41. ◯ Sep–Jun: Sat & Sun; Jul–Aug: daily; by appt weekdays. 🖼

Sigüenza ❷

Guadalajara. 🏠 5,000. 🚆 🚹 Calle Serrano Sanz 9, 949 34 70 07. 🚆 Sat. 🎉 San Vicente (22 Jan), San Juan (24 Jun), Fiestas Patronales (mid-Aug). **www**.siguenza.es

Dominating the hillside town of Sigüenza is its impressive castle-parador *(see p587)*. The **cathedral**, is Romanesque, with later additions, such as the Gothic-Plateresque cloisters. In one of the chapels is the Tomb of El Doncel, built

Semi-recumbent figure of El Doncel on his tomb in Sigüenza Cathedral

for Martín Vázquez de Arce, Isabel of Castile's page *(see p56)*. He was killed in battle against the Moors in 1486. The sacristy has a ceiling carved with flowers and cherubs.

Molina de Aragón ❸

Guadalajara. 🏠 3,900. 🚹 C/ Carmen 1, 949 83 20 98. 🚆 Thu. 🎉 Día del Carmen (16 Jul), Ferias (30 Aug –5 Sep).

Molina's attractive medieval quarter is at the foot of a hill next to the Río Gallo. The town was disputed during the Reconquest and captured from the Moors by Alfonso I of Aragón in 1129. Many monuments were destroyed during the War of Independence *(see p63)*, but the 11th-century hilltop castle preserves seven original towers. It is possible to visit the Romanesque-Gothic **Iglesia de Santa Clara.**

Environs

West of Molina is the **Virgen de la Hoz** chapel, set in a rust-red ravine. Further sout’ west is a nature reserve, the **Parque Natural del Alto Tajo**

Arab ramparts above Molina de Aragón's old town

La Alcarria ❹

Guadalajara. 🚆 Guadalajara. 🚹 Pastrana, Palacio Ducal, 949 37 0 (closed Mon). **www**.pastrana.or

This vast stretch of undula olive groves and fields eas Guadalajara is still evocati of Camilo José Cela's *(see p35)* classic book *Journey the Alcarria*. Driving throu the rolling hills, it seems t little has changed since th account of the hardship o Spanish rural life was writ in the 1940s.

Towards the centre of th Alcarria are three immens adjoining reservoirs called the **Mar de Castilla** (Sea o

Olive groves in La Alcarria in the province of Guadalajara

For hotels and restaurants in this region see pp586–8 and pp636–8

Castile). The first reservoir was built in 1946, and holiday homes have subsequently sprung up close to the shores and on the outskirts of villages.

Historic **Pastrana**, 45 km (28 miles) southeast of Guadalajara, is one of the prettiest towns in the Alcarria. The town developed alongside the **Palacio Mendoza**, and by the 17th century was larger and more affluent than Guadalajara. The **Iglesia de la Asunción** contains four 16th-century Flemish tapestries and paintings from El Greco's school.

Brihuega, 30 km (19 miles) northeast of Guadalajara, has a pleasant old centre.

Guadalajara ❺

Guadalajara. 🏠 75,000. 🚌 🚉 ℹ *Plaza de los Caídos 6, 949 21 16 26.* 🏪 *Tue, Sat.* 🎎 *Virgen de la Antigua (Sep).* **www**.guadalajara.es

Guadalajara's history is largely lost within the modern city, although traces of its Renaissance splendour survive. The **Palacio de los Duques del Infantado**, built between the 14th and 17th centuries by the powerful Mendoza dynasty, is an outstanding example of Gothic-Mudéjar architecture *(see p24)*. The main façade and patio are adorned with carving. The restored palace now houses the Museo Provincial. Among the churches in the town is the **Iglesia de Santiago**, with a Gothic-Plateresque chapel by

Detail of the façade of the Palacio Los Duques del Infantado

Sculpted rock figures in Ciudad Encantada

Alonso de Covarrubias. The 15th-century **Iglesia de San Francisco** is home to the mausoleum of the Mendoza family; it cannot, however, be visited. The cathedral is built on the site of a mosque.

Environs
At **Lupiana**, 11 km (7 miles) east of Guadalajara, is the two-storey Monasterio de San Bartolomé, which was founded in the 14th century.

🏛 **Palacio de los Duques del Infantado**
Avenida del Ejército. *Tel 949 21 33 01.* ☐ *Tue–Sun.*

Serranía de Cuenca ❻

Cuenca. 🚉 *Cuenca.* ℹ *Cuenca, 969 24 10 51.* **www**.cuenca.es

To the north and east of Cuenca stretches the vast *serranía*, a mountainous area of forests and pastures dissected by deep gorges. Its two most popular beauty spots are the

Ciudad Encantada (Enchanted City), where the limestone has been eroded into spectacular shapes, and the moss-clad waterfalls and rock pools of the **Nacimiento del Río Cuervo** (Source of the River Cuervo).

The main river flowing through the area, the Júcar, carves a gorge near Villalba de la Sierra. The viewpoint of the **Ventana del Diablo** gives the best view of the gorge.

Between Beteta and Priego (known for its pottery and canework), to the north, is another spectacular river canyon, the **Hoz de Beteta**, where the Río Guadiela has cut its way through the surrounding cliffs. There are good views from the convent of **San Miguel de las Victorias**. A small road leads to the 18th-century royal spa of **Solán de Cabras**.

In the emptier eastern and southern tracts is **Cañete**, a pretty, fortified old town with a parish church displaying 16th-century paintings. To the southeast of Cañete are the eerie ridgetop ruins of the abandoned town of **Moya**.

Street-by-Street: Cuenca ❼

Cuenca's picturesque old town sits astride a steeply
sided spur which drops precipitously on either side to
the deep gorges of the Júcar and Huécar rivers. Around
the Moorish town's narrow, winding streets grew the
Gothic and Renaissance city, its monuments built with
with the profits of the wool and textile trade. The main
sight is the cathedral, one of the most original works
of Spanish Gothic, with Anglo-Norman influences.
One of the picturesque Hanging Houses,
which jut out over the Huécar ravine, has
been converted into the excellent
Museum of Abstract Art.

The Plaza de la Merced
buildings contrast with
the modern Museo de las
Ciencias (Science Museum

**Museo de las
Ciencias**

CALLE DE SANTA MARÍA

CALLE DE ALFONSO VIII

CALLE MOSEN DIEGO DE VALERA

Torre Mangana
*This ruined lookout tower at
the top of the town is all that
remains of an Arab fortress.
There are wonderful pano-
ramic views from the top.*

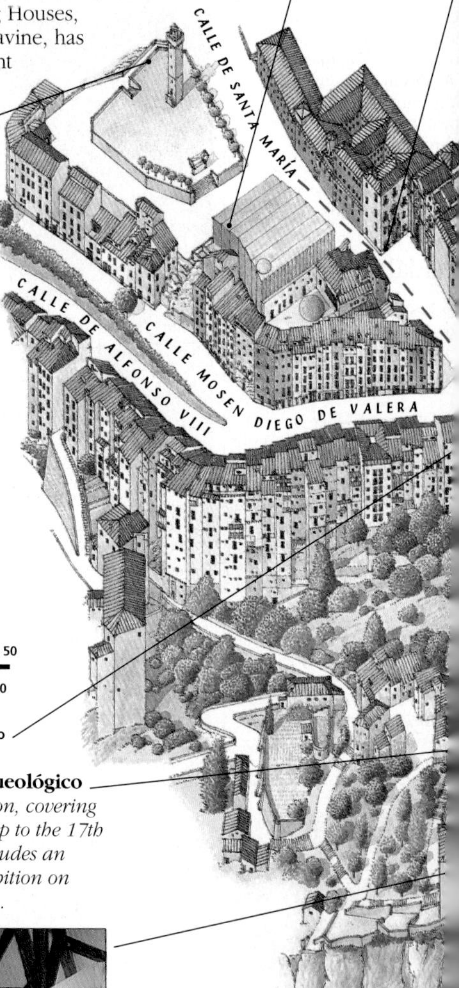

| 0 metres | 50 |
| 0 yards | 50 |

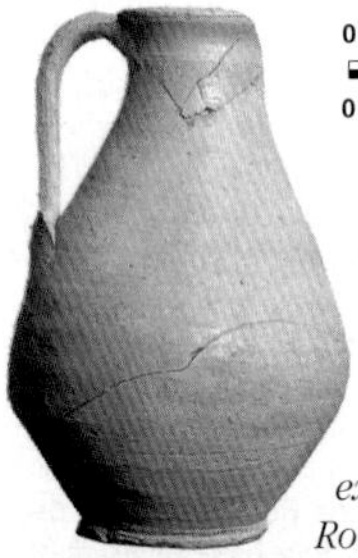

Ayuntamiento

Museo Arqueológico
*The collection, covering
prehistory up to the 17th
century, includes an
excellent exhibition on
Roman Cuenca.*

KEY

– – – Suggested route

★ Museo de Arte Abstracto
*Spain's abstract art museum is inside
of the Hanging Houses. It contains wor
the movement's leading artists, includ
Antoni Tàpies and Eduardo Chillida.*

Plaza Mayor
This café-lined, arcaded square is in the heart of the old town. The 18th-century Baroque town hall (ayuntamiento), built with arches, stands at the south end.

VISITORS' CHECKLIST

Cuenca. 🔟 52,000. 🚂 Calle Mariano Catalina, 902 24 02 02. 🚌 Calle Fermín Caballero 20, 969 22 70 87. 🛈 Plaza Mayor 1, 969 24 10 51. 🕭 Tue. **Museo Diocesano** 🕭 Tue–Sun. 🖾 **Museo de Arte Abstracto** 🕭 Tue–Sun. 🖾 🏛 **Museo de las Ciencias** 🕭 Tue–Sun. 🖾 🏛 **Museo Arqueológico** 🕭 Tue–Sun. 🖾 www.cuenca.es

The Iglesia de San Miguel, perched over the Júcar gorge, was built in the Romanic style.

PLAZA MAYOR

SEVERO CATALINA

CALLE DE SAN PEDRO

CALLE DE JULIÁN ROMERO

VALERO

To Parador de Cuenca

Museo Diocesano
The cathedral's treasures, which are housed in the Palacio Episcopal, include paintings by El Greco.

★ Cathedral
Highlights of the 12th- to 18th-century building are the decorated altar, chapterhouse and the side chapels.

STAR SIGHTS

★ Museo de Arte Abstracto

★ Hanging Houses

★ Cathedral

★ Hanging Houses
The 14th-century beamed Casas Colgadas were once used as a summer residence for the royal family.

Remains of a Roman building in Segóbriga

Segóbriga ❽

Saelices (Cuenca). **Tel** 629 75 22 57. ⬜ Tue–Sun. **Museum** ● *public hols, 24, 25 & 31 Dec.* 📷

The small ruined Roman city of Segóbriga, near the town of Saelices, is located in open, unspoiled countryside close to the Madrid–Valencia motorway. The Romans who lived here exploited the surrounding area, growing cereals, felling timber and mining minerals.

Many parts of the city can be explored. The 1st-century theatre – which has a capacity of 2,000 people – is sometimes used for dramatic performances today. Segóbriga also had a necropolis, an amphitheatre, a temple to Diana and public baths. The quarries which supplied the stone to build the city can also be seen.

Nearby, there is a small museum containing some of the site's finds, although the best statues are in Cuenca's Museo Arqueológico *(see p384)*.

Monasterio de Uclés ❾

Uclés (Cuenca). **Tel** 969 13 50 58. ⬜ *10am–dusk daily.* ● *1 & 6 Jan, 25 Dec.* 📷

The small village of Uclés, to the south of the Alcarria, is dominated by its impressive castle-monastery, nicknamed "El Escorial de La Mancha" for the similarity of its church's profile to that of El Escorial *(see pp330–31)*. Originally an impregnable medieval fortress, Uclés became the monastery seat of the Order of Santiago

from 1174, because of its central location. The austere building you see today, used as a seminary school, is mainly Renaissance, but overlaid with ornamental Baroque detail. It has a magnificent carved wooden ceiling and staircase.

Illescas ❿

Toledo. 🏘 *15,000.* 🚉 🚌 *Plaza Mercado 14, 925 51 10 51.* ⬛ *Thu.* 📷 *Fiesta de Milagro (11 May); Fiesta Patronal (31 Aug).* **www**.illescas.com

Just off the Madrid–Toledo motorway, Illescas was the summer location for Felipe II's court. While there is little to see of its old town, the 16th-century **Hospital de la Caridad**, near the Iglesia de Santa María (built in the 12th and 13th centuries and renovated in the 15th), is important for its art collection. The hospital has five

Ceramics in Talavera workshop

outstanding late El Grecos *(see p373).* The subjects of three of these are the Nativity, the Annunciation and the Coronation of the Virgin.

🏛 **Hospital de la Caridad**
Calle Cardenal Cisneros 2. **Tel** 925 54 00 35. ⬜ *daily.* 📷 ♿

Talavera de la Reina ⓫

Toledo. 🏘 *80,000.* 🚉 🚌 🚌 *C/ Palenque 2, 925 82 63 22.* ⬛ *Wed & 1st Sat of month.* 📷 *Feria de San Isidro (15–18 May), Virgen del Prado (8 Sep), Feria de San Mateo (20–23 Sep), Las Mondas (Sat after Easter).*

A ruined 15th-century bridge across the Tagus marks the entrance to the old part of the busy market town. From the bridge you can walk past the surviving part of the Moorish and medieval wall to the 12th-century **collegiate church**. It has a small but beautiful Gothic cloister, and the belfry is from the 18th century.

Talavera's ceramic workshops still produce the blue and yellow *azulejos* (tiles) which have been a trademark of the town since the 16th century; but nowadays they also make domestic and decorative objects.

A good selection of *azulejos* can be seen in the large **Ermita de la Virgen del Prado** by the river. Many of the interior walls have superb 16th- to 20th-century tile friezes of religious scenes.

Part of a frieze of tiles in Talavera's Ermita del Virgen del Prado

aditional embroidery work in
garteria, near Oropesa

)ropesa ⑫

ledo. 🏛 2,871. 🚉 🚻 Plaza del
varro 9, 925 45 00 02. 🚌 Mon &
u. 🎪 Virgen de Peñitas (8–10 Sep),
ato Alonso de Orozco (19 Sep).

opesa's medieval and Re-
issance splendour as one
Toledo's satellite com-
nities has left a charming
d quarter at the centre of
lay's small farming town.
circular Ruta Monumental
rts from the massive, mainly
h-century **castle** on the top
the hill. A Renaissance
ension – thought to be the
rk of Juan de Herrera, co-
hitect of El Escorial *(see
330–31)* – was added to
castle in the 16th century
the wealthy and influential
arez family. A large part of
castle has been converted
o a parador *(see p587)*.
he Ruta Monumental con-
es around the town, taking
a number of churches, con-
ts, a small ceramics mu-
m and the town hall which
sides over the main square.

irons

area around Oropesa is
ellent for buying handicrafts.
artera, just to the west of
town, is famous for the
roidery and lacework by
women in the village and **El
te del Arzobispo**, 12 km (7
s) south of Oropesa, is a
d source of painted ceramics
esparto (grass-weaving)
k. **Ciudad de Vascos**, further
heast, is a ruined 10th-
ury Arab city in splendid
tryside around Azután.

Montes de Toledo ⑬

Toledo. 🚉 *Pueblo Nuevo del
Bullaque.* 🚻 *Parque Nacional de
Cabañeros, 926 78 32 97.*

To the southwest of Toledo
a range of low mountains
sweeps towards Extremadura.
In medieval times the Montes
de Toledo were owned by
bishops and the kings. They
cover an area of approximately
1,000 sq km (386 sq miles).

The attractive new nature reserve of the **Parque Nacional
de Cabañeros** *(see pp30–1)*
encloses a sizeable area of
woodland and pastures used
for grazing sheep. The easiest
access to the park is from
Pueblo Nuevo del Bullaque.
From here it is possible to
make four-hour guided trips
in Land Rovers, during which
you may spot wild boar, deer
and imperial eagles. In the
pasturelands stand *chozos*,
conical refuges for shepherds.

In the eastern foothills of the
Montes de Toledo is **Orgaz**,
with a parish church which
contains works by El Greco.
Nearby villages, such as **Los
Yébenes** and **Ventas con Peña
Aguilera**, are known for their
leather goods and restaurants
serving game.

On the plains stands the
small church of **Santa María
de Melque**, believed to date
back to the 8th century. Close
by is the Templar castle of
Montalbán, a vast but ruined
12th-century fortress. Nearer
to Toledo, at **Guadamur**, there
is another handsome castle.

A *chozo* (shepherd's cabin) in the
Parque Nacional de Cabañeros

CASTILLA-LA MANCHA'S FIESTAS

La Endiablada *(2–3 Feb)*
Almonacid del Marquesado
(Cuenca). At the start of
the two-day-long "Fiesta
of the Bewitched", men
and boys, gaudily dressed
as "devils", with cowbells
strapped to their backs,
gather in the house of
their leader, the *Diablo
Mayor*. They accompany
the images of the Virgen
de la Candelaria (Virgin of
Candlemas) and St Blaise
in procession. As the devils
dance alongside the floats
bearing the saints' images,
they ring their bells loudly
and incessantly.

One of the so-called "devils" in
La Endiablada fiesta

**Romería del Cristo del
Sahúco** *(Pentecost, May/
Jun)*, Peñas de San Pedro
(Albacete). A cross-shaped
coffin bearing a figure of
Christ is carried 15 km (9
miles) here from its shrine
by men dressed in white.
La Caballada *(early Jun)*,
Atienza (Guadalajara).
Horsemen follow the route
across country taken by the
12th-century muleteers of
Atienza, who are said to
have saved the boy King
Alfonso VIII of Castile from
his uncle, Fernando II.
Corpus Christi *(May/Jun)*,
Toledo. One of Spain's
most dramatic Corpus
Christi *(see p38)* processions. The cathedral
monstrance *(see p392)* is
paraded in the streets.

Street-by-Street: Toledo ⑭

Damascene work, typical of Toledo

Picturesquely sited on a hill above the River Tagus is the historic centre of Toledo. Behind the old walls lies much evidence of the city's rich history. The Romans built a fortress on the site of the present-day Alcázar. The Visigoths made Toledo their capital in the 6th century AD, and left behind several churches. In the Middle Ages, Toledo was a melting pot of Christian, Muslim and Jewish cultures, and it was during this period that the city's most outstanding monument – its cathedral – was built. In the 16th century the painter El Greco came to live in Toledo, and today the city is home to many of his works.

Puerta Cristo de la Cruz

The Iglesia de San Román, of Visigothic origin, now contains a museum relating the city's past under the Visigoths.

| 0 metres | | 100 |
| 0 yards | | 100 |

CARDENAL LORENZANA

CALLE DE SAN ROMÁN

CALLE DE ALFONSO X

CALLE DE ALFONSO XII

CALLE DE LA TRINIDAD

★ **Iglesia de Santo Tomé**
This church, with a beautiful Mudéjar tower, houses El Greco's masterpiece, The Burial of the Count of Orgaz *(see p32).*

To Sinagoga de Santa María la Blanca and Monasterio de San Juan de los Reyes

To Sinagoga del Tránsito and Casa-Museo de El Greco

Archbishop's Palace

Taller del Moro
This Mudéjar palace houses a museum of Mudéjar ceramics and tiles. It is currently closed for renovation but due to reopen in 2009.

STAR SIGHTS

★ Iglesia de Santo Tomé

★ Cathedral

★ Museo de Santa Cr[...]

erta de Sol
as a double
sh arch and
wo towers.

Mezquita del Cristo de la Luz

This mosque, one of the city's two remaining Muslim buildings, dates from around AD 1000.

To Estación de Autobuses
and Estación de RENFE

VISITORS' CHECKLIST

Toledo. 🏠 75,500. ✈ 🚉
Paseo de la Rosa, 925 22 30 99.
🚌 Avenida de Castilla-La
Mancha, 925 21 58 50. 🛈 Plaza
del Consistorio 1, 925 25 40 30.
🗓 Tue. 🎉 Corpus Christi
(Easter/May/Jun); Virgen del
Sagrario (15 Aug). **Iglesia de San
Román** ⬭ Tue–Sun. 🎟 **Taller
del Moro** ⬤ renovations.
www.toledoweb.org

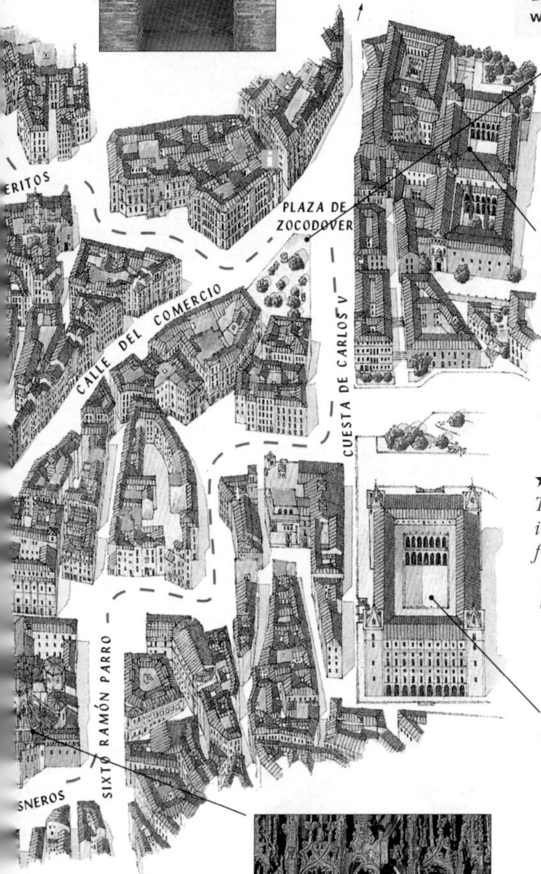

The Plaza de Zocodover is
named after the market
which was held here in
Moorish times. It is still the
city's main square, with
many cafés and shops.

PLAZA DE
ZOCODOVER

ERITOS

CALLE DEL COMERCIO

CUESTA DE CARLOS V

SIXTO RAMÓN PARRO

SNEROS

Y

- - Suggested route

★ Museo de Santa Cruz

*This fine arts collection
includes several tapestries
from Flanders, including
this 15th-century
zodiac tapestry.
Restoration work is in
progress in one part of
the museum.*

★ Cathedral

*lt on the site of a Visigothic
bedral and a mosque, this
pressive structure is one of
ristendom (see pp392–3).
e Flamboyant Gothic high
altar reredos (1504) is the
work of several artists.*

Alcázar

*In the central patio is a
replica of the statue* Carlos
V y el Furor. *Alcázar is
closed for restoration
until sometime in 2009.*

Toledo Cathedral rising above the rooftops of the medieval part of the city

Exploring Toledo

Toledo is easily reached from Madrid by rail, bus or car, and is then best explored on foot. To visit all the main sights you need at least two days, but it is possible to walk around the medieval and Jewish quarters in a long morning. To avoid the heavy crowds, go midweek and stay for a night, when the city is at its most atmospheric.

♠ Alcázar

Cuesta de Carlos V. **Tel** 925 22 16 73. ○ for expansion until 2009.
Charles V's fortified palace stands on the site of former Roman, Visigothic and Muslim fortresses. Its severe square profile suffered damage by fire three times before being almost completely destroyed in 1936 when the Nationalists survived a 70-day siege by the Republicans. Restoration followed the original plans and the siege headquarters have been preserved as a monument to Nationalist heroism. The building is currently closed while undergoing renovations in order to house the Museo del Ejército (see p287), which will then be transferred from Madrid, making this the main army museum in Spain.

The Borbón-Lorenzana Library (open to the public) contains 100,000 books and manuscripts from the 16th to 19th centuries.

⑪ Museo de Santa Cruz

Calle Miguel de Cervantes 3.
Tel 925 22 10 36. ○ daily.
This museum is housed in a 16th-century hospital founded by Cardinal Mendoza. The building has some outstanding Renaissance architectural features, including the main doorway, staircase and cloister. The four main wings, laid out in the shape of a Greek cross, are dedicated to the fine arts. The collection is especially strong in medieval and Renaissance tapestries, paintings and sculptures. There are also works by El Greco, including one of his last paintings, *The Assumption* (1613), still in its original altarpiece. Decorative

The Assumption by El Greco (1613) in the Museo de Santa Cruz

arts on display include two typically Toledan crafts: armo and damascened swords, ma by inlaying blackened steel with gold wire. Damascene work, such as plates and jewellery (as well as swords is still produced in the city.

♠ Iglesia de Santo Tomé

Calle Santo Tomé.
Tel 925 25 60 98. ○ daily. 🎟️ (free Wed pm for EU residents).
www.santotome.org
Visitors come to Santo Tom mainly to admire El Greco's masterpiece, *The Burial of the Count of Orgaz (see p3.* The Count paid for much o the 14th-century building th stands today. The painting, commissioned in his memo by a parish priest, depicts t miraculous appearance of S Augustine and St Stephen at burial, to raise his body to heaven. It has never been moved from the setting for which it was painted, nor restored. Nevertheless, it is remarkable for its contrast glowing and sombre colou In the foreground, alleged are the artist and his son (I looking out) as well as Cer tes. The church is thought date back to the 11th cent and its tower is a fine exam of Mudéjar architecture.

Nearby is the **Pastelería Santo Tomé**, a good place buy locally made marzipa

⛩ Sinagoga de Santa María la Blanca

Calle de los Reyes Católicos 4. *Tel 925 22 72 57.* ◯ *daily.* ● *24 (pm), 25, 31 (pm) Doc & 1 Jan* 🎫 ♿

The oldest and largest of the city's original synagogues, this monument dates back to the 12–13th century. In 1405 it was taken over as a church by San Vincente Ferrer after the expulsion of the Jews. Restoration has returned it to its original beauty – carved stone capitals and wall panels stand out against white horse-shoe arches and plaster-work. In the main chapel is a Plater-esque altarpiece. In 1391 a massacre of Jews took place on this site, a turning point after years of religious tolerance in the city.

Mudéjar arches in the Sinagoga de Santa María la Blanca

⛩ Sinagoga del Tránsito, Museo Sefardi

Calle Samuel Leví. *Tel 925 22 36 65.* ◯ *Tue–Sun (Sun am only).* ● *public s.* 🎫 *(free Sat pm & Sun am).*

The most elaborate Mudéjar interior in the city is hidden behind the deceptively humble facade of this former synagogue, built in the 14th century by Samuel Ha-Leví, the Jewish treasurer to Pedro the Cruel. The interlaced frieze of the lofty prayer hall harmoniously combines Islamic, Gothic and Hebrew geometric motifs below a wonderful coffered ceiling. Alongside the synagogue is a museum of Sephardi (Spanish Jewish) culture. The manuscripts, costumes and sacred objects of worship date from both before and after the Jews' expulsion from Spain in the 15th century *(see p57).*

Ornate ceiling in the Monasterio de San Juan de los Reyes

🏰 Monasterio de San Juan de los Reyes

Calle San Juan de los Reyes Católicos 2. *Tel 925 22 38 02.* ◯ *daily.* 🎫 ♿ *(free Wed pm, for EU members).*

A wonderful mixture of architectural styles, this monastery was commissioned by the Catholic Monarchs in honour of their victory over the Portuguese at the battle of Toro in 1476 *(see p357).* Originally, it was intended to be their burial place, but they were actually laid to rest in Granada *(see p486).* Largely the work of Juan Guas, the church's main Isabelline structure was completed in 1496. Although it was badly damaged by Napoleon's troops in 1808 *(see p63),* it has been restored to its original splendour with features such as a Gothic cloister (1510) which has a multicoloured Mudéjar ceiling. Near to the church is a stretch of the Jewish quarter's original wall.

🏛 Museo del Greco

Calle Samuel Leví. *Tel 925 22 40 46.* ◯ *Tue–Sun.* 🎫 *(free Sat pm, Sun).* ● *in 2009.*

It is not clear whether El Greco actually lived in or simply near to this house in the heart of the Jewish quarter, now a museum housing a collection of his works. Canvases on display include *View of Toledo*, a detailed depiction of the city at the time, and the superb series *Christ and the Apostles.* Underneath the museum, on the ground floor, is a domestic chapel with a fine Mudéjar ceiling and a collection of art by painters of the Toledan School, such as Luis Tristán, a student of El Greco.

🏰 Iglesia de Santiago del Arrabal

Calle Arrabal

This is one of Toledo's most beautiful Mudéjar monuments. It can be easily identified by its tower, which dates from the 12th-century Reconquest *(see pp54–5).* The church, which was built slightly later, has a beautiful woodwork ceiling. The ornate Mudéjar pulpit and Plateresque altarpiece stand out against the otherwise plain Mudéjar interior.

⛩ Puerta Vieja de Bisagra

When Alfonso VI conquered Toledo in 1085, he entered it through this gateway, alongside El Cid. It is the only gateway in the city to have kept its original 10th-century military architecture. The huge towers are topped by a 12th-century Arab gatehouse.

EL GRECO

Born in Crete in 1541, El Greco ("the Greek") came to Toledo in 1577 to paint the altarpiece in the convent of Santo Domingo el Antiguo. Enchanted by the city, he stayed here, painting religious portraits and altarpieces for other churches. Although El Greco was trained in Italy and influenced by masters such as Tintoretto, his works are closely identified with the city where he settled. He died in Toledo in 1614.

Domenikos Theotocopoulos, better known as El Greco

Toledo Cathedral

The splendour of Toledo's massive cathedral reflects its history as the spiritual heart of the Church in Spain and the seat of the Primate of all Spain. The Mozarabic Mass, which dates back to Visigothic times, is still said here today. The present cathedral was built on the site of a 7th-century church. Work began in 1226 and spanned three centuries, until the completion of the last vaults in 1493. This long period of construction explains the cathedral's mixture of styles: pure French Gothic – complete with flying buttresses – on the exterior; with Spanish decorative styles, such as Mudéjar and Plateresque work, used in the interior.

★ **Sacristy**
El Greco's The Denuding of Christ, *above the marble altar, was painted especially for the cathedral. Also here are works by Titian, Van Dyck and Goya.*

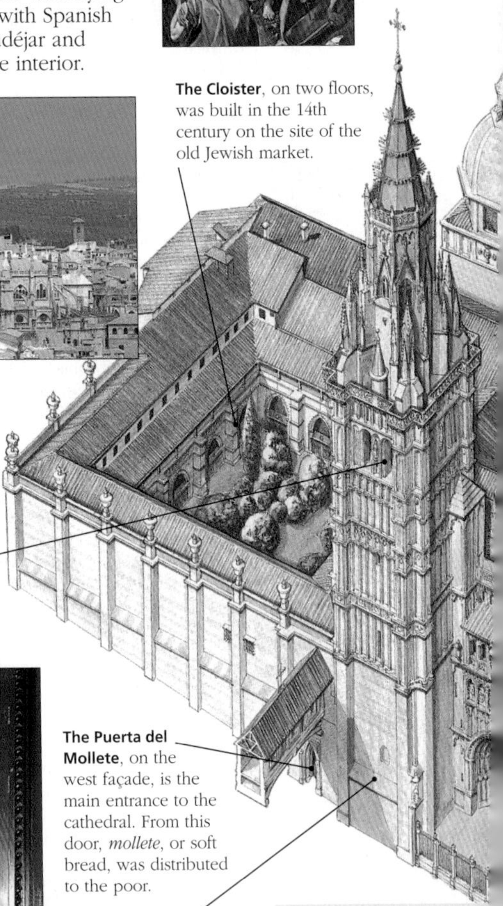

The Cloister, on two floors, was built in the 14th century on the site of the old Jewish market.

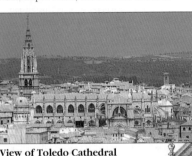

View of Toledo Cathedral
Dominating the city skyline is the Gothic tower at the west end of the nave. The best view of the cathedral, and the city, is from the parador (see p588).

The belfry in the tower contains a heavy bell known as *La Gorda* ("the Fat One").

The Puerta del Mollete, on the west façade, is the main entrance to the cathedral. From this door, *mollete*, or soft bread, was distributed to the poor.

Monstrance
In the Treasury is the 16th-century Gothic silver and gold monstrance. It is carried through the streets of Toledo during the Corpus Christi celebrations (see p387).

STAR FEATURES

★ Sacristy

★ Choir

★ High Altar Reredos

★ Transparente

★ **Transparente**
This Baroque altarpiece of marble, jasper and bronze, by Narciso Tomé, is illuminated by an ornate skylight. It stands out from the mainly Gothic interior.

VISITORS' CHECKLIST

Plaza del Ayuntamiento. **Tel** 925 22 22 41. ☐ 10:30am–6:30pm Mon–Sat, 2–6:30pm Sun. ✝ 8am, 9am, 10am, 10:30am, 5:30pm, 6:30pm Mon–Sat; 8am, 9am, 10am, 10:30am, noon, 1pm, 5:30pm, 6:30pm Sun (Catholic); 8:45am Mon–Sat, 9:45am Sun (Monzarabic). **Choir, Treasury, Sacristy and Chapterhouse** ☐ see cathedral. 📷 📹 ♿ 📠 arranged by tourist office.

Capilla de Santiago

The Capilla de San Ildefonso contains the superb Plateresque tomb of Cardinal Alonso Carrillo de Albornoz.

Chapterhouse
Above 16th-century frescoes by Juan de Borgoña is this multicoloured Mudéjar ceiling, unique in the city.

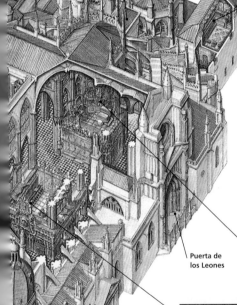

Puerta de los Leones

Puerta Llana

The Puerta del Perdón, or Door of Mercy, has a tympanum decorated with religious characters.

The Capilla Mozárabe has a beautiful Renaissance ironwork grille, carved by Juan Francés in 1524.

★ **High Altar Reredos**
The polychrome reredos, one of the most beautiful in Spain, depicts scenes from Christ's life.

★ **Choir**
The carvings on the wooden lower stalls depict scenes of the fall of Granada. The alabaster upper ones show figures from the Old Testament.

Windmills on the ridge above Consuegra, overlooking the plains of La Mancha

Tembleque ⓯

Toledo. 🏠 2,200. 🛈 Plaza Mayor 1, 925 14 55 53. 🚍 Wed. 🎭 Jesús de Nazareno (23–27 Aug).

The well-preserved stone Plaza Mayor (see p27) at Tembleque dates from the 17th century. It is decorated with the red cross of the Knights Hospitallers, the military order which once ruled the town.

Environs
Ocaña, 30 km (20 miles) north of Tembleque, centres on the huge yet elegant, late 18th-century *plaza mayor*, the third largest town square in Spain, after Madrid and Salamanca.

Consuegra ⓰

Toledo. 🏠 10,500. 🚍 🛈 Calle Molino de Viento Bolero s/n, Cerro Calderico, 925 47 57 31. 🚍 Sat. 🎭 Consuegra Medieval (mid Aug), La Rosa de Azafrán (last weekend Oct).

Consuegra's 11 windmills (see p27) and restored castle stand on a ridge, overlooking the plains of La Mancha. One windmill which has working machinery is set in motion every year during the town's festival to celebrate the autumn harvest of saffron (see p338). During the fiesta, pick-ers compete to see who can strip petals from the saffron crocus the fastest.

Environs
About 4 km (2 miles) on the road to **Urda** is a Roman dam. An old restaurant (see p638) at **Puerto Lápice**, off the A4 20 km (13 miles) south of Consuegra, claims to be the inn in which Don Quixote was "knighted" by the landlord.

Campo de Criptana ⓱

Ciudad Real. 🏠 14,700. 🚍 🛈 Calle Barbero 1, 926 56 22 31. 🚍 Tue. 🎭 Virgen de Criptana (Easter Mon), Cristos de Villejos (first Thu in Aug), Ferias (23–28 Aug).

The remaining ten windmills of what was once La Mancha's largest group – 32 – stand on a hillcrest in the town. Three are 16th-century and have their original machinery intact. One is the tourist information office, and three others are museums.

Environs
More windmills stand above **Alcázar de San Juan** and **Mota del Cuervo**, a good place to buy *queso Manchego*, local sheep's cheese (see p339).

El Toboso ⓲

Toledo. 🏠 2,200. 🛈 C/ Daoíz y Velarde 3, 925 56 82 26. 🚍 Wed. 🎭 Carnival (17–20 Jan), Cervantes Days (23 Apr), San Agustín (27–30 Aug).

Of all the villages of La Mancha claiming links to Don Quixote, El Toboso has the clearest ties. It was chosen by Cervantes as the birthplace Dulcinea, Don Quixote's sweetheart. The **Casa de Dulcinea**, the home of Doña Ana Martínez Zarco, on whom Dulcinea was allegedly based, has been refurbished in its original 16th-century style.

Considered of such cultural importance, the French army allegedly refused to attack the village during the War of Independence (see pp62–3).

🏛 **Casa de Dulcinea**
Tel 925 19 72 88. 🕐 Tue–Sun. 🎟 (free pm Sat & am Sun). 🔲

Belmonte ⓳

Cuenca. 🏠 2,500. 🚍 🛈 Castillo de Belmonte, 690 203 076. 🚍 M 🎭 San Bartolomé (24 Aug); Virgen de Gracia (second weekend of Se

Belmonte's magnificent 15th-century **castle** (see p344) is of the best preserved in the region. It was built by Juan Pacheco, Marquis of Villena after Enrique IV gave him town in 1456. Inside it has orative carved coffered ceilings, and Mudéjar plaster work. The **collegiate churc** especially remarkable for

Belmonte's splendid 15th-century castle

richly decorated chapels and Gothic choir stalls, which were brought here from Cuenca cathedral (see p385). There is also outstanding ironwork, a Renaissance reredos and the font at which the Golden Age poet Fray Luis de León (1527–91), was baptized.

Environs

Two villages near Belmonte also flourished under the Marquis of Villena. The church at **Villaescusa de Haro**, 6 km (4 miles) to the northeast, has an outstanding 16th-century reredos. **San Clemente**, some 40 km (25 miles) further southeast, clusters around two near-perfect Renaissance squares. There is a Gothic alabaster cross in the Iglesia de Santiago Apóstol.

Castillo de Belmonte
Tel 690 203 076. ☐ Tue–Sun. 🎫

castle of Alarcón, which has been converted into a parador

Alarcón ⑳

[Cuen]ca. 🏠 200. 🚍 Calle Posadas 1, [9]33 03 01. 🎉 Cristo de la Fé (14 [May],) San Sebastian (20 Jan), Fiesta [del E]migrante (2nd weekend in Aug).

[Perf]ectly preserved, the [forti]fied village of Alarcón [guar]ds a narrow loop of the [Río] Júcar from on top of a [hill]. As you drive through its [defe]nces, you may have the [impr]ession of entering a film-[set f]or a medieval epic. [The] village dates back to the [8th] century. It became a key [milit]ary base for the Recon-[ques]t (see pp54–5) and was [reca]ptured from the Moors by [Alfon]so VIII in 1184 following [a nin]e-month siege. It was

The chalk cliffs of Alcalá del Júcar, honeycombed with tunnels

later acquired by the Marquis of Villena. Alarcón has dramatic walls and three defensive precincts. The small, triangular **castle**, high above the river, has been turned into a parador (see p586), preserving much of its medieval atmosphere.

The **Iglesia de Santa María** is a lovely Renaissance church, with a fine portico and an altarpiece attributed to the Berruguete school. The nearby **Iglesia de Santísima Trinidad** is in Gothic-Plateresque style (see p25).

Alcalá del Júcar ㉑

Albacete. 🏠 1,500. 🚍 Avenida de los Robles 1, 967 47 30 90. 🚍 Sun 🎉 San Lorenzo (7–15 Aug).

Where the Río Júcar runs through the chalk hills to the northeast of Albacete, it cuts a deep, winding gorge, the

Hoz de Júcar, along which you can drive for a stretch of 40 km (25 miles). Alcalá del Júcar is dramatically sited on the side of a spur of rock jutting out into the gorge. The town is a warren of steep alleys and flights of steps. At the top of the town, below the castle, houses have been extended by digging caves into the soft rock. Some of these have been transformed into tunnels cut from one side of the spur to the other.

Environs: To the west, the gorge runs past fertile orchards to the Baroque **Ermita de San Lorenzo**. Further on is the picturesque village of **Jorquera**, which was an independent state for a brief period during the Middle Ages, refusing to be ruled by the crown. It retains its Arab walls. A collection of shields is on display in the Casa del Corregidor.

DON QUIXOTE'S LA MANCHA

Cervantes (see p333) doesn't specify where his hero was born but several places are mentioned in the novel. Don Quixote is knighted in an inn in Puerto Lápice, believing it to be a castle. His sweetheart, Dulcinea, lives in El Toboso. The windmills he tilts at, imagining them to be giants, are thought to be those at Campo de Criptana. Another adventure takes place in the Cueva de Montesinos (see p397).

Illustration from a 19th-century edition of Don Quixote

Albacete ㉒

Albacete. 🏙 160,000. 🚉 ✈ ℹ
Calle del Tinte 2, 967 58 05 22. 🚌
Tue. 🎉 Virgen de los Llanos (8 Sep).

Despite being labelled one of Spain's least interesting cities, this provincial capital is not without its attractions. The main one is the excellent **Museo Provincial**, which has exhibits ranging from Iberian sculptures and unique Roman amber and ivory dolls to 20th-century paintings. The city's **cathedral**, begun in 1515, has Renaissance altarpieces.

Albacete is also known for its daggers and jackknives, crafted here since Muslim times, and the agricultural fair, held each September.

> 🏛 **Museo Provincial**
> Parque Abelardo Sánchez.
> **Tel** 967 22 83 07. ◯ Tue–Sun.
> 🎟 free Sat & Sun. ♿

The castle of Chinchilla de Monte Aragón, overlooking the town

Environs
Chinchilla de Monte Aragón, 12 km (7 miles) to the southeast, has a well-preserved old quarter around a main square. Above the town is the picturesque shell of its 15th-century castle.

Almansa, 70 km (43 miles) further east, is dominated by another imposing castle, which is of Moorish origin.

Alcaraz ㉔

Albacete. 🏙 2,000. ℹ Plaza Mayor 967 38 08 27. 🚌 Wed. 🎉 Canto a Los Mayos (30 Apr–1 May), Feria (4–9 Sep), La Romería de la Virgen (2 Aug, 8 Sep). www.turalcaraz.com

An important Arab and Christian stronghold, Alcaraz's military power waned after the Reconquest but its economy flourished around its (now defunct) carpet-making industry.

Standing in the attractive Renaissance Plaza Mayor are the "twin towers" of **Tardón**

Sierra de Alcaraz ㉓

Where the Sierras of Segura and Alcaraz push northwards into the southeastern plains of La Mancha, they form spectacular mountains, broken up by dramatic gorges and fertile valleys. The source of the Río Mundo is a favourite beauty spot. Nearby Riópar, perched on the side of the mountain, has a 15th-century parish church. Among the less-explored villages, Letur, Ayna, Yeste and Liétor are especially picturesque. Their narrow, winding streets and craft traditions clearly reflect their Muslim origins.

Source of the Río Mundo ⑤
The river begins as a waterfall, inside the Cueva de Los Chorros, and tumbles down a dramatic cliff face into a bubbling spring at the bottom.

0 kilometres 5

0 miles 5

KEY
▬▬ Tour route
═══ Other roads
🎦 Viewpoint

Yeste ④
The village of Yeste, which stands at the foot of the Sierra de Ardal, is crowned by a hilltop Arab castle. It was reconquered under Fernando III, and was later ruled by the Order of Santiago.

and **Trinidad**, and an 18th-century commodity exchange, the **Lonja del Corregidor**, with Plateresque decoration. The square is surrounded by lively, narrow streets. On the outskirts of the town are the castle ruins and surviving arch of a Gothic aqueduct. Alcaraz makes a good base for touring the sierras of Alcaraz and Segura.

The twin towers of Tardón and Trinidad on Alcaraz's main square

Lagunas de Ruidera ㉕

Ciudad Real. 🚉 Ruidera.
🛈 Ruidera (Sep–Jun: Wed–Sun, Jul–Aug: daily), 926 52 81 16.
www.lagunasruidera.info

Once nicknamed "The Mirrors of La Mancha", the 15 inter-connected lakes which make up the Parque Natural de las Lagunas de Ruidera stretch for 39 km (24 miles) through a valley. They allegedly take their name from a story in *Don Quixote (see p395)* in which a certain Mistress Ruidera, her daughters and her nieces are said to have been turned into lakes by a magician.

Although La Mancha's falling water table has led to a decline in the amount of water in the lakes, they are still worth visiting for their wealth of wildlife, which includes great and little bustards, herons and many types of duck. The wildlife has recently come under threat due

One of the lakes in the Parque Natural de las Lagunas de Ruidera

to the increasing number of tourists, and the development of holiday chalets on the lakes' shores. Near one of the lakes, the Laguna de San Pedro, is the **Cueva de Montesinos**, a deep, explorable cave which was also used as the setting for an episode in *Don Quixote*.

To the northwest, the lakes link up with the Embalse de Peñarroya reservoir.

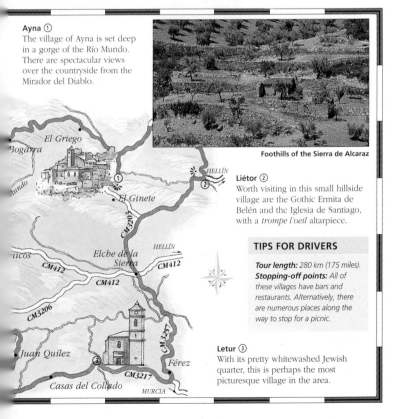

Ayna ①
The village of Ayna is set deep in a gorge of the Río Mundo. There are spectacular views over the countryside from the Mirador del Diablo.

Foothills of the Sierra de Alcaraz

Liétor ②
Worth visiting in this small hillside village are the Gothic Ermita de Belén and the Iglesia de Santiago, with a *trompe l'oeil* altarpiece.

TIPS FOR DRIVERS

Tour length: 280 km (175 miles).
Stopping-off points: All of these villages have bars and restaurants. Alternatively, there are numerous places along the way to stop for a picnic.

Letur ③
With its pretty whitewashed Jewish quarter, this is perhaps the most picturesque village in the area.

Villanueva de los Infantes 26

Ciudad Real. 🚶 6,000. 🚌 🛈 *Plaza Mayor 3, 926 36 13 21.* 🚆 *Fri.* 🎉 *Cruz de Mayo (2–3 May), Ferias (late Aug), Virgen de Antigua (8 Sep), Santo Tomás (18 Sep).* **www**.infantes.org

Villanueva's old town, which centres on the graceful Neo-Classical Plaza Mayor, is one of the most attractive in La Mancha. Many buildings on the square have wooden balconies and arcades. Also on the square is the **Iglesia de San Andrés**, which has a Renaissance façade. Inside are a Baroque altarpiece and organ, as well as the now empty tomb of the Golden Age author Francisco de Quevedo. He lived and died in the **Convento de los Domínicos**.

Environs
The village of **San Carlos del Valle**, 25 km (15 miles) to the northwest, has an 18th-century square and galleried houses of rust-red stone.

Valdepeñas 27

Ciudad Real. 🚶 30,000. 🚌 🚆 🛈 *Pl de España, 926 31 25 52.* 🚆 *Thu.* 🎉 *Grape Harvest (1–8 Sep).*

Valdepeñas is the capital of La Mancha's vast wine region, the world's largest expanse of vineyards, producing vast quantities of red wine *(see pp202–3)*. This largely modern town comes alive for its September wine festival. In the network of

older streets around the café-lined Plaza de España are the **Iglesia de la Asunción** and the municipal museum.

Valdepeñas has over 30 bodegas which can be visited. One of them, **Bodega Museo**, has some of the few remaining traditional cellars, with huge earthenware jars, *tinajas*.

🍷 Bodega Museo
Calle Torrecillas 116. *Tel 926 31 28 49.* ⬜ *daily.* 🎫 ♿

Courtyard of the Palacio del Viso in Viso del Marqués

Viso del Marqués 28

Ciudad Real. 🚶 3,000. 🚌 🛈 *Calle Real 39, 926 33 68 15 (am only).* 🚆 *Tue.* 🎉 *San Andrés (second Sun of May), Feria (24–8 Jul).*

The small village of Viso del Marqués in La Mancha is the unlikely setting of the **Palacio del Viso**, a grand Renaissance building. This mansion was

commissioned in 1564 by the Marquis of Santa Cruz, the admiral of the fleet which defeated the Turks at Lepanto in 1571 *(see p59)*. One of the main features of the house is a Classical patio. Inside, the principal rooms have been decorated with Italian frescoes.

Environs
About 25 km (16 miles) to the northeast of Viso del Marqués is Spain's oldest bullring at **Las Virtudes**. Square and galleried, it was built in 1641 next to a 14th-century church which has a Churrigueresque altarpiece.

🏛 Palacio del Viso
Plaza del Pradillo 12. *Tel 926 33 60 08.* ⬜ *Tue–Sun.*

Calatrava la Nueva 29

Ciudad Real. Aldea de Rey. *Tel 926 69 31 19.* ⬜ *Tue–Sun, times vary, call ahead.*

Magnificent in its isolated hilltop setting, the ruined castle-monastery of Calatrava la Nueva is reached by a stretch of original medieval road.

It was founded in 1217 by the Knights of Calatrava, Spain's first military-religious order *(see p54)*, to be their headquarters. The complex of huge proportions, with a double patio and a church with a triple nave. The church has been restored and is illuminated by a beautiful rose window above the entrance.

Expanse of vineyards near Valdepeñas

For hotels and restaurants in this region see pp586–8 and pp636–8

Calatrava la Nueva castle-monastery, dominating the plains of La Mancha

After the Reconquest, the building continued to be used as a monastery until it was abandoned in 1802 following fire damage.

Opposite the castle are the ruins of a Muslim frontier fortress, **Salvatierra**, which was captured from the Moors by the Order of Calatrava in the 12th century.

Almagro ③⓪

Ciudad Real. 🏠 9,000. 🚊 🚌 🅘 Plaza Mayor 1, 926 86 07 17. 🛏 Wed. 🎉 Virgen de las Nieves (5 Aug), San Bartolomé (23–24 Aug). www.ciudad-almagro.com

Almagro was disputed during the Reconquest, until the Order of Calatrava captured it and built the castle of Calatrava la Nueva to the southwest of the town. The rich architectural heritage of the atmospheric old town is partly the legacy of the Fugger brothers, the Habsburgs' bankers who settled in nearby Almadén during the 16th century.

The town's main attraction is its colonnaded stone plaza, with characteristic enclosed, green balconies. On one side is a 17th-century courtyard-theatre – the **Corral de Comedias** – where a drama festival is held for the Festival de Teatro Clásico every summer. Other monuments worth visiting include the Fuggers' Renaissance warehouse and former university, and also a parador (see p586).

Environs
To the northwest is **Ciudad Real**, founded by Alfonso X the Learned in 1255. Its sights include the Iglesia de San Pedro and the Mudéjar gateway, the Puerta de Toledo.

Raised walkway in the Parque Nacional de Las Tablas de Daimiel

Tablas de Daimiel ③①

Ciudad Real. 🚌 Daimiel. 🅘 Daimiel, Santa Teresa, s/n 1, 926 26 06 39. www.lastablasdedaimiel.com

The marshy wetlands of the Tablas de Daimiel, northeast of Ciudad Real, are the feeding and nesting grounds of a huge range of aquatic and migratory birds. Despite being national parkland since 1973, they have become an ecological *cause célèbre* due to the growing threat from the area's lowering water table. This has affected the area's wildlife in recent years.

One corner of the park is open to the public, with walking routes to islets and observation towers. Breeding birds here include great crested grebes and mallards. Otters and red foxes are among the mammals found in the park.

Valle de Alcudia ③②

Ciudad Real. 🚌 Fuencaliente. 🅘 Almadén, 926 71 04 38.

Alcudia's lush lowlands, which border the Sierra Morena foothills to the south, are among central Spain's most unspoiled countryside. The area is used largely as pasture land. In late autumn it is filled with sheep, whose milk makes the farmhouse cheese for which the valley is known.

The mountain village of **Fuencaliente** has thermal baths that open in the summer. Further north, **Almadén** is the site of a large mercury mine with a museum. **Chillón**, to the northwest, has a late Gothic church.

Small isolated farmhouse in the fertile Valle de Alcudia

EXTREMADURA

CÁCERES · BADAJOZ

O f all the Spanish regions, far-flung Extremadura – "the land beyond the River Douro" – is the most remote from the modern world. Green sierras run southwards through rolling hills strewn with boulders. Forests and reservoirs shelter rare wildlife. The towns, with their atmospheric old quarters, have a romantic, slow-paced charm. In winter, storks nest on their spires and belltowers.

The finest monuments in Extremadura are the ruins of ancient settlements scattered across the region. Many are exceptionally well preserved. Some of Spain's finest Roman architecture is to be seen in Mérida, capital of the Roman province of Lusitania, which has an aqueduct and a magnificent theatre. Other Classical remains dot the countryside – notably a Tartessan temple at Cancho Roano and a Roman bridge at Alcántara. Smaller finds are displayed in Badajoz museum.

Modern development has bypassed the old town of Cáceres, whose ancient walls, winding streets and nobles' mansions are still marvellously intact. Trujillo, Zafra and Jerez de los Caballeros have medieval and Renaissance quarters; and there are small, splendidly decorated cathedrals in Plasencia, Coria and Badajoz.

The castles and stout walls of Alburquerque and Olivenza mark frontiers embattled through history. Many cathedrals and monasteries were built in the troubled times during and after the Reconquest by the large military-religious orders which then governed the region for the crown.

Extremadura was the birthplace of many conquistadors and emigrants to the New World; the riches they found there financed a surge of building. Guadalupe monastery, in the eastern hills, is the most splendid monument to the region's New World ties.

View over the rooftops of the historic town of Cáceres

An old stone cross in the woods near Yuste, a Hieronymite monastery founded in 1404

Exploring Extremadura

Extremadura is ideal for nature lovers and those who
want to get off the beaten track to discover the old
Spain. It offers beautiful driving and walking country
in its northern sierras and valleys, and exceptional
wildlife in Monfragüe Natural Park. Some of
the best Roman ruins in Spain can be found
throughout Extremadura, especially in the
regional capital, Mérida. The walled old
town of Cáceres, with its well-preserved
Jewish quarter, and the monasteries of
Guadalupe and Yuste, are other historic
sights not to be missed. To the south, the
Templar towns in the Sierra Morena,
such as Jerez de los Caballeros, have
fine old buildings, while the small,
historic towns of Coria, Zafra and
Llerena all make charming bases
for excursions.

SIGHTS AT A GLANCE

Alcántara ⑫
Arroyo de la Luz ⑪
Badajoz ⑮
Cáceres pp408–9 ⑩
Cancho Roano ⑰
Coria ④
Guadalupe ⑧
Hervás ③
Las Hurdes ①
Jerez de los Caballeros ⑲
Llerena ⑳
Mérida ⑭
Monasterio de Yuste ⑥
Olivenza ⑯
Parque Natural de
  Monfragüe ⑦
Plasencia ⑤
Sierra de Gata ②
Tentudía ㉑
Trujillo ⑨
Valencia de Alcántara ⑬
Zafra ⑱

Orchards near Hervás in the Valle del Ambroz

EE ALSO

Where to Stay pp588–90

Where to Eat pp638–40

Ávila

de Montemayor

·S

ONASTERIO DE YUSTE

Cuacos de Yuste

araiz de la Vera

Talayuela

Navalmoral de *Madrid*
la Mata

la

NV-AS

E NATURAL
NFRAGÜE

Embalse de
Valdecañas

Tajo

cejo

Almonte

Castañar de Ibor

Sierra de
Villuercas

LO

GUADALUPE

adroñera

8

Alía

Sierra de
Guadalupe

N502

Zorita

Logrosán

Embalse de
García de Sola

Castilblanco

Embalse
de Cijara

Herrera del Duque

Navalvillar de Pela

N430

Embalse
de Orellana

Ciudad
Real

iana

ieva de la Serena

Puebla de Alcocer

o

ario

Embalse de
Zújar

Embalse de
La Serena

Cabeza del
Buey

Castuera

17

Zalamea
de la Serena

Helechal

Zújar

aleda del
Zaucejo

N432

Córdoba

0 kilometres   25

0 miles   15

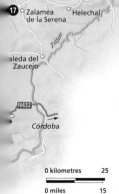
Cattle grazing in the fields near Cáceres

KEY

▬▬	Motorway
▬▬	Major road
══	Secondary road
▬▬	Scenic route
▭▬▭	Main railway
—	Minor railway
▬▬▬	International border
▬▬▬	Regional border
△	Summit

GETTING AROUND

Extremadura is not very well
connected by air or rail services.
Badajoz has the only (domestic)
airport in the region, while the
region's main rail link is the line from
Madrid to Cáceres, Mérida and
Badajoz. Coach services are infrequent,
and in many areas, such as the northern
sierras, they are non-existent. It is generally
much more convenient to travel by car.
Be aware that as Spain has recently changed its
road numbering system some of the roads
featured here may differ from new road signs.

Roman bridge crossing the Río Guadiana at Mérida

Beehives, a common sight in Las Hurdes

Las Hurdes **❶**

Cáceres. 🚍 Pinofranqueado, Caminomorisco, Nuñomoral. 🛈 Pinofranqueado, 927 67 41 81.

Las Hurdes' slate mountains, goats and beehives were memorably caught in the 1932 Luis Buñuel film, *Tierra sin Pan (Land without Bread)*. The area's legendary poverty disappeared with the arrival of roads in the 1950s, but the black slopes, riverbeds and hill terraces remain.

From Pinofranqueado or Vegas de Coria, roads climb past picturesque "black" villages like Batuequilla, Fragosa, and El Gasco, which sits under an extinct volcano. The more developed **Lower Hurdes** area, crossed by the Río Hurdano and the main access route (C512), is dotted with camp sites and restaurants serving traditional cuisine.

Sierra de Gata **❷**

Cáceres. 🚍 Cáceres. 🛈 Hoyos, 927 51 45 85. **www**.sierradegata.es

There are 40 hamlets in the Sierra de Gata, scattered between olive groves, orchards and fields. The area has retained its old-fashioned rural charm by conserving hunters' paths for woodland walking, and its local crafts, most notably lace-making. In the lowland towns of **Valverde de Fresno** and **Acebo**, the local dialect, *chapurriau*, is still spoken. On the higher slopes, **Eljas**, **Gata** and **Villamiel** have remains of medieval fortresses. The old granite houses have carved family crests on the front and distinctive outside staircases.

Coat of arms on a house front in Acebo

Hervás **❸**

Cáceres. 🏠 4,000. 🛈 C/ Braulio Navas 6, 927 47 36 18. 🗓 Sat. 🎉 Las Ferias Cristo de la Salud (15–16 Sep). **www**.valleambroz.org

Sitting at the top of the wide Valle del Ambroz, Hervás is known for its medieval Jewish quarter, with its whitewashed houses. The tiny streets, dotted with taverns and craft workshops, slope down towards the Río Ambroz. Just off the main plaza is the **Museo Pérez Comendador-Leroux**, named after the town's noted 20th-century sculptor and his wife, whose work is exhibited here.

The next town up towards the Béjar pass is **Baños de Montemayor**, whose name comes from its sulphurous baths, which date back to Roman times. They were revived in the early 1900s and are open to the public. At **Cáparra**, southwest of Hervás, four triumphal arches stand on the Roman road, the Vía de la Plata *(see p352)*.

🏛 **Museo Pérez Comendador-Leroux**
C/ Asensio Neila 5. **Tel** 927 48 16
🕐 pm Tue–Fri, am Sat, Sun. 🎟

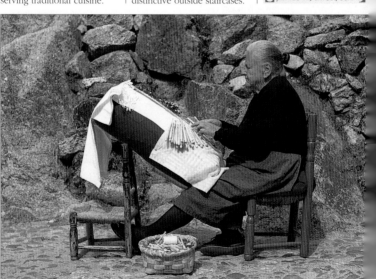

Traditional lace-making in one of the villages of the Sierra de Gata

For hotels and restaurants in this region see pp588–90 and pp638–40

Ancient wall and olive groves in the Valle del Ambroz

...oria ❹

...ceres. 🏠 14,000. 🚉 🛈 Avenida ...Extremadura 39, 927 50 13 51. ...Thu. 🎉 Día de la Virgen (2nd ...n in May), San Juan (23–29 Jun).

...ria's walled old town, ...rched above the Río ...gón, boasts a Gothic-...naissance **cathedral** with ...n Plateresque carving, and ...16th-century **Convento de ...Madre de Dios**, which has a ...e Renaissance cloister. ...orming part of the town ...ls, which are a Muslim ...d medieval patchwork, are ...impressive castle tower, ...d four gates, two of which ...e back to Roman times. ...e gates are closed during ...fiesta of San Juan in June ...night-time bullrunning. ...ated below the old town ...e **Puente Seco**, or Puente ...o, a Roman bridge.

...sencia ❺

...res. 🏠 40,500. 🚉 🚌 ...anta Clara 2, 927 42 38 43. ...ue. 🎉 Ferias (6–8 Jun).

...encia's golden-grey walls, ...g above a curve in the ...s of the Río Jerte, tell of ...own's past as a military ...on. Nowadays Plasencia ...st known for its Tuesday ...et, dating back to the ...century, which is held in ...nain square. ...short walk away are the ...'s two cathedrals, which ...uilt back-to-back. The ...16th-century **Catedral**

Nueva has a Baroque organ and carved wooden choir stalls. The Romanesque **Catedral Vieja**, next to it, has a museum with works by Ribera, and a late 14th-century Bible.

The nearby **Museo Etnográfico y Textil**, housed in a 14th-century hospital, has displays of crafts and costumes.

The rest of the Jerte valley has pockets of outstanding beauty, such as the **Garganta de los Infiernos**, a nature reserve with dramatic, rushing waterfalls.

🏛 **Museo Etnográfico y Textil**
Plaza del Marqués de la Puebla. **Tel** 927 42 18 43. ◯ Wed–Sun.

Monasterio de Yuste ❻

Cuacos de Yuste (Cáceres). **Tel** 927 17 21 30. ◯ Tue–Sun. 🎥 ♿

The Hieronymite monastery of Yuste, where Charles V (see p59) retired from public life in 1556 and died two years later, is remarkable for its simplicity and its lovely setting in the wooded valley of La Vera.

The church's Gothic and Plateresque cloisters and the austere palace are open to visitors. Just below it is **Cuacos de Yuste**, the most unspoiled of La Vera's old villages, where peppers, for making paprika, hang outside the houses.

Paprika peppers hanging up around a door in Cuacos de Yuste

A Carantoña, during the fiesta of St Sebastian, Acehuche

EXTREMADURA'S FIESTAS

Carantoñas (20–21 Jan), Acehúche (Cáceres). During the fiesta of St Sebastian, the Carantoñas take to the streets of the town dressed up in animal skins, with their faces covered by grotesque masks designed to make them look terrifying. They represent the wild beasts which are said to have left the saint unharmed.

Pero Palo (Carnival Feb/Mar), Villanueva de la Vera (Cáceres). In this ancient ritual a wooden figure dressed in a suit and representing the devil is paraded around the streets and then destroyed – except for the head, which is reused the year after.

Los Empalaos (Maundy Thursday), Valverde de la Vera (Cáceres). Men do penance by walking in procession through the town with their arms outstretched and bound to small tree trunks.

La Encamisá (7–8 Dec), Torrejoncillo (Cáceres). Riders on horseback parade around town, where bonfires are set alight for the occasion.

Los Escobazos (7 Dec), Jarandilla de la Vera (Cáceres). At night, the town is illuminated by bonfires in the streets, and torches are made from burning brooms.

Parque Natural de Monfragüe ❼

Cáceres. 🚉 *Villareal de San Carlos*. 🛈 *Villareal de San Carlos, 927 19 91 34.*

To the south of Plasencia, rolling hills drop from scrubby peaks through wild olive, cork and holm oak woods to the dammed Tagus and Tiétar river valleys. In 1979, some 500 sq km (200 sq miles) of these hills were granted natural park status in order to safeguard the area's outstandingly varied wildlife species, which includes a large proportion of Spain's protected bird species *(see pp342–3)*.

The many species of bird which breed here include the black-winged kite, black vulture and, most notably, the black stork, as well as more

Birdwatchers in the Parque Natural de Monfragüe

common aquatic species on and near the water. Mammals living here include the lynx, red deer and wild boar. At **Villareal de San Carlos**, a hamlet founded in the 18th century, there is parking and an information centre which gives out maps of walks. An ideal time to visit the park is September, when many migrating birds stop off here.

Guadalupe ❽

Cáceres. 🏘 2,500. 🚉 🛈 *Plaza Mayor, 927 15 41 28.* **Monasterio** ◯ *daily.* 🔲 *guided tour only.* ◯ *Wed.* 🎉 *Cruz de Mayo (3 May), La Virgen y Día de la Comunidad (8 Sep).* **www.**monasterioguadalupe.com

This village grew around the magnificent Hieronymite **Monasterio de Guadalupe**, founded in 1340. In the main square there are shops that sell handmade ceramics and beaten copper cauldrons, both traditional monastic crafts, now made as souvenirs.

The turreted towers of the monastery, which is set in a deep wooded valley, help give it a fairy-tale air. According to legend, a shepherd found a wooden image of the Virgin Mary here in the early 14th century. The monastery grew to splendour under royal patronage, acquiring schools of grammar and medicine, three hospitals, an important pharmacy and one of the largest libraries in Spain.

The 16th-century *hospedería* where royalty once stayed was destroyed by fire; the 20th-century reconstruction is now a hotel run by the monks *(see p589)*. The old hospital has been converted into a parador. In the car park is a plaque commemorating Spain's first human dissection, which took place here in 1402.

By the time the New World was discovered, the monastery was very important and in 1496 was the site of the baptism of some of the first native Caribbeans brought to Europe by Columbus *(see pp56–7)*.

The monastery was sacked by Napoleon in 1808 but was refounded by Franciscans a century later. It is a major centre of Catholicism, visited by thousands of pilgrims.

Guided tours (in Spanish only) begin in the museum of illuminated manuscripts, embroidered vestments and fine art. They continue to the choir and the magnificent Baroque sacristy, nicknamed "the Spanish Sistine Chapel" because of Zurbarán's portraits of monks hanging on the highly decorated walls. For many, the chance to touch or kiss the tiny Virgin's dress in the *camarín* (chamber) behind the altar is the highlight of the tour. The 16th-century Gothic cloister has two tiers of horseshoe arches around an ornate central pavilion. The church, with a magnificent 16th-century iron grille partly forged from the chains of freed slaves, may be visited separately.

Environs
The surrounding **Sierra de Villauercas** and **Los Ibores** sierras, where herbs were once picked for the monastery pharmacy, have good woodland walks. The road south also gives access to the pasture lands of **La Serena**, a vital breeding ground for birds of the steppe *(see pp342–3)* and the huge reservoir of **Cíjara**, surrounded by a game reserve.

Monasterio de Guadalupe, overlooking the town

Trujillo 9

Cáceres. 🏠 10,000. 🚌 ℹ️ Plaza
Mayor, 927 32 26 77. 🚏 Thu. 🎉
Chíviri (Easter Sun), Feria del Queso
(weekend of 1 May). www.trujillo.es

When the Plaza Mayor of the
medieval hilltop town of
Trujillo is floodlit at night, it
is one of the most beautiful
squares in Spain. By day, there
is much to visit, including the
**Iglesia de Santa María la
Mayor**, on one of the town's
winding streets, which contains
various sarcophagi.

At the top of the hill there
is an Islamic fortress, which
defended the town against
the Christian advance during
the Reconquest (see pp54–5);
but in 1232 it was retaken by
the forces of Fernando III.
Trujillo was the birthplace of

**Statue of Francisco Pizarro in
Trujillo's main square**

several conquistadors, most
notably Francisco Pizarro, who
conquered Peru (see p58), of
whom there is a statue in the
main square. His brother,
Hernando Pizarro, founded

the **Palacio del Marqués de la
Conquista**, one of several
palaces and convents built
with New World wealth. It has
an elaborate corner window
with carved stone heads of
the Pizarro brothers and their
Inca wives. The beautiful 16th-
century **Palacio de Pizarro-
Orellana** was built by descendants of Francisco de Orellana,
the explorer of Ecuador and
the Amazon. It has a fine
Plateresque patio.

In late April or early May,
gourmets flock here for the
four-day cheese fair.

🏛️ **Palacio del Marqués de
la Conquista**
Plaza Mayor. 🚫 to the public.

🏛️ **Palacio de Pizarro-Orellana**
Plaza de Don Juan Tena. **Tel** 927 32
11 58. ⏰ 10am–1pm, 4–6pm Tue–
Fri; 11am–2pm, 4:30–7pm Sat, Sun.

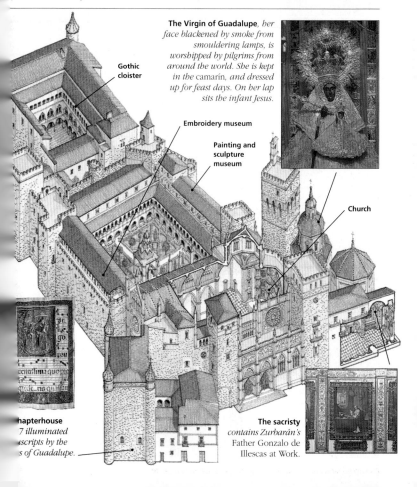

The Virgin of Guadalupe, her
face blackened by smoke from
smouldering lamps, is
worshipped by pilgrims from
around the world. She is kept
in the camarín, and dressed
up for feast days. On her lap
sits the infant Jesus.

Gothic cloister

Embroidery museum

Painting and sculpture museum

Church

Chapterhouse 7 illuminated manuscripts by the s of Guadalupe.

The sacristy contains Zurbarán's Father Gonzalo de Illescas at Work.

Street-by-Street: Cáceres ⑩

After Alfonso IX of Leon conquered Cáceres
in 1227, its growing prosperity as a free trade
town attracted merchants, and later aristocracy,
to settle here. They rivalled each other with stately
homes and palaces fortified by watchtowers,
most of which Isabel and Fernando, the reigning
monarchs *(see pp56–7)*, ordered to be demolished
in 1476 to halt the continual jostling for power.
Today's serene Renaissance town dates from
the late 15th and 16th centuries, after which
economic decline set in. Untouched by the wars
of the 19th and 20th centuries, Cáceres became
Spain's first listed heritage city in 1949.

★ **Casa de los Golfines de Abaj**
*The ornamental façade of this
16th-century mansion displays th
shield of one of the town's leadin
families, the Golfines.*

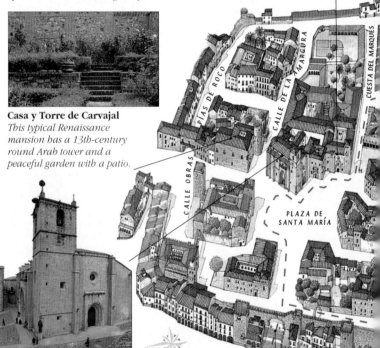

Casa y Torre de Carvajal
*This typical Renaissance
mansion has a 13th-century
round Arab tower and a
peaceful garden with a patio.*

★ **Iglesia de Santa María**
*Facing the Palacio Episcopal,
this Gothic-Renaissance
church has a beautiful
cedarwood reredos and a
15th-century crucifix – the
Cristo Negro (Black Christ).*

Arco de la Estrell
*This low-arched ga
way was built by
Manuel Churrigue
in 1726. It leads
through the city we
from the Plaza Ma
into the old town a
is flanked by a 15
century watchtowe*

0 metres	50
0 yards	50

KEY

- - - Suggested route

Barrio de San Antonio

This quaint old Jewish quarter, with narrow streets of whitewashed houses restored to their original condition, takes its name from the nearby hermitage of St Anthony.

VISITORS' CHECKLIST

Cáceres. 82,000. Avenida de Alemania, 927 23 50 61. C/ de Sevilla, 927 23 25 50 Plaza Mayor 3, 927 01 08 34. Wed. San Fernando (30 May), San Jorge (23 Apr).
Museo de Cáceres Tel 927 01 08 77. Tue–Sun.

★ Museo de Cáceres

Housed in the Casa de las Veletas, this museum has contemporary art and archaeology from the region.

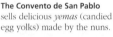

The Convento de San Pablo sells delicious *yemas* (candied egg yolks) made by the nuns.

Casa y Torre de las Cigüeñas

The slender, battlemented tower of the House of the Storks was allowed to remain after 1476 because of the owner's loyalty to Isabel. It is now owned by the army and not open to the public.

STAR SIGHTS

- ★ Casa de los Golfines de Abajo

- ★ Iglesia de Santa María

- ★ Museo de Cáceres

The Iglesia de San Mateo, built between the 14th and 17th centuries, is one of Cáceres' earliest churches.

Casa del Sol (Casa de los Solis) façade of this elegant Renaissance ...ng, once home of the Solis family, ...blazoned with a sun (sol) motif.

Arroyo de la Luz ⓫

Cáceres. 👥 6,650. 🚌 ℹ️ Travesía
Regajal 12, 927 27 16 23.
🗓️ Thu. 🎉 Día de la Patrona
(Easter Mon), Fiestas (15 Aug).

The small town of Arroyo de
la Luz is home to one of the
artistic masterpieces of
Extremadura. Its **Iglesia de la
Asunción**, completed in 1565,
contains a spectacular altarpiece which incorporates 20
paintings by the mystical religious painter Luis de Morales.

Environs
The area has a large population of white storks *(see p343)*.
Nearby **Malpartida** is home to
the largest colony, whose nests
adorn the church roof. There
are some good picnic spots in
the surrounding countryside.

**Alterpiece in the Iglesia de la
Asunción, Arroyo de la Luz**

Alcántara ⓬

Cáceres. 👥 1,720. 🚌 ℹ️ Avenida de
Mérida 21, 927 39 08 63. 🗓️ Tue. 🎉
Classic Drama Festival (first 2 weeks in
Aug); San Pedro (18–19 Oct).

Alcantara has two important
sights. One is the drystone
Roman bridge, above the
Tagus River, with its honorary
arch and a temple. The other
the restored **Convento de San
Benito**. This was built as the
headquarters of the Knights of
the Order of Alcántara during
the 16th century and was sacked by Napoleon. Its surviving
treasures are in the **Iglesia de
Santa María de Almocovar**.

**Walls of the 16th-century Convento
de San Benito, Alcántara**

Valencia de Alcántara ⓭

Cáceres. 👥 6,000. 🚌 🚌 ℹ️ Calle
de Hernán Cortés 3, 927 58 21 84.
🗓️ Mon. 🎉 San Isidro (15 May), San
Bartolomé (24 Aug).

The Gothic quarter of this hilltop frontier town is given an
elegant air by its fountains and
orange trees. The **Castillo de
Piedra Buena** was built near
the town by the Knights of the
Order of Alcántara and on the
outskirts of the town there are
more than 40 dolmens, or
megalithic burial sites.

Environs
Alburquerque, to the southeast,
is sited on a rocky outcrop
with a panoramic view from
the ramparts and keep of its
castle. Below is the old town
and the 15th-century Iglesia
de Santa María del Mercado.

Mérida ⓮

Badajoz. 👥 53,100. 🚆 🚌 ℹ️
C/Santa Eulalia 64, 924 33 07 22.
🗓️ Tue. 🎉 Easter Week, Classic
Drama Festival (Jul–Aug), Feria (10
Sep). **www**.extremadura.com

Founded by Augustus in
25 BC, Augusta Emerita grew
into the cultural and economi
capital of Rome's westernmo
province, Lusitania, but lost i
eminence under the Moors.
Though a small city, Mérida,
the capital of Extremadura, h
many fine Roman monumen
   The best approach is from
the west of town, via the mod
ern suspension bridge over th
Río Guadiana, bringing you
the original entrance of the
Roman city and Arab fortres
   The city's centrepiece is th
Roman theatre *(see pp50–1)*
One of the best-preserved
Roman theatres anywhere, i
is still used in summer for th
city's drama festival and is
part of a larger site with an
amphitheatre *(anfiteatro)*
and gardens. Nearby are the
remains of a Roman house,
the **Casa del Anfiteatro**,
where there are undergrou
galleries and large areas of
well-preserved mosaics.
   Opposite stands Rafael
Moneo's stunning red-brick
**Museo Nacional de Arte
Romano**. The semicircular
arches of its main hall are b
to the same height as the ci
Los Milagros aqueduct. Off
hall, which features sculptu
from the Roman theatre, th
are three galleries exhibitir
ceramics, mosaics, coins a
statuary. There is also an

Megalithic tomb on the outskirts of Valencia de Alcántara

Mérida's well-preserved Roman theatre, still used as a venue for classical drama

excavated Roman street. Near the museum are several other monuments, namely two villas with fine mosaics, and a racecourse.

A chapel in front of the 3rd-century **Iglesia de Santa Eulalia** is dedicated to the child saint who was martyred on this site in Roman times. Towards the centre of the town are the **Templo de Diana** (1st century AD), with tall, fluted

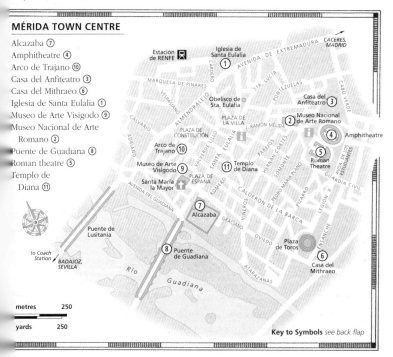

Sculpture of **Emperor Augustus**

columns, and the **Arco de Trajano**. The **Museo de Arte Visigodo** (Museum of Visigothic Art) is in the Convento de Santa Clara, which is situated off the main square. From the huge **Puente de Guadiana** there is a good view of the massive walls of the **Alcazaba**, one of Spain's oldest Moorish buildings (AD 835), whose precinct includes towers, a cistern and

Roman ruins. To the east stands the **Casa del Mithraeo**, with its Pompeiian-style frescoes and fine mosaics.

The magnificent, ruined Los Milagros aqueduct, with its granite and brick arches, is off the N630 towards Cáceres.

Museo de Arte Visigodo
C/ Sta Julia. **Tel** 924 30 01 06.
Tue–Sun. public hols.

Museo Nacional de Arte Romano
C/ José Ramón Mélida. **Tel** 924 31 16 90. Tue–Sun. (free Sat pm & Sun am). www.mnar.es

MÉRIDA TOWN CENTRE

Alcazaba ⑦
Amphitheatre ④
Arco de Trajano ⑩
Casa del Anfiteatro ③
Casa del Mithraeo ⑥
Iglesia de Santa Eulalia ①
Museo de Arte Visigodo ⑨
Museo Nacional de Arte Romano ②
Puente de Guadiana ⑧
Roman theatre ⑤
Templo de Diana ⑪

metres 250
yards 250

Key to Symbols see back flap

Badajoz **⑮**

Badajoz. 🚶 150,000. ✈ 🚌 🚃
ℹ️ *Pasaje de San Juan, 924 22 49 81.*
🗓️ *Tue & Sun.* 🎉 *Feria (24 Jun).*

Badajoz is a plain, modern city, though it retains traces of its former importance. It was a major city under the Moors but centuries of conflict robbed Badajoz of its former glories.

The Alcazaba now houses the **Museo Arqueológico**, which has over 15,000 pieces from around the province, as far back as Paleolithic times. Nearby is the cathedral, dating from the 13th–18th centuries, with a stunning tiled cloister. A museum of contemporary art is situated on Calle Museo and is open every day except Sunday evening and Monday.

🏛️ **Museo Arqueológico**
Pl José Álvarez Saez de Buruaga.
Tel *924 00 19 08.* ⏰ *Tue–Sun.* ♿

Olivenza **⑯**

Badajoz. 🚶 12,000. 🚌 ℹ️ *Plaza de España, 924 49 01 51.* 🗓️ *Sat.*
🎉 *Muñecas de San Juan (23 Jun).*

A Portuguese enclave until 1801, Olivenza has a colourful character. Within the walled town are the medieval castle, housing the **Museo Etnográfico Gonzalez Santana**, a museum of rural life, and three churches. **Santa María del Castillo** has a naive family tree of the Virgin Mary. **Santa María Magdalena**, is a fine example of the 16th-century Portuguese

Interior of Santa María Magdalena church, Olivenza

Manueline style. The 16th-century **Santa Casa de Misericordia** has blue and white tiled friezes. In one, God is shown offering Adam and Eve 18th-century coats to cover their nakedness.

Off the main square is the **Pasteleria Fuentes**, which sells *Pécula Mécula* cake.

🏛️ **Museo Etnográfico Gonzalez Santana**
Plaza de Santa María. ***Tel*** *924 49 02 22.* ⏰ *Tue–Sun am.* 🎨 ♿

Cancho Roano **⑰**

Zalamea de la Serena, Carretera Zalamea-Quintana km 3. ***Tel*** *629 23 52 79.* ⏰ *daily (except Sun pm).*

This sanctuary-palace, which is thought to have been built under the civilization of Tartessus *(see p49)*, was discovered in 1978. Excavations on this small but unique site have revealed a moated temple

that was rebuilt three times – many of the walls and slate floors are still intact. Each temple was constructed on a grander scale than the previous one and then burned in the face of invasion during the 6th century BC.

Most of the artifacts unearthed from the site are on display in the archaeological museum at Badajoz.

Environs
A Roman funereal monument stands next to the church in nearby **Zalamea de la Serena**. The town comes alive during the August fiestas, when the townsfolk act out the classic 17th-century play, *The Mayor of Zalamea*, by Calderón de la Barca *(see p34)*, which was supposedly based on a local character. Shops in the town also sell *torta de la Serena*, cheese made of sheep's milk

Remains of the Tartessan sanctuary at Cancho Ruano

Zafra **⑱**

Badajoz. 🚶 16,000. 🚌 🚃
ℹ️ *Plaza de España 8, 924 55 10*
🗓️ *Sun.* 🎉 *San Miguel (end Sep–early Oct).* **www**.turismozafra.c

At the heart of this graceful town, nicknamed "little Seville" because of its similar to the capital of Andalusia, are two arcaded squares. **Plaza Grande**, the larger of two, near the **Iglesia de la Candelaria**, was built in the 15th century. The older square is **Plaza Chica**, which used to be the marketplace. On Calle Sevilla is the 15

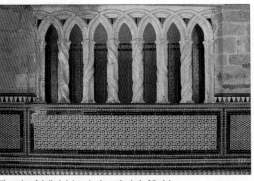
The colourful tiled cloister in the cathedral of Badajoz

Altarpiece by Zurbarán in the Iglesia de la Candelaria at Zafra

century Convento de Santa
Clara. Nearby is the **Alcázar
de los Duques de Feria**, now a
parador *(see p590)* with a
patio of Herriano style.

Environs
Some 25 km (16 miles) to the
south, in **Fuente de Cantos**, is
the house in which the painter
Francisco de Zurbarán was
born in 1598.

Jerez de los Caballeros ⑲

Badajoz. 🏘 9,600. 🚌 🚹 *Plaza
Constitucion 4, 924 73 03 72.* 🕑 *Wed.*
🎉 *Easter week, Feria del Jamón (early
Sep).* www.jerezdeloscaballeros.es

The hillside profile of Jerez,
which is broken by three
Baroque church towers, is one of
the most picturesque in
Extremadura. This small town
was also historically important –
Vasco Núñez de Balboa, who
discovered the Pacific, was
born here. In the **castle**, now

laid out as gardens, knights of the
Order of Knights Templar were
beheaded in the Torre Sangrienta
(Bloody Tower) in 1312. The old
quarters of the town grew up
around three churches: **San
Bartolomé**, its façade studded
with glazed ceramics; **San
Miguel**, whose brick tower dominates the Plaza de España; and
Santa María de la Encarnación.

Environs
Fregenal de la Sierra, 25 km
(16 miles) to the south, is
an attractive old town with
a bullring and a castle.

Llerena ⑳

Badajoz. 🏘 5,900. 🚊 🚌 🚹 *Calle
Aurora 2, 924 87 05 51.* 🕑 *Thu.* 🎉
*Nuestra Señora de la Granada (1–15
Aug).* www.llerena.org

Extremadura's southeastern
gateway to Andalusia, the
town of Llerena, is a mixture
of Mudéjar and Baroque buildings. In the pretty square,

lined with palm trees, stands
the arcaded, whitewash-and-
stone church of **Nuestra
Señora de la Granada**, its
sumptuous interior reflecting
its former importance as a seat
of the Inquisition *(see p274)*.
At one end of the square is a
fountain designed by Zurbarán, who lived here for 15
years. Also worth seeing is
the 16th-century **Convento de
Santa Clara**, on a street leading out of the main square.

Environs
At **Azuaga**, 30 km (20 miles)
to the east, is the Iglesia de la
Consolación, containing Renaissance and Mudéjar tiles.

Tentudía ㉑

Badajoz. 🚌 *Calera de León.* 🚹 *Calera
de León, 924 584 084* **Monasterio** 🕘
Tue–Sun. 🖥 www.caleradeleon.es

Where the Sierra Morena
runs into Andalusia, fortified
towns and churches founded
by the medieval military
orders stand among the
wooded hills of Tentudía.
Here, on a hilltop, stands the
tiny **Monasterio de Tentudía**.
Founded in the 13th century
by the Order of Santiago, the
monastery contains a superb
Mudéjar cloister, and reredos
with Seville *azulejos* (tiles).
At **Calera de León**, just 6 km
(4 miles) north of Tentudía,
there is a Renaissance convent,
which was also founded by
the Order of Santiago. The
convent has a Gothic church
and a cloister on two floors.

Bullring at Fregenal de la Sierra

SOUTHERN SPAIN

INTRODUCING SOUTHERN SPAIN 416–425
SEVILLE 426–446
SEVILLE STREET FINDER 447–453
SHOPPING IN SEVILLE 454–455
ENTERTAINMENT IN SEVILLE 456–457
ANDALUSIA 458–501

Southern Spain at a Glance

One large region – Andalusia – extends across
the south of Spain. Its landscape varies from the
deserts of Almería in the east, to the wetlands of
Doñana National Park in the west; and from the
snow-capped peaks of the Sierra Nevada to the
beaches of the Costa del Sol. Three inland cities
between them share the greatest of Spain's
Moorish monuments: Granada, Córdoba and
Seville, the capital, which stands on the banks of
the Río Guadalquivir. Andalusia has many other
historic towns as well as attractive, whitewashed
villages, important nature reserves and the sherry-
producing vineyards around Jerez de la Frontera.

Córdoba's Mezquita *(see pp480–81)
has a remarkable forest of arches in i
interior and an exquisitely decorated
mihrab (prayer niche) facing Mecca.*

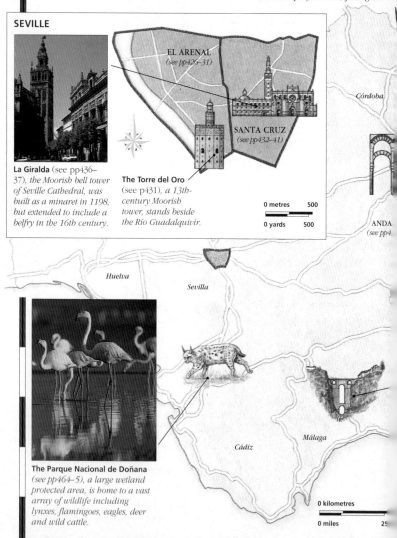

SEVILLE

EL ARENAL
(see pp426–31)

SANTA CRUZ
(see pp432–41)

Córdoba

ANDA
(see pp4

La Giralda (see pp436–
37), *the Moorish bell tower
of Seville Cathedral, was
built as a minaret in 1198,
but extended to include a
belfry in the 16th century.*

The Torre del Oro
(see p431), *a 13th-
century Moorish
tower, stands beside
the Río Guadalquivir.*

| 0 metres | 500 |
| 0 yards | 500 |

Huelva

Sevilla

Málaga

Cádiz

The Parque Nacional de Doñana
*(see pp464–5), a large wetland
protected area, is home to a vast
array of wildlife including
lynxes, flamingoes, eagles, deer
and wild cattle.*

| 0 kilometres | |
| 0 miles | 25 |

◁ Whitewashed houses with red-tiled roofs in Montefrío, near Granada

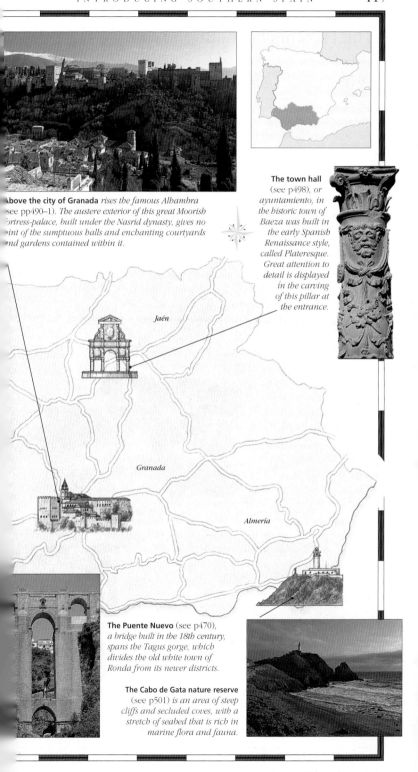

Above the city of Granada rises the famous Alhambra (see pp490–1). The austere exterior of this great Moorish fortress-palace, built under the Nasrid dynasty, gives no hint of the sumptuous halls and enchanting courtyards and gardens contained within it.

The town hall (see p498), or ayuntamiento, in the historic town of Baeza was built in the early Spanish Renaissance style, called Plateresque. Great attention to detail is displayed in the carving of this pillar at the entrance.

Jaén

Granada

Almería

The Puente Nuevo (see p470), a bridge built in the 18th century, spans the Tagus gorge, which divides the old white town of Ronda from its newer districts.

The Cabo de Gata nature reserve (see p501) is an area of steep cliffs and secluded coves, with a stretch of seabed that is rich in marine flora and fauna.

The Flavours of Southern Spain

Andalusia is vast, bordered on one side by the Mediterranean and on the other by the Atlantic. Inland are lofty mountains and undulating hills, endless olive groves and bright fields of sunflowers. The cuisine is as varied as the terrain, with a huge array of seafood, superb meat and game, and a harvest of sun-ripened fruit and vegetables. The *tapeo* (tapas-bar-hopping) is a regional institution, and around Granada, these little morsels are still served free with drinks. Along the coast, especially the Costa del Sol, the influx of foreigners has brought glamorous international restaurants but, inland, traditional recipes are still the norm at old-fashioned inns.

Olives and olive oil

Diners choosing from a selection at a tapas bar

TAPAS

The *tapeo*, or tapas crawl, is an intrinsic part of daily life in Andalusia. Each bar is usually known for a particular speciality: one might be well known for its home-made *croquetas* (potato croquettes, usually filled with ham or cod), while another will serve exceptional hams, and yet another might make the best *albóndigas* (meatballs) in the neighbourhood. Tapas are often accompanied by a glass of chilled, refreshing sherry, or perhaps a cold draught beer *(una caña)*. Tapas were once free, but that tradition has largely died out.

SEAFOOD

It's not surprising, given its extensive coastline, that southern Spain offers every imaginable variety of seafood including cod, hake, prawns, crayfish, clams, razor clams, octopus, cuttlefish, sole and tuna. Almost every seaside resort will offer *pescaíto frito* (fried fish) originally a Malaga dish, made with the freshest catch of the day. In Cádiz, they are served appealingly in a paper cone, and in nearby Sanlúcar do not miss the sweet and juicy *langostinos* (king prawns).

Jamón iberico belota   Morcilla with onion   Morcilla with rice   Salchichón iberico belot...   Chorizo rosario pica...   embuc...

Selection of delicious Spanish *embutidos* (cured meats)

REGIONAL DISHES AND SPECIALITIES

Pomegranates

Andalusia embodies many of the images most closely associated with Spain – the heady rhythms of flamenco, striking white villages and bullfighting. And tapas – in Andalusia, you can easily make a meal of these delectable treats, and every bar has an excellent range. Don't miss the mouthwatering hams from Jabugo and Trevélez which are famed throughout Spain, or the platters of freshly fried fish liberally doused with lemon juice. An ice-cold sherry (the word comes from Jérez, where most sherry is produced) is deliciously refreshing in the searing summer heat and is the most popular tipple at southern fiestas. While pork remains the most appreciated local meat, duck, beef and lamb are also favourites, subtly flavoured with aromatic bay leaves.

Gazpacho *This famous chilled soup is made with plump, ripe tomatoes, garlic and red peppers.*

Andalusian vegetable seller displaying fresh local produce

used in Andaluz cuisine, and the typical southern breakfast is toasted country bread topped with thin slices of tomato and drizzled with olive oil – utterly delicious. The hot climate is perfect for fruit and vegetables, including luscious peaches, papayas, persimmons, and mangoes, as well as tomatoes, asparagus, aubergines (eggplants) and artichokes. The chilled tomato soup, *gazpacho*, is a classic, but *salmorejo*, which is thicker and topped with a sprinkling of chopped boiled eggs and ham, is even tastier.

MEAT AND GAME

Pork and beef are the most popular meats in Andalusia. Glossy black bulls (some raised for bull-fighting but most for meat) are a common sight, and one of the most popular local dishes is *rabo de toro* (bull's tail). The famous hams of Jabugo (in the southwest) and Trevélez (near Granada) are among the finest produced in Spain, and are made with free-range, black-footed pigs fed on a diet of acorns. All kinds of cured meats are made here, often to traditional recipes which have remained unchanged for centuries. In the wild inland Sierras, you will find an abundance of game in season, along with the traditional country staples of lamb and rabbit.

FRUIT AND VEGETABLES

The undulating Andalusian fields and hillsides are densely covered with beautiful olive groves, and the best oils are graded as carefully as fine wines. Olive oil is liberally

Prawns and sardines on display at a fishmarket

ON THE MENU

Chocos con habas Cuttlefish is cooked with beans, white wine and plenty of bay leaves.

Pato a la Sevillana Succulent duck, cooked slowly with onion, leeks, carrots, bayleaf and a dash of sherry, this is a speciality of Seville.

Rabo de Toro An Andaluz classic, made with chunks of bull's tail, slowly braised with vegetables, bay leaf and a dash of sherry until tender.

Salmorejo Cordobés A creamy tomato dip thickened with breadcrumbs.

Torta de Camarones Delicious fritters filled with tiny, whole shrimp.

Tortilla del Sacromonte A speciality of Granada: omelette with brains, kidney or other offal, peppers and peas.

Huevos a la Flamenca *Eggs baked in a terracotta dish with vegetables, ham and chorizo sausage.*

Pescaíto Frito *A seaside favourite, this is a platter of small fish tossed in batter and fried in olive oil.*

Tocino de Cielo *This is a creamy custard dessert with a caramel topping. Its name means "heavenly bacon".*

Wines of Southern Spain

Andalusia is a land of fortified wines, and the best of these is *Jerez* (sherry). Andalusians drink the light, dry fino and manzanilla styles of sherry as wines (they only have 15.5 per cent alcohol) – always chilled, and often as an accompaniment to tapas *(see pp606–7)*. The longer-aged, richer, yet still dry styles of amontillado and oloroso sherry go well with the cured *jamón serrano (see p604)*. Other wines include fino, which may or may not be fortified, and Madeira-like Málaga.

González Byass logo

Working the soil in Jerez

Tio Pepe *is one of the finos of Jerez, which are noted for their bouquet of flor (yeast), pale colour and appetizing finish.*

WINE REGIONS

The Jerez wine region covers the chalky downs between the towns of Jerez, Sanlúcar and El Puerto de Santa María. South of the Montilla-Moriles region are Málaga's vineyards, which have been reduced by urban development.

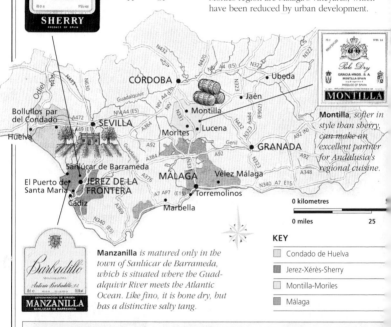

Montilla, *softer in style than sherry, can make an excellent partner for Andalusia's regional cuisine.*

KEY

- Condado de Huelva
- Jerez-Xérès-Sherry
- Montilla-Moriles
- Málaga

0 kilometres 25

0 miles 25

Manzanilla *is matured only in the town of Sanlúcar de Barrameda, which is situated where the Guad-alquivir River meets the Atlantic Ocean. Like fino, it is bone dry, but has a distinctive salty tang.*

KEY FACTS ABOUT WINES OF SOUTHERN SPAIN

Location and Climate
The Jerez region has one of the sunniest climates in Europe – summer heat tempered by ocean breezes. The best type of soil is white, chalky *albariza*. In Montilla it is more clayey.

Grape Varieties
The best dry sherry is produced from the Palomino grape. Pedro Ximénez is used for the sweeter styles and is the main grape in Montilla and Málaga. Moscatel is also grown in Málaga.

Good Producers
Condado de Huelva: Manuel Sauci Salas (Riodiel), A.Villarán (Pedro Ximénez Villarán). *Jerez:* Barbadillo (Solear), Blázquez (Carta Blanca), Caballero (Puerto), Garvey (San Patricio), González Byass (Alfonso, Tío Pepe), Hidalgo (La Gitana, Napoleón), Lustau, Osborne (Quinta), Pedro Domecq (La Ina), Sandeman. *Montilla-Moriles:* Alvear (C.B., Festival), Gracia Hermanos, Pérez Barquero, Tomás García. *Málaga:* Scholtz Hermanos, López Hermanos.

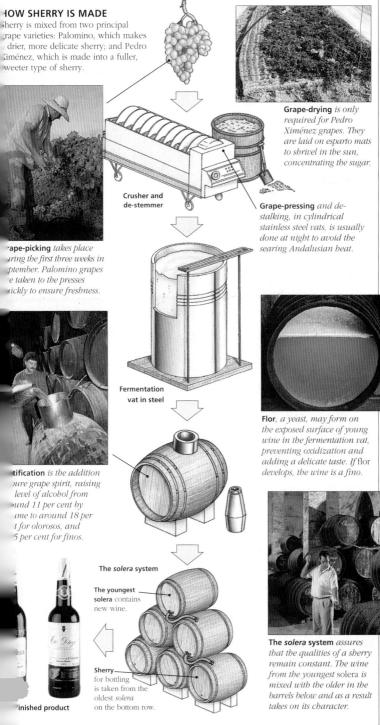

HOW SHERRY IS MADE

Sherry is mixed from two principal grape varieties: Palomino, which makes a drier, more delicate sherry; and Pedro Ximénez, which is made into a fuller, sweeter type of sherry.

Grape-drying *is only required for Pedro Ximénez grapes. They are laid on esparto mats to shrivel in the sun, concentrating the sugar.*

Crusher and de-stemmer

Grape-pressing *and destalking, in cylindrical stainless steel vats, is usually done at night to avoid the searing Andalusian heat.*

Grape-picking *takes place during the first three weeks in September. Palomino grapes are taken to the presses quickly to ensure freshness.*

Fermentation vat in steel

Flor, *a yeast, may form on the exposed surface of young wine in the fermentation vat, preventing oxidization and adding a delicate taste. If flor develops, the wine is a fino.*

Fortification *is the addition of pure grape spirit, raising the level of alcohol from around 11 per cent by volume to around 18 per cent for olorosos, and 15 per cent for finos.*

The *solera* system

The youngest solera contains new wine.

Sherry for bottling is taken from the oldest *solera* on the bottom row.

Finished product

The *solera* system *assures that the qualities of a sherry remain constant. The wine from the youngest solera is mixed with the older in the barrels below and as a result takes on its character.*

Moorish Architecture

The first significant period of Moorish architecture arrived with the Cordoban Caliphate. The Mezquita was extended lavishly during this period and possesses all the enduring features of the Moorish style: arches, stucco work and ornamental use of calligraphy. Later, the Almohads imported a purer Islamic style, as can be seen in La Giralda *(see pp436–7)*. The Nasrids built the superbly crafted Alhambra *(see pp490–1)* and the Mudéjares *(see p55)* used their skill to create beautiful Moorish-style buildings such as the Palacio Pedro I in Seville's Real Alcázar *(see pp440–1)*.

Reflections *in water, combined with an overall play of light, we central to Moorish architecture*

Moorish domes *were frequently unadorned on the outside. Inside, an intricate lattice of stone ribs supported the dome's weight. Like this one in the Mezquita* (see pp480–1)*, they were inlaid with multicoloured mosaics featuring stylized flowers.*

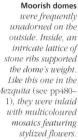

Defensive walls

Moorish gardens were often arranged around gently rippling pools and channels.

DEVELOPMENT OF MOORISH ARCHITECTURE

Pre-Caliphal era 710–929	Caliphal era 929–1031	Almoravid and Almohad era 1091–1248	Nasrid era c.1238–1492
	1031–91 *Taifa period (see p54)*		**c.1350** Alhambra palace

700	800	900	1000	1100	1200	1300	1400
	785 Mezquita in Córdoba begun			**1184** La Giralda in Seville begun		**c.1350** Palacio Pedro I	
		936 Medina Azahara near Córdoba begun			**Mudéjar era, after c.1215**		

Azulejos (see p438), *tiles, often adorned geometric patterns, the Real Alcázar (p*

MOORISH ARCHES

The Moorish arch was developed from the horseshoe arch that the Visigoths used in the construction of churches. The Moors modified it and used it as the basis of great architectural endeavours, such as the Mezquita. Subsequent arches show more sophisticated ornamentation and the slow demise of the basic horseshoe shape.

Caliphal arch, Medina Azahara *(see p477)*

Almohad arch, Real Alcázar *(see p440)*

Mudéjar arch, Real Alcázar *(see p440)*

Nasrid arch, the Alhambra *(see p490)*

MOORISH PALACE

The palaces of the Moors were designed with gracious living, culture and learning in mind. The imaginary palace here shows how space, light, water and ornamentation were combined to harmonious effect.

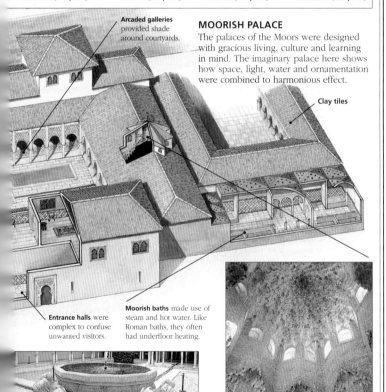

Arcaded galleries provided shade around courtyards.

Clay tiles

Entrance halls were complex to confuse unwanted visitors.

Moorish baths made use of steam and hot water. Like Roman baths, they often had underfloor heating.

Elaborate stucco work *typifies the Nasrid style of architecture. The Sala de los Abencerrajes in the Alhambra (see p491) was built using only the simplest materials, but it is nevertheless widely regarded as one of the most outstanding monuments of the period of the Moorish occupation.*

Water *cooled the Moors' elegant courtyards and served a contemplative purpose, as here in the Patio de los Leones in the Alhambra (see p491).*

Flamenco, the Soul of Andalusia

Seville feria poster 1953

More than just a dance, flamenco is a forceful artistic expression of the sorrows and joys of life. Although it has interpreters all over Spain and even the world, it is a uniquely Andalusian art form, traditionally performed by gypsies. There are many styles of *cante* (song) from different parts of Andalusia, but no strict choreography – dancers improvise from basic movements, following the rhythm of the guitar and their feelings. Flamenco was neglected in the 1960s and 1970s, but recent years have seen a revival of serious interest in traditional styles and the development of exciting new forms.

Sevillanas, *a folk dance strongly influenced by flamenco, is danced by Andalusians in their bars and homes.*

At a *tablao* (flamenco club) there will be at least four people on stage, including the hand clapper.

The origins of flamenco *are hard to trace. Gypsies may have been the main creators of the art, mixing their own Indian-influenced culture with existing Moorish and Andalusian folklore, and with Jewish and Christian music. There were gypsies in Andalusia by the early Middle Ages, but only in the 18th century did flamenco begin to develop into its present form.*

THE SPANISH GUITAR

The guitar has a major role in flamenco, traditionally accompanying the singer. The flamenco guitar developed from the modern classical guitar, which evolved in Spain in the 19th century. Flamenco guitars have a lighter, shallower construction and a thickened plate below the soundhole, used to tap rhythms. Today, flamenco guitarists often perform solo. One of the greatest, Paco de Lucía, began by accompanying singers and dancers, before making his debut as a soloist in 1968. His inventive style, which combines traditional playing with Latin, jazz and rock elements, has influenced many musicians outside the realm of flamenco, such as the group Ketama, who play flamenco-blues.

Classical guitar

Expert guitarist Paco de Lucía

Singing is an integral part of flamenco and the singer often performs solo. Camarón de la Isla (1950–92), a gypsy born near Cádiz, was among the most famous contemporary cantaores (flamenco singers). He began as a singer of expressive cante jondo (literally, "deep song"), from which he developed his own distinctive style. He has inspired many singers.

WHERE TO ENJOY FLAMENCO

Madrid has several good *tablaos*, flamenco venues, (see p321). In Granada, Sacromonte's caves (p489) are an exciting location. In Seville, the Barrio de Santa Cruz (pp432–41) has good *tablaos*.

The proud yet graceful posture of the *bailaora* is suggestive of a restrained passion.

A harsh, vibrating voice is typical of the singer.

The bailaora *(female dancer) is renowned for amazing footwork as well as intensive dance moments. Eva Yerbabuena and Sara Baras are both famous for their personal styles. Both lead their own acclaimed flamenco companies. Another flamenco star is Juana Amaya.*

Traditional polka-dot dress

The bailaor *(male dancer) plays a less important role than the* bailaora. *However, many have achieved fame, including Antonio Canales. He has introduced a new beat through his original foot movements.*

THE FLAMENCO TABLAO

These days it is rare to come across spontaneous dancing at a *tablao*, but if dancers and singers are inspired, an impressive show usually results. Artists performing with *duende* ("magic spirit") will hear appreciative *olés* from the audience.

FLAMENCO RHYTHM

The unmistakable rhythm of flamenco is created by the guitar. Just as important, however, is the beat created by hand-clapping and by the dancer's feet in high-heeled shoes. The *baila-ora* may also beat a rhythm with castanets; Lucero Tena (born in 1939) became famous for her solos on castanets. Graceful hand movements are used to express the dancer's feelings of the moment – whether pain, sorrow, or happiness. Like the movements of the rest of the body, they are not choreo-graphed, and the styles used vary from person to person.

Castanets made of wood

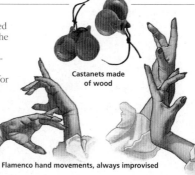

Flamenco hand movements, always improvised

EL ARENAL

Bounded by the Río Guadalquivir and guarded by the 13th-century Torre del Oro, El Arenal used to be a district of munitions stores and shipyards. Today this quarter is dominated by the

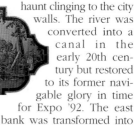

Torre del Oro shown on 20th-century tiles

dazzling white bullring, the Plaza de Toros de la Maestranza, where the Sevillians have been staging corridas for more than two centuries. The many bars and bodegas in the neighbouring streets are especially busy during the summer bullfighting season.

Once central to the city's life, the influence of the Guadalquivir declined as it silted up during the 17th century. By then El Arenal had become a notorious underworld

haunt clinging to the city walls. The river was converted into a canal in the early 20th century but restored to its former navigable glory in time for Expo '92. The east bank was transformed into a tree-lined promenade with excellent views of Triana and La Isla de la Cartuja across the water *(see p446)*.

The Hospital de la Caridad testifies to the city's continuing love affair with the Baroque. Its church is filled with famous paintings by Murillo, and the story of the Seville School is told in the immaculately restored Museo de Bellas Artes further north. The city's stunning collection of art includes great works by Zurbarán, Murillo and Valdés Leal.

SIGHTS AT A GLANCE

Historic Buildings
Hospital de la Caridad ④
Plaza de Toros de la Maestranza ③
Torre del Oro ⑤

Museums
Museo de Bellas Artes ①

Churches
Iglesia de la Magdalena ②

GETTING THERE

Plenty of orange or red and black buses. The C4 runs along the Paseo de Colón. A tram runs from Prado de San Sebastian to Plaza Nueva.

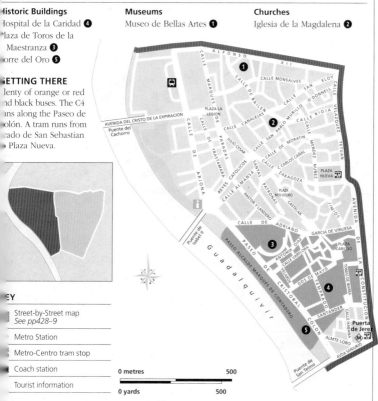

KEY

| | Street-by-Street map *See pp428–9* |
| Metro Station |
| Metro-Centro tram stop |
| Coach station |
| Tourist information |

| 0 metres | 500 |
| 0 yards | 500 |

Putting up an advertisement for a bullfight on the walls of the Plaza de Toros de la Maestranza

Street-by-Street: El Arenal

Once home to the port of Seville, El Arenal also housed the ammunition works and the artillery headquarters. Now its atmosphere is set by the city's bullring, the majestic Plaza de Toros de la Maestranza. During the bullfighting season *(see p430)* the area's bars and restaurants are packed, but for the rest of the year El Arenal's backstreets remain quiet. The riverfront is dominated by one of Seville's best-known monuments, the Moorish Torre del Oro, while the long, tree-lined promenade beside the Paseo de Cristóbal Colón is perfect for a slow, romantic walk along the Guadalquivir.

Statue of Carmen

★ **Plaza de Toros de la Maestr**
Seville's 18th-century bullring, o…
Spain's oldest, has a Baroque fa…
in white and ochre ❸

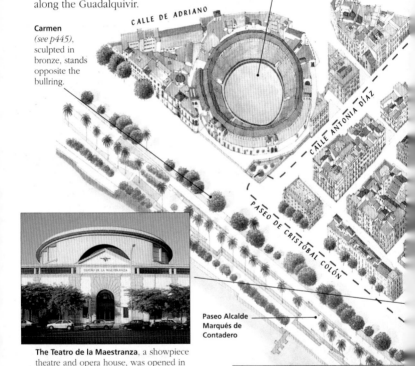

CALLE DE ADRIANO

Carmen
(see p445),
sculpted in bronze, stands opposite the bullring.

CALLE ANTONIA DÍAZ

PASEO DE CRISTÓBAL COLÓN

Paseo Alcalde Marqués de Contadero

The Teatro de la Maestranza, a showpiece theatre and opera house, was opened in 1991. Home of the Orquesta Sinfónica de Sevilla, the theatre also features international opera and dance companies.

STAR SIGHTS

★ Plaza de Toros de la Maestranza

★ Hospital de la Caridad

★ Torre del Oro

The Guadalquivir used to cause catastrophic inundations. Following floods in 1947 a barra… was constructed. Today, tourists enjoy peacef… boat trips, starting from the Torre del Oro.

El Buzo ("The Diver") is one of many traditional tapas bars and *freidurías* on or just off Calle Arfe. Nearby is Meson Cinco Jotas, a bar where *jamón ibérico (see p462)* is served.

LOCATOR MAP
See Street Finder map 3

El Postigo is an arts and crafts market.

GARCÍA VINUESA

ARTE

MAYO

TEMPRADO

TOMÁS DE IBARRA

AVENIDA DE LA CONSTITUCIÓN

CALLE SANTANDER

To the Cathedral

El Torno, in the secluded Plaza de Cabildo, sells sweets made in a convent.

★ **Hospital de la Caridad**
The walls of this Baroque hospital church are hung with fine paintings by Bartolomé Esteban Murillo and Juan de Valdés Leal ④

To Reales Alcázares

Maestranza de Artillería

| 0 metres | 75 |
| 0 yards | 75 |

KEY

– – – Suggested route

★ **Torre del Oro**
Built in the 13th century to protect the port, this crenellated Moorish tower now houses a small maritime museum ⑤

Madonna and Child in the Baroque Iglesia de la Magdalena

Museo de Bellas Artes ❶

Plaza del Museo 9. **Map** 1 B5. **Tel** 95 478 65 00. B2, C3, C4. 2:30–8:30pm Tue, 9am–8:30pm Wed–Sat, 9am–2:30pm Sun, public hols. Groups of 20: by appt. (free for EU citizens)

The Convento de la Merced Calzada has been restored to create one of the best art museums in Spain. Completed in 1612 by Juan de Oviedo, the building is designed around three patios. The Patio Mayor is the largest of these, remodelled by the architect Leonardo de Figueroa in 1724. The convent church is notable for its Baroque domed ceiling, painted by Domingo Martínez.

The museum's collection of Spanish art and sculpture, from the medieval to the modern, focuses on the work of Seville School artists. Among the star attractions is *La Servilleta*, a Virgin and Child (1665–8), which is said to be painted on a napkin *(servilleta)*. One of Murillo's most popular works, it may be seen in the restored convent church.

The boisterous *La Inmaculada* (1672) by Juan de Valdés Leal is on display in a gallery devoted to the artist's forceful religious

San Jerónimo Penitente in the Museo de Bellas Artes

paintings. The museum also contains several fine works by Zurbarán including San *Hugo en el Refectorio* (1655), which was painted for the monastery at La Cartuja *(see p446)*.

Iglesia de la Magdalena ❷

Calle San Pablo 10. **Map** 3 B1. **Tel** 95 422 96 03. Plaza Nueva. 43. 7:30–11am, 6:30–9pm Mon–Sat, 7:30am–1:30pm, 6:30–9pm Sun.

This immense Baroque church by Leonardo de Figueroa, completed in 1709, is gradually being restored to its former glory. In its southwest corner stands the Capilla de la Quinta Angustia, a Mudéjar chapel with three cupolas. This chapel survived from an earlier church where the great Seville School painter Bartolomé Murillo was baptized in 1618. The font that was used for his baptism is now in the baptistry of the present building. The church's west front is topped by a belfry which is painted in vivid colours.

Among the religious works in the church are a painting by Francisco de Zurbarán, St *Dominic in Soria*, housed in the Capilla Sacramental (to the right of the south door), and frescoes by Lucas Valdés over the sanctuary. On the wall of the north transept there is a cautionary fresco of a medieval *auto-da-fé (see p274)*.

Plaza de Toros de la Maestranza ❸

Paseo de Cristóbal Colón 12. **Map** 3 B2. **Tel** 95 422 45 77. Puerta Jerez. Archivo de Indias. 9am–7pm daily.

Seville's famous bullring, built between 1761–1881, is well worth a visit.

The arcaded arena holds up to 14,000 spectators. Guided tours of this immense building start from the main entrance on Paseo de Cristóbal Colón. On the west side is the Puerta del Príncipe (Prince's Gate), through which the triumphant matadors are carried aloft by admirers from the crowd.

Just beyond the *enfermería* (emergency hospital) is a museum of portraits, posters and costumes, including a purple cape painted by Pablo Picasso. The tour continues on to the chapel where matadors pray for success, and then to the stables where the horses of the *picadores* (lance-carrying horsemen) are kept.

The bullfighting season starts on Easter Sunday and continues intermittently until October. Most *corridas* take place on Sunday evenings. Tickets can be bought from the *taquilla* (booking office) at the bullring.

Next door to the Plaza de Toros, and echoing its circular bulk, is the Teatro de la Maestranza. Seville's austere opera house and theatre, designed by Luis Marín de Terán and Aurelio de Pozo, opened in 1991. Fragments of ironwork from the 19th-century ammunition works that first occupied the site adorn the river façade.

Arcaded arena of the Plaza de Toros de la Maestranza, begun in 1761

Finis Gloriae Mundi by Juan de Valdés Leal in the Hospital de la Caridad

Hospital de la Caridad ❹

Calle Temprado 3. **Map** 3 B2. **Tel** 95 422 32 32. 🚇 🚊 Puerta Jerez. 🚌 🚊 □ 9am–1:30pm, 3:30–6:30pm Mon–Sat, 9am–1pm Sun & public hols. 🎫 🛇

This charity hospital was founded in 1674 and it is still used today as a sanctuary for elderly and infirm people. In the gardens stands a statue of its benefactor, Miguel de Mañara, whose dissolute life before he joined a brotherhood is said to have inspired the story of Don Juan. The facade of the hospital church, with its whitewashed walls, reddish stonework and framed *azulejos*, provides a glorious example of Sevillian Baroque. Inside are two square patios decorated with plants, 18th-century Dutch tiles, and fine fountains with Italian statues depicting Charity and Mercy. At their northern end a passage to the right leads to another patio, containing a 13th-century arch which survives from the city's shipyards.

Inside the church there are a number of original canvases by some of the leading painters of the 17th century, despite the fact that some of the greatest artworks were looted by Marshal Soult during the Napoleonic occupation of 1808–14 *(see p62)*. Directly above the entrance is the ghoulish *Finis Gloriae Mundi* (The End of the World's Glory) by Juan de Valdés Leal, and opposite hangs his morbid *In Ictu Oculi* (In the Blink of an Eye). Many of the other works that can be seen are by Murillo, including *St John of God Carrying a Sick Man* and portraits of the Child Jesus and *St John the Baptist as a Boy*.

Torre del Oro ❺

Paseo de Cristóbal Colón. **Map** 3 B2. **Tel** 95 422 24 19. 🚇 🚊 Puerta Jerez. 🚌 C2, C3, C4, 21. □ 10am–2pm Tue–Fri, 11am–2pm Sat & Sun. ● Aug & Mon. 🎫 *(free Tue & for EU citizens)*. 🛇

In Moorish Seville the Tower of Gold formed part of the walled defences, linking up with the Real Alcázar *(see pp440–1)*. It was built as a defensive lookout in 1220, with a companion tower on the opposite bank. A metal chain stretched between them to prevent hostile ships from sailing upriver. The turret was added in 1760. The gold in its name may be the gilded *azulejos* that once clad its walls, or treasures from the Americas unloaded here. The tower has had many uses, such as a chapel and a prison. Now, as the Museo Marítimo, it exhibits maritime maps and antiques.

The Torre del Oro, built by the Almohads

SEVILLE'S FIESTAS

April Fair *(two weeks after Easter)*. Life in the city moves over the river to the fairground for a week. Here, members of clubs, trade unions and neighbourhood groups meet in numerous *casetas* (entertainment booths) to drink and dance all night to the infectious, non-stop rhythm of sevillanas. (Access to booths may be limited to private parties.) Every day, from around 1pm, elegant, traditionally dressed riders on horseback and mantilla-crowned women in open carriages show off their finery in parades. During the afternoons, bullfights are often staged in the Maestranza bullring.

Float in Holy Week procession

Holy Week *(Mar/Apr)*. Over 100 gilded *pasos* (floats bearing religious images) are borne through the streets between Palm Sunday and Easter Day. Singers in the crowds often spontaneously burst into *saetas*, fragments of song in praise of Christ or the Virgin. Emotions are high in the early hours of Good Friday as the images of the Virgen de la Macarena and the Virgen de la Esperanza of Triana emerge from their churches.

Corpus Christi *(May/Jun)*. The *Seises*, boys dressed in Baroque costume, dance before the main altar of the cathedral *(see p437)*.

SANTA CRUZ

Seville's old Jewish quarter, the Barrio de Santa Cruz, is a warren of white alleyways and patios that has long been the most picturesque corner of the city. Many of the best-known sights are located here: the cavernous Gothic cathedral with its landmark tower, La Giralda; the splendid Real Alcázar, with the royal palaces and lush gardens of Pedro I and Carlos V; and the Archivo de Indias, whose documents tell of Spain's exploration and conquest of the Americas.

Ornate streetlamp, Plaza del Triunfo

Spreading northeast from these great monuments is an enchanting maze of whitewashed streets. The Golden Age artist Bartolomé Esteban Murillo lived here in the 17th century, while his contemporary, Juan de Valdés Leal, decorated the Hospital de los Venerables with superb Baroque frescoes. Further north is one of Seville's favourite shopping streets, the Calle de las Sierpes. The market squares around it, such as the charming Plaza del Salvador, provided backdrops for some of the stories of Cervantes. Nearby, the ornate façades and interiors of the Ayuntamiento (town hall) and the Casa de Pilatos, a gem of Andalusian architecture, testify to the great wealth that flowed into the city from the New World during the 16th century, much of it spent on art.

SIGHTS AT A GLANCE

Historic Buildings
Archivo de Indias ⑥
Ayuntamiento ②
Casa de Pilatos ④
Hospital de los Venerables ⑤
Real Alcázar pp440–1 ⑦

Churches
Cathedral and La Giralda pp436–7 ①

Streets and Plazas
Calle de las Sierpes ③

GETTING THERE
This area is well served by orange, red and black buses. Buses 21, 22, 23, 25, 26, 30, 31, 33, 34, 40, 41, 42, C3 and C4 will take you to Puerta de Jerez. Metro-Centro tram runs along Avenida de la Constitución.

KEY
- Street-by-Street map (pp434–5)
- ⓂMetro Station
- Metro-Centro tram stop
- Tourist information

0 metres 400
0 yards 400

Giralda seen from the gardens of the Real Alcázar

Street-by-Street: Santa Cruz

Window grille, Santa Cruz

The maze of narrow streets to the east of Seville Cathedral and the Real Alcázar represents Seville at its most romantic and compact. As well as the expected souvenir shops, tapas bars and strolling guitarists, there are plenty of picturesque alleys, hidden plazas and flower-decked patios to reward the casual wanderer. Once a Jewish ghetto, its restored buildings, with characteristic window grilles, are now a harmonious mix of upmarket residences and tourist accommodation. Good bars and restaurants make the area well worth an evening visit.

Plaza Virgen de los Reyes is often lined by horse-drawn carriages. In the centre of the square is an early 20th-century fountain by José Lafit

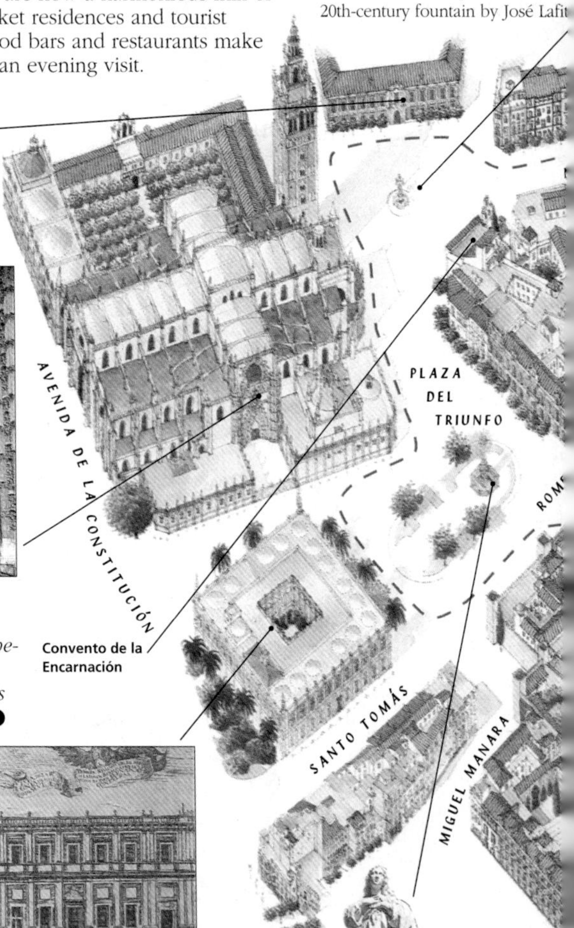

Palacio Arzobispal, the 18th-century Archbishop's Palace, is still used by Seville's clergy.

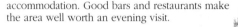

AVENIDA DE LA CONSTITUCIÓN

PLAZA DEL TRIUNFO

ROM

★ Cathedral and La Giralda
This huge Gothic cathedral and its Moorish bell tower are Seville's most popular sights ❶

Convento de la Encarnación

SANTO TOMÁS

MIGUEL MANARA

Archivo de Indias
Built in the 16th century as a merchants' exchange, the Archive of the Indies now houses documents relating to the Spanish colonization of the Americas ❻

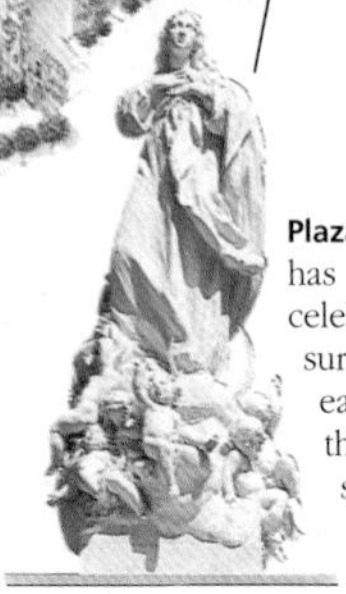

Plaza del Triunfo has a Baroque col celebrating the cit survival of the g earthquake of 1 the centre is a statue of the V Mary (Immac Conception)

For hotels and restaurants in this region see pp590–91 and pp640–42

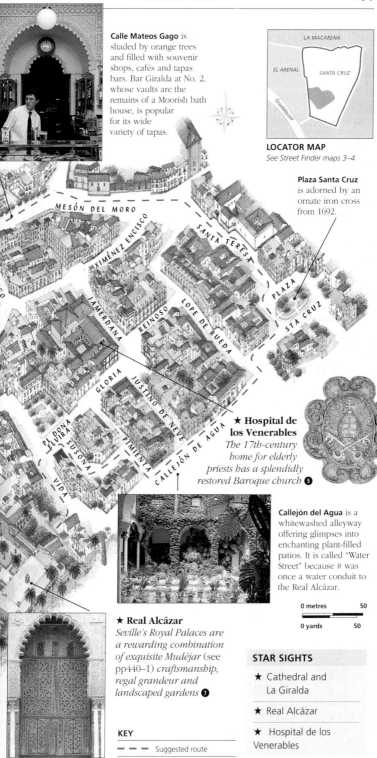

Calle Mateos Gago is shaded by orange trees and filled with souvenir shops, cafés and tapas bars. Bar Giralda at No. 2, whose vaults are the remains of a Moorish bath house, is popular for its wide variety of tapas.

LOCATOR MAP
See Street Finder maps 3–4

LA MACARENA

EL ARENAL   SANTA CRUZ

Guadalquivir

Plaza Santa Cruz is adorned by an ornate iron cross from 1692.

MESÓN DEL MORO

XIMÉNEZ ENCISO

SANTA TERESA

JAMERDANA

REINOSO

LOPE DE RUEDA

PLAZA

STA CRUZ

GLORIA

JUSTINO DE NEVE

PL DONA ELVIRA

SUSONA

PIMIENTA

CALLEJÓN DE AGUA

VIDA

★ Hospital de los Venerables
The 17th-century home for elderly priests has a splendidly restored Baroque church ❺

Callejón del Agua is a whitewashed alleyway offering glimpses into enchanting plant-filled patios. It is called "Water Street" because it was once a water conduit to the Real Alcázar.

| 0 metres | 50 |
| 0 yards | 50 |

★ Real Alcázar
Seville's Royal Palaces are a rewarding combination of exquisite Mudéjar (see pp440–1) craftsmanship, regal grandeur and landscaped gardens ❼

STAR SIGHTS

★ Cathedral and La Giralda

★ Real Alcázar

★ Hospital de los Venerables

KEY

– – – Suggested route

Seville Cathedral and La Giralda ❶

16th-century stained glass

Seville's cathedral occupies the site of a great mosque built by the Almohads *(see p54)* in the late 12th century. La Giralda, its bell tower, and the Patio de los Naranjos are a legacy of this Moorish structure. Work on the Christian cathedral, the largest in Europe, began in 1401 and took just over a century to complete. As well as enjoying its Gothic immensity and the works of art in its chapels and sacristy, visitors can climb La Giralda for stunning views over the city.

★ La Giralda
The bell tower is crowned by a bronze weathervane (giraldillo) portraying Faith, from which it takes its name. A replica has replaced the original vane.

Group Entrance

★ Patio de los Naranjos
In Moorish times worshippers would wash their hands and feet in the fountain under the orange trees before praying.

THE RISE OF LA GIRALDA

The tower was built as a minaret in 1198. In the 14th century the bronze spheres at its top were replaced by Christian symbols. A new belfry was planned in 1557, but built to a more ornate design by Hernán Ruiz in 1568.

1198

1400

1557 (plan)

1568

Puerta del Perdón (Exit)

Roman pillars brought from Itálica *(see p476)* surround the cathedral steps.

Retablo Mayor
Santa María de la Sede, the cathedral's patron saint, sits at the high altar below a waterfall of gold. The 44 gilded relief panels of the reredos were carved by Spanish and Flemish sculptors between 1482 and 1564.

VISITORS' CHECKLIST

Avenida de la Constitución. **Map** 3 C2. **Tel** 954 21 49 71. 🚇 *Puerta Jerez.* 🚌 *Archivo de Indias.* 🚍 21, 22, 23, 31, 33, 40. **Cathedral & La Giralda** ⬜ *Sep–Jun: 11am–5pm Mon–Sat; 2:30–6pm Sun; Jul–Aug: 9:30am–3:30pm Mon–Sat, 2:30–6pm Sun.* 🎫 *(discounts for students & over 65s).* 🕐 *8:30am, 9am, 10am, noon, 5pm Mon–Sat (Sat also 8pm); 8:30am, 10am, 11am, noon, 1pm, 5pm, 6pm Sun* **www**.catedralsevilla.es

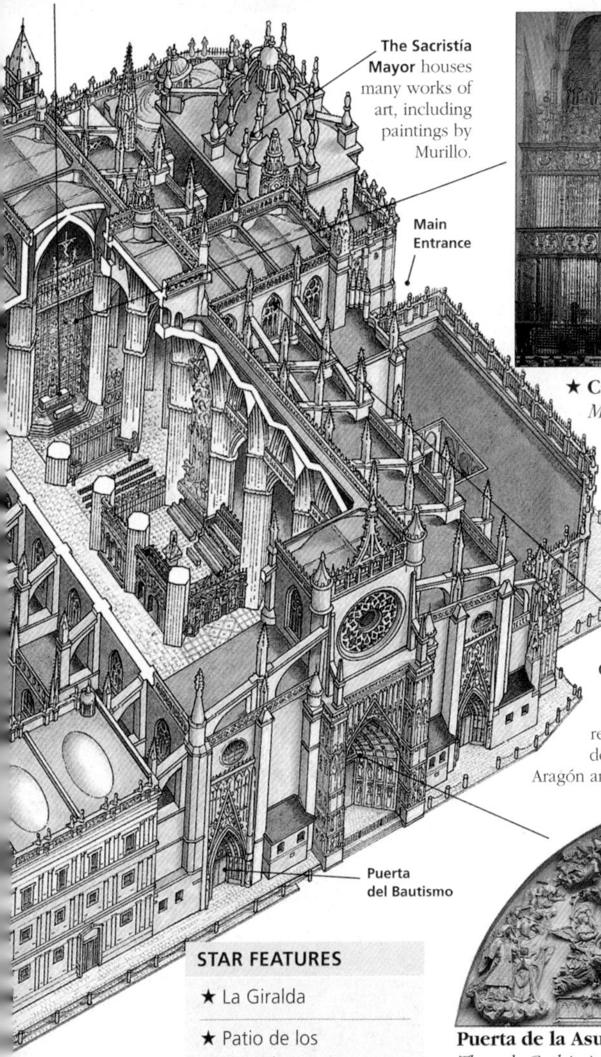

The Sacristía Mayor houses many works of art, including paintings by Murillo.

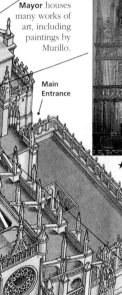

Main Entrance

★ **Capilla Mayor**
Monumental iron grilles forged in 1518–32 enclose the main chapel, which is dominated by the overwhelming Retablo Mayor.

The Tomb of Columbus dates from the 1890s. His coffin is carried by bearers representing the kingdoms of Castile, León, Aragón and Navarra *(see p54).*

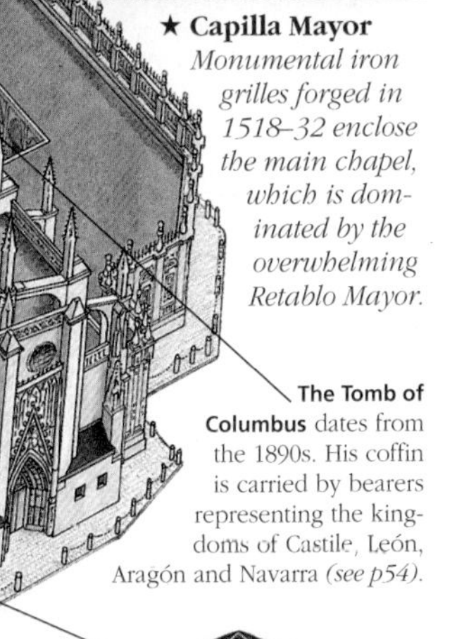

Puerta del Bautismo

STAR FEATURES

★ La Giralda

★ Patio de los Naranjos

★ Capilla Mayor

glesia del Sagrario, large 17th-century hapel, is now used s a parish church.

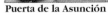

Puerta de la Asunción
Though Gothic in style, this portal was not completed until 1833. A stone relief of the Assumption of the Virgin decorates the tympanum.

Genoese fountain in the Mudéjar Patio Principal of the Casa de Pilatos

Ayuntamiento ❷

Plaza Nueva 1. **Map** 3 C1. **Tel** 95 459 01 01. 🚌 *Plaza Nueva.* ◯ *5:30, 6:30pm Tue Wed, & Thu.* ◖ *Aug & Jul.* ⬚ ▨ www.ayunt-sevilla.es

Seville's City Hall stands between the Plaza de San Francisco, where *autos-da-fé* (public trials of heretics) were held, and the Plaza Nueva.

Building was completed between 1527 and 1534. The side bordering the Plaza de San Francisco is a fine example of ornate Plateresque style *(see p25)* favoured by the architect Diego de Riaño. The west front is Neo-Classical, built in 1891. Sculpted ceilings survive in the vestibule and the lower Casa Consistorial (Council Meeting Room), containing Velázquez's *Imposition of the Chasuble on St Ildefonso.* The upper Casa Consistorial has a dazzling coffered ceiling and paintings by Zurbarán and Valdés Leal.

Calle de las Sierpes ❸

Map 3 C1. 🚌 *21, 30.* **Casa de la Condesa Lebrija. Tel** 95 422 78 02. 🚌 *Plaza Nueva.* ◯ *10am– 7:30pm Mon-Fri.* ▨ www. palaciodelebrija.com

Seville's main shopping promenade, the "Street of the Snakes", runs north from Plaza de San Francisco. Long-established stores selling hats, fans and traditional *mantillas* (lace headdresses) stand alongside clothes and souvenir shops. The parallel streets of

Cuna and Tetuán also offer some enjoyable window-shopping. Halfway up the road walking north, Calle Jovellanos to the left leads to the 17th-century Capillita de San José. Further on at the junction with Calle Pedro Caravaca is the Real Círculo de Labradores, a private men's club founded in 1856.

Opposite – with its entrance in Calle Cuna – is a 15th-century private mansion, the **Casa de la Condesa Lebrija**. Among the Lebrija family's treasures on display is a Roman mosaic from the ruins of nearby Itálica *(see p476)* and a collection of *azulejos*.

Right at the end of the street is La Campana, Seville's best-known *pastelería*.

Casa de Pilatos ❹

Plaza de Pilatos 1. **Map** 4 D1. **Tel** 95 422 52 98. 🚌 *C3, C4.* ◯ *9am– 6:30pm daily.* ▨ ▨ *first floor.* ⬚ ⬚ *ground floor.*

Enraptured by by the architectural and decorative wonders of High Renaissance Italy and the Holy Land, the first Marquis of Tarifa built the Casa de Pilatos. So called because it was thought to resemble Pontius Pilate's home in Jerusalem, today it is the residence of the Dukes of Medinaceli and is one of the finest palaces in Seville.

Visitors enter through a marble portal, commissioned by the Marquis in 1529 from Genoese craftsmen. Across the arcaded Apeadero (carriage yard) is the Patio Principal. The courtyard is essentially Mudéjar *(see p55)* in style and decorated with *azulejos* and intricate plasterwork. In its corners are three Roman statues, depicting Minerva, a dancing muse and Ceres, and a Greek statue of Athena, dating from the 5th century BC.

In its centre is a fountain which was imported from Genoa. To the right, through the Salón del Pretorio with its coffered ceiling and marquetry is the Corredor de Zaquizamí

AZULEJOS

Colourful *azulejos*, glazed ceramic tiles, are a striking feature of Seville. The craft was introduced to Spain by the Moors, who created fantastic mosaics in sophisticated geometric patterns for palace walls – the word *azulejo* derives from the Arabic for "little stone". New techniques were introduced in the 16th century and later mass production extended their use to decorative signs, shop façades and advertising hoardings.

Azulejo billboard for Studebaker Motor Cars (1924), Calle Tetuán

Fresco by Juan de Valdés Leal in the Hospital de los Venerables

Valdés. Other highlights of the church include sculptures of St Peter and St Ferdinand by Pedro Roldán, flanking the east door; and *The Apotheosis of St Ferdinand* by Lucas Valdés, top centre in the reredos of the main altar. Its frieze (inscribed in Greek) advises to "Fear God and Honour the Priest".

In the sacristy, the ceiling has an effective *trompe l'oeil* depicting *The Triumph of the Cross* by Juan de Valdés Leal.

Archivo de Indias **6**

Avda de la Constitución. **Map** 3 C2. **Tel** 95 421 12 34. Puerta Jerez. Archivo de Indias. 10am–4pm Mon–Sat.

The Archive of the Indies illustrates Seville's pre-eminent role in the colonization and exploitation of the New World. Built between 1584–98 to designs by Juan de Herrera, co-architect of El Escorial *(see pp330–31)*, it was originally a lonja (exchange), where merchants traded. In 1785, Carlos III had all Spanish documents relating to the "Indies" collected under one roof. Among the archive's 86 million handwritten pages and 8,000 maps and drawings are letters from Columbus, Cortés, and Cervantes and the extensive correspondence of Felipe II.

Upstairs, the library rooms contain regularly changing displays of drawings, maps and facsimile documents.

The antiquities on display in adjacent rooms include a bas-relief of *Leda and the Swan* and two Roman reliefs commemorating the Battle of Actium of 31 BC.

Coming back to the Patio Principal, you turn right into the Salón de Descanso de los Jueces. Beyond is a rib-vaulted Gothic chapel, with Mudéjar plasterwork walls and ceiling. On the altar is a copy of a 16th-century sculpture in the Vatican, *The Good Shepherd*. Left through the Gabinete de Platos, with its small central fountain, is the Jardín Grande. Returning once more to the main patio, behind the statue of Ceres, a tiled staircase leads to the upper floor. It is roofed with a wonderful *media naranja* (half orange) cupola built in 1537. Here are Mudéjar ceilings in some rooms, full of family portraits and antiques.

Hospital de los Venerables **5**

Plaza de los Venerables 8. **Map** 3 C2. **Tel** 95 456 26 96. Archivo de Indias. 10am–1:30pm, 4–7:30pm daily. 25 Dec, 1 Jan, Good Friday.

Set in the heart of the Barrio de Santa Cruz, this home for elderly priests was begun in 1675 and completed around 20 years later by Leonardo de Figueroa. It has recently been restored as a cultural centre by FOCUS (Fundación Fondo de Cultura de Sevilla).

Stairs from the central, rose-coloured, sunken patio lead to the upper floors, which, along with the infirmary and cellar, are used as exhibition galleries.

The Hospital church, a showcase of Baroque splendours, has frescoes by both Juan de Valdés Leal and his son Lucas

Façade of the Archivo de Indias by Juan de Herrera

Real Alcázar ❼

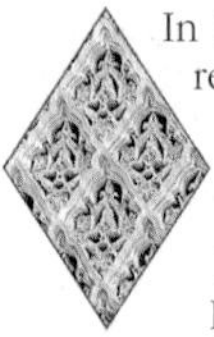

Mudéjar stucco

In 1364 Pedro I ordered the construction of a royal residence within the palaces which had been built by the city's Almohad *(see p54)* rulers. Within two years, craftsmen from Granada and Toledo had created a jewel box of Mudéjar patios and halls, the Palacio Pedro I, now at the heart of Seville's Real Alcázar. Later monarchs added their own distinguishing marks: Isabel I *(see p56)* dispatched navigators to explore the New World from her Casa de la Contratación, while Carlos I (the Holy Roman Emperor Charles V – *see p58*) had grandiose, richly decorated apartments built.

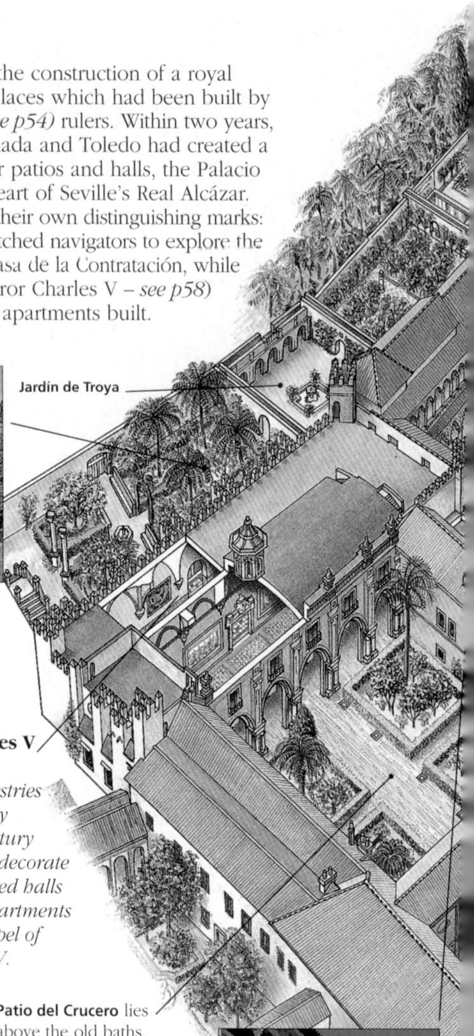

Jardín de Troya

Gardens of the Alcázar
Laid out with terraces, fountains and pavilions, these gardens provide a delightful refuge from the heat and bustle of Seville.

★ Charles V Rooms
Vast tapestries and lively 16th-century azulejos *decorate the vaulted halls of the apartments and chapel of Charles V.*

Patio del Crucero lies above the old baths.

PLAN OF THE REAL ALCÁZAR
The complex has been the home of Spanish kings for almost seven centuries. The palace's upper floor is used by the royal family today.

KEY

▢ Area illustrated above

▢ Gardens

★ Patio de las Doncellas
The Patio of the Maidens boasts plasterwork by the top craftsmen of Granada.

★ Salón de Embajadores

Built in 1427, the dazzling dome of the Ambassadors' Hall is of carved and gilded, interlaced wood.

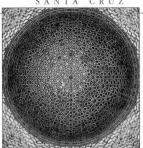

VISITORS' CHECKLIST

Patio de Banderas. **Map** 3 C2. **Tel** 95 450 23 23. 🚇 Puerta Jerez. 🚉 Archivo de Indias. ⏱ 9:30am–8pm Tue–Sat (to 6pm Oct–Mar), 9:30am–6pm Sun & hols (to 2:30pm Oct–Mar). 📷

Horseshoe Arches

Azulejos and complex plasterwork decorate the Ambassadors' Hall, which has three symmetrically arranged, ornate archways, each with three horseshoe arches.

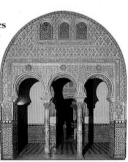

Casa de la Contratación

The Patio de la Montería was where the court met before hunting expeditions.

Patio de las Muñecas

The Patio of the Dolls and its surrounding bedrooms formed the domestic heart of the palace. It derives its name from two tiny faces on one of its arches.

The façade of the Palacio Pedro I is a prime example of Mudéjar style.

Puerta del León (entrance)

STAR FEATURES

- ★ Charles V Rooms
- ★ Patio de las Doncellas
- ★ Salón de Embajadores

io del Yeso

e Patio of Plaster, a garden with flower beds d a water channel, retains features of the lier, 12th-century Almohad Alcázar.

FURTHER AFIELD

The north of Seville, La Macarena, is a characterful mix of decaying Baroque and Mudéjar churches, and old-style tapas bars. The place to visit here is the Basílica de la Macarena, a shrine to Seville's much-venerated Virgen de la Esperanza Macarena. Among the many convents and churches in the area, the Convento de Santa Paula offers a rare opportunity to peep behind the walls of an enclosed community.

The area south of the city is dominated by the extensive, leafy Parque María Luisa. A large part of the park originally formed the grounds of the Baroque Palacio de San Telmo. Many of the historic buildings in the park were erected for the Ibero-American Exposition of 1929. The grand five-star Hotel Alfonso XIII and the crescent-shaped Plaza de España are the most striking legacies of this upsurge of Andalusian pride. Nearby is the Royal Tobacco Factory, forever associated with the fictional gypsy heroine Carmen, who toiled in its sultry halls. Today, it is part of the Universidad, Seville's university. There is more to see across the river from the city centre. With its cobbled streets and shops selling ceramics, the Triana quarter retains the feel of old Seville. In the 15th century a Carthusian monastery, the Monasterio de Santa María de las Cuevas, was built north of Triana. Columbus resided there and the area around it, the Isla de la Cartuja, was chosen as the site for Expo '92. Today the site is home mainly to offices but the Isla Mágica amusement park and Teatro Central are also located here.

Roman column, Alameda de Hércules

SIGHTS AT A GLANCE

Historic Buildings
Palacio de San Telmo ❹
Universidad ❺

Churches and Convents
Basílica de la Macarena ❶
Convento de Santa Paula ❷
Iglesia de San Pedro ❸

Historic Areas
Isla de la Cartuja ❽
Parque María Luisa ❻
Triana ❼

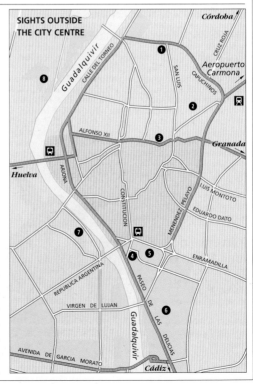

SIGHTS OUTSIDE THE CITY CENTRE

Córdoba
Aeropuerto Carmona
Granada
Guadalquivir
CALLE DEL TORNEO
CRUZ ROJA
SAN LUIS
CAPUCHINOS
ALFONSO XII
Huelva
ARJONA
CONSTITUCION
MENENDEZ Y PELAYO
LUIS MONTOTO
EDUARDO DATO
ENRAMADILLA
REPUBLICA ARGENTINA
VIRGEN DE LUJAN
PASEO DE LAS DELICIAS
Guadalquivir
AVENIDA DE GARCIA MORATO
Cádiz

0 kilometres 1

0 miles 0.5

KEY

☐ City centre

☐ Parks and open spaces

🚌 Coach station

🚆 Railway station

━ Major road

═ Minor road

Pabellón de Andalucía, built on the Isla de la Cartuja for Expo '92

St John the Baptist by Montañés
in the Convento de Santa Paula

Basílica de la Macarena ❶

Calle Bécquer 1. **Map** 2 D3.
Tel 95 437 01 95. ▥ C1, C2, C3,
C4, 2, 10, 13, 14. ◐ 5–9pm daily.
◑ Easter Fri. **Treasury** ◐ 9:30am–
2pm, 5–8pm daily.

The Basílica de la Macarena
was built in 1949 in the Neo-
Baroque style by Gómez
Millán as a new home for the
much-loved Virgen de la
Esperanza Macarena. It butts
on to the 13th-century Iglesia
de San Gil, where the image
was housed until a fire in 1936.

The image of the Virgin,
standing above the main altar
amid waterfalls of gold and
silver, has been attributed to
Luisa Roldán (1656–1703), the
most talented female artist of
the Seville School. The wall-
paintings, by Rafael Rodríguez
Hernández, date from 1982.

The Virgin's magnificent processional gowns and jewels are
held in the Treasury museum.

Convento de Santa Paula ❷

C/ Santa Paula 11. **Map** 2 E5. **Tel** 95
453 63 30. ▥ 10, 11. ◐ 10am–
1pm, 4:30–6:30pm Tue–Sun. ▨ ▣

Founded in 1475, Santa Paula
is a working convent and
home to 40 nuns. The museum
consists of two galleries filled
with religious artifacts and
paintings. Marmalades and

jams, made by the nuns, are
sold in a room by the exit.
The nave of the convent
church has an elaborate
wooden roof, dating from
1623. Among the statues in
the church are St John the
Evangelist and St John the
Baptist, both the work of Juan
Martínez Montañés.

Iglesia de San Pedro ❸

Plaza San Pedro. **Map** 2 D5.
Tel 954 22 91 24. ▥ 10, 11, 12,
24, 27, 32. ◐ 8:30–11:30am,
7–8:30pm Mon–Sat, 9:30am–
1:30pm, 7–8:30pm Sun. ♿

Diego Velazquez, the Golden
Age painter *(see p32)*, was baptized in this church in 1599. It
is built in a typically Sevillian
mix of architectural styles.
Mudéjar elements survive in
the lobed brickwork of its
tower, which is surmounted
by a Baroque *(see p25)* belfry.
The principal portal – facing
the Plaza de San Pedro – is
also Baroque, and was added
by Diego de Quesada in 1613.

The poorly lit interior has a
Mudéjar wooden ceiling and
west door. The vault of one
of its chapels is decorated
with exquisite geometric
patterns of interlacing bricks.

Behind the church, in Calle
Doña María Coronel, cakes
are sold from a revolving
drum in the wall of the 14th-
century Convento de Santa
Inés. Fronting its church is an
arcaded patio, decorated with
17th-century frescoes by
Francisco de Herrera.

**Modern tilework adorning the
front of the Iglesia de San Pedro**

Palacio de San Telmo ❹

Avenida de Roma. **Map** 3 C3. **Tel** 95
503 55 05. ◈ ▤ Puerta de Jerez. ▥
C3, C4, 5, 34. ◐ for renovation until
mid-2009. ♿ ▨ ▣

This imposing palace, named
after the patron saint of navigators, was built in 1682 as a
university to train ships' pilots
navigators and high-ranking
officers. In 1849 it became the
residence of the Dukes of
Monpensier and until 1893 its
grounds included what is now
Parque María Luisa. Today it is
the presidential headquarters
of the Junta de Andalucía (the
regional government).

The most striking feature of
the Palacio de San Telmo is the

Parque María Luisa ❻

Map 4 D4. ◈ ▤ Prado de San
Sebastián. ♿ **Museo Arqueológic**
Tel 95 423 24 01. ◐ 3–8pm Tue,
9am– 8pm Wed–Sat, 9am–2pm Sun
▨ (free for EU citizens). ▨ **Muse**
de Artes y Costumbres Populare
Tel 95 423 25 76. ◐ as above.
▨ ▨ ♿

Princess Maria Luisa
donated part of the
grounds of the Palacio
de San Telmo to the city
for this park in 1893.

Plaza de España
was built in a
theatrical style by
Aníbal González.

The Glorieta de Bécquer
is an arbour with sculpted
figures depicting the phases
of love – a tribute to poet
Gustavo Adolfo Bécquer.

exuberant Churrigueresque portal designed by Leonardo de Figueroa, and completed in 1734. Surrounding the Ionic columns are allegorical figures representing the Sciences and Arts. St Telmo, holding a ship and charts, is flanked by the sword-bearing St Ferdinand and St Hermenegildo, with a cross. On the north façade is ranged a row of sculptures of Sevillian celebrities, added by Susillo in 1895. Among them are artists such as Montañés, Murillo and Velázquez.

Opposite is Seville's most famous hotel, the Alfonso XIII, dating from the 1920s. Its centrepiece is a grand patio with fountain and orange trees. Non-residents are welcome to visit the bar and the restaurant.

Universidad ❺

Calle San Fernando 4. **Map** 3 C3. **Tel** 95 455 10 00. ⚇ Puerta de Jerez. 🚏 Puerta de Jerez or Prado de San Sebastian. 🚌 C3, C4, 5, 25. ⬜ 8am–8:30pm Mon–Fri. ⬤ public hols. **www**.us.es

The former Real Fábrica de Tabacos (Royal Tobacco Factory) is now part of Seville University. In the 19th century, three-quarters of Europe's cigars were manufactured here, rolled by 10,000 *cigarreras* (female cigar-makers) – the inspiration for French author Mérimée's *Carmen*.

Built in 1728–71, the factory complex is the largest building in Spain after El Escorial (see pp330–31) near Madrid.

Baroque fountain in one of the patios in the Universidad

The moat and watchtowers are evidence of the importance given to protecting the king's lucrative tobacco monopoly.

landscaped by Jean Forestier, director of the Bois de Boulogne in Paris, the park was the leafy setting for the 1929 Ibero-American Exposition. The legacies of this extravaganza are the Plaza de España, decorated with regional scenes on ceramic tiles, and the Plaza de América, both the work of Aníbal González. On

the latter, in the Pabellón Mudéjar, the Museo de Artes y Costumbres Populares displays traditional Andalusian folk arts. The Neo-Renaissance Pabellón de las Bellas Artes houses the provincial Museo Arqueológico. Exhibits devoted to the Roman era include statues and fragments found at Itálica (see p476).

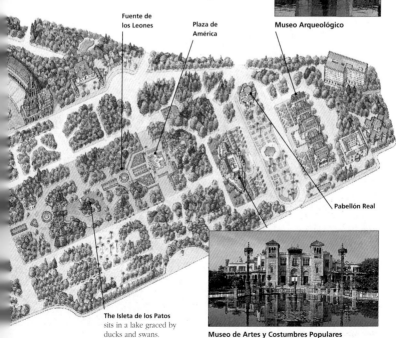

Fuente de los Leones

Plaza de América

Museo Arqueológico

Pabellón Real

The Isleta de los Patos sits in a lake graced by ducks and swans.

Museo de Artes y Costumbres Populares

Decorative tiles at Cerámica Santa Ana, a popular ceramics shop in Triana

Triana ❼

Map 3 A2. 🚇 *Plaza de Cuba, Parque de los Príncipes.*

This close-knit area, named after the Roman Emperor Trajan, was once Seville's gypsy quarter. Triana remains a traditional working-class district, with compact, flower-filled streets and a tangibly independent atmosphere. For centuries it has been famous for its potteries. The best-known of its ceramics shops today is Cerámica Santa Ana at No. 31 Calle San Jorge.

A good way to approach Triana is across the Puente de Isabel II, leading to the Plaza del Altozano. This square has glass-fronted, wrought-iron balconies called *miradores*. Nearby is one of the characteristic streets of the area, the Calle Rodrigo de Triana, named after the Andalusian sailor who was the first to sight the shores of the New World on Columbus's momentous voyage of 1492.

The Iglesia de Santa Ana, founded in the 13th century and splendidly renovated, is Triana's most popular church. In the baptistry is the Gypsy Font, which is believed to pass on the gift of flamenco song to the children of the faithful.

Isla de la Cartuja ❽

Map 1 B3. www.caac.es 🚌 C1, C2. **Monasterio de Santa María de las Cuevas** ⬤ Oct–Mar: 10am–8pm Tue–Fri, 11am–8pm Sat, 10am–3pm Sun; Apr–Sep: 10am–9pm Tue–Fri, 11am–9pm Sat, 10am–3pm Sun. 🖼 ♿ **Centro Andaluz de Arte Contemporáneo Tel** 95 503 70 70 ⬤ as above. 🖼 (free Tue for EU citizens). **Isla Mágica Tel** 902 16 17 16. ⬤ Apr–May: 11am–7pm Wed–Sun (to 10pm Sat, Sun); Jun: 10:30am–7:30pm Tue–Fri, 11am–11pm Sat, Sun; Jul: 11am–11pm Tue–Sun (to midnight Sat); Aug–mid-Sep: 11am–11pm & Tue–Fri (& Mon in Aug), 11am–midnight Sat; mid-Sep–Oct: 11am–9pm Sat, Sun; Nov: 11am–9pm Sat, Sun; Dec: noon–7:30pm Sat, Sun; Jan: noon–7:30pm daily. ⬤ 24, 25, 31 Dec, 1 Jan, last 3 weeks of Jan–Mar. 🖼 ♿ www.islamagica.es

The site of Expo '92 *(see pp68–9)*, this area has since been transformed into a complex of exhibition halls, museums and leisure spaces.

The 15th-century Carthusian Monasterio de Santa María de las Cuevas, inhabited by monks until 1836, is at the heart of the area. Columbus stayed and worked here, and it was restored as a central exhibit for Expo '92 and houses the Centro Andaluz de Arte Contemporáneo, which contains works by Andalusian artists, as well as Spanish and international art.

The centrepiece of Expo, the Lago de España, is now part of the Isla Mágica theme park. This re-creates the journeys and exploits of the explorers who left Seville in the 16th century for the New World.

Main entrance of the Carthusian Monasterio de Santa Maria de las Cuevas, founded in 1400

SEVILLE STREET FINDER

The map references given with the sights described in the Seville section of the guide refer to the maps on the following pages. Map references are also given for Seville hotels *(see pp590–91)* and restaurants *(pp640–42)*. The schematic map below shows the area of Seville covered by the *Street Finder*. The symbols used for the sights and other features are listed in the key at the foot of the page.

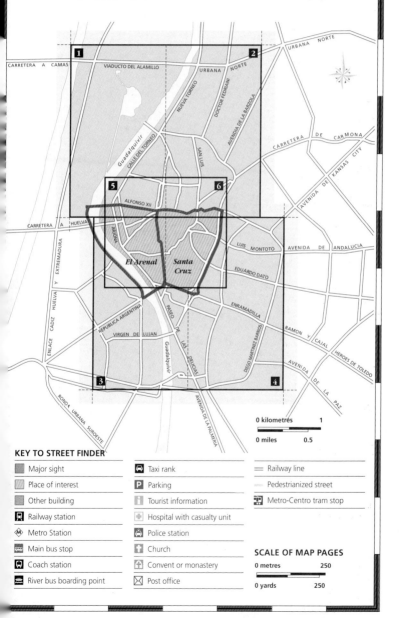

KEY TO STREET FINDER

▇	Major sight	🚕	Taxi rank	═	Railway line
▨	Place of interest	P	Parking	—	Pedestrianized street
▧	Other building	ℹ	Tourist information	🚋	Metro-Centro tram stop
🚉	Railway station	✚	Hospital with casualty unit		
Ⓜ	Metro Station	🚔	Police station		
🚏	Main bus stop	✝	Church		**SCALE OF MAP PAGES**
🚌	Coach station	⛪	Convent or monastery		0 metres 250
🛥	River bus boarding point	⊠	Post office		0 yards 250

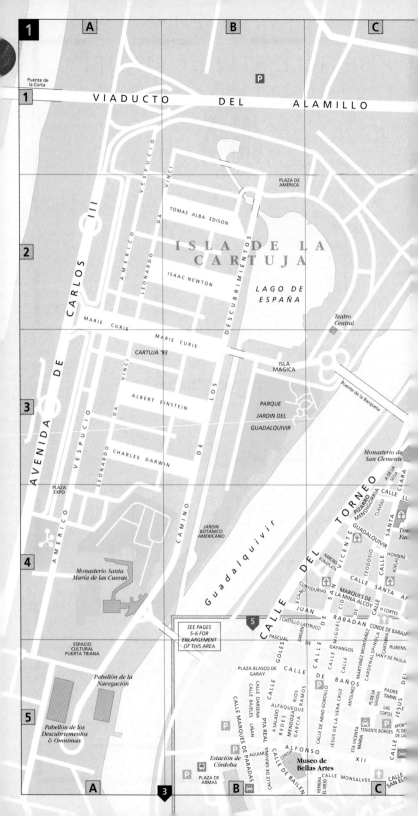

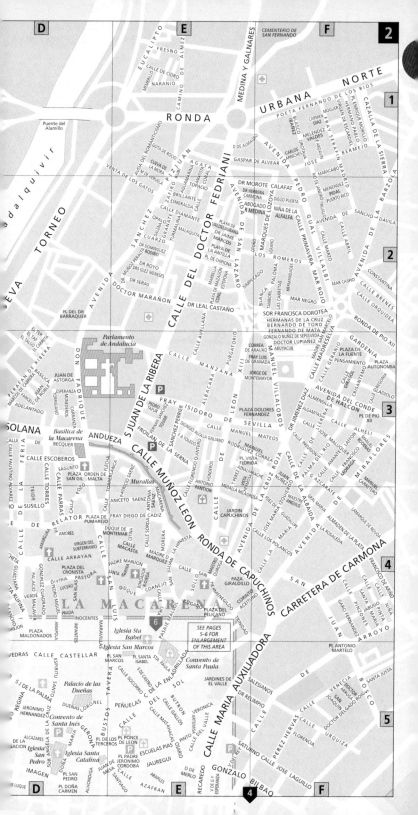

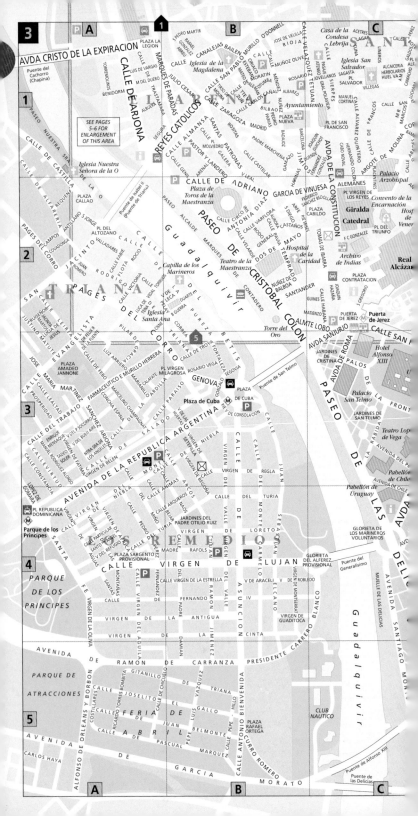

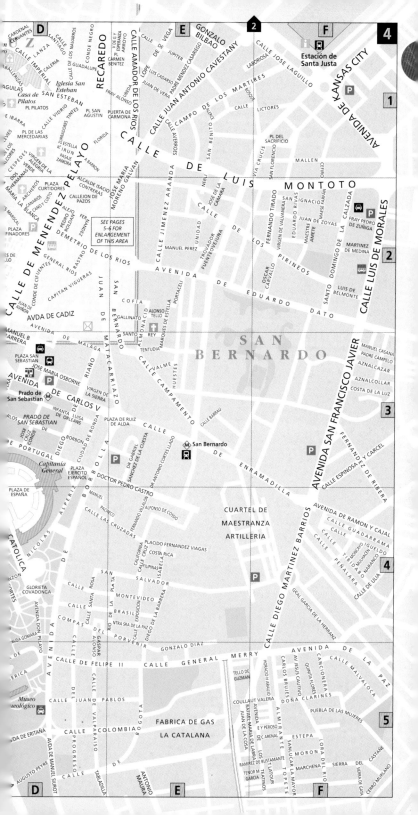

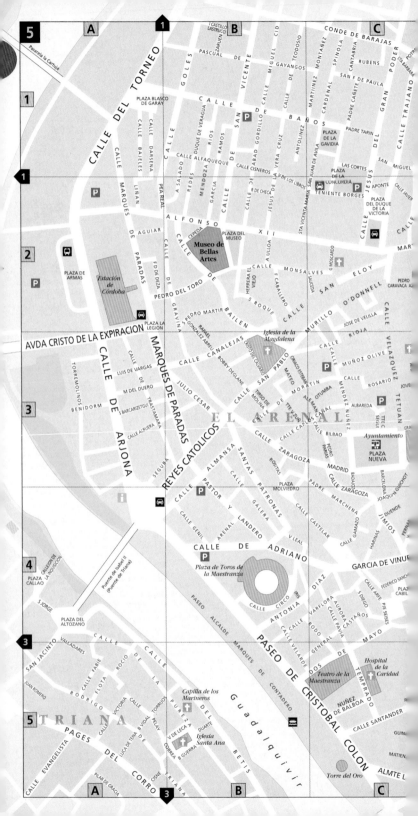

SHOPPING IN SEVILLE

The shopping experience in Seville is influenced by its culture – bustling with energy until the moment the siesta arrives, then relaxing over lunch before the frenzy begins again. Seville has a good mix of well-known chain stores and independently owned shops, and the stores in this vibrant city are as colourful and diverse as the people themselves. The main shopping district winds through

One of several styles of plate made in Seville

Calle Tetuán and Calle Sierpes and flows on towards Plaza Nueva and over to Plaza Alfalfa, where you will find a fantastic range of goods – anything from the latest fashions to unique Spanish arts and crafts. Yet more diverse items can be found while strolling along Amor de Dios toward Alameda de Hercules, where there are many wonderful Moroccan, Indian and African import shops to explore.

SPECIALIST SHOPS

The streets of Calle Cuna, Calle Francos and Calle Lineros are lined with shops that capture the flamenco spirit. **Lina Boutique** has impeccably styled, unique dresses as well as accessories. **Calzados Mayo** sells flamenco dance shoes, while beautiful handmade shawls and intricate lace *mantillas* (veils) can be found at **Juan Foronda**. Handmade *sombreros* (hats), in addition to tasteful men's accessories, are available at **Maquedano**. For a fabulous range of leather goods and fashions, **El Caballo** is the place to shop.

To relive the spirit of Semana Santa (Easter Week), religious items can be bought at **Casa Rodríguez**. If you are enraptured by the aroma of orange blossom, visit **Agua de Sevilla**, known for its scintillating range of perfumes that capture the scents of the region.

Stylish handmade *sombreros*

An array of fans at Díaz, Calle Sierpes, Seville

DEPARTMENT STORES AND GALERIAS

El Corte Inglés, Spain's national department store, has two main locations in the centre – Plaza Duque de la Victoria and Plaza Magdalena. The larger building at Plaza Duque offers clothes, shoes, cosmetics, sporting goods, a gourmet shop and a supermarket, while the smaller building stocks a good selection of music, books and art supplies. The outlet in Plaza Magdalena sells kitchenware, fine china, appliances and houses a supermarket. Formerly a train station, Plaza de Armas is the only shopping centre located in the heart of town, with shops, restaurants, bars, a nightclub, cinema and a supermarket. Nervion Plaza, the largest shopping hub close to the city centre, is lined

with shops, restaurants, bars, a cinema and a mall. All shopping centres are open from Monday to Saturday, 10am–8:30pm.

OPEN-AIR MARKETS

The lively and colourful open-air markets feature a dazzling display of unique wares and are a great way to spend a leisurely morning. Distinctive accessories and clothing can be found in the markets of Plaza Duque de Victoria and Plaza Magdalena, open all day, Thursday to Saturday.

The markets at Plaza Encarnación, El Arenal and Calle Fería (open Monday to Saturday) offer local produce, fish, meat and cheese whilst the Thursday market at Calle Fería specializes in bric-a-brac. On Sundays, stamps, coins and other collectibles are traded in Plaza del Cabildo, and the painters' market in Plaza del Museo has some beautiful displays of local art.

ANTIQUES AND CRAFTS

Antique shops are scattered throughout the city centre, mainly in Barrio Santa Cruz and Alfalfa. **Antigüedades Angel Luis Friazza** has classic Spanish furnishings, while handmade goods can be found at **El Postigo**, an arts and crafts centre. **Ocre y Imagra** boasts unique paintings, ceramics and functional artwork with Andalusian influences. Seville's great ceramic tradition is visible in the Triana district, which still has several operating ceramic workshops. Ceramic shops can also be found along Calle Sierpes and Calle Tetuán.

FOOD AND WINE

To bring home some of Seville's gastronomic specialities or to prepare a nice picnic, visit **Baco**. The gourmet shop of El Corte Inglés has exquisite luxuries for the discerning palate, as well as an ample wine cellar. For general groceries try the supermarket downstairs. Every area has several small convenience stores. For out-of-hours shopping **Open Cor** is open 9am–2am daily.

FASHION

The shops of Calle Tetuán and Calle Sierpes bustle with an exciting range of the latest fashions. For avant-garde *haute couture* with Andalusian flare, visit the Sevillian designers' boutique, **Victorio y Lucchino**. **Luchi Cabrera** has exclusive women's clothes and accessories. **Loewe** offers classic lines of clothing, luggage and accessories for both men and women, while **Zara** stocks all the latest high-street trends. For the latest styles in baby clothes, pay a visit to **Marco y Ana**.

The well-heeled of Seville shop at the vast array of shoe stores in the area as well as at the well-stocked "shoe street" of Calle Córdoba.

BOOKS AND MUSIC

Small bookshops are tucked into numerous corners of the city, but for the biggest selection of books in multiple languages, go to **Casa del Libro**. Music aficionados can find regional sounds of flamenco, Rock Andaluz and Semana Santa music at **Compás Sur Flamenco** with their impressive collection of

CDs, DVDs, books and sheet music. Also, a large selection of musical instruments and equipment can be found at **Sevilla Musical**.

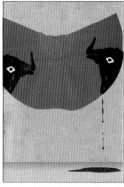

A poster advertising the quirky Flamenco Cool store

GIFTS AND SOUVENIRS

Typical souvenir shops are abundant along Avenida de la Constitución, Calle Mateos de Gago and all throughout Barrio Santa Cruz. For a truly unique experience, check out **Flamenco Cool** where local tradition morphs with the outrageous in this "Pop Flamenco" store.

DIRECTORY

SPECIALIST SHOPS

Agua de Sevilla
San Fernando 3. **Map** 3 C3, 5 D5. **Tel** 954 50 15 38.

Calzados Mayo
Alfalfa 2. **Map** 3 C1, 5 D3. **Tel** 954 22 55 55.

Casa Rodríguez
Francos 35. **Map** 3 C1, 5 D3. **Tel** 954 22 78 42.

Caballo
Plaza Nueva 12. **Map** 3 B1, 5 C3. **Tel** 954 50 08 42.

Juan Foronda
Tetuan 28. **Map** 3 C1, 5 C3. **Tel** 954 22 60 60.

Lina Boutique
Lineros 17. **Map** 3 C1, 5 D3. **Tel** 954 21 24 23.

Maquedano
Sierpes 40. **Map** 3 C1, 5 C3. **Tel** 954 56 47 71.

DEPARTMENT STORES AND GALERIAS

El Corte Inglés
Pl Duque de la Victoria 8, 13B. **Map** 1 C5, 5 C2. **Tel** 954 59 70 00.
One of several branches.

ANTIQUES AND CRAFTS

Antigüedades Angel Luis Friazza
C/ Zaragoza 48.
Map 3 B1, 5 B3.
Tel 954 22 35 67.

El Postigo
C/ Arfe s/n. **Map** 3 B2, 5 B4. **Tel** 954 56 00 13.

Ocre y Almagra
C/ Sierpes 83. **Map** 3 B2.
Tel 954 21 27 48.

FOOD AND WINE

Baco
C/ Cuna 4. **Map** 3 C1, 6 D2. **Tel** 954 21 66 73.

Open Cor
Av Sanjurjo.
Map 3 C3, 5 C5.

FASHION

Loewe
Pl Nueva 12. **Map** 3 B1, 5 C3. **Tel** 954 22 52 53.

Luchi Cabrera
C/ Cerrajería 18. **Map** 3 C1, 5 C2. **Tel** 954 21 65 17.

Marco y Ana
C/ Cuna 24. **Map** 4 C1, 6 D2. Tel 954 21 30 38.

Victorio y Lucchino
Pl. Nueva 10. **Map** 3 B1, 5 C3. **Tel** 954 50 26 60.

Zara
C/ Rioja 10. **Map** 3 B1, 5 C3. **Tel** 954 21 10 58.
One of several branches.

BOOKS AND MUSIC

Casa del Libro
C/ Velázquez 8. **Map** 3 C1, 5 C3. **Tel** 954 50 29 50.

Compás Sur Flamenco
Cuesta del Rosario 7E.
Map 3 C1, 6 D3.
Tel 954 21 56 62.

Sevilla Musical
C/ Cardinal Spinola 3. **Map** 1 C5. **Tel** 954 91 57 55.

GIFTS AND SOUVENIRS

Flamenco Cool
Amor de Diós 14. **Map** 1 C5. **Tel** 954 91 51 94.

ENTERTAINMENT IN SEVILLE

Flamenco dancer in traditional dress

Seville is universally famed as being a city of celebration and vitality, and this is reflected in its two spring festivals, Semana Santa and Feria de Abril (*see p431*). In fact, the city has a year-round programme of interesting cultural events. The modern Teatro de la Maestranza and Teatro Lope de Vega, along with a number of independent venues, host a range of dance, music, theatre and arts festivals, while the world's most important flamenco festival, the Bienal de Flamenco, takes place in the city. Seville also has an enviable selection of night spots, from the quiet, more relaxed area surrounding the cathedral to the buzzing bars of Calle Betis and the Alfalfa district. For sports fans, a local derby between Real Betis and Sevilla FC is an absolute must-see.

Decorative tile commemorating Seville's Real Betis football club

SEASONS AND TICKETS

In Seville, the arts season usually starts in September, lasting until June–July. From April to the end of the summer, the streets and open-air stages also host shows.

Two of the city's biggest events – the Bienal de Flamenco and the Bienal de Arte Contemporáneo – are biannual and take place in the autumn in even numbered years.

Tickets for major sports events, opera, concerts and festivals should be booked in advance – details can be provided by the city's tourist information offices. Football matches are very popular, so buy these in advance too.

ENTERTAINMENT GUIDES

A monthly events guide, *El Giraldillo* covers film, music, theatre, clubs, art, sport, books, gay life, travel and much more. *La Teatral*, a bimonthly publication, is specifically focused on theatre and dance.

FLAMENCO

One of the richest forms of music, flamenco embraces a broad spectrum of dancing, singing and musical styles. One venue with high-quality performances is **Los Gallos**. For something really authentic, venture out to **La Anselma**, across the river in the Triana quarter – the traditional home of the gypsy community. **La Carbonería** is an enchanting informal bar where free flamenco shows are performed daily by amateur artists.

Promoting semi-professional local artists, **Casa Carmen** in El Arenal district presents varied shows daily. As the venue is quite small, it is recommended you buy tickets in advance, or show up early to get a seat.

In Calle Betis, there are bars where the public can watch and join in with *Sevillanas*, a popular Andalusian folk dance. The **Museum of Flamenco Dance** is a good place to learn about the origins of the dance and current developments.

MUSIC AND DANCE

The setting of Bizet's *Carmen*, Rossini's *The Barber of Seville* and Mozart's *Don Giovanni* and *Figaro*, Seville is a city of opera lovers. Prestigious international opera companies perform at the elegant **Teatro de la Maestranza**, starting in December and lasting until May. This theatre is home to the Real Orquesta Sinfónica de Sevilla, whose performances are highly regarded. The annual programme of the theatre also includes chamber and classical music seasons.

A live performance of flamenco at Los Gallos

...sario Flores, the famous Andalusian singing star, ...rforming at one of her concerts

...atro Lope de Vega and ...nservatorio Superior de ...úsica Manuel Castillo are ...o other remarkable venues ...r classical music.

The Maestranza and Teatro ...ntral are the main venues ...sting a wide range of ...tional and international ...ssical and contemporary ...nce performances. Sala ...danza is the ideal venue ... smaller productions.

...CK, JAZZ AND BLUES

...w international rock ...rs make it to Seville, ...Barcelona and Madrid tend ...attract all the big names. ...wever, large concerts are ...netimes held at Estadio ...mpico. Some of Spain's

most popular groups and singers in the flamenco pop genre, such as Niña Pastori and Rosario Flores, are from Andalusia. Café Naima and Café Daoiz, have live music from local bands, including jazz, folk and rock, but the highlight of the jazz calendar in Seville has to be the International Jazz Festival, held in November at the Teatro Central.

NIGHTLIFE

The nightlife of Seville offers an endless array of possibilities for tourists and locals alike. Calle Betis, along the Triana side of the river, has many bars, restaurants and clubs. Alameda de Hércules is one of the liveliest areas, with Café Habanilla and Café Central as main bohemian hotspots. Las Columnas is the most popular tapas bar in Barrio de Santa Cruz district and Bar Garlochi is recommended for the first drink of the night. Buddha del Mar is a

fashionable nightclub in Plaza de Armas next to El Arenal. The streets surrounding Plaza de la Alfalfa overflow with youthful revellers. Frequented by Spanish celebrities, Antique in Isla de la Cartuja is the place to dance till dawn.

BULLFIGHTING

The Maestranza Bullring is mythical among fans of bullfighting and some of the most important bullfights in Spain are held here at during the Feria de Abril. The season runs from April to October. It is advisable to book in advance if the matadors are famous, and also if you want a seat in the *sombra* (shade). Tickets are sold at the *taquilla* (box office) at the bullring.

AMUSEMENT PARKS

Isla Mágica re-creates the exploits of 16th-century New World explorers. The first of the eight zones which visitors experience is Seville, port of the Indies, followed by Quetzal, the Fury of the Gods, the Gateway to the Americas, Amazonia, the Pirate's Lair and El Dorado. Fun for children of all ages.

DIRECTORY

...AMENCO

...asa Carmen
...Marqués de Paradas, 30
...ap 1B5, 5B3
...l 954 212 889.

...a Anselma
...Pages del Corro 49.
...ap 3 A2, 5 A5.

...Carbonería
...evíes 18. **Map** 3 D1,
...3. **Tel** 954 21 44 60.

...s Gallos
...de Santa Cruz 11.
...ap 3 D2, 5 E4.
...954 21 69 81.

...JSIC AND DANCE

...nservatorio
...perior de Música
...anuel Castillo
...años 48. **Map** 1 C5, 5
...**Tel** 954 91 56 30.

Sala Endanza
C/San Luís 40. **Map** 1 E4.
Tel 954 56 26 16.

Teatro de la Maestranza
Paseo de Colón 22.
Map 5 C5, 3 B2.
Tel 954 22 65 73.

Teatro Central
Av José Gálvez s/n,
Isla de la Cartuja.
Map 1 C2.
Tel 955 03 72 00.

Teatro Lope de Vega
Av María Luisa s/n.
Map 3 C3.
Tel 954 59 08 67.

ROCK, JAZZ AND BLUES

Estadio Olímpico
Isla de la Cartuja, s/n.
Map 1 B1.

Café Naima
C/Trajano 47. **Map** 1 C5,
5 C1. **Tel** 954 38 24 85.

Café Daoiz
C/Jesus del Gran Poder 27.
Map 1 C5, 5 C1.
Tel 954 22 65 73.

NIGHTLIFE

Antique
Matemáticos Rey Pastor y
Castro s/n. **Map** 1 B3. **Tel**
954 46 44 07.

Bar Garlochi
C/Boteros 26.
Map 3 C1, 6 E3.

Buddha del Mar
Pl de Armas. **Map** 3 A1, 5
A2. **Tel** 954 56 17 11.

Café Central
Pl Alameda de Hércules 64.
Map 1 D4.
Tel 954 38 73 12.

Café Habanilla
Pl Alameda de
Hércules 63.
Map 1 D4.
Tel 954 90 27 18.

Las Columnas
C/Rodrigo Caro 1.
Map 3 C2, 5 2E4.

BULLFIGHTING

Plaza de Toros de la Maestranza
Paseo de Colón 12.
Map 3 B2, 5 B4.
Tel 954 22 45 77.

AMUSEMENT PARKS

Isla Mágica
Pabellón de España,
Isla de la Cartuja.
Map 1 B2.
Tel 902 16 17 16.

ANDALUSIA

HUELVA · CÁDIZ · MÁLAGA · GIBRALTAR · SEVILLA
CÓRDOBA · GRANADA · JAÉN · ALMERÍA

*ndalusia is where all Spain's stereotypes meet. Bullfighters,
beaches, flamenco, white villages, cave houses, gaudy fiestas,
religious processions, tapas and sherry are all here in
abundance. But each is part of a larger whole, which includes great
art and architecture, nature reserves and an easy-going way of life.*

The eight provinces of Andalusia stretch across Southern Spain from the deserts of Almería to the Portuguese border. One of Spain's longest rivers, the Guadalquivir, bisects the region. Andalusia is linked to the central tableland by a pass, t h e Desfiladero de Despeñaperros. The highest peaks on the Spanish mainland are in Andalusia's Sierra Nevada.

Successive invaders left their mark on Andalusia. The Romans built cities in this southern province, which they called Baetica, among them Córdoba, its capital, and the well-preserved Itálica near Seville. It was in Andalusia that the Moors lingered longest and left their greatest buildings – Córdoba's Mezquita and the splendid palace of the Alhambra in Granada.

Inevitably, perhaps, the most visited places are the great cities and the busy Costa del Sol, with Gibraltar, a geographical and historical oddity, at its western end. But there are many attractions tucked into other corners of the region. Many of the sights of Huelva province, bordering Portugal, are associated with Christopher Columbus, who set sail from here in 1492. Film directors have put to good use the atmospheric landscapes of Almería's arid interior, which are reminiscent of the Wild West or Arabia. Discreetly concealed among the countless olive groves that cover Jaén province, but not to be missed, are Andalusia's two lovely Renaissance towns, Úbeda and Baeza.

The city of Jaén surrounded by olive groves, seen from the Castillo de Santa Catalina

Doorway into the *mihrab* (prayer niche) in the Mezquita at Córdoba

Exploring Andalusia

Andalusia is Spain's most varied region. It offers dramatic desert scenery at Tabernas, water sports on the Costa del Sol, skiing in the Sierra Nevada and sherry tasting in Jerez. Of the many nature reserves, the vast, watery Doñana teems with birdlife, while Cazorla is a rugged limestone massif. Granada and Córdoba are unmissable for their Moorish heritage; Úbeda and Baeza are Renaissance gems; and Ronda is one of dozens of superb white towns.

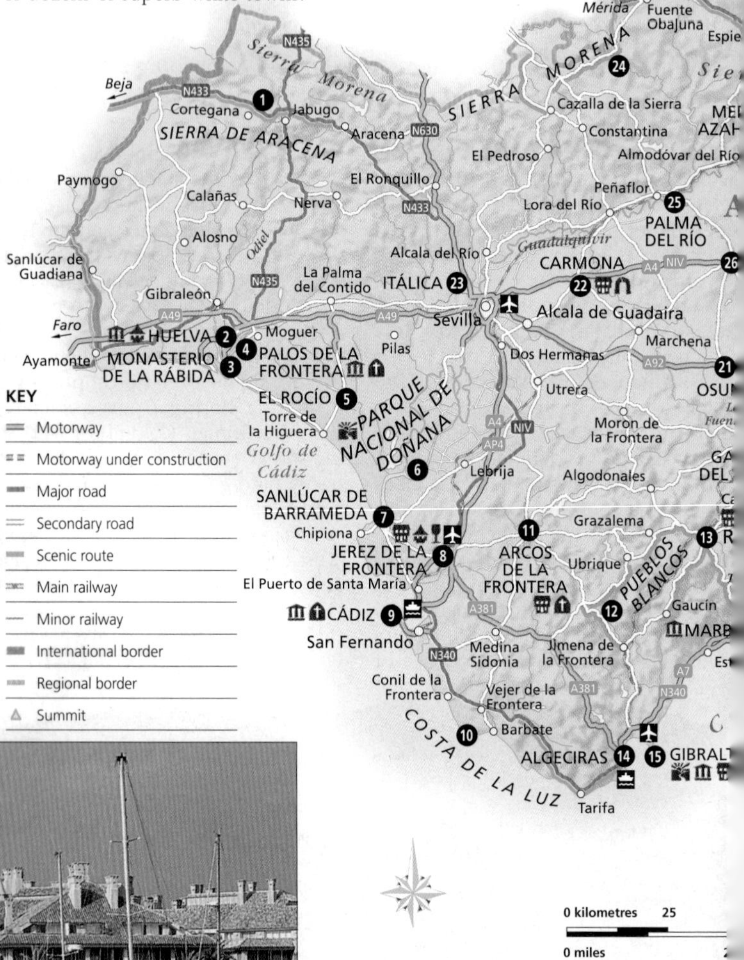

KEY

Motorway
Motorway under construction
Major road
Secondary road
Scenic route
Main railway
Minor railway
International border
Regional border
△ Summit

The smart marina at Sotogrande

0 kilometres 25

0 miles

GETTING AROUND

Andalusia has a modern motorway network, with the principal NIV A4 (E5) from Madrid following the Guada valley to Córdoba, Seville and Cádiz. The fast AVE trai links Seville and Córdoba with Madrid. Coaches cover of the region. The main airports are Málaga, Seville, Je and Gibraltar. Be aware that as Spain is in the process changing its road numbering system some of the road featured here may differ from new road signs.

SEE ALSO

- **Where to Stay** pp591–7
- **Where to Eat** pp642–8

Singers in festive spirit at a village christening

SIGHTS AT A GLANCE

Algeciras 🄌
Almería 🄺
Almuñécar 🅛
Andújar 🅜
Antequera 🄌
Arcos de la Frontera 🄌
Baeza pp498–9 🅜
Cádiz 🄌
Carmona 🄌
Córdoba pp478–81 🅜
Costa de la Luz 🄌
Écija 🄌
Garganta del Chorro 🄌
Gibraltar 🄌
Granada pp486–92 🄌
Guadix 🄌
Huelva 🄌
Itálica 🄌
Jaén 🄌

Jerez de la Frontera 🄌
La Calahorra 🄌
Lanjarón 🄌
Laujar de Andarax 🄌
Málaga 🄌
Marbella 🄌
Medina Azahara 🄌
Mojácar 🄌
Monasterio de la Rábida 🄌
Montefrío 🄌
Montilla 🄌
Nerja 🄌
Osuna 🄌
Palma del Río 🄌
Palos de la Frontera 🄌
Parque Nacional de Doñana
    pp464–5 🄌
Parque Natural de Cabo de
    Gata 🄌

Parque Natural de Cazorla 🄌
Priego de Córdoba 🄌
El Rocío 🄌
Ronda pp470–1 🄌
Sanlúcar de Barrameda 🄌
Seville see pp426–457
Sierra de Aracena 🄌
Sierra Morena 🄌
Sierra Nevada 🄌
Tabernas 🄌
El Torcal 🄌
Úbeda 🄌
Vélez Blanco 🄌

Tours
Las Alpujarras 🄌
Pueblos Blancos 🄌

The famed *jamón ibérico* hanging in a bar in Jabugo, Sierra de Aracena

Sierra de Aracena ❶

Huelva. 🚉 *El Repilado.* 🚌 *Aracena.*
🛈 *Plaza de San Pedro, s/n, Aracena,
959 12 82 06.* 🗓 *Sat.*

This wild mountain range is one of the most remote and least visited corners of Andalusia. On the hillside are the ruins of a Moorish fort. The hill is pitted with caverns and in one, the **Gruta de las Maravillas**, is a lake in a chamber hung with many stalactites.

The village of **Jabugo** is famed for its ham, *jamón ibérico*, or *pata negra (see p419)*.

Off the A–471 are the giant opencast mines at Minas de Riotinto, where iron, copper and silver have been exploited since Phoenician times. The **Museo Minero** traces the history of the Rio Tinto Company.

Bronze jug, Museo Provincial, Huelva

🦇 **Gruta de las Maravillas**
Pozo de la Nieve. **Tel** *959 12 83 55*
(for info about availability). 🕐
10am–1:30pm, 3–6pm. 🎫 🗹

🏛 **Museo Minero**
Plaza del Museo. **Tel** *959 59 00 25.* 🕐
daily. ⬤ *25 Dec, 1 & 6 Jan.* 🗹 🗹

Huelva ❷

Huelva. 🚶 *130,000.* 🚉 🚌 🛈
Avda Alemania 12, 959 25 74 03.
🗓 *Fri.* 🎉 *Las Columbinas (3 Aug).*

Founded as Onuba by the Phoenicians, Huelva had its grandest days as a Roman port. It was almost wiped out in the great Lisbon earthquake of 1755. It is an industrial city today, sprawling around the quayside on the Río Odiel.

Columbus's departure for the New World *(see p56)* from Palos de la Frontera, across the Río Odiel estuary, is celebrated in the excellent **Museo Provincial**, which also charts the history of the Rio Tinto mines.

To the east of the centre, the Barrio Reina Victoria is a bizarre example of English mock-Tudor suburban bungalows built by the Rio Tinto Company for its workers in the early 20th century. South of the town, at Punta del Sebo, the Monumento a Colón, a rather bleak statue of Columbus created by Gertrude Vanderbilt Whitney in 1929, dominates the Odiel estuary.

Environs

There are three resorts with sandy beaches near Huelva: **Punta Umbria**, on a promontory next to the bird-rich wetlands of the Marismas del Odiel; **Isla Cristina**, which is also an important fishing port and has excellent seafood restaurants; and **Mazagón** with miles of windswept dunes.

The hilly region east of Huelva known as **El Condado** produces several of Andalusia's finest wines, and Bollullos del Condado has the largest wine cooperative in the region. **Niebla**, nearby, has a Roman bridge. The town walls and 12th-century **Castillo de los Guzmanes** are both Moorish.

🏛 **Museo Provincial**
Alameda Sundheim 13. **Tel** *959 65 04 24.* 🕐 *Tue –Sun.* ♿

♟ **Castillo de los Guzmanes**
C/ Campo Castillo, Niebla. **Tel** *959 36 22 70.* 🕐 *daily.*

Monasterio de la Rábida ❸

Huelva. 🚌 *from Huelva.* **Tel** *959 35 04 11.* 🕐 *Tue–Sun.* ♿ 🗹 🗹

Four kilometres (2 miles) to the north of Palos de la Frontera is the Franciscan **Monasterio de la Rábida**, founded in the 15th century.

In 1491, a dejected Columbus sought refuge here after his plans to sail west to find the East Indies had been rejected by the Catholic Monarchs. Its prior, Juan Pérez, fatefully used his considerable influence as Queen Isabella's confessor to reverse the royal decision.

Inside, frescoes painted by Daniel Vásquez Díaz in 1930 glorify the explorer's life and discoveries. Also worth seeing are the Mudéjar cloisters, the flower-filled gardens and the beamed chapterhouse.

Frescoes depicting the life of Columbus at the Monasterio de la Rábida

For hotels and restaurants in this region see pp591–7 and pp642–8

Palos de la Frontera ❹

Huelva. 🏠 *12,000.* 🚉 ℹ️ *Parque Botánico José Celestino Mutis Paraje de la Rábida, 959 53 05 97.* 🚌 *Sat.* 🎉 *Santa María de la Rábida (3 &16 Aug).*

Columbus put to sea on 3 August 1492 from Palos, the home town of his two captains, the brothers Martín and Vicente Pinzón. Martín's former home, the **Casa Museo de Martín Alonso Pinzón**, is now a small museum of exploration, and his statue stands in the main square.

The 15th-century **Iglesia de San Jorge** has a fine portal, through which Columbus left after hearing Mass before boarding the *Santa María.* The pier is now silted up.

Environs
In the beautiful white town of **Moguer** are treasures such as the 16th-century hermitage of Nuestra Señora de Monte-mayor, and the Neo-Classical town hall *(ayuntamiento).* The **Convento de Santa Clara** and the Monasterio de San Francisco have pretty cloisters.

🏛 **Casa Museo de Martín Alonso Pinzón**
Calle Colón 24. **Tel** *959 35 01 99.* ◐ *Mon–Sat.*

⛪ **Convento de Santa Clara**
Plaza de las Monjas. **Tel** *959 37 01 07.* ◐ *Tue–Sat.* ◐ *public hols.* 🎫 ▣

El Rocío ❺

Huelva. 🏠 *2,500.* 🚉 ℹ️ *Avda de la Canaliega, 959 44 38 08.* 🎉 *Romería (May/Jun).*
www.turismodedonana.com

Bordering the Parque Nacional de Doñana *(see pp464–5)*, El Rocío is famous for its annual *romería*, which sees almost a million people converge on the village. Many of the pilgrims travel from distant parts of Spain, some on gaudily decorated ox-carts, to visit the **Iglesia de Nuestra Señora del Rocío**. A statue of the Virgin in the church is believed to have performed miraculous healings since 1280. Early on the Monday morning, men from Almonte fight to carry the statue in procession, and the crowd clambers on to the float to touch the image.

Iglesia de Nuestra Señora del Rocío, El Rocío

Crowds following the image of the Virgin at El Rocío

ANDALUSIA'S FIESTAS

Carnival *(Feb/Mar)*, Cádiz. The whole city puts on fancy dress for one of Europe's largest and most colourful carnivals. Groups of singers practise for many months to perform ditties satirizing current fashions, celebrities and politicians.
Romería de la Virgen de la Cabeza *(last Sun in Apr)*, Andújar (Jaén). A mass pilgrimage to a lonely sanctuary in the Sierra Morena.
Día de la Cruz *(first week in May)*, Granada and Córdoba. Neighbourhood groups compete to create the most colourful crosses adorned with flowers on squares and street corners.
Córdoba Patio Fiesta *(mid-May)*. Flower-decked patios in old Córdoba are opened to the public with displays of flamenco.
El Rocío *(May/Jun)*. More than 70 brotherhoods of pilgrims arrive at the village of El Rocío to pay homage to the Virgen del Rocío.
Columbus Festival *(late Jul/early Aug)*, Huelva. This celebration of Columbus's voyage is dedicated to the native music and dance of a different Latin American country every year.
Exaltación al Río Guadalquivir *(mid-Aug)*, Sanlúcar de Barrameda (Cádiz). Horses are raced on the beach at the mouth of the Río Guadalquivir.

Parque Nacional de Doñana ❻

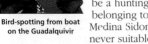

Doñana National Park is ranked among Europe's greatest wetlands. Together with its adjoining protected areas, the park covers in excess of 50,000 hectares (123,000 acres) of marshes and sand dunes. The area used to be a hunting ground *(coto)* belonging to the Dukes of Medina Sidonia. As the land was never suitable for human settlers, wildlife was able to flourish. In 1969, this large area became officially protected. In addition to a wealth of endemic species, thousands of migratory birds stop over in winter when the marshes become flooded again, after months of drought.

Bird-spotting from boat on the Guadalquivir

Shrub Vegetation
Backing the sand dunes is a thick carpet of lavender, rock rose and other low shrubs.

Prickly Juniper
This species of juniper (Juniperus oxycedrus) *thrives in the wide dune belt, putting roots deep into the sand. The trees may get buried beneath the dunes.*

Palacio del Acebrón

El Ro

La Rocina

H612

El Acebuche

Matalascañas

Palacio de Doña

Laguna de Sant

Coastal Dunes
Softly rounded, white dunes, up to 30 m (100 ft) high, fringe the park's coastal edge. The dunes, ribbed by prevailing winds off the Atlantic, shift constantly.

Monte de Doñana, the wooded area behind the sand dunes, provides shelter for lynx, deer and boar.

The Interior
The number of visitors to the park's interior is strictly controlled to ensure minimal environmental impact. The only way to view the wildlife here is on officially guided day tours.

KEY

▢	Marshes
▢	Dunes
•••	Parque Nacional de Doñana
•••	Parque Natural de Doñana
▬	Road
⋇	Viewpoint
🛈	Visitors' centre
P	Parking
🚌	Coach station

For hotels and restaurants in this region see pp591–7 and pp642–8

Deer
Fallow deer (Dama dama) *and larger red deer* (Cervus elaphus) *roam the park. Stags engage in fierce contests in late summer as they prepare for breeding.*

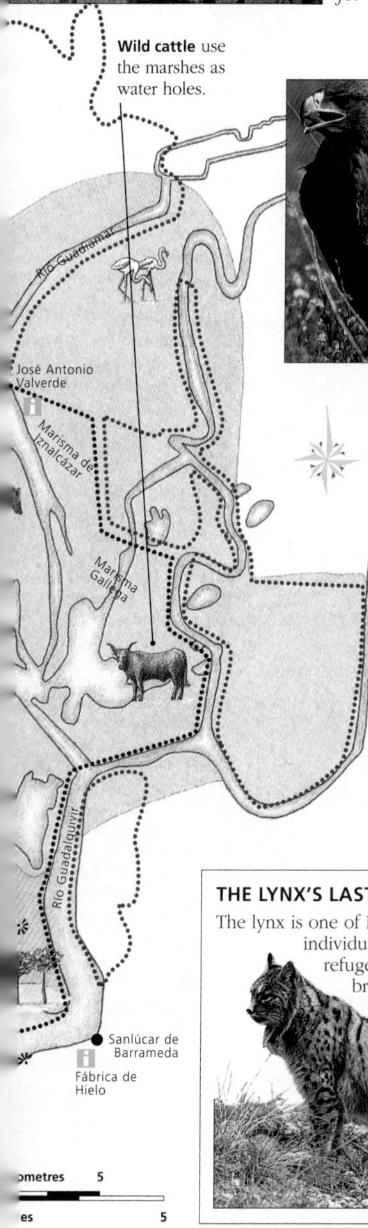

Wild cattle use the marshes as water holes.

VISITORS' CHECKLIST

Huelva & Sevilla. **Marginal areas**
⬜ daily. 🚫 1 Jan, 6 Jan, Pentecost, 25 Dec. 🚹 **La Rocina** *Tel*
959 44 23 40. 🚹 **Palacio del
Acebrón** : exhibition "Man and
Doñana". 🚹 **El Acebuche:**
reception, audiovisual exhibition,
café and shop. *Tel 959 44 87 11.*
Self-guided paths: La Rocina
and Charco de la Boca (90 min); El
Acebrón from Palacio del Acebrón
(45 min); Laguna del Acebuche
from Acebuche (45 min). **Inner
park areas** ⬜ May–Sep: Mon–
Sat; Oct–Apr: Tue–Sun. Guided
tour only. Jeeps leave from El
Acebuche at 8:30am & 3pm. Bookings *Tel 959 448 711.* 🖰 www.
turismodedonana.com

Imperial Eagle
The imperial eagle (Aquila adalberti) *is one of Doñana's rarest birds.*

Greater Flamingo
During the winter months, the salty lakes and marshes provide the beautiful, pink greater flamingo (Phoenicopterus ruber) *with crustaceans, its main diet.*

José Antonio Valverde

Marisma de IznalCázar

Marisma Gallega

Río Guadiamar

Río Guadalquivir

Sanlúcar de Barrameda

Fábrica de Hielo

ometres   5

es   5

THE LYNX'S LAST REFUGE
The lynx is one of Europe's rarest mammals. In Doñana about 30 individual Spanish lynx *(Lynx pardellus)* have found a refuge. They have yellow-brown fur with dark brown spots and pointed ears with black tufts. Research is under way into this shy, nocturnal animal, which tends to stay hidden in scrub. It feeds mainly on rabbits and ducks, but might catch an unguarded fawn.

The elusive lynx, only glimpsed with patience

Sanlúcar de Barrameda ❼

Cádiz. 🏠 *63,000.* 🚉 **ℹ** *Calzada del Ejército, 956 36 61 10.* 🛒 *Wed.* 🎉 *Exaltación al Río Guadalquivir and horse races (mid-Aug).*

A fishing port at the mouth of the Río Guadalquivir, Sanlúcar is overlooked by a Moorish **castle**. This was the departure point for Columbus's third voyage in 1498 and also for Magellan's 1519 expedition to circumnavigate the globe.

Sanlúcar is best known for its light, dry manzanilla sherry made by, among other producers, **Bodegas Barbadillo**. Boats from the quay take visitors across the river to the Parque Nacional de Doñana (*see pp464–5*).

Environs

Chipiona, along the coast, is a lively little resort town with an excellent beach. The walled town of **Lebrija**, inland, enjoys views over vineyards. Its Iglesia de Santa María de la Oliva is a reconsecrated 12th-century Almohad mosque.

🍷 **Bodegas Barbadillo**
C/ Luis de Eguilaz 11. **Tel** *956 38 55 00.* ⭘ *Tue–Sat.* 🎫 🎥 ♿

Entrance to the Barbadillo bodega in Sanlúcar de Barrameda

Jerez de la Frontera ❽

Cádiz. 🏠 *190,000.* ✈ 🚉 🚌 **ℹ** *Alameda Cristina 7, 956 34 17 11.* 🛒 *Mon.* 🎉 *Grape Harvest (Sep).*

Jerez is the capital of sherry production (*see pp420–1*) and many bodegas can be visited. Among the well-known names are **González Byass** and **Pedro Domecq**.

The city is also famous for its **Real Escuela Andaluza de Arte Ecuestre**, a school of equestrian skills. There are public dressage displays on Thursdays. If you visit on another day you may be able to watch the horses being trained. The **Palacio del Tiempo**, nearby, has one of the largest clock collections in Europe. On the Plaza de San Juan, the 18th-century **Palacio de Penmartín** houses the Centro Andaluz de Flamenco, where exhibitions give a good introduction to this music and dance tradition (*see pp424–5*). The partially restored, 11th-century **Alcázar** encompasses well-preserved mosque, now church. Just to the north is the **cathedral**. *The Sleeping Girl* by Zurbarán, is in the sacristy.

Environs

The port of **El Puerto de Santa María** exports great quantities of sherry. Here, too, several bodegas can be visited, including **Osborne** and **Terry**. The town also has a 13th-century castle and one of the largest and most famous bull rings in Spain.

🎠 **Real Escuela Andaluza de Arte Ecuestre**
Duque de Abrantes. **Tel** *956 31 96 35 (by appt).* ⭘ *Mon–Fri.* 🎫 ♿ **www**.realescuela.org

🏛 **Palacio del Tiempo**
Calle Cervantes 3. **Tel** *956 18 21 00.* ⭘ *Tue–Sun.* 🎫 ♿

🎠 **Palacio de Penmartín**
Plaza de San Juan 1. **Tel** *956 34 92 65.* ⭘ *Mon–Fri.* ● *public hols.*

♣ **Alcázar**
Alameda Vieja. **Tel** *956 31 97 98.* daily. ● *1 & 6 Jan, 25 Dec.* 🎫 ♿

🍷 **Sherry Bodegas**
⭘ *phone for tour times.* 🎫
González Byass, C/ Manuel María González 12, Jerez. **Tel** *956 35 70 00.* **Pedro Domecq,** C/ San Ildefonso 3, Jerez. **Tel** *956 15 15 00.* **Sandeman,** C/ Pizarro 10, Jerez. **Tel** *956 15 17 00.* **Osborne,** C/ de los Moros, Puerto de Santa María. **Tel** *956 85 91 00.* **Terry,** C/ Tonelero, Puerto Santa María. **Tel** *956 85 77 00.*

Real Escuela Andaluza de Arte Ecuestre, Jerez de la Frontera

For hotels and restaurants in this region see pp591–7 and pp642–8

Cádiz 9

Egyptian mask, Museo de Cádiz

Jutting out of the Bay of Cádiz, and almost entirely surrounded by water, Cádiz lays claim to being Europe's oldest city. Legend names Hercules as its founder, although history credits the Phoenicians with establishing the town of Gadir in 1100 BC. Occupied by the Carthaginians, Romans and Moors in turn, the city also prospered after the Reconquest *(see pp54–5)* on wealth taken from the New World. In 1587 Sir Francis Drake sacked the city in the first of many British attacks in the war for world trade. In 1812 Cádiz briefly became Spain's capital when the nation's first constitution was declared here *(see p63)*.

VISITORS' CHECKLIST

Cádiz. 155,000. Plaza de Sevilla, 902 24 02 02. Plaza de la Hispanidad, 902 19 92 08. Plaza de San Juan de Diós 11, 956 24 10 01. Mon. Carnival (Feb/ Mar). www.cadizturismo.com

Exploring Cádiz

The joy of visiting Cádiz is to wander along the waterfront with its well-tended gardens and open squares before exploring the old town, which is full of narrow alleys busy with market and street life.

The pride of the city is its Carnival *(see p463)* – a riotous explosion of festivities, fancy dress, singing and drinking.

Catedral

Known as the Catedral Nueva (New Cathedral) and built on the site of an older one, this Baroque and Neo-Classical church, with its dome of golden-yellow tiles, is one of Spain's largest. In the crypt is the tomb of composer Manuel de Falla (1876–1946), native of Cádiz. The cathedral's treasures are stored in the Casa de la Contaduria, behind the cathedral.

Museo de Cádiz

Plaza de Mina. **Tel** 956 21 22 81. 2:30–8:30pm Tue; 9am–8:30pm Wed–Sat; 9am–2:30pm Sun & hols.

The museum has archaeological exhibits charting the history of Cádiz and the largest art gallery in Andalusia, with works by Rubens, Zurbarán and Murillo. On the third floor is a collection of puppets made for village fiestas.

Torre Tavira

Calle Marqués del Real Tesoro 10. 956 21 29 10. daily. The city's official watchtower in the 18th century has now been converted into a camera obscura, and offers great views.

Oratorio de San Felipe Neri

This 18th-century church has been a shrine to liberalism since 1812. In that year, as Napoleon tightened his grip on Spain during the War of Independence *(see pp62–3)*, a provisional government assembled here to try to lay the foundations of Spain's first constitutional monarchy. The liberal constitution it declared was bold but ineffectual.

Zurbarán's *Saint Bruno in Ecstasy*, in the Museo de Cádiz

CÁDIZ CATHEDRAL

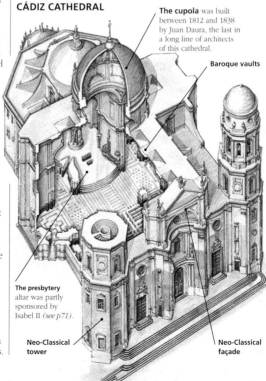

The cupola was built between 1812 and 1838 by Juan Daura, the last in a long line of architects of this cathedral.

Baroque vaults

The presbytery altar was partly sponsored by Isabel II *(see p71)*.

Neo-Classical tower

Neo-Classical façade

7ª CA-5-18-93

Fishing boats at the resort of Zahara de los Atunes on the Costa de la Luz

Costa de la Luz ⑩

Cádiz. *Cádiz.* *Cádiz, Tarifa.*
Plaza San Antonio, 956 80 70 61.

The Costa de la Luz (Coast of Light) between Cádiz and Tarifa, at Spain's southernmost tip, is an unspoiled, windswept stretch of coast characterized by strong, pure light – the source of its name. From the Sierra del Cabrito, to the west of Algeciras, it is often possible to see the outline of Tangier and the parched Moroccan landscape below the purple-tinged Rif mountains across the narrow Strait of Gibraltar.

Tarifa is named after an 8th-century Moorish commander, Tarif ben Maluk, who landed there with his forces during the Moorish conquest *(see pp52–3)*. Later, Tarifa and its 10th-century castle were defended by the legendary hero, Guzmán, during a siege by the Moors in 1292.

Tarifa has since become the windsurfing capital of Europe The breezes that blow on to this coast also drive the numer ous wind turbines visible in the hills above Tarifa.

Off the N340 (E5), at the en of a long, narrow road which strikes out across a wildernes of cacti, sunflowers and lone cork trees, is **Zahara de los Atunes**, a modest holiday resort with a few hotels. **Coni de la Frontera**, to the west, is busier and more built up.

The English admiral Nelson defeated a Spanish and Frenc fleet off **Cabo de Trafalgar** in 1805, but died in the battle.

A Tour Around the Pueblos Blancos ⑫

Instead of settling on Andalusia's plains, where they would have fallen prey to bandits, some Andalusians chose to live in fortified hilltop towns and villages. These are known as *pueblos blancos* (white towns) because they are whitewashed in the Moorish tradition *(see p26)*. They are working agricultural towns today, but touring them will reveal a host of references to the past.

Jimena de la Frontera ⑨
Set amid hills, where wild bulls graze among cork and olive trees, this town has a ruined Moorish castle.

Ubrique ②
Nestling at the foot of th Sierra de Ubrique, this *pueblo* is known for its flourishing leather indus

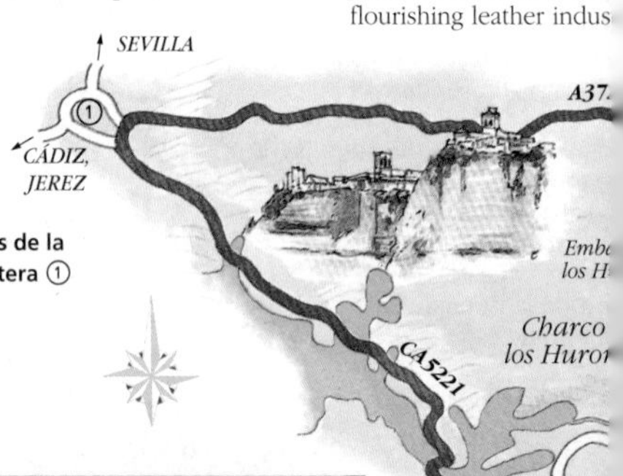
SEVILLA
CÁDIZ, JEREZ
Arcos de la Frontera ①
A37
Emb los H
Charco los Huror
CA5221
CA503
La Saucedo
0 kilometres
0 miles
5

Arcos de la Frontera ①

KEY

- Tour route
- Other roads

Gaucín ⑧
From here there are unsurpassed vistas over the Mediterranean, the Atlantic, the Rock of Gibraltar and across the strait to the Rif mountains of North Africa.

TIPS FOR DRIVERS

Tour length: *205 km (127 miles).*
Stopping-off points: *There are places to stay and eat at all of these pueblos, but Ronda has the widest range of hotels* (see p595) *and restaurants* (see p647). *Arcos has a parador* (see p592).

Arcos de la Frontera ⓫

Cádiz. 🏛 *30,000.* 🚌 ℹ️ *Plaza del Cabildo, 956 70 22 64.* 🚉 *Fri.* 🎭 *Toro del Domingo de Resurreccion (last day of Easter), Velada de Nuestra Señora de las Nieves (4–6 Aug), Semana Santa, Feria de San Miguel (end of Sep).* **www.**ayuntamientoarcos.org

Although legend has it that a son of Noah founded Arcos it is more probable that it was the Iberians. It gained the name Arcobriga in the Roman era and, under the Caliphate of Córdoba *(see p52),* became the Moorish stronghold of Medina Arkosh. It is an archetypal white town, with a labyrinthine old quarter.

On the Plaza de España, at the top of the town, are the parador *(see p592)* and the Iglesia de Santa María de la Asunción, a Late Gothic-Mudéjar building noted for its choir stalls and altarpiece. The huge, Gothic **Iglesia de San Pedro**, perched on the edge of a cliff formed by the Río Guadalete, is a striking building. Nearby is the **Palacio del Mayorazgo**, which has an ornate Renaissance façade. The **town hall** *(ayuntamiento)* has a fine Mudéjar ceiling.

Environs

In the 15th-century the Guzmán family was granted the dukedom of **Medina Sidonia**, a white west of Arcos de la Frontera. The area became one of the most important ducal seats in Spain. The Gothic Iglesia de Santa María la Coronada is the town's finest building. It contains a notable collection of Renaissance religious art.

Iglesia de Santa María de la Asunción in Arcos de la Frontera

🏛 **Palacio del Mayorazgo**
C/ San Pedro 2. **Tel** *956 70 30 13 (Casa de Cultura).* 🕘 *9am–2pm Mon–Fri.* ♿

🏛 **Ayuntamiento**
Plaza del Cabildo. **Tel** *956 70 00 02.* 🕘 *Mon–Fri.* ⬤ *public hols.*

Zahara de la Sierra ③
Fanning out below a castle ruin, this fine *pueblo blanco* has been declared a national monument.

Grazalema ④
This village in the Sierra de Grazalema has the highest rainfall in Spain.

Ronda la Vieja ⑤
Significant remains of the Roman town of Acinipo, including a theatre, can be visited.

Setenil ⑥
Some of the streets of this unusual white town, which climbs up the sides of a gorge, are covered by rock overhangs. The gorge was carved out of volcanic tufa rock by the Río Trejo.

Ronda ⑦
(see pp470–71)

Street-by-Street: Ronda ⓭

Plate hand-painted in Ronda

One of the most spectacularly located cities in Spain, Ronda sits on a massive rocky outcrop, straddling a precipitous limestone cleft. Because of its impregnable position this town was one of the last Moorish bastions, finally falling to the Christians in 1485.

On the south side perches a classic Moorish *pueblo blanco (see pp468–9)* of cobbled alleys, window grilles and dazzling whitewash – most historic sights are in this part of the town. Located in El Mercadillo, the newer town, is one of the oldest bullrings in Spain.

★ Puente Nuevo
An impressive feat of 18th-century civil engineering, the "New Bridge" over the 100-m (330-ft) deep Tajo gorge joins old and new Ronda.

Convento de Santo Domingo was the local headquarters of the Inquisition *(see p274).*

To El Mercadillo, Plaza de Toros, parador *(see p595)* and tourist information

Casa del Rey Moro
From this 18th-century mansion, built on the foundations of a Moorish palace, 365 steps lead down to the river.

Mirador El Campillo (viewpoint)

SANTO DOMI

CALLE ARMIÑ

TENORIO

PLAZA DEL CAMPILLO

0 metres   75
0 yards   75

★ Palacio Mondragón
Much of this palace was rebuilt following the Reconquest (see pp54–55), but its arcaded patio is adorned with original Moorish mosaics and plasterwork.

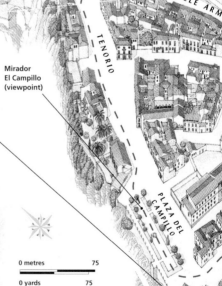

STAR SIGHTS

★ Puente Nuevo

★ Palacio Mondragón

For hotels and restaurants in this region see pp591–7 and pp642–8

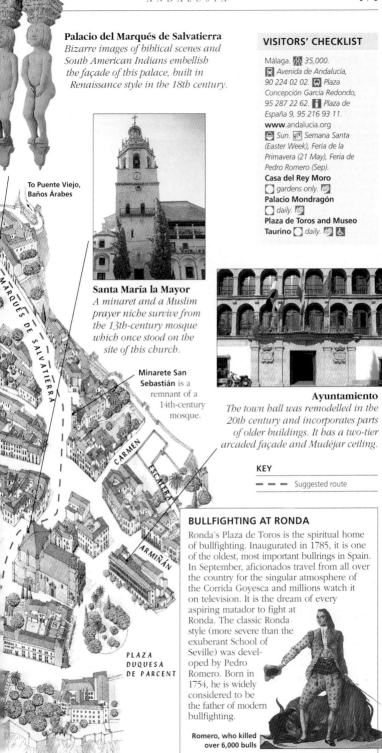

Palacio del Marqués de Salvatierra
Bizarre images of biblical scenes and South American Indians embellish the façade of this palace, built in Renaissance style in the 18th century.

To Puente Viejo, Baños Árabes

MARQUÉS DE SALVATIERRA

Santa María la Mayor
A minaret and a Muslim prayer niche survive from the 13th-century mosque which once stood on the site of this church.

Minarete San Sebastián is a remnant of a 14th-century mosque.

CARMEN

ESCALERA

ARMIÑÁN

PLAZA DUQUESA DE PARCENT

VISITORS' CHECKLIST

Málaga. 35,000. Avenida de Andalucia, 90 224 02 02. Plaza Concepción García Redondo, 95 287 22 62. Plaza de España 9, 95 216 93 11. www.andalucia.org Sun. Semana Santa (Easter Week), Feria de la Primavera (21 May), Feria de Pedro Romero (Sep).
Casa del Rey Moro gardens only.
Palacio Mondragón daily.
Plaza de Toros and Museo Taurino daily.

Ayuntamiento
The town hall was remodelled in the 20th century and incorporates parts of older buildings. It has a two-tier arcaded façade and Mudéjar ceiling.

KEY

--- Suggested route

BULLFIGHTING AT RONDA

Ronda's Plaza de Toros is the spiritual home of bullfighting. Inaugurated in 1785, it is one of the oldest, most important bullrings in Spain. In September, aficionados travel from all over the country for the singular atmosphere of the Corrida Goyesca and millions watch it on television. It is the dream of every aspiring matador to fight at Ronda. The classic Ronda style (more severe than the exuberant School of Seville) was developed by Pedro Romero. Born in 1754, he is widely considered to be the father of modern bullfighting.

Romero, who killed over 6,000 bulls

Algeciras ⑭

Cádiz. 🏛 *200,000.* 🚉 ℹ *Calle Juan de la Cierva, 956 78 41 31.* 🚌 *Tue.* 🎪 *Feria Real (24 Jun–2 Jul).*

From the industrial city of Algeciras, there are spectacular views of Gibraltar, 14 km (9 miles) away across its bay. The city is a major fishing port and Europe's main gateway for ferries to North Africa, especially Tangier and Spain's territories of Ceuta and Melilla.

Gibraltar ⑮

British Crown Colony. 🏛 *35,000.* 🚉 ℹ *Duke of Kent House, Cathedral Square, 9567 749 50.* 🎪 *Nat Day (10 Sep).* **www**.*gibraltar.gi*

The high, rocky headland of Gibraltar was signed over to Britain "in perpetuity" at the Treaty of Utrecht in 1713 *(see p62).* Today, about 4 million people stream across the border annually from La Línea de la Concepción in Spain.

Among the chief sights of Gibraltar are those testifying to its strategic military importance over the centuries. Halfway up the famous Rock are an 8th-

St Michael's Cave, which served as a hospital during World War II

century Moorish castle, whose **keep** is still used as a prison, and 80 km (50 miles) of **siege tunnels** housing storerooms and barracks. **St Michael's Cave**, which served as a hospital during World War II, is now used for classical concerts.

The **Apes' Den**, near Europa Point, Gibraltar's southern-most tip, is home to the tailless apes. Legend says that the British will keep the Rock only as long as the apes remain there, despite the machinations of politicans.

A cable car takes visitors to the **Top of the Rock** at 450 m (1,475 ft). **Gibraltar Museum** charts the colony's history.

🏰 **The Keep, Siege Tunnels, St Michael's Cave, Apes' Den**
Upper Rock Area. *Tel 9567 749 50.* ⏰ *daily.* ⬤ *1 Jan, 25 Dec.* 🎫

🏛 **Gibraltar Museum**
18 Bombhouse Lane. *Tel 9567 742 89.* ⏰ *Mon–Sat.* ⬤ *public hols.* 🎫

The Costa del Sol

Thanks to its average of 300 days' sunshine a year and its varied coastline, the Costa del Sol, between Gibraltar and Málaga, offers a full range of beach-based holidays and water sports. Complementing the sophistication and luxury of Marbella are many other popular resorts aimed at the mass market. More than 30 of Europe's finest golf courses lie just inland.

Puerto Banús is Marbella ostentatious marina. The expensive shops, restaur and glittering nightlife re the wealth of its clientel

Estepona's quiet evenings make it popular with families with young children. Behind the big hotels are old squares shaded by orange trees.

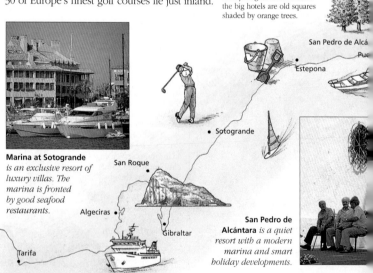

San Pedro de Alcá
Pue
Estepona
Sotogrande
San Roque
Algeciras
Gibraltar
Tarifa

Marina at Sotogrande *is an exclusive resort of luxury villas. The marina is fronted by good seafood restaurants.*

San Pedro de Alcántara *is a quiet resort with a modern marina and smart holiday developments.*

Yachts and motorboats in the exclusive marina of Marbella – the summer home of the international jet set

Marbella ⓖ

Málaga. 120,000. Glorieta de la Fontanilla, Paseo Marítimo, 95 77 14 42. Mon. San Bernabé (Jun). **www**.marbella.com

Marbella is one of Europe's most exclusive holiday resorts, frequented by royalty and film stars. In winter, the major attraction is the golf. Among the delights of the old town, with its spotlessly clean alleys, squares, and smart shops and restaurants, is the **Iglesia de Nuestra Señora de la Encarnación**.

The **Museo del Grabado Español Contemporáneo** displays some of Picasso's least-known work. The beaches are named Babaloo, Victor's, Don Carlos, Cabopino and Las Dunas.

🏛 Museo del Grabado Español Contemporáneo
C/ Hospital Bazan. Tel 95 276 57 41.
Tue–Sat. public hols.

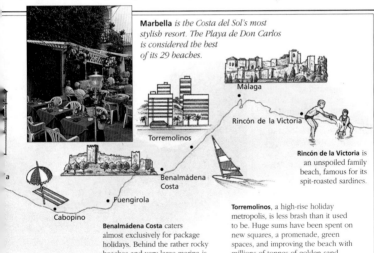

Marbella *is the Costa del Sol's most stylish resort. The Playa de Don Carlos is considered the best of its 29 beaches.*

Málaga

Rincón de la Victoria

Torremolinos

Rincón de la Victoria is an unspoiled family beach, famous for its spit-roasted sardines.

Benalmádena Costa

Fuengirola

Cabopino

Benalmádena Costa caters almost exclusively for package holidays. Behind the rather rocky beaches and very large marina is a plethora of tourist attractions.

Torremolinos, a high-rise holiday metropolis, is less brash than it used to be. Huge sums have been spent on new squares, a promenade, green spaces, and improving the beach with millions of tonnes of golden sand.

Cabopino, on a not-too-crowded stretch of coast, is a wide, sandy nudist beach beside a modern marina.

kilometres   10

miles   10

Fuengirola *still has an active fishing port – as these boxes of fresh fish suggest – although it is better known today as a package-holiday resort with a chiefly British clientele. It has a spectacular backdrop of steep, ochre mountains.*

473

The main façade of Málaga's cathedral, consecrated in 1588

Málaga ⑰

Málaga. 🏠 650,000. 🛫 🚂 🚌 🚢
🛈 Avda de Cervantes, 1 Paseo del
Parque, 95 221 41 20. 🚌 Sun. 🎭
Carnival (Feb/Mar), Feria (second
Sat–third Sun of Aug).
www.malagaturismo.com

Málaga, the second largest city in Andalusia, is today a thriving port, just as it was in Phoenician times, and again under the Romans and then the Moors. It also flourished during the 19th century, when sweet Málaga wine *(see p420)* was one of Europe's most popular drinks – until phylloxera ravaged the area's vineyards in 1876.

The **cathedral** was begun in 1528 by Diego de Siloé, but it is a bizarre mix of styles. The half-built second tower, abandoned in 1765 when funds ran out, gave the cathedral its nickname: La Manquita ("the one-armed one").

Málaga's former Museo de Bellas Artes is being adapted to house a new **Museo Picasso** displaying works by the native artist. The **Casa Natal de Picasso**, where the painter spent his early years, is now the Picasso Foundation.

Málaga's vast **Alcazaba** *(see p53)* was built between the 8th and 11th centuries. There is a partially excavated Roman amphitheatre by its entrance, but the real attraction is the display of Phoenician, Roman and Moorish artifacts in the **Museo Arqueológico**

On the hill directly behind the Alcazaba are the ruins of the **Castillo de Gibralfaro**, a 14th-century Moorish castle.

Environs
In the beautiful hills to the north and east of Málaga is the **Parque Natural de los Montes de Málaga**. Wildlife, such as eagles and wild boars, thrive here amid the scent of lavender and wild herbs. Walkers can follow a number of scenic marked trails. Going north on the C345 you can also visit a small preserved winery of the 1840s.

🏛 **Museo de Picasso**
Calle San Agustín 8. **Tel** 95 260 27 31.
🕐 Tue–Sat. 🔴 25 Dec & 1 Jan 🈲

⚓ **Alcazaba and Museo Arqueológico**
Calle Alcazabilla. **Tel** 95 221 60 05.
🕐 Tue–Sun.

Garganta del Chorro ⑱

Málaga. 🚂 El Chorro. 🚌 Parque
Ardeles. 🛈 Avenida de la
Constitución, Álora, 95 249 55 77.

Up the fertile Guadalhorce valley, beyond the village of El Chorro, is one of the geographical wonders of Andalusia.

The Garganta del Chorro is an immense chasm, 180 m (590 ft) deep and in places only 10 m (30 ft) wide, cut by the river through a limestone mountain. Downstream, a hydroelectric plant detracts from the wildness of the place.

The **Camino del Rey** is a catwalk clinging to the rock face which leads to a bridge across the gorge. It is, however, closed to the public.

Environs
Álora, a classic white town *(see p468)* with a ruined Moorish castle and an 18th-century church, lies 12 km (7 miles) down the valley.

Along the twisting MA441 from Álora is the village of **Carratraca**. In the 19th and early 20th centuries, Europe's highest society travelled here for the healing powers of the sulphurous springs. These days, Carratraca has a faded glory – water still gushes out at 700 litres (155 UK and 185 US gal) a minute and the outdoor baths remain open, but they are little used.

The Garganta del Chorro, rising high above the Guadalhorce River

/eathered limestone formations in El Torcal

:l Torcal 19

ʼálaga. Antequera. Ante-
ɹera. Antequera, 95 270 25 05.

massive exposed hump of mestone upland, which has een slowly weathered into izarre rock formations and ıves, the Parque Natural del ɔrcal is very popular with ːkers. Footpaths lead from a sitors' centre in the middle. /alks of up to two hours are ıarked by yellow arrows; ·nger walks by red.

The park is also a pleasure ·r natural historians, with fox ıd weasel populations, and ɔlonies of eagles, hawks and ılltures. It also protects rare ants and flowers, among em species of wild orchid.

ntequera 20

ʼılaga. 42,000. Pl
ı Sebastián 7, 95 270 25 05.
ɜ. Ferias (end May & mid-Aug).
ww.aytoantequera.com

ıis busy market town was ategically important first as ɔman Anticaria and later as Moorish border fortress fending Granada.

Of its many churches, the **ıesia de Nuestra Señora del rmen**, with its vast Baroque arpiece, is not to be ssed. At the opposite end the town is the 19th-ntury **Plaza de Toros**, with a ıseum of bullfighting.

The hilltop **castle** was built the 13th century on the site a Roman fort. Visitors can ılk round the castle walls by proaching through the 16th-century Arco de los Gigantes. There are excellent views of Antequera from the Torre del Papabellotas on the best-preserved part of the wall.

In the town below, the 18th-century **Palacio de Nájera** is the setting for the Municipal Museum, the star exhibit of which is a splendid Roman bronze statue of a boy.

The massive **dolmens**, just outside the town, are thought to be the burial chambers of tribal leaders and date from around 2500–2000 BC.

Environs

Laguna de la Fuente de Piedra, north of Antequera, teems with bird life, including huge flocks of flamingoes, which arrive to breed after wintering in West Africa. A road off the N334 leads to a lakeside viewing point. There is a visitors' centre in Fuente de Piedra village. To the east, also off the N334, is **Archidona**, with its 18th-century, octagonal Plaza Ochavada built in French style, but which also incorporates traditional Andalusian features.

The triumphal, 16th-century Arco de los Gigantes, Antequera

Plaza de Toros
Carretera de Sevilla. ***Tel*** *95 270 81 42.* *Tue–Sun.* **Museo Taurino** *Sat, Sun, public hols.*

Palacio de Nájera
Coso Viejo. ***Tel*** *95 270 40 21.*
Tue –Sun. *Mon.*

Osuna 21

Sevilla. *17,500.*
Plaza Mayor, 95 481 57 32.
Mon. *San Alcadio (12 Jan), Virgen de la Consolación (8 Sep).*

Palacio del Marqués de la Gomera, in Osuna, completed in 1770

Osuna was once a key Roman garrison town. It rose again to prominence in the 16th century under the Dukes of Osuna, who wielded immense power. In the 1530s they founded the **Colegiata de Santa María**, a grand church with a Baroque reredos and paintings by José de Ribera. This was followed in 1548 by the **University**, a rather severe building with a beautiful patio. Some fine mansions, among them the **Palacio del Marqués de la Gomera**, also reflect the town's former glory.

Environs

To the east lies **Estepa**, whose modern-day fame rests on its biscuits – *polvorones* and *mantecados* *(see p419)*. The Iglesia del Carmen has a black and white, Baroque façade.

Tomb of Servilia in the Roman necropolis in Carmona

Carmona ㉒

Sevilla. 👥 25,000. 🚍 🚹 Alcázar de la Puerta de Sevilla, 95 419 09 55. 🚍 Mon & Thu. 🎪 Feria (May), Fiestas Patronales (8–16 Sep). **www**. turismo.carmona.org

Carmona is the first major town east of Seville, its old quarter built on a hill above the suburbs on the plain. Beyond the **Puerta de Sevilla**, a gateway in the Moorish city walls, is a dense cluster of mansions, Mudéjar churches, and winding streets.

The Plaza de San Fernando has a feeling of grandeur which is characterized by the Renaissance façade of the old **Ayuntamiento**. The present town hall, set just off the square, dates from the 18th century; in its courtyard are some Roman mosaics. Close by is the **Iglesia de Santa María la Mayor**. Built in the 15th century over a mosque, whose patio still survives, this is the finest of Carmona's churches.

Dominating the town are the ruins of the **Alcázar del Rey Pedro**, once a palace of Pedro I, known as Pedro the Cruel. Parts of it now form a parador *(see p592)*.

Just outside Carmona is the **Necrópolis Romana**, the extensive remains of a Roman burial ground. A site museum displays some of the items found in the graves, including statues, glass and jewellery.

🏛 **Ayuntamiento**
Calle Salvador 2. **Tel** 95 414 00 11. 🕐 Mon–Fri. ⬤ public hols.

🏛 **Necrópolis Romana**
Avenida Jorge Bonsor 9. **Tel** 95 414 08 11. 🕐 Tue–Sun. ⬤ Mon & Sun in summer; public hols.

Itálica ㉓

Sevilla. **Tel** 95 562 22 66. 🚍 from Seville. 🕐 Apr–Sep: 8:30am–8:30pm Tue–Sat, 9am–3pm Sun; Oct–Mar: 9am–5:30pm Tue–Sat, 10am–4pm Sun. 🖼

Roman mosaic from Itálica

Itálica was founded in 206 BC by Scipio Africanus. One of the earliest Roman cities in Hispania *(see pp50–1)*, it grew to become important in the 2nd and 3rd centuries AD. Emperor Hadrian, who was born in the city and reigned from AD117–138, added marble temples and other grand buildings.

Archaeologists have speculated that the changing course of the Río Guadalquivir may have led to Itálica's later demise during Moorish times.

Next to the vast but crumbling **amphitheatre** is a display of finds from the site. More treasures are displayed in the Museo Arqueológico in Seville *(see p445)*.

The traces of Itálica's streets and the mosaic floors of some villas can be seen. However, little survives of the city's temples or of its baths as most of the stone and marble has been plundered over the centuries.

Some well-preserved Roman baths and a theatre can be seen in **Santiponce**, a village just outside the site.

Sierra Morena ㉔

Sevilla and Córdoba. 🚍 Cazalla, 95 883 562, & Constantina, 955 881 297. 🚍 Constantina, Cazalla. 🚹 El Robledo, 95 588 15 97.

The Sierra Morena, clad in oak and pine woods, runs across the north of the provinces of Sevilla and Córdoba It forms a natural frontier between Andalusia and the plain of neighbouring Extremadura and La Mancha. Smaller sierra (ranges of hills) within the Sierra Morena chain are also named individually.

Fuente Obejuna, north of Córdoba, was immortalized Lope de Vega *(see p290)* in h play about an uprising in 14 against a local overlord. The Iglesia de San Juan Bautista **Hinojosa del Duque** is a vast church in both Gothic and R naissance styles. **Belalcázar** i dominated by the huge tow of a ruined 15th-century cast Storks nest on the church towers of the plateau of **Val de los Pedroches**, to the east

Cazalla de la Sierra, the main town of the sierra nort of Seville, is cosmopolitan, and popular with young *Sevillanos* at weekends. A unique concoction of cherry liqueur and aniseed, Liquor Guindas, is produced here. **Constantina**, to the east, is more peaceful and has supe views across the countryside

A cow grazing in the pastures of the Sierra Morena north of Sevil

Palma del Río ㉕

Córdoba. 🏛 19,400. 🚇 🚌
🚉 Cardenal Portocarrero, 957 64 43
0. 🛍 Tue. 🎪 Ferias (19–21 May &
13–20 Aug). www.palmadelrio.es

The Romans sited a strategic
settlement here, on the road
between Córdoba and Itálica,
almost 2,000 years ago. The
remains of the 12th-
century city walls are a
reminder of the town's
frontier days under the
Almohads (see p54).

The **Iglesia de
la Asunción**, a
Baroque church,
dates from the 18th
century. The **Mona-
sterio de San
Francisco** is now a
hotel (see p595),
and guests can eat
dinner in the 15th-
century refectory
of the Franciscan
monks.

Palma del Río is
the home town of
El Cordobés, one
of Spain's most
famous matadors. His
biography, Or I'll Dress You in
Mourning, paints a vivid
picture of life in the town and
the hardship which followed
the end of the Civil War.

**Tower,
Asunción**

Environs

One of the most dramatic
silhouettes in Southern Spain
breaks the skyline of
Almodóvar del Río. The
Moorish castle – parts of it
dating from the 8th century –
stands on a hilltop over-
looking the whitewashed
town and fields of cotton.

Castillo de Almodóvar
Río
957 63 51 16. ⭘ daily. 🎫

Écija ㉖

Sevilla. 🏛 40,000. 🚌 🛈 Plaza de
España 1, Ayuntamiento 95 590 29
33 🛍 Thu. 🎪 Feria (21–24 Sep).
www.turismoecija.com

Écija is nicknamed "the frying
pan of Andalusia" owing to
its famously torrid climate. In
the searing heat, the palm
trees on the Plaza de España

provide blissful shade. An
ideal place to sit and observe
daily life passing by, this is
also a spot for evening strolls.

Écija has 11 Baroque church
steeples, many adorned with
gleaming azulejos (see p438),
and together they make a
very impressive sight. The
most florid of these is the
Iglesia de Santa María, which
overlooks the Plaza de España.
The **Iglesia de San Juan**, with
its exquisite, brightly coloured
bell tower, is a very close rival.

Of the many mansions along
Calle Caballeros, the Baroque
Palacio de Peñaflor is worth a
visit. Its pink marble doorway
is topped by twisted columns,
while an attractive wrought-
iron balcony runs along the
whole front façade.

🏛 Palacio de Peñaflor
C/ Caballeros 32. **Tel** 95 483
02 73. ⭘ daily (courtyard only).

Medina Azahara ㉗

Córdoba. **Tel** 957 35 55 06. 🚌 Córdoba. ⭘ 10am–6:30pm Tue–Sat (to
8:30pm 16 Sep–30 Apr), 10am–2pm
Sun & public hols. 🎫

Just a few kilometres north of
Córdoba lies this once
glorious palace. Built in the
10th century for Caliph Abd al
Rahman III, it is named after
his favourite wife, Azahara. He
spared no expense, employ-

Detail of wood carving in the
main hall of Medina Azahara

ing more than 15,000 mules,
4,000 camels and 10,000 workers to bring building materials
from as far as North Africa.

The palace is built on three
levels and includes a mosque,
the caliph's residence and fine
gardens (see pp422–23).
Marble, ebony, jasper and
alabaster once adorned its
many halls, and it is believed
that shimmering pools of
quicksilver added lustre.

The glory was short-lived.
The palace was sacked by Berber invaders in 1010 and over
subsequent centuries it was
ransacked for its building materials. Now, the ruins give only
glimpses of its former beauty
– a Moorish main hall, for
instance, decorated with
marble carvings and a carved
wood ceiling. The palace is
currently being restored.

Trompe l'oeil on the ornate Baroque façade of the Palacio de Peñaflor, Écija

Street-by-Street: Córdoba ⑳

Statue of Maimónides

The heart of Córdoba is the old Jewish quarter, situated to the west of the Mezquita's towering walls. A walk around this area gives the sensation that little has changed since the 10th century when this was one of the greatest cities in the Western world. Wrought ironwork decorates cobbled streets too narrow for cars, where silversmiths create fine jewellery in their workshops. Most of the chief sights are here, while modern city life takes place some blocks north, around the Plaza de Tendillas. To the east of this square is the Plaza de la Corredera, a 17th-century arcaded square with a daily market.

Sinagoga
Hebrew script covers this 14th-century synagogue. Spain's other synagogues are in Toledo, Madrid and Barcelona.

The Capilla de San Bartolome
This small Church was built in the Gothic-Mudéjar style. It is decorated with elaborate plasterwork and tiles.

Museo Taurino, the museum of bullfighting, is closed for renovation.

★ Alcázar de los Reyes Cristianos
Water terraces fountains add to the tranquil atmosphere of the gardens belonging to the palace-fortress of the Catholic Monarchs (see pp56–7), built in the 14th century.

KEY

– – – Suggested route

STAR SIGHTS

★ Alcázar de los Reyes Cristianos

★ Mezquita

The Callejón de las Flores
brims with colourful geraniums, which contrast with the whitewashed walls of this alley, leading to a tiny square.

VISITORS' CHECKLIST

Córdoba. 🕎 330,000. 🚉
Glorieta de las Tres Culturas, 902
24 02 02. 🚌 Glorieta de las Tres
Culturas, 957 40 40 40. 🚹
Palacio de Congresos, Calle Torri-
jos 10, 957 35 51 79. 🚩 Tue, Fri
& Sun. 🎉 Semana Santa (Easter
Week), Festival de los Patios
(5–11 May), Feria (late May).
Sinagoga ◯ Tue–Sun. 🗺
Museo Taurino ⬤ renovations.
🗺 **Alcázar de los Reyes
Cristianos** ◯ Tue–Sun. 🗺
www.andalucia.org

The Palacio
Episcopal
now houses
the tourist
office.

MAGISTRAL GONZÁLEZ FRANCÉS

QUEBRADO

CORREGIDOR

**Puerta del
Puente**

The Puente Romano
spans the Río Guadal-
quivir and is still sup-
ported by its original
Roman foundations.

HERRERO

BOSCO

TORRIJOS

DOR DE LOS RÍOS

RONDA DE ISASA

RESA DE JORNET

★ **Mezquita**
*The mighty walls
of the Great Mosque
(see pp480 –81) hide
delicate arches, pillars
and a dazzling* mihrab.

metres   100
yards   100

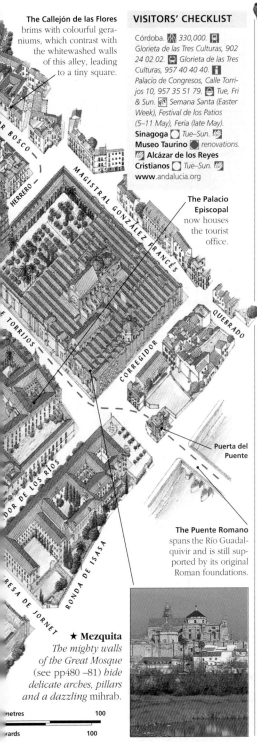

Moorish bronze stag from Medina
Azahara, Museo Arqueológico

Exploring Córdoba
Córdoba lies on a sharp bend
in the Río Guadalquivir, which
is spanned by a Roman bridge
linking the 14th-century Torre
de la Calahorra and the old
town. One of the most atmospheric squares in Andalusia is
the Plaza de los Capuchinos.
With its haunting stone calvary
surrounded by wrought-iron
lamps, it is particularly evocative when seen by moonlight.

🏛 Museo de Bellas Artes
Plaza del Potro 2. **Tel** 957 47 13 14.
◯ Tue–Sun.
Exhibits in a former charity
hospital include sculptures
by local artist Mateo Inurria
(1867–1924) and works by
Valdés Leal, Zurbarán and
Murillo of the Seville School.

🏛 Museo Arqueológico
Plaza Jerónimo Páez 7. **Tel** 957 47
40 11. ◯ Tue–Sat. 🗺
Located in a Renaissance
mansion, displays include
Roman mosaics, pottery and
relief carvings, and impressive
finds from the Moorish era.

🏛 Palacio de Viana
Plaza Don Gome 2. **Tel** 957 49 67
41. ◯ Mon–Sat. ⬤ Sun, for 15
days in June, public hols. 🗺 📷
Furniture, tapestries, paintings
and porcelain are displayed in
the 17th-century former home
of the Viana family.

🏛 Museo Romero de Torres
Plaza del Potro 1. **Tel** 957 49 19 09.
◯ Tue–Sun. 🗺 (free Fri).
Julio Romero de Torres (1874–
1930), who was born in this
house, captured the soul of
Córdoba in his paintings.

Córdoba: the Mezquita

Córdoba's Great Mosque, dating back 12 centuries, embodied the power of Islam on the Iberian Peninsula. Abd al Rahman I *(see p52)* built the original mosque between 785 and 787. The building evolved over the centuries, blending many architectural forms. In the 10th century al Hakam II made some of the most lavish additions, including the elaborate *mihrab* (prayer niche) and the *maqsura* (caliph's enclosure). During the 16th century a cathedral was built in the heart of the reconsecrated mosque, part of which was destroyed.

Patio de los Naranjos
Orange trees grow in the courtyard where the faithful washed before prayer.

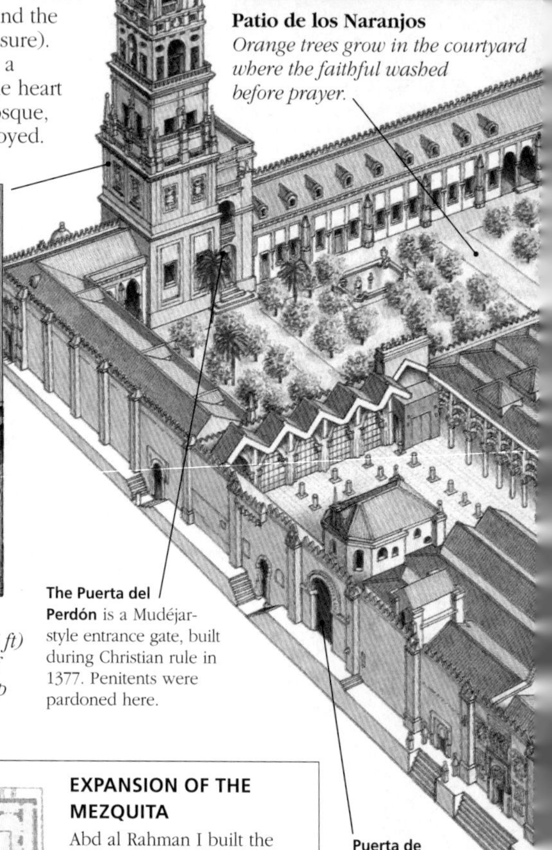

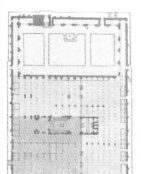

Torre del Alminar
This bell tower, 93 m (305 ft) high, is built on the site of the original minaret. Steep steps lead to the top for a fine view of the city.

The Puerta del Perdón is a Mudéjar-style entrance gate, built during Christian rule in 1377. Penitents were pardoned here.

Puerta de San Esteban is set in a section of wall from an earlier Visigothic church.

EXPANSION OF THE MEZQUITA

Abd al Rahman I built the original mosque. Extensions were added by Abd al Rahman II, al Hakam II and al Mansur.

KEY TO ADDITIONS

- ☐ Mosque of Abd al Rahman I
- ☐ Extension by Abd al Rahman II
- ☐ Extension by al Hakam II
- ☐ Extension by al Mansur
- ☐ Patio de los Naranjos

STAR FEATURES

★ Mihrab

★ Capilla de Villaviciosa

★ Arches and Pillars

Cathedral
Part of the mosque was destroyed to accommodate the cathedral, started in 1523. Featuring an Italianate dome, it was designed chiefly by members of the Hernán Ruiz family.

VISITORS' CHECKLIST

Calle Torrijos 10. **Tel** 957 47 05 12. ☐ Apr–Jun: 10am–7:30pm; Jul– Oct: 10am–7pm; Nov & Feb: 10am–6pm, Dec & Jan: 10am–5:30pm, Mar: 10am–7pm Mon–Sat. ☐ ☐ 9:30am Mon–Sat; 11am, noon & 1pm Sun & hols.

The cathedral choir has Churrigueresque stalls carved by Pedro Duque Cornejo in 1758.

Capilla Mayor

Capilla Real

★ **Arches and Pillars**
More than 850 columns of granite, jasper and marble support the roof, creating a dazzling visual effect. Many were taken from Roman and Visigothic buildings.

★ **Mihrab**
This prayer niche, richly ornamented, held a gilt copy of the Koran. The worn flag-stones indicate where pilgrims circled it seven times on their knees.

★ Ca
*The f
was b
in 13
p55) c
lobed a*

Baroque statuary in the Fuente del Rey at Priego de Córdoba

Montilla ㉙

Córdoba. ⚑ *23,000*. 🚍 🚆 ❟ *Capitán Alonso de Vargas 3, 957 65 24 62.* ⛺ *Fri.* ⚑ *Grape Harvest (late Aug).*

Montilla is the centre of an important wine region that produces an excellent smooth white fino *(see p420)*. Unlike sherry, it is not fortified with alcohol. Several bodegas, including **Alvear** and **Pérez Barquero**, will show visitors around by prior arrangement.

The Mudéjar **Convento de Santa Clara** dates from 1512. The town library is in the **Casa del Inca**, so named because Garcilaso de la Vega, who wrote about the Incas, lived there in the 16th century.

Environs

Aguilar, 13 km (8 miles) to the south, has the unusual, eight-sided Plaza de San José (built in 1810) and several seigneurial houses.

Baena, 40 km (25 miles) to the west of Montilla, has been famous for its olive oil since Roman times. On the Plaza de la Constitución is the Casa del Monte, a mansion dating from the 18th century. At Easter thousands of costumed drummers take to the streets.

Bodega Alvear
┆a María Auxiliadora 1. **Tel** *957 66*
◯ *Mon–Sat.* ⬤ *public hols.*

┐a Pérez Barquero
┆dalucía 27. **Tel** *957 65*
┐–Fri. ⬤ *public hols.*

Priego de Córdoba ㉚

Córdoba. ⚑ *23,000*. 🚍 ❟ *Calle del Río 33, 957 70 06 25.* ⛺ *Sat.* ⚑ *Feria Real (1–5 Sep).* **www**.aytopriegodecordoba.es

Priego de Córdoba's claim to be the capital of Cordoban Baroque is borne out by the dazzling work of carvers, ironworkers and gilders in the many houses, and especially churches, built with wealth generated by a prosperous 18th-century silk industry.

A restored Moorish fortress stands in the whitewashed medieval quarter, the **Barrio de la Villa**. Close by is the outstanding **Iglesia de la Asunción**, converted from Gothic to Baroque style by Jerónimo Sánchez de Rueda. Its pièce de résistance is the sacristy, created in 1784 by local artist Francisco Javier Pedrajas. The main altar is Plateresque *(see p25)*.

At midnight every Saturday the brotherhood of another Baroque church, the **Iglesia de la Aurora**, parades the streets singing songs in praise of the Virgin.

La Asunción, Priego de Córdoba

Silk merchants built many of the splendid mansions that follow the curve around the Calle del Río. At the street's end is the Baroque Fuente del Rey (The King's Fountain). The 139 spouts splash water into three basins adorned with a riot of statuary.

Environs

Zuheros, perched on a crag in the limestone hills northwest of Priego, is one of Andalusia's prettiest villages. **Rute**, to the southwest, is known for its *anís (see p607)*.

Alcalá la Real, in the lowlands east of Priego, is overlooked by the hilltop ruins of a castle and a church. There are two hand some Renaissance buildings on its central square: the Fuente de Carlos V and the Palacio Abacia

Montefrío ㉛

Granada. ⚑ *7,000*. 🚍 ❟ *Plaza España 1, 958 33 60 04.* ⛺ *Mon.* ⚑ *Fiesta patronal (14–18 Aug).*

The approach to Montefrío from the south offers wonder ful views of its tiled rooftops and pretty whitewashed hous es running up to a steep crag

This archetypal Andalusian town is topped by the remains of its Moorish fortifications and the 16th-century Gothic **Iglesia de la Villa**, attributed to Diego de Siloé. In the centre of town i the Neo-Classical **Iglesia de la Encarnación**, identifiable by its large dome. The architect Ventu Rodríguez (1717–85 is credited with its design. Th town is known for its chorize

Environs

Santa Fé was built by the Catholic Monarchs at the en of the 15th century. Their arn

Barrels of Montilla, the sherry-like wine from the town of the same name

urants in this region see pp591–7 and pp642–8

he castle overlooking the resort of Almuñécar on the Costa Tropical

amped here while laying
ege to Granada, and this was
e site of the formal surrender
the Moors in 1492 *(see*
56–7). A Moor's severed
ead, carved in stone, adorns
e spire of the parish church.
Sited above a gorge, **Alhama
Granada** was named Al hamma
ot springs) by the Moors. Their
ths, close to the spot where
e hot water gushes from the
ound just outside town, can
seen in the Hotel Balneario.
Loja, on the Río Genil, near
s Infiernos gorge, is known
"the city of water" because
its spring-fed fountains.

erja ❷

aga. 👥 *18,000.* 🚌 **ℹ** *Calle
rta del Mar 2, 95 252 15 31.*
Sun. 🎭 *Feria (9–12 Oct).*
w.nerja.org

s well-established resort,
t on a cliff above sandy
es, lies at the foot of the
utiful Sierra de Almijara.
re are sweeping views up
down the coast from the
y promontory known as
alcón de Europa (the
ony of Europe). Along it
a promenade lined with
s and restaurants.
st of the town are the
as de Nerja, a series of
caverns which were dis-
red in 1959. Wall paint-
found here are believed
about 20,000 years old.
a few of the many cathe-
sized chambers are open
blic view. One of these
een converted into an
essive auditorium which
capacity of several
red people.

Environs
In **Vélez-Málaga**, the ruins of the
Fortaleza de Belén, a Moorish
fortress set dramatically on a
rocky outcrop, dominates the
medieval Barrio de San Sebastián.

🎟 **Cuevas de Nerja**
Carretera de las Cuevas de Nerja.
Tel *95 252 95 20.* 🕐 *daily.* 🖼

Almuñécar ❸

Granada. 👥 *22,000.* 🚌 **ℹ** *Avda
Europa, 958 63 11 25.* 🚌 *Fri, 1st Sat
of each month.* 🎭 *Virgen de la Antigua (15 Aug).* **www**.almunecar.info

Almuñécar lies on the Costa
Tropical, so named because its
climate allows the cultivation of

exotic fruit. Just inland, mountains rise to more than 2,000
m (6,560 ft). The Phoenicians
founded the first settlement
here, called Sexi, and the
Romans constructed an aqueduct, the remains of which can
be seen today. Almuñécar is
now a popular holiday resort.
Above the old town is the
castle, which was built by the
Moors and altered in the 16th
century. Below it is the **Parque
Ornitológico** (comprising an
aviary and botanic gardens)
and the ruins of a Roman fish-
salting factory. The **Museo
Arqueológico** displays a variety of Phoenician artifacts.

Environs
The ancient white town of
Salobreña is set amid fields
of sugar cane. Narrow streets
lead up a hill, first fortified by
the Phoenicians, to a restored
Arab castle with fine views of
the Sierra Nevada *(see p485)*.
Modern buildings now line
part of Salobreña's beach.

🌳 **Parque Ornitológico**
Plaza de Abderraman. **Tel** *958 63
11 25.* 🕐 *daily.* 🖼

🏛 **Museo Arqueológico**
Casco Antiguo. 🕐 *Tue–Sun.* 🖼

⛪ **Castillo de Salobreña**
Calle Andrés Segovia. **Tel** *958 61 03
14.* 🕐 *Tue–Sun.* 🖼 📷

One of the succession of sandy coves that make up the resort of Nerja

The majestic peaks of the Sierra Nevada towering, in places, to over 3,000 m (9,800 ft) above sea level

Lanjarón ㉞

Granada. 🏘 24,000. 🚉 🛈 *Plaza de la Constitución 29, 958 77 00 02.* 🗓 *Tue & Fri.* 🎉 *San Juan (24 Jun).*

Scores of clear, snow-fed springs bubble from the slopes of the Sierra Nevada; their abundance at Lanjarón, on the southern side of this great range of mountains, has given the town a long history as a health spa. From June to October, visitors flock to take the waters for arthritic, dietary and nervous ailments. Bottled water from Lanjarón is sold all over the country.

A major festival begins on the night of 23 June and ends in an uproarious water battle in the early hours of 24 June, the Día de San Juan. Every-one in the streets gets douse◦

The town is on the thresho◦ of Las Alpujarras, a scenic u◦ land area of dramatic land-scapes, where steep, terrace◦ hillsides and deep-cut valley◦ conceal remote, whitewashe◦ villages. Roads to and from Lanjarón wind slowly and d◦ zily around the slopes.

A Tour of Las Alpujarras ㉟

The fertile, upland valleys of Las Alpujarras, clothed with chestnut, walnut and poplar trees, lie on the southern slopes of the Sierra Nevada. The architecture of the quaint white villages which cling to the hillsides – compact clusters of irregularly shaped houses with tall chimneys sprouting from flat, grey roofs – is unique in Spain. Local specialities are ham cured in the cold, dry air of Trevélez and brightly coloured, handwoven rugs.

Trevélez ④
Trevélez, in the shadow of Mulh◦ Spain's highest mountain, is fam◦ for its cured ham.

Poqueira Valley ②
Capileira, Bubión and Pampaneira are three villages typical of Las Alpujarras in this pretty river valley.

▲ *MULHACÉN*
3,479 m
11,410 ft

S I E◦

Pórtugos

Pitres

Guade◦

GR421

GR413

A348
LANJARÓN ①
GRANADA

A5◦

S I E R R A   D E

Orgiva ①
This is the largest town of the region, with a Baroque church in the main street and a lively Thursday market.

Fuente Agria ③
People come to this spring to drink the iron-rich, naturally carbonated waters.

Laujar de Andarax ㊱

Almería. 🏘 *2,000.* 🚌 ℹ️
*Carretera Laujar–Berja km 1, 950 51
35 48.* 📅 *3 & 17 of each month.*
🎉 *San Vicente (22 Jan), San Marcos
(25 Apr), Virgen de la Salud (19 Sep).*

Laujar, in the arid foothills
of the Sierra Nevada
looks southwards
across the Andarax
valley towards the
Sierra de
Gádor.
  Andarax
was founded
by one of the
grandsons of
Noah. In the
16th century, Abén
Humeya, leader of
the greatest Morisco
rebellion *(see p59),*
made his base here.
The revolt was
crushed by Christian troops
and Abén Humeya was killed
by his own followers. Inside

Laujar's 17th-century church,
La Encarnación, is a statue of
the Virgin by Alonso Cano.
Next to the Baroque **town hall**
(ayuntamiento) is a fountain
inscribed with some lines
written by Francisco
Villespesa, a dramatist and
poet who was born in Laujar
in 1877: *"Six fountains has my
    pueblo/He who drinks
      their waters/ will never
        forget them/so heav-
          enly is their taste."*
            El Nacimiento,
          a park to the
        east of Laujar,
        is a suitable
        place to have
        a picnic. You
        can accompa-
ny it with one of
the area's hearty
red wines. **Ohanes**,
above the Andarax

**Painting, Iglesia de
la Encarnación**

valley further to the
east, is an attractive
hill town of steep streets and
whitewashed houses known
for its crops of table grapes.

Sierra Nevada ㊲

Granada. 🚌 *from Granada.*
ℹ️ *Plaza de Andalucía, Cetursa
Sierra Nevada, 958 24 91 19.*
www.sierranevadaski.com

Fourteen peaks more than
3,000 m (9,800 ft) high crown
the Sierra Nevada. The snow
lingers until July and begins
falling again in late autumn.
One of Europe's highest
roads, the GR411, runs past
Solynieve, an expanding ski
resort at 2,100 m (6,890 ft),
and skirts the two highest
peaks, **Pico Veleta** at 3,398 m
(11,149 ft) and **Mulhacén** at
3,482 m (11,420 ft).
  The Sierra's closeness to the
Mediterranean and its altitude
account for the great diversity
of the indigenous flora and
fauna found on its slopes – the
latter including golden eagles
and some rare butterflies.
  There are several mountain
refuges for the use of serious
hikers and climbers.

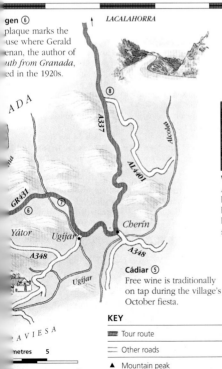

gen ⑥
plaque marks the
use where Gerald
enan, the author of
uth from Granada,
ed in the 1920s.

Puerto de la Ragua ⑧
This pass, which leads across the
mountains to Guadix, is nearly
2,000 m (6,560 ft) high and is often
snowbound in winter.

Válor ⑦
Abén Humeya, leader of a rebellion
by Moriscos in the 16th century, was
born here. A commemorative battle
between Moors and Christians is
staged each year in mid-September.

Cádiar ⑤
Free wine is traditionally
on tap during the village's
October fiesta.

TIPS FOR DRIVERS

Tour length: 85 km (56 miles).
Stopping-off points: There are
bars and restaurants in Orgiva,
Capileira, Bubión (see p643) and
Trevélez. Orgiva, Bubión and
Trevélez have good hotels (see
pp592–96). Orgiva is the last
petrol stop before Cádiar.

KEY

▬▬ Tour route

═══ Other roads

▲ Mountain peak

Granada ③⑧

Stone relief, Museo Arqueológico

The guitarist Andrés Segovia (1893–1987) described Granada as a "place of dreams, where the Lord put the seed of music in my soul". It was first occupied by the Moors in the 8th century, and its golden period came during the rule of the Nasrid dynasty *(see p55)* from 1238 to 1492, when artisans, merchants, scholars and scientists all contributed to the city's international reputation as a centre for culture. Under Christian rule, following its fall to the Catholic Monarchs in 1492 and the expulsion of the Moors *(see pp56–7)*, the city blossomed in Renaissance splendour. There was a period of decline in the 19th century, but Granada has recently been the subject of renewed interest and efforts are being made to restore parts of it to their past glory.

Façade of Granada Cathedral

Exploring Granada

The old city centre around the cathedral is a maze of narrow one-way streets. It contains the Alcaicería – a reconstruction of a Moorish bazaar that burned down in 1843. Granada's two main squares are the Plaza Bib-Rambla, near the cathedral, and the Plaza Nueva. From the latter, Cuesta de Gomérez leads up to the city's two principal monuments: the Alhambra and the Generalife. On a hill opposite is the Albaicín district.

Churches well worth a visit are the Iglesia de San Juan de Dios, almost overwhelming in its wealth of Baroque decoration, and the Renaissance Iglesia de San Jerónimo.

🔒 Cathedral

C/ Gran Vía 5. **Tel** 958 22 29 59.
⬜ daily. 🖼
On the orders of the Catholic Monarchs, work on the cathedral began in 1523 to plans in a Gothic style by Enrique de

Egas. It continued under the Renaissance maestro, Diego de Siloé, who also designed the façade and the magnificent Capilla Mayor. Under its dome, 16th-century windows depict Juan del Campo's *The Passion*. The west front was designed by Alonso Cano, who was born in the city. His grave can be seen in the cathedral.

🔒 Capilla Real

C/ Oficios 3. **Tel** 958 22 78 48.
⬜ daily. ⬤ Dec 25, Jan 1, Good Fri.
The Royal Chapel was built for the Catholic Monarchs between 1506 and 1521 by Enrique de Egas. A magnificent *reja* (grille) by Maestro Bartolomé de Jaén encloses the high altar and the Carrara marble figures of Fernando and Isabel, their daughter Juana la Loca (the Mad) and her husband Felipe el Hermoso (the Fair). Their coffins are in the crypt. In the sacristy there are art treasures, including paintings by Botticelli and Van der Weyden.

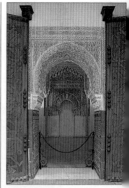

Entrance to the Moorish *mihrab* in the Palacio de la Madraza

🏛 Palacio de la Madraza

Calle Oficios 14. **Tel** 958 24 34 84.
⬜ Mon–Fri 8am–10pm.
Originally an Arab university (now part of Granada University), this building later became the city hall. The façade is 18th century. The Moorish hall has a finely decorated *mihrab* (prayer niche).

🏛 Corral del Carbón

Calle Mariana Pineda. **Tel** 958 22 5
90. ⬜ 10.30am–1.30pm, 5pm–8p
Mon–Sat; 9am–2pm Sun.
This galleried courtyard, onc
a storehouse and inn, is a re
of the Moorish era. In Christi
times it was a theatrical venu
and later a coal exchange.
Today it houses craft shops a
a cultural centre.

🏛 Casa de los Tiros

Calle Pavaneras. **Tel** 958 22 10 72
⬜ 2:30pm–8.30pm Tue, 9am–
8:30pm Wed–Sat, 9am–2.30pm Su
This palace was built in
Mudéjar style in the 1500s.
It originally belonged to the
family that was awarded th
Generalife after the fall of

Grille by Maestro Bartolomé de Jaén enclosing the altar of the Capilla

Cupola in the sanctuary of the Monasterio de la Cartuja

VISITORS' CHECKLIST

Granada. 241,000. 12 km
(7 miles) southwest of city.
Avenida Andaluces, 902 24
02 02. Carretera de Jaen,
958 18 54 80. Santa Ana 4,
958 57 52 02. Sat & Sun.
Semana Santa (Easter), Día de
la Cruz (3 May), Corpus Christi
(May/Jun). www.granadatur.com

Granada. Among their possessions was a sword that had belonged to Boabdil. This is carved on the façade, along with statues of Mercury, Hercules, and Jason. The building owes its name to the muskets projecting from its battlements: *tiro*, meaning shot.

Alhambra and Generalife
See pp490–92.

El Bañuelo
Carrera del Darro 31. *Tel 958 22 97 38.* 10am–2pm Tue–Sat. public hols.
These Arab baths were built in the 11th century. The columns are topped by Visigothic, Roman and Arab capitals.

Museo Arqueológico
Carrera del Darro 43. *Tel 958 22 56 40.* Tue–Sun. public hols.

This museum occupies the Casa de Castril, a Renaissance mansion with a Plateresque (*see p25*) portal. It displays Iberian, Phoenician and Roman finds from Granada province.

Monasterio de la Cartuja
Paseo de la Cartuja. *Tel 958 16 19 32.* Founded in 1516 by Christian warrior, El Gran Capitán, this monastery outside Granada has a dazzling cupola by Antonio Palomino, and a Churrigueresque (*see p25*) sacristy by Luis de Arévalo and Luis Caballo.

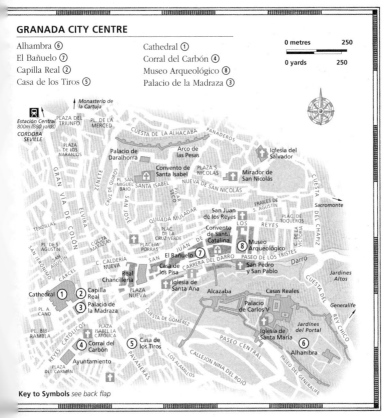

GRANADA CITY CENTRE

Alhambra ⑥
El Bañuelo ⑦
Capilla Real ②
Casa de los Tiros ⑤
Cathedral ①
Corral del Carbón ④
Museo Arqueológico ⑧
Palacio de la Madraza ③

Key to Symbols see back flap

Street-by-Street: the Albaicín

Ornate plaque on a house in the Albaicín

This corner of the city, clinging to the hillside opposite the Alhambra, is where one feels closest to Granada's Moorish ancestry. A fortress was first built here in the 13th century and there were once over 30 mosques. Most of the city's churches were built over their sites. Along the cobbled alleys stand *cármenes*, villas with Moorish decoration and gardens, secluded from the world by their high walls. In the jasmine-scented air of evening, take a walk up to the Mirador de San Nicolás. The view over the maze of rooftops of the Alhambra glowing in the sunset is magical.

Street in the Albaicín
Steep and sinuous, the Albaicín's streets are truly labyrinthine. Many street names start with Cuesta, *meaning slope.*

Real Chancillería
Built in 1530 by the Catholic Monarchs, the Royal Chancery has a beautiful Renaissance façade.

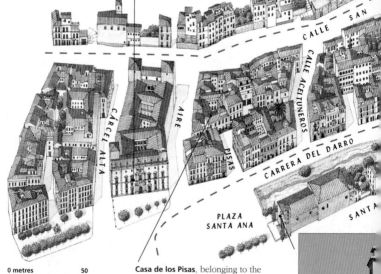

CALLE SAN
CALLE ACEITUNEROS
CÁRCEL ALTA
AIRE
PISAS
CARRERA DEL DARRO
PLAZA SANTA ANA
SANTA

0 metres 50
0 yards 50

Casa de los Pisas, belonging to the Knights Hospitallers, displays works of art – some depicting St John of God, who died here in 1550.

STAR SIGHTS
★ Iglesia de Santa Ana
★ El Bañuelo
★ Museo Arqueológico

★ **Iglesia de Santa Ana**
At the end of the Plaza Nueva stands this 16th-century brick church in Mudéjar style. It has an elegant Plateresque portal and, inside, a coffered ceiling.

Carrera del Darro
The road along the Río Darro leads past crumbling bridges and the fine façades of ancient buildings, now all restored.

★ **Museo Arqueológico**
The ornate Plateresque carvings on the museum's façade include this relief of two shields. They show heraldic devices of the Nasrid kings of Granada, who were defeated by the Catholic Monarchs in 1492 (see pp56–7).

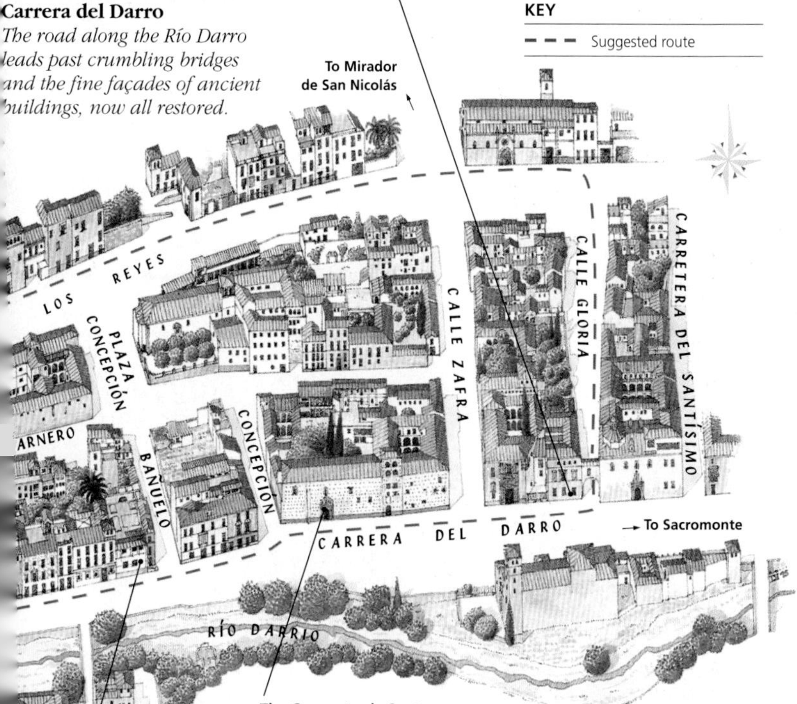

To Mirador de San Nicolás

KEY
- - - Suggested route

LOS REYES

PLAZA CONCEPCIÓN

ARNERO

BAÑUELO

CONCEPCIÓN

CALLE ZAFRA

CALLE GLORIA

CARRETERA DEL SANTÍSIMO

CARRERA DEL DARRO

To Sacromonte

RÍO DARRO

The **Convento de Santa Catalina** was founded in 1521.

El Bañuelo
-shaped openings in the ults let light into these well-erved Moorish baths, which e built in the 11th century.

SACROMONTE

Granada's gypsies formerly lived in the caves honey-combing this hillside. In the past, travellers would go there to enjoy spontaneous outbursts of flamenco. Today, virtually all the gypsies have moved away, but touristy flamenco shows of variable quality are still performed here in the evenings (see pp424–5). Sitting at the very top of the hill is the Abadía del Sacromonte, a Benedictine monastery. The ashes of St Cecilio, Granada's patron saint, are kept inside.

Gypsies dancing flamenco, 19th century

The Alhambra

A magical use of space, light, water and decoration characterizes this most sensual piece of architecture. It was built under Ismail I, Yusuf I and Muhammad V, caliphs when the Nasrid dynasty *(see pp54–5)* ruled Granada. Seeking to belie an image of waning power, they created their idea of paradise on Earth. Modest materials were used (plaster, timber and tiles), but they were superbly worked. Although the Alhambra suffered pillage and decay, including an attempt by Napoleon's troops to blow it up, in recent times it has undergone extensive restoration and its delicate craftsmanship still dazzles the eye.

Sala de la Barca

★ Salón de Embajadores
The ceiling of this sumptuous throne room, built from 1334 to 1354, represents the seven heavens of the Muslim cosmos.

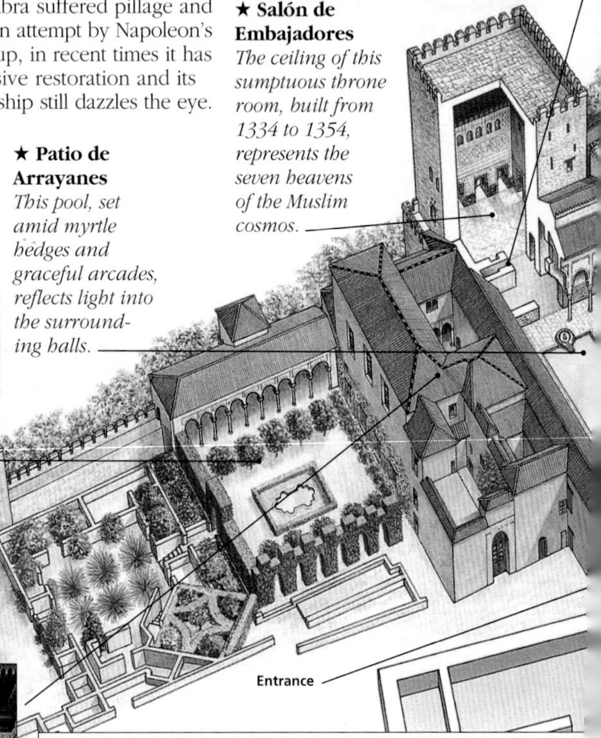

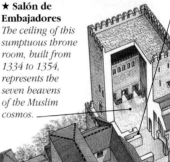

★ Patio de Arrayanes
This pool, set amid myrtle hedges and graceful arcades, reflects light into the surrounding halls.

Patio de Machuca

Entrance

Patio del Mexuar
This council chamber, completed in 1365, was where the reigning sultan listened to the petitions of his subjects and held meetings with his ministers.

PLAN OF THE ALHAMBRA

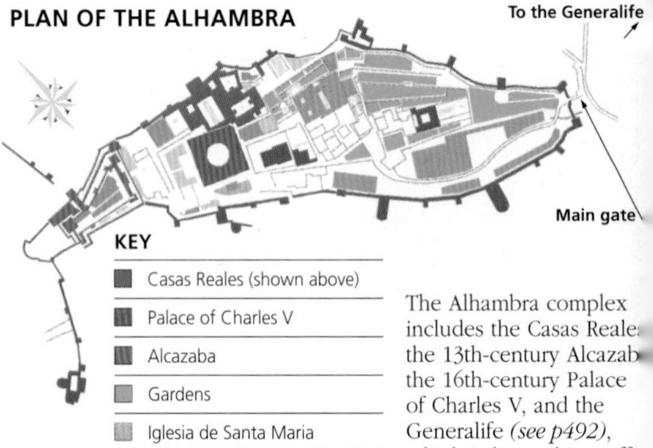

To the Generalife

Main gate

KEY

- ■ Casas Reales (shown above)
- ■ Palace of Charles V
- ■ Alcazaba
- ■ Gardens
- ■ Iglesia de Santa Maria
- ■ Other buildings

The Alhambra complex includes the Casas Reales, the 13th-century Alcazaba, the 16th-century Palace of Charles V, and the Generalife *(see p492)*, which is located just off the map.

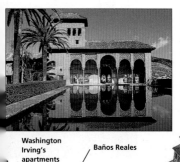

Palacio del Partal

A pavilion with an arched portico and a tower is all that remains of this palace, the oldest building in the Alhambra.

VISITORS' CHECKLIST

For the Alhambra and Generalife. **Tel** 902 44 12 21. **Reservations** (essential) **Tel** 902 22 44 60. www.alhambratickets.com 🔲 2. ⏰ Mar–Oct: 8:30am–8pm daily; Nov–Feb: 8:30–6 daily. **Last adm:** 1 hr before closing. **Night visits:** Mar–Oct: 10 & 10:30pm Tue–Sat; Nov–Feb: 8 & 8:30pm Fri–Sat. 🔳 📷 🍴 www.alhambra-patronato.es

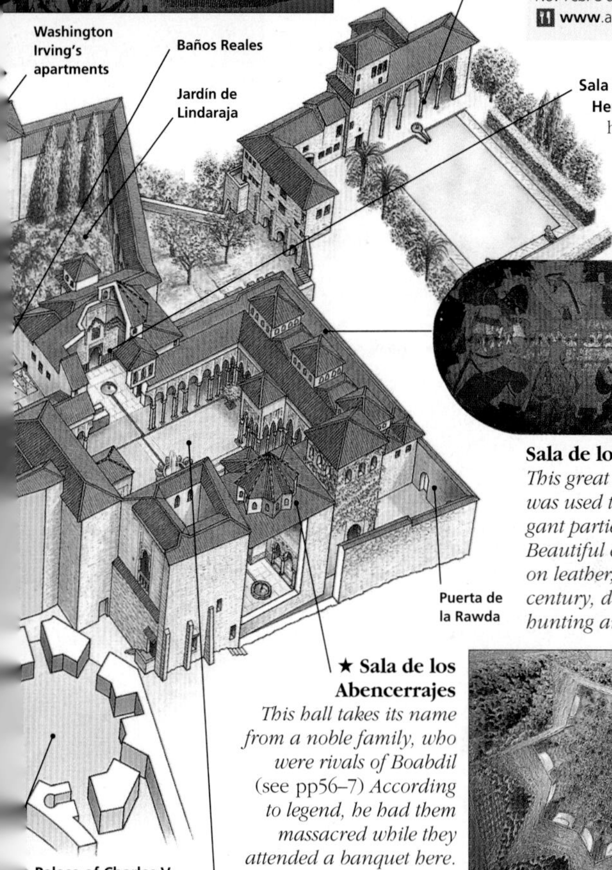

Washington Irving's apartments

Baños Reales

Jardín de Lindaraja

Sala de las Dos Hermanas, with its honeycomb dome, is regarded as the ultimate example of Spanish Islamic architecture.

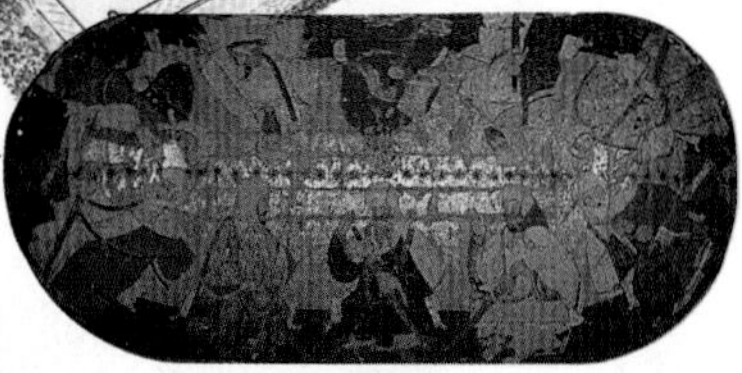

Sala de los Reyes

This great banqueting hall was used to hold extravagant parties and feasts. Beautiful ceiling paintings on leather, from the 14th century, depict tales of hunting and chivalry.

Puerta de la Rawda

★ Sala de los Abencerrajes

This hall takes its name from a noble family, who were rivals of Boabdil (see pp56–7) According to legend, he had them massacred while they attended a banquet here. The geometrical ceiling pattern was inspired by Pythagoras' theorem.

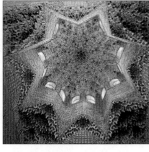

e Palace of Charles V
26) houses a collection
Spanish-Islamic art,
ose highlight is the
ambra vase (see p52).

★ Patio de los Leones

The patio, which is lined by arcades supported by slender columns, is open to the public, although the lion statues and fountain are being restored.

STAR FEATURES

★ Salón de Embajadores

★ Patio de Arrayanes

★ Patio de los Leones

★ Sala de los Abencerrajes

Granada: Generalife

From the Alhambra's northern side, a footpath leads to the Generalife, the country estate of the Nasrid kings. Here, they could escape from palace intrigues and enjoy tranquillity high above the city, a little closer to heaven. The name Generalife, or Yannat al Arif, has various interpretations, perhaps the most pleasing being "the garden of lofty paradise". The gardens, begun in the 13th century, have been modified over the years. They originally contained orchards and pastures. The Generalife provides a magical setting for Granada's annual music and dance festival *(see p41)*.

The Patio de la Acequia *is an enclosed oriental garden built round a long central pool. Rows of water jets on either side make graceful arches above it.*

Sala Regia

Jardines Alto (Upper Gardens

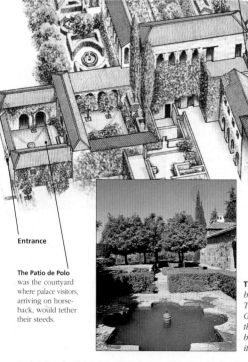

The Escalera Agua is a staircase water flowing gently dow

The Patio de los Cipreses, otherwise known as the Patio de la Sultana, was the secret meeting place for Zoraya, wife of the Sultan Abu-l-Hasan, and her lover, the chief of the Abencerrajes.

Entrance

The Patio de Polo was the courtyard where palace visitors, arriving on horseback, would tether their steeds.

The Patio del Generalife *lies just before the entrance to the Generalife. The walk from the Alhambra to the Generalife gardens passes first through the Jardines Bajos (lower gardens), before crossing this Moorish patio with its characteristically geometric pool.*

The forbidding exterior of the castle above La Calahorra

Castillo de La Calahorra ❸

La Calahorra (Granada). **Tel** 958 67 71 32. 🚌 Guadix. ⏰ 10am–1pm, 4–6pm Wed. 📷

Grim, immensely thick walls and stout, cylindrical corner towers protect the castle on a hill above the village of La Calahorra. Rodrigo de Mendoza, son of Cardinal Mendoza, had the castle built for his bride: the work was carried out between 1509 and 1512 by Italian architects and craftsmen. Inside is an ornate, arcaded Renaissance courtyard over two floors with pillars and a Carrara marble staircase.

Guadix ❹

Granada. 🚶 20,100. 🚌 🚉 🛈 Avenida Mariana Pineda, 958 69 95 74. 🗓 Sat. 🎉 Fiesta & Feria (31 Aug–5 Sep). www.guadixymarquesado.org

The troglodyte quarter, with its 2,000 caves, is the town's most remarkable sight. The Cueva-Museo Al Fareria and Cueva-Museo Costumbres Populares shows how people live underground.

The **cathedral** was begun in 1594 and finished between 1701 and 1796. Relics of San Torcuato, who founded Spain's first Christian bishopric, are kept in the cathedral museum. Near the Moorish **Alcazaba** is the fine Mudéjar-style Iglesia de Santiago.

Cueva-Museo Al Fareria
San Miguel 46. **Tel** 958 66 47 67. ⏰ 10am–2pm, 4–7pm Mon–Sun. 📷

Cueva-Museo Costumbres Populares
Plaza de Ermita Nueva. **Tel** 958 66 93 00. ⏰ daily. 📷

Jaén ❹

🚶 115,000. 🚌 🚉 🛈 Calle Maestra 13, 953 31 32 81. 🗓 Thu. 🎉 Nuestra Señora de la Capilla (11 Jun), San Lucas (18 Oct), Romería de Santa Catalina (25 Nov).

The Moors called Jaén *Geen* – meaning "way station of caravans" – because of its strategic site on the road between Andalusia and Castile. Their hilltop fortress was rebuilt as the **Castillo de Santa Catalina** after it was captured by King Fernando III in 1246. Part of it is now a parador *(see p594)*.

Andrés de Vandelvira, who was responsible for many of Úbeda's fine buildings *(see pp496–7)*, designed Jaén's **cathedral** in the 16th century. Later additions include the two 17th-century towers that now flank the west front.

An old mansion, the **Palacio Villardompardo**, houses a museum of arts and crafts, and also gives access to the **Baños Árabes**, the 11th-century baths of Ali, a Moorish chieftain. These have horseshoe arches, ceilings with small, star-shaped windows and two ceramic vats in which bathers once immersed themselves. Tucked away in an alley is the **Capilla de**

San Andrés, a Mudéjar chapel founded in the 16th century by Gutiérrez González who, as treasurer to Pope Leo X, was endowed with extensive privileges. A gilded iron screen by Maestro Bartolomé de Jaén is the highlight of the chapel.

The **Real Monasterio de Santa Clara** was founded in the 13th century and has a lovely cloister dating from the late 16th century. Its church, which has a coffered ceiling, contains a bamboo image of Christ made in Ecuador.

The **Museo Provincial** displays Roman mosaics and sculptures, and Iberian, Greek and Roman ceramics.

Horseshoe arches supporting the dome at the Baños Árabes, Jaén

🏰 **Castillo de Santa Catalina**
Carretera al Castillo.
Tel 953 12 07 33. ● Mon.

🏛 **Palacio Villardompardo**
Plaza Santa Luisa de Marillac. **Tel** 953 24 80 68. ⏰ Tue–Sun. ● public hols. www.promojaen.es

🏛 **Museo Provincial**
Paseo de la Estación 29. **Tel** 953 25 06 00. ⏰ Tue–Sun. ● public hols.

Whitewashed cave dwellings in the troglodyte quarter of Guadix

Roman bridge spanning the Guadalquivir at Andújar

Andújar **42**

Jaén. 🏠 40,000. 🚌🚇ℹ️ Pl Santa María. Torre del Reloj, 953 50 49 59. 🏛️ Tue. 🎉 Romería (last Sun of Apr).

Andújar is known for its olive oil and its pottery. It stands on the site of an Iberian town, Iliturgi, which was destroyed in the Punic Wars (see p50) by Scipio. The Roman conquerors built the 15-arched bridge spanning the Río Guadalquivir.

In the central square is the Gothic **Iglesia de San Miguel**, with paintings by Alonso Cano. The **Iglesia de Santa María** la Mayor has a Renaissance façade and a Mudéjar tower. Inside it is El Greco's *Christ in*

the Garden of Olives (c.1605). A pilgrimage to the nearby **Santuario de la Virgen de la Cabeza** takes place in April.

Environs
The mighty fortress of **Baños de la Encina** has 15 towers and ramparts built by Caliph Al Hakam II in AD 967. Further north, the road and railway between Madrid and Andalusia squeeze through a spectacular gorge in the eastern reaches of the Sierra Morena, the **Desfiladero de Despeñaperros.**

Baeza **43**

See pp498–9.

Úbeda **44**

Jaén. 🏠 35,000. 🚇 ℹ️ Palacio Marqués de Contadero, C/ Baja del Marqués 4, 953 75 08 97. 🏛️ Fri. 🎉 San Miguel (28 Sep). **www.** ubedainteresa.com

Úbeda is a showcase of Renaissance magnificence, thanks to the patronage of some of Spain's most influential men of the 16th century, including such dignitaries as Francisco de los Cobos, secretary of state, and his greatnephew, Juan Vázquez de Molina, who gave his name to Úbeda's most historic square. The old town is contained within city walls that were first raised by the Moors in 852. The town was designated a UNESCO World Heritage Site in 2003.

Created on the orders of the Bishop of Jaén around 1562, the colossal former **Hospital de Santiago** was designed by Andrés de Vandelvira, who refined the Spanish Renaissance style into its more austere characteristics. The façade is flanked by square towers, one topped with a blue-and-white-tiled spire. Today the building is a conference centre

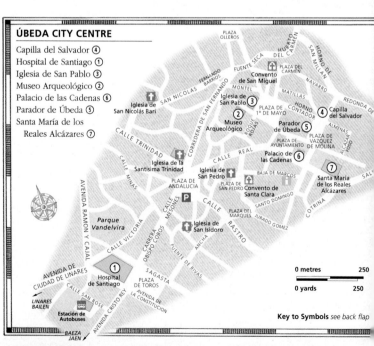

ÚBEDA CITY CENTRE

Capilla del Salvador ④
Hospital de Santiago ①
Iglesia de San Pablo ③
Museo Arqueológico ②
Palacio de las Cadenas ⑥
Parador de Úbeda ⑤
Santa María de los
   Reales Alcázares ⑦

0 metres 250
0 yards 250

Key to Symbols *see back flap*

◁ **Fields of poppies and olive groves south of Andújar in the province of Jaén**

Laguna de Valdeazores in the Parque Nacional de Cazorla

Sited in the 15th-century Casa Mudéjar, the **Museo Arqueológico** exhibits artifacts from Neolithic to Moorish times.

The **Iglesia de San Pablo** has a 13th-century apse and a beautiful 16th-century chapel by Vandelvira. It is surmounted by a Plateresque tower that was completed in 1537.

A monument to the poet and mystic St John of the Cross (1549–91) stands in the **Plaza de Vázquez de Molina**. The **Capilla del Salvador**, on the square, was designed by three 16th-century architects – Diego de Siloé, Andrés de Vandelvira and Esteban Jamete – as the personal chapel of Francisco de los Cobos. Behind it stand Cobos' palace, with a Renaissance façade, and the Hospital de los Honrados Viejos (Hostal of the Honoured Elders), looking on to the Plaza de Santa Lucía. From here, the Redonda de Miradores follows the line of the city walls and offers views of the countryside. Plaza Vázquez de Molina also holds Úbeda's **parador** *(see p596)*. Built in the 16th century, but much altered in the 17th, it was the residence of Fernando Ortega Salido, Dean of Málaga and chaplain of the Capilla del Salvador. Úbeda's town hall and tourist office occupy the **Palacio de Cadenas**, a mansion built by Vázquez de Molina by Vandelvira. It gets its name from the iron chains *(cadenas)* once attached to the columns supporting the main doorway. Also on the square are the church of **Santa María de los Reales Alcazares**, which dates mainly from the 13th century, and the **Cárcel del Obispo** (Bishop's Jail), where nuns who had been punished by the bishop were confined.

🏛 **Museo Arqueológico**
Casa Mudéjar, Calle Cervantes 6.
Tel 953 77 94 32. 🕐 *Tue–Sun.* ♿

🏥 **Hospital de Santiago**
Calle Obispo Cobos. *Tel 953 75 08 42.* 🕐 *daily.*

Capilla del Salvador, Úbeda, one of Spain's finest Renaissance churches

Parque Natural de Cazorla 🄯

Jaén. 🚉 *Cazorla.* 🚶 *C/ Martínez Farelo 11, 953 72 01 25.*

First-time visitors are amazed by the spectacular scenery of this 214,336-ha (529,409-acre) nature reserve with thickly wooded mountains rising to peaks of 2,000 m (6,500 ft) and varied, abundant wildlife.

Access to the Parque Natural de Cazorla, Segura y Las Villas is via the town of Cazorla. Its imposing Moorish **Castillo de la Yedra** houses a folklore museum. From Cazorla, the road winds upwards beneath the ruins of the clifftop castle at **La Iruela**. After crossing a pass it drops down to a crossroads (El Empalme del Valle) in the valley of the Río Guadalquivir. Roads lead to the source of the river and to the peaceful modern parador *(see p593)*.

The main road through the park follows the river. The information centre at Torre del Vinagre is 17 km (11 miles) from the crossroads.

Environs
There is a well-restored Moorish castle at **Segura de la Sierra**, 30 km (19 miles) from the reserve's northern edge. Below it is an unusual rockhewn bullring.

🏰 **Castillo de la Yedra**
Tel 953 71 00 39. 🕐 *Tue–Sun.* 🔒 *17 Sep, 24, 25, 31 Dec & 1 Jan.* 🎫 *(free for EU citizens).*

CAZORLA'S WILDLIFE
More than 100 bird species live in this nature reserve, some very rare, such as the golden eagle and the griffon vulture. Cazorla is the only habitat in Spain, apart from the Pyrenees, where the lammergeier lives. Mammals in the park include the otter – active at dawn and dusk – mouflon and wild boar, and a small remaining population of Spanish ibex. The red deer was reintroduced in 1952. Among the flora supported by the limestone geology is the indigenous *Viola cazorlensis*.

Wild boar foraging for roots, insects and small mammals

For hotels and restaurants in this region see pp591–7 and pp642–8

Street-by-Street: Baeza ㊸

**Coat of arms,
Casa del Pópulo**

Nestling amid the olive groves that characterize much of Jaén province, beautiful Baeza is a small town, unusually rich in Renaissance architecture. Called Beatia by the Romans and later the capital of a Moorish fiefdom, Baeza is portrayed as a "royal nest of hawks" on its coat of arms. It was conquered by Fernando III in 1226 – the first town in Andalusia to be definitively won back from the Moors – and was then settled by Castilian knights. An era of medieval splendour followed, reaching a climax in the 16th century, when Andrés de Vandelvira's splendid buildings were erected. The town was designated a UNESCO World Heritage Site in 2003.

★ Palacio de Jabalquinto
An Isabelline-style (see p24) façade, flanked by elaborate, rounded buttresses, fronts this splendid Gothic palace.

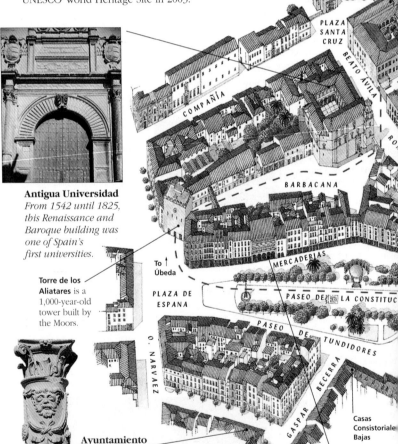

Antigua Universidad
From 1542 until 1825, this Renaissance and Baroque building was one of Spain's first universities.

Torre de los Aliatares is a 1,000-year-old tower built by the Moors.

To ↑ Úbeda

PLAZA DE ESPAÑA

O. NARVAEZ

COMPAÑÍA

PLAZA SANTA CRUZ

SAN FEL

BEATO AVILA

ROM

BARBACANA

MERCADERIAS

PASEO DE LA CONSTITUC

PASEO DE TUNDIDORES

GASPAR BECERRA

Ayuntamiento
Formerly a jail and a courthouse, the town hall is a dignified Plateresque structure (see p25). The coats of arms of Felipe II, Juan de Borja and of the town of Baeza adorn its upper façade.

Casas Consistoriale Bajas

La Alhóndiga, the old corn exchang has impressive tr tier arches runnin along its front.

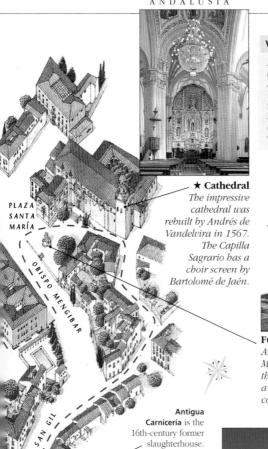

VISITORS' CHECKLIST

Jaén. 19,000. Linares-Baeza, 902 24 02 02. Avenida Alcalde Puche Pardo, 953 74 04 68. Plaza del Pópulo, 953 77 99 82. Tue. Semana Santa (Easter), Feria (mid-Aug), Romería de la Yedra (early Sep). www.todosobrebaeza.com

★ **Cathedral**
The impressive cathedral was rebuilt by Andrés de Vandelvira in 1567. The Capilla Sagrario has a choir screen by Bartolomé de Jaén.

Fuente de Santa María
Architect-sculptor Ginés Martínez of Baeza designed this fountain in the form of a triumphal arch. It was completed in 1564.

Antigua Carnicería is the 16th-century former slaughterhouse.

Puerta de Jaén y Arco de Villalar
This gateway in the city ramparts is adjoined by an arch erected in 1521 to appease Carlos I (see p58) after a rebellion.

0 metres	75
0 yards	75

KEY

Tourist information

– – – Suggested route

★ **Plaza del Pópulo**
The Casa del Pópulo, a fine Plateresque palace, now the tourist office, overlooks this square. In its centre is the Fuente de los Leones, a fountain with an Ibero-Roman statue flanked by lions.

To Jaén

STAR SIGHTS

★ Palacio de Jabalquinto

★ Plaza del Pópulo

★ Cathedral

Renaissance castle overlooking the village of Vélez Blanco

Vélez Blanco 46

Almería. 2,200. Vélez Rubio. Avenida Marqués de los Vélez, 950 41 53 54. Wed. Cristo de la Yedra (second Sun of Aug).

Dominating this pleasant village is the mighty **Castillo de Vélez Blanco**. It was built between 1506–13 by the first Marquis de Los Vélez. The Renaissance interiors are now displayed in the Metropolitan Museum in New York, but there is a reconstruction of one of the patios.

Just outside Vélez Blanco, the **Cueva de los Letreros** contains paintings from c.4000 BC. One depicts the Indalo, a figure holding a rainbow and believed to be a deity with magical powers, now adopted as the symbol of Almería.

⋔ **Cueva de los Letreros**
Camino de la Cueva de los Letreros. **Tel** 617 88 28 08. daily.

Mojácar 47

Almería. 7,000. Calle Glorieta 1, 950 61 50 25. Wed, Sun. Moors and Christians (second weekend of Jun), San Agustin (28 Aug).

From a distance, Mojácar shimmers like the mirage of a Moorish citadel, its white houses cascading over a lofty ridge, 2 km (1 mile) inland from long, sandy beaches.

Following the Civil War (see pp66–7), the village fell into ruin as most of its inhabitants emigrated, but in the 1960s it was discovered by tourists, which gave rise to a new era of prosperity. The old gateway in the walls still remains, but otherwise the village has been completely rebuilt and holiday complexes have grown up along the nearby beaches. The coast south from Mojácar is among the least built up in Spain, with only small resorts and villages along its length.

Tabernas 48

Almería. 3,000. Carretera Nacional 340 km 364, 950 52 50 30. Wed. Virgen de las Angustias (11–15 Aug).

Tabernas is set in Europe's only desert. The town's Moorish fortress dominates the harsh surrounding scenery of cactus-dotted, rugged, eroded hills and dried-out riverbeds, which has provided the setting for many classic spaghetti westerns, such as A Fistful of Dollars. Two film sets can be visited: **Mini-Hollywood** and

Texas Hollywood, 1 km (1 mile) and 4 km (2 miles) from Tabernas respectively.

Not far from town is a solar energy research centre, where heliostats follow the course of Andalusia's powerful sun.

Environs
Sorbas sits on the edge of the chasm of the Río de Aguas. It has two notable buildings: the 16th-century Iglesia de Santa María and a 17th-century mansion said to have been a summer retreat for the Duke of Alba.

Nearby is the karst scenery, honeycombed with hundreds of cave systems, of the **Yesos de Sorbas** nature reserve. Permission to explore them is required from Andalusia's environmental department.

🎬 **Mini-Hollywood**
Carretera N340. **Tel** 950 36 52 36. daily. Mon in winter.

🎬 **Texas Hollywood**
Carretera N340, Tabernas. **Tel** 950 16 54 58. daily.

Desert landscape around Tabernas reminiscent of the Wild West

SPAGHETTI WESTERNS

Two Wild West towns lie off the N340 highway west of Tabernas. Here, visitors can re-enact classic film scenes or watch stuntmen performing bank hold-ups and saloon brawls. The poblados del oeste were built during the 1960s and early 1970s when low costs and eternal sunshine made Almería the ideal location for spaghetti westerns. Sergio Leone, director of The Good, the Bad and the Ugly, built a ranch here and filmsets sprang up in the desert. Local gypsies played Indians and Mexicans. The deserts and Arizona-style badlands are still used for television commercials and series, and by film directors such as Steven Spielberg.

Still from For a Few Dollars More by Sergio Leone

The 10th-century Alcazaba, which dominates Almería's old town

Almería ⑲

Almería. 🏛 *170,000.* 🚃 🚗
Estación Intermodal 🚩 *Parque
Nicolás Salmerón, 950 27 43 55.* 🛍
Tue, Fri & Sat. 🎭 *Feria (last week of
Aug).* www.andalucia.org

Almería's colossal **Alcazaba**,
dating from AD 995, is the
largest fortress built by the
Moors in Spain. The huge
structure bears witness to the
city's golden age, when it was
an important port under the
Caliphate of Córdoba *(see
pp52–3)*. The Moorish city,
known as Al Mariyat (Mirror
of the Sea), exported mainly
brocade, silk and cotton.

During the Reconquest, the
Alcazaba withstood two major
sieges before eventually falling
to the armies of the Catholic
Monarchs *(see pp56–7)* in
1489. The royal coat of arms
can be seen on the Torre del
Homenaje, built during their
reign. The Alcazaba also has
a Mudéjar chapel and gardens.

Adjacent to the Alcazaba is
the old fishermen's and gypsy
quarter of **La Chanca**, where
some families live in caves
with brightly painted façades
and modern interiors. On
Mondays a lively street market
is held. Although this district is
picturesque, it is also des-
perately poor and it is unwise
to walk around here alone or
at night with valuables.

Berber pirates from North
Africa often raided Almería.
Consequently, the **cathedral**
looks almost more like a castle
than a place of worship, with
its four towers, thick walls and
small windows. The site was
originally a mosque. This was
converted into a church, but

in 1522 it was destroyed in an
earthquake. Work on the present building began in 1524
under the direction of Diego
de Siloé, who designed the
nave and high altar in Gothic
style. The Renaissance façade
and the carved walnut choir
stalls are by Juan de Orea.

Brightly coloured entrance to a
gypsy cave in La Chanca district

Traces of Moorish Almería's
most important mosque can be
seen in the **Templo San Juan**.
The **Plaza Vieja** is an attractive
17th-century arcaded square.
On one side is the **town hall**
(ayuntamiento), with a cream
and pink façade (1899).

Environs
One of Europe's most important examples of a Copper Age
settlement lies at **Los Millares**,
near Gádor, 17 km (11 miles)
north of Almería. As many as
2,000 people may have occupied the site around 2500 BC.

⚓ **Alcazaba**
Calle Almanzor. **Tel** *950 17 55 00.*
⏰ *Tue–Sun.* ⬤ *1 Jan, 25 Dec.*
🎫 *(free for EU citizens).*

⌂ **Los Millares**
Santa Fé de Mondújar. **Tel** *677 90 34
04.* ⏰ *Wed–Sun.* ⬤ *public hols.*

Parque Natural de Cabo de Gata ㊿

Almería. 🚌 *San José.* 🚩 *Centro de
Visitantes de las Amoladeras,
Carretera–Cabo de Gata km 6, 950
16 04 35.* ⏰ *daily.*

Towering cliffs of volcanic
rock, sand dunes, salt flats
and secluded coves characterize the 29,000-ha (71,700-
acre) Parque Natural de Cabo
de Gata. Within its confines
are a few fishing villages, and
the small resort of San José. A
lighthouse stands at the end
of the *cabo* (cape), which can
be reached by road from the
village of Cabo de Gata. The
park includes a stretch of seabed 2 km (1 mile) wide and
the marine flora and fauna
protected within it attract
scuba-divers and snorkellers.

The dunes and saltpans between the cape and the Playa
de San Miguel are a habitat
for thorny jujube trees. Many
migrating birds stop here, and
among the 170 or so bird
species recorded are flamingoes, avocets, griffon vultures
and Dupont's larks.

Environs
Set amid citrus trees on the
edge of the Sierra de Alhamilla, **Níjar's** fame stems from
the pottery and the hand-
woven *jarapas* – blankets and
rugs – that are made here. The
barren plain between Níjar
and the sea has been brought
under cultivation using vast
plastic greenhouses to
conserve the scarce water.

The dramatic, dark volcanic rocks at
Cabo de Gata, east of Almería

SPAIN'S ISLANDS

INTRODUCING SPAIN'S ISLANDS 504–505
THE BALEARIC ISLANDS 506–527
THE CANARY ISLANDS 528–551

Introducing Spain's Islands

Spain's two groups of islands lie in separate seas –
the Balearics in the Mediterranean and the Canaries in
the Atlantic, off the African coast. Both are popular
package-tour destinations blessed with warm climates,
good beaches and clear waters. But each has more to
offer than high-rise hotels, fast-food restaurants and
discos. The Balearics have white villages, wooded
hills, caves and prehistoric monuments, while the
extraordinary volcanic landscapes of the Canaries are
unlike any other part of Spain. Four of Spain's national
parks (see pp30–1) are in the Canary Islands.

Ibiza (see pp510–12) is the liveliest
of the Balearic Islands. Ibiza town
and Sant Antoni are the main touris
centres, offering world-famous
nightlife and excellent beaches.

Eivissa
(Ibiza)

Formentera

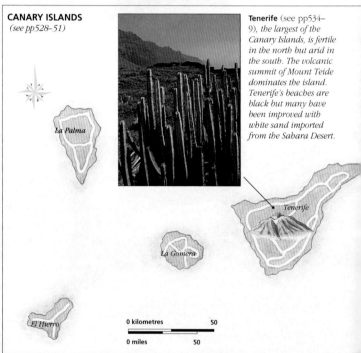

CANARY ISLANDS
(see pp528–51)

Tenerife (see pp534–
9), the largest of the
Canary Islands, is fertile
in the north but arid in
the south. The volcanic
summit of Mount Teide
dominates the island.
Tenerife's beaches are
black but many have
been improved with
white sand imported
from the Sahara Desert.

La Palma

Tenerife

La Gomera

El Hierro

0 kilometres 50

0 miles 50

◁ Vines growing in the volcanic soil of Lanzarote, protected by drystone walls

In Menorca (see pp522–7) *tourism has developed more slowly than in Mallorca and Ibiza, and the island has largely avoided being over-commercialized. Scattered across the countryside are the ruins of unique Bronze Age buildings.*

BALEARIC ISLANDS
(see pp506–27)

Menorca

Mallorca

Mallorca (see pp514–21) *best known for its beaches, has caves and other natural features to explore. The most spectacular of the island's historic sights is the great Gothic cathedral in Palma, which rises above the boats moored in the old harbour.*

kilometres | 50
miles | 50

Lanzarote (see pp548–50) *is the most attractive of the Canary Islands, even though the landscape is strikingly bare. White houses contrast starkly with black volcanic fields. The most dramatic attraction is Timanfaya National Park, including the Montañas del Fuego.*

Lanzarote

Fuerteventura

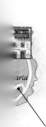

Gran Canaria (see p542–5) *centres on a symmetrical volcanic cone. The capital city of Las Palmas has some interesting museums and monuments. In contrast, the sprawling Maspalomas, on the south coast, is the biggest holiday resort in Spain.*

THE BALEARIC ISLANDS

IBIZA · FORMENTERA · MALLORCA · MENORCA

*C*hic resorts and attractive coves and beaches, combined with a
climate which is hot but never uncomfortably so, have made
tourism the mainstay of life along the coasts of the Balearic
Islands. Inland, there is peace and quiet in abundance, and a great
variety of sights to seek out: wooded hills, pretty white villages,
monasteries, country churches, caves and prehistoric monuments.

Standing at a crossroads
in the Mediterranean, the
Balearic Islands have been
plundered or colonized
in turn by Phoenicians,
Greeks, Carthaginians, Romans, Moors and Turks.
In the 13th century Catalan
settlers brought their language, a
dialect of which is widely spoken today.

The islands can justifiably claim to
cater for all tastes: from sun-seekers on
package holidays, for whom the larger
resorts serve as brash fun factories, to
jet-setters and film stars, who head for
luxurious but discreet hideaways in the
hills. The largest island, where tourism
has been established the longest, is

Mallorca. A massive
Gothic cathedral stands
near the waterfront of
Palma, the capital.

The green country-
side of Menorca is dotted
with prehistoric monuments and
its towns full of noble, historic mansions. The coast of Ibiza is notched by
innumerable rocky coves. The island's
hilly interior is characterized by brilliant white farmhouses and robust
churches. On Formentera, small and
relatively undeveloped, the pace of
life is slow. The islets surrounding the
four principal islands are mainly uninhabited; one of them, Cabrera (off
Mallorca), is a national park.

w through the window of one of Ibiza's traditional, whitewashed farmhouses

e massive, heavily buttressed cathedral overlooking Palma de Mallorca's harbour

Exploring the Balearics

Though the Balearic islands are often associated with high-density, inexpensive package tourism, they offer enough variety to satisfy everyone's tastes. For those unattracted by the bustle of the coastal resorts and their beautiful beaches, the countryside and the old towns of Palma, Ibiza, Maó and Ciutadella are relatively undisturbed. Mallorca is by far the most culturally rich of the Balearics, with its distinguished collection of modern and traditional galleries, and interesting museums. Menorca is strong on Neolithic remains and Neo-Colonial architecture, while Ibiza is for lovers of clear, painterly light and rustic peasant houses; it also has some of the wildest nightclubs in Europe. Formentera – for many, the most alluring island – has crystal water, white sand, a pure, parched landscape and total tranquillity.

Poblat des Pescadors in the tourist village of Binibeca

MALLO

🛈 **VALLDEMOSS**

Estellencs ○

ANDRATX ➐ **PAL** 🏛 🏛
Port d'Andratx ○
Palma Nova

Early-morning mist on the waters of Port de Pollença in Mallorca

| 0 kilometres | 25 |
| 0 miles | 15 |

IBIZA

ELS AMUNTS

SANT ANTONI ➊   ➍   ➎ **SANTA EULÀRIA** 🏛 🛈

Sant Vicenç

○ Jesús

SANT JOSEP ➋
Sa Talaiassa
475m
➌ **IBIZA (EIVISSA)** 🏛 🛈

Ses Salines 🏖 🏛 🛈

FORMENTERA ➏
Sant Francesc ○
Cala Saona
Cap de Barbaria   *Platja de Migjorn*   *Punta Roja*
Es Caló ○

GETTING AROUND

Nearly all foreign visitors to the Balea arrive by plane – the no-frills airlines making it all the more popular. Mallo Menorca and Ibiza connect to major E pean cities as well as Madrid, Barcelo and Valencia. Several airlines fly to r other Spanish cities out of Son Sant J airport in Palma. Another way of arri is by boat from Barcelona, Valencia, Alicante or Dénia. Between the islan there are regular ferry services, run b Transmediterránea, Balearia and Fleb Mallorca is the only island with rail services, which run between Palma a Inca, and between Palma and Sóller, v is now extended to Sa Pobla and Mar Roads vary from excellent to poor. T best way to get around is by car, ex on Formentera, where cycling is bes

SIGHTS AT A GLANCE

Alfàbia ⑩
Els Amunts ④
Andratx ⑦
Cabrera ⑰
Cales Coves ㉔
Capocorb Vell ⑯
Ciutadella ⑳
Coves del Drac ⑲
Felanitx ⑱
Ferreries ㉑
Formentera ⑥
Ibiza (Eivissa) ③

La Granja ⑧
Maó ㉓
Es Mercadal ㉒
Palma (pp518–21) ⑭
Pollença ⑬
Puig de Randa ⑮
Santa Eulària ⑤
Sant Antoni ①
Sant Josep ②
Santuario de Lluc ⑫
Sóller ⑪
Valldemossa ⑨

A peaceful stroll on the sands of Ibiza's Sant Miquel beach

MENORCA

Cap de Cavalleria
Fornells
🏛 🖼 CIUTADELLA ⑳ C721 FERRERIES
Cala Sta Galdana ㉑ ㉒ ES MERCADAL
Cap d' Artrutx Alaior
🏛 🖼
MAÓ
CALES COVES ⛪ ㉔
Binibeca ✈ ㉓ Sant Lluís

Cap de
Formentor
Port de Pollença
⑬ POLLENÇA 🏛 ⓘ
SANTUARIO ᵒAlcúdia
DE LLUC
Badia
d'Alcúdia
C713 Sa Pobla
C712 Capdepera
ᵒca Santa ᵒCala Rajada
Sineu Margalida Artà
Petra C715 ᵒCoves d'Artà
Son Servera
tuiri Manacor
PUIG DE Coves dels ᵒPortocristo
⑤ RANDA Hams
C714 ⑲ COVES DEL DRAC
acmajor ⑱ FELANITX
mpos Castell de Santueri
C717 ᵒPortopetro
ORB
Santanyí
ia ᵒ ᵒCala Figuera
rdi
Cap de
ses Salines

⑦ CABRERA

SEE ALSO

- *Where to Stay* pp597–9
- *Where to Eat* pp648–51

The rocky coast around the Coves d'Artà in Mallorca

KEY	
	Motorway
	Major road
	Secondary road
	Scenic route
	Minor railway
	Summit

Ibiza

This small island, the nearest of the Balearics to the coast of Spain, was unknown and untouched by tourism until the 1960s, when it suddenly appeared in Europe's holiday brochures along with Benidorm and Torremolinos. There is still a curious, indefinable magic about Ibiza (Eivissa) and the island has not entirely lost its character. The countryside, particularly in the north, is a rural patchwork of groves of almonds, olives and figs, and wooded hills. Ibiza town retains the air of a 1950s Spanish provincial borough. At once package-tour paradise, hippie hideout and glamour hot spot, this is one of the Mediterranean's mythical destinations.

An Ibizan shepherdess

The bustling harbour of the resort of Sant Antoni

Sant Antoni ❶

Baleares. 🏃 17,500. 🔛 🚢
ℹ️ Passeig de Ses Fonts, 971 34 33 63. 🎭 Sant Antoni (17 Jan), Sant Bartolomé (24 Aug).
www.illesbalears.es

Ibiza's second town, Sant Antoni was known by the Romans as Portus Magnus because of its large natural harbour. Formerly a tiny fishing village, it has turned into a sprawling and exuberant resort. Although it was once notoriously over-commercialized, the town has recently undergone a dramatic facelift. Nevertheless, the 14th-century parish church of Sant Antoni is practically marooned in a sea of modern high-rise hotels.
   To the north of Sant Antoni, on the road to Cala Salada, is the chapel of **Santa Agnès**, an unusual early Christian temple (not to be confused with the village of the same name). When this catacomb-like chapel was discovered, in 1907, it contained Moorish weapons and fragments of pottery.

Sant Josep ❷

Baleares. 🏃 13,500. ℹ️ Carrer Pedro Escanellas 33-39, 971 34 33 63. 🎭 Sant Josep (19 Mar).

The village of Sant Josep, the administrative centre of south-west Ibiza, lies in the shadow of Ibiza's highest mountain. At 475 m (1,560 ft) Sa Talaiassa offers a panorama of all Ibiza, including the islet of **Es Vedrà**, rising from the sea like a rough-

The salt lakes of Ses Salines, a haven for many bird species

cut pyramid. For the most accessible view of this enormous rock, take the coastal road to the sandy cove of Cala d'Hort where there are a number of good restaurants and a quiet beach.

Environs

Before tourism, salt was Ibiza's main industry, most of it coming from the salt flats at **Ses Salines** in the southeast corner of the island. Mainland Spain is the chief consumer of this salt, but much goes to the Faroe Islands and Scandinavia for salting fish. It is loaded on to ships at Ibiza's southernmost port, La Canal. Ses Salines is also an important refuge for birds, including the flamingo. **Es Cavallet**, 3 km (2 miles) east, is an unspoiled stretch of soft, white sand.

Ibiza ❸

Baleares. 🏃 35,000. ✈️ 🔛 🚢
ℹ️ Calle Antonio Riquer 2, Andenes del Puerto, 971 30 19 00. 🛒 Mo... Sat. 🎭 Fiestas Patronales (1-8 Aug), San Juan Bautista (24 Jun).
www.illesbalears.es

The old quarter of Ibiza (Eivissa), known also as Da... Vila, or upper town, is a miniature citadel guarding ... mouth of the almost circular bay. The **Portal de ses Taule** a magnificent gateway in the north wall of the 16th-cent... fortifications, carries the fir... carved coat of arms of the kingdom of Aragón, to wh... the Balearic Islands belong... in the Middle Ages (see p2... Inside the walls is the 16th-century **Església de Santo**

Domingo with its three red-tiled domes. The Baroque interior, with its barrel-vaulted ceiling and frescoed walls, has been restored to its former glory. Works of art by Erwin Bechtold, Barry Flanagan and other artists connected with Ibiza are on display in the **Museu d'Art Contemporani**, just inside the Portal de ses Taules. Crowning the whole Dalt Vila is the **cathedral**, a 13th-century Catalan Gothic building with 18th-century additions. The cathedral's Museo de la Sacristia houses assorted works of art.

Under the Carthaginians, the soil of Ibiza was considered holy. The citizens of Carthage deemed it an honour to be buried in the **Necrópolis Única del Puig des Molins**. Part of it can be visited by the public. The museum is currently closed for restoration.

The crossroads village of Jesús, 3 km (2 miles) north, is

A backstreet in the Sa Penya district of Ibiza town

worth a visit for its 16th-century church. Originally built as part of a Franciscan monastery, it has a 16th-century altarpiece by Rodrigo de Osona the Younger.

ⓜ Museu d'Art Contemporani
Ronda Narcís Puget s/n. **Tel** 971 302 723. ⬭ Tue–Sun. ⬤ Mon & public hols. ⬛ ⬛

ⓝ Necrópolis Púnica del Puig des Molins
Via Romana 31. **Tel** 971 301 771. ⬭ Tue–Sun. ⬤ Mon & public hols.

Els Amunts ❹

Baleares. ⬚ Sant Miquel. ⬚ Santa Eulària d'es Riu, 971 33 07 28.

Els Amunts is the local name for the uplands of northern Ibiza, which stretch from Sant Antoni on the west coast to Sant Vicenç in the northeast. Though hardly a mountain range – Es Fornás is the highest point, at a mere 450 m

view across the port towards za's upper town

(1,480 ft) – the area's inaccessibility has kept it unspoiled. There are few special sights here, apart from the landscape: pine-clad hills sheltering fertile valleys whose rich red soil is planted with olive, almond and fig trees, and the occasional vineyard. Tourist enclaves are also scarce – except for a handful of small resorts, such as Port de Sant Miquel, Portinatx and Sant Vicenç. Inland, villages like Sant Joan and Santa Agnès offer an insight into Ibiza's quiet, rural past.

The architectural highpoints of northern Ibiza are several beautiful white churches, like the one in **Sant Miquel** which, on Thursdays in summer, is host to a display of Ibizan folk dancing. Outside Sant Llorenç is the tranquil, fortified hamlet of **Balàfia**, with flat-roofed houses, tiny whitewashed alleys, and a watchtower that was used as a fortress during raids by the Turks.

IBIZA'S HOTTEST SPOTS

Ibiza's reputation for extraordinary summer nightlife is largely justified. The main action takes place in two areas: the Calle de la Virgen in the old harbour district, with its bars, fashion boutiques and restaurants; and the mega-discos out of town – Privilege, Pachá, Amnesia and Es Paradis. When the last of these is closing, at about 7am, the wildest club of them all, Space, is only just opening its doors. Ibiza has long been a magnet for the rich and famous. Celebrities seem to have become more elusive of late, but a few well-known faces can often be glimpsed dining in the restaurant Las Dos Lunas, and taking the rays the next day on the beach at Ses Salines.

Nightclubbers enjoying a bubble bath at Amnesia

One of the many beautiful beaches along the unspoiled shores of the island of Formentera

Santa Eulària **❺**

Baleares. 🏠 *28,000.* 🚌 🚤 ℹ *Carrer Mariano Riquer Wallis 4, 971 33 07 28.* 🏠 *Wed & Sat.* 🎪 *Fiesta (12 Feb), Cala Llonga (14–15 Aug).*

Despite catering for tourism, the town of Santa Eulària d'es Riu (Santa Eulalia del Río), situated on the island's only river, has managed to hold on to its character far more than many other Spanish resorts.

The 16th-century church, with its pretty covered courtyard, and the surrounding old town, were built on the top of a little hill, the **Puig de Missa**, because this site was more easily defended in times of war than the shore below.

Ajdacent to the church is the **Museu Etnològic**, a folk museum, which is housed in an ancient but tastefully adapted Ibizan farmhouse. Included in the exhibits (labelled in Catalan only) are traditional costumes,

The domed roof of Santa Eulària's 16th-century church

farming implements, toys and an olive press. A collection of photographs covering 50 years show how Ibiza has changed.

🏛 **Museu Etnològic**
Can Ros, Puig de Missa. **Tel** *971 33 28 45.* 🕐 *Mon–Sat.* ⬤ *Sun, mid-Dec– mid-Jan.* 📷 🎫 *(by appt).*

Formentera **❻**

Baleares. 🏠 *7,000.* 🚤 *from Ibiza.* ℹ *Calle Calpe, La Savina, 971 32 20 57.* 🏠 *Sun.* 🎪 *Fiesta Sant Jaume (25 Jul).*

An hour's boat ride from Ibiza harbour will bring you to this largely unspoiled island where the waters are blue and the way of life slow.

From the small port of La Savina, where the boat docks, there are buses to other parts of the island, or you can hire a car, moped or bicycle from one of the shops nearby.

Sant Francesc Xavier, Formentera's tiny capital, is situated 3 km (2 miles) from La Savina. Most of the island's amenities are in this town, plus a pretty 18th-century church in the main square, and a folk museum.

From Sant Francesc, a bumpy minor road leads for 9 km (6 miles) southwards, ending at Cap de Barbaria, the site of an 18th-century defensive tower and a lighthouse.

Formentera is entirely flat, apart from the small plateau of **La Mola**, which takes up the whole eastern end of the island. From the fishing port of Es Caló the road winds up-

wards past the Restaurante E: Mirador, with its panoramic view of western Formentera, t village of Nostra Senyora del Pilar de la Mola on top o the plateau. About 3 km (2 miles) to the east is a lighthouse, Far de la Mola, sited on the highest point of the island. Nearby stands a monument to Jules Verne (1828–1905), who used Formentera for the setting of on of his novels, *Hector Servada*

Although there are many purple road signs indicating places of cultural interest on Formentera, most lead only disappointment. But one sig well worth seeking out is th megalithic sepulchre of **Ca N Costa** (2000 BC) near Sant Francesc, the only one of its kind in the Balearics. This monument, a circle of uprig stone slabs, pre-dates the Carthaginians (*see pp49–50*)

However, the island's great strength is not its history an culture, but its landscape, which has a spare and delic beauty and some of the Me terranean's last unspoiled shorelines. More than 60% the island's landscape is protected by law. The fines beaches are, arguably, Migjc and Cala Sahona, southwes of Sant Francesc. Nearly all beaches have nudist areas.

Illetes and Llevant are tw beautiful beaches on either of a long sandy spit in the north of the island. To the north, between Formentera Ibiza, is the island of **Espa mador**, with its natural spri

The Flavours of the Balearics

This quartet of beautiful islands, strategically positioned on ancient trading routes, has been fought over for thousands of years. Each occupying force – Arabs, Catalans, French and British among them – has left its mark and the local cuisine reflects this. Mediterranean seafood, particularly spectacular lobster and crayfish, remains the most prominent local ingredient, but the islands are also known for their delicious pastries and desserts, like the feather-light *ensaimada* from Mallorca and the typical Ibizan *flaó*. Cured meats *(embutits)* and traditionally made cheeses are also local specialities.

Locally grown oranges

Seafood from the Mediterranean in a Mallorcan fish market

MALLORCA AND MENORCA

Seafood predominates in the Balearic islands. Menorca is renowned for *caldereta de langosta* (spiny lobster stew), once a simple fishermen's dish but now an expensive delicacy. The classic Mallorcan dish is *pa amb oli*, a slice of toasted country bread rubbed with garlic and drizzled with local olive oil. Menorca's creamy garlic sauce *all i oli* is a delicious accompaniment to meat and seafood dishes, and the island also produces fine cheese, *formatge de Maó*.

IBIZA AND FORMENTERA

Seafood also reigns supreme on Ibiza and its quieter little sister, Formentera, especially in *calders* (stews) such as *borrida de rajada* (skate with potatoes, eggs and pastis), and *guisat de peix*. Pork is the staple meat. For a picnic, try *cocarrois*, pastries filled with meat, fish or vegetables and *formatjades*, soft-cheese-filled pastries flavoured with cinnamon. Delicious local desserts include *gató* (almond cake served with ice-cream) and Ibizan *flaó*, made with creamy cheese and eggs, and flavoured with mint.

Cuscussó Menorquin (bread pudding)

Ensaimadas

Flaó Ibicenco

Galletas de Alaior (aniseed biscuits)

Formatjades

El Gató (almond tart)

Appetizing selection of delicious Balearic pastries

REGIONAL DISHES AND SPECIALITIES

All i oli

Fish and shellfish (particularly the revered local lobster) are omnipresent in the Balearics, particularly along the coast. Try them simply grilled to fully appreciate their freshness (many seaside restaurants have their own fishing boats), but you'll also find wonderful, slow-cooked stews which are bursting with flavour. The rugged inland regions provide mountain lamb and kid, along with pork, which is also used to make *embutits* including spicy Mallorcan *sobrassada* which is delicious with *pa amb oli*. The tourist industry hasn't killed off the long-standing farming tradition on the Balearics, which produce plentiful fruit and vegetables. Mallorca makes its own robust wines, particularly around the village of Binissalem, while Menorca, thanks to the long British occupation of the island, makes its own piquant gin.

Tumbet de peix *A fish pie, made with layers of firm white fish, peppers, aubergine (eggplant) and sliced boiled egg.*

Mallorca

Mallorca is often likened to a continent rather than simply an island. Its varied nature never fails to astonish, whether you are looking for landscape, culture or just entertainment. No other European island has a wider range of scenery, from the fertile plains of central Mallorca to the almost alpine peaks of the Tramuntana. The island's mild climate and lovely beaches have made it one of Spain's foremost package tour destinations but there is a wealth of culture, too, evident in sights like Palma Cathedral (*see pp520–1*). Mallorca's appeal lies also in its charm as a living, working island: the cereal and fruit crops of the central plains, and the vineyards around Binissalem are vital to the island's economy.

Terraced orange grove in the Sierra Tramuntana

Andratx ❼

Baleares. 🏘 *10,500.* 🚌 🛈
*Avinguda de la Cúria 1, 971 62 80
19.* 🅿 *Wed.* 🎉 *San Pedro
(29 Jun).*

This small town lies amid a valley of almond groves in the shadow of Puig de Galatzó, which rises to 1,026 m (3,366 ft). With its ochre and white shuttered houses and the old watchtowers perched high on a hill above the town, Andratx is a very pretty place.

The road southwest leads down to **Port d'Andratx** 5 km (3 miles) away. Here, in an almost totally enclosed bay, expensive yachts are moored in rows along the harbour and luxury holiday homes pepper the surrounding hillsides. In the past, Port d'Andratx's main role was as the fishing port and harbour for Andratx, but since the early 1960s it has gradually been transformed into an exclusive holiday resort for the rich and famous. When visiting Port d'Andratx, it is a good

idea to leave all thoughts of the real Mallorca behind and simply enjoy it for what it is – a chic and affluent resort.

La Granja ❽

Carretera de Esporlas. **Tel** *971 61 00
32.* 🚌 🔘 *daily.* 🎫 ♿
www.lagranja.net

La Granja is a private estate, or *possessió*, near the little country town of Esporles. Formerly a Cistercian convent, it is now the property of the Seguí family, who have opened their largely unspoiled 18th-century house to the public as a kind of living museum. Peacocks roam the gardens, salt cod and hams hang in the kitchen, *The Marriage of Figaro* plays in the ballroom, and the slight air of chaos just adds to the charm of the place.

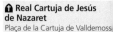

Bust of Frédéric Chopin at Valldemossa

Valldemossa ❾

Baleares. 🏘 *1,800.* 🚌 🛈 *Avenida
Palma 7, 971 61 21 06.* 🅿 *Sun.*
🎉 *Santa Catalina Thomás (28 Jul),
San Bartolomé (24 Aug).*
www.valldemossa.com

This pleasant mountain town will forever be linked with the name of George Sand, the French novelist who stayed here during the winter of 1838–9 and later wrote unflatteringly of the island in *Un Hiver à Majorque*. Dearer to Mallorcans is the Polish composer Frédéric Chopin (1810–49) who stayed with Sand at the **Real Cartuja de Jesús de Nazaret**. "Chopin's cell", off the monastery's main courtyard, is where a few of his works were written, and still houses the piano on which he composed.

Nearby is a 17th-century pharmacy displaying outlandish medicinal preparations such as "powdered nails of the beast". In the cloisters is an art museum with works by Tàpies, Miró and the Mallorcan artist Juli Ramis (1909–90), and a series of Picasso illustrations, *The Burial of the Count of Orgaz*, inspired by the El Greco painting of the same name (*see p32*).

🔒 **Real Cartuja de Jesús de Nazaret**
Plaça de la Cartuja de Valldemossa.
Tel *971 61 21 06.* 🔘 *daily.* 🎫 ♿

A view across the harbour of Port d'Andratx

Alfàbia ⑩

Carretera de Sóller km 17. **Tel** 971
61 31 23. 🚌 tour bus from Palma.
◐ Sat pm & Sun. ⓖ

Very few *possessicós* in
Mallorca are open to the
public, which makes Alfàbia
worth visiting. The house and
garden are an excellent example of a typical Mallorcan
aristocratic estate and exude a
Moorish atmosphere. Very little
remains of the original 14th-
century architecture, so it is
well worth looking out for the
Mudéjar inscription on the ceiling of the entrance hall and the
Hispano-Arabic fountains and
pergola. The garden is a sumptuous 19th-century creation,
making imaginative use of
shade and the play of water.

Sóller ⑪

Baleares. 🏘 9,100. 🚉🚌 ℹ Plaza
España, 971 63 80 08. 🅿 Sat. 🎉
Sa Fira & Es Firó (2nd week May).
www.a-soller.es

Sóller is a little town grown
fat on the produce of its olive
groves and orchards, which
climb up the slopes of the
Sierra Tramuntana. In the
19th century Sóller traded its
oranges and wine for French
goods, and the town retains a
faintly Gallic, bourgeois feel.

One of Sóller's best-known
features is its delightfully old-
fashioned narrow-gauge railway, complete with quaint
wooden carriages. The town,
whose station is in the Plaça
Espanya, lies on a scenic
route between Palma and the
fishing village of Port de Sóller
5 km (3 miles) to the west.

Environs
From Sóller a road winds southwards along the spectacular
west coast to **Deià** (Deyá). This
village was once the home of
Robert Graves (1895–1985), the
English poet and novelist,
who came to live here in 1929.
His simple tombstone can be
seen in the small cemetery.

The **Museu Arqueològic**, curat-
ed by the archaeologist William
Waldren, offers a glimpse into
prehistoric Mallorca. Outside
the village is **Son Marroig**, the

Houses and trees crowded together on the hillside of Deià

estate of Austrian Archduke
Ludwig Salvator (1847–1915),
who documented the Balearics
in a series of books included in
a display of his possessions.

🏛 Museu Arqueològic
Calle Teix 4, Es Clot Deià. **Tel** 971
63 90 01. ◐ Tue, Thu, Sun. ⓖ

Statue of La Moreneta at the
Santuario de Lluc

Santuario de Lluc ⑫

Lluc. 🚌 from Palma. **Tel** 971 87 15
25. ◐ daily. ⓖ museum only.
www.lluc.net

High in the mountains of the
Sierra Tramuntana, in the
remote village of Lluc, is an
institution regarded by many
as the spiritual heart of
Mallorca. The Santuario de
Lluc was built mainly in the
17th and 18th centuries on the
site of an ancient shrine. The
monastery's Baroque church,

with its imposing façade,
contains the stone image of
La Moreneta, the Black Virgin
of Lluc, supposedly found by
a young shepherd boy on a
nearby hilltop in the 13th
century. The altar and sanctuary of one chapel are by
Catalan architect and designer
Antoni Gaudí *(see pp140–1)*.
Along the Camí dels Misteris,
the paved walkway up to this
hilltop, there are some bronze
bas-reliefs by Pere Llimona.
Just off the main Plaça dels
Pelegrins are a café and bar, a
pharmacy and a shop. The
museum, situated on the first
floor, includes Mallorcan paintings and medieval manuscripts.
The monastery incorporates a
guest house *(see p598)*.

From Lluc, 13 km (8 miles)
of tortuous road winds through
the hills and descends towards
the coast, ending at the beautiful rocky bay of **Sa Calobra**.
From here, it is just 5 minutes'
walk up the coast to the deep
gorge of the Torrent de Pareis.

Sheer cliff face rising out of the
sea at Sa Calobra

The cloisters of the Convent de Santo Domingo in Pollença

Pollença ⓑ

Baleares. 🏘 *15,500.* 🚌 🛈 *Calle Guillem Cife de Colonya, 971 53 50 77.* 🚌 *Sun.* 🎉 *Sant Antoni (17 Jan), Patron Saint (2 Aug).* **www**.ajpollenca.net

Although Pollença has become one of Mallorca's most popular tourist spots, it still appears unspoiled. The town, with its ochre-coloured stone houses and winding lanes, is picturesquely sited on the edge of fertile farmland. The Plaça Major, with its bars frequented mainly by locals, has an old-world atmosphere.

Pollença has fine churches, including the 18th-century **Parròquia de Nostra Senyora dels Angels** and the Convent de Santo Domingo, containing the **Museu de Pollença**, with its displays of archaeology and art. It also holds Pollença's Classical Music Festival in July and August. A chapel on the hilltop, **El**

Calvari, is reached either by road or a long climb of 365 steps. On the altar there is a Gothic Christ, carved in wood.

Environs
Alcúdia, 10 km (6 miles) to the east, is surrounded by 14th-century walls with two huge gateways. Near the town centre is the **Museu Monografico de Pollentia**, exhibiting statues, jewellery and other remains found in the Roman settlement of Pollentia, 2km (1 mile) south of Alcúdia.

🏛 **Museu de Pollença**
Calle Guillem Cife de Colonya 33.
Tel *971 53 11 66.* ☐ *Tue–Sun.* 🎫

🏛 **Museu Monografico de Pollentia**
Calle San Jaume 30, Alcúdia.
Tel *971 54 70 04.* ☐ *Tue–Sun.* 🎫

Palma de Mallorca ⓒ

See pp518–21.

Puig de Randa ⓕ

8 km (5 miles) northeast of Llucmajor. 🚌 *to Llucmajor, then taxi.* 🛈 *Llucmajor Plaça Reina María Cristina s/n, 971 44 04 14.*

In the middle of a fertile plain called the *pla* rises a mini mountain 543 m (1,780 ft) high, the Puig de Randa. It is said that Mallorca's greatest son, the 14th-century theologian and mystic Ramon Llull, came to a hermitage on this mountain to meditate and write his religious treatise, *Ars Magna*. On the way up Puig de Randa there are two small monasteries, the 14th-century Santuari de Sant Honorat and the Santuari de Nostra Senyora de Gràcia. The latter, built on a ledge under an overhanging cliff, contains a 13th-century chapel with fine Valencian tiles inside.

On the mountain top is the **Santuari de Cura**, built to commemorate Llull's time on the *puig*, and largely devoted to the study of his work. Its central courtyard is built in the typical beige stone of Mallorca. A small museum, housed in a 16th-century former school off the courtyard, contains some of Llull's manuscripts.

The philosopher Ramon Llull

Capocorb Vell ⓖ

C/ Llucmajor–Cap Blanc km 23. 🚌 *El Arenal.* ☐ *Fri–Wed.* 🎫

Mallorca is not as rich in megalithic remains as Menorca, but this *talaiotic* village *(see p527)* in the stony flatlands of the southern coast is worth seeing – particularly on a quiet day when you can wander among the stones in peace. The settlement, which dates back to around 1000 BC, originally consisted of five *talaiots* (stone tower-like structures with timbered roofs) and another 28 smaller dwellings. Little is known about its inhabitants and the uses for some of the rooms inside the buildings, such as the tiny underground gallery. Too small for living in, this room may have been used to perform magic rituals.

Part of the charm of this place lies in its surroundings among fields of fruit trees and dry stone walls, a setting that somehow complements the ruins. Apart from a snack bar nearby, the site remains mercifully undeveloped.

...e of the *talaiots* of Capocorb Vell

abrera 🔟

...eares. 🚢 from Colònia Sant ...di. 🛈 Carrer Doctor Barraquer 5, ...ònia Sant Jordi, 971 65 60 73.

...om the beaches of Es Trenc ...d Sa Ràpita, on the south ...ast of Mallorca, Cabrera ...oms on the horizon. The ...gest island in an archipelago ...the same name, it lies 18 ...(11 miles) from the most ...utherly point of Mallorca. ...brera is home to several ...e plants, reptiles and ...birds, such as Eleonora's ...on. The waters are ...ortant for marine life. All ...has resulted in it being ...lared a national park *(see ...0–1)*. For centuries ...rera was used as a milit...base and it has a small ...ulation. On it stands a ...-century castle.

A street in Felanitx

Felanitx 🔞

Baleares. 👥 14,200. 🚌 🛈 Avenida Cala Marsas 15, 971 82 60 84. 🚢 Sun. 🎭 Sant Joan Pelós (24 Jun).

This bustling agricultural town is the birthplace of Renaissance architect Guillem Sagrera (1380–1456) and the 20th-century painter Miquel Barceló. Felanitx is visited mainly for three reasons: the imposing façade of the 13th-century church, the **Esglesia de Sant Miquel**; its *sobrassada de porc negre* (a spiced raw sausage made from the meat of the local black pig) and its lively religious fiestas including Sant Joan Pelós *(see p523)*.

About 5 km (3 miles) southeast is the **Castell de Santueri**, founded by the Moors but rebuilt in the 14th century by the kings of Aragón, who ruled Mallorca. Though a ruin, it is worth the detour for the views to the east and south from its vantage point, 400 m (1,300 ft) above the plain.

Coves del Drac 🔟

1 km (1 mile) south of Porto Cristo. 🚌 from Porto Cristo. **Tel** 971 82 07 53. ☐ daily. ⬤ 1 Jan, 25 Dec. 🎫

Mallorca has innumerable caves, ranging from mere holes in the ground to cathedral-like halls. The four vast chambers of the **Coves del Drac** are reached by a steep flight of steps, at the bottom of which is the beautifully lit cave known as "Diana's Bath". Another chamber holds the large underground lake, Martel, which is 29 m (95 ft) below ground level and is 177 m (580 ft) long. Music fills the air of the cave, played from boats plying the lake. Equally dramatic are the two remaining caves, charmingly named "The Theatre of the Fairies" and "The Enchanted City".

Environs

The **Coves d'Hams** is so called because some of its stalactites are shaped like hooks – hams in Mallorcan. The caves are 500 m (1,640 ft) long and contain the "Sea of Venice", an underground lake on which musicians sail in a small boat.

The entrance to the **Coves d'Artà**, near Capdepera, is 40 m (130 ft) above sea level and affords a wonderful view. The caves' main attraction is a stalagmite 22 m (72 ft) high.

🎫 **Coves d'Hams**
11 km (7 miles) from Manacor towards Porto Cristo. **Tel** 971 82 09 88. ☐ daily. ⬤ 1 Jan, 25 Dec. 🎫

🎫 **Coves d'Artà**
Carretera Canyamel. **Tel** 971 84 12 93. ☐ daily. ⬤ 1 Jan, 25 Dec. 🎫

The dramatically lit stalactites of the Coves d'Artà

Street-by-Street: Palma ⑭

**Forn des Teatre
pastry shop**

On an island whose name has become synonymous with mass tourism, Palma surprises by its cultural richness. Under the Moors it was already a prosperous town of fountains and cool courtyards. After he had conquered it in 1229, Jaime I wrote, "It seemed to me the most beautiful city we had ever seen". Signs of Palma's past wealth are still evident in the sumptuous churches, grand public buildings and fine private mansions that crowd the old town. The hub of the city is the old-fashioned Passeig des Born, whose cafés invite you to try one of Mallorca's specialities, the ensaimada, a spiral of pastry dusted with icing sugar.

The Forn des Teatre is an old pastry shop noted for its *ensaimadas* and *gató* (almond cake).

The Fundació la Caixa, once the Gran Hotel, is now a cultural centre.

Palau Reial de l'Almudaina
This palace belongs to the Spanish royal family and houses a museum, whose highlights include the chapel of Santa Ana, with its Romanesque portal, and the Gothic tinell *or salon.*

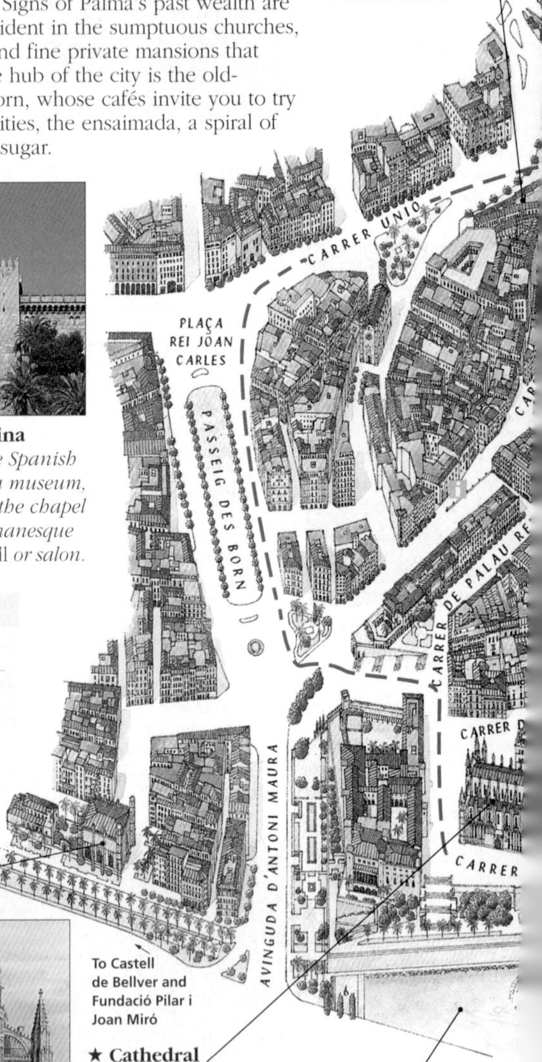

STAR SIGHTS

★ Cathedral

★ Basílica de Sant Francesc

La Llotja is a beautiful 15th-century exchange with tall windows and delicate tracery.

To Castell de Bellver and Fundació Pilar i Joan Miró

★ Cathedral
Built of golden limestone quarried from Santanyi, Palma's huge Gothic cathedral stands in a dramatic location near the waterfront.

Parc de la Mar

CARRER UNIÓ

PLAÇA REI JOAN CARLES

PASSEIG DES BORN

CARRER DE PALAU R

CARRER D

CARRER

AVINGUDA D'ANTONI MAURA

CAR

KEY

– – – Suggested

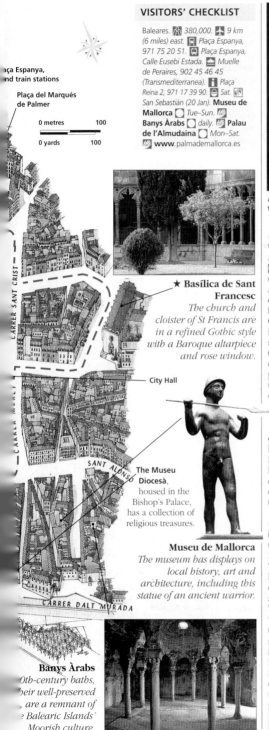

aça Espanya,
nd train stations

Plaça del Marqués
de Palmer

0 metres   100

0 yards   100

VISITORS' CHECKLIST

Baleares. **⚐** 380,000. **✈** 9 km
(6 miles) east. **🚉** Plaça Espanya,
971 75 20 51. **🚌** Plaça Espanya,
Calle Eusebi Estada. **⛴** Muelle
de Peraires, 902 45 46 45
(Transmediterranea). **🛈** Plaça
Reina 2, 971 17 39 90. **⛱** Sat. **⚑**
San Sebastián (20 Jan). **Museu de
Mallorca** ⬜ Tue–Sun. **⚑**
Banys Àrabs ⬜ daily. **⚑ Palau
de l'Almudaina** ⬜ Mon–Sat.
⚑ www.palmademallorca.es

**A view along the circular walls of
the Castell de Bellver**

★ **Basílica de Sant
Francesc**
*The church and
cloister of St Francis are
in a refined Gothic style
with a Baroque altarpiece
and rose window.*

City Hall

**The Museu
Diocesà**,
housed in the
Bishop's Palace,
has a collection of
religious treasures.

Museu de Mallorca
*The museum has displays on
local history, art and
architecture, including this
statue of an ancient warrior.*

Banys Àrabs
*0th-century baths,
heir well-preserved
, are a remnant of
e Balearic Islands'
Moorish culture.*

♟ Castell de Bellver

West side of Palma Bay, C/ Camilo
José Cela 17. **Tel** *971 73 06 57.*
⬜ *Apr–Oct: 8:15am–9pm Mon–Sat;
Oct–Mar: 8:15am–7pm Mon–Sat.* ⚑
About 5 km (3 miles) from the
city centre, standing 113 m (370
ft) above sea level, is Palma's
Gothic castle. It was commissioned by Jaime II during the
short-lived Kingdom of Mallorca
(1276–1349) as a summer residence, but soon after became a
prison, and remained as such
until 1915. The castle, on a hill
overlooking the bay of Palma, is
of an unusual circular design.
Three of its towers are set
into the main castle wall; the
other is set apart from it, but
linked by a high walkway.
From some angles the castle
looks more decorative than
defensive: witness the cloister
of delicate arches that rings
the central courtyard.

♟ Fundació Pilar
i Joan Miró

Carrer Joan de Saridakis 29. *Tel 971
70 14 20.* ⬜ *Tue–Sun.* ⚑ ♿ 🛍
When Joan Miró died in 1983,
his wife took on the task of
converting his former studio
and gardens into an art centre.
The building – christened
"the Alabaster Fortress" by
the Spanish press – is a
stunning example of modern
architecture designed by
Navarrese architect Rafael
Moneo. It incorporates Miró's
original studio (complete with
unfinished paintings), a
permanent collection of the
painter's work, a shop, a
library and an auditorium.

Palma Cathedral

According to legend, when Jaime I of Aragón was caught in a storm on his way to conquer Mallorca in 1229, he vowed that if God led him to safety he would build a great church in his honour. In the following years the old mosque of Medina Mayurqa was torn down and architect Guillem Sagrera (1380–1456) drew up plans for a new cathedral. The last stone was added in 1587, and in subsequent years the cathedral has been rebuilt, notably early last century when parts of the interior were remodelled by Antoni Gaudí *(see pp140–1)*. Today Palma Cathedral, or Sa Seu, as Mallorcans call it, is one of the most breathtaking buildings in Spain, combining vast scale with typically Gothic elegance *(see p24)*.

Bell Tower
This robust tower was built *
1389 and houses nine bells,
the largest of which is know
as N'Eloi, mean-
ing "praise".

Palma Cathedral
*One of the best-sited
cathedrals anywhere, it is
spectacularly poised high on
the sea wall, above what was
once Palma's harbour.*

STAR FEATURES

★ Great Rose Window

★ Baldachino

19th-century tower

Entrance to cathedral museum

Portal Major

Cathedral Museum
*One of the highlights of the
beautifully displayed collection
in the Old Chapterhouse is a
15th-century reliquary of
the True Cross which is
encrusted with jewels and
precious metals.*

Flying buttresses

★ Great Rose Window

The largest of seven rose windows looks down from above the High Altar like a gigantic eye. Built in 1370 with stained glass added in the 16th century, the window has a diameter of over 11 m (36 ft).

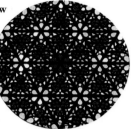

VISITORS' CHECKLIST

Plaça Almonia. **Tel** 902 022 445/6. ☐ Apr–May & Oct: 10am–5:15pm Mon–Fri (3pm Nov–Mar, 6:15pm Jun–Sep); 10am–2pm Sat all year. ● public hols. ✝ 9am, Mon–Sat, 9am, 10:30am, noon, 1pm, 7pm Sun. ♿
www.catedraldemallorca.org

The Great Organ was built with a Neo-Gothic case in 1795, and restored in 1993 by Gabriel Blancafort.

Capella de la Trinitat
This tiny chapel was built in 1329 as the mausoleum of Jaime II and III of Aragón. It contains their alabaster tombs.

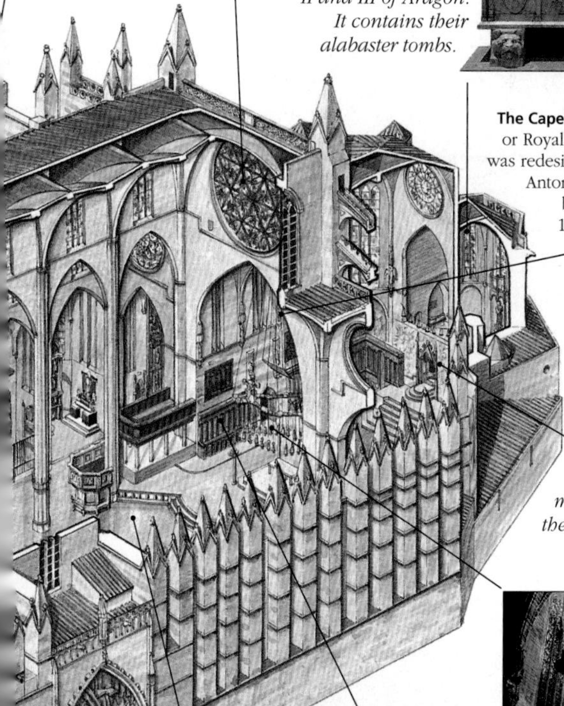

The Capella Reial, or Royal Chapel, was redesigned by Antoni Gaudí between 1904 and 1914.

Bishop's Throne
Built in 1269 and made of Carrara marble, the chair is embedded in a Gothic vaulted niche.

Choir stalls

Portal del Mirador

Nave
The magnificent ceiling, 44 m (144 ft) high, is held up by 14 slender pillars. At over 19 m (62 ft) wide, it is one of the broadest naves in the world.

★ Baldachino
Gaudí's bizarre wrought-iron canopy above the altar incorporates lamps, tapestries and a multicoloured crucifix.

Menorca

Menorca is the Balearic island furthest from the mainland and it is set apart from the rest of the country in many other ways. The coastline of Menorca is, arguably, more unspoiled than in any other part of Spain. Its countryside remains largely green and pleasant with cows roaming the meadows. The old towns of Maó – the island's capital – and Ciutadella are filled with noble, historic buildings and beautiful squares. Menorca also has abundant reminders of its more distant history: the island boasts a spectacular hoard of Bronze Age stone structures, which provide an invaluable insight into its prehistoric past. The Menorcans are often more inclined to drink the locally brewed gin *(ginebra)* than the wine which is favoured elsewhere in Spain.

Fishermen mending their nets in Ciutadella's harbour

The peaceful seafront of Ciutadella at twilight

Ciutadella [20]

Baleares. 🏘 *22,000* 🚌 🚢 🛈
Plaça de la Catedral 5, 971 38 26 93.
🕎 *Fri & Sat.* 🎊 *Sant Joan (23–24 Jun).* **www**.illesbalears.es

The key date in the history of Ciutadella is 1558. In that year the Turks, under Barbarossa, entered and decimated the city, consigning 3,495 of its citizens to the slave markets of Constantinople. Of Ciutadella's main public buildings, only the fine Catalan Gothic **Església Catedral de Menorca** managed to survive this fearsome onslaught in more or less its original condition, only later to be stripped of all its paintings, ornaments and other treasures by Republican extremists during the Civil War.

The nearby **Plaça d'es Born** was built as a parade ground for Moorish troops and from 1558 was gradually rebuilt in Renaissance style. Today it is one of Spain's most impressive squares, containing pleasant cafés and bordered by shady palm trees. At the centre of the Plaça d'es Born is an obelisk which commemorates the "Any de sa Desgràcia" (Year

The historic Plaça d'es Born in the centre of Ciutadella

of Misfortune), when the Turks invaded the city. Around the square are the Gothic-style **town hall** *(ajuntament)*, the late 19th-century **Teatre Municipal d'es Born**, and a series of aristocratic mansions with Italianesque façades, the grandest of which is the early 19th-century **Palau de Torre-Saura**. From the northern end of the square there is a fine view over the small harbour.

If you walk up the Carrer Major d'es Born past the cathedral, you come to **Ses Voltes**, an alley lined on both sides by whitewashed arches. Turn right along the Carrer del Seminari for the Baroque **Església dels Socors** and the **Museu Diocesà** with its displays of ecclesiastical paraphernalia. In the narrow street of the old town there are many impressive palaces, but only the early 19th-century **Palau Salort**, on the Carrer Major d'es Born, is open to the public. The Art Nouveau **market** (1895), its ironwork painted in smart municipal dark green, stands nearby.

The peace of Ciutadella is disturbed every June by the Festa de Sant Joan, a spectacular ritual of horsemanship. During the festival the local gin *(ginebra)* is drunk copiously and the city grinds to a halt.

🏛 **Museu Diocesà**
Carrer del Seminari 5. **Tel** *971 48 ...
97.* ☐ *Tue–Sat.* 🎟 ♿ 🅿 *(by ap...*

🏛 **Palau Salort**
Carrer Major d'es Born 9. **Tel** *97...
38 00 56.* ☐ *May–Oct: 10am–2...
Mon–Sat.* 🎟

Ferreries ㉑

Baleares. 🏛 *3,100.* 🚌 🛈 *Carrer Sant Bartomeu 55, 971 37 30 03.* 🚤 *Tue, Fri, Sat.* 🎭 *Sant Bartomeu (23–5 Aug).*

Ferreries lies in between Mercadal and Ciutadella and sprang up when a road was built to connect the two towns. Today Ferreries is an attractive village of white houses, built against the slope of a hill. The simple church, Sant Bartomeu, dates from 1770.

The bay of **Santa Galdana**, 10 km (6 miles) to the south, is even prettier. You can take a pleasant walk from the beach inland through the fertile riverbed of Barranc d'Algendar.

Courtyard in the Santuari del Toro

Es Mercadal ㉒

Baleares. 🏛 *3,700.* 🚌 🛈 *Carrer Major 16, 971 37 50 02.* 🚤 *Sun.* 🎭 *Sant Martí (third Sun of Jul).*

Es Mercadal is a small country town – one of the three, with Maior and Ferreries, that are strung out along the main road from Maó to Ciutadella.

The town is unremarkable in itself, but within reach of it are three places of interest.

El Toro, 3 km (2 miles) to the east, is Menorca's highest mountain, at 350 m (1,150 ft). It is also the spiritual heart of the island and at its summit is the Santuari del Toro, built in 1670, which is run by nuns.

About 10 km (6 miles) north of Es Mercadal, the fishing village of **Fornells** transforms itself every summer into an outpost of St Tropez. In the harbour, smart yachts jostle with fishing boats, and the local jet-set crowd into the Bar Palma. Fornells' main culinary speciality is the *caldereta de llagosta* (lobster casserole), but the quality varies and prices can be high.

The road-cum-dirt track to the **Cap de Cavalleria**, 13 km (8 miles) north of Es Mercadal, passes through one of the Balearics' finest landscapes. Cavalleria is a rocky promontory, whipped by the tramontana wind from the north. It juts out into a choppy sea which, in winter, looks more like the North Atlantic than the Mediterranean. At the western edge of the peninsula are the remains of Sanisera, a Phoenician village mentioned by Pliny in the 1st century AD. The road leads to a headland, with a lighthouse and cliffs 90 m (295 ft) high, where peregrine falcons, sea eagles and kites ride the wind.

Further west along the coast is a string of fine, unspoiled beaches, though with difficult access: Cala Pregonda, Cala del Pilar and La Vall d'Algaiarens are three of the most beautiful.

Horse rearing in the fiesta of Sant Lluís

THE BALEARIC ISLANDS' FIESTAS

Sant Antoni Abat *(16– 17 Jan)*, Mallorca. This fiesta is celebrated with parades and the blessing of animals all over Mallorca and in Sant Antoni in Ibiza.

Sant Joan *(24 Jun)*, Ciutadella (Menorca). The horse plays a major part in Menorca's festivals. In the streets and squares of Ciutadella on 24 June, the Day of St John the Baptist, elegantly dressed riders put their horses through ritualized medieval manoeuvres. The fiesta reaches a climax when the horses rear up on their hind legs and the jubilant crowds swarm around them trying to hold them up with their hands. Similarly, the annual fiesta in Sant Lluís, which takes place at the end of August, sees many of the locals taking to the streets on horseback.

Sant Joan Pelós *(24 Jun)*, Felanitx (Mallorca). As part of this fiesta, a man is dressed in sheepskins to represent John the Baptist.

Romeria de Sant Marçal *(30 Jun)*, Sa Cabeneta (Mallorca). A feature of this fiesta is a market selling *siurells*, primitive Mallorcan whistles.

Our Lady of the Sea *(16 Jul)*, Formentera. The island's main fiesta honours the Virgen del Carmen, patroness of fishermen, with a flotilla of fishing boats.

Quiet stretch of beach at Santa Galdana

The steep hillside of Maó running up from the harbour

Maó ㉓

Baleares. 🖼 24,000. 🛬 🚉 ⛴ ℹ
Sa Rovellada de Dalt 24, 971 36 37 90.
🅿 Tue, Sat. 🎪 Fiestas de Gràcia (7–8
Sep), Fiesta de Sant Antoni (17 Jan).

The quietly elegant town of
Maó has lent its Spanish
name, Mahón, to mayonnaise.
It was occupied by the British
three times during the 18th
century. The legacy of past
colonial rule can be seen in
sober Georgian town houses,
with their dark green shutters
and sash windows.

Maó's harbour is one of the
finest in the Mediterranean.
Taking the street leading from
the port to the upper town,
the S-shaped Costa de Ses
Voltes, you come to the 18th-
century **Església del Carme**, a
former Carmelite church
whose cool white cloister now
houses an attractive fruit and
vegetable market. Behind the
market is the **Col·lecció
Hernández Sanzy Hernández
Mora**, which houses
Menorcan art and antiques.
The nearby Plaça Constitució
is overlooked by the church
of Santa Maria, which has a
huge organ. Next door is the
town hall (ajuntament) with
its Neo-Classical façade, into
which is mounted the famous
clock donated by Sir Richard
Kane (1660–1736), the first
British governor of Menorca.

Located at the end of the
Carrer Isabel II is the **Església
de Sant Francesc**, with an
intriguing Romanesque doorway and Baroque façade. The
church houses the newly
refurbished Museu de
Menorca, which is open daily
except Monday. Two minutes'
walk south of here will take
you to Maó's main square, the
Plaça de S'Esplanada, behind
which is the **Ateneu Científic
Lliterat Artistic**, a centre of
Menorca-related culture and
learning. Inside are collections
of local ceramics and maps,
and a library. It is advisable
to obtain permission before
looking around. On the north
side of the harbour is a mansion known as **Sant Antoni** or
the Golden Farm. As Maó's
finest example of Palladian
architecture, it has an arched
façade, painted plum red, with
white arches, in the traditional
Menorcan style. The British
admiral, Nelson, is thought to
have stayed here. The house
has a collection of Nelson
memorabilia and a fine library
but is closed to the public.

🏛 **Col·lecció Hernández
Sanzy Hernández Mora**
Claustre del Carme 5. **Tel** 971 35
05 97. 🕐 10am–1pm Mon–Sat.

🏛 **Ateneu Científic Literari i
Artistic**
C/ Rovellada de Dalt 25. **Tel** 971 36
05 53. 🌑 Sun, public hols.

Cales Coves ㉔

Baleares. 🚌 Sant Climent, then
25 mins walk. **Tel** Maó, 971 36 37 90

On either side of a pretty
bay can be found Cales Coves
– the site of Neolithic
dwellings of up to 9 m (30 ft)
in length, hollowed out of the
rock face. The caves, thought
to have been inhabited since
prehistoric times, are today
occupied by a community of
people seeking an alternative
lifestyle. Some of the caves
have front doors, chimneys
and even butane cookers.

About 8 km (5 miles) west,
along the coast, lies Binibeca,
a tourist village built in a style
sympathetic to old Menorca.
The jumble of white houses
and tiny streets of the Poblat
de Pescadors, an imitation
fishing village, have the look
of the genuine article.

**Modern sculpture outside one of
the dwellings at Cales Coves**

◁ The clear blue waters of Cala Turqueta in Menorca

Ancient Menorca

Menorca is exceptionally rich in prehistoric remains – the island has been described as an immense open-air museum. The majority of the sites are the work of the "talayot" people who lived between 2000–1000 BC and are named after the *talaiots* or huge stone towers that characterize the Menorcan landscape. There are hundreds of these Bronze Age villages and structures dotted around the island. Usually open to the public and free of charge, these sites provide an invaluable insight into the ancient inhabitants of the Balearics.

Huge *talaiot* amid the settlement of Trepucó

DIFFERENT STRUCTURES

The ancient stone structures scattered around the countryside of Menorca and, to a lesser extent, Mallorca can be placed into three main categories: *taulas, talaiots* and *navetas*.

Taulas *are two slabs of rock, one placed on top of the other, in a "T" formation. Suggestions as to their possible function range from a sacrificial altar to a roof support.*

Talayots *are circular or square buildings that may have been used as meeting places and dwellings.*

Navetas *are shaped like upturned boats and apparently had a dual role as dwellings and burial quarters. At least ten of these remain in Menorca.*

Spectacular *taula* at Talatí de Dalt, standing 3 m (10 ft) high

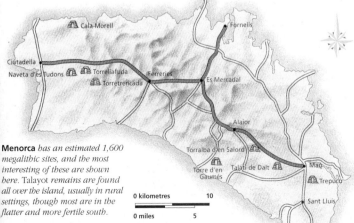

Menorca *has an estimated 1,600 megalithic sites, and the most interesting of these are shown here. Talayot remains are found all over the island, usually in rural settings, though most are in the flatter and more fertile south.*

0 kilometres 10

0 miles 5

THE CANARY ISLANDS

LA PALMA · EL HIERRO · LA GOMERA · TENERIFE
GRAN CANARIA · FUERTEVENTURA · LANZAROTE

*P*oised on the edge of the tropics west of Morocco, the Canaries
enjoy a generous supply of sunshine, pleasantly tempered by
the trade winds. Their scenery ranges from lava desert to
primeval forest and from sand dunes to volcanic peaks. The old towns
on the main islands have colonial centres, full of character.

Seven islands and half a dozen islets make up the Canary archipelago. They are the tips of hundreds of volcanoes that first erupted from the sea bed 14 million years ago. Teneguía on La Palma last erupted in 1971.

In the 14th and 15th centuries, when navigators discovered the islands and claimed them for Spain, they were inhabited by the Guanches, who practised a stone culture. Sadly, little evidence of them remains.

Today the islands are divided into two provinces. The four western isles, making up the province of Santa Cruz de Tenerife, are all mountainous; Tenerife's colossal dormant volcano, Mount Teide, casts the world's biggest sea-shadow. La Palma, El Hierro and La Gomera, where Columbus stayed on his voyages, are all small, unspoiled islands, not yet developed for mass tourism.

The eastern islands belong to the province of Las Palmas. Forested Gran Canaria is the biggest and its capital, Las Palmas de Gran Canaria, is a colonial town. Lanzarote, by contrast, is flat, with lunar landscapes, while Fuerteventura has long, virgin beaches.

Protected area of sand dunes at Maspalomas, next to the busy Playa del Inglés, Gran Canaria

La Rambla banana plantation on the north coast of the island of Tenerife

Exploring the Western Islands

Tenerife has the widest range of holiday attractions
of any of the Canary Islands. The province of Santa
Cruz de Tenerife also includes the three tiny westerly
islands of La Palma, La Gomera and El Hierro, which
are scarcely developed for tourism and have no large
resorts. Gradually, more visitors are discovering these
peaceful, green havens. If you enjoy walking, wildlife
and mountain scenery, visit one of these hideaways.
All three islands have comfortable hotels, including
paradors. But compared with Gran Canaria and the
eastern islands, there are fewer sandy beaches here,
and little organized entertainment or sightseeing.

**Las Teresitas artificial beach, Santa
Cruz de Tenerife**

LA PALMA

- Los Sauces
- Puntagorda
- *Caldera de Taburiente*
- C830
- C832
- Breña Alta
- Santa Cruz de la Palma
- Los Llanos de Aridane
- El Paso
- Tazacorte
- **LA PALMA**
- ❶
- C832
- Fuencaliente

SIGHTS AT A GLANCE

Candelaria ❽
Los Cristianos ❹
La Gomera ❸
El Hierro ❷
La Laguna ❾
Montes de Anaga ❿
La Orotava ❼
La Palma ❶
Parque Nacional del Teide
pp538–9 ❺
Puerto de la Cruz ❻
Santa Cruz de Tenerife ⓫

Roque Bonanza on the rocky east coast of El Hierro

LA GO

- Villahermoso
- Valle Gran Rey
- **LA GO**
- Allajero

EL HIERRO

- Valverde
- *Ermita de los Reyes*
- Frontera
- Puerto de la Estaca
- ❷
- **EL HIERRO**
- La Restinga

KEY

▭	Motorway
▬	Major road
▭	Secondary road
▬	Scenic route
△	Summit

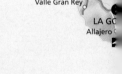

Terraced hillside, maximizing cultivation in the lush green Valle Gran Rey, in western La Gomera

GETTING AROUND

From mainland Spain there are flights *(see p676)* and ferries *(see p677)* to the Canary Islands. Transport to the small islands is mainly from Tenerife. La Gomera is easily reached by ferry or hydrofoil from Los Cristianos, or by plane from Gran Canaria or Tenerife. Airports on La Palma and El Hierro are served by regular flights from Tenerife's northern airport of Los Rodeos. Unless you take an organized coach trip, a car is essential to see the island scenery. Roads are improving, but great care is needed for mountain driving.

TENERIFE

MONTES DE ANAGA

LA LAGUNA ⑩ 🌊 *Playa de Las Teresitas*
Tacoronte ○ 🏛🎪 ⑨
TF5
✈ ⑪ SANTA CRUZ DE TENERIFE

PUERTO DE LA CRUZ ⑥ 🍃
🏛🎪 El Rosario
TF1
Buenavista del Norte ○ Garachico ○ LA OROTAVA ⑦
Punta de Teno C820 C824
C821
Guía ○
C823 Pico del Teide 3718m 🌋 ⑤ PARQUE NACIONAL DEL TEIDE
Parador de Cañadas del Teide C822
Vilaflor ○
Adeje ○ C821 Granadilla de Abona
○ Arona Punta de Abona

Güímar ○

⑧ CANDELARIA

...ián
Playa de las Américas ○
LOS CRISTIANOS ④ ○ El Medano
TF1 Punta Roja
Punta de la Rasca Costa del Silencio

Kilometres 25
Miles 10

SEE ALSO

Where to Stay pp591–601

Where to Eat pp651–3

The wild landscape of Punta de Teno in western Tenerife

La Palma ❶

Santa Cruz de Tenerife. ⚇ 80,000.
✕ ⌂ Santa Cruz de la Palma.
ℹ Calle O'Daly 22, Santa Cruz de la
Palma, 922 41 21 06.
www.lapalmaturismo.com

Reaching an altitude of 2,426 m (7,959 ft) on a land base of less than 706 sq km (280 sq miles), La Palma is the world's steepest island. It lies on the northwestern tip of the archipelago and has a cool, moist climate and lush vegetation. The mountainous interior is covered with forests of pine, laurel and giant fern.

The centre of the island is dominated by **La Caldera de Taburiente**, a volcano's massive crater, more than 8 km (5 miles) wide. National park status (see pp30–1) is an indication of its botanical and geological importance. The International Astrophysics Observatory crowns the summit. A couple of roads traverse

Pastel façades and delicate wooden balconies in Santa Cruz, La Palma

The Parque Nacional de la Caldera de Taburiente, La Palma

La Palma's dizzy heights, offering spectacular views of the craters of La Cumbrecita and Roque de los Muchachos.

Santa Cruz de la Palma, the island's main town and port, is an elegant place of old houses with balconies, some fine churches and several 16th-century buildings. In the cobbled street behind the seafront, Calle O'Daly (named after an Irish banana trader), are the Iglesia El Salvador, boasting a Mudéjar coffered ceiling, and the town hall (ayuntamiento), which is housed in a cardinal's palace. A full-sized cement replica of the Santa María, Columbus's flagship, stands at the end of the Plaza Alameda.

The tortuous mountain road southwest of Santa Cruz winds over Las Cumbres mountains via Breña Alta to **El Paso** in the centre of the island. A relatively sizeable community, the village is known for its silk production and hand-rolled cigars.

Among the almond terraces and vineyards of southern La Palma, solidified lava from the Teneguia volcano is a reminde of its recent activity (see p551,

Craters on El Hierro, Spain's most western territory

El Hierro ❷

Santa Cruz de Tenerife. ⚇ 10,50C
✕ ⌂ Puerto de la Estaca.
ℹ C/ Doctor Quintero 4,
Valverde, 922 55 03 02.

Due to a dearth of sandy beaches, El Hierro has escaped tourist invasions. Instead it has caught the atte tions of naturalists. Its hilly landscape and unusual faur and flora are part of its appe El Hierro is the smallest of Canaries, and the furthest w consequently it is the last pl in Spain where the sun sets

Valverde, the island's capi stands inland at 600 m (2,0 ft) above sea level. Canary pines and peculiarly twiste juniper trees cover El Hierr

LA GOMERA'S WHISTLE LANGUAGE

The problems of communication posed by La Gomera's rugged terrain produced an unusual language, known as El Silbo. This system of piercing whistles probably developed because its sounds carry across the great distances from one valley to the next. Its origins are mysterious, but it was allegedly invented by the Guanches (see p547). Few young Gomerans have any use for El Silbo today, and the language would probably be dead if it were not for the demonstrations of it still held for interested visitors at the parador, and in the restaurant at Las Rosas.

El Silbo practised on La Gomera

juniper trees cover El Hierro's mountainous interior, best seen from the many footpaths and scenic viewpoints along the roads. A ridge of woodland, curving east-west across the island, marks the edge of a volcano. The crater forms a fertile depression known as El Golfo.

In the far west is the **Ermita de los Reyes**, a place of pilgrimage and the starting point of the island's biggest fiesta, held in July every four years. The turquoise seas off the south coast are popular with skin-divers, who base themselves in the small fishing village of **La Restinga**.

La Gomera ❸

anta Cruz de Tenerife. 🏠 *21,400.*
✕ 🚢 🛈 *Calle Real 4, San Seba-*
tián de la Gomera, 922 14 15 12.
www.gomera-island.com

a Gomera is the most ccessible of the smaller western islands, only 40 minutes by hydrofoil from Los ristianos on Tenerife (90 minutes by ferry), or by plane rom Tenerife or Gran Canaria. Many come to La Gomera for a day only, taking a coach ip. Others hire a car and xplore on their own: a cenic but exhausting drive or a single day as the terrain intensely buckled, and the entral plateau is deeply ored by dramatic ravines. riving across these gorges volves negotiating countless zzying hairpin bends.

The best way to enjoy the and is to stay awhile and

Terraced hillsides in the fertile Valle Gran Rey, La Gomera

explore it at leisure, preferably doing some walking. On a fine day, La Gomera's scenery is glorious. Rock pinnacles jut above steep slopes studded with ferns while terraced hillsides glow with palms and flowering creepers. The best section, the **Parque Nacional de Garajonay**, is a UNESCO World Heritage Site.

San Sebastián, La Gomera's main town and ferry terminal, is situated on the east coast, a scattering of white buildings around a small beach. Among its sights are some places associated with Columbus (*see pp58–9*), who topped up

his water supplies here before setting out on his adventurous voyages. A well in the customs house bears the grand words "With this water America was baptized". According to legend he also prayed in the Iglesia de la Asunción, and stayed at a local house.

Beyond the arid hills to the south lies **Playa de Santiago**, the island's only real resort, which has a grey pebble beach. **Valle Gran Rey**, in the far west, is a fertile valley of palms and staircase terraces. These days it is colonized by foreigners attempting alternative lifestyles. In the north, tiny roads weave a tortuous course around several pretty villages, plunging at intervals to small, stony beaches. **Las Rosas** is a popular stop-off for coach parties, who can enjoy the visitors' centre and a restaurant with a panoramic view.

The road towards the coast from Las Rosas leads through the town of **Vallehermoso**, dwarfed by the huge **Roque de Cano**, which is an impressive mass of solidified lava. Just off the north coast stands **Los Órganos**, a fascinating rock formation of crystallized basalt columns resembling the pipes of an organ.

per trees on El Hierro, twisted and bent by the wind

Tenerife

In the language of its aboriginal Guanche inhabitants Tenerife means "Snowy Mountain", a tribute to its most striking geographical feature, the dormant volcano of Mount Teide, Spain's highest peak. The largest of the Canary Islands, Tenerife is a roughly triangular landmass rising steeply on all sides towards the cloud-capped summit that divides it into two distinct climatic zones: damp and lushly vegetated in the north, sunny and arid in the south. Tenerife offers a more varied range of attractions than any of the other Canary Islands, including its spectacular volcanic scenery, water sports and a vibrant atmosphere after dark. Its beaches, however, have unenticing black sand and are rather poor for swimming. The main resorts are crowded with high-rise hotels and apartments, offering nightlife but little peace and quiet.

Bananas in northern Tenerife

Los Cristianos **❹**

Santa Cruz de Tenerife. 🏘 *60,000.*
🚌 🚢 🛈 *Plaza del Pescador 1, 922 75 71 37.* 🛒 *Sun.* 🎭 *Fiesta del Carmen (first Sun of Sep).*
www.arona.org

The old fishing village of Los Cristianos, on Tenerife's south coast, has grown into a town spreading out along the foot of barren hills. Ferries and hydrofoils make regular trips from its little port to La Gomera and El Hierro *(see pp532–3).*

To the north lies the modern expanse of **Playa de las Américas**, Tenerife's largest development. It offers visitors a cheerful, relaxed, undemanding cocktail of sun and fun.

A brief sortie inland leads to the much older town of **Adeje** and to the **Barranco del Infierno**, a wild gorge with an attractive waterfall (two hours' round walk from Adeje).

Along the coast to the east, the **Costa del Silencio** is a pleasant contrast to most of

the other large resorts, with its bungalow developments surrounding fishing villages. Los Abrigos has lively fish restaurants lining its harbour.

Further east, **El Médano** shelters below an ancient volcanic cone. Its two beaches are popular with windsurfers.

Parque Nacional del Teide **❺**

See pp538–39.

Puerto de la Cruz **❻**

Santa Cruz de Tenerife. 🏘 *27,500.*
🚌 🛈 *Plaza Europa, 922 38 60 00.*
🛒 *Sat.* 🎭 *Carnival (Feb–Mar), Fiesta del Carmen (second Sun of Jul).*

Puerto de la Cruz, the oldest resort in the Canaries, first sprang to prominence in 1706, when a volcanic eruption obliterated Tenerife's principal port of Garachico. Puerto de

la Cruz took its place, later becoming popular with genteel English convalescents. The town's older buildings give it much of its present character.

The beautiful Lago Martiánez lido, designed by the Lanzarote architect César Manrique *(see p548)*, compensates for a lack of good beaches with its sea water pools, palms and fountains. Other attractions include the tropical gardens of **Loro Parque**, where visitors can also see parrots and dolphins.

Outside town, the **Bananera El Guanche** plantation has an exhibition on bananas and other tropical crops. **Icod de los Vinos**, a short drive west, attracts crowds for its spectacular ancient dragon tree.

🌿 **Loro Parque**
Avenida Loro Parque
Tel 922 37 38 41. 🕐 *daily.* 🔲&

🌿 **Bananera El Guanche**
Carretera Botánico, La Orotava.
Tel 922 33 18 53. 🕐 *daily.* 🔲&

THE DRAGON TREE

The Canary Islands have many unusual plants, but the dragon tree *(Dracaena draco)* is one of the strangest. This primitive creature looks a little like a giant cactus, with swollen branches that sprout multiple tufts of spiky leaves. When cut, the trunk exudes a reddish sap once believed to have magical and medicinal properties. Dragon trees form no annual rings, so their age is a mystery. Some are thought to be hundreds of years old. The most venerable surviving specimen can be seen at Icod de los Vinos.

The landscaped Lago Martiánez lido, Puerto de la Cruz

La Orotava ●

Santa Cruz de Tenerife. ⌂ 40,000.
🚌 🛈 *Carrera del Escultor Estévez 2, 922 32 30 41.* 🎭 *Carnival (Feb/Mar), Corpus Christi (May/Jun), Romeria San Isidoro Labrador (Jun).*

A short distance from Puerto de la Cruz, in the fertile hills above the Orotava valley, La Orotava makes a popular excursion. The old part of this historic town clusters around the large **Iglesia de Nuestra Señora de la Concepción**. This domed Baroque building with twin towers was built in the late 18th century to replace an earlier church that was destroyed in earthquakes at the beginning of that century.

In the surrounding streets and squares are many old churches, convents and grand houses with elaborate wooden balconies. The **Casas de los Balcones** and **Casa del Turista** have interior courtyards that are open to the public.

Statue of a Guanche chief on the seafront of Candelaria

Nuestra Señora de la Candelaria, patron saint of the Canary Islands

Candelaria ●

Santa Cruz de Tenerife. ⌂ 17,000.
🛈 *Plaza del Cit, 922 50 04 15.* 🚌 *Sat, Sun.* 🎭 *Nuestra Señora de Candelaria (14–15 Aug).*

This coastal town is famous for its shrine to Nuestra Señora de la Candelaria, the Canary Islands' patron saint, whose image is surrounded by flowers and candles in a modern church in the main square. This gaudy Virgin, supposedly washed ashore in pagan times, was venerated before Christianity reached the island. In 1826 a tidal wave returned her to the sea, but a replica draws pilgrims to worship here every August. Outside, stone effigies of Guanche chiefs line the sea wall.

La Laguna ●

Santa Cruz de Tenerife. ⌂ 141,000.
🚌 🛈 *Plaza Adelantado s/n, 922 63 11 94.* 🚌 *daily.* 🎭 *San Benito (15 Jul), Santísimo Cristo de la Laguna (14 Sep).*

A bustling university town and former island capital, La Laguna is the second largest settlement on Tenerife and a UNESCO World Heritage Site.

In its old quarter, best explored on foot, there are many atmospheric squares, historic buildings and good museums. Most of the sights lie between the bell-towered **Iglesia de Nuestra Señora de la Concepción** (1502), and the Plaza del Adelantado, on which stand the town hall, a convent and the **Palacio de Nava.**

Montes de Anaga ●

Santa Cruz de Tenerife. 🚌 *Santa Cruz de Tenerife, La Laguna.*

The rugged mountains north of Santa Cruz are kept green and lush by a cool, wet climate. They abound with a wide variety of interesting birds and plants, including cacti, laurels and tree heathers. Walking the mountain trails is very popular, and maps showing many of the best paths are readily available from the tourist office. A steep road with marker posts climbs up from the village of San Andrés by the beautiful but artificial beach of Las Teresitas. On clear days there are marvellous vistas along the paths, especially from the viewpoints of Pico del Inglés and Bailadero.

Winding down through the laurel forests of Monte de las Mercedes and the colourful valley of Tejina you reach **Tacoronte** with its interesting churches, an ethnographic museum and a bodega, where you can sample local wines.

THE CANARY ISLANDS' FIESTAS

Carnival *(Feb/Mar)*, Santa Cruz de Tenerife. One of Europe's biggest carnivals, this grand street party is a lavish spectacle of extravagant costumes and Latin American dance music to rival that of Rio de Janeiro. For years under the Franco regime, Carnival was suppressed for its irreverent frivolity. It begins with the election of a queen of the festivities and builds up to a climax on Shrove Tuesday when there is a large procession. The "funeral" of an enormous mock sardine takes place on Ash Wednesday. Carnival is also celebrated on the islands of Lanzarote and Gran Canaria.

Revellers in Carnival outfits on Tenerife

Corpus Christi *(May/Jun)*, La Orotava (Tenerife). The streets of the town are filled with flower carpets in striking patterns, while the Plaza del Ayuntamiento is covered in copies of works of art, formed from coloured volcanic sands.
Descent of the Virgin of the Snows *(Jul, every five years: 2005, 2010)* Santa Cruz de La Palma.
Romería de la Virgen de la Candelaria *(15 Aug)*, Candelaria (Tenerife). Pilgrims come here in their thousands to venerate the Canary Islands' patroness.
Fiesta del Charco *(7–11 Sep)*, San Nicolás de Tolentino (Gran Canaria). People leap into a large saltwater pond to catch mullet.

Large ships moored at the busy port of Santa Cruz de Tenerife

Santa Cruz de Tenerife ⓫

Santa Cruz de Tenerife. 🏘 220,000.
🚌 🚢 🛈 Plaza de España 1, 922 23 95 92. 🖪 Sun. 🎉 Carnival *(Feb/Mar)*, Día de la Cruz (3 May).
www.turismosantacruz.com

Tenerife's capital city is an important regional port, with a deep-water harbour suitable for large ships. Its most attractive beach, **Las Teresitas**, lies 7 km (4 miles) to the north. Completely artificial, it was created by importing millions of tonnes of golden Saharan sand and building a protective reef just offshore. Shaded by palms, backed by mountains and so far devoid of concrete hotel developments, the result improves on anything nature has bestowed on Tenerife.

Santa Cruz can boast many handsome historic buildings. The hub of the town is around the **Plaza de España**, situated near the harbour. Just off it is the Calle de Castillo, the main shopping street. Its two most noteworthy churches are the **Iglesia de Nuestra Señora de la Concepción**, with parts dating from 1500, and Baroque **Iglesia de San Francisco**.

Particularly interesting is the **Museo de la Naturaleza y el Hombre**, in the Palacio Insular, where Guanche mummies grin in glass cases. Inside the museum you can also see the cannon which is alleged to have removed the arm of the British admiral Nelson during an unsuccessful raid on the city in the late 18th century.

Other attractions include the **Museo de Bellas Artes** which features old masters as well as modern works. Many of its paintings focus on local events and landscapes. Contemporary sculptures adorn the **Parque Municipal García Sanabria**, a pleasant park with shady paths, laid out in 1926.

In the morning, visit the **Mercado de Nuestra Señora de África**, which combines a bazaar with a food market. Outside stalls sell domestic goods; those inside offer an eclectic mix of live chickens, spices and cut flowers. Santa Cruz is especially worth a vis during its flamboyant carniva

🏛 **Museo de la Naturaleza y el Hombre**
Calle Fuentes Morales. **Tel** 922 53 58 16. ☐ Tue–Sun. 🎟 ♿

🏛 **Museo de Bellas Artes**
Calle José Murphy 12. **Tel** 922 24 43 58. ☐ Tue–Fri.

The artificial beach of Las Teresit in Santa Cruz

The Flavours of the Canary Islands

The exotic fruits and vegetables that grow in the sub-tropical Canaries climate, and the unusual fish that are caught in local waters, have led to a cuisine very different from that of the Iberian Peninsula. From the original inhabitants, the Guanche, culinary traditions survive in local staples like *gofio* (maize meal). Over the centuries, Spanish, Portuguese and North African influences have been incorporated into the local cuisine, but the underlying theme is always one of simplicity and a reliance on ultra-fresh local produce. All kinds of unusual delicacies are available, from sweet-fleshed parrot-fish to succulent tropical fruits.

Maize (corn)

Fish straight from the ocean, being dried in the sun to preserve them

SEAFOOD AND MEAT

The Canaries offer an incredible array of seafood, with varieties unknown on the Spanish mainland. Delicacies like *lapas* (limpets) are around only for a few months during the summer, and are usually served simply grilled (*a la plancha*). Other unusual varieties include wreckfish, damselfish, dentex and parrot-fish. These, along with more common varieties, are usually fried, baked in a salt crust, or dried in the sun.

Meats include standard Iberian favourites like pork, kid and beef, but they are often prepared according to ancient Guanche traditions.

FRUIT AND VEGETABLES

The mild, stable Canarian climate is perfect for growing luscious tropical fruits (the most famous crop of the islands being bananas). Exotic vegetables thrive, too, as well as potatoes and tomatoes, which were introduced here 500 years ago from the newly discovered Americas. The islands boast varieties of potato unknown elsewhere, and these feature in the local favourite *papas arrugadas* ("wrinkly potatoes"), which are made by boiling potatoes in their skins in very salty water – sometimes seawater.

Dates   Bananas   Pineapple   Papayas (paw paw)

Mangoes   Guavas

Mouthwatering fresh fruits from the Canary Islands

CANARIAN DISHES AND SPECIALITIES

The Greeks named the Canaries "the fortunate islands", and they are certainly blessed in terms of the freshness and abundance of the local produce. What ever you choose to eat, you can be sure of encountering a bowl of the ubiquitous *mojo* sauce. This aromatic Canarian creation accompanies almost every dish, and appears in countless versions: the main ones are red *picón*, which is spiced up with pepper and paprika, and green *verde*, with parsley and coriander. The Canarian staple, *gofio* (roasted maize meal), is served for breakfast and used in local dishes such as *gofio de almendras*, a rich almond dessert. The islands are also known for delicious pastries like the honey-drizzled *bienmesabes* (meaning "tastes good to me") and traditional cheeses.

Almonds

Sopa de pescados tinerfeña
This Tenerife fish soup of sea bass and potatoes is scented with saffron and cumin.

Parque Nacional del Teide ❺

Towering over Tenerife, Mount Teide, surrounded by a wild volcanic landscape, is an awesome sight. 180,000 years ago a much larger adjacent cone collapsed leaving behind the devastation of Las Cañadas, a 16-km (10-mile) wide caldera, and the smaller volcano, Teide, on its northern edge. Today volcanic material forms a wilderness of weathered, mineral-tinted rocks, ash beds and lava streams. A single road crosses the plateau of Las Cañadas, passing a parador, cable car station, and visitors' centre. Follow the marked paths for unforgettable views of this unique, protected area.

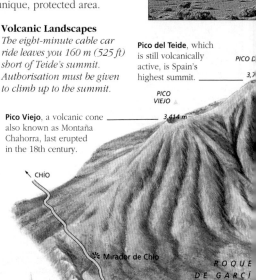

Volcanic Landscapes
The eight-minute cable car ride leaves you 160 m (525 ft) short of Teide's summit. Authorisation must be given to climb up to the summit.

Pico del Teide, which is still volcanically active, is Spain's highest summit. _____ PICO D

3,7

PICO VIEJO

Pico Viejo, a volcanic cone _____ 3,414 m
also known as Montaña Chahorra, last erupted in the 18th century.

CHÍO

Mirador de Chío

ROQUE DE GARCÍ

C823

Mirado de La F

LLANO DE UCANC

Mirador de Boca Tauce

VILAFLOR

C821

0 kilometres 2

0 miles 1

KEY

═══ Road

━━━ Track

- - - Footpath

Los Roques de García
These flamboyantly shaped lava rocks near the parador are some of the most photographed in the whole park. The rocks of Los Azulejos, nearby, glitter blue-green because of the copper deposits within them.

WILD FLOWERS

The inhospitable badlands of Las Cañadas are inhabited by some rare and beautiful plants. Many of these are unique to the Canary Islands. Most striking is the tall *Echium wildprettii*, a kind of viper's buglos whose red flowers reach 3 m (9 ft) in early summer. Other common plants include Teide broom, the Teide daisy, and a uniqu species of violet. The best time of year for flower-spotting is May to June. Displays housed in the visitors' centre will help identify them. Don't take any plants away with you: all vegetation within the park is strictly protected and must not be uproote or picked.

La Caldera de Las Cañadas

A rim of fractured crags forms a pie-crust edge to the sides of this enormous caldera – a wide volcanic crater (see p551). Now collapsed and intensely eroded, the perimeter of the caldera measures 45 km (28 miles).

VISITORS' CHECKLIST

Tel *922 29 01 29.* 342 & 348 *from Puerto de la Cruz.* **El Portillo Visitors' Centre & cable car** *(to NE of park on C821).* 9am–4:30pm daily.

At El Portillo Visitors' Centre, a video film and exhibition chart the origins of the park.

SANTA CRUZ
DE TENERIFE

El Portillo

jio de Altavista

C821

Mirador
de San José

Mirador del
Tabonal Negro

LAS CAÑADAS

Las Cañadas

The flat expanses of the seven cañadas (small sandy plateaux) were created by the collapse of ancient craters. Several colourful plants have managed to colonize this dusty, barren wasteland.

Parador

The recently refurbished visitor centre and Parador de Cañadas del Teide (see p601) is set in the surreal scenery, and makes an excellent base for those who want to explore the park thoroughly.

mustard
ainia
uana)

eide
wer
num
ium)

Teide violet
(Viola cheiranthifolia)

Teide viper's bugloss
(Echium wildpretii)

Exploring the Eastern Islands

The Eastern Province of the Canary Islands – Las
Palmas – comprises the islands of Gran Canaria,
Lanzarote and Fuerteventura. All feature unusual and
spectacular scenery, plenty of sunshine and excellent
sandy beaches, but each has a very different atmosphere. Gran Canaria boasts the only really large
town, Las Palmas de Gran Canaria, which is also the
administrative centre for the eastern islands. It also
offers the biggest resort, Maspalomas, with its Playa
del Inglés, which has a package holiday feel. As a
contrast, the white beaches of Fuerteventura have
been left fairly undeveloped and it is still possible to
find privacy among their sand dunes. Lanzarote has
fine beaches, too, while its interior is dominated by a
volcanic landscape which makes for great excursions.

**Corralejo's beach, in the north
of Fuerteventura**

The marina at Puerto Rico, in southern Gran Canaria

GETTING AROUND

Most people travel from mainlan
Spain to the eastern islands by ai
(see p676). The alternative is a lo.
sea crossing from Cádiz (see p67
There are flights between all the
islands, mainly from Gran Canar
There are also regular inter-islan
ferries. Taxis and public transpo
are fine within resorts, but expe
sive over long distances. Cars ca
be hired on all the islands, usua
at airports or ferry terminals. Th
main roads are well-surfaced an
fast on the flatter sections, thou
traffic in Gran Canaria can be
heavy in places. A four-wheel dr
Jeep is advisable to reach some
remoter beaches.

Cenobio de Valerón
Gáldar
AGAETE **15** Firgas   Arucas
Teror
CRUZ
San Nicolás   DE TEJEDA **18**   Vega de San Mateo
de Tolentino   Roque Nublo   Telde
Pico de las Nieves
1949m
Mogán   Santa Lucía
PUERTO DE   Agüimes
MOGÁN **12**
13 PUERTO RICO
14 MASPALOMAS

17 LAS PALMAS
DE GRAN CANARIA
16 TAFIRA

GRAN CANARIA

KEY

═══ Motorway

━━━ Major road

═══ Secondary road

━━━ Scenic route

△ Summit

0 kilometres   2

0 miles   10

SIGHTS AT A GLANCE

Agaete ⑮
Arrecife ㉗
Betancuria ⑳
Caleta de Fuste ㉑
Corralejo ㉓
Costa Teguise ㉘
Haría ㉚
Jameos del Agua ㉛
Maspalomas ⑭
Las Palmas de
  Gran Canaria ⑰
Parque Nacional de
  Timanfaya ㉕
Península de Jandía ⑲

Playa Blanca ㉔
Puerto del Carmen ㉖
Puerto de Mogán ⑫
Puerto del Rosario ㉒
Puerto Rico ⑬
Tafira ⑯
Teguise ㉙

Tour
Cruz de Tejeda ⑱

Isla Alegranza

Isla de Montaña Clara

Isla Graciosa

○ Orzola

JAMEOS DEL AGUA ㉛

HARÍA ㉚

Tinajo

㉙ TEGUISE

Mozaga

PARQUE NACIONAL
DE TIMANFAYA ㉕

San

COSTA
TEGUISE

Bartolomé

Yaiza

㉘

㉗ ARRECIFE

Tias

Salinas de Janubio

㉖

PUERTO
DEL CARMEN

PLAYA BLANCA ㉔

*Playa del
Papagayo*

LANZAROTE

*Isla de
los Lobos*

CORRALEJO ㉓

La Oliva

Tindaya

㉒ PUERTO DEL ROSARIO

BETANCURIA ⑳

Antigua

㉑ CALETA DE FUSTE

Pájara

Tuineje

Gran Tarajal

Tarajalejo

PENÍNSULA DE JANDÍA

FUERTEVENTURA

⑲

○ Morro Jable

SEE ALSO

• *Where to Stay* pp599–601

• *Where to Eat* pp651–3

Volcanoes of Montañas de Fuego in Parque Nacional de Timanfaya, Lanzarote

Gran Canaria

Gran Canaria is the most popular of the Canary Islands, with over 3 million holidaymakers visiting it each year. The island offers a surprising range of scenery, climate, resorts and attractions within its compact bounds. Winding roads follow the steep, ruggedly beautiful terrain which rises to a symmetrical cone at the centre of the island. Las Palmas, Gran Canaria's capital and port, is the largest city in the Canaries, and Maspalomas/Playa del Inglés, in the south, is one of the biggest resorts in Spain. Both tourist meccas are packed with high-rise hotels and villa complexes, but not far away there is some marvellous scenery to discover.

Farmer and donkey

Holiday-makers on the golden sands of Puerto Rico beach

Puerto de Mogán ⑫

Las Palmas. 🚶 1,500. 🛈 Avenida de Mogán, Puerto Rico, 928 15 88 04. 🚌 Fri. 🎭 Virgen del Carmen (Jul).

Situated at the end of the verdant valley of Mogán, this is one of Gran Canaria's most appealing and successful developments – an idyll to many visitors after the brash concrete of Playa del Inglés. Based around a small fishing port, it consists of a village-like complex of pretty, white, creeper-covered houses and a similarly designed hotel built around a marina. Boutiques, bars and restaurants add an ambience without any of the accompanying rowdiness.

The sandy beach, sheltered between the cliffs, is scarcely big enough for all visitors; a car is recommended to reach more facilities at Maspalomas. Ferries provide a leisurely way to get to nearby resorts.

Sun worshippers in Puerto Rico

Puerto Rico ⑬

Las Palmas. 🚶 1,800. 🛈 Avenida de Mogán, 928 15 88 04. 🎭 Maria de Auxiliadora (May), San Antonio (13 Jun), Carmen (16 Jul).

The barren cliffs west of Maspalomas now sprout apartment complexes at every turn. Puerto Rico is an over-developed resort, but has one of the more attractive beaches on the island, a firm crescent of imported sand supplemented by lidos and excellent water sports facilities. It is a great place to learn sailing, diving and windsurfing, or just to soak up the ultraviolet – Puerto Rico enjoys the best sunshine record in the whole of Spain.

Maspalomas ⑭

Las Palmas. 🚶 33,000. ✈ 🛈 Centro Comercial Anexo II, Playa del Inglés, 928 76 84 09. 🚌 Wed & Sat. 🎭 Santiago (25 Jul), San Bartolomé (24 Aug).

When the fast motorway from Las Palmas airport first tips you into this bewildering mega-resort, it seems like a homogeneous blur, but gradually three separate communities emerge. **San Agustín**, the furthest east, is sedate compared with the others. It has a series of beaches of dark sand, attractively sheltered by low cliffs and landscaped promenades, and a casino.

The next exit off the coastal highway leads to **Playa del Inglés**, the largest and liveliest resort, a triangle of land jutting into a huge belt of golden sand. Developed from the end of the 1950s, the area is built up with giant blocks of flats linked by a maze of roads. Many hotels lack sea views, though most have spacious grounds with swimming pools

Floral arches decorating a street of apartments in Puerto de Mogán

For hotels and restaurants in this region see pp599–601 and pp651–3

At night the area pulsates with bright disco lights and flashing neon. There are more than 300 restaurants and over 50 discos.

West of Playa del Inglés the beach undulates into the **Dunas de Maspalomas**. A relieving contrast to the hectic surrounding resorts, these dunes form a nature reserve protected from further development. The western edge of the dunes (marked by a lighthouse) is occupied by a cluster of luxury hotels. Just behind the dunes lies a golf course encircled by bungalow estates.

Everything is laid on for the package holiday: water sports, excursions, fast food, as well as go-karts, camel safaris and funfairs. Best of these include **Palmitos Park,** with exotic birds in subtropical gardens; and **Sioux City**, a fun-packed Western theme park.

Palmitos Park
Barranco de los Palmitos. *Tel* 928 14 02 76. ⬤ *daily.* 🖼 ♿
www.palmitospark.es

Sioux City
Cañón del Águila. *Tel* 928 76 25 73. ⬤ *Tue–Sun.* 🖼 ♿

The rocky shore and steep cliffs of the northeast coast near Agaete

Agaete 🕔

Las Palmas. 🏘 5,600. 🛈 *Avenida Señora de las Nieves 1, 928 55 43 82.* 🎭 *Fiesta de las Nieves (5 Aug).* www.aytoagaete.es

The cloudier northern side of the island is far greener and lusher than the arid south, and banana plantations take up most of the coastal slopes. Agaete, on the northwest coast, a pretty scatter of white houses round a striking rocky bay,

is growing into a small resort. Every August, Agaete holds the Fiesta de la Rama, a Guanche *(see p547)* rain-making ritual which dates from long before the arrival of the Spanish. An animated procession of villagers bearing green branches heads from the hills above the town down to the coast and into the sea. The villagers beat the water to summon the rain.

The **Ermita de las Nieves** contains a fine 16th-century Flemish triptych and model

sailing ships, and the **Huerto de las Flores**. This botanical garden is being extended. Until completion, access is by key, held at the town hall.

Environs
A brief detour inland up along the Barranco de Agaete takes you through a fertile valley of papaya, mango and citrus trees. North of Agaete are the towns of Guía and Gáldar. Though there is little to see here, both parish churches do contain examples of the religious statuary of the celebrated 18th-century sculptor, José Luján Pérez.

Nearby, towards the north coast, lies the **Cenobio de Valerón**. One of the most dramatic of the local Guanche sights, this cliff-face is pockmarked with nearly 300 caves beneath a basalt arch. These are believed to have been hideaways for Guanche priestesses, communal grainstores and refuges from attack.

Huerto de las Flores
Calle Huertas. ⬤ *Mon–Fri.* ♿ 🖼

…les of wind-sculptured sand: the dunes at Maspalomas

Tafira ⑯

Las Palmas. 🏠 *23,000.* 🚉 🚌 *Calle León y Castillo 322, 928 44 68 24.* 🎭 *San Francisco (Oct).*

The hills southwest of Las Palmas have long been desirable residential locations. A colonial air still wafts around Tafira's patrician villas. The **Jardín Canario**, a botanical garden founded in 1952, is the main reason for a visit. Plants from all of the Canary Islands can be studied in their own, re-created habitats.

Near La Atalaya lies one of Gran Canaria's most impressive natural sights – the **Caldera de la Bandama**. This is a volcanic crater 1,000 m (3,300 ft) wide, best seen from the Mirador de Bandama where you gaze down into the green depression about 200 m (660 ft) deep. Some of the inhabited caves in the **Barranco de Guayadeque**, a valley of red rocks to the south, were dug in the late 15th century. A few of them have electricity.

🌱 **Jardín Canario**
Carretera de Dragonal, Tafira. **Tel** *928 21 95 80.* ◻ *daily.* ● *1 Jan & Good Fri.* ♿

Las Palmas de Gran Canaria ⑰

Las Palmas. 🏠 *378,000.* 🚉 🚢 🚌 *Calle León y Castillo 322, 928 446 824.* 🎭 *Carnival (Feb/Mar).*

Las Palmas is the largest city in the Canary Islands. A bustling seaport and industrial city, it sees 1,000 ships docking

Palm trees in a natural setting in the Jardín Canario, Tafira

each month. Las Palmas has faded somewhat from the days when wealthy convalescents flocked here in winter and glamorous liners called in on transatlantic voyages. But it remains a vibrant place to visit.

Las Palmas is a sprawling city built around an isthmus and its layout can be confusing. The modern commercial shipping area, Puerto de la Luz, takes up the eastern side of the isthmus, which leads to the former island of La Isleta, a sailors' and military quarter. On the other side of the isthmus is the crowded **Playa de las Canteras**, a 3-km (2-mile) long stretch of golden beach. The promenade behind has been built up with bars, restaurants and hotels.

The town centre stretches along the coast from the isthmus. For a pleasant scenic tour, begin in the **Parque Santa Catalina**, near the port. This is a popular, shady square of

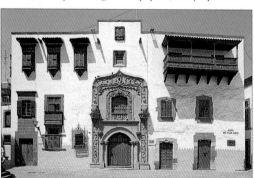
Bronze dog at Plaza Santa Ana

cafés and newspaper kiosks. In the leafy residential quarter of Ciudad Jardín are the Parque Doramas and the traditional casino hotel of Santa Catalina.

The **Pueblo Canario** is a tourist enclave where visitors can watch folk dancing, and browse in the craft shops and the small art gallery. All this can be viewed from above by walking uphill towards the Altavista district and the Paseo Cornisa.

At the end of town is the Barrio Vegueta, an atmospheric quarter which dates back to the Spanish conquest. At its heart stands the **Catedral de Santa Ana**, begun in 1500. The adjacent **Museo Diocesano de Arte Sacro** contains works of religious art. The square in front is guarded by Canarian dogs in bronze.

Nearby, the **Casa de Colón** is a 15th-century governor's residence where Columbus stayed. A museum dedicated to his voyages displays charts, models and diary extracts.

Early history can be seen in the **Museo Canario**, which contains Guanche mummies, skulls, pottery and jewellery.

🏛 **Museo Diocesano de Arte Sacro**
Calle Espíritu Santo 20. **Tel** *928 31 4 89.* ◻ *Mon–Sat.* 🗓

🏛 **Casa de Colón**
Calle Colón 1. **Tel** *928 31 23 73.* ◻ *daily.* 🗓 *(by appointment for group.*

🏛 **Museo Canario**
Calle Doctor Verneau 2. **Tel** *928 33 4 00.* ◻ *daily.* ● *1 Jan, 25 Dec.* 🗓 🛈

The Casa de Colón museum, Las Palmas, dedicated to Columbus

Tour of Cruz de Tejeda ⑱

Gran Canaria's mountainous interior makes for an ideal day tour, from any part of the island. Choose a fine day or the views may be obscured. The route from Maspalomas leads through dry ravines of bare rock and cacti, becoming more fertile with altitude. Roads near the central highlands snake steeply through shattered, tawny crags, past caves and pretty villages to panoramic viewpoints from which you can see Mount Teide (see pp538–9) on Tenerife. On the north side, the slopes are much lusher, growing citrus fruits and eucalyptus trees.

White farmhouses en route to Teror

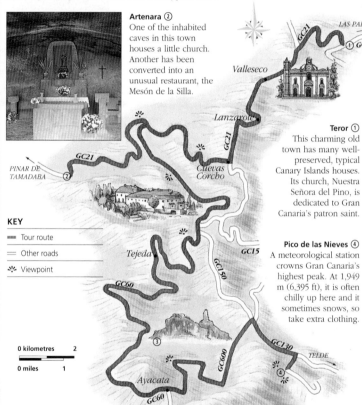

Artenara ②
One of the inhabited caves in this town houses a little church. Another has been converted into an unusual restaurant, the Mesón de la Silla.

Teror ①
This charming old town has many well-preserved, typical Canary Islands houses. Its church, Nuestra Señora del Pino, is dedicated to Gran Canaria's patron saint.

Pico de las Nieves ④
A meteorological station crowns Gran Canaria's highest peak. At 1,949 m (6,395 ft), it is often chilly up here and it sometimes snows, so take extra clothing.

KEY

■■■ Tour route

= Other roads

✲ Viewpoint

0 kilometres 2
0 miles 1

LAS PALMAS

Valleseco

Lanzarote

Cuevas Corcho

Tejeda

PINAR DE TAMADABA

Ayacata

MASPALOMAS

TEIDE

Roque Nublo ③
This 60-m (195-ft) high jagged spike of basalt tops a 1,700-m (5,578-ft) peak. Together with nearby Roque Bentayga, it was sacred to the Guanches. It's a stiff climb to the summit.

TIPS FOR DRIVERS

Length: 35–45 km (22–28 miles).
Stopping-off points: the Mesón de la Silla cave-restaurant in Artenara is a popular lunch spot.
Note: roads can be narrow with few passing places; sudden patches of cloud or mist may loom without warning.

Fuerteventura

Lying just 100 km (60 miles) off the Atlantic coast of Morocco, leaf-shaped Fuerteventura is continually battered by coastal winds. It is the second largest of the Canary Islands after Tenerife, and the most sparsely populated: its 69,500 inhabitants are outnumbered by goats. The island used to be densely wooded, but European settlers cut down the timber for shipbuilding; the dry climate and the goats have since reduced the vegetation to parched scrub. It is so dry that water has to be shipped over from the mainland. The only significant revenue is tourism, but the tourist industry is still in its infancy compared with the other main islands. However, visitors are increasing in number as thousands of sun-worshippers flock to more than 150 splendid beaches. The island is popular with water sports fans and naturists.

A herd of goats near the airport on Fuerteventura

Península de Jandía ⓳

Las Palmas. 🚌 *Costa Calma, Morro Jable.* ⛴ *(jetfoil) from Gran Canaria.* ℹ *Centro Comercial Cosmo, Local 88, 928 54 07 76.*

Excellent beaches of pale sand fringe the elongated Jandía Peninsula in the south of Fuerteventura. A string of *urbanizaciones* (apartment complexes) now takes up much of the peninsula's shel-tered east coast (Sotavento).

Costa Calma, a burgeoning cluster of modern complexes, offers the most interesting beaches with long stretches of fine sand interrupted by low cliffs and coves. **Morro Jable**, a fishing village now swamped by new developments, lies at the southern end of a vast, glittering strand. Beyond Morro Jable, the access road dwindles away into a potholed track leading towards the lonely lighthouse at Punta de Jandía.

Expanses of deserted sand, accessible only by four-wheel drive vehicle, line the westerly, windward coast (Barlovento) – too exposed for all but the hardiest beach lovers. Some of the island's best subtropical marine life can be found in this area, however, making it popular with skin divers.

From 1938 to the early 1960s, Jandía belonged to a German entrepreneur and was out of bounds to locals. Even today, rumours of spies, submarines and secret Nazi bases still circulate.

Betancuria ⓴

Las Palmas. 🚗 *740.* 🚌 ℹ *Calle Amador Rodríguez 6, 928 87 80 92.* 🎉 *San Buenaventura (14 Jul), Romería de La Peña (3rd Sat of Sep).*

Inland, rugged peaks of extinct volcanoes, separated by wide plains, present a scene of austere grandeur. Scattered, stark villages and obsolete windmills occupy the lowlands, which are occasionally fertile enough to nurture a few crops or palm trees. Beyond, devoid of vegetation, the hills form stark outlines. From a distance they appear brown and grey, but up close the rocks glow with an astonishing range of mauves, pinks and ochres. The richness of colour in this

The gilded interior of the Iglesia Santa María in Betancuria

interior wilderness is at its most striking at sunset, when a leisurely drive can reveal some breathtaking scenes.

Betancuria, built in a valley surrounded by mountains in the centre of the island, is named after Jean de Béthen-court, Fuerteventura's 15th-century conqueror, who moved his capital inland to thwart pirates. Nestling in the moun-tains, this peaceful oasis is now the island's prettiest village. The **Iglesia de Santa María** contains gilded altars, decorated beams and sacred relics. The **Museo Arqueológico** houses many local artifacts.

Environs

To the south, the village of **Pájara** boasts a 17th-century church with a curiously decorated doorway. Its design of serpents and strange beasts is believed to be of Aztec in-fluence. Inside, the twin aisles both contain statues: one of a radiant Madonna and Child in white and silver, the other a Virgen de los Dolores in black.

La Oliva, to the north, was the site of the Spanish military headquarters until the 19th cen-tury. The Casa de los Coroneles (House of the Colonels) is a faded yellow mansion with a grand façade and hundreds of windows. Inside it has coffered ceilings. The fortified church and the arts centre displaying works of Canary Islands artists are also worth a visit.

🏛 **Museo Arqueológico**
Calle Roberto Roldán. *Tel 928 87 82 41.* ⬤ *Tue–Sun.* 🎨 ♿

Caleta de Fuste ㉑

Las Palmas. 🏠 *1,600.* 🚌 🅸 *Calle Juan Ramón Soto Morales 10, El Castillo, 928 16 32 86.* 🛍 *Sat.* 🎉 *Día del Carmen (16 Jul), Nuestra Señora de Antigua (8 Sep).*

South of Puerto del Rosario about halfway down the eastern coast, lies Caleta de Fuste. The attractive low-rise, self-catering holiday centres surround a horseshoe bay of soft, gently shelving sand. The largest complex, El Castillo, takes its name from an 18th-century watchtower situated by the harbour.

There are many water sports facilities, including diving and windsurfing schools, as well as the Pueblo Majorero, an attractive "village" of shops and restaurants around a central plaza near the beach. These features make Caleta de Fuste one of Fuerteventura's most relaxed and pleasant resorts.

Fishing boats on a beach on the Isla de Lobos, near Corralejo

Puerto del Rosario ㉒

Las Palmas. 🏠 *16,500.* ✈ 🚌 🚢 🅸 *Avenida de la Constitución 5, 928 53 08 44.* 🎉 *El Rosario (7 Oct).*

Fuerteventura's commercial and administrative capital was founded in 1797. It was originally known as Puerto de Cabras (Goats' Harbour), after a nearby gorge that was once used for watering goats, but was rechristened to smarten up its image in 1957. As Puerto del Rosario is the only large port on Fuerteventura, it is the base for inter-island ferries and a busy fishing industry. The town is also enlivened by the presence of the Spanish Foreign Legion, which occupies large barracks here.

Corralejo ㉓

Las Palmas. 🏠 *7,200.* 🚢 🅸 *Avenida Marítima 2, 928 86 62 35.* 🛍 *Mon & Fri.* 🎉 *Día del Carmen (16 Jul).*

This much-expanded fishing village is now (together with the Jandía Peninsula) one of the island's two most important resorts. Its main attraction is a belt of glorious sand dunes stretching to the south, resembling the Sahara in places, and protected as a nature reserve. This designation arrived too late, however, to prevent the construction of two obtrusive hotels right on the beach.

The rest of the resort, mostly consisting of apartments and hotels, spills out from the town centre. The port area is lively, with busy fish restaurants and an efficient 40-minute ferry service to Lanzarote.

Offshore is the tiny Isla de los Lobos, named after the once abundant monk seals (*lobos marinos*). Today, scuba divers, snorkellers, sport fishers and surfers claim the clear waters. Glass-bottomed cruise boats take less adventurous excursionists to the island for barbecues and swimming trips.

THE GUANCHES

When Europeans first arrived in the Canary Islands in the late 14th century, they discovered a tall, white-skinned race, who lived in caves and later in small settlements around the edges of barren lava fields. Guanche was the name of one tribe on Tenerife, but it came to be used as the European name for all the indigenous tribes on the islands, and it is the one that has remained. The origins of the Guanches are still unclear, but it is probable that they arrived on the islands in the 1st or 2nd century BC from Berber North Africa. Within 100 years of European arrival the Guanches had been subdued and virtually exterminated by the ruthless conquistadors. Very few traces of their culture remain today.

Reminders of the Guanches can be seen in many places in the Canaries. Specimens of their mummified dead, as well as baskets and stone and bone artifacts, are on display in several museums and there are statues of chiefs in Candelaria (see p535) on Tenerife.

Guanche bowl for preparing *gofio* (see p537)

A Guanche basket

Lanzarote

The easternmost and fourth largest of the Canary Islands is virtually treeless and relies on desalination plants for some of its water. Yet many visitors consider Lanzarote the most attractive of all the islands for the vivid shapes and contrasting colours of its volcanic landscapes. Despite low rainfall, carefully tended crops flourish in its black volcanic soil. Locals pride themselves on the way their island has been preserved from the worst effects of tourism; there are no garish billboards, overhead cables or high-rise buildings. Its present-day image owes much to the artist César Manrique. Touring the spectacular volcanic Timanfaya National Park is a favourite trip.

Wind turbines harnessing Lanzarote's winds for power

Playa Blanca ㉔

Las Palmas. 🏘 4,500. 🔁 ⛴
🛈 Calle El Varadero 2, 928 51 90 18. 🎭 Nuestra Señora del Carmen (16 Jul).

The fishing village origins of this resort are readily apparent around its harbour. Although it has expanded in recent years, Playa Blanca remains an agreeably family-oriented place with some character. It has plenty of cafés and restaurants, shops and bars, and several large hotels. However, the buildings are well dispersed and the resort is rarely noisy at night. Visitors converge here not for nightlife or contrived entertainment, but for relaxing beach holidays. There are one or two good stretches of sand near to the town, but the most enticing lie hidden around the rocky

headlands to the east, where the clear, warm sea laps into rocky coves, and clothes seem superfluous. **Playa Papagayo** is the best known of these, but a diligent search will probably gain you one all to yourself. A four-wheel drive vehicle is advisable to negotiate the narrow, unsurfaced roads which lead to these beaches.

Parque Nacional de Timanfaya ㉕

Las Palmas Yaiza. 🛈 Ctra L2–67, Mancha Blanca, 928 84 08 39.
◌ daily. 🎫

From 1730–36, a series of volcanic eruptions took place on Lanzarote. Eleven villages were buried in lava, which eventually spread over 200 sq km (77 sq miles) of Lanzarote's most fertile land. Miraculously, no one was killed, though many islanders emigrated.

Today, the volcanoes that once devastated Lanzarote provide one of its most lucrative and enigmatic attractions, aptly known as the **Montañas del Fuego** (Fire Mountains). They are part of the Parque Nacional de Timanfaya, established in 1974 to protect a fascinating and important geological record. The entrance to the park lies just north of the small village of Yaiza. Here you can pause and take a 15-minute camel ride up the volcanic slopes for wonderful views across the park. Afterwards, you pay the entrance fee and drive through haunting scenery of dark, barren lava cinders topped by brooding red-black

Las Coloradas beach near Playa Blanca in southern Lanzarote

CÉSAR MANRIQUE (1919–92)

Local hero César Manrique trained as a painter, and spent time in mainland Spain and New York before returning to Lanzarote in 1968. He campaigned for traditional and environmentally friendly development on the island for the remaining part of his life, setting strict building height limits and colour requirements. Dozens of tourist sites throughout the Canaries benefited from his talents and enthusiasm.

César Manrique in 1992

Camel rides from Yaiza across the Montañas de Fuego

volcano cones. Finally, you will reach **Islote de Hilario**. You can park at El Diablo panoramic restaurant. From here, buses take visitors for exhilarating 30 minute tours of the desolate, lunar-like landscapes.

Afterwards, back at Islote de Hilario, guides will provide graphic demonstrations that this volcano is not extinct but only dormant brushwood pushed into a crevice bursts instantly into a ball of flame, while water poured into a sunken pipe shoots out in a scorching jet of steam.

The road from Yaiza to the coast leads to the **Salinas de Janubio** where salt is extracted from the sea. At **Los Hervideros** the rough coast can create spectacular seas and further north, at **El Golfo**, is an eerie emerald-coloured lagoon.

Puerto del Carmen 26

Las Palmas. 🚶 13,700. 🚌 🛳 ℹ *Avenida de la Playa, 928 51 53 37.* 🎉 *Nuestra Señora del Carmen (16 Jul).* **www**.turismolanzarote.com

More than 60 per cent of Lanzarote's tourists stay in this resort, which stretches several kilometres along the seafront. The coastal road curves its way through a solid slab of holiday infrastructure: car hire offices, banks, bureaux de change, shops, bars, restaurants and discos. Behind the roadside arcades lie countless villas, apartments and hotels. Though dense, the buildings are pleasantly designed and unoppressive. All have easy access to a long golden beach, Playa Blanca, which in places

is very wide. Another beach nearby is Playa de los Pocillos. The original village lies west of the port, away from the hustle and bustle of the resort.

Fishing boat in Arrecife port

Arrecife 27

Las Palmas. 🚶 46,900. ✈ 🚌 ℹ *Blas Cabrera Felipe, 928 81 17 62.* 🎉 *San Ginés (25 Aug).*

Arrecife, with its modern buildings and lively streets, is the commercial and administrative centre of the island.

Despite its modern trappings, the capital retains much of its old charm, with palm-lined promenades, a fine beach and two small forts. Only the 18th-century **Castillo de San José**, now a museum of contemporary art, is open to the public. The fort was renovated by César Manrique, and one of his paintings is on display here. An historic house, **La Casa de los Arroyo**, is noted for its scientific library and is open to the public.

🏛 **La Casa de los Arroyo**
Avda Coll 3, Arrecife. **Tel** *928 80 17 29.* ⬜ *Mon–Fri.*

🏛 **Castillo de San José**
Puerto de Naos. **Tel** *928 81 23 21.* ⬜ *daily.* ● *1 Jan, 25 Dec.*

Costa Teguise 28

10 km (6 miles) north of Arrecife. 🚌 ℹ *Avda Islas Canarias, Centro Comercial los Charcos, local 11, 928 82 71 30.*

This resort, largely financed by a mining conglomerate, has transformed the arid, low-lying terrain north of Arrecife into an extensive cluster of timeshare accommodation, leisure clubs and luxury hotels. The contrast between old town Teguise, Lanzarote's former capital, and the exclusive, new Costa Teguise is striking. Fake greenery and suburban lamps line boulevards amid barren ashlands. White villas line a series of small sandy beaches. The high level of investment has succeeded in attracting jet-set clientele. King Juan Carlos also has a villa here.

Umbrellas on the beach, Puerto del Carmen

Iglesia de San Miguel on the main square in Teguise

Teguise ㉙

Las Palmas. 🏠 12,300. 🚌 🛈 *Plaza General Franco 1, 928 84 50 72.* 🚌 *Sun.* 🎊 *Dia del Carmen (16 Jul), Las Nieves (5 Aug).*

Teguise, the island's capital until 1852, is a well-kept, old-fashioned town with wide, cobbled streets and patrician houses grouped around the **Iglesia de San Miguel**. The best time to visit is on a Sunday, when there is a lively handicrafts market and folk dancing. Just outside Teguise, the castle of Santa Bárbara contains the **Museo del Emigrante Canario**, which tells the story of Canarian emigrants to South America.

Environs
To see more of inland Lanzarote, follow the central road south of Teguise, through the strange farmland of **La Geria**. Black volcanic ash has been scooped into protective, crescent-shaped pits which trap moisture to enable vines and other crops to flourish. **Mozaga**,

one of the main villages in the area, is a major centre of wine production. On the roadside near Mozaga is the *Monumento al Campesino*, Manrique's *(see p548)* striking modern sculpture dedicated to Lanzarote's farmers.

Halfway between Teguise and Arrecife is the **Fundación César Manrique**. The fascinating former home of the artist incorporates five lava caves. It contains some of his own work and his collection of contemporary art.

🏛 **Museo del Emigrante Canario**
Montaña de Guanapay. *Tel 928 84 50 01.* ☐ *Mon–Fri.* 🗞

🏛 **Fundación César Manrique**
Taro de Tahiche. *Tel 928 84 31 38.* ☐ *daily.* 🗞

Haría ㉚

Las Palmas. 🏠 4,000. 🚌 🛈 *Plaza de la Constitución 1, 928 83 52 51.* 🚌 *Sat.* 🎊 *San Juan (24 Jun).*

Palm trees and white, cube-shaped houses distinguish this picturesque village. It acts as a gateway to excursions round the northern tip of the island. The road to the north gives memorable views over exposed cliffs, and the 609-m (2,000-ft) high Monte Corona.

Environs
From Manrique's **Mirador del Río** you can see La Graciosa, and the northernmost of the Canary Islands, Alegranza. **Orzola** is a delightful fishing village providing fish lunches as well as boat trips to La Graciosa. To the south are the Mala prickly pear plantations, where cochineal (crimson dye)

is extracted from the insects which feed on the plants. Nearby is the **Jardín de Cactus**, a well-stocked cactus garden, which has a smart restaurant, again designed by Manrique.

🎋 **Mirador del Río**
Haria. *Tel 928 52 65 48.* ☐ *daily.* 🗞

🌵 **Jardín de Cactus**
Guatiza. *Tel 928 52 93 97.* ☐ *daily.* 🗞

Landscaped pool on top of the caves of Jameos del Agua

Jameos del Agua ㉛

Las Palmas. *Tel 928 84 80 20.* ☐ *daily.* 🗞

An eruption of the Monte Corona volcano formed the Jameos del Agua lava caves on Lanzarote's northeast coast. In 1965–8, these were landscaped by César Manrique into an imaginative subterranean complex containing a restaurant, night club, a swimming pool edged by palm trees, and gardens of oleander and cacti. Steps lead to a shallow seawater lagoon where a rare species of blind white crab, unique to Lanzarote, glows softly in the dim light. An exhibition on volcanology and Canarian flora and fauna also deserves a look. Folk-dancing evenings are regularly held in this unusual setting.

Environs
Another popular attraction is the nearby **Cueva de los Verdes**, a tube of solidifed lava stretching 6 km (4 miles) underground. Guided tours of the caves are available.

🎋 **Cueva de los Verdes**
Haria. *Tel 928 84 84 84.* ☐ *daily.*

Volcanic ash swept into crescent-shaped pits for farming, La Geria

Volcanic Islands

The volcanic activity which formed the Canary Islands has created a variety of scenery, from distinctive lava formations to enormous volcanoes crowned by huge, gaping craters. The islands are all at different stages in their evolution. Tenerife, Lanzarote, El Hierro and La Palma are still volcanically active; dramatic displays of flames and steam can be seen in Lanzarote's Montañas de Fuego *(see p548)*. The last eruption was on La Palma in 1971.

Origin of the Islands
The Canaries are situated above faults in the earth's crust, which is always thinner under the oceans than under the continents. When magma (molten rock) rises through these cracks volcanoes are formed.

Atlantic Ocean — Transform fault — Atlas Fault
Canary Islands
Thin oceanic crust
Upper mantle
Africa
Continental mantle between crust and earth's core
Dense lower mantle — Thick continental crust

EVOLUTION OF THE CANARY ISLANDS

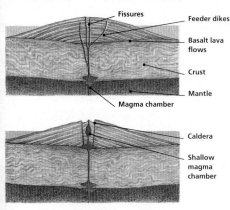

Fissures — Feeder dikes
Basalt lava flows
Crust
Mantle
Magma chamber

1 **Lanzarote, El Hierro and La Palma** *are wide, gently sloping shield volcanoes standing on the sea floor. All of them are composed of basalt formed by a hot, dense magma. The flexible crust is pressed down by the weight of the islands.*

Caldera
Shallow magma chamber

2 **An explosive eruption** *can empty the magma chamber, leaving the roof unsupported. This collapses under the weight of the volcano above to form a depression, or caldera, such as Las Cañadas on Tenerife. There are thick lava flows during this stage of the island's evolution.*

Sea level
Exposed solidified magma chamber

3 **If eruptions cease** *a volcano will be eroded by the action of the sea, and by wind and rain. Gran Canaria's main volcano is in the early stages of erosion, while the volcano on Fuerteventura has already been deeply eroded, exposing chambers of solidified magma.*

Rope lava near La Restinga, El Hierro

Pico Viejo crater, next to Mount Teide, Tenerife *(see p538)*

TRAVELLERS'
NEEDS

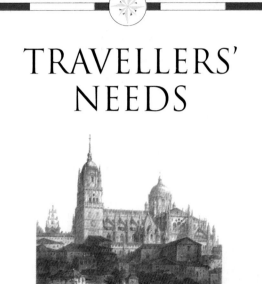

WHERE TO STAY 554–601

RESTAURANTS AND BARS 602–653

WHERE TO STAY

Medieval castles turned into luxury hotels and mansions converted into youth hostels typify the variety of places to stay in Spain. The tourists who sustain Spain's economy have almost 10,000 establishments to choose from, offering around one million beds. Suites in once-royal palaces are at the top of the scale. Then there are luxury beach hotels on the

Logo for a luxury five-star hotel

Costa del Sol and in the Balearic and the Canary Islands. Visitors can also stay on remote farms, or in villas and old houses let for self-catering. For budget travel there are pensions, family-run *casas rurales* and guest houses, camp sites, and refuges with stunning views for mountaineers. Some of the best hotels in all these categories and in every style and price range are listed on pages 560–601.

Hotel de la Reconquista, Oviedo, an 18th-century mansion *(see p563)*

HOTEL GRADING AND FACILITIES

All of Spain's hotels are classified into categories and awarded stars by the country's regional tourist authorities. Hotels (indicated by an H on a blue plaque near the hotel door) are awarded from one to five stars. Hostals (Hs) and pensions (P) offer fewer comforts but are correspondingly cheaper than hotels.

Spain's star-rating system reflects the number and range of facilities available – whether the hotel has air conditioning, for instance, or a lift – rather than the quality of service.

Most hotels have restaurants that are open to non-residents. Although hotel-residencias (HR) and hostal-residencias (HsR) do not have dining rooms, some serve breakfast. Among Spain's largest hotel chains are **Grupo Sol Meliá, Grupo Riu** and **NH**. Many large tour operators book rooms in Spain's best hotels.

PARADORS

Paradors are government-run hotels, classified from three to five stars. Spain's first parador opened in the Sierra de Gredos in 1928 *(see p584)*; there is now a wide network of them on the mainland and the islands. They are located close together so that there is never more than a day's drive to the nearest one. The best are in former royal hunting lodges, monasteries, castles and other monuments; some modern paradors have been purpose-built, often in spectacular scenery or in towns of historic interest *(see pp558–9)*.

A parador is not necessarily the best hotel in town, but it can be counted on to

deliver a predictably high level of comfort. Each parador is furnished in its own individual style, and the bedrooms are usually spacious and comfortable.

If you plan to tour in high season or to stay in the smaller paradors, it is wise to reserve a room. The paradors may be booked through the **Central de Reservas** in Madrid or through their London agent, **Keytel International**.

PRICES

Spanish law requires all hotel managements to display their prices behind reception and in every room. As a rule, the higher a hotel's star-rating, the more you pay. Rates for a double room can be as little as 20–25 euros a night for a cheap one-star hostal; a five-star hotel will cost more than 220 euros a night, but a room price higher than 300 euros a night is exceptional.

Prices usually vary according to room, region and season. A suite or a very spacious room or one with a view, a balcony or other special feature, may cost more than average. Rural and suburban hotels are generally less expensive than those in the city centre.

All the prices given on pages 560–601 are based on mid-season or high-season rates.

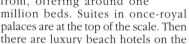

Jaén's parador, a modern extension of the medieval castle *(see p594)*

◁ *Madrileños* enjoying afternoon sunshine, drinks and conversation in the Plaza Mayor

High season covers July and August, but in some areas it runs from April to October and in the Canary Islands the winter is high season.

Many of Spain's city hotels charge especially inflated rates for their rooms during major fiestas, such as the April Fair in Seville *(see p431)*, Los Sanfermines in Pamplona *(see p132)*, Carnival in Santa Cruz de Tenerife and Easter Week *(see p38)* in many places.

Most hotels quote prices per room and meal prices per person without including VAT *(IVA)*, which is 7 per cent in most of Spain, but 5 per cent in the Canary Islands.

The glass-domed foyer of the Palace Hotel, Madrid *(see p581)*

BOOKING AND CHECK-IN

Off-season in rural or small towns you are unlikely to need to book ahead; but if you plan to travel in high season or want to stay in a particular hotel, you should reserve a room by phone, e-mail or through a travel agent. You will need to reserve if you want a special room: one with a double bed (twin beds are the norm); on the ground floor; away from a noisy main road; or a room with a view. The resort hotels often close from autumn to spring. Before you travel, it is always advisable to check that your preferred hotels will be open at that time of year.

You will not normally be asked for a deposit when you book a hotel room. However, a deposit of 20–25 per cent

may be requested if you book during a peak period or for a stay of more than a few nights. Send it by credit card or giro in Spain and by credit card or banker's draft from outside the country. If you have to cancel, do so at least a week before the booking date or you may lose all or some of the deposit.

Most hotels will honour a booking only until 8pm unless business is poor. If you are delayed, call the hotel to assure them you are coming and to tell them when to expect you.

When you check in you will be asked for your passport or identity card to comply with Spanish police regulations. It will normally be returned to you promptly as soon as your details have been copied.

You are expected to check out of your room by noon on the last day of your stay, or to pay for another night.

PAYING

Unless otherwise indicated, the hotels in the listings on pages 560–601 accept credit cards. In some large, busy hotels you may be asked to sign a blank credit card pay slip on arrival. Under Spanish law it is illegal to ask this; you should refuse.

Eurocheques are accepted in some hotels, but personal cheques are not accepted in Spanish hotels, even if backed by a cheque guarantee card or drawn on a Spanish bank. Many people pay cash and in some cheap hotels this may be the only payment accepted.

Around 1.5–2 euros is the usual tip for all hotel staff.

The pretty beach of Meliá Salinas Hotel, Lanzarote *(see p601)*

CASAS RURALES

The owners of some country houses *(casas rurales)* accept a few visitors, usually in high season. They are most numerous in Asturias, Navarra, Aragón and Catalonia (where they are called *cases de pagès*). They are becoming common in Galicia and Cantabria (where they are called *casonas*), and in Andalusia.

Casas rurales range from manor houses to small, isolated farms. Some offer bed and breakfast; some an evening meal or full board. Most are self-catering. Do not expect hotel service or lots of facilities. You may, however, be given a friendly welcome and good home cooking, all at an affordable price. You can book *casas rurales* directly or through regional associations, such as **RAAR** in Andalusia, **Ruralia** in Asturias, **TVR (Turismo Verde y Rural)** in Huesca, Aragón, **Ruralverd** in Catalonia and **Asociación Gallega de Turismo Rural** in Galicia.

El Nacimiento, Turre, a charming Andalusian *casa rural* *(see p596)*

SELF-CATERING

Villas and holiday flats let by the week are plentiful along the Spanish coasts. In scenic areas of the countryside there are many *casas rurales* (farm and village houses) for rent by the day. To obtain information about the *casas rurales*, contact their regional organizations *(see p555)*. They also take bookings.
The Individual Traveller's Spain is a UK organization that acts as an agent for owners of holiday houses and flats in Spain, as does **Hometours International Inc.** in the US. Other organizations and owners of holiday homes advertise in the travel sections of UK Sunday newspapers. Tour operators offer a range of self-catering accommodation.

The prices for self-catering accommodation vary according to the location, the property and the season. A four-person villa with a pool can cost under 240 euros for a week if it is inland and 960 euros a week or more if it is on the coast.

An apartment hotel is a new type of accommodation; in Andalusia it is called a *villa turística*. Half hotel, half holiday flats, it gives guests a choice between self-catering (all rooms have a kitchen) or eating in the hotel restaurant. Holiday villages are similar, often catering for specialist interests. One example is the village of Ainsa in the mountain sports region of Aragón *(see p574)*, which offers a mix of camping and hostel accommodation, with restaurants and bars.

Typical holiday villas in Lanzarote's Puerto del Carmen, the Canary Islands

YOUTH HOSTELS AND MOUNTAIN REFUGES

To use the network of *albergues juveniles* (youth hostels) in Spain you need to show a YHA (Youth Hostel Association) card from your country or an international card, which you can buy from any hostel. Prices per person for bed and breakfast are lower than hotel prices.

Youth hostels can be booked directly or via the **Red Española de Albergues Juveniles** (Spanish Network of Youth Hostels). Despite the name, there is no age limit.

Mountaineers heading for the more remote areas may use the *refugios* (refuges). These are shelters with a dormitory, cooking facilities and heating. Some are huts with about six bunks; others are mountain houses with up to 50 beds.

The *refugios* are marked on large-scale maps of mountain areas and national parks and administered by the regional mountaineering associations.

The **Federación Española de Deportes de Montaña y Escalada (FEDME)** and the local tourist offices will supply their addresses.

La Oliva Monastery, Navarra *(see p130)*, welcomes paying guests

MONASTERIES AND CONVENTS

If you have a taste for peace and austerity you may enjoy a night in one of Spain's 150 religious houses where guests are welcome. Most belong to the Benedictine and the Cistercian orders. Room prices are inexpensive. They are not hotels, however; you have to book ahead by writing or by phone; and few have private telephones or television. The guests may be asked to tidy their rooms, observe the same strict mealtimes as the monks or nuns and to help with the washing up. Some convents admit only women and some monasteries only men.

Youth hostel in rustic style on the edge of Cazorla nature reserve, Jaén

CAMP SITES

There are nearly 1,200 camp sites scattered across Spain. Most of them are on the coasts, but there are also some outside the major cities and in the most popular areas of countryside. Most sites have electricity and running water; some also have launderettes, playgrounds, restaurants, shops, a swimming pool and other amenities.

It is sensible to carry a camping carnet with you. This can be used instead of a passport to check in at sites and it covers you for third-party insurance. Carnets are issued in the UK by the AA, RAC and **The Camping and Caravanning Club**.

Every year, the *Guía Oficial de Campings* is published by Turespaña. Information about camp sites is available from the **Federación Española de Empresarios de Campings y Ciudades de Vacaciones**

Sign for a camp site

(Spanish Camp Site and Holiday Camp Federation). In Spain, camping is only permitted on official sites.

DISABLED TRAVELLERS

Hotel managers will advise on access for people in wheelchairs, and the staff will help, but few hotels are well equipped for disabled guests, although some of the youth hostels are. **COCEMFE** (the Confederación Coordinadora Estatal de Minusválidos Físicos de España) runs a hotel in Madrid for disabled people's groups.

COCEMFE and Viajes 2000 *(see p665)* advise on hotels for guests with special needs. A UK charity, Holiday Care Service, produces a fact sheet on Spain. **IHD** (International Help for the Disabled), which is based in France, will arrange transport, hotels and other help for visitors to the Costa del Sol and Mallorca.

View from the Cabina Verónica mountain refuge, Picos de Europa

FURTHER INFORMATION

Every spring, Turespaña publishes the *Guía Oficial de Hoteles*, which is sold in Spanish bookshops and newsstands and can be consulted in Spanish tourist offices. It lists every pension, hostal and hotel in Spain and gives their star-rating, their prices and a resumé of their facilities.

Each *comunidad autónoma* distributes a list of the hotels and other accommodation in its area via the tourist offices.

DIRECTORY

HOTEL CHAINS

Grupo Riu
Tel 902 40 05 02.
Fax 971 74 38 98.
www.riu.com

Grupo Sol-Meliá
Tel 902 14 44 40.
Fax 91 579 13 92.
www.solmelia.com

NH-Hoteles
Tel 902 11 51 16.
www.nh-hotels.com

PARADORS

Central de Reservas
Calle Requena 3, 28013 Madrid.
Tel 902 54 79 79.
Fax 902 52 54 32.
www.parador.es

Keytel International
402 Edgware Road, London W2 1ED.
Tel 020 7616 0300 in UK.
www.keytel.co.uk

SELF-CATERING AND BED AND BREAKFAST

Asociación Gallega de Turismo Rural
Recinto Ferial, Apdo 26, Silleda 36540 Pontevedra.
Tel 986 58 00 50.
www.agatur.org

Hometours International Inc.
1108 Scottie Lane, Knoxville, TN 37919,USA.
Tel 865 690 84 84.
@ hometours@aol.com

The Individual Traveller's Spain
Spring Mill, Earby, Barnoldswick, Lancs BB94 0AA. *Tel 087007 80194.*

RAAR
Sagunto 8, 04004 Almería. *Tel 902 44 22 33.* www.raar.es

Ruralia
C/ Marques de Canillejas 12, Bajo, 33500 Llanes (Asturias). *Tel 902 10 70 70.* www.ruralia.com

Ruralverd
C/ del Pí 11, Principal 3, 08002 Barcelona.
Tel 93 304 37 74.
Fax 93 481 42 09.
www.ruralverd.es

TVR
C/ Miguel Servet 12, 22002 Huesca.
Tel 902 29 41 41.
www.turismoverde.es

YOUTH HOSTELS

Red Española de Albergues Juveniles
Tel 915 22 70 07.
www.reaj.com

MOUNTAIN REFUGES

FEDME
C/ Floridablanca 84, 08015 Barcelona. *Tel 93 426 42 67.* www.fedme.es

CAMPING

The Camping and Caravanning Club
Tel 0845 130 7633 in UK.

Federación de Empresarios de Campings

C/Valderibas 48, 1° C, 28007 Madrid.
Tel 91 448 12 34.
Fax 91 448 12 67.
www.fedcamping.com

DISABLED TRAVELLERS

COCEMFE
C/ Luis Cabrera 63, 28002 Madrid.
Tel 91 744 36 00.
Fax 91 413 19 96.

SATH
347 Fifth Ave, Suite 610, New York, NY 10016
Tel 212 447 7284.
www.sath.org

FURTHER INFORMATION

Spanish Tourist Office
Tel 020 7486 8077 in UK.
www.spain.info
Tel 212 265-8822 in US.
www.spain.info

Spain's Best: Paradors

Parador is an old Spanish word for a lodging place for travellers of respectable rank. In the late 1920s a national network of state-run hotels called paradors was established. Many of the 90 or so paradors are converted castles, palaces or monasteries, although some have been purpose-built in strategic tourist locations. They are generally well signposted and the prices are comparable with other luxury hotels. All offer a high degree of comfort and service, and have restaurants which offer regional cuisine.

Hotel de los Reyes Católicos, *one of the sights of Santiago de Compostela (see p90), may be the world's oldest hotel. It was founded as a hospital in 1499 (see p562).*

Parador de León *is housed in the Hostal San Marcos, one of Spain's finest Renaissance buildings (see p25). The main hall has a magnificent coffered ceiling (see p584).*

Hotel de los Reyes Católicos

Parador de León

Parador de Guadalupe is a 16th-century former hospice for pilgrims. It stands beside a famous monastery in Extremadura *(see p589).*

Parador de Arcos de la Frontera *is situated in one of the archetypal* pueblos blancos *(white towns). Its wide, semicircular terrace offers panoramic views of the Moorish castle, the Guadalete river and the rolling farmland beyond* (see p592).

Parador de Guadalupe

Parado Grana

Parador de Arcos de la Frontera

Parador de Granada *is a captivating 15th-century convent built in the beautiful gardens of the Alhambra at the instruction of the Catholic Monarc. Antique Spanish furniture fills the ba and rooms of this atmospheric parado and an old roofless chapel forms a pat Advance booking is essential (see p59*

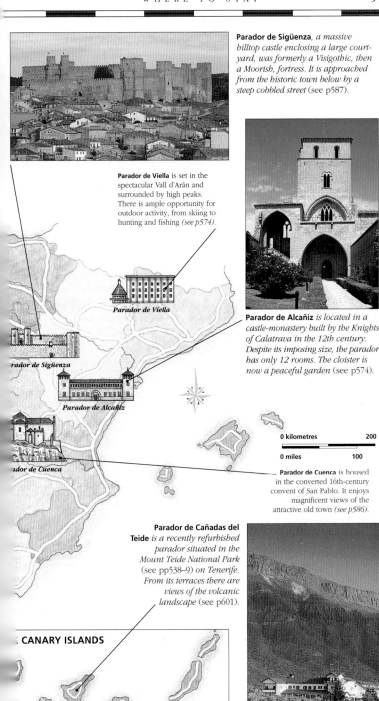

Parador de Sigüenza, *a massive hilltop castle enclosing a large courtyard, was formerly a Visigothic, then a Moorish, fortress. It is approached from the historic town below by a steep cobbled street* (see p587).

Parador de Viella is set in the spectacular Vall d'Arán and surrounded by high peaks. There is ample opportunity for outdoor activity, from skiing to hunting and fishing *(see p574)*.

Parador de Viella

rador de Sigüenza

Parador de Alcañiz

ador de Cuenca

Parador de Alcañiz *is located in a castle-monastery built by the Knights of Calatrava in the 12th century. Despite its imposing size, the parador has only 12 rooms. The cloister is now a peaceful garden* (see p574).

| 0 kilometres | 200 |
| 0 miles | 100 |

Parador de Cuenca is housed in the converted 16th-century convent of San Pablo. It enjoys magnificent views of the attractive old town *(see p586)*.

Parador de Cañadas del Teide *is a recently refurbished parador situated in the Mount Teide National Park* (see pp538–9) *on Tenerife. From its terraces there are views of the volcanic landscape* (see p601).

CANARY ISLANDS

Choosing a Hotel

The hotels in this guide have been selected across a wide price range for excellent facilities and location. Many also have a highly recommended restaurant. The chart lists hotels by region, starting in the north and moving to the south. For more details on restaurants *see pages 608–653.*

PRICE CATEGORIES
Standard double room per night, with tax and service charge included.

€ under 75 euros
€€ 75–125 euros
€€€ 125–175 euros
€€€€ 175–225 euros
€€€€€ over 225 euros

GALICIA

A CORUÑA Ciudad de la Coruña
€€

Paseo Adormideras s/n, 15002 **Tel** *981 21 21 00* **Fax** *981 22 46 10* **Rooms** *131*

Situated in the residential district of Adormideras, close to San Amaro beach, this hotel offers views of A Coruña bay. It has spacious bedrooms, meeting rooms, a gym and Jacuzzi. It also provides indoor and outdoor parking. The Torremar restaurant specializes in lobster and seafood. **www.hotelciudaddelacoruna.com**

A ESTRADA Fonteclara
€

Sta Marina de Ribeira 6, 36685 (Pontevedra) **Tel** *986 57 32 09* **Fax** *981 36 49 99* **Rooms** *8*

A 17th-century Galician country house, peacefully located in the valley of the Río Ulla, close to both Santiago de Compostela and the Rías Baixas. This hotel offers reasonably priced bed and breakfast and the use of a sitting room with an open fireplace. Extensive garden. Closed mid-Jan–mid-Feb. **www.casafonteclara.com**

A GUARDA Convento San Benito
€€

Plaza de San Benito, 36780 (Pontevedra) **Tel** *986 61 11 66* **Fax** *986 61 15 17* **Rooms** *24*

A converted 16th-century convent, where the nuns' cells, surrounding a small cloister with a palm tree and a stone fountain, have been transformed into bedrooms for the guests. Two rooms have their own sitting rooms; there is also a suite. All rooms have Internet access. Closed start Jan–early Feb. **www.hotelsanbenito.es**

BAIONA Pazo de Mendoza
€€

C/ Elduayen 1, 36300 (Pontevedra) **Tel** *986 38 50 14* **Fax** *986 38 59 88* **Rooms** *12*

This 18th-century town house on the seafront is close to the beach and Baiona's shops. The former residence of the dean of Santiago de Compostela, it was converted into a hotel in 1998. The restaurant serves "New Galician" cuisine. Its cafeteria, with a variety of imported coffees, has tables set out on the Paseo Marítimo. **www.pazodemendoza.es**

BAIONA Parador de Baiona
€€€€€

Castillo Monterreal, 36300 (Pontevedra) **Tel** *986 35 50 00* **Fax** *986 35 50 76* **Rooms** *122*

This parador, built in an old Galician *pazo* (manor house) style, is located within the walls of Monterreal Castle *(see p96)*. The restaurant serves seafood accompanied by the local Ribeiro wine. Some rooms have four-poster beds and offer sea views, while others look out onto the gardens. **www.parador.es**

BARREIROS Casa do Merlo
€€

C/ Sargendez 4, 27793 (Lugo) **Tel** *982 13 49 06* **Fax** *982 13 49 07* **Rooms** *10*

A walled 17th-century country *pazo* in a small coastal village. The decoration is reminiscent of English colonial style and the rooms are bright; some have sea views. Breakfast is served in a winter garden with tropical plants. There is also an inner patio and several public rooms, including a library and a games room. **www.casadomerlo.com**

BENTRACES Pazo Bentraces
€€

Ctra 540, Celanobas km 7/ Bentraces Bardadas, 32890 (Ourense) **Tel** *988 38 33 81* **Fax** *988 38 33 81* **Rooms** *7*

This 15th-century *pazo*, a short way southwest of Ourense city, was transformed into a palace by an aristocratic Portuguese family. It has since been refurbished, keeping the original features of wood and marble and part of the family's furniture. Its restaurant has a one-star Michelin rating. Closed 22 Dec–22 Jan. **www.pazodebentraces.co**

BRIÓN Casa Rosalía
€

Soigrexa 29 Os Anxeles Brion, 15280 (A Coruña) **Tel** *981 88 75 80* **Fax** *981 88 75 57* **Rooms** *30*

A country house hotel, stone-built and surrounding a cloister, and named after the "national" poetess of Galicia. It offers simple accommodation 25 km (16 miles) from the coast and Santiago de Compostela. Its restaurant offers "gourmet days". A fire is lit in the sitting room in winter. Closed 23 Dec–23 Jan. **www.hotelcasarosalia.com**

CAMBADOS Parador de Cambados
€€€€

Paseo de la Calzada, 36630 (Pontevedra) **Tel** *986 54 22 50* **Fax** *986 54 20 68* **Rooms** *57*

Sited in the middle of the Rías Baixas coast, this parador occupies a handsome *pazo* built around a large courtyard garden, surrounding a fountain where drinks are served. Within easy reach of beaches and pleasant places to walk. Galician specialities and local wines (Cambados is a production centre) are served in the restaurant. **www.parador.e**

Key to Symbols *see back cover flap*

CERVO Pousada O'Almacen

Ctra de Sargadelos 2, 27891 (Lugo) **Tel** *982 55 78 36* **Fax** *982 55 78 94* **Rooms** *7*

A restored 18th-century building on the north coast of Galicia. Once an *almacén* (food store) for nearby hamlets, it is now run by a family as a homely rural hotel. It makes a good base for walking or horse riding, or from which to discover the lesser known parts of Galicia. The best bedrooms look on to the Río Xunco. Closed 10–31 Jan.

CORNIDE Casa Grande de Cornide

Calo, Teo, 15886 (A Coruña) **Tel** *981 80 55 99* **Fax** *981 80 57 51* **Rooms** *12*

A welcoming bed-and-breakfast hotel in a renovated house, 10 minutes by car from Santiago de Compostela. It is beautifully decorated with antiques and has a library and a garden with two traditional *hórreos* (granaries), an old magnolia and an 18th-century dovecote. International wines. **www.casasgrandesdegalicia.com**

MIÑO Casa Grande Fontao

C/ Fontao 1A, 15639 (A Coruña) **Tel** *981 78 27 72* **Fax** *981 78 27 17* **Rooms** *7*

A traditional Galician stone and whitewashed country house built in the 17th century with a bay window that overlooks the garden and fields. The interior is welcoming and warm and has a well-equipped library. The bedrooms are decorated in white with traditional furniture and have comfortable beds. **www.casagrandefontao.com**

NOIA Pesqueria del Tambre

Central del Tambre, Santa Maria de Roo, 15211 (A Coruña) **Tel** *981 05 16 20* **Fax** *981 05 16 29* **Rooms** *16*

On the bank of Río Tambre, and surrounded by a forest, this is a place to get lost in nature. The main building was a hydroelectric plant built in the early 20th century. The bedrooms, elegantly restored and decorated using traditional fabrics, are in a group of houses near the river. Closed 23–29 Dec. **www.pesqueriadeltambre.com**

O GROVE Gran Hotel de la Toja

Isla de la Toja, 36991 (Pontevedra) **Tel** *986 73 00 25* **Fax** *986 73 00 26* **Rooms** *199*

This majestic hotel, built at the turn of the 19th century, stands on its own small island planted with palm and pine trees, and is reached from the mainland by a bridge. It has an old-fashioned feel to it with a ballroom and a piano bar. Offers lovely sea views, and has good beaches nearby. It also has a spa.

O SAVIÑAO Torre Vilariño

Lugar de Vilariño 47, Fión, 27548 (Lugo) **Tel** *982 45 22 60* **Fax** *982 45 22 60* **Rooms** *9*

A 18th-century inn converted into a hotel offering bed and breakfast, mainly to tourists following Galicia's "Romanesque Route". The owners serve home-made food and wine. The large garden is populated by peacocks, pheasants and geese. Bicycles are available for touring. Closed Nov–early Dec. **www.torrevilarino.com**

POBRA DE TRIVES Casa Grande de Trives

C/ Marqués de Trives 17, 32780 (Ourense) **Tel** *988 33 20 66* **Fax** *988 33 20 66* **Rooms** *9*

A *posada* (small hotel) in a 17th-century stone manor, with a coat of arms on its central tower, in the hills of eastern Galicia. Antiques and old paintings decorate the cosy interior. There is a chapel with a magnificent reredos. Also has three sitting rooms and a garden in which to relax. Serves breakfast only. **www.casagrandetrives.com**

POBRA DE TRIVES Pazo A Freiria

C/ A Freiria, 32780 (Ourense) **Tel** *696 05 71 94* **Fax** *988 33 70 86* **Rooms** *7*

Beautifully located in hills and surrounded by chestnut forests, this old stone *pazo* was originally a 12th-century monastery. It has been restored respecting the unique structure, which incorporates exposed stone, ancient chestnut timbers and wrought iron details. One of the rooms is a suite with magnificent views. **www.pazoafreiria.com**

PONTEVEDRA Parador de Pontevedra

Rua del Barón 19, 36002 **Tel** *986 85 58 00* **Fax** *986 85 21 95* **Rooms** *45*

A parador in a 16–18th-century Renaissance palace, which was once a school, granary, masonic lodge and an aristocratic residence. The decor incorporates antiques, gilt mirrors, chandeliers and tapestries. Some rooms are in a new wing. The restaurant specializes in seafood of the Rías Baixas. **www.parador.es**

RIBADEO Casa de Doñano

Vilela (Cubelas), 27714 (Lugo) **Tel** *982 13 74 29* **Fax** *982 13 48 00* **Rooms** *9*

This country house, built in 1907, has since been converted into a homely hotel surrounded by its own land. There is a large public area downstairs, and the library, which offers fine views from its windows, has telescopes for star gazing. Two rooms have double beds. One room is suitable for disabled guests. Breakfast included. **www.casadonano.com**

RIBADUMIA Pazo Carrasqueira

Carrasqueira, 36638 (Pontevedra) **Tel** *986 71 00 32* **Fax** *986 71 00 32* **Rooms** *9*

A thick-walled 18th-century country mansion, with a stone staircase outside and a coat of arms set into its façade. Some of the bedrooms are cosy and all have heating and TV. Seafood and Albariño wine (produced on the estate) are served in the dining room. Also has a laundry service, a library and Internet access. **www.pazocarrasqueira.com**

SAN PEDRO DE VIANA Pazo As Casas

Pantada, 27513 (Lugo) **Tel** *600 66 91 14* **Tel/Fax** *982 44 05 53* **Rooms** *12*

A restored 17th-century house north of Ourense, eclectically decorated with original heavy furniture of dark wood and exposed stone. It has a pleasant terrace for relaxing in the summer. All the bedrooms are distinctly styled with brilliant white and have baths, TV and heating. The salon doubles as a library. **www.pazoascasas.com**

SANTIAGO DE COMPOSTELA As Artes 　　　　　　　　🅿️ 　€€

Trav de Dos Puertas 2, 15707 (A Coruña) **Tel** *981 57 25 90* **Fax** *981 577 823* **Rooms** *7*

Each room in this comfortable small hotel, close to the cathedral, is dedicated to one of the arts: theatre, sculpture, dance, architecture, painting, music or cinema. The place is decorated with flair, and has parquet floors and wrought-iron beds. A small cafeteria offers breakfast. Hospitable and friendly owners. Closed 9–18 Dec. **www.asartes.com**

SANTIAGO DE COMPOSTELA Pazo Cibrán 　　　　　　　　　　€€

San Xulian de Sales, Vedra, 15885 (A Coruña) **Tel** *981 51 15 15* **Fax** *981 81 47 66* **Rooms** *11*

This noble house, with its own chapel, is situated in a very peaceful hamlet a short way from Santiago de Compostela. It has belonged to the same family since the 18th century and has been lovingly restored. Lunch is not served but the breakfast is particularly good. **www.pazocibran.com**

SANTIAGO DE COMPOSTELA Hesperia Peregrino 　　🄿🈯🅿️🍴🈺 　€€€€

Av Rosalia de Castro s/n, 15706 (A Coruña) **Tel** *981 52 18 50* **Fax** *981 52 17 77* **Rooms** *150*

A hotel in the new city area, a ten minute walk from the historical centre and very close to the university and the train station. The interior decoration is modern. There is a bar and a restaurant, TV, heating and laundry service. Internet and meeting rooms are available as well. **www.hesperia-compostela.com**

SANTIAGO DE COMPOSTELA Parador Hostal Dos Reis Catolicos 　🄿🈯🍴🈺 　€€€€€

Praza do Obradoiro 1, 15705 (A Coruña) **Tel** *981 58 22 00* **Fax** *981 56 30 94* **Rooms** *137*

Built under the Catholic monarchs as a hostel for poor pilgrims, this luxurious 16th-century parador, on the same square as Santiago de Compostela's famous cathedral, is one of the world's grandest hotels. It is built around four arcaded courtyards with fountains. The public rooms have regal touches such as hanging tapestries. **www.parador.es**

TUI Parador de Tui 　　　　　　　　　　🄿🈯🍴🈺🈺🈺 　€€€

Av de Portugal, 36700 (Pontevedra) **Tel** *986 60 03 00* **Fax** *986 60 21 63* **Rooms** *32*

This pretty parador is a perfect replica of a traditional Galician *pazo* combining granite with chestnut beams. The public and guest rooms have superb views of the town of Tui and across the Río Miño, which forms the frontier with Portugal. It has a lovely garden. Dishes on the menu include baby eels and scallops. **www.parador.es**

VILAGARCIA DE AROUSA Pazo O'Rial 　　　　　　🈯🍴🅿️🈺🈺 　€€€

C/ El Rial 1, 36600 (Pontevedra) **Tel** *986 50 70 11* **Fax** *986 50 16 76* **Rooms** *60*

A beautiful 17th-century manor with a tower, tiled floors, stone walls and arches, just outside Vilagarcía de Arousa and a walk away from the seashore. It is stylishly decorated with fine furnishings and comfortable armchairs, and has its own chapel. There are four lounges-cum-reception-rooms, one with a massive old fireplace. **www.pazorial.com**

VILALBA Parador de Vilalba 　　　　　　　　🄿🈯🅿️🍴🈺🈺🈺 　€€€

Valeriano Valdesuso, 27800 (Lugo) **Tel** *982 51 00 11* **Fax** *982 51 00 90* **Rooms** *48*

Six rooms of this hotel are found in a medieval octagonal tower which was built between the 11th and 13th centuries and restored in the 15th century. Other rooms as well as the bar and restaurant are in a modern stone building beside it. The castle preserves its moat and portcullis. Facilities include a gym, sauna and Turkish bath. **www.parador.es**

ASTURIAS AND CANTABRIA

CAMALEÑO El Jisu 　　　　　　　　　　　🍴🈯🅿️🈺 　€€

Ctra Potes–Fuente Dé, 39570 (Cantabria) **Tel** *942 73 30 38* **Fax** *942 73 03 15* **Rooms** *9*

A modern, purpose-built chalet hotel in the heart of the Picos de Europa *(see p108–9)* . It stands in its own grounds in the Liébana Valley, on the road to Fuente Dé, close to Liébana monastery. El Jisu enjoys great mountain views and makes a good base for walking or exploring the Picos by car. The sitting rooms have rustic furniture. Closed 20 Dec–1 Feb.

CANGAS DE ONIS Aultre Naray 　　　　　　　　　　　€€

Peruyes, 33457 (Asturias) **Tel** *985 84 08 08* **Fax** *985 84 08 48* **Rooms** *10*

This country hotel, in a renovated 19th-century Asturian house, has superb views of the mountains of the Sierra de Escapa and the Picos de Europa from the first-floor bedrooms. The second floor has cosy attic rooms. The sitting room has a warm atmosphere and big windows. Also has a library with a fireplace and a bar. **www.aultrenaray.com**

CANGAS DE ONIS Parador de Cangas de Onis 　　🈯🄿🍴🈺🈺🈺 　€€€€€

Villanueva (km 2 from Cangas), 33550 (Asturias) **Tel** *985 84 94 02* **Fax** *985 84 95 20* **Rooms** *64*

A restored 12th-century Benedictine monastery with magnificent cloisters, located on the bank of the Río Sellar just outside the town of Cangas de Onis. The rooms are spacious and comfortable, and the restaurant serves regional dishes. Includes facilities such as meeting rooms. **www.parador.es**

CARAVIA El Babú 　　　　　　　　　　　　🍴 　€€

Carrales, 33343 (Asturias) **Tel** *985 85 32 72* **Fax** *985 85 32 73* **Rooms** *8*

A small and intimate hotel in a 19th-century country house, which has been renovated and decorated in modern style using neutral colours. The rooms have mountain or garden views: the cosiest ones are in the attic. A filling breakfast is served. The hotel has grounds to walk around. Also has a library, bar and elevator chair. **www.elbabu.com**

Key to Price Guide *see p560* **Key to Symbols** *see back cover flap*

COLOMBRES La Casona de Villanueva   **P** **⑪**   €€

Villanueva de Colombres, 33590 (Asturias) **Tel** *985 41 25 90* **Fax** *985 41 25 14* **Rooms** *8*

An 18th-century village house restored in traditional style and dotted with antiques and works of art. It is well located for visits either to the Picos de Europa or to the beaches of the Asturian coast. They serve home-made jams at breakfast, which is included. **www.lacasonadevillanueva.com**

COMILLAS Hostal Esmeralda   🛌 **⑪**   €€

C/ Antonio López 7, 39520 (Cantabria) **Tel** *942 72 00 97* **Fax** *942 72 22 58* **Rooms** *12*

This simple and traditional hostal is situated in a beautiful townhouse dating back to 1874, with exterior glass and wooden galleries. Rooms are basic but comfortable, and all come complete with Internet and security boxes. The restaurant serves local cuisine and has a cosy fireplace. **www.lacasonadevillanueva.com**

ESCALANTE (CANTABRIA) San Román de Escalante   🛌 **⑪** 🏊 🗐   €€€€

Ctra Escalante–Castillo km 2, 39795 (Cantabria) **Tel** *942 67 77 45* **Fax** *942 67 76 43* **Rooms** *16*

A Relais et Châteaux hotel in an exquisitely decorated 17th-century manor house overlooking trees and meadows. All the rooms are different, and one of them has a terrace. An indoor swimming pool, horse riding, water-skiing and golf are also available. The restaurant has an impressive wine list. Closed 6–20 Nov. **www.sanromandeescalante.com**

FIGUERAS DEL MAR Palacete Peñalba   **⑪**   €€€

C/ Granda, Figueras del Mar, 33794 (Asturias) **Tel** *985 63 61 25* **Fax** *985 63 62 47* **Rooms** *23*

Made up of two beautiful Art Nouveau mansions, the Palacete Cotalerelo and the Palacete Granada, this hotel is near the Ria de Eo. The Granada is a magnificent fantasy, with a façade of oval windows and two curved staircases to the front door. Inside it has much of its original furniture. Closed Jan. **www.hotelpalacetepenalba.com**

FUENTE DÉ (CANTABRIA) Parador de Fuente Dé   🖥 🛌 🏊 **⑪** 🗐   €€€

Ctra Fuente Dé, a 3.5 km de Espinama, 39588 (Cantabria) **Tel** *942 73 66 51* **Fax** *942 73 66 54* **Rooms** *78*

This modern parador stands in an unbeatably dramatic location in the rock amphitheatre of Fuente Dé, at the foot of the Picos de Europa cable car. It has pleasant bedrooms and long galleries with huge windows. There is only one road in and out, so it is peaceful at night. This hotel makes an ideal base for walking. Closed Nov–Feb. **www.parador.es**

GIJÓN La Casona de Jovellanos   🖥 **⑪**   €€

Plazuela de Jovellanos 1, 33201 (Asturias) **Tel** *985 34 20 24* **Fax** *985 35 61 51* **Rooms** *13*

A small hotel in an 18th-century building overlooking a little square in the old part of the city, near San Lorenzo beach. One of its two dining rooms incorporates the remains of the old city wall which was discovered during restoration work. A five-person aparthotel is also available. **www.lacasonadejovellanos.com**

GIJÓN Parador de Gijón   🖥 🛌 🏊 **⑪** 🗐   €€€€

Parque de Isabel la Católica, 33203 (Asturias) **Tel** *985 37 05 11* **Fax** *985 37 02 33* **Rooms** *40*

A modern parador in the grounds of an 18th-century watermill, located in a corner of what has been described as one of Spain's prettiest parks. The old watercourse in the grounds has been preserved. The speciality of the restaurant is the regional stew, *fabada Asturiana*, but choice seafood is also served. **www.parador.es**

LIÉRGANES Balneario de Liérganes   🖥 **P** **⑪** 🏊   €€

C/ J.A. Primo de Rivera, 39722 (Cantabria) **Tel/Fax** *942 52 80 11* **Rooms** *97*

This 20th-century mountain house, now a spa hotel near the Río Miera, has a covered heated swimming pool and offers various beauty treatments at extra cost. During the high season the minimum stay is three nights. Liérganes is also close to Santillana del Mar *(see p112)*. Closed 24 Dec–early Feb. **www.relaistermal.com**

LLANES La Posada de Babel   **⑪**   €€€

La Pereda, 33509 (Asturias) **Tel** *985 40 25 25* **Fax** *985 40 26 22* **Rooms** *13*

The spectacular Picos de Europa peaks lie behind this small, family-run hotel. It is partly modern, but has huge, traditional fireplaces and one bedroom is a converted *hórreo* (granary). It has a modern suite, recently built, in the garden. Also has a small library and a bar. Closed 1 Nov–1 Mar. **www.laposadadebabel.com**

MOLLEDA, VAL DE SAN VICENTE Casona de Molleda   🚶   €€

Barrio la Fuente 7, 39569 (Cantabria) **Tel** *942 71 95 67* **Fax** *942 71 95 79* **Rooms** *14*

A renovated village house decorated in warm colours and using lots of textiles. The bedrooms are spacious and some have sitting areas with relaxing views of the Río Deva and the mountains. The hotel is suitably located close to the Picos de Europa. Most rooms have a lounge separate from the bedroom. Closed 10 Dec–12 Feb.

OVIEDO Hotel de la Reconquista   🖥 **P** 🛌 **⑪** 🗐   €€€€€

C/ Gil de Jaz 16, 33004 (Asturias) **Tel** *985 24 11 00* **Fax** *985 24 11 66* **Rooms** *142*

A luxury hotel in a magnificent 18th-century building, originally an orphanage, with a massive stone coat of arms above the main entrance. Its name commemorates the Reconquest of Spain, which was launched from Asturias. The public rooms are arranged around several courtyards. **www.hoteldelareconquista.com**

PECHÓN Don Pablo   **P** 🛌   €

El Cruce, 39594 (Cantabria) **Tel** *942 71 95 00* **Fax** *942 71 95 23* **Rooms** *34*

Three houses joined together make up this family-run rural hotel along the coast from San Vicente de la Barquera, which is close to the sea and the Picos de Europa. The rooms are cosy, with old beams of oak and chestnut, and have marble bathrooms. The hotel also has large sitting rooms and pretty terraces. **www.donpablohotel.com**

PRAVIA Casa del Busto   🕭🛇   €€

Plaza del Rey Don Silo 1, 33120 (Asturias) **Tel** *985 82 27 71* **Fax** *985 82 27 72* **Rooms** *30*

In a town 10 km (6 miles) from the beaches of the Asturian coast, is this hotel in a typical 16th-century Asturian house where the Spanish writer Jovellanos spent his summers. The bedrooms overlook a central patio. The hotel is decorated with period pieces. An Asturian breakfast buffet is served. **www.casonadelbusto.es**

QUIJAS Casona Torre de Quijas   🅿🕭🛇   €€

Barrio Vinueva 76, 39590 (Cantabria) **Tel** *942 82 06 45* **Fax** *942 83 82 55* **Rooms** *22*

This hotel is in a restored, 19th-century stone house near Santillana del Mar. It has bay windows and a large garden, and is decorated with Art Nouveau furniture. There are some attic rooms, a sitting room with a library and two rooms have disabled access. The restaurant offers only light dinners. Closed 15 Dec–end Jan. **www.casonatorredequijas.com**

QUIJAS Hostería de Quijas   🅿🛇🏊   €€

Barrio Vinueva, 39590 (Cantabria) **Tel** *942 82 08 33* **Fax** *942 83 80 50* **Rooms** *19*

A family-run hotel in an 18th-century stone-built mansion on the Santander–Oviedo road, close to Santillana del Mar and the Altamira caves. It has bay windows, timbered ceilings and a garden. Six of the rooms are suites. The menu is strong on seafood, and breakfast can be served outdoors. Closed 20 Dec–15 Jan. **www.hosteriadequijas.com**

RIBADEDEVA Mirador de la Franca   🛇🚶   €€

Playa de la Franca, 33590 (Asturias) **Tel** *985 41 21 45* **Fax** *985 41 21 53* **Rooms** *61*

A beach hotel, popular with families, with spacious sitting areas, a tennis court and great views from the lounge and restaurant. The waters of the bay are safe for water sports and fishing. Close to the Picos de Europa. Minimum three nights stay during the high season. Closed Nov–Mar. **www.arceahoteles.com**

RIBADESELLA Gran Hotel del Sella   🅿🕭🖥🛇🏊   €€€

Ricardo Cangas 17, 33560 (Asturias) **Tel** *985 86 01 50* **Fax** *985 85 74 49* **Rooms** *81*

The former summer palace of the Marquis of Argüelles is dwarfed by the new hotel wing, but it still lends this family-run beach hotel some class. It is sited at the mouth of the Río Sella, on Santa Marina beach and has vast gardens. Four of the rooms are suites. The restaurant specializes in seafood. Closed Jan–Feb. **www.granhoteldelsella.com**

SAN VICENTE DE TORANZO Posada del Pas   🅿🛇🏊   €

Ctra N623 Burgos–Santander, 39699 (Cantabria) **Tel** *942 59 44 11* **Fax** *942 59 43 86* **Rooms** *32*

An 18th-century stone mountain house standing in a green valley beside the Santander–Burgos road, which is used as a stopover by travellers arriving or departing on the ferry between Plymouth and Santander. The restaurant specializes in regional Cantabrian dishes. There is a private garage. **www.hotelposadadelpas.com**

SANTANDER Las Brisas   €€

La Braña 14, El Sardinero, 39005 (Cantabria) **Tel** *942 27 50 11* **Fax** *942 28 11 73* **Rooms** *13*

A recently-refurbished homely hotel in a 19th-century white turret-shaped villa, close to the popular Sardinero beach. Each room is different with floral fabrics predominating. Breakfast, included in the price, can be served on a seaside terrace. The hotel also has five self-catering apartments. Closed 22 Dec–15 Jan. **www.hotellasbrisas.net**

SANTANDER Hotel Real   🅿🖥🛇🛏📺🏊 €€€€€

Paseo Pérez Galdós 28, 39005 (Cantabria) **Tel** *942 27 25 50* **Fax** *942 27 45 73* **Rooms** *114*

An elegant, formal hotel visible on the city's highest hill. It was built in the early 20th century for nobility accompanying the royal family on holiday. Its chandeliers and moulded plaster still testify to its status. The balconies offer spectacular views of the bay, especially those on the top floor. The hotel has its own spa. **www.hotelreal.es**

SANTILLANA DEL MAR Altamira   🛇   €€€

C/ Cantón 1, 39330 (Cantabria) **Tel** *942 81 80 25* **Fax** *942 84 01 36* **Rooms** *32*

A town-centre hotel in a restored 16th-century palace very close to the Romanesque church of La Colegiata. The old wooden staircase leads to bedrooms with beams and polished floors, two of them with private sitting rooms. Also well located for the visitor centre of the famous caves after which the hotel is named. **www.hotelaltamira.com**

SANTILLANA DEL MAR Los Infantes   🅿🛇   €€€

Avda Le Dorat 1, 39330 (Cantabria) **Tel** *942 81 81 00* **Fax** *942 84 01 03* **Rooms** *88*

The 18th-century country mansion, comprising three buildings, houses this hotel that was formerly the residence of the Calderons family. It is set slightly back from the road. The massive beams, stone floors, carved chests and leather armchairs in the lobby give it an old-fashioned feel. Closed 24–31 Dec. **www.hotel-santillana.com**

SANTILLANA DEL MAR Parador Gil Blas   🅿🖥🕭🛇🛏 €€€€

Plaza Ramón Pelayo 11, 39330 (Cantabria) **Tel** *942 02 80 28* **Fax** *942 81 83 91* **Rooms** *28*

This stone mansion, begun in the 15th century, blends perfectly into the unspoiled medieval town, which is busy with tourists during the day but quiet at night. The building has a pretty patio. Inside bare walls and tiled floors enhance the medieval atmosphere. Rooms are spacious and tastefully decorated. **www.parador.es**

SOLARES Hostería Palacio de los Marqueses de Valbuena   🛇📺   €€

General Mola 6, 39710 (Cantabria) **Tel** *942 52 28 66* **Fax** *942 52 21 76* **Rooms** *27*

A late 17th-century Baroque mansion with imposing façade and its own chapel, built by the Inquisitor General of Spain. It is conveniently located for an overnight stop, just off the Bilbao–Santander motorway. The public rooms are spacious and the bedrooms comfortable. It has a cafeteria and a restaurant. **www.marquesesdevalbuena.com**

Key to Price Guide *see p560* **Key to Symbols** *see back cover flap*

TARAMUNDI La Rectoral   🅿️🖥🍴📺🖥   €€€

Taramundi, 33775 (Asturias) **Tel** *985 64 67 60* **Fax** *985 64 67 77* **Rooms** *18*

An 18th-century former priest's house, built of stone and timber with a slate roof, deep in the Asturian countryside. It has been tastefully converted into a quiet and atmospheric hotel. All the bedrooms have mountain views. An alternative to the main house are some cottages with room service. Closed 24 Dec. **www.larectoral.com**

VILLACARRIEDO Palacio Soñanes   🛗🖥🅿️🍴   €€€€

Barrio del Quintanal 1, 39640 (Cantabria) **Tel** *942 59 06 00* **Fax** *942 59 06 14* **Rooms** *30*

An imposing 18th-century Baroque palace of beautiful golden stone that dominates this quiet rural town. Inside, it has a superb Renaissance main staircase. The bedrooms are very comfortable, all different, and decorated in a rich variety of colours. The verdant Valle de la Pas is a good area for gentle walking. **www.palaciodevillacarriedo.com**

THE BASQUE COUNTRY, NAVARRA AND LA RIOJA

ANGUIANO Abadía de Valvanera   🍴   €

Monasterio de Valvanera, Hospital Viejo, 26323 (La Rioja) **Tel** *941 37 70 44* **Fax** *941 37 71 94* **Rooms** *28*

This old Benedictine abbey with simple rooms offers no-frills accommodation, good food and lots of history. Queen Isabel I stayed in the cells here in 1482. It is located in the beautiful surroundings of one of Spain's least-known range of hills, the Sierra de la Demanda. Closed 22 Dec–10 Jan. **www.abadiavalvanera.com**

ARGOMÁNIZ Parador de Argomániz   🅿️🎿🛗🍴   €€€

Ctra Nal Madrid-Irún km 363, 01192 (Alava) **Tel** *945 29 32 00* **Fax** *945 29 32 87* **Rooms** *53*

Sited in a splendid 17th-century Renaisance stone palace, complete with coat of arms, this parador is located on the slopes of Mount Zabalgaña, just outside Vitoria. It is a peaceful spot with good views. The common areas are spacious and rooms tastefully decorated. Basque cuisine is served in the dining room. **www.parador.es**

ARNEDILLO Hospedería Las Pedrolas   🛗🖥   €€

Plaza Felix Merino 16, 26589 (La Rioja) **Tel** *941 39 44 01* **Fax** *941 39 44 04* **Rooms** *7*

An 18th-century whitewashed town house with a coat of arms set into the façade. It has been restored and decorated simply but elegantly. There is an inner patio with a fountain and flowers. The bedrooms are spacious and comfortable. The only noise to disturb you will be the bells of the Gothic church next door. **www.rusticae.es**

AXPE-ATXONDO Mendi Goikoa   🍴   €€

Barrio de San Juan 33, 48291 (Vizcaya) **Tel** *946 82 08 33* **Fax** *946 82 11 36* **Rooms** *12*

Ancient twin stone-built Basque farmhouses, lovingly converted into a pleasant rural hotel and restaurant, in the peaceful heart of the Valle de Atxondo in the hills southeast of Durango. The hotel's slogan is "where you can hear the silence". Ideal for relaxing or taking gentle strolls. One of the rooms has a balcony. Closed 22 Dec–22 Jan.

BAKIO Hostería del Señorío de Bizkaia   🅿️🍴   €€

José María Cirarda 4, 48130 (Vizcaya) **Tel** *946 19 47 25* **Fax** *946 19 47 25* **Rooms** *16*

A stone building with wooden balconies houses this hotel in the resort of Bakio on the Basque coast not far from Bilbao. Guests can play the local racket game of pelota, take a guided tour or visit the nearby beach. The restaurant serves typical Basque cuisine. Closed 10 Jan–15 Feb. **www.hosteriasreales.com**

BERUETE Peruskenea   🛗🍴🖥   €€

Diseminado, Beruete (Basaburua Mayor), 31866 (Navarra) **Tel** *948 50 33 70* **Fax** *948 50 32 84* **Rooms** *9*

An "enchanted house" in which all the bedrooms are named after local fairies or nature spirits. Peruskenea is located in the heart of the Beruete forest between Pamplona and San Sebastián, where there are walking trails to dolmens and craft workshops. The restaurant prepares deliciously creative dishes. **www.peruskenea.com**

BILBAO Carlton   🖥🍴📺🖥   €€

Plaza Federico Moyúa 2, 48009 (Vicaya) **Tel** *944 16 22 00* **Fax** *944 16 46 28* **Rooms** *142*

This luxury hotel, with a domed stained-glass ceiling, is one of the landmarks of Bilbao. Built in 1919, it was formerly the seat of the Basque government. Kings, opera singers, poets and celebrities (including Einstein and Pierce Brosnan) have stayed here. Bedrooms are decorated in classical style. Disabled access **www.aranzazu-hoteles.com**

BILBAO Iturrienea Ostatua   €€

Santa Maria 14, 48005 (Vicaya) **Tel** *944 16 15 00* **Fax** *944 15 89 29* **Rooms** *21*

A small hotel occupying the first and second floors of an old house in the lively old quarter of the city centre, the Casco Viejo – ideal for bar hopping. It is clean and welcoming, combining rustic decorations with some modern flourishes in its large bedrooms. Street-facing rooms, however, catch the noise from below. **www.iturrieneaostatua.com**

BILBAO Ercilla   🖥🛗🍴📺🖥   €€€

Ercilla 37–9, 48011 (Vicaya) **Tel** *944 70 57 00* **Fax** *944 43 93 35* **Rooms** *354*

Bilbao's largest hotel, a modern tower block in the main business district, is close to the Plaza Moyúa. It is comfortable and bustling with life, and has a well-known restaurant, the Bermeo. There is also a bar, a coffee shop and a nightclub. All rooms have wireless Internet. **www.ercillahoteles.com**

BILBAO Mirohotel   �̲🛇̲🅿̲🛏̲🖫̲   €€€€
Alameda Mazarredo 77, 48009 (Vicaya) **Tel** *946 61 18 80* **Fax** *944 25 51 82* **Rooms** *50*

This glass-fronted boutique hotel designed by Antonio Miró is located between the Guggenheim and Fine Arts
Museums. Facilities include a library, a gym and a spa. The bar, which hosts jazz or other live music some evenings,
acts as a meeting point for art lovers. **www.mirohotelbilbao.com**

BRIÑAS Hospedería Señorío de Briñas   🛇̲🅿̲   €€€
Travesía de la Calle Real 3, 26290 (La Rioja) **Tel** *941 30 42 24* **Fax** *941 30 43 45* **Rooms** *14*

This beautifully restored 18th-century palace near the wine town of Haro was used during the Spanish Civil War as
barracks for Italian troops. It is decorated with antiques, frescoes and works of art by a Polish artist. The bedrooms are
spacious and colourful. Close to the Basque Country and Burgos. Closed 15 Dec–15 Jan. **www.hotelesconencanto.org**

CASALARREINA Hospedería Señorío de Casalarreina   🖫̲   €€€
Plaza Sto Domingo de Guzmán 6, 26230 (La Rioja) **Tel** *941 32 47 30* **Fax** *941 32 47 31* **Rooms** *15*

This austere but welcoming 16th-century Plateresque monastery has been refurbished, retaining old architectural
elements. Innovative touches create a warm, elegant and cosy atmosphere. Bedrooms are big and well equipped,
and all the bathrooms have hydromassage baths. Closed 24–25, 31 Dec & 1 Jan. **www.hotelesconencanto.org**

DONAMARIA Donamaria'ko Benta   🍽̲🅿̲   €€
Barrio Ventas 4, 31750 (Navarra) **Tel** *948 45 07 08* **Fax** *948 45 07 08* **Rooms** *5*

This is a small, family-run hotel with a pleasant atmosphere in a stone-built Pyrenean mountain house north of
Pamplona. Close to the Señorío de Bertiz, this is a good base for walking. The antique-furnished rooms are in an
annexe. Cookery courses are also held. Closed 10 Dec–4 Jan. **www.donamariako.com**

FITERO Gustavo Adolfo Bécquer   🚰̲🛇̲🍽̲♨̲🖫̲🖫̲   €€
Baños de Fitero, Extramuros, 31593 (Navarra) **Tel** *948 77 61 00* **Fax** *948 77 62 25* **Rooms** *328*

On the site of the Roman baths south of Navarra, the hotel is named after the Spanish poet who supposedly
recovered from ill health here in the 19th century and was inspired to write two poems. A thermal spring provides spa
bathing, massage and a range of other treatments. Closed mid-Dec–mid-Jan. **www.fitero.com/balneario**

HARO Los Agustinos   🚰̲🅿̲🛏̲🖫̲🖫̲   €€€
C/ San Agustín 2, 26200 (La Rioja) **Tel** *941 31 15 62* **Fax** *941 30 31 48* **Rooms** *62*

A lounge in a vast, arched chamber hung with tapestries is one of the highlights of this hotel in a former Augustinian
monastery. Another is the grand central patio in the old cloister. In the middle of La Rioja's main wine town, the in-
house restaurant, El Campanario, serves good Basque and Riojan dishes. **www.aranzazu-hoteles.com**

HONDARRIBIA Pampinot   🍽̲   €€€€
Kalea Nagusia 5, 20280 (Guipúzcoa) **Tel** *943 64 06 00* **Fax** *943 64 51 28* **Rooms** *8*

An atmosphere of warmth and elegance is achieved by the team of women who run this hotel in a 16th-century
palace, which has been declared a historic national monument. It is located in the heart of old Hondarribia. The
bedroom ceilings are hand painted with images of angels, birds and clouds. Closed Jan. **www.hotelpampinot.com**

HONDARRIBIA Parador de Hondarribiae   🅿̲🛇̲🛇̲   €€€€€
Plaza de Armas 14, 20280 (Guipúzcoa) **Tel** *943 64 55 00* **Fax** *943 64 21 53* **Rooms** *36*

An elegant parador in a 10th-century restored fortress that occupies the highest point of this historic town. It has a
beautiful inner patio incorporating a ruined part of the castle and a terrace overlooking the Bidasoa estuary.
Weapons and other memorabilia of its colourful history adorn the walls of the public rooms. **www.parador.es**

LAGUARDIA Castillo El Collado   🅿̲🛇̲🍽̲🛅̲🖫̲   €€€
Paseo El Collado 1, 01300 (Alava) **Tel** *945 62 12 00* **Fax** *945 60 08 78* **Rooms** *8*

In an unusual building with a Gothic tower reminiscent of a folly, the bedrooms of this small hotel offer views of the Sierra
de Cantabria and the vineyards surrounding the wine town of Laguardia. Bodega visiting is the biggest attraction, but it is
handily located also for Estella and other sights in southern Navarra. Closed 24 Dec–1 Jan. **www.hotelcollado.com**

LAGUARDIA Posada Mayor de Migueloa   🅿̲🍽̲🖫̲   €€€€
C/ Mayor 20, 01300 (Alava) **Tel** *945 62 11 75* **Fax** *945 62 10 22* **Rooms** *8*

Occupying the beautiful 17th-century Baroque Palacio de Viana, this hotel is in the pedestrianized old wine-making
town of Laguardia. It has been refurbished keeping many of its original features. It has its own bodega and one of
the best restaurants of Northen Spain, offering both Basque and La Rioja cuisine. **www.mayordemigueloa.com**

LOGROÑO Herencia Rioja   🚰̲🅿̲🛇̲🍽̲🛏̲🖫̲   €€
Marqués de Murrieta 14, 26005 (La Rioja) **Tel** *941 21 02 22* **Fax** *941 21 02 06* **Rooms** *83*

A modern chain hotel close to the Paseo del Espolon and near Logroño's historic quarter. It has comfortable
bedrooms and a restaurant serving *haute cuisine*. Rooms have wireless Internet and guests are supplied with pay-per-
view films and video games. Other services include a gym, dry cleaning and car rental. **www.nh-hotels.com**

MUNDAKA El Puerto   €€
Portu Kalea 1, 48360 (Vizcaya) **Tel** *946 87 67 25* **Fax** *946 87 67 26* **Rooms** *12*

A fisherman's house in one of the prettiest towns on the Basque coast. Located at the mouth of the Genika estuary,
which is renowned for its surfing beaches, the windows offer great views of the sea. Converted into a simple, cosy
hotel it is decorated in contemporary style. It has a cafeteria and a bar. Close to Bilbao. **www.hotelelpuerto.com**

Key to Price Guide *see p560* **Key to Symbols** *see back cover flap*

MUNDAKA Atalaya

Itxaropen Kalea 1, 48360 (Vizcaya) **Tel** *946 17 70 00* **Fax** *946 87 68 99* **Rooms** *11*

This hotel, in a pretty early 20th-century English-inspired villa next to the fishing port, has small but pleasant bedrooms, large window galleries with views of the sea and a terrace. A good area for strolling on the beach, surfing or lingering over lunch. **www.hotel-atalaya-mundaka.com**

OLITE Parador de Olite

Plaza de los Teobaldos 2, 31390 (Navarra) **Tel** *948 74 00 00* **Fax** *948 74 02 01* **Rooms** *43*

Occupying a wing of the 15th-century castle and palace of Carlos III, king of Navarra, this parador is decorated on a medieval theme with armour, tapestries, stained glass and wrought-iron lamp brackets. The most atmospheric (and pricey) rooms are in the old part of the castle; there are also some modern bedrooms. **www.parador.es**

PAMPLONA Ciudad de Pamplona

Iturrama 21, 31007 (Navarra) **Tel** *948 26 60 11* **Fax** *948 17 36 26* **Rooms** *117*

An ultra-modern luxury hotel, decorated in warm tones and scattered with avant-garde furniture. It has four sitting rooms and ample facilities for business people. The hotel is at some distance from the old part of Pamplona, in one of the streets behind the Ciudadela fortress. The restaurant serves classic Navarran dishes. **www.ac-hotels.com**

RONCESVALLES La Posada

Ctra de Francia, 31650 (Navarra) **Tel** *948 76 02 25* **Fax** *948 76 02 66* **Rooms** *19*

This historic inn opened in 1612 to cater for pilgrims to Santiago de Compostela – Roncesvalles being one of the main crossing points from France. It has been renovated but its austere bedrooms with tiled floors are simply furnished and still cheap. The restaurant serves Basque cuisine and game. Closed Nov. **www.laposadaderoncesvalles.com**

SAN MILLÁN DE LA COGOLLA Hostería del Monasterio de San Millán

Monasterio de Yuso, 26326 (La Rioja) **Tel** *941 37 32 77* **Fax** *941 37 32 66* **Rooms** *25*

A hotel occupying a wing of the Monasterio de Yuso, which is inhabited by Augustinian friars. The bedrooms are soberly decorated and have thick walls to guarantee complete peace. Three of the rooms are suites. Best of all is the Royal Room, which has a balcony over the inner patio. Closed 7–31 Jan. **www.sanmillan.com**

SAN SEBASTIÁN La Galería

Infanta Cristina 1–3, 20008 (Guipúzcoa) **Tel** *943 31 75 59* **Fax** *943 21 12 98* **Rooms** *23*

This late 19th-century French-style building is situated on Ondarreta beach and offers views of La Concha bay. The bedrooms are dedicated to famous painters such as Renoir, Picasso, Dali, Miró and Regoyos, and contain replicas of their works. It has two charming attic rooms. Internet and bicycles are available. **www.hotellagaleria.com**

SAN SEBASTIÁN Niza

C/ Zubieta 56, 20007 (Guipúzcoa) **Tel** *943 42 66 63* **Fax** *943 44 12 51* **Rooms** *40*

Niza is a beautiful seafront hotel in *belle époque* style in the middle of La Concha beach, not far from the city centre. The bedrooms are warm and airy and 18 of them have sweeping views of the bay. All have wireless Internet. The hotel has a bar and an Italian restaurant, La Pasta Gansa, on the beachfront. **www.hotelniza.com**

SAN SEBASTIÁN Mercure Monte Igueldo

Paseo del Faro 134, 20008 (Guipúzcoa) **Tel** *943 21 02 11* **Fax** *943 21 50 28* **Rooms** *125*

Superbly located on Monte Igueldo, one of the hills marking the end of La Concha bay, this Mercure chain hotel has panoramic views across the city and the bay. The restaurant, enjoying the same views, serves Basque *haute cuisine*. It also has a rooftop swimming pool. Next door is San Sebastian's amusement park. **www.monteigueldo.com**

SAN SEBASTIÁN Abba de Londres y de Inglaterra

C/ Zubieta 2, 20007 (Guipúzcoa) **Tel** *943 44 07 70* **Fax** *943 44 04 91* **Rooms** *148*

This classical-style luxury hotel with grand public spaces within occupies a 19th-century palace on La Concha beach. It was transformed into a hotel in 1902. Twelve of the rooms are suites. The Mari Galant brasserie in the hotel serves buffet meals and offers a children's menu. Five salons double as meeting rooms. **www.hlondres.com**

SAN SEBASTIÁN María Cristina

C/ Oquendo 1, 20004 (Guipúzcoa) **Tel** *943 43 76 00* **Fax** *943 43 76 76* **Rooms** *136*

Built in 1912 and named after Queen Maria Cristina, this is a landmark of the city and one of the most historic hotels in Spain. It was designed by the architect of the London and Paris Ritz hotels and is decorated in *belle époque* style. It is also the venue of the San Sebastián film festival. **www.mariacristina.es**

SANTO DOMINGO DE LA CALZADA Parador de Santo Domingo

Plaza del Santo 3, 26250 (La Rioja) **Tel** *941 34 03 00* **Fax** *941 34 03 25* **Rooms** *61*

A hospital founded in the 12th century for pilgrims on the road to Santiago de Compostela, now converted into a parador. Next to Santo Domingo's cathedral, it has an imposing lounge divided by Gothic arches and a carved timber ceiling. The restaurant serves stuffed Piquillo peppers and has a good list of wines from La Rioja. **www.parador.es**

UDABE Venta Udabe

Udabe-Basaburua, 31869 (Navarra) **Tel** *948 50 31 05* **Fax** *948 50 34 00* **Rooms** *9*

Decorated in country style, this small hotel in a typical old Basque farmhouse stands in a unique natural setting at the heart of the Basaburua Valley, just off the Pamplona to San Sebastián motorway. The owners are hospitable and can organize "an infinity of activities" for their guests. Closed 24 Dec–24 Jan. **www.hotelventaudabe.com**

VERA DE BIDASOA Churrut   P 🅿 🚾 🚐   €€€€
Plaza de los Fueros 2, 31780 (Navarra) **Tel** *948 62 55 40* **Fax** *948 62 55 41* **Rooms** *17*

A beautifully renovated family-run hotel in an 18th-century house. Downstairs there is a gallery with wicker armchairs and plants arranged beside a glass wall with relaxing views of the garden. The bedrooms are comfortable and homely. Churrut has a good restaurant and a small gym in the attic. The rooms include two suites. **www.hotelchurrut.com**

VITORIA General Álava   🔁 ♿ 🍴 🚐   €€
Av Gasteiz 79, 01009 (Alava) **Tel** *945 21 50 00* **Fax** *945 24 83 95* **Rooms** *114*

A modern hotel with comfortable bedrooms in a spectacular spot in the new town, near the Palacio de Congresos, making it suitable for business travellers. The restaurant serves regional dishes and avant-garde cuisine, with a daily changing menu. The buffet breakfast includes fruit salads and home marinated salmon. **www.hga.info**

YESA Hospedería de Leyre   P 🚾 📧 ♿ 🍴   €
Monasterio de Leyre, 31410 (Navarra) **Tel** *948 88 41 00* **Fax** *948 88 41 37* **Rooms** *32*

This hotel occupies part of an 11th-century Benedictine monastery, located beneath crags. The rooms are plain and clean, some looking onto the garden. The monastery can be busy by day but is quiet at night. Typical Navarran cuisine is served. Men can stay in the monastery by written request. Closed 10 Dec–1 Mar. **www.hospederiadeleyre.com**

ZARAUTZ Karlos Arguiñano   🍴 📧   €€€€€
C/ Mendilauta 13, 20800 (Guipúzcoa) **Tel** *943 13 00 00* **Fax** *943 13 34 50* **Rooms** *12*

A stone tower-cum-mansion on the beach of Zarautz, this is a restaurant-with-rooms owned by a celebrated TV chef. The bedrooms are decorated with antiques and traditional furniture; some have terraces and sea views. There are two restaurants: one traditional, one *haute cuisine*. Closed 20 Nov–1 Feb. **www.hotelka.com**

BARCELONA

OLD TOWN Downtown Paraiso   📧   €
C/ Junta de Comerç 13, 08001 **Tel** *93 302 61 34* **Fax** *93 302 61 34* **Rooms** *8*   **Map** *2 F3*

Established by four former travellers in a renovated townhouse on a quiet street in the lively Raval area, this friendly hostal is a hit with young backpackers. Centrally located, there is no curfew and there is a range of rooms, with or without bathrooms. Wi-Fi access and a kitchen are available for guests' use. **www.downtownparaisohostel.com**

OLD TOWN Rembrandt   🔁   €
Carrer de Portaferrissa 23, 08002 **Tel** *933 18 10 11* **Fax** *933 18 10 11* **Rooms** *28*   **Map** *5 A2*

A simple, clean hotel in the Barri Gòtic, popular with students. The rooms have old-fashioned wicker furniture, but are all spotlessly clean and the best have wrought-iron balconies overlooking the shopping street below. It is quiet, considering the city centre location. Some bedrooms share bathrooms. **www.hostalrembrandt.com**

OLD TOWN Gat Xino   🏃 📧   €€
C/ Hospital 149–155, 08001 **Tel** *93 324 88 33* **Fax** *93 324 88 34* **Rooms** *34*   **Map** *2 E2*

This is the second hostal from the Gat Accommodation group, and it repeats the successful formula that has worked so well: simple, modern design and great prices. Its worth splashing out on the suite, which has its own private terrace. All rooms have free Wi-Fi. Family rooms are available. **www.gataccommodation.com**

OLD TOWN Hotel Urquinaona   🚾 🍴 📧   €€
Ronda de Sant Pere 24, 08010 **Tel** *932 68 13 36* **Fax** *932 95 41 37* **Rooms** *18*   **Map** *5 B1*

This has a perfect city centre location, close to the Plaça de Catalunya. A modest hotel, Hotel Urquinaona has been recently renovated and offers bright, well-equipped rooms with modern furnishings. There is also a good restaurant and free Internet access for guests. Triple and quadruple rooms are also available. **www.hotelurquinaona.com**

OLD TOWN Jardí   🚾 📧   €€
Plaça Sant Josep Oriol 1, 08002 **Tel** *933 01 59 00* **Fax** *933 42 57 33* **Rooms** *42*   **Map** *5 A2*

A popular hostal overlooking a pretty leafy square in the heart of the Barri Gòtic quarter. Some bedrooms have been renovated and have good views of the square and the handsome Gothic church of Santa María del Pi; others are cheaper but not as atmospheric. Because of its location, this is the best place for night owls.

OLD TOWN Chic and Basic   ♿ 🚾 🍴 🏃 📧   €€€
C/ Princesa 50, 08003 **Tel** *93 295 46 52* **Fax** *93 295 46 53* **Rooms** *31*   **Map** *5 C2*

This converted 19th-century townhouse is popular with visiting fashionistas. Rooms are a rather blinding white, with contemporary glass and steel bathrooms, but they are given a touch of kitsch glamour with colourful LED lighting. The White Bar is very hip. **www.chicandbasic.com**

OLD TOWN Hotel 54 Barceloneta   ♿ 🚾 🍴 🏃 📧   €€€
Passeig de Borbó 54, 08003 **Tel** *93 225 00 54* **Fax** *93 225 00 80* **Rooms** *28*   **Map** *5 B5*

This hotel has simple, modern decor and rooms (which are a touch on the small side) and is located in the Barceloneta area, in front of Port Vell and close to the beach. The Gothic Quarter is only a fifteen-minute stroll away. Free Wi-Fi in all rooms and views over the port and sea. **www.hotel54barceloneta.com**

Key to Price Guide *see p560* **Key to Symbols** *see back cover flap*

OLD TOWN Jazz Hotel €€€

Carrer Pelai 3, 08001 **Tel** *935 52 96 96* **Fax** *935 52 96 97* **Rooms** *108* **Map** 5 A1

A glassy ultra-modern hotel, close to the Plaça de Catalunya, Jazz offers better facilities than its three-star rating would suggest. There is a rooftop pool with sun deck, and the rooms (all soundproofed) are stylishly decorated with contemporary furniture and fabrics. **www.hoteljazzbarcelona.com**

OLD TOWN Montecarlo €€€

La Rambla 124, 08002 **Tel** *934 12 04 04* **Fax** *933 18 73 23* **Rooms** *55* **Map** 5 A2

This beautiful hotel right on La Rambla in the centre of Barcelona occupies a former 19th-century palace. The lobby is a gorgeous whirl of gilt and marble, while the rooms are smart and modern. Staff are particularly helpful here, and there are fantastic deals available on the website. **www.montecarlobcn.com**

OLD TOWN Park Hotel €€€€

Carrer de Marqués de l'Argentera 11, 08003 **Tel** *933 19 60 00* **Fax** *933 19 45 19* **Rooms** *91* **Map** 5 C3

A rare gem of 1950s architecture, designed by Antonio Moragas in 1951 and well preserved by his son's award-winning renovations in 1990. The slim wraparound staircase is a highlight. Rooms are small but smartly furnished and the best have balconies. The restaurant, Abac, is outstanding. **www.parkhotelbarcelona.com**

OLD TOWN Petit Palace Opera Garden €€€

C/ La Bouqueria 10, 08002 **Tel** *93 302 00 92* **Fax** *93 302 15 66* **Rooms** *61* **Map** 5 A2

A smart new boutique hotel in a handsomely converted town house just off La Rambla. Modern, colourful rooms have a musical theme (the city's Opera House is around the corner). The large and shady interior garden with its ancient trees and candle-lit corners is deeply romantic. **www.hthoteles.com**

OLD TOWN Arts €€€€€

Carrer de Marina 19–21, 08005 **Tel** *932 21 10 00* **Fax** *932 21 10 70* **Rooms** *455* **Map** 6 E4

Set in a soaring tower overlooking the Port Olímpic, Arts is one of the most luxurious and glamorous hotels in Europe. Huge rooms boast spectacular views along with every imaginable modern convenience. There are stunning suites on the upper floors for those with very deep pockets. **www.hotelartsbarcelona.com**

OLD TOWN Neri €€€€€

Carrer de Sant Server 5, 08002 **Tel** *933 04 06 55* **Fax** *933 04 03 37* **Rooms** *22* **Map** 5 A2

An enchanting hotel, which stunningly combines the architectural features of the original 18th-century palace with sleek contemporary fittings. Airy, stylish rooms are draped in sensuous fabrics, and there is a magnificent rooftop terrace with views of the Gothic cathedral. Fabulous restaurant too. **www.hotelneri.com**

EIXAMPLE Felipe II €€

Carrer de Mallorca 329, 08037 **Tel** *934 58 77 58* **Fax** *932 07 21 04* **Rooms** *21* **Map** 3 C4

Completely renovated in 2005, this is a basic, clean hotel in an old apartment block in the Eixample, with a fine antique elevator. You will get a good welcome from the friendly owners, and all the rooms come complete with TV and either shared or *en suite* facilities. Breakfast is not available. **www.hotelfelipe2.com**

EIXAMPLE Hotel Paseo de Gracia €€

Passeig de Gràcia 102, 08008 **Tel** *932 15 58 24* **Fax** *932 15 37 24* **Rooms** *33* **Map** 3 B3

There are few budget choices in the chichi Eixample district, but this modest little hotel is a good option. It has a fabulous location on the city's most desirable boulevard, close to the finest Gaudí buildings. Some of the simple rooms have views over the Plaça de Catalunya. **www.hotelpaseodegracia.com**

EIXAMPLE Windsor €€

Rambla Catalunya 84, 08007 **Tel** *932 15 11 98* **Rooms** *15* **Map** 3 A4

A rickety old-fashioned hostal on an elegant tree-lined boulevard, this has pretty streetside rooms with balconies. Interior rooms are quieter but lack charm and can be stuffy in summer. All are decorated in plain, traditional style. The Windsor is a stone's throw from the Gaudí buildings on the Passeig de Gràcia.

EIXAMPLE Alexandra €€€

Carrer de Mallorca 251, 08008 **Tel** *934 67 71 66* **Fax** *934 88 02 58* **Rooms** *109* **Map** 3 A4

A stylish, modern interior behind a 19th-century façade sets the tone at this hotel, which is well equipped for business meetings. It offers rooms and suites, all comfortably and tastefully furnished. There is a good restaurant, and the website offers excellent weekend packages. **www.hotel-alexandra.com**

EIXAMPLE Granados 83 €€€

Enric Granados 83, 08008 **Tel** *93 492 96 70* **Fax** *93 492 96 90* **Rooms** *77* **Map** 3 A3

The rooms at this designer hotel are stylishly decorated with African zebrawood, chocolate brown leather and original pieces of Buddhist and Hindu art. Suites have private terraces overlooking a small plunge pool. There is an excellent restaurant and a small rooftop area with a very fashionable bar. **www.derbyhotels.es**

EIXAMPLE Hostal Palacios €€€

Rambla Catalunya 27, 08007 **Tel** *933 01 3079* **Fax** *933 01 3792* **Rooms** *11* **Map** 3 A3

This friendly hostal is housed in a magnificent Modernista building. Many of the original fittings, including the huge carved doors and colourful tiles, have been retained, and are stylishly complemented by modern fabrics and contemporary bathrooms. Guests can use the piano in the comfortable lounge. **www.hostalpalacios.com**

EIXAMPLE Actual

🅿️ 🔲 🔲 📧   €€€€

Carrer Rosselló 238, 08008 **Tel** *935 52 05 50* **Fax** *935 52 05 55* **Rooms** *29*   **Map** *3 B3*

This modern hotel is fashionably decorated in sleek minimalist style. It has a superb location on the same block as Gaudí's La Pedrera, and the upmarket boutiques of the Passeig de Gràcia are on the doorstep. Like many hotels in this area, it is geared towards business travellers, which means good weekend deals. **www.hotelactual.com**

EIXAMPLE Axel

🔲 🔲 🍴 ≅ 📺 📧   €€€€

Carrer Aribau 33, 08011 **Tel** *933 23 93 93* **Fax** *933 23 93 94* **Rooms** *66*   **Map** *2 F1*

Axel is Barcelona's best gay hotel, a chic four-star establishment with a wealth of excellent facilities. The rooms are sleek and modern, there is a fabulous rooftop bar, and business facilities are available in the small library. There is also a dipping pool, and a good restaurant (with drag shows). **www.hotelaxel.com**

EIXAMPLE Clarís

🔲 🅿️ 🍴 ≅ 📺 📧   €€€€€

Carrer Pau Clarís 150, 08009 **Tel** *934 87 62 62* **Fax** *932 15 79 70* **Rooms** *124*   **Map** *3 B4*

Antique kilims and elegant English and French furniture ornament this hotel off the Passeig de Gràcia. Clarís occupies the converted Vedruna Palace, and is scattered with fabulous artworks from around the world. There's a panoramic rooftop pool and sun deck, and guests may use the hotel's Smart cars. **www.derbyhotels.es**

EIXAMPLE Condes de Barcelona

🔲 🔲 🍴 ≅ 📺 📧   €€€€€

Passeig de Gràcia 73–75, 08008 **Tel** *934 45 00 00* **Fax** *934 45 32 32* **Rooms** *235*   **Map** *3 A4*

This hotel is located in two handsomely renovated Modernista palaces, with marble lobbies and creamy façades. The rooms in both locations are cool and contemporary, and some have Jacuzzis. Choose a room with a terrace to admire Gaudí's "La Pedrera" building directly across the street. **www.condesdebarcelona.com**

EIXAMPLE Gallery

🔲 🅿️ 🔲 🍴 ≅ 📺 📧   €€€€

Carrer Rosselló 249, 08008 **Tel** *934 15 99 11* **Fax** *934 15 91 84* **Rooms** *115*   **Map** *3 A3*

A modern, efficient and comfortable hotel that is well situated and retains the personal atmosphere of a family-run business. Soundproofed rooms are smartly furnished with contemporary black and white decor and have large, marble bathrooms. An attractive garden restaurant leads into a public garden. **www.galleryhotel.com**

EIXAMPLE Majèstic

🔲 🍴 🅿️ 🔲 ≅ 📺 📧   €€€€€

Passeig de Gràcia 68, 08007 **Tel** *934 88 17 17* **Fax** *934 88 18 80* **Rooms** *303*   **Map** *3 A4*

A grand, traditional hotel in Neo-Classical style in a chic street (adjoining Carrer de València). The stylish bedrooms are decorated with plush drapes and elegant prints, and are all equipped with five-star amenities. There are also some very luxurious suites, and a superb rooftop pool with spectacular views. **www.hotelmajestic.es**

EIXAMPLE NH Calderón

🔲 🅿️ 🔲 ≅ 📺 📧   €€€€€

Rambla de Catalunya 26, 08007 **Tel** *933 01 00 00* **Fax** *934 12 41 93* **Rooms** *253*   **Map** *3 A5*

Calderón is a modern hotel from the reliable NH chain, near the Plaça de Catalunya, offering spacious, comfortable rooms and suites. The excellent facilites include indoor and rooftop pools (with panoramic views), and a good restaurant. **www.nh-hoteles.es**

EIXAMPLE Omm

🔲 🅿️ 🔲 🍴 ≅ 📧   €€€€€

Carrer Rosselló 265, 08008 **Tel** *934 45 40 00* **Fax** *934 45 40 04* **Rooms** *59*   **Map** *3 B3*

From the glistening ultra-modern façade with its peeled-back balconies, to the fluid, glassy public spaces, Omm is the epitome of sleek Barcelona design. The fashionably minimalist rooms are very comfortable, and the slick bar and club make it popular with fashionistas. Also has spa facilities. **www.hotelomm.es**

EIXAMPLE Palace

🔲 🍴 📺 📧   €€€€€

Gran Via de les Corts Catalanes 668, 08010 **Tel** *935 10 11 30* **Fax** *933 18 01 48* **Rooms** *125*   **Map** *3 B5*

Palace has recently been refurbished and is the most elegant of Barcelona's grand hotels. The large luxurious bedrooms are decorated in classical style and boast huge marble bathrooms. Contains a health club and a beauty parlour. Famous guests have included the Spanish royal family and Frank Sinatra. **www.hotelpalacebarcelona.com**

EIXAMPLE Prestige Paseo de Gracia

🔲 🔲 📧   €€€€€

Passeig de Gracia 62, 08007 **Tel** *932 72 41 80* **Fax** *932 72 41 81* **Rooms** *45*   **Map** *3 A4*

Zen meets Modernism in this luxury hotel near Gaudí's most important buildings. Rooms are filled with light and have up-to-the-minute amenities including Bang and Olufsen TVs and music systems. In the Zeroom, you can browse through art and design books. There's also an Oriental garden. Breakfast included. **www.prestigehotels.com**

FURTHER AFIELD (POBLE NOU) Hostel Poble Nou

📧   €€

Carrer Taulat 30, 08005 **Tel** *932 21 26 01* **Fax** *932 21 26 01* **Rooms** *5*

This charming little hostal is located in a colourful 1930s town house in the traditional neighbourhood of Poble Nou. It's close to the city's best beaches and well connected by metro and tram to the city centre. The *en suite* rooms are simple, and there is a pretty breakfast terrace as well. Breakfast is included in the price. **www.hostalpoblenou.com**

FURTHER AFIELD (VALLVIDRERA) Gran Hotel La Florida

🔲 🅿️ 🔲 🍴 ≅ 🔲 📧   €€€€€

Carretera Vallvidrera al Tibidabo 83–93, 08035 **Tel** *932 59 30 00* **Fax** *932 59 30 01* **Rooms** *74*

In a luxurious palace in the hills above Barcelona, this outstanding hotel is set in beautiful gardens offering great views of the whole city. The suites are all equipped with every imaginable facility, and there is a wonderful spa and restaurant. A shuttle service takes you to the heart of the city in minutes. **www.hotellaflorida.com**

Key to Price Guide *see p560* **Key to Symbols** *see back cover flap*

CATALONIA

ANDORRA LA VELLA Andorra Park Hotel
€€€€€

Les Canals 24 **Tel** *376 87 77 77* **Fax** *376 82 09 83* **Rooms** *40*

One of Andorra's most luxurious hotels, this modern structure is built into a steep, wooded hillside. There is a library, a swimming pool hewn out of rock, and a pleasant bar-restaurant. Rooms come with satellite TV and a mini-bar, and the hotel also provides a laundry and ironing service. **www.andorraparkhotel.com**

ARTIES Parador Don Gaspar de Portolà
€€€

Ctra Bequeira-Beret, 25599 (Lleida) **Tel** *973 64 08 01* **Fax** *973 64 10 01* **Rooms** *57*

A modern, comfortable parador, Don Gaspar de Portolà is built in the local traditional stone and slate. It is located in one of the prettiest villages of the Vall d'Aran, with attractive narrow streets dotted with medieval chapels. The parador is handy for local ski resorts, and makes a good base for mountain walkers. **www.parador.es**

AVINYONET DE PUIGVENTÓS Mas Pau
€€€

Ctra Figueres-Besalú, 17742 (Girona) **Tel** *972 54 61 54* **Fax** *972 54 63 26* **Rooms** *20*

A beautiful hotel in a 16th-century house, surrounded by gardens and farmland. Many of the luxurious bedrooms and suites are located in the 25-m (82-ft) high tower, and have splendid views. There is a spectacular restaurant, secluded terraces and a separate swimming pool and games area for children. Closed 6 Jan–Feb. **www.maspau.com**

BANYOLES Mirallac
€€€

Passeig Darder 50, 17820 (Girona) **Tel** *972 624 562* **Fax** *972 571 039* **Rooms** *27*

Mirallac is a cheerful, old-style hotel overlooking the vast lake at Banyoles, offering traditionally decorated rooms with their own balcony/terrace, a huge swimming pool and lots of lakeside activities. Also houses a good restaurant serving tasty, local specialities. Guests also have use of a bar and a reading room. **www.hotelmirallac.com**

BEGUR Aigua Blava
€€€€

Platja de Fornells, 17255 (Girona) **Tel** *972 62 45 62* **Fax** *972 62 21 12* **Rooms** *86*

This charming whitewashed Mediterranean-style hotel overlooks Fornells Bay, one of the prettiest spots on the Costa Brava. Surrounded by pine trees and gardens, the arched windows of the hotel frame beautiful sea views. The rooms are light and airy. Aigua Blava also offers 10 fully-equipped apartments. Closed Nov–Feb. **www.aiguablava.com**

BEQUEIRA-BERET Royal Tanau
€€€€€

Ctra de Beret, 25598 (Lleida) **Tel** *973 64 44 46* **Fax** *973 64 43 44* **Rooms** *30*

A luxurious boutique hotel in the Tanau skiing area that has all kinds of amenities, including indoor and outdoor jacuzzis and a spa. In winter, a private ski lift whisks guests directly to the pistes. There are full après-ski facilities are available. Elegant, fully-equipped suites as well as rooms. **www.solmelia.com**

BOLVIR DE CERDANYA Torre del Remei
€€€€€

Camí Reial s/n, 17539 (Girona) **Tel** *972 14 01 82* **Fax** *972 14 04 49* **Rooms** *20*

One of the most deluxe hotels in the region, this opulent Modernista mansion is set in magnificent gardens with a stunning mountain backdrop. The classically decorated rooms are perfectly equipped with up-to-the-minute gadgetry, and the extensive facilities include a new spa and a gym. **www.torredelremei.com**

CADAQUÈS Hotel Llane Petit
€€€

Platja Llane Petit, 17488 (Girona) **Tel** *972 25 10 20* **Fax** *972 25 87 78* **Rooms** *37*

Llane Petit is a delightful seaside hotel with a peaceful and welcoming ambience, set right on the beach in the white-washed village of Cadaquès. Simple, friendly and family-run, the best rooms boast terraces where you can relax in a hammock and soak up the sun. The restaurant is open in summer only. Closed Nov–end Feb. **www.llanepetit.com**

CARDONA Parador de Cardona
€€€€

Carrer de Castell s/n, 08261 (Barcelona) **Tel** *938 69 12 75* **Fax** *938 69 16 36* **Rooms** *54*

One of the most striking paradors in Spain, this luxuriously converted medieval castle dominates Cardona and offers spectacular views of the countryside. Many of the elegant rooms boast four-poster beds. The parador has a fine Catalan restaurant as well. **www.parador.es**

CASTELLÓ D'EMPURIES Allioli
€€

Carrer Paborderia s/n, 17486 (Girona) **Tel** *972 25 03 20* **Fax** *972 25 03 00* **Rooms** *42*

A 17th-century Catalan farmhouse, just off the main Roses-Figueres road, with simple rooms, some suitable for families. The restaurant, open all year round, is popular for Sunday lunch among locals. The swimming pool is only open in the summer, and the hotel is closed from mid-December until the end of February. **www.hotelallioli.com**

FIGUERES Hotel Durán
€€

Carrer de Lasauca 5, 17600 (Girona) **Tel** *972 50 12 50* **Fax** *972 50 26 09* **Rooms** *60*

Established in 1855, this ochre-and-pink hotel is set above one of the finest restaurants in the region. It is still owned by the same family, who are warm and friendly. Rooms are attractively, if simply, furnished, and many have pretty wrought-iron balconies overlooking the street below. **www.hotelduran.com**

GIRONA Pensión Bellmirall

Carrer de Bellmirall 3, 17004 (Girona) **Tel** *972 20 40 09* **Rooms** *7*

Pensión Bellmirall is a rickety, old-fashioned charmer tucked away in the ancient heart of Girona. The old house ha preserved its massive stone walls, and bedrooms are individually decorated with traditional furniture and original a A huge breakfast is served in a pretty garden area. Closed Jan and Feb.

GRANOLLERS Fonda Europa

Carrer Anselm Clavé 1, 08400 (Barcelona) **Tel** *938 70 03 12* **Fax** *938 70 79 01* **Rooms** *7*

This small hotel has been an inn for travellers since 1714, and is still owned by the same family. The bedrooms, on the second floor, have been completely modernized and are simply decorated. The restaurant is the big draw here with its hearty Catalan specialities prepared using traditional recipes.

LA SEU D'URGELL El Castell

Ctra N 260 km 229, 25700 (Lleida) **Tel** *973 35 00 00* **Fax** *973 35 15 74* **Rooms** *38*

This extravagant hotel is a low, modern building beneath the medieval castle of Seu d'Urgell. It has plenty of facilities, including an outdoor Jacuzzi and an immense covered pool. There are impressive views across the mountains of El Cadí and the ski slopes of Andorra are nearby. **www.hotelelcastell.com**

LA SEU D'URGELL Parador de La Seu d'Urgell

Carrer Sant Domènec 6, 25700 (Lleida) **Tel** *973 35 20 00* **Fax** *973 35 23 09* **Rooms** *79*

Only the Renaissance cloister, now used as the lounge, remains of a convent that occupied this site close to the 12th-century cathedral of La Seu. The modern parador has good facilities, including a covered pool, and there are excellent opportunities on the doorstep for hiking and skiing. **www.parador.es**

L'ESCALA El Roser

Plaça L'Eglésia 7, 17130 (Girona) **Tel** *972 77 02 19* **Fax** *972 77 45 29* **Rooms** *22*

El Roser is a charming, old-fashioned seaside hotel right on the beach, in the heart of the historic centre of L'Escal The restaurant is smart and elegant, with old wood and stone walls, and is one of the best in the area. Rooms are immaculate and brightly furnished, if somewhat basic. Closed Sun–Mon in winter. **www.elroserhostal.com**

L'ESPLUGA DEL FRANCOLÍ Hostal del Senglar

Plaça de Montserrat Canals 1, 43440 (Tarragona) **Tel** *977 87 01 21* **Fax** *977 87 01 27* **Rooms** *34*

A three-storey, whitewashed hotel with simply furnished, traditional rooms including family rooms. There is a delightful shady garden where barbecues are held in summer. A menu of delicious dishes, traditional to the area, i served in the restaurant. **www.hostaldelsenglar.com**

LLORET DE MAR Santa Marta

Platja Santa Cristina, 17310 (Girona) **Tel** *972 36 49 04* **Fax** *972 36 92 80* **Rooms** *76*

This low, white-painted modern hotel overlooks a beautiful cove on the fringes of the frenetic resort of Lloret de N Rooms vary from rustic to contemporary decor with up-to-the-minute amenities. Pine woods and gardens extend the shore, and there are tennis courts and other sporting facilities. Closed 15 Dec–mid Feb. **www.hstamarta.com**

MONTSENY Sant Bernat

Finca El Clot, Ctra Sant Maria de Palautordera a Seva, km 20.8, 08460 (Barcelona) **Tel** *938 47 30 11* **Rooms** *23*

A gorgeous country house in the Serra de Montseny, the old stone walls of which are cloaked in greenery. The roo and suites are stylishly decorated with traditional prints and rustic furniture. The house is surrounded by extensive gardens with lawns and a pond. All kinds of outdoor activities can be arranged. **www.santbernat.com**

MONTSERRAT Abat Cisneros

Plaça del Monestir, 08199 (Barcelona) **Tel** *938 77 7 01* **Fax** *938 7 77 24* **Rooms** *82*

Part of the celebrated monastery complex at Montserrat, Abat Cisneros is where Catalan newly-weds come to ensure that they have the blessing of La Moreneta, the miraculous figure of the Virgin. Rooms are modest but mo comfortable than the ascetic setting would suggest. **www.montserratvisita.com**

PERAMOLA Can Boix de Peramola

Carrer Afores s/n, 25790 (Lleida) **Tel** *973 47 02 66* **Fax** *973 47 02 81* **Rooms** *41*

This good value, traditional mountain hotel has been in the same family for 10 generations. It has charming room and apartments with breathtaking views, a quiet garden and a swimming pool. Can Boix de Peramola is very convenient for walking in the Pyrenean foothills. Closed Jan–mid-Feb. **www.canboix.com**

REGENCÓS Hotel del Teatre

Plaça Major s/n, 17214 (Girona) **Tel** *972 30 62 70* **Fax** *972 30 62 73* **Rooms** *7*

In the heart of a rambling, medieval village, this boutique-style hotel is located in a pair of handsomely restored 18 century mansions. Sleek minimalism and charming original features are stylishly combined in the bedrooms. Has a lovely semi-shaded pool in the garden. **www.hoteldelteatre.com**

SA TUNA (BEGUR) Hotel Sa Tuna

Platja Sa Tuna, 17255 (Girona) **Tel** *972 62 21 98* **Fax** *972 62 41 82* **Rooms** *5*

Sa Tuna is a simple, whitewashed small hotel on one of the Costa Brava's prettiest coves. Recent improvements by the grandson of the original owner have added to its charms. Some rooms have their own terrace overlooking the bay. The restaurant is well known in the area. Open from April to September only. **www.hostalsatuna.com**

Key to Price Guide *see p560* **Key to Symbols** *see back cover flap*

SADURNI D'ANOIA Sol i Vi

Ctra San Sadurni–Vilafranca km 4, Lavern, 08739 (barcelona) **Tel** 938 99 32 04 **Fax** 938 99 34 35 **Rooms** 25

A cheery, traditional hotel set amid a sea of vines, thus making this a good base for exploring the wine and cava-producing region southwest of Barcelona. It offers comfortable, simple rooms and boasts a superb restaurant, which specializes in traditional Catalan cuisine. **www.solivi.com**

S'AGARÓ Hostal de la Gavina

Plaça de la Rosaleda, 17248 (Girona) **Tel** 972 32 11 00 **Fax** 972 32 15 73 **Rooms** 74

This elegant Mediterranean-style beach mansion is set in its own exclusive estate with beautiful gardens and a sea water pool. Bedrooms are splendidly decorated with silk-lined walls and burnished antiques. The many facilities include a luxurious spa and a fine restaurant. **www.lagavina.com**

SANTA CRISTINA D'ARO Mas Torrellas

Ctra Santa Cristina-Platja d'Aro, 17246 (Girona) **Tel** 972 83 75 26 **Fax** 972 83 75 27 **Rooms** 17

An attractive 18th-century country house hotel, with ancient stone walls and flower-filled gardens. Its most comfortable bedroom is in the distinctive yellow tower, built at a later date. There is a pool and tennis courts and horse riding can be arranged. The restaurant is excellent. Closed from October to March.

SITGES Romàntic

Carrer Sant Isidre 33, 08870 (Barcelona) **Tel** 938 94 83 75 **Fax** 938 94 81 67 **Rooms** 58

Well known in Sitges, this memorable hotel lives up to its name. Bedrooms are simple, but attractively decorated with antiques and paintings. There is a gloriously shady garden with tinkling fountains which is perfect for breakfast and evening cocktails. **www.hotelromantic.com**

SITGES San Sebastián Playa

Carrer de Port Alegre 53, 08870 (Barcelona) **Tel** 938 94 86 76 **Fax** 938 94 04 30 **Rooms** 51

This modern hotel on the beach near the old part of the town has attentive staff and comfortable bedrooms, many directly overlooking the sea. There is also a decent restaurant and good facilities for business travellers, including meeting rooms. **www.hotelsansebastian.com**

SOLDEU (ANDORRA) Sport Hotel Village

Ctra General s/n **Tel** 376 87 05 55 **Fax** 376 87 05 55 **Rooms** 165

Sport Hotel Village is the best-equipped hotel in the popular ski resort of Soldeu, and many of the comfortable rooms overlook the slopes. The four-star facilities include a pool and Jacuzzi, and – best of all – the lift to the top of the slopes leaves directly from the hotel. Closed for two weeks in October. **www.sporthotels.ad**

TARRAGONA Lauria

Rambla Nova 20, 43004 (Tarragona) **Tel** 977 23 67 12 **Fax** 977 23 67 00 **Rooms** 72

A modern, functional hotel in the town centre and close to the sea, with an elegant entrance under balustraded stone stairs. Although the decor is dated, the rooms are large and the hotel offers good amenities for the price, including a pool and facilities for business travellers. **www.hlauria.es**

TARRAGONA Imperial Tarraco

Passeig Les Palmeres s/n, 43004 (Tarragona) **Tel** 977 23 30 40 **Fax** 977 21 65 66 **Rooms** 170

The plushest option in Tarragona, this large, modern hotel has a panoramic location right on the balcón del Mediterrani (the balcony of the Mediterranean). Many of the spacious, elegant rooms and suites have large terraces. The hotel is conveniently close to the historic centre of the city. **www.husa.es**

TAVERTET El Jufré

isbe Galzeran Sacosta 1, 08511 (Barcelona) **Tel** 938 56 51 67 **Fax** 938 56 51 67 **Rooms** 8

This converted farmhouse is now a delightful casa rural with stunning mountain views. It has been in the same family for over 800 years, and warm comfortable rooms have replaced what were previously animal quarters. A perfect base for walking and exploring nearby Osona. Price includes dinner, bed and breakfast.

TORRENT Mas de Torrent

fueras, 17123 (Girona) **Tel** 972 30 32 92 **Fax** 972 30 32 93 **Rooms** 39

superbly converted 18th-century country house, Mas de Torrent offers handsome accommodation in ten beautiful rooms in the main house, or in elegant bungalows scattered around the extensive gardens. There are also deluxe suites with private pools available, and a new spa facility. **www.mastorrent.com**

TORTOSA Parador Castillo de la Zuda

astillo de la Zuda, 43500 (Tarragona) **Tel** 977 44 44 50 **Fax** 977 44 44 58 **Rooms** 72

medieval Moorish castle makes a superb hilltop parador with views of the town and valley of the Riu Ebre. The fine restaurant offers al fresco dining on the terrace, and there are plenty of luxurious extras including a swimming pool – in summer only, however. **www.parador.es**

TOSSA DE MAR Diana

aça d'Espanya 6, 17320 (Girona) **Tel** 972 34 11 16 **Fax** 972 34 11 03 **Rooms** 21

fine Modernista mansion is the gorgeous setting for this delightful hotel. There are nice views of the castle from the terrace and the best of the modest rooms have private balconies. The elegant lobby is full of original details and has been converted into a comfortable lounge area. **www.diana-hotel.com**

TREDÒS Hotel de Tredòs
Ctra a Baqueira-Beret km 177.5, 25598 (Lleida) **Tel** *973 64 40 14* **Fax** *973 64 43 00* **Rooms** *42*

Skiers and mountain walkers find the Hotel de Tredòs in the Val d'Aran good value. It is built of stone and slate in the local style, and offers attractive rooms with wooden beams. There is a heart-shaped outdoor pool to cool off in summer. Minimum five-night stay during the high skiing season. **www.hoteldetredos.com**

VIC Parador de Turismo de Vic-Sau
Paratge Bac de Sau, 08500 (Barcelona) **Tel** *938 12 23 23* **Fax** *938 12 23 68* **Rooms** *36*

This recently refurbished and comfortable stone-built parador, 14 km (9 miles) from Vic, has magnificent views of the Sau reservoir. It is a peaceful retreat amid pine forests and dramatic rock formations. Facilities include a tennis court and an outdoor pool (in summers only). **www.parador.es**

VIELHA (VIELLA) Parador Valle de Arán
Ctra de Túnel s/n, 25530 (Lleida) **Tel** *973 64 01 00* **Fax** *973 64 11 00* **Rooms** *118*

Valle de Arán is a modern parador that has a panoramic circular lounge dominated by a large window from which there are magnificent mountain views. There is a wonderful spa and a fine restaurant, and the rooms are bright, spacious and well appointed. **www.parador.es**

ARAGÓN

AÍNSA Casa Cambra
Ctra A-138 Barbastro–Ainsa km 42, Morillo de Tou s/n, 22395 (Huesca) **Tel** *974 50 07 93* **Fax** *974 50 07 93* **Rooms** *17*

Casa Cambra is a modest farmhouse in the picturesque medieval village of Morillo de Tou. A perfect location for visiting historical sites as well as natural wonders. The rooms are spacious and many feature original exposed brick arches. More basic accommodation is also available. Closed two weeks in Feb. **www.morillodetou.com**

ALBARRACÍN Posada del Adarve
Portal de Molina 23, 44100 (Teruel) **Tel** *978 70 03 04* **Fax** *978 70 03 04* **Rooms** *5*

In the heart of the Albarracín, Teruel's one-time Moorish stronghold, this hotel used to be a nobleman's home. Each room has its own character and decoration. Try the "Fogón" suite, which used to be the house's kitchen, or the "La Alcoba" suite, with its countless stars painted on the deep blue ceiling. **www.posada-adarve.com**

ALBARRACÍN Casa de Santiago
C/ Subida a las Torres 11, 44100 (Teruel) **Tel** *978 70 03 16* **Fax** *978 71 01 41* **Rooms** *9*

Close to the city's main square, this small hotel was once a residence of the Knights of Santiago, who used to protect the pilgrims from roaming bandits. The rooms are modest (only the suite possesses a TV), but the owners are friendly and the home-cooked meals are good. Closed three weeks in Feb, 13–17 Sep. **www.casadesantiago.net**

ALBARRACÍN La Casona del Ajimez
C/ San Juan 2, 44100 (Teruel) **Tel** *978 71 03 21* **Fax** *978 70 03 26* **Rooms** *6*

This 16/17th-century residence has been decorated in the style of the three religions that once resided in Teruel's old town – Judaism, Islam and Christianity. The pretty pink and red façade houses rooms with king-size beds, eclectic antiques and period knick-knacks. The garden has fabulous views of the cathedral. **www.casonadelajimez.com**

ALCAÑIZ Parador de Alcañiz
Castillo Calatravos s/n, 44600 (Teruel) **Tel** *978 83 04 00* **Fax** *978 83 03 66* **Rooms** *37*

This used to be the castle of the 12th-century Knights of Calatrava, a particularly violent and independent order who ruled the area with an iron fist. Now, it is a luxurious parador, with many atmospheric corners, including a keep, a bell tower and a chapel; just be careful you do not end up in the dungeon while exploring. **www.parador.es**

ALQUÉZAR Santa María
Arrabal s/n, 22145 (Huesca) **Tel** *974 31 84 36* **Fax** *974 31 84 35* **Rooms** *21*

A simple hotel set inside a heavily altered and extended medieval palace offering comfortable accommodation with wonderful views of the Colegiata and Vero rivers. The hotel's lounge has an open, cosy fireplace, and the staff can also organize "adventure sports". Closed Jan–Feb but can open for groups. **www.hotel-santamaria.com**

BENASQUE Hotel Hospital de Benasque
Camino Real s/n, 22440 (Huesca) **Tel** *974 55 20 12* **Fax** *974 56 05 03* **Rooms** *56*

A huge old hospital and pilgrims' shelter has been converted into a hotel with various types of lodging available, from duplexes to suites. Nestled in a gorgeous valley (and prime cross-country skiing territory), the in-house restaurant is also well known. **www.llanosdelhospital.com**

BIELSA Parador de Bielsa
Valle de Pineta s/n, 22350 (Huesca) **Tel** *974 50 10 11* **Fax** *974 50 11 88* **Rooms** *39*

The name of the mountain which rises above this parador – Monte Perdido (Lost Mountain) – gives an idea of its isolated location in one of the most beautiful spots of Northern Spain. The modern building has been tastefully built with wooden beams and offers great views of the Ordesa National Park. Closed end Jan–Feb. **www.parador.es**

Key to Price Guide *see p560* **Key to Symbols** *see back cover flap*

DAROCA Posada del Almudí 🖼️🍴 €

C/ Grajera 5–7–9, 50360 (Zaragoza) **Tel** *976 80 06 06* **Fax** *976 80 11 41* **Rooms** *13*

The rooms in this converted 16th-century palace are situated around a stunning Renaissance patio. After a grand entrance, the rooms themselves lack a bit in character, but are comfortable enough for the price. There is a lovely garden terrace, library and a decent restaurant serving local cuisine. Closed 24–25 Dec.

FUENTESPALDA La Torre del Visco 🍴📧 €€€€€

Fuentespalda, 44587 (Teruel) **Tel** *978 76 90 15* **Fax** *978 76 90 16* **Rooms** *15*

The King of Spain, Juan Carlos I, has been known to use this beautiful, solitary and labyrinthine 15th-century estate house, overlooking 220 acres of rose gardens, olive and almond trees. This hotel prides itself on offering a relaxing and quiet environment with no TVs or phones in the rooms. Dinner and breakfast included. **www.torredelvisco.com**

HUESCA Pedro I de Aragón 🖼️🍴🏊📧 €€

Calle del Parque 34, 22003 **Tel** *974 22 03 00* **Fax** *974 22 00 94* **Rooms** *130*

This comfortable, if slightly soulless, hotel is conveniently located in the centre of the city and is a good bet for those who want to spend some time exploring Huesca. The rooms are large and pleasant and some have terraces. The hotel's restaurant is justifiably popular for its hearty Aragonese stews. **www.gargallo-hotels.com**

JACA Conde Aznar 🖼️🅿️🍴 €€

Paseo Constitución 3, 22700 (Huesca) **Tel** *974 36 10 50* **Fax** *974 36 07 97* **Rooms** *34*

Conde Aznar is a traditional, double-story residence that was renovated in 2004; each room has pretty ceramic tiled bathrooms, lace curtains and embroidered bedspreads. Exposed beams and polished floors complete the rustic look. Perfect for taking advantage of Jaca's excellent access to all the Aragonese ski resorts. **www.condeaznar.com**

JACA Hotel Chalet Puigdefabregas ♿🏊📧 €€

Calle Pico Collarada 59, 22700 (Huesca) **Tel** *974 36 01 74* **Rooms** *12*

This traditional villa has been converted into a charming boutique hotel and offers excellent service and attention to detail. The twelve rooms are all decorated according to feng shui principles and have exterior views of the surrounding gardens and nearby mountains as well as Wi-Fi access and plasma TVs. **www.hotelchaletpuigdefabregas.com**

LANUZA-SALLENT DE GÁLLEGO La Casueña 🍴 €€

Troniecho (Lanuza), 22640 (Huesca) **Tel** *974 48 85 38* **Fax** *974 33 73 49* **Rooms** *10*

The literary inclinations of the owners of La Casueña are evident by the dedication of each of the rooms to a Spanish writer. The austere stone walls of this country house give way to a luxuriously decorated interior, with dramatic murals on the slanted roofs. The rooms have comfy king-size beds and a huge bath. **www.lacasuena.com**

PANTICOSA Gran Hotel de Panticosa 🖼️🅿️♿🍴🏊📧 €€€€€

Ctra del Balneario km 10, 22650 (Huesca) **Tel** *902 25 25 22* **Fax** *902 25 25 32* **Rooms** *42*

Situated next to a lake and surrounded by the stunning mountain scenery of the Panticosa resort, this old spa was converted in 2004 into a five-star hotel by the renowned architect Rafael Moneo. Its luxurious facilities include a hairdresser, a spa and a private skiing piste, which takes you right up to the front door. **www.panticosa.com**

SALLENT DE GÁLLEGO Almud 🍴🅿️ €

Espadilla 11, 22640 (Huesca) **Tel** *974 48 83 66* **Fax** *974 48 81 43* **Rooms** *11*

Conveniently placed in a pretty village near the Formigal and Panticosa ski resorts, this family-run hotel occupies an 18th-century building which used to be the village stables. Visitors will find welcoming staff, comfortable rooms furnished with rustic furniture and the atmosphere of a typical Aragonese mountain retreat. **www.hotelalmud.com**

SOS DEL REY CATÓLICO Parador Sos del Rey Católico 🖼️🅿️♿🍴📧 €€€

Arquitecto Sainz de Vicuña s/n, 50680 (Zaragoza) **Tel** *948 88 80 11* **Fax** *948 88 81 00* **Rooms** *58*

This reconstructed Aragonese home offers modern accommodation. All rooms have large windows and are decorated in a somewhat heavy, faux-Castilian style. The in-room facilities are abundant and include Internet. The restaurant is a good place to sample the non-diet friendly local cuisine. **www.parador.es**

TARAZONA Condes de Visconti 🖼️🅿️♿🍴📧 €€

Visconti 15, 50500 (Zaragoza) **Tel** *976 64 49 08* **Fax** *976 64 18 58* **Rooms** *15*

A rather grand hotel, which borders on being overdone with its Provençal decorative touches; frescoes, stucco and enough throws to bury yourself in. Facilities include in-room hydro-massage tubs, Internet and satellite TV. Extras include the super-friendly staff and a great in-house restaurant. **www.condesdevisconti.com**

TERUEL Torico Plaza 🖼️🍴♿📧 €

Yagüe de Salas 5, 44001 **Tel** *978 60 86 55* **Fax** *978 60 86 55* **Rooms** *31*

An attractive, functional and central hotel overlooking a 16th-century Mudéjar tower. It offers plenty of natural light, cheery decor in earthy tones and family-size rooms. Three of the rooms are suites with balconies. Closed 24–25 Dec. **www.bacohoteles.com**

TERUEL Parador de Teruel 🖼️♿🍴🏊📧 €€€

Ctra Sagunto–Burgos N234 km 122, 44003 **Tel** *978 60 18 00* **Fax** *978 60 86 12* **Rooms** *62*

On the outskirts of the city in an Arabesque palace inspired by the culture of the Mudéjars, this highly impressive parador offers spacious rooms, an excellent restaurant, a landscaped garden and a pool. With its fanciful tilework, swathes of marble and arches, staying here is like taking a trip into the Arabian Nights. **www.parador.es**

TORRE DEL COMPTE Parada del Compte 🔳🅿🔳🏊🔳   €€€
Finca la Antigua Estación del Ferrocarril, 44597 (Teruel) **Tel** *978 76 90 72* **Fax** *978 76 90 74* **Rooms** *11*

Parada del Compte is a quirky hotel located in a disused railway station. Each room is named after a famous international city train station with supposedly "matching" decor, ranging from a minimalist "loft" treatment in the New York suite to a lush Oriental Istanbul suite. **www.hotelparadadelcompte.com**

UNCASTILLO Posada La Pastora   €€
Roncesvalles 1, 50678 (Zaragoza) **Tel/Fax** *976 67 94 99* **Rooms** *8*

This charmingly renovated 18th-century country retreat offers just eight rooms with exposed brick walls contrasted with bright furnishings. Breakfast features fresh produce from local farmers. Fishing, golfing, rafting and horse riding facilities are also available close by. Two-night minimum stay. **www.lapastora.net**

ZARAGOZA Hotel Avenida 🔳🅿🔳   €
Avda César Augusto 55, 50003 **Tel** *976 43 93 00* **Fax** *976 43 93 64* **Rooms** *85*

What this hotel may lack in character it more than makes up for in comfort and in its location in the historical and commercial centre of Zaragoza. The rooms are well equipped with Internet and satellite TV and some have a terrace. Well placed for those who want to visit all of Zaragoza's major sites on foot. **www.hotelavenida-zaragoza.com**

ZARAGOZA Palafox 🔳🅿🔳🔳🏊🔳🔳🔳   €€€€€
Casa Jiménez s/n, 50004 **Tel** *976 23 77 00* **Fax** *976 23 47 05* **Rooms** *179*

The Spanish architect Pascua Ortega went to town on his design for this luxurious hotel. The grand entrance is flanked by full-scale representations of the old gates to the city. The rooms, on the other hand, are tasteful and minimalist. In terms of location and facilities this is one of the best places in the city. **www.palafoxhoteles.com**

VALENCIA AND MURCIA

ÁGUILAS Carlos III 🔳🅿🔳   €
C/ Rey Carlos III 22, 30880 (Murcia) **Tel** *968 41 16 50* **Fax** *968 41 16 58* **Rooms** *32*

This modern, town-centre hotel is located close to the beach, and offers spectacular views of a beautiful bay, dramatic volcanic cliffs and nearby islands. Rooms are comfortably, if simply, furnished. The hotel's restaurant is a good place to try the local seafood dishes. **www.hotelcarlosiii.com**

ALICANTE Les Monges Palace 🔳🅿🔳   €
San Augustín 4, 03002 (Alicante) **Tel** *965 21 50 46* **Fax** *965 14 71 89* **Rooms** *18*

Ideal for budget travellers, this hotel is often fully booked well in advance. Situated in the heart of Alicante's old town, it features original Modernista details, including colourfully tiled floors, and rooms with antique furnishings. Two slightly more expensive rooms with a sauna and Jacuzzi are also available. **www.lesmonges.net**

ALICANTE Hotel Albahia 🔳🅿🔳🔳🔳   €€
Sol Naciente 6, 03016 (Alicante) **Tel** *965 15 59 79* **Fax** *965`15 53 73* **Rooms** *93*

This modern hotel, five minutes from the city centre, has a beachfront location with sea views and offers various luxuries and comforts, including tennis, a business centre and babysitting facilities. They also have a Mediterranean restaurant specializing in regional rice dishes. Access for disabled guests. **www.albahia.com**

ALICANTE Amerigo 🔳🔳🔳🏊🔳🔳   €€€€
C/ Rafael Altamira 7, 03002 (Alicante) **Tel** *965 14 65 70* **Fax** *965 14 65 71* **Rooms** *80*

What was once a Dominican convent has now been spectacularly converted into Alicante's smartest and most stylish hotel. A striking fusion of ancient and ultra-modern, it offers minimalist rooms, an excellent restaurant, a fashionable bar and a health centre. The rooftop pool has great views of the old city. **www.hospes.es**

ALICANTE Sidi San Juan 🔳🔳🔳🏊🔳🔳🔳   €€€€
La Doblada 8, Playa San Juan, 03540 (Alicante) **Tel** *965 16 13 00* **Fax** *965 16 33 46* **Rooms** *176*

A gleaming, modern luxury hotel overlooking the lively and popular San Juan beach on the outskirts of the city centre. Surrounded by beautiful gardens, the hotel hosts a spa, health centre and various sports facilities, as well as play area and paddling pool for kids. **www.hotelessidi.es**

ARCHENA Termas 🔳🔳🏊🔳   €
Ctra Balneario, 30600 (Murcia) **Tel** *902 33 32 22* **Fax** *968 68 80 22* **Rooms** *67*

This spa hotel boasts an elegant and charming complex set amid flower-filled gardens and palm trees. The spa treatment areas are decorated in a glorious Mudéjar style and feature ornate plasterwork, domes and Moorish arches. The outdoor pool has massaging jets. **www.balneariodearchena.com**

BENISSA Casa del Maco 🔳🏊🔳   €
Pou Roig s/n, 03720 (Alicante) **Tel** *965 73 28 42* **Fax** *965 73 01 03* **Rooms** *4*

An exquisite rural retreat, this hotel is located on a beautifully restored, 18th-century *finca* (farm estate). Surrounded by groves of olives, almonds and oranges, each of the rooms is stylishly decorated. The terrace and pool provide splendid views of the mountains. Also has a romantic French restaurant. Closed Jan. **www.casadelmaco.com**

Key to Price Guide *see p560* **Key to Symbols** *see back cover flap*

CALABARDINA Al Sur · P · €€

Torre de Cope 24, 30889 (Near Águilas, Murcia) **Tel** 968 41 94 66 **Rooms** 8

Situated in a tiny village, this cosy, whitewashed hotel overlooks one of the wildest and most beautiful stretches of the Murcian coast. The rooms are painted in soothing shades of blue and green. Ideal for those looking for an intimate and relaxing getaway. Breakfast included in rate. Closed 15 Dec–22 Feb. **www.halsur.com**

CALPE Gran Hotel Sol y Mar · €€€€

C/ Benidorm 3, 03710 (Alicante) **Tel** 965 87 50 55 **Fax** 965 83 31 82 **Rooms** 327

This modern hotel has a great location next to the beach and close to the village, and all the mod-cons, including a spa, a swimming pool and gym facilities. The more expensive rooms have spectacular views over the sea and some have private terraces. The two restaurants cater for children and the health-conscious. **www.granhotelsolymar.com**

CARTAGENA Los Habaneros · €€

C/ San Diego 60, 30202 (Murcia) **Tel** 968 50 52 50 **Fax** 968 50 91 04 **Rooms** 90

At the entrance to Cartagena's old quarter, this long-established hotel offers modern and well-equipped rooms at affordable prices. Has a great restaurant and tapas bar. The town's famous Roman and Carthagenian antiquities are located close by. **www.hotelhabaneros.com**

CARTAGENA Regency Hyatt La Manga · €€€€

La Manga Club, 30385 (Murcia) **Tel** 968 33 12 34 **Fax** 968 33 12 35 **Rooms** 189

A luxurious hotel, part of an exclusive resort complex built in the style of a Spanish village. Frequented by several celebrities, the hotel is surrounded by palm and olive groves, and has three golf courses, 28 tennis courts and four swimming pools. Also boasts a Centre for Professional Football among other amenities. **www.lamangaclub.com**

CASTELL DE CASTELLS Pensión Castells · €

C/ San Vicente 18, 03793 (Alicante) **Tel** 965 51 82 54 **Rooms** 4

A 200-year-old house in an inland village not far from the Costa Blanca. The stone walls keep the rooms cool even at the height of summer. The charming British owners offer bed and breakfast and can prepare packed lunches and dinners for patrons. Guests are also taken for walks in the surrounding hills. **www.mountainholidays-spain.com**

CHULILLA Balneario de Chulilla · €€

Afueras s/n, 46167 (Valencia) **Tel** 902 74 74 02 **Fax** 961 65 70 13 **Rooms** 100

This spa hotel, surrounded by gardens and set in a tranquil location on the banks of the Río Túria, is an inexpensive place to stop while exploring the woods and hills of inland Valencia. It has all the facilities for a rest-cure, including massage and vapour baths, a gym and a beauty centre. Closed 22 Dec–Jan. **www.balneariodechulilla.com**

DENIA Rosa · €€

C/ Congre 3, Las Marinas, 03700 (Alicante) **Tel** 965 78 15 73 **Fax** 966 42 47 74 **Rooms** 40

A modern, white villa with a perfect location close to the beach. It was built and is run by a hospitable Parisian expat who has several repeat customers. Comfortable rooms have sun-trapping, Florentine-style balconies. Guests can also opt for one of the garden bungalows. The family-friendly pool has a section for toddlers. **www.hotelrosadenia.com**

EL SALER Parador de El Saler · €€€€€

Avda de los Pinares 151, 46012 (Valencia) **Tel** 961 61 11 86 **Fax** 961 62 70 16 **Rooms** 58

A contemporary parador, situated beside the sea near L'Albufera and surrounded by a renowned golf course. It overlooks one of Valencia's loveliest and least crowded beaches. The rooms are light and modern. Features a football pitch. The restaurant serves Valencian cuisine, specializing in *paella*. **www.parador.es**

ELX (ELCHE) Huerto del Cura · €€€

Porta de la Morera 14, 03203 (Alicante) **Tel** 966 61 20 50 **Fax** 966 61 20 60 **Rooms** 81

A secluded hotel in Europe's largest palm tree forest, surrounded by landscaped grounds. The bedrooms are located in Mediterranean-style bungalows. Furnishings and fittings are somewhat dated, but the hotel's reputation rests on its extraordinary array of sports facilities, which remain top-notch. **www.huertodelcura.com**

BENICARLÓ Parador de Benicarló · €€€

Avenida Papa Luna 5, 12580 (Castellón) **Tel** 964 47 01 00 **Fax** 964 47 09 34 **Rooms** 106

Situated only 30 minutes from the sea on the Azahar coast, this recently refurbished hotel has a swimming pool and "pitch and putt" golf course, and is popular with families with young children (there is a children's play area). All rooms face the beautiful garden and some have private terraces. **www.parador.es**

FORTUNA Balneario Leana · €€€

C/ Balneario, 30630 (Murcia) **Tel** 902 44 44 10 **Fax** 968 68 50 87 **Rooms** 58

This is the oldest hotel in Murcia and has the ambience of a former grand hotel. Many of the original Modernista details, including swirling woodwork and original doors, have been retained. Also boasts a splendid staircase. An array of spa and health treatments, as well as a series of thermal pools are available. **www.leana.es**

XÀTIVA (XÀTIVA) Hostería Mont Sant · €€€€

Sra de Castillo, 46800 (Valencia) **Tel** 962 27 50 81 **Fax** 962 28 19 05 **Rooms** 17

A country hotel in a magnificently restored mansion. There are just six elegant rooms in the main building, and the remaining are located in charming wooden bungalows scattered throughout the beautiful gardens. It offers all kinds of amenities, including a spa and gym, and the restaurant is superb. Closed 7–20 Jan. **www.mont-sant.com**

JÁVEA (XABIA) Hotel Jávea

€€

Calle Pio X 5, 03730 (Alicante) **Tel** *965 79 54 61* **Fax** *965 79 54 63* **Rooms** *24*

A cheerful, simple, typically Spanish seaside hotel. This good-value option is just a stone's throw from the pebbly beach in Jávea's picturesque port. The restaurant serves local specialities and offers wonderful views over the bay from its large picture windows. **www.hotel-javea.com**

JÁVEA (XABIA) Parador de Jávea

€€€€

Avda Mediterráneo 233, 03730 (Alicante) **Tel** *965 79 02 00* **Fax** *965 79 03 08* **Rooms** *70*

A large, modern parador surrounded by lush Mediterranean gardens right on the beach. The rooms are bright and spacious and almost all have balconies overlooking the sea. Offers a wide range of sports facilities, including horse riding, diving, sailing and golf. The restaurant serves regional cuisine. Lunch or dinner included. **www.parador.es**

LA VILA JOIOSA El Montiboli

€€€€

Partida El Montiboli, 03570 (Alicante) **Tel** *965 89 02 50* **Fax** *965 89 38 57* **Rooms** *86*

This beautiful, cliff-side luxury hotel overlooks a secluded beach. The rooms are decorated in warm Mediterranean colours, and most have spacious terraces offering glorious sea views. There are a handful of plush suites as well, and guests can also stay in one of the romantic bungalows in the gardens. **www.redhoteles.com/montiboli**

MORATALLA Cenajo

€€

Embalse del Cenajo, 30440 (Murcia) **Tel** *968 72 10 11* **Fax** *968 72 06 45* **Rooms** *42*

At night, silence descends on this creamy-yellow hotel beside the Cenajo dam. Few tourists stray into this lovely, remote corner of Murcia, but the surrounding hills and wealth of animal and bird life attract many hikers and nature enthusiasts. The hotel offers several activities, including horse riding. Closed 18 Dec–21 Jan. **www.hotelcenajo.com**

MORELLA Cardenal Ram

€€

Cuesta Suñer 1, 12300 (Castellón) **Tel** *964 17 30 85* **Fax** *964 17 32 18* **Rooms** *19*

This country hotel, housed in a 16th-century mansion with stone arches and beamed ceilings, overlooks the main porticoed street. Rooms have sturdy wooden furniture and colourful local prints, and there is an excellent restaurant. Newly renovated bathrooms include hydromassage baths or showers. Closed 24–26 Dec. **www.cardenalram.com**

MÚRCIA Conde de Floridablanca

€€

C/ Princesa 18, 30002 (Murcia) **Tel** *968 21 46 26* **Fax** *968 21 32 15* **Rooms** *82*

A comfortable, good-value hotel, situated across the river from the old city centre and overlooking the manicured Floridablanca gardens. The rooms are well furnished. A wide range of services makes it popular among business travellers. Offers excellent deals on their website. **www.hoteles-catalonia.es**

MÚRCIA Arco de San Juan

€€€

Plaza de Ceballos 10, 30003 (Murcia) **Tel** *968 21 04 55* **Fax** *968 22 08 09* **Rooms** *100*

The award-winning restoration of this old palace combines contemporary materials with antique furnishings. This luxury hotel is often chosen for wedding dinners and other celebrations by local Murcians. Rooms are large and comfortable, although they lack character. Also has a popular restaurant and bar. **www.arcosanjuan.com**

OLIVA Pensión Oliva

€

C/ San Luis 35, 46780 (Near Gandia, Valencia) **Tel** *653 60 69 14* **Rooms** *5*

A delightful guesthouse, located in a restored, stone-built cottage close to the coast. The rooms are comfortable with modern amenities such as a TV, minibar and tea and coffeemakers. Also has two family rooms and one especially adapted for disabled guests. Serves a daily breakfast buffet. **www.hotelitooliva.com**

ONTINYENT Hotel Kazar

€€

C/ Dos de Mayo 117, 46870 (Valencia) **Tel** *962 38 24 43* **Fax** *962 38 23 18* **Rooms** *19*

The hotel is located in a picturesque palace built by the Mompo family in the 19th century following the style of a Moorish fortress and surrounded by a garden filled with palm trees. Very comfortable and elegant bedrooms all with mini-bar and free Wi-Fi. **www.hotelkazar.com**

ORIHUELA (ORIOLA) Hotel Meliá Palacio Tudemir

€€€

C/ Alfonso XIII, 03300 (Alicante) **Tel** *966 73 80 10* **Fax** *966 73 80 70* **Rooms** *51*

This hotel is housed in a superbly restored, 18th-century palace. The coat-of-arms of the original owner still sits proudly over the main door, and the interior is palatial. The latest modern conveniences have been added, but many original details have been retained. Also has a good restaurant. **www.solmelia.com**

PENÁGUILA Mas de Pau

€

Ctra Alcoi-Penáguila km 9, 03815 (Alicante) **Tel** *965 51 31 11* **Fax** *965 51 31 09* **Rooms** *23*

A 19th-century house set amid a remote and striking landscape of almond and olive trees, and located halfway between Guadalest and Alcoi. The rooms are a little small, but most offer splendid views of the beautiful Sierra de Penáguila. The hotel is popular with families. The restaurant serves regional cuisine. Closed 24–25 Dec.

PENÍSCOLA Benedicto XIII

€€

C/ Dinamarca 2, Urbanización Las Atalayas, 12598 (Castellón) **Tel** *686 45 32 99* **Fax** *964 48 95 23* **Rooms** *30*

A white villa in a quiet private estate on a hillside near Peñíscola, with views of the sea and castle. The rooms are plain and functional, but spotlessly clean and equipped with modern conveniences and large bathrooms. Most have spacious terraces. Features two tennis courts, and the beach is just a 10-minute walk away.

Key to Price Guide *see p560* **Key to Symbols** *see back cover flap*

PENÍSCOLA Hostería del Mar

€€€

Av Papa Luna 18, 12598 (Castellón) **Tel** *964 48 06 00* **Fax** *964 48 13 63* **Rooms** *86*

A medieval Castilian style, beachfront hotel. The rooms and suites are equipped with modern amenities, including Internet facilities and a minibar. Note that from mid-June to mid-September guests are required to stay a minimum of seven nights and to take the half-board, which includes lunch or dinner. **www.hosteriadelmar.net**

VALENCIA Ad Hoc

€€€

C/ Boix 4, 46003 (Valencia) **Tel** *963 91 91 40* **Fax** *963 91 36 67* **Rooms** *28*

This chic hotel is housed in a renovated, soundproofed, 19th-century building near the Río Turia gardens. The bedrooms are furnished in a mixture of old and new styles, with brick walls, antiques and modern fabrics. Book early for one with a terrace. The restaurant offers an excellent, fixed-price lunch. **www.adhochoteles.com**

VALENCIA Hotel Venecia

€€€

C/ En Llop 5, 46002 (Valencia) **Tel** *963 52 42 67* **Fax** *963 52 44 21* **Rooms** *54*

An excellent, modestly priced hotel in the centre of the city. Although set in an old building, the hotel's interior is modern. The rooms are functionally decorated and provide basic amenities such as a TV, telephone and electronic safe. Several eateries can be found within walking distance. A breakfast buffet is served. **www.hotelvenecia.com**

VALENCIA Meliá Inglés

€€€

C/ Marqués de Dos Aguas 6, 46002 (Valencia) **Tel** *963 51 64 26* **Fax** *963 94 02 51* **Rooms** *63*

This convenient and stylish city-centre hotel is in the old palace of the Dukes of Cardona, next to the National Ceramics Museum. The rooms and suites overlook the street, and are equipped with amenities such as Internet access, a TV, a minibar and a safe. The restaurant serves regional specialties. **www.meliainges.solmelia.com**

VALENCIA Reina Victoria

€€€€

C/ Barcas 4, 46002 (Valencia) **Tel** *963 52 04 87* **Fax** *963 52 27 21* **Rooms** *96*

The grande dame of Valencia's hotels retains its splendid early 20th-century decor in the public salons, which are a dazzling whirl of gilt and marble. Rooms are disappointingly bland in comparison, but all are reasonably spacious and comfortably equipped. They were renovated in 2004 and offer Internet facilities. **www.husa.es**

MADRID

OLD MADRID Hostal Buenos Aires

€

Gran Vía 61, 28013 **Tel** *915 42 22 50* **Fax** *915 42 28 69* **Rooms** *30*   **Map** *2 D5*

A simple, economical hotel, conveniently located on the busy Gran Vía. The public rooms are pleasantly decorated, and almost all the bedrooms have their own balcony or small terrace. Moreover, the rooms are soundproofed against the capital's noisy nightlife. No breakfast. **www.hoteleshn.com**

OLD MADRID Hostal Madrid

€€

C/ Esparteros 6–2°, 28012 **Tel** *915 22 00 60* **Fax** *915 32 35 10* **Rooms** *15*   **Map** *4 F2*

One of the best budget options in Madrid, this hotel is set in the heart of the old city. Offers both rooms and apartments decorated in a mixture of traditional and modern styles, with amenities such as Wi-Fi. The staff is friendly, and the city's sights, restaurants, bars and nightlife are right on the doorstep. No breakfast. **www.hostal-madrid.info**

OLD MADRID Hostal San Lorenzo

€€

C/ Clavel 8, 28004 **Tel** *915 21 30 57* **Fax** *915 32 79 78* **Rooms** *40*   **Map** *7 A1*

A smart, well-kept hostal conveniently located on the Gran Vía, within walking distance of several sightseeing attractions and shopping areas. The crisply decorated rooms have attached bathrooms; some of the rooms feature balconies as well. Also offers a family room with two interconnected bedrooms. **http://hotel-sanlorenzo.com**

OLD MADRID Hotel Mario

€€

C/ Campomanes 4, 28004 **Tel** *915 48 85 48* **Fax** *915 59 12 88* **Rooms** *54*   **Map** *4 D2*

Hotel Mario is situated close to many major sights, as well as great shopping and dining. The rooms are small, but slickly decorated in black-and-white minimalist style with splashes of colour and high-tech gadgets. A self-service buffet breakfast is also available until late. **www.room-matehoteles.com**

OLD MADRID Hotel Plaza Mayor

€€

C/ Atocha 2, 28012 **Tel** *913 60 06 06* **Fax** *913 60 06 10* **Rooms** *34*   **Map** *7 A3*

Just around the corner of Madrid's central square, this popular hotel fills up fast, so book well in advance. Rooms vary in size and decor, but are spotless and brightly painted. The attic suite is more expensive, but offers fine views from its private terrace. Also has a reading room. Free wireless Internet in cafeteria. **www.h-plazamayor.com**

OLD MADRID Reyes Católicos

€€

C/ del Ángel 18, 28005 **Tel** *913 65 86 00* **Fax** *913 65 98 67* **Rooms** *38*   **Map** *3 C4*

Set in the trendy La Latina district, this modern hotel is very popular and always busy. Children are made welcome, and there are board games to keep them amused. The bedroom windows are double-glazed for soundproofing, and five of the rooms have their own terraces. **www.hotelreyescatolicos.es**

OLD MADRID Carlos V
€€€

C/ Maestro Victoria 5, 28013 **Tel** 915 31 41 00 **Fax** 915 31 37 61 **Rooms** 67   **Map** 4 E2

A city-centre hotel in a pedestrian street beside the Puerta del Sol. This hotel has interconnecting bedrooms as well as family rooms. Some of the rooms also have balconies and sun terraces. A generous buffet breakfast is served in the café bar, and the staff are friendly and helpful. **www.hotelcarlosv.com**

OLD MADRID Hotel Moderno
€€€

C/ Arenal 2, 28013 **Tel** 915 31 09 00 **Fax** 915 31 35 50 **Rooms** 97   **Map** 4 E2

A comfortable, modern hotel in a central location. The rooms are decorated with chintzy prints and traditional furniture; some have terraces with a view of the city's skyline. Offers free Wi-Fi access, and is popular with both business travellers and tourists. A range of restaurants can be found nearby. **www.hotel-moderno.com**

OLD MADRID Hotel Petit Palace Londres
€€€

C/ Galdo 2, 28013 **Tel** 915 31 41 05 **Fax** 915 31 41 01 **Rooms** 76   **Map** 4 F2

Behind the façade of this turn-of-the-20th-century mansion is a modern hotel with many rooms and suites. The four hi-tech rooms offer everything the business traveller could require, including a personal computer, an excercise bike and a business centre. Two specially-adapted rooms are also available for disabled travellers. **www.hthoteles.com**

OLD MADRID Tryp Gran Vía
€€€

Gran Vía 25, 28013 **Tel** 915 22 11 21 **Fax** 915 21 24 24 **Rooms** 175   **Map** 2 D5

A large, chain hotel on one of the city's busiest streets, close to main sightseeing and shopping areas. The service is brisk and efficient, and the rooms, although blandly decorated, are reasonably comfortable. Some are better than others, and are worth checking in advance. The hotel's website offers good discounts. **www.solmelia.com**

OLD MADRID Tryp Rex
€€€

Gran Vía 43, 28013 **Tel** 915 47 48 00 **Fax** 915 47 12 38 **Rooms** 145   **Map** 2 D5

This expansive hotel, renovated in 2004, is situated in an old building between the Plaza del Callao and the Plaza de España, close to a large public car park. It has spacious public rooms and well-equipped bedrooms, each with its own safe. Offers good value for money considering the central location and reasonable amenities. **www.solmelia.com**

OLD MADRID Casa de Madrid
€€€€€

C/ Arrieta 2, 28013 **Tel** 915 59 57 91 **Fax** 915 40 11 00 **Rooms** 7   **Map** 4 D1

Housed in an 18th-century palace, this stylish little hotel is ideal for a romantic getaway. The seven rooms – two of which are suites – are exquisitely decorated with antiques. The hotel has a small library. The breakfast includes freshly squeezed juice and home-made marmalade. Highly recommended. **www.casademadrid.com**

BOURBON MADRID Hostal Bianco II
€

C/ Echegaray 5, 1° D, 28014 **Tel** 913 69 13 32 **Fax** 913 69 13 32 **Rooms** 15   **Map** 7 A2

A well-kept hostal with a convenient location right off Gran Vía – all the museums and other attractions are close by. The rooms are simply decorated with all the basic amenities including TVs and a safety box. The friendly staff can speak some English. No breakfast. **www.hostalbianco.com**

BOURBON MADRID Hostal Gonzalo
€

C/ Cervantes 34, 28014 **Tel** 914 29 27 14 **Fax** 914 20 20 07 **Rooms** 15   **Map** 7 B3

A family-run hostel, which often fills up well in advance. Provides good facilities, immaculate bedrooms and excellent value for money. The multi-lingual owners are hospitable and offer helpful information regarding nearby attractions and entertainments. Several restaurants can be found within walking distance. **www.hostalgonzalo.com**

BOURBON MADRID Hostal Martín Cervelo
€

C/ Atocha 43, 28012 **Tel** 914 29 95 94 **Fax** 914 29 09 64 **Rooms** 24   **Map** 7 A3

A simple pension with a friendly atmosphere, close to three museums and the lively bars and cafés of the Santa Ana neighbourhood. The rooms are clean, decorated with flowery prints and well equipped – all have free Internet connections and en suite facilities. No breakfast. **www.hostalcervelo.com**

BOURBON MADRID Hotel Miau
€€

C/ Príncipe 26, 28012 **Tel** 913 69 71 20 **Fax** 914 29 74 60 **Rooms** 20   **Map** 7 A2

This modest hotel, housed in a handsome 19th-century building, is located in the famous Plaza Santa Ana Square at the heart of Madrid's literary quarter. The rooms are simply, but comfortably decorated, with basic amenities. In addition, all the rooms are soundproofed. Breakfast is included. **www.hotelmiau.com**

BOURBON MADRID Mora
€€

Paseo del Prado 32, 28014 **Tel** 914 20 15 69 **Fax** 914 20 05 64 **Rooms** 62   **Map** 7 C2

A 1930s hotel with an attractive entrance and a lobby with an original glass skylight. The recently renovated rooms are modern, functional and brightly furnished. Located near the Prado, the hotel offers very good value for money. Families can request an extra bed in the room for a small surcharge. **www.hotelmora.com**

BOURBON MADRID Santander
€€

C/ de Echegaray 1, 28014 **Tel** 914 29 66 44 **Fax** 913 69 10 78 **Rooms** 35   **Map** 7 A2

This small, popular, family-run hotel is situated in Madrid's literary quarter, which is filled with lively tapas bars and cafés. Opened in the 1920s, the hotel has neat, comfortable rooms, decorated in a traditional Spanish style. The staff are very helpful, and are happy to arrange theatre and flamenco tickets. **www.hotelsantandermadrid.com**

Key to Price Guide see p560 **Key to Symbols** see back cover flap

BOURBON MADRID Hotel Liabeny

C/ Salud 3, 28013 **Tel** *915 31 90 00* **Fax** *915 32 74 21* **Rooms** *220*

Map *4 F2*

An elegant, modern hotel, located just a short walk from the main sights, yet away from the hubbub of the city centre. The extensively renovated hotel features traditionally decorated rooms and suites with every modern amenity, a good restaurant and excellent service. The private parking and disabled access is a plus. **www.hotelliabeny.com**

BOURBON MADRID Inglés

C/ de Echegaray 8, 28014 **Tel** *914 29 65 51* **Fax** *914 20 24 23* **Rooms** *58*

Map *7 A2*

A good-value, family-run hotel with its own garage (for which there is a fee). Situated in the city's literary and theatre district, the hotel is a little rundown, but remains a bargain thanks to its location. The bedrooms facing the street are sunny but the rooms at the back are quieter. **www.hotel-ingles.net**

BOURBON MADRID Suite Prado

Manuel Fernández y González 10, 28014 **Tel** *914 20 23 18* **Fax** *914 20 05 59* **Rooms** *18*

Map *7 A3*

A stylish apartment-hotel of luxurious suites, all fully equipped with a kitchen, dining room, telephone lines and marble bathrooms. The hotel is very popular with business travellers, but its proximity to attractions such as the Prado and the Museo Thyssen-Bornemisza makes it a good choice for tourists as well. **www.suiteprado.com**

BOURBON MADRID ME Madrid Reina Victoria

Plaza de Santa Ana 14, 28012 **Tel** *917 01 60 00* **Fax** *915 22 03 07* **Rooms** *192*

Map *7 A3*

This ultra-stylish and innovative hotel is situated in the majestic building of the former Gran Hotel Reina Victoria. Each of the contemporary rooms offers a fully-stocked martini bar and the latest entertainment technology, including iPod sound systems and WiFi, and the trendy Penthouse bar has fantastic views over the city. **http://memadrid.travel**

BOURBON MADRID Ritz

Plaza de la Lealtad 5, 28014 **Tel** *917 01 67 67* **Fax** *917 01 67 76* **Rooms** *167*

Map *7 C2*

Inaugurated in 1910 as a hotel for aristocrats, the Ritz is still one of Spain's most elegant hotels. Close to the Prado, the hotel has an ornate, circular foyer and a terraced garden, and serves tea and brunch along with live music. Rooms are luxurious and offer every imaginable comfort. **www.ritz.es**

BOURBON MADRID Villa Real

Plaza de las Cortes 10, 28014 **Tel** *914 20 37 67* **Fax** *914 20 25 47* **Rooms** *115*

Map *7 B2*

Close to the Prado and the Retiro gardens, this stylish hotel is based in an opulent, early 19th-century building. One of Madrid's smartest hotels, the spacious rooms and suites are decorated in a tasteful mixture of traditional and contemporary styles, and scattered with ancient Roman art. Some suites even have a Jacuzzi. **www.derbyhotels.es**

BOURBON MADRID Westin Palace

Plaza de las Cortes 7, 28014 **Tel** *913 60 80 00* **Fax** *913 60 81 00* **Rooms** *465*

Map *7 B2*

This *belle époque* hotel with a glass dome and a colonnade has accommodated statesmen, as well as Mata Hari, the spy. The decor features marble columns, chandeliers and huge oil paintings and statues. Rooms are nicely decorated, and the service is charmingly old-fashioned and efficient. They also have a wine cellar. **www.palacemadrid.com**

FURTHER AFIELD (EAST) NH Alcalá

C/ de Alcalá 66, 28009 **Tel** *914 35 10 60* **Fax** *914 35 11 05* **Rooms** *146*

Map *4 F2*

A large, chain hotel close to the lovely Retiro gardens. Features spacious, well-equipped rooms with amenities that include Wi-Fi and Internet access. This reasonably priced hotel also has a café, bar and private car park. It is within walking distance to the up-market shopping district in Salamanca, and three museums. **www.nh-hotels.com**

FURTHER AFIELD (NORTH) Hostal Sil

C/ Fuencarral 95, 28004 **Tel** *914 48 89 72* **Fax** *914 47 48 29* **Rooms** *20*

Map *2 F3*

This comfortable hostal is situated in one of the city's liveliest nightlife districts, which is also a prominent gay neighbourhood. Offers simple, but adequate bedrooms, with *en suite* facilities at a reasonable price. There are plenty of fashionable bars, cafés, shops and restaurants nearby. **www.silserranos.com**

FURTHER AFIELD (NORTH) Intercontinental Castellana

Paseo de la Castellana 49, 28046 **Tel** *917 00 73 00* **Fax** *913 19 58 53* **Rooms** *307*

Map *6 D1*

This glossy, modern chain hotel in Madrid's business and financial district centre is a favourite with business travellers. The rooms and suites offer several amenities. The hotel also hosts a well-equipped business centre, as well as a cocktail lounge for relaxing after work, and a baby-sitting service. **www.intercontinental.com**

FURTHER AFIELD (NORTH) Occidental Miguel Ángel

Miguel Ángel 31, 28010 **Tel** *914 42 00 22* **Fax** *914 42 53 20* **Rooms** *263*

Map *6 D2*

Located beside the Paseo de la Castellana, this large hotel combines modern comfort with classic style. It is popular with both business travellers, who appreciate the business centre and related amenities, as well as tourists, who enjoy the central location and luxurious extras. **www.miguelangelhotel.com**

FURTHER AFIELD (NORTH) Santo Mauro

Zurbano 36, 28010 **Tel** *913 19 69 00* **Fax** *913 08 54 77* **Rooms** *51*

Map *5 C2*

This palace, built in 1894 on one of Madrid's most elegant streets, is surrounded by beautiful wooded gardens. The rooms and suites are stylishly decorated, and the two fine restaurants offer romantic outdoor dining in summer. Also houses a swimming pool in the vaulted cellars. **www.ac-hotels.com**

FURTHER AFIELD (NORTH) Villamagna Park Hyatt   🖥️🅿️⛾🍴🛏️🐾🕳️🔲   €€€€€

Paseo de la Castellana 22, 28046 **Tel** *915 76 75 00* **Fax** *915 75 31 58* **Rooms** *151*   **Map** *6 D1*

Set in attractive, tree-filled gardens, the luxurious Villamagna combines 18th-century decor with 21st-century amenities. Features spacious and comfortable rooms, decorated with antiques and contemporary furnishings. It also offers an excellent business centre, a health club and a choice of restaurants and bars. **www.madrid.hyatt.com**

FURTHER AFIELD (NORTHEAST) Hotel Galiano   🖥️🍴🔲   €€€

C/ Alcalá Galiano 6, 28010 **Tel** *913 19 20 00* **Fax** *913 19 99 14* **Rooms** *29*   **Map** *5 C2*

A charming hotel in the city's quiet embassy district, close to the Paseo Castellana and the Prado. The hotel was once a convent and then a palace – part of it is still a private mansion – and is scattered with fine antiques. The decor is flowery and flouncy, and rooms are spacious. Offers good value for money. **www.hotelgaliano.com**

FURTHER AFIELD (NORTHEAST) NH Príncipe de Vergara   🖥️🅿️🍴🕳️🛏️🔲   €€€€

C/ Príncipe de Vergara 92, 28006 **Tel** *915 63 26 95* **Fax** *915 63 72 53* **Rooms** *173*   **Map** *4 D2*

Part of a chain of well-appointed hotels, this large, modern property is extremely popular with business travellers. Offers a range of luxuries, including a sauna and massage service and baby-sitting facilities. The hotel's website offers excellent weekend deals. **www.nh-hotels.com**

MADRID PROVINCE

ARANJUEZ El Cocherón 1919   🖥️🍴🔲   €€

C/ Montesinos 22, 28300 **Tel** *918 75 43 50* **Fax** *918 75 43 47* **Rooms** *18*

This small, charming family-run hotel is set around a historic *corrala* (central courtyard), but has been decorated in a fine mixture of contemporary and traditional styles. The bedrooms look out onto the ochre-painted courtyard. Perfectly located in the city centre, it has a small café for guests. Serves breakfast only. **www.rusticae.es**

CERCEDILLA Hotel Rural Luces del Poniente   🖥️🍴🐾🔲   €€

C/ Lina de Avila 4, Cercedilla, Madrid, 28470 **Tel** *918 52 55 87* **Fax** *918 52 32 47* **Rooms** *11*

Sited in a picturesque chalet town on the fringes of the Sierra de Guadarrama, this place provides respite from the summer heat. The rooms are chic and stylish in their decor, yet provide a warm inviting ambience. It is an ideal base for nearby ski resorts and additionals include mountain bikes and horseback riding. **www.lucesdelponiente.com**

CHINCHÓN Parador de Chinchón   🍴🅿️🏊🔲   €€€

C/ de los Huertos 1, 28370 **Tel** *918 94 08 36* **Fax** *918 94 09 08* **Rooms** *38*

Housed in a 17th-century monastery, this stunning parador is set around a tree-filled courtyard, and adorned with frescoes, *azulejos* (tiles) and antiques. The handsome bedrooms have immensely thick stone walls, and the restaurar serves traditional Castilian fare, including garlic soup and roast suckling pig. **www.parador.es**

RASCAFRÍA Santa María de El Paular   🖥️🍴🏊🐾🛏️🔲   €€

Ctra M–604, km 26.5, 28741 **Tel** *918 69 10 11* **Fax** *918 69 10 06* **Rooms** *56*

A relaxing retreat in the beautiful Sierra de Guadarrama, this hotel occupies a section of a 15th-century Benedictine monastery. Part of the Sheraton chain of hotels, it offers several facilities, from tennis courts and an outdoor pool to an elegant restaurant and an informal tavern. Closed January. **www.hotelsantamariapaular.com**

SAN LORENZO DEL ESCORIAL El Botánico   🅿️🖥️🍴🔲   €€

C/ Timoteo Padrós 16, 28200 **Tel** *918 90 78 79* **Fax** *918 90 81 58* **Rooms** *20*

An appealing hotel, housed in a handsome, whitewashed country mansion. A stone's throw from the vast El Escori monastery, it is surrounded by beautiful gardens and is situated opposite the golf course. The bedrooms are decorated with modern furnishings, and offer great views. Breakfast included. **www.valdesimonte.com**

TORREJÓN DE ARDOZ La Casa Grande   🍴🔲   €€€

C/ Madrid 2, 28850 **Tel** *916 75 39 00* **Fax** *916 75 06 91* **Rooms** *8*

This luxurious hotel is located in a 16th-century former convent. The ornate suites are decorated with antiques which on belonged to the Russian royal family – Catherine the Great is said to have slept in the bed now in the main suite. The ho also houses two art museums and a gourmet grocery shop and hosts medieval-themed dinners. **www.lacasagrande.e**

CASTILLA Y LEÓN

ASTORGA Asturplaza   🅿️🖥️⛾🍴🔲   €

Plaza España 2–3, 24700 **Tel** *987 61 89 00* **Fax** *987 61 89 49* **Rooms** *37*

A popular hotel with striking views of some of Astorga's best sites, including the cathedral, the city wall and the Episcopal palace. The rooms are comfortably furnished. Those overlooking the Plaza España can get noisy at night during the holiday season, but offer guests the chance to soak up the town's atmosphere. **www.asturplaza.com**

ÁVILA Rey Niño

Plaza José Tomé 1, 05001 **Tel** *920 25 52 10* **Fax** *920 22 62 80* **Rooms** *24*

Located within the city's medieval walls, in a tranquil pedestrian street, this hotel proves the old adage – "Ávila, the city where one hears the silence". The building was completely renovated in 2001 and offers spacious and comfortable rooms. **www.hotelreynino.com**

ÁVILA Hospedería la Sinagoga

Reyes Católicos 22, 05001 **Tel** *920 35 23 21* **Fax** *920 35 34 74* **Rooms** *22*

This 15th-century building, situated in the centre of the old town, was formerly a synagogue serving Ávila's thriving Jewish commmunity. Some decorative elements from the original structure remain, lending an atmospheric touch to this well-equipped and comfortable hotel.

ÁVILA Parador de Ávila

C/ Marqués Canales de Chozas 2, 05001 **Tel** *920 21 13 40* **Fax** *920 22 61 66* **Rooms** *61*

Ideal for history lovers, this hotel is set in a 16th-century palace, next to the walls that surround Ávila's old town. Refurbished with stone and adobe, the hotel is furnished with many antiques. It also boasts a covered interior patio and a garden replete with archaeological remains. **www.parador.es**

BURGOS La Puebla

La Puebla 20, 09004 **Tel** *947 20 00 11* **Fax** *947 20 47 08* **Rooms** *15*

A grand 19th-century building houses this good-value hotel, equipped with comfortable but no-frills rooms. With its excellent location near the Teatro Principal, La Puebla offers its guests a great all-round package, which includes free bicycles. The old-fashioned atmosphere and friendly staff give this place a timeless feel. **www.hotellapuebla.com**

BURGOS NH Palacio de la Merced

C/ de la Merced 13, 09002 **Tel** *947 47 99 00* **Fax** *947 26 04 26* **Rooms** *110*

Part of the NH chain, this spectacular hotel is set in a 17th-century palace. Tastefully renovated, it comes complete with its own Gothic cloister. Modern amenities and luxuries, such as saunas, massage services and baby-sitting facilities are also available. **www.nh-hotels.com**

BURGOS Landa Palace

Ctra Al (E-5) de Madrid a Irún km 235, 09001 **Tel** *947 25 77 77* **Fax** *947 26 46 76* **Rooms** *39*

Considered one of the best hotels in the region, this family-run establishment offers guests a taste of luxurious living with large, elegant and comfortable rooms equipped with DVD players and other creature comforts. Some rooms have Jacuzzis. The highlight, however, is the magnificent swimming pool covered by Gothic arches. **www.landapalace.es**

CARRIÓN DE LOS CONDES Hotel Monasterio de San Zoilo

Obispo Souto Vizoso s/n, 34120 **Tel** *979 88 00 49* **Fax** *979 88 10 90* **Rooms** *50*

Situated along the Santiago pilgrimage route, this former Benedictine monastery has been welcoming travellers for centuries. It provides a perfect place to relax after a long day exploring the stunning surroundings. The restaurant serves elaborate Castilian seasonal cuisine. **www.sanzoilo.com**

CIUDAD RODRIGO Parador de Ciudad Rodrigo

Plaza Castillo 1, 37500 (Salamanca) **Tel** *923 46 01 50* **Fax** *923 46 04 04* **Rooms** *35*

Located in a castle on a hill overlooking the river, this comfortable parador is famous for the medieval Homenaje Tower, which provides great views of the local scenery. The rooms are decorated with traditional Castilian furniture, and the garden and patio offer guests an ideal spot to spend some quiet time. **www.parador.es**

COVARRUBIAS Hotel Doña Sancha

Avenida Victor Barbadillo, 09346 (Burgos) **Tel** *947 40 64 00* **Fax** *947 40 05 04* **Rooms** *14*

This small hotel offers peace and tranquillity in a natural setting, surrounded by mountains. The bedrooms are comfortable and well equipped, and all have a balcony with views over the valley. The breakfast includes home-made breads and jams made from the fruit trees that grow in the garden. **www.hoteldonasancha.com**

EL BURGO DE OSMA Virrey II

Mayor 2, 42300 (Soria) **Tel** *975 34 13 11* **Fax** *975 34 08 55* **Rooms** *52*

Housed in a section of an ancient hospital for ailing pilgrims, this hotel has been luxuriously refurbished. The decor features classical busts, a grand piano, chandeliers, a grandfather clock and a range of other lavish flourishes. The staff are friendly, and the rooms are comfortable and clean. Closed 21 Dec–9 Jan. **www.virreypalafox.com**

HOYOS DEL ESPINO El Milano Real

Toleo s/n, 05634 (Ávila) **Tel** *920 34 91 08* **Fax** *920 34 91 56* **Rooms** *21*

This recently-renovated hotel with spa has managed to maintain its rustic charm and is ideal for those in search of a relaxing and tranquil retreat. Guests can explore the scenic beauty of the surrounding Gredos mountains by foot or on horseback. Spectacular views of the mountains are available from some rooms. **www.elmilanoreal.com**

LA ALBERCA Hotel Antiguas Eras

Las Batuecas 29 bajo, 37624 (Salamanca) **Tel** *923 41 51 13* **Fax** *923 41 51 13* **Rooms** *34*

This unique building is a mishmash of different and somewhat clashing architectural styles. The rooms are large, comfortable and functional. Some of them offer views of the Béjar mountain range, while others have a terrace and a bath with hydromassage. **www.antiguaseras.com**

LEÓN Alfonso V

Padre Isla 1, 24002 **Tel** *987 22 09 00* **Fax** *987 22 12 44* **Rooms** *62*

This hotel, built in the 1920s to accommodate tourists passing through, has retained some of its "golden age" charm in the lobby with the glass dome that floods the entrance with natural light. The lift also dates from the 1920s. The rooms are large and comfortable, if a little old-fashioned. **www.lesein.es/alfonsov**

LEÓN Paris

C/ Ancha 18, 24003 **Tel** *987 23 86 00* **Fax** *987 27 15 72* **Rooms** *55*

Most Spanish towns seem to have a hotel called "Paris" and, generally, they are as different from the Parisian style as can be imagined. León's version is very Spanish, with simple, unsophisticated decor and an efficient, if not overly-enthusiastic, staff. **www.hotelparisleon.com**

LEÓN Parador de San Marcos

Plaza de San Marcos 7, 24001 **Tel** *987 23 73 00* **Fax** *987 23 34 58* **Rooms** *226*

The dramatic Renaissance façade of this former San Marcos monastery gives way to an interior full of stone work and wooden masterpieces by medieval maestros. The rooms are comfortable and luxurious. A stay at this museum-like hotel is an experience in itself. **www.parador.es**

MOLINASECA La Posada de Muriel

Plaza Santo Cristo s/n, 24413 (León) **Tel** *987 45 32 01* **Fax** *987 45 31 35* **Rooms** *8*

A small and welcoming country inn on the Santiago pilgrimage route. This renovated farmhouse offers simple and well-equipped rooms with traditional furnishings. The two rooms on the upper floor are smaller, but have a beautiful view through the skylight windows. Closed 7–31 Jan. **www.laposadademuriel.com**

NAVARREDONDA DE GREDOS Parador de Gredos

Ctra. Barraco-Béjar, 05635 (Ávila) **Tel** *920 34 80 48* **Fax** *920 34 82 05* **Rooms** *74*

Built in 1928, this is considered by many as one of Spain's best paradors. The hotel is decorated in a sober, no-frills Castilian style, and offers excellent views over the Tormes valley and the nearby peaks of the Gredos mountains. Some of the rooms have their own terrace. The restaurant serves local cuisine. **www.parador.es**

PALENCIA AC Palencia

Av de Cuba 25, 34004 **Tel** *979 16 57 01* **Fax** *979 16 57 02* **Rooms** *65*

This modern hotel is located near the town centre, and is very popular with both business travellers and weekend tourists. The hotel gives guests the chance to unwind in its sauna, and enjoy the buffet at its restaurant. The rooms are equipped with high-speed Internet and cable TV and free mini-bar. **www.ac-hotels.com**

PEDRAZA Hospedería de Santo Domingo

Matadero 3, 40172 (Segovia) **Tel** *921 50 99 71* **Fax** *921 50 86 83* **Rooms** *17*

The coat of arms on the façade of this converted 18th-century manor reads "Jesus and Mary's slaves. Year 1703". What was once an austere establishment is now a comfortable, modern hotel, which tastefully incorporates the numerous remaining historical elements with contemporary touches. **www.hospederiadesantodomingo.com**

PONFERRADA AC Ponferrada

Avda de Astorga 2, 24400 **Tel** *987 40 99 73* **Fax** *987 40 99 74* **Rooms** *60*

A steep climb up paved alleys takes guests to the entrance of this recently refurbished hotel, situated near the city's castle. Offers comfortable, well-equipped rooms and adequate service at a good price. Also has parking facilities for those who find the walk too challenging. **www.ac-hotels.com**

POZAL DE GALLINAS La Posada del Pinar

Finca Pinar de San Rafael s/n, 47450 (Valladolid) **Tel** *983 48 10 04* **Fax** *983 48 10 04* **Rooms** *19*

Very close to Valladolid and less than an hour from Ávila, Salamanca and Segovia, this country house comes with a beautiful, expansive garden. The cosy living room, library and dining room give this hotel a homely touch. Bikes are available for guests and there is a children's pool. Breakfast is included. **www.laposadadelpinar.com**

SALAMANCA Hostería Casa Vallejo

San Juan de la Cruz 3, 37001 **Tel** *923 28 04 21* **Fax** *923 21 31 12* **Rooms** *14*

This comfortable hostal near the Plaza Mayor is one of town's oldest hotels. The staff are friendly and willing to help guests make the most of their stay by pointing them in the right direction and suggesting some hidden corners off the well-beaten tourist track. Closed two weeks in Feb & last two weeks in Jul. **www.hosteriacasavallejo.com**

SALAMANCA AC Palacio de San Esteban

Arroyo de Santo Domingo 3, 37001 **Tel** *923 26 22 96* **Fax** *923 26 88 72* **Rooms** *51*

The AC hotel chain took over this old convent in 2002 and converted it into one of the city's finest hotels. The original character of the building has been kept alive within the context of a modern hotel. The vaulted ceilings and stone walls breathe history, while the comfortable rooms do not lack any amenities and offer a free mini-bar. **www.ac-hotels.com**

SALAMANCA Rector

Paseo Rector Esperabé 10, 37008 **Tel** *923 21 84 82* **Fax** *923 21 40 08* **Rooms** *13*

This hotel is set in an elegant building with a beautiful, wide entrance hall with stained-glass windows in an Art Nouveau style. Tastefully designed rooms with mahogany furniture and white marble bathrooms make this one of the town's best-looking places to stay. **www.hotelrector.com**

Key to Price Guide *see p560* **Key to Symbols** *see back cover flap*

SAN ROMÁN DE LOS INFANTES Posada Dehesa Congosta   €€

Finca la Congosta, 49281 (Zamora) **Tel** *615 21 76 42* **Fax** *980 98 05 04* **Rooms** *10*

Welcoming and friendly inn located in a natural environment. Offers cosy and beautifully decorated rooms, each priced individually. One of the rooms is in an adjacent building, separate from the main hotel. Activities such as trekking, mountain biking, canoeing and horse riding are also available. Closed 8 Jan–8 Feb. **www.dehesacongosta.com**

SANTA MARÍA DE MAVE El Convento   €

Monasterio de Santa María de Mave s/n, 34402 (Palencia) **Tel** *979 12 36 11* **Fax** *979 12 54 92* **Rooms** *25*

Located in the Montaña Palentina Natural Park, close to Aguilar de Campoo. The rooms are comfortable, even if they do occasionally resemble a nun's cell, and are well equipped with amenities such as minibars, TVs and hairdryers. The restaurant serves up some satisfying Castilian stews. **www.hosteriaelconvento.com**

SANTO DOMINGO DE SILOS Santo Domingo de Silos   €

Santo Domingo de Silos 12–22, 09610 (Burgos) **Tel** *947 39 00 53* **Fax** *947 39 00 52* **Rooms** *60*

A modest and functional hotel, located in front of the Santo Domingo de Silos monastery. The rooms evoke the seriousness and austerity of Castilian monastic life with forged-iron bedsteads and solid wooden furniture. The hotel's restaurant serves some good, hearty local fare. **www.hotelsantodomingodesilos.com**

SEGOVIA Parador de Segovia   €€€

Ctra de Valladolid s/n, 40003 **Tel** *921 44 37 37* **Fax** *921 43 73 62* **Rooms** *113*

This country house is just a short distance from the aqueduct and offers magnificent views of Segovia. The abstract art in the large lobby forms a nice contrast to the sober lines of the classical interior. The restaurant is one of the best places to sample the city's favourite dish, *cochinillo* (suckling pig). **www.parador.es**

SORIA Hostería Solar de Tejada   €

Claustrilla 1, 42002 **Tel** *975 23 00 54* **Fax** *975 23 00 54* **Rooms** *18*

Situated in the heart of the city, this hotel is equipped with comfortable and modern facilities. The bright and somewhat chintzy rooms have a special charm and offer amenities such as TVs, hairdryers and iron-forged headboards by Luis Saénz, a local artist. Breakfast is not available. **www.hosteriasolardetejada.com**

SORIA Parador de Soria   €€€

Parque del Castillo s/n, 42005 **Tel** *975 24 08 00* **Fax** *975 24 08 03* **Rooms** *67*

The highlight of this parador is, without doubt, its privileged location on a hill overlooking Soria and the Duero valley. The hotel itself is surrounded by ancient oaks and green pastures. The rooms have been renovated recently and are modern in style. **www.parador.es**

TORDESILLAS Parador de Tordesillas   €€€

Ctra de Salamanca 5, 47100 (Valladolid) **Tel** *983 77 00 51* **Fax** *983 77 10 13* **Rooms** *68*

An ancestral home located in a beautiful pine forest. The hotel's spectacular location is complemented by its numerous facilities, including sauna, gym, winter and summer swimming pools and conference room. The large and comfortable rooms are luxuriously furnished with Castilian antiques. **www.parador.es**

VALLADOLID Hostal París   €

Especería 2, 47001 **Tel** *983 37 06 25* **Fax** *983 35 83 01* **Rooms** *37*

A simple, four-storey building conveniently set in the heart of the city, near the Plaza Mayor. This friendly, family-run hotel has comfortable bedrooms with all modern facilities, and offers good value for those travelling on a budget. The service here is impeccable. **www.hostalparis.com**

VALLADOLID Meliá Recoletos   €€

Acera de Recoletos 13, 47004 **Tel** *983 21 62 00* **Fax** *983 21 62 10* **Rooms** *80*

This recently opened hotel is situated in Valladolid's beautiful historical city centre, and offers great views of the Campo Grande park. The hotel is well equipped with all modern conveniences. What it lacks in character, it makes up with its excellent location close to the town's main train station. **www.solmelia.com**

VILLAFRANCA DEL BIERZO Parador del Bierzo   €€€

Avda Calvo Sotelo 28, 24500 (León) **Tel** *987 54 01 75* **Fax** *987 54 00 10* **Rooms** *39*

An unassuming and welcoming hotel near the entrance to the town. The surrounding landscapes of the Ancares mountain range create a tranquil atmosphere. Large and comfortable rooms with traditional Castilian decor and a good restaurant make this one of the best-value paradors around. Closed 22 Dec–1 Feb. **www.parador.es**

ZAMORA NH Palacio del Duero   €€

Plaza de la Horta1, 49002 **Tel** *980 50 82 62* **Fax** *980 53 37 22* **Rooms** *49*

The Duero Palace once used to house one of the city's first distilleries, and remains a good place to indulge in a tipple at the hotel's restaurant. Like all NH chain properties, the decor here follows a modern, minimalist style that contrasts nicely with the ancient stone walls. Modern amenities and good value for money. **www.nh-hotels.com**

ZAMORA Parador de Zamora   €€€

Plaza de Viriato 5, 49001 **Tel** *980 51 44 97* **Fax** *980 53 00 63* **Rooms** *52*

Located in a 15th-century palace, this hotel's medieval decor features aristocratic tapestries, armour and beds with canopies (in some rooms). The Renaissance patio, embellished with heraldic motifs, is a perfect place to sample some of the restaurant's star dishes, including a mouthwatering almond custard. **www.parador.es**

CASTILLA-LA MANCHA

ALARCÓN Parador de Alarcón
€€€€

Avda Amigos de los Castillos 3, 16214 (Cuenca) **Tel** *969 33 03 15* **Fax** *969 33 03 03* **Rooms** *14*

A medieval fortress stunningly located above the Júcar valley. The lounge and dining rooms are vaulted chambers with thick walls. However, modern artworks by some of Spain's most renowned artists create a contemporary look. The large suites are all spectacular; the one in the lookout tower is the best. **www.parador.es**

ALBACETE Parador de Albacete
€€€

Ctra N301 km 251, 02000 (Albacete) **Tel** *967 24 53 21* **Fax** *967 24 32 71* **Rooms** *68*

This parador is set in expansive gardens, with shady terraces, a large outdoor pool and a pitch and putt course. Provides a perfect setting for activities such as walking, fishing and horse riding. The public spaces are decorated with ox yokes and other rural implements, and the fine restaurant serves local cuisine. **www.parador.es**

ALMAGRO Posada de Almagro
€

C/ Gran Maestre 5, 13270 (Ciudad Real) **Tel** *926 26 12 01* **Fax** *926 26 12 01* **Rooms** *11*

This lovely, 16th-century *posada* has been prettily renovated into a simple and charming guesthouse. Features a timbered gallery and cool, rustically-decorated rooms, overlooking a delightful courtyard. Also has a typical tavern serving regional specialities. **www.laposadadealmagro.es**

ALMAGRO Parador de Almagro
€€€€

Ronda de San Franciso 31, 13270 (Ciudad Real) **Tel** *926 86 01 00* **Fax** *926 86 01 50* **Rooms** *54*

An exquisite parador, housed in a 16th-century convent, and set around a series of courtyards and cloisters. The former cells have been converted into bedrooms, though their austerity has been replaced by modern comforts. A lace-maker works in one of the courtyards, keeping the town's tradition alive. **www.parador.es**

AYNA Felipe II
€

Avenida Manuel Carrera s/n, 02125 (Albacete) **Tel** *967 29 50 83* **Fax** *967 29 50 83* **Rooms** *41*

This modern hotel is set in a charming village in the mountains of Albacete. Its semi-circular layout allows a panoramic view of the town and the valley from every bedroom. The staff are friendly and can arrange various outdoor activities, including rafting, horse riding and even stargazing. Closed Jan. **www.hotelfelipeiiayna.com**

BALLESTEROS DE CALATRAVA Palacio de la Serna
€€€

C/ Cervantes 18, 13432 (Ciudad Real) **Tel** *926 84 22 08* **Fax** *926 84 22 24* **Rooms** *24*

An 18th-century farmhouse in the plains of La Mancha, decorated in a mix of Castilian and modern styles. The rooms are large and painted in bold, contemporary colours. The staff can arrange horseback and mountain bike excursions into the surrounding hills. Also has art galleries and a sculpture garden. **www.palaciodelaserna.com**

BELMONTE Palacio Buenavista
€

C/ La Iglesia 2, 16640 (Cuenca) **Tel** *967 18 75 80* **Fax** *967 18 75 88* **Rooms** *36*

A charming country hotel in a renovated 15th-century palace. Features spacious rooms, decorated in a traditional style, wooden galleries and a delightful garden. Some of the rooms have views of Belmonte's magnificent castle. A primrose-yellow dining room serves delicious oven-roasted lamb and steak. **www.palaciodebuenavista.es**

CUENCA La Cueva del Fraile
€€

Ctra Cuenca-Buenache km 7, 16001 (Cuenca) **Tel** *969 21 15 71* **Fax** *969 25 60 47* **Rooms** *76*

Set in a green valley outside Cuenca, this 16th-century hotel is built around a white patio and surrounded by vast gardens. The rooms are elegantly furnished with all modern comforts. The special duplex apartments are ideal for families. Also has tennis courts, and guests can rent bicycles. Closed Jan. **www.hotelcuevadelfraile.com**

CUENCA Leonor de Aquitania
€€€

C/ San Pedro 58–60, 16001 (Cuenca) **Tel** *969 23 10 00* **Fax** *969 23 10 04* **Rooms** *49*

Named after a medieval princess, this hotel is located in a historic building in the heart of old Cuenca. The spacious bedrooms and suites are decorated in a traditional style, and the public areas are adorned with tapestries and hunting trophies. Some rooms offer panoramic views. **www.hotelleonordeaquitania.com**

CUENCA Posada de San José
€€

C/ Julián Romero 4, 16001 (Cuenca) **Tel** *969 21 13 00* **Fax** *969 23 03 65* **Rooms** *22*

Run by a Canadian-Spanish couple, this hotel is set in a 17th-century convent. Perched vertiginously above the gorge it is one of Cuenca's famous hanging houses *(see pp384–5)* . The rooms are stylishly decorated with white fabrics, and offer splendid views. Curiously labyrinthine, it showcases many antiques and frescoes. **www.posadasanjose.cor**

CUENCA Parador de Cuenca
€€€€

Subida de San Pablo s/n, 16001 (Cuenca) **Tel** *969 23 23 20* **Fax** *969 23 25 34* **Rooms** *63*

The 16th-century convent of San Pablo has been transformed into an elegant parador. The town's famous old hanging houses, draped vertiginously over the gorge, can be seen from some of the bedrooms. Offers a range of modern facilities, including a fine regional restaurant. **www.parador.es**

Key to Price Guide *see p560* **Key to Symbols** *see back cover flap*

EL TOBOSO Casa de la Torre

C/ Antonio Machado 16, 45820 (Toledo) **Tel** *925 56 80 06* **Fax** *925 56 80 06* **Rooms** *14*

A rural inn in the heart of Don Quixote country, El Toboso was once home to Dulcinea, the object of the knight's affections. The inn is set in a 17th-century mansion, built around a typical Manchegan galleried courtyard. The rooms and suites are attractively decorated. Three dining areas serve regional specialities. **www.casadelatorre.com**

GUADALAJARA España

C/ Teniente Figueroa 3, 19001 (Guadalajara) **Tel** *949 21 13 03* **Fax** *949 21 13 05* **Rooms** *40*

A family-run hotel in a modernized, 19th-century mansion located in the centre of the city. Offers excellent amenities, including a small sauna. The simple, spotlessly clean rooms are decorated in a traditional style. The restaurant serves local specialities, and the staff can advise on nearby attractions.

MANZANARES Parador de Manzanares

Autovía de Andalucía km 174, 13200 (Ciudad Real) **Tel** *926 61 04 00* **Fax** *926 61 09 35* **Rooms** *44*

Set in the heart of the city's principal wine region, this parador is a good base for exploring Don Quixote country. With two natural parks just a short distance away, it is also perfect for nature enthusiasts. The hotel is modern, but built in traditional Manchegan style, and is surrounded by extensive gardens. **www.parador.es**

OROPESA Parador de Oropesa

Plaza de Palacio 1, 45560 (Toledo) **Tel** *925 43 00 00* **Fax** *925 43 07 77* **Rooms** *48*

The Sierra de Gredos forms a scenic backdrop to this medieval fortress rising above a plain of olive groves and vineyards. The bedrooms are spacious. The parador also arranges activities such as pheasant hunting and horse riding excursions. The romantic restaurant serves regional cuisine. **www.parador.es**

OSSA DE MONTIEL Albamanjón

Laguna de San Pedro 16, 02611 (Albacete) **Tel** *926 69 90 48* **Fax** *926 69 91 20* **Rooms** *12*

A tranquil retreat by the Lagunas de Ruidera, La Mancha's attractive string of turquoise lakes. This modern complex has been built in a traditional style, and is beautifully decorated with colourful tiles and climbing plants. The bedrooms are elegant and comfortable, and present far-reaching countryside views. Closed 24–25 Dec. **www.albamanjon.net**

PASTRANA Hospedería Real de Pastrana

Convento del Carmen, Ctra Pastrana-Zorita km 1, 19100 (Guadalajara) **Tel/Fax** *949 37 10 60* **Rooms** *27*

This hotel occupies a wing of the Monasterio del Carmen, founded by St Teresa of Ávila. Located near the picturesque town of Pastrana, it overlooks the Río Tajo, and offers simple rooms. Trips to sights associated with the famous saint, as well as hunting, fishing and sailing can also be arranged. **www.hosteriasreales.com**

SAN CLEMENTE Casa de los Acacio

C/ Cruz Cerrada 10, 16600 (Cuenca) **Tel** *969 30 03 60* **Fax** *969 30 00 67* **Rooms** *8*

This hotel is housed in a carefully restored, 17th-century stone mansion in a historical village. The rooms and suites are set around a graceful patio, and decorated with traditional Castilian furniture. The restaurant is for hotel guests only, book in advance. On Saturday evenings there is a *degustación* dinner with wine tasting. **www.casadelosacacio.es**

SIGÜENZA El Molino de Alcuneza

Ctra de Alboreca km 0.5, 19264 (Guadalajara) **Tel** *949 39 15 01* **Fax** *949 34 70 04* **Rooms** *11*

A restored mill in the Alcarria now contains this intimate country hotel. Each room has been stylishly decorated with traditional furnishings and pretty prints, and many feature the original beams and cool stone walls. A stream burbles beneath the public lounge. Dinner includes fresh produce from the kitchen garden. **www.molinodealcuneza.com**

SIGÜENZA Parador de Sigüenza

Plaza del Castillo, 19250 (Guadalajara) **Tel** *949 39 01 00* **Fax** *949 39 13 64* **Rooms** *81*

Sigüenza's massive castle overlooks the city from a hilltop – its crenellated towers and battlements are a stirring sight. Former VIP guests here include the Catholic Monarchs *(see pp56–7)* . Bedrooms are handsomely furnished with every modern amenity and overlook a striking courtyard. **www.parador.es**

TOLEDO La Almazara

Ctra Toledo-Argés km 3.4, 45080 (Toledo) **Tel** *925 22 38 66* **Fax** *925 25 05 62* **Rooms** *28*

This 16th-century country-house hotel is set high on a wooded hilltop oustide Toledo, and has a magnificent view. Renowned artist, El Greco, was reputedly a frequent guest here. The hotel is surrounded by olive trees, oaks and junipers, and has simple rooms; some with a terrace. Closed 10 Dec–1 Mar. **www.hotelalmazara.com**

TOLEDO Hostal del Cardenal

Paseo de Recaredo 24, 45004 (Toledo) **Tel** *925 22 49 00* **Fax** *925 22 29 91* **Rooms** *27*

Now a historic hotel near the city walls, this 18th-century mansion was once the residence of Toledo's archbishop. It has sculpted ceilings and brick courtyards, and the bedrooms and suites are traditionally decorated with plush fabrics and every modern comfort. Some overlook the lovely, jasmine-scented gardens. **www.hostaldelcardenal.com**

TOLEDO Pintor El Greco

C/ Alamillos del Tránsito 13, 45002 (Toledo) **Tel** *925 28 51 91* **Fax** *925 21 58 19* **Rooms** *33*

A 17th-century bakery in Toledo's former Jewish quarter has been discreetly extended behind the original façade and patio. Wrought iron, traditional ceramics and lots of flowering plants add character to the hotel. The bedrooms are modern, yet in keeping with the historic surroundings. **www.hotel-pintorelgreco.com**

TOLEDO Parador de Toledo   🏦 P 🍴 🏊 🗐   €€€€
Cerro del Emperador s/n, 45002 (Toledo) **Tel** *925 22 18 50* **Fax** *925 22 51 66* **Rooms** *77*

The terrace of this graceful, stone-built parador, which is located on the brow of a hill overlooking the city, offers a spectacular view of Toledo. The hotel is popular with sightseers and photographers, so book well in advance. It is currently undergoing refurbishment work but will remain open. **www.parador.es**

TRAGACETE Hotel El Gamo   🗐 🍴 🗐   €
C/ Fernando Royuela s/n, 16150 (Cuenca) **Tel** *969 28 90 11* **Fax** *969 28 92 28* **Rooms** *39*

A good-value hostal in a peaceful village, among the hills and woods in the Serranía de Cuenca, near the Río Cueryo's source. The bedrooms are simply furnished, but more than adequate. The hotel is ideally located for hiking, mountain biking and other active pursuits. The restaurant serves generous portions of local cuisine. **www.elgamo.org**

UCLÉS Casa Palacio Fernández Contreras   🍴 🏊 🗐   €€
C/ Angustias 2, 16450 (Cuenca) **Tel** *969 13 50 65* **Fax** *969 13 50 11* **Rooms** *7*

This historic mansion, built in 1546 in the centre of the beautiful town of Uclés, has been transformed into an intimate and stylish hotel. Great care has been taken with the decor, which presents a perfect blend of original details and contemporary furnishings. **www.lacasapalacio.com**

VALDEPEÑAS Hotel Central   🗐 🍴   €
C/ Capitán Fillol 4, 13300 (Ciudad Real) **Tel** *926 31 33 88* **Fax** *926 31 35 09* **Rooms** *25*

A modest but reliable hotel in the centre of Castilla-La Mancha's largest wine-producing town. This modern establishment is tucked behind a historic façade, and makes a good base for touring the local bodegas. The rooms are simply yet comfortably decorated, with amenities such as 24-hour room service. **www.hotelcentralval.com**

VALVERDE DE LOS ARROYOS El Nido de Valverde   🍴 🗐   €€€€€
C/ Escuelas 1, 19224 (Guadalajara) **Tel/Fax** *949 85 42 21* **Rooms** *3*

This exceptional little hotel is set in a storybook village of black slate-roofed houses in the northernmost tip of Guadalajara, and has just three rooms. The owners of this stone-built cottage offer creative, home-cooked meals – dinner and breakfast are included. A magical and unforgettable spot. **www.nidodevalverde.com**

VILLANUEVA DE LOS INFANTES Hospederia Real de Quevedo   🍴 P 📺 🗐   €
C/ Frailes 1, 13320 (Ciudad Real) **Tel** *926 36 17 88* **Fax** *926 36 17 88* **Rooms** *24*

Originally a 16th-century Dominican convent, this appealing country inn has traditional bedrooms decorated with local wrought-iron furniture and a fine patio in the former cloister. The hotel is named after Francisco de Quevedo, a famous 17th-century Spanish author, who died here in 1645. **www.hosteriasreales.com**

EXTREMADURA

ALMENDRAL Monasterio de Rocamador   ♿ 🍴 🏊 🎿 🗐   €€€€
Ctra Badajoz-Huelva km 41, 06171 (Badajoz) **Tel** *924 48 90 00* **Fax** *924 48 90 01* **Rooms** *30*

An enchanting country hotel, in a restored former monastery, built in honey-coloured stone. The rooms at this stylish, romantic retreat retain many of their original details, and are beautifully furnished in a mixture of contemporary and traditional styles. Most have their own fireplaces, and all enjoy breathtaking views. **www.rocamador.com**

BADAJOZ Río   🗐 P ♿ 🍴 🏊 🗐   €€
Av Adolfo Díaz Ambrona 13, 06006 (Badajoz) **Tel** *924 27 26 00* **Fax** *924 27 38 74* **Rooms** *101*

A large, comfortable modern hotel in the city centre, with spacious, spotlessly clean rooms decorated in bland chain-hotel style. It is geared towards business travellers, which means that rates drop impressively at weekends. The facilities include a café, airy public lounges and even a bingo hall. **www.gruporiodehoteles.com**

CÁCERES Meliá Cáceres   🗐 🍴 🗐   €€€
Plaza de San Juan 11, 10003 (Cáceres) **Tel** *927 21 58 00* **Fax** *927 21 40 70* **Rooms** *86*

This 16th-century mansion beside the city walls has been renovated by a hotel chain, though it retains the feel of a chic boutique hotel. Rooms are decorated with light, modern furnishings, and some have vaulted stone ceilings. Also showcases many antique hunting implements. Several outdoor activities can be arranged. **www.solmelia.com**

CÁCERES Parador de Cáceres   🗐 🍴 🗐   €€€
C/ Ancha 6, 10003 (Cáceres) **Tel** *927 21 17 59* **Fax** *927 21 17 29* **Rooms** *33*

A small parador in the converted 14th-century Palace of Torreorgaz. Inside a labyrinth of stairs, doors, patios and corridors unfolds. The rooms are elegantly decorated in creamy fabrics and understated floral prints. Some boast coffered ceilings. Also has extensive, well-maintained gardens. **www.parador.es**

CUACOS DE YUSTE La Casona de Valfrío   🍴 🏊 🗐   €€
Ctra Cuacos de Yuste–Valfrío km 4, 10430 (Cáceres) **Tel** *927 19 42 22* **Rooms** *6*

Relax in tranquillity in this beautifully restored country guesthouse surrounded by oak woods and cherry trees. Facilities include an outdoor swimming pool, a relaxation room offering massages, and mountain bike hire. Several outdoor activities can be arranged. The restaurant serves dinner only for guests. **www.lacasonadevalfrio.com**

Key to Price Guide *see p560* **Key to Symbols** *see back cover flap*

GUADALUPE Hospedería del Real Monasterio

€

Plaza de Juan Carlos I, 10140 (Cáceres) **Tel** *927 36 70 00* **Fax** *927 36 71 77* **Rooms** *47*

This hotel is part of the 16th-century Franciscan monastery which dominates Guadalupe. Many of the rooms, which surround the Gothic stone courtyard, were originally pharmacies, and are simply decorated with traditional, carved wooden furnishings. Also has several public lounges. Closed mid-Jan to mid-Feb. **www.monasterioguadalupe.com**

GUADALUPE Parador de Guadalupe

€€€

C/ Marqués de la Romana 12, 10140 (Cáceres) **Tel** *927 36 70 75* **Fax** *927 36 70 76* **Rooms** *41*

Located in a 16th-century hospital and convent, this beautiful parador is set in flower-filled gardens very close to the monastery. The elegant bedrooms overlook whitewashed patios full of citrus trees. The rooms in the annexe are larger, but those in the original building have much more character. **www.parador.es**

JARANDILLA DE LA VERA Parador de Jarandilla

€€€

Av de García Prieto 1, 10450 (Cáceres) **Tel** *927 56 01 17* **Fax** *927 56 00 88* **Rooms** *53*

This imposing 15th-century castle, where Emperor Carlos V stayed for a year, has been modernized without losing its medieval feel. The swimming pool is surrounded by olive trees and rose gardens, and there is a tennis court and children's play area. It boasts one of the region's best restaurants, along with a café-bar. **www.parador.es**

JERÉZ DE LOS CABALLEROS Los Templarios

€€

Ctra de Villanueva, 06380 (Badajoz) **Tel** *924 73 16 36* **Fax** *924 75 03 38* **Rooms** *49*

A modern hotel named after the Knights Templar, who played an important part in the history of the area. All the bedrooms have views over the valley and are decorated with contemporary furnishings. A wide terrace surrounds the pool. The friendly staff can arrange biking and horse riding excursions. **www.hotellostemplarios.net**

LOSAR DE LA VERA Antigua Casa del Heno

€

Finca Valdepimienta, 10460 (Cáceres) **Tel** *927 19 80 77* **Rooms** *7*

A farmhouse surrounded by oak trees and meadows in a beautiful setting near the Sierra de Gredos. Offers B&B, and is popular during spring when the cherry trees bloom. The bedrooms are simply decorated, and the old stone walls and wooden beams add a rustic charm. Dinner is provided on request. **www.antiguacasadelheno.com**

LOSAR DE LA VERA Hostería Fontivieja

€

C/ Mártires 11, 10460 (Cáceres) **Tel** *927 57 01 08* **Fax** *927 57 01 08* **Rooms** *16*

A small, family-run hotel in a peaceful olive grove outside the town. Built in the traditional style, it offers rooms in the main building, as well as luxurious suites in the bungalows scattered in the gardens. All are comfortable and decorated with locally made furniture. The amenities are excellent. **www.hosteriafontivieja.com**

MALPARTIDA DE PLASENCIA Cañada Real

€€

Ctra Ex-108 km 42, 10680 (Cáceres) **Tel** *927 45 94 07* **Fax** *927 45 94 34* **Rooms** *61*

This modern hotel is located within easy distance of Plasencia and nearby nature reserves. The bedrooms are comfortable and spacious, and there are three suites with Jacuzzis. All are decorated with floral prints and traditional furniture. A children's play area and board games are also available, as well as a library. **www.hotelcreal.es**

MÉRIDA Meliá Mérida Boutique Hotel

€€

Plaza España 19, 06800 (Badajoz) **Tel** *924 38 38 00* **Fax** *924 38 38 01* **Rooms** *76*

One of the newest hotels in the Meliá chain, this charming retreat is housed in a pair of elegant historic palaces. Illustrious former guests include three Spanish monarchs. The hotel maintains a regal atmosphere with a profusion of antiques and original architectural details. All modern conveniences are available. **www.meliamerida.solmelia.com**

MÉRIDA Parador de Mérida

€€€

Plaza de la Constitución 3, 06800 (Badajoz) **Tel** *924 31 38 00* **Fax** *924 31 92 08* **Rooms** *82*

A converted, 17th-century Baroque convent, which was built on the ruins of an ancient Roman temple. Roman columns, inscriptions in Arabic and Visigothic capitals have been preserved and incorporated into the wonderful "Garden of Antiquities". Also arranges activities such as hunting, golf, fishing and tennis. **www.parador.es**

MÉRIDA Velada Mérida

€€€

Av Reina Sofia s/n, 06800 (Badajoz) **Tel** *924 31 51 10* **Fax** *924 31 15 52* **Rooms** *99*

Conveniently located near the cultural centre of Mérida, this hotel has good transport links to the rest of the city. Its modern design draws inspiration from classical temples. The rooms are large, traditionally decorated and have every modern convenience. The restaurant offers regional cuisine. **www.veladahoteles.com**

PLASENCIA Alfonso VIII

€€€

Av Alfonso VIII 32, 10600 (Cáceres) **Tel** *927 41 02 50* **Fax** *927 41 80 42* **Rooms** *55*

A modern hotel, centrally located near the Parque de la Isla. Offers all the expected four-star facilities. The rooms are large and bright, with contemporary furnishings, and the staff is attentive. The hotel itself is ideally situated for exploring this beautiful, rural region. **www.hotelalfonsoviii.com**

TRUJILLO Mesón La Cadena

€

Plaza Mayor 8, 10200 (Cáceres) **Tel** *927 32 14 63* **Fax** *927 32 31 16* **Rooms** *9*

This restaurant-with-rooms, in an attractive granite house on the main square, is a good budget option. The bedrooms, decorated with locally-made textiles, are on the second floor, and the best offer spectacular views over Trujillo's beautiful Plaza Mayor. The eatery on the ground floor is a classic in the city, serving regional specialities.

TRUJILLO Parador de Trujillo
€€€

C/ Santa Beatriz de Silva 1, 10200 (Cáceres) **Tel** *927 32 13 50* **Fax** *927 32 13 66* **Rooms** *50*

This charming parador and former chapel, where breakfast is now served, incorporates parts of a 16th-century convent. The hotel is within the spellbinding old city of Trujillo, but located on a quiet street away from the noise. The elegant rooms look out onto a series of lovely patios, filled with orange trees. **www.parador.es**

ZAFRA Huerta Honda
€€

Av López Asme 30, 06300 (Badajoz) **Tel** *924 55 41 00* **Fax** *924 55 25 04* **Rooms** *48*

Many regular guests feel that the accommodation at this hotel is as good as that at the parador next door. Set around patios with fountains and flowers, the hotel's construction is stylish, yet traditional. The chic bedrooms are decorated in a contemporary style and are extremely comfortable. Some have a Jacuzzi. **www.hotelhuertahonda.com**

ZAFRA Parador de Zafra
€€€

Pl del Corazón de María 7, 06300 (Badajoz) **Tel** *924 55 45 40* **Fax** *924 55 10 18* **Rooms** *51*

This fairytale castle, with its round towers, was built in the 15th century on the ruins of a Moorish fortress. A beautiful staircase leads from the courtyard, with an arcaded gallery, to the bedrooms. These are regally fitted with traditional furnishings, which evoke the ducal palace of former times. It is set in elegant gardens. **www.parador.es**

SEVILLE

EL ARENAL Hotel Adriano
€€

C/ Adriano 12, 41001 **Tel** *954 29 38 00* **Fax** *954 22 89 46* **Rooms** *34*   **Map** *3 B2*

A recently renovated hotel in an excellent location for sightseeing, close to Plaza de Toros, the cathedral and the riverfront, as well as Giralda and Real Alcázar. The spacious, comfortable rooms have modern facilities. Some have courtyard views and others have balconies overlooking the street. **www.adrianohotel.com**

EL ARENAL NH Plaza de Armas
€€

C/ Marqués de Paradas, 41001 **Tel** *954 90 19 92* **Fax** *954 90 18 32* **Rooms** *262*   **Map** *1 B5*

A reliable, modern chain hotel built in 1992 and refurbished in 1999 in a functional, minimalist style. Offers excellent facilities for business travellers, and tourists can benefit from the hotel's hefty weekend discounts. This city-centre hotel is handily located for sightseeing. **www.nh-hotels.com**

EL ARENAL Simón
€€

C/ García de Vinuesa 19, 41001 **Tel** *954 22 66 60* **Fax** *954 56 22 41* **Rooms** *29*   **Map** *3 B2*

A central hotel in an 18th-century mansion built around a pretty patio planted with ferns and covered with local *azulejos* (tiles). The public areas are tiled and hung with chandeliers, but the bedrooms are simpler and vary in size and quality. A buffet breakfast is available. The hotel is very popular, so book early. **www.hotelsimonsevilla.com**

EL ARENAL Petit Palace Marques Santa Ana
€€€

C/ Jimios 9–11, 41001 **Tel** *954 22 18 12* **Fax** *954 22 89 93* **Rooms** *57*   **Map** *3 B1*

In a quiet street close to the cathedral, this mid-19th century building has been spectacularly renovated to offer a luxurious oasis in the heart of the city. The decor is sleek and modern, and the rooms are equipped with hi-tech features, such as hydro-showers, Internet access and flat-screen TVs. **www.hotelmarquessantaana.com**

EL ARENAL Vincci La Rabida
€€€

C/ Castelar 24, 41001 **Tel** *954 50 12 80* **Fax** *954 21 66 00* **Rooms** *81*   **Map** *3 B1*

Located in El Arenal district, close to shops, restaurants and a bullring, this 18th-century palace was restored and opened as a four-star hotel in 2003. The guestrooms combine warm, earthy tones with dark furnishings and wrought-iron beds. Some rooms have views of the central courtyard. **www.vinccihoteles.com**

SANTA CRUZ Alcántara
€€

C/ Ximenez de Enciso 28, 41004 **Tel** *954 50 05 95* **Fax** *954 50 06 04* **Rooms** *21*   **Map** *6 E4*

This 18th-century mansion can be accessed through the old coach entrance, which takes guests into a modern, welcoming hotel. The rooms are simple, with stripped pine floors and painted headboards, but comfortable and clean. They vary in size and some are suitable for families. **www.hotelalcantara.net**

SANTA CRUZ Murillo
€€

C/ Lope de Rueda 7 & 9, 41004 **Tel** *954 21 60 95* **Fax** *954 21 96 16* **Rooms** *57*   **Map** *4 D2*

A pleasant, reasonably-priced hotel in an ochre-and-white building off Plaza Alfaro, a short walk from the cathedral. The public areas are decorated with antiques, hand-carved furniture, coffered ceilings and even suits of armour. The bedrooms are plain and functional, and are located on a quiet pedestrian street. **www.hotelmurillo.com**

SANTA CRUZ Hotel Posada del Lucero
€€€

C/ Almirante Apodaca 7, 41003 **Tel** *954 50 24 80* **Fax** *954 22 54 20* **Rooms** *40*   **Map** *6 E2*

Located in the heart of Seville, this unique hotel stunningly combines traditional and modern architecture. Its minimalist interior uses dark walnut wood, white stucco and black slate, with exposed brick walls and neutral colour scheme. All rooms face the central courtyard. **www.posadadellucero.com**

Key to Price Guide *see p560* **Key to Symbols** *see back cover flap*

SANTA CRUZ La Casa del Maestro

C/ Almudena 5, 41002 **Tel** *954 50 00 07* **Fax** *954 50 00 06* **Rooms** *11*

Map *6 E2*

Once the home of celebrated flamenco guitarist Niño Ricardo, this charming yellow-and-ochre painted town house is built around a patio bursting with plants and flowers. Rooms are on the small side, but full of thoughtful touches such as a jug of iced water and chocolates placed by the bed. Has a lovely roof terrace. **www.lacasadelmaestro.com**

SANTA CRUZ Casa Numero Siete

C/ Virgenes 7, 41004 **Tel** *954 22 15 81* **Fax** *954 21 45 27* **Rooms** *7*

Map *6 E3*

One of the loveliest and most romantic hotels in Seville. This elegant guesthouse occupies a mansion and features just a handful of rooms. The decor includes a range of antiques and family heirlooms. Also has an opulent sitting room with a bar. The breakfasts here are delicious. **www.casanumero7.com**

SANTA CRUZ Las Casas del Rey de Baeza

Plaza Jesús de la Redención 2, 41003 **Tel** *954 56 14 96* **Fax** *954 56 14 41* **Rooms** *41*

Map *4 D1*

Located in a beautiful unique setting, this hotel expertly fuses the past and present. Bright, whitewashed walls blend with the ochres and reds of the courtyard, shaded by arched walkways. Indoors, cool stone flooring and natural tones lead to the rooms, where chic interiors pay tribute to modernity. **www.hospes.es**

SANTA CRUZ Alfonso XIII

C/ San Fernando 2, 41004 **Tel** *954 91 70 00* **Fax** *954 91 70 99* **Rooms** *147*

Map *3 C2*

Seville's legendary grand hotel, built in Neo-Mudéjar style as a royal guesthouse, is still fit for kings. Elegance and formal service are assured, and bedrooms are decorated with opulent furnishings. Crystal chandeliers, marble columns and palm trees adorn the public spaces. Also has a posh cocktail bar. **www.alfonsoxiii.com**

TRIANA Abba Triana Hotel

Plaza Champina s/n, 41010 **Tel** *954 28 80 00* **Rooms** *137*

Map *3 A1*

Enjoy spectacular riverfront views from the spacious rooms of this modern hotel, built in 2006 with the latest technological advances and contemporary decor. Amenities include a rooftop pool and terrace and a full breakfast buffet. Close to all public transport. **www.abbatrianahotel.com**

FURTHER AFIELD (LA MACARENA) Alcoba del Rey de Sevilla

C/ Bécquer 9, 41002 **Tel** *954 915 800* **Fax** *95 491 56 75* **Rooms** *15*

Map *2 D3*

This is a stylish little hotel, full of small details which create a romantic atmosphere. Furnishings include lovely glasswork, tiles, silk cushions, objets d'art and beds – all of which are for sale. Each of the rooms is named after a personality from the Moorish period and are elegantly decorated. **www.alcobadelrey.com**

FURTHER AFIELD (LA MACARENA) Casa Romana Hotel Boutique

C/ Trajano 15, 41003 **Tel** *954 91 51 70* **Fax** *954 37 31 91* **Rooms** *26*

Map *4 D5*

Rooms are distributed around the picturesque central courtyard, with all the comforts you would expect of a four-star hotel. All the rooms are tastefully decorated in subdued elegance while some have Jacuzzis. Website offers specials including flamenco tickets with reservations. **www.hotelcasaromana.com**

FURTHER AFIELD (SOUTH) Ciudad de Sevilla

Av Manuel Siurot 25, 41003 **Tel** *954 23 05 05* **Fax** *954 23 85 39* **Rooms** *94*

Map *4 D5*

Located in a residential neighbourhood on the outskirts of the city, this luxurious chain hotel occupies a mansion. Behind the old façade is a contemporary hotel with all modern conveniences, including business facilities, a small rooftop pool and a sun terrace. The hotel's website offers some good deals. **www.ac-hoteles.com**

ANDALUSIA

ALCALÁ DE GUADAIRA Hacienda La Boticaria Hotel

Ctra Alcalá–Utrera km 2, 41500 (Sevilla) **Tel** *955 69 88 20* **Fax** *955 69 87 55* **Rooms** *120*

In the village of Alacalá de Guadaira, just 20 km (13 miles) from Seville, this elegant hotel is surrounded by lush gardens with an artificial lake, large courtyards and an outdoor pool. The rooms are well-equipped and facilities include an indoor pool, spa, golf course and two restaurants. **www.laboticaria-hotel.com**

ALMERÍA AM Torreluz

Plaza Flores 5, 04001 (Almería) **Tel** *950 23 49 99* **Fax** *950 23 47 09* **Rooms** *109*

Smart and modern, this is the grandest of the Torreluz group of hotels, all sited in the centre of Almería. A grand spiral staircase sweeps up to bedrooms with every imaginable amenity, including interactive TVs. There is also a rooftop pool and a little sun terrace with loungers. The nearby sister hotels are cheaper. **www.amhoteles.com**

ARACENA Sierra de Aracena

Gran Vía 21, 21200 (Huelva) **Tel** *959 12 61 75* **Fax** *959 12 62 18* **Rooms** *43*

This quiet hotel is in the centre of the attractive town of Aracena. Although it is a modern building, the design integrates pretty Arabic-style details. The rooms are simply furnished, and some have views of the town's castle. Staff can arrange outdoor activities such as hiking, rafting, and horse riding. **www.hsierraaracena.es**

ARACENA Finca Buen Vino   €€€

Los Marines, 21293 (Huelva) **Tel** *959 12 40 34* **Fax** *959 50 10 29* **Rooms** *4*

A wonderful guesthouse located in an elegant villa on a hilltop surrounded by chestnut and cork oak trees. The owners grow their own organic produce – used for breakfasts, afternoon teas and cordon bleu cuisine served at dinner (guests only). Stay in the villa, or rent a cottage in the grounds. **www.fincabuenvino.com**

ARCOS DE LA FRONTERA Casa Grande   €

C/ Maldonado 10, 11630 (Cádiz) **Tel** *956 70 39 30* **Fax** *956 71 70 95* **Rooms** *7*

A charming little hotel set in a whitewashed 18th-century mansion, which still bears the escutcheon of its original owner. Each of the originally decorated rooms is full of character. Family-run, it is warm, intimate and full of details such as home-made marmalade for breakfast. Offers splendid views from the roof terrace. **www.lacasagrande.net**

ARCOS DE LA FRONTERA Parador de Arcos de Frontera   €€€

Plaza del Cabildo s/n, 11630 (Cádiz) **Tel** *956 70 05 00* **Fax** *956 70 11 16* **Rooms** *24*

Formerly a magistrate's house, this mansion perched on a cliff above the old city is now a smart parador. A huge terrace offers great views of ancient spires and rooftops below, and the rooms are set around a series of beautifully tiled patios with wells and fountains. Rooms are plush and comfortable and some have Jacuzzis. **www.parador.es**

AYAMONTE Vincci Selección Canela Golf   €€

Golf Norte s/n, Campo de Golf Isla Canela, 21409 (Huelva) **Tel** *959 47 78 30* **Fax** *959 47 78 31* **Rooms** *58*

In the heart of Isla Canela golf course and close to the beach, this small hotel offers luxury in a charming Andalusian style. The spacious rooms are sleek and modern, and all have a terrace or balcony. Facilities include a fitness centre, spa, tennis courts and preferential access to, and rates on, green fees at three golf courses. **www.vinccihoteles.com**

BAEZA Hotel Fuentenueva   €€

Calle del Carmen 15, 23440 (Jaén) **Tel** *953 74 31 00* **Fax** *953 74 32 00* **Rooms** *13*

Located in to a 19th-century house, this hotel offers all the mod-con facilities. These include a library, cafeteria, conference hall, a Japanese Garden and wireless Internet. Rooms boast hydromassage baths and sleek modern decor. **www.fuentenueva.com**

CAÑOS DE MECA La Breña   €€

Av Trafalgar 4, 11160 (Cádiz) **Tel** *956 43 73 68* **Fax** *956 43 73 68* **Rooms** *7*

The beaches of the Costa de la Luz are some of the most beautiful and unspoilt in Spain. This charming beachside hotel is painted a crisp blue and white, and the rooms and suites are simple and spacious. Most offer sea views. The excellent restaurant has a modern Andalusian menu, and a shady terrace. Closed mid–Oct—mid–Mar. **www.hotelbrena.com**

CARMONA Casa de Carmona   €€€€

Plaza de Lasso 1, 41410 (Sevilla) **Tel** *954 19 10 00* **Fax** *954 19 01 89* **Rooms** *34*

A 16th-century palace, decorated in a blend of contemporary and period styles, has been converted into a hotel which has featured in numerous fashion magazines. The luxurious rooms and suites are filled with art and opulent furniture, and there is a superb restaurant. A good base for exploring Seville province. **www.casadecarmona.com**

CARMONA Parador de Carmona   €€€€

C/ Alcázar, 41410 (Sevilla) **Tel** *954 19 10 00* **Fax** *954 14 17 12* **Rooms** *63*

This magnificent clifftop parador was built as a fortress by the Moors and became the palace of the Christian king, Pedro the Cruel. It is hung with tapestries and scattered with antiques, and the plush rooms have superb views of the countryside. There is a huge outdoor pool, and one of the best parador restaurants. **www.parador.es**

CASTELLAR DE LA FRONTERA Casa Convento La Almoraima   €€

Finca La Almoraima, 11350 (Cádiz) **Tel** *956 69 30 02* **Fax** *956 69 32 14* **Rooms** *23*

Surrounded by a protected forest of Mediterranean cork trees, this stunning mansion and former convent is now a tranquil rural hotel. The cloisters are now a flower-filled patio, and the public areas are decorated with antiques. The rooms are simple, and the hotel can arrange tours of the estate and the region. **www.la-almoraima.com**

CAZALLA DE LA SIERRA Las Navezuelas   €

Ctra Cazalla-Ed Pedroso, 41370 (Sevilla) **Tel** *954 88 47 64* **Fax** *954 88 45 94* **Rooms** *10*

The spacious rooms in this family-run farmhouse are furnished with handworked fabrics. Staying here gives visitors a rare opportunity to experience living in an authentic Andalusian *cortijo* (farmstead). The rooms look out over vast orchards of olive trees and cork oaks, and home-cooked meals are served. **www.lasnavezuelas.com**

CAZALLA DE LA SIERRA Hospedería La Cartuja   €€

Ctra Cazalla-Constantina km 2.5, 41370 (Sevilla) **Tel** *954 88 45 16* **Fax** *954 88 47 07* **Rooms** *12*

An old monastery has been converted into a charming refuge for artists by its crusading owner. Painters, sculptors and musicians sometimes offer their art in exchange for their stay, and there is a gallery exhibiting work by resident artists, which can be purchased. Choose from rooms, suites or a cottage. **www.cartujadecazalla.com**

CAZORLA Molino de la Farraga   €

Camino de la Hoz s/n, 23470 (Jaén) **Tel** *953 72 12 49* **Fax** *953 72 12 49* **Rooms** *9*

A recently-renovated, 200-year-old mill on the fringes of the lovely rural village of Cazorla, this is perfect for anyone seeking tranquility. Shrouded by abundant greenery, the whitewashed mill is surrounded by rambling gardens, and the rooms are simple but very pretty. They also have an annexe. Closed 10 Dec–1 Mar. **www.molinolafarraga.com**

CAZORLA Parador de Cazorla ⬛🏔 €€€

Sierra de Cazorla, 23470 (Jaén) **Tel** *953 72 70 75* **Fax** *953 72 70 77* **Rooms** *34*

The forests and mountains of the Sierra de Cazorla, a major Andalusian nature reserve, are the superb setting for this parador. It is modern, but has been designed with the rural setting in mind. Nestled into the side of the hill, it offers fine views from the well-equipped bedrooms. The restaurant serves local game in season. **www.parador.es**

COLMENAR Casa Rural Ahora ⬛📧 €

C/ Lepanto 40, Bda El Colmenar, Cortes de la Frontera, 29390 (Málaga) **Tel/Fax** *952 15 30 46* **Rooms** *7*

A relaxed rural retreat located in a quiet, picturesque valley, close to a river. Ahora is a small, comfortable villa with rustic decor and a natural therapy centre offering a range of therapies, including clay treatments, massages, saunas and Turkish baths. Weekend specials combine therapies with meals in the restaurant. **www.ahoraya.es**

CÓRDOBA Maestre 🔲⬛📧 €

C/ Romero Barros 4–6, 14003 (Córdoba) **Tel** *957 47 24 10* **Fax** *957 47 53 95* **Rooms** *26*

Near the Mezquita in the centre of Córdoba, this is a simple hotel with basic amenities. It is set around a series of pretty Andalusian patios with colourful tiles, fountains and trailing plants, and is perfectly placed for sightseeing. They offer both rooms and self-catering apartments. Private underground parking. **www.hotelmaestre.com**

CÓRDOBA Casa de los Azulejos ⬛📧 €€

C/ Fernando Colón 5, 14002 (Córdoba) **Tel** *957 47 00 00* **Fax** *957 47 54 96* **Rooms** *8*

The "House of the Tiles" is an enchanting 17th-century mansion set around a typical patio with exquisite local tiles, pretty wrought iron and lush greenery. The pretty rooms are cool and modern, with extras such as Internet. A terrific restaurant offers a fusion of Andalusian and South American cuisine. **www.casadelosazulejos.com**

CÓRDOBA Hospes Palacio del Bailío 🔲⬛🆓📧🔅📧 €€€€

Ramírez de las Casas Deza, 10-12 14001 (Córdoba) **Tel** *957 49 89 93* **Fax** *957 49 89 94* **Rooms** *53*

Situated in the historic centre of the city, this hotel consists of converted granaries, coach-houses and stables, surrounded by beautiful gardens and courtyards, which have been decorated in a stylish fusion of rustic stone walls and modern furnishings. There is a spa with full services and indoor and outdoor pools. **www.hospes.es**

CÓRDOBA Maciá Alfaros 🔲⬛📧📧 €€€€

C/ Alfaros 18, 14001 (Córdoba) **Tel** *957 49 19 20* **Fax** *957 49 22 10* **Rooms** *133*

In a busy street, but soundproofed against traffic noise, the Alfaros is a sleek contemporary hotel built around three courtyards in Neo-Mudéjar style. One of the marble courtyards contains an elegant swimming pool. Geared towards business travellers, it offers good facilities including Wi-Fi. Rooms and suites are comfortable. **www.maciahoteles.com**

EL ROCÍO Hotel Toruño ⬛📧 €

Plaza Acebuchal 22, 21750 (Huelva) **Tel** *959 44 23 23* **Fax** *959 44 23 38* **Rooms** *30*

A charming whitewashed villa just a short distance from the hermitage containing the image of the virgin of El Rocío. It is set on the fringes of the Doñana National Park *(see pp464–5)*, one of the important wetlands and wildlife refuges in Europe. Popular with bird-watchers. Prices double during the El Rocío pilgrimage. **www.toruno.es**

GERENA Hotel Cortijo el Esparragal ⬛🆓📧📧 €€

Autovía A66 Sevilla–Merida, exit 795, 41860 (Sevilla) **Tel** *955 78 27 02* **Fax** *955 78 27 83* **Rooms** *21*

Situated within beautiful grounds on a working farm, this hotel in a converted 17th-century farmhouse offers relaxation in an historical setting. The rooms have all the comforts of a modern hotel and are decorated with antiques. Activities include horseriding, fishing and mountain biking. Excellent restaurant. **www.elesparragal.com**

GIBRALTAR The Rock 🔲⬛📧📧 €€€€€

3 Europa Road, **Tel** *956 77 30 00* **Fax** *956 77 35 13* **Rooms** *104*

Built in 1932 by the Marquess of Bute, Gibraltar's first five-star hotel still trades on its old-fashioned colonial style and service. Perched on the cliff-side, high above the town and harbour, it offers all imaginable amenities from a hair and beauty centre to a casino. Popular with both business travellers and tourists. **www.rockhotelgibraltar.com**

GRANADA Pensión Landázuri 📧⬛ €

Cuesta de Gomérez 24, 18009 (Granada) **Tel** *958 22 14 06* **Rooms** *15*

Perhaps the nicest budget option in Granada, this tiled little pension has two terraces offering great city views. All the rooms are simple, but surprisingly spacious, and those on the top floor (book in advance) enjoy magical views of the Alhambra. Not all rooms have *en suite* facilities, but those without are extremely cheap. **www.pensionlandazuri.com**

GRANADA Posada Pilar del Toro 🔲📧🆓📧 €€

C/ Elvira 25, 18010 (Granada) **Tel** *958 22 73 33* **Fax** *958 21 62 18* **Rooms** *15*

Rustic charm and a historic ambience are combined with modern comforts in this welcoming hotel which is located close to Albaicin, Plaza Nueva and the cathedral. Rooms have hydromassage showers and the internet, and there is an attractive central courtyard where guests can relax. **www.posadapilardeltoro.com**

GRANADA El Ladron de Agua 🔲🆓⬛📧 €€€

Carrera del Darro 13, 18010 (Granada) **Tel** *958 21 50 40* **Fax** *958 22 43 45* **Rooms** *15*

This 16th-century mansion was opened as a hotel in 2004. Each room is tastefully decorated with features such as terracotta floors, oriental rugs and wood-beamed ceilings. Eight of the rooms have views of the Alhambra. There is also a lovely inner courtyard and reading room. **www.ladrondeagua.com**

GRANADA Parador de Granada   🗺🍴🗐   €€€€€
C/ Real de la Alhambra, 18009 (Granada) **Tel** *958 22 14 40* **Fax** *958 22 22 64* **Rooms** *36*

This parador in the jasmine-scented gardens of the Alhambra was once a convent, and the cloister has been transformed into a tree-filled oasis filled with flowers. From the elegant bedrooms, you can hear the fountains of the Generalife and enjoy blissful views of the city and the ancient palace. Book well in advance. **www.parador.es**

JAÉN Parador de Jaén   🗺🍴🏊🗐   €€€
Ctra Sta Catalina, 23001 (Jaén) **Tel** *953 23 00 00* **Fax** *953 23 09 30* **Rooms** *45*

Looming massively from the hills above Jaén, this medieval castle is now a pretty parador which evokes the Middle Ages with its sturdy walls and crenellated battlements. There are great views across the Sierra Morena. Dine on local fare in the restaurant, which retains its Arabic detailing. An excellent base for hiking. **www.parador.es**

LA HERRADURA Hotel La Tartana   ♿🍴   €€
Urbanización San Nicolas, 18697 (Granada) **Tel** *958 64 05 35* **Fax** *958 64 05 35* **Rooms** *7*

In a quiet beachside village, this is the only hotel on the Costa Tropical in true Andalusian style, with all the rooms situated around a central courtyard and fountain. The best of traditional architecture is combined with modern facilities in spacious and airy rooms. Restaurant and bar with terrace overlooking the sea. **www.hotellatartana.com**

LAS CABEZAS Hotel Cortijo Soto Real   🗺🍴🏊🎾🗐   €€€€€
Ctra Las Cabezas-Villamartin km 13, 41730 (Sevilla) **Tel** *955 86 92 00* **Fax** *955 86 92 02* **Rooms** *25*

A luxury retreat, this exquisite country mansion is one of the finest hotels in Andalusia. You can explore the extensive grounds in a horse and carriage, indulge in outdoor activities, including hunting or bike excursions, or simply laze by the pool. The elegant rooms and suites are ultra-stylish, and there is a fine restaurant. **www.hotelcortijosotoreal.com**

LOJA La Bobadilla   🗺🍴🏊🎠🎾🗐   €€€€€
Finca La Bobadilla, 18300 (Granada) **Tel** *958 32 18 61* **Fax** *958 32 18 10* **Rooms** *62*

Looking rather like a labyrinthine Andalusian village surrounded by its own vast estate, this is one of the most luxurious hotels in Europe. Each of the rooms and suites is different, but all are fitted with every imaginable amenity. There is a lake-size pool, and guests can take part in a wide range of activities. **www.barcelolabobadilla.com**

MÁLAGA Don Curro   🗺🍴🗐   €€
C/ Sancha de Lara 7, 29015 (Málaga) **Tel** *952 22 72 00* **Fax** *952 21 59 46* **Rooms** *118*

The exterior may not be attractive, but this hotel's interior is charming and comfortable, with a welcoming ambience. Rooms are tastefully furnished with dark wood and marble, and they offer some thoughtful extras, including a valet parking service. Houses a simple bar-restaurant and is popular with business travellers. **www.hoteldoncurro.com**

MARBELLA El Fuerte   🗺🍴🏊🎾🗐   €€€
Av El Fuerte, 29600 (Málaga) **Tel** *952 92 00 00* **Fax** *952 82 44 11* **Rooms** *263*

El Fuerte was the first purpose-built hotel in Marbella and is still one of the best. It is unmissable – a big pink building surrounded by tropical gardens. Some rooms have mountain views but the best look out to sea. Next to the beach-front, it has a heated, glassed-in pool, an outdoor pool and a health and beauty centre. **www.fuertehoteles.com**

MARBELLA Marbella Club Hotel   🗺🍴🏊🎾🗐   €€€€€
Blvr Principe von Hohenlohe, 29600 (Málaga) **Tel** *952 82 22 11* **Fax** *952 82 98 84* **Rooms** *137*

Built for a prince in the 1950s, this is now an ultra-luxurious beachside complex with two pools (one indoors) and extensive subtropical gardens. Located in the Golden Mile (between Marbella and Puerto Banus), it includes a world-class golf course and a spa. The rooms, suites and villas have private heated pools. **www.marbellaclub.com**

MAZAGÓN Parador de Mazagón   🗺🍴🏊🎾🗐   €€€
Ctra San Juan del Puerto, A Matalascañas km 30, 21130 (Huelva) **Tel** *959 53 63 00* **Fax** *959 53 62 28* **Rooms** *63*

A modern parador on the Huelva coast with a perfect location right on the seafront. Draped in ivy and surrounded by gardens, it has bright, modern rooms and is well-located for visiting the wildlife reserve of Doñana National Park. Offers outdoor sports and activities such as cycling, horse riding, golf, and windsurfing. **www.parador.es**

MECINA BOMBARÓN Casas Rurales Benarum   🍴🏊🎠   €
C/ Casas Blancas 1, 18450 (Granada) **Tel** *958 85 11 49* **Rooms** *12*

Nestled in the mountain town of Mecina Bombarón, these rustic yet elegant cabins for up to five people are luxurious and fully equipped with a kitchen, living room with fireplace, TV and DVD player, laundry facilities and full bathroom. Pool and spa in grounds, and outdoor activities available. Minimum seven night stay in high season. **www.benarum.com**

MIJAS Club Puerta del Sol   🗺🍴🏊🎠🎾🗐   €
Ctra Fuengirola-Mijas km 4, 29650 (Málaga) **Tel** *952 48 64 00* **Fax** *952 48 54 62* **Rooms** *130*

A whitewashed modern hotel complex in the foothills of the Sierra de Mijas offering spacious rooms. There are impressive views of Fuengirola and the coast. Facilities include tennis courts, a gym, indoor and outdoor pools and a host of other sports amenities. It is child friendly, and the beaches are nearby. **www.hotelclubpuertadelsol.com**

MOJÁCAR Mamabel's   🍴🗐   €
C/ Embajadores 5, 04638 (Almeria) **Tel** *950 47 24 48* **Fax** *950 47 24 48* **Rooms** *9*

Mamabel's restaurant has long been an institution in Mojácar, and the addition of guestrooms (and a suite) has given it an added bonus. The rooms are simple and small, but they are decorated with traditional furnishings and Moorish-style arches. The best rooms have sea views, and the suite contains a Jacuzzi. **www.mamabels.com**

MOJÁCAR Parador de Mojácar
Playa de Mojácar s/n, 04638 (Almería) **Tel** *950 47 82 50* **Fax** *950 47 81 83* **Rooms** *98*

The architecture of this purpose-built parador on the dry sunny coast of Almería echoes that of the dazzling white cube houses in nearby Mojácar. It has excellent facilities for all manner of water sports. The light, airy bedrooms have terraces with wonderful sea views, and the restaurant offers local specialities. **www.parador.es**

MONACHIL Hotel Vincci Rumaykiyya
Urbanización Sol y Nieve, 18196 (Granada) **Tel** *958 48 25 08* **Fax** *958 48 00 32* **Rooms** *57*

In the heart of the Sierra Nevada ski area, this luxurious hotel offers comfortable, spacious rooms with typically alpine decoration. All rooms have free Internet access, a safe, mini-bar and bathrobes. Ski lockers are provided and a chairlift starts at the door of the hotel. Restaurant and English pub. Closed May–Nov. **www.vinccihoteles.com**

MOTRIL Casa de los Bates
Ctra Nacional 340 km 329.5, 18600 (Granada) **Tel** *958 34 94 95* **Fax** *958 83 41 31* **Rooms** *4*

A country villa set in its own gardens, with stunning views of the sea, the mountains and the castle of Salobreña. It is a chic retreat with an aristocratic ambience – antiques, family portraits and even a grand piano. The rooms are furnished in soothing pastel tones, and for breakfast you can enjoy fresh tropical juices. **www.casadelosbates.com**

NIGUELAS Alquería de los Lentos
Camino de los Molinos s/n, 18657 (Granada) **Tel** *958 77 78 50* **Fax** *958 77 78 48* **Rooms** *16*

This hotel offers a sumptuous retreat, convenient to Las Alpujarras, Sierra Nevada and Granada. All rooms are suites and are well-appointed and pleasantly decorated. Romantics can check out the "Corral de la Luna" (stable of the moon), which provides a perfect mixture of intimacy and warmth. **www.loslentoshotel.com**

NÉRJA Hostal Miguel
C/ Almirante Ferrándiz 31, 29780 (Málaga) **Tel & Fax** *952 52 15 23* **Rooms** *9*

This friendly, eclectic hostal with Moroccan touches first opened in the 1960s. The rooms are decorated in subdued styles and all have ceiling fans, mini-fridges and airy balconies. Breakfast can be taken on the rooftop terrace, and the lounge has a selection of books and magazines. **www.hostalmiguel.com**

ORGIVA Taray
Ctra Tablate-Albuñol km 18, 18400 (Granada) **Tel** *958 78 45 25* **Fax** *958 78 45 31* **Rooms** *15*

A whitewashed rural hotel set in lovely gardens, with olive groves and orange trees. The bedrooms are large enough to be small apartments, but they have even larger suites. A good base for walking or pursuing outdoor activities such as horse riding. The hotel is also equipped for disabled visitors, with specially adapted rooms. **www.hoteltaray.com**

PALMA DEL RÍO Hospedería de San Francisco
Av de Pío XII 35, 14700 (Córdoba) **Tel** *957 71 01 83* **Fax** *957 71 02 36* **Rooms** *35*

Built in the 15th century as a Franciscan monastery and located in the centre of the pretty country town of Palma del Río. This hotel has some bedrooms in former monks' cells, furnished with hand-painted basins and bedcovers woven by nuns. The kitchen uses its own organic produce and meals are served in the old refectory. **www.casasypalacios.com**

PECHINA Balneario de Sierra Alhamilla
Pechina, 04359 (Almería) **Tel** *950 31 74 13* **Fax** *950 31 75 51* **Rooms** *19*

This spa hotel in the peaceful hills of the Sierra de Alhamilla has been beautifully restored to its 18th-century glory. The thermal waters have long been known for their healing properties – the Romans and then the Arabs built spas on this spot. Treatments include soaking in an outdoor thermal pool with underwater jets, mudpacks and massages.

PRADO DEL REY Cortijo Huerta Dorotea
Ctra Vilamartín-Ubrique km 12, 11660 (Cádiz) **Tel** *956 72 42 91* **Fax** *956 72 42 89* **Rooms** *25*

On a hill surrounded by olive trees, near the white town of Prado del Rey, sits this tranquil rural hotel. Guests can choose from simply decorated rooms to cosy log cabins. There are large gardens with lakes, paths and swimming pools, and plenty of outdoor activities are available. Good regional restaurant. **www.huertadorotea.com**

RONDA Husa Reina Victoria
C/ Doctor Fleming 25, 29400 (Málaga) **Tel** *952 87 12 40* **Fax** *952 87 10 75* **Rooms** *89*

The Reina Victoria, perched on the edge of the famous gorge which divides Ronda, was built in 1906. It remains the grand dame of Ronda's hotels, although its facilities have been eclipsed by modern upstarts. Rooms are traditionally decorated, and the restaurant offers more panoramic views. **www.husa.es**

RONDA Parador de Ronda
Plaza España, 29400 (Málaga) **Tel** *952 87 75 00* **Fax** *952 87 81 88* **Rooms** *78*

Edging up to Ronda's famous cliff, yet close to the town centre, this modern, purpose-built parador has stunning views over the gorge, especially from the top-floor suites. The bedrooms are full of light and stylishly decorated. The parador is surrounded by huge gardens with an outdoor pool right on the cliff edge. **www.parador.es**

ROTA Hotel Playa de la Luz
Avda de la Diputación s/n, 11520 (Cádiz) **Tel** *956 81 05 00* **Fax** *956 81 06 06* **Rooms** *235*

A beautiful two-storey Andalusian hotel on a secluded beach in the quaint village of Rota, near Puerto de Santa María and Jerez. The rooms offer modern, elegant decor, and most have a large terrace or balcony. Junior suites provide the ultimate luxury, being directly on the beach. **www.hotelplayadelaluz.com**

SAN JOSÉ Cortijo El Sotillo ▮▮▮▮ €€€

Ctra San José s/n, 04118 (Almería) **Tel** *950 61 11 00* **Fax** *950 61 11 05* **Rooms** *20*

An elegant 18th-century farmhouse set in the beautiful countryside of the natural parks of Cabo de Gata and Níjar. The perfect place for a walking holiday, with hikes into the volcanic hills, with the beaches of this stunning stretch of coastline just a short drive away. The restaurant uses produce from the estate. Disabled access. **www.cortijoelsotillo.com**

SANLÚCAR DE BARRAMEDA Los Helechos ▮▮▮ €€

Plaza Madre de Diós 9, 11540 (Cádiz) **Tel** *956 36 13 49* **Fax** *956 36 96 50* **Rooms** *54*

Decorated with tiles and potted plants, Los Helechos is a delightful, relaxing seaside hotel. Rooms are light, spacious and prettily, if simply, decorated, and are set around a plant-filled courtyard. The friendly staff are very informative and can arrange visits to the nearby Doñana National Park. **www.hotelloshelechos.com**

SANLÚCAR LA MAYOR Hacienda de Benazuza ▮▮▮▮▮ €€€€€

Virgen de las Nieves, 41800 (Sevilla) **Tel** *955 70 33 44* **Fax** *955 70 34 10* **Rooms** *44*

This ultra-luxurious hotel is part of the El Bulli empire, and contains an exceptional restaurant *(see p647)* among other five-star comforts. Set in an ancient Moorish farmhouse, the opulent rooms and suites contain original vaulted ceilings. The hotel offers myriad excursions, from river cruises to tours of the sherry bodegas. **www.elbullihotel.com**

SIERRA NEVADA Hotel El Lodge ▮▮▮▮▮▮ €€€€€

Maribel 8, Sierra Nevada, 18196 (Granada) **Tel** *958 48 06 00* **Fax** *958 48 13 14* **Rooms** *20*

This warm and welcoming hotel is perfectly located for enjoying a ski holiday in winter or a mountain escape in summer. It looks like a typical alpine ski lodge with picturesque wooden frame and rustic decor. Ski rental and classes can be arranged, as well as bike rental in summer. **www.ellodge.com**

TARIFA Hurricane ▮▮▮▮ €€€

Ctra N340 km 77, 11380 (Cádiz) **Tel** *956 68 49 19* **Fax** *956 68 03 29* **Rooms** *33*

Tarifa is a mecca for windsurfers and the Hurricane is a temple to the sport. It is an imaginative, open-plan building set in subtropical gardens, which lead out onto the beach. Rooms are decorated in Andalusian style. It is one of the least crowded corners of the Spanish coast, with fine views across the sea to Africa. **www.hotelhurricane.com**

TOLOX Cerro de Hijar ▮▮ €€

Cerro de Hijar s/n, 29019 (Málaga) **Tel** *952 11 21 11* **Fax** *952 11 97 45* **Rooms** *18*

This hotel offers stunning views of the surrounding natural beauty and the pretty white village of Tolox. The estate is Andalusian in style with a central patio and spacious rooms. All kinds of outdoor pursuits can be arranged, including horse riding and excursions. The restaurant serves local specialities and their own wines. **www.cerrodehijar.com**

TORREMOLINOS Hotel Miami ▮▮ €

C/ Aladino 14, 29620 (Málaga) **Tel & Fax** *952 38 52 55* **Rooms** *26*

The Miami offers welcome respite from the Costa del Sol's modern growth. It has whitewashed walls, tiles, iron grilles, balconies and potted plants. Rooms are simple, and vary in terms of size and amenities, but they are all comfortable and the staff are friendly and helpful. The pool is an added bonus. **www.residencia-miami.com**

TREVÉLEZ Hotel La Fragua ▮ €

C/ San Antonio 4, 18417 (Granada) **Tel** *958 85 86 26* **Fax** *958 85 86 14* **Rooms** *24*

This simple whitewashed *mesón* (inn) is in what claims to be the highest village in Spain. There are great views from the rooftop terrace. The rooms vary considerably in size and character, but most have lovely beamed ceilings, terracotta tiled floors and simple decor. There is a wonderful open fire in winter. **www.hotellafragua.com**

TURRE El Nacimiento ▮▮ €

Cortijo El Nacimiento, 04639 (Almería) **Tel** *950 52 80 90* **Rooms** *5*

A friendly couple runs this remote and lovely old farmhouse set in unspoilt rolling countryside. They offer bed and breakfast and home-cooked vegetarian dinners (on request) using organic produce from their farm. Rooms are cosy and pretty. Best of all is the natural swimming pool in the grounds.

TURRE Finca Listonero ▮▮▮ €€

Cortijo Grande, 04639 (Almería) **Tel** *950 47 90 94* **Rooms** *7*

This beautifully restored farmhouse, run by two Australian restauranteurs, is in the hills behind Mojácar. The rooms are individually and stylishly decorated, and all open out onto terraces overlooking the mountains or the pool and gardens. The breakfasts are generous, and home-grown vegetables are served at meals. **www.fincalistonero.com**

ÚBEDA María de Molina ▮▮▮▮▮ €€

Plaza del Ayuntamiento s/n, 23400 (Jaén) **Tel** *953 79 53 56* **Fax** *953 79 36 94* **Rooms** *27*

Located in the heart of the historic centre of Úbeda, next to the City Hall, this hotel is housed in a 16th-century palace. Rooms, clustered around the central courtyard with a marble fountain, are decorated in Renaissance style with all the modern amenities. Enjoy local cuisine in the cafeteria. **www.hotel-maria-de-molina.com**

ÚBEDA Parador de Úbeda ▮▮ €€€

Plaza Vázquez de Molina 1, 23400 (Jaén) **Tel** *953 75 03 45* **Fax** *953 75 12 59* **Rooms** *36*

Presiding over Úbeda's monumental central square, this parador is in a former 16th-century aristocratic palace. Blue and white tiles adorn the façade and the house surrounds a Renaissance two-storeyed patio. The spacious, high-ceilinged rooms are decorated with traditional furniture, and the restaurant serves regional cuisine. **www.parador.es**

VÉJER DE LA FRONTERA Casa Cinco

€€

C/ Sancho IV el Bravo 5, 11150 (Cádiz) **Tel** *956 45 50 29* **Fax** *956 45 11 25* **Rooms** *4*

This beautiful little hostal on the town's hilltop aims to stimulate all five senses. All the rooms are decorated individually with a mixture of contemporary and traditional furnishings from around the world. Thoughtful details such as CD players add to its charm. Bookings are for a minimum of two nights. **www.hotelcasacinco.com**

ZUHEROS Zuhayra

€

C/ Mirador 10, 14870 (Córdoba) **Tel** *957 69 46 93* **Fax** *957 69 47 02* **Rooms** *19*

The principal charm of this simple rural hotel is its location in a white town on the edge of a range of high hills. The building is modern, but imitates the style of the noble mansion it replaced. It is a perfect base for hiking in the Sierra Subbética, and the hotel rents mountain bikes. The restaurant serves local specialities. **www.zercahoteles.com**

THE BALEARIC ISLANDS

FORMENTERA Hotel Cala Saona

€€

Cala Saona, 07860 (Formentera) **Tel** *971 32 20 30* **Fax** *971 32 25 09* **Rooms** *116*

A modern hotel, this is the only option in the secluded Playa Cala Saona, one of the prettiest of Formentera's wild and unspoilt beaches. The interior is classic Spanish beach-hotel style with chintzy fabrics and TVs. Also has a pool with a sun terrace and good facilities for children including a play area. Open Apr–Oct. **www.hotelcalasaona.com**

FORMENTERA, ES PUJOLS Sa Volta

€€

C/ Miramar 94, 07871 (Formentera) **Tel** *971 32 81 25* **Fax** *971 32 82 28* **Rooms** *25*

A family-run *hostal* in a modern block close to the beach in one of Formentera's main resorts. The standard rooms are simple, but comfortable. It is worth splashing out on one of the three semi-suites, which have plush modern decor, including canopied beds and spacious private terraces. Charming staff. Open Mar–Dec. **www.savolta.com**

IBIZA (EIVISSA), IBIZA TOWN Hostal La Marina

€€

C/ Barcelona 7, 07800 (Formentera) **Tel** *971 31 01 72* **Fax** *971 31 48 94* **Rooms** *25*

A classic on the seafront, Hostal La Marina is located in a modernized 19th-century building, which retains some charming original details. Rooms are brightly painted in Mediterranean colours and the best have lovely sea views. In high season, it is a little overpriced, but a good deal otherwise. **www.hostal-lamarina.com**

BIZA (EIVISSA), IBIZA TOWN Hotel Royal Plaza

€€€

Pere Frances 27-29, 07800 (Ibiza) **Tel** *971 31 00 00* **Fax** *971 31 40 95* **Rooms** *117*

This hotel, in the centre of Ibiza's old town, has clean lines and classic decor and provides all the comforts you may require, such as Wi-Fi in all rooms, a mini-bar and a pillow menu. There is also a well-being centre with Jacuzzi, sauna, gym and treatments. Open Apr–Oct. **www.royalplaza.es**

IBIZA (EIVISSA), SANTA EULÀRIA D'ES RIU Les Terrasses

€€€€

Apto 1235 Ctra Santa Eulalia km 1, 07600 (Ibiza) **Tel** *971 33 26 43* **Fax** *971 33 89 78* **Rooms** *8*

A country house decorated simply but beautifully in Ibizan style, painted white, blue and sunshine yellow. Each room is individually styled with a perfect mixture of traditional and contemporary influences. It is a tranquil place with flower-filled gardens. Dinner is prepared with organic produce from the kitchen garden. **www.lesterrasses.net**

IBIZA, BAHÍA DE SANT ANTONI Osiris Ibiza

€€

Playa Es Puet s/n, 07820 (Ibiza) **Tel** *971 34 16 88* **Fax** *971 34 16 85* **Rooms** *97*

A family-run modern hotel in the popular resort of Sant Antoni, this is a great place for families on a budget. Osiris Ibiza is close to the beach and various water sports facilities, and has its own pool with a section for young children. The rooms are large and bright and offer views of the sea or the gardens. Open May–Oct. **www.hotelosiris.com**

IBIZA, CALA MOLÍ Hostel Cala Molí

€€

Cala Molí, 07830 (Ibiza) **Tel** *971 80 60 02* **Fax** *971 80 61 50* **Rooms** *8*

This is a family-friendly little hostal overlooking a lovely bay. All the rooms face a tree-shaded terrace, and there is a swimming pool if you cannot make the walk to the nearby beach. The rooms are whitewashed and simply furnished with private balconies. The cheerful staff will give you tips on what to see. Open May–Oct. **www.calamoli.com**

IBIZA, IBIZA TOWN Casa de Huéspedes Vara de Rey

€€

C/ Vara de Rey 7, 07800 (Ibiza) **Tel** *971 30 13 76* **Rooms** *15*

In the heart of the whitewashed maze of Ibiza's old town, this is an intimate little pension with quirkily decorated rooms painted by young artists from the island. None have private facilities, but this means bargain prices, making it ideal for travellers on a budget. All the rooms enjoy fine views. Friendly staff. Open Mar–Nov. **www.hibiza.com**

MALLORCA, ALCÚDIA Cas Ferrer Nou Hotelet

€€

Pou Nou 1, 07400 (Mallorca) **Tel** *971 89 75 42* **Fax** *971 89 75 49* **Rooms** *6*

This cosmopolitan boutique hotel has six unique rooms which mix natural decor elements with the avant-garde. The "Pafo" room has a private terrace complete with a double bed for sleeping under the stars, while three of the rooms come with their own Jacuzzi. **www.nouhotelet.com**

MALLORCA, BANYALBUFAR Sa Baronia   🍴🏧📧   €

C/ Sa Baronia 16, 07191 (Mallorca) **Tel** *971 61 81 46* **Fax** *971 14 87 38* **Rooms** *39*

Situated in a small village on the island's unspoilt, northwest coast, this simple family-run hotel was built as a modern extension onto a 17th-century baronial tower. The extension itself is unattractive, but the warm welcome and the tranquility of the area makes up for it. The simple bedrooms have terraces with sea views. **www.hbaronia.com**

MALLORCA, BINISSALEM Scott's Hotel   🍴🏧📧   €€€

Plaza de la Iglesia 12, 07350 (Mallorca) **Tel** *971 87 01 00* **Fax** *971 87 02 67* **Rooms** *78*

This restored and elegantly decorated 18th-century town house in the wine-producing town of Binissalem has won countless awards. The charming owners have given thought to every detail, right down to the handmade beds. Try their excellent bistro for dinner. Also has an indoor pool. All rooms are non-smoking. **www.scottshotel.com**

MALLORCA, DEIÀ La Residencia   🏊🍴🏧🍽📧   €€€€€

Son Canals s/n, 07179 (Mallorca) **Tel** *971 63 90 11* **Fax** *971 63 93 70* **Rooms** *64*

Two magnificently restored 16th- and 18th-century manors have been combined into a legendary hotel, which has long been a favourite hideaway of celebrities. The rooms and suites (some with private pools) are beautifully done with traditional Mallorcan furniture and pale linen. It also has a spa and a restaurant. **www.hotel-laresidencia.com**

MALLORCA, LLUC Santuari de Lluc   🍴   €

Santuari de Lluc, 07315 (Mallorca) **Tel** *971 87 15 25* **Fax** *971 51 70 96* **Rooms** *129*

The spectacular Santuari de Lluc in the Tramuntana mountains is Mallorca's most important place of pilgrimage, and home to a much-venerated statue of the Madonna, the island's patron saint. If you are seeking spiritual calm then book yourself into one of the austere former monks' cells. They also offer simple apartments. **www.lluc.net**

MALLORCA, PALMA DE MALLORCA Born   📧   €

C/ Sant Jaume 3, 07012 (Mallorca) **Tel** *971 71 29 42* **Fax** *971 71 86 18* **Rooms** *30*

The Marquis of Ferrandell's town mansion, built in the 16th century and restored in the 18th, makes a splendid little hotel. The simple but comfortable bedrooms are set around a typical Mallorcan courtyard with palms and a grand staircase. A few have tiny balconies overlooking the courtyard. One of the best budget options. **www.hotelborn.com**

MALLORCA, PORT D'ANDRATX Villa Italia   🏊🍴🏧🍽📧   €€€€€

Camino Sant Carles 13, 07157 (Mallorca) **Tel** *971 67 40 11* **Fax** *971 67 33 50* **Rooms** *16*

A pink, Florentine-style villa, built in the 1920s by an Italian millionaire, has been lovingly restored to house this ultra-luxurious hotel. Inside there are stucco ceilings and marble floors, and the huge gardens – with fountains, tiles and Italianate balustrades – offer great sea views. Has a fine restaurant and a spa. **www.hotelvillaitalia.com**

MALLORCA, PORT DE POLLENÇA Formentor   🏊🍴🏧🏌🍽📧   €€€€

Playa de Formentor, 07470 (Mallorca) **Tel** *971 89 91 00* **Fax** *971 86 51 55* **Rooms** *127*

Writers, opera singers, film stars and the Dalai Lama have signed the visitors' book of this luxury hotel on the island's northwest tip. No longer quite the celebrity haunt that it was, it still remains an elegant retreat. The rooms are traditionally decorated. Superb sports facilities available and the beach is on the doorstep. **www.hotelformentor.net**

MALLORCA, PORT DE SÓLLER Hostal Brisas   📧🏊🍴   €

Camino de Muleta 15, 07108 (Mallorca) **Tel** *971 63 13 52* **Rooms** *46*

A simple seaside hostal, built in the 1960s in traditional style. Rooms are basic, but more than adequate, and the best have views of the sea from private terraces. It is perfectly located for a relaxed beach holiday, just metres from the sands, and has a simple café-bar that serves local dishes. **www.mallorcahotelguide.com**

MALLORCA, RANDA Es Recó de Randa   🍴🏧📧   €€€

C/ Font 21, 07629 (Mallorca) **Tel** *971 66 09 97* **Fax** *971 66 25 58* **Rooms** *14*

A restaurant-with-rooms in an old stone house in a quiet village at the foot of the Puig de Randa mountain. The rustically decorated rooms have wooden beams and traditional furnishings, and many offer breathtaking views of the mountains and citrus groves. There is a lovely outdoor pool and a terrace. **www.esrecoderanda.com**

MALLORCA, SES SALINES Es Turó   🍴🏧📧   €€€

Camí Casperets, 07640 (Mallorca) **Tel** *971 64 95 31* **Fax** *971 64 95 48* **Rooms** *10*

Rural calm, tasteful comfort and timeless Mallorcan life are combined in this romantic stone-built hotel. Converted from an old farmhouse, it is surrounded by almond and olive groves and is just a short drive (8 km) to Es Trenc beach. All the suites are spacious and nicely decorated in traditional style. Has a fine restaurant. **www.esturo.com**

MALLORCA, SÓLLER Ca N'Aí   🏊🍴🏧📧   €€€€€

Camí de Son Sales, 07100 (Mallorca) **Tel** *971 63 24 94* **Fax** *971 63 18 99* **Rooms** *11*

This enchanting hotel has been converted from an old Mallorcan mansion, built into the side of the Sóller valley and surrounded by orange and palm groves. Inside, the decor is a refined mixture of local and contemporary styles. The service has a personal touch and the cooking is excellent. Garden and pool. Open mid-Feb–Oct. **www.canai.c**

MALLORCA, VALLDEMOSSA Cases de C'as Garriguer   🏧📧   €€

Ctra de Valldemossa-Andratx km 2-5, 07170 (Mallorca) **Tel** *971 61 23 00* **Fax** *971 61 25 83* **Rooms** *10*

A peaceful rural hotel located in a series of stone-built country houses, erected early in the 20th century. The spacious bedrooms are furnished with antiques and have wooden-beamed ceilings. Most have private terraces, with spellbinding views of the hills. A perfect destination for walkers. Open Mar–Oct. **www.vistamarhotel.es**

Key to Price Guide *see p560* **Key to Symbols** *see back cover flap*

MENORCA, CIUTADELLA Hostal Ciutadella

C/ San Eloi 10, 07760 (Menorca) **Tel** *971 38 34 62* **Fax** *971 48 48 58* **Rooms** *17*

Just around the corner from the Plaça de Alfons III, this simple, modern hotel offers good-value, no-frills lodging.
Renovated in 2005, the rooms are plainly furnished and spotless, and are cooled with ceiling fans in summer.
Simple meals are served in the family-friendly café-bar on the ground floor. **www.hostalciutadella.com**

MENORCA, CIUTADELLA Hostal Sa Prensa

Plaça de Madrid s/n, 07760 (Menorca) **Tel** *971 38 26 98* **Rooms** *7*

Probably the best of the cheaper hotels in Ciutadella, which has a shortage of good budget accommodation.
Book early to get one of the four bedrooms which have terraces with great views of the port; the other three rooms
are plain and overlook nondescript apartments. A café-bar downstairs serves breakfast. Closed 15 Dec–15 Jan.

MENORCA, CIUTADELLA Patricia

Paseo San Nicolás 90–92, 07760 (Menorca) **Tel** *971 38 55 11* **Fax** *978 48 11 20* **Rooms** *44*

A modern, cream-coloured chain hotel with white bay windows near the harbour. Rooms are spacious and blandly
furnished. Geared towards business travellers, it has conference facilities and a business centre. The convenient
location and efficient staff make it a good bet for tourists. Offers weekend discounts. **www.hesperia-patricia.com**

MENORCA, MAÓ Hostal Jumé

C/ Concepció 6, 07701 (Menorca) **Tel** *971 36 32 66* **Fax** *971 36 48 78* **Rooms** *35*

A very basic pension, run by a charming elderly couple, offering functional rooms (all *en suite*) with no frills at low
prices. It is conveniently central (close to the port and the market) and the owners go out of their way to make
guests comfortable. There is a simple, old-fashioned café-bar serving breakfast and local dishes.

MENORCA, MAÓ Del Almirante

Ctra de Es Castell, 07720 (Menorca) **Tel** *971 36 27 00* **Fax** *971 36 27 04* **Rooms** *39*

Built in the 18th century in classic Georgian style, this fine mansion house became the home of Admiral Lord
Collingwood, a friend of Lord Nelson. Some bedrooms are in a modern annexe overlooking the swimming pool
and a pretty terrace has views of Port Mahón. Disabled access. **www.hoteldelalmirante.com**

MENORCA, MAÓ Port Mahón

C/ Fort de l'Eau 13, 07701 (Menorca) **Tel** *971 36 26 00* **Fax** *971 35 10 50* **Rooms** *82*

Housed in an attractive red and white colonial-style building, this hotel – probably the most luxurious in the city –
overlooks Maó harbour. Its grounds include wide terraces and a curving swimming pool surrounded by lawns.
The best rooms, comfortably furnished in chain-hotel style, have private terraces. **www.sethotels.org**

MENORCA, MAÓ Capri

C/ San Esteban 8, 07703 (Menorca) **Tel** *971 36 14 00* **Fax** *971 35 08 53* **Rooms** *75 & 7 apartments*

This is a central hotel in a modern block, five floors high, close to shops, the harbour and the beach. Although the
exterior is unappealing, the interior is light and modern. The hotel offers exceptionally good facilities, including a
fully equipped spa, a health centre and a swimming pool. Some rooms have Jacuzzis. **www.rtmhotels.com**

MENORCA, MAÓ Casa Alberti

C/ Isabel II 9, 07701 (Menorca) **Tel** *971 35 42 10* **Fax** *971 35 42 10* **Rooms** *6*

Located in a handsome 18th-century mansion, this is perhaps the most charming hotel in Maó. All the rooms are
beautifully and individually decorated in chic, modern style. The winding, whitewashed staircase leads to a glorious
roof terrace with good views of the sea. The charismatic owner is full of local information. **www.casalberti.com**

THE CANARY ISLANDS

EL HIERRO, FRONTERA Ida Inés

Camino del Hoyo Belgara Alta 2, 38911 **Tel** *922 55 94 45* **Fax** *922 55 60 88* **Rooms** *12*

Located in the valley of El Golfo, roughly in the middle of the island, this small and cosy hotel looks onto the Atlantic
Ocean and the bedrooms have superb views of either the sea or the hills inland. The small swimming pool has a
solarium and guests have Internet access. A good base for walking or mountain biking. **www.hotelitoidaines.com**

EL HIERRO, VALVERDE Parador de El Hierro

Las Playas 15, 38910 **Tel** *922 55 80 36* **Fax** *922 55 80 86* **Rooms** *47*

Black cliffs are the backdrop for this modern, pantiled parador which stands in a peaceful spot on an isolated beach
facing the Roque de Bonanza. It has an elegant colonial decor with white walls, and wooden balconies with sea
views. An ideal option for walking or relaxing. El Hierro specialities served in the restaurant. **www.parador.es**

FUERTEVENTURA, ANTIGUA Era de la Corte

Corte 1, 35630 **Tel** *928 87 87 05* **Fax** *928 87 87 10* **Rooms** *11*

A low-lying 19th-century house in a residential area of Antigua village, mostly painted in gleaming white, with
exposed stone walls inside, but with some touches of striking colour here and there. All the rooms are individually
decorated and two have four-poster beds. It has two sitting areas. Gay friendly. **www.eradelacorte.com**

FUERTEVENTURA, PÁJARA Casa Isaitas   🍴   €€

Pájara, 35626 **Tel** *928 16 14 02* **Fax** *928 16 14 82* **Rooms** *4*

This tiny rural B&B in a 200-year old Canarian house is located in a village in the middle of the island. Offering simple lodging and home-made food, Casa Isaitas has only four bedrooms and an inner patio. A room which was formerly used as a corn mill now houses a lounge-library and bar where snacks are available. **www.casaisaitas.com**

FUERTEVENTURA, VILLAVERDE Mahoh   🍴🛏   €

Sitio de Juan Bello, 35660 **Tel** *928 86 80 50* **Fax** *928 86 86 12* **Rooms** *9*

Mahoh (a Guanche word meaning "my land, my country") is an early 19th-cenrury traditional rural house in the north of Fuerteventura, built of the island's volcanic stone and local timber. The bedrooms are simply decorated, often with bare stone walls. Some of them have four-poster beds. The hotel has horses for hire. **www.mahoh.com**

GRAN CANARIA, AGAETE Finca Las Longueras Hotel Rural   🍴🛏🏊   €€

Finca Las Longueras, 35480 **Tel** *928 89 81 45* **Fax** *928 89 87 52* **Rooms** *10*

This 19th-century colonial manor in the Agaete Valley, also known as the "Red House", is located in a plantation of bananas, oranges, papayas and avocados. It is tastefully decorated, with its own gardens and a chapel. In the grounds a self-catering house for rent sleeps four. Close to the ferry terminal of Tenerife. **www.laslongueras.com**

GRAN CANARIA, AGAETE Hotel Puerto de las Nievas   🛏🅿🍴🛏🏋🍽   €€

Avda. Alcalde Joses de Armas, 35480 **Tel** *928 88 62 56* **Fax** *928 88 62 67* **Rooms** *30*

A tranquil retreat, in the unbeatable surroundings of Puerto de las Nieves, offering luxurious pampering. Indulge in one of the health treatments at the hydrotherapy centre, and enjoy dining at the á la carte restaurant. There is also a sport and leisure centre. **www.hotelpeurtodelasnievas.es**

GRAN CANARIA, ARUCAS Hacienda del Buen Suceso   🍴🏊🍽   €€€

Finca del Buen Suceso, Ctra de Arucas a Bañaderos km 1, 35400 **Tel** *928 62 29 45* **Fax** *928 62 29 42* **Rooms** *18*

An elegant hotel occupying a 16th-century colonial farmhouse, once the residence of the Marquis of Arucas. Located on the way up to Arucas town from the coast, it is surrounded by a banana plantation and is very quiet at night. There are various outdoor spaces, and a heated swimming pool. **www.haciendabuensuceso.com**

GRAN CANARIA, CRUZ DE TEJEDA El Refugio   🍴🏊🍽   €€

Cruz de Tejeda, 35328 **Tel** *928 66 65 13* **Fax** *928 66 65 20* **Rooms** *17*

This hotel stands on the remote Cruz de Tejeda crossroads at a high point in the middle of the island. It can be busy with trippers during the day but is peaceful at night. Offers sauna, mini golf, pool, sundeck and gardens. A long way from the coast and the nearest nightlife, but a great area for walking or horse riding. **www.hotelruralelrefugio.com**

GRAN CANARIA, LAS PALMAS Aldiana Mirador   🛏🍴🏊🍽🍽   €€

Oficial Mayor José Rubio, San Bartolomé de Tirajana, 35290 **Tel** *928 12 30 00* **Fax** *928 12 30 23* **Rooms** *60*

High above the brash and noisy resorts on Gran Canaria's southern coast, this spa hotel is on the edge of an ancient caldera and enjoys breathtaking mountain scenery. A suitable place to unwind or use as base for walking. It also has a restaurant serving Canarian cuisine, a covered pool and a gym. Open May–Oct. **www.aldiana.com**

GRAN CANARIA, LAS PALMAS Santa Catalina   🛏🍴🏊🍽🍽   €€€€

C/ León y Castillo 227, 35005 **Tel** *928 24 30 40* **Fax** *928 24 27 64* **Rooms** *202*

This traditional Canarian building with its wooden balconies and Colonial atmosphere has been a classic hotel since it opened in 1890. Many of the rooms have either a park or sea view. Among them are 14 junior suites and 2 senior suites. Facilities include an opulent casino and a well-equipped spa centre. **www.hotelsantacatalina.com**

GRAN CANARIA, MASPALOMAS Riu Grand Palace Maspalomas Oasis   🛏🍴🏊🏋🍽🍽   €€

Plaza de las Palmeras, 35106 **Tel** *928 14 14 48* **Fax** *928 14 11 92* **Rooms** *332*

In a prime, palm-shaded spot by Maspalomas' renowned (and unspoilt) sand dunes is this secluded, modern, grand hotel, surrounded by subtropical gardens. The guests are stylishly accommodated in split-level suites with spacious bedrooms. The staff are efficient and pleasant. The restaurant has a no-smoking section. **www.riu.com**

GRAN CANARIA, VEGA DE SAN MATEO Las Calas   🍴   €€

El Arenal 36, La Lechuza, 35320 **Tel** *928 66 14 36* **Fax** *928 66 07 53* **Rooms** *9*

This small, friendly, countryside hotel is in a 17th-century Canarian building, located down a winding lane at La Lechuza. It has been tastefully decorated with traditional furniture, while keeping some unusual features of the house such as a bread oven in one of the rooms. There are good walks up and down the hills. **www.hotelrurallascalas.com**

LA GOMERA, PLAYA DE SANTIAGO Jardín Tecina   🛏🍴🏊🏋🍽🍽   €€€

Lomada de Tecina, 38811 **Tel** *922 14 58 50* **Fax** *922 14 58 51* **Rooms** *434*

The main reason to stay at this attractive hotel is to go walking around the island of La Gomera. Its many facilities and entertainments make the complex, which is in the hills behind the Playa de Santiago, virtually a self-contained resort. It is surrounded by gardens. A cliff-side lift takes guests down to the beach club. **www.jardin-tecina.com**

LA GOMERA, SAN SEBASTIÁN Parador de la Gomera   🛏🍴🏊🍽   €€€

San Sebastián de La Gomera, 38800 **Tel** *922 87 11 00* **Fax** *922 87 11 16* **Rooms** *60*

On a clifftop above La Gomera's main town and port, this traditional parador is decorated with a variety of maritime paraphernalia. The bedrooms have dark wood fittings and tiled bathrooms. From the hotel and its luxuriant subtropical gardens there are impressive views across the sea to Mt Teide on Tenerife. **www.parador.es**

Key to Price Guide *see p560* **Key to Symbols** *see back cover flap*

LA PALMA, BARLOVENTO La Palma Romántica
€€

Las Llanadas s/n, 38726 **Tel** *922 18 62 21* **Fax** *922 18 64 00* **Rooms** *41*

Nestling into a hillside in the northeast tip of the island, high above the sea, is this airy hotel with spacious rooms. Apart from double and single rooms there are some suites and rooms in bungalows. It has both indoor and outdoor swimming pools, a sauna, a solarium and a fitness centre. Pets are allowed. **www.hotellapalmaromantica.com**

LA PALMA, SANTA CRUZ DE LA PALMA Parador de la Palma
€€€

Ctra de el Zumacal, Breña Baja, 38720 **Tel** *922 43 58 28* **Fax** *922 43 59 99* **Rooms** *78*

This new, purpose-built parador, in the traditional Canarian style, looks out on to the sea and is surrounded by a lovely garden. It is located near the island's main town and the airport. Various excursions and activities are available. The restaurant excels in fish and other Canarian specialities and wine made on the island. **www.parador.es**

LANZAROTE, ARRECIFE Lancelot
€€

Av Mancomunidad 9, 35500 **Tel** *928 80 50 99* **Fax** *928 80 50 39* **Rooms** *112*

This modern hotel stands on Arrecife's Reducto beach, a tempting stretch of soft, pale sand with coral reefs lying just offshore. The hotel has all the standard services including a reception desk open 24 hours. The restaurant has sea views and is also close to other good restaurants in the town. **www.hotellancelot.com**

LANZAROTE, COSTA TEGUISE Gran Meliá Salinas
€€€

Av Islas Canarias, Urbanización Costa Teguise, 35509 **Tel** *928 59 00 40* **Fax** *928 59 03 90* **Rooms** *316*

A vast atrium with central water gardens and ornamental plants is the focus of this modern luxury hotel in the northern area of Costa Teguise. It has two bars and five restaurants offering a wide choice of food and drink. A swimming pool, three tennis courts, a gym, mini-golf and a newsagent are add-ons. **www.solmelia.com**

LANZAROTE, PLAYA BLANCA H10 Lanzarote Princess
€€

C/ Maciot Urb Playa Blanca, 35570 **Tel** *928 51 71 08* **Fax** *928 51 70 11* **Rooms** *407*

A resort hotel popular with families in the south of Lanzarote facing Fuerteventura. It is cool and light, with split-level areas ornamented with water gardens. Of the two swimming pools, one is heated. Tennis and golf are available and there are bikes for hire. They also have evening entertainments and a "miniclub" for children. **www.h10hotels.com**

LANZAROTE, PUERTO DEL CARMEN Los Fariones
€€

C/ Roque del Este 1, 35510 **Tel** *928 51 01 75* **Fax** *928 51 02 02* **Rooms** *248*

This seven-storey hotel has direct access to an attractive beach. All the rooms are spacious and have sea views. The hotel has a good range of facilities including a dive centre and two swimming pools. Outside is a large tropical garden. Two bars offer a range of snacks and live music most evenings. **www.grupofariones.com**

TENERIFE, GARACHICO Hotel San Roque
€€€€

C/ Esteban de Ponte 32, 38450 **Tel** *922 13 34 35* **Fax** *922 13 34 06* **Rooms** *20*

This charming hotel decorated with avant-garde art occupies an 18th-century house built around two pretty patios, in a historic north coast town away from the island's tourist resorts. All rooms have Jacuzzi, flat-screen TVs and video and DVD players. Dinner and breakfast are served at tables set by the poolside. **www.hotelsanroque.com**

TENERIFE, LA LAGUNA Costa Salada
€€

Camino La Costa, Finca Oasis, Valle de Guerra, 38270 **Tel** *922 69 00 00* **Fax** *922 54 10 55* **Rooms** *13*

A pretty rural hotel standing on a series of terraces over the rocky northern coast of Tenerife, at the end of a subtropical nursery for plants. The hotel has cosy bedrooms, mostly with terraces and sea views. It also has a wine cellar in a natural cave. Located off the coast road between Tejina and Valle de Guerra. **www.costasalada.com**

TENERIFE, LA OROTAVA Hotel Rural La Orotava
€€

C/ Carrera 17, 38300 **Tel** *922 32 27 93* **Fax** *922 32 27 25* **Rooms** *8*

This 16th-century house, with cosy bedrooms around an attractive Canarian patio, was formerly the home of the Marquis of La Florida. Now transformed into a hotel, it is one of the historic buildings that forms the compact, harmonious centre of La Orotava. It also has a wine cellar. Breakfast included in price. **www.saborcanario.net**

TENERIFE, LA OROTAVA Parador de Cañadas del Teide
€€€

Las Cañadas del Teide, 38300 **Tel** *922 37 48 41* **Fax** *922 38 23 52* **Rooms** *37*

This modern parador, which looks like an Alpine chalet, is the only place to stay inside the national park. It stands in an otherwise uninhabited volcanic landscape looking out at the Roques de Garcia and towards Mt Teide. In the daytime its cafeteria caters for day-trippers but at night the guests have the park to themselves. **www.parador.es**

TENERIFE, SANTA CRUZ DE TENERIFE Pelinor
€

C/ Bethencourt Alfonso 8, 38002 **Tel** *922 24 68 75* **Fax** *922 24 08 33* **Rooms** *73*

Pelinor is a comfortable and recently renovated modern hotel, mainly frequented by business people. Well located in a pedestrian street in the centre of Santa Cruz and close to the Teresitas beach. It only offers a cafeteria and a snack bar. There is a public car park a very short distance away. **www.hotelpelinor.com**

TENERIFE, SANTA CRUZ DE TENERIFE Taburiente
€€

C/ Dr José Navieras 24A, 38001 **Tel** *922 27 60 00* **Fax** *922 27 05 62* **Rooms** *171*

An elegant hotel in the city centre facing the beautiful Parque Garcia Sanabria. The bedrooms are well equipped and the hotel has its own boutique, a shop and a restaurant offering international cuisine. They also have a swimming pool, Jacuzzi, sauna and a solarium. Completely renovated and expanded. **www.hoteltaburiente.com**

RESTAURANTS AND BARS

One of the joys of eating out in Spain is the sheer sociability of the Spanish. Family and friends, often with children in tow, can be seen eating out from early in the day until after midnight.

Spanish food has a regional bias. Traditional restaurants originated as taverns and tapas bars serving dishes based on local produce. Spain also has

Wall tile advertising a Barcelona restaurant

its fair share of top-quality gourmet restaurants, notably in the Basque Country.

The restaurants listed on pages 608–53 have been selected for their food and conviviality. Pages 604–7 illustrate some of the best tapas and drinks; and each of the book's five regional sections includes features on the area's unique food and wines.

An elaborately decorated bar in Barcelona

RESTAURANTS AND BARS

The cheapest and quickest places to eat are the bars and cafés that serve tapas. Some bars, however, especially pubs (late-opening bars for socializing) serve no food.

Family-run bar-restaurantes, ventas, posadas, mesones and fondas – all old words for the different types of inn – serve inexpensive, sit-down meals. Chiringuitos are beachside bars. They open only during the summer season.

Spain's top restaurants tend to be clustered in the Basque Country, Galicia, Barcelona, Catalonia and Madrid.

Most restaurants close one day a week, some for lunch or dinner only, and most for an annual holiday. They also close on some public holidays. The main closing times of the restaurants on pages 608–53 are listed at the end of each entry. Always check these opening times, however, when phoning to book a table.

EATING HOURS IN SPAIN

The Spanish often have two breakfasts (*desayunos*). The first is a light meal of biscuits or toast with olive oil or butter and jam and café con leche (milky coffee). A more substantial breakfast may follow between 10 and 11am, perhaps in a café. This may consist of a savoury snack, such as a *bocadillo* (sandwich) with sausage, ham or cheese, or a thick slice of *tortilla de patatas* (potato omelette). Fruit juice, coffee or beer are the usual accompaniments.

From about 1pm people will stop in the bars for a beer or a *copa* (glass) of wine with tapas. By 2pm those who can will have arrived home from work for *la comida* (lunch), which is the main meal of the day. Others will choose to have lunch in a restaurant.

The cafés, *salones de té* (tea rooms) and *pastelerías* (pastry shops) fill up by about 5:30 or

Decoration, Barcelona bar

6pm for *la merienda* (tea) of sandwiches, pastries or cakes, with coffee, tea or juice. Snacks like *churros* (fried batter sticks) can also be bought from stalls.

By 7pm, bars are crowded with people having tapas with sherry, wine or beer. In Spain *la cena* (dinner or supper), begins at about 10pm. Restaurants sometimes begin their evening service earlier for tourists. In summer, however, Spanish families and groups of friends often do not sit down to eat until as late as midnight. At weekend lunch times, especially in summer, you may find that restaurants are filled by large and noisy family gatherings.

HOW TO DRESS

A jacket and tie are rarely required, but the Spanish dress smartly, especially for city restaurants. Day dress is casual in beach resorts, but shorts are frowned on in the evenings.

The elegant Egaña Oriza restaurant in Seville *(see p641)*

Pavement tables outside a cafeteria, in Cadaqués on the Costa Brava

READING THE MENU

Aside from tapas, perhaps the cheapest eating options in Spanish restaurants are the fixed-price *platos combinados* (meat or fish with vegetables and, usually, chips) and the *menú del día*. A *plato combinado* is only offered by cheaper establishments. Most restaurants – but not all – offer an inexpensive, fixed-price *menú del día* at lunch time, normally of three courses, but with little choice. Some restaurants offer a *menú de degustación* consisting of a choice of six or seven of the head chef's special dishes.

The Spanish word for menu is *la carta*. It starts with *sopas* (soups), *ensaladas* (salads), *entremeses* (hors d'oeuvres), *huevos y tortillas* (eggs and omelettes) and *verduras y legumbres* (vegetable dishes).

Main courses are *pescados y mariscos* (fish and shellfish) and *carnes y aves* (meat and poultry). Daily specials are chalked on a board or clipped to menus. Paella and other rice dishes may be served as the first course. A useful rule is to follow rice with meat, or start with serrano ham or salad and then follow with a paella.

Desserts are called *postres* in Spanish. All restaurants offer fresh fruit (the usual dessert in Spain) but otherwise the range of *postres* is generally poor. The better restaurants offer a limited choice, perhaps *natillas* (custard) and *flan* (crème caramel). Gourmet restaurants have more creative choices.

Vegetarians are rather poorly catered for in Spain, but in big cities such as Madrid there are a handful of vegetarian restaurants. Most menus have a vegetable or egg dish.

Most eating places welcome children and will serve small portions if requested.

The modern, elegant Cinc Sentits in Barcelona *(see p619)*

WINE CHOICES

Dry fino wines go with shellfish, serrano ham, olives, soups and most first courses. Main courses are usually accompanied by wines from Ribera del Duero, Rioja, Navarra or Penedès. A bar might serve wines from Valdepeñas or the local vineyards. Oloroso wines (see p607) are often ordered as a digestif.

SMOKING

All restaurants, bars and cafés larger than 100m² (1100 sq ft) are non-smoking unless they have a separate smoking area. Smaller venues have a sign at the door stating whether they are smoking or non-smoking.

PRICES AND PAYING

If you order from *la carta* in a restaurant, your bill can soar way above the price of the *menú del día*, especially if you order pricey items, such as fresh seafood, fish or ibérico ham (see p462). If there is an expensive fish such as sole or swordfish on the menu at a bargain price, it may be frozen. Sea bass and other popular fish and shellfish, such as large prawns, lobster and crab, are priced by weight as a rule.

La cuenta (the bill) includes service charges and perhaps a small cover charge. Prices on menus do not include 7 per cent VAT (IVA), which is usually added when the bill is totalled. The Spanish hardly ever tip restaurant waiters more than 5 per cent, often just rounding up the bill.

Cheques are rarely used in Spain. Traveller's cheques are usually accepted but you may be given a poor rate of exchange. The major credit cards and international direct debit cards are now accepted in most restaurants, but not in smaller places like tapas bars, cafés or *bodegas*.

WHEELCHAIR ACCESS

Since restaurants are rarely designed for wheelchairs, phone in advance (or ask the hotel staff to call) to check on access to tables and toilets.

Designer tapas bar Comerç 24 in Barcelona *(see p618)*

Choosing Tapas

Tapas, sometimes called *pinchos*, are small snacks that originated in Andalusia in the 19th century to accompany sherry. Stemming from a bartender's practice of covering a glass with a saucer or *tapa* (cover) to keep out flies, the custom progressed to a chunk of cheese or bread being used, and then to a few olives being placed on a platter to accompany a drink. Once free of charge, tapas are usually paid for nowadays, and a selection makes a delicious light meal. Choose from a range of appetizing varieties, from cold meats to elaborately prepared hot dishes of meat, seafood or vegetables.

Mixed green olives

Patatas bravas *is a piquant dish of fried potatoes with a spicy red sauce.*

Albóndigas *(meatballs) are a hearty tapa, often served with a spicy tomato sauce.*

Almendras fritas *are fried, salted almonds.*

Banderillas *are canapés skewered on toothpicks. The entire canapé should be eaten at once.*

Calamares fritos *are squid rings and tentacles which have been dusted with flour before being deep fried in olive oil. They are usually served garnished with a piece of lemon.*

Jamón serrano *is salt-cured ham dried in mountain (serrano) air.*

ON THE TAPAS BAR

Almejas Clams

Berenjenas horneadas Roasted aubergines (eggplants)

Boquerones Anchovies

Boquerones al natural Fresh anchovies in garlic and olive oil

Buñuelos de bacalao Salt cod fritters

Butifarra Catalonian sausage

Calabacín Rebozado Battered courgettes (zucchini)(Catalan)

Calamares a la romana Fried squid rings

Callos Tripe

Caracoles Snails

Champiñones al ajillo Mushrooms fried in white wine with garlic

Chistorra Spicy sausage

Chopitos Cuttlefish fried in batter

Chorizo al vino Chorizo sausage cooked in red wine

Chorizo diablo Chorizo served flamed with brandy

Costillas Spare ribs

Criadillas Bulls' testicles

Croquetas Croquettes

Diabolitos picantes Spicy mini hamburgers

Empanada Pastry filled with tomato, onion and meat or fish

Ensaladilla rusa Potatoes, carrots, red peppers, peas, olive boiled egg, tuna and mayonnais

Gambas pil pil Spicy, garlicky fried king prawns (shrimp)

Longaniza roja Spicy red pork sausage from Aragón (Longaniz blanca is paler and less spicy.)

Magro Pork in a paprika and tomato sauce

TAPAS BARS

Even a small village will have at least one bar where the locals go to enjoy drinks, tapas and conversation with friends. On Sundays and holidays, favourite places are packed with whole families enjoying the fare. In larger towns it is customary to move from bar to bar, sampling the specialities of each. A tapa is a single serving, whereas a *ración* is two or three. Tapas are usually eaten standing or perching on a stool at the bar rather that sitting at a table, for which a surcharge is usually made.

Diners make their choice at a busy tapas bar

Chorizo, *a popular sausage flavoured with paprika and garlic, may be eaten cold or fried and served hot.*

Salpicón de mariscos *is a luxurious cold salad of assorted fresh seafood in a zesty vinaigrette.*

Gambas a la plancha *is a simple but flavourful dish of grilled prawns (shrimp).*

Tortilla española *is the ubiquitous Spanish omelette of onion and potato bound with egg.*

Queso manchego *is a sheep's-milk cheese from La Mancha.*

Pollo al ajillo *consists of small pieces of chicken (often wings) sautéd and then simmered with a garlic-flavoured sauce.*

Manitas de cerdo Pig's trotters

Mejillones Mussels

Merluza a la romana Hake fried in a light batter

Morcilla Black (blood) pudding

Muslitos del mar Crab-meat roquette, on a claw skewer

Orejas de cerdo Pig's ear

Pa amb tomàquet Bread rubbed with olive oil and tomatoes

Paella Rice dish made with meat, fish and/or vegetables

Pan de ajo Garlic bread

Patatas a lo pobre Potato chunks sautéd with onions and red and green peppers

Patatas alioli Potato chunks in a garlic mayonnaise

Pescaditos Small fried fish

Pimientos rellenos Stuffed peppers

Pinchos morunos Pork skewers

Pisto Thick ratatouille of diced tomato, onion and courgette

Pulpitos Baby octopus (Catalan)

Quesos A selection of Spanish cheeses

Rabo de toro Oxtail

Revueltos Scrambled eggs with asparagus or mushrooms

Sepia a la plancha Grilled cuttlefish

Sesos Brains, usually lamb or calf

Surtido de Ibéricos Assortment of pork products

Tortilla riojana Ham, sausage and red pepper omelette

Tostas Bread with various toppings such as tuna or brie

Verdura a la plancha Grilled vegetables

What to Drink in Spain

Spain is one of the world's largest wine-producing countries and many fine wines are made here, particularly reds in La Rioja and sherry in Andalusia. Many other beverages – alcoholic and non-alcoholic – are served in bars and cafés, which provide an important focus for life in Spain. The Spanish are also great coffee drinkers. In the summer, a tempting range of cooling drinks is on offer, in addition to beer, which is always available. Brandy and a variety of liqueurs, such as *anís*, are drunk as apéritifs and *digestifs*, as is chilled pale gold fino sherry.

Customers enjoying a drink at a terrace café in Seville

Hot chocolate

A plate of *churros* (batter sticks)

Café con leche

Camomile

Lime flower

HOT DRINKS

Café con leche is a large half-and-half measure of milk and espresso coffee; *café cortado* is an espresso with a splash of milk; *café solo* is a black coffee. Hot chocolate is also popular and is often served with *churros* (batter sticks). Herbal teas include *manzanilla* (camomile) and *tila* (lime flower).

COLD DRINKS

In most Spanish towns and cities it is safe to drink the tap water, but people generally prefer to buy bottled mineral water, either still *(sin gas)* or sparkling *(con gas)*. Besides soft drinks, a variety of other thirst-quenching summer beverages is available, including *horchata (see p253)*, a sweet, milky drink made from ground *chufas* (earth almonds). Another popular refreshing drink is *leche merengada* (lemon and cinnamon flavoured milk ice cream). *Gaseosa*, fizzy lemonade, can be drunk either on its own or as a mixer, usually with wine. *Zumo de naranja natural* (freshly squeezed orange juice) is an excellent thirst quencher.

Horchata, made from *chufas*

Sparkling and still mineral water

SPANISH WINE

Wine has been produced in Spain since pre-Roman times and there is a great variety on offer today, including famous types such as Rioja. The key standard for the industry is the *Denominación de Origen* (DO) classification, a guarantee of a wine's origin and quality. *Vino de la Tierra* is a classification of wines below that of DO in which over 60 per cent of the grapes come from a specified region. *Vino de Mesa*, the lowest category, covers basic unclassified wines. For more detailed information on Spain's principal wine-producing regions, refer to the following pages: Northern Spain (*see pp78–9*), Eastern Spain (*see pp202–3*), Central Spain (*see pp340–1*), and Southern Spain (*see pp420–1*).

Penedès white wine

Rioja red wine

Sparkling wine (*cav*

SPIRITS AND LIQUEURS

Spanish brandy, which comes mainly from the sherry bodegas in Jerez, is known as *coñac*. Most bodegas produce at least three different labels and price ranges. Magno is a good middle-shelf brandy; top-shelf labels are Cardenal Mendoza and Duque de Alba. *Anís*, which is flavoured with aniseed, is popular. *Pacharán*, made from sloes, is sweet and also tastes of aniseed. Licor 43 is a vanilla liqueur. Ponche is brandy that has been aged and flavoured with herbs.

Anís

Pacharán

Licor 43

Ponche

BEER

Most Spanish beer *(cerveza)* is bottled lager, although you can almost always find it on draught. Popular brands include San Miguel, Cruzcampo, Mahou and Estrella. To order a glass of beer in a bar ask for *una caña*. Alcohol-free lager *(cerveza sin alcohol)* is also available in most bars in Spain.

Bottled beers

SHERRY

Sherry is produced in bodegas in Jerez de la Frontera (Andalusia) and in nearby towns Sanlúcar de Barrameda and El Puerto de Santa María *(see pp420–1)*. Although not officially called sherry, similar kinds of wine are produced in Montilla near Córdoba. Pale fino is dry and light and excellent as an apéritif. Amber amontillado (aged fino) has a strong, earthy taste while oloroso is full-bodied and ruddy.

Two brands of fino sherry

MIXED DRINKS

Red wine and lemonade

Sangria is a refreshing mixture of red wine, *gaseosa* (lemonade) and other ingredients including chopped fruit and sugar. Wine diluted with lemonade is called *vino con gaseosa*. Another favourite drink is *Agua de Valencia*, a refreshing blend of *cava* (sparkling wine) and orange juice. Young people will often order the popular *cubalibres*, cola with rum.

Sangria

Cubalibre

Vino con gaseosa

HOW TO READ A WINE LABEL

f you know what to look for, the abel will provide a key to the wine's lavour and quality. It will bear the name of the wine and its producer or bodega, its vintage if there is one, and show its *Denominación de Origen* (DO) if applicable. Wines abelled *cosecha* are recent vintages and the least expensive, while *crianza* and *reserva* wines are aged a minimum of two or three years – part of that ime in oak casks – and therefore more expensive. Table wine *(Vino de Mesa)* may be *tinto* (red), *blanco* (white) or osado (rosé). *Cava* is a sparkling wine made by the *méthode champenoise* in pecified areas of origin.

Brand name

Company's crest

Capacity of the bottle

Estate-bottled rather than cooperative

The wine's *Denominación de Origen*

75 cl.   13% Alc

MARQUÉS DE MURRIETA
Embotellado por: BODEGAS MARQUÉS DE MURRIETA, S.A. - YGAY

Vinos de Rioja

YGAY   (LOGROÑO)

RESERVA
COSECHA 1970

The vintage   Symbol for region

Choosing a Restaurant

The restaurants in this guide have been selected across a wide range of price categories for their good value, exceptional food and interesting location. This chart lists the restaurants by region. Within each town or city, entries are listed by price category, from the least expensive to the most expensive.

PRICE CATEGORIES
For a three-course evening meal for one including a half bottle of house wine, service and taxes:

€ under 25 euros
€€ 25–35 euros
€€€ 35–50 euros
€€€€ over 50 euros

GALICIA

A CORUÑA La Penela   €

Plaza de María Pita 12, 15001 **Tel** *981 20 92 00*

In the square dedicated to a Galician heroine, and very close to the harbour, is this simple, unpretentious but very popular restaurant which serves traditional Galician fare. The roast veal, tripe with *garbanzos* (chickpeas), Spanish omelette and Galician-style monkfish are specialities. Closed Sun & two weeks in Jan.

A CORUÑA Taberna Pil-Pil   *Tapas*   €

C/ Pelamios 7, 15001 **Tel** *981 21 27 12*

Located in front of the Escuela de Artes Picasso, this pleasant, though rather small, taberna restaurant uses the freshest local produce in season to create simple dishes, with sauces or spices that enhance the main ingredients. Choose from about 12 dishes and five desserts. Closed Sun & 15–31 Oct.

A CORUÑA Casa Pardo   €€€€

C/ Novoa Santos 15, 15006 **Tel** *981 28 00 21*

High-quality cooking and an extensive menu of Galician dishes are the characteristics of this restaurant by the fishing port. It is renowned for its monkfish, *caldeirada de rape*, a dish which does not always get mentioned on the menu but is always available. Try the hot chocolate soufflé with nougat ice cream. Closed Sun. Reservation recommended.

A GUARDA Anduriña   €€€

C/ Rúa Do Porto 58, 36780 (Pontevedra) **Tel** *986 61 11 08*

Watch the fishing boats bring in their catch as you enjoy fresh hake, turbot or roasted mixed fish from the covered terrace of this port-side restaurant. It also serves traditional *empanada gallega* (a pie stuffed with cod, tuna or shellfish), a good stew with monkfish and clams, and a fair variety of desserts. Closed Nov, Sun evenings Sep–Jul.

ALLARIZ Casa Tino Fandiño   *Tapas*   €€€

C/ Rúa do Carcere 1, 32660 (Ourense) **Tel** *988 44 22 16*

A famous restaurant, specializing in traditional Galician cooking with modern touches. It is a good place to try *pulpo* (octopus) or *empanada* (pie). For something more elaborate try the *lubina* (sea bass) with mushroom sauce or the veal stew. Good wine list. Closed on Mon and for two weeks in Oct.

BAIONA Moscón   €€

C/ Alférez Barreiro 2, 36300 (Pontevedra) **Tel** *986 35 50 08*

This restaurant in Baiona serves mainly Galician cuisine with fish stews predominating on the menu. These include a tasty fish *caldeirada* (casserole) spiced with paprika. There is also seafood from the estuary; all complemented by a good selection of Galician wines. The harbour view makes for a pleasant dining experience. Outside tables in summer.

BETANZOS La Casilla   €€

Ctra de Castilla 90, 15300 (A Coruña) **Tel** *981 77 01 61*

Located in an old-stone house, this restaurant is famous throughout Spain for its omelettes, especially the potato variety – *tortilla de patata* – but it also serves traditional Galician food, tripe and grilled meat. It is very busy during the summer and at weekends. Closed Sun evenings except in summer, Mon & 20 days in Nov.

BUEU A Centoleira   *Tapas*   €€€

Playa de Beluso 27, 36937 (Pontevedra) **Tel** *986 32 34 81*

What started as an old fishermen's inn 120 years ago is now a popular restaurant run by the same family, serving Galician food such as *guisotes marineros* (fish stews), *empanada de maiz* (sweetcorn pie) and cheese mousse over tomato compote. Closed Mon (except summer), Sun evenings & 15 Oct–15 Nov and Christmas.

CAMBADOS Ribadomar   €€

C/ Valle Inclán 17, 36630 (Pontevedra) **Tel** *986 54 36 79*

A welcoming family-run restaurant offering mainly seafood and traditional dishes, although there are a few innovations as well, such as the *Perdiz* (partridge). Try the *vieiras al horno* (oven-baked scallops) and sole with scallops; and for dessert the home-made almond pie. Open daily in summer; closed Sun & Tue evenings, 15 days Sep–Oct & 15 days end of Feb–Mar.

Key to Price Guide *see p608* **Key to Symbols** *see back cover flap*

CAMBADOS María José 🗎📶　€€€

C/ San Gregorio 2– 1º, 36630 (Pontevedra) **Tel** *986 54 22 81*

Situated on the first floor of the building opposite the Parador de Cambados, this restaurant offers experimental cooking, combining traditional dishes with modern creations. It has a good selection of Albariño wines. Try the *langostino* (king prawn) salad wrapped in bacon. Closed Sun evenings & Mon (except Jul & Aug).

COMBARRO Taberna de Alvariñas　*Tapas* 🗎♿🏠📶　€€€

C/ Mar 63, 36993 (Pontevedra) **Tel** *986 77 20 33*

Located in a picturesque fishing village, famous for its *hórreos* (granaries) on the seafront, this restaurant has three lovely terraces. Try the roasted scallops with lobster ragu with Alvariño wine, the *lomos de merluza* (hake) and the *filloas* (Galician crêpes) filled with cream and toffee. Closed Mon except in summer & 10 Dec–31 Jan.

LUGO Mesón de Alberto　*Tapas* 🗎♿📶　€€€

C/ Cruz 4, 27001 **Tel** *982 22 83 10*

An institution of Galician cooking, located in a stone house in the monumental area of town. Award-winning chef Alberto García offers a selection of traditional delicacies and more modern creations. The fish and shellfish are excellent, including small squid and sea bass with baby eels. Wide selection of Galician cheeses and wines. Closed Sun.

LUGO Verruga　*Tapas* 🗎♿📶🅿　€€€

C/ Cruz 12, 27001 **Tel** *982 22 95 72*

This restaurant, in the heart of the old town, has been serving good classic and uncomplicated Galician fare for more than 50 years. It also offers a wide variety of seafood from its own aquarium. Try the red peppers stuffed with crab meat and the delicious home-made *filloas rellenas fritas* (Galician crêpes). Closed Sun evenings & Mon.

O GROVE El Crisol　♿🗎　€€€

C/ Hospital 10–12, 36980 (Pontevedra) **Tel** *986 73 00 29*

A restaurant renowned for its traditional Galician cooking as well as creative dishes. It serves mainly fish and seafood and is a good place to discover new species of fish such as sargo, dentón or pinto, or sample traditional ones such as sea bass and turbot. The dining room overlooks the sea. Closed Mon, but open Mon for dinner in Jul–Aug.

OURENSE A Rexidora　🗎♿🏠📶　€€€

Ctra N540 Bentraces-Celanova, km 7, Bentraces, 32890 **Tel** *988 38 30 78*

An award-winning restaurant in an old building in Bentraces offering modern Galician cuisine prepared in a personal and adventurous way. It is worth having the *empanada con masa de castañas* (chestnut pie), the sea bass or the wild boar with leeks and pumpkin. Closed Sun evenings, Mon, two weeks in Jan and two weeks in Sep.

OURENSE San Miguel　*Tapas* 🗎🏠📶🅿　€€€

C/ San Miguel 12–14, 32005 **Tel** *988 22 07 95*

One of the best restaurants in Ourense, run by the same family for more than half a century. Soberly decorated, it has a wide choice of fish and seafood dishes. Its meats are also excellent, notably the veal medallions with truffles and foie gras. Try the chocolate cream with pineapple juice and mint for dessert. Closed Jan.

PADRÓN Casa Ramallo　🅿🏠♿🗎　€

C/ Castro 5, Rois, 15900 (A Coruña) **Tel** *981 80 41 80*

A short way from Padrón, this pleasant *casa de comidas* has been serving good value traditional Galician fare for more than 100 years. Especially good are its *guisos marineros*, shellfish and seasonal dishes including lamprey. Casa Ramallo also has a good selection of meats and home-made pie for dessert. Closed Mon and evenings daily.

PADRÓN Chef Rivera　*Tapas* 🗎🅿📶　€€€

C/ Enlace Parque 7, 15900 (A Coruña) **Tel** *981 81 04 13*

In this restaurant, chef Jose Antonio Rivera's varied menu offers fish, seafood, game specialities and traditional Galician cooking with a French touch. Particularly good are his seasonal dishes, among them lamprey, a freshwater fish from the Río Ulla. Wide variety of port wine and cigars. Closed Sun evenings & Mon evenings (except Aug).

PONTEVEDRA Alameda de Doña Antonia　🗎📶　€€€

C/ Soportales de la Herrería 4–1º, 36002 **Tel** *986 84 72 74*

Regional cuisine in a refined and beautiful setting overlooking the lovely Plaza de la Herrería. Monkfish salad, marinated sea bass salad, oven-cooked lamb with honey, and *mero al vapor* (grouper) with vegetables and olive oil are favourites. Closed Sun & Mon evening (except December and August), two weeks in Sep and May.

PONTEVEDRA Alameda 10　♿🗎📶　€€€

C/ Alameda 10, 36001 **Tel** *986 85 74 12*

An efficient restaurant preparing good traditional seafood and excellent fish, including seasonal varieties such as lamprey and eels from the Río Miño. Try the *croquetas de marisco* (fish balls), the famous *bacalao* (cod) Alameda or the *solomillo de cerdo ibérico* (pork steak). Try *tarta del abuelo con frutos secos* for dessert. Closed Sun.

PONTEVEDRA Casa Román　🗎♿　€€€

C/ Augusto García Sánchez 12, 36003 **Tel** *986 84 35 60*

A busy restaurant with fast and efficient service serving traditional cuisine prepared with the best quality produce. It specializes in rice dishes, and in elvers and lamprey from the Río Miño, when in season. Favourites are the turbot stew, monkfish in green sauce and *lubina a la sal* (sea bass baked in salt). Closed Sun evenings & Mon (except Aug).

RAXO Pepe Víeíra Camiño da Serpe   🍽️🛢️🏮🍷🅿️   €€€
Camiño da Serpe s/n, 36992 (Pontevedra) **Tel** *986 74 13 78*

A small restaurant run by the award-winning Torres Cannas brothers, who offer creative cooking combining unusual tastes and textures, with surprisingly good results. These include the *pulpo en su sangre* (octopus in its own blood) or *rape en emulsión de almendras* (monkfish in almond sauce) when in season. Open Tue–Sun lunch & Fri–Sat dinner.

SAN SALVADOR DE POIO Casa Solla   🛢️🍽️🍷   €€€€
Av Sineiro 7, 36163 (Pontevedra) **Tel** *986 87 28 84*

In a lovely old *pazo* (manor house) outside Pontevedra, this restaurant is worth the journey. It serves modern "designer" Galician cuisine based on traditional recipes. Try the *bacalao confitado con crema de quesos* (confit of cod with cheese sauce) or the *costilla de cerdo deshuesada y confitada* (confit of boned pork rib). Closed Sun & Thu evenings & Mon.

SANTIAGO DE COMPOSTELA Moncho Vilas   *Tapas* 🍽️ 🍷   €€
Av de Villagarcía 21, 15706 (A Coruña) **Tel** *981 59 83 87*

Exemplary Galician dishes are served at this long-standing restaurant, which was one of the best in Santiago de Compostela and has picked up again after a rather downish period. The fish and seafood, such as clams, scallops and spiny lobster, are ultra-fresh, and the meat and *empanadas* excellent. Closed Sun evenings and Mon.

SANTIAGO DE COMPOSTELA La Tacíta D'Juan   🍽️🛢️🍷   €€€
C/ Hórreo 31, 15702 (A Coruña) **Tel** *981 56 20 41*

The service is careful and professional in this busy restaurant serving classical Galician meat, fish and seafood dishes. They prepare a famous seasonal *cocido* (stew), but otherwise try the *lenguado* (filet of sole) or the *entrecot de buey* (ox steak). End with the *filloas rellenas de crema pastelera* (custard cream filled crêpes). Closed Sun and Aug.

SANTIAGO DE COMPOSTELA Casa Marcelo   🍽️🛢️🍷   €€€€
C/ Hortas 1, 15705 (A Coruña) **Tel** *981 55 85 80*

Recently awarded a Michelin star, this is undoubtably one of the best restaurants in Galicia. Chef Marcelo Tejedor creates his own interpretations of Galician cuisine, and the daily fixed-price menu, served in an intimate, candle-lit dining room, is based on what is available in the town's morning market. Closed Sun–Tue & Oct–Mar.

SANTIAGO DE COMPOSTELA Toñi Vicente   🍽️🛢️🍷   €€€€
C/ Rosalía de Castro 24, 15706 (A Coruña) **Tel** *981 59 41 00*

Worshippers of Galician *haute cuisine* flock faithfully to Toñi Vicente's culinary temple. Among her creations are the marinated sea bass salad, the duck liver sautéed with apple, the red tuna fish in pickle and the carpaccio of venison with truffle oil, salad and parmesan. Closed Sun & some weeks during the year (call ahead).

SANXENXO La Taberna de Rotílio   🍽️🍷   €€€€
Av del Puerto 7–9, 36960 (Pontevedra) **Tel** *986 72 02 00*

Located in the Hotel Rotilio, this restaurant is famous for its innovative approach to Galician cuisine. The chef's creations include monkfish *caldeirada*, fried oysters and an unusual original rice dish. There is also a cheaper menu. Home-made desserts. Closed Sun evenings (except summer), Mon & mid-Dec–mid-Jan.

VEDRA Roberto   🍽️🛢️🏮🍷   €€€€
San Julián de Sales-Vedra, 15880 (A Coruña) **Tel** *981 51 17 69*

Housed in a magnificent *pazo*, 7 km (4.5 miles) from Santiago de Compostela, the emphasis of this restaurant is fish and vegetables. Owner Roberto Crespo uses home-grown produce to create dishes such as sea bass with tomato compote and mushroom stew or scallops over potato purée with balsamic vinegar. Closed Sun evenings, Mon & Jan.

VIGO La Oca   🍷   €€
C/ Purificación Saavedra 8, 36207 (Pontevedra) **Tel** *986 37 12 55*

A cosy restaurant specializing in modern Galician cuisine, using fresh ingredients from the nearby Teis market. *Erizo de mar revuelto con huevos de la casa* (sea urchin omelette), lamprey salad and oven-baked suckling pig are the delicacies here. Only six tables. Closed Sat–Sun, Mon–Thu evenings, Easter and three weeks in Aug.

VIGO Casa Alfredo   🍽️🛢️🍷   €€€
C/ Tameiga 87–88, Mos, 36415 (Pontevedra) **Tel** *986 33 85 40*

This restaurant is in Mos, 10 km (6 miles) from Vigo (take exit 660 from the Vigo-Portugal motorway). It specializes i game dishes and organizes game days. Try the partridge cooked differently in summer or winter. It also has excellent *lubina* and a good selection of breads and desserts. Closed Sun, Mon & Tue evenings, 15–31 Aug & Christmas.

VILAGARCÍA DE AROUSA Casa Bóveda   🍽️🛢️🏮   €€€
Av La Marina 2, Carril, 36610 (Pontevedra) **Tel** *986 51 12 04*

It is better to book in advance to eat in this busy restaurant situated on Carril harbour, a short way from Vilagarcía d Arousa. It specializes in fish and shellfish from the Rias Baixas and also prepares excellent *guisos* and rice dishes. Closed Sun evenings & Mon (except Aug) and 20 Dec–20 Jan.

VILANOVA DE AROUSA O'Paspallas   🛢️🏮   €€
Ctra Nacional, Cambados–Vilagarcía km 320, C/ A Cerca 46, 36620 (Pontevedra) **Tel** *986 55 52 21*

Sited in the Ria de Arousa, near Vilagarcía de Arousa, a popular resort with a pretty promenade and water sports facilities, this small family restaurant is so popular that advanced booking is advised. Sit on the terrace to try the *filloas de mejillón a la albahaca* (mussel crêpes with basil). Closed Sun evenings & Mon (Oct–May).

Key to Price Guide *see p608* **Key to Symbols** *see back cover flap*

ASTURIAS AND CANTABRIA

AJO La Casona de la Peña
Barrio de la Peña, Ajo, 39170 (Cantabria) **Tel** *942 67 05 67*

Located in Ajo, a village east of Santander, this restaurant and hotel in a 17th-century house has an extraordinary dining room which doubles as an exhibition of paintings and antiques. La Casona serves fairly modern cuisine with traditional sauces such as prawns with curry sauce and mango ravioli. Closed Sun evenings, Mon, Christmas & Jan.

AVILÉS La Cofradia del Puerto
Av Los Telares 11, 33400 (Asturias) **Tel** *985 56 12 30*

This is a typical no-frills, no-fuss *sidreria* (cider bar), where you can sample Asturias' famous beverage and eat excellent fish and seafood fresh from the Cantabrian sea. If you are more inclined to meat, they offer a selection of red meats cooked over embers, as well as *frixuelos* (crêpes typical of the region). Closed Sun, 2 weeks end Jun & 2 weeks in Nov.

CANGAS DEL NARCEA Blanco
C/ Mayor 11, 33800 (Asturias) **Tel** *985 81 03 16*

Despite its unprepossessing appearance, the food here is of a very good quality. The seasonal Asturian dishes include *bacalao confitado* (confit of cod) and partridge with vegetables. There are Asturian cheeses and desserts such as ice cream with red fruits and mango purée. Closed Sun evenings, Mon in winter & Sun in summer.

CANGAS DE ONIS El Molín de la Pedrera
C/ Rio Güeña 2, 33550 (Asturias) **Tel** *985 84 91 09*

A stylish *sidreria*, decorated with traditional objects and implements which give it a rustic air. It serves original combinations such as *crujiente de cabrales con avellanas* (Cabrales cheese from the Picos de Europa with hazelnuts) and more traditional dishes such as *bonito* and *frixuelos* (crêpes). Closed Wed except in summer & Jan.

CASTAÑEDA Hostería de Castañeda
C/ Barrio de San Juan, 39660 (Cantabria) **Tel** *942 59 81 13*

After seeing the nearby caves at Puente Viesgo, which are very close to Castañeda, relax in the converted stables of this 17th-century mansion with its own chapel and terrace. Tuck into the hake with green asparagus or the sirloin steak with mushrooms. Or try the white beans with wild boar. Orange jelly for dessert is a must.

CASTRO URDIALES El Ruso
C/ Allendelagua 2, 39700 (Cantabria) **Tel** *942 87 06 18*

A modest restaurant in Allendelagua, a village outside Castro Urdiales, serving quality cooking. There is no written menu; you will need to ask the waiter to reel off what is available and the prices. Dishes include traditional stews, seafood and grilled fish, all in sizeable portions. Home-made desserts. Closed Sun evenings & Oct.

CASTRO URDIALES Mesón del Marinero
C/ Correria 23, 39700 (Cantabria) **Tel** *942 86 00 05*

This listed historic building, decorated as its name suggests in a maritime theme, houses a stylish seafood restaurant. The portions are generous and its proximity to the fishing port is evident in the freshness of the produce. It also serves excellent *ternera* (veal) and other local meats. The traditional *leche frita* is a sweet ending to the meal.

COMILLAS La Rabia
C/ Barrio de la Rabia 8, 39520 (Cantabria) **Tel** *942 72 02 75*

The terrace of this restaurant enjoys views of the estuary in the Oyambre nature reserve making it a popular place for a pre-lunch apéritif. The menu is focused on fish, including *almejas a la marinera* (clams), *rape al ajillo* (monkfish with garlic). Choice of classic desserts. Lunch-time menu for 16 euros. Closed Mon except in summer & Jan.

COMILLAS El Capricho de Gaudí
C/ Barrio de Sobrellano, 39520 (Cantabria) **Tel** *942 72 03 65*

Antoni Gaudí's architectural wonder (see p111), clad in green tiles and sunflowers, provides a unique setting for this sophisticated restaurant. Recommended are the salmon in mustard cream and the turbot with tomato vinaigrette and garlic sprouts. End with chestnuts with caramel ice cream. Closed Sun evenings in winter & Mon.

COSGAYA Mesón del Oso
Ctra C621 Potes-Fuente Dé, km 14, 39539 (Cantabria) **Tel** *942 73 30 18*

Delightful country hotel and restaurant by the Río Deva in the peaceful Liebana Valley, with dramatic views of the Picos de Europa. The veal steaks and *cocido lebaniego* (a rich stew with chickpeas and pork) are local specialities. The *arroz con leche* (rice pudding) makes a traditional dessert. Closed Jan.

CUDILLERO La Casona de Pio
C/ Riofrío 3, 33150 (Asturias) **Tel** *985 59 15 12*

This small hotel and restaurant occupies a renovated old fish-salting factory in the heart of Cudillero, a resort on the Asturian coast with lovely beaches and impressive cliffs. It serves traditional Asturian food, based mainly on fish and seafood. Choices for dessert include grandmother's home-made pie. Closed 7 Jan–7 Feb.

CUDILLERO Mariño
Tapas 🚗🍴🍷 €€

C/ Concha de Artedo, 33155 (Asturias) **Tel** *985 59 11 88*

Located west of the lively seaside resort of Cudillero, with views of the beach, this restaurant-with-rooms serves fish casseroles, delicious *almejas a nuestro modo* (clams "cooked our way") and *curadillo*, a typical dish made with a fish from the shark family. Closed Sun evenings & Mon (except Jul & Aug, Christmas and Easter).

ESCALANTE San Román de Escalante
🚗P🍴🍷 €€€€

Ctra Escalante–Castillo, km 2, 39795 (Cantabria) **Tel** *942 67 77 28*

This lovely old mountain house is set in gardens and woodland in front of a 12th-century chapel. The dining room, decorated with paintings, is the setting for modern seasonal cuisine inspired by traditional recipes. Dishes include fried clams with spinach and pine kernels and hake with clam ravioli. Home-made desserts.

GIJÓN Casa Victor
🚗🍴🍷 €€€

C/ Carmen 11, 33206 (Asturias) **Tel** *985 35 00 93*

This restaurant is an institution in Gijón. It specializes in dishes based on fish caught in the Cantabrian sea. Try the *lomos de salmonete rellenos de marisco* (red mullet filled with seafood). For dessert there is chocolate soufflé with raspberry ice cream. It offers various menus at cheaper prices. Closed Sun & 20 Dec–20 Jan.

LAREDO El Camarote
Tapas 🍴🚗🍷🍷 €€

Av de la Victoria, 39770 (Cantabria) **Tel** *942 60 67 07*

This restaurant, decorated with marine paraphernalia, offers simple cooking based on seasonal market produce. There is a wide range of fish and seafood, cooked in an uncomplicated way. Try the home-style clams and for dessert millefeuille with strawberries and cream. Closed Sun evenings except Jul & Aug.

LAREDO Casa Felipe
Tapas 🍴 €€€

C/ Travesía José Antonio 5, 39770 (Cantabria) **Tel** *942 60 32 12*

A simple restaurant in Laredo, one of Cantabria's most popular holiday resorts with a long sandy beach and an attractive old town. It serves simple traditional food, emphasizing good fresh fish and seafood. It also specializes in local cheeses, mainly made from cow's milk. Closed Mon, Sun evening & 15 Dec–15 Jan.

LUGONES La Máquina
🍴🚗 €€

Av Conde de Santa Bárbara 59, 33420 (Asturias) **Tel** *985 26 36 36*

Although La Máquina is about 6 km (4 miles) from the Asturian capital, it is a good place for an excellent *fabada* Asturiana, the region's typical hearty stew made with white beans and chorizo. For dessert try the delicious home-made *arroz con leche* (rice pudding). Open for lunch only. Closed Sun, mid-Jun–mid-Jul and 16–26 Dec.

OVIEDO Casa Fermín
🍴🚗🍷 €€€€

C/ San Francisco 8, 33003 (Asturias) **Tel** *985 21 64 52*

The cosy Casa Fermín is one of Oviedo's most classic restaurants offering a combination of traditional and modern, seasonal cuisine. Try the caramelized black sausage with plum sauce and the venison with sweet purée. For dessert, try the chocolate cylinder with raspberry textures. Closed Sun.

POTES El Cenador del Capitán
🍷 €

C/ Cervantes 3, 39570 (Cantabria) **Tel** *942 73 21 61*

On the top floor of a big stone house in the centre of Potes is this restaurant with a beamed ceiling and decorated in a simple rustic fashion. It specializes in local food, especially *cocido lebaniego* and game dishes. It offers a cheap *Menú del Peregrino* ("pilgrim's" menu). Closed Mon–Thu in winter, Sun evening all year.

POTES Paco Wences
P🍴🚗🍴 €€

C/ Roscabao 5, 39570 (Cantabria) **Tel** *942 73 00 25*

The restaurant of the Picos de Valdecoro hotel, in the Picos de Europa, offers simple traditional food from the Liebana Valley, with filling *cocidos* made from quality locally-grown ingredients. Try the *cocido lebaniego* or the *solomillo al queso de Tresviso* (steak cooked with a local cheese). Typical Cantabrian desserts. Closed Jan.

PRAVIA Balbona
🍴🚗 €€€

Calle Pico Merás 2, 33120 (Asturias) **Tel** *985 82 11 62*

A superb restaurant located at the heart of Pravia which provides traditional Asturian cuisine with modern touches. They also have excellent home-made desserts, many of which must be ordered at the beginning of the meal, such as creamy hazelnut cake with spicy bread. Closed Tue.

PRENDES Casa Gerardo
P🍴🚗🍷 €€€€

Ctra AS–19 km 8, 33438 (Asturias) **Tel** *985 88 77 97*

This delightful restaurant is run by the fifth generation of the same family since its opening. It reputedly serves the best *fabada Asturiana* and also offers other delights such as king prawn with fresh pasta and Asturian cabbage. Closed Sun–Thu evenings (except Tue–Thu evenings in summer), Mon and two weeks in Jan.

RAMALES DE LA VICTORIA Cenador de Amós
🚗🍴🍷🍴 €€€€

Villaverde de Pontones, 39750 (Cantabria) **Tel** *942 50 82 43*

This restaurant, which has had a Michelin star since 1993, is housed in an 18th-century country palace surrounded by a pleasant garden with outside tables in summer. The menu fuses traditional and creative Cantabrian cuisines. Closed Sun evening, Mon, Christmas and one week in Jun.

Key to Price Guide *see p608* **Key to Symbols** *see back cover flap*

SALINAS Real Balneario de Salinas
Tapas 🍽️ ♿ 🏧 🍷   €€€€

Av Juan Sitges 3, 33400 (Asturias) **Tel** *985 51 86 13*

This lovely restaurant in the seaside resort of Salinas is owned by a family of restaurateurs who work together in the kitchen and the dining room. They offer a combination of classical and modern cuisine using high-quality ingredients. Try the *mero con alcachofas* (grouper with artichokes). Closed Sun evenings & Mon.

SAN VICENTE DE LA BARQUERA Augusto
Tapas 🍽️ ♿ 🏧 🍷   €€€€

C/ Mercado 1, 39540 (Cantabria) **Tel** *942 71 20 40*

Located in the porticoed part of town, this renovated tavern specializes in fresh fish, seafood and rice. You can also eat in a lovely shaded terrace in summer. Try the *ensalada de mariscos* (seafood salad), *almejas con arroz* (clams with rice), *calamares en su tinta* (squid cooked in its own ink) and other delicacies. Closed Mon (except Jun–Sep).

SAN VICENTE DE TORANZO Casona de Toranzo
Tapas 🍽️ 🏧 🍷   €

Ctra N623, Burgos-Santander km 115, 39699 **Tel** *942 59 44 11*

The restaurant of the hotel Posada del Pas (see p564) has a separate entrance for non-residents beside the main road between Santander and Burgos. The menu is strong on Cantabrian food and includes an excellent *cocido montañes* (mountain stew), as well as entrecôte with Treviso cheese sauce and lovely sorbet.

SANTANDER Bodega del Riojano
Tapas 🍽️ ♿   €€

C/ Río de la Pila 5, 39003 (Cantabria) **Tel** *942 21 67 50*

This colourful bodega (wine cellar) is as famous for its decorative wine barrels, painted by Spanish artists, as it is for its delicious food. The red peppers stuffed with anchovies and other ingredients are renowned. It also serves a tasty leek salad and oxtail stew. Closed Sun evenings & Mon except in summer.

SANTANDER Hostería de Adarzo
🅿️ 🍽️ 🏧   €€

C/ Adarzo 68, 39011 (Cantabria) **Tel** *942 33 23 11*

A restaurant and hotel serving traditional cooking using fresh, seasonal market produce, with special emphasis on red meats and daily caught fish. Adarzo serves dishes such as octopus salad with vegetables, cod loin with tomatoes, trotters and veal chinstraps. Has its own parking which is an advantage in the capital. Closed Mon & Sun evening.

SANTANDER El Nuevo Molino
🅿️ 🍽️ ♿ 🏧 🍷   €€€€

Ctra N611 Santander Torrelavega km 13, Barrio Monseñor 18, Puente Arce, 39478 (Cantabria) **Tel** *942 57 50 55*

Sited in Puente Arce, this ancient mill belongs to El Serbal in Santander. It offers creative cooking with dishes such as cod salad with mushrooms and *pil pil* (a creamy parsley sauce) and monkfish ravioli filled with king prawn and cream. There is a divine ice cream with sultanas and brandy over toffee cream. Closed Sun evenings & Tue.

SANTANDER El Serbal
🍽️ ♿ 🍷   €€€€

C/ Andrés del Río 7 (Puerto Chico), 39004 (Cantabria) **Tel** *942 22 25 15*

A nice restaurant that is becoming very popular for its innovative cuisine, created by adding personal touches to traditional dishes. It also offers some originals such as oven-baked ray in mushroom *pil pil* and creamy rice and a distinctive chicken curry. For dessert, strawberries with apple jelly and basil. Closed Sun evenings & Mon.

SANTILLANA DEL MAR La Joraca
♿   €€

Los Hornos 20, 39330 (Cantabria) **Tel** *942 84 01 37*

The restaurant of the Hotel Colegiata may be uninspiringly furnished and decorated, and lacking the beautiful views of the hotel, but it is still a good place to eat excellent food made with local produce. Choice dishes are grilled monkfish with salad onions *pil pil* and ham. For dessert, order cream of smoked cheese. Closed Sun evenings & Mon.

SOLARES Casa Enrique
Tapas 🍽️ ♿ 🏧 🍷   €€

Paseo de la Estación 20, 39710 (Cantabria) **Tel** *942 52 00 73*

Casa Enrique hotel's restaurant is popular with locals and tourists alike. It is a decent place to sample traditional home cooking, which results in tasty stews and dishes such as *albóndigas de ternera* (veal meatballs) or *ventresca de bonito con cebolla y pimiento* (tuna fish with onions and peppers). Closed Sun evenings & 20 Sep–10 Oct.

THE BASQUE COUNTRY, NAVARRA & LA RIOJA

AMOREBIETA Juantxu
🅿️ 🍽️ ♿ 🏧 🍷   €€€

C/ Barrio Enartze 2, 48340 (Vizcaya) **Tel** *946 73 26 50*

Housed in a traditional Basque rural house on the road between Amorebieta and Gernika, this restaurant with a garden specializes in both fish (particularly cod) and meats including roast lamb. Good choice of salads and vegetarian options. The dessert menu includes a selection of home-made ice creams. Closed Sun–Thu evenings, Tue & Christmas.

AOIZ Beti Jai
Tapas 🍽️ ♿ 🏧 🍷   €€€

C/ Santa Agueda 2, 31430 (Navarra) **Tel** *948 33 60 52*

A well-known restaurant with bar in an old house on the main square of the town, with views of the river. Beti Jai serves high-quality Navarrese cuisine and some modern and creative dishes based on seasonal market produce. Try the *menudicos* (tripe) and any of the excellent home-made desserts. Closed Sun evenings & weekends of 15–31 Aug.

AZPEITIA Kiruri
Tapas 📋 ♿ 🏧 🍷   €€

Barrio Loiola Hiribidea 24, 20730 (Guipúzcoa) **Tel** *943 81 56 08*

Located in front of the shrine of Loyola, this family-run restaurant offers simple cooking and traditional Basque dishes such as *txangurro* (spider crab baked and served in the shell) and *menestra de verduras* (vegetable stew) and a choice of pies for dessert. The car park is convenient for visiting the shrine. Closed Mon evenings & 24 Dec–7 Jan.

BERMEO Jokin
Tapas 📋 ♿ 🏧 🍷   €€€

C/ Eupeme Deuna 13, 48370 (Vizcaya) **Tel** *946 88 40 89*

Jokin, with pretty views of Bermeo's fishing port, specializes in seasonal fish dishes such as *habitas frescas con bacalao fresco* (small broad beans with fresh cod) or *rollitos de merluza confitados en aceite de oliva* (hake in olive oil). Meat-eaters can try the crispy trotters in sauce. Closed Sun evenings.

BILBAO Café Iruña
Tapas 🏧   €

C/ Berastegi 5, 48001 (Vizcaya) **Tel** *944 23 70 21*

The classic café opened in 1903 opposite the Jardines de Albia. It has a marvellous, ornately decorated mock-Mudéjar interior of ceramic tiles evocative of the age of Islamic Spain. The *menú del día* is good and surprisingly inexpensive for such a charming place. A place worth dipping into even if you only feel like drinking coffee.

BILBAO Café La Granja
Tapas   €

Plaza Circular, 40001 (Vizcaya) **Tel** *944 230 813*

An old-fashioned café created in "the French style" of the 1920s. It stands in the centre of Bilbao, amidst office blocks, facing the statue of the city's founder. A full and inexpensive *menú del día* is served, but the café also does a good breakfast. Snacks and sandwiches are available throughout the day. Closed Sun.

BILBAO Ein Prosit
Tapas 📋 ♿ 🍷   €

Plaza Ensanche 7, 48009 (Vizcaya) **Tel** *944 24 13 11*

An authentic German restaurant run by the descendants of a renowned Saxon *charcutier* (butcher) who settled in Bilbao in the early 20th century. The specialities are all meaty except for salmon marinaded in vodka. Serves draught German beer and a selection of different types of schnapps. Closed Sun and Tue evenings, Mon and Easter.

BILBAO Xukela
Tapas   €

C/ Perro 2, 48005 (Vizcaya) **Tel** *944 15 97 72*

A refreshingly informal place to eat snacks or a light meal in the Casco Viejo. Choice morsels include fine Spanish ham, crab meat, cheeses, peppers with anchovies and caviar and mushrooms topped with smoked cod and a dollop of apple purée.

BILBAO Víctor
Tapas 📋 🏧 🍷   €€€

Plaza Nueva 2, 48005 (Vizcaya) **Tel** *944 15 16 78*

A classic restaurant located in the historic square of the old quarter. Specialities are cod dishes, *chipirones* (Cantrabrian squid), green peppers filled with spider crab, *lenguado a la plancha* (grilled sole), ostrich in mushroom sauce and, for dessert, *tarta capuchina* (syrup-soaked cake) Closed Sun, second week in Jan, Easter week & 1–15 Sep.

BILBAO Zortziko
📋 🛗 🍷   €€€€

C/ Alameda Mazarredo 17, 48001 (Vizcaya) **Tel** *944 23 97 43*

Contemporary *haute cuisine* served in a beautiful building, not far from the Guggenheim Museum. The menu is seasonal with creative Basque touches. Among the specialities are *pintada a baja temperatura* (guinea fowl cooked at a low temperature), foie gras, turbot and a delicious tiramisu. Closed Sun, Mon & 20 Aug–15 Sep.

CINTRUÉNIGO Maher
📋 🏧 🍷   €€€€

La Ribera 19, 31592 (Navarra) **Tel** *948 81 11 50*

Innovative cuisine is impeccably presented in the Hotel Maher restaurant, although the service can be variable. Salad with different kinds of lettuces, asparagus pudding, rice with hare and suckling lamb in mushroom sauce, are all house specialities. Order bitter chocolate soufflé with caramel ice cream. Closed Sun evenings, Mon & 20 Dec–20 Jan.

ESTELLA Navarra
Tapas 📋 ♿ 🏧   €€

C/ Gustavo de Maeztu 16, 31200 (Navarra) **Tel** *948 55 00 40*

Traditional regional cuisine is served in this grand house, with tiles depicting Navarra's former kings. The *Blanca de Navarra* (a lemon and honey ice cream, served with fresh cream and nuts) is superb. Other specialities are *espárragos rellenos* (stuffed asparagus), roast piglet and lamb, and *crema tostada* for dessert. Closed Sun evenings & Mon.

EZCARAY El Rincón del Vino
📋 🅿 ♿ 🏧 🍷   €€

C/ Jesús Nazareno 2, 26280 (La Rioja) **Tel** *941 35 43 75*

Vino serves traditional Riojan cuisine with an emphasis on seasonal produce including mushrooms and truffles. During the hunting season, it offers good game dishes. Vino also has a shop selling local wines, including 2,000 different Riojas, and other delicacies typical of the region. Closed Mon–Thu evenings in winter & Wed except in Jul & Aug.

EZCARAY El Portal del Echaurren
📋 🅿 ♿ 🍷   €€€€

Hèroes del Alcázar 2, 26280 (La Rioja) **Tel** *941 35 40 47*

One of La Rioja's emblematic restaurants, run by the Paniego family who also have a small hotel. Special dishes include *solomillos de rape negro sobre purrusalda* (monkfish with leeks). There is also a great variety of Rioja and Albariño wines. Closed Sun evenings, Mon, Tue evenings Jul–Dec, two weeks in Jun & 9–25 Dec.

Key to Price Guide *see p608*   **Key to Symbols** *see back cover flap*

GETARIA Elkano
📋🍴 €€€€

C/ Herrerieta 2, 20808 (Guipúzcoa) **Tel** 943 14 00 24

Elkano is famous for its grilled fish dishes and seafood. The baby squid and the turbot are excellent. Also good are the local grilled hake cheeks and small squid Pelayo style. The best Basque brand of Txacoli wine, Txomín Echaniz, is available. Closed Sun evenings, Mon and Tue evenings in winter, two weeks after Easter & two weeks in Nov.

GERNIKA Zallo Barri
📋♿🍴 €€€

C/ Juan Calzada 79, 48300 (Vizcaya) **Tel** 946 25 18 00

Barri offers both traditional Basque cuisine and innovative dishes. Only the freshest produce is used and the menu changes with the season so options might include *cordero a la parrilla con patata y foie gras a la plancha* (grilled lamb with foie gras) and *bizcocho de almendra* (almond sponge cake). Closed Sun–Thu evenings.

HARO Beethoven
📋 €€

C/ Santo Tomás 8–10, 26200 (La Rioja) **Tel** 941 31 11 81

The Fresno family owns the two restaurants Beethoven I and Beethoven II in the same street at Haro. Both use local Riojan products to prepare traditional fare, with emphasis on local seasonal vegetables and *chuletillas de cordero* (lamb chops). *Torrijas* (slices of bread soaked in milk and egg and then fried) make a popular dessert.

HARO Terete
📋♿ €€€

C/ Lucrecia Arana 17, 26200 (La Rioja) **Tel** 941 31 00 23

An ancient wood-burning oven has been roasting lamb here since 1877. Sit at the long wooden tables and savour the Riojan specialities, accompanied by a bottle of house wine. You can start with asparagus, and end the meal with traditional *cuajada*, a fresh cheese similar to yoghurt. Closed Sun evenings, Mon, 1–15 Jul & 15–31 Oct.

HONDARRIBIA Sebastián
📋♿🍴 €€€€

C/ Mayor 11, 20280 (Guipúzcoa) **Tel** 943 64 01 67

A 16th-century house in the historic part of town. The traditional cuisine is based on seasonal produce and is cooked by chef Miguel Soto. Try the *Ensalada de Txangurro* (spider crab salad) or the monkfish with scallops and king prawns cooked in the local txacolí wine. Game dishes are available in season. Closed Sun evenings, Mon.

LAGUARDIA Posada Mayor de Migueloa
Tapas 📋♿🏠🍴🍴 €€€€

C/ Mayor de Migueloa 20, 01300 (Alava) **Tel** 945 62 11 75

The restored 17th-century palace of Viana now houses a small hotel and one of northern Spain's best restaurants. The cuisine is a Basque-La Rioja fusion, strong on fish and seafood (try the baked hake), meat (roast lamb or venison) and vegetables. Excellent choice of home-made desserts, one made with sweet peppers. Closed mid-Dec–7 Jan.

LASARTE Martin Berasategui
🅿📋♿🏠🍴🍴 €€€€

C/ Loidi 4, 20160 (Guipúzcoa) **Tel** 943 36 64 71

One of the top restaurants of Spain is located in a converted farmhouse, 7 km (4.5 miles) from San Sebastián. The specialities change with the season but Martín Berasategui, a trendsetter among chefs, always surprises with his creations. Reservations essential especially for terrace tables. Closed Sun evenings, Mon, Tue & mid-Dec–mid-Jan.

LEITZA Basa Kabi
Tapas 📋 €€

C/ Alto de Leiza, 31880 (Navarra) **Tel** 948 51 01 25

In the middle of lovely woodland and mountain scenery, Basa Kabi serves traditional food with modern touches. Try the sautéed broad beans and peas with grilled bacon and cauliflower cream, grilled tuna with mushroom sauce or, for dessert, vanilla rice pudding with cherries and chocolate cream. Special children's menu. Open only in summer, Jul–Aug.

LOGROÑO Cachetero
♿📋🍴 €€€

C/ Laurel 3, 26001 (La Rioja) **Tel** 941 22 84 63

Tasty home cooking is served in this cosy restaurant, well known in the city for its basic dishes capturing the best of each season. Standards include vegetable stews and stuffed peppers. Desserts include *helado de queso de roquefort con nueces* (Roquefort cheese ice cream with walnuts). Closed Sun, Wed evenings & one week end of Aug.

LOGROÑO Casa Emilio
♿📋🍴 €€€

Av República Argentina 8, 26002 (La Rioja) **Tel** 941 25 88 44

A good-value restaurant in the heart of the city specializing in high-quality roasted red meats, grilled fish and oven-baked kid. Particular specialities are *ensalada de perdiz* (partridge salad) and *taco de rape con crema suave de ajos confitados* (creamed monkfish) and venison served with grape and plum sauce. Closed Sun except in May, Aug.

OIARTZUN Zuberoa
🅿♿📋🏠🍴🍴 €€€€

Plaza Bekosoro 1, 20180 (Guipúzcoa) **Tel** 943 49 12 28

The celebrated restaurant of the Arbelaitz brothers is in a 600-year-old farmhouse. Among the dishes are Cantabrian squid cooked in a traditional sauce and roast piglet with ginger and potato purée. Exquisite desserts to follow. They also have a sampler menu. Closed Sun, Wed, 30 Dec–15 Jan, two weeks after Easter & 15–30 Oct.

OLITE Casa Zanito
📋🍴 €€€€

Rúa Mayor 16, 31390 (Navarra) **Tel** 948 74 00 02

Probably the best option for a lunch of traditional Navarrese cuisine with a few modern touches. One speciality is a salad of fried artichokes with prawns. Desserts include apple pie with cinnamon ice cream. They also have a reasonable fixed lunch and dinner menu. The service is good. Closed Mon, Tue (in winter) & mid-Dec–mid-Jan.

PAMPLONA Alhambra   🖼️🚻📶❄️   €€€€
C/ Francisco Bergamín 7, 31003 (Navarra) **Tel** *948 24 50 07*

Typical Navarrese cooking as well as some unusual combinations are the hallmark of this welcoming and elegant restaurant. The artichokes, the truffle and vegetable purée and the mushroom risotto are all delicious appetizers. Dessert could be the hot chocolate soufflé with saffron ice cream and pumpkin seeds. Closed Sun & Easter week.

PAMPLONA Europa   🖼️❄️   €€€€
C/ Espoz y Mina 11, 31002 (Navarra) **Tel** *948 22 18 00*

Located in the Hotel Europa, in the old part of the city near the cathedral, is one of Pamplona's best places to eat. It offers a range of traditional Navarrese dishes such as *menestra de verduras* (vegetable stew), *sopa de castañas* (chestnut soup) and *chateaubriand de lomo de ciervo con mango a la parrilla* (grilled deer with mango). Closed Sun.

PASAI DONIBANE Casa Camara   ♿   €€€
C/ Donibane 79, 20110 (Guipúzcoa) **Tel** *943 52 36 99*

A restaurant with wonderful views of Pasai Donibane port (just outside San Sebastián), where you can dine watching the boats and choose your own live lobster from the aquarium. Try the baked mushrooms with crunchy vegetables or the Basque speciality of *txangurro al horno*. Alternatively, there are steaks. Closed Sun evenings & Mon.

PUENTE LA REINA Mesón del Peregrino   🅿️🖼️🚻❄️   €€€€
Irumbidea, Puente la Reina, 31100 (Navarra) **Tel** *948 34 00 75*

The restaurant-cum-hotel of a well-known chef is sited on the pilgrimage route to Santiago de Compostela. The cuisine combines Mediterranean and Navarrese influences. Try the *cochinillo en salsa de trufas* (suckling pig in a truffle sauce). Closed 8–31 Jan, Sun evenings & Mon.

SAN SEBASTIÁN Bar Sport   *Tapas* 🖼️   €
C/ Fermín Calbetón 10, 20001 (Guipúzcoa) **Tel** *943 42 68 88*

One of several bars lining the streets of the old part of San Sebastián, which have counters stacked with *pinchos* (tapas). For an informal meal, point to what you want and keep going until you are full, then settle the bill. It is an enjoyable way of having your meal but beware that the price can add up to more than you expect.

SAN SEBASTIÁN Akelarre   🖼️♿🚻❄️   €€€€
Paseo Padre Orkolaga 56, Barrio de Igueldo, 20008 (Guipúzcoa) **Tel** *943 31 12 09*

One of the famous restaurants of Spain, a gourmet temple with great views of rolling hills which plunge into the sea. If you have room for it, choose the seven-course *menú de degustación* (a sampler menu). Spectacular desserts. Closed Sun evenings, Mon (and Tue Jan–Jun), 1–15 Oct and Feb.

SAN SEBASTIÁN Arzak   🖼️♿🚻❄️   €€€€
Av Alcalde José Elósegui 273, 20015 (Guipúzcoa) **Tel** *943 27 84 65*

Celebrity chef Juan Mari Arzak has earned a reputation beyond Spain for his perfectly presented, creative dishes. His daughter Elena works here as well. They even run a "laboratory" where a team of cooks experiment. Closed Sun, Mon and for two weeks in Jun & Nov.

SAN VICENTE DE LA SONSIERRA Casa Toni   🖼️♿❄️   €€€
C/ Zumalacárregui 27, 26338 (La Rioja) **Tel** *941 33 40 01*

Book in advance for this restaurant serving modern Riojan cuisine based on traditional dishes. Its best-known speciality is the *crema de patatas a la riojana con espuma de piquillos y láminas de chorizo* (Riojan cream of potatoes with peppers and chorizo). Closed Sun–Thu evenings (winters), Mon (except in summer), 15–30 Jun & 15–30 Sep.

SANTO DOMINGO DE LA CALZADA El Rincón de Emilio   🖼️❄️   €€
Plaza Bonifacio Gil 7, 26250 (La Rioja) **Tel** *941 34 09 90*

This classic restaurant offers both traditional and contemporary Riojan cuisine. Specialities are *solomillo al vino tinto* (fillet steak in red wine), *bacalao a la riojana* (Riojan cod) and *arroz con leche con helado de caramelo* (rice pudding with caramel ice cream). Closed Tue evenings & Feb.

SORAUREN Txarrantxena   🖼️❄️   €€€
C/ del Medio 3, 31194 (Navarra) **Tel** *948 33 18 05*

In Sorauren, 7 km (4.5 miles) from Pamplona, in a beautiful 18th-century house, this restaurant offers modern Navarrese cuisine.Try the goats' cheese millefeuille with caramelised onions and roasted peppers and hot chocolate cake with white chocolate ice cream. Closed Sun evenings, Mon; two weeks in Feb; Sun–Thu evenings Sep–Apr.

TAFALLA Túbal   🖼️♿🚻❄️   €€€
Plaza de Navarra 4, 31300 (Navarra) **Tel** *948 70 08 52*

Túbal, one of the best restaurants in Navarra, is housed in a historic building with 18 balconies overlooking the square. If you are not sure what to have they will prepare a personalized *menú de degustación* for you. Its forté is regional cuisine with seasonal vegetables. Closed Sun evenings, Mon, 21 Aug–4 Sep & the Christmas period.

TUDELA Restaurante 33   🖼️♿❄️   €€€
C/ Capuchinos 7, 31500 (Navarra) **Tel** *948 82 76 06*

A busy restaurant in the largest town of the Ribera region, where the menu reflects the local skill of growing vegetables. Try the *menú de degustación*, which includes the choice of the season's crop. One speciality is *lomo de lubina salvaje asado con verduritas* (roasted wild sea bass with vegetables). Closed Mon and Tue evenings, Sun & 1–21 Aug.

VIANA Borgia ⬛ €€€€
C/ Serapio Urra, 31230 (Navarra) **Tel** *948 64 57 81*

Located in the centre of Viana, this family-run restaurant only opens for lunch, except on Fridays and Saturdays when it is open all day. Borgia offers varied and refreshingly eclectic dishes. Try the *espárragos frescos con crema de remolacha* (fresh asparagus with creamed beetroot) and roast lamb with gin sauce. Closed Sun & Aug.

VINIEGRA DE ABAJO Venta de Goyo 🅿⬛⬛⬛ €€
Puente Río Neila 3, 26325 (La Rioja) **Tel** *941 37 80 07*

Part of an old *venta* (inn), also a hotel, in the Sierra de la Demanda, about 40 km (25 miles) southwest of Nájera, this simple restaurant offers good value. The menu is based on the culinary heritage of the Sierra with good game dishes. Try the red beans, the *cordero a la cazuela* (lamb casserole) and the *tarta de manzana* (apple pie). Closed Christmas.

VITORIA Casa Felipe **Tapas** ⬛⬛ €€€
C/ Fueros 28, 01005 (Alava) **Tel** *945 13 45 54*

This bar-restaurant is a traditional, no-nonsense *casa de comidas* and a classic in Vitoria. It serves mainly Basque fare, with some standards such as *merluza rebozada* (batter hake) and lamb stew. Other specialities are grilled mushrooms and clams. For dessert try *tarta de la casa* (home-made pie). Closed Mon, Sun evenings & mid-Jun–mid-Jul.

VITORIA Dos Hermanas ⬛⬛ €€€
C/ Madre Vedruna 10, 01008 (Alava) **Tel** *945 13 29 34*

A pleasant and cosy restaurant serving classic dishes with innovative touches. From the seasonally-changing menu try the pig's trotters stuffed with foie gras, served with *berza* (a local vegetable) and violet potatoes. The home-made desserts might include cocoa jelly with rice pudding cream and peanut crisps. Closed Sun evenings.

BARCELONA

OLD TOWN Bar Pinotxo **Tapas** 🔲 €
C/ Mercat de la Boqueria (La Rambla 89), 08002 **Tel** *933 17 17 31*   **Map** 5 A2

The most famous of all the bars in the Boqueria. Steel buckets hold chilled bottles of *cava* (Catalan champagne-style wine), and fresh ingredients from neighbouring market stalls are cooked and served hot on the spot. Try the squid cooked in diverse styles and the fresh oysters. The bar is closed on Sundays and in the evenings after 6pm.

OLD TOWN Elisabets **Tapas** ⬛⬛⬛ €
C/ Elisabets 2, 08001 **Tel** *933 17 58 26*   **Map** 2 F2

A local institution, this homely bustling restaurant specializes in traditional Catalan cuisine. It is a favourite for diners in search of hearty, home-cooked mid-day meals and Friday night tapas. Dishes include rabbit stew, chicken cooked in beer and a variety of *bocadillos* (sandwiches). Closed Sun (the bar is open) & three weeks in Aug.

OLD TOWN Mosquito **Tapas** ⬛ €
C/ Carders 46, 08003 **Tel** *932 68 75 69*   **Map** 5 C2

A laid-back bar, frequented by a healthy mix of Catalans and resident expats. Trendy music, friendly staff, cheap drinks and a solid array of Asian favourites such as chicken tikka brochettes, Singapore noodles and *gyoza* dumplings. Try the exotic tapas that can change in the middle of the evening from Indian to Japanese. Closed Mon.

OLD TOWN Organic ⬛⬛ €
C/ Junta de Comerç 11, 08001 **Tel** *933 01 09 02*   **Map** 2 F3

Spacious, clean and pleasantly lit, this good-value vegetarian restaurant offers an imaginative menu of Asian dishes, lasagnes, stews and an all-you-can-eat salad buffet. The home-made bread with nuts is a must. They also have a small shop selling organic products. Has an excellent lunch set menu.

OLD TOWN El Salón ⬛⬛ €€
C/ Hostal d'en Sol 6–8, 08002 **Tel** *933 15 21 59*   **Map** 5 B3

The Baroque-style interior gives this establishment the feel of an 18th-century boudoir. The menu changes constantly but promises sumptuous ingredients and inventive dishes, often featuring French and Catalan specialities. Closed Sun & for lunch.

OLD TOWN Euskal Etxea **Tapas** ⬛⬛⬛⬛ €€
C/ Placeta Montcada 1–3, 08003 **Tel** *933 10 21 85*   **Map** 5 B3

Home to the Basque Cultural Institute, the Euskal Etxea is one of the best places in town for Basque *pintxos* (small rounds of bread with a myriad of toppings). Other specialities include fish and meat stews, roasted meat and fresh seafood dishes. It also serves exceptionally good à la carte meals. Closed Sun & Mon lunch.

OLD TOWN Inopia ⬛⬛⬛ €€
C/Tamarit 104, 08015 **Tel** *93 424 52 31*   **Map** 5 D5

It's off the beaten track, but dedicated foodies are advised to seek this restaurant out. Owner Albert Adria (brother of Ferran, of El Bulli fame) has gone back to basics, and the bar serves classic tapas – *croquetas, patatas bravas* – all prepared with the finest of local ingredients. He also has a sweet shop. Closed on Sun.

OLD TOWN Kaiku

P ⊞ 目 🖫 €€

Plaça del Mar 1, 08003 **Tel** *93 221 90 82* **Map** 5 B5

Despite its humble exterior this unassuming, apparently simple beach-front restaurant makes what is probably the best paella in the city. Described on the menu as *arròs del xef*, it is prepared with smoked rice and succulent shellfish. Book the terrace in summer, for sea views and a breeze. Great desserts too. Open Tue–Sun lunch only. Closed Mon & Aug.

OLD TOWN Mam i Teca

Tapas 目 🖫 €€

C/ Lluna 4, 08001 **Tel** *934 41 33 35* **Map** 2 F2

Tiny, sunflower-yellow bar that plays well-known jazz, blues and rock tunes. The tapas are superb, and include locally sourced cheeses, organic sausages and country dishes such as ham and broad beans. They also have an excellent wine list and a good range of Scottish single malts. Closed Tue, Sat lunch and two weeks in Aug.

OLD TOWN 7 Portes

🖫 目 & 🖫 €€€

Passeig Isabel II 14, 08003 **Tel** *933 19 30 33* **Map** 5 B3

A long-standing Barcelona institution since 1836, with a who's who of past guests, including Winston Churchill and Che Guevara. It is famed for its classic marble tiles and wood-panelled dining room, and most of all for paella, which comes in 10 different varieties. They serve a different paella every day of the week.

OLD TOWN Agua

目 & 🖫 🖫 €€€

Passeig Marítim de la Barceloneta 30, 08003 **Tel** *932 25 12 72* **Map** 6 D4

Classy seafront restaurant with floor-to-ceiling windows and abstract fish sculptures. It is popular with a young crowd and serves excellent fish and rice dishes. Specials include steamed mussels, butan potatoes, Norway lobsters au gratin and grilled fish. Agua is also known for cooking rice over coal. There is an appealing terrace too.

OLD TOWN Biblioteca

目 & 🖫 €€€

C/ Junta de Comerç 28, 08001 **Tel** *934 12 62 21* **Map** 2 F3

Elegant restaurant-cum-cookbook shop with Modernista tiles and an open kitchen. The cooking focuses on seasonal ingredients. Specialities include rice with pigeon and black pudding, black spaghetti with *calçots* (leek-sized green onions) and poached egg. Service can be erratic. Closed Sun, Mon & two weeks in Aug.

OLD TOWN Café de l'Academia

🖫 目 🖫 🖫 €€€

C/ Lledó 1, Plaça Sant Just, 08002 **Tel** *933 19 82 53* **Map** 5 B3

An intimate, candle-lit restaurant with exposed brick walls and a pretty terrace in the lovely Plaça Sant, in the centre of Barri Gòtic. The menu offers superb Catalan fare, interesting salads and home-made pasta. The cod dishes, from raw to baked, are excellent. The desserts are top-notch. Closed Sat, Sun and for three weeks in Aug.

OLD TOWN Cal Pep

Tapas 目 🖫 €€€

Plaça de les Olles 8, 08003 **Tel** *933 10 79 61* **Map** 5 B3

Arguably the best bar in town for fresh fish and seafood, right off the boats. Cal Pep has an excellent selection of tapas as well. The long, narrow, standing bar means it gets crowded at peak times. Arrive early for one of five tables out back. Closed Sat dinner, Sun, Mon lunch & Aug.

OLD TOWN Can Majó

🖫 目 🖫 🖫 €€€

C/ Almirall Aixada 23, 08003 **Tel** *932 21 54 55* **Map** 5 B5

As places for paella go, this is one of the best, especially when eaten on a warm summer's day on the terrace with sea views. If you start getting into the shellfish, prices hike right up, but it is worth it for freshness and quality of produce, cooked to perfection. Closed Sun evenings and Mon.

OLD TOWN Pla de la Garsa

& 目 🖫 €€€

C/ Assaonadors 13, 08003 **Tel** *933 15 24 13* **Map** 5 B2

Situated in the stables of a 17th-century palace, the cosy atmosphere of this pretty, split-level restaurant makes it a good place for romantic evenings. For cheese-lovers the 40-strong list is a winner. There is also an interesting selection of red wines. Closed for lunch daily.

OLD TOWN Taxidermista

目 & 🖫 🖫 €€€

Plaça Reial 8, 08002 **Tel** *934 12 45 36* **Map** 5 A3

Soft colour schemes and high ceilings give this trendy restaurant an edge over the touristy competition on the bustling Plaça Reial. Inventive market cooking offers a wide range of dishes from around the Mediterranean Rim, including *baba ghanoush* (Lebanese eggplant purée), sardine tarts and duck confit. Closed Mon & for two weeks in Jan.

OLD TOWN Carballeira

P 🖫 目 & 🖫 €€€€

C/ Reina Cristina 3, 08003 **Tel** *933 10 10 06* **Map** 5 B3

The first Galician seafood restaurant in Barcelona, Carballeira is well known for its simply grilled fish and seafood, perfect paellas and the house special – Galician-style tender octopus sprinkled with paprika. The *vieiras* (escallops) are a popular dish. Lobsters and sea crabs are brought live from the Galician coasts. Closed Sun evenings & Mon.

OLD TOWN Comerç 24

Tapas 目 & 🖫 €€€€

C/ Comerç 24, 08003 **Tel** *933 19 21 02* **Map** 5 C3

Designer tapas bar with charcoal grey walls and primary colour accents, serving some of the most inventive tapas in town. A "festival" of tapas is served for groups of six or more. Try the *arròs a banda* (rice with fish) or the *tortilla de patatas* (potato omelette). Reservations necessary. Closed Sun & Mon.

Key to Price Guide *see p608* **Key to Symbols** *see back cover flap*

EIXAMPLE Cata 1.81

Tapas 🗐 🖥 €€

C/ València 181, 08011 **Tel** *933 23 68 18* **Map** *3 A4*

Long, slim and blindingly white, this modern tapas bar was one of the pioneers of Post-Modernist *pinchos*, turning classics such as Russian salad into state-of-the-art taste explosions. The excellent wine list is on offer by the glass. A top choice for those interested in the wonders of New Catalan cuisine. Closed daily for lunch, Sun & three weeks in Aug.

EIXAMPLE Madrid-Barcelona

Tapas 🛗🗐🖥🖥 €€

C/ Aragó 282, 08007 **Tel** *932 15 70 27* **Map** *3 A4*

This smart, split-level restaurant with its cast-iron balustrades and polished wood looks more expensive than it is. It is hugely popular, often with long queues coming out the door, for Málaga-style *pescaditos fritos* (fried fish) and other good-value tapas.

EIXAMPLE Thai Lounge

🖥🛗🗐 €€

C/ València 205, 08007 **Tel** *934 54 90 32* **Map** *3 A4*

Typical of a Thai restaurant with lots of Buddhas and teakwood furniture, Thai Lounge succeeds where others have failed in bringing the flavour of the country to Barcelona. The curries are the house speciality, but there is also a good range of less obvious dishes. The reasonably priced evening menu special is a bargain.

EIXAMPLE Shibui

🗐🖥 €€€

C/ Comte d'Urgell 272–274, 08036 **Tel** *933 21 90 04* **Map** *2 E1*

With its sleek blonde wood fittings, Japanese cardboard-brick walls and trim waiting staff, this excellent sushi bar has Tokyo written all over it. The basement dining room also has custom-made tatami mat areas and sliding screens, making them a brilliant choice for parties. Closed Sun.

EIXAMPLE Alkimia

🗐🖥🍷🖥 €€€€

C/ Indústria 79, 08025 **Tel** *932 07 61 15* **Map** *3 C2*

One of the rising stars of Barcelona's gastronomic scene, this small designer restaurant revitalizes traditional Catalan dishes with new techniques and foreign flavours. Signature dishes include creamy rice with crayfish and nyora peppers, sticky, slow roasted bull tail and mandarin essence with *hortchata* (tiger nut) foam. Closed Sat, Sun, Aug & Easter.

EIXAMPLE Casa Calvet

🗐🖥🍷🖥 €€€€

C/ Casp 48, 08010 **Tel** *934 12 40 12* **Map** *3 B5*

A beautiful restaurant that was originally designed by Gaudí as a private home and offices for a wealthy textile merchant. The cosy seating booths, formal table settings and old-school service set the ambience. Try the lamb meatballs with creamy risotto and pine nut tart with foamed *crema catalana*. Closed Sun.

EIXAMPLE Cinc Sentits

🗐🖥 €€€€

C/ Aribau 58, 08011 **Tel** *933 23 94 90* **Map** *2 F1*

This warm yet minimal restaurant offers impeccable service. Try the duck and pear salad or "6-hour" tender suckling pig. Meticulously sourced products are cooked with flair and creativity. The chef's choice tasting menu is recommended. Kids are welcome during the week and at lunch. Closed Mon evenings, Sun, Easter and two weeks in Aug.

EIXAMPLE Moo

Tapas 🗐🖥🍷🖥 €€€€

C/ Rosselló 265, 08008 **Tel** *934 45 40 00* **Map** *3 A3*

In the short time that Moo has been open it has walked away with a string of accolades, thanks to the inspired cooking of the Roca brothers, who manage the restaurant. The tasting menu with matching wines is magical: Dublin bay prawns with rose and licorice; sea bass with lemon thyme. Closed Sun.

EIXAMPLE Noti

🗐🖥 €€€€

C/ Roger de Llúria 35–37, 08009 **Tel** *93 342 66 73* **Map** *3 B4*

In a city where style often triumphs over substance, Noti stands out as a glorious exception. The decor is as slinky and glamorous as the crowd, but doesn't detract from the fantastic food - Mediterranean and French cuisine prepared with flair and originality. The Goodbar next door is popular too. Closed Sat lunch and all day Sun.

FURTHER AFIELD (GRÀCIA) Chido One

🗐 €

C/ Torrijos 30, 08012 **Tel** *932 85 03 35* **Map** *3 C2*

Lined floor to ceiling with Mexican Day of the Dead artifacts and trophies, as well as retro jalapeño chilli cans, this trendy eatery serves excellent regional fare including steaming bowls of heart-warming *pozole* (soup made with pork and hominy), soft fat *enchiladas* slathered with chilli sauce, *tacos* and lethal margaritas.

FURTHER AFIELD (GRÀCIA) Envalira

🖥🛗🗐 €€

Plaça del Sol 13, 08012 **Tel** *932 18 58 13* **Map** *3 B1*

A real neighbourhood joint in the spirited Plaça del Sol, Envalira is noisy, raucous and fun with a laid-back, anything-goes ambience. Intimate it is not, but it is a great place for hearty, no-nonsense fare with rice dishes topping the bill. Specialities include the black squid rice and the Milanese rice. Closed Sun evenings, Mon and Aug.

FURTHER AFIELD (GRÀCIA) La Rosa del Desierto

🗐🖥🖥 €€€

Plaça Narcís Oller 7, 08006 **Tel** *932 37 45 90* **Map** *3 A2*

This was Barcelona's first ever Moroccan restaurant and is still widely regarded to be the best. With its atmospheric decor it is a fun place for couscous and delicious *tagines*. They have interesting meat dishes, soups and salads on their menu. Also try one of their typical Arab teas. Closed Sun evenings, Mon and 15 Aug–15 Sep.

FURTHER AFIELD (GRÀCIA) Botafumeiro

Tapas 🍽️♿🌳🎵🍷🍴   €€€€

C/ Gran de Gràcia 81, 08012 **Tel** *932 18 42 30*   **Map** 3 A2

A legendary seafood restaurant with ice-banks piled high with boat-fresh fish and seafood at the entrance. A-listers from Woody Allen to Madonna have all made this a favourite haunt while in town, thanks to discreet management and luxury surroundings. Try the tender *pulpo Gallego* (Galician octopus). Reservations essential.

FURTHER AFIELD (GRÀCIA) Hofmann

🅿️🍽️♿   €€€€

C/ La Granada del Penedès 16 **Tel** *93 218 71 65*   **Map** 5 B2

Talented, Michelin-star-chef Mey Hofmann has been at the forefront of Barcelona's restaurant scene for many years. Her restaurant-cum-cooking school produces high-quality creative cuisine in a sophisticated locale and with attentive service. Closed Sat, Sun and Aug.

FURTHER AFIELD (GRÀCIA) Roig Robí

🍽️🔲🍷🍴   €€€€

C/ Sèneca 20, 08006 **Tel** *932 18 92 22*   **Map** 3 A2

This little and friendly restaurant, with a pretty interior courtyard for summer dining, is a classic for genuine Catalan cuisine. The menu boasts a good selection of *bacalao* dishes as well as typical vegetable preparations of broad beans and artichokes. Also two tasting menus. Closed Sat lunch & Sun.

FURTHER AFIELD (HORTA) Can Travi Nou

♿🌳🔲🍴   €€€€

C/ Jorge Manrique, 08035 **Tel** *934 28 03 01*

Few people venture so far from the centre for their supper, but this 14th-century farmhouse is well worth the trek to soak up the atmosphere of yesteryear, and the rolling terraces are wonderful for al fresco dining. Roast meats, rice dishes and fresh fish are on the menu. Closed Sun evenings.

FURTHER AFIELD (POBLENOU) Els Pescadors

🍽️♿🌳🔲🍴   €€€

Plaça Prim 1, 08005 **Tel** *932 25 20 18*

The multiple-spaced restaurant – terrace, formal dining room and old-fashioned tiled cafeteria – is named after the fishermen that used to frequent it. It is an excellent place for a catch of the day special, zingy-fresh mussels and other fishy delights. Also try the anchovies. Closed Easter & Christmas.

FURTHER AFIELD (SANT GERVASI) La Balsa

🔲🍷🍴   €€€

C/ Infanta Isabel 4, 08060 (Barcelona) **Tel** *932 11 50 48*

Much-loved by Barcelona's glitterati; sportspersons, artists, actors and politicians are all in attendance at this uptown eatery. Service is discreet, the decor tasteful and the terraces among the best in town for enjoying Basque, Catalan and Mediterranean food at its finest. Closed Sun dinner, Mon lunch, Aug & Easter.

FURTHER AFIELD (TIBIDABO) L'Orangerie

🍽️♿🎵🔲🍷🍴   €€€€

La Florida Hotel, Ctra de Vallvidrera 83–93, 08035 (Barcelona) **Tel** *932 59 30 00*

Perched high on the mountain above Barcelona and the sea, this beautiful restaurant has wonderful views and is well worth the 30-minute taxi ride. Try the lobster *carpaccio* with tomato bread or grilled sea-bream in a clam and potato *caldereta* stew. Live music on special days. Closed Sun dinner and Mon.

CATALONIA

ALCANAR Taller de Cuina Carmen Guillemot

🅿️🍽️   €€€

C/ Colón 26, 43530 (Tarragona) **Tel** *977 73 03 23*

A series of elegant dining rooms spread over three floors, each individually but classically decorated. The cuisine is Mediterranean, with French influences, and the menu choices depend on what is freshest at the market. Among several fixed-price menus, they also offer a vegetarian option. Closed Mon, Tue, Sun evenings & Christmas.

ALELLA Restaurante 1789

🌳🍽️   €€€€

Rambla Ángel Guimerá 1, 08328 (Barcelona) **Tel** *935 55 34 55*

Restaurante 1789 is an intimate and romantic restaurant situated in the centre of Alella. It serves good-quality, creative Mediterranean cuisine based on fresh local fare. Be sure to leave some space for the delicious homemade desserts. Closed Sun dinner, Wed and 21 Aug–15 Sep.

ALTAFULLA Faristol

🌳🔲🍴   €€

C/ Sant Martí 5, 43893 (Tarragona) **Tel** *977 65 00 77*

Experience traditional Catalan fare at this charming 18th-century farmhouse. The English-Catalan couple that run it are welcoming and it makes for a romantic getaway from the bustle of Barcelona. Rooms are also available. They usually have music on Friday and Saturday nights. Open Fri dinner–Sun lunch (Oct–May) & for dinner only in summer

ANDORRA LA VELLA Borda Estevet

♿🌳🍽️🔲🍴   €€€

Ctra de la Comella 2, 23500 **Tel** *376 86 40 26*

This old-country manor is still used for the traditional practice of drying tobacco that is grown nearby, and oozes an old-world atmosphere. Extensive menu of Andorran-Catalan and French fare. The meat dishes are exceptional, particularly *carns a la llosa* (lamb or beef) which arrive sizzling on a hot slate.

Key to Price Guide *see p608* **Key to Symbols** *see back cover flap*

ARENYS DE MAR Hispania
📠♿📺🖥 €€€€

C/ Real 54, Ctra NII, 08350 (Barcelona) **Tel** *937 91 04 57*

A famous bistro that has earned numerous awards for the quality of its cooking. People travel from far and wide for its *clam suquet* (fish stew) and home-made *crema catalana* (traditional vanilla custard with a burnt, caramel crust). Closed Sun evenings, Tue, Easter & Oct.

BERGA Sala
Tapas ♿🖥🖥 €€€€

Passeig de la Pau 27, 08600 (Barcelona) **Tel** *938 21 11 85*

A good choice for hearty winter dishes that feature freshly picked mushrooms from the nearby forests; wild game is available in season. Sala offers extremely innovative cuisine, and they also have a set tasting menu. Try partridge in vinegar sauce or the roasted young goat. Closed Sun evenings & Mon.

BOLVIR DE CERDANYA Torre del Remei
♿🖥📠🍴🖥 €€€€

C/ Camí Reial, 17539 (Girona) **Tel** *972 14 01 82*

One of the region's finest hotels (see p571) and restaurants, set in a summer palace and surrounded by verdant countryside. The chef of cuisine uses regional products to create meals such as melting veal cheeks with sweet and sour berries, fresh scallops in Priorato sauce, desserts and local cheeses.

CADAQUÉS Casa Nun
📠🖥 €€€

Plaça Port Ditxos 6, 17488 (Girona) **Tel** *972 25 88 56*

In an old town house, this prettily decorated seafood restaurant overlooks one of the most charming towns of the Catalan coast. The fish couldn't be fresher as the restaurant has its own fishing boat. Book a table on the balcony for perfect views of the harbour. Closed Tue–Thu lunch (Jun–Oct except Aug); & Tue–Wed & Thu lunch (Nov–May) except Easter.

CAMBRILS Can Bosch
🖥🖥 €€€€

Rambla Jaume I 19, 43850 (Tarragona) **Tel** *977 36 00 19*

A classic and highly-respected restaurant serving superb fish, seafood and rice dishes. Their *arroz negro* (rice cooked in squid ink) is justly famous; also try sole with crayfish and black rice with lobster. Patrons rave about their wine list almost as much as the food. Closed Sun evening, Mon & 22 Dec–1 Feb.

CERCS Estany Clar
🖥📠🖥 €€€€

Ctra C 16 km 99.4, 08698 (Barcelona) **Tel** *938 22 08 79*

A little off the beaten track, this much-praised restaurant is set in a restored Catalan farmhouse near Berga. The contemporary Catalan cuisine includes dishes such as rice with lobster and foie gras, snails with local ham, roasted Iberian suckling pig and for dessert order *cuajada*. Exquisite service. Closed Mon & 21 Dec–1 Mar.

COLLSUSPINA Can Xarina
🖥🖥 €€

C/ Mayor 30, 08178 (Barcelona) **Tel** *938 30 05 77*

A friendly welcome awaits at this lovely old-village house, now a cosy little restaurant and guesthouse. In the vaulted dining room, you can enjoy rustic mountain cuisine, charcuterie and cheeses, grilled local lamb and rabbit, as well as fresh fish. Features classic wines from around Spain. Opening times vary call ahead.

CORCA Bo.TiC
🅿🖥♿📠🖥 €€€€

Ctra C-66 Girona-Palermos km 11,5 (Palermos) 17121 **Tel** *972 63 08 69*

Chef Albert 'Tito' Strasreneger has converted this old *masia* (farmhouse) into an elegant, modern restaurant, where he serves creative Catalan cuisine. There is a reasonably priced tasting menu, which consists of two tapas, four starters, two main dishes (one fish and one meat) and two desserts for €49. Good wine list. Closed Tues evening, Wed & Nov.

ESPONELLÀ Can Roca
🖥♿📠 €€

Avda Carles de Fortuny 1, 17832 (Girona) **Tel** *972 59 70 12*

A miniature village, 10 km (6 miles) from Banyoles, hosts this family-run restaurant. This remote inland region is known for its *embutits* (Catalan charcuterie), and the menu features delicious locally made cured hams and sausages. Excellent fixed-price lunch menu. Open for dinner Fri and Sat only. Closed Tue, 15–30 Sep & 1–15 Mar.

FIGUERES Hotel Empordà
🖥📠🍴🖥 €€€€

Hotel Empordà, Ctra Antigua de Francia km 7.4, 17600 (Girona) **Tel** *972 50 05 62*

A legendary restaurant that played a great part in putting Catalan cuisine on the map for travelling gourmets. Established in 1961, folks still gather here to enjoy the legacy of chef Jaime Subirós's cuisine including classic dishes such as *mar y muntaña* (produce of sea and mountain).

GIRONA El Celler de Can Roca
🖥♿🍴🖥 €€€€

Can Sunyer 46, 17007 (Girona) **Tel** *972 22 21 57*

Celler de Can Roca offers a fusion of Catalan and French *nouvelle cuisine* cooking. A must on the list of dedicated food enthusiasts, the Roca brothers turn out innovative, technically brilliant dishes at terrifying speed. This is a place to wow and be wowed. Closed Sun, Mon, 1–15 July & Christmas.

GOMBREN Fonda Xesc
🖥♿🖥 €€€

Plaça del Roser 1, 17531 (Girona) **Tel** *972 73 04 04*

Picasso drew inspiration from this lovely mountain village near Berga. Fonda Xesc is a charming, low-key restaurant-with-rooms, serving good Catalan food. Everything is fresh and locally sourced, from the tender lamb to the artisanal cheeses. In season, you can try a dizzying variety of wild mushrooms. Closed Mon & Sun, Tue & Wed evenings.

GRANOLLERS El Trabuc
P 目 & 雨 ♀   €€€

Ctra de Masnou km 15.3, 08400 (Barcelona) **Tel** *938 708 657*

A restored *masia* (farmhouse) on the outskirts of Granollers, El Trabuc offers an extensive menu of classic Catalan dishes. The sautéed wild mushrooms make a wonderful starter, and there is a fine wine selection. You might spot the odd Formula One driver during the annual Catalan Grand Prix. Closed Sun evenings & three weeks in Aug.

GRATALLOPS El Celler de Gratallops
Tapas P 目 & ♀   €€€

C/ Piró 32 (Priorat), 43737 (Tarragona) **Tel** *977 83 90 36*

This smart village restaurant is owned by the Clos l'Obac vineyard, one of pioneers of new Priorato wines. It serves their entire range, along with local olive oils and an excellent Moroccan influenced menu; for example duck confits and foie gras. Well worth seeking out during a trip to wine country. Closed Mon & evenings (except Fri & Sat).

LA SEU D'URGELL El Castell de Ciutat – Tàpies
目 雨 ♀   €€€€

Ctra N260 km 229, 25700 (Lleida) **Tel** *973 35 00 00*

Situated at the foot of La Seu d'Urgell castle, lies this idyllic hotel-restaurant. El Castell serves top-flight modern Catalan cuisine and superlative wines. Many of the dishes include a variety of wild local mushrooms from the Pyrenean mountains and meat from the region. A different menu is served to outside tables.

LA VALL DE BIANYA Ca L'Enric
目 & 雨 ♀   €€€€

Ctra de Camprodón s/n, 17813 (Girona) **Tel** *972 29 00 15*

This restaurant serves some of the finest cuisine in the region and has won numerous accolades. It has justly become a place of pilgrimage during the hunting season, when they offer Catalan specialities from wild boar to venison, all finely prepared by chef Maria Isabel Juncá. Booking advisable. Closed Mon, Sun evenings & two weeks in Jul & Dec.

LLAGOSTERA Els Tinars
目 & 雨 ♀   €€€

Ctra Sant Feliú-Girona km 7, 2, 17240 (Girona) **Tel** *972 83 06 26*

A classic, Els Tinars offers exceptionally fresh modern Catalan cuisine, including the house speciality of trotter salad served with calamari and prawns. Less adventurous diners can try grilled fish, but the charm of this place is in the details: home-baked bread, served warm and crusty and great desserts. Closed Sun evenings, Mon and 8 Jan–8 Feb.

LLEIDA Gardeny
目 卉 &   €€

C/ Salmerón 10, 25004 (Lleida) **Tel** *973 23 45 10*

Excellent regional cooking including chargrilled red peppers and aubergines (eggplants) and snails Gardeny style. Specialities include *xatonada* with beans, mushrooms and cod and a Basque salad of smoked fish, tomatoes and olives with cod and elvers. It has a cheaper fixed-price menu Monday to Friday. Closed Mon evenings and Tue.

LLORET DE MAR El Trull
P 目 & ♫ 雨 ♀   €€€€

Ronda Europa 1, Cala Canyelles, 17310 (Girona) **Tel** *972 36 49 28*

Should your travels take you through the uninspiring Lloret de Mar, this characterful rustic dining room is handy at a pinch. It serves good grilled lobster, fresh fish, *fideuá* (Catalan noodle) and paella. They also have a wide range of wines and sparkling wines. Live piano music in summer only.

MANRESA Sibar
目 & 雨 ♀   €€

C/ Carrasco i Formiguera 18, 08242 (Barcelona) **Tel** *938 74 81 71*

This modern establishment has a cafeteria on the ground floor for coffee and cakes, and a sleek elegant restaurant in the basement for formal dining. The *chuletón* (T-bone steak), for a minimum of two people, is exquisite, as are the unlikely sounding fried eggs and potatoes. Regional wines are a must. Closed Christmas.

MARTINET Boix
P 目 & 雨 ♀   €€€

Ctra N260 Lleida-Puigcerdá km 204.5, 25724 (Lleida) **Tel** *973 51 50 50*

A famous Catalan restaurant located on the banks of the Río Segre. Boix serves a slow-roasted leg of lamb so tender you could eat it with a spoon, complemented perfectly by a bottle of soft luscious local wine from the Costers del Segre. The meat stews are also very popular. Closed Sun evenings, Mon and for 2 weeks in Feb.

MONTSENY Can Barrina
目 & 雨 ♀   €€

Ctra Palautordera–Montseny km 12.6, 08560 (Barcelona) **Tel** *938 47 30 65*

In the hills of the Montseny natural park, this restored 17th-century *masia* is now a fine country hotel and restaurant Dine in the stone-walled dining room or out on the garden terrace, on delicious Catalan specialities, including wild mushrooms and game in season, kid with honey and aniseed and home-made desserts. Closed Sun evenings.

PALS Sa Punta
P 目 & 雨 ♀   €€€€

C/ des Forns 65, 17256 (Girona) **Tel** *972 63 64 10*

The cuisine of the Empordá region in Catalonia is known for its mixture of seafood and meat – known here as *mar y muntaña*. This elegant hotel-restaurant is a good place to try classic Empordan dishes such as chicken with local prawns. The dessert selection will have you drooling, and the service is impeccable. Excellent wine list too.

PERALADA Castell de Peralada
P 目 ♀ ♀   €€€€

Hotel Castell de Peralada, C/ Sant Joan, 17491 (Girona) **Tel** *972 53 81 25*

The setting of this medieval castle makes for a truly special lunch or dinner. It specializes in traditional Empordan cuisine, while the castle's own bodegas provide the wine. As the restaurant is inside a casino, under-18s are not allowed. Kids are allowed in July and August when a buffet is served outside. Closed Mon & Tue (15 Sep–May).

Key to Price Guide *see p608* **Key to Symbols** *see back cover flap*

ROSES El Bulli

Cala Montjoi Ap 30, 17480 (Girona) **Tel** *972 15 04 57* **Fax** *972 15 07 17*

Critics and foodies alike widely believe this bistro to be, not only the best in Spain, but one of the best in the world. Super-chef Ferran Adrià produces state-of-the-art dishes in one of Spain's prettiest beachside settings. They have a fixed tasting menu. Reservations required one year in advance! Closed Oct–Mar.

SANT CELONI El Racó de Can Fabes

C/ de Sant Joan 6, 08470 (Barcelona) **Tel** *938 67 28 51*

Santi Santamaría is one of Spain's most emblematic chefs and this country restaurant, in the house where he was born, is a gastronomic wonderland. The seasonal menu is full of delights including fennel cream with crab, sweetbreads with mashed potato and wild duck in cocoa bean sauce. Reservations essential. Closed Sun evenings & Mon.

SANT FELÍU DE GUÍXOLS La Taverna del Mar

Platja de s'Agaró s/n, 17220 (Girona) **Tel** *972 32 38 00*

This century-old tavern serves a dazzling array of spectacularly cooked fresh fish. Recipes include Mediterranean classics such as spiny lobster stew and fish baked in a salt crust. Comfortable wicker armchairs and whitewashed arches frame perfect sea views. Bookings essential. Closed Mon & Tue from Oct–Apr, 15 Dec–2 Jan.

SANT POL DE MAR Sant Pau

C/ Nou 10, 08395 (Barcelona) **Tel** *937 60 06 62*

This three-Michelin-starred restaurant is an hour-long train ride from Barcelona. The bounty of earth and sea make for some wonderful dishes created from courgette (zucchini) flowers, sea cucumbers and wild boar. Only apéritif and coffee is served at the outside tables. Closed Sun evenings, Mon, Thu lunch & three weeks in May & Nov.

SANTES CREUS Grau

C/ Pere el Gran 3, 43815 (Tarragona) **Tel** *977 63 83 11*

The honey-coloured stone monastery of Santes Creus is one of the most beautiful places in Catalonia, and is part of the great Cistercian monastery route. This simple hostel and restaurant offers great home cooking, which you can enjoy in the garden terrace. Try the wonderful roasted *calçots* in season. Closed Mon.

SITGES El Velero

Passeig de la Ribera 38, 08870 (Barcelona) **Tel** *938 94 20 51*

A seaside restaurant whose imaginative creations are a cut above more standard offerings of paella and grilled fish. Here sole comes on a bed of wild mushrooms and is drizzled with unctuous crab sauce, lobster comes with chickpea cream and boat-fresh razor clams are the best starters. Closed Mon, Sun evenings & Tue lunch in winter & 22 Dec–22 Jan.

TARRAGONA El Merlot

C/ Cavallers 6, 43003 (Tarragona) **Tel** *977 22 06 52*

Situated in the old part of town, this restaurant serves classical Mediterranean dishes. House specials include game in season, fresh fish and home-made desserts. Specialities include flower salad with vinaigrette of seeds and apples, tartar with foie gras and anise ice cream. Also good wines. Closed Sun & Mon lunch, 1–15 Feb & Christmas.

TORRENT (PALAFRUGELL) Mas de Torrent

C/ Afores s/n, 17123 (Girona) **Tel** *902 55 03 21*

An elegant country hotel, the Mas de Torrent has a wonderful restaurant under the direction of renowned chef Joan Piqué. The 18th-century mansion and gardens provide the perfect backdrop for a romantic dinner on the terrace. Go for the spectacular *menú de degustación*, a showcase for Piqué's dazzling talents.

TORROELLA DE MONTGRÍ Palau Lo Mirador

Passeig l'Esglesia 1, 17257 (Girona) **Tel** *972 75 80 63*

For royal treatment head to this hotel, the residence of Catalonia's most powerful King Jaume I. The dining rooms, with their stone walls, vaulted ceilings and chandeliers are truly palatial. Fine regional cuisine with international touches – Indian spices and Oriental flavours appear on the menu alongside classic Catalan dishes. Closed Mon.

TORTOSA Rosa Pinyol

C/ Hernán Cortés 17, 43500 (Tarragona) **Tel** *977 50 20 01*

One of the most creative restaurants in the area, Rosa Pinyol serves deftly prepared Catalan cuisine with Italian and Mediterranean influences. The sautéed baby squid with wild mushrooms melt in the mouth, and the desserts, particularly anything made with chocolate, are heavenly. Outstanding service. Closed Sun & Mon evenings.

TOSSA DE MAR La Cuina de Can Simón

C/ Portal 24, 17320 (Girona) **Tel** *972 34 12 69*

A delightful family-run restaurant, serving very good contemporary Mediterranean cuisine. In summer, you can dine al fresco on the terrace. Try the rice cooked in squid ink with a mouthwatering *romesco* sauce (made with crushed almonds, peppers and garlic). Closed Mon, Tue (except Aug), Sun evenings, 15–30 Nov & 7–25 Jan.

VALLS Masia Bou

Ctra Lleida km 21.5, 43800 (Tarragona) **Tel** *977 60 04 27*

A large and noisy country house with room for more than 600 people. The specialities here are game, wild mushrooms and *calçots*, chargrilled over hot vines and served with a scrumptious almond, hazelnut and red pepper dipping sauce. Closed Tue in summers.

VIC Cardona 7　　　　　　　　　📋🏃🍷　　€€€

Cardona 7, 08500 (Barcelona) **Tel** *938 86 38 15*

Chef Jordi Parramón is well known in Vic for his creative cooking based on fresh, seasonal produce. This restaurant is located in a 16th-century building decorated with contemporary art and modern furniture right in the heart of Vic. Closed Mon, Sun dinner and Tue–Fri for lunch & for two weeks in Feb and Sep.

VIELHA Era Lucana　　　　　　　📋♿🍷　　€€

Avda Calbetó Barra 10, 25530 (Lleida) **Tel** *973 64 17 98*

With its warm wood panelling, locally made lace tablecloths and roaring fires, this is a cosy and welcoming place to rest after a day on the slopes. The menu offers creative renditions of classic Catalan fare, including succulent meats grilled over charcoal, served with wild mushroom sauce. Closed Mon & 1–15 Nov.

VILAFRANCA DEL PENEDÉS Cal Ton　　📋🔧🍷　　€€€

C/ Casal 8, 08720 (Barcelona) **Tel** *938 90 37 41*

Capital of Catalonia's main wine-producing region, Vilafranca del Penedès is a tranquil little town. Cal Ton is an old-fashioned favourite in the centre, with rustically furnished dining rooms serving sturdy Catalan classics such as *butifarra amb mongetes* (a classic bean and sausage dish) and local lamb. Closed Sun & Tue evenings, Mon & Easter.

ARAGÓN

AÍNSA Bodegas del Sobrarbe　　　　　📋🍷🔧　　€€€

Plaza Mayor 2, 22330 (Huesca) **Tel** *974 50 02 37*

Located in medieval cellars under the Plaza Mayor of Aínsa town, with a beautiful courtyard. They serve regional cuisine based on game, wild mushrooms and the Aragónese veal, cooked over a wood fire, accompanied by wine. The home-made desserts are not to be missed, especially the apple pastry with strawberry sauce. Closed Jan–Feb.

ALBARRACÍN El Bodegón　　　　*Tapas* 📋🔧　　€

C/ Azagra 2, 44100 (Teruel) **Tel** *978 70 03 55*

El Bodegón is located in one of the typical "hanging houses". Apart from the fine views, traditional Aragonese fare such as trout with *jamón*, roast lamb and bull's tail stew is offered. Finish off with a *cuajada*, a bitter yoghurt sweetened with honey and cinnamon, known for its digestive properties. Excellent value. Closed Wed & last week in Jun.

ALCAÑIZ (TERUEL) La Oficina　　　*Tapas* 📋　　€

Avda de Aragón 12, 44600 (Teruel) **Tel** *978 87 08 01*

Situated in the historic town of Alcañiz, renowned for its Easter celebrations, this small, excellent value *mesón* (inn) specializes in traditional, home-made food using local produce, including the area's famed olive oil. They specialize in meat dishes with options such as the succulent steak with Roquefort sauce. Closed Sun.

BARBASTRO El Portal del Somontano　*Tapas* 🏃📋🔧🍷　　€

Ctra N 240 Tarragona-San Sebastian km 162, 22300 (Huesca) **Tel** *974 31 53 68*

Restaurant, cellar and delicatessen shop in a renovated building with a fireplace in the dining room. It offers fixed-price and children's menus, with simple dishes based on lentils, free-range chicken, home-made *morcilla*, local lamb, artichokes and foie gras and grilled fish. It also offers an extensive list of *cavas*, champagne and cigars.

BIESCAS Casa Ruba　　　　　　*Tapas* 📋🔧♿　　€

C/ Esperanza 18–20, 22630 (Huesca) **Tel** *974 48 50 01*

This simple dining room, founded in 1884, is the best choice for traditional cuisine. Try the cod wrapped in pastry and served with artichokes or the tender local steaks cooked to perfection. Desserts include caramelized custard with ice cream and hot chocolate sauce. Good value lunchtime fixed menu. Closed Sun evenings & mid-Oct–mid-Nov.

BORJA La Bóveda del Mercado　　　　📋🍷　　€€

Plaza del Mercado 4, 50540 (Zaragoza) **Tel** *976 86 82 51*

In a 17th-century cellar, in the historic centre of Borja, you will find this magnificently decorated little gem, serving traditional dishes perfectly cooked, at prices that belong to yesteryear. Try the *morcilla* crêpe or peaches in wine. Closed Sun evenings, Mon & Jan or Feb.

CARIÑENA La Rebotica　　　　　🅿📋♿　　€€

C/ San José 3, 50400 (Zaragoza) **Tel** *976 62 05 56*

This lovely eatery retains vestiges of its old life as a pharmacy. Salads, vegetable and pasta dishes are the order of the day. Favourites include rice salad with duck ham and foie gras and *morcilla* lasagne. The atmosphere is friendly. La Rebotica is open for lunch only (except Saturdays). Closed Mon.

ESQUEDAS Venta del Sotón　　　　📋♿🔧🍷　　€€€

Ctra Tarragona a San Sebastian km 227, 22810 (Huesca) **Tel** *974 27 02 41*

Very pleasant, homespun restaurant located 14 kms (8.6 miles) from Huesca in a typical Pyrenean chalet. The cuisine is traditional and includes such local treats as cod *pil pil*, baby lamb with potatoes or beef baked in rock salt. They also have a good fixed-price menu. Closed Sun evenings, Mon & mid-Jan–mid-Feb.

Key to Price Guide *see p608* **Key to Symbols** *see back cover flap*

HUESCA Lillas Pastia

Tapas 📋 🚶 ♿ 🍴 🍷   €€€€

Plaza de Navarra 4, 22002 Tel 974 21 16 91

Located in the salon of the casino, this is one of the most popular restaurants in Huesca. A highly creative "market" cuisine is on offer, using the freshest seasonal produce. Try the honey-baked cod served with milk foam or new potatoes with wild mushrooms. Closed Sun, Mon evenings (in winter only) & Oct–Nov (variable).

JACA Lilium

📋 ♿ 🍴 🍷   €€

Avda Primer Viernes de Mayo 8, 22700 (Huesca) Tel 974 35 53 56

This split-level eatery has a split personality; contemporary upstairs and reassuringly rustic in the basement. The cuisine is typical of Aragón's high country and features dishes such as chargrilled lamb chops with wild mushrooms and lettuce hearts filled with goat's cheese. Rich home-made desserts. Closed Mon, two weeks in spring & autumn.

LA IGLESUELA DEL CID Casa Amada

📋   €

C/ Fuente Nueva 10, 44142 (Teruel) Tel 964 44 33 73

This simple, quality restaurant offers a good fixed menu from Monday to Friday and a more varied à la carte on the weekends. Its specialities include stuffed potatoes, bean stew, garlic chickpeas, partridge and grilled meats and trout. The home-made desserts are excellent. There are a few rooms available. Closed Sun evenings (except Aug).

NUÉVALOS Reyes de Aragón

📋 🚶 ♿ 🍴   €€

Ctra Monasterio de Piedra, 50210 (Zaragoza) Tel 976 84 90 11

Located in a 12th-century monastery complex inside Monasterio de Piedra, and surrounded by cascades and grottos, the setting is perfect for enjoying Aragonese specialities such as local trout stuffed with *jamón* (ham) and roasted suckling lamb and much more. Leave room for the tasty desserts; baked apples or chocolate and almond mousse.

PANTICOSA Restaurante del Lago

📋 ♿ 🍷   €€€€

Ctra del Balneario km 10, 22650 (Huesca) Tel 974 48 71 61

Part of the Panticosa Resort, Restaurante del Lago is top class. Chef Pedro Subijana fuses Basque and Navarran cuisines in dishes such as *bogavante con especias y ravioli de epio* (lobster with spices and celery ravioli), eggs with caviar over a cauliflower mousse and gin and tonic jelly with lemon sorbet. Reservations recommended.

RUBIELOS DE MORA El Castillo

📋 ♿ 🍴 🍷   €€€€

Plaza del Carmen 2, 44415 (Teruel) Tel 978 80 46 40

This restaurant occupies a unique Neo-Gothic palace, located in a charming and quiet medieval square. It serves traditional local cuisine with an original touch, for example *migas a la pastora*, a soup of bread, garlic, onions and ham, and venison with spaghetti and truffles. Closed Sun dinner & Mon.

SENEGÜE Casbas

Tapas 📋 🚶 ♿ 🍴 🍷   €€

Ctra N260 Biescas s/n, 22666 (Teruel) Tel 974 48 01 49

Casbas specializes in cod, which can be combined with imaginative starters such as warm salad with goat's cheese, walnuts and a honey vinaigrette, all washed down with a well-sourced selection of local wines. Skiers gather here in the mornings for a hearty cooked breakfast and there are also rooms for rent on the upper floors. Closed Sep.

TERUEL La Menta

📋 ♿ 🍷   €€€

C/ Bartolomé Esteban 10, 44001 Tel 978 60 75 32

One of the most charming restaurants with paintings from celebrated local artists adorning the walls. The seasonal cuisine includes crêpes filled with spinach and cured ham, partridge *escabechada* and a caramelized cheese cake with pine nuts. Attentive table service. Reservations recommended. Closed Mon, Sun, 7–27 Jan & 20 days in July.

UNCASTILLO Un-Castello

Tapas 📋 🍷   €

Plaza de la Villa 24, 50678 (Zaragoza) Tel 976 67 91 05

Next to the city hall in a rustic building, Un-Castello offers surprisingly innovative Basque and Aragonese cuisine. Try the aubergines with mushrooms wrapped in pastry, stuffed leg of lamb or roast beef with mustard sauce. Great choice of local wines. It is recommended to ring first to check opening times.

ZARAGOZA Casa Juanico

Tapas 📋   €

Plaza de Santa Cruz 21, 50003 Tel 976 39 72 52

In Zaragoza's old town, close to the famous Pilar Cathedral, this perpetually crowded, classic bar offers the best tapas in town. Grilled meats, a great selection of *pinchos* and cold cod salad are the highlights. There is also a rear dining room for more formal eating, for which reservations are recommended. Closed Sun evening.

ZARAGOZA Espejo

📋 🍴   €€

C/ Santiago 30–32, 50003 Tel 976 29 34 32

Near to the soaring Pilar Cathedral and frequented by artists, politicians and Zaragoza's intelligentsia. The speciality of the house is foie gras sautéed in modena vinegar – particularly memorable when eaten on the lovely outside terrace. Closed Sat lunch, Sun, three weeks in Aug & public holidays.

ZARAGOZA La Rinconada de Lorenzo

Tapas 📋 ♿ 🍷   €€

C/ La Salle 3, 50006 Tel 976 55 51 08

This emblematic restaurant, decorated in the colourful tiles typical of the area, offers excellent home-style cooking. Specialities include chickpeas with lobster, ham and grapes and other hearty meat and fish dishes. There is a distinctly fun and family-friendly atmosphere here. Closed Sun evenings & Mon in summer & Easter week.

ZARAGOZA Don Pascual   🖩♿🍴📶   €€€

C/ Residencial Paraíso 48, 50008 **Tel** *976 21 87 14*

Inside this romantic, intimate space, creative cooking wows the regulars. The promise of using only the freshest market ingredients is reflected in the dishes. The king prawns in curry and the steak tartar are very popular choices. Closed Sun (except May & Dec), Easter & 1–15 Aug.

ZARAGOZA Las Lanzas   🖩♿📶   €€€

Avda César Augusto 13 (Meliá Hotel), 50004 **Tel** *976 28 55 22*

This award-winning restaurant has large rooms and a refined, Provençal atmosphere. It offers an avant-garde creative cuisine with attention to every detail. Highlights include the watercress and oyster soup with liquid bomb of red pearls and the chef's home-made foie gras. Excellent wine list. Closed Sun evenings, Holy Week, first two weeks in Aug.

VALENCIA AND MURCIA

ALICANTE Mesón de Labradores   *Tapas* 🖩   €

C/ Labradores 19, 03001 (Alacant) **Tel** *965 20 48 46*

Decorated with colourful tiles and huge wine barrels, Mesón de Labradores is one of the best and most authentic of Alicante's many tapas bars. Cheerful waiters breeze between the crowded tables, with platters of deliciously fresh snacks held aloft. Try the *croquetas* (meat-stuffed rolls), a speciality of the house. Closed Mon & 15–30 Nov.

ALICANTE Dársena   *Tapas* 🖩♟♿📶   €€€

Marina Deportiva, Muelle Levante 6, Puerto, 03001 (Alacant) **Tel** *965 20 75 89*

A classic restaurant overlooking the port, Dársena has an elegant interior, with crisp white linen. The nautical-style brass lamps give it the feel of a luxurious ocean liner. Gaze out at the sea of yachts through the enormous picture windows, and choose from around 150 delicious rice dishes. Do not miss the *arròs a banda* (rice with fish).

ALICANTE Nou Manolín   *Tapas* 🖩♿📶   €€€€

C/ Villegas 3, 03001 (Alacant) **Tel** *965 20 03 68*

An Alicantino favourite, this attractive restaurant is tucked away in the old quarter in the former home of local author Gabriel Miró. There is an excellent tapas bar downstairs, while upstairs you can dine in an elegant brick-lined salon on classic Valencian seafood, rice dishes, accompanied by an extensive wine list.

ALTEA Racó de Toni   *Tapas* 🖩♿📶   €€€

C/ de la Mar 127, 03590 (Alicante) **Tel** *965 84 17 63*

An old-fashioned charmer, this cosy, traditional *mesón* serves good regional specialities including excellent rice dishes and locally caught fish. Specialities include rice with salt cod and vegetables and peppers stuffed with anchovies. There's a good-value *menú del día*, or you can join the lively crowd of locals in the tapas bar. Closed 20–30 Nov.

BENIDORM Ulía   🖩🍴📶   €€

C/ Vicente Llorca Alós 15, 03502 (Alicante) **Tel** *965 85 68 28*

This old-fashioned seaside restaurant is one of the best places in Benidorm to try an authentic paella. The good food, made with the freshest local produce, makes it popular with families that flock from the beach on Sundays for long lunches on the lovely, breezy terrace. Closed Mon, Sun evenings & 22 Dec–22 Jan.

BENIDORM La Palmera-Casa Paco Nadal   🖩♿🍴   €€€

Av Severo Ochoa, Rincón de Loix, 03503 (Alicante) **Tel** *965 85 32 82*

La Palmera is one of the best places to try the huge range of rice dishes for which Valencia is famous. A large, typically Spanish seaside restaurant with a flower-filled terrace, it's a popular place for long Sunday lunches with the family. There is a reasonably priced *menú de degustación*. Closed Mon.

BENIMANTELL L'Obrer   🖩♿🍴📶   €€

Ctra de Alcoi 27, 03516 (Alicante) **Tel** *965 88 50 88*

L'Obrer's popularity rests on its great food, bargain prices and welcoming ambience. A rustic-style restaurant, decorated with locally made ceramics, it serves home-cooked country dishes such as baked lamb or roasted rabbit. Home-made desserts include almond tart with chocolate. Closed Fri, evenings (except Fri–Sat in Aug) & end Jun–1 Aug.

BENIMANTELL Venta la Montaña   🖩♿🍴   €€

Ctra de Alcoi 9, 03516 (Alicante) **Tel** *965 88 51 41*

This mountain inn, decorated with antique farming implements, serves wholesome dishes such as the typical *olleta de trigo* (a broth made with pork, vegetables and wheat). Accompany it with a sturdy local wine and finish with caramel soufflé. If you do not want a big meal, try the tapas at the bar. Closed last week of Jun & Mon.

BENISSANO Levante   🖩♿📶   €

C/ Virgen del Fundamento 27, 46181 (Valencia) **Tel** *962 78 07 21*

You cannot leave Valencia without trying Levante's excellent paellas, cooked to perfection over a wood fire. Other house recommendations include the delicious *croquetas de atún* (home-made tuna croquettes). The restaurant boasts one of the region's largest and best wine cellars. Open for lunch only. Closed Tue, Holy Week, mid Jul–mid Aug.

BUÑOL Venta L'Home
🖥 ♿ 🍽 🍷 · €€€

Autovía A3 Madrid-Valencia km 306 (exit Venta Mina), 46360 (Valencia) **Tel** *962 50 35 15*

A whitewashed 18th-century staging post is the setting for this attractive country restaurant. You can dine on great regional cuisine, such as rabbit with honey, or artichokes with baby squid, in a rustically decorated dining room. There is a good wine list, which features an interesting selection of regional wines.

CABO DE PALOS Miramar
Tapas 🖥 ♿ 🍽 🍷 €

Paseo del Puerto 14, 30370 (Murcia) **Tel** *968 56 30 33*

Every seaside resort in Spain has a Miramar restaurant, and the lively town of Cabo de Palos is no exception. It is a family-friendly seafood restaurant with huge picture windows overlooking the port and the bay. Specialities include local rice dishes, and fish baked in salt. Try the local desserts, particularly the *pan de Calatrava*. Closed 7–30 Jan.

CARAVACA DE LA CRUZ Los Viñales
Tapas 🖥 ♿ 🍽 🍷 €

Av Juan Carlos I 41, 30400 (Murcia) **Tel** *968 70 84 58*

An old-fashioned, down-to-earth inn, Los Viñales is justly famous for its fine *guisos* (mountain stews), prepared with locally-reared lamb or pork and the delicious vegetables for which Murcia is famous. These stews are perfect for the cool nights in this enchanting hill-top town. Closed Mon evening, Tue & 25–31 Jan.

CARTAGENA Los Sauces
Tapas 🖥 ♿ 🍽 🍷 €€€

Ctra La Palma km 4.5, 30300 (Murcia) **Tel** *968 53 07 58*

Stylish and intimate, Los Sauces is set in a pretty chalet-style building on the outskirts of Cartagena. The menu features Spanish and international haute cuisine, prepared with a creative twist. Try the confit of suckling pig with black olive caramel and for dessert, toffee mousse. Closed Sun evenings and Mon.

CASTELLÓ DE LA PLANA Rafael
🖥 🍷 🍷 €€€€

C/ Churruca 28, 12100 (Castellón) **Tel** *964 28 21 85*

Rafael has long been a fixture on Castellón's port, El Grao, close to the main city centre. Welcoming and unfussy, the restaurant has always focused on the quality of its ingredients, particularly the incredibly fresh fish. Service is excellent and the wine list offers a good range of regional labels. Closed Sun, 1–15 Sep, bank holidays & 23 Dec–8 Jan.

COCENTAINA L'Escaleta
🖥 ♿ 🍽 🍷 🍷 €€€€

Subida Estación Norte 205, 03824 (Alicante) **Tel** *965 59 21 00*

One of the best restaurants in the Cocentaina region, L'Escaleta is situated in a chalet decorated in classic, elegant style. The freshest produce from the market is used to prepare creative interpretations of classic dishes. The wine list has both Spanish and international wines. Closed Sun, Mon and Tue evenings and 7–21 Jan.

CULLERA Casa Salvador
Tapas 🖥 ♿ 🍽 🍷 €€€

L'Estany de Cullera, 46400 (Valencia) **Tel** *961 72 01 36*

Sitting pretty on the edge of the *estany* (lake) of Cullera, this family-run restaurant has a beautiful wooden terrace overlooking the lake. Choose from a wide variety of traditional rice dishes, locally-caught seafood, and vegetables grown in their own orchard. Paella with duck is a speciality. The wine cellar has more than 4,000 bottles of wine.

DENIA El Poblet
🖥 ♿ P 🍽 🍷 €€€€

Ctra Las Marinas km 3, 03700 (Alicante) **Tel** *965 78 41 79*

El Poblet offers exceptional and highly creative Spanish cuisine, created by Enrique Dacosta, one of the most exciting chefs in Spain. This is one of the best places to try Dénia's famous prawns. There is a wonderful *menú de degustación*. Parking facilities are available. Closed Mon (except Aug), Sun evening, three weeks starting end Feb & two weeks in Oct.

ELCHE (ELX) Asador Ilicitano
P 🖥 ♿ 🍷 €€€

C/ Maestro Giner 9, 03201 (Alicante) **Tel** *965 43 58 64*

A fine old *mesón*, with handsome traditional decor and ancient wooden beams, Asador Ilicitano serves succulent roasted meats prepared over charcoal to give them a delicate smoky flavour. Specialities include roast kid and lamb, but they also serve some delicious seafood dishes such as Basque-style cod. Closed Sun & 16–31 Aug.

FORCALL Mesón de la Vila
🖥 ♿ €€

Plaza Mayor 8, 12310 (Castellón) **Tel** *964 17 11 25*

Right on Forcall's expansive main square, this handsome *mesón* is located in the 16th-century cellars of the Ayuntamiento (Town Hall). In the elegant vaulted dining rooms, you can try affordable regional dishes such as the *sopa forcallana* (broth with vegetables, boiled eggs, ham and meatballs). Closed Mon.

GANDIA Gamba
P 👫 🖥 ♿ 🍽 €€€

Carretera Nazaret-Oliva s/n, Gandia-Playa, 46730 (Valencia) **Tel** *962 84 13 10*

Although you cannot see the sea from here, the fish and shellfish are straight from the fishermen's nets. There are three airy dining areas, where you can enjoy grilled shrimps, home-style aubergines or squid cooked in diverse ways. Open lunch (winter); lunch & dinner (Easter, summer). Closed Sun evening, Mon and Nov.

JÁTIVA (XÀTIVA) Casa La Abuela
🖥 €€€

C/ Reina 17, 46800 (Valencia) **Tel** *962 27 05 25*

Tucked away in the higgledy-piggledy maze in the centre of Játiva, this pretty turn-of-the-19th-century house is now a delightful restaurant set around a plant-filled interior patio. The cuisine is refined and creative: try the magret of duck with red fruits, or the lamb with rosemary mousse. A *menú del día* is available. Closed Sun and 15–30 Jul.

LORCA El Teatro
Plaza de Colón 12, 30800 (Murcia) **Tel** *968 46 99 09*

El Teatro is a simple little restaurant with a good range of Murcian dishes, many featuring delicious local vegetables as well as variations of the classic rice dishes for which Eastern Spain is famous. Seafood is freshly caught in the nearby bay of Águilas. Try the aubergine gratin with a tasty meaty sauce. Closed Sun evenings, Mon & Aug.

MORAIRA La Sort
Avda Madrid 1, 03724 (Alicante) **Tel** *966 49 11 61*

This smart, modern restaurant prides itself on serving Mediterranean cooking using the freshest ingredients from local suppliers. Daily fresh fish from Moraira market may be used in such dishes as the red mullet with tempura leeks. Meat dishes include the Iberian lamb with cranberry sauce. Game in season. Closed 23 Dec–15 Jan.

MORELLA Casa Roque
C/ Cuesta de San Juan 1, 12300 (Castellón) **Tel** *964 16 03 36*

An old stone mansion houses this classic restaurant in mountainous Maestrat. Diners come from near and far to savour Roque Guttiérez's fillet steak with truffles in puff pastry. Fixed-price menu includes an excellent *menú de degustación*. Closed Sun evenings, Mon (in Aug opens daily), two weeks in Jan or Feb, 24–25 Dec, & 1 Jan.

MURCIA La Tapa
Plaza de las Flores 13, 30004 (Murcia) **Tel** *968 21 13 17*

Upbeat and brightly lit, with a terrace out on one of Murcia's liveliest squares, La Tapa is a classic on the Murciano tapas route. There is an excellent range of tasty snacks, especially fried prawns, usually washed down with an ice-cold beer or a glass of crisp local wine. It may be wise to arrive early to grab a table on the square. Open daily.

MURCIA Rincón de Pepe
Apóstoles 34, 30001 (Murcia) **Tel** *968 21 22 39*

Some of the best regional cuisine in the city is served at one of Murcia's most famous restaurants. Its seasonal menu includes a wide range of Spanish and international dishes. Try the pig's trotters with white beans or the mouthwatering platter of assorted grilled fish and seafood. Reservations recommended. Closed Sun evening.

MURCIA Acuario
Plaza Puxmarina 3, 30004 (Murcia) **Tel** *968 21 99 55*

This enchanting restaurant is the perfect place for a romantic dinner. The cuisine is contemporary, highly original and based on the extraordinary range of local produce available in Murcia – delicious vegetables, fresh seafood and succulent meat. Unusually, they also offer a vegetarian menu. Closed Sun & Mon evenings, Easter, 15–31 Aug.

MURCIA Hispano
C/ Radio Murcia 3, 30001 (Murcia) **Tel** *968 21 61 52*

A long-established restaurant in the centre of old Murcia, Hispano is known for its delicious regional cooking, with specialities such as *caldero marinero del Mar Menor* (a typical seafood casserole), and dorada baked in salt. A stalwart on Murcia's lively tapas scene, it has a bustling bar. Closed Sun evenings (winter) & Sat evenings & Sun (summer)

MURCIA Hostería Palacete Rural La Seda
Vereda del Catalan s/n, km 6.5 from Murcia City, 30162 (Murcia) **Tel** *968 87 08 48*

Housed in an 18th-century mansion, this restaurant is one of Murcia's most prestigious. Dine on elegant contemporary cuisine made with the highest quality seasonal produce. The innovative menu changes four times a year. The wine list was recently voted the finest in all of Spain. Closed Sun.

ORIHUELA Cabo Roig
Urbanización Cabo Roig, Playas de Orihuela, 03189 (Alicante) **Tel** *966 76 02 90*

Perched on top of the cliff with magnificent views of the Costa Blanca, Cabo Roig offers a great variety of seafood and rice dishes. Some of the best are the simplest, particularly the wonderfully fresh fish of the day which is served grilled to perfection. The ancient watchtower houses a historic wine collection of more than 20,000 bottles.

PEÑÍSCOLA Casa Jaime
Av Papa Luna 5, 12598 (Castellón) **Tel** *964 48 00 30*

With spectacular views of the castle of Papa Luna, this reliable seafood restaurant sits right on the seafront. Freshly-caught fish is served either simply grilled or in one of the many paellas and rice dishes. Try the prawn carpaccio, or *arroz de la huerta* (rice flavoured with local vegetables). Closed Sun evenings, Wed (except Jul–Sep), 20 Dec–20 Jan.

POLOP DE LA MARINA Ca l'Ángeles
C/ Gabriel Miró 12, 03520 (Alicante) **Tel** *965 87 02 26*

Run by the same family for two generations, Ca l'Ángeles is a charming country restaurant with dining rooms that have ancient beams and lovely, rustic decoration. The menu offers sophisticated regional fare, including kid baked with roasted garlic, or oven-baked locally-caught fish. Closed Tue, 15 Jun–15 Jul & Sun–Thu evenings in winter.

SAGUNTO L'Armeler
C/ Subida al Castillo 44, 46500 (Valencia) **Tel** *962 66 43 82*

In the old Jewish quarter of Sagunt, a historic house contains this chic restaurant. There are two dining areas, with wooden beams and colourful tiles. The menu offers innovative Mediterranean cuisine, with signature dishes such as duck with figs and aniseed sauce. Closed Mon–Wed evenings (open Tue–Wed evenings Jul–Aug) and Sun all day.

SANTA POLA El Faro

P 🚹 🗓 🏤 🍽   €€€

Ctra N-332 Alicante-Cartagena km 81, 03130 (Alicante) **Tel** 965 41 21 36

El Faro is a typical Spanish seaside restaurant with a good range of delicious regional rice dishes and wonderful fresh fish caught locally. On the edge of town, near the hill of Santa Pola, it is a lovely walk to the tip of the headland, with beautiful views. The wine list has a fine selection from all around Spain. Good value fixed-price menu. Closed 24 Dec.

VALENCIA Bar Pilar

Tapas 🗓 🏤   €

C/ Moro Zeit 13, 46001 (Valencia) **Tel** 963 91 04 97

Although Valencia has been shooting up in the style stakes in recent years, wonderful El Pilar has remained untouched by the whims of fashion. A cheerful, noisy tapas bar where customers shout their orders to the waiters, who shout them to the kitchen, it is justly famous for mussels. Chuck the shells in the buckets under the bar. Closed 25 Dec–1 Jan.

VALENCIA 33 Lounge

🗓 🚻 🍽   €

C/ San Dionisio 8, 46003 (Valencia) **Tel** 963 92 41 61

Located close to the IVAM museum, this is the perfect place to stop and have a bite to eat before or after a visit to the museum. Dishes are based on Mediterranean cuisine with original touches, from baby squid carpaccio to crispy goat's cheese with mushrooms. Paellas for one person are also available. Closed Sun dinner & Mon.

VALENCIA Ca Sento

🗓 🚹 🍽   €€€€

C/ Méndez Núñez 17, 45024 (Valencia) **Tel** 963 30 17 75

Probably the finest restaurant in Valencia, Ca Sento is renowned for its exquisite regional and international cuisine. The decor is sleek and subtle. The dishes, imaginatively cooked by a chef-and-wife team, use spectacularly fresh produce and are immaculately presented. The *menú de degustación* for 145 euros is excellent. Closed Sun, Mon, Easter & Aug.

VILLENA Warynessy

Tapas 🗓 🍽   €€€

C/ Isabel la Católica 13, 03400 (Alicante) **Tel** 965 80 10 47

This chic restaurant-bar comes as a pleasant surprise in the otherwise sleepy mountain town of Villena. The decor is elegant with contemporary furnishings and clean lines. The menu offers creative, yet unfussy, local dishes prepared with flair and imagination. The bar is a lively spot for a pre-dinner cocktail. Closed Mon, Easter & second half of Jul.

VINARÒS El Faro

P 🗓 🚹 🏤 🍽   €€€

Zona Portuaria, 12500 (Castellón) **Tel** 964 45 63 62

Overlooking the port, this smart restaurant in a 19th-century villa has a pretty garden. Dine in the classy salons with sea views, or out on the less formal summer terrace. The menu changes regularly and offers sophisticated and highly creative Spanish and international cuisine, which leans towards seafood. Closed Sun evenings & Mon.

MADRID

OLD MADRID Casa Patas

Tapas 🗓 🚹 🎵   €

C/ Cañizares 10, 28012 **Tel** 913 69 04 96   **Map** 7 A3

Casa Patas is primarily known for its flamenco shows in the evenings, which are among the best in the city. It is also an original place to eat in the heart of Old Madrid, with a well-stocked tapas bar and an unbeatable fixed-price lunch menu. Wheelchair-users must call in advance for assistance. There is an admission charge. Closed Sun.

OLD MADRID El Estragón

🗓 🚹   €

Plaza de la Paja 21, 28005 **Tel** 913 65 89 82   **Map** 4 D3

El Estragón is located in a pretty spot, overlooking one of Madrid's loveliest and most fashionable squares. *Madrileño* cuisine is decidedly meaty, but this long-standing vegetarian restaurant provides a welcome break for veggies. The menu features a variety of delectable vegetable- and soy-based dishes. Note that there are two sittings for dinner.

OLD MADRID Taberna Los Cuatro Robles

Tapas 🗓   €

Plaza de Celenque 1, 28013 **Tel** 915 23 08 09   **Map** 4 E2

A simple, brightly-lit tapas bar, lined with colourful tiles, this tavern brings a taste of Andalusia to the capital. Although it is in the heart of the city, it isn't on the well-trodden tourist route. You can try the delicious croquettes and all kinds of seafood specialities in the company of *Madrileño* workers. Closed Sun.

OLD MADRID Casa Ciriaco

Tapas 🗓 🚹 🏤 🍽   €€

C/ Mayor 84, 28013 **Tel** 915 48 06 20   **Map** 3 C3

A traditional Castilian-style tavern near the Royal Palace, Casa Ciriaco is renowned for its *gallina en pepitoria* (a chicken stew with egg and saffron), which it has been making for more than a century. Other home-made delights include game in season, and *cocido Madrileño*. Book in advance. Closed Wed & Aug.

OLD MADRID Cornucopia

🚹 🗓 🍽   €€

C/ Navas de Tolosa 9, 28013 **Tel** 915 21 38 96   **Map** 4 E1

Charming and intimate, Cornucopia has an interesting cuisine that blends European and American flavours. Ultra-fresh ingredients are used in the cooking, with a plenty of choice for vegetarians. Do not miss the wonderful desserts, especially the strawberry mousse. There is a reasonable lunch menu from Mon–Sat and a well-considered wine list.

OLD MADRID Delic

Tapas 🖼️📧♿🖼️   €€

Plaza de la Paja s/n, 28005 **Tel** *913 64 54 50*   **Map** 4 D3

Stylish Delic is a popular café-bar, doubling as a hip local drinking hole. It serves everything from delicious breakfasts, to light snacks and more substantial cuisine with an exotic touch. With a perfect location on the trendy Plaza de la Paja, the terrace is a good place to watch a smart crowd of locals hang out on hot summer nights.

OLD MADRID Malacatín

Tapas 📧🖼️   €€

C/ de la Ruda 5, 28005 **Tel** *913 65 52 41*   **Map** 4 D4

This bar is full of bullfighting memorabilia, such as paintings, photographs and even bulls' heads, reflecting the owner's former occupation as a bullfighter. To try their star dish *cocido Madrileño* (meat and vegetable stew). Other favourites include tripe cooked Madrid-style. Closed Sat evenings, Sun & Aug.

OLD MADRID Naïa

Tapas 📧🖼️🖼️   €€

Plaza de la Paja 3, 28005 **Tel** *913 66 27 83*   **Map** 4 D3

The newest arrival on the ultra-trendy Plaza de la Paja, this glassy modern restaurant is currently a favourite with Madrid's fashionistas. Dine on deftly prepared Mediterranean cuisine out on the terrace – a perfect vantage point to admire the beautiful old square. There is also a reasonably priced *menú del día*. Closed Sun evenings & Mon.

OLD MADRID Taberna Bilbao

Tapas 📧♿🖼️   €€

C/ Costanilla de San Andrés 8, 28005 **Tel** *913 65 61 25*   **Map** 3 C3

A hugely popular Basque tavern, Taberna Bilbao serves home-made specialities such as *bacalao* cooked in a range of styles. The *chipirones* (baby squid), prepared in their own ink, are excellent. Definitely worth trying is the typical Basque wine, *txakoli*, which is light, tart and very refreshing. Reservations are highly recomended. Closed Mon.

OLD MADRID Belalúa

📧♿🖼️🖼️   €€€

C/ San Nicolás 8, 28012 **Tel** *915 47 22 22*   **Map** 3 C2

Belalúa is a modern, glassy designer restaurant, with slick minimalist furnishings and an excellent menu featuring cuisine from Spain's Northern coast. Fish is served predominantly, but there are plenty of meat specialities too. Try the hake stuffed with shellfish or the meaty seared tuna. A short but interesting wine list. Closed Sun evenings.

OLD MADRID Botín

📧♿🖼️   €€€

C/ de Cuchilleros 17, 28011 **Tel** *913 66 42 17*   **Map** 4 E3

Dating back to 1725, Botín is reputedly the oldest restaurant in the world. With its brick-lined vaults and heavy wooden beams, it has changed little since. Even the original wood-burning oven is still used to cook the traditional roast lamb and suckling pig. There is a reasonable fixed-price lunch menu. Book well in advance.

OLD MADRID Casa Lucio

Tapas 🅿️📧♿🖼️   €€€€

C/ Cava Baja 35, 28005 **Tel** *913 65 32 52*   **Map** 4 D4

Casa Lucio is a historic tavern serving Castilian specialities. The *huevos estrellados* (fried eggs with potatoes) are so exquisite that they have even made it into a celebrated Spanish poem. The typical *Madrileño* tripe and rice pudding are equally renowned. The wine list has some fine wines from around Spain. Closed Sat lunch & Aug.

OLD MADRID Lhardy

Tapas 🅿️📧🖼️🖼️   €€€€

Carrera de San Jerónimo 8, 28014 **Tel** *915 21 33 85*   **Map** 4 F2

Established in 1839 and preserving its character with chandeliers, mirrors and dark wood-panelled walls, this restaurant serves what is arguably the most classic *cocido Madrileño*. Legend has it that Isabel II once entertained her lovers in the upstairs dining rooms. Downstairs is a celebrated cake shop, delicatessen and tapas area. Closed Sun evenings & Aug.

BOURBON MADRID Arrocería Gala

Tapas 🖼️📧♿   €

C/ Moratín 22, 28014 **Tel** *914 29 25 62*   **Map** 7 B3

Admire the indoor patio and chandeliers and enjoy a generous set menu with Catalan specialities, such as paellas and other rice dishes, at an unbelievably reasonable price. Accompany them with one of the excellent range of Catalan wines or *cavas*. They also serve tapas, including snails and grilled prawns. Closed Mon.

BOURBON MADRID Casa Labra

Tapas 📧   €

C/ Tetuán 12, 28013 **Tel** *915 32 14 05*   **Map** 4 F2

Open since 1860, Casa Labra is one of Madrid's most atmospheric tapas bars. Tucked away on a small street close to the Puerta del Sol, it retains the old wood panels and pretty tiles. Once a meeting place for the Spanish Socialist party, the restaurant has been in the same family since 1947 and is renowned for its *bacalao*. Closed 1 Jan.

BOURBON MADRID El Txoko

Tapas 🖼️📧🖼️   €

C/ Jovellanos 3, 28014 **Tel** *915 32 34 43*   **Map** 7 B2

There is no better place to try delicious Basque delicacies than the Eusko-Etxea (a Basque club). The restaurant is simple but appealing, and offers a good fixed-price lunch menu and *menu degustacion*, which is so popular with local workers that it is sometimes hard to get a seat. Try the stuffed peppers and baby squid. Closed Sun evenings, Mon & Aug.

BOURBON MADRID The Grill Club Café

♿📧🎵   €

C/ Jorge Juan 8, 28001 **Tel** *915 78 01 08*   **Map** 6 E5

Situated close to the Museo Arqueologico in stylish Barrio de Salamanca, The Grill Club Café is a New York-style eater with minimalist decor and moderate prices. Specialising in grilled steaks, the kitchen also churns out staples such as pasta, pizza and salads. The special muffin breakfast is recommended. They also have a weekday lunch menu.

BOURBON MADRID La Fábrica

Tapas €

C/ Jesús 2, 28014 **Tel** *913 69 06 71*

Map *7 B3*

A down-to-earth tapas bar, which is always crammed with customers, La Fábrica has long counters groaning with a bewildering array of fresh tapas. The octopus, which sits steaming on the bar-top, is particularly good, as are the freshly made *montaditos* (crusty bread with delicious toppings). Try them with the Cabrales, pungent Asturian cheese.

BOURBON MADRID Las Bravas

Tapas €

C/ Álvarez Gato 5, 28012 **Tel** *915 32 26 20*

Map *4 F3*

Patatas bravas (chunks of fried potato doused in a lurid orange sauce) are now found everywhere in Spain, but they were created at Las Bravas. There are four locations, all within a stone's throw of each other, and they are always packed. The generous portions and low prices particularly attract local students.

BOURBON MADRID Terra Mundi

Tapas €

C/ Lope de Vega 32, 28014 **Tel** *914 29 52 80*

Map *7 B3*

A friendly restaurant with rustic decor, Terra Mundi serves specialities from Galicia. The *pulpo* is a favourite, along with home-made *empanadas* (pies filled with tuna, meat or vegetables). They serve tapas from Sunday to Thursday, with restaurant service only on other days. There's a good *menú del día*. Closed Mon evenings.

BOURBON MADRID Café Gijón

Tapas €€

Paseo Recoletos 21, 28007 **Tel** *915 21 54 25*

Map *7 C1*

A legendary café, established in 1888 and still decorated with original Art Nouveau style furnishings, Café Gijón is perfect for breakfast, a fixed-price lunch or afternoon tea with cakes. Specialities include hake with cider and seafood paella. There is an elegant terrace, frequented by the well-heeled.

BOURBON MADRID La Castafiore

Tapas €€€

C/ Marqués de Monasterio 5, 28004 **Tel** *915 32 21 00*

Map *5 C5*

A charming Italian restaurant, this unique dining spot features singing waiters. All trained opera singers, they burst into magnificent arias as they serve fine Italian cuisine. The food may play second fiddle to the service, but it remains consistently good. Booking is recommended. Closed Sun.

BOURBON MADRID Teatriz

Tapas €€€

C/ Hermosilla 15, 28001 **Tel** *915 77 53 79*

Map *6 D4*

Formerly a theatre, Teatriz was completely transformed by French designer Philippe Starck in 1989 and now houses a chic restaurant and a stylish tapas bar. In the restaurant, you can dine on fresh Mediterranean cuisine with Italian influences, while the tapas bar offers gourmet tapas. Prices reflect the glamorous setting. Closed Aug.

BOURBON MADRID Thai Gardens

€€€

Paseo de la Habana 3, 28036 **Tel** *915 77 88 84*

Spain's first-ever Thai restaurant, Thai Gardens is beautifully decorated with wicker furniture, exquisite orchids and spectacular Thai artwork. The award-winning food has been toned down to suit Spanish palates, but the delicate authentic spices are deftly handled. It is a romantic spot, ideal for an intimate dinner.

BOURBON MADRID El Amparo

€€€€

Callejón de Puigcerdá 8, 28001 **Tel** *914 31 64 56*

Map *6 E5*

Enjoy new Basque cuisine in what many consider to be Madrid's nicest setting, with a skylight that lets you gaze up at the stars. The dining rooms are spread out over three levels, and the cuisine is assured and highly creative, such as tuna mousse with lobster and parsley oil. Closed Sat lunch, Sun & Easter.

BOURBON MADRID Paradis

€€€€

C/ Marques de Cubas 14, 28014 **Tel** *914 29 73 03*

Map *7 B2*

Part of a successful Catalan chain, Paradis offers high-quality Mediterranean cuisine. The grilled vegetables and the rice dishes make delicious starters, followed by any of the fresh fish available. The restaurant has two other branches in the Casa de América (Paseo Recoletos 2) and the Thyssen museum. Closed Sat lunch, Sun & bank holidays.

BOURBON MADRID Viridiana

€€€€

C/ Juan de Mena 14, 28014 **Tel** *915 23 44 78*

Map *7 C2*

Innovative Spanish cuisine, complemented by an encyclopedic wine list, is offered in this restaurant decorated with stills from Luís Buñuel's film, *Viridiana*. The creative menu changes frequently, and features elaborate creations prepared with the best seasonal produce. The wine list was recently voted one of the best in the world. Closed Sun.

FURTHER AFIELD (EAST) La Taberna de la Daniela

Tapas €€

C/ General Pardiñas 21, 28001 **Tel** *915 75 23 29*

In the heart of the smart Salamanca district, this authentic Castilian tavern is famous for its excellent tapas. It also serves an excellent *cocido* (the typical Madrid stew) at lunch and has a short menu of other traditional *Madrileño* dishes, including *callos* (tripe) and lamb chops. Make your reservation a day in advance.

FURTHER AFIELD (EAST) Los Timbales

Tapas €

C/ Alcalá 227, 28028 **Tel** *917 25 07 68*

Conveniently located near to the Las Ventas bullring, Los Timbales is the classic meeting place for bullfighting aficionados. Posters, photographs and bulls' heads deck the walls. Tuck into tapas, including good hams, or enjoy the substantial fixed-price lunch menu. The wine list features some excellent Riojas.

FURTHER AFIELD (NORTH) Chantarella
P 🗐 🍷 €€€

C/ Doctor Fleming 7, 28036 **Tel** *913 44 10 04*

A little way out of the centre in the Chamartín district, this small and chic restaurant is well worth the trek. Its sleek, minimalist decor is the perfect showcase for the excellent contemporary Spanish cuisine, prepared with the freshest seasonal produce available. Impeccable service and an interesting wine list. Closed Sat lunch & Sun.

FURTHER AFIELD (NORTH) Goizeko Kabi
P 🗐 🕭 🍴 🍷 €€€€

C/ Comandante Zorita 37, 28020 **Tel** *915 33 01 85*

At Goizeko Kabi, traditional Basque cuisine is served in a refined setting. Excellent fresh produce and seafood are the basis of the chef's creations, winning plaudits from gourmets across Europe. The spider crab is outstanding, and the *chipirones encebollados* (baby squid) remains a signature dish. There is an excellent wine list. Closed Sun.

FURTHER AFIELD (NORTH) Jockey
P 🗐 🕭 🍴 🍷 €€€€

C/ Amador de los Ríos 6, 28010 **Tel** *913 19 24 35*

Map 6 D4

Among Madrid's top five restaurants, frequented by gourmets and celebrities, Jockey offers a seasonal menu which specializes in top-of-the-range Castilian cuisine. There are excellent poultry and game dishes. The place has the air of a sophisticated gentleman's club, complete with equestrian paintings. Closed Sun, Aug & bank holidays.

FURTHER AFIELD (NORTH) Santceloni
P 🗐 🕭 🍷 €€€€

Hotel Hesperia, Paseo de la Castellana 57, 28046 **Tel** *912 10 88 40*

Map 6 D1

Sister to the famous Santi Santamaría in Catalonia, Santceloni is one of the best places in Madrid to appreciate Spain's culinary revolution over the last few years. The menu is short, but exquisite: try the fabulous *menú gastronómico* which features their finest dishes. Outstanding wine list. Closed Sat lunch, Sun, Easter & Aug.

FURTHER AFIELD (NORTH) Zalacain
P 🗐 🕭 🍴 🍷 €€€€

C/ Álvarez de Baena 4, 28006 **Tel** *915 61 59 35*

Considered Madrid's finest restaurant, Zalacaín has a splendidly formal setting, attentive service and superb Basque-oriented cuisine. The menu changes four times a year and features the finest seasonal produce. The *menú de degustación* features house specialities. Closed Sat lunch, Sun, Easter, Aug & bank holidays.

FURTHER AFIELD (NORTHEAST) Asador Aguinaga
🗐 🍴 🍷 €€€

C/ Velázquez 102, 28036 **Tel** *915 77 15 91*

A rather formal restaurant in the chichi Salamanca district, this restaurant offers delicious Basque specialities, including *angulas* (eels) from Aguinaga, a sought-after Basque delicacy, and salads made with spider crab or prawns. Although seafood features prominently, the meat dishes are also excellent. Closed Sat lunch, Sun & Aug.

FURTHER AFIELD (NORTHEAST) El Olivo
🗐 🍷 €€€

C/ General Gallegos 1, 28036 **Tel** *913 59 15 35*

El Olivo is popular for its top-of-the-line Mediterranean cuisine using excellent-quality seasonal produce. Olive oil is the underlying culinary theme, and there's even an olive oil and honey ice cream on the menu. The wine list includes a range of sherries. They also own a shop with a range of olive oils across the street. Closed Mon evening, Sun & 15–30 Aug.

FURTHER AFIELD (NORTHEAST) Sacha
🗐 🕭 🔛 🍷 €€€

C/ Juan Hurtado de Mendoza, 11 (entrance by the back garden), 28036 **Tel** *913 45 59 52*

Decorated like a cosy bistro, this charming and much-lauded restaurant serves sensational, creative cuisine including specialities such as partridge with rice and mushrooms and marinated oysters. Book early to get a table out on the lovely terrace, shaded with pines and cypress trees. Excellent wines and unmissable desserts. Closed Sun.

FURTHER AFIELD (WEST) Casa Ricardo
🗐 🕭 €€

C/ Fernando el Católico 31, 28015 **Tel** *914 47 61 19*

Map 2 D1

Inaugurated in 1935, this delightful *Madrileño* restaurant has changed little since. It is crammed with bullfighting memorabilia and is popular with an arty crowd as well as local politicians. Try typical dishes such as *callos a la Madrileña* (tripe in a spicy white wine sauce). Disabled access is limited to the downstairs salon. Closed Sun evenings.

MADRID PROVINCE

ALCALÁ DE HENARES Gran Mesón La Casa Vieja
Tapas 🗐 🔛 €

C/ San Felipe Neri 7, 28302 **Tel** *918 83 62 81*

A wonderful old inn in the heart of the beautiful and historic town of Alcalá de Henares, La Casa Vieja has wooden-beamed dining areas spread over three floors, and a charming summer terrace out on the patio. Juicy grilled meats, *migas* (breadcrumbs fried with chunks of pork) and other hearty Castilian favourites are on the menu. Closed Mon.

ARANJUEZ Casa Pablo
Tapas 🗐 🕭 🍷 €€€

C/ Almibar 42, 28300 **Tel** *918 91 14 51*

A centrally located tavern, Casa Pablo has been offering solid home cooking for more than 60 years. You can dine or typical dishes such as pheasant with grapes, taste the asparagus and strawberries for which Aranjuez is famous, or pile into the tapas area with everyone else for generous *raciones* (large portions) of Castilian favourites. Closed Aug.

CHINCHÓN Mesón de la Virreina
Tapas 🖽 👌 🛋 €€

Plaza Mayor 28, 28370 **Tel** *918 94 00 15*

Under the porticoes of Chinchón's celebrated Plaza Mayor, this classic *mesón* serves traditional fare such as *sopa castellana* (a garlic soup with chickpeas). Located in a handsome 16th-century building, it also has a terrace on the square, which has appeared in countless films. Wheelchair access is limited to the lower level.

MORALZARZAL El Cenador de Salvador
🅿 🖽 👌 🎵 🛋 🍴 €€€€

Av de España 30, 28411 **Tel** *918 57 77 22*

Many gourmets make the trek from Madrid to Moralzarzal just for the pleasure of dining in this lovely chalet. The exquisite seasonal cooking has won several prestigious international awards. Try the house speciality: hake in the style of grandmother Salvadora. A pianist entertains diners in summer. Closed Sun evenings; Mon; Tue lunch.

NAVACERRADA La Fonda Real
Tapas 🅿 🖽 👌 🎵 €€

Ctra N-601 km 12.5, 28491 **Tel** *918 56 03 05*

This 18th-century country house was once a staging post on the royal route from Madrid to the palace at La Granja. With sturdy furnishings and a welcoming fireplace, it's the perfect setting for Castilian country cooking. The house speciality is roasted suckling pig. Closed Sun evenings & Mon in Jul & Aug; Mon & Sun–Thu evenings rest of the year.

PATONES DE ARRIBA El Poleo
🅿 🖽 🍴 €€€

Travesia del Arroyo 2–3, 28189 **Tel** *918 43 21 01*

Set in a picturesque town with slate-roofed houses, El Poleo is a wonderful restaurant serving Navarrese-style dishes. Try the crab-stuffed crêpes with a wild mushroom sauce. The same owner runs El Jardin del Poleo on the same street, which is cheaper. Opens Thu–Sat all day & Sun lunch. Closed 15 Jul–5 Aug & 21–25 Dec.

RASCAFRÍA Barondillo
Tapas 👌 €€

Cuesta del Chorro 4, 28740 **Tel** *918 69 18 19*

Brick walls, wooden beams, and hefty iron chandeliers decorate this country restaurant in a mountain town. The menu features whatever is in season, from wild mushrooms in spring to game in autumn. Home-made bread and desserts are also available. If you are too full to make it home, they also have rooms. Closed Tue & two weeks in Jun.

SAN LORENZO DE EL ESCORIAL Taberna La Cueva
Tapas 🛋 🍴 €€

C/ San Antón 4, 28200 **Tel** *918 90 15 16*

Juan de Villanueva, architect of the Prado, designed this 18th-century inn whose specialities include the *huevos a la cueva* (fried eggs and ham served in a nest of straw potatoes). A cool stone house, it is cosy in winter and cool in summer, when you can also tuck into tapas out on the terrace. A good range of local wines. Closed Mon.

SAN LORENZO DE EL ESCORIAL Charolés
🖽 👌 🛋 🍴 €€€€

C/ Floridablanca 24, 28200 **Tel** *918 90 59 75*

A well-established classic in San Lorenzo de el Escorial, this elegant restaurant serves polished Castilian cuisine with creative touches. Nonetheless, the trademark dish here is the authentic *cocido Madrileño*, served on Wednesdays and Fridays when you would be well advised to book. The thoughtfully chosen wine list has around 300 labels.

CASTILLA Y LEÓN

AMPUDIA Restaurante Arambol-Casa del Abad
Tapas 🖽 🛋 🍴 €€€€

Plaza Francisco Martín Gromaz 12, 34191 (Palencia) **Tel** *979 76 80 08*

Located in the wine press of the old residence of the Colegiata of San Miguel's Abbot, this spectacular setting offers decorative elements dating back to the 17th century. Exquisite cuisine from the Michelin-starred chef, Joachim Koerper, is based on local vegetables, game, spring lamb, fresh fish and various rice dishes. Closed Sun from Sep–Mar & Mon.

ARANDA DE DUERO Mesón de la Villa
Tapas 🖽 👌 🍴 €€

La Sal 3, 09400 (Burgos) **Tel** *947 50 10 25*

Mesón de la Villa is renowned throughout the province, and serves up typical Castilian cuisine. Amongst the favourites are the famous roasted baby lamb and the creative pork, lentil, bean and chickpea combinations. A great selection of wines is stocked in their underground cellar. Closed Mon & 15–30 Oct.

ARÉVALO Asador Las Cubas
🖽 🍴 €

Figones 11, 05200 (Avila) **Tel** *920 30 01 25*

Complete with period furniture and fittings, Asador las Cubas is a popular carvery serving roast meats at reasonable prices. Veal is the star here. The dining room is tiny, so reservations are recommended. Closed evenings, last 15 days of Jun & 24 Dec–2 Jan.

ASTORGA La Peseta
Tapas 🖽 👌 🍴 €

Plaza de San Bartolomé 3, 24700 (León) **Tel** *987 61 72 75*

This 100-year-old restaurant is a classic in Astorga for its high-quality traditional cooking. Among its specialities are *maragato* stew (a heavy dish of nine different meats, chickpeas and vegetables), local beans with chorizo and conger. There is a decent wine list. Closed Sun evening, 15–31 Jan & 15–31 Oct.

ÁVILA El Almacén
Crta Salamanca 6, 05002 **Tel** 920 25 44 55

This restaurant, located in an old warehouse, is generally regarded as one of the best in all of Castilla, and is particularly noted for its wine cellar. It offers creative cooking with high-quality local produce, all cooked to perfection. There are views of Ávila's famous wall from the dining room. Closed Sun evenings, Mon & Sep.

BENAVENTE El Ermitaño
Ctra de Benavente-León km 1.2, 49600 (Zamora) **Tel** 980 63 22 13

This 18th-century house is a great family option with plenty of outdoor space. There are various rooms to explore as well as an attic for coffee. The menu is typical of the area's rural cooking with some hints of modernity in the salads and desserts, and there is a good *menu degustación*. Closed Sun evenings, Mon & 24 Dec–15 Jan.

BURGOS Mesón del Cid
Plaza Santa María 8, 09003 **Tel** 947 20 87 15

In a 15th-century edifice located in front of the cathedral, this rustic place is named after Spain's most notorious conqueror. A favourite among locals, it is celebrated for its home-style cooking. The menu features traditional fare such as roast lamb, garlic soup and cod cooked with garlic. There is an excellent house wine. Closed Sun evenings.

CANEDO Prada a Tope-Palacio de Canedo
Tapas
La Iglesia s/n, 24546 (León) **Tel** 902 40 01 01

Prada a Tope is a popular restaurant located in a grand 17th-century palace. The food, however, is more down to earth. Some of the best dishes to try are *chorizo* with potatoes, *botillo* (vegetable stew), tuna or vegetables and preserves. The house wine is made on the premises. Closed Sunday evening.

COVARRUBIAS Casa Galín
Tapas
Plaza Doña Urraca 4, 09346 (Burgos) **Tel** 947 40 65 52

This modest little eatery, in the medieval village of Covarrubias, is an ideal place to sample Castilian home-cooked fare such as organic chicken with peppers, thick and hearty bean-based soups and the ominous sounding *olla podrida*, a slow-cooked stew of pigs' ears and feet, black sausage and vegetables. Closed Sun evenings, Tue & 8 Dec–9 Jan.

EL BURGO DE OSMA Virrey Palafox
Tapas
Universidad 7, 42300 (Soria) **Tel** 975 34 02 22

The most popular time to dine at Virrey Palafox is January to March, the months when suckling pig is in season. For wine buffs interested in trying the local wines from the Ribera del Duero region, this is the best place to start, with over 1,000 varieties to choose from. Reservations recommended. Closed Sun evenings, Mon & 22 Dec–10 Jan.

FRÓMISTA Hostería de los Palmeros
Tapas
Plaza San Telmo 4, 34440 (Palencia) **Tel** 979 81 00 67

An excellent restaurant housed in an ancient building, which formerly served as a pilgrims' hospital and is now a rural hostal. Travellers can enjoy hearty cooking based on fresh products, such as *morcilla*, *chorizo* and peppers, in a lovely garden setting if weather permits. Closed Tue (except at Easter, in summer and at Christmas) and Jan.

LEÓN Vivaldi
Platerías 4, 24003 **Tel** 987 26 07 60

In the historic Húmedo district, Vivaldi is one of the better-known restaurants in León. Original creations include fresh pasta with fungi and foie gras, sautéed vegetables with octopus and chickpeas with garlic prawns. There is a bar for pre-dinner drinks. Closed Sun evenings and Mon (except in Jul & Aug).

MOLINASECA Casa Ramón
Tapas
Jardines Ángeles de Balboa 2, 24413 (León) **Tel** 987 45 31 53

Casa Ramón is a popular rural restaurant in a beautiful village near Ponferrada, surrounded by a river which is also a popular swimming spot. The varied menu includes Cantabrian fish dishes, lentils *a la Marinara*, king prawns with clams and entrecôte with Bierzo peppers. Closed Mon & 24–30 Sep.

MORALES DEL TORO Chivo
Tapas
Av Comuneros s/n, 49810 (Zamora) **Tel** 980 69 82 62

Located 8 km (5 miles) from the village of Toro on the vineyard belt, El Chivo is regularly frequented by workers in the area, who come here for the satisfying meat and fish creations, washed down with local wine. The focus is on Basque and Castilian-style cooking, and there is a good value fixed-price menu. Closed Sun evenings and 1–15 Nov.

NAVALENO El Maño
Tapas
Calleja del Barrio 5, 42149 (Soria) **Tel** 975 37 42 01

Set in an old, rambling country home, El Maño has a large and lively dining room. The daily menu features regional cooking based on local game, wild mushrooms and river fish, and truffles. The attentive staff will make you feel more than welcome. A popular and busy restaurant. Closed Mon evenings & 1–15 Sep.

NAVALONGUILLA El Remanso de Gredos
Iglesia s/n, 05668 **Tel** 920 34 38 98

In the Sierra de Gredos park, guests staying at the hotel can sample the satisfying local bean dishes or fresh and succulent steaks from the region's famed livestock. Afterwards, take a stroll through the surrounding peaceful natural parkland (only for guests of the hotel).

Key to Price Guide see p608 **Key to Symbols** see back cover flap

PALENCIA Casa Lucio
Tapas 📋 🔖 €€

Don Sancho 2, 34001 **Tel** *979 74 81 90*

Traditional cooking is at its best in this classic restaurant in the centre of Palencia. At lunch time businessmen flock here for the meats roasted in a firewood oven. Fish is also on offer and specialities include chickpeas with crab and wild turbot *a la gallega*. Home-made desserts. Closed Sun & 1–15 Jul.

PEDRAZA DE LA SIERRA La Olma de Pedraza
📋 🖼 🔖 €€€

Plaza del Ganado 1, 40172 (Segovia) **Tel** *921 50 99 81*

If it is suckling pig you are after, this 16th-century mansion in a pretty square is the place to visit, although ordering it in advance is required. Fish dishes, such as baby squid cooked in its own ink, and peppers stuffed with hake, also feature. A pleasant covered terrace looks out onto the square for outdoor dining. Closed Tue & second week of Sep.

PONFERRADA Menta y Canela
📋 ♿ 🔖 €€

Alonso Cano 10, 24400 (León) **Tel** *987 40 32 89*

This carvery offers succulent dishes from local livestock, with the best grilled meats in the province. The menu varies according to availability and prices. Other ingredients are celebrated in their "thematic weeks". In March, there's a special menu of rice dishes. Welcoming atmosphere and friendly staff. Closed Mon.

SALAMANCA Momo
Tapas 📋 🖼 🔖 €€

San Pablo 13, 37002 **Tel** *923 28 07 98*

Momo is a retro-modern eatery complete with furniture from the mid-20th century. Tapas are served downstairs, while on the first floor, you can indulge in beautifully prepared dishes such as the imaginative salads, *solomillo* with Arbequina olive oil, cod in garlic and chilli oil and cheesecake with wild berries. Closed Sun (Jul) & Aug.

SALAMANCA El Río de la Plata
Tapas 📋 🔖 €€€

Plaza del Peso 1, 37001 **Tel** *923 21 90 05*

Located in the heart of the old town, this traditional restaurant, run by the locally celebrated Andrés brothers, serves slow-cooked lamb, pork and veal stews and suckling pig. Lighter eaters may wish to stick to the excellent selection of tapas. Amongst the tasty desserts is apple baked in a secret sauce! Closed Mon, 8–20 Jan & 15–20 days in Jul.

SALAMANCA Víctor Gutiérrez
📋 ♿ 🔖 €€€€

San Pablo 66, 37008 **Tel** *923 26 29 73*

This romantic and cosy restaurant in Salamanca's old town, with views over the San Esteban church, offers creative and modern cooking using seasonal products. The restaurant is particularly noted for its perfectly cooked game, interesting vegetable dishes and excellent wine list. Closed Sun & Tue evenings, 7–14 Jan & 1–15 Jul.

SANTA MARÍA DE MAVE Hostería el Convento
📋 ♿ 🔖 €€

Santa María de Mave, 34492 (Palencia) **Tel** *979 12 36 11*

Once a Benedictine convent in the Montaña Palentina Natural Park, this Romanesque jewel is the setting for a charming restaurant that combines traditional dishes with modern influences. Try their scrambled eggs with wild mushrooms and foie gras, game loin with oatmeal cream and wild fruits or the vegetable stew. Closed 24–25 Dec.

SARDÓN DE DUERO Sardón
Tapas 📋 🔖 €€

Ctra Valladolid-Soria km 335, 47340 (Valladolid) **Tel** *983 68 03 07*

A pleasant restaurant in the heart of the Ribera del Duero wine-growing area, Sardón is located very close to some of the most famed bodegas. The extensive, high-quality menu features local products with original touches. The wine list is top-notch and you can purchase some to take home from their adjoining shop. Closed Sun evenings.

SEGOVIA Mesón de Cándido
Tapas 📋 ♿ 🖼 🔖 €€€

Azoguejo 5, 40001 **Tel** *921 42 59 11*

One of the region's better-known restaurants, Mesón de Candido is located in a 15th-century home, close to the Roman aqueduct. The restaurant is famed for its roast suckling pig (so tender they carve it for you with the side of a plate) and hearty Castilian soups. A favourite amongst locals, it is always busy, so reservations are recommended.

SEPÚLVEDA Cristóbal
Tapas 📋 🔖 €€

Conde de Sepúlveda 9, 40300 (Segovia) **Tel** *921 54 01 00*

Renovated in 2005 and located just near the information centre of the Hoces del Río Duratón National Park, Cristóbal is the best restaurant in the village. The extensive menu features regional dishes that can be savoured in the fittingly rustic setting of an underground cave. Closed Mon–Thu evenings, Tue, 1–15 Sep & 15–30 Dec.

SORIA Casa Augusto
📋 🖼 🔖 €€€

Plaza Mayor 5, 42002 **Tel** *975 21 30 41*

This emblematic restaurant in the centre of Soria is tastefully decorated with period furniture and offers a fusion of traditional and original dishes. Specialities include spring lamb's breast, stuffed Piquillo peppers, and aubergines with wild mushrooms. The staff are more than happy to recommend an accompaniment from the list of local wines.

TORDESILLAS El Torreón
📋 ♿ 🔖 €€€€

Dimas Rodríguez 11, 47100 (Valladolid) **Tel** *983 77 01 23*

This restaurant, founded in 1981, has a reputation for excellent meats grilled in an open kitchen. The highlights are the grilled ox steaks, deliciously succulent lamb chops, fresh duck liver, anchovies with leeks and cheese, and tasty, original salads. There is also an excellent selection of wines. Closed Sun & 10–22 Sep.

VALLADOLID Vinotinto
Tapas 📋 🍷   €€

Campanas 4, 47001 **Tel** *983 34 22 91*

In a neighbourhood famous for its bars and bodegas, this modest eatery serves well-portioned tapas on the ground floor, while the cellar is reserved for slightly more formal sit-down dining. Satisfying dishes, such as steaks, spring lamb and duck breast, are used in simple, traditional recipes that are cooked to perfection. Closed 15–30 Aug.

VALLADOLID Trigo
📋 ♿ 🚻 🍷   €€€€

C/ Los Tintes 8, 47002 **Tel** *983 11 55 00*

Victor Martin has been the head chef of many prestigious restaurants, including Sant Celoni, but opened his own restaurant to great acclaim in 2007. Traditional ingredients are used to create dishes with *haute cuisine* influences but a lighter touch; for example artichokes in a cod sauce. Closed Sun and Mon evenings.

VILLAFRANCA DEL BIERZO Casa Méndez
📋   €

Plaza de la Concepción s/n, 24500 (León) **Tel** *987 54 24 08*

This welcoming family-run restaurant is located 20 km (12.4 miles) from Ponferrada, a village on the famous Santiago Route. Among its homespun specialities are stuffed Bierzo peppers and trout. For dessert, try the delicious *tarta de Santiago*, a cake made of almond flour bearing the cross of St James, or Santiago. Closed Mon in winter.

ZAMORA Serafín
Tapas 📋 🎴 🍷   €€€

Plaza del Maestro Maedo 2, 49003 (Zamora) **Tel** *980 53 14 22*

Located in the centre of the city, Serafín has an exhaustive menu offering all that the regional cuisine is famous for. Especially good are the fish and rice dishes, and the eggs and chicken come straight from the restaurant's own farm. Tapas are also available and there is a lovely terrace for al fresco dining. Closed Thu.

CASTILLA-LA MANCHA

ALBACETE Nuestro Bar
Tapas ♿ 📋 🍷   €€€

C/ Alcalde Conangla 102, 02002 (Albacete) **Tel** *967 24 33 73*

Decorated with local handicrafts, this welcoming local restaurant has three dining areas serving regional dishes, one from each of the villages in the province. The *menú de degustación* includes specialities of La Mancha such as *gazpacho manchego* (a rich game stew thickened with biscuits). Closed Sun evenings & July.

ALCÁZAR DE SAN JUAN Casa Paco
Tapas 📋 ♿ 🎴   €

Av Álvarez Guerra 5, 13600 (Ciudad Real) **Tel** *926 54 06 06*

Casa Paco, a comfortable, traditional restaurant, has been going for more than 80 years. On the menu are delicious local dishes such as scrambled eggs with wild mushrooms and ham, lamb baked in a brick oven, and traditional regional desserts. There is a bargain lunch menu which can be enjoyed out on the terrace. Closed Mon & 15–30 Sep.

ALMAGRO El Corregidor
Tapas 📋 ♿ 🎴 🍷   €€€€

C/ Jerónimo Ceballos 2, 13270 (Ciudad Real) **Tel** *926 86 06 48*

This delightful 18th-century house near Plaza Mayor, with many dining rooms and a central patio, is one of Castilla-La Mancha's prettiest restaurants. Menu features creative, regional cuisine, including the town's speciality, pickled aubergines. Try the Manchego menu or the more elaborate *menú de degustación*. Closed Mon (except Jul).

ALMANSA Mesón de Pincelín
Tapas ♿ 📋 🍷   €€€

C/ Las Norias 10, 02640 (Albacete) **Tel** *967 34 00 07*

Mesón de Pincelín is considered by many to be one of the region's best restaurants, with traditional Castilian decor. Try authentic regional dishes prepared with a dash of creativity, including their famous *gazpacho manchego*. Home-made desserts are excellent and the wine list is very good. Closed Sun evenings, Mon, 7–14 Jan & three weeks in Aug.

ATIENZA Restaurante El Mirador
📋 🍷   €€

C/ Barruelo s/n, 19270 (Guadalajara) **Tel** *949 39 90 38*

This sophisticated restaurant specializes in *ollas* and *pucheros*, the hearty stews and casseroles which are typical of this mountainous region. Fresh seasonal vegetables and excellent local meats are prominently used in the cooking. The cosy dining room is decorated with antlers, brass knick-knacks and paintings. Closed Sun evenings & 23 Dec–7 Jan.

BELMONTE Palacio Buenavista Hospedería
Tapas 📋 ♿ 🎴   €€

C/ La Iglesia 2, 16640 (Cuenca) **Tel** *967 18 75 80*

The elegant restaurant at this stylish and graceful hotel, in a beautifully restored 16th-century palace, has ochre walls and wooden beams. The subtle decor complements the refined regional cuisine, which includes oven-baked lamb and steaks and a wonderful array of Manchegan cheeses and country pâtés.

BRIHUEGA Asador El Tolmo
Tapas 📋 ♿   €€

Av de la Constitución 26, 19400 (Guadalajara) **Tel** *949 28 11 30*

A restaurant-bar popular with locals, Asador El Tolmo is located in a pretty, walled Alcarrian village. The traditional Castilian decor is in keeping with the cuisine, which includes roast kid, beans with partridge and other regional favourites. There's a good fixed-price lunch menu and delicious home-made desserts.

Key to Price Guide *see p608* **Key to Symbols** *see back cover flap*

CHINCHILLA DE MONTEARAGÓN Montearagón
Tapas 🖿 🕭 🖾   €

C/ Arenal 35 (7 km from Albacete), 02520 (Albacete) **Tel** *967 26 05 97*

In a historic town, praised for its loyalty by the Catholic Monarchs and dominated by a ruined castle, this is a very popular local café-bar. An easy jaunt from Alabacete, it is an ideal stopover for lunch. Serves a wide range of tapas along with some sturdy local dishes and a cheap and filling fixed lunch menu. Closed Tue & 15–31 Aug.

CIUDAD REAL Gran Mesón
🖿 🕭 🖟   €€€

Ronda de Ciruela 34, 13004 (Ciudad Real) **Tel** *926 22 72 39*

Friendly, charming and recommended by locals, Gran Mesón offers an ample set menu with regional specialities such as *gachas* (gruel), *pisto* (a kind of ratatouille), suckling pig and local cheese and wines. The seasonal meat and game are roasted over charcoal and the wine list has more than 200 hundred varieties. Closed Sun evenings.

CUENCA Marlo
🖿 🖟   €€€

C/ Colón 41, 16002 **Tel** *969 21 11 73*

Fish and shellfish feature predominantly on Marlo's modern menu, created by adventurous young chef, Maripaz Martínez. Recommended dishes include confit of lamb with wild mushroom sauce, or the stuffed partridge in season. Service is impeccable and there is an interesting choice of reasonably priced wines as well. Closed Sun evenings.

CUENCA Mesón Casas Colgadas
Tapas 🖿   €€€

C/ Canonigos s/n, 16001 **Tel** *969 22 35 09*

Dine in one of Cuenca's famous hanging houses, an upside-down medieval skyscraper that clings to the gorge. There are unbeatable views to go with great regional cuisine. There is a tapas bar downstairs, and a dining room up a narrow medieval staircase. Staff are utterly delightful. Closed Mon evenings & Tue.

DAIMIEL Mesón El Bodegón
Tapas 🖿 🕭 🎵 🖟   €€€

C/ Luchana 20, 13250 (Ciudad Real) **Tel** *926 85 26 52*

An atmospheric 18th-century cellar and olive oil press is the setting for this charming restaurant, on the fringes of the lakes of Daimiel, a natural park. Dine on typical Manchego cuisine, accompanied by a spectacular wine list. Flamenco performances take place on some Friday nights. Check in advance for more details. Closed Sun–Tue evenings.

GUADALAJARA Minaya
Tapas 🖿   €€

C/ Mayor 23, 19001 (Guadalajara) **Tel** *949 21 22 53*

Minaya is a reasonably priced, elegant restaurant housed in a romantic 16th-century mansion. There is a dining area upstairs, with several fixed-price menus, while downstairs houses a tapas bar. The house speciality is *carnes a la brasa* (meat grilled over charcoal). The home-made desserts are excellent. Service, sadly, is patchy. Closed Sun.

GUADALAJARA Amparito Roca
🖿 🕭 🖾 🖟   €€€€

C/ Toledo 19, 19002 (Guadalajara) **Tel** *949 21 46 39*

The chefs of Amparito Roca, the finest restaurant in the region, reinvent classic Spanish recipes with flair. Traditional Castilian suckling pig is served boned and caramelized. Other highlights are veal stew with white truffle. The desserts are outstanding and the service impeccable. Closed Sun, Easter & 15–30 Aug.

ILLESCAS El Bohío
🅿 🕭 🖿 🖟   €€€€

Av Castilla La Mancha 81, 45200 (Toledo) **Tel** *925 51 11 26*

Two brothers have taken over this once-traditional restaurant, and transformed it into a place of pilgrimage for local gastronomes. Sophisticated and creative versions of Manchegan recipes include pigeon with wild rice. The magnificent *menú de degustación* is a real treat. Closed Sun, Mon evenings & Aug.

JADRAQUE El Castillo
Tapas 🖿 🖾 🖟   €€

Ctra de Soria km 46, 19240 (Guadalajara) **Tel** *949 89 02 54*

After visiting the 10th-century castle, stop here for classic Castilian dishes prepared in this typical *mesón*. The traditional, delightfully old-fashioned decor matches the menu, which features dishes such as kid roasted in a brick oven (the house speciality). Finish up with home-made desserts. Closed Wed & 22 Dec–2 Jan.

LAS PEDROÑERAS Las Rejas
🖿 🕭 🖟   €€€€

C/ General Borreros 49, 16660 (Cuenca) **Tel** *967 16 10 89*

This chic restaurant has won countless international gourmet awards. Manuel de la Osa's superb, highly creative cuisine is prepared with the finest and freshest local produce. Do not miss the fresh Manchego cheese salad. A *menú de degustación* is available. Closed Sun evenings, Mon & two weeks in Jun or Jul.

MANZANARES Mesón Sancho
Tapas 🖿 🕭   €

C/ Jesús del Perdón 26, 13200 (Ciudad Real) **Tel** *926 61 10 16*

This simple, down-to-earth restaurant serves typical robust dishes such as garlic soup, *duelos y quebrantos* (scrambled eggs with pork) and rabbit *a la Manchega* (in a sauce), washed down with local wine. There is a good-value *menú del día*. Also offers accommodation.

OROPESA La Hostería
Tapas 🖿 🕭 🖾 🖟   €

Paseo Escolar 5, 45560 (Toledo) **Tel** *925 43 08 75*

A charming stone-built inn nudged up against the castle walls, La Hostería is a typical, traditional restaurant. Try the *revuelto de morcilla* (scrambled eggs flavoured with pungent blood sausage) or the *bacalao a la plancha* (grilled cod). Choose from a good range of local and national wines, and finish up with a home-made dessert. Closed 24–25 Dec.

PUERTO LÁPICE Venta del Quijote
Tapas 目 ⬤ 🖼 ⓔⓔⓔ

C/ El Molino 4, 13650 (Ciudad Real) **Tel** *926 57 61 10*

Set in the heart of Don Quixote country, this legendary inn evokes Cervantes' masterpiece, and the episode is recreated in a colourful tile. Sit around the pebbled courtyard and enjoy any of the Manchegan specialities, or try some of the tasty tapas and a glass of the robust local wine.

SIGÜENZA El Motor
目 ⬤ 🖼 🍷 ⓔ

Av Juan Carlos I 2, 19250 (Guadalajara) **Tel** *949 39 08 27*

A hostal-restaurant in a classic, stone-built house, El Motor specializes in elegant versions of regional dishes including roast suckling pig and lamb, *migas* (breadcrumbs fried with pork) or *sopa castellana* (garlic soup). The menu also features seafood, prepared to traditional Basque recipes. Closed Sun evening and Mon.

TALAVERA DE LA REINA Antonio
Tapas 目 ⬤ ⓔ

Av de Portugal 8, 45600 (Toledo) **Tel** *925 80 40 17*

A simple hostal with a popular local bar, Antonio serves good-quality tapas at reasonable prices. It is well-known for its chickpeas and vegetable stews. A separate dining room offers typical regional fare. Fill up on the hearty lunchtime *menú del día*, after exploring the old-fashioned, ceramic-producing town. Closed Sun evenings & 1–15 Jul.

TOLEDO Hostal del Cardenal
目 🖼 ⓔⓔ

Paseo de Recadero 24, 45004 (Toledo) **Tel** *925 22 08 62*

Once the summer residence of Cardinal Lorenzana, this 18th-century palace retains its beautiful Arabic-style gardens, enclosed by the city walls. It serves suckling pig, traditionally roasted in a brick oven, along with game (particularly pheasant) in season. Desserts always feature the famous Toledo *mazapán*.

TOLEDO Locum
目 🍷 ⓔⓔⓔ

C/ Locum 6, 45001 (Toledo) **Tel** *925 22 32 35*

An elegant fusion of old and new, both in the cuisine and decor, this relative newcomer to Toledo's culinary scene is located in a beautifully restored 17th-century mansion. Classic Castilian recipes, such as roast suckling pig, are superbly reinvented. The desserts are splendid: try the pear tart with hazelnut caramel. Closed Mon evenings, Tue & Aug.

TOLEDO Adolfo
目 ⬤ 🍷 ⓔⓔⓔⓔ

C/ de la Granada 6 and at C/ Hombre de Palo 7, 45001 (Toledo) **Tel** *925 25 24 72*

Set in the heart of Toledo's old quarter, the Adolfo, with its tiles, columns, antiques and a wonderful 15th-century coffered Mudehar ceiling, serves game in winter and fresh trout from the Río Tajo. The wine list is exceptional. There is a fine *menú de degustación*. Closed Sun evenings, Mon & 15–30 Jul.

TRAGACETE El Gamo
目 ⬤ 🖼 ⓔ

Plaza de los Caídos 2, 16150 (Cuenca) **Tel** *969 28 90 08*

This mountain inn in the heart of the attractive town of Tragacete enjoys superb views over the countryside. It has a simple family-run restaurant where you can try home-style cooking, such as venison stew and *migas ruleras* (a local version of Castilian breadcrumbs fried with pork). There is a good-value lunch menu. Closed 24–25 Dec.

VALDEPEÑAS Venta la Quinteria
Tapas 🅿 目 ⬤ 🖼 🍷 ⓔⓔ

A4 Madrid-Cádiz km 197, 4, 13300 (Ciudad Real) **Tel** *926 33 82 93*

Set in a pretty garden and cobbled courtyard, this old country inn has a rustic decor. The menu offers tasty specialities from the La Mancha region, including hearty stews, and home-made desserts such as pears poached in local wine. Located in the heart of wine country, it has a great wine list. Closed evenings and Tue.

EXTREMADURA

ALMENDRALEJO Nando
Tapas 目 ⓔ

C/ Ricardo Romero 12, 06200 (Badajoz) **Tel** *924 66 12 71*

A comfortable country inn, with wooden beams and a rustic interior, Nando serves generous portions of rice with rabbit – the house speciality, *judiones* (locally-grown beans prepared with pig's knuckle or partridge) and fresh fish. There is also a good tapas bar for trying local dishes.

BADAJOZ Aldebarán
目 ⬤ 🖼 🍴 🍷 ⓔⓔⓔⓔ

Av de Elvas, Urbanización Guadiana, 06006 (Badajoz) **Tel** *924 27 42 61*

Deep red walls, crisp white linen, chandeliers and antiques adorn the dining rooms of this formal, elegant restaurant. The menu offers superb contemporary Spanish and Extremaduran cuisine. The *menú de degustación* features highlights from the chef's repertoire. An impressive wine and cigar list. Closed Sun, Mon evenings & two weeks in Aug.

CÁCERES El Pato
Tapas 目 🖼 🍴 🍷 ⓔ

Plaza Mayor 12, 10003 (Cáceres) **Tel** *927 24 87 36*

An atmospheric, classic inn right on the main square with all kinds of tasty local tapas, including *migas* and unusual partridge croquettes at the bar. Relish the home-cooked Extremaduran specialities in the old-fashioned dining room with whitewashed, brick-lined walls.

Key to Price Guide *see p608* **Key to Symbols** *see back cover flap*

CÁCERES El Figón de Eustaquio 🖽♿🛗📶 €€

Plaza de San Juan 14, 10003 (Cáceres) **Tel** *927 24 43 62*

In the heart of Cáceres' beautiful old centre, this long-standing and resolutely old-fashioned restaurant has been preparing genuine Extremaduran food since 1947. Try traditional dishes like trout *a la extremeña* (stuffed with ham) and the house speciality, *sopa 'el Figón* (tomato soup with poached egg).

CÁCERES Atrio 🖽♿🛗📶 €€€€

Av de España 30, Bloque 4, 10002 (Cáceres) **Tel** *927 24 29 28*

One of the finest restaurants in Spain, with countless international gourmet awards to prove it, Atrio serves innovative, contemporary cuisine. Try tender kid with rosemary or the monkfish. Stylish, modern decor and perfect service make this restaurant a memorable gourmet experience. Closed Sun evenings & 1–15 Sep.

GUADALUPE Hospedería del Real Monasterio 🖽♿📶 €€

Plaza de Juan Carlos I, 10140 (Cáceres) **Tel** *927 36 70 00*

Owned by the Franciscan order, this restaurant (linked to a simple *hospedería*) offers simple regional cooking in the unforgettable surroundings of a magnificent monastery. The tomato soup, the roast kid, the *migas extremeñas* and the fixed-price menu are all recommended. There is also a simple café-bar. Closed 15 Jan–15 Feb.

GUADALUPE Posada del Rincón Tapas 🖽♿📶 €€

Plaza Santa María de Guadalupe 11, 10140 (Cáceres) **Tel** *927 36 71 40*

Part of a charming rural hotel, Posada del Rincón is a delightful restaurant and café-bar. Inside, there are brick-lined walls, wooden beams and wrought-iron furniture out on the plant-filled patio. Fine regional cuisine, prepared with the freshest seasonal produce, has touches of creativity. Try the roasted suckling kid. Good fixed-price menu.

JARANDILLA DE LA VERA Puta Parió II Tapas 🖽 €€

C/ Francisco Pizarro 8, 10450 (Cáceres) **Tel** *927 56 03 92*

This old stone house was once home to Don Luis de Quijada, major domo to Emperor Charles V (Carlos I). It is now a lively and popular tavern with good regional dishes, including tomato soup and lamb casserole, and locally-produced house wine. There is a good value fixed-price lunch menu. Closed Mon & second half of Sep.

JEREZ DE LOS CABALLEROS La Ermita Tapas 📶 €€

C/ Doctor Benítez 9, 06380 (Badajoz) **Tel** *924 73 14 76*

Housed in a 17th-century chapel converted into a wine cellar, La Ermita serves authentic local dishes. Sample the partridge stew or the typical *revuelto de espárragos*, made with scrambled eggs and asparagus tips. They also have fabulous tapas, including the delectable Iberian hams, made from pigs raised on acorns.

LOSAR DE LA VERA Carlos V Tapas 🖽♿📶 €€

Av de Extremadura 45, 10460 (Cáceres) **Tel** *927 57 06 36*

Local home cooking and lovely views of the Sierra de Gredos mountains are the fare at this charming rural inn, which is decorated with antlers and hunting trophies. Specialities include scrambled eggs with white truffles, roast kid and steaks. There is a good-value lunch menu. Finish up with *helado frito* (fried ice cream). Closed Mon & 15–30 Oct.

MÉRIDA Nicolás Tapas 🖽📶 €€

C/ Félix Valverde Lillo 13, 06800 (Badajoz) **Tel** *924 31 96 10*

Nicolás is a long-standing restaurant in a handsome historic mansion in the heart of Mérida. You might want to visit the brick wine cellar for an apéritif before tucking into the regional specialities such as the delicious lamb with plums or the pork sirloin with pepper. There is also a pretty garden terrace. Closed Sun evenings & two weeks in Jul.

MÉRIDA Rufino Tapas 🖽♿📶 €€€

Plaza Santa Clara 2, 06800 (Badajoz) **Tel** *924 31 20 01*

With a terrace out on a delightful pedestrianized square, this much-loved local institution is the perfect place to start the *tapeo* (a pub crawl from tapas bar to tapas bar). Try the delicious local hams. It also serves typical Extremaduran cuisine, including *revuelto con criadillas de tierra* (scrambled eggs with mushrooms). Closed Sun & Aug.

MÉRIDA Altair 🖽♿📶 €€€€

Av José Fernández López s/n, 06800 (Badajoz) **Tel** *924 30 45 12*

Sleekly mimimalist in design, this fashionable, glassy restaurant overlooks Santiago Calatrava's gleaming modern bridge, also echoed in the crisp white furnishings. Altair is linked to the spectacular Atrio in Cáceres, and offers fine contemporary cuisine, best appreciated in the good-value *menú de degustación*. Closed Sun.

OLIVENZA Alcañices Tapas 🖽♿📶 €€

C/ Colón 3, 06100 (Badajoz) **Tel** *924 49 15 70*

Elegant, yet informal, Alcañices is a charming restaurant in the attractive border town of Olivenza. The light and creative cuisine uses fresh local produce: try the *lasaña de morcilla* (black pudding lasagne), or the succulent game in season. Offers a good *menú de degustación*. Closed two weeks in Oct; check timings.

PLASENCIA Puerta Talavera Tapas 🖽🎵📶 €€

C/ Talavera 30, 10600 (Cáceres) **Tel** *927 42 15 45*

A stylish, modern restaurant with a wide-ranging menu and several fixed-price options to suit all pockets. The cuisine is based on fresh local ingredients, and includes delicacies, such as local veal, lamb and game, as well as a range of tapas at the informal bar. The wine list has plenty of regional wines to choose from. Live music Fri evening. Closed Mon & Jul.

PLASENCIA Alfonso VIII
Tapas 🍴 ♿ 🍷 €€€€

Avenida Alfonso VIII 32–34, 10600 (Cáceres) **Tel** *927 41 02 50*

This smart hotel-restaurant offers creative cuisine that relies heavily on local produce and updated traditional recipes. Try the kid stew, or the cod with courgette (zucchini) ratatouille and finish up with a delicious flan made with pine nuts and chestnuts. A relaxed tapas bar serves wonderful Iberian hams. Fixed-price menu available.

PUEBLA DE LA REINA Mesón La Jara-Casa Andrés
🍴 ♿ 🍷 €

Calle Luis Chamizo 14, 06228 (Badajoz) **Tel** *924 36 00 05*

This charming *mesón* has become a sanctuary of authentic regional food, often prepared using ancient recipes. The classic dish here is rabbit in "La Jara" sauce – flavoured with onion, garlic, bay leaf and wine, though the partridge is also good. There is a cheap lunch menu and a more complete *menú de degustación*. Closed 15–30 Sep.

TRUJILLO Mesón La Troya
Tapas 🍴 ♿ 🍴 €

Plaza Mayor 10, 10200 (Cáceres) **Tel** *927 32 13 64*

A typical 16th-century *mesón*, on the main square of the magnificent Renaissance town, La Troya serves regional food in hearty portions in a pair of old-fashioned dining rooms with lacy curtains and ceramics. The *migas* with pork are recommended. The tapas bar, with photographs lining the wall, is worth visiting.

TRUJILLO Corral del Rey
🍴 ♿ 🍴 🍷 €€

Plaza Corral del Rey (Plaza Major) 2, 10200 (Cáceres) **Tel** *927 32 17 80*

One of the best in the city, Corral del Rey is a classic *asador* specializing in roasted meat and fish. Traditional decor consists of brick walls and wooden beams. Recommended delicacies include wild sea bass baked in salt and beef seared on the grill. They also have a cigar list and a good liqueur menu. Closed Sun & 1–10 Jul.

TRUJILLO Pizarro
🍴 🍷 €€

Plaza Mayor 13, 10200 (Cáceres) **Tel** *927 32 02 55*

On Trujillo's beautiful central square, this restaurant has retained much of its decor since it opened before the Civil War. Enjoy traditional dishes such as tomato soup with figs and grapes; chicken stuffed with truffles; and potatoes cooked in Extremaduran style. Family run, it is friendly and welcoming. Closed Tue, two weeks in Feb & Jun.

ZAFRA Josefina
🍴 🍴 🍷 €€

Av López Asme 1, 06300 (Badajoz) **Tel** *924 55 17 01*

A warm welcome awaits in this delightful family-run restaurant, which serves typical Extremeño cuisine with a dash of creativity. Try the mushroom and prawn ravioli or the green bean salad with foie gras. A good-value lunch menu on weekdays. Closed Sun evenings & Mon.

ZAFRA La Rebotica
🍴 ♿ 🍷 €€

C/ Boticas 12, 06300 (Badajoz) **Tel** *924 55 42 89*

In the heart of lovely, whitewashed Zafra, chic little La Rebotica has a series of intimate dining areas linked by arches. The deftly prepared local dishes include a wonderful partridge soup, and codfish served with baby squid. Fabulous home-made desserts include a refreshing orange and fig ice cream. Closed Sun evenings, Mon & 1–15 Aug.

SEVILLE

ALAMEDA La Eslava
Tapas 🍴 €€€

C/ Eslava 3, 41002 **Tel** *954 90 65 68*

Map *1 C4*

La Eslava is a favourite local haunt with no cutesy decor geared towards tourists. Instead, the emphasis is firmly on assured Andalusian cuisine with touches of creativity. The dining area has a full menu of seafood dishes and some excellent salads, while the bar serves up tasty, fresh tapas. Go early for a table. Closed Sun evenings & Mon.

EL ARENAL As-Sawirah
🍴 ♿ 🍷 €

C/ Galera 5, 41001 **Tel** *954 56 22 68*

Map *3 B1 (5 B3)*

Rustic Moroccan decor and traditional Moroccan cuisine are combined in this restaurant near the Mercado de El Arenal. Dishes include kebabs, lamb couscous, tagines and *pastelas* (meat pastries). Try the *menú de degustación* for a weekday lunch. Closed Sun evening, Mon & Aug.

EL ARENAL El Cabildo
🍴 €€

Plaza del Cabildo, 41001 (Seville) **Tel** *954 22 79 70*

Map *3 C2 (5 C4)*

Part of the ancient Arabic walls have been conserved in this classic and delightfully old-fashioned restaurant. All the traditional favourites are on the menu, excellently cooked with fresh local ingredients. Try a platter of fresh fried fish, *Sevillian revueltos* (scrambled eggs with different fillings) accompanied by sturdy local wine.

EL ARENAL Enrique Becerra
Tapas 🍴 ♿ 🍷 €€€

C/ Gamazo 2, 41001 **Tel** *954 21 30 49*

Map *3 B1 (5 C4)*

Housed in a beautifully renovated 19th-century mansion, this plush restaurant-bar offers a fine selection of fish and meat dishes. The daily specials feature Andalusian home-style cooking. The classic apéritif is a wonderful ice-cold Manzanilla sherry, which you can follow with tapas or specialities like roast lamb with pine nuts. Closed Sun.

Key to Price Guide *see p608* **Key to Symbols** *see back cover flap*

EL ARENAL La Isla

Tapas 📋 🖼 🍷   €€€€

C/ Arfe 25, 41001 **Tel** *954 21 26 31*   **Map** *3 B2 (5 C4)*

This attractive, centrally located restaurant features superb seafood specialities from Galicia, including turbot, bream and delicacies such as *percebes* (sea barnacles). Some Andalusian dishes, such as a meaty beef stew, also feature. There is a small tapas bar where you can enjoy fabulous prawns, oysters and a wide range of local hams.

SANTA CRUZ Ajoblanco

Tapas 📋 📋   €

C/ Alhóndiga 19, 41004 **Tel** *954 22 93 20*   **Map** *2 D5 (6 E2)*

Tucked away down a narrow street, this relaxed, boho-chic café-bar is fully covered with jazz posters. Good for a coffee, it also serves great tapas – everything from standards such as *patatas bravas*, to more unusual offerings such as fried Camembert with raspberry sauce, and even spicy burritos and *tacos*. Closed Mon evenings.

SANTA CRUZ El Rincón de Anita

Tapas 📋 ♿ 🖼 🍷   €

Plaza del Cristo de Burgos 23, 41004 **Tel** *954 21 74 61*   **Map** *6 E2*

This delightful little restaurant is decorated with colourful tiles, polished wood, images of the Semana Santa processions, and lots of plants. This is the perfect place to tuck into tasty Andalusian specialities. Try the *cola de toro* (bull's tail), kidneys cooked in sherry, and home-made desserts. Classic tapas can be enjoyed at the bar.

SANTA CRUZ Mesón de la Infanta

Tapas 📋   €

C/ Dos de Mayo 26, 41002 **Tel** *954 22 19 09*   **Map** *3 B2 (5 C5)*

Set in a restored historic building in the heart of the lively Arenal district, Mesón de la Infanta offers an excellent choice of traditional dishes, including delicious *guisos*. The tapas bar is a classic on the Sevillano tapas route, with a bewildering array of fine local hams and *embutidos* (charcuterie) and the usual favourites. Closed Tue.

SANTA CRUZ Modesto

Tapas 📋 ♿ 🖼 🍷   €€

C/ Cano y Cueta 5 (Puerta de la Carne), 41004 **Tel** *954 41 68 11*   **Map** *4 D2*

The traditional Andalusian cuisine at El Modesto includes an excellent assortment of tapas, served at the spacious bar; try shrimps with garlic or *coquinas* (tiny clams). In the more formal upstairs dining room dishes include home-made paella and *frito variado* (a selection of fried fish). Plenty of outside tables with views of the Jardines de Murillo.

SANTA CRUZ Becerrita

Tapas 📋 ♿ 🖼 🍷   €€€

C/ Recaredo 9, 41004 **Tel** *954 41 20 57*   **Map** *2 E5 (6 F3)*

Becerrita is a beautiful restaurant, warmly decorated in modern Andalusian style. Delicious Andaluz specialities include outstanding croquettes made with bull's tail, or kid flavoured with thyme. At the bar, you can choose from a superb range of tapas that changes daily, depending on the season. Closed Sun evenings & Aug.

SANTA CRUZ Casa Robles

📋 ♿ 🖼   €€€

C/ Álvarez Quintero 58, 41001 **Tel** *954 56 32 72*   **Map** *3 C1 (6 D3)*

Right in the heart of Seville, close to the cathedral, this elegant restaurant is decorated with oil paintings, statuary and pretty tiles. Although the menu leans towards seafood, there are also plenty of local meat dishes to choose from, all exquisitely presented. The desserts, in particular, are miniature works of art.

SANTA CRUZ Corral del Agua

📋 🖼   €€€

Callejón del Agua 6, 41004 **Tel** *954 22 48 41*   **Map** *3 C2 (6 D/E5)*

Dine on the cool patio in a lee of the Reales Alcázares gardens, with plants trailing romantically around wrought-iron grilles and a marble fountain burbling quietly. Antique furniture and paintings adorn the dining room, and the menu emphasizes seasonal specialities, traditionally prepared. Closed Sun.

SANTA CRUZ La Albahaca

📋 🖼 🍷   €€€

Plaza de Santa Cruz 12, 41004 **Tel** *954 22 07 14*   **Map** *4 D2 (6 E4)*

Overlooking a charming, verdant square dominated by a wrought-iron cross, La Albahaca is one of the most authentic restaurants in the Barrio Santa Cruz. Its fine setting in a 1920s mansion furnished with 17th-century antiques, makes it a perfect place to enjoy Basque-influenced food, along with excellent local dishes. Closed Sun.

SANTA CRUZ Egaña Oriza

📋 ♿ 🖼 🍷   €€€€

C/ San Fernando 41, 41004 **Tel** *954 22 72 11*   **Map** *3 C2 (6 D5)*

Tucked against the walls of the Alcázar gardens, Egaña Oriza is located in a beautiful early 20th-century mansion. The dining room is in an elegant light-filled conservatory, and the sophisticated modern Basque cuisine leans heavily towards fish. Meat dishes and desserts are equally delicious. The wine list is superb. Closed Sat lunch & Sun.

FURTHER AFIELD (SOUTH) Salvador Rojo

📋 ♿ 🖼 🍷   €€€€

C/ San Fernando 23, 41004 **Tel** *954 22 97 25*   **Map** *3 C2 (6 D5)*

A stylish, modern little restaurant opposite the old Fábrica de Tabaco, Salvador Rojo offers contemporary Spanish cuisine. The freshest local produce is used with innovation: try the stir-fried prawns with Thai rice. Leave room for the fabulous desserts. Classic Spanish wines feature along with some excellent but lesser-known labels. Closed Sun.

FURTHER AFIELD (WEST) El Faro de Triana

Tapas ♿ 🖼   €€

C/ Betis (Triana), 41010 **Tel** *954 33 61 92*   **Map** *3 A2 (5 A5)*

A long-standing institution on the banks of the Guadalquivir, with sublime views of the old city from the terrace. This old-fashioned ochre building, tucked into the side of the emblematic Triana bridge, is a historic *freiduría*, where heaped platters of fried fish have been the classic dish for more than 70 years.

FURTHER AFIELD (WEST) Sol y Sombra
Tapas 🗐 🔧 €€

C/ Castilla 149 (Triana), 41010 **Tel** *954 33 39 35* **Map** *3 A1*

A sea of hams suspended from the ceiling and peeling bullfighting posters adorn the walls of this historic tavern. Though tucked away in Triana, the restaurant is well worth seeking out for the authentic Sevillano ambience. Visit the tapas bar for freshly prepared large portions of tapas, or dine more substantially at the adjoining restaurant.

FURTHER AFIELD (WEST) Río Grande
Tapas 🗐 🕭 🔧 🔧 €€€€

C/ Betis s/n, 41010 **Tel** *954 27 39 56* **Map** *3 A2 (5 A5)*

Río Grande has a terrific location on the liveliest steet in the old sailor's barrio of Triana. Enjoy the *rabo de toro* on a terrace overlooking the Guadalquivir with views of the Torre del Oro. There is a formal, English-style dining area and an ever-lively tapas bar, where shellfish is the speciality. Good range of wines.

ANDALUSIA

ALJARAQUE Las Candelas
🗐 🕭 🔧 €€€

Av de Huelva 3, 21110 (Huelva) **Tel** *959 31 84 33*

A long-established classic in a village 6 km (3.7 miles) from Huelva, this restaurant is decorated with maritime motifs. Seafood, unsurprisingly, dominates the Mediterranean menu, with delicacies such as monkfish in almond sauce, but there is a range of good local meat dishes as well. Traditional Spanish wines. Closed Sun & 24–5, 31 Dec.

ALMERÍA Rincón de Juan Pedro
Tapas 🗐 €

C/ Federico Castro 2, 04130 (Almería) **Tel** *950 23 58 19*

A much-loved stalwart on Almería's busy tapas scene, this Andalusian bar serves a wonderful range of tapas – still included in the price of a drink. You can dine more substantially on *raciones*, as well as meat and seafood specialities, and local dishes, such as *trigo a la cortijera* (a stew with wheat berries, meat and sausage). Closed Mon.

ALMERÍA Bodega Bellavista
🗐 🕭 🔧 🔧 €€

Urbanización Bellavista, Llanos del Alquián, 04130 (Almería) **Tel** *950 29 71 56*

In an unlikely location in a housing complex near the airport, this charmingly old-fashioned restaurant offers a range of classic and innovative Andalusian dishes prepared with top-quality local products. Fish and shellfish predominate, but you can also try good beef and kid. A huge range of wines from all around Spain. Closed Sun evenings & Mon.

ALMERÍA Club de Mar
🗐 🕭 🔧 €€

Playa de la Almadrabillas 1, 04007 (Almería) **Tel** *950 23 50 48*

Enjoy fresh fish and shellfish right on the seafront at the Almerían yacht club, where well-heeled locals and sailors mingle on the breezy terrace. The fresh seafood complements the views over the port, and the *bullabesa* (Spanish bouillabaisse) and *fritura* (mixed fried fish) are specialities. Also offers a good-value lunch menu.

ANTEQUERA La Espuela
Tapas 🗐 🕭 🔧 €€

C/ San Agustín 1, 29200 (Málaga) **Tel** *952 70 30 31*

Uniquely situated in a bullring, this restaurant prepares Andalusian dishes including the town speciality, *porra* (a thick gazpacho). With its brightly coloured tiles, brick walls and perpetually busy tapas bar, it offers a taste of authentic Andalusia. It is enormously popular with tourists and locals alike, so be sure to book ahead. Closed Mon.

ARCOS DE LA FRONTERA Parador Restaurant
🗐 🕭 🔧 🔧 €€€

Plaza Cabilda s/n, 11630 (Cádiz) **Tel** *956 70 05 00*

Spain's parador hotels are known for their high standards, and this traditional, elegant example located in the historic centre of Cádiz is no exception. The restaurant has been beautifully decorated and has an excellent menu. Try the *corvina a la roteña* (rota-style fish) or the tasters' menu, which features 12 tantalising dishes.

BAEZA Juanito
🗐 €€

Paseo Arca del Agua s/n, 23440 (Jaén) **Tel** *953 74 00 40*

A comfortable family-run hotel and restaurant in the heart of the olive belt. The good home cooking is based on traditional regional recipes which feature plenty of olive oil. Try the artichokes or the *patatas a lo pobre*, a tasty potato dish flavoured with ham. The home-made desserts are scrumptious. Closed Sun–Thu evenings & Mon.

BAEZA Vandelvira
🗐 🕭 🔧 🔧 €€

C/ San Francisco 14, 23440 (Jaén) **Tel** *953 74 81 72*

Located in a 16th-century monastery built by Andrés de Vandelvira, Jáen's Renaissance architect, this beautiful, classically decorated restaurant serves typical regional food: *cardos* (cardoons, a type of artichoke) in a cream sauce, partridge salad and a mouthwatering pine-nut ice cream. Closed Sun–Thu evenings & Mon.

BAILÉN Zodíaco Libra
Tapas 🗐 🕭 🔧 🔧 €€

Antigua Ctra Madrid-Cádiz km 294, 23710 (Jaén) **Tel** *953 67 10 58*

A modern hotel with a large and popular restaurant. Cold soups are on the menu in summer, such as *ajo blanco* (white garlic) with almonds. Other specialities include the scrambled eggs with ham, asparagus, prawn/shrimp and elvers and partridge. Has a lovely, tree-shaded garden terrace in summer.

Key to Price Guide *see p608* **Key to Symbols** *see back cover flap*

BENAHAVIS Los Abanicos 🔲♿🎔🅿 €€
C/ Málaga 15, 29679 (Málaga) **Tel** *952 85 51 31*

A well known and consistently good restaurant decorated with pretty painted *abanicos* (fans) in the heart of the lovely village of Benahavís. Dine on tasty regional dishes. The house speciality, *paletilla de cordero* (shoulder of lamb) is particularly good. It is a favourite for Sunday lunch, so book early. Closed Tue except Jul & Aug.

BUBIÓN Teide *Tapas* ♿🎔 €
C/ Carretera 70, 18412 (Granada) **Tel** *958 76 30 37*

Lost in the beautiful wilderness of the Alpujarras, this is a simple, stone-built restaurant surrounded by a charming, informal garden with pots of flowers and shady trees. They serve traditional dishes such as roast kid and generous salads of local vegetables. It also serves free tapas with a drink in the time-honoured Andalusian tradition. Closed Tue.

CÁDIZ Freiduria Cerveceria Las Flores *Tapas* 🔲🔲♿🎔 €
Plaza Topete 4, 11009 (Cádiz) **Tel** *956 22 61 12*

The classic Andalusian dish is *pescaíto frito*, and every town has several *freiduria*.(fried-fish shops) This is the best in Cádiz. Order your fish (anything from shark to squid), which is fried on the spot and wrapped up to takeaway for a picnic. You can also eat it out on the terrace near the square. Non-fish snacks include croquettes and *empanadas*.

CÁDIZ Balandro 🔲♿🎔 €€
C/ Alameda Apodaca 22, 11004 (Cádiz) **Tel** *956 22 09 92*

The Balandro is an elegant local restaurant with creative and sophisticated cuisine. The house speciality is seafood from the Bay of Cádiz, fresh and prepared with imagination, but there are plenty of local meat (especially beef) dishes too. Try octopus salad or the beef medallions with port. Closed Sun evenings & Mon (only Sun in Jul & Aug).

CÁDIZ El Faro *Tapas* 🔲♿🅿 €€€
C/ San Félix 15, 11011 (Cádiz) **Tel** *956 21 10 68*

El Faro restaurant has a warm atmosphere in the old fishermen's barrio of Cádiz. The menu, a wonderful blend of modern and traditional, changes daily but always features local seafood, such as the *tortillitas de camarones* (fritters of tiny shrimps), or the rice dishes flavoured with shellfish from the bay. There is a popular tapas bar too.

CÁDIZ Ventorillo del Chato 🔲♿🎔🅿 €€€€
Vía Augusta Julia s/n, 11011 (Cádiz) **Tel** *956 25 00 25*

A picturesque inn, in an 18th-century staging post next to the sea, this place offers Andalusian cuisine. Recipes use superbly fresh fish from the bay, local meat and fresh vegetables, often combined in one of the restaurant's *guisos*. A very popular spot for Sunday lunch, when families pile off the glorious beach for a huge feast. Closed Sun.

CARMONA Ancla *Tapas* 🔲♿🎔🅿 €€
C/ Bonifacio IV 8, 41410 (Sevilla) **Tel** *954 14 38 04*

Sturdy home cooking is served at this friendly family-run restaurant, which takes pride in choosing the freshest local ingredients. There is an excellent lunch menu which you can enjoy on the terrace, and specialities include prawns in garlic sauce, roast lamb and *pescaíto frito* (fried fish platter). Closed Wed and 2nd & 3rd weeks of Sep.

CARMONA San Fernando 🔲🅿 €€
C/ Sacramento 3, 41410 (Sevilla) **Tel** *954 14 35 56*

An exquisite mansion, built in 1700, houses this elegant restaurant, which offers fresh seasonal cuisine from the region. The *salmorejo*, a thick tomato soup garnished with boiled egg and ham, is particularly good, and the *bacalao* is prepared in myriad ways, including with a delectable squid ink and garlic sauce. Closed Sun evening & Mon.

CÓRDOBA Federación de Peñas *Tapas* 🔲 €
C/ Conde y Luque, 14003 (Córdoba) **Tel** *957 47 54 27*

Located right next to the Mezquita, Peñas offers simple but excellent local food. Try the *rabo de toro*, a house speciality or the *cardos* with clams. There's always a good variety of seafood and prices are exceptionally reasonable. The city has awarded it a gold medal in recognition of its high standards.

CÓRDOBA Almudaina 🔲♿ €€€
Jardines de los Santos Mártires 1, 14004 (Córdoba) **Tel** *957 47 43 42*

Once the palace of Bishop Leopold of Austria, this mansion serves typical local dishes which draw on the cuisines from the distinct cultures that have shaped Córdoba. The Córdoban *salmorejo* is excellent here, also try angler fish with stewed tomatoes. Closed Sun evenings.

CÓRDOBA Caballo Rojo *Tapas* 🔲🎔🅿 €€€
C/ Cardenal Herrero 28, 14003 (Córdoba) **Tel** *957 47 53 75*

Right next to the Mezquita, this lovely restaurant has a central patio with wrought-iron balconies thickly hung with brightly coloured flowers. The dishes are based on ancient recipes, many adapted from Moorish and Sephardic recipes. Enjoy lamb with honey or Sephardi salad of wild mushrooms, asparagus, roasted peppers and salt cod.

CÓRDOBA Casa Pepe de la Judería *Tapas* 🔲♿🎔 €€€
C/ Romero 1, 14003 (Córdoba) **Tel** *957 20 07 44*

This has been one of Córdoba's most appealing restaurants since it opened in 1928. Dine on a lovely Córdoban patio blazing with flowers, or sit in the dining rooms festooned with photos of notable customers. Try the *flamenquín* (fried rolls of veal and ham), or the unusual cherry gazpacho flavoured with mint. Closed 24–31 Dec.

CÓRDOBA El Blasón
Tapas 📋 🔳   €€€

C/ José Zorrilla 11, 14008 (Córdoba) **Tel** *957 48 06 25*

A typical Andalusian mansion, set around a magical tiled patio, this is a perfect place to try a wide range of Córdoban specialities, including seafood, sturdy meat stews and wonderful home-made desserts. It is also a lively and very popular tapas bar and café – and has a handy location close to the main shopping district.

CÓRDOBA El Churrasco
Tapas 📋 ♿ 🔳 🔳   €€€

C/ Romero 16, 14003 (Córdoba) **Tel** *957 29 08 19*

A traditional Andalusian mansion, the speciality here is charcoal-grilled meat, but vegetable dishes and soups such as *salmorejo* are also good. The dining rooms are set around two patios: in the lovely Patio del Limonera you can eat under a fragrant lemon tree. Sip an apéritif in the nearby wine cellars. Closed Easter, Aug & Christmas.

EL PUERTO DE SANTA MARÍA Aponiente
📋 ♿ 🔳   €

C/ Puerto Escondido 6, 11500 (Cádiz) **Tel** *956 85 18 70*

Head to this modern restaurant for some delicious gourmet cuisine created by head chef Ángel León. Try the fresh catch of the day roasted over olive stones, or the taster menu (€48) of the chef's signature dishes, such as venison sirloin with plums and spring garlic. There is also a large selection of teas, dessert wines and a cigar menu. Closed Sun.

EL PUERTO DE SANTA MARÍA Casa Flores
Tapas 📋 ♿ 🔳   €€€

C/ Ribera del Río 9, 11500 (Cádiz) **Tel** *956 54 35 12*

A family-run traditional restaurant, with a series of intimate dining rooms decorated with pretty tiles, paintings and a smattering of bullfighting memorabilia. Seafood and shellfish are the house specialities, with a spectacular array, which includes everything from the local sweet striped prawns to unusual delicacies such as sea urchins.

ESTEPONA La Alborada
📋 ♿ 🔳   €€

Puerto Deportivo de Estepona, 29680 (Málaga) **Tel** *952 80 20 47*

This quayside eatery serves excellent paella and other rice dishes, such as *arroz a la banda* (a kind of fish risotto). It also serves delicious *pescaíto frito* and has tasty home-made desserts such as the *pudin de almendras* (creamy almond pudding). There are lovely views of the yacht-filled harbour from the terrace. Closed Wed.

ESTEPONA Lido
📋 ♿ 🔳 🔳 🔳   €€€€

Hotel Las Dunas, Urb La Boladilla Baja, 29680 (Málaga) **Tel** *952 79 43 45*

In the opulent surroundings of the luxurious Las Dunas Hotel, this is a stylish restaurant serving contemporary international cuisine. It has magnificent outdoor seating on a balustraded terrace overlooking gardens, or in an elegant conservatory. Signature dishes include a foie gras mousse and seafood cannelloni. Closed Mon & Sun.

FUENGIROLA Portofino
📋 ♿ 🔳   €€

Edificio Perla 1, Paseo Marítimo 29, 29640 (Málaga) **Tel** *952 47 06 43*

This seafront restaurant is popular for its friendly service and good international food, such as the fish brochette or delicious pastas with rich sauces. It also prepares traditional Andalusian dishes, all served in generous portions. The terrace has views over the glossy, yacht-filled port. Closed Mon & Jul.

GRANADA Bodegas Castañeda
Tapas 📋 ♿   €

C/ Almireceros 1–3, 18010 (Granada) **Tel** *958 215 464*

With its time-worn tiles, huge wooden barrels and battered air, Castañeda is one of the most delightful and authentic of Granada's tapas bars. Try the melt-in-the-mouth Trevélez ham (which has its own *denominación de origen*) or the wide variety of seafood conserves. A glass of ice-cold sherry is the perfect way to begin the evening.

GRANADA Chikito
Tapas 📋 ♿ 🔳 🔳   €€

Plaza del Campillo 9, 18009 (Granada) **Tel** *958 22 33 64*

Built on the site of a café where Lorca and his contemporaries used to meet, Chikito serves broad beans with ham and Sacromonte omelette (prepared with brains, but tastier than you might think) as specialities. At the brick bar, inset with painted tiled scenes, you can enjoy the tapas. Closed Wed.

GRANADA Mirador de Morayma
📋 ♿ 🎵 🔳   €€

C/ Pianista García Carrillo 2, 18010 (Granada) **Tel** *958 22 82 90*

Situated in the Albaícin with views of the Alhambra, this charming patio-restaurant specializes in typical dishes of Granada, such as *remojón* (a salad of oranges and codfish) and lamb sautéed with garlic. The wine list includes organic wines produced on the restaurant's own estate. Flamenco on Tuesdays, call to confirm times. Closed Sun evenings.

GRANADA Carmen de San Miguel
📋 ♿ 🔳   €€€

Plaza Torres Bermejas 3, 18009 (Granada) **Tel** *958 22 67 23*

The Andalusian specialities at this pretty restaurant with Moorish-style decor include the seabass with aubergine and the ox loin in a juniper and red wine sauce. Everything is fresh and prepared with imagination by a talented young chef. There are wonderful views of the whitewashed maze of the Albaícin from the terrace. Closed Sun.

GRANADA Ruta del Veleta
📋 ♿ 🔳 🔳   €€€

Ctra Sierra Nevada 136, km 5,400 Cenes de la Vega, 18190 (Granada) **Tel** *958 48 61 34*

Out on the winding old road to the Sierra Nevada, on the fringes of Granada, this traditional restaurant has an excellent reputation for its hearty regional cuisine. The decoration, with typical Alpujarran textiles and ceramic jugs, goes well with dishes such as roast baby kid and good seafood. Be sure to try the game in season. Closed Sun evenings.

Key to Price Guide *see p608* **Key to Symbols** *see back cover flap*

GRANADA Velázquez
Tapas 📋 ♿ 🔖   €€€

C/ Profesor Emilio Orozco 1, 18010 (Granada) Tel 958 28 01 09

The ambience here is warm and the food imaginative, with modern interpretations of such Moorish dishes as *pastela*, a pigeon pastry with pine nuts and almonds and savoury almond cream soup. Velázquez has an old-fashioned lively tapas bar where you can enjoy tapas along with good local wines and Andalusian sherries. Closed Sun & Aug.

HUELVA Restaurante San Sebastián
📋 🔖   €€

C/ Ricardo Velázquez 39, 21003 (Huelva) Tel 959 25 08 24

This traditional restaurant, situated in the town centre and close to the Parque de la Esperanza, offers an ample selection of fresh fish and seafood from the Atlantic coast. Try the delicious Galician oysters. Staff are friendly and very welcoming. Closed Sun.

HUELVA El Portichuelo
Tapas 📋 ♿ 🔖   €€€

Gran Vía 1, 21110 (Huelva) Tel 959 24 57 68

A simple spot in the centre of the city, serving traditional Andalusian cuisine in the dining room and at the bar, where there is a range of tapas. The excellent local hams feature prominently, as does seafood and shellfish. There are no culinary surprises, just well-cooked food made with fresh regional products. Staff are cheerful. Closed Sun.

HUELVA Las Meigas
📋 ♿ 🔖   €€€

Avda Guatemala 44, 21003 (Huelva) Tel 959 27 19 58

Some of the freshest seafood can be found at this crisply decorated Galician restaurant. The Gallegos are famed throughout the country for their skill with seafood, and here it is simply prepared – grilled, baked in a salt crust or served Gallego style – in order to appreciate its exquisite freshness. Fabulous home-made desserts. Closed Sun.

ISLA CRISTINA Casa Rufino
Tapas 📋 🔖 🔖   €€

Av de la Playa, 21410 (Huelva) Tel 959 33 08 10

A popular beachside place whose *el tonteo* (for four) menu comprises eight different fish in eight different sauces, including angler fish in raisin sauce. It has a well-deserved reputation for outstandingly fresh seafood and shellfish, and excellent wines including all the classics. Closed 22 Dec–2 Feb & evenings except Jul–Oct & Easter.

JABUGO Mesón 5 Jotas
Tapas 📋 ♿ 🔖   €€€

Ctra San Juan del Puerto s/n, 21290 (Huelva) Tel 959 12 10 71

Fine Jabugo hams are made here and the adjoining bar-restaurant is a good place to sample them. This is the original and best of a Spanish chain of tapas bars, which have mushroomed across the country. Besides ham and sausage dishes, you can also try the fresh Iberian pork dishes, such as *presa de paletilla al mesón*. Closed Sun evening.

JAÉN Casa Vicente
Tapas 📋 ♿ 🔖   €€

C/ Francisco Martín Mora 1, 23002 (Jaén) Tel 953 23 22 22

A classic restaurant with a bullfighting theme in an Andalusian mansion, Vicente serves typical dishes from Jaén. A good *menú de degustación* features local specialities such as lamb stew or artichokes in a delicate sauce. Have an apéritif at the bar, which has just a few simple tapas. Closed Sun evening and Aug.

JAÉN Casa Antonio
📋 ♿ 🔖   €€€€

C/ Fermín Palma 3, 23008 (Jaén) Tel 953 270 262

An elegant restaurant with bold contemporary art and blonde wood panelling serving excellent contemporary Andalusian cuisine. Traditional recipes are reinvented with style and creativity: try the *carpaccios* (Huelva prawns or tuna). They have an excellent *menú de degustación*. Closed Sun evenings, Mon and Aug.

JEREZ DE LA FRONTERA Bar Juanito
Tapas 📋 ♿ 🔖   €

C/ Pescadería Vieja 8, 11403 (Cádiz) Tel 956 33 48 38

This atmospheric tapas bar and restaurant has a heady reputation for its exceptionally large portions of tapas. A fabulous array is offered, of which the local artichokes remain the star dish. You can also dine more substantially on traditional stews and casseroles and a fine *pescaito frito* from the Bay. Closed Sun evenings.

JEREZ DE LA FRONTERA La Mesa Redonda
📋   €€

C/ Manuel de la Quintana 3, 11402 (Cádiz) Tel 956 34 00 69

A charming, family-run restaurant, which remains a favourite with locals for the quality and excellence of its cuisine. The creative menu changes with the seasons offering seafood, meat dishes and game. Try the *mojama* (cured tuna) as a starter, and do not miss the spectacular beef *salteado* (sautéed with black sausage). Closed Sun, 15 Jul–16 Aug.

LOJA La Finca
📋 ♿ 🔖 🔖   €€€€

Hotel La Bobadilla, Autovía Granada-Sevilla, 18300 (Granada) Tel 958 32 18 61

Worth a detour off the Autovía, this exceptional restaurant in a luxury hotel is a place for fine dining. The chef makes creative use of farm-fresh vegetables, capon and pork, game (in season) and seafood. Splash out on the wonderful *menú de degustación*, and soak up the romance of the garden terrace.

LOS BARRIOS Mesón El Copo
📋 ♿ 🔖 🔖   €€€

Autovía Cádiz-Málaga km 111 Palmones, 11370 (Cádiz) Tel 956 67 77 10

In the village of Palmones, 9 km (5.6 miles) from Los Barrios, Mesón El Copo is one of the most reliable restaurants on this stretch of coastline. Dine on superb seafood, from fried anchovies to lobster and sea bass. Order a few shell-fish dishes to share as a starter, and follow with the *dorada al horno* (bream casserole with potatoes). Closed Sun.

MÁLAGA Antigua Casa de Guardia
Tapas 🖼️📋 €

C/ Alameda Principal 18, 29015 (Málaga) **Tel** *952 21 46 80*

This is Málaga's oldest bar, housed in the fomer guard post which gives it its name. The speciality is sherry, poured straight from one of the vast barrels stacked behind the bar. Accompany it with a few simple tapas – a plate of prawns or mussels, or silvery *boquerones* (anchovies) which bear no resemblance to their salty cousins. Closed Sun.

MÁLAGA Mesón Astorga
Tapas 📋♿🖼️ €€

C/ Gerona 11, 29006 (Málaga) **Tel** *952 34 25 63*

Using Málaga's superb local produce with flair, makes this classically decorated and typically Andalusian restaurant popular. Try the fried aubergine (eggplant) drizzled with molasses or the salad of fresh tuna with sherry vinegar dressing. At the lively tapas bar, you can join the locals tucking into generous *raciones*. Closed Sun.

MÁLAGA Café de Paris
📋♿🍷🍴 €€€€

C/ Vélez Málaga 8, 29016 (Málaga) **Tel** *952 22 50 43*

An unprepossessing exterior conceals this elegant, classically decorated restaurant, which serves sublime, contemporary Spanish and Mediterranean cuisine. Creative dishes are exquisitely presented, particularly in the exceptional *menú de degustación*. Excellent wine list and immaculate service. Closed Sun evening & Mon.

MANILVA Macues
📋♿🖼️ €€€€

Puerto Deportivo de la Duquesa Local 13, 26961 (Málaga) **Tel** *952 89 03 95*

At this upmarket restaurant at the very tip of the Costa del Sol, you can dine on good international and Spanish cuisine on a shaded terrace, overlooking the sea of masts in the impressive yacht harbour below. House specialities include all kinds of fish baked in salt and juicy local meat grilled over charcoal. Opens for dinner only. Closed Mon.

MARBELLA Altamirano
📋🖼️ €

Plaza Altamirano 3, 29600 (Málaga) **Tel** *952 82 49 32*

In the heart of Marbella's lovely, whitewashed old town, this is a welcoming, family-run restaurant with a pretty terrace. Tasty home-cooked dishes include plenty of local seafood such as a platter of freshly fried fish, typical of the area. Staff are charming. This is one of the best-value options in the old town. Closed Wed.

MARBELLA Toni Dalli
📋♿🎵🖼️🍴 €€

El Oasis, Ctra de Cádiz km 176, 29600 (Málaga) **Tel** *952 77 00 35*

This handsome white palace flanked by palms makes for a great night out. It has been a classic on Marbella's Golden Mile since 1981. The Italian-influenced food includes home-made pastas, meat and fish. Live music is sometimes provided by Tony – formerly a popular singer with his own show in California – himself. Opens for dinner only.

MARBELLA El Portalón
Tapas 📋♿🖼️🍷🍴 €€€€

Ctra Cádiz-Málaga (N340) km 178, 29600 (Málaga) **Tel** *952 82 78 80*

Elegantly decorated dining rooms overlooking flower-filled gardens is the setting of this classic Andalusian restaurant. The highlight here is the meat and seafood cooked in a traditional brick oven, and you can also enjoy tapas and a glass of local wine in the attractive adjoining Vinoteca. Closed Sun except Aug.

MARBELLA La Meridiana
📋♿🖼️🍷🍴 €€€€

C/ Camino de la Cruz s/n km 3,5, 29600 (Málaga) **Tel** *952 77 61 90*

Situated in Marbella's rarified heights, La Meridiana is a magnificent restaurant with a canopied garden room and an adjoining patio bar. This is creative Mediterranean cuisine at its finest: recommendations include the ox stroganoff, or the monkfish with red pepper confit. Opens daily.

MARBELLA Santiago
Tapas 📋♿🖼️🍴 €€€€

C/ Paseo Marítimo 5, 29600 (Málaga) **Tel** *952 77 00 78*

This is probably the best place for seafood on the Costa del Sol. On any day, there might be 40 or 50 fish and shellfish dishes, all very fresh. Famous for more than 50 years, it's essential to book your table well in advance. Tapas are served at the bar, but there is a huge variety (more than 500) on offer at the adjoining Tabernita de Santiago.

MIJAS El Castillo
📋🖼️🍴 €€

Plaza de la Constitución, Pasaje de los Pescadores 2, 29650 (Málaga) **Tel** *952 48 53 48*

This rustic-style restaurant is right on the main square of the enchanting white village. It serves both typically Andalusian and international dishes, which you can enjoy out on the breezy terrace. Try the *ajoblanco*, a traditional cold soup made with an almond base, bread and garlic, and garnished with Malaga raisins. Closed Fri.

MOTRIL Tropical
📋 €€€

Av Rodríguez Acosta 23, 18600 (Granada) **Tel** *958 60 04 50*

A simple hostal with a good restaurant, serving a wide choice of typical Andalusian dishes in a classic Spanish seaside setting. Both seafood, such as bass with *ajo verde* (green garlic), and meat, such as *choto a la brasa* (roast baby kid) are specialities here. For dessert try the sorbet made with *chirimoya* (custard apple). Closed Sun & Jun.

OSUNA Casa del Marqués
📋♿🖼️🍴 €€€

C/ San Pedro 20, 41640 (Sevilla) **Tel** *954 81 22 23*

A luxurious hotel in the heart of historic Osuna, Casa del Marqués is located in a flamboyant Baroque mansion set in gardens. The restaurant offers superb, highly creative Andalusian cuisine which reinvents traditional recipes. The scallops sautéed with broad beans and ham and the cod fillet with baby squid are signature dishes. Closed Mon evenings.

PALMA DEL RÍO El Refectorio (Hospedería de San Francisco)　📋♿🔲🍷　€€

Av Pío XII 35, 14700 (Córdoba) **Tel** *957 71 01 83*

Dine in the 15th-century refectory of this out-of-the-way former monastery, now an elegant hotel. The restaurant has an ever-changing menu, which features Andalusian cuisine, with lots of typically Córdoban dishes. In autumn and winter, game features prominently, and in summer dinner is served on an enchanting candle-lit patio.

PALOS DE LA FRONTERA El Bodegón　*Tapas* 📋🔲　€

C/ Rábida 46, 21810 (Huelva) **Tel** *959 531 105*

An atmospheric former wine cellar now houses this cosy, informal restaurant, where the menu features local culinary stalwarts such as fish baked in a salt crust and meat grilled traditionally over holm oak firewood. The menu is short, but care is taken over selecting fresh local ingredients, and the result is always delicious. Closed Tue & 16–30 Sep.

RONDA Traga Tapas　*Tapas* 📋♿🔲🍷　€

C/ Nueva 4, 29400 (Málaga) **Tel** *952 87 72 09*

Located in the town centre, Traga Tapas is the sister restaurant to Tragabuches, and also offers an innovative menu, but at more reasonable prices. The imaginative tapas dishes include salmon marinated in lemon and vanilla, and wild mushrooms sautéed with Spanish onions and garnished with serrano ham. Closed Mon.

RONDA Del Escudero　📋♿🔲🍷　€€€

Paseo de Blás Infante 1, 29400 (Málaga) **Tel** *952 87 13 67*

With an incomparable garden setting near Ronda's famous bullring, this elegant restaurant offers spectacular views over the valley to go with its traditional Andalusian cuisine. Go for the good-value fixed-price lunch menu, which you can enjoy on the panoramic garden terrace. Closed Sun evenings.

RONDA Tragabuches　📋♿🔲🍷　€€€€

C/ José Aparicio 1, 29400 (Málaga) **Tel** *952 19 02 91*

A stylish fusion of contemporary and traditional, the dining room at this fabulous restaurant has red-brick walls and chunky industrial-chic fittings. The Andalusian cuisine is simply superb, and the *menú de degustación* (70 euros) allows diners to appreciate the chef's skilful handling of textures and flavours. Closed Sun evenings & Mon.

SAN FERNANDO Venta de Vargas　*Tapas* 📋♿🎵🔲　€€

Plaza de San Juan Vargas s/n, 11100 (Cádiz) **Tel** *956 88 16 22*

This popular small-town eatery has lots of flamenco atmosphere, and was immortalized by the mythical Camarón de la Isla. Order *raciones* of classics such as *aliñadas* (potato salad), or tuck into typical local stews and fresh fish from the bay. Finish up with creamy *tocino de cielo* ("heavenly bacon") for dessert. Closed Mon & Sun evening.

SAN ROQUE Villa Victoria (Los Remos Rest)　📋🔲🍷　€€

Ctra San Roque-La Línea 351 km 2.8, Campamento, 11314 (Cádiz) **Tel** *956 69 84 12*

Housed in a restored Victorian mansion with Mediterranean decor, this restaurant serves exquisite dishes. The focus is on first-rate seafood and a *menú de degustación* includes shrimp fritters and sea nettles. There is always a good list of seasonal specialities, including wild mushrooms. Closed Sun evenings & Mon.

SANLÚCAR DE BARRAMEDA Casa Bigote　*Tapas* 📋♿🔲🍷　€€€

C/ Bajo de Guía 10, 11540 (Cádiz) **Tel** *956 36 26 96*

At the mouth of the Río Guadalquivir, this typical sailor's tavern is legendary throughout Andalusia. The tapas bar, hung with hams and piled up with wooden barrels, offers fabulous seafood tapas, or you can dine in the wooden-beamed *comedor* on *langostinos de Sanlúcar* (large, sweet striped prawns) and fresh fish. Closed Sun & Nov.

SANLÚCAR LA MAYOR La Alquería　*Tapas* 📋♿🔲🍷　€€€€

Hacienda de Benazuza, C/ Virgen de las Nieves s/n, 41800 (Sevilla) **Tel** *955 70 33 44*

A luxurious hotel (part of the El Bulli empire) with a spectacular restaurant, where the cuisine is modelled on the culinary fireworks of celebrity chef, Ferran Adriá. Expect the unexpected and prepare to be dazzled: go for the *menú de degustación*, a series of miniature marvels. Closed Sun, Mon; check days for summer & winter.

TARIFA Mesón de Sancho　*Tapas* 📋　€€

Ctra Cádiz-Málaga km 94, 11380 (Cádiz) **Tel** *956 68 49 00*

A classic inn, just outside Cádiz on the road to Algeciras. Warm and friendly, it is decorated in typical *mesón* style, and offers set menus featuring sturdy Andalusian meats such as beef with mushrooms. It also serves a range of generous *raciones* in the bar. Sancho is a popular spot for family outings, particularly Sunday lunch.

TARIFA Miramar　📋♿🔲🍷　€€

Dos-Vida Hotel, Ctra Nacional 340 km 79.3, 11380 (Cádiz) **Tel** *956 68 52 46*

This is a fabulous hotel, set in dunes right on Tarifa's endless beach. Its pretty restaurant-café with a stylishly simple blue-and-white decor serves fresh salads, pizzas and grilled seafood, along with a few more exotic dishes such as Thai coconut soup. They also do cakes, delicious brownies and coffee. The views reach all the way to Africa.

TORREMOLINOS Bar Restaurante Casa Juan　*Tapas* 📋🔲　€€€

C/ San Ginés 18–24, 29620 (Málaga) **Tel** *952 37 35 12*

A popular beachfront restaurant with an expansive terrace offering home-cooked favourites such as fish baked in salt and *fritura Malagueña*, which are based on old family recipes (provided by Juan's mother and grandmother). It has been going since the tourist boom first transformed this former fishing village. Closed Mon.

TORREMOLINOS Frutos
Tapas 🍽 ♿ 🎴 🍷   €€€

Av de la Riviera 80, 29620 (Málaga) **Tel** *952 38 14 50*

The grande dame of Costa del Sol restaurants, serving superb meat and fish. There is a terrace, and two glassy dining areas where you can enjoy suckling pig, followed by *arroz con leche*. The remarkable wine cellar in the basement can be visited. An informal tapas bar at the entrance serves lighter meals. Closed Sun evenings.

ÚBEDA El Seco
Tapas 🍽 ♿   €€

C/ Corazon de Jesús 8, 23400 (Jaén) **Tel** *953 79 14 52*

A delightful find in the lovely Renaissance town of Úbeda. A charming, family-run restaurant, with a modest, but spick and span dining room, El Seco serves fresh and tasty home cooking, including delicious croquettes, game in season and country soups and stews. Opens daily for lunch and also for dinner on Fri & Sat. Closed Sun evenings & Jul.

VÉJER DE LA FRONTERA Venta Pinto
Tapas 🍽 ♿ 🎴 🍷   €€€€

La Barca de Véjer s/n, 11150 (Cádiz) **Tel** *956 45 08 77*

Véjer de la Frontera is a magical, hill-top town on the Costa de la Luz with a shadowy maze of narrow alleys, which evoke its Moorish past. This pretty restaurant, in a former staging post 3 km (1.8 miles) from the town centre, serves creative versions of local dishes, and has a popular tapas bar where you can also buy local specialities.

VERA Terraza Carmona
Tapas 🍽 ♿ 🎴 🍷   €€€

C/ Mar 1, 04620 (Almería) **Tel** *950 39 07 60*

A simple roadside hotel, with a fine restaurant that has won several local awards. The specialities here are excellent seafood, and unusual regional dishes such as *gurullos con conejo* (pasta with rabbit). In season, game dishes feature prominently, including wild boar with olives and almonds. Houses a pretty tapas bar. Closed Mon & 8–21 Jan.

ZAHARA DE LOS ATUNES Casa Juanito
Tapas 🍽 🎴 🍷   €€

C/ Alcalde Jose Ruiz Cana 7, 11393 (Cádiz) **Tel** *956 43 92 11*

In a pretty fishing village and low-key seaside resort, this is a charming, typically Andalusian restaurant with an airy, expansive terrace just steps from the beach. Seafood is the house speciality, particularly the tuna, which gives the town its name. It also has a dining area with tapas bar. Closed Wed (except Aug), Nov, Dec & Jan.

THE BALEARIC ISLANDS

FORMENTERA Restaurante Pascual
🍽 ♿ 🎴 🍷   €

C/ Es Caló, 07872 (Formentera) **Tel** *971 32 70 14*

A friendly, family-run restaurant in the pretty little bay of Es Caló, this is one of the most popular seafood restaurants on Formentera. Tucked behind a grove of pines only steps from the beach, it is enjoyably chaotic and informal, but the seafood dishes, particularly the stews and rice are exceptionally good.

FORMENTERA Juan y Andrea
🍽 🎴 🍷   €€€

Playa de Illetas s/n, 07860 (Formentera) **Tel** *971 18 71 30*

Dine on beautifully fresh fish and shellfish, including lobster, caught by the restaurant's own fishing boat, in this wonderful beach restaurant. It overlooks the Playa de Illetas, one of the wildest and most beautiful beaches in the Mediterranean. Local rice dishes are a speciality here. Opens daily 1–8pm & closed 15 Nov–1 Apr.

FORMENTERA, ES PUJOLS Sa Palmera
🍽 ♿ 🎴 🍷   €

Playa Es Pujols, C/Aguadulce 15–31, 07871 (Formentera) **Tel** *971 32 83 56*

Freshly caught seafood is served at this classic seafront restaurant, which specializes in traditionally prepared regional cuisine. Try the mixed fish paella or the *zarzuela de mariscos* (shellfish casserole), although you will also find a few meat dishes on the menu. You can eat out on the breezy terrace and enjoy great sea views. Closed Dec–Feb.

IBIZA (EIVISSA), SANT ANTONI Sa Capella
🍽 ♿ 🎴   €€

Ctra de Cala Salada km 1, 07840 (Ibiza) **Tel** *971 34 00 57*

Exquisitely housed in a former chapel, this elegant restaurant offers a wide range of fresh Mediterranean cuisine. There are lots of good fish dishes, including grilled sea bream, sea bass baked in a salt crust as well as juicy steaks cooked over charcoal. For dessert, try the delicious *tarte tatin*. Opens for dinner only from Easter to Oct.

IBIZA (EIVISSA), SANT JOSEP Can Pujol
🍽 ♿ 🍷   €€€

C/ Escalo s/n, 07839 (Ibiza) **Tel** *971 34 14 07*

Highly recommended by locals and tourists alike, this restaurant is known for its excellent seafood. Try the *parrillada de pescado* (variety of grilled fish), or one of the many paellas on offer. Finish with the house flan, made with bananas and pine nuts. It is located on the beach, and fills up quickly, so be sure to book in advance. Closed Wed & Dec.

IBIZA (EVISSA), SANTA GERTRUDIS Ama Lur
🍽 ♿ 🎴 🍷   €€€

Ctra San Miguel km 2.3, 07815 (Ibiza) **Tel** *971 31 45 54*

One of the best restaurants on the island, in a villa with Mediterranean decor. The menu features refined Basque cuisine, with the emphasis on fresh seafood, although Balearic meat dishes appear too. Try the sea bream with almonds and pistachios or local spring lamb with honey. Closed Wed (except Jul & Aug) & Jan–Mar.

Key to Price Guide *see p608* **Key to Symbols** *see back cover flap*

IBIZA (EIVISSA), SANTA GERTRUDIS Ca'n Pau 　　　€€€€
Ctra de Sant Miquel km 2.9, 07814 (Ibiza) **Tel** *971 19 70 07*

A beautifully restored Ibizan *masía* surrounded by gardens, Ca'n Pau serves fine Catalan and Mediterranean cuisine. The house speciality is *bacalao* prepared in several different ways, but tender roast kid, quail with cabbage and rabbit are also on the menu. A good selection of Catalan wines and *cavas*. Closed 1 Jan–10 Feb; check timings.

IBIZA, CALA BENIRRÀS Roca y Mar 　　　€€
Cala Benirràs, 07815 (Ibiza) **Tel** *971 33 35 32*

This restaurant is located on one of Ibiza's loveliest coves, with a small curving beach of golden sand. You can watch sunsets from the palm-shaded terrace, where simple snacks and more substantial Mediterranean cuisine, often featuring local seafood, is offered. The beach is hidden between Sant Miquel and Sant Joan. Closed Nov–mid-Apr.

IBIZA, IBIZA TOWN La Masía d'en Sort 　　　€€€
Ctra San Miguel km 1, 07814 (Ibiza) **Tel** *971 31 02 28*

A sturdy Ibizan *masía* set in orange groves is home to this elegant restaurant, with stylish dining rooms which double as art galleries for local artists. The food is no less artistic, and features dynamic reinventions of classic Balearic cuisine prepared with fresh local ingredients. Try the refreshing *langoustine* salad. Closed Mon (except in Jul & Aug) & Nov–Mar.

IBIZA, IBIZA TOWN La Oliva 　　　€€€
C/ Santa Cruz 2–4, 07800 (Ibiza) **Tel** *971 30 57 52*

An intimate restaurant tucked away in Ibiza town's labyrinthine old quarter, serving Mediterranean, French and Balearic cuisine. Try the sea bream baked in a salt crust, a flaky pie filled with goat's cheese, and finish up with the creamy chocolate Charlotte for dessert. Opens only for dinner. Closed 15 Oct to Easter.

IBIZA, SAN RAFEL DE FORCA Clodenis 　　　€€€
Plaza de la Iglesia s/n, 07816 (Ibiza) **Tel** *971 19 85 45*

A lovely country house, surrounded by shady gardens, Clodenis serves elegant Provençal and Mediterranean cuisine and offers lots of vegetarian specialities. Dine out on the romantic terrace under tendrils of trailing greenery, on tender marinated chicken or a fragrant au gratin of local vegetables. Closed Sun in winter & Nov.

MALLORCA, ALCÚDIA Mesón Los Patos 　　　€€
C/ Camí Can Blau 42, 07400 (Mallorca) **Tel** *971 89 02 65*

An agreeably decorated family restaurant with a garden and children's playground, close to the Parque Natural de la Albufera. It offers simple and traditional Mallorcan dishes, including *arroz brut* (a soupy rice served with meat), or roast shoulder of lamb. There is a good-value lunch menu. Closed Tue & 7 Jan–1 Mar.

MALLORCA, CALA RATJADA Ses Rotges 　　　€€€€
C/ Rafael Blanes 21, 07590 (Mallorca) **Tel** *971 56 31 08*

An enchanting family-run rural hotel, this lovely stone mansion is an ideal setting for dining on Mediterranean cuisine prepared with prime local produce. They offer a range of fixed-price menus, including a Medieval Menu that features ancient Balearic recipes. Booking essential. Opens Mon, Wed, Fri & Sat evenings only. Closed Nov–15 Mar.

MALLORCA, DEIÀ Ca'n Costa 　　　€€
Ctra Valldemossa-Deià km 2.5, 07170 (Mallorca) **Tel** *971 61 22 63*

An attractive, rural restaurant located in a prettily restored olive oil mill, Ca'n Costa serves honest Mallorcan cuisine at reasonable prices. Traditional *sopas Mallorquinas* (thick broths) and barbecued meats are the specialities here. You can also enjoy glorious mountain views from the terrace, and there is a playground for kids. Closed Tue in winters.

MALLORCA, DEIÀ El Olivo 　　　€€€€
Hotel la Residencia, Finca Son Canals, 08179 (Mallorca) **Tel** *971 63 93 92*

A magnificent hotel set in a fine 16th-century mansion houses this excellent restaurant, where you can dine on cool stone patios with breathtaking views of the mountains and sea. The delicious *nouvelle cuisine* incorporates Mediterranean influences, with dishes such as lamb baked with mustard croustade. Excellent wine list. Closed Mon & Tue.

MALLORCA, DEIÀ / PORT DE SÓLLER Bens d'Avall 　　　€€€€
Urbanización Costa Deià, Ctra Sóller-Deià s/n, 07100 (Mallorca) **Tel** *971 63 23 81*

This cliff-top restaurant offers wonderful views of the magnificent stretch of coastline, pocketed with turquoise-blue bays. The superb, contemporary cuisine reinvents traditional Mediterranean recipes with style and originality, and uses the finest regional produce. Go for the *menú de degustación*. Closed Mon, Tue & Dec–Feb.

MALLORCA, INCA Celler Ca'n Amer 　　　€€€
Pau 39, 07300 (Mallorca) **Tel** *971 50 12 61*

This wonderful old wine cellar, lined with battered wine barrels, is now home of one of the island's most authentic regional dishes, *sopes Mallorquinas*, made with bread and braised vegetables. They also have delicious local lamb, prepared with aubergine and *sobrasada* (Mallorcan sausage). Closed Sun evenings & all day Sun in Jun–Sep.

MALLORCA, PALMA La Bóveda **Tapas** 　　　€€
Botería 3, 07012 (Mallorca) **Tel** *971 71 48 63*

The most popular and characterful tapas bar in Palma, this has lazy paddle fans, multi-coloured tiles and huge wooden barrels. The menu ranges from simple *pa amb oli*, country bread rubbed with garlic and tomato and drizzled with olive oil to fresh seafood like the *bacalao al pil pil* (cod in a Basque sauce) and succulent grilled prawns. Closed Sun & Feb.

MALLORCA, PALMA DE MALLORCA Ca'n Carlos   ▣🏛️   €€

C/ del Aigua 5, 07011 (Mallorca) **Tel** *971 71 38 69*

Old Balearic recipes have been revived, providing diners with an authentic version of the island's food, with a new touch of creativity from the original owner's son. This is a much-loved local favourite, and bookings are essential. The oven-roasted suckling lamb and the hake with cabbage are particularly good. Great local wines. Closed Sun.

MALLORCA, PALMA DE MALLORCA Porto Pí   ▣♿🏛️🍴🍷   €€€

C/ Garita 25, 07015 (Mallorca) **Tel** *971 40 00 87*

This elegant old house, surrounded by gardens, is an ideal spot to savour creative Mediterranean and international cuisine using first-class ingredients. Try the sea bream cooked in wine or the duck with lime and curry spices. They also offer a range of elaborate dishes using foie gras. Delicious desserts. Closed Sat lunch & Sun.

MALLORCA, PEGUERA La Gran Tortuga   ▣🏛️   €€€

Urb Aldea Cala Fornells I, 07160 (Mallorca) **Tel** *971 68 60 23*

The spellbinding sea views from the terrace stretch all the way to the Magrat islands at this seaside restaurant overlooking a lovely bay. Try home-made foie gras, hake stuffed with salmon in a spinach sauce or lamb, all creatively prepared with fresh local ingredients. The set-price lunch and tasting menus are good value.

MALLORCA, PORT D'ANDRATX Layn   ▣♿🏛️🍷   €€

C/ Almirall Riera Alemany 20, 07157 (Mallorca) **Tel** *971 67 18 55*

This charming seaside villa is home to a delightful, simple restaurant, where the fish arrives straight from local fishing boats. The fabulous views of the sea from the terrace are the perfect accompaniment to the wonderfully fresh fish, but there are also meat specialities including roast suckling pig and beef with cabbage. Closed Mon.

MALLORCA, PORT DE POLLENÇA Stay   ▣♿🏛️🍷   €€

C/ Muelle Nuevo s/n, 07470 (Mallorca) **Tel** *971 86 40 13*

With tables right on the bay, this popular local restaurant serves tasty regional cuisine with emphasis on fish and seafood. Try the *salsa de eneldo*, filets of white fish grilled with vegetables and served with a dill sauce. They also have a cheap and cheerful snack bar (for sandwiches and burgers), good for families coming off the beaches.

MALLORCA, PORTOCOLOM Celler Sa Sinia   ▣♿🏛️   €€€

C/ Pescadors 5, 07670 (Mallorca) **Tel** *971 82 43 23*

Exceptional Mallorcan cuisine at modest prices. With a perfect location overlooking the port, it specializes in fresh seafood such as the wonderful salmon and prawn brochettes. It also serves delicious local meats. Try the duck with orange. Desserts include tiramisu made with *ensaimada*, Mallorca's famous pastry. Closed Mon, Nov, Dec & Jan.

MALLORCA, SÓLLER Sa Cova   *Tapas* ▣♿🏛️   €

Plaça de la Constitució 7, 07100 (Mallorca) **Tel** *971 63 32 22*

On Sóller's main square, shaded by vast plane trees, this is a simple, welcoming restaurant serving honest home cooking. The menu of classic Mallorcan dishes changes every three months, according to what is in season, and they also offer delicious home-made desserts. There is a good fixed-price lunch menu.

MALLORCA, SÓLLER El Guía   ▣🏛️🍷   €€

C/ Castanyer 2, 07100 (Mallorca) **Tel** *971 63 02 27*

A pretty, old-fashioned hotel with a delightful flower-filled garden, El Guía's dining room is a popular local favourite. The charming dining rooms retain some of its original Modernista details, and the good, home-cooked food include tasty dishes such as locally grown artichokes stuffed with spinach. Reasonably priced. Closed Mon & Nov–Mar.

MENORCA, CIUTADELLA Café Balear   *Tapas* ▣♿🏛️   €

C/ Pla de Sant Joan 15, 07760 (Menorca) **Tel** *971 38 00 05*

A legendary restaurant right on the port, Café Balear specializes in fish and seafood including *caldera de langosta* (lobster casserole) and *fritada de gambas* (fried prawns). The fish arrives on the restaurant's own boat, and is prepared with the minimum of fuss to better appreciate its freshness. Reservations essential. Closed Sun evening & Mon.

MENORCA, CIUTADELLA Cas Ferrer de Sa Font   ▣♿🏛️   €€€

C/ Portal de Sa Font 16, 07760 (Menorca) **Tel** *971 48 07 84*

A rustically decorated 18th-century mansion set around a patio, Cas Ferrer de Sa Font offers a range of set menus, including a special children's one. The focus is on Menorcan and Mediterranean cuisine, with local ingredients prepared with touches of creativity. Try the stuffed courgettes (zucchinis) with prawns. Closed Mon & Mar.

MENORCA, ES MERCADAL Ca'n Olga   ▣♿🏛️   €

C/ Pont de na Macarrana, 07740 (Menorca) **Tel** *971 37 54 59*

A pretty country cottage, which doubles as an exhibition space for local artists, is the attractive setting for this charming restaurant. Delicious, sophisticated Menorcan and Mediterranean cuisine is on offer, accompanied by so sturdy local wines. In summer, dine in the garden terrace at the back. Closed Nov–Mar; Mon & Tue Apr–May.

MENORCA, ES MIGJORN GRAN S'Engolidor   ▣🏛️   €€

C/ Major 3, 07749 (Menorca) **Tel** *971 37 01 93*

An old country house, now a small rural inn, is home to this restaurant which serves home-cooked Menorcan specialities at very reasonable prices. The menu features refreshing salads and simple but delicious local meat and fish. The garden terrace overlooks the gorge of S'Engolidor, which gives the restaurant its name. Closed Mon & Nov–Easte

Key to Price Guide *see p608* **Key to Symbols** *see back cover flap*

MENORCA, FORNELLS Es Cranc

C/ Escoles 31, 07748 (Menorca) **Tel** *971 37 64 42*

Fornells has long been associated with the typically Menorcan dish of lobster *caldereta* (spiny lobster stew), once a poor fishermen's dish and now a pricey delicacy. No other place does it better than this traditional bar-restaurant. It also offers a good-value lunch menu. Closed Wed (except Aug), Dec, Jan & Feb.

MENORCA, MAÓ Cap Roig

Urb Cala Mesquida 14, 07700 (Menorca) **Tel** *971 18 83 83*

A classic, informal seafood restaurant right on the beach, which has an imaginative set menu at lunch time and tasty specialities with fresh fish and lobster. The *pescado frito* is outstandingly good, and they also do a wonderful version of the *caldereta de langostinos*, Menorca's famous stew of spiny lobsters. Closed Mon.

MENORCA, MAÓ Jágaro

Moll de Levant 334, 07701 (Menorca) **Tel** *971 36 23 90*

A classic restaurant right on the harbour, with a cosy dining room filled with knick-knacks and a popular breezy terrace. It serves fine Mediterranean seafood dishes, including the Menorcan speciality *caldereta de langosta* lobster stew). There are over 100 wines on their wine list. Closed Mon, Feb & Sun evenings in winter.

MENORCA, SANT CLIMENT Es Molí de Foc

C/ Sant Llorenç 65, Sant Climent, 07712 (Menorca) **Tel** *971 15 32 22*

A country-house restaurant located in a tiny village a few kilometres southeast of Maó. Delicious creative Menorcan and international cuisine makes excellent use of varied local produce, and includes rice and seafood dishes. There is an attractive garden terrace, where sea shanties are sung in summer. Closed Jan, Sun evenings & Mon in winter.

THE CANARY ISLANDS

EL HIERRO, VALVERDE La Higuera de la Abuela

C/ Tajanis Caba 10, Echedo, 38900 **Tel** *922 55 10 26*

A low-lying building with colourful walls and a courtyard planted with cactuses, this restaurant is 10 km (6 miles) to the north of Valverde. It serves no-frills traditional, home-made island cooking, notably *cordero herreño a la herreña* (El Hierro lamb in El Hierro style) and a variety of local fish. Also try bass with mojo sauce. Closed Tue in winters.

EL HIERRO, VALVERDE El Mirador de la Peña

Ctra General Norte 40, Guarazoca, 38916 **Tel** *922 55 03 00*

This house hanging from a rock on the north coast of the island with spectacular views of the Valle del Golfo was designed by celebrated Canarian architect César Manrique. It serves typical El Hierro food such as *ensalada templada* de ventresca de bonito (warm tuna salad) and *mousse de gofio*, made with the typical Guanche cereal. Closed Mon.

FUERTEVENTURA, BETANCURIA Casa Santa María

Plaza de la Concepción, 35510 **Tel** *928 87 82 82*

Situated on the same square as the 15th-century Iglesia de Santa María (now Fuerteventura's cathedral), this restaurant-cum-museum, in a 16th-century house, is worth a visit. It has its own bodega and a garden. A good place to try the traditional *puchero canario* (Canarian stew) and, for dessert, the *crema Canaria*.

FUERTEVENTURA, PUERTO DEL ROSARIO La Barca del Pescador

Franchi Roca, El Castillo, Caleta de Fuste, 35510 **Tel** *928 16 35 00*

Built on two levels and decorated with maritime paraphernalia, this restaurant offers traditional cuisine based mainly on fish and seafood brought directly from Galicia. They do a good salt-crusted sea bass. For starters try the *crema de* berros (watercress soup) and for dessert *tocino de cielo*. Pescador serves classic Spanish wines as well.

FUERTEVENTURA, PUERTO DEL ROSARIO Fabiola

Caserío de Ampuyenta 43, 35510 **Tel** *928 17 46 05*

An old country house, decorated with antiques, and with an atmosphere somewhat evocative of the Belle Epoque. It's run by two Belgian men who offer creative cuisine based on market produce. Try the warm salad of endives with bacon and goat's cheese or the John Dory fillets. For dessert there is cheese cake. Closed for lunch Mon–Wed.

GRAN CANARIA, AGÜIMES La Farola

Alcalá Galiano 3, 35118 **Tel** *928 18 04 10*

On Arinaga beach, down the coast from the airport, is this restaurant with a sea-inspired decor, which specializes in fish and seafood. Worth trying, in particular, is the oven-baked salted fish or the *paella* made with fish or shellfish. Desserts are home made, including a pleasing *tarta de turrón*. Open lunchtime only except Fri–Sat. Closed Sun evening.

GRAN CANARIA, ARUCAS Casa Brito

Paraje Teror 17, Ctra Arucas-Teror km 1.3, 35400 **Tel** *928 62 23 23*

Meat is the specialty of this rustic restaurant in Visvice, just outside Arucas, but the fish dishes are just as good. Both are cooked in a wood-fired oven. Start with *setas salteadas con langostinos* (wild mushrooms sautéed with prawns) and finish with flaky pastry made with almonds and honey. Closed Mon, Tue, Sun evening, Easter week & first fortnight of Sep.

GRAN CANARIA, ARUCAS El Mesón de la Montaña ▤ ♿ ▦   €€

C/ Montaña de Arucas, 35400 **Tel** *928 60 08 44*

A spiralling road leads to this restaurant perched on the top of a mountain outside Arucas offering great views of the northern part of the island. It serves a selection of international and Canarian dishes – some of the latter need to be ordered in advance. Good fish and seafood, including cod and prawns. Also has a playground. Caters largely for groups.

GRAN CANARIA, LAS PALMAS Kamakura *Tapas* ▤   €€

C/ Galileo Galilei 4, 35010 **Tel** *928 22 26 70*

A small Japanese restaurant near the Playa de las Canteras, with Oriental decor. Choose between the sushi bar or one of the tables. The specialities include tempura (lightly battered vegetables and prawns), fish tartare with aromatic herbs and sushimi (a plate of slices of raw fish), all served with an attention to detail. Closed Mon lunch, Sun & Aug.

GRAN CANARIA, LAS PALMAS Amaiur ▤ ♿ ▦ ▯   €€€

C/ Péréz Galdós 2, 35002 **Tel** *928 37 07 17*

Housed in a 19th-century colonial home in the Barrio de Tirana, this restaurant is run by two brothers who offer traditional Basque cooking with innovations, depending upon the fresh market produce available. Among the tempting items on the menu are foie gras with grape sauce and Armagnac and hake with seafood. Closed Sun & Aug

GRAN CANARIA, LAS PALMAS La Hacienda ▤ ♿ ▯   €€€

Edificio Venegas, Profesor Agustín Millares Carló 9, 35003 **Tel** *928 37 31 97*

The serious approach to food is accentuated by a minimalist decor. It offers creative cuisine of Mediterranean origin. On the menu is duck with ginger and moschatel and cod with fried green tomatoes. Do not miss the souffle *cremos* made with Tanzanian chocolate. *Menú de degustación* at lunchtime. Closed Sun & Mon–Thu evenings.

GRAN CANARIA, SANTA BRIGIDA Las Grutas de Artiles ♿ ▦   €€

Las Meleguinas, Valle de la Angostura, 35300 **Tel** *928 64 05 75*

More a leisure complex built around two natural caves and various outdoor spaces, including terraces and a pool, than a mere restaurant. The food is Canarian, with specialities including *pescado al mojo verde* (fish with a spicy green sauce) and *buñuelos de plátano al vino tinto* (banana dumplings in red wine). Also has pool-side tables.

LA GOMERA, AGULO La Vieja Escuela ♿   €

C/ Poeta Trujillo Armas 2, 38830 **Tel** *922 14 60 04*

The old village school, a charming whitewashed cottage with beamed ceilings, is home to this simple restaurant-bar Try typical local dishes, including home-made soups, fresh seafood, goat and *almogrote*, a piquant pâté made with cured Gomeran cheese, tomatoes and hot pepper.

LA GOMERA, SAN SEBASTIÁN El Silbo *Tapas* ▦   €

Ctra General 102, Hermigua, 38800 **Tel** *922 88 03 04*

This restaurant on the Hermigua beach offers no-frills dining. Instead, it serves simple food and a small selection of mainstream wines. For a typical lunchtime meal, you can start with the *croquetas de pescado* (fish croquettes), followed by *filetes de atun en adobo* (tuna fish in sauce) and finish with bananas covered with the local palm hone

LA GOMERA, SAN SEBASTIÁN Marqués de Oristano *Tapas* ♿ ▯   €

C/ del Medio 24, 38800 **Tel** *922 87 29 01*

On the second floor of a beautiful old house, this restaurant offers modern Canarian food using traditional produc both from the land and the sea. It has a grill and a bar on the ground floor. If you like rabbit, try the *conejo con verduras y plátanos verdes*. For dessert order the *cilindro de chocolate blanco con almendras*. Closed Sun & Mon lunc

LA PALMA, LOS LLANOS DE ARIDANE El Bernegal ♿   €

C/ Díaz Suárez 5, Santo Domingo, Garafía, 38760 **Tel** *922 40 04 80*

This restaurant, sited in an old house with an inner patio on the west coast of the island, serves traditional Canary Islands cuisine and vegetarian dishes, notably *potaje de berros* and, if you like kid, *cabrito palmero*. For dessert the is *delicias con naranja* (a kind of biscuit with orange). Open only at lunchtime. Closed Mon & mid-May–early Jul.

LA PALMA, LOS LLANOS DE ARIDANE La Casona de Argual ♿ ▦   €€

Plaza Sotomayor 6, 38760 **Tel** *922 40 18 16*

A restaurant-with-rooms in a noble house built in 1732, with a romantic garden. It serves international cuisine wit creative touch such as the cream of pumpkin soup and the chicken with tropical fruits. Another good bet is a selection of pâtés with home-made delicacies. For dessert try tiramisu. Closed Sun lunch, Thu & 15 May–15 Jun.

LA PALMA, SANTA CRUZ Chipi Chipi ♿ ▦ ▯   €€

C/ Velhoco 42, 38700 **Tel** *922 41 10 24*

Around 6 km (4 miles) out of the island capital, this good-value restaurant with a pretty patio adorned with tropic plants, specializes in grilled meats and local dishes such as chickpea soup, roasted cheese with *mojo verde* and kic Good selection of wines from the island. Private room available. Closed Sun, Wed & Oct–mid-Nov.

LA PALMA, SANTA CRUZ La Ola ♿ ▦   €

Aparthotel Las Olas, Los Cancajos, Breña Baja, 38700 **Tel** *637 41 17 18*

In a small tourist resort 4 km (2.5 miles) down the coast from Santa Cruz, this restaurant has good sea views. It se international food using fresh market products such as *tosta de anchoas y pimientos* (toasted bread with anchovies peppers). For dessert try the local *bienmesabe* (an almond sweet) with vanilla ice cream. Closed Sun evening & M

Key to Price Guide *see p608* **Key to Symbols** *see back cover flap*

LANZAROTE, ARRECIFE Castillo de San José
Tapas 🍽 €

Castillo de San José, Ctra de Puerto Nao, 35340 **Tel** *928 81 23 21*

Puerto Nao's converted fortress was built in 1779 by King Carlos III and restored by the Lanzarote architect César Manrique. It now houses a contemporary art gallery and a restaurant. Enjoy international and regional specialities as you admire the art and views of the harbour. Ironically the castle has always been known locally as the "Hungry Fort".

LANZAROTE, COSTA TEGUISE Mesón La Jordana
Tapas 🍽 ♿ 🍴 🍷 €€

Centro Comercial de Lanzarote Bay, Av de los Geranios, 35509 **Tel** *928 59 03 28*

A popular restaurant in one of Costa Teguise's shopping centres, King Hussein of Jordan was once a customer here, where local fare is given a French touch. For starters there are Burgundy snails. Main course includes stewed partridge, braised duck and sole with almonds. Desserts include papaya sorbet and crêpe suzette. Closed Sun & Sep.

LANZAROTE, COSTA TEGUISE Neptuno
Tapas 🍽 ♿ 🍴 🍷 €€

Av del Jabillo, Centro Comercial Neptuno, local 6, 35509 **Tel** *928 59 03 78*

This airy restaurant in a shopping centre serves traditional Canary Islands cooking. The menu is strong on all types of meat but there are also some excellent fresh fish dishes such as *atun adobado al horno* (oven-cooked tuna fish) and *salmón ahumado de Uga* (smoked salmon). Wines and cheeses from the island. Closed Sun and 20 Jun–22 Jul.

LANZAROTE, YAIZA La Era
🍽 ♿ €€

C/ El Barranco 3, 35340 **Tel** *928 83 00 16*

La Era occupies one of the few old houses to survive the island's volcanic eruptions of 1730–36. It was built in the 17th century and restored as a restaurant by César Manrique, who created murals for it. Enjoy a salad of octopus and Canary-style potatoes, stew and fish caught fresh at Playa Blanca and cooked to the customer's orders. Closed Mon.

TENERIFE, ADEJE El Patio
🍽 ♿ 🎵 🍴 🍷 🕐 🍷 €€€€

Hotel Jardín Tropical, Urbanización San Eugenio, C/ Gran Bretaña s/n, 38670 **Tel** *922 74 60 01*

The restaurant of the luxurious Hotel Jardín Tropical provides an enchanting setting for a special evening. Imaginative, modern dishes are created using local produce. Try the lobster on a pyramid of fresh pasta or the roasted young pigeon with walnut cream and wild mushroom sauce. Open for dinner only, closed Sun & Mon. Reservation recommended.

TENERIFE, EL SAUZAL Casa del Vino La Baranda
🍴 🍷 €€€

Autopista general del Norte km 21 (Enlace de El Sauzal, La Baranda), 38360 **Tel** *922 56 38 86*

Tenerife's wine industry is explained by this museum in an old house on the northwest coast near Tacoronte. The restaurant serves modern Canary Islands cuisine based on fresh local market produce though, of course, the wine is the centre of focus here. There are sometimes concerts in summer on the central patio. Closed Mon & May.

TENERIFE, GRANADILLA DE ABONA Bodega El Jable
🍽 ♿ 🍷 €€

C/ Betejüi 9, San Isidro, 38611 **Tel** *922 39 06 98*

A Canary Islands' *casa de comidas* serving both traditional and creative cooking, particularly fish. The menu includes *potaje de berros*, warm fish salad with thyme, roasted cheese with *mojo verde* and bass with tomato vinagrette and lentils.Try the *tarta de millo* for dessert. Only local wines served. Closed Sun, Mon lunch & 1–15 July.

TENERIFE, PUERTO DE LA CRUZ Régulo
🍽 ♿ €€

C/ Pérez Zamora 16, 38400 **Tel** *922 38 45 06*

An old house dating from the 18th century, with an agreeable inner patio which attempts to recreate a traditional decor. It is close to the Plaza del Charco in the centre of town. The menu is noted for its locally caught grilled fish and Argentinian roast lamb. Try the fig mousse for dessert. Closed Sun, Mon lunch & Jul.

TENERIFE, SANTA CRUZ El Coto de Antonio
🍽 ♿ 🍷 €€

C/ General Goded 13, 38006 **Tel** *922 27 21 05*

One of Tenerife's most celebrated restaurants where you can expect excellent food and good service but, of course, there is a price to match. A serious place which welcomes business people and VIPs. The black potato salad with salt cod, peppers and olive oil and the bass in a coriander sauce are favourites. Closed Sun evenings & three weeks in Sep.

TENERIFE, SANTA CRUZ El Rincón de Elis
🍽 🍷 €€

C/ Ángel Guimerá 38 (Puerta Canseco), 38003 **Tel** *922 27 58 93*

Creative Lebanese and Mediterranean cuisine is served in El Rincón de Elis, which is run by a well-travelled chef who also adds exotic touches from around the world. The staff are charming and helpful. Reservation recommended. Closed Sun, Mon & Sep.

TENERIFE, SANTA CRUZ El Bacalao de la Cazuela
🍽 🍷 €€€

C/ General Goded 11, 38006 **Tel** *922 29 32 49*

A union of Basque cuisine, with emphasis on multiple ways of cooking cod, and Canarian ideas. Try the toast served with home-made foie gras and onion marmalade and, instead of fish, order the *cerdo ibérico en salsa de vino tinto* (pork in red wine sauce). End with *tarta de queso fresco y mango* (cheesecake with mango). Closed Sun & Sat lunch.

TENERIFE, TEGUESTE Mesón El Drago
♿ 🍴 🍷 €€€€

Marqués de Celada 2, Urbanización San Gonzalo, El Socorro, 38293 **Tel** *922 54 30 01*

A 18th-century farmhouse provides a rustic setting for creative Canary Islands cooking including watercress soup, stew, fish casserole and rabbit with Canarian-style potatoes. There is a gourmet tasting menu and a selection of Canarian cheeses. Vegetarian menu available. Reservation only. Closed Mon, Tue, Aug & evenings (except Fri & Sat).

SHOPPING IN SPAIN

Spain has a thriving shopping culture, with many unique, family-run boutiques as well as a few reliable chain stores and big department stores. Good buys include leather, fashion, wine and ceramics, though these days it is possible to find anything you are looking for, from traditional gifts to designer clothes. Spain has its own rules of etiquette when it comes to shopping. In small shops, most merchandise is behind the counter, and the clerk will retrieve whatever you need, making for a time-consuming, but friendly way to shop. It is considered polite to greet the shop owner and fellow shoppers with a "*buenos dias*" as you enter, and to call out "*adios*" as you leave.

A traditional fan

Fresh produce in a market in Pollença (Mallorca)

OPENING HOURS

Most shops in Spain, barring some supermarkets or department stores, close at midday. Small shops are open Monday to Saturday (10am–2pm and 5–8pm). Service-related shops such as dry cleaners usually open an hour earlier and close an hour later. Nearly all shops are closed on Sunday and holidays, except during the Christmas season and sales.

PAYMENT METHODS

Cash is still the payment of choice in Spain. Cheques are rarely accepted, and credit cards may not be accepted in small shops or markets. Even in large stores, there may be a minimum purchase required for credit card users.

ATMs are widely available throughout the country, even in small towns, so getting cash should not be a problem.

VAT & VAT EXEMPTION

Value added tax (VAT), known as *IVA* in Spanish, is included in the price of nearly everything in Spain. However, non-EU residents are eligible for a VAT refund. Before leaving a shop, request a VAT refund form. If you buy goods worth a total of €90.15 or more, you can get the form stamped at a Spanish customs office, usually located in the airport. Present the stamped form at a Spanish Bureau de Change in the airport for a same-day refund, or mail it for the refund to be credited to your credit card.

SALES

Spain's twice-annual *rebajas* (sales) are a fantastic opportunity to find good deals on everything from shoes and clothes to linens, electronics and household goods. Some stores offer a reduction of 50% or more.

The first *rebajas* of the year begin on 7 January (the day after Three Kings Day) and last until mid-February.

Summer *rebajas* start in early July and last until mid-August.

MARKETS

A visit to a Spanish market is a great lesson in local culture. Every town, large or small, has at least one fresh market, where you can buy local produce, Spanish cheeses and sausages and other foods.

Markets in the cities follow regular store opening hours, but in smaller towns, they may only be open in the morning, or on certain days of the week.

Speciality markets for antiques, arts and crafts are popular in Spain, as are the *rastros* (flea markets). These are usually open only at weekends, though the times vary across markets and towns.

The country's most celebrated market is El Rastro (*see p302*), a massive flea market in Madrid, which has been running for many generations. It is frequented by locals and tourists alike. Watch out for pickpockets.

Display of hand-painted ceramics in Toledo

Shopping in Barcelona pp186–9; in Madrid pp316–9; in Seville pp454–5

REGIONAL PRODUCTS

Spain has a strong artisan heritage, and the best places to buy authentic traditional items are the artisan markets and speciality shops. All over Spain, you'll find great pottery and ceramics. Spain's pottery is sturdy and colourful and each region puts its own spin on the traditional forms. Andalusia, El Bisbal in Catalonia, Paterna and Manises near Valencia and Talavera de la Reina in Castilla-La Mancha are the main centres for ceramic production.

Leather goods are another traditional craft. Reasonably-priced shoes, wallets and accessories are available almost everywhere.

In Toledo, filigree metalwork and swords are sold on almost every street corner. Other sought-after products include guitars, traditional fans, Lladró porcelain figures and Majorica pearls.

A Madrid branch of the fashionable Camper shoe store

ONE-STOP SHOPPING

Small family-run shops are quaint, but when you're in a hurry department stores and one-stop shops are more convenient. Spain's most famous department store, El Corte Inglés, is found in every major city in Spain, sometimes with multiple branches. This mega store sells everything from clothes and sports goods, to furniture

Basketware, sold in all parts of Spain

and food. Other one-stop shops include hypermarkets such as Carrefour (the Walmart of Europe) and Hipercor.

American-style malls, called *centros comerciales* in Spain, are gaining popularity and can be found on the outskirts of most large cities.

FASHION

Spain has a long textile history, so it's no surprise to find good quality clothing here. In large cities such as Madrid and Barcelona, you'll find boutiques of major Spanish labels, including Antonio Miro, Lydia Delgado, Josep Font, Adolfo Dominguez and Loewe. Spanish fashion may not be on par with Paris or Milan yet, but designers here are increasingly gaining a reputation for quality and originality.

For something trendy and a bit easier on the wallet, Spanish-owned chains such as Zara, Mango and Massimo Dutti are great places to shop.

Mallorca is a good place to buy shoes, home to Spain's most famous shoe company, Camper. Along with branded shoes, *Espadrilles* (traditional Spanish rope-soled shoes) are a good informal option.

FOOD & DRINK

Spain is second only to Italy in wine production, and Spanish wine is rated to be of the best value in Europe. Major wine regions are Penedès (reds, whites and cava), Priorat (reds), Rias Baixas (whites), Ribera del Duero (reds), Rioja (reds) and Toro (whites). Sherry from Jerez is another popular Spanish drink.

A gourmet's paradise, Spain is great for food shopping. Olives and olive oil are always a good buy. Prominent olive-growing areas include Andalusia, Aragón and southern Catalonia. You can also buy Spain's famous *jamón Ibérico* (Iberian cured ham), or one of the many region-specific sausages such as Catalan *butifarra* and Castilian *morcilla*.

Gourmet chocolate shops are becoming popular now, especially in the cities. Escribà in Barcelona has a good reputation for producing exquisite confectionery.

SIZE CHART

Women's dresses, coats and skirts

European	36	38	40	42	44	46	48
British	10	12	14	16	18	20	22
American	8	10	12	14	16	18	20

Women's shoes

European	36	37	38	39	40	41
British	3	4	5	6	7	8
American	5	6	7	8	9	10

Men's suits

European	44	46	48	50	52	54	56	58 (size)
British	34	36	38	40	42	44	46	48 (inches)
American	34	36	38	40	42	44	46	48 (inches)

Men's shirts (collar size)

European	36	38	39	41	42	43	44	45 (cm)
British	14	15	15½	16	16½	17	17½	18 (inches)
American	14	15	15½	16	16½	17	17½	18 (inches)

Men's shoes

European	39	40	41	42	43	44	45	46
British	6	7	7½	8	9	10	11	12
American	7	7½	8	8½	9½	10½	11	11½

ENTERTAINMENT IN SPAIN

Spain has always been known for its vibrant, colourful culture – wherever you are, there is usually a fiesta going on somewhere nearby, or some impromptu celebration taking place in the street. So while there's usually no need to seek out formal entertainment, those who do want to plan a day or night out will find plenty of choice, ranging from

Traditional singers in Santa Cruz, Seville

raucous cabarets to live flamenco and high-brow cultural events. Although Madrid, Barcelona and, to a lesser extent, Seville have the widest selection of programmes, the other regional capitals are not far behind. The coastal resorts also witness a lot of action in the summer months. Regular annual events in various parts of Spain are detailed on pages 38–9.

the Spanish music scene is also enriched by influences from South America and Africa.

The Benicassim festival in August is fast becoming the preferred live event for those in search of new music. Keep an eye out for show posters as big international jazz artists can surprisingly turn up in small town stadiums and bullrings.

The Spanish music channel RNE 3 broadcasts an eclectic selection of Spanish as well as international music.

FLAMENCO

Flamenco *(see pp424–5)* is a traditional art form that combines song, music and dance. Infused with sensuality and emotion, it originated in Andalusia but is performed all over Spain. It is a highly varied musical form, and acts can range from spontaneous performances in gypsy patios to international spectacles in major concert halls.

However, note that shows are often adapted to tourists'

tastes. To see and hear flamenco that even purists admire, try the smaller venues or catch a performance during an Andalusian fiesta, particularly in the provinces of Seville and Jerez.

Córdoba hosts the National Flamenco Competition in May every third year. The next two will be held in 2010 and 2013.

CLASSICAL MUSIC, OPERA AND BALLET

Opera, classical music and ballet are performed in all the major cities in imposing concert halls. The best-known venues include the Auditorio Nacional de Música in Madrid *(see p322)*, Palau de la Música in Valencia *(see p242)*, Teatro de la Maestranza *(see p456)* and Gran Teatre del Liceu *(see p191)* in Barcelona.

For a more unusual concert setting, look out for performances in Spain's spectacular caves such as those found in Nerja *(see p483)* Drac *(see p517)* and the Cuevas of

Preparing for a dressage display at the equestrian school in Jerez

TRADITIONAL MUSIC AND DANCE

Spain's rich musical heritage is marked by typical regional instruments, musical styles and dance forms. The *txistu*, a small wind instrument is typical to the Basque Country, Galicia and Asturias lilt to the notes of the *gaita* (bagpipes), while Valencia is proud of its countless brass bands.

Andalusia is the home of flamenco, while Aragón's rhythm comes from the hop-step of its folk dance, *jota*. In Catalonia, the famous *sardana* *(see p205)* is accompanied by a *flabiol* (flute), *tabal* (drum) and *gralla* (a type of oboe).

JAZZ, ROCK AND POP

Television talent shows tend to dominate the Spanish pop industry, but many creative bands fail to get international recognition only because they sing in Spanish. At the cultural crossroads of southern Europe,

Palau de la Música, Valencia

Entertainment in Barcelona pp190–95; in Madrid pp320–25; in Seville pp456–7

A performance at the beautifully preserved Roman theatre in Mérida, Extremadura

Canelobre near Alicante. Sacred music can still be heard in some of Spain's many functioning monasteries. Montserrat *(see p219)* is famous for its all-boy choir. In Leyre monastery *(see p135)*, the Gregorian plainchant is performed during mass.

THEATRE

Spain has a great repertoire of classical theatre and although most performances are in Spanish, it may be worth going to a show for the venue alone.

Corral de Comedias in Almagro *(see p417)* is a perfectly preserved 17th-century Golden Age theatre. Mérida's stunning Roman theatre *(see pp54–5 and pp428–9)* serves as the splendid backdrop for an annual summer festival of classical theatre.

CINEMA

Spain's thriving film scene has gained international exposure in recent years. The country makes around 100 feature films a year with directors such as Pedro Almodóvar and Alejandro Amenábar.

Most foreign-language films are dubbed in Spanish, but select cinemas in university cities and areas with a large number of foreign residents show films in their original language. San Sebastián hosts an acclaimed international film festival *(see p127)* in

September and the Sitges Film Festival, which takes place in October or November.

The open-air summer cinemas in some coastal resorts are an experience in themselves, but do remember to carry a mosquito repellent.

NIGHTLIFE

Spain's prodigious nightlife starts later than in most other countries, with 11pm considered an early start for most revellers. The idea is to spend the first part of the evening in pubs or *bares de copas*: sparsely decorated drinking dens, usually with loud music blaring. Then move on to the clubs and discos, often located out of town, where the noise will not bother anyone.

You can enjoy a floorshow while dining out at coastal package-holiday resorts such as Lloret del Mar on the Costa Brava, Maspalomas on Gran Canaria, Torremolinos on the Costa del Sol and Benidorm on the Costa Blanca.

SPECTATOR SPORTS

Football is Spain's favourite sport and is centred on the battle between the two top teams, Real Madrid and Barcelona. Other teams with large followings include Real Betis from Seville, Deportivo La Coruña, FC Valencia and Real Zaragoza. Cycling, tennis, basketball and golf are also popular.

BULLFIGHTING

For an authentic spectacle of Spain's most recognized traditional sport *(see pp36–7)*, watch a bullfight in a large arena – Madrid *(see p306)*, Seville *(see p430)*, Valencia, Bilbao and Zaragoza have the best bullrings. All bullfights start in the early evening at around 5pm. Tickets should be bought directly at the venue to avoid the mark-up of touts and ticket agencies.

ENTERTAINMENT FOR CHILDREN

Spain's big theme parks are Port Aventura on the Costa Daurada *(see p224)* and Terra Mítica outside Benidorm *(see p260)*. Other amusements suitable for kids include the cowboys of Mini-Hollywood *(see p500)* and the dancing horses of Jerez *(see p466)*.

Rollercoaster ride at Port Aventura on the Costa Daurada

OUTDOOR ACTIVITIES & SPECIALIST HOLIDAYS

Spain is one of Europe's most geographically varied countries, with mountain ranges, woodlands and river deltas suitable for scenic tours and sports holidays. The options are endless and include sailing on the Mediterranean or surfing in the Atlantic, mountain climbing in the Pyrenees or rambling through

Golfer preparing to tee off

the plains of Castille, snow skiing in the Sierra Nevada or water skiing off the coast of Mallorca. To focus on just one activity, sign up for a specialist holiday. Weekend or week-long holidays, featuring everything from yoga to horse riding, are gaining popularity in Spain. Local tourist offices can provide information on outdoor activities.

WALKING AND TREKKING

Spain offers exciting choices for a challenging week-long trek through the Pyrenees, or a gentle walk along the coast. Look out for the wide, well-marked GR (*Grandes Recorridos* meaning long-distance) trails, which criss-cross Spain. Though most people usually choose to walk only a small portion of each GR trail, long-distance trekkers use them to traverse all the way across the country.

Nearly 8 per cent of Spain's total terrain is protected parkland, and the countless natural parks and 13 large national parks are the most popular and attractive hiking options. Some of the best parks for walking include Aragón's Parque Nacional de Ordesa (*see pp232–3*), Catalunya's Parque Nacional d'Aigüestortes (*see pp210–11*), and Asturias' Parque Nacional de los Picos de Europa (*see pp108–9*). For details about

trails in the parks, contact the **Environment Ministry of Spain**. For information on other trails, contact the **Federación Española de Deportes de Montaña y Escalada**.

AIR SPORTS

The best way to take in Spain's landscape is to view it from above. Options for thrilling aerial views include hot-air ballooning, skydiving, paragliding and hang-gliding. One of the well-known hot-air balloon companies is **Kon-Tiki**, which began flying in the Costa Brava and now covers the whole country. **Glovento Sur** operates in southern Spain. Standard rides cost €150–€300, depending on the trip's length. For details contact the **Real Federación Aeronáutica Española**.

For those who have forever been fascinated by the birds' ability to fly, paragliding and hang-gliding are two excellent options. The Real

Federación Aeronáutica Española can provide information on schools and outfitters across Spain.

When it comes to a real thrill, nothing surpasses skydiving. Reputable companies offering skydiving courses or tandem jumps include **Skydive Lillo** in Madrid and **Skydive Spain** near Seville. Expect a single tandem jump (a jump made while attached to a qualified instructor) to cost between €150 and €200.

WATER SPORTS

Spain is virtually surrounded by water, so it is little surprise that sailing is popular here. The country's most celebrated yacht ports are those of up-scale resorts including Palma de Mallorca and Marbella, and in 2007 the port of Valencia hosted the prestigious America's Cup sailing tournament. Mooring a private yacht or sailboat in a top-notch marina is expensive and often impossible. A much easier alternative is to rent a sailboat by the day or week, or to sign up for a half- or full-day sailing excursion. Most other seaside towns also have small recreational ports offering sailboats and yacht charters which can be rented by providing a sailing licence. For details, contact the **Real Federación Española de Vela**.

Scuba diving is available up and down the coast of Spain and on nearly all the islands. However, the best places for underwater exploration are around the Canary Islands.

Paragliding above the Vall d'Aran in the eastern Pyrenees

Whitewater rafting in the Spanish Pyrenees

Just off the island of El Hierro are the warm, calm waters of the Mar de las Calmas, which is full of colourful coral and dozens of marine species. In the Mediterranean, head to the Balearic Islands or to the Illes Medes, seven tiny islets off the Costa Brava that are home to some of the most diverse marine life in all the Mediterranean. The local Illes Medes information office, **Estació Nàutica**, will provide detailed information about area outfitters.

Surfing and windsurfing are other popular sports. On mainland Spain the best places for either kind of surfing are the Basque coast (especially towns such as Zarautz and Mundaka) and Tarifa, on the Costa de la Luz. In the Canary islands, try Lanzarote or Fuerteventura for surfing and El Médano (Tenerife) for windsurfing. El

Windsurfing off Fuerteventura in the Canary Islands

Médano's **Surf Center Playa Sur** is a useful place to look for rentals and information.

Sea kayaking is becoming very popular and kayak rental is now available in many Mediterranean resort towns. Since rentals are cheap and little prior experience is necessary, kayaking is a great option for boating novices who might want to spend some time out on the water.

ADVENTURE SPORTS

Since Spain is Europe's second-most mountainous country after Switzerland, mountain climbing is a natural sport here. Head to the Aragon Pyrenees or the Catalan Pyrenees for a wide range of challenging rock faces. Other popular spots include the mountain of Montserrat in Catalonia, the Parque Natural de los Cañones y Sierra de Guara in Aragón, the Sierra Nevada in Andalusia and the Picos de Europa in Asturias. For more information, contact the **Federación Española de Deportes de Montaña y Escalada**.

If mere mountain climbing doesn't sound interesting enough, go for *barranquismo* (canyoning), a thrilling adventure sport that lets you explore canyons, cliffs and rivers with a combination of hiking, climbing, rappelling and swimming.

The undisputed capital of canyoning is Parque Natural de la Sierra y los Cañones de Guara, a park and natural area in central Aragón that is

home to dozens of "wet" and "dry" canyons. Outfitters such as **Camping Lecina** provide wetsuits and experienced guides – a must for novices – for €40 per person. Most services and lodging are in, or near, the pretty town of Alquezar.

Another fun way to explore rivers is whitewater rafting. Although Spain is not known for its raging rivers, there are a few places where some white water can be found. Head for the rivers: Noguera Pallaresa in Catalunya, the Carasa in Asturias, or the Miño in Galicia. Late spring and early summer are the best times for rafting, since run-off from melted snow ensures a good deal of water and big rapids.

Fly-fishing in the rivers of Castilla y León, famous for their trout

FISHING

Deep-sea fishing excursions are offered all along Spain's coasts. Fishing in the Mediterranean or the Atlantic is unregulated except for marine reserves and some parks. Trout fishing in lakes and streams is possible; some of the best trout rivers are in Asturias, Rioja and Castilla y León. It is challenging to fish in the narrow, tree-lined streams of the Pyrenees.

It is essential to acquire a seasonal or a daily permit specifying if the fishing area is *sin muerte* (catch and release). Bring your own equipment, as only a few companies offer guided trips. For details on fishing sites and regulations, contact **Federación Española de Pesca y Casting**.

CYCLING

Road biking and mountain biking are both popular in Spain. Helmets are recommended while cycling, especially on highways where extreme caution should be exercised. Drivers here are not accustomed to sharing the road and accidents on highways are not uncommon. The **Real Federación Española de Ciclismo** will provide useful information as well as advice on how to plan a safe cycling excursion.

Mountain bikers will find plenty of trails to keep them busy pedalling in Spain. Several walking paths are also suitable for mountain biking, which are referred to as "BTT" (Bici Todo Terreno or all-terrain bikes). Throughout Catalunya, Centros BTT are set up to inform bikers about trails and conditions. In other regions, where this service is not available, trail information and maps can be found at tourist offices.

For young or inexperienced cyclers, *vias verdes* (rail trails) are a fantastic option. These flat, long-distance trails follow the paths of discontinued rail lines, ideal for those who want lovely views without making an effort. Many *vias verdes* cut through historic towns, making interesting pit stops along the way. The **Fundación de los Ferrocarriles Españoles** has detailed information about routes.

GOLF

Golf is popular throughout Spain, though most courses can be found near the coasts and coastal resort areas. There are too many important golfing areas to highlight just one; the **Real Federación Española de Golf** has detailed information on all the courses. Some of the golf courses offer activities for non-golfers as well. For year-round golf head to the island of Tenerife, where nearly a dozen courses, including the beautifully situated **Golf Las Américas**, are huddled in the southern corner of the island.

SNOW SKIING AND WINTER SPORTS

Spain's mountainous terrain makes it an excellent place for skiing, and resorts here are often cheaper than those in the Alps or other places in Europe. The top ski resorts are the Sierra Nevada in Granada, and the Spanish royal family's favourite skiing spot, Baqueria-Beret, in the Pyrenean Val d'Aran. It is also possible to ski in the Sierra de Guadarrama, just north of Madrid, and in a handful of other high-altitude areas. Details are available through the **Real Federación Española de Deportes de Invierno**.

BIRD-WATCHING

Spain's mild climate attracts a huge variety of fowl year-round. In winter, one can observe birds native to northern Europe; in spring, native Mediterranean species come to nest. There are numerous natural parks working to conserve Spain's diverse bird population. The top bird-watching site is Extremadura's Parque Natural Monfragüe, where big birds of prey can be seen swooping and hunting. Other excellent places to observe birds in their natural habitat are Andalusia's Parque Nacional de Doñana, Guadalquivir Delta and Laguna de Fuente de Piedra, and Delta de l'Ebre in southern Catalonia.

SPAS

Health and wellness spas, or *balnearios*, are nothing new in Spain. As far back as Roman times residents here were enjoying the healthy benefits of mineral-rich waters along the Mediterranean or in the interior. Day spas offering a range of beauty and therepeutic treatments are popular as well, especially in cities and resorts. The **Asociación Nacional de Estaciones Termales** website (National Association of Thermal Resorts) has details on reputable spas throughout the country.

NATURISM

Specially designated nudist, or naturist, beaches are not hard to find in Spain. Contact the various coastal tourist offices for details of nudist beaches. Alternatively, log on to the official website of the **Federación Española de Naturismo (FEN)** (www. naturismo.org), which has a comprehensive list.

SPECIALIST HOLIDAYS

A weekend or week-long specialist holiday provides the luxury of practising a favourite hobby, or probably learning a new one.

Food and wine holidays are more popular than ever in Spain with its varied cuisine and excellent wines. A growing number of companies – many of them owned by expat British – have opened in recent years, offering everything from tours of well-known wine regions to the chance to harvest grapes or olives. For upscale, made-to-order tours of wine regions all over Spain, contact the Madrid-based company **Cellar Tours**. For daily cooking classes and an in-depth look at local Spanish cuisines and customs, try a cooking holiday like those offered by the Priorat-based **Catacurian** or the Granada-based **Alhambra Travel**.

The scenic landscapes of Spain are a wonderful inspiration to indulge the artistic temperament. A painting holiday offers the chance to escape to the quiet countryside and paint. Companies including **Andalucian Adventures** offer multi-day holidays for artists of all levels. Holidays include instruction with an experienced painter as well as practising independently. Sculpture or drawing classes are often available too.

Activity-focused holidays are a great option as well. Spain's pleasant weather is particularly favourable for walking, biking, water skiing or horseback riding. The holiday company **On Foot in Spain** offers a variety of walking holidays in northern Spain, while **Switchbacks Mountain Bike Vacations** has cycling holidays for all levels in Andalusia. For water sports enthusiasts, **Xtreme Gene** specializes in water skiing holidays. Those interested in dance can try **Club Dance**, a London-based company offering dancing holidays. **Fantasia Adventure Holidays** specializes in horseback riding holidays in southern Spain.

To relax, a yoga holiday may be ideal. There are some great alternatives for getting away from the stress of daily life, such as **Kaliyoga** that offers yoga instruction in a pristine setting. A healthy menu and ample free time for hiking or meditating add to the general feel-good factor of a yoga holiday.

A specialist holiday is also a great opportunity to learn Spanish. Language holidays are available in many parts of Spain, where the Spanish language can be learnt in the best way possible – by immersing oneself completely in the country's culture. Language holidays provide the chance to observe the Spanish way of life from close quarters, for an extended period of time. The **Instituto Cervantes** has information on schools and classes across Spain.

DIRECTORY

WALKING AND TREKKING

Environment Ministry of Spain
Pl San Juan de la Cruz, Madrid. **Tel** 915 97 60 00.
www.mma.es

Federación Española de Deportes de Montaña y Escalada
C/ Floridablanca 84, Barcelona.
Tel 934 26 42 67.
www.fedme.es

AIR SPORTS

Glovento Sur
Placeta Nevot 4 1ºA, Granada.
Tel 958 29 03 16.
www.gloventosur.com

Kon-Tiki
Igualada, Barcelona.
Tel 690 83 07 13.
www.globuskontiki.com

Real Federación Aeronáutica Española
Carretera de la Fortuna, Madrid. **Tel** 915 08 29 50.
www.rfae.org

Skydive Lillo
Aeródromo Don Quijote, Lillo, Toledo. **Tel** 902 36 62 09. www.skydivelillo.com

Skydive Spain
Bullullos de la Mitación, Seville. **Tel** 687 72 63 03.
www.skydivespain.com

WATER SPORTS

Estació Náutica
C/ de la Platja 10–12, L'Estartit. **Tel** 972 75 06 99. www. enestartit.com

Real Federación Española de Vela
C/ Luis de Salazar 9, Madrid. **Tel** 915 19 50 08.
www.rfev.es

Surf Center Playa Sur
El Médano, Tenerife.
Tel 922 176 688.
www.surfcenter.info

ADVENTURE SPORTS

Camping Lecina
Lecina, Sierra de Guara.
Tel 974 318 386.
www.campinglecina.com

FISHING

Federación Española de Pesca y Casting
C/ Navas de Tolosa 3, Madrid.
Tel 915 32 83 52.
www.fepyc.es

CYCLING

Fundación de los Ferrocariles Españoles
C/ Santa Isabel 44, Madrid. **Tel** 911 51 10 62.
www.viasverdes.com.

Real Federación Española de Ciclismo
C/ Ferraz 16, 5º, Madrid.
Tel 915 40 08 41.
www.rfec.com

GOLF

Golf Las Américas
Playa de las Américas, Tenerife.
Tel 922 75 20 05.
www.golf-tenerife.com

Real Federación Española de Golf
C/ Provisional Arroyo del Fresno Dos 5, Madrid.
Tel 915 552 682. www. golfspainfederacion.com

SNOW SKIING AND WINTER SPORTS

Real Federación Española de Deportes de Invierno
C/ Madroños 36A, Madrid.
Tel 913 769 930.
www.rfedi.es

SPAS

Asociación Nacional de Estaciones Termales
C/ Rodriguez San Pedro 56, Madrid. **Tel** 902 117 622. www.balnearios.org

NATURISM

Federación Española de Naturismo (FEN)
www.naturismo.org

SPECIALIST HOLIDAYS

Alhambra Travel
C/ San Luis 23, Upper Albaycin, Granada.
Tel 958 20 15 57.
www.alhambratravel.com

Andalucian Adventures
15 Merretts Mill, Woodchester, Glos (UK). **Tel** 00 44 (0) 1453 834 137.
www.andalucian-adventures.co.uk

Catacurian
C/ Progrés 2, El Masroig, Tarragona. **Tel** 977 82 53 41. www.catacurian.com

Cellar Tours
C/ Infantas 27, 3º derecha, Madrid. **Tel** 915 21 39 39.
www.cellartours.com

Club Dance Holidays
108 New Bond Street, London (UK). **Tel** 00 44 (0) 207 099 4816.
www.danceholidays.com

Fantasia Adventure Holidays
C/ Martin Machuca P7–3A, Barbate, Cadiz.
Tel 610 94 36 85. www. fantasiaadventureholidays.com

Instituto Cervantes
C/ Alcalá 49, Madrid.
Tel 914 36 76 00.
www.cervantes.es

Kaliyoga
Las Alpujarras, Granada.
Tel 958 78 44 96 or 647 379 888.
www.kaliyoga.com

On Foot in Spain
Rosalia de Castro 29, Teo, A Coruña.
Tel 686 94 40 62.
www.onfootinspain.com

Switchbacks Mountain Bike Vacations
Barrio La Ermita s/n, Bubion, Granada.
Tel 660 62 33 05.
www.switch-backs.com

Xtreme Gene
C/ Rosario 5, Almodovar del Río, Córdoba.
Tel 957 635 437.
www.xtreme-gene.com

SURVIVAL
GUIDE

PRACTICAL INFORMATION 664–673

TRAVEL INFORMATION 674–683

PRACTICAL INFORMATION

Spain has finally begun to market itself beyond the attractions of its coastline, and now has a solid tourist information infrastructure. There are national tourist offices in every large city, and regional offices in the smaller towns. All offer help with finding accommodation, restaurants and activities in their area. August is Spain's main holiday month.

Old street signs

Many businesses close for the whole month and roads are very busy at the beginning and end of this period. At any time of year, try to find out in advance if your visit coincides with local fiestas, because although these are attractions, they often entail widespread closures. It is a good idea to plan leisurely lunches, as most of Spain stops from 2pm to 5pm.

ERRESERBATUA

BIZKAIKO FORU ALDUNDIA

RESERVADO

DIPUTACION FORAL DE BIZKAIA

A bilingual Basque/Castilian reserved parking sign

LANGUAGE

The main language of Spain, *Castellano* (Castilian), is spoken by almost everyone. There are three main regional languages: Catalan, spoken in Catalonia, *Gallego* (Galician) in Galicia and *Euskera* (Basque) in the Basque Country. Variants of Catalan are spoken in the Valencia region and also in the Balearic Islands.

People who speak English are often employed in places that deal with tourists.

MANNERS

The Spanish greet and say goodbye to strangers at bus stops and in lifts, shops and other public places. They often talk to people they do not know. Men shake hands when introduced and whenever they meet. Women usually kiss on both cheeks when they meet, and friends and family members may kiss or embrace briefly.

VISAS AND PASSPORTS

Visas are not required for citizens of EU countries, Iceland, Norway or Switzerland.

A list of entry requirements, which is available from Spanish embassies, specifies 44 other countries, including New Zealand, Canada, the USA and Australia, whose nationals do not need to apply for a visa if visiting Spain for less than 90 days. Thereafter they may apply to the *Gobierno Civil* (a local government office) for an extension. You need proof of employment or of sufficient funds to support yourself during a long stay. Visitors from other countries must obtain a visa before travelling.

If you intend to stay for a long time in Spain, you should contact your nearest Spanish embassy several months in advance about your needs.

British visitors should note that a Visitor's Passport is no longer available. A full passport must be obtained.

TAX-FREE GOODS AND CUSTOMS INFORMATION

Non-EU residents can reclaim *IVA* (VAT) on single items worth over 90 euros bought in shops displaying a "Tax-free for Tourists" sign. (Food, drink, tobacco, cars, motorbikes and medicines are exempt.) You pay the full price and ask the sales assistant for a *formulario* (tax exemption form). On leaving Spain, you

ask customs to stamp your *formulario* (this must be within six months of the purchase). You receive the refund by mail or on your credit card account.

Banco Exterior branches at Barcelona, Madrid, Málaga, Mallorca, Oviedo, Santander and Seville airports will give refunds on *formularios* stamped by customs.

TOURIST INFORMATION

All major cities and towns have *oficinas de turismo*. They will provide town plans, lists of hotels and restaurants, information about the locality and details of activities and events for tourists.

There is a **Spanish National Tourist Office** in several large cities abroad.

OPENING HOURS

Most monuments and museums close on Mondays. On other days they generally open from 10am to 2pm, close from 2pm to 5pm, and in some cases, reopen from 5pm to 8pm. Churches may follow these hours or only be opened for services. Admission is charged for most museums and monuments. Public museums are free on Sundays. In smaller towns it is common for churches, castles and other sights to be kept locked. The key, available to visitors on request, will be lodged with a caretaker in a neighbouring house, in the town hall, or perhaps at the local bar.

 OFICINA DE TURISMO *i*

Spanish tourist office sign with distinctive " i " logo

◁ The old town of Ibiza enclosed by its 16th-century walls, seen from the harbour

Students enjoy reduced admission fees to many museums and galleries

FACILITIES FOR THE DISABLED

Spain's national association for the disabled, the Confederación Coordinadora Estatal de Minusválidos Físicos de España (COCEMFE), publishes guides to facilities in Spain and will help plan a holiday to individual needs *(see p557)*. Tourist offices and the social services departments of town halls can provide information on local conditions and facilities. A travel agency, **Viajes 2000**, specializes in holidays for disabled people. Holiday Care Service in the UK (www.holidaycare.org.uk) offers limited information on facilities for the disabled in Spanish resorts, as does SATH in the USA *(see p557)*.

COCEMFE sign
disabled access

SPANISH TIME

In winter, Spain is one hour ahead of Greenwich Mean Time (GMT) and in summer an hour ahead of British Summer Time (BST). The Canary Islands are on GMT in winter and an hour ahead in summer. Spain uses the 24-hour clock, so 1pm = 13:00.

La madrugada is the small hours. *Mañana* (morning) lasts until the Spanish lunch time at about 2pm and *mediodía* (midday) from about 1–4pm. *La tarde* is the afternoon and *a noche* evening.

STUDENT INFORMATION

Holders of the International Student Identity Card (ISIC) are entitled to benefits, such as discounts on travel and reduced entrance charges to museums and galleries. Information is available from all national student organizations and, in Spain, from the local government-run **Centros de Información Juvenil (CIJ)** in large towns. **Turismo y Viajes Educativos (TIVE)** specializes in student travel.

ELECTRICAL ADAPTORS

Spain's electricity supply is 220 volts, but the 125-volt system still operates in some old buildings. Plugs for both have two round pins. A three-tier standard travel converter enables you to use appliances from abroad on both supplies. Heating appliances should be used only on 220 volts.

CONVERSION CHART

Imperial to metric
1 inch = 2.54 centimetres
1 foot = 30 centimetres
1 mile = 1.6 kilometres
1 ounce = 28 grams
1 pound = 454 grams
1 pint = 0.6 litre
1 gallon = 4.6 litres

Metric to imperial
1 millimetre = 0.04 inch
1 centimetre = 0.4 inch
1 metre = 3 feet 3 inches
1 kilometre = 0.6 mile
1 gram = 0.04 ounce
1 kilogram = 2.2 pounds
1 litre = 1.8 pints

DIRECTORY

EMBASSIES

United Kingdom
Paseo Recoletos 7 & 9,
28004 Madrid.
Tel 91 524 97 00.
www.ukinspain.com

United States
Calle Serrano 75, 28006 Madrid.
Tel 91 587 22 00.
www.embusa.es

SPANISH TOURIST OFFICES

Australia (consulate)
Level 24, St Martin's Tower, 31 Market St, Sydney NSW 2000.
Tel 29 261 2433.

Barcelona
Palau Robert, Paseo de Gràcia 107,
08008 Barcelona.
Tel 93 238 40 00.

Madrid
Calle Duque de Medinaceli 2,
28014 Madrid.
Tel 91 429 49 51.

Seville
Avenida de la Constitución 21b,
41004 Seville.
Tel 95 478 75 78.
www.andalucia.org

United Kingdom
79 New Cavendish Street,
London W1W 6XB.
Tel 020 7486 8077.
www.tourspain.co.uk

United States
666 Fifth Ave, 35th floor,
New York NY 10103.
Tel (212) 265 8822.
www.okspain.org

DISABLED

Viajes 2000
Paseo de la Castellana 228–230,
28046 Madrid.
Tel 91 323 10 29.
www.viajes2000.com

YOUTH/STUDENT

CIJ
Gran Via 10, 28013 Madrid.
Tel 901 510 610.
www.madrid.org/inforjoven

TIVE
Calle Fernando el Católico 88,
28015 Madrid.
Tel 91 543 74 12.
www.madrid.org/inforjoven

Personal Security and Health

In Spain, as in most European countries, rural areas are generally safe, but certain parts of cities are subject to petty crime. Carry cards and money in a belt and never leave anything visible in your car when you park it.

Taking out medical insurance cover is advisable, but for minor health problems pharmacists are a good source of assistance. Emergency phone numbers vary – the most important ones are on the opposite page. If you lose your documents, contact your consulate or the local police.

Spanish pharmacy sign

IN AN EMERGENCY

Only the *Policía Nacional* operate a nationwide emergency phone number. Call it even if you need some other service and they will assist you in getting help. Telephone directories list local emergency numbers under *Servicios de Urgencia,* and they appear on tourist maps and leaflets.

For emergency medical treatment call the Cruz Roja (Red Cross), look under *Ambulancias* in the phone book, or go to a hospital casualty department *(Urgencias).*

exactly what health care you are entitled to and where and how to claim. You may find you have to pay and reclaim the money later.

Not all treatments are covered by the card and some are costly, so arrange for medical cover before travelling.

If you want private medical care in Spain, ask at a tourist

Urgencias

Sign identifying a Cruz Roja (Red Cross) emergency treatment centre

MEDICAL TREATMENT

All EU nationals are entitled to Spanish social security cover. To claim, you must obtain the European Health Insurance Card from the UK Department of Health or from a post office before you travel. You give this card to anyone who treats you and it comes with a booklet, *Health Advice for Travellers,* which explains

office, or at your embassy or hotel for the name and number of a doctor. If necessary, ask for one who speaks English.

PHARMACIES

Spanish pharmacists have wide responsibilities. They can advise and, in some cases, prescribe without consulting a doctor. In a non-emergency a *farmacéutico* is a good

person to see first. It is easy to find one who speaks English.

The *farmacia* sign is a green or red illuminated cross. Those open at night in a town are listed in the windows of all the local pharmacies. Do not confuse them with *perfumerías,* which sell toiletries only.

PERSONAL SECURITY

Violent crime is rare in Spain but visitors should avoid walking alone in poorly lit areas. Wear a bag or camera across your body, not on your shoulder. Men occasionally make complimentary remarks *(piropos)* to women in public, particularly in the street. This is an old custom and not intended to be intimidating.

SPANISH POLICE

There are essentially three types of police in Spain. The *Guardia Civil* (National Guard) mainly police rural areas. Their uniform is olive green but there are local and regional variations. They impose fines for traffic offences.

The *Policía Nacional,* who wear a blue uniform, operate in towns with a population of more than 30,000. The *Policía Nacional* have been replaced with a regional force, the *Ertzaintza,* in the Basque country, and with the *Mossos d'Esquadra* in Catalonia. These can be distinguished by their respective red and blue berets.

The *Policía Local,* also called *Policía Municipal* or *Guardia Urbana,* dress in blue. They operate independently in each town and also have a separate branch for city traffic control.

All three services will direct you to the relevant authority in the event of an incident requiring police help.

Guardia Civil

Policía Nacional

Policía Local

DIRECTORY

EMERGENCY NUMBERS

Emergency: all services
Tel 112 (in most important cities).

Policía
Tel 091 Nacional (nationwide).

**Fire Brigade
(Bomberos)**
Tel 080 (in most major cities).

**Ambulance:
(Red Cross, Cruz Roja)**
*Tel 112 or 91 522 22 22. (This
Madrid number is now the nat-
ional number for the Red Cross).*

*For other cities' emergency services,
consult the local phone directory.*

Patrol car of the Policía Nacional, Spain's main urban police force

Policía Local patrol car, mainly seen in small towns

Cruz Roja (Red Cross) ambulance

The emergency number on the side of fire engines varies regionally

LEGAL ASSISTANCE

Some insurance policies
cover legal costs, for instance
after an accident. If you are
not covered, telephone your
nearest consulate.

   You can also contact the
Colegio de Abogados (lawyers'
association) of the nearest
town or city, which can advise
you where to obtain legal advice or representation locally.

   If you need an interpreter,
consult the *Páginas Amarillas
(Yellow Pages)* telephone directory for the region under
Traductores or *Intérpretes.*
Both *Traductores Oficiales*
and *Traductores Jurados* are
qualified to translate legal or
official documents.

PERSONAL PROPERTY

Holiday insurance is there
to protect you financially
from the loss or theft of your
property, but it is always best
to take obvious precautions
against loss and theft.

   If you have to carry large
sums of money with you, take
traveller's cheques and, if you
have two credit cards, do not
carry them together. Never
leave a bag or handbag un-
attended anywhere and do
not put down a purse or handbag on the tabletop in a café.
Take particular care at markets,
tourist sights and stations.

   The moment you discover a
loss or theft, report it to the
local police station. To claim
insurance you must do this
immediately, as many com-

panies give you 24 hours only.
Ask for a *denuncia* (written
statement), which you need to
make a claim. If your passport
is stolen, or if you lose it,
report it to your consulate.

PUBLIC CONVENIENCES

Public pay-toilets are rare in
Spain. Department stores are
good places to try, as are bars
and restaurants where you are
a customer. On motorways,
there are toilets at service
stations. You may have to ask
for a key (*la llave*), not only
at the service stations but also
in some bars in country areas.
It is best to bring your own
tissues. The term generally
used for toilets is *los servicios.*

OUTDOOR HAZARDS

Spain is prey every summer
to forest fires fanned by
winds and fuelled by bone-
dry vegetation. Be sensitive to
fire hazards and use car ash-
trays. Broken glass can start a
fire so be careful to take your
empty bottles away with you.

   The sign *coto de caza* in
woodland areas identifies a
hunting reserve where you
must follow the country codes.
Toro bravo means "fighting
bull" – do not approach. A
camino particular sign indicates a private driveway.

   If you are climbing or hill-
walking go properly equipped
and let someone know when
you expect to return.

Banking and Local Currency

You may enter Spain with any amount of money, but if you intend to export more than 6,000 euros, you should declare it. Traveller's cheques may be exchanged at banks, *cajas de cambio* (foreign currency exchanges), some hotels and some shops. Banks generally offer the best exchange rates. The cheapest exchange may be offered on your credit or direct debit card, which you can use in cash dispensers (automated teller machines, ATMs) displaying the appropriate sign.

24-hour cash dispenser

BANKING HOURS

Spanish banks are beginning to extend their opening hours, but expect extended hours only at large central branches in the big cities.

Generally, banks are open from 8am to 2pm during the week. Some open until 1pm on Saturdays. Most close on Saturdays in August; in some areas they also close on Saturdays from May to September.

CHANGING MONEY

BBVA

Logo for BBVA, the Banco Bilbao Vizcaya Argentaria

Most banks have a foreign exchange desk with the sign *Cambio* or *Extranjero*, which will accept traveller's cheques and cash. Always take your passport as identification to effect any transaction.

You can draw up to €300 on major credit cards at a bank. If you bank with **Barclays** or **Lloyds TSB**, it is possible to cash a cheque in the usual way at one of their branches in Spain.

Bureaux de change, with the sign *Caja de Cambio* or "Change", may state that they charge no commission but their exchange rates are invariably worse than those found at banks. One benefit is that they are often open outside normal banking hours. They are usually located throughout the major cities and at many popular tourist areas. They can also usually be found at airports and mainline rail stations. *Cajas de Ahorro* (savings banks) also exchange money. They open from 8:30am to 2pm on weekdays and also on Thursday afternoons from 4:30pm to 7:45pm.

CHEQUES AND CARDS

Traveller's cheques can be purchased at **American Express** (AmEx), **Travelex** or your bank. All are accepted in Spain. If you exchange AmEx cheques at an AmEx office, commission is not charged.

Banks require 24 hours' notice to cash cheques larger than €3,000. If you draw more than €600 on traveller's cheques, you may be asked to show the purchase certificate as proof.

The most widely accepted card in Spain is the **VISA** card, although **MasterCard** (Access)/ Eurocard and American Express are also useful currency. The major banks will allow cash withdrawals on credit cards. All cash dispensers accept most foreign cards, and will often give you a choice of several languages, including English. However, the level of commission charged on your withdrawal will depend on your own bank, and some credit cards may charge an additional fee.

When you pay with a card, cashiers will usually pass it through a card-reading machine. In shops you will always be asked for additional photo ID. As leaving your passport in the hotel safe is preferable, make sure you have an alternative original document on hand (photocopies will rarely do) such as a driver's licence.

As is common throughout Europe, cards are not always accepted in some smaller bars and restaurants. Checking first will avoid unnecessary embarrassment.

CASH DISPENSERS

If your card is linked to your home bank account, you can use it with your PIN to withdraw money from cash dispensers. Nearly all take VISA or Mastercard (Access).

When you enter your PIN, instructions are displayed in English, French, German and Spanish. These days, many dispensers are inside buildings and to gain access you will have to run your card through a door-entry system.

Cards with Cirrus and Maestro logos can also be widely used to withdraw money from cash machines.

DIRECTORY

FOREIGN BANKS

Barclays Bank
Plaza de Colón 1, 28046 Madrid.
Tel 91 336 10 00.

Citibank
C/ Velázquez 31, 28001 Madrid.
Tel 91 426 07 82.

LOST CARDS AND TRAVELLER'S CHEQUES

American Express
Tel 902 37 56 37.

Diners Club
Tel 901 10 10 11.

MasterCard
Tel 900 97 12 31 (toll free).

Travelex
Tel 900 94 89 71 (toll free).

VISA
Tel 900 99 12 16 (toll free).

THE EURO

Introduction of the single European currency, the euro, has taken place in 16 of the 27 member states of the EU. Austria, Belgium, Finland, Cyprus, France, Germany, Slovakia, Greece, Ireland, Italy, Malta, Luxembourg, The Netherlands, Portugal, Slovenia, and Spain have adopted the new currency; the UK, Denmark and Sweden stayed out, with an option to review the decision. Euro banknotes and coins came into circulation on 1 January 2002. After a transition period allowing the use of both national currencies and the euro, Spain's own currency, the peseta, was completely phased out by March 2002. All euro banknotes and coins can be used anywhere within the participating member states.

Banknotes

Euro banknotes, each a different colour and size, have seven denominations. The 5-euro note (grey in colour) is the smallest, followed by the 10-euro note (pink), 20-euro note (blue), 50-euro note (orange), 100-euro note (green), 200-euro note (yellow) and 500-euro note (purple).

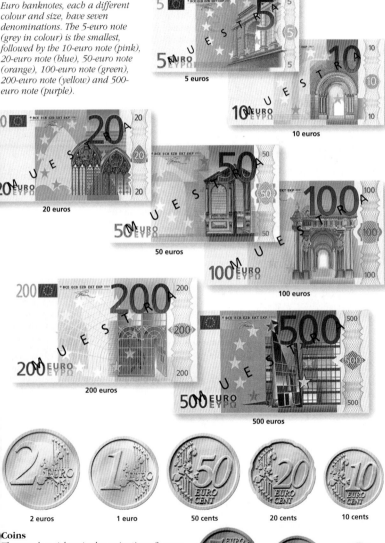

5 euros

10 euros

20 euros

50 euros

100 euros

200 euros

500 euros

2 euros

1 euro

50 cents

20 cents

10 cents

Coins

The euro has eight coin denominations: 2 euros and 1 euro (silver and gold); 50 cents, 20 cents and 10 cents (gold); and 5 cents, 2 cents and 1 cent (bronze). The reverse (number) side of euros are the same in all euro-zone countries, but the front is different in each state.

5 cents

2 cents

1 cent

Communications

Telefónica, the Spanish telecommunications company, has improved its service since it was digitized in 1995, and the state monopoly was removed in 1998. Public telephones are easy to find, but most now operate with a card not coins. International calls have a high charge.

The postal service, Correos, is identified by a crown insignia in blue on a yellow background. Registered post and telegrams can be sent from all Correos offices *(see pp672–3)* . They sell stamps as well, but most people buy them from *estancos* (tobacconists). There are no public phones in Correos offices.

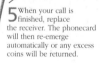

Logo of the Spanish telecom system

TELEPHONING IN SPAIN

As well as public telephone boxes (*cabinas*), there are nearly always payphones in Spanish bars. Very few now take coins. Phonecards are far more convenient and can be bought at newsstands and *estancos*. Generally, there will be a high minimum connection charge, especially for international calls, so make sure that you have plenty of units on your card. Some phones are equipped with multilingual electronic instruction displays.

There are public telephone offices called *locutorios* where you can make a call and pay for it afterwards. They are usually quieter and cheaper than phone booths and you do not need a phonecard. Telefónica run the official ones, which are the cheapest type; private ones, often located in shops, are more expensive.

There are four charge bands for international calls, which are: European Union countries; non-European Union countries and Northwest Africa; North and South America; and the rest of the world. With the exception

USING A PUBLIC TELEPHONE

1 Lift the receiver, and wait for the dialling tone and for the display to show *Inserte monedas o tarjeta*.

2 Insert a card *(tarjeta)*. Or if coins are still accepted, insert, using the button on the top right if there is one.

3 Key in the number firmly, but not too fast – Spanish phones require a pause between each digit.

4 As you press the digits, the number you are dialling will appear on the display. You will also be able to see how much money or how many units are left. The display will indicate when you need to deposit more coins.

5 When your call is finished, replace the receiver. The phonecard will then re-emerge automatically or any excess coins will be returned.

Spanish phonecard

USEFUL SPANISH DIALLING CODES

- When calling within a city, within a province, or to call another province, dial the entire number. The province is indicated by the initial digits: Barcelona numbers, for example, start with 93, Girona with 972 and Tarragona 977.
- To make an international call, dial 00, then dial the country code, the area code and the number.
- Country codes are: UK 44; Eire 353; France 33; USA and Canada 1; Australia 61; New Zealand 64. It may be necessary to omit the initial digit of the destination's area code.

- For operator/directory service, dial 11818.
- For international directories, dial 11825.
- To make a reversed-charge (collect) call within the EU, dial 900 99 00 followed by the country code; to the USA or Canada, dial 900 99 00 followed by 11 or 15 respectively. Numbers for other countries can be found in the front of the A-K telephone directory under *Modalidades del Servicio Internacional*.
- To report technical faults, dial 1002.
- For the speaking clock dial 093, for a wake-up dial 096.

of local calls, using the telephone system can be expensive, especially when making calls from a hotel, which may add a surcharge. A call from a *cabina* costs 35 per cent more than one made from a private phone in someone's home. Reverse-charge (collect) calls made to European Union countries may be dialled directly, but most other reverse-charge calls must be made through the operator.

Spain abolished provincial area codes in 1998, so the full number, including the initial 9, must always be dialled even from within the area.

When calling Spain from abroad, first dial the international code for Spain (34) followed by the area code. So, to call Barcelona, you dial 34 93.

Public payphone booth, easily visible in a city street

TELEVISION AND RADIO

Televisión Española, Spain's state television company, broadcasts two channels, which are called TVE1 and TVE2.

Several of the *comunidades* (see pp672–3) have their own publicly owned television channels, which broadcast in the language of the region.

There are two national independent television stations: Antena 3 and Tele-5 (Teleinco). New channels La Sexta and Cuatro are also free of

Daily papers report Spanish news

charge. Several digital channels are available on payment of a subscription for a decoder.

Most foreign films shown on Spanish television (and in cinemas) are dubbed and subtitled films are listed as *V.O. (versión original).*

Several satellite channels, such as CNN, Eurosport and Cinemanía, can be received throughout Spain.

The state radio station, Radio Nacional de España has four stations plus the World Service. News programmes are on R1, classical music on R2, pop music on R3 and news on R5. Local stations also rebroadcast the BBC World Service. They are: Onda Cero Radio in Marbella and Tenerife; Radio Maspalomas in Gran Canaria; and Sunshine Capital Radio in Palma de Mallorca.

NEWSPAPERS AND MAGAZINES

Newsagents and kiosks in town centres often stock periodicals in English. The newspapers available on publication day are the *International Herald Tribune,* the *Financial Times* and the *Guardian International.* Other English-language and European titles are on sale, but usually not until a day after they have been published.

The European newspaper and popular

Logo of Radio Nacional de España

weekly news magazines such as *Time, Newsweek* and *The Economist* are readily available throughout the country. The most widely read of the Spanish newspapers, in descending number of sales, are *El País, El Mundo, ABC, La Razon,* and *La Vanguardia* (in Catalonia). *El Mundo* is feature led and aimed at a younger market than the other three, which cover international news in more depth. Several free newspapers are distributed in all of the big cities as well as in some larger towns. *Metro, Qué* and *20 Minutos,* for example, are usually found on or near public transport.

Weekly listings magazines for arts and events are published in Barcelona *(see p190),* Madrid *(see p320)* and Seville. They are the *Guía del Ocio* in Barcelona and *El Giraldillo* in Seville. Several other cities also have listings magazines. Local newspapers in Spanish, such as *Levante* in Valencia and *La Gaceta de Canarias* in the Canary Islands, are a useful source of information on local and regional events.

Foreign-language periodicals are published by expatriates in Madrid and in the country's main tourist areas. Examples in English include *Sur* on the Costa del Sol, the *Costa Blanca News* and the *Mallorca Daily Bulletin.* One of the longest-running magazines is *Lookout.* Published in Fuengirola, it features in-depth reports covering all aspects of life in Spain.

A *prensa* (press) sign identifies a newsstand

POSTAL SERVICE

Correos is the name of Spain's postal service. Mail sent to an address in the city where it is posted usually takes a day to arrive. Deliveries between cities take between two to three days. Urgent or important post can be sent by *urgente* (express) or *certificado* (registered) mail. To be sure of fast delivery it is wise to use the Correos Postal Express Service or a private courier.

Shops with this sign sell stamps

Post can be registered and telegrams sent from all Correos offices. However, it is much easier to buy stamps for letters and postcards from an *estanco* (tobacconist). Postal rates fall into three price bands: Spain; Europe and North Africa; the rest of the world. Parcels have to be weighed and stamped at Correos offices and must be securely tied with string.

The main Correos offices open 8:30am–9:30pm from Monday to Friday and 9:30am–1pm on Saturday. Branches in the suburbs and small towns and villages open 8:30am–8:30pm from Monday to Friday and 9:30am–1pm on Saturday.

Spanish stamps

ADDRESSES

In Spanish addresses the house number follows the name of the street. The floor of a block of flats comes after a hyphen. Therefore 4-2° means a flat on the second floor of number four. All postcodes have five digits, the first two being the province number.

SPAIN'S LOTTERIES

Lottery fever is greater in Spain than in any other European country. The Lotería Nacional runs prize draws most Saturdays, plus a few special ones, the *extraordinarios*, of which the biggest is El Gordo ("the Fat One") at Christmas *(see p43)* . It is common to buy a *décimo* (one-tenth of a number), rather than a full ticket. Punters can also try their luck with the ONCE lottery, which has draws daily, the twice-weekly Lotería Primitiva, and the Bono-loto, with four draws a week.

ONCE lottery booth

LETTERS AND FAXES

Letters posted at a central post office usually arrive more quickly than if posted in a postbox *(buzón)*. Postboxes in cities are yellow pillar boxes; in towns and villages they are small, wall-mounted postboxes. Poste restante letters should be addressed care of the *Lista de Correos* and the town. You can collect them from main offices. To send and receive money by post ask for a *giro internacional*.

When dealing with businesses in Spain, it is best to phone or fax. The post tends to be used only as a last resort. There are fax facilities in some *locutorios (see p670)* and in hotels and many private shops. Look for a *telefax* sign.

Spanish postbox

LOCAL GOVERNMENT

Spain is one of Europe's most decentralized states. Many powers have been devolved to the 17 regions, *comunidades autónomas,* which have their own elected parliaments. These regions have varying degrees of independence from Madrid, with the Basques and Catalans enjoying the most autonomy. The *comunidades* provide some services – such as the promotion of tourism – which were once carried out by central government.

The country is subdivided into 50 provinces, each with its *diputación* (council). The affairs of each of the Balearic and Canary islands are run by an island council.

Every town, or group of villages, is administered by an *ayuntamiento* (town council – the word also means town hall) which is supervised by an elected *alcalde* (mayor) and a team of councillors.

Murcia's town hall *(ayuntamiento or casa consistorial)*

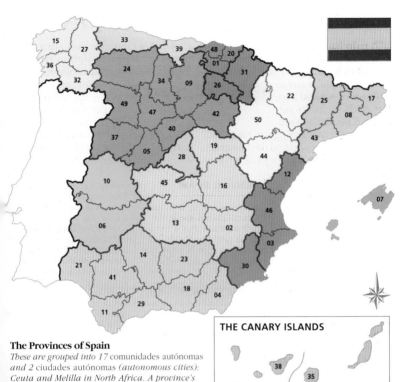

The Provinces of Spain

These are grouped into 17 comunidades autónomas and 2 ciudades autónomas (autonomous cities): Ceuta and Melilla in North Africa. A province's number is used as the first two digits of its postcode.

THE CANARY ISLANDS

THE COMUNIDADES OF SPAIN AND THEIR PROVINCES

NORTHERN SPAIN

Galicia
15 A Coruña
27 Lugo
32 Ourense
36 Pontevedra

Asturias   **Cantabria**
33 Asturias
39 Cantabria

Basque   **Navarra**   **La Rioja**
Country
Basque Country (Euskadi)
01 Álava
20 Guipúzcoa
48 Vizcaya
Comunidad Foral de Navarra
31 Navarra
La Rioja
26 La Rioja

EASTERN SPAIN

Catalonia
08 Barcelona
17 Girona
25 Lleida
43 Tarragona

Aragón
22 Huesca
44 Teruel
50 Zaragoza

Valencia   **Murcia**
Comunidad Valenciana
03 Alicante
12 Castellón
46 Valencia
Murcia
30 Murcia

CENTRAL SPAIN

Madrid
28 Comunidad de Madrid

Castilla-La Mancha
02 Albacete
13 Ciudad Real
16 Cuenca
19 Guadalajara
45 Toledo

Extremadura
06 Badajoz
10 Cáceres

Castilla y León
05 Ávila
09 Burgos
24 León
34 Palencia
37 Salamanca
40 Segovia
42 Soria
47 Valladolid
49 Zamora

SOUTHERN SPAIN

Andalusia
04 Almería
11 Cádiz
14 Córdoba
18 Granada
21 Huelva
23 Jaén
29 Málaga
41 Sevilla

SPAIN'S ISLANDS

The Balearic Islands (Islas Baleares)
07 Baleares

The Canary Islands (Islas Canarias)
35 Las Palmas
38 Santa Cruz de Tenerife

TRAVEL INFORMATION

Spain has an increasingly efficient transport system. All the major cities have airports and flights from all over the globe arrive at those of Madrid and Barcelona. Both the road and rail networks were greatly improved during the 1980s and in the run-up to Expo and the Olympics in 1992 *(see p69)*. Intercity rail services are efficient, but coaches are a faster and more frequent option between smaller towns. In much of rural Spain, however, public transport is limited and a car is the most practical solution for getting about. Ferries connect mainland Spain with the UK, North Africa and the Balearic and Canary islands.

Sign for an airport

ARRIVING BY AIR

Spain is served by most international airlines. **Iberia**, the national airline, has scheduled flights daily into Madrid and Barcelona from all west European capitals, and once or twice weekly from most east European capitals.

British Airways offers flights to Madrid and Barcelona daily from Heathrow and Gatwick. Many budget airlines, such as **easyJet, Bmibaby, Ryanair,** Clickair, Jetz and Flyglobespan fly to mainland and island Spain from airports throughout the UK.

US airlines **Delta Airlines** and Continental both fly direct to Madrid and Barcelona. **American Airlines** flies direct to Barcelona, and also offers a non-direct flight to Madrid. Iberia has a comprehensive service from the USA. Its flights from Toronto and Montreal to Spain involve a change in the USA or London.

Shopping at Barcelona's El Prat airport

BARAJAS AIRPORT, MADRID

Madrid-Barajas' airport is 13 km (8 miles) from the city centre. The airport has rearranged the distribution of airlines among its four terminals, which are all connected by a shuttle bus. Iberia, British Airways and American Airlines are in Terminal 4. Most of the low-cost airlines plus Delta and Continental are in Terminal 1. It only takes 12 minutes by metro to reach the central station of Neuvos Ministerios from Terminals 2 or 4, where numerous airlines have set up check-in facilities. Taxis are also widely available and a shuttle bus runs every 10 minutes to the city centre.

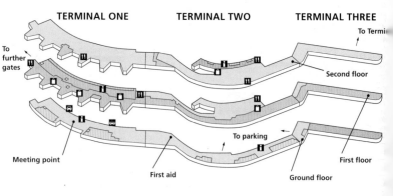

TERMINAL ONE　　**TERMINAL TWO**　　**TERMINAL THREE**

To Termi

To further gates

Second floor

To parking

Meeting point

First aid

First floor

Ground floor

KEY

Departures	Passport control/Customs	No public access
Arrivals	Public access	Restricted access
Check-in	Ticket sales	

INTERNATIONAL AIRPORTS

The most regular international services operate from Madrid and Barcelona. The busiest international airports for scheduled and charter flights in Spain are marked on the map on pages 14–15.

Palma de Mallorca, Tenerife Sur, Las Palmas de Gran Canaria, Málaga, Lanzarote, Ibiza, Alicante, Fuerteventura and Menorca handle large amounts of holiday traffic. The first four are especially busy – Palma topped 23 million passengers in 2007. Most is seasonal traffic, mainly from north European countries, and at peak summer holiday time these airports can get crowded. Details of public transport to and from Spain's most important airports are given on page 676.

All the Balearic and Canary islands have international air ports, except Hierro and La Gomera which have domestic

Iberia plane on the tarmac of Seville airport

ones. Melilla and Ceuta are also served by domestic flights only.

AIR FARES

Air fares for flights to Spain vary through the year, depending on demand. They are generally highest during the summer months. Special deals, particularly for weekend city breaks, are often offered in the winter and may include a number of nights at a hotel. Look out for Iberia's reduced air fares, and for **easyJet**,

Bmibaby, **Ryanair**, Jetz, Flyglobespan and Clickair for competitive deals. Christmas and Easter flights are often booked up well in advance.

Charter flights from the UK serve airports such as Alicante, Málaga and Girona near beach resorts. These can be very cheap, but less reliable, and often fly at unsociable hours. Make sure your agent is ABTA bonded before booking. Local car hire companies may offer good deals at resort airports, but read rental terms carefully.

EL PRAT AIRPORT, BARCELONA

Barcelona's airport is 12 km (7 miles) from the city centre. Terminal A handles international arrivals and foreign airlines' departures. Terminals B and C are for departures on Spanish airlines and arrivals from European Union countries. Trains to the Passeig de Gràcia and Estació de Franca leave every 30 minutes. For intercity rail services get off at Sants mainline station. There is also a shuttle bus, the Aerobús, running every 6 minutes, which will leave you in Plaça de Catalunya.

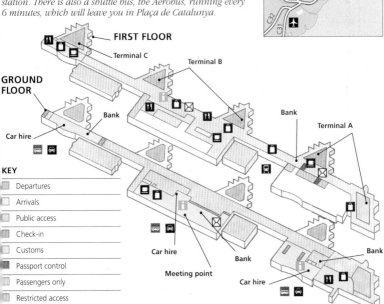

FIRST FLOOR
Terminal C
Terminal B
GROUND FLOOR
Bank
Bank
Terminal A
Car hire
Car hire
Bank
Meeting point
Bank
Car hire
Bank

KEY

- Departures
- Arrivals
- Public access
- Check-in
- Customs
- Passport control
- Passengers only
- Restricted access

Insignia of Spain's national airline

DOMESTIC FLIGHTS

Most of Spain's domestic flights have traditionally been operated by **Iberia**. In recent years, this monopoly has been broken. The main alternative carriers include **Air Europa**, **Spanair**, **Vueling** and **Clickair**.

The most frequent shuttle service is the Puente Aéreo, run between Barcelona and Madrid by Iberia. It flies every 15 minutes at peak business times, and half-hourly or hourly at other times. A self-check-in machine helps speed up the checking-in process. When a flight is full, waiting passengers are always offered a seat on the next available shuttle. The flight usually takes 50 minutes.

Air-Nostrum, Air Europa and Spanair services between Madrid and the regional capitals are not as frequent as the Puente Aéreo, but their prices are usually slightly lower. They operate in a similar way to Apex tickets:

the earlier the booking is made, the greater the discount. The cheapest ticket, which must be booked a week in advance, can save up to one-third of the full price. Flights to the provincial cities usually operate in the morning and evening. They can be expensive, costing as much as €120 for a one-way trip. Pressure from the intercity rail services may eventually result in lower air fares.

Self-ticketing machine

Flights to the Canary islands, and island-hopping flights between them, are operated by an Iberia-affiliated company: **Binter**. Travel agencies often offer a variety of special deals on internal flights, which may include one night or more in a hotel. It is worth shopping around. These deals are advertised in the Spanish press. Some flights from domestic airports are billed as international flights but they do not go directly to foreign destinations. Instead, they stop en route at major cities like Madrid or Barcelona.

The departures concourse in Seville Airport

AIRPORT	INFORMATION	DISTANCE TO CITY CENTRE	TAXI FARE TO CITY CENTRE	PUBLIC TRANSPORT TIME TO CITY CENTRE
Alicante	902 40 47 04	10 km (6 miles)	14 euros	Bus: 20 mins
Barcelona	902 40 47 04	14 km (9 miles)	22 euros	Rail: 25 mins Bus: 25 mins
Bilbao	902 40 47 04	12 km (7 miles)	20 euros	Bus: 30 mins
Madrid	902 40 47 04	16 km (10 miles)	25 euros	Bus: 20 mins Metro: 30–40 mins
Málaga	902 40 47 04	8 km (5 miles)	17 euros	Rail: 15 mins Bus: 20 mins
Palma de Mallorca	902 40 47 04	9 km (6 miles)	18–20 euros	Bus: 15 mins
Las Palmas de Gran Canaria	902 40 47 04	18 km (11 miles)	24 euros	Bus: 60 mins
Santiago de Compostela	902 40 47 04	10 km (6 miles)	18 euros	Bus: 20–30 mins
Seville	902 40 47 04	10 km (6 miles)	17–20 euros	Bus: 25–30 mins
Tenerife Sur – Reina Sofía	902 40 47 04	64 km (40 miles) to Santa Cruz	52 euros	Bus: 60 mins
Valencia	902 40 47 04	9 km (5 miles)	15–20 euros	Bus: 20 or 60 mins

ARRIVING BY SEA

Ferries connect the Spanish mainland to the Balearic and Canary islands, to North Africa and to the UK. All the important routes are served by car ferries. It is always wise to make an advance booking, especially in summer.

Two routes link Spain with the UK. **Brittany Ferries** sails between Plymouth in the UK and Santander in Cantabria; and **P&O European Ferries** sails from Portsmouth into Santurce harbour, near Bilbao in the Basque Country. The crossings take over 24 hours. Each ship has cabins, chairs to sleep on, restaurants, cafés and cinemas. Discos are sometimes held on board.

Ferry in port at Los Cristianos (Tenerife) in the Canary Islands

FERRIES TO THE ISLANDS

Frequent crossings run from Barcelona and Valencia to the three main Balearic islands. On **Acciona Trasmediterránea** ferries the crossings take from four hours (using the fast ferry from Barcelona) to eight hours. The same company also operates frequent inter-island services; and small operators take day-trippers (passengers only) from Ibiza to Formentera.

Acciona Trasmed-iterránea logo

Acciona Trasmediterránea operates a weekly service from Cádiz to the main ports of the Canary Islands. Crossings normally take 32 hours. Car ferries link the islands with each other. There are also passengers-only services between the islands of Gran Canaria, Tenerife and Fuerteventura, and between Tenerife and La Gomera.

Balearia is a ferry company operating from Barcelona and Valencia to the Balearic Islands and from Algeciras to Cueta or Tangier.

The ferries to Spain's islands have cabins, cafés, restaurants, bars, shops, cinemas, pools and sunbathing decks. They are also fitted with lifts and other facilities for people with special needs, and even have kennels. Entertainment is provided on crossings from the mainland to the Canary Islands.

FERRIES TO AFRICA

Acciona Trasmediterránea has daily services to the Spanish territories in North Africa: from Málaga and Almería to Melilla, and from Algeciras to Ceuta, as well as to Tangier in Morocco from Algeciras and Tarifa.

Balearia car ferry to the Balearic Islands

DIRECTORY

AIRLINES

Air Europa
Tel 902 40 15 01 in Spain.
www.aireuropa.com

American Airlines
Tel 902 11 55 70 in Spain.
Tel 1 800 433 7300 in USA.
www.aa.com

Bmibaby
Tel 902 100 737 in Spain.
Tel 0871 224 0224 in UK.
www.bmibaby.com

British Airways
Tel 902 111 333 in Spain.
Tel 08708 509 850 in UK.
www.ba.com

Clickair
Tel 902 254 252 in Spain.
www.clickair.com

Delta Air Lines
Tel 901 11 69 46 in Spain.
Tel 800 221 12 12 in USA.
www.delta.com

easyJet
Tel 807 07 00 70 in Spain.
Tel 0871 244 2366 in UK.
www.easyjet.com

Iberia
Tel 902 400 500 in Madrid.
Tel 0870 609 0500 in UK.
www.iberia.com

Ryanair
Tel 807 22 00 32 in Spain.
Tel 0871 246 0000 in UK.
www.ryanair.com

Spanair
Tel 902 13 14 15 in Spain.
www.spanair.com

Vuelair
Tel 902 33 39 33 in Spain.
www.vueling.com

FERRIES

Acciona Trasmediterránea
Tel 902 454 645 in Spain.
www.trasmediterranea.es

Balearia
Tel 902 16 01 80 in Spain.
www.balearia.com

Brittany Ferries
Tel 0870 907 61 03 in UK.
Tel 942 36 06 11 in Spain.
www.brittany-ferries.com

P&O European Ferries
Tel 0871 664 5645 in UK.
Tel 902 02 04 61 in Spain.
www.poferries.com

Travelling by Train

Logo of the Spanish national railways

The Spanish state railway, **RENFE** *(Red Nacional de Ferrocarriles Españoles)*, operates a service that is continually improving, particularly between cities. The fastest intercity services are called the TALGO and the AVE – their names are acronyms for the high-speed, luxury trains that run on these routes. *Largo recorrido* (long-distance) and *regionales y cercanías* (regional and local) trains are notoriously slow, many stopping at every station on the way. They are much cheaper than the high-speed trains but journey times can be hours longer.

ARRIVING BY TRAIN

There are several routes to Spain from France. The main western route runs from Paris through Hendaye in the Pyrenees to San Sebastián. The eastern route from Paris runs via Cerbère and Port Bou to Barcelona. The trains from London, Brussels, Amsterdam, Geneva, Zurich and Milan all reach Barcelona via Cerbère. At Cerbère there are connections with the TALGO and the *largo recorrido* (long-distance) services to Valencia, Málaga, Seville and Madrid, and other major destinations. If you book a sleeper on the TALGO from Paris, you travel to your destination without having to change trains. There are direct trains from Paris to Madrid and Barcelona, and from Milan, Geneva and Zurich to Barcelona.

EXPLORING BY TRAIN

Spain offers many options for train travellers. In the last ten years, the TALGO high-speed services have belied Spain's reputation for inefficiency and it is now possible to travel the long distances between the main cities extremely quickly. Ticket prices compare very favourably with the cost of high-speed train fares in many other countries in Europe. Efficient high-speed AVE rail services currently link Madrid with Seville in two and a half hours and with Barcelona in three hours. The AVE from

AVE high-speed trains at Estación de Santa Justa in Seville

Madrid to Zaragoza is one and a half hours and from Madrid to Málaga two hours 40 minutes.

The *largo recorrido* (long-distance) trains are so much slower you usually need to travel overnight. You can choose between a *cochecama* (compartment with two or four *camas* or beds) or a *litera*, one of six seats in a compartment which converts into a bunk bed. You reserve these when booking and pay a supplement. Book at least a month in advance.

Regionales y cercanías (the regional and local services) are frequent and very cheap. You buy the tickets from machines on the station. Some cities have more than one station. In Madrid the major stations for regional and long-distance trains are Atocha and Chamartín. The AVE runs from Atocha, the TALGO from

AVE Logo for a high-speed rail service

both. Sants and Francia are Barcelona's two principal stations. In Seville Santa Justa is the only station for regional and international services.

FARES

Fares for rail travel in Spain are structured according to the speed and quality of the service. Tickets for the TALGO and AVE cost the most.

Interrail tickets for people under 26, and Eurail tickets for non-EU residents are available from major travel agencies in Europe and from RENFE ticket offices in Spain. Always take proof of your identity when booking.

Holidays on Spain's two luxury trains *(see p679)* are expensive but offer high standards of comfort.

REGIONAL RAILWAYS

Three of the *comunidades autónomas* have regional rail companies. Catalonia and Valencia each has its own *Ferrocarrils de la Generalitat*: respectively the

DIRECTORY

NATIONAL ENQUIRIES AND RESERVATIONS

Al Andalus Express
Tel 800 09 92 40.
www.alandalusexpreso.com

El Transcantábrico
Tel 985 98 17 11.
www.transcantabrico.com

RENFE
Tel 902 24 02 02.
www.renfe.es

REGIONAL RAILWAYS

ET
Tel 902 54 32 10.
www.euskotren.es

FEVE
Tel 985 29 76 56.
www.feve.es

FGC
Tel 93 205 15 15.
www.fgc.net

FGV
Tel 96 526 27 31.
www.fgv.es

SPAIN'S PRINCIPAL RENFE NETWORK

Spain's Rail Network operates a wide variety of services. Study a RENFE brochure or train time-table before you buy your ticket.

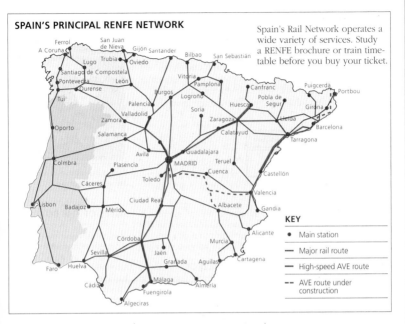

KEY

● Main station

— Major rail route

— High-speed AVE route

-- AVE route under construction

FGC and the **FGV**; and the Basque Country has the **ET** *(Eusko Trenbideak).*

Tickets for two special trains, similar to the Orient Express, can be obtained from travel agents. Tickets for **Al Andalus Express**, which tours Andalusia, including Seville and Granada, can also be bought through RENFE. While *FEVE (Ferro-carriles de Vía Estrecha)* run **El Transcantábrico**, which travels Spain's north coast between León and Santiago de Compostela. Passengers travel in style in 14 period carriages built between 1900–30 and since restored.

The regional tourist offices publicize unusual rail services, such as the narrow-gauge lines to Inca and Sóller in Mallorca.

BOOKING TICKETS

TALGO, AVE and any other tickets for *largo recorrido* travel by train may be booked and bought at any of the major railway stations from the *taquilla* (ticket office). They are also sold by all travel agents in Spain, who will charge a commission. RENFE tickets are sometimes sold by travel agents in other countries. Tele-phone reservations may be made directly to all RENFE

Ticket machine for local and regional lines

ticket offices with a credit card. Tickets can also be bought via the RENFE internet site. They must be collected in person.

Tickets for local and regional services are purchased from the station *taquilla*. In larger stations they can be bought from ticket machines. Tickets for *cercanías* (local services) cannot be reserved. For a one-way journey ask for *ida* and for a return ask for *ida y vuelta.* Return tickets offer discounts.

TIMETABLES

RENFE timetables change in May and October each year. Your travel agent will be able to provide the correct times of trains for your journey. Timetables can also be accessed in English via the RENFE internet site. In Spain timetables are available from RENFE offices. Most come as leaflets and are broken down into the various types of jour-ney: intercity, *largo recorrido* and *regionales. Cercanías* time-tables are posted on boards at local railway stations.

Atocha, one of Madrid's largest mainline railway stations

Travelling by Road

Spain's fastest roads are its *autopistas*. They are normally dual carriageways and are subsidized by *peajes* (tolls). *Autovías* are similar but have no tolls. The *carretera nacional* is the countrywide network of main roads or highways with the prefix N. Smaller minor roads are generally less well kept but are often a more leisurely and enjoyable way to see rural areas of Spain. These pages tell you how to use the roads, tolls and parking meters, how to buy petrol, and explain important driving regulations.

Sign for national highway N110

Cambio de sentido (slip road) 300 m (330 yd) ahead

ARRIVING BY CAR

Many people drive to Spain via the French motorways. The most direct routes across the Pyrenees, using the motorways, pass through Hendaye on the western flank and Port Bou in the east. Other, rather more tortuous routes may be used, from Toulouse through the Vall d'Aran, for instance. From the UK there are car ferries from Plymouth to Santander and from Portsmouth to Bilbao in northern Spain *(see p677)*.

WHAT TO TAKE

A Green Card from your motor insurance company is needed in order to extend your comprehensive cover to Spain. The RAC, the AA and Europ Assistance have sound rescue and recovery policies with European cover.

Spanish law requires you to carry with you at all times your vehicle's registration document, a valid insurance certificate and your driving licence. You must always be able to show a passport or a valid identity card as ID. You must also display a sticker with the car's country of registration on the rear of the vehicle.

The headlights of right-hand drive vehicles will have to be adjusted or deflected. This is done with stickers that can be bought at ferry ports and on ferries. You risk on-the-spot fines if you do not carry a red warning triangle, spare light bulbs and a first-aid kit.

In winter you should carry chains if you intend to drive in mountain areas. In summer, it is a good idea to take drinking water with you if you are travelling in a remote area.

BUYING PETROL

In Spain *gasolina* (petrol) and *gasóleo* (diesel) are priced by the litre. *Gasolina sin plomo* (unleaded petrol) is available everywhere. All cost more at the *autopista* service stations. Self-service stations, where you fill up yourself, are common. You must wait for service if there are attendants. They will ask *¿cuánto?* (how much?); you should reply *lleno* (fill the tank) or specify an amount in euros: *dos euros por favor*. Small stations do not all accept credit cards. If you use your credit card to pay at a motorway service station you will be asked to show your passport or ID. Modern pumps sometimes operate by credit card. You run your card through the machine, press the buttons to indicate the amount of petrol you want in euros, and then serve yourself.

Speed limit 50 km/h (31 mph)

Pedestrian crossing sign

RULES OF THE ROAD

Most traffic regulations and warnings to motorists are represented on signs by easily recognized symbols. But Spain has a few road rules and signs that may be unfamiliar to some drivers from other countries.

To turn left at a busy junction or across oncoming traffic you may have to turn right first and cross a main road, often by way of traffic lights, a bridge or an under-pass. If you are going the wrong way on a motorway or a main road with a solid white line, you are allowed to turn round where you see a sign for a *cambio de sentido*.

At any crossing you must give way to the right unless a sign indicates otherwise. It is compulsory always to wear seat belts if they are fitted in front and rear seats. Oncoming drivers may flash their headlights at you to mean "you go"; "danger"; "your lights are on unnecessarily"; or (most often) "speed trap ahead".

A filling station run by a leading chain with branches throughout Spain

SPEED LIMITS AND FINES

Speed limits on the roads in Spain for cars without trailers are as follows:
• 120 km/h (75 mph) on *autopistas* (toll motorways).
• 100 km/h (62 mph) on *autovías* (non-toll motorways).
• 90 km/h (56 mph) on *carreteras nacionales* (main roads) and *carreteras comarcales* (secondary roads).
• 40 km/h (31 mph) in built-up areas.

Speeding fines are imposed on the spot at the rate of six euros for every kilometre per hour over the limit. Fines for other traffic offences (such as turning the wrong way into a one-way street) depend on the severity of the offence and the whim of a police officer.

Tests for drink-driving and fines for drivers over the blood alcohol legal limit, which is 30 mg per millilitre, are now imposed frequently throughout the country.

MOTORWAYS

Spain has more than 2,000 km (1,240 miles) of *autopistas*, and many more are planned. They are generally toll roads and can be expensive to use.

Be aware that Spain has recently changed its road numbering system so some of the roads featured here may differ from new road signs. However, you can establish whether a motorway is toll or toll-free by the letters that prefix the number of the road: A = free motorway, AP = toll motorway.

The long-distance tolls are calculated per kilometre and the rate varies from region to region. Among the busiest and most expensive are the AP7 along the south coast to Alicante and the AP68 Bilbao-Zaragoza *autopista*.

There are service stations every 40 km (25 miles) or so along the *autopistas*, marked by a blue and white parking sign (P) or a sign indicating the services available. About 1 km (550 yd) from a service station, a sign indicates the distance to the next one and lists its services. Most have fuel, toilets, a shop for maps,

Driving through the Sierra Nevada along one of Europe's highest roads

coffee and snacks, and a café which serves full meals.

Emergency telephones occur every 2 km (2 miles) along the *autopistas*.

USING AUTOPISTA TOLLS

If you are travelling a long distance on the *autopista* you pick up a ticket from a toll booth *(peaje)* as you drive on to it and give it up at a booth as you exit. Your toll will be calculated according to the distance you have covered. Over some short stretches of motorways near to cities a fixed price is charged. Tolls can be paid either in cash or by credit card.

You must join one of three channels at the *peaje* leading to different booths. Do not drive into *telepago*, a credit system for which a chip on your windscreen is required. *Tarjetas* has machines for you to pay by credit card. In *manual* an attendant in the booth will take your ticket and your money.

**PEAJE
TOLL**

Autopista **toll booths ahead**

OTHER ROADS

Carreteras nacionales, Spain's main roads, have black and white signs and are designated N *(Nacional)* plus a number. Those with Roman numerals (NIII) start at the Puerta del Sol, Madrid. The distance from the Kilometre Zero mark in the Puerta del Sol *(see p272)* appears on kilometre markers. Those with ordinary numbers (N6) have kilometre markers giving the distance from the provincial capital. Some *carreteras nacionales* are dual carriageways, but most are single-lane roads and can be slow. They tend to be least busy at lunch time, from 2–5pm, when many lorry drivers stop for lunch.

Autovías are new roads built in recent years to motorway standard to replace N roads. They have blue signs similar to *autopista* signs. Because they have no tolls they are busier than *autopistas*.

Carreteras comarcales, secondary roads, have a number preceded by a letter C. Other minor roads have numbers preceded by letters representing the name of the province, such as the LE 1313 in Lleida. On any road in winter, watch out for signs indicating whether a mountain pass ahead is open *(abierto)* or closed *(cerrado)*.

The *peaje manual* channel, with attendant

CAR HIRE

As well as the international car hire companies, a few Spanish companies, such as **Atesa**, operate nationwide. You can probably negotiate the best deal with an international company from home. There are also fly-drive and other package deals, including car hire. Fly-drive, an option for two or more travellers, can be arranged by travel agents.

There are car hire desks at airports, train stations and offices in the large towns. If you wish to hire a car locally for, say, a week or less, you can arrange it with a local travel agent. A car for hire is called a *coche de alquiler*.

For chauffeur-driven cars in Spain, **Avis** offer deals from major cities. Car-hire prices and conditions vary according to the region and locality.

Some of the leading car-hire companies operating in Spain

MAPS

Fold-out road maps can be obtained at airports, on the ferries and from tourist offices. The Spanish Ministry of Transport publishes a comprehensive road map in book form, the *Mapa Oficial de Carreteras*. Campsa, the oil company, publishes the *Guía Campsa*, a road map and restaurant guide in one book. Michelin publishes a useful series of maps (440–448, with orange covers) at a scale of 1:400,000 (1 cm:4 km), which covers Spain in eight sections, including the islands. They are sold at bookshops and petrol stations all over Spain.

A series of more detailed maps at 1:200,000 for cycling, walking and other specialist uses is published by Plaza y Janés. Military maps at scales of 1:50,000 and 1:100,000 are available from **Stanfords Travel Bookshop** in London and from specialist bookshops

City taxis with their logo and official numbers

and some local bookshops in Spain, such as **Altaïr** in Barcelona. Tourist offices in towns and cities usually have a giveaway street map.

There are detailed street maps of central Barcelona on pages 180–85, of Madrid on pages 308–15 and of Seville on pages 448–53 of this guide.

PARKING

The hours for which drivers have to pay for parking in Spain are 8am until 2pm and 4pm until 8pm on Mondays to Saturdays.

As a rule, you may not park where the pavement edge is painted yellow or where a no parking sign is displayed. Occasionally there is a no parking sign on both sides of a city street, one saying "1–15" and the other "16–30". This means that you can park on one side of the street only for the fortnight indicated on the sign.

In the cities, non-metered, on-street parking is generally hard to find, but there are blue pay and display parking spaces. To use them you buy a ticket from the machine and display it on the inside of your windscreen. The cost varies, but averages about 1–2 euros per hour. You can usually park at the same spot for up to two hours. The penalties for infringements vary from town to town.

Major cities have many large underground car parks. You collect a ticket when you enter, retain it, and pay the attendant as you drive out.

A parking ticket machine

TAXIS

There is no central system for taxis in Spain. Every city and/or region has its own design and tariffs for its taxis. All will display a green light if they are free. Most taxis are metered and at the start of the journey a minimum fee will be shown on the meter. In smaller villages the taxi service may well be run by a resident driving an unmetered private car. Ask at the hotel reception or in a nearby shop for the name and number of a local driver. It is best to negotiate a price for the trip before you set off.

In the cities there are taxi ranks at the airports, the railway and bus stations and usually in the main shopping areas. Tips of about 1 euro will be acceptable.

ROAD CONDITIONS AND WEATHER FORECASTS

To hear recorded road and traffic information call the national toll-free number for **Información de Tráfico de Carreteras**. This service is in Spanish only. Ask your hotel receptionist to call for you if you need a translation. The RAC offers route-planning services tailored to individual requirements, which may include current road conditions. The weather information service, **Teletiempo**, gives forecasts for the regions and provinces, as well as the national and international weather. It also gives information on maritime and mountain conditions.

No parking at any time of day

ARRIVING BY COACH

Often the cheapest way to reach and travel around Spain is by coach. **Eurolines** operates routes throughout Europe and runs daily services to Barcelona.

Coaches from the UK depart from London Victoria Coach Station. Tickets may be bought from National Express offices or travel agents, or a credit card booking may be made by telephone. The journey takes about 24 hours.

TRAVELLING AROUND SPAIN BY COACH

There is no Spanish national coach company, but private regional companies operate routes around the country. The largest coach company in Spain is **Alsa**, which operates in all of the regions and has routes and services that cover most of the country. Other coach companies operate in particular regions – Alsina Graells, for instance, covers most of the south and east of Spain. Tickets and information for long-distance travel are available at all main coach stations as well as from travel agents but it is not always possible to book tickets in advance. In Madrid

CYCLING

Cycling is popular in Spain and there are bicycles for hire in most tourist spots but there are few cycle lanes, even in towns. Bicycles may be carried on *cercanías* trains after 2pm on Fridays until the last train on Sunday night, on any *regional* train

Cycle touring, a popular holiday activity

with a goods compartment, and on all long-distance overnight trains. If you need to take your bicycle long-distance at other times, you should check it in an hour before the train departs. You may have to send it as luggage and pay a baggage charge based on its weight. It might not travel with you so you will have to collect it when it arrives.

Alsa, a regional coach service

the biggest coach stations are **Estación Sur**, which serves the whole of Spain; **Intercambiador des Autobuses**, for terminals in the north; and **Terminal Auto Res**, serving Valencia, Extremadura and parts of Castilla-León.

LOCAL BUSES

Local bus routes and timetables are posted at bus terminuses and stops. You pay on the bus or buy strips of ten tickets called *billetes bonobus* from *estancos* (tobacconists).

Indicators for Seville's circular bus routes

DIRECTORY

CAR HIRE

Atesa
Tel 902 10 01 01.
www.atesa.es

Avis
Tel 0844 581 0147 in UK.
Tel 902 13 55 31 in Spain.
www.avisworld.com
www.avis.es

Europcar
Tel 0845 758 5375 in UK.
Tel 902 10 50 30 in Spain.
www.europcar.com
www.europcar.es

Hertz
Tel 0870 844 8844 in UK.
Tel 901 10 10 01 in Spain.
www.hertz.co.uk
www.hertz.es

COACH OPERATORS

Alsa
Tel 902 42 22 42.
www.alsa.es

Eurolines
Tel 0870 580 8080 in UK.
Tel 902 40 50 40 in Spain. www.eurolines.es

COACH STATIONS

Madrid
Estación Sur, Calle Méndez Álvaro, 83. *Tel* 91 468 42 00. www.estacionauto busesmadrid.com
Intercambiador de Autobuses, Avenida de América, 9. *Tel* 902 42 22 42 (Alsa).
Terminal Auto Res
Calle Fernández Shaw 1.

Tel 902 02 09 99.
www.auto-res.net

Barcelona
Estació del Nord, Calle Ali Bei 80. *Tel* 902 26 06 06.
www.barcelonanord.com
Estació de Sants
Calle Viriato.

Seville
Estación Plaza de Armas, Calle Cristo de la Expiración. *Tel* 95 490 80 40.

MAPS

Altaïr S.A.
Gran Vía 616, 08007 Barcelona. *Tel* 93 342 71 71.

Guía Campsa
www.guiacampsa.com

Michelin
www.viamichelin.es

Stanfords
12–14 Long Acre, London WC2E 9LP.
Tel 020 7836 1321.
www.stanfords.co.uk

WEATHER FORECASTS

Teletiempo Nacional
Tel 807 170 365.

Teletiempo Provincial
Tel 807 17 03 65.

TRAFFIC AND ROAD CONDITIONS

Información de Tráfico de Carreteras
Tel 900 12 35 05 toll-free.

General Index

Page numbers in **bold** type refer to
main entries.

A

ABC Serrano (Madrid) 318
Abd al Rahman I, Caliph 52, 53, 480
Abd al Rahman II, Caliph 52, 480
Abd al Rahman III, Caliph 477
Los Abrigos 534
Abu-l-Hasan, Sultan 492
Accessories shops 188, 189
   Madrid 318, 319
Accident (Ponce de León) 298
Acebo 404
Aceúche, fiestas 405
Addresses, postcodes 672, 673
Adeje 534
   restaurants 653
The Adoration of the Magi
   (Campaña) 354
The Adoration of the Shepherds (El
   Greco) 293
Adrian of Utrecht 58
Adventure sports 659, 661
Africa, ferries 677
Agaete **543**
   hotels 600
Agatha Ruíz de la Prada 318
Agres 259
Agriculture **28–9**
   New World crops 59
Agüero 234
Aguilar 482
Aguilar, Marquises of 369
Aguilar de Campoo 369
Águilas 263
   hotels 576
Agüimes, restaurants 651
Aigüestortes, Parc Nacional d' 30,
   207, **211**
Ainsa **231**
   hotels 574
Air sports 658, 661
Air travel 674–7
Airlines 676–7
Airports 674–5
   Barajas (Madrid) 674
   El Prat (Barcelona) 675
Ajo, restaurants 611
Alacant *see* Alicante
Alameda del Valle, hotels 582
Alaraque, restaurants 642
Alarcón **395**
   hotels 586
Álava 115
Alba de Tormes 361
Alba, Duchess of 286
Alba, Dukes of 361, 500
Alba family 304
Albacete **396**
   hotels 586
   restaurants 636
Albacete province 379
Albarracín **241**
   hotels 574
   restaurants 624

La Alberca **356**
   festivals 43
   hotels 583
Albornoz, Alonso Carrillo de 393
L'Albufera (La Albufera) 244, **254**
Albuquerque 410
Alcalá de Guadaira, hotels 591
Alcalá de Henares **332–3**
   restaurants 632
Alcalá del Júcar 380, **395**
Alcalá la Real 482
Alcalá de la Selva 240
Alcanar, restaurants 620
Alcañiz **239**
   hotels 574
   restaurants 624
Alcántara 51, 410
Alcanyis 252
Alcaraz **396–7**
La Alcarria **382–3**
Alcazaba (Almería) 501
Alcazaba (Málaga) **52–3**, 474
Alcázar (Jerez de la Frontera) 466
Alcázar (Segovia) 344–5
Alcázar (Toledo) 389, **390**
Alcázar de los Duques de Feria
   (Zafra) 413
Alcázar de San Juan 394
   restaurants 636
Alcázar de los Reyes Cristianos
   (Córdoba) 478
Los Alcázares 262
Alcoi (Alcoy) 243, **259**
   festivals 38, 40, 255
Alcossebre 247
Alcoy *see* Alcoi
Alcúdia 516
   hotels 597
   restaurants 649
Alella, restaurants 620
Alella wine region 202–3
Alemán, Rodrigo 357
Alexander VI, Pope 254–5
Alfàbia 515
Alfonso I, King of Aragón 382
Alfonso I, King of Asturias 52
Alfonso II, King of Aragón
   captures Teruel 240
   Monasterio de Piedra 238
   Puigcerdà 212
   Santiago de Compostela
   cathedral 92
   tomb of 222
   unites Catalonia and Aragón 54
Alfonso III, the Great, King of
   Asturias
   casket of 352
   Zamora city walls 356
Alfonso VI, King of Castile
   captures Toledo 54
   and El Cid 370–71
   and Madrid 269
   Puerta Antigua de Bisagra
   (Toledo) 391
Alfonso VIII, King of Castile
   Alarcón 395

Alfonso VIII. King of Castile (cont.)
   Battle of Las Navas de Tolosa 54
   La Caballada (Atienza) 387
   Real Monasterio de las Huelgas
   (Burgos) 371
Alfonso IX, King of León
   captures Cáceres 408
   Universidad (Salamanca) 360
Alfonso X the Learned, King of
   Castile
   Cantigas 55
   and the Castilian language 34
   Ciudad Real 399
   poetry 330
Alfonso XI, King of Castile,
   Convento de Santa Clara
   (Tordesillas) 366
Alfonso XII, King of Spain 71
   portrait 64
   statue 297
Alfonso XIII, King of Spain
   abdication 64, 65
   Hotel Ritz (Madrid) 286
   marriage 290
   Palacio Real (Madrid) 276
   Palau Reial de Pedralbes
   (Barcelona) 177
   portrait 71
   and Primo de Rivera 65
   Santander summer palace 113
Algeciras 472
Algorta 119
Alhama de Granada 483
Alhambra (Granada) 54, 422–3,
   490–91
Ali ben Yusuf 275
Alicante (Alacant) **260–61**
   airport 676
   beach 258
   hotels 576
   restaurants 626
Alicante province 243
Alicante wine region 202–3
All Saints' Day 42, 43
Allariz 98
   restaurants 608
Almadén 399
Almagro **399**
   festivals 41
   hotels 586
   restaurants 636
Almansa 396
   restaurants 636
Almansa wine region 340–41
Almendral, hotels 588
Almendralejo, restaurants 638
Almería **501**
   hotels 591
   restaurants 642
Almería province 459
Almodóvar, Pedro 21, 22
   *Women on the Verge of a Nervous
   Breakdown* 305
Almodóvar del Río 477
Almohads 54
   architecture 422–3

Almonacid del Marquesado 387
Almond trees 29
Almoravids 54
   architecture 422
Almuñécar 483
Alonso Martinez (Madrid), nightlife
   324–5
Álora 474
Alpuente 248
Las Alpujarras 484–5
Alquézar 235
   hotels 574
Altafulla, restaurants 620
Altamira Caves *see* Cuevas de
   Altamira
Altea 260
   beach 258
   restaurants 626
Alto Campoo 111
Alto Turia 248
Álvarez family 387
Amadeo I, King of Savoy 63, 71
Amandi 107
Amargós, Josep 155
Ambulances 667
Amenabar, Alejandro 21
Amorebieta, restaurants 613
Amposta 225
Ampudia, restaurants 633
Ampurdán-Costa Brava wine region
   202–3
Ampurias *see* Empúries
Els Amunts 511
Amusement parks
   Tibidabo (Barcelona) 178, **192**
   see also Theme parks
Anarchism 47, **64–5**, 67
Anaya, Diego de, tomb of 3 60
Ancient Music Festival (Seville) 43
Al Andalus 47, **52–3**
   Reconquest 54–5
Andalusia **458–501**
   character 13
   climate 44
   Exploring Andalusia 460–61
   fiestas 463
   food and drink 418–19
   hotels 591–7
   restaurants 642–8
Andorra **212**
Andorra la Vella **212**
   hotels 571
   restaurants 620
Andratx 514
Andújar **496**
   fiestas 463
Aneto 231
Angelico, Fra, *The Annunciation*
   293
Anguiano
   fiestas 132
   hotels 565
Anís 607
The Annunciation (Fra Angelico)
   293
Año Nuevo 43

Ansó 230
Antequera **475**
   restaurants 642
Antigua, hotels 599
Antique shops
   Barcelona 188, 189
   Madrid 302, 317, 319
   Seville 455
Anual, Battle of (1921) 6 5
Aoiz, restaurants 613
Apartment hotels 556
Apes' Den (Gibraltar) 472
Apolo (Barcelona) 194, 195
April Fair (Seville) 40, 431
Aquarium (San Sebastián) 122
Aqueduct (Segovia) 51, 364, **365**
Aqüeducte de les Ferreres 225
Arabs 52
Aracena **462**
   hotels 591–2
Aragón **226–41**
   character 11
   climate 45
   Exploring Aragón 228–9
   fiestas 239
   food and drink 200–1
   hotels 574–6
   restaurants 624–6
Aragón, River 135
Aranda de Duero 377
   restaurants 633
Aranjuez
   hotels 582
   restaurants 632
Aranjuez, Palacio Real de *see*
   Palacio Real de Aranjuez
Arantza 134
Arantzazu 124
Arazas, River 232
Arc de Berà 225
Arc del Triomf (Barcelona) 154
Arce, Martín Vázquez de 382
Archena, hotels 576
Arches, Moorish 423
Archidona 475
Archivo de Indias (Seville) 434, **439**
ARCO (Madrid) 43
Arcos de la Frontera 468, **469**
   hotels 592
   restaurants 642
El Arenal (Seville) **426–31**
   area map 427
   hotels 590
   restaurants 640–41
   Street-by-Street map 428–9
Arenys de Mar, restaurants 621
Ares del Maestre 246
Arévalo 365
   restaurants 633
Arévalo, Luis de 487

Arfe, Antonio de 3 67
El Argar civilization 48
Argomániz, hotels 565
Argüelles (Madrid), nightlife 324–5
Arias, Eugenio 328
Arizkun 134
Armada 59, 89
Arnedillo 129
   hotels 565
Arrecife **549**
   hotels 601
   restaurants 653
Arribas, Alfredo 173
Arroyo de la Luz 410
Arroyuelo 111
Art **32–3**
Art Nouveau 25
   Barcelona 159
   Modernisme 140–41
Art shops
   Barcelona 188, 189
   Madrid 317
Artenara 545
Arties 210
   hotels 571
Arts, performing 21–2
   see also Cinema; Dance; Music;
   Theatre
Arucas
   hotels 600
   restaurants 651–2
Assumption Day 41, 43
The Assumption (El Greco) 390
Astorga **352**
   hotels 582
   restaurants 633
   The Road to Santiago 82
Astún 230
Asturias and Cantabria **100–13**
   character 10
   climate 44
   Exploring Asturias and Cantabria
   102–3
   fiestas 110
   food and drink 76
   hotels 562–5
   restaurants 611–13
Ateneo de Madrid 291
Atienza **382**
   fiestas 387
   restaurants 636
Atlético de Madrid 321
Auditorio Nacional de Música
   (Madrid) 322
Augustus, Emperor
   captures Cantabria and Asturias 50
   and Lugo 99
   Mérida 410, 411
   Ausetan tribe 220
Auto-da-fé in the Plaza Mayor (Rizi)
   274
Autol 129
Autumn Landscape in Oldenburg
   (Schmidt-Rottluff) 289
Autumn in Spain 42
   fiestas 39

Ávila **362–3**
  hotels 583
  restaurants 634
Ávila province 347
Avilés **105**
  restaurants 611
Avinyonet de Puigventós, hotels 571
Axpe-Atxondo, hotels 565
Ayamonte, hotels 592
Ayllón 365
Ayna **397**
  hotels 586
Ayub 238
Ayuntamiento 672
Ayuntamiento (Seville) 438
Azahar, Costa del *see* Costa del Azahar
Azca (Madrid), nightlife 325
Aznar, José María 69
Azpeitia, restaurants 614
Aztecs 58
Azuaga 413
Azulejos (ceramic tiles) 24, 422, **438**

B

Bacall, Lauren 123
Bacon, Francis 118
Badajoz **412**
  hotels 588
  restaurants 638
Badajoz province 401
Baena 482
Baetica (Roman province) 50
Baeza 417, **498–9**
  hotels 592
  restaurants 642
  Street-by-Street map 498–9
Bagur *see* Begur
Baílen, restaurants 642
Baiona (Bayona) **96**
  hotels 560
  restaurants 608
Bakio 119
  hotels 565
Balàfia 511
Balboa, Vasco Núñez de 4 13
El Balcón de Europa 483
Ballesteros de Calatrava, hotels 586
Ballet 656
Balloons, hot-air 658
Bank notes 669

Banks 668
Baños Árabes (Jaén) 493
Baños de Cerrato 368
Baños de la Encina 496
Baños de Montemayor 404
El Bañuelo (Granada) 489
Banyalbufar (Bañalbufar), hotels 598
Banyoles, hotels 571
Banyoles, lake 213
Baqueira-Beret **211**
  hotels 571
Barajas Airport (Madrid) 674
Barbarossa 522
Barbastro 235
  restaurants 618
Barceló, Miquel 517
Barcelona **136–95**
  cathedral 139, 144, **148–9**
  character 11
  coach stations 683
  Eixample 158–67
  entertainment 190–95
  exhibitions 64, 65
  fiestas 40, 41, **157**
  Further Afield 174–8
  hotels 568–70
  Introducing Barcelona 138–9
  Jewish community 146
  Montjuïc 168–73
  nightlife 194–5
  Old Town 142–57
  Olympic Games 23, 69
  Palau Güell 140–41
  Picasso in 153
  El Prat Airport **675**, 676
  Las Ramblas 139, **150–51**
  restaurants 617–20
  Sagrada Família 166–7
  shopping 186–9
  Spanish Civil War 66
  Street-by-Street maps
    Barri Gòtic 144–5
    Montjuïc 170–71
    Quadrat d'Or 160–61
  Barcelona Football Club 177
  Barcelona province 207
  Barceloneta (Barcelona) 156
  Bárcena Mayor 102, 111
  Bardem, Javier 21
  Baroja, Pío 35, **64**
  Bárdenas Reales 130
  Barlovento, hotels 601
  Baroque architecture 25, 63
  Barranc d'Algendar 523
  Barranco de Guayadeque 544
  Barranco del Infierno 534
  Barreiros, hotels 560
  Barri Gòtic (Barcelona) **144–5**
    nightlife 194, 195
    Street-by-Street map 144–5
  Barri Xinès (Barcelona) 150
  Los Barrios, restaurants 645
  Barruera 211
  Bars **602**
    Barcelona 194–5
    Madrid 320, 323, 324–5

Bars (cont.)
  tapas bars 605
Bartolomé de Jaén, Maestro 486, 493
Basílica de la Macarena 444
Basílica Pontificia de San Miguel (Madrid) 270
Basílica de Santa Maria del Mar (Barcelona) 153
Basque Country, Navarra and La Rioja **114–23**
  character 10–11
  climate 45
  Communist demonstrations 64–5
  exploring 116–17
  fiestas 132
  food and drink 77
  hotels 565–8
  independent kings of Navarra 130
  restaurants 613–17
Basques 19–20, 115
  culture 125
  ETA 67, 68
  Guernika-Lumo 118–19
  independence movement 23
  language 115, 664
  literature 34
Bassá, Ferrer 177
  Virgin and Child 32
Battle of the Flowers (Laredo) 110
Las Batuecas 356
Bayeu, Francisco 302
  tapestry designs 306
Bayona *see* Baiona
Bayonne Treaty (1386) 55
Beaches
  Costa Blanca 258
  Costa Brava 217
  Costa del Sol 472–3
Bears, brown 104
Beatus of Liébana, St, *Commentary on the Apocalypse* 110, 212, 215
Becerra, Gaspar 352
Bechtold, Erwin 511
Bécquer, Gustavo Adolfo 444
Bed and breakfast 555, 557
Beech forests 80
Beer 607
Begur (Bagur)
  beach 217
  hotels 571
Béjar 357
Belaguer, José María Escrivá de 235
Belalcázar 476
Belchite 239
Belén, Ana 69
Belmonte 344, **394–5**
  hotels 586
  restaurants 636
Benahavis, restaurants 643
Benalmádena Costa 473
Benasque **231**
  hotels 574
Benavente, restaurants 634
Benedict XIII, Pope 247

Benedictine order
  accommodation 556
  Monastir de Montserrat 218–19
Benet, Joan 35
Benicarló 247
Benicassim (Benicasim) 247
Benidorm **260**
  beach 258
  restaurants 626
Benimantell, restaurants 626
Benissa, hotels 5 76
Benissano, restaurants 626
Bentraces, hotels 5 60
Bera (Vera) 134
Berbers 53
Berceo, Gonzalo de 34
Berenguer, Francesc 178
Berga
  fiestas 221
  restaurants 621
Berlanga de Duero 377
Bermejo, Bartolomé 32
  St Dominic of Silos Enthroned as
    Abbot 294
Bermeo 119
Berruguete, Alonso, Natividad 367
Berruguete, Pedro de 32, 294
Beruete, hotels 565
Besalú 213
Betancuria **546**
  restaurants 651
Betanzos **88**
  restaurants 608
Béthencourt, Jean de 546
Biasteri see Laguardia
Biblioteca de Catalunya (Barcelona)
  150
Bicycles 683
Bielsa
  fiestas 239
  hotels 574
Bienal de Arte Flamenco (Seville)
  42
Bienvenida, Antonio 306
El Bierzo 350
Bierzo wine region 340–41
Biescas, restaurants 618
Bigarny, Philippe de 368, 373
Bilbao (Bilbo) **118**
  airport 676
  festivals 41
  hotels 565–6
  opera 43
  restaurants 614
Bilbao (Madrid), nightlife 324–5
Binibeca 508, 526
Binissalem, hotels 598
Bird-watching 660, 661
Birds
  L'Albufera 254
  Central Spain 342–3
  Delta de l'Ebre 225
  Lagunas de Ruidera 397
  Tablas de Daimiel 399
Bizkaia see Vizcaya
Blanca of Navarra 129

Blancafort, Gabriel 521
Blanes 216
Blay, Miquel 173, 213
  St George 152
Boabdil 56, 57, 487, 491
Bocairent 259
Bodega Alvear (Montilla) 482
Bodega Pérez Barquero (Montilla)
  482
Bodegas 602
Bodegas Barbadillo (Sanlúcar de
  Barramedo) 466
Bofill, Guillem 214
Bofill, Ricardo 173
Bolnuevo 263
Bolvir de Cerdanya
  hotels 571
  restaurants 621
Bonaparte, Joseph see José I
Bonastre, Maestro de 252
Bookshops
  Barcelona 188, 189
  Madrid 318, 319
  Seville 455
La Boqueria (Barcelona) 186
Borges, José Luis 35
Borgia, Cesare 366
Borgia family 254–5
Borgoña, Juan de 393
Borja, restaurants 618
Borja, Juan de 498
Borja, St Francis 255
El Born (Barcelona) 153
Borrassa, Luis 32
Bort, Jaime 262
Bosch, Hieronymus 252
  Ecce Homo 305
  The Garden of Delights 292
  The Haywain 295
  Temptation of St Anthony 295
Bossòst 210
Botticelli, Sandro 295, 486
Bourbon dynasty 61, **62**, 70
  Castell de Montjuïc 173
  restoration of 71
Bourbon Madrid 282–99
  area map 283
  hotels 580–81
  restaurants 630–31
Bous en la Mar (Dénia) 255
Breakfast 602
Brenan, Gerald 485
Brihuega 383
  restaurants 636
Briñas, hotels 566
Brión, hotels 560
Briviesca 369
Brown bears 104
Brueghel, Pieter the Elder 281, 295
Bubión
  hotels 592
  restaurants 643
Buen Amor, castle of 361
Bueu, restaurants 608
Buigas, Carles 173
Buigas, Gaietà 156

Buitrago del Lozoya 328
Bulevard Rosa (Barcelona) 187
Bullfighting 22, **36–7**, 657
  Museo Taurino (Antequera) 475
  Museo Taurino (Córdoba) 478
  Museo Taurino (Madrid) 306
  Museo Taurino (Seville) 457
  Plaza de Toros (Antequera) 475
  Plaza de Toros de la Maestranza
    (Seville) 428, **430**, 457
  Plaza de Toros de Las Ventas
    (Madrid) 300, **306**, 321, 323
  Ronda 471
Bulnes 109
Buñol
  fiestas 248–9, 255
  restaurants 627
Buñuel, Luis 356, 404
El Burgo de Osma **377**
  hotels 583
  restaurants 634
Burgos **370–73**
  cathedral 337, 372–3
  hotels 583
  map 371
  restaurants 634
Burgos province 347
"Burgos trials" 67
The Burial of the Count of Orgaz
  (El Greco) 32, 388, 390
Buses 683
Bush, George 69
Butterflies, Vall d'Aran 210
El Buzo (Seville) 429

C

Ca Na Costa 512
La Caballada (Atienza) 387
Caballé, Montserrat 22, 191
Caballero Bonald, José Manuel 35
Caballo, Luis 487
Cabañeros National Park 31, 387
Sa Cabaneta, fiestas 523
Las Cabezas, hotels 594
Cable cars
  Barcelona 169
  Fuente Dé 109
  Parque Nacional del Teide 538–9
Cabo Fisterra 85, **89**
Cabo de Gata, Parque Natural de
  417, **501**
Cabo de Palos, restaurants 627
Cabo Tinoso 263
Cabo de Trafalgar 468
Cabopino 473
O Cabreiro see Cebreiro
Cabrera 507, **517**
Cabrera, Archipiélago de 30, 517
Cabuérniga, Valle de see Valle de
  Cabuérniga
Cáceres 401, **408–9**
  hotels 588
  restaurants 638–9
  Street-by-Street map 408–9
Cáceres province 401
Cadalso 111

Cadaqués 206, 207, **216**
  beach 217
  hotels 571
  restaurants 621
Cadí-Moixeró 212
Cádiar 485
Cádiz **467**
  festivals 39, 43, 463
  history 49
  restaurants 643
Cádiz province 459
Caesar, Julius 50
Café de Chinitas (Madrid) 321
Café Gijón (Madrid) 321
Cafés, Madrid 320, 323, 324–5
Cala Benirràs, restaurants 649
Cala Ratjada, restaurants 649
Cala Turqueta 524–5
Calabardina, hotels 576
La Calahorra (Elx) 261
Calatañazor 346, 377
Calatayud 238
  wine region 202–3
Calatrava, Santiago 253
Calatrava la Nueva 398–9
Calderón, Rodrigo 273
Calderón de la Barca, Pedro 34, 60
  La Estátua de Prometeo 61
  The Mayor of Zalamea 412
Caldes de Boí 211
Calera de León 413
Cales Coves 526
Caleta de Fuste 547
Calle Mateos Gago (Seville) 435
Calle de Serrano (Madrid) 296
Calle de las Sierpes (Seville) 438
Callejón del Agua (Seville) 435
Callosa D'en Sarria, fiestas 42
Sa Calobra 515
Calp (Calpe) 242, **259**
  hotels 577
Camariñas 89
Cambados 95
  hotels 560
  restaurants 608–9
Cambarro, restaurants 609
Cambrils 224
  restaurants 621
Camp Nou (Barcelona) 176
Camp sites 557
Campaña, Pedro de, *The Adoration of the Magi* 354
Campin, Robert 295
Camping and Caravanning Club 557
Campisábalos 382
Campo, Juan del 486
Campo del Agua 350
Campo de Borja wine region 202–3
Campo de Criptana 379, **394**
Campo del Moro (Madrid) 275
Camprodon 213
Canalejas, José 65, 272

Canales, Antonio 425
Canary Islands 15, 504–5, **528–51**
  character 13
  climate 45
  Exploring the Eastern Islands 540–41
  Exploring the Western Islands 530–31
  ferries 677
  fiestas 536
  Fuerteventura 546–7
  Gran Canaria 542–5
  hotels 599–601
  International Music Festival 43
  Lanzarote 548–50
  map 17, 504–5
  regional food 537
  restaurants 651–3
  Tenerife 534–9
  volcanoes 551
Cancho Roano 412
Candas 104
Candelaria **535**
  fiestas 536
Candelario 357
Canedo, restaurants 634
Cañete 383
Cangas de Onís **107**
  fiestas 110
  hotels 562
  restaurants 611
Cano, Alonso 304, 485, 486, 496
Caños de Meca, hotels 592
Cánovas del Castillo, Antonio 64, 286
Cantabria *see* Asturias and Cantabria
Cantabrian mountains 111
El Cantar del Mío Cid 34, 370
Cantavieja 246
Canyoning 659
Cap de Cavalleria 523
Cáparra 404
Capek, Karl 34
Capocorb Vell 516–17
El Capricho (Comillas) **111**, 141
Car hire **682**, 683
Carantoñas (Aceúche) 405
Caravaca de la Cruz **263**
  restaurants 627
Caravaggio 294
  David Victorious over Goliath 295
Caravans 557
Caravia, hotels 562
Carbonero, José Moreno 35
Cardona **220**
  hotels 571
Cardona, Dukes of 2 20
Carducho, Vicente 280
Cares, River 1 08
Cariñena 239
  restaurants 624
Cariñena wine area 202–3
Carlist Wars 62, 63, 64
Carlos I, King of Spain *see* Charles V
Carlos II, King of Spain
  death 61
  portrait 70, 106

Carlos III, King of Spain 62, 71
  Archivo de Indias (Seville) 439
  becomes king 63
  Bourbon Madrid 283
  expels Jesuits 62, 272
  Illa de Tabarca 261
  Museo del Prado (Madrid) 292
  Palacio Real (Madrid) 276, 277
  Paseo de la Castellana (Madrid) 306
  Paseo del Prado (Madrid) 284
  Plaza Cánovas del Castillo (Madrid) 286
  Plaza Mayor (Madrid) 273
  portraits 295
  Puerta de Alcalá (Madrid) 287
  Puerta del Sol (Madrid) 272
  Real Jardín Botánico (Madrid) 297
  statue of 297
  tomb of 133
Carlos III the Noble, King of Navarra 130
Carlos IV, King of Spain 62, 239
  The Family of King Charles IV (Goya) 33
  Monestir de Poblet 222
  Palacio Real (Madrid) 276
  Palacio Real de Aranjuez 333
  portraits 71, 276
Carlos V, Emperor *see* Charles V, Emperor
Carlos de Viana, Prince 130
Carmen, statue of 428
Carmona (Andalusia) **476**
  hotels 592
  restaurants 643
Carmona (Cantabria) 111
Carnival **39**, 43
  Bielsa 239
  Cádiz 463
  Santa Cruz de Tenerife 536
Carracedo del Monasterio 351
Carratraca 474
Carreño, Juan 106
Carrer Montcada (Barcelona) **154**
Carreras, José 22, 190–91
Carrero Blanco, Admiral 67
Carrión de los Condes 368
  hotels 583
Cars **680–83**
  see also Tours by car
Cartagena **263**
  hotels 577
  restaurants 627
Carthaginians 47, 48, 49
Cartuja de Miraflores (Burgos) 371
Casa de l'Ardiaca 144, **146**
La Casa de los Arroyo (Arrecife) 549
Casa Batlló (Barcelona) 140
Casa de Campo (Madrid) 302
Casa de Cervantes (Valladolid) 367
Casa de la Ciutat (Barcelona) 144, 147
Casa de Colón (Las Palmas de Gran Canaria) 544

Casa de las Conchas (Salamanca) 24, **361**
Casa de la Condesa Lebrija (Seville) 438
Casa de Dulcinea (El Toboso) 394
Casa de Lope de Vega (Madrid) 290
Casa Milà (Barcelona) 138, 140, 161, **165**
Casa Modernista (Novelda) 260
Casa de las Muertes (Salamanca) 361
Casa Museo de Martín Alonso Pinzón (Palos de la Frontera) 463
Casa Patas (Madrid) 321
Casa de Pilatos (Seville) 438–9
Casa Terrades (Barcelona) 161, **165**
Casa de los Tiros (Granada) 486–7
Casa Vicens (Barcelona) 141
Casa-Museo de Cervantes (Alcalá de Henares) 333
Casalarreina, hotels 566
Casals, Pau, Museu Pau Casals (El Vendrell) 224
Casas, Father Bartolomé de las 58
Casas rurales **555**, 556
Cash dispensers 668
Casino, Murcia 262
Casón del Buen Retiro (Prado) 295
Castañeda, restaurants 611
Castelao, Alfonso 94
Castelar, Emilio 64
Castell de Castells, hotels 577
Castellar de la Frontera, hotels 592
Castelló de la Plana **247**
  restaurants 627
Castelló d'Empúries, hotels 571
Castellón 243
Castile, Kingdom of 54
Castile and León, Kingdom of 54, 55
Castilian *see* Spanish language
Castilla-La Mancha **378–99**
  character 12
  climate 45
  Exploring Castilla-La Mancha 380–81
  fiestas 387
  food and drink 339
  hotels 586–8
  restaurants 636–8
Castilla y León **346–77**
  castles of Castile 344–5
  character 12
  climate 44
  Exploring Castilla y León 348–9
  fiestas 368
  food and drink 338–9
  hotels 582–5
  restaurants 633–6
Castles
  Alarcón 395
  Alcalá de la Selva 240
  Alcañiz 239
  Alcazaba (Almería) 501
  Alcazaba (Málaga) **52–3**, 474

Castles (cont.)
  Alcázar (Jerez de la Frontera) 466
  Alcázar (Segovia) **344–5**, 364, 365
  Alcázar (Toledo) 389, **390**
  Alcázar del Rey Pedro 476
  Almodóvar del Rio 477
  Almuñécar 483
  Arévalo 365
  Bellver (Palma) 519
  Belmonte 344, 394
  Berlanga del Duero 377
  Buen Amor 361
  Buitrago del Lozoya 328
  Calatañazor 346, 377
  Calatrava la Nueva 398–9
  Caravaca de la Cruz 263
  Castell del Papa Luna (Peñíscola) 247
  Castile 344–5
  Castillo Árabe (Antequera) 475
  Castillo de la Concepción (Cartagena) 263
  Castillo de Gibralfaro (Málaga) 474
  Castillo de los Guzmanes (Niebla) 462
  Castillo de la Mota (Medina del Campo) 344, **366**
  Castillo de San José (Arrecife) 549
  Castillo de Santa Bárbara (Alicante) 260
  Castillo de Santa Catalina (Jaén) 493
  Castillo de Santa Cruz de la Mota (San Sebastián) 122
  Castillo de la Yedra (Cazorla) 497
  Chinchilla de Monte Aragón 396
  Coca 344, 365
  Dénia 255
  Guadalest 259
  Hondarribia 123
  Javier 135
  Jerez de los Caballeros 413
  Keep (Gibraltar) 472
  Lacalahorra 493
  Loarre 234–5
  Manzanares el Real 332
  Medina de Pomar 369
  Mendoza 127
  Monterrei (Verín) 97
  Montjuïc (Barcelona) 138, **173**
  Onda 248
  Oropesa 387
  Palacio Real de Olite 131
  Pedraza de la Sierra 365
  Peñafiel 345, 367
  Peñaranda de Duero 349, 376
  Ponferrada 351
  Sagunt 249
  Salobreña 483
  Santueri (Felanitx) 517
  Simancas 367

Castles (cont.)
  Tarifa 468
  Valderrobres 240
  Vélez Blanco 500
  Xàtiva 254
  see also Palaces
Castrillo de Murcia, fiestas 368
Castro, Rosalia de, Museo Rosalia de Castro (Padrón) 94
Castro de Coaña 104
Castro Urdiales **113**
  restaurants 611
Castropol 104
  hotels 563
Catalan language 212, 664
Catalans 19–20
  independence movement 23
Catalonia (Catalunya) **206–25**
  character 11
  climate 45
  Exploring Catalonia 208–9
  fiestas 221
  food and drink 200
  hotels 571–4
  restaurants 620–24
Cathedrals
  Albacete 396
  Albarracín 241
  Almería 501
  de la Almudena (Madrid) 275
  Astorga 352
  Ávila 362–3
  Badajoz 412
  Baeza 499
  Barcelona 139, 144, **148–9**
  Bilbao 118
  El Burgo de Osma 377
  Burgos 337, 370, **372–3**
  Cádiz 467
  Ciudad Rodrigo 357
  Ciutadella 522
  Colegiata de San Isidro (Madrid) 271, **272**
  Córdoba 481
  Coria 405
  Cuenca 385
  Girona 214–15
  Granada 486
  Guadalajara 383
  Guadix 493
  Huesca 235
  Ibiza 511
  Jaca 231
  Jaén 493
  Jerez de la Frontera 466
  León 24, 57, 336, **354–5**
  Lleida 220
  Logroño 129
  Lugo 99
  Málaga 474
  Mondoñedo 88
  Murcia 198, 262
  Orihuela 261
  Ourense 98
  Oviedo 106
  Palencia 368

Cathedrals (cont.)
Palma 518, **520–21**
Las Palmas de Gran Canaria 544
Pamplona 132–3
Plasencia 405
Roda de Isábena 236
Salamanca 358, **360**
Santander 113
Santiago de Compostela 84, 85, 91, **92–3**
Santo Domingo de la Calzada 128
Segovia 364
La Seu d'Urgell 212
Seville 434, **436–7**
Sigüenza 382
Tarazona 229, 236
Tarragona 225
Teruel 55, 240, **241**
Toledo 337, 389, **392–3**
Tortosa 225
Tudela 130
Tui 96–7
Valencia 250–51
Valladolid 367
Vic 220
Vitoria 126
Zamora 356
Zaragoza 237
Catholic Church 21
Inquisition 274
religious art 32
Catholic Monarchs *see* Fernando II, King of Aragón; Isabel I, Queen of Castile
Cava 606, 607
Es Cavallet 510
cave dwellings 27
Caves
Albarracín 241
Cales Coves 526
Coves d'Artà 509
Coves d'Artá **517**
Coves del Drac 517
Coves dels Hams 517
Coves de Sant Josep 248
Les Covetes dels Moros 259
Cueva del Buxu 107
Cueva de El Monte Castillo 112
Cueva de los Letreros 500
Cueva de Montesinos 397
Cueva de Tito Bustillo 107
Cueva de Valporquero 352
Cueva de los Verdes (Jameos de los Verdes) 550
Cuevas de Águila 362
Cuevas de Altamira 48, 49, **112**
Cuevas de Nerja 483
Cuevas de Santimamiñe 119
Gruta de las Maravillas 462
Guadix 485
Ramales de la Victoria 113
St Michael's Cave (Gibraltar) 472
Yesos de Sorbas 500
Cayón, Gaspar 493
Cazalla de la Sierra 476
hotels 592–3

Cazorla
hotels 593
Parque Natural de 497
O Cebreiro (O Cabreiro) **99**
The Road to Santiago 82
Cedeira 88
Cehegín 263
Cela, Camilo José 35, 382
Celanova 97
Cella 241
Celts 48
Castro de Coaña 104
O Cebreiro 99
Monte de Santa Tecla 96
Cenobio de Valerón 543
Central de Reservas (paradors) 557
Central Spain **334–413**
birds 342–3
Castilla-La Mancha 378–99
Castilla y León 346–77
Extremadura 400–13
Introducing Central Spain 336–7
regional food 338–9
wines 340–41
Centre de Cultura Contemporània (Barcelona) 150
Centre del Disseny 154
Centre Excursionista de Catalunya (Barcelona) 145
Centro de Arte Reina Sofía (Madrid) 267, **298–9**
Ceramics Museum (Valencia) 251
Cercedilla 329
Cercle de Pessons 212
Cercs, restaurants 621
Cerdà i Sunyer, Ildefons 140, 159
Cerdanya valley 212
Cereal farming 28
Cerler 231
Cermeño, Juan Martín de 156
Ceroni, Juan Antonio 360
Cerralbo, 17th Marquis of, Museo Cerralbo (Madrid) 304
Certamen Internacional de Habaneras y Polifonía (Torrevieja) 41
Cervantes, Miguel de **333**
Archivo de Indias (Seville) 439
Casa de Cervantes 367
Casa-Museo de Cervantes (Alcalá de Henares) 333
Don Quixote 34, 60, 394, **395**
statue of 268, 280
Cervatos 111
Cervera de Pisuerga 369
Cervo, hotels 561
Chagall, Marc 216
La Chanca 425
Charlemagne, Emperor
Battle of Roncesvalles 52, 134
Girona cathedral 214–15
Charles V, Emperor (Carlos I) **59**, 305
Alcázar (Toledo) 389, 390
and Baeza 499
coronation 58
El Escorial 331

Charles V, Emperor (cont.)
empire 58
homage to Tarazona 236
illegitimate son 157
Monasterio de Yuste 405
Palace of Charles V, Alhambra (Granada) 490–91
Palacio Real (Madrid) 277
portrait 70
Real Alcázar (Seville) 440
Simancas castle 367
Charles Martel, King of the Franks 52
Cheeses
Manchego 338, 605
Northern Spain 76
Chelva 248
Cheques 668
Chestnut forests 81
Children, entertainment 657
Children at the Beach (Sorolla) 295
Chillida, Eduardo 119
Chillida-Leku museum (San Sebastián) 123
The Comb of the Winds 122
Toki-Egin 299
Chillón 399
Chinchilla de Monte Aragón 396
restaurants 637
Chinchón **333**
hotels 582
restaurants 633
Chipiona 466
Chocolatería San Ginés (Madrid) 324, 325
Chopin, Frederic 514
Christ at the Column (Siloé) 372
Christianity 51
Reconquest **54–5**
Christmas **39**, 43
Christus, Petrus, *Our Lady of the Dry Tree* 2, 88
Chulilla, hotels 577
Churches
opening hours 664
Romanesque architecture 83
see also Cathedrals; Convents; *individual towns and cities*; Monasteries
Churriguera brothers 25, 358
Arco de la Estrella (Cáceres) 408
Iglesia-Convento de San Esteban (Salamanca) 360
Medina de Rioseco altarpiece 367
Plaza Mayor (Salamanca) 360
Real Academia de Bellas Artes (Madrid) 281
San Cayetano (Madrid) 302
Churrigueresque architecture 25
El Cid **370**
captures Alpuente 248
captures Valencia 54
epic poems 34
exile 371
Puerta Antigua de Bisagra (Toledo) 391

El Cid (cont.)
  statue of 370
  sword of 287
  tomb of 373
  and Valencia 250
Cider Festival (Nava) 41
Cigales wine region 340–41
CIJ 665
Cíjara 406
Cinco Villas 230
Cinema 21, 657
  Barcelona **192**, 193
  Madrid **322**, 323
  San Sebastián Film Festival
  42, **123**
  Spaghetti Westerns 500
Cintruénigo, restaurants 614
Cirauqui 131
Cisneros, Cardinal 57, 273, 332
Cistercian order 99, 556
"Cistercian triangle" 199, 221, 222
Ciudad Encantada 383
Ciudad Real 399
  restaurants 637
Ciudad Rodrigo **357**
  hotels 583
Ciudad de Vascos 387
Ciutadella (Ciudadela) **522**
  fiestas 523
  hotels 599
  restaurants 650
Ciutat (de les) Arts i de les Ciències
  (Valencia) 253
Clameño, hotels 562
Clarín, Leopoldo Alas 35, 106
Classical music 656–7
  Barcelona **191**, 193
  Madrid **322**, 323
  Seville 456–7
Classical Theatre Festival (Mérida)
  41
Claude Lorrain 295
Clavé, Josep Anselm 152
Clement X, Pope 255
Climate 44–5
Climbing 659
The Clothed Maja (Goya) 293
Clothes
  in restaurants 602
  size chart 655
Clothes shops 655
  Barcelona 187–8, 189
  Madrid 318, 319
  Seville 455
Cloud and Chair (Tàpies) 160
Clubs
  Barcelona 194–5
  Madrid 324–5
  Seville 457
Coach Travel 683
Cobos, Francisco de los 496, 497
Coca, Castillo de 344, **365**
COCEMFE 557, 665
Cocentaina, restaurants 627
Cocido madrileño 338
Cock and hen of St Dominic 128

Coello, Claudio 33, 281, 360
Coffee 606
Coins 669
Cola de Caballo 233
El Colacho (Castrillo de Murcia)
  368
Colegiata de San Isidoro 353
Colegiata Real (Roncesvalles) 134
Colegiata de Santa María (Toro)
  356–7
La Colegiata (Santillana del Mar)
  112
Colegio del Patriarca (Valencia)
  251
Colegio de San Ildefonso (Alcalá de
  Henares) 332–3
Coll 211
Collage (Miró) 33
Collet, Charles 219
Collsuspina, restaurants 621
Colmenar, hotels 593
Colmenar Viejo 332
Colombres, hotels 563
Las Colorades 548
Colossus of Rhodes (Dalí) 33
Columbus, Christopher 144, 406
  Archivo de Indias (Seville) 439
  Barcelona Cathedral 148
  Burgos 370
  Casa de Colón (Las Palmas de
  Gran Canaria) 544
  death 366
  explorations 47, 56, **57**
  festival (Huelva) 463
  and Huelva 462
  Monasterio de la Rábida 462
  Monasterio de Santa María de las
  Cuevas (Seville) 446
  Monument a Colón (Barcelona)
  150, **156**
  and Palos de la Frontera 463
  Pinta 96
  Plaza de Colón (Madrid) 296
  Quincentenary 69
  return to Spain 146
  San Sebastián (La Gomera) 533
  and Sanlúcar de Barrameda 466
  Santa María 532
  statues of 138, 462
  tomb of 437
The Comb of the Winds (Chillida)
  122
Combarro 95
Comendador-Leroux, Pérez, Museo
  Pérez Comendador-Leroux
  (Hervás) 404
Comillas **110–11**
  hotels 563
  restaurants 611
Communications 670–73
Communist Party 64, 67, 68
Companys, Lluís 173
Compostela *see* Santiago de
  Compostela
Comunidad de Madrid (Madrid
  province) 266, 272, 327

Comunidad Valenciana 241, 243
Comunidades 673
Conca de Barberà wine region
  202–3
Concierto de Aranjuez (Joaquín
  Rodrigo) 333
El Condado 462
Condado de Huelva wine region
  420
The Condesa Mathieu de Noailles
  (Zuloaga) 118
Congosto de Ventamillo 231
Congreso de los Diputados
  (Madrid) 284, 291
Conil de la Frontera 468
Conquistadors 58–9
Conservatorio Superior
  de Música Manuel Castillo
  (Seville) 457
Constable, John 305
Constantina 476
Constantine I, Emperor 51
Constitution Day 43
Consuegra 21, 27, **394**
  festivals 42
Convents
  accommodation in 556
  Convento de las Dueñas
  (Salamanca) 359, 361
  Convento de San Martiño
  Pinario (Santiago de
  Compostela) 90
  Convento de Santa Clara
  (Moguer) 463
  Convento de Santa Paula
  (Seville) 444
Conversion chart 665
Copa del Rey 41
Córdoba **478–81**
  fiestas 40, 41, 463
  hotels 593
  Mezquita 53, 416, 458, 459, 479,
  480–81
  Moors 52
  restaurants 643–4
  Street-by-Street map 478–9
Córdoba province 459
El Cordobés 477
Coria 405
Cornejo, Pedro Duque 481
Cornide, hotels 561
Corpus Christi
  La Orotava 536
  Seville 431
  Toledo 387
Corral, Jerónimo del 367
Corral del Carbón 486
Corral de Comedias (Almagro)
  399
Corralejo 540, **547**
El Corte Inglés
  Barcelona 187
  Madrid 316, 317
  Seville 454
Cortés, Hernán 58, 287, 439
Cortes (parliament) 291

Corullón 351
A Coruña (La Coruña) **89**
  hotels 560
  restaurants 608
A Coruña province 85
Cosgaya, restaurants 611
Costa del Azahar 247
Costa Blanca 199, 243
  beaches 258
Costa Brava 199, 207
  beaches 217
Costa Cálida 263
Costa Calma 546
Costa Daurada (Costa Dorada)
  224
Costa de la Luz 468
Costa da Morte 89
Costa del Silencio 534
Costa del Sol 472–3
Costa Teguise **549**
  hotels 601
  restaurants 653
Costa Tropical 483
Costa Vasca 119
Costa Verde 104–5
Costers del Segre wine region
  202–3
Coullaut-Valera, Lorenzo, statue of
  Cervantes 268
Counter-Reformation, and literature
  34
Covadonga 108, 109
  fiestas 110
Covarrubias **370**
  hotels 583
  restaurants 634
Coves d'Artà 509, **517**
Coves del Drac 517
Coves d'Hams 517
Coves de Sant Josep (Grutas de San
  José) 248
Les Covetes dels Moros 259
Craft shops
  Madrid 318, 319
  Seville 455
Cranach, Lucas 295
Credit cards 668
  in hotels 555
  in restaurants 603
  in shops 654
Crime 666–7
Los Cristianos **534**
Cro-Magnon people 48, 119, 125
Cruz, Juanita 306
Cruz Roja 667
Cruz de Tejeda
  hotels 600
  tour of 545
Cuacos de Yuste 405
  hotels 588
Cuban War of Independence 65
Cubero, José 306
Cudillero 104
  restaurants 611–12
Cuenca 337, 378, **384–5**
  festivals 40

Cuenca (cont.)
  hotels 586
  restaurants 637
  Street-by-Street map 384–5
Cuenca, Serranía de see Serranía de
  Cuneca
Cuenca province 379
Cuervo, River 383
Cueva de Brujas 134
Cueva del Buxu 107
Cueva de los Letreros 500
Cueva de Montesinos 397
Cueva de Tito Bustillo 107
Cueva de Valporquero 352
Cueva de los Verdes (Jameos de los
  Verdes) 550
Cuevas de Águila 362
Cuevas de Altamira 48, 49, **112**
Cuevas de Nerja 483
Cuevas de Santimamiñe 119
Cullera, restaurants 627
Currency 669
Customs information 664
Cycling 658, 661, 683

D

Daimau, Luis 32
Daimicl, restaurants 637
Dalí, Salvador **215**, 261, 281
  Cadaqués 216
  Casa Museu Salvador Dalí
    (Cadaqués) 216
  Colossus of Rhodes 33
  Landscape at Cadaqués 298
  Rainy Taxi 215
  Tarot cards 127
  Teatro-Museo Dalí (Figueres)
    215
La Dama de Elche **48**, 49, 261
Dance 656
  Barcelona **190–91**, 192, 193
  flamenco **424–5**, 656
  Madrid **321**, 323
  Sardana 225
  Seville 456–7
Dance of Death (Verges) 221
Danza de los Zancos 132
Daoíz 304
Daroca 227, **238**
  hotels 575
David Victorious over Goliath
  (Caravaggio) 295
Degrain, Antonio Muñoz 252
Deià (Deyá) 515
  hotels 598
  restaurants 649
Delaunay, Robert 118
Delgado, Alvaro 35
Delta de l'Ebre 225
Deltebre 225
Demetrius, St 235
Denia 245, **255**
  beach 258
  fiestas 39, 255
  hotels 577
  restaurants 627

The Denuding of Christ (El Greco)
  392
Department stores 655
  Barcelona **187**, 189
  Madrid 317, 319
  Seville 454
The Deposition (van der Weyden)
  295
Descent of the River Miño 97
Descent of the River Sella 41
Descent of the Virgin of the Snows
  (Santa Cruz de la Palma) 536
Desfiladero de los Beyos 108
Desfiladero de Despeñaperros 496
Desfiladero de la Hermida 110
Desfiladero del Río Cares 108
Design shops
  Barcelona 188, 189
  Madrid 318, 319
Designer labels, Barcelona 187, 189
Deyá see Deià
Día de la Constitución 43
Día de la Cruz (Granada and
  Córdoba) 463
Día de la Hispanidad 42, 43
Día del Pilar (Zaragoza) 42, 239
Día de los Reyes 43
Día de Sant Ponç (Barcelona) 157
Día de los Santos Inocentes (All
  Fools' Day) 39, 43
La Diada (Barcelona) 157
Dialling codes **670**, 671
Díaz, Daniel Vásquez 462
Dinosaur footprints 129
Dios, Juan de 488
Disabled travellers 665
  in hotels 557
  in restaurants 603
Discounts
  railway 678
  students 665
Diving and snorkelling 658–9
Domènech i Montaner, Lluís 140
  Casa de l'Ardiaca (Barcelona)
    146
  Casa Lleó Morera (Barcelona)
    160, **164**
  Fundació Tàpies (Barcelona) 160,
    164
  Hospital de la Santa Creu i de
    Sant Pau (Barcelona) 159, **165**
  Museu de Zoologia (Barcelona)
    155
  Palau de la Música Catalana
    (Barcelona) 152
  Universidad Pontificia (Comillas)
    111
Domènech i Montaner, Pere 165
Domènech i Roura, Pere 173
Domingo, Plácido 22
Domínguez, Adolfo 296
Dominic, St **128**
  tomb of 376
Don Quixote see Cervantes
Doña i Ocell (Miró) 176
Donamaria, hotels 566

Doñana National Park 30, 416, **464–5**
El Doncel, tomb of 56
Donostia *see* San Sebastián
Dos de Mayo (Madrid) 290
Dragon tree 534
Drake, Sir Francis 467
Drassanes (Barcelona) 157
Drinks *see* Food and drink
Dumas, Alexandre 34
Dunas de Maspalomas 543
Duratón, River 365
Dürer, Albrecht 295
Durro 211
Durruti, Buenaventura 286

E

Easter **38**, 43
Eastern Spain **196–263**
Aragón 226–41
Catalonia 206–25
flowers of the *matorral* 204–5
Introducing Eastern Spain 198–9
regional food 200–1
Valencia and Murcia 242–63
wildlife of the *matorral* 205
wines 202–3
Ebro, River 111, 225
Ecce Homo (Bosch) 305
Ecce Homo (Juanes) 252
Echagüe, Antonio Ortiz 123
Echalar *see* Etxalar
Écija **477**
Economy 23
Edificio Metrópolis (Madrid) 284
Egas, Enrique de 486
Eiffel, Gustave 97
Eivissa *see* Ibiza
Eixample (Barcelona) **158–67**
area map 159
hotels 569–70
nightlife 194, 195
restaurants 619
Ejea de los Caballeros 230
Elche *see* Elx
Electrical adaptors 665
Elizabeth, Empress of Austria 261
Elizondo 134
Eljas 404
Elx (Elche) **261**
fiestas 38, 41, 255
hotels 577
restaurants 627
Embalse de Puentes Viejas 328
Embassies 665
Emergencies 666–7
Emiliano, St 129
Los Empelaos (Valverde de la Vera) 405
Empúries (Ampurias) 51, **216**
La Encamisá (Torrejoncillo) 405
Encants Vell (Barcelona) 186
Enciso 129
La Endiablada (Almonacid del Marquesado) 387

Enlightenment 35, 47, **62**
Enrique IV, King of Castile 56, 394
Enrique, Prince of Asturias 369
Entertainment 656–7
Barcelona 190–95
Madrid 320–25
Seville 456–7
Epiphany 39, 43
Ercina, Lago de la 101, 108
Erill-la-Vall 211
Ermita 27
Ermita de los Reyes (El Hierro) 533
Ermita de San Antonio de la Florida (Madrid) 303
Ermita de San Lorenzo 395
Ermita de San Marcial 123
L'Escala 217
hotels 572
Escalante
hotels 563
restaurants 612
Los Escobazos (Jarandilla de la Vera) 405
El Escorial (Madrid) 59, 266, **330–31**
Escunhau 210
Espartero, General 63
L'Espluga de Francolí, hotels 571
Esponellà, restaurants 621
Esquedas, restaurants 624
Estació de Atocha (Madrid) 297
Estació del Norte (Valencia) 252
Estadi Olímpic de Montjuïc (Barcelona) 173
Estadio Bernabéu 306
L'Estartit, beach 217
La Estàtua de Prometeo (Calderón de la Barca) 61
Estella (Lizarra) **132**
restaurants 614
Estepa 475
Estepona 472
restaurants 644
A Estrada, hotels 560
ETA 23, 67, 68, 69
Etiquette 664
Etxalar (Echalar) 134
Eulalia, St 148
sarcophagus 149
Eunate 131
Euro, the 669
European Union 23, 68
Euskadi *see* Basque Country
Euskera language 115, 664
Exaltación al Río Guadalquivir (Sanlúcar de Barrameda) 463
Expo '92 (Seville) 23, **68–9**, 446
Extremadura **400–13**
character 12
climate 44
Exploring Extremadura 402–3
fiestas 405
food and drink 339
hotels 588–90
restaurants 638–40
Ezcaray, restaurants 614

F

Fabada 76
Fairs, annual, Madrid 317
The Fall of Granada (Pradilla) 56–7
Falla, Manuel de, tomb of 467
Las Fallas (Valencia) 40, 255
Falqués, Pere 160
The Family of King Charles IV 33
Family life 20–21
Farming *see* Agriculture
Fashion shops 655
Barcelona 187–8, 189
Madrid 318, 319
Seville 455
Father Gonzalo de Illescas at Work (Zurbarán) 407
Faust, Karl 216
Faxes 672
FC Barcelona 177, 191
Federación Española de Deportes de Montaña y Escalada 556, 557, 658
Federación Española de Empresarios de Campings 557
Federación Española de Pesca 659
Felanitx **517**
fiestas 523
Felipe II, King of Spain 70, 498
Archivo de Indias (Seville) 439
Armada 89
armour 59
birthplace 366
citadel (Pamplona) 133
empire 58
El Escorial 330–31
Illescas 386
Madrid 269
marriage 58
Museo del Prado (Madrid) 295
Palacio Real (Madrid) 277
tomb of 330
Felipe III, King of Spain 70, 376
expels Moriscos 60
Iglesia de San Antonio de los Alemanes (Madrid) 304
statue of 273
Felipe IV, King of Spain 61, 70
Castell de Montjuïc 173
Monasterio de las Descalzas Reales (Madrid) 281
Parque del Retiro (Madrid) 297
statue of 275
Felipe V, King of Spain
abdication 62, 71
becomes king 61
and Catalan language 212
Cinco Villas 230
La Granja de San Ildefonso 363
Lleida Cathedral 220
Palacio Real (Madrid) 276
Parc de la Ciutadella 154
Plaza Mayor (Salamanca) 360
portraits 62, 71
Real Fábrica de Tapices 306
siege of Barcelona 62
and Xàtiva 254

Felipe el Hermoso (the Fair) 486
Felix, St, tomb of 214
Feria del Caballo (Jerez de la Frontera) 40
Feria Nacional del Queso 40
Fernández, Gregorio 280
  Recumbent Christ 367
Fernández de Moratín, Leandro 35
Fernando I of Castilla-León 369
  ivory crucifix 296
  unites Castile and León 54
Fernando II of Aragón (the Catholic) **56–7**
  and Almería 501
  birthplace 230
  and Cáceres 408
  and Columbus 146
  Granada 486
  Inquisition 274
  marriage 227, 366
  Monasterio de San Juan de los Reyes (Toledo) 391
  and Orihuela 261
  Real Chancillería (Granada) 488
  Santa Fé 482–3
  unification of Spain 47, **70**
Fernando II of Castile 387
  annexes Navarra 130
Fernando III of Castile
  Burgos cathedral 372
  conquers Baeza 498
  reunites Castile and León 55
  and Trujillo 407
  and Yeste 396
Fernando VI, King of Spain 71
  Arnedillo 129
  death 63
Fernando VII, King of Spain 71
  Colegiata de San Isidro (Madrid) 272
Ferrer, Pere 147
Ferrer, St Vincent 246
Ferreries (Ferreries) 523
Ferrero, Juan Carlos 22
Ferries 677
Ferrol 88
Festa Major (Barcelona) 157
Festivals *see* Fiestas and festivals
Fiestas and festivals 38–43
  Andalusia 463
  Aragón 239
  Asturias and Cantabria 110
  Balearic Islands 523
  Barcelona 157
  Basque Country, Navarra and La Rioja 132
  Canary Islands 536
  Castilla-La Mancha 387
  Castilla y León 368
  Catalonia 221
  Extremadura 405
  Galicia 98
  Madrid 290
  Seville 431
  Valencia and Murcia 255
  see also individual towns by name

Figueras (Asturias) 104
Figueres (Figueras) (Catalonia) **215**
  hotels 571
  restaurants 621
Figueroa, Antonio Matías de 445
Figueroa, Leonardo de
  Convento de la Merced Calzada (Seville) 430
  Hospital de los Venerables (Seville) 439
  Iglesia de la Magdalena (Seville) 430
Films *see* Cinema
Fines, driving 681
Finis Gloriae Mundi (Valdés Leal) 431
Finisterre *see* Fisterra
Fire Brigade 667
Fire hazards 667
Fire-walking fiesta (San Pedro Manrique) 368
First Republic 62, **64**, 71
Fish and seafood, Northern Spain 76
Fishing 97, 659
Fisterra (Finisterre) 89
Fitero 130
  hotels 566
Fiveller, Joan 147
Flame in Space and Naked Woman (Miró) 172
Flamenco **424–5**, 656
  Barcelona **192**, 193
  Madrid **321**, 323
  National Flamenco Competition (Córdoba) 40
  Seville 456
Flanagan, Barry 511
Flandes, Juan de 368
Floguera, Françesc 218
Florentino, Nicolás 360
Flores, Rosario 457
Floridablanca, Count of 62
Flower pavements (Ponteareas) 98
Flowers
  matorral 204–5
  Parque Nacional del Teide 538–9
Fluvià, River 213
FNAC (Madrid) 318
Foix, Counts of 212
La Folía (San Vicente de la Barquera) 110
Fonseca, Alonso de 359, 368
  tomb of 361
Font de Canaletes (Barcelona) 151
Font i Carreras 173
Font Màgica (Barcelona) 168, 169, 171
Fontibre 111
Fontseré, Josep 155
Food and drink
  Andalusia 418–19
  Aragón 200–1
  Asturias and Cantabria 76
  Balearic islands 513

Food and drink (cont.)
  Basque Country, Navarra and La Rioja 77
  Canary Islands 537
  Castilla-La Mancha 339
  Castilla y León 338–9
  Catalonia (Catalunya) 200
  Central Spain 338–9
  Eastern Spain 200–1
  Extremadura 339
  Galicia 76
  Madrid 338
  Northern Spain 76–7
  shops 655
  shops in Barcelona 186, 186–7, 189
  shops in Madrid 316–17, 319
  shops in Seville 455
  Southern Spain 418–19
  Valencia and Murcia 201
  what to drink in Spain 606–7
  wines of Central Spain 340–41
  wines of Eastern Spain 202–3
  wines of Northern Spain 78–9
  wines of Southern Spain 420–21
  see also Restaurants
Football 22, 657
  FC Barcelona 177, 191
  Museu del Futbol Club Barcelona 176
  Real Madrid 321, 323
Forcall 246
  hotels 577
  restaurants 627
Foreign exchange 668
Forestier, Jean 155, 445
Forests, Northern Spain 80–81
Forment, Damià 223, 235
Formentera 507, **512**
  fiestas 523
  food and drink 513
  hotels 597
  restaurants 648
El Formigal 230
Fornells 523
  restaurants 651
Fortuna, hotels 577
Foster, Sir Norman 118, 177
Fournier, Heraclio 127
Foz 88
Francés, Juan 393
Francés, Nicolás 354, 355
Franco, General Francisco 47, **66–7**, 71
  Asturian miners' revolt 65
  birthplace 88
  bombing of Gernika-Lumo 118
  Burgos 370
  death 23, 67, 68
  Palacio de El Pardo 332
  Santa Cruz del Valle de los Caídos 329
  Spanish Civil War 66–7
  statues of 88
François I, King of France 272
Franks 51

Fray Pedro Machado (Zurbarán) 281
Fregenal de la Sierra 413
Freire, Oscar 22
Freud, Lucian, *Portrait of Baron Thyssen-Bornemisza* 288
Frías 369
Frómista **368–9**
  restaurants 634
Frontera, hotels 599
Fruit
  Canary Islands 537
  Southern Spain 419
Fuencaliente 399
Fuendetodos 238–9
Fuengirola 473
  restaurants 644
Fuente Agria 484
Fuente Dé
  cable car 109
  hotels 563
Fuente de Cantos 413
Fuente de Neptuno (Madrid) 284
Fuente Obejuna 476
Fuenterabbía *see* Hondarribia
Fuentespalda, hotels 575
Fuerteventura **546–7**
  hotels 599–600
  map 541
  restaurants 651
Fugger brothers 399
Fundació Joan Miró (Barcelona) 171, **172**
Fundació Tàpies (Barcelona) 160, **164**
Funfairs *see* Amusement parks; Theme parks

G

Gainsborough, Thomas 305
Gáldar 543
Galdiano, Lázaro, Museo Lázaro Galdiano (Madrid) 305
Galerías
  Barcelona 187, 189
  Seville 454
Galicia **84–99**
  character 10
  climate 44
  Exploring Galicia 86–7
  fiestas 39, 98
  food and drink 76
  hotels 560–62
  restaurants 608–10
Gallego, Fernando 294
Gallego language 85, 664
Galleons 58–9
Galleries *see* Museums and galleries
  Galters, Charles 148, 149
Ganchegui, Luis Peña 176
Gandesa 209
Gandía **254–5**
  beach 258
  restaurants 627
Gañinas 368
Garajonay, Parque Nacional 31, 533

García Lorca, Federico 35, **67**, 291
  Blood Wedding 67
  on bullfighting 36
García Márquez, Gabriel 35
Garcilaso de la Vega 482
The Garden of Delights (Bosch) 292
Gardens *see* Parks and gardens
Gargallo, Pablo (Pau) 152, 165
  Museuo Pablo Gargallo (Zaragoza) 237
Garganta de Añisclo 233
Garganta del Chorro 474
Garganta de los Infiernos 405
Garganta de la Yecla 376
Garona, River (Garonne) 210
Gasparini 276
Gasteiz *see* Vitoria
Gata 404
Gaucín 468
Gaudí, Antoni **140–41**, **164**, 172
  bronze bas-reliefs (Lluc) 515
  El Capricho (Comillas) 111, 141
  Casa Batlló (Barcelona) 140, 164
  Casa de Botines (León) 353
  Casa Milà (Barcelona) 25, 140, 161, **165**
  Casa Vicens (Barcelona) 141, 164
  Casa-Museu Gaudí (Barcelona) 178
  materials 141
  Modernisme 140–41
  Palacio Episcopal (Astorga) 352
  Palau Güell (Barcelona) **140–41**, 151
  Palau Reial de Pedralbes (Barcelona) 177
  Palma Cathedral 520, 521
  Parc de la Ciutadella (Barcelona) 139, **154–5**
  Parc Güell (Barcelona) 141, **178**
  Plaça Reial lampposts (Barcelona) 151
  Sagrada Família (Barcelona) 139, 140, 141, 158, 159, **166–7**
Gaugin, Paul, *Mata Mua* 289
Gazpacho 418
Gehry, Frank 120
Generalife (Granada) 492
Generation of 27 35
Generation of 1898 64
Gerena Hotels 592
La Geria 550
Gernika-Lumo (Guernica) **118–19**
  restaurants 615
Gerona *see* Girona
Getaria (Guetaria) 119
  restaurants 615
Getxo, fiestas 41
Giaquinto 277
Gibraltar 459, **472**
  hotels 593
Gift shops
  Barcelona 188, 189
  Madrid 318
  Seville 455
Gijón **105**

Gijón (cont.)
  hotels 563
  restaurants 612
Gin, Balearic Islands 513
Giordano, Luca 295
  El Escorial fresco 331
  Iglesia de San Antonio de los Alemanes (Malasaña) frescoes 304
Giovanni de Bologna 273
Gipuzkoa *see* Guipúzcoa
La Giralda (Seville) 416, 422, 432, 433, 434, **436–7**
Giralte, Francisco 302
Girona (Gerona) **214–15**
  hotels 572
  map 214
  restaurants 621
Girona province 207
Godoy, Manuel 62, 281
Goicoa, José 122
Golden Age 60–61
Golf 660, 661
Golfines family 408
El Golfo 549
Golondrinas (Barcelona) 157
Gombren, restaurants 621
La Gomera 530, 531, **533**
  hotels 600
  restaurants 652
  whistle language 532
Góngora, Luis de 34
González, Anibal 444, 445
González, Felipe 23, 68, **69**
González, Fernán, tomb of 370
González, Gutiérrez 493
González, Julio 252
Good Friday 43, 255, 368
Gorbachev, Mikhail 69
El Gordo 43
Gormaz 377
Gothic architecture 24, 57
Gothic Quarter (Barcelona) *see* Barri Gòtic
Government, local 672–3
Goya, Francisco de 32, **239**, 252
  altar painting (Chinchón) 333
  Black Paintings 294
  Burial of the Sardine 281
  Casa-Museo de Goya (Fuendetodos) 238–9
  The Clothed Maja 293
  The Duchess of Alba 304
  Ermita de San Antonio de la Florida (Madrid) 303
  The Family of King Charles IV 33
  Madhouse 281
  Museo Camón Aznar (Zaragoza) 237
  Museo de Navarra (Pamplona) 133
  The Naked Maja 259, 293
  Portrait of Carlos IV 276
  Queen María Luisa 62
  Saturn Devouring One of his Sons 294
  Self-Portrait 239

Goya, Francisco de (cont.)
  statue of 290
  tapestry designs 306, 332
  The Procession of the Flagellants 274
  The Third of May **62–3**, 294
  tomb of 303
Gràcia (Barcelona), nightlife 195
Gran Canaria 505, **542–5**
  hotels 600
  restaurants 651–2
El Gran Capitán 487
Gran Teatre del Liceu (Barcelona) 151
Gran Vía (Madrid) 280–81
Granada **486–92**
  Alhambra 54, 417, **490–91**
  fiestas 38, 41, 463
  Generalife 492
  hotels 593–4
  map 487
  Reconquest 56–7
  restaurants 644–5
  Street-by-Street map: Albaicín 488–9
Granada province 459
Grandas de Salime 104
La Granja 514
La Granja de San Ildefonso 363
Granollers
  hotels 572
  restaurants 621
Grape Harvest (Jerez de la Frontera) 42
Gratallops, restaurants 622
Graus 236
Graves, Robert 515
Grazalema 469
Grec Arts Festival (Barcelona) 41
El Greco 252, 281, **391**
  The Adoration of the Shepherds 293
  The Assumption 390
  The Burial of the Count of Orgaz 32, 388, 390
  Casa-Museo de El Greco (Toledo) 391
  Christ in the Garden of Olives 496
  The Denuding of Christ 392
  The Ecstasy of St Francis of Assisi 304
  The Nobleman with his Hand on his Chest 294
Gredos, Sierra de *see* Sierra de Gredos
Greek colonizers 47, 48, 49
Gregorian plainchant 376, 657
Gregory I, Pope 376
Grimau, Julián 272
Gris, Juan, *Jug and Glass* 33
O Grove (El Grove) 94
  hotels 561
  restaurants 609
Grupo Riu 557
Grupo Sol-Meliá 557

Gruta de las Maravillas 462
Gruta de San José *see* Coves de Sant Josep
Guadalajara **383**
  hotels 587
  restaurants 637
Guadalajara province 379
Guadalest 259
Guadalhorce, River 474
Guadalquivir, River 428, 476
Guadalupe **406–7**
  hotels 589
  restaurants 639
Guadamur 387
Guadiela, River 383
Guadix 493
Guanches 49, **547**
A Guarda (La Guardia) 49, **96**
  hotels 560
  restaurants 608
Guardamar del Segura, beach 258
La Guardia *see* (A) Guarda
Güas, Juan 367, 391
Güell, Count Eusebi 141, 177, 178
Guernica *see* Gernika-Lumo
Guernica (Picasso) **66–7**, 118, **299**
Guerra, Juan Carlos 123
Guetaria *see* Getaria
Guía 543
Guifré el Pélos (Wilfred the Hairy) 212, 213
Guipúzcoa (Gipuzkoa) 115
Guitar Festival (Córdoba) 41
Guitars 424
Guzmán 468
Guzmán family 469
Gypsies 424, 489

H

Ha-Leví, Samuel 391
Habsburg dynasty 47, 60, 70
Hadrian, Emperor 476
Al Hakam II, Caliph 480, 496
Hams, Southern Spain 419
Hang-gliding 658
Hanging Houses (Cuenca) 385
Hannibal 50, 249
Haría 550
Harlem Jazz Club (Barcelona) 192
Harlequin with a Mirror (Picasso) 288
Haro 78, **128**
  fiestas 132
  hotels 566
  restaurants 615
Hat shops, Barcelona 188, 189
Hayedo de Montejo de la Sierra 328
Hayedo de Montejo de Tejera Negra 382
The Haywain (Bosch) 295
Healthcare 666
Hecho 230
Hemingway, Ernest 34, 132
Hercules 467
Hermosilla, José 286
Hernández, Rafael Rodríguez 444

La Herradura Hotels 595
Herrera, Francisco de 444
Herrera, Juan de 273
  Archivo de Indias (Seville) 439
  El Escorial 331
  Oropesa Castle 387
  Valladolid Cathedral 367
Herrería de Compludo 350
Hervás 404
Los Hervideros 549
El Hierro 530, **532–3**
  hotels 599
  restaurants 651
  volcanoes 551
Hinojosa del Duque 476
Hío 95
La Hiruela 328
Hisham II, Caliph 52
Hispania 50
History 47–71
Hitler, Adolf 66
HM the King's International Cup (Palma de Mallorca) 41
Holanda, Cornelis de 98
Holiday Care Service 557
Holidays, public 43
Holm oak 205
The Holy Children with the Shell (Murillo) 33
Holy Grail 234
Holy Week (Seville) 431
Homo erectus 48
Hondarribia (Fuenterabbía) **123**
  hotels 566
  restaurants 615
Hopper, Edward, *Hotel Room* 288
Hórreo 27
Horse riding, Real Escuela Andaluza de Arte Ecuestre (Jerez de la Frontera) 466
Hospital de la Caridad (Illescas) 386
Hospital de la Caridad (Seville) 429, **431**
Hospital de la Santa Creu i de Sant Pau (Barcelona) 159, **165**
Hospital de Santiago (Úbeda) 496
Hospital de los Venerables (Seville) 435, **439**
Hostal de los Reyes Católicos (Santiago de Compostela) 90
Hostal de San Marcos (León) 25, **353**
Hostels, youth 554, **556**, 557
Hotel Ritz (Madrid) 285, **286**
Hotel Room (Hopper) 288
Hotels **554–601**
  Andalusia 591–7
  Aragón 574–6
  Asturias and Cantabria 562–5
  Balearic Islands 597–9
  Barcelona 568–70
  Basque Country, Navarra and La Rioja 565–8
  booking and check-in 555
  Canary Islands 599–601
  casas rurales 555
  Castilla-La Mancha 586–8

Hotels (cont.)
Castilla y León 582–5
Catalonia 571–4
disabled travellers 557
Extremadura 588–90
Galicia 560–62
grading and facilities 554
hotel chains 557
Madrid 579–82
Madrid Province 582
monasteries and convents 556
mountain refuges 556
paradors **554**, 557, **558–9**
paying 555
prices 554–5
self-catering 556
Seville 590–91
Valencia and Murcia 576–9
youth hostels 556
Hoyos, Cristina 425
Hoyos del Espino, hotels 583
Hoz de Arbayún 135
Hoz de Beteta 383
Hoz de Lumbier 135
Huelva **462**
fiestas 42, 463
restaurants 645
Huelva province 459
Huertas (Madrid), nightlife 324–5
Huesca **235**
hotels 575
restaurants 625
Huesca province 227
Huguet, Jaume 147
Human towers (Catalonia) 221
Humeya, Abén 485
Las Hurdes 404
Hurtado, Francisco de 329
Hypermarkets 655

I

Iberian tribes 48
Ibiza (Eivissa) 504, 507, **510–12**
food and drink 413
hotels 597
map 508
nightlife 511
restaurants 648–9
Ibiza Town **510–11**, 662–3
hotels 597
restaurants 649
Los Ibores, Sierra de 406
Icod de los Vinos 534
Igantzi (Yanci) 134
Iglesia de la Magdalena (Seville)
430
Iglesia de Nuestra Señora del Rocío
(El Rocío) 463
Iglesia de San Antolín (Tordesillas)
366
Iglesia de San Jerónimo el Real
(Madrid) 290
Iglesia de San Juan Bautista (Baños
de Cerrato) 368
Iglesia de San Miguel de Escalada
(León) 353

Iglesia de San Nicolás de Bari
(Madrid) 275
Iglesia de San Pedro (Seville) 444
Iglesia de Santa Ana (Granada) 488
Iglesia de Santa María de Eunate
(near Puente la Reina) 131
Iglesia-Convento de San Esteban
(Salamanca) 359, 360
La Iglesuela del Cid, restaurants 625
Ignatius of Loiola, St
Jesuit Order 124
Santiario de Loiola 124
La Illa (Barcelona) 187, 189
Illa de la Discòrdia (Barcelona)
160, 164
Illa de Tabarca **261**
beach 258
Illas Cíes 95
Illes Medes (Islas Medes) 217
Illescas **386**
restaurants 637
Inca, restaurants 649
Incas 58
The Individual Traveller's Spain
556, 557
Induráin, Miguel 22
Infantado, Dukes of 3 32
Inmaculada Concepción 43
Inquisition 56, **274**
Palau Reial (Barcelona) 147
Institut Amatller d'Art Hispanic 164
Instituto Cervantes 661
Insurance
car 680
holiday 667
Interior design shops
Barcelona 188, 189
Madrid 318, 319
International Classical Theatre
Festival (Almagro) 41
International Exhibition, Barcelona
(1929) 169, 170, 172, 173
International Festival of Music and
Dance (Granada) 41
International Festival of Santander 41
International Folklore Gala 42
International Jazz Festival 41
International Vintage Car Rally 40
Interpreters 667
Inurria, Mateo 479
Irache 132
Iranzu 132
Irati, Selva de 135
Iregua Valley 129
La Iruela 497
Iruña see Pamplona
Irving, Washington 491
Isaba 135
Isabel I, Queen of Castile (the
Catholic) **56–7**
and Almería 501
Arévalo castle 365
Battle of Toro 357
and Cáceres 408, 409
and Columbus 146, 462
Granada 486

Isabel I, Queen of Castile (cont.)
Iglesia de San Jerónimo el Real
(Madrid) 290
Inquisition 274
Madrigal de las Altas Torres 366
marriage 366
Medina del Campo 366
Monasterio de San Juan de los
Reyes (Toledo) 391
and Orihuela 261
Real Alcázar (Seville) 440
Real Chancillería (Granada) 488
Santa Fé 482–3
unification of Spain 47, **70**
Isabel II, Queen of Spain
abdication 63
Museo Arqueológico Nacional
(Madrid) 296
portraits 62, 71
Teatro Real (Madrid) 275
Isabel of Portugal, tomb of 371
Isabel Clara Eugenia, Princess 281
Isidore, St 271, 272, 273
Isla 104
Isla de la Cartuja (Seville) 446
Isla Cristina 462
restaurants 645
Isla Mágica (Seville) 457
Isla Vedra see (Es) Vedrá
Islands **502–51**
Balearic Islands 506–27
Canary Islands 528–51
Introducing Spain's Islands 504–5
Islas Canarias see Canary Islands
Islote de Hilario 549
Ismail I 490
Isozaki, Irata 173
Itálica 51, 476

J

Jabugo 462
restaurants 645
Jaca **231**
festivals 41
hotels 575
restaurants 625
Jadraque, restaurants 637
Jaén 459, **493**
hotels 594
restaurants 645
Jaén, Bartolomé de 499
Jaén province 459
Jaime (Jaume) I, King of Aragón
Monasterio de El Puig 249
and Palma 518, 520
statue of 147
and Valencia 239, 250
Jaime II, King of Aragón
Barcelona cathedral 148, 149
Castell de Bellver (Palma) 519
tomb of 221, 521
Jaime III, King of Aragón, tomb 521
Jameos del Agua 550
James, St 55
and Padrón 94
Santiago de Compostela 92–3

James, St (cont.)
  statue of 129
  The Road to Santiago **82–3**, 85
  tomb of 52, 91, 93
Jamete, Esteban 497
Jandía, Península de 546
Jarama, River 333
Jarandilla de la Vera
  fiestas 405
  hotels 589
  restaurants 639
El Jardín de Serrano (Madrid)
  317
Játiva *see* Xàtiva
Jávea *see* Xàbia
Jazz 656
  Barcelona 192, 193
  Madrid **322**, 323
  Seville 457
Jerez de los Caballeros **413**
  hotels 589
  restaurants 639
Jerez de la Frontera **466**
  festivals 40, 42
  restaurants 645
Jerez-Xérès-Sherry wine region
  420–21
Jesuit Order **124**
  Carlos III expels 62
  Colegiata de San Isidro (Madrid)
  272
Jesús 511
Jewellery shops
  Barcelona **188**, 189
  Madrid 318, 319
Jews
  in Barcelona 146
  Centre Bonastruc Ça Porta
  (Girona) 214
  forced conversions 56
Jiloca, River 241
Jimena de la Frontera 468
Jiménez, Juan Ramón 35
Joan, Pere 225
John of the Cross, St 34, 363, 497
Jorquera 395
José I (Joseph Bonaparte) 63, 71,
  275
Joselito 37
Jovellanos, Gaspar Melchor de 105
Juan I, King of Aragón 369
Juan II, King of Aragón, tomb of
  222
Juan II, King of Castile, tomb of 371
Juan, King of Portugal 55
Juan, Prince, tomb of 3 63
Juan of Austria, Don 157
Juan Carlos I, King of Spain 23, 71
  and attempted coup d'état 68
  coronation 290
  Costa Teguise 549
  as Franco's successor 67
  Zarzuela Palace (Madrid) 276
Juan de la Cruz, San *see* John of the
  Cross, St
Juana, Doña 281

Juana la Beltraneja 56, 361
Juana la Loca (the Mad), Queen of
  Castile 57, 70
  Capilla Real (Granada) 486
  Castillo de la Mota (Medina del
  Campo) 366
Juanes, Juan de, *Ecce Homo* 252
Júcar (Xúquer), River 248, 383, 395
Jug and Glass (Gris) 33
Jujol, Josep Maria
  Casa Milà (Barcelona) 165
  Parc Güell (Barcelona) 178
  Plaça d'Espanya fountain
  (Barcelona) 173
Juliana, St, tomb of 112
Juliobriga 111
Jumilla wine region 202–3
Juni, Juan de 367, 377

K

Kane, Sir Richard 5 26
Kayaking 659
Ketama 424
Keytel International 557
Kingdom of Castile 54
Kingdom of Castile and León 54, 55
Knick-knack shops, Barcelona 188,
  189
The Knight's Dream (Pereda) 60–61
Knights Hospitallers 394, 488
Knights of Montesa 246
Knights of the Order of Alcántara
  410
Knights of the Order of Toisón del
  Oro 148
Knights Templar
  Castell del Papa Luna (Peñíscola)
  247
  Castro Urdiales 113
  Iglesia del Crucifijo (Puente la
  Reina) 131
  Jerez de los Caballeros castle 413
  El Maestrat 246
  Ponferrada Castle 351
Kokoschka, Oskar 118
Kolbe, Georg 170
  Morning 173
Kursaal (San Sebastián) 123

L

La Isla, Camarón de 425
Labels, wine 607
Labour Day 43
La Calahorra 493
Laga 119
Lagartera 387
Lago de Carucedo 350
Lago de Sanabria 351
Laguardia (Biastieri) **127**
  hotels 566
  restaurants 615
La Laguna 535
  hotels 601
Laguna de la Fuente de Piedra 475
Laguna Negra de Urbión 377
Lagunas de Peñalara 329

Lagunas de Ruidera 397
Laida 119
Lalique, René 361
Landscape at Cadaqués (Dalí) 298
Language **664**
  Basque (*Euskera*) 115
  Catalan 212
  Gallego 85
  La Gomera's whistle language
  532
  Valenciano dialect 243
Lanjarón 484
Lanuza-Sallent de Gállego, hotels
  575
Lanzarote 505, **548–50**
  hotels 601
  map 541
  restaurants 653
  volcanoes 551
Laredo **113**
  fiestas 110
  restaurants 612
Larouco 42
Larra 35
Las Cinco Villas Del Valle de
  Bidasoa 134
Lasarte, restaurants 615
Lastres 104
Latin American Film Festival
  (Huelva) 42
La Latina (Madrid) **302**
  nightlife 325
Laujar de Andarax 485
Lavapiés (Madrid), nightlife 324–5
Laza, fiestas 98
El Lazarillo de Tormes 34
Leather goods, Madrid 318, 319
Lebrija 466
Ledesma 361
Legal assistance 667
Léger, Fernand 118
Leitza, restaurants 615
Lekeitio (Lequeitio) 119
León **353–5**
  Cathedral 24, 57, 336, **354–5**
  hotels 584
  restaurants 634
  The Road to Santiago 82
León, Fray Luis de 395
León province *see* Castilla y León
Leonardo da Vinci 294, 305
Leone, Sergio 500
Leonor, Queen 133
Lepanto, Battle of (1571) 59
Lequeitio *see* Lekeitio
Lérida *see* Lleida
Lerma 376
Lerma, Duke of 60, 376
Lesaka 134
Letters and stamps 672
Letur 397
Leyre, Monasterio de 75, 135
Lichtenstein, Roy 156
Liérganes, hotels 563
Liétor 397
Linares, Marquis of 286

Linares de Mora 240
Liqueurs 607
Literature 34–5
Lizarra see Estella
Llafranc, beach 217
Llagostera, restaurants 6 22
Llamazares, Julio 35
Llanes 105
  hotels 563
Los Llanos de Aridane, restaurants
  652
Lleida (Lérida) **220–21**
  restaurants 622
Lleida (Lérida) province 207
Llerena 413
Llívia 212
Lloret de Mar
  beach 217
  hotels 572
  restaurants 622
La Llotja (Barcelona) 152
Lluc, hotels 598
Llull, Ramon 516
Llúria, Roger de, statue of 199
Local government 672–3
Logroño **129**
  hotels 566
  restaurants 615
Loiola, St Ignatius see Ignatius of
  Loiola, St
Loja 483
  hotels 594
  restaurants 645
La Lonja (Valencia) 251
Lope de Rueda 291
Lope de Vega see Vega, Lope de
López, Antonio López y 110
Lorca **263**
  fiestas 255
  restaurants 628
Los Vélez, Marquis of 500
Losar de la Vera
  hotels 589
  restaurants 639
Lotteries 672
Louis XIV, King of France 61
Lovers of Teruel 241
Lozoya 329
Luarca 104
Lucan 34
Lucía, Paco de 424
Ludwig Salvator, Archduke 515
Lugo 51, **99**
  restaurants 609
Lugo province 85
Lugones, restaurants 612
Luis I, King of Spain 62, 71
Luis de León, Fray 360
Luke, St 219
Lupiana 383
Lusitania (Roman province) 50

M

Maceo, Antonio 65
Machado, Antonio 35, 377, 498
Machuca, Pedro 294

Madrid **264–333**
  Autumn Festival 42
  Barajas Airport **674**, 676
  Bourbon Madrid 282–99
  Centro de Arte Reina Sofía 267,
  298–9
  character 12
  climate 44
  coach stations 683
  entertainment 320–25
  fiestas and festivals 40, 42, 43, 290
  food and drink 338
  French occupation 63
  hotels 579–82
  Introducing Madrid 266–7
  Museo del Prado 292–5
  Museo Thyssen-Bornemisza
  288–9
  nightlife 324–5
  Old Madrid 268–81
  Palacio Real 266, 276–7
  restaurants 629–32
  shopping 316–19
  Street-by-Street maps
  Old Madrid 270–71
  Paseo del Prado 284–5
  Street Finder 307–15
Madrid Province **326–33**
  hotels 582
  restaurants 632–3
Madrigal de la Altas Torres 366
El Maestrat (El Maestrazgo) 246
Magazines 671
Magellan, Ferdinand 58, 466
Os Magostos 42
Mahón see Maó
Majorca see Mallorca
Málaga **474**
  airport 676
  Alcazaba 52–3
  festivals 38
  hotels 594
  restaurants 646
Málaga province 459
Málaga wine region 420
Malasaña (Madrid) **304**
  nightlife 324–5
Maldonado, Rodrigo 361
Mallorca (Majorca) 505, 507,
  514–21
  fiestas 523
  food and drink 413
  hotels 597–8
  map 508–9
  restaurants 649–50
Malpartida de Plasencia 410
  hotels 589
Malpica 89
Mañara, Miguel de 431
La Mancha see Castilla-La Mancha
La Mancha wine region 340–41
Manchego cheese 338, 605
La Manga del Mar Menor, hotels
  578
Manilva, restaurants 646
Manises 253

Mannerists 294
Manners 664
Manolete 37, 306
Manresa, restaurants 622
Manrique, César 534, **548**, 549
  Fundación César Manrique
  (Teguise) 550
  Jameos del Agua 550
  Monumento al Campesino 550
Al Mansur 53, 377, 480
Manzanares
  hotels 587
  restaurants 637
Manzanares, River 276
Manzanares el Real **332**
Maó (Mahón) **526**
  hotels 599
  restaurants 651
Maps
  Las Alpujarras tour 484–5
  Ancient Menorca 527
  Andalusia 460–61
  Aragón 228–9
  Asturias and Cantabria 102–3
  Baeza 498–9
  Balearic Islands 504–5, 508–9
  Barcelona 138–9
  Barcelona: Barri Gòtic 144–5
  Barcelona: Eixample 159
  Barcelona: Further Afield 175
  Barcelona: Montjuïc 169, 170–71
  Barcelona: Old Town 143
  Barcelona: Quadrat d'Or 160–61
  Barcelona: Las Ramblas 151
  Barcelona: Street Finder 179–85
  Basque Country, Navarra and La
  Rioja 116–17
  birds of Central Spain 342
  broad-leaved forests 81
  Burgos 371
  Cáceres 408–9
  Canary Islands 17, 504–5
  Canary Islands: Eastern Islands
  540–41
  Canary Islands: Western Islands
  530–31
  Castilla-La Mancha 380–81
  Castilla y León 348–9
  castles of Castilla y León 345
  Catalonia 208–9
  Central Spain 336–7
  Córdoba 478–9
  Costa Blanca 258
  Costa del Sol 472–3
  Cruz de Tejeda tour 545
  Cuenca 384–5
  driving maps **682**, 683
  Eastern Spain 198–9
  Extremadura 402–3
  Galicia 86–7
  Girona 214
  Granada: Albaicín 488–9
  Granada: city centre 487
  legacy of Spanish colonization
  64
  Madrid 266–7

Maps (cont.)
Madrid: Bourbon Madrid 283
Madrid: Further Afield 301
Madrid: Old Madrid 269, 270–71
Madrid: Paseo del Prado 284–5
Madrid: Street Finder 307–15
Madrid Province 266, **326–33**
Mérida 411
national parks 31
Northern Spain 74–5
Palma 518–19
Pamplona 133
paradors 558–9
Parque Nacional de Ordesa
232–3
Parque Nacional de Picos de
Europa 108–9
Parque Nacional del Teide 538–9
prehistoric Spain 48
provinces of Spain 673
Pueblos Blancos tour 468–9
railways 679
Regional Spain 16–17
Rías Baixas 95
The Road to Santiago 82–3
Roman Spain 50
Ronda 470–71
Salamanca 358–9
Santiago de Compostela 90–91
Segovia 364
Seville: El Arenal 427, 428–9
Seville: Further Afield 443
Seville: Santa Cruz 433, 434–5
Seville: Street Finder 447–53
Sierra de Alcaraz 396–7
Sierra de Francia and Sierra de
Bejar tour 356–7
Southern Spain 416–17
Spain 14–15
Spain in 1714 62
Spain in July 1936 66
Spain today 68
Spain's exploration of the New
World 56
Spanish Empire in 1580 58
Spanish Empire in 1647 60
Toledo 388–9
Úbeda 496
Valencia 251
Valencia and Murcia 244–5
Vitoria 126
Wines of Eastern Spain 202–3
Wines of Northern Spain 78–9
Zaragoza 237
Mar de Castillo 382–3
Mar Menor 262
Maragatos 353
Marbella **473**
hotels 594
restaurants 646
Marcilla, Diego de 241
Marès i Deulovol, Frederic 223
Museu Frederic Marès 145, **146**
Margaret of Austria 280, 287
María Cristina, Queen
Palacio Miramar 122

María Cristina, Queen (cont.)
regency 63, 71
María Luisa, Princess 444
María Luisa, Queen **62**, 239
María Teresa, Queen of France 61
Mariscal, Javier 173
Markets 654
Barcelona 151, 154, **186**, 189
Madrid 302, 316–17, 319
Seville 454
Valencia 251
Vic 220
Marsé, Juan 35
Martí the Humanist 147
Martial 34
Martinet, restaurants 622
Martínez, Conchita 22
Martínez, Domingo 430
Martínez, Ginés 499
Martorell, Bernat 32
Transfiguration 149
Martorell, Joan 110–11
The Martyrdom of St Philip (Ribera)
292
Mary Tudor, Queen of England 58
Maspalomas 529, **542–3**
hotels 600
Mata Mua (Gaugin) 289
Matadors 36–7
Matarana, Bartolomé 251
Mateo, Maestro 92
Mateu, Pau 1 47
Matorral
flowers 204–5
wildlife 205
Matxitxaco 119
Maundy Thursday 43
Mauricio, Bishop 372
Mayonnaise 526
The Mayor of Zalamea (Calderón
de la Barca) 412
Mazagón 462
hotels 594
Mecina Bombarón Hotels 595
El Médano 534
Medical treatment 666
Medina Azahara 53, **477**
Medina del Campo 366
Medina de Pomar 369
Medina de Rioseco 367
Medina Sidonia, Dukes of 464, 469
Medinaceli **377**
Medinaceli, Dukes of 438
Las Médulas 350
Megaliths, Menorca 527
Meier, Richard 150
Mendizábal 63, 328
Mendoza, Cardinal 390, 493
Mendoza, Castillo de 127
Mendoza, Rodrigo de 493
Mengs, Anton Raffael 295
Las Meninas (Picasso) 32, 153
Las Meninas (Velázquez) **32–3**, 294
Menorca (Minorca) 505, 507, **522–7**
Ancient Menorca 49, **527**
fiestas 523

Menorca (Minorca) (cont.)
food and drink 513
hotels 599
map 509
restaurants 650–51
Méntrida wine region 340–41
Menus 603
Es Mercadal **523**
restaurants 650
Mercado Central (Valencia) 251
Mercado de San Miguel (Madrid)
270
Mercat del Born (Barcelona) 154
Mercat de las Flors (Barcelona)
191
Mercat de San Josep (Barcelona)
151
La Mercé (Barcelona) 157
Mérida 403, **410–11**
festivals 41
history 50
hotels 589
map 411
restaurants 639
Roman Theatre 50–51
Mérimée, Prosper 445
Mezquita (Córdoba) 416, 422, 479,
480–81
Midsummer's Eve (Catalonia) 221
Mies van der Rohe, Ludwig, Pavelló
Mies van der Rohe (Barcelona)
170, **173**
Es Migjorn Gran, restaurants 650
Mijas
hotels 594
restaurants 646
Milà, Casa 165
Milà family 165
Millán, Gómez 444
Los Millares 48, 501
Mini-Hollywood (Tabernas) 500,
657
Miño, hotels 561
Minorca *see* Menorca
Mirador del Río 550
Mirambel 246
Miranda del Castañar 357
Miró, Joan 261
Collage 33
Doña i Ocell 176
*Flame in Space and Naked
Woman* 172
Fundació Joan Miró (Barcelona)
171, **172**
Fundació Pilar y Joan Miró
(Palma) 519
Plaça de la Boqueria mosaic
(Barcelona) 151
Portrait II 298
Misteri d'Elx 41, 255
Mitjans, Francesc 176
Modernisme (Modernismo) 25,
140–41
Barcelona 159
Illa de la Discòrdia 164
Moguer 463

Mojácar **500**
　hotels 594–5
Molina de Aragón 382
Molinaseca
　hotels 584
　restaurants 634
Molleda, Val de San Vicente 563
Mombeltrán 362
Monachil, hotels 595
Monasteries
　accommodation in 556
　Monasterio de la Cartuja
　　(Granada) 63, 487
　Monasterio de las Descalzas
　　Reales (Madrid) 281
　Monasterio de La Encarnación
　　(Madrid) 280
　Monasterio de Guadalupe 406–7
　Monasterio de Iranzu 132
　Monasterio de Leyre 75, **135**
　Monasterio de Nuestra Señora de
　　Irache 132
　Monasterio de la Oliva 130
　Monasterio de Oseira 99
　Monasterio de Piedra 238
　Monasterio de El Puig 249
　Monasterio de la Rábida 462
　Monasterio de Ribas de Sil 86, **98**
　Monasterio de San Juan de Duero
　　377
　Monasterio de San Juan de la
　　Peña **234**, 251
　Monasterio de San Juan de los
　　Reyes (Toledo) 391
　Monasterio de San Millán de Suso
　　129
　Monasterio de San Millán de
　　Yuso 129
　Monasterio de San Pedro de
　　Cardeña 371
　Monasterio de San Salvador
　　(Celanova) 97
　Monasterio de Santa Clara (Olite)
　　131
　Monasterio de Santa Clara
　　(Tordesillas) 366
　Monasterio de Santa María (A
　　Guarda) 96
　Monasterio de Santa María de
　　Huerta 377
　Monasterio de Santa María de las
　　Cuevas (Seville) 446
　Monasterio de Santa María
　　(Fitero) 130
　Monasterio de Santa María de El
　　Paular 326, **328–9**
　Monasterio de Santa María la Real
　　129
　Monasterio de Santo Domingo de
　　Silos 376
　Monasterio Sobrado de los
　　Monjes 99
　Monasterio de Tentudia 413
　Monasterio de Uclés 386
　Monasterio de Veruela 236
　Monasterio de Yuste 400, **405**

Monasteries (cont.)
　Monestir de Montserrat 218–19
　Monestir de Poblet 199, **222–3**
　Monestir de Santa Maria de
　　Pedralbes (Barcelona) 177
　Monestir de Santes Creus 221
Moncloa (Madrid)
　nightlife 324–5
Mondoñedo 88
Moneo, Rafael 292, 519
Monestir see Monasteries
Money 668–9
Monfragüe, Parque Natural de 406
Monpensier, Dukes of 4 44
Monreal del Campo 238
Mont-Ras, restaurants 622
Montalbán 387
Montañas del Fuego 541, 548, 551
Montañés, Juan Martínez 61, 444
Montblanc (Montblanch) 221
El Monte Castillo 112
Monte Igueldo 122
Monte de Santa Tecla 96
Monte Ulía 122
Monte Urgull 122
Montefrío 414–15, **482–3**
Montejo de la Sierra 328
Montes de Anaga 535
Montes de León 350
Montes de Málaga, Parque Natural
　de los 474
Montes de Toledo 381, **387**
Montes Universales 241
Montgolfier brothers 62
Montilla **482**
Montilla-Moriles wine region 420
Montjuïc (Barcelona) **168–73**
　area map 169
　Street-by-Street map 170–71
Montseny
　hotels 572
　restaurants 622
Montserrat
　hotels 572
　Monestir de 218–19
Monturiol i Estarriol, Narcís, statue
　of 215
Monument a Colom (Barcelona)
　156
Monument del Dos de Mayo
　(Madrid) 285
Moore, Henry 119
Moore, Sir John 89
Moorish architecture 24, **422–3**
Moors 47
　converts 59
　expulsion from Spain 56–7
　expulsion of Moriscos 60, 61
　Granada 486
　history 52–3
　Reconquest **54–5**, 101
Moors and Christians (Alcoi) 40,
　255
Moors and Christians (Callosa D'en
　Sarria) 42
Mora de Rubielos **240**

Mora, Juan Gómez de
　Monasterio de la Encarnación
　　(Madrid) 280
　Plaza de la Villa (Madrid) 273
　Plaza Mayor (Madrid) 273
Moraira
　hotels 578
　restaurants 628
Morales del Toro, restaurants 634
Morales, Luis de 294, 361, 410
Moralzarzal, restaurants 633
Moratalla 263
　hotels 578
Morella **246**
　hotels 578
　restaurants 628
Moriscos 59
　expulsion of 60, 61
Morning (Kolbe) 173
Morro Jable 546
Mosques
　Mezquita (Córdoba) 416, 422,
　　458, 459, **480–81**
　Mezquita del Cristo de la Luz
　　(Toledo) 389
Mosteiro de Oseira see Monasterio
　de Oseira
Mosteiro de San Estevo de Rivas do
　Sil see Monasterio de Ribas del Sil
La Mota Castle (Medina del Campo)
　344, **366**
Mota del Cuervo 394
Motorways 681
Motril
　hotels 595
　restaurants 646
Mountain refuges 556
Mountain sports 659
Mountains 30
La Movida 305
Movies see Cinema
Moya 383
Mozaga 550
Mozarabic architecture 24, 353
Mudéjar architecture 24, 55, 422
Muela de Cortes 248
Muhammad II al Nasir 54
Muhammad V 490, 491
Muhammad ben Abd al Rahman
　269
Mulhacén 485
Mundaka 119
　hotels 566–7
Mundo, River 396
Muñoz Molina, Antonio 35
Muralla Bizantina (Cartagena) 263
Murat, Marshal 63
Murcia **262**
　Cathedral 198, 262
　festivals 38
　hotels 578
　restaurants 628
Murcia province see Valencia and
　Murcia
Murillo, Bartolomé Esteban 252,
　281, 437

Murillo, Bartolomé Esteban (cont.)
baptism 430
The Holy Children with the Shell 33
Hospital de la Caridad (Seville)
paintings 429
St John the Baptist as a Boy 431
*St John of God Carrying a Sick
Man* 431
*San Diego de Alcalá Giving Food
to the Poor* 61
La Servilleta 430
Muros 95
Museums and galleries
admission charges 664
Ateneu Científic Literari i Artistic
(Maó) 526
Bodega Museo (Valdepeñas) 398
Casa de l'Ardiaca (Barcelona)
144, **146**
Casa del Batle (Villafamés) 247
Casa de Cervantes (Valladolid) 367
Casa de Colón (Las Palmas de
Gran Canria) 544
Casa de Juntas (Gernika-Lumo)
119
Casa-Museo de Cervantes (Alcalá
de Henares) 333
Casa-Museo Gaudí (Barcelona)
178
Casa-Museo de Goya
(Fuendetodos) 239
Casa Museo de Martín Alonso
Pinzón (Palos de la Frontera) 463
Casa Museu Salvador Dalí
(Cadaqués) 216
Casa-Museo de Unamuno
(Salamanca) 361
Casa Natal de Picasso 474
Castillo de la Yedra (Cazorla) 497
Castro de Coaña 104
Cathedral Museum (Murcia) 262
Cathedral Museum (Palma) 520
Cathedral Museum (Santiago de
Compostela) 92
Centre Bonastruc Ça Porta
(Girona) 214
Centre de Cultura Contemporània
(Barcelona) 150
Centre del Disseny 154
Centro Andaluz de Arte
Contemporaneo (Seville) 446
Chillida-Leku (San Sebastián) 123
Ciutat de les Arts i de les
Ciències (Valencia) 253
Collecció Hernández Sanzy
Hernández Mora (Maó) 526
Conjunt Monumental de la Plaça
del Rei (Barcelona) 143, 145,
146–7
Cosmocaixa – Museu de la
Ciència (Barcelona) **178**
Cueva-Museo Al Fareria (Guadix)
493
Cueva-Museo Costumbres
Populares (Guadix) 493
Eco-Museo (Deltebre) 225

Museums and galleries (cont.)
Fundació Pilar i Joan Miró
(Palma) 519
Fundació Tàpies (Barcelona) 160,
164
Fundación César Manrique
(Teguise) 550
Gibraltar Museum (Gibraltar) 472
Herrería de Compludo (El Bierzo)
350
Iglesia de San Antolín
(Tordesillas) 366
Instituto Valenciano de Arte
Moderno (IVAM, Valencia) 252
León Cathedral 354
Monasterio de El Puig 249
Museo de América (Madrid) 303
Museo de Armería (Vitoria) 127
Museo de Arqueología (Vitoria)
126
Museu Arqueològic (Barcelona)
171, **172**
Museu Arqueològic (Sóller) 515
Museo Arqueológico (Almuñécar)
483
Museo Arqueológico (Badajoz) 412
Museo Arqueológico (Betancuria)
546
Museo Arqueológico (Córdoba)
479
Museo Arqueológico (Cuenca) 384
Museo Arqueológico, Etnografico
de Histórico Vasco (Bilbao) 118
Museo Arqueológico (Granada)
487, 489
Museo Arqueológico (Málaga)
474
Museo Arqueológico Nacional
(Madrid) 296
Museo Arqueológico (Oviedo)
106, 107
Museo Arqueológico Provincial
(Huesca) 235
Museo Arqueológico (Seville) 445
Museo Arqueológico (Úbeda) 497
Museu d'Art Contemporani
(Barcelona) **150**
Museu d'Art Contemporani
(Ibiza) 511
Museum of Art (El Escorial) 331
Museu d'Art (Girona) 215
Museo Art Nouveau y Art Deco
(Salamanca) 361
Museo de Arte Abstracto
(Cuenca) 384
Museo de Arte Contemporáneo
(Alicante) 261
Museu de Arte Visigodo 411
Museo de Artes y Costumbres
Populares (Seville) 445
Museu de Arts Decoratives
(Barcelona) 177
Museu d'Automates (Barcelona)
178
Museo de Bellas Artes (Bilbao)
118

Museums and galleries (cont.)
Museo de Bellas Artes (Córdoba)
479
Museo de Bellas Artes (Oviedo)
106, 107
Museo de Bellas Artes (Santa
Cruz de Tenerife) 536
Museo de Bellas Artes
(Santander) 113
Museo de Bellas Artes (Seville) 430
Museo de Bellas Artes (Valencia)
252
Museo de Burgos 371
Museo de Cádiz 467
Museo Camón Aznar (Zaragoza)
237
Museo Canario (Las Palmas de
Gran Canaria) 544
Museu Cau Ferrat (Sitges) 224
Museu de Cera (Barcelona) 151
Museu de Ceràmica (Barcelona)
177
Museo Cerralbo (Madrid) 304
Museo de Ciencias Naturales El
Carmen (Onda) 248
Museu Comarcal de la Conca de
Barberà (Montblanc) 221
Museu Comarcal de la Garrotxa
(Olot) 213
Museu Diocesà (Ciutadella) 522
Museo Diocesà (Palma) 519
Museu Diocesà (La Seu d'Urgell)
212
Museu Diocesà i Comarcal
(Solsona) 220
Museo Diocesano (Cuenca) 385
Museo Diocesano (Mondoñedo)
88
Museo Diocesano (Santillana del
Mar) 112
Museo Diocesano de Arte Sacro
(Las Palmas de Gran Canaria) 544
Museo Diocesano de Arte Sacro
(Vitoria) 127
Museo del Emigrante Canario
(Teguise) 550
Museu Episcopal de Vic 220
Museo Etnográfico (Grandas de
Salime) 104
Museu Etnográfico (O Cebreiro) 99
Museo Etnográfico Gonzalez
Santana (Olivenza) 412
Museo Etnográfico y Textil
(Plasencia) 405
Museu Etnològic (Barcelona) 171
Museu Etnològic (Santa Eulària)
512
Museo Etnológico de la Huerta
de Murcia (Murcia) 262
Museu Frederic Marès 145, **146**
Museo del Futbol Club Barcelona
176
Museo de Geologia (Barcelona)
155
Museo del Grabado Español
Contemporáneo (Marbella) 473

Museums and galleries (cont.)
Museo del Greco (Toledo) 391
Museo Guggenheim (Bilbao) 118, **120–21**
Museo Heráldica (Castillo de Mendoza) 127
Museu d'Història de la Ciutat (Barcelona) 146–7
Museu d'Història de la Ciutat (Girona) 215
Museo de Historia Valencia 253
Museo de Ignacio Zuloaga (Zumaia) 119
Museo del Joguet (Figueres) 215
Museo Lázaro Galdiano (Madrid) 305
Museo de León 353
Museu de Mallorca (Palma) 519
Museu Marítim and Drassanes (Barcelona) 157
Museo Marítimo (Santander) 113
Museo de Micro-Miniaturas (Guadalest) 259
Museo Minero (Riotinto) 462
Museu Monografico de Pollentia (Alcúdia) 516
Museo de Monte de Santa Tecla (A Guarda) 96
Museo Municipal (Madrid) 25, **304–5**
Museu Municipal (Pollença) 516
Museu Municipal (Tossa del Mar) 216
Museo Municipal (Xàtiva) 254
Museo Nacional Arqueología Marítima (Cartagena) 263
Museu Nacional Arqueològic (Tarragona) 224–5
Museu Nacional d'Art de Catalunya (Barcelona) 170, **172**
Museo Nacional de Arte Romano (Mérida) 336, 410–11
Museu Nacional de Artes Decorativas (Madrid) 285, **287**
Museo Nacional Centro de Arte Reina Sofía (Madrid) 267, **298–9**
Museo Nacional de Céramica Gonzalez Martí (Valencia) 251
Museo Nacional de Escultura (Valladolid) 367
Museo de Naipes (Vitoria) 127
Museo de la Naturaleza y el Hombre (Santa Cruz de Tenerife) 536
Museo de Navarra 133
Museo Numantino (Soria) 377
Museo Pablo Gargallo (Zaragoza) 237
Museu Pau Casals (El Vendrell) 224
Museo Pérez Comendador-Leroux (Hervás) 404
Museo del Pescador 119
Museu Picasso (Barcelona) 153
Museo Picasso (Buitrago del Lozoya) 328
Museo de Picasso (Málaga) 474

Museums and galleries (cont.)
Museo de Pontevedra 94
Museo del Prado (Madrid) 267, **292–5**
Museo de Prehistoria y Arqueología (Santander) 113
Museo Pretori i Circ Romans (Tarragona) 224–5
Museo Provincial (Albacete) 396
Museo Provincial (Cáceres) 409
Museo Provincial (Huelva) 462
Museo Provincial (Jaén) 493
Museo Provincial (Lugo) 99
Museo Provincial (Teruel) 241
Museo Provincial de Bellas Artes (Castelló de la Plana) 247
Museo de Ricas Telas (Burgos) 371
Museo Romero de Torres (Córdoba) 479
Museo Rosalia de Castro (Padrón) 94
Museo de San Gil (Atienz) 382
Museo San Juan de Dios (Orihuela) 261
Museo de San Telmo (San Sebastián) 123
Museo de Santa Cruz (Toledo) 389, **390**
Museo de Semana Santa (Zamora) 356
Museo Sorolla (Madrid) 305
Museo Taurino (Antequera) 475
Museo Taurino (Córdoba) 478
Museo Taurino (Madrid) 306
Museo Taurino (Seville) 457
Museu Tèxtil i de la Indumentària (Barcelona) 177
Museo Thyssen-Bornemisza (Madrid) 267, 284, 286, **288–9**
Museu de la Vall d'Aran (Vielha) 210
Museu del Vi (Vilafranca del Penedès) 221
Museu de la Xocolata (Barcelona) 154
Museo de Zaragoza 237
Museu de Zoologia (Barcelona) 155
Necropolis de Puig d'es Molins (Ibiza) 511
New Museum (Monastery of Montserrat) 218
opening hours 664
Palacio Episcopal (Astorga) 352
Palacio de Nájera (Antequera) 475
Patio Herreriano Museo de Arte Español Contemporáneo (Valladolid) 367
Real Academia de Bellas Artes (Madrid) 281
Ruinas de Santo Domingo (Pontevedra) 94

Museums and galleries (cont.)
Salón de Reinos (Madrid) 285, 287
Teatre-Museu Dalí (Figueres) 215
Tesoro de Villena (Villena) 260
Villa Romana la Olmeda 369
Music 656–7
Barcelona 191–3
flamenco **424–5**, 656
Gregorian plainchant 376
Madrid 321–3
Seville 456–7
Music shops
Barcelona 188, 189
Madrid 318, 319
Seville 455
Muslim Spain 52–3
Mussolini, Benito 66

N

Nacimento del Río Cuervo 383
Nagel, Andrés 176
Nàjera 129
The Naked Maja (Goya) 259, 293
Napoleon I, Emperor 47
and Alcántara 410
and the Alhambra (Granada) 490
and Guadalupe 406
invasion of Madrid 239
occupation of Spain 63
War of Independence 467
Naranjo de Bulnes 109
Narcissus, St, tomb of 214
Nasrid architecture 422–3
Nasrid dynasty 490, 492
National Day 43
National parks 30–31
Parc Nacional d'Aigüestortes 30, 207, **211**
Parque Nacional de Cabañeros 31, 387
Parque Nacional de Doñana 30, 416, **464–5**
Parque Nacional de Garajonay 31, 533
Parque Nacional de la Caldera de Taburiente (La Palma) 31 532
Parque Nacional de Ordesa 30, 198, 226, 227, **232–3**
Parque Nacional de los Picos de Europa 30, **108–9**
Parque Nacional del Teide **538–9**, 551
Parque Nacional de Timanfaya 31, 541, **548–9**
walking in 658
Nationalists, Spanish Civil War 66–7
Natividad (Berruguete) 367
NATO 68
Nature reserves
Parc Natural del Delta de l'Ebre 225
Parque Natural del Alto Tajo 382
Parque Natural de Cabo de Gata 417, **501**

Nature reserves (cont.)
Parque Natural de Cazorla 497
Parque Natural de las Hoces del Duratón 365
Parque Natural de Moncayo 236
Parque Natural de Monfragüe 406
Parque Natural de los Montes de Málaga 474
Parque Natural de Somiedo 105
Parque Natural del Torcal 475
Reserva Nacional de los Ancares Leoneses 350
Reserva Nacional de Fuentes Carrionas 369
Reserva Nacional de Gredos 362
Naturism 660, 661
Nava, festivals 41
Navacerrada 329
restaurants 633
Navarra see Basque Country, Navarra and La Rioja
Navarra wine region 78–9
Navarredonda de Gredos, hotels 584
Las Navas de Tolosa, Battle of (1212) 54–5
La Naveta d'es Tudons 49
Nazis 66
Neanderthal man 48
Necrópolis Romana (Carmona) 476
Nelson, Admiral 62, 63, 526
Nerja 483
hotels 595
New Year 39, 43, 290
Newspapers 671
NH-Hoteles 557
Nicolau, Pere 32, 252
Niebla 462
Nightlife 657
Barcelona 194–5
Ibiza 511
Madrid 324–5
Seville 457
Níjar 501
Noche Buena (Christmas Eve) 43
Noche Vieja (New Year's Eve) 43
Noelithic 48
Noia (Noya) 94, 95
hotels 561
North Africa, ferries 677
Northern Spain 72–135
Asturias and Cantabria 100–13
Basque Country, Navarra and La Rioja 114–23
forests 80–81
Galicia 84–99
map 74–5
regional food 76–7
The Road to Santiago 82–3
wines 78–9
Novaleno, restaurants 634
Novalonguilla, restaurants 634
Novelda 260
Nudism 660

Nuestra Señora de Covadonga 110
Nuévalos, restaurants 625
Numantia 377

O
Oak forests 81
Ocaña 394
Ochagavia 135
Oia, fiestas 90
Oiartzun, restaurants 615
Old Madrid 268–81
area map 269
restaurants 629–30
Street-by-Street map 270–71
Old Town (Barcelona) 142–57
restaurants 617–18
Olite (Herriberri) 130–31
hotels 567
restaurants 615
La Oliva 546
Oliva, hotels 578
Oliva, Abbot 220
Olivares, Count-Duke 60, 304
Oliveira, Juan José 96
Olivenza 412
restaurants 639
Olleros de Pisuerga 369
La Olmeda 369
Olot 213
Olympic Games, Barcelona (1992) 23, 156, 173
Oña 369
Oñati (Oñate) 124
Onda 248
Ondarroa 119
Ontinyent, hotels 578
Opening hours 664
banks 668
restaurant 602
shops 316, 654
Opera 22, 656
Barcelona 191, 193
Bilbao 43
Madrid 322, 323
Seville 456
Opus Dei 235
Oranges 29, 200
Oratorio de San Felipe Neri (Cádiz) 467
Order of Calatrava 54
Alcañiz 239
Almagro 399
Calatrava la Nueva 398–9
Sinagoga de Santa María la Blanca 391
Order of Santiago
Casa de las Conchas (Salamanca) 361
Hostal de San Marcos (León) 353
Monasterio de Tentudia 413
Monasterio de Uclés 386
Vilar de Donas 99
Yeste 396
Ordesa, Parque Nacional de 30, 198, 226, 227, 232–3

Orea, Juan de 501
Orellana, Francisco de 407
Orense see Ourense
Los Órganos 533
Orgaz 387
Orgiva 484
hotels 595
Ori, Monte 135
Orihuela (Oriola) 261
hotels 578
restaurants 628
Oropesa 247, 387
hotels 587
restaurants 637
La Orotava 535
fiestas 536
hotels 601
Orreaga see Roncesvalles
Ortega, Gómez 297
Ortiguera, Ría de 88
Ortiguera (Asturias) 104
Orzola 550
Los Oscos 104
Oseira, Monasterio de 99
Osona, Rodrigo de (the Younger) 511
Ossa de Montiel, hotels 587
Osuna 475
restaurants 646
Osuna, Dukes of 475
Our Lady of the Dry Tree (Christus) 288
Our Lady of the Sea (Formentera) 523
Ourense (Orense) 98
restaurants 609
Ourense (Orense) province 85
Outdoor activities 658–61
Oviedo 74, 106–7
hotels 563
restaurants 612
Oviedo, Juan de 430

P
Pabellón de Andalucia (Seville) 442
Pacheco, Francisco de 61
Padilla, Juan de, tomb of 371
Padilla, María de 366
Padrón 94
restaurants 609
Paella 201
Paintings 32–3
El País 69
Pájara 546
Palaces
Alcázar de los Reyes Cristianos (Córdoba) 478
Alfajería (Zaragoza) 237
Alhambra (Granada) 54, 422–3, 490–91
Casa del Cordón (Zamora) 356
Casa de los Momos (Zamora) 356
El Escorial (Madrid) 266, 330–31
La Granja de San Ildefonso 363
Medina Azahara 53, 477
Moorish architecture 423

Palaces (cont.)
Palacio Arzobispal (Seville) 434
Palacio de Avellaneda (Peñaranda de Duero) 376–7
Palau Baro de Quadras (Barcelona) 161
Palacio de las Cadenas (Úbeda) 25, **497**
Palacio de Cristal (Madrid) 297
Palau Ducal (Gandia) 255
Palacio de los Duques del Infantado (Guadalajara) 383
Palacio de El Pardo 332
Palacio Episcopal (Astorga) 352
Palau de la Generalitat (Barcelona) 144, **147**
Palau de la Generalitat 250
Palau Güell (Barcelona) **140–41**, 150–51
Palacio de Jabalquinto (Baeza) 498
Palacio de Liria (Madrid) 304
Palacio de la Madraza (Granada) 486
Palacio de la Magdalena (Santander) 113
Palacio del Marqués de la Conquista (Trujillo) 407
Palacio Miramar (San Sebastián) 122
Palau Moja (Barcelona) 151
Palacio Mondragón (Ronda) 470
Palacio de Monterrey (Salamanca) 358
Palau de la Música (Valencia) 252
Palau de la Música Catalana (Barcelona) 142, **152**, 191
Palacio de la Música y Congresos Euskalduna (Bilbao) 118
Palau Nacional (Barcelona) 138
Palacio de Nájera (Antequera) 475
Palacio de Navarra 133
Palacio Pedro I (Seville) 422, 440
Palacio de Peñaflor (Écija) 477
Palacio de Penmartín (Jerez de la Frontera) 466
Palacio de Pizarro-Orellana (Trujillo) 407
Palacio Real (Madrid) 266, **276–7**
Palacio Real de Aranjuez 333
Palau Reial (Barcelona) 146–7
Palau Reial de l'Almudaina (Palma) 518
Palau Reial de Pedralbes (Barcelona) 177
Palacio de Revillagigedo 105
Palacio de Sada (Sos del Rey Católico) 230
Palau Salort (Ciutadella) 522
Palacio de San Telmo (Seville) 444–5
Palacio de Santa Cruz 271
Palacio Sobrellano (Comillas) 110–11

Palaces (cont.)
Palacio del Tiempo (Jerez de la Frontera) 466
Palacio de Velázquez (Madrid) 297
Palacio de Viana (Córdoba) 479
Palacio Villardompardo (Jaén) 493
Palau de la Virreina (Barcelona) 151
Palacio del Viso (Viso del Marqués) 398
Real Alcázar (Seville) 435
see also Castles
Palacio, León Gill de 305
Palaeolithic 48
Palamós, beach 217
Palau see Palaces
Palencia **368**
hotels 584
restaurants 635
Palencia province 347
Palloza 350
Palm Sunday processions 38
La Palma 530, **532**
hotels 601
restaurants 652
volcanoes 551
Palma de Mallorca 506, **518–21**
airport 676
Cathedral 520–21
festivals 41
hotels 598
restaurants 649–50
Street-by-Street map 518–19
Palma del Río **477**
hotels 595
restaurants 647
Las Palmas de Gran Canaria **544**
airport 676
festivals 40
hotels 600
restaurants 652
La Paloma (Barcelona) 194, 195
Palomino, Antonio 487
Palos de la Frontera 463
Pals, restaurants 622
Pamplona (Iruña) **132–3**
bull run 75
fiestas 20, 39, 132
hotels 567
map 133
restaurants 616
The Road to Santiago 83
Pantaleon, St 280
Panteón Real (León) 353
Panticosa, hotels 575
Panxón 95
Paradores **554**, 557, **558–9**
Paragliding 658
Paraja, hotels 600
Paris School 33
Parking 682
Parks and gardens
Alcázar de los Reyes Cristianos (Córdoba) 478

Parks and gardens (cont.)
Balcón de Mediterráneo (Benidorm) 260
Bananera El Guanche (Puerto de la Cruz) 534
Campo del Moro (Madrid) 275
Casa de Campo (Madrid) 302
Generalife (Granada) 492
La Granja de San Ildefonso 363
Huerto del Cura (Elx) 261
Huerto de las Flores (Agaete) 543
Jardí Botànic Mar i Murtra (Blanes) 216
Jardín de Cactus (Guatiza) 550
Jardín Canario (Tarifa) 544
Jardines del Río Turia (Valencia) 252
Loro Parque (Puerto de la Cruz) 534
Moorish gardens 422
Palacio Miramar (San Sebastián) 122
Palacio Real de Aranjuez 333
Palmitos Park (Maspalomas) 543
Parque de l'Aigüera (Benidrom) 260
Parc d'Atraccions (Barcelona) 178, **192**
Parc de la Ciutadella (Barcelona) 139, **154–5**
Parc de l'Espanya Industrial (Barcelona) 176
Parc Güell (Barcelona) 141, **178**
Parc de Joan Miró (Barcelona) 176
Parque María Luisa (Seville) 444–5
Parque Municipal García Sanabria (Santa Cruz de Tenerife) 536
Parque del Oeste (Madrid) 303
Parque Ornitológico (Almuñécar) 483
Parque del Retiro (Madrid) 267, 282, 283, **297**
Parc Zoològic (Barcelona) 155
Real Alcázar (Seville) 440
Real Jardín Botánico 297
see also Amusement parks; National parks; Nature reserves; Theme parks
Pas Valley 112
Pasaia Donibane 123
restaurants 616
Pasarela Cibeles (Madrid) 43
Paseo de la Castellana (Madrid) 306
Paseo del Prado (Madrid), Street-by-Street map 284–5
El Paso 532
Passeig de Gràcia (Barcelona) 160
The Passion (Chinchon) 290
Passports 664
lost 667
Pastori, Niña 457
Pastrana 383
hotels 587
Patio Fiesta (Córdoba) 463
Patones de Arriba 328
restaurants 633

La Patum (Berga) 221
Paul III, Pope 124
Pavelló Mies van der Rohe (Barcelona) 170, **173**
Pazo de Oca 94
Pazos 85
Pechina, hotels 595
Pechón, hotels 563
Pedrajas, Francisco Javier 482
Pedraza de la Sierra **365**
    hotels 584
    restaurants 635
La Pedriza 332
Pedro I the Cruel, King of Castile 391
    Alcázar del Rey Pedro (Carmona) 476
    Convento de Santa Clara (Tordesillas) 366
    Real Alcázar (Seville) 440
Pedro II, King of Aragón 54
Pedro de Osma, San, tomb of 377
Las Pedroñeras, restaurants 637
Peguera, restaurants 650
Pelayo 52, 107, 108, **109**
Pelayo, Marcelino Menéndez 291
Os Peliqueiros (Laza) 98
Peña Cortada 248
La Peña de Francia 356
Peñafiel 20, 345, 367
Penáguila, hotels 578
Peñalba de Santiago 351
Peñaranda de Duero 349, **376–7**
Peñarroya 240
Peñas de San Pedro, fiestas 387
Penedès wine region 202–3
Península de Jandía 546
Peninsular War *see* War of Independence
Peñíscola **247**
    hotels 578–9
    restaurants 628
Peñón de Ifach *see* Penyal d'Ifach
Pensions 554
Penyal d'Ifach (Peñón de Ifach) 242, **259**
Peral, Isaac 263
Peralada, restaurants 622
Peramola, hotels 572
Peratallada 216
Perdido, Monte 233
Pere the Ceremonious 215, 222
Pereda, Antonio de, *The Knight's Dream* 60–61
Pérez, José Luján 543
Pérez, Juan 462
Pérez de Andrade, Count Fernán 88
Pérez Galdós, Benito 35
Pero Palo (Villanueva de la Vera) 405
Personal security 666–7
Peter, St 219
Peter of Aragón 235
Petrol 680
Petronila of Aragón 54

Pharmacies 666
Phoenicians 47, 48, 49
Phone cards 670
Picadores 36
Picasso, Pablo **32**, **65**, 261
    in Barcelona 153
    The Burial of the Count of Orgaz 514
    Casa Natal de Picasso (Málaga) 474
    Guernica **66–7**, 118, **299**
    Harlequin with a Mirror 288
    in Madrid 281
    matador's cape 430
    Las Meninas 32, 153
    Museu Picasso (Barcelona) 153
    Museo Picasso (Buitrago del Lozoya) 328
    Museo Picasso (Málaga) 474
    Self Portrait 153
    Woman in Blue 298
Pico de las Nieves 545
Pico del Remedio 248
Pico de Tres Mares 111
Pico Veleta 485
Pico Viejo 551
Picos de Europa 74, 101, 102
    Parque Nacional de Picos de Europa 30, **108–9**
Pilgrims, The Road to Santiago 82–3
Pinazo, Ignacio 252
Piños, Elisenda de Montcada de 177
Pinzón, Martín, Casa Museo de Martín Alonso Pinzón (Palos de la Frontera) 463
Pinzón, Vicente 463
Pizarro, Francisco 58, 407
Pizarro, Hernando 407
Plaça de la Boqueria (Barcelona) 151
Plaça d'Espanya (Barcelona) 173
Plaça Reial (Barcelona) 151
Plainchant, Gregorian 376, 657
Planetariums, El Planetario (Castelló de la Plana) 2 47
Plasencia **405**
    hotels 589
    restaurants 639–40
Plateresque architecture 25
La Platja d'Aro (Playa de Aro), beach 217
Platja de Sant Joan (Playa de San Juan), beach 258
Playa de las Américas 534
Playa d'Aro *see* La Platja d'Aro
Playa Blanca 548
    hotels 601
Playa del Camello (Santander) 102
Playa de las Canteras 544
Playa de la Concha (San Sebastián) 122
Playa del Inglés 542–3
Playa de Ondarreta (San Sebastián) 117, 122

Playa Papagayo 548
Playa de San Juan *see* Platja de Sant Joan
Playa de Santiago 533
    hotels 600
Playa de la Zurriola (San Sebastián) 122
La Plaza 105
Plaza Cánovas del Castillo (Madrid) 284, 286
Plaza de Cibeles (Madrid) 267, 285, **286**
Plaza de Colón (Madrid) 296
Plaza de la Constitución (San Sebastián) 122
Plaza de España (Madrid) 280
Plaza de los Fueros (Tudela) 130
Plaza mayor 27
Plaza Mayor (Madrid) 61, 266, 270, **273**
Plaza Mayor (Salamanca) 359, 360
Plaza de Oriente (Madrid) 275
Plaza de la Paja (Madrid) 302
Plaza del Pópulo (Baeza) 499
Plaza de Toros (Antequera) 475
Plaza de Toros de la Maestranza (Seville) 36, 426, 427, 428, **430**
Plaza de Toros de Las Ventas (Madrid) 300, **306**, 321
Plaza del Triunfo (Seville) 434
Plaza de la Villa (Madrid) 270, **272–3**
Plaza Virgen de los Reyes (Seville) 434
Plentzia 119
Poble Espanyol (Barcelona) 170, **173**
Poble Sec (Barcelona), nightlife 194–5
Poblet, Monestir de 199, **222–3**
Pobra de Trives, hotels 561
Poetry 34
Police 666–7
Pollença (Pollensa) 516
Polop de la Marina, restaurants 628
Pompey 50
Ponce de León, Alfonso, *Accident* 298
Ponferrada **351**
    hotels 584
    restaurants 635
Ponteareas, fiestas 98
Pontedeume (Puentedeume) 88
Pontevedra 86, **94**, 95
    festivals 40
    hotels 561
    restaurants 609
Pontevedra province 85
Ponticosa, restaurants 625
Pop music 656
Poqueira Valley 484
Port d'Andratx 514
    hotels 598
    restaurants 650
Port Aventura 224, 657

Port Olímpic (Barcelona) 156
  nightlife 194, 195
Port de Pollença (Pollensa) 508
  hotels 598
  restaurants 650
Port Vell (Barcelona) 156
  nightlife 194, 195
Pórtico da Gloria (Santiago de
  Compostela) 92
Portinaxt 511
Portocolom, restaurants 650
*Portrait of Baron Thyssen-
  Bornemisza* (Freud) 288
Portrait II (Miró) 298
Posets 231
Postal services 672
Potes **110**
  restaurants 612
Poussin, Nicolas 295
Poxal de Gallinas, hotels 584
Pozo, Aurelio de 430
Pradilla, Francisco, *The Fall of
  Granada* 56–7
Prado, Museo del (Madrid) 267,
  292–5
Prado del Rey, hotels 595
El Prat (Barcelona) 675
Pravia
  hotels 564
  restaurants 612
Praza do Obradoiro (Santiago de
  Compostela) **90**, 92
Pre-Romanesque architecture 24, 106
Prehistoric Spain **48–9**
  Cales Coves 526
  Capocorb Vell 516–17
  Cueva de El Monte Castillo 112
  Cuevas de Altamira 112
  Menorca 527
  Los Millares 501
Prendes, restaurants 611
Priatorio wine region 202–3
Priego de Córdoba 482
Prim, General 63, 155
Primo de Rivera, José Antonio 329
  military coup 65
  portrait 64
  resignation 65
Príncipe Pío (Madrid) 317
Provinces 673
PSOE (Socialist Workers' Party) 68,
  69
Public conveniences 667
Public holidays 43
Pubs 602
Puebla de la Reina, restaurants 640
Puebla de Sanabria 351
Puebla de la Sierra 328
Pueblo Nuevo del Bullaque 387
Pueblos Blancos, tour of 468–9
El Puente del Arzobispo 387
Puente Internacional (Tui) 97
Puente Nuevo (Ronda) 470
Puente la Reina **131**
  restaurants 616
  The Road to Santiago 83

Puente Romano (Córdoba) 479
Puente Romano (Salamanca) 358
Puente Viesgo 112
Puentedeume *see* Pontedeume
Puerta de Alcalá (Madrid) 285,
  287
Puerta de Europa (Madrid) 306
Puerta del Sol (Madrid) 271, **272**
Puerto Banús 472
Puerto del Carmen **549**
  hotels 601
Puerto de la Cruz **534**
  restaurants 653
Puerto Lápice 394
Puerto de Mazarrón 263
Puerto de Mogán **542**
Puerto de la Ragua 485
Puerto Rico 540, **542**
Puerto del Rosario **547**
  restaurants 651
El Puerto de Santa María 466
  restaurants 644
Puerto de Somport 230
Puig i Cadafalch, Josep 140
  Casa Amatller (Barcelona) 164
  Casa Terrades (Barcelona) 161,
    165
  Palau Baro de Quadras
    (Barcelona) 161
Puig de Missa 512
Puig de Randa 516
Puigcerdà 212
Es Pujols
  hotels 597
  restaurants 648
Punta de Teno 531
Punta Umbria 462
Pyrenees
  Folklore Festival (Jaca) 41
  Parque Nacional de Ordesa
    232–3
  wildlife 232
Pyrenees, Peace of the (1659) 61

Q
Quadrat d'Or (Barcelona), Street-by-
  Street map 160–61
Quesada, Diego de 444
Quevedo, Francisco de 34, 398
Quijas, hotels 564
Quintanilla de las Viñas 370
Quixote, Don *see* Cervantes

R
RAAR 555, 557
Radio 671
Rail travel 678–9
Rainfall 44–5
Rainy Taxi (Dalí) 215
Ramales de la Victoria 113
  restaurants 612
Las Ramblas 139, **150–51**
Ramiro I, King of Aragón 106
Ramiro II, King of Aragón 235
Ramis, Julie 514

Ramon Berenguer I, King of
  Catalonia 149
Ramon Berenguer IV, King of
  Catalonia 54
  Monestir de Poblet 222
  Monestir de Santes Creus 221
Ranc, Jean 295
Randa, hotels **598**
A Rapa das Bestas (Oia,
  Pontevedra) 40, 98
Raphael 281
  Christ Falls on the Way to Calvary
    295
Rascafría 329
  hotels 582
  restaurants 633
El Rastro (Madrid) **302**, 317
El Raval (Barcelona) **150**
  nightlife 194, 195
Raventós, Ramon 173
Real Academia de Bellas Artes
  (Madrid) 281
Real Academia de la Historia
  (Madrid) 291
Real Alcázar (Seville) 422, 435,
  440–41
Real Cartuja de Jesús de Nazaret
  (Valldemossa) 514
Real Chancillería (Granada) 488
Real Escuela Andaluza de Arte
  Ecuestre (Jerez de la Frontera)
  466
Real Fábrica de Tapices (Madrid)
  306
Real Federación Aeronáutica
  Española 658
Real Federación Española de
  Ciclismo 660
Real Federación Española de Golf
  660
Real Federación Española de Vela
  658
Real Madrid 177, 321
Real Monasterio de las Huelgas
  (Burgos) 371
Real Monasterio de Santo Tomás
  (Ávila) 363
Rebull, Joan, *Three Gypsy Boys*
  144
Reccared, King 51
Recceswinth, King 367
Reconquest **54–5**, 101
Recumbent Christ (Fernández) 367
Red Cross 667
Red Española de Albergues
  Juveniles 557
Refuges, mountain 556
Regencós, hotels 572
Reial Acadèmia de Ciències i Arts
  (Barcelona) 151
La Reineta 118
Reinosa 111
Religion 21
Religious art 32
Religious Music Week (Cuenca)
  40

Rembrandt 295, 304
Renaissance architecture 25
RENFE 678–9
Republicans **64–5**, 66
Requena 248
Reserva Nacional de los Ancares Leoneses 350
Reserva Nacional de Fuentes Carrionas 369
Reserva Nacional de Gredos 362
Restaurants **602–53**
  Andalusia 642–8
  Aragón 618–20
  Asturias and Cantabria 611–13
  Balearic Islands 648–51
  Barcelona 617–20
  bars 602
  Basque Country, Navarra and La Rioja 613–17
  Canary Islands 651–3
  Castilla y León 633–6
  Castilla-La Mancha 636–8
  Catalonia 620–24
  dress in 602
  eating hours 602
  Extremadura 638–40
  Galicia 608–10
  in hotels 554
  Madrid 629–32
  Madrid Province 632–3
  prices and paying 603
  reading the menu 603
  Seville 640–42
  smoking in 603
  tapas 604–5
  Valencia and Murcia 626–9
  what to drink in Spain 606–7
  wheelchair access 603
  wine choices 603
  see also Food and drink
La Restinga 533
Retiro Park (Madrid) 267, 282, 283, **297**
Reus 225
Reynés, Josep 154
Reynolds, Joshua 305
Riaño, Diego de 438
Rías Altas 88
Rías Baixas (Rías Bajas) 74, **95**
  wine region 78–9
Ribadedeva, hotels 564
Ribadeo, hotels 561
Ribadeo, Ría de 88
Ribadesella **107**
  hotels 564
Ribadumia, hotels 561
Ribalta, Francisco 32, 252
  Christ Embracing St Bernard 294
  The Last Supper 251
Ribas de Sil, Monasterio de 86, **98**
Ribeiro wine region 78–9
Ribera, José de 280, 281, 294, 475
  The Martyrdom of St Philip 292
  The Saviour 32

Ribera, Pedro de
  Cuartel del Conde-Duque (Madrid) 304
  Museo Municipal (Madrid) 304–5
  San Cayetano (Madrid) 302
Ribera Sacra wine region 78
Ribero del Duero wine region 340–41
De Ricci, Francisco, *Auto-da-fé in the Plaza Mayor* 274
Rice growing 29
Rincón de Ademuz 241
Rincón de la Victoria 473
Río Cárdenas valley 116
Rio Tinto Company 462
Riofrío 364–5
La Rioja *see* Basque Country, Navarra and La Rioja
Rioja wine region 78–9
Rioja wines 78
Ripoll 212
Road to Santiago 82–3
Road travel 680–83
  road conditions and weather forecast 682, 683
El Rocío **463**
  festivals 38
  hotels 593
Rock of Gibraltar 472
Rock music
  Barcelona 192, 193
  Madrid 322, 323
  Seville 457
Rocroi, Battle of (1643) 6 0
Roda de Isábena 236
Rodrigo, Joaquín, *Concierto de Aranjuez* 333
Rodríguez, Ventura
  Basílica de Nuestra Señora del Pilar (Zaragoza) 237
  Catedral de San Isidro 272
  Iglesia de la Encarnación (Montefrío) 482
  Monasterio de la Encarnación (Madrid) 280
  Monasterio de Santo Domingo de Silos 376
  Palacio de Liria (Madrid) 304
  Plaza Cánovas del Castillo (Madrid) 286
  Plaza de Cibeles (Madrid) 286
Roig i Soler 155
Rojas, Fernando de 34
Roldán, Luisa 444
Roldán, Pedro 439
Romanesque architecture 24
  churches 83
Romans 47, **50–51**
  Barcelona 147
  Carmona 476
  Empúries 216
  Itálica 476
  Juliobriga 111
  Lugo 99
  Mérida 410–11
  Sagunt 249
  Segóbriga 386

Romans (cont.)
  Segovia 51, 364, **365**
  Tarragona 224–5
Romanticism 35
Romería del Cristo del Sahúco (Peñas de San Pedro) 387
Romeria de Sant Marçal (Sa Cabaneta) 523
Romería de Santa Orosia (Yebra de Basa) 239
Romería de la Virgen de la Cabeza (Andújar) 463
Romería de la Virgen de la Candelaria 536
Romerías 38
Romero, Pedro 471
Romero de Torres, Julio, Museo Romero de Torres (Córdoba) 479
Roncal 114, 134
Roncesvlles (Orreaga) **134**
  Colegiata Real stained-glass 54–5
  hotels 567
Ronda 417, 469, **470–71**
  bullfighting 471
  festivals 42
  hotels 595
  restaurants 647
Ronda la Vieja 469
Roque Bonanza (El Hierro) 530
Roque de Cano 533
Roque Nublo 545
Las Rosas 533
Roses
  beach 217
  restaurants 623
Rota Hotels 593
Rubens, Peter Paul 304, 467
  The Adoration of the Magi 295
  The Three Graces 292
  The Toilet of Venus 289
  The Triumph of the Eucharist 281
Rubielos de Mora 240
  restaurants 625
Rueda, Jerónimo Sánchez de 482
Rueda wine region 340–41
Ruidera, Lagunas de 397
Ruiz, Hernán 436, 481
Ruiz, Juan 34
Rulers 70–71
Rum, Canary Islands 5 37
Rural architecture 27
Ruralia 555, 557
Ruralverd 555, 557
Rusiñol, Santiago 224
Rute 482

S
Sábada 230
Sabartes, Jaime 153
Sabatini, Francesco
  Palacio de El Pardo (Madrid) 332
  Palacio Real (Madrid) 277
  Puerta de Alcalá (Madrid) 287
Sacromonte 489
Sadurni d'Anoia, hotels 573
Saffron (*azafrán*) 339

Saffron (cont.)
  Saffron Festival (Consuegra) 42
Safont, Marc 147
S'Agaró
  hotels 573
  restaurants 623
Sagnier, Enric 178
Sagrada Família (Barcelona) 139,
  140, 141, 158, 159, **166–7**
Sagrera, Guillem 517, 520
Sagunt (Sagunto) **249**
  restaurants 628
Sahagún 353
Sailing 658
St Agatha's Day (Zamarramala) 368
Saint Bruno in Ecstasy 467
St Casilda (Zurbarán) 289
*St Dominic of Silos Enthroned as
  Abbot* (Bermejo) 294
St George's Day (Catalonia) 221
St James's Day (Santiago de
  Compostela) 98
St Michael's Cave (Gibraltar) 472
Saja 111
Salamanca 336, **358–61**
  hotels 584
  restaurants 635
  Street-by-Street map 358–9
  University 55, 360
Salamanca province 347
Salardú 210
El Saler, hotels 577
Salido, Fernando Ortega 497
Salinas, restaurants 613
Salinas de Añana 127
Salinas de Janubio 549
Ses Salines (Las Salinas) 510
  hotels 598
Sallent de Gállego 230
  hotels 575
Salobreña 483
Salón de Reinos (Madrid) 287
Salou 224
Salzillo, Francisco 262
San Agustín (Sant Agustí) 542
San Andrés de Teixido 88
San Antonio see Sant Antoni
San Carlos del Valle 398
San Césareo de Arles 129
San Clemente 395
  hotels 587
*San Diego de Alcalá Giving Food to
  the Poor* (Murillo) 61
San Fernando, restaurants 647
San Francisco see Sant Françesc
San Isidro (Madrid) 290
San José (Almería), hotels 596
San Juan de la Cruz see St John of
  the Cross
San Juan de Gaztelugatxe 119
San Juan de la Peña, Monasterio de
  234, 251
San Julián de los Prados 107
San Lorenzo de El Escorial
  hotels 582
  restaurants 633

San Martín de Castañeda 351
San Martín de Frómista 83
San Martín de Oscos 104
San Miguel, see also Sant Miquel
San Miguel de Escalada 353
San Miguel de Lillo 107
San Miguel de las Victorias 383
San Millán de la Cogolla 116, **129**
  hotels 567
San Nicolás de Tolentino, fiestas
  536
San Pedro de Alcántara 472
San Pedro de Arlanza 370
San Pedro Manrique, fiestas 368
San Pedro de la Nave 356
San Pedro de Viana, hotels 561
San Rafel de Forca, restaurants 649
San Román de los Infantes, hotels
  585
San Roque, restaurants 647
San Salvador de Poyo, restaurants
  610
San Sebastián (Donostia) 75, **122–3**
  festivals 41
  Film Festival 42, **123**
  hotels 567
  restaurants 616
San Sebastián (La Gomera) 533
  hotels 600
  restaurants 652
San Vicente de la Barquera 111
  fiestas 110
  restaurants 613
San Vicente de la Sonsierra,
  restaurants 616
San Vicente de Toranzo, hotels 564
Sancha, Doña 296
Sánchez, Arantxa 22
Sancho I, King of Aragón 235
Sancho I, King of Navarra 53
Sancho I Garcés, King of Pamplona
  130
Sancho II, King of Castilla y León
  370
  death 356, 371
Sancho III the Great, King of
  Navarra 130, 135
Sancho VI the Wise, King of
  Navarra 130
Sancho VII the Strong, King of
  Navarra 54, 55
  tomb of 134
Sand, George 514
Los Sanfermines (Pamplona) 20,
  132
Sangria 607
Sangüesa (Zangotxo) 135
Sanjeno see Sanxenxo
Sanlúcar de Barrameda **466**
  fiestas 463
  hotels 596
  restaurants 647
Sanlúcar la Mayor
  hotels 596
  restaurants 647
Sant Agustí see San Agustín

Sant Antoni (San Antonio) **510**
  hotels 597
  restaurants 648
Sant Antoni Abat (Mallorca) 523
Sant Carles de la Ràpita 225
Sant Celoni, restaurants 623
Sant Climent, restaurants 651
Sant Francesc Xavier 512
Sant Gertrudis de Fruitera,
  restaurants 649
Sant Joan (Ciutadella) 523
Sant Joan de les Abadesses 213
Sant Joan Pelós (Felanitx) 523
Sant Josep (San José) **510**
  restaurants 648
Sant Martí (La Cortinada) 212
Sant Miquel (San Miguel) 509, **511**
Sant Pol de Mar, restaurants 623
Sant Sadurní 221
Santa Ana (Madrid), nightlife 324–5
Santa Brígida, restaurants 652
Santa Comba de Bande 97
Santa Cristina d'Aro, hotels 573
Santa Cruz, Marquis of 398
Santa Cruz (Seville) **432–41**
  area map 433
  hotels 590–91
  restaurants 641
  Street-by-Street map 434–5
Santa Cruz de la Palma 532
  fiestas **536**
  hotels 601
  restaurants 652
Santa Cruz de Tenerife 530, **536**
  fiestas 39, 43, 536
  hotels 601
  restaurants 653
Santa Cruz del Valle de los Caídos
  329
Santa Eulalia 99
Santa Eulària d'es Riu (Santa Eulalia
  del Río) **512**
  hotels 597
Santa Fé 482–3
Santa Galdana 523
Santa Gertrudis, restaurants 648
Santa María de Huerta 377
Santa María de Mave
  hotels 585
  restaurants 635
Santa María de Melque 387
Santa María del Naranco **106**, 107
Santa Pola
  beach 258
  restaurants 629
Santander **113**
  festivals 41
  hotels 564
  restaurants 613
Santes Creus 221
  restaurants 623
Santiago de Compostela 74, **90–93**
  airport 676
  cathedral 84, 85, 91, **92–3**
  fiestas 98
  hotels 562

Santiago de Compostela (cont.)
pilgrimages 85
restaurants 610
Street-by-Street map 90–91
The Road to Santiago 82–3
Santiago de la Ribera 262
Santillana del Mar 75, 100, 101, **112**
hotels 564
restaurants 613
Santiponce 476
Santo Domingo de la Calzada **128**
hotels 567
restaurants 616
The Road to Santiago 83
Santo Domingo de Silos **376**
hotels 585
Santo Toribio de Liébana 110
Santos Inocentes 43
Santuario de Arantzazu 124
Santuario de Lluc 515
Santuario de Loiola 124
Santuario de Torreciudad 235
Santuario de la Vera Cruz (Caravaca de la Cruz) 263
Sanxenxo (Sangenjo), restaurants 610
Saportella, Francesca 177
Sardana 225
El Sardinero 113
Sardón de Duero, restaurants 635
Saturn Devouring One of his Sons (Goya) 294
Saturrarán 119
Saura, Antonio 33
El Sauzal, restaurants 653
O Saviñao, hotels 561
The Saviour (Ribera) 32
Scacchi, Greta 123
Schmidt-Rottluff, Karl, *Autumn Landscape in Oldenburg* 289
Scipio Africanus 476
Scipio the Elder 50, 496
Sea travel 677
Seafood
Canary Islands 537
Southern Spain 418
Second Republic **64–5**, 71
Second-hand fashion, Barcelona **187**, 189
Segóbriga 386
Segovia 337, **364–5**
Acázar 344–5
aqueduct 51, 364, **365**
hotels 585
map 364
restaurants 635
Roman remains 51
Segovia, Andrés 486
Segovia province 347
Seguí family 514
Segura, Isabel de 241
Segura, River 262
Segura de la Sierra 497
Self-catering accommodation **556**, 557

Self-Portrait (Picasso) 153
Sella, River 41, 108
Selva de Irati 135
Semana Santa *see* Easter
Semana Trágica, Barcelona (1909) 65
Semanas Grandes 41
Sempere, Eusebio 261
Senegüe, restaurants 625
Séneca 34, 50
Septembrina Revolution (1868–70) 71
Sepúlveda **365**
restaurants 635
La Serena 406
Serna, Ramón Gómez de la 305
Serra brothers 32
Serra, Josep Maria
Casa de la Ciutat (Barcelona) murals 147
Murals of Basque Life 123
Vic cathedral murals 220
Setenil 469
La Seu d'Urgell 208, **212**
hotels 572
restaurants 618
Seville **426–57**
airport 676
El Arenal 426–31
Cathedral 434, **436–7**
character 12–13
coach stations 683
entertainment 456–7
exhibitions 65
Expo '92 68–9
fiestas and festivals 38, 40, 42, 43, 431
Further Afield 443–6
La Giralda 416, 432, 433, 434, **436**
hotels 590–91
nightlife 457
Real Alcázar 440–41
restaurants 640–42
Santa Cruz 432–41
shopping 454–5
Street Finder 447–53
Street-by-Street map: El Arenal 428–9
Street-by-Street map: Santa Cruz 434–5
Seville province 459
Seville School 61, 444, 479
Shakespeare, William 333
Sheep farming 28
Sherry **421**, 607
Jerez de la Frontera 466
Shoes
shops 655
shops in Barcelona **188**, 189
shops in Madrid 318, 319
size chart 655
Shops **654–5**

Barcelona 186–9
Madrid 316–19
opening hours 654
Seville 454–5
Sierra de Alcaraz 396–7
Sierra de Aracena 462
Sierra de Béjar 356–7
Sierra Centro de Guadarrama 43, 329
Sierra de la Demanda 376
Sierra de Francia 356–7
Sierra de Gata 404
Sierra de Gredos **362**
Sierra de Gúdar 240
Sierra Mariola 259
Sierra Morena 476
Sierra Nevada 484, **485**
hotels 596
Sierra Norte 328
Sigüenza **382**
hotels 587
restaurants 638
Sil, River 98
El Silbo (whistle language) 532
Siloé, Diego de 367
Almería Cathedral 501
Burgos Cathedral 372
Capilla del Salvador (Úbeda) 497
Christ at the Column 372
Granada Cathedral 486
Iglesia de la Villa (Montefrío) 482
Málaga Cathedral 474
Siloé, Gil de 368
Adoration of the Magi 370
altarpieces 371, 372
tomb of Juan de Padilla 371
Simancas 367
Simon of Cologne 368, 370
Siresa 230
Sitges 209, **224**
hotels 573
restaurants 618
Size chart 655
Skiing 660, 661
Skydiving 658
Smoking, in restaurants 603
Sobrado de los Monjes, Monasterio 99
Socialist Workers' Party (PSOE) 68, 69
Sofía, Queen 23
Solán de Cabras 383
Solana, José Gutiérrez, *La Tertulia del Café de Pombo* 299
Solares
hotels 564
restaurants 613
Soldeu, hotels 573
Soler, Frederic 155
Solis family 409
Sóller **515**
hotels 598
restaurants 650
Solsona 220
Solynieve 485

Somiedo, Parque Natural de 105
Somontano wine region 202–3
Son Marroig 515
Sorauren 616
Sorbas 500
Soria **377**
  hotels 585
  restaurants 635
Soria province 347
Sorolla, Joaquín 33, 252, 253
  Children at the Beach 295
  Museo Sorolla (Madrid) 305
Sos del Rey Católico **230**
  hotels 575
Sotogrande 460, 472
Soult, Marshal 431
Southern Spain **414–501**
  Andalusia 458–501
  Flamenco 424–5
  Moorish architecture 422–3
  regional food 418–19
  Seville 426–57
  Southern Spain at a Glance 416–17
  wines 420–21
Souvenir shops, Seville 455
Spaghetti Westerns 500
Spanish Armada 59
Spanish Civil War 47, **66–7**
  Santa Cruz del Valle de los Caídos 329
Spanish Formula One Grand Prix (Barcelona) 40
Spanish Inquisition *see* Inquisition
Spanish language 664
Spanish Motorcycle Grand Prix (Jerez de la Frontera) 40
Spanish Tourist Office 557
Spanish-American War 64
Spas 660, 661
Specialist holidays 660–61
Speed limits 681
Spirits 607
Sports 22, **658–61**
  Barcelona 193
  spectator 657
Sports fashion, Barcelona **187**, 189
Spring in Spain 40
  fiestas 38
Stained glass, León Cathedral 355
Still Life with Four Vessels (Zurbarán) 294
Storks 343
Student information 665
Suárez, Adolfo 68
Subirachs, Josep Maria 166
Summer in Spain 41
  fiestas 38–9
Sunshine 44–5
Surfing 658
Surrealism 172, 215
Surrender of Breda (Velázquez) 61
Susillo 445

Synagogues
  Barcelona 146
  Córdoba 478
  Toledo 391

T

Tabarca island *see* Illa de Tabarca
Tabernas 500
Tablas de Daimiel National Park 30, **399**
Tacca, Pietro
  statue of Felipe III 273
  statue of Felipe IV 275
Tacoronte 535
Tafalla, restaurants 616
Tafira 544
Tagus (Tajo), River 333, 386
Talavera, Battle of (1809) 63
Talavera de la Reina **386**
  restaurants 638
Talayots 527
Las Tamboradas (Teruel) 239
Tapas **604–5**
  Andalusia 418
Tapia de Casariego 104
Tàpies, Antoni 33, 514
  Cloud and Chair 160
  Fundació Tàpies 160, **164**
Taramundi **104**
  hotels 565
Tarantino, Quentin 123
Tarazona 229, **236**
  hotels 575
Tarif ben Maluk 468
Tarifa 468
  hotels 596
Tarifa, Marquis of 438
Tariq 52
Tarraconensis (Roman province) 50
Tarragona 51, 199, **224–5**
  hotels 573
  restaurants 618
Tarragona province 207
Tarragona wine region 202–3
Tarrasa *see* Terrassa
Tartessus 49
Taüll 24, 211
Tauste 230
Taveret, hotels 573
Tax-free goods 664
Taxis 682
Teatre Grec (Barcelona) 171
Teatre Nacional de Catalunya 191
Teatro Albéniz (Madrid) 321
Teatro Central (Seville) 457
Teatro de la Comedia (Madrid) 322
Teatro Español (Madrid) 291
Teatro Lope de Vega (Seville) 457
Teatro de la Maestranza (Seville) 428, 456
Teatro María Guerrero (Madrid) 322
Teatro Pavón (Madrid) 322
Teatro Real (Madrid) 322
Teatro de la Zarzuela (Madrid) 322
Tegueste, restaurants 653
Teguise 550

Teide, Mount 31, **538–9**
Teide, Parque Nacional del **538–9**, 551
Teito 27
Tejero, Colonel Antonio 68, 291
Telephones 670–71
Television 22, 671
Tembleque 394
Temperatures 44–5
Templo de Debod (Madrid) 303
Temptation of St Anthony (Bosch) 295
Tena, Lucero 425
Tenerife 504, 528, **534–9**
  airport 676
  hotels 601
  map 531
  restaurants 653
  volcanoes 551
Tentudía 413
Terán, Luis Marín de 430
Teresa of Ávila, St
  Ávila 362–3, **363**
  tomb of 361
Las Teresitas (Santa Cruz de Tenerife) 530, **536**
Teror 545
Terra Alta wine region 202–3
Terra Mítica 657
La Tertulia del Café de Pombo (Solana) 299
Teruel **240–41**
  cathedral 55
  fiestas 239
  hotels 575
  Lovers of Teruel 241
  restaurants 625
Teruel province 227
Teverga 105
Texas-Hollywood (Tabernas) 500
Texeiro, Pedro 305
The Procession of the Flagellants (Goya) 274
Theatre 657
  Barcelona 190–91, 193
  Madrid 322, 323
  see also Teatre; Teatro
Theft 667
Theme parks 657
  Isla Mágica (Seville) 446, 457
  Mini-Hollywood (Tabernas) 500, 657
  Port Aventura 224
  Sioux City (Maspalomas) 543
  Texas-Hollywood (Tabernas) 500
  see also Amusement parks
The Third of May (Goya) **62–3**, 294
Thirty Years War 61
The Three Graces (Rubens) 292
Three Gypsy Boys (Rebull) 144
Thyssen-Bornemisza, Baron Heinrich 288
  portrait 288
Thyssen-Bornemisza, Hans Heinrich 288
Tibaldi 330

Tibidabo (Barcelona) **178**, 192
nightlife 195
Tickets
entertainment, Barcelona 190,
193
entertainment, Madrid **320**, 323
entertainment, Seville 456
railways 679
Tiepolo, Giovanni Battista 295
Tiermes 365
Tierra de Campos 347
Tiles, *azulejos* 24, 422, **438**
Timanfaya, Parque Nacional de 31,
541, **548–9**
Time zones 665
Timetables, railway 679
Tintoretto 295, 391
Tipping
in hotels 555
in restaurants 603
Titian 281, 304
*The Emperor Charles V at
Mühlberg* 295
TIVE 665
El Toboso 394
hotels 587
Todos los Santos 43
The Toilet of Venus (Rubens) 289
Toilets 667
La Toja *see* (A) Toxa
Toki-Egin (Chillida) 299
Toledan School 391
Toledo **388–93**
Cathedral 337, 389, **392–3**
fiestas 38, 387
hotels 587–8
restaurants 638
Street-by-Street map 388–9
Toledo, Juan Bautista de 331
Toledo, Montes de *see* Montes de
Toledo
Toledo province 379
Tolls, motorway 681
Tolox, hotels 596
La Tomatina (Buñol) **248–9**, 255
Tomé, Narciso 366, 393
El Torcal 475
Torcal, Parque Natural del 475
Torcuato, San 493
Tordesillas **366**
hotels 585
restaurants 635
Tordesillas, Treaty of (1494) 57
Torla 226, 232
Toro 357
El Toro 523
Toro wine region 340–41
Toros de Guisando 362
Torquemada, Tomás de 56, 236
tomb of 363
Torre del Clavero (Salamanca) 359,
361
Torre de Collserola (Barcelona) 177
Torre del Compte, hotels 576
Torre de Hércules (A Coruña) 89
Torre del Infantado (Potes) 110

Torre de los Lujanes (Madrid) 270,
272, 273
Torre del Oro (Seville) 429, **431**
Torre de Picasso (Madrid) **25**, 306
Torre Tavira (Cádiz) 467
Torrejón de Ardoz, hotels 582
Torrejoncillo, fiestas 405
Torremolinos 473
hotels 596
restaurants 647–8
Torrent
hotels 573
restaurants 623
Torres de Serranos (Valencia) 252
Torrevieja (Torrevella) **261**
beach 258
festivals 41
Torroella de Montgrí, restaurants
623
Tortosa **225**
hotels 573
restaurants 623
Tossa de Mar 23, **216**
beach 217
hotels 573
restaurants 623
Tourism 23, **69**
Tourist offices **664**, 665
Tours by car
Las Alpujarras 484–5
Cruz de Tejeda 545
Pueblos Blancos 468–9
Sierra de Alcaraz 396–7
Sierra de Francia and Sierra de
Bejar 356–7
A Toxa (La Toja) 94
Trafalgar, Battle of (1805) 62, 63
Traffic regulations 680
Tragacete
hotels 588
restaurants 638
Trains 678–9
Trajan, Emperor 50, 446
Transfiguration (Martorell) 149
Travel **674–83**
air 674–7
Andalusia 460
Aragón 229
Asturias and Cantabria 103
Balearic Islands 508
Basque Country, Navarra and La
Rioja 117
bus 683
Canary Islands: Eastern Islands
540
Canary Islands: Western Islands
531
Castilla-La Mancha 381
Castilla y León 349
Catalonia 208
coach 683
cycling 683
Extremadura 403
ferries 677
Galicia 87
golondrinas (Barcelona) 157

Travel (cont.)
rail 678–9
regional capitals 16
road 680–83
taxis 682
Valencia and Murcia 244
Travellers' cheques 668
in restaurants 603
Tredòs, hotels 574
Trekking 658, 661
Trepucó 527
Els Tres Tombs (Barcelona)
157
Trevélez 484
hotels 596
Triana (Seville) 446
Tristán, Luis 391
The Triumph of Bacchus
(Velázquez) 292
The Triumph of the Cross (Valdés
Leal) 439
Trofeo Conde de Godó (Barcelona)
40
Trujillo **407**
fiestas 40
hotels 589–90
restaurants 640
Tudela (Tutera) **130**
restaurants 616
Tuesta 127
Tui (Tuy) **96–7**
hotels 562
Sa Tuna, hotels 572
Turégano 365
Turia, River 248, 250, 254
Turner, JMW 305
Turner, Lana 42, 123
Turre, hotels 596
Tutera *see* Tudela
Tuy *see* Tui
TVR 557
Txacoli (chacolí) 78
Txacoli de Guetaria wine region
78–9

U

Úbeda **496–7**
hotels 596
map 496
restaurants 648
Ubrique 468
Uclés
hotels 588
Monasterio de 386
Udabe, hotels 567
Ujué 130
Ulla, River 94
Unamuno, Miguel de 35, 361
Uncastillo 230
hotels 576
restaurants 625
UNESCO 178, 533
Unification of Spain 70
United Nations 67
Universal Exhibition, Barcelona
(1888) 64, 65, 154, 156

Universidad (Salamanca) 358, 360
Universidad (Seville) 445
Universidad Pontificia 111
Universidad de Sancti Spiritus
   (Oñati) 124
Urda 394
Urraca of Navarra, Doña 54
   tomb of 368
Utiel-Requena wine region 202–3
Utrecht, Treaty of (1713) 62, 472

V

La Vaguada (Madrid) 317
Valdediós 107
Valdelinares 240
Valdeorras 42
Valdepeñas **398**
   hotels 588
   restaurants 638
Valdepeñas wine region 340–41
Valderrama, golf 42
Valderrobres 240
Valdés Leal, Juan de 479
   Ayuntamiento (Seville) paintings
      438
   Finis Gloriae Mundi 431
   Hospital de la Caridad (Seville)
      paintings 429
   In Ictu Oculi 431
   La Inmaculada 430
   The Triumph of the Cross 439
Valdés, Lucas 430, 439
Valencia 198, 243, **250–53**
   airport 676
   beaches 253
   festivals 38, 40
   horchata 253
   hotels 579
   map 251
   restaurants 629
Valencia and Murcia **242–63**
   character 11
   climate 45
   Exploring Valencia and Murcia
      244–5
   fiestas 255
   food and drink 201
   hotels 576–9
   restaurants 626–9
Valencia wine region 202–3
Valencia de Alcántara 410
Valencia de Don Juan 353
Valenciano dialect 243
La Vall de Bianya, restaurants 622
Vall d'Aran (Valle de Arán) **210**
   butterflies 210
Vall de Boí (Valle de Bohí) 211
Valladolid **366–7**
   fiestas 38, 368
   history 60
   hotels 585
   restaurants 636
Valladolid province 347
Valldemossa **514**
   hotels 598
Valle de Alcudia 399

Valle del Amboz 402
Valle de Arán see Vall d'Aran
Valle de Bohí see Vall de Boí
Valle de Cabuérniga 111
Valle de los Caídos, Santa Cruz del
   329
Valle de Fuenfría 329
Valle Gran Rey 531, 533
Valle de Ordesa 232
Valle de los Pedroches 476
Valle de Roncal 134–5
Valle de Salazar 135
Valle de Silencio 351
Valle-Inclán, Ramón María del 35
Vallehermoso 533
Los Valles 230
Valley of the Fallen see Valle de los
   Caídos
Valls, restaurants 618
Valmaseda 368
Válor 485
Valporquero, Cuevas de see Cuevas
   de Valporquero
Valverde 532
   hotels 599
   restaurants 651
Valverde de los Arroyos, hotels 588
Valverde de Fresno 404
Valverde de la Vera, fiestas 405
Van der Weyden, Rogier 486
   The Deposition 295
   The Calvary 331
Van Dyck, Anthony 252, 281
Van Gogh, Vincent 156
Van Loo, Louis-Michel 295
Vandals 51
Vandelvira, Andrés de
   Baeza 498, 499
   Capilla del Salvador (Úbeda) 497
   Hospital de Santiago (Úbeda) 496
   Iglesia de San Pablo (Úbeda) 497
   Jaén Cathedral 493
   Palacio de las Cadenas (Úbeda)
      497
Vasarely, Viktor 118
VAT 654, 664
   in restaurants 603
Vayreda, Joaquim 213
Vázquez de Molina, Juan 496, 497
Vedra, restaurants 610
Es Vedrà (Isla Vedra) 510
Vega, Félix Lope de 34, 60, 333
   Casa de Lope de Vega (Madrid)
      290
   Fuente Obejuna 476
Vega de Pas 112
Véjer de la Frontera
   hotels 597
   restaurants 648
Velarde 304
Velázquez, Diego de 32, 60, 61,
   281, 287
   baptism 444
   *Imposition of the Chasuble on St
   Ildefonso* 438
   Las Meninas **32–3**, 153, 294

Velázquez, Diego de (cont.)
   Self-Portrait 252
   statue of Felipe IV 275
   Surrender of Breda 61
   *The Temptation of St Thomas
   Aquinas* 261
   The Triumph of Bacchus 292
Velázquez Bosco 297
Vélez Blanco 500
Vélez-Málaga 483
El Vendrell 224
Ventana del Diablo 383
Ventas con Peña Aguilera 387
Venus and Cupid (Rubens) see
   Toilet of Venus
Vera (Andalusia), restaurants 648
Vera (Basque Country) see Bera
   Vera de Bidasoa, hotels 568
Veral, River 230
Verdaguer, Jacint 212
Vergara, Ignacio 251
Verges, fiestas 221
Verín 97
Vernacular architecture **26–7**
Verne, Jules 512
Veronese, Paolo 295
Vespasian, Emperor 50
Vespucci, Amerigo 157
Vía de la Plata 352
Viajes 2000 665
Viana, restaurants 617
Viana family 479
Vic (Vich) **220**
   hotels 574
   restaurants 618
Victoria Eugenia, Queen 290
Vielha (Viella) **210**
   hotels 574
   restaurants 624
Vigo **96**
   restaurants 610
   Video Festival 43
La Vila Joiosa (Villajoyosa) 260
   hotels 578
Vilafamés 247
Vilafranca del Penedès **221**
   restaurants 618
Vilagarcía de Arousa 95
   hotels 562
   restaurants 610
Vilalba see Villalba
Vilanova de Arousa, restaurants 610
Vilar de Donas 99
Vilaseca i Casanovas, Josep 154
Villacarriedo 112
   hotels 565
Villaescusa de Haro 395
Villafranca del Bierzo **350–51**
   hotels 585
   restaurants 636
Villajoyosa see La Vila Joiosa
Villalba (Vilalba), hotels 562
Villamiel 404
Villanueva 105
Villanueva, Juan de 273
   Museo del Prado (Madrid) 292

Villanueva, Juan de (cont.)
  Real Academia de la Historia (Madrid) 291
  Real Jardín Botánico 297
  Teatro Español (Madrid) 291
Villanueva de Alcolea, festivals 39
Villanueva de los Infantes 398
Villanueva de la Vera, fiestas 405
El Villar de Álava 70
Villar i Lozano, Francesc de Paula 167
Villareal de San Carlos 406
Villaverde, hotels 600
Villaviciosa 107
Villena, restaurants 629
Villena, Juan Pachero, Marquis of 344, 394, 395
Villena Treasure **48–9**, 260
Villespesa, Francisco 485
Villuercas, Sierra de 406
Vinaròs 247
  restaurants 629
Vincent, St, tomb of 363
Viniegra de Abajo, restaurants 617
Vinos de Madrid wine region 340–41
Vintage fashion, Barcelona 188, 189
La Virgen Blanca Vitoria (Vitoria) 132
Virgen de la Hoz 382
Virgin and Child (Bassá) 32
Virgin of Guadalupe 407
Virgin of Montserrat 219
Las Virtudes 398
Visas 664
Visigoths 47, 50, **51**, 52
  architecture 423
Viso del Marqués 398
Vitoria (Gasteiz) **126–7**
  fiestas 41, 132
  hotels 568
  map 126
  restaurants 617
Viveiro (Vivero) 88
Vizcaya (Bizkaia) 115
Volcanic islands (Canary Islands) 31, **551**
Volvo Masters Golf Championship (Valderrama) 42
Vuelta Ciclista a España 40, 42

W

Waldren, William 515
Walking 658, 661
  in national parks 233, 658
Wamba 367
War of Independence 62, 63
War of the Spanish Succession 62, 70
Water, drinking 606
Water sports 658–9
Watteau, Antoine 288, 295
Weather 44–5
  forecasts **682**, 683
Wellington, Duke of
  siege of Ciudad Rodrigo 357
  War of Independence 63, 126
Wetlands 30

Wheelchair access *see* Disabled travellers
Whistle language, La Gomera 532
Whitewater rafting 659
Whitney, Gertrude Vanderbilt 4 62
Wildlife 30–31
  L'Albufera 254
  Birds of Central Spain 342–3
  brown bears 104
  Butterflies of the Vall d'Aran 210
  Delta de l'Ebre 225
  Forests of Northern Spain 80–81
  Lagunas de Ruidera 397
  matorral 205
  Parque Nacional de Doñana 464–5
  Parque Natural de Cabo de Gata 501
  Parque Natural de Cazorla 497
  Parque Natural de Monfragüe 406
  Pyrenees 232
  Tablas de Daimiel 399
  see also National parks; Nature reserves; Zoos
Windmills 27, 394
Windsurfing 659
Wine 655
  Balearic Islands 513
  Central Spain 340–41
  Eastern Spain 202–3
  labels 607
  Northern Spain 78–9
  in restaurants 603
  Southern Spain 420–21
  vineyards 29
  What to Drink in Spain 606
Wine Battle (Haro) 132
Winter in Spain 43
  fiestas 39
Winter sports 660, 661
Woman in Blue (Picasso) 298
Woods and forests 31
World Cup 68
World Music, Madrid **322**, 323
World War II 66
Wornum, Selden 122

X

Xàbia (Jávea) 245, **255**
  beach 258
  hotels 577
Xàtiva (Játiva) 254
  hotels 577
  restaurants 627
Xavier, St Francis 135
Xúquer, River *see* Júcar, River

Y

Yaiza, restaurants 653
Yanci *see* Igantzi
Yáñez de la Almedina, Fernando 294
Los Yébenes 387
Yecla wine region 202–3
Yegen 485

Yemas 339
Yerba de Basa, fiestas 239
Yesa, hotels 568
Yesos de Sorbas 500
Yeste 396
Youth hostels **556**, 557
Yuste, Monasterio de 400, **405**
Yusuf I 490

Z

Zafón, Carlos Ruiz 35
Zafra **412–13**
  hotels 590
  restaurants 640
Zahara de los Atunes 468
  restaurants 648
Zahara de la Sierra 469
Zalamea de la Serena 412
Zamarramala, fiestas 39, 368
Zamora **356–7**
  hotels 585
  restaurants 636
Zamora province 347
Zangotza *see* Sangüesa
Zapatero, José Luis Rodríguez **69**
Zaragoza 198, **236–7**
  fiestas 42, 239
  hotels 576
  map 237
  restaurants 625–6
Zaragoza province 227
Zarautz 119
  hotels 568
Zarco, Doña Anna Martínez 394
Zarzuela **322**, 323
Zoos, Parc Zoològic (Barcelona) 155
Zoraya 492
Zorrilla, José 35, 366
Zuázola, Bishop of Ávila 124
Zuheros 482
  hotels 597
Zuloaga, Ignacio 123
  The Condesa Mathieu de Noailles 118
  Museo de Ignacio Zuloaga (Zumaia) 119
  Pedraza de la Sierra 365
Zumaia (Zumaya) 119
Zurbarán, Francisco de 32, 61, 247, 287
  Ayuntamiento (Seville) paintings 438
  birthplace 413
  Father Gonzalo de Illescas at Work 407
  fountain (Llerena) 413
  Fray Pedro Machado 281
  Saint Bruno in Ecstasy 467
  St Casilda 289
  St Dominic in Soria 430
  San Hugo en el Refectorio 430
  Still Life with Four Vessels 294
  Zafra altarpiece 412

Acknowledgments

Dorling Kindersley would like to thank the following people whose contributions and assistance made preparation of this book possible.

Main Contributors

John Ardagh is a journalist and writer, and the author of several books on modern Europe.

David Baird, resident in Andalusia from 1971 to 1995, is the author of *Inside Andalusia*.

Vicky Hayward, a writer, journalist and editor, lives in Madrid, and has travelled extensively in Spain.

Adam Hopkins is an indefatigable travel writer and author of *Spanish Journeys: A Portrait of Spain*.

Lindsay Hunt has travelled widely and has contributed to several Eyewitness Travel Guides.

Nick Inman writes regularly on Spain for books and magazines.

Paul Richardson is the author of *Not Part of the Package*, a book on Ibiza, where he lives.

Martin Symington is a regular contributor to the *Daily Telegraph*. He also worked on the *Eyewitness Travel Guide to Great Britain*.

Nigel Tisdall, contributor to the *Eyewitness Travel Guide to France*, is the author of the *Insight Pocket Guide to Seville*.

Roger Williams has contributed to Insight Guides on Barcelona and Catalonia, and was the main contributor to the *Eyewitness Travel Guide to Provence*.

Additional Contributors

Mary Jane Aladren, Sarah Andrews, Pepita Aris, Emma Dent Coad, Rebecca Doulton, Harry Eyres, Josefina Fernández, Anne Hersh, Nick Rider, Mercedes Ruiz Ochoa, David Stone, Clara Villanueva, Christopher Woodward, Patricia Wright.

Additional Illustrations

Arcana Studio, Richard Bonson, Louise Boulton, Martine Collings, Brian Craker, Jared Gilbey (Kevin Jones Associates), Paul Guest, Steven Gyapay, Claire Littlejohn.

Additional Photography

David Cannon, Tina Chambers, Geoff Dann, Phillip Dowell, Mike Dunning, Neil Fletcher, Steve Gorton, Frank Greenaway, Derek Hall, Colin Keates, Alan Keohane, Dave King, Ella Milroy, D Murray, Cyril Laubsouer, Ian O'Leary Stephen Oliver, J Selves, Mathew Ward, P. Wojcik.

Cartography

Lovell Johns Ltd (Oxford), ERA-Maptec Ltd.

Design And Editorial Assistance

Sam Atkinson, Pilar Ayerbe, Rosemary Bailey, Vicky Barber, Teresa Barea, Claire Baranowski, Cristina Barrallo, Jill Benjamin, Vandana Bhagra, Sonal Bhatt, Julie Bond, Chris Branfield, Gretta Britton, Daniel Campi, Paula Canal (Word on Spain) Lola Carbonell, Peter Casterton, Elspeth Collier, Carey Combe, Jonathan Cox, Martin Cropper, Linda Doyle, Nicola Erdpresser, Anna Freiberger, Rhiannon Furbear, Aruna Ghose, Elena González, Des Hemsley, Tim Hollis, Juliet Kenny, Michael Lake, Erika Lang, Maite Lantaron, Rebecca Lister, Sarah Martin, Caroline Mead, Sam Merrell, Kate Molan, Jane Oliver, Simon Oon, Mary Ormandy, Mike Osborn, Malcolm Parchment, Pollyanna Poulter, Anna Pirie, Tom Prentice, Mani Ramaswamy, Ellen Root, Sadie Smith, Anna Streiffert, Leah Tether, Helen Townsend, Andy Wilkinson, Suzanne Wales, Robert Zonenblick.

Proofreader Huw Hennessy, Stewart J Wild.

Indexer Helen Peters.

Special Assistance

Dorling Kindersley would like to thank the regional and local tourist offices, *ayuntamientos*, shops, hotels, restaurants and other organizations in Spain for their invaluable help. Particular thanks also to Dr Giray Ablay (University of Bristol); María Eugenia Alonso and María Dolores Delgado Peña (Museo Thyssen-Bornemisza); Ramón Álvarez (Consejería de Educación y Cultura, Castilla y León); Señor Ballesteros (Santiago de Compostela Tourist Office); Carmen Brieva, Javier Campos and Luis Esteruelas (Spanish Embassy, London); Javier Caballero Arranz; Fernando Cañada López; The Club Taurino of London; Consejería de Turismo, Castilla-La Mancha; Consejería de Turismo and Consejería de Cultura, Junta de Extremadura; Mònica Colomer and Montse Planas (Barcelona Tourist Office); María José Docal and Carmen Cardona (Patronato de Turismo, Lanzarote); Edilesa; Klaus Ehrlich; Juan Fernández, Lola Moreno and others at El País-Aguilar; Belén Galán (Centro de Arte Reina Sofía); Amparo Garrido; Adolfo Díaz Gómez (Albacete Tourist Office); Professor Nigel Glendinning (Queen Mary and Westfield College, University of London); Pedro Hernández; Insituto de Cervantes, London; Victor Jolín (SOTUR); Joaquim Juan Cabanilles (Servicio de Investigación Prehistórica, Valencia); Richard Kelly; Mark Little (*Lookout* Magazine); Carmen López de Tejada and Inma Felipe (Spanish National Tourist Office, London); Caterine López and Ana Roig Mundi (ITVA); Julia López de la Torre (Patrimonio Nacional, Madrid); Lovell Johns Ltd (Oxford); Josefina Maestre (Ministerio de Agricultura, Pesca y Alimentación); Juan Malavia García and Antonio Abarca (Cuenca Tourist Office); Mario (Promoción Turismo, Tenerife); Janet Mendel; Javier Morata (Acanto Arquitectura y Urbanismo. Madrid); Juan Carlos Murillo; Sonia Ortega and Bettina Krücken (Spain Gourmetour); Royal Society for the Protection of Birds (UK); Alícia Ribas Sos; Katusa Salazar-Sandoval (Fomento de Turismo, Ibiza); María Ángeles Sánchez and Marcos; Ana Sarrieri (Departamento de Comercio, Consumo y Turismo, Gobierno Vasco); Klaas Schenk; María José Sevilla (Foods From Spain); The Sherry Institute of Spain (London); Anna Skidmore (Fomento de Turismo, Mallorca); Philip Sweeney; Rupert Thomas; Mercedes Trujillo and Antonio Cruz Caballero (Patronato de Turismo, Gran Canaria); Gerardo Uarte (Gobierno de Navarra); Fermín Unzue (Dirección General de Turismo, Cantabria); Puri Villanueva.

Artwork Reference

Sr Joan Bassegoda, Catedral Gaudí (Barcelona); José Luis Mosquera Muller (Mérida); Jorge Palazón, Paisajes Españoles (Madrid).

Photography Permissions

The Publisher would like to thank the following for their kind assistance and permission to photograph at their establishments:© Patrimonio Nacional, Madrid; Palacio de la Almudaina, Palma de Mallorca; El Escorial, Madrid; La Granja de San Ildefonso; Convento de Santa Clara, Tordesillas; Las Huelgas Reales, Burgos; Palacio Real, Madrid; Monasterio de las Descalzas; Bananera "El Guanche S.L."; Museo Arqueológico de Tenerife-OACIMC del Excmo. Cavildo Insular de Tenerife; Asociación de Encajeras de Acebo-Cáceres; Museo de Arte Abstracto Español, Cuenca; Fundación Juan March; Pepita Alia Lagartera; Museo Naval de Madrid; © Catedral de Zamora; Museo de Burgos; Claustro San Juan de Duero, Museo Numantino, Soria; San Telmo Museoa Donostia-San Sebastián; Hotel de la Reconquista, Oviedo; Catedral de Jaca; Museo de Cera, Barcelona; Museu D'Història de la Ciutat, Barcelona; © Capitol Catedral de Lleida; Jardí Botànic Marimurtra, Estació Internacional de Biologia Mediterrània, Girona; Museo Arqueológico Sagunto (Teatro Romano-Castillo); Museo Municipal y Ermita de San Antonio de la Florida, Madrid. Also all the other churches, museums, hotels, restaurants, shops, galleries and sights too numerous to thank individually.

Picture Credits

Key: t=top; tl=top left; tlc=top left centre; tc=top centre; trc=top right centre; tr=top right; cla=centre left above; ca=centre above; cra=centre right above; cl=centre left; c=centre; cr=centre right; clb=centre left below; crb=centre right below; cb=centre below; bl=bottom left; br=bottom right; b=bottom; bc=bottom centre; bcl=bottom centre left; bcr=bottom centre right; (d)=detail.

Every effort has been made to trace the copyright holders. Dorling Kindersley apologizes for any unintentional omissions and would be pleased, in such cases, to add an acknowledgment in future editions.

Works of art have been published with the permission of the following copyright holders: *Dona i Ocell* Joan Miró © Succession Miró/ADAGP, Paris & DACS, London 2006 176tl; *Guernica* Pablo Ruiz Picasso 1937 © Succession Picasso/DACS, London 2006 299cb; *Morning* George Kolbe © DACS London 2006 170tr, 173tl; *Peine de los Vientos* Eduardo Chillida © DACS, London 2006 122b; Various works by Joaquín Sorolla © DACS, London 1996 305tl; *Rainy Taxi* Salvador Dalí © Kingdom of Spain, Gala - Salvador Dalí Foundation, DACS, London 2006 215tr; *Tapestry of the Foundation* Joan Miró 1975 © Succession Miró/ADAGP, Paris & DACS, London 171crb; *Three Gypsy Boys* © Joan Rebull 1976 144bl.

The publisher would like to thank the following individuals, companies and picture libraries for their kind permission to reproduce their photographs: ACE PHOTO AGENCY: Bob Masters 26b; Mauritius 23t; Bill Wassman 320b; AISA ARCHIVO ICONOGRÁFICO, Barcelona: 22t, 36bl, 46l, 48ca, 48cb, 49bl, 49br, 50cra, 50cb, 51tl, 52cla, 52bl(d), 54bl, 54br, 54cla, 54–55, 55cl,

55cra, 55bl, 56bl, 61br, 65tr, 67tl, 67b, 274t, 303b, 355bl, 423bl, 423br, 424cl, 489br; Biblioteca Nacional, Madrid *Felipe V* Luis Meléndez 71bl; Catedral de Sevilla *Ignacio de Loyola* Alonso Vázquez 124bl(d); *Camilo José Cela* Álvaro Delgado 1916 © DACS, London 2006 35br (d); *La Tertulia del Pombo* José Gutiérrez Solana 1920 © DACS, London 2006 299t; Museo de América, Madrid *Vista de Sevilla* Alonso Sánchez Coello 58cb; Museo de Bellas Artes, Seville *Sancho Panza y El Rucio* Moreno Carbonero 60ca; Museo de Bellas Artes, Valencia *Ecce Homo* Juan de Juanes 252br; Museo Frankfurt *La Armada* 59tl; Museo de Historia de México *Hernán Cortés* S.E. Colane 58bl(d); Museo Histórico Militar, San Sebastián *Guerra Carlista* 63br(d); Museo Lázaro Galdiano, Madrid *Lope de Vega* Caxes 290tr; Museo Nacional del Teatro *Poster for "Yerma"* (FG Lorca) Juan Antonio Morales y José Caballero © DACS, London 2006 35tr; Museo del Prado, Madrid *La Rendición de Breda* Diego Velázquez 61cb, *El Tres de Mayo de 1808 en Madrid* Francisco de Goya y Lucientes 62-63(d), La Reina María Luisa María Francisco de Goya 62cla, *Carlos IV* Francisco de Goya 71bc, *Los Borrachos* Diego de Velázquez 292t, *Saturno devorando a un hijo* Francisco de Goya 294tr, *El Descendimiento* Van der Weyden 295b; Real Academia de Bellas Artes de San Fernando, Madrid *El Sueño del Caballero* Antonio de Pereda 60–61(d); ALAMY IMAGES: Paul Hardy Carter 200cla; Michelle Chaplow 456b; Ian Dagnall 11br; Expuesto/Nicholas Randall 656b; Mike Finn-Kelcey 679c; Robert Harding Picture Library 419cr, 656cla; paulbourdice 513cla; Profimedia. CZ s.r.o. 537cl; Alex Segre 77t, 605tr; Peter Titmuss 201t; Vario Images GmbH 69br; Renaud Visage 418cla; Ken Welsh 665tl; ALSA GROUP S.L.L.C: 683c; AKG, London: 67cr; Allsport: Stephen Munday 42cr; AQUILA: Adrian Hoskins 210cla, 210clb; Mike Lane 343clb; James Pearce 205bl; ARCAID: Paul Raftery 120bl; ARXIU MAS: 36br, 37bl, 51crb, 54tl, 57cl, 53br(d); Museo del Prado, Madrid *Felipe II* Sánchez Coello 70br(d); Patrimonio Nacional, Madrid 59cl, 59b(d); THE ART ARCHIVE: Museo del Prado Madrid/Dagli Orti (A) *St Cecilia patron saint of music* Nicholas Poussin (1594–1665) 295cr.

JAUME BALANYA: 167crb; BALEARIA: 677bl; BIOFOTOS: Heather Angel 80cla, 80bl; BRIDGEMAN ART LIBRARY: *St Dominic enthroned as Abbot* Bartolomé Bermejo 294tl; Index/ Museo del Prado, Madrid *Auto-da-fé in the Plaza Mayor* Francisco Rizi 274c; Musée des Beaux Artes, Berne *Colossus of Rhodes* Salvador Dalí 1954 © Kingdom of Spain, Gala – Salvador Dalí Foundation, DACS, London 2006 33tr; Museo del Prado, Madrid *Charles IV and his Family* Francisco de Goya y Lucientes 33cb, *The Adoration of the Shepherds* El Greco 292cl, *The Annunciation* Fra Angelico 293bc, *The Clothed Maja* Francisco de Goya y Lucientes 293t, *The Naked Maja* Francisco de Goya y Lucientes 293ca, *The Three Graces* Peter Paul Rubens 292crb, *The Martydom of St Philip* José de Ribera 293crb; Museo Picasso, Barcelona *Las Meninas, Infanta Margarita* Pablo Ruiz Picasso 1957 © Succession Picasso/DACS, London 2006 32tl; Phoenix Galleries, London *Rooftops, Fortna Luxt, Majorca* Frederick Gore 8-9; MICHAEL BUSSELLE: 207r, 209b, 210t.

CAMPER STORE, Madrid: 655tr; CENTRO DE ARTE REINA SOFÍA: *Bertsolaris* Zubiaurre © DACS, London 2006 125cb, *Paisaje de Cadaqués* Salvador Dalí 1923 ©

Kingdom of Spain, Gala - Salvador Dalí Foundation, DACS, London 2006 298cb, *Accidente* Ponce de León 298b, *Toki-Egin (Homenaje a San Juan de la Cruz)* Eduardo Chillida 1952 © DACS, London 2006 299bl; CEPHAS: Mick Rock 29bl, 42t, 78t, 202tr, 202cl, 203tr, 340tr, 420tr, 421br, 421cr; Roy Stedall 421tr; CINC SENTITS: 603c; BRUCE COLEMAN: Eric Crichton 204tr; José Luis González Grande 205tr; Werner Layer 343tl; Andy Purcell 31ca; Hans Reinhard 80crb; Norbert Schwirtz 205tl; Colin Varndell 205crb; Dee Conway: 425cl, 425cr; COMERÇ 24: 603br; CORBIS: Ric Ergenbright 456t; Owen Franken 77c, 201c, 338cl, 339c, 419t; Carloine Penn 339t; Jose Fuste Raga 10cr; Reuters/Marcelo del Pozo 12br; SYLVIA CORDAIY PHOTO LIBRARY: Chris North 40tl; JOE CORNISH: 28ca, 346, 364b, 372tr; GIANCARLO COSTA: 37bc; COVER: Genin Andrada 40b, 43b; Austin Catalan 70bl; Juan Echeverria 31cra, 41br, 545bl; Pepe Franco 185c; Quim Llenas 125ca, 317tl; Matías Nieto 43c; F J Rodríguez 125bl; CUIDAD DE LAS ARTES Y LAS CIENCAS (CACSA): Javier Yaya Tur 253t; Cocomfe: 665b.

J D DALLET: 70tr, 464tl, 605br.

EDEX: 51bl, 405b; EDILESA: 352b; EL DESEO: Pedro Almodóvar 305b; EGANA ORIZA RESTAURANT, Seville: Manolo Manosalbas 602b; ELEPHANT CLUB: 602cr; PACO ELVIRA: 30crb; EMI: Hispavox 376b; EQUIPO 28: 425t; ET ARCHIVE: 52br; EUROPA PRESS: 23c, 68tl, 69ca; MARY EVANS PICTURE LIBRARY: 9t, 56cla, 63bl, 73t, 137r, 197t, 265r, 274bl, 335, 415r, 471b, 503, 553t, 663r; Explorer 424t; EYE UBIQUITOUS: James Davis Travel Photography 21t, 218br.

FIRO FOTO: 157c; 533t; FLAMENCOCOOL: Seville, 455tr; FUNDACIÓN CÉSAR MANRIQUE Manrique: 548br; FUNDA-CIÓN COLECCIÓN THYSSEN-BORNEMISZA: *Madonna of Humility* Fra Angelico 177t, *La Virgen del Árbol* Petrus Christus 288tr, *Mata Mua* Paul Gauguin 1892 289crb, *Harlequin with a Mirror* Pablo Ruiz Picasso 1923 © Succession Picasso/DACS, London 2006 288cl, *Hotel Room* © Edward Hopper 1931 288bl, *Portrait of Baron HH Thyssen-Bornemisza* © Lucian Freud 1981–82 288br, *Venus y Cupido* Peter Paul Rubens (after 1629) 289tl, *Santa Casilda* Francisco de Zurbarán 1640–1645 289cra, *Autumn Landscape in Oldenburg* Karl Schmidt-Rottluff 1907 © DACS, London 2006 289b; Fundació Joan Miró, Barcelona: *Flama en L'espai i dona nua* Joan Miró 1932 © Succession Miró/ADAGP, Paris and DACS, London, 2006 172t.

GODO FOTO: 220b, 221t, 225t, 249b, 255t, 333bl; RONALD GRANT ARCHIVE: *For a Few Dollars More* © United Artists 500b; © FMGB GUGGENHEIM BILBAO MUSEOA. Erica Barahona Ede. All rights reserved. Partial or total reproduction is prohibited 120t, *The Matter of Time* Richard Serra © ARS, NY and DACS, London 2006 120br, 121t, 121b.

ROBERT HARDING PICTURE LIBRARY: 19t, 141tr, 160ca, 172b, 173b, 249t, 303t, 511br; Julia Bayne 196– 197; Nigel Blythe 19b, 149c; Bob Cousins 26clb; Robert Frerck 439tr; James Strachan 270tl; MARÍA VICTORIA HERNÁNDEZ: 533b; HULTON DEUTSCH COLLECTION: 66b, 391br.

IBERDIAPO: Triangle 524–525; THE IMAGE BANK, London: Andra Pistolesi 174; Mark Romanelli 140bl; Mathew Weinreb 161b; IMAGES COLOUR LIBRARY: A.G.E Fotostock 28tr, 29tr, 30cra, 30ca, 30br, 36tr,

37ca, 40c, 42cl, 122b, 168, 187t, 187c, 211br, 233ca, 233br, 316t, 335c, 343cla, 349 tr, 421cl, 424br, 466b, 497t, 531t, 557tr, 659c, 659b; Horizon International 36-37, 140cb; INCAFO: J A Fernández & C De Noriega 75bl, 125br; Juan Carlos Muñoz 396b, 497b; A Ortega 30bl; INDEX: 34tl, 48c, 48b, 49c, 49cb, 50tl, 50b, 54cra, 56br (d), 59tr, *Los Moriscos suplicando al rey Felipe III* 61c, 64–65, 65b, 67 cl, *Carlos I* 70tc, 70bl, 71br, 491ca; Bridgeman, London 58cra; CCJ 23b; X Correa 48tl; *Garrote Vil* José Gutiérrez Solana 1931 © DACS, London 2006 65clb(d); Galería del Ateneo, Madrid *Lucio Anneo Seneca* Villodas 50cla (d); Galeria Illustres Catalonia, Barcelona *Joan Prim I Prats* J Cusachs 63ca(d); Image *José Zorilla* 35bl; Instituto Valencia de Don Juan, Madrid *Carlos V* Simón Bening 59crb; Iranzo 56cra; Mithra 52clb, 58br (d), 64tl; Museo de América, Madrid *Indio Yumbo y Frutas Tropicales* 59cra; Museo Lázaro Galdiano, Madrid *Lope de Vega* Anonymous 34c, *Félix Lope de Vega* Francisco Pacheco 60br(d); Museo Municipal, Madrid *Fiesta en la Plaza Mayor de Madrid* Juan de la Corte 61tl; Museo del Prado, Madrid *Ascensión de un globo Montgolfier en Madrid* Antonio Carnicero 62cra(d), *José Moreño Conde de Floridablanca* Francisco de Goya 62br(d), *Flota del Rey Carlos III de España* A Joli 63tl(d); National Maritime Museum, Greenwich *Batalla de Trafalgar* Chalmers 62cb; A Noé 56cb; Palacio del Senado, Madrid *Alfonso X "El Sabio"* Matías Moreno 34b(d), *Rendición de Granada* Francisco Pradilla 56–57(d); Patrimonio Nacional 51br; Private Collection, Madrid *Pedro Calderón de la Barca* Antonio de Pereda 61bl(d); Real Academia de Bellas Artes de San Fernando, Madrid *San Diego de Alcalá dando de comer a los pobres* Bartolomé Esteban Murillo 61ca(d), *Fernando VII* Francisco de Goya 71tl(d), *Isabel II* 71tc, *Self-Portrait* Francisco de Goya 239b; A Tovy 69cb; NICK INMAN: 204bc, 253tr, 664t, 667cb, 672tr, 679b; INSTITUT TURÍSTIC VALENCIÁ: 245br.

CÉSAR JUSTEL: 353b.

ANTHONY KING: 291t.

L'ESTARTIT TOURIST BOARD: 217c; LIFE FILE PHOTOGRAPHIC: 217c; Tony Abbott 342cla; Xavier Catalan 141cb; Emma Lee 141cra, 420tl, 683tr; NEIL LUKAS: 464cb, 464b.

MAGNUM: S Franklin 68cb; Jean Gaumy 68br, 69tl; MARKA, Milan: Sergio Pitamitz 154t; Imagen Mas, Leon: 355tr; John Miller: 206l, 502–503, 505cb, 529r, 538b, 543b, 548t, 549b; MUSEO ARQUEOLÒGIC DE BARCELONA: 171c; MUSEO ARQUEOLÓGICO DE VILLENA: 48–49; MUSEO NACIONAL DEL PRADO: *El Jardín de las Delicias* 292b; MUSEU PICASSO, Barcelona: *Auto Retrato* Pablo Ruiz Picasso 1899–1900 © Succession Picasso/DACS, London 2006 153b; MUSEU TEXTIL I D'INDUMENTÀRIA : 154bl;.

NATURAL SCIENCE PHOTOS: Nigel Charles 108tl; C Dani & I Jeske 104b, 343br; Richard Revels 342br; Brian Sutton 342bl; W Tarboton 342tl; P & S Ward 232br; NATURPRESS: Oriol Alamany 31bl; J L Calvo & J R Montero 343crb; José Luis Grande 465b; Walter Kwaternik 30clb, 81bc, 342cra, 343cra; Francisco Márquez 465cb, 416bl; Aurelio Martín 31br, Sebastián Martín 343bc; José A Martínez 80tr, 207b, 342clb, 342crb; © NATIONAL MARITIME MUSEUM: 58–59; Network: Bilderberg/W Kunz 421tl; NHPA: Laurie

Campbell 80cra; Stephen Dalton 81cl; Vicente García Canseco 31cla, 465ca; Manfred Daneggar 80br, 81br.

OMEGA FOTO: 110tl, Manuel Pinilla 42b, 123b; ORONOZ: 4, 33br, 36cl, 37br, 47b, 49t, 50b, 53t, 53clb, 53crb, 54tl, 54cb, 55t, 55br, 59tl, 58cla, 60cb, 65tl, 68ca, 82tl, 112t, 305cr, 355br, 363br, 370b, 434bl, 441bl, 467tl, 478cl, 479t, 480l, 489bl, 657t; Biblioteca Nacional, Madrid *Isabel la Católica* Luis Madrazo 70tl(d); Iglesia Santo Tomé, Toledo *El Entierro del Conde de Orgaz* El Greco 32ca; *Portrait II* Joan Miró 1938 © Succession Miró/ ADAGP, Paris and DACS, London 298; Monasterio Santa Maria, Barcelona *Virgen con Niño* Ferrer Bassa 32clb(d); Museo de Bellas Artes, Cádiz *San Bruno en Éxtasis* Zurbarán 467tr; Museo Casa Gredo, Toledo *Carlos II* Miranda Correño 70tr(d); Museo del Ejército, Madrid *Isabel II* Madrazo 62tl; Museo Municipal de Bellas Artes, Tenerife *Retrato de Boabdil o Abu Abdala* 57tr(d); Museo Nacional de Escultura, Valladolid *Natividad* Berruguete 367tr; Museo Naval, Madrid *Desembarco de Colón* José Garnelo 57tl; Museo Naval Laminas, Madrid *Carabelas de Colón* Monleón 57bl(d); Museo del Prado, Madrid *El Salvador* José de Ribera 32crb, *Las Meninas o Familia de Felipe V* Diego Velázquez 32–33, *Felipe III* Pedro A Vidal 60bl, *Felipe V* 62bl, Guernica Pablo Ruiz Picasso 1937 © Succession Picasso/DACS, London 2006, 66–67, *Felipe IV* Diego Velázquez 66bc(d), *Bodegón* Zurbarán 294b, *David Vencedor de Goliat* Caravaggio 295t; Palacio Moncloa *Interior de la Catedral de Santiago* Villaamil Pérez 82–83; *Mujer en Azul* Pablo Ruiz Picasso 1901 © Succession Picasso/DACS, London 2006 298ca; Private Colection, Palma *Oleo Sobre Lienzo* Joan Miró 1932 © Succession Miró/ADAGP, Paris and DACS, London, 2006 33ca; Real Academia de Bellas Artes de San Fernando *Fray Pedro Machado* Zurbarán 281tr.

PANOS PICTURES: Adrian Evans 68–69; José M Pérez De Ayala: 30cr, 464tr, 464ca, 465t, 465ca; THE PHOTO- GRAPHERS LIBRARY: 523tr; PICTURES COLOUR LIBRARY: 22b, 30tr, 162-163, 258b, 416cl; PRISMA: 64ca, 65crb, 66ca, 66cb, 67tr, 97t, 140br, 239c, 250t, 321t, 475tl, 459, 516br, 532cl, 539clb, 539cb, 539crb, 539bl, 543t, 551bl, 551br; *Franco* Aguiar 71tr; *El ingenioso hidalgo Don Quixote de la Mancha* 1605 Ricardo Balaca 395br; Diputación de Madrid *Francisco Bahamonde Franco* Enrique Segura 66tl; Domènech & Azpiliqueta 118t; Albert Heras 186b; Marcel Jaquet 531b, 541b; Hans Lohr 483b; *Los Niños de la Concha* Bartolomé Esteban Murillo 33bl(d); Museo de Arte Moderno, Barcelona *Pío Baroja* Ramón Casas 64cb(d); Museo de Bellas Artes, Bilbao *Condesa Mathieu de Noailles* Ignacio Zuloaga y Zubaleta © DACS, London 2006 118b; Museo de Bellas Artes, Zaragoza *Príncipe de Viana* José Moreno Carbonero 130b (d); Mateu 191c; Palacio del Senado, Madrid *Alfonso XIII* Aquino © DACS, London 2006 71cr; Patrimonio Nacional Palacio de Riofrío, Segovia: 64br; *Auto Retrato* Pablo Ruiz Picasso 1907 © Succession Picasso DACS, London 2006 65ca; Marta Povo 674t; Real Academia de Bellas Artes de San Fernando, Madrid *Las Bodas de Camacho* José Moreno Carbonero 35tl(d), *Procession of the Flagellants* Francisco de Goya 274br(d); PURE ESPANA: Port Aventura 657br.

RENFE: 678tl; REX FEATURES: Sipa Press 215cb; © ROYAL MUSEUM OF SCOTLAND: Michel Zabé 47t; JOSE LUCAS RUIZ: 440br, 456cl.

MARÍA ÁNGELES SÁNCHEZ: 38tr, 39b, 43t, 79t, 98cl, 18l, 290tl, 304b, 387c, 405tr, 532t, 532cr, 532b, 536c, 547t; SCIENCE PHOTO LIBRARY: Geospace 14l; 6 TOROS 6: 37cb; SPANISH TOURIST BOARD: 255c; SPECTRUM COLOUR LIBRARY: 136–137, 140tr, 552–553; STOCKPHOTOS, Madrid: Marcelo Brodsky 40t; Campillo 659t; Heinz Hebeisen 41bl; Mikael Helsing 658b, 332tl; David Hornback 21b; Javier Sánchez 332tl; Werner Otto Reisefotografie 663t; James Strachan: 291b, 302t, 302c, 304t; TONY STONE WORLDWIDE: Doug Armand 20b; Jon Bradley 316bl; Robert Everts 440ca; SUPERSTOCK: Pixtal 76cl.

VISIONS OF ANDALUCÍA: Michelle Chaplow 424–425; J D Dallet 397tr; VU: Christina García Rodero 2–3, 20c, 38b, 39c, 39t, 132cl, 256–257, 368l, 431cr.

CHARLIE WAITE: 494–495; WERNER FORMAN ARCHIVE: Museo de Arte Hispanomusulmán 52t; Museum of Catalan Art, Barcelona 344tl; National Maritime Museum, Greenwich 52cr; ALAN WILLIAMS: 78b; PETER WILSON: 264–265, 282, 468b, 469c, 475t, 481t; WORLD PICTURES: 317b, 512t. ZEFA: 1.

Front endpaper: All special photography except JOE CORNISH cbl; JOHN MILLER tr; SPECTRUM COLOUR LIBRARY ca; PETER WILSON cbr.

JACKET

Front - MARY EVANS PICTURE LIBRARY: Explorer/Courau bl; GETTY IMAGES: Taxi/Peter Adams main image. Back - AGENCE VU: Cristina Garcia Roberto tl; DK IMAGES: Max Alexander clb; Neil Lukas cla; JOHN MILLER: bl. Spine - : DK IMAGES Max Alexander b; GETTY IMAGES: Taxi/Peter Adams t.

All other images © Dorling Kindersley. For further information see www.DKimages.com

SPECIAL EDITIONS OF DK TRAVEL GUIDES

DK Travel Guides can be purchased in bulk quantities at discounted prices for use in promotions or as premiums. We are also able to offer special editions and personalized jackets, corporate imprints, and excerpts from all of our books, tailored specifically to meet your own needs.

To find out more, please contact: (in the United States) **SpecialSales@dk.com** (in the UK) **travelspecialsales@uk.dk.com** (in Canada) DK Special Sales at **general@tourmaline.ca** (in Australia) **business.development@pearson.com.au**

Phrase Book

In an Emergency

Help!	¡Socorro	soh-**koh**-roh
Stop!	¡Pare!	**pah**-reh
Call a doctor!	¡Llame a un médico!	**yah**-meh ah **oon meh**-dee-koh
Call an ambulance!	¡Llame a una ambulancia!	**yah**-meh ah **oonah** ahm-boo-**lahn**-thee-ah
Call the police!	¡Llame a la policía!	**yah**-meh ah lah poh-lee-**thee**-ah
Call the fire brigade!	¡Llame a los bomberos!	**yah**-meh ah lohs bohm-**beh**-rohs
Where is the nearest telephone?	¿Dónde está el teléfono más próximo?	**dohn**-deh ehs-**tah** ehl teh-**leh**-foh-noh mahs **prohx**-ee-moh
Where is the nearest hospital?	¿Dónde está el hospital más próximo?	**dohn**-deh ehs-**tah** ehl ohs-pee-**tahl** mahs **prohx**-ee-moh

Communication Essentials

Yes	Sí	see
No	No	noh
Please	Por favor	pohr fah-**vohr**
Thank you	Gracias	**grah**-thee-ahs
Excuse me	Perdone	pehr-**doh**-neh
Hello	Hola	**oh**-lah
Goodbye	Adiós	ah-dee-**ohs**
Goodnight	Buenas noches	**bweh**-nahs **noh** chehs
Morning	La mañana	lah mah-**nyah**-nah
Afternoon	La tarde	lah **tahr**-deh
Evening	La tarde	lah **tahr**-deh
Yesterday	Ayer	ah-**yehr**
Today	Hoy	oy
Tomorrow	Mañana	mah-**nya**-nah
Here	Aquí	ah-**kee**
There	Allí	ah-**yee**
What?	¿Qué?	keh
When?	¿Cuándo?	**kwahn**-doh
Why?	¿Por qué?	pohr-**keh**
Where?	¿Dónde?	**dohn**-deh

Useful Phrases

How are you?	¿Cómo está usted?	**koh**-moh ehs-**tah** oos-**tehd**
Very well, thank you.	Muy bien, gracias.	mwee bee-**ehn grah**-thee-ahs
Pleased to meet you.	Encantado de conocerle.	ehn-kahn-**tah**-doh deh koh-noh-**thehr**-leh
See you soon.	Hasta pronto.	ahs-tah **prohn**-toh
That's fine.	Está bien.	ehs-**tah** bee-**ehn**
Where is/are ...?	¿Dónde está/están ...?	**dohn**-deh ehs-**tah**/ehs-**tahn**
How far is it to ...?	Cuántos metros/ kilómetros hay de aquí a ...?	**kwahn**-tohs **meh**-trohs/kee-**loh**-meh-trohs **eye** deh ah-**kee** ah pohr **dohn**-deh
Which way to ...?	¿Por dónde se va a ...?	seh bah ah
Do you speak English?	¿Habla inglés?	**ah**-blah een-**glehs**
I don't understand	No comprendo	noh kohm-**prehn**-doh
Could you speak more slowly please?	¿Puede hablar más despacio por favor?	pweh-deh ah-**blahr** mahs dehs-pah-thee-oh pohr fah-**vohr**
I'm sorry.	Lo siento.	loh see-**ehn**-toh

Useful Words

big	grande	**grahn**-deh
small	pequeño	peh-**keh**-nyoh
hot	caliente	kah-lee-**ehn**-the
cold	frío	**free**-oh
good	bueno	**bweh**-noh
bad	malo	**mah**-loh
enough	bastante	bahs-**tahn**-te
well	bien	bee-**ehn**
open	abierto	ah-bee-**ehr**-toh
closed	cerrado	thehr-**rah**-doh
left	izquierda	eeth-key-**ehr**-dah
right	derecha	deh-**reh**-chah
straight on	todo recto	toh-doh **rehk**-toh
near	cerca	**thehr**-kah
far	lejos	**leh**-hohs
up	arriba	ah-**ree**-bah
down	abajo	ah-**bah**-hoh

early	temprano	tehm-**prah**-noh
late	tarde	**tahr**-deh
entrance	entrada	ehn-**trah**-dah
exit	salida	sah-**lee**-dah
toilet	lavabos, servicios	lah-**vah**-bohs sehr-**bee**-thee-ohs
more	más	mahs
less	menos	**meh**-nohs

Shopping

How much does this cost?	¿Cuánto cuesta esto?	**kwahn**-toh kwehs-tah **ehs**-toh
I would like ...	Me gustaría ...	meh goos-ta-**ree**-ah
Do you have?	¿Tienen?	tee-**yeh**-nehn
I'm just looking, thank you.	Sólo estoy mirando, gracias.	**soh**-loh ehs-**toy** mee-**rahn**-doh **grah**-thee-ahs
Do you take credit cards?	¿Aceptan tarjetas de crédito?	ah-**thehp**-tahn tahr-**heh**-tahs deh **kreh**-dee-toh
What time do you open?	¿A qué hora abren?	ah **keh** oh-rah **ah**-brehn
What time do you close?	¿A qué hora cierran?	ah keh oh-rah thee-**ehr**-rahn
This one.	Éste	**ehs**-the
That one.	Ése	**eh**-she
expensive	caro	**kahr**-oh
cheap	barato	bah-**rah**-toh
size, clothes	talla	**tah**-yah
size, shoes	número	no∅-mehr-oh
white	blanco	**blahn**-koh
black	negro	**neh**-groh
red	rojo	**roh**-hoh
yellow	amarillo	ah-mah-**ree**-yoh
green	verde	**behr**-deh
blue	azul	ah-**thool**
antiques shop	la tienda de antigüedades	lah tee-**ehn**-dah deh ahn-tee-gweh-**dah**-dehs
bakery	la panadería	lah pah-nah-deh-**ree**-ah
bank	el banco	ehl **bahn**-koh
book shop	la librería	lah lee-breh-**ree**-ah
butcher's	la carnicería	lah kahr-nee-theh-**ree**-ah
cake shop	la pastelería	lah pahs-teh-leh-**ree**-ah
chemist's	la farmacia	lah fahr-**mah**-thee-ah
fishmonger's	la pescadería	lah pehs-kah-deh-**ree**-ah
greengrocer's	la frutería	lah froo-teh-**ree**-ah
grocer's	la tienda de comestibles	lah tee-**yehn**-dah deh koh-mehs-**tee**-blehs
hairdresser's	la peluquería	lah peh-loo-keh-**ree**-ah
market	el mercado	ehl mehr-**kah**-doh
newsagent's	el kiosko de prensa	ehl kee-**ohs**-koh deh **prehn**-sah
post office	la oficina de correos	lah oh-fee-**thee**-nah deh kohr-**reh**-ohs
shoe shop	la zapatería	lah thah-pah-teh-**ree**-ah
supermarket	el supermercado	ehl soo-pehr-mehr-**kah**-doh
tobacconist	el estanco	ehl ehs-**tahn**-koh
travel agency	la agencia de viajes	lah ah-**hehn**-thee-ah deh bee-**ah**-hehs

Sightseeing

art gallery	el museo de arte	ehl moo-**seh**-oh deh **ahr**-the
cathedral	la catedral	lah kah-teh-**drahl**
church	la iglesia la basílica	lah ee-**gleh**-see-ah lah bah-**see**-lee-kah
garden	el jardín	ehl hahr-**deen**
library	la biblioteca	lah bee-blee-oh-**teh**-kah
museum	el museo	ehl moo-**seh**-oh
tourist information office	la oficina de turismo	lah oh-fee-**thee**-nah deh too-**rees**-moh
town hall	el ayuntamiento	ehl ah-yoon-tah-mee-**ehn**-toh
closed for holiday	cerrado por vacaciones	thehr-**rah**-doh pohr bah-kah-thee-**oh**-nehs
bus station	la estación de autobuses	lah ehs-tah-thee-**ohn** deh owtoh-**boo**-sehs
railway station	la estación de trenes	lah ehs-tah-thee-**ohn** deh **treh**-nehs

Staying in a Hotel

Do you have a vacant room?	¿Tienen una habitación libre?	tee-**eh**-nehn **oo**-nah ah-bee-tah-thee-**ohn lee**-breh
double room	habitación doble	ah-bee-tah-thee-**ohn doh**-bleh
with double bed	con cama de matrimonio	kohn **kah**-mah deh mah-tree-**moh**-nee-oh
twin room	habitación con dos camas	ah-bee-tah-thee-**ohn** kohn dohs **kah**-mahs
single room	habitación individual	ah-bee-tah-thee-**ohn** een-dee-vee-doo-**ahl**
room with a bath	habitación con baño	ah-bee-tah-thee-**ohn** kohn bah-nyoh
shower	ducha	**doo**-chah
porter	el botones	ehl boh-**toh**-nehs
key	la llave	lah **yah**-veh
I have a reservation.	Tengo una habitación reservada.	tehn-goh **oo**-na ah-bee-tah-thee-**ohn** reh-sehr-**bah**-dah

Eating Out

Have you got a table for ...?	¿Tienen mesa para ...?	tee-**eh**-nehn **meh**-sah **pah**-rah
I want to reserve a table.	Quiero reservar una mesa.	kee-eh-roh reh-sehr-**bahr oo**-nah **meh**-sah
The bill please.	La cuenta por favor.	lah **kwehn**-tah pohr fah-**vohr**
I am a vegetarian	Soy vegetariano/a	soy beh-heh-tah-ree-**ah**-no/na
waitress/ waiter	camarera/ camarero	kah-mah-**reh**-rah kah-mah-**reh**-roh
menu	la carta	lah **kahr**-tah
fixed-price menu	menú del día	meh-**noo** dehl **dee**-ah
wine list	la carta de vinos	lah **kahr**-tah deh **bee**-nohs
glass	un vaso	oon **bah**-soh
bottle	una botella	oo-nah boh-**teh**-yah
knife	un cuchillo	oon koo-**chee**-yoh
fork	un tenedor	oon teh-neh-**dohr**
spoon	una cuchara	oo-nah koo-**chah**-rah
breakfast	el desayuno	ehl deh-sah-**yoo**-noh
lunch	la comida/ el almuerzo	lah koh-**mee**-dah/ ehl ahl-**mwehr**-thoh
dinner	la cena	lah **theh**-nah
main course	el segundo plato	ehl pree-**mehr plah**-toh
starters	los primeros	lohs ehn-treh **meh**-sehs
dish of the day	el plato del día	ehl **plah**-toh dehl **dee**-ah
coffee	el café	ehl kah-**feh**
rare	poco hecho	**poh**-koh **eh**-choh
medium	medio hecho	**meh**-dee-oh **eh**-choh
well done	muy hecho	mwee **eh**-choh

Menu Decoder

al horno	ahl **ohr**-noh	baked
asado	ah-**sah**-doh	roast
el aceite	ah-**thee-eh**-teh	oil
las aceitunas	ah-theh-**toon**-ahs	olives
el agua mineral	**ah**-gwa mee-neh-**rahl**	mineral water
sin gas/con gas	seen gas/kohn gas	still/sparkling
el ajo	**ah**-hoh	garlic
el arroz	ahr-**rohth**	rice
el azúcar	ah-**thoo**-kahr	sugar
la carne	**kahr**-neh	meat
la cebolla	theh-**boh**-yah	onion
la cerveza	thehr-**beh**-thah	beer
el cerdo	**thehr**-doh	pork
el chocolate	choh-koh-**lah**-teh	chocolate
el chorizo	choh-**ree**-thoh	red sausage
el cordero	kohr-**deh**-roh	lamb
el fiambre	fee-**ahm**-breh	cold meat
frito	**free**-toh	fried
la fruta	**froo**-tah	fruit
los frutos secos	**froo**-tohs **seh**-kohs	nuts
las gambas	**gahm**-bahs	prawns
el helado	eh-**lah**-doh	ice cream
el huevo	oo-**eh**-voh	egg
el jamón serrano	hah-**mohn** sehr-**rah**-noh	cured ham

el jerez	heh-**rehz**	sherry
la langosta	lahn-**gohs**-tah	lobster
la leche	**leh**-cheh	milk
el limón	lee-**mohn**	lemon
la limonada	lee-moh-**nah**-dah	lemonade
la mantequilla	mahn-teh-**kee**-yah	butter
la manzana	mahn-**thah**-nah	apple
los mariscos	mah-**rees**-kohs	seafood
la menestra	meh-**nehs**-trah	vegetable stew
la naranja	nah-**rahn**-hah	orange
el pan	pahn	bread
el pastel	pahs-**tehl**	cake
las patatas	pah-**tah**-tahs	potatoes
el pescado	pehs-**kah**-doh	fish
la pimienta	pee-mee-**yehn**-tah	pepper
el plátano	**plah**-tah-noh	banana
el pollo	**poh**-yoh	chicken
el postre	**pohs**-treh	dessert
el queso	**keh**-soh	cheese
la sal	sahl	salt
las salchichas	sahl-**chee**-chahs	sausages
la salsa	**sahl**-sah	sauce
seco	**seh**-koh	dry
el solomillo	soh-loh-**mee**-yoh	sirloin
la sopa	**soh**-pah	soup
la tarta	**tahr**-tah	pie/cake
el té	teh	tea
la ternera	tehr-**neh**-rah	beef
las tostadas	tohs-**tah**-dahs	toast
el vinagre	bee-**nah**-greh	vinegar
el vino blanco	**bee**-noh **blahn**-koh	white wine
el vino rosado	**bee**-noh roh-**sah**-doh	rosé wine
el vino tinto	**bee**-noh **teen**-toh	red wine

Numbers

0	cero	**theh**-roh
1	uno	**oo**-noh
2	dos	dohs
3	tres	trehs
4	cuatro	**kwa**-troh
5	cinco	**theen**-koh
6	seis	says
7	siete	**see**-eh-the
8	ocho	**oh**-choh
9	nueve	**nweh**-veh
10	diez	dee-**ehth**
11	once	**ohn**-theh
12	doce	**doh**-theh
13	trece	**treh**-theh
14	catorce	kah-**tohr**-theh
15	quince	**keen**-theh
16	dieciséis	dee-eh-thee-**seh**-ees
17	diecisiete	dee-eh-thee-see-**eh**-the
18	dieciocho	dee-eh-thee-**oh**-choh
19	diecinueve	dee-eh-thee-**nweh**-veh
20	veinte	**beh**-een-the
21	veintiuno	beh-een-tee-**oo**-noh
22	veintidós	beh-een-tee-**dohs**
30	treinta	**treh**-een-tah
31	treinta y uno	treh-een-tah ee **oo**-noh
40	cuarenta	kwah-**rehn**-tah
50	cincuenta	theen-**kwehn**-tah
60	sesenta	seh-**sehn**-tah
70	setenta	seh-**tehn**-tah
80	ochenta	oh-**chehn**-tah
90	noventa	noh-**vehn**-tah
100	cien	thee-**ehn**
101	ciento uno	thee-**ehn**-toh **oo**-noh
102	ciento dos	thee-**ehn**-toh dohs
200	doscientos	dohs-thee-**ehn**-tohs
500	quinientos	khee-nee-**ehn**-tohs
700	setecientos	seh-teh-thee-**ehn**-tohs
900	novecientos	noh-veh-thee-**ehn**-tohs
1,000	mil	meel
1,001	mil uno	meel **oo**-noh

Time

one minute	un minuto	oon mee-**noo**-toh
one hour	una hora	**oo**-na **oh**-rah
half an hour	media hora	meh-dee-a **oh**-rah
Monday	lunes	**loo**-nehs
Tuesday	martes	**mahr**-tehs
Wednesday	miércoles	mee-**ehr**-koh-lehs
Thursday	jueves	hoo-**weh**-vehs
Friday	viernes	bee-**ehr**-nehs
Saturday	sábado	**sah**-bah-doh
Sunday	domingo	doh-**meen**-goh

DATE DUE

BARCELONA TRANSPORT MAP

Barcelona's metro runs from 5am–11pm Mon–Thu; 5am–11pm Fri and Sat; and 6:30am–12pm Sun. The lines are identified by number and colour; platform signs display the name of the last station on the line. A multi-journey (for example a T-10) card allows the traveller to interchange between different modes of transport. The *Barcelona Card*, available in one-day to five-day values offers unlimited travel on metro and bus. Tickets for the interconnecting FF CC suburban rail network, which runs from the city centre out to the airport and to Barcelona's environs, and for the funiculars, must be purchased separately.

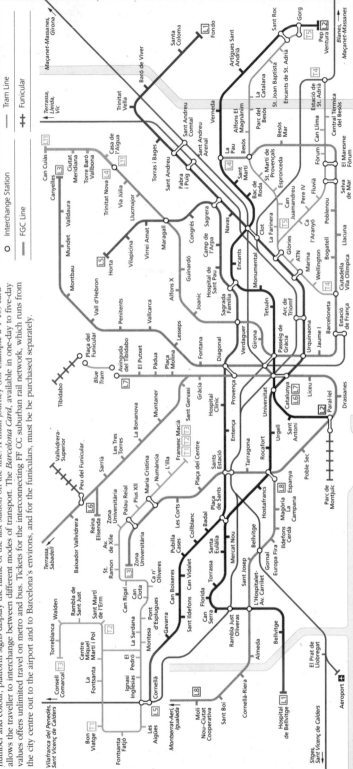

KEY

— Renfe Line
— Tram Line
— Funicular
L1 Metro Line
○ Interchange Station
— FGC Line